UNDERSTANDING
ANIMAL LAW

(2015–Pub.3364)

UNDERSTANDING ANIMAL LAW

Adam P. Karp

CAROLINA ACADEMIC PRESS

Durham, North Carolina

ISBN: 978-0-7698-5420-5

Library of Congress Control Number: 2016914967

Carolina Academic Press, LLC
700 Kent Street
Durham, NC 27701
Telephone (919) 489-7486
Fax (919) 493-5668
www.caplaw.com

Printed in the United States of America

Dedication

1984, Miami Beach, Florida: At the age of 11, preoccupied by *Choose Your Own Adventure* books, body surfing, playing shuffleboard with my grandmother, and oblivious to the treatment of animals, I received my first exposure to the concept of animal suffering. After years of dining on veal parmigiana at an Italian restaurant on Collins Ave., my father stated that he would no longer order veal. When asked why, he explained that he could not eat baby calves who were forcibly separated from their mothers shortly after birth and conscripted to a short, brutish life before being slain for the premium placed upon their pale flesh. From that point forward, I, too, swore off veal. While my ageist speciesism persisted, I thank my father for planting a small seed of compassion.[1]

About 13 years later, while attending law school and then graduate school, a convergence of ethical storms buffeted my senses. No matter how hard I tried to batten down the hatches and pump the bilge of my mind (a desperate effort to remain afloat upon the bloody waters of gastronomic ignorance), humane messages continued to seep in: whether it was Brandyn Miller, vegetarian peer at the University of Washington School of Law (and now practicing Washington attorney) who made me rethink my misperceptions; or Erik Sundin, former Swedish merchant mariner turned vegan and electric vehicle entrepreneur, whose decades of righteous living set me on the right path; or Dave Bemel, founder of Action for Animals, whose campus kiosk with looping video footage finally made inroads the fiftieth day I passed by; or PETA's *Seven Minutes of Reality* (https://new.vk.com/video-5044443_171287108?list=072aea63f2e80752cd) that I watched, wanting desperately to turn away, but unable to do so;[2] or gems found in Peter Singer's classic *Animal Liberation* and James Serpell's *In the Company of Animals*, which, while not a book on vegetarianism *per se*, drew attention to the cognitive dissonance in the curious and confoundingly inconsistent treatment of animals by various human societies; so many personalities and opportunities for enlightenment aided my transition.

Having become vegan at the age of 26, I decided to make personal commitments a professional endeavor, joining the Animal Legal Defense Fund as a young attorney member willing to take on cases pro bono and putting up my shingle as a self-employed solo practitioner in Seattle. In 2001, then-ALDF Board member Steve Ann Chambers met with me to introduce me to the basics of practical legal practice and, from there, my first case. A referral through ALDF, I co-represented Cindy Foster, who rescued an unidentified and ailing Beagle only to be sued over a year later and forced to return her (sans ovaries and uterus) after a bench trial. I handled the appeal from an award against her in the sum of $5,000 for allegedly "wrongfully spaying" the dog, and prevailed. *Williams v. McMahan*, 110 Wash. App. 1031 (II, 2002, unpub.) Since then, I have come

---

[1] Many years later, my father, a physician, confessed guilt using rabbits as part of his graduate medical research studies. Though he did not kill them, I know he was discomfited by this quite common practice in the 1960s.

[2] A much longer, more thorough, and modern cinematic treatment of the subject, which only strengthened my resolve, was the 2005 documentary *Earthlings*, which I recommend to everyone. http://www.nationearth.com/earthlings-1/. Indeed, I donated copies to high schools where I had been invited to speak to students about animal rights.

Dedication

to know and respect the many involved in organizing and furthering the goals of ALDF, to whom I owe a huge debt of gratitude: Joyce Tischler, David Favre, Steven Wise, Bruce Wagman, and Scott Heiser.

While I dedicate this book to the above-identified individuals, and many others not listed, the primary dedication goes to my wife, Kim — beautiful, intelligent, and ethically impassioned, a vegan of 25 years, a former shelter worker, and an animal rights activist — with deepest gratitude. Her abiding love and profound patience made this book possible.

Bhavatu sabba mangalam,

Adam P. Karp
Bellingham, Wash.
July 4, 2016

Preface

Since the first attorney sent a dunning letter or made an opening statement, counsel have bemoaned the increasing incivility of colleagues whose cutthroat tactics confirm the nasty prejudices held by the public and drive morally upstanding lawyers from its fold. Yet, for those who remain, the promise of animal law is both jurisprudentially substantive and ethically normative. For if, as the *Preamble to the Rules of Professional Conduct* state, we desire "the respect and confidence of the members of the legal profession and the society which the lawyer serves," while aspiring to the "highest possible degree of ethical conduct," what better way to revise the notion of the lawyer as barbarian than to replace it with the archetype of lawyer as benevolent gendarme for all creation?

Altruist and philanthropist Albert Schweitzer's magnanimity benefited all species. Despite his harried life, it has been said that Schweitzer, while traversing a sidewalk, encountered an earthworm directly in his path. Languishing under the oppressive sun, he bent down to remove it from the hot pavement and place it on cool grass. If one were to begin this vignette by swapping an "average lawyer" for Albert Schweitzer, how would most finish the tale? Instead of weaving through lush greenery, the earthworm would likely end up in court, squished under the heel of the lawyer's expensive shoes. This is not to say that all lawyers must rescue insects from going down the drain or practice with a Jainist's discipline. But our profession must grapple with this worrisome truth — in the eyes of non-lawyers, we are not trusted. Far from preserving the sanctity of the law, we are seen as the key saboteurs willing to prostitute dignity for pecuniary gain. We may reconstitute ourselves as impassioned warriors, engaging in adversarial combat with an honor and vision lost among many. Reaching back to core principles, that is, in our conduct toward nonhuman animals, we might find a way to reestablish professional respectability.

If asked to share the moments in my life where perfect clarity and joyful endeavor align, I describe a bay in Western Washington into which I routinely cold-plunged, wading out to waist depth. From the corner of my eye, I sensed almost imperceptible movement breaking the smoothness of the water. Adrift what must have seemed like miles from shore was a completely unexpected creature clinging to flotsam, water droplets beading on fragile wings, delicate legs and antennae curled into a ball, and the current slowly pulling him out to certain death in the sound — a *malacosoma constrictum*, or a Pacific tent caterpillar moth (a much-scorned defoliator of deciduous trees). Cupping my palms around him, I withdrew from the bay and set him down on a dry log. Slowly his antennae poked at the air, his legs got under him, and the beautiful wings started to vibrate — a happy, preflight systems check before he took to the safety of the sky.

Since the *malacosoma* experience, I continue to lend aid to creatures great and small, including the stinging or biting variety, without casualty to myself or the subject of my compassion, and in spite of the inevitable eye-rolling and harrumphing of those who fail to approach life in more principled, humane, karmic, and respectful fashion, who refuse to stretch Hobbes's social compact theory (see his comments in *Leviathan*, Ch. III on the prudent beast)[3] to encompass all species. And being vegan for 16 years illustrates this commitment.

These same impulses that motivate rescue of the voiceless from a linguistically and culturally impenetrable sea of law, sacrifices made while rendering aid to the derelict, and rejuvenation that follows the consummated endeavor translate to the practice of animal law save one key difference: scale matters. As lawyers, we have the ability and privilege to turn each individual plight into a precedential miracle, what I call the *malacosoma* principle in honor of the little moth who saved me. May this book guide you through your career and the animal lives you touch.

---

[3] Hobbes claimed that humans could not enter into contracts with "brute beasts," calling it "impossible, because not understanding our speech, they understand not, nor accept of any translation of right, nor can translate any right to another: and without mutual acceptation, there is no covenant." *Leviathan*, Ch. XIII. Yet consider the latest peer-reviewed research by psychologist John Pilley, who proved that his Border Collie named Chaser knew over one thousand words and demonstrated both inferential reasoning and an ability to communicate beyond the capability of a toddler. John Pilley and Hilary Hinzmann, *Chaser: Unlocking the Genius of the Dog Who Knows a Thousand Words* (Houghton Mifflin Harcourt: 2013).

Table of Contents

Table of Contents

Table of Contents

Table of Contents

Table of Contents

Table of Contents

Table of Contents

Table of Contents

Table of Contents

Table of Contents

Table of Contents

Chapter 1

INTRODUCTION

A. THE ORIGIN OF SPECIES (WHAT *WAS* AN ANIMAL LAW CASE?)

Constantin Stanislavski and Lee Strasberg introduced method acting as a technique to render credible performances representing the emotional turmoil of the character portrayed on stage. Such "method" in the theatrical arts bears out on the legal stage as well, for while humans cannot summon from a reservoir of personal experiences without making anthopomorphical errors, the conceptual switch of a nonhuman species with a human, in such categories of *victim, perpetrator, witness, party seeking relief, party resisting relief, tortfeasor, agent,* and *beneficiary*, drives a deep analytic process that, in the course of detecting germane dissimilarities, allows one to better comprehend and apply the law to all subjects of a life.[1] In this regard, animal (animacentric) law is the understudy for non-animal (or homocentric) law. Regardless of the dramatic or comedic overtones, or the lighting, staging, and props that fill the federal or state court theater, the legal actor who devotes him- or herself to this area of law serves dual roles, for he or she achieves mastery over a diverse range of disputes that touch upon the lives of humans and nonhumans alike. While lawyers undergo extensive training to represent and remedy injustices inflicted upon the human condition, in representing the nonhuman, they assume the role of storyteller with the added task of surrogate translator trying to give voice to another species incapable of conversing in human language and whose feelings are at best extrapolated from scientific studies. This text attempts to instruct the reader in "method" lawyering for issues involving nonhuman animals, nonhuman-Americans to be precise.

Animal law did not earn the appellation of a distinct, legal practice area until the late 1970s. See the godmother of animal law and Animal Legal Defense Fund ("ALDF") founder Joyce Tischler's *The History of Animal Law, Part I (1972-1987)*, 1 Stan. J. Animal L. & Pol'y 1 (2008) and *A Brief History of Animal Law*

---

[1] Ethicist Tom Regan authored *The Case for Animal Rights* (1983), taking a modified Kantian view that moral rights ascribe to human and certain nonhuman "subjects-of-a-life," regardless of rationality, eschewing irrelevant dissimilarities between them. *Id.*, at 243 ("They have beliefs and desires; perception, memory, and a sense of the future, including their own future; an emotional life together with feelings of pleasure and pain; preference — and welfare — interests; the ability to initiate action in pursuit of their desires and goals; a psychophysical identity over time; and an individual welfare in the sense that their experiential life fare well or ill for them, logically independently of their utility for others, and logically independently of their being the object of anyone else's interests.") David Degrazia, in *Taking Animals Seriously: Mental Life and Moral Status* (Cambridge Univ. Press, 1996), extends Regan's subject-of-a-life precept to birds, some fish, reptiles, and amphibians.

(1985-2011), 5 STAN. J. ANIMAL L. & POL'Y 27 (2012). Nonetheless, virtually every first-year law student encountered an "animal law" case upon reading *Pierson v. Post*, 3 Cai. R. 175 (N.Y. Sup. Ct. 1805), a personalty-based dispute over capture rights in *ferae naturae*, specifically a fox. Professor Bethany R. Berger describes *Pierson* as one of many notable cases featured in a student's rite of passage in her article *It's Not About the Fox: The Untold History of* Pierson v. Post, 55 DUKE L. J. 1089 (2006), comprehensively historicizing the 208-year-old case by focusing not on perceived rights to hunt and kill the fox but instead on a "growing conflict over who could regulate and use the common resources of the town, and over whether agricultural traditions or commerce and wealth would define its social organization." *Id.*, at 1089.

While questioning its staying power within the American legal pedagogical pantheon and among those who claim its doctrinal similarity to disputes over transgendered discrimination, fugitive homerun balls, groundwater aquifers, and America's Cup trophies, *Id.*, at 1091–92, Prof. Berger's excellent essay ignores the case's most obvious utility — i.e., not the socioeconomic undercurrents of the opinion, or the rumored staging of the case as a jurisprudential exercise, *Id.*, at 1133 fn. 256, nor even in resolving which hunter has the right to skin and sell the tortured creature, but instead to use the case as an opportunity to discuss its modern application, where it really *is* about the fox.

Though he urges that the matter "should have been submitted to the arbitration of sportsmen," *Pierson*'s dissenting Justice Livingston makes the all-too-common rhetorical move of trivializing and caricaturing the animal at issue while mock-personalizing the only one in the entire dispute who lost everything (i.e., his life), the "poor *reynard*" of whose "carcass" Livingston speaks. After describing the fox as a "pirate" and hostile to humanity, Livingston disregards the "maxim of our profession" not to speak ill of the dead by proceeding to disparage "the memory of the deceased." He does so all but calling for open season by giving "the greatest possible encouragement to the destruction of an animal, so cunning and ruthless in his career." *Pierson*, at 180.

This book brings focus to the fox. While the extrinsic factors discussed by Prof. Berger undoubtedly warrant consideration, they remain ancillary here. Legal education and conceptual understanding requires not just answering old questions in new ways, but posing new questions altogether. In making *Pierson* "about the fox," one asks such questions as:

1. Was the fox causing property damage when killed or in the act of depredating when slain (i.e., should we *de mortuis nil nisi bonum* of this fox)?

2. Does the fox have any rights against pursuit, wounding, and capture worthy of legal protection?

3. If the fox may be killed lawfully, must it be done in a noncruel fashion?

4. Is the fox protected as an endangered species under state or federal law?

5. Should any person or entity be entitled to claim damages for the wrongful killing of the fox?

Long before Pierson and Post bickered over who had the right to claim the fox's broken body, the law pertaining to animals took shape. Take Davidic law, for instance. In 2 Samuel 12, Nathan tells the parable of the ewe lamb, whom a destitute man adored "like a daughter," sharing his meager resources for her to dine with his family at the dinner table instead of slaughtering her for his family to dine on. A rich man seized the poor man's "daughter" rather than cull from his own abundant flock in order to feed a traveler. King David indignantly concluded that the rich man should die for such transgression, only to have Nathan turn the parable against the King who had betrayed his soldier Uriah in order to cover up the adulterous affair he had with Uriah's wife, Bathsheba. To read more of biblical prophecy and relational justice, see Carolyn J. Sharp, Assistant Professor of Old Testament, Yale Divinity School, *The Lamb That Was Slain: Rereading "Dominion" in Scriptural Traditions*, www.all-creatures.org/gcm/articles-thelamb.html.

Animal law reaches further back than even King David's time, however. Section 224 of the Mesopotamian Code of Hammurabi prescribed, "The animal surgeon who has performed a successful operation on a beast or an ass should be given 6 shekels as a fee. If, however, due to the operation, the animal dies, the surgeon must pay compensation for ¼ of the animal's price to the owner." DENES KARASSZON, A CONCISE HISTORY OF VETERINARY MEDICINE 20 (E. Farkas, trans., Budapest: Akademaiai Kiado 1988). More than a millennium later, King Asoka issued an edict stating, "If a veterinarian was careless in providing treatment to a horse, or found to have used improper medicines, and the condition of the horse worsened, he could be fined double the cost of treatment." J.F. SMITHCORS, EVOLUTION OF THE VETERINARY ART: A NARRATIVE ACCOUNT TO 1850, 18 (Veterinary Med. Publg. Co. 1957).

Historically, an animal law case literally placed the nonhuman on trial. In the middle ages, nonhuman animal defendants were dressed in formal wear and tried for murder; notably, they were assigned counsel. The earliest such known case dates from 1266 in Fontenay, France, where a pig was burned to death for eating a child. Ecclesiastical courts also dealt with lawsuits against groups of pests accused of destroying crops. After summoning each class of unwanted pests before the tribunal, and due deliberation, the result was often anathema and excommunication (albeit by default). The earliest case is found in the Valley of Aosta in 824, when the priest excommunicated moles. *See* E.P. EVANS, THE CRIMINAL PROSECUTION AND CAPITAL PUNISHMENT OF ANIMALS (Faber & Faber: 1906, 1987).[2]

But times have changed. Today, the accused await sentencing from a concrete run at the local animal shelter. With increasing frequency, however, their owners, guardians, and trustees lodge "appeals" before hearing examiners, boards of

---

[2] *See also* Hampton Carlson, *The Trials of Animals and Insects*, American Philosophical Transactions (1917); Jen Girgen, *The Historical and Contemporary Prosecution and Punishment of Animals*, 9 Animal L. 97 (2003); Paul Schiff Berman, *Rats, Pigs, and Statues on Trial: The Creation of Cultural Narratives in the Prosecution of Animals and Inanimate Objects*, 69 N.Y.U. L. REV. 288 (1994); Steven M. Wise, *The Legal Thinghood of Nonhuman Animals*, 23 B.C. ENVTL. AFF. L. REV. 471 (1996); Karl von Amira, *Thierstrafen and Thierprocesse (Animal Trials and Animal Punishment)*, 12 Mitteilungen des Osterreichischen Instituts fur Geschichtsforschung 545–601 (1891); E.P. Evans, *Bugs and Beasts before the Law*, 54 The Atlantic Monthly 235 (Aug. 1984); Piers Beirne, *A note on the facticity of animal trials in early modern Britain; or, the curious prosecution of farmer Carter's dog for murder*, 55 CRIME L. & SOC. CHANGE 359 (2011).

equalization, municipal and district courts, and even the occasional chief of police, exercising rights to due process and reasonable searches and seizures for the benefit of the animal whose life hangs in the balance of the fact finder following a contested hearing.

B. THE STATUS QUO OF SPECIES (WHAT *IS* AN ANIMAL LAW CASE?)

Animal law, while taught as a discrete area of law, is perhaps better described as a thread woven through all substantive, procedural, ethical, and evidentiary aspects of jurisprudence. One leading casebook defines animal law as "in its simplest (and broadest) sense, a combination of statutory and decisional law in which the nature — legal, social, or biological — of nonhuman animals is an important factor." WAGMAN ET AL., ANIMAL LAW: CASES AND MATERIALS (Carolina Academic Press, 3d ed. 2006). This definition serves academicians well, but for the average practitioner it may be a bit too restrictive or abstract. The field embraces the mundane (dog bites), perfunctory (failure to license), rarefied (constitutional violations), and graphic (equine bestiality), not to mention cutting-edge advancements in nearly every practice area recognized by state bar sections.

While many working definitions exist, textualism provides the greatest utility and ease of application. Within the four corners of the complaint, petition, information, motion or any legal pleading, does one find any reference to a nonhuman animal? If not, it is not an animal law case. But merely using the word "cria" or "kit" in an allegation does not decide the question either. Something more must exist. That is, the nonhuman animal must materially affect a genuine issue in the dispute. Trivial or passing references do not suffice.

Further, animal law questions may arise in a non-animal law case. While subordinate to the core claims or contentions in the action, these animal-related problems still call for analytical resolution. For instance, a criminal defendant may object to the presence of a dog in the witness box giving moral support to a child victim of sexual molestation. While no criminal charge pertains to a nonhuman animal, the nonhuman animal's in-trial appearance, and any aura of credibility or sympathy the dog may lend to the child witness, could increase the likelihood of conviction.

The animal kingdom occasionally serves as the raw material for judicial metaphor. Courts sometimes invoke animal fable or stereotype to lambaste, belittle, or pun. Infrequently, the bench pays a compliment to nonhuman species, though the praise is faint. In and of themselves, whatever demystification, crystallization, illustration, contextualization, or animation of the facts they afford do not an animal case make. *See* Douglas R. Richmond, *Bullies on the Bench*, 72 LA. L. REV. 325, 351 (2012) (discussing use of humor and figurative language by court). For example, Justice Rehnquist invoked the fairy tale Little Red Riding Hood in *FCC v. League of Women Voters*, 468 U.S. 364, 402–03 (1984), analogizing the federal government to a wolf. For further discussion, see Richard Delgado & Jean Stefancic, *Scorn*, 35 WILLIAM & MARY L. REV. 1061, n.49 (1994) and Saul P. Levmore, *Fables, Sagas, and Laws*, 33:3 WILLAMETTE L. REV. (1997) (describing foxes as cunning and wolves as predators).

In other instances, subject matter and allusion align to create a bona fide animal law case — albeit with less-than-flattering treatment of the nonhuman at the center of the dispute. Commentator Marshall Rudolph examines the prolific judicial writing of Judge John S. Wilkes in *Judicial Humor: A Laughing Matter?*, 41 Hastings L. J. 175, 180–81 (1989), noting how he "reveled in [his] infamy" writing on animals, "[h]is favorite subjects for humor[.]" In *Citizens' Rapid Transit Co. v. Dew*, 45 S.W. 790, 792 (Tenn. 1897), Judge Wilkes wrote of a dog struck by a train:

> It is attempted to show that this dog's descent may not have been entirely pure, and it is intimated that he may have had terrier blood in him, but the only foundation for this inference [was] that he 'tarried' so long on the track when the car was approaching. But it appears from the record that it is a characteristic of the pointer, when he sets, to become oblivious to all earthly surroundings, and the bluer his blood the more absent-minded he becomes on such an occasion.

In *Nashville & K.R. Co. v. Davis*, 78 S.W. 1050 (Tenn. 1902), Judge Wilkes characterized a goose as an "obstruction" on a train track:

> But the line must be drawn somewhere, and we are of the opinion that the goose is a proper bird to draw it at . . . . Snakes, frogs, and fishing worms, when upon railroad tracks, are, to some extent, obstructions; but it was not contemplated by the statute that for such obstructions as these trains should be stopped, and passengers delayed.

Adalberto Jordan, who assumed office as Eleventh Circuit Federal Appeals Court Judge in 2012, authored an article titled *Imagery, Humor, and the Judicial Opinion*, 41 U. Miami L. Rev. 693 (1987) during his last year of law school. The article devotes an entire section to the use of animals to "provide judges with comic material." In the section titled "The Animal Menagerie," he describes three cases. In *U.S. v. Dowden*, 139 F. Supp. 781 (W.D. La. 1956) (wherein Judge Dawkins concluded the hornless deer was not a fawn, acquitting the defendant of the wildlife crime), he quotes:

> A tiny tempest in a tinier teapot has brought forth here all the ponderous powers of the Federal Government, mounted on a Clydesdale in hot pursuit of a private citizen who shot a full-grown deer in a National Forest.
>
> Not content with embarrassing defendant by this prosecution, and putting him to the not inconsiderable expense of employing counsel, the Government has compounded calumny by calling the poor dead creature a 'fawn.' Otherwise fully equipped with all the accounterments of virile masculinity, the deceased, alas, was a 'muley.' Unlike other young bucks, who could proudly preen their points in the forest glades or the open meadows, this poor fellow was foredoomed to hide his head in shame: by some queer quirk of Nature's caprice, he had no horns, only 'nubbins,' less than an inch in length.

Instead of giving him a quiet, private internment and a 'requiescat in pace,' which decency should have dictated as his due, the Government has filed his blushing head in evidence for all to see. Pointing to the lack of points, to prove its point, it now insists that, whatever his status may have been in other climes, in Louisiana our departed friend is officially puerile.

Id., at 781–82. In *U.S. v. Sentovich*, 677 F.2d 834 (11th Cir. 1982), he quotes Judge Johnson in his zest to evaluate the probative value of "human sniff" evidence in a drug crime prosecution:

The ubiquitous DEA Agent Paul Markonni once again sticks his nose into the drug trade. This time he is on the scent of appellant Mitchell Sentovich's drug courier activities. We now learn that among Markonni's many talents is an olfactory sense we in the past attributed only to canines. Sentovich argues that he should have been able to test, at a magistrate's hearing on issuance of a search warrant, whether Markonni really is the human bloodhound he claims to be. Sentovich's claims, however, have more bark than bite. In fact, they have not a dog's chance of success. Zeke, Rocky, Bodger and Nebuchadnezzar, and the drug dogs of the southeast had best beware. Markonni's sensitive proboscis may soon put them in the dog pound . . . .

Markonni emerges with his nose unbloodied and his tail wagging. Sentovich's claims are without merit. Having also reviewed the evidence, we find it sufficient for his conviction.

Id., at 835–36, 838. Finally, he quotes Judge Mulligan in his opinion on the theft of rare swans in *U.S. v. Byrnes*, 644 F.2d 107 (2d Cir. 1981):

Canadian geese have been regularly crossing, exiting, reentering and departing our borders with impunity, and apparently without documentation, to enjoy more salubrious climes. Those unwilling or unable to make the flight either because of inadequate wing spans, lack of fuel or fear of buck shot, have become prey to unscrupulous traffickers who put them in crates and ship them to American ports of entry with fraudulent documentation in violation of a host of federal statutes.

Id., at 109. In a footnote, Adalberto also refers to the Seventh Circuit case involving pigeons, dogs, and macaws, *Kirchoff v. Flynn*, 786 F.2d 320 (7th Cir. 1986), where Judge Easterbrook, at 321, made light of the dog at-large charge.

In litigation, sometimes against their better judgment, parties let slip the dogs of war. In so doing, they unfurl animal insults or draw from animal fables to elucidate the argument. While they may aid in understanding complex legal concepts, metaphoric extensions do not give birth to an animal law case. A common judicial rebuke urging attorneys to furnish pinpoint citations, "Judges are not like pigs, hunting for truffles buried in briefs," has more than 400 judicial references according to scholar.google.com. The porcine reference, however, does not convert the opinion into one to be reported in the annals of animal law. One example for the hungry reader includes the "cat's paw doctrine," described in *Cook v. IPC International Corp.*, 673 F.3d 625, 628 (7th Cir. 2012) by Federal Circuit Judge Richard Posner as a "judicial attractive nuisance." Jean de La Fontaine wrote the fable *Le Singe et le Chat* in the collection *Fables Choisies* in 1679. Distilled to its essence, a *cat's paw* is a "patsy" or one victimized as a means to serve another's ends. According to the fable, a monkey desiring chestnuts roasting in the noble's fireplace persuaded a cat to remove them from the fire with his bare paw. This way, the monkey reasoned, he would enjoy the bounty without the blame. In taking this risk, the monkey assured the cat his fair share. One at a time, the cat snatches the chestnut from the burning embers, the cat injuring his paw and the monkey devouring the tidbit. In the legal arena, "cat's paw" amounts to a rubber stamp theory, whereby the formal decisionmaker, or employer (here the monkey), suffers liability for the acts of a prejudiced subordinate or employee (here the cat) by serving as the conduit of the prejudicial mistreatment of the plaintiff.

The "stalking horse" theory provides another example. In *U.S. v. Watts*, 67 F.3d 790, 794 (9th Cir. 1995), *rev. e.g.*, 519 U.S. 148 (1997), the Ninth Circuit examined the constitutional limits of collaboration between law enforcement and a third party, where the third party obtains incriminating evidence against a criminal defendant without law enforcement having independently complied with probable cause and warrant requirements of the Fourth Amendment. In bypassing the conditions for perfecting a lawful search by using such a "decoy," or "stalking horse," the court will suppress inculpatory evidence:

> A probation officer acts as a stalking horse if he conducts a probation search on prior request of and in concert with law enforcement officers. However, collaboration between a probation officer and police does not in itself render a probation search unlawful. The appropriate inquiry is whether the probation officer used the probation search to help police evade the Fourth Amendment's usual warrant and probable cause requirements or whether the probation officer enlisted the police to assist his own legitimate objectives.

According to WEBSTER'S THIRD INTERNATIONAL DICTIONARY, at 2221 (1976), a *stalking horse* is "a horse or figure like a horse behind which a hunter stalks game; something used to cover up a secret project: MASK, PRETENSE."

A third example is the Dutch cross-border, patent infringement "spider in the web" doctrine, whereby Dutch courts assume subject matter jurisdiction only where the lead defendant (spider) domiciled or transacted business in the Netherlands while controlling other defendants within or outside the Netherlands (the web) as part of common business plan even if the disputed patent was issued outside the Netherlands.

Trademark infringement law has proved accommodating of animal subject matter, both totemically and in parody. *Jordache Enterprises, Inc. v. Hogg Wyld, Ltd.*, 828 F.2d 1482 (10th Cir. 1987), for instance, tasked the court with contrasting the stylistic inconsistency of the Jordache equine head with the "large, brightly colored pig head and two hooves, giving the appearance that a pig is peering over the back pocket." And *PETA v. Doughney*, 263 F.3d 359 (4th Cir. 2001), resulted in claims against Michael Doughney for cybersquatting, trademark infringement, and trademark dilution when, in 1995, he registered peta.org and created the site "People Eating Tasty Animals," mocking the 1980-incorporated animal rights organization People for the Ethical Treatment of Animals. As turnabout is fair play,

PETA courted litigation when it released online, and no charge, the download *Pokemon: Black and Blue*, parodying Nintendo's *Pokemon 2: Black and White 2*, in an effort to critique alleged themes of animal abuse and illicit fighting within the popular game and draw parallels to such practices as chaining circus elephants. The PETA-Nintendo dispute arguably constitutes an "animal law" case even though the copyright and trademark issues pertain to fictional, nonhuman characters, for the gravamen of the message urged by PETA embraces the First Amendment right in using Nintendo as a vehicle for public education about animal cruelty.

Merely comparing animals to legal phenomena does not suffice, such as comparing boycotts to "blood-thirsty tigers," as discussed briefly by Gary Minda in *The Law and Metaphor of Boycott*, 41 BUFFALO L. REV. 807, 865 (1993). And while purple prose, poetic license, or complimentary allusions to nonhumans do not alone whelp or queen an animal law litter, judges habitually adorn *bona fide* animal legal opinions with them. For instance, *City of Canadian v. Gutherie*, 87 S.W.2d 316 (Tex. App. 1932) evaluates the death of Mr. Gutherie's impounded, one-eyed bay mare, shot "between the bad eye and the one not so bad," describing the manner of her killing with alliterative excess by stating, "in the vernacular of gangland, when Panhandle Pete's pistol popped, she petered, for which the poundmaster paid Pete a pair of pesos." Despite the doggerel, this case represents a Depression-era statement of the law on equine valuation, concluding in a moment of seriousness: "The measure of damages in the case of a wrongful killing of an animal is its market value, if it has one, and if not, then its actual or intrinsic value, with interest. . . . Appellee's counsel suggested that this being the rule, it is cheaper to kill a mare in Texas than it is to cripple her. The same seems to be true with reference to men, but this court must declare the law as it exists." *Id.*, at 318.

Occasionally, an issue as mundane as a business license dispute can excite judicial inquiry into uncharted territory. Take the case of Blackie the Talking Cat, which sought to resolve whether street performers teaming up with nonhuman animals required a business license in the City of Augusta. It resulted in the district judge's disclosure of *ex parte* interaction with the talking cat followed by a rich encomium to the cat:

> That a talking cat could generate interest and income is not surprising. Man's fascination with the domestic feline is perennial. People of western cultures usually fall into two categories. Generally, they are ailurophiles or ailurophobes. Cats are ubiquitous in the literature, lore and fiber of our society and language. The ruthless Garfield commands the comic strips, the Cat in the Hat exasperates even Dr. Seuss, and who hasn't heard of Heathcliff, Felix or Sylvester? Historically, calico cats have eaten gingham dogs, we are taught that "a cat can look at a king" and at least one cat has "been to London to see the Queen."
>
> It is often said that imitation is the sincerest form of flattery. To the animal world, I am sure that the sincerest form is anthropomorphosis. The ailurophobes contend that anthropomorphosis abounds, and that it is the work of ailurophiles. The ailurophiles say that they do not anthropomorphize cats but, rather, that cats have such human qualities as they may condescend to adopt for their own selfish purposes. Perhaps such was the

case with Saki's ill-fated Tobermory, the cat who knew too much and told all, who, when asked if the human language had been difficult to learn, ". . . looked squarely at [Miss Resker] for a moment and then fixed his gaze serenely on the middle distance. It was obvious that boring questions lay outside his scheme of life."

For hundreds, perhaps thousands of years, people have carried on conversations with cats. Most often, these are one-sided and range from cloying, mawkish nonsense to topics of science and the liberal arts. Apparently Blackie's pride does not prevent him from making an occasional response to this great gush of human verbiage, much to the satisfaction and benefit of his "owners." Apparently, some cats do talk. Others just grin.

Miles v. City Council of Augusta, 551 F. Supp. 349, 350–51 n.2 (S.D. Ga. 1982), *affirmed, Miles v. City Council of Augusta*, 710 F.2d 1542 (11th Cir. 1983). The Eleventh Circuit made passing reference to Blackie's First Amendment right to freedom of speech, thereby giving the *Miles* case its "animal law" bona fides:

> This Court will not hear a claim that Blackie's right to free speech has been infringed. First, although Blackie arguably possesses a very unusual ability, he cannot be considered a "person" and is therefore not protected by the Bill of Rights. Second, even if Blackie had such a right, we see no need for appellants to assert his right *jus tertii*. Blackie can clearly speak for himself.

Id., at 1544 n.5.

Rife with purple passages, perhaps due to this being a small claims court appeal, Suffolk County District Court Judge Rockwell Colaneri examined the "sad tale (or is it tail) of the noble, but late, toco toucan bird (hereinafter Bird), which the plaintiff, Debra Bazzini, purchased from the defendants doing business as Sexy Sadie's Exotic Bird House. For Bird, a youthful creature of but four months, the plaintiff paid the not insubstantial sum of $1,200." *Bazzini v. Garrant*, 116 Misc. 2d 119 (N.Y. Dist. Ct. 1982). In spite of the humor, the opinion reaffirms the status of birds as chattel and "goods" under the Uniform Commercial Code, which warranty of merchantability defendant breached, necessitating full reimbursement.

Finally, animal cases need not boast a "rights" pedigree or possess a pro-animal flavor, but may simply seek to classify animals according to statutory or common law definitions, to circumscribe the legitimate contours for their fair use by humans, or, occasionally, to attempt to decide legal disputes between animals on their own terms. In reversing an award of $50 to the owner of a dog killed by another dog, Judge William F. Allen of the New York Supreme Court, 5th District, in *Wiley v. Slater*, 22 Barb. 506 (N.Y. Gen. Term 1856), wrote of the dueling code of the canine:

> The branch of the law, therefore, applicable to direct conflicts and collisions between dog and dog is entirely new to me, and this case opens up to me an entire new field of investigation. I am constrained to admit total ignorance of the code duello among dogs, or whatever constitutes a just cause of offense and justifies a resort to the *ultima ration regem*, a resort to arms, or rather to teeth, for redress; whether jealousy is a just cause of war, or what different degrees and kinds of insult or slight, or what

violation of the rules of etiquette entitle the injured or offended beast to insist upon prompt and appropriate satisfaction, I know not, and am glad to know that no nice question upon the conduct of the conflict on the part of the principal actors arises in this case.

Judge Allen even anticipated a matter of first impression: excess force by one animal against another.

The defense is not rested upon the principle of self-defense, or defense of the possession of the master of the victorious dog. Had this defense been interposed, a serious and novel question would have arisen, as to the liability of the offending dog for excess of force, and whether he would be held to the same rules which are applied to human beings in like cases offending; whether he would be held strictly to the proof of the necessity and reasonableness of all the force exerted, under the plea that in defense of his carcase or the premises committed to his watch and care, "he did necessarily a little bite, scratch, wound, tear, devour and kill the plaintiff's dog, doing no unnecessary damage to the body or hide of the said dog."

C.   THE DESTINY OF SPECIES (WHAT *WILL BE* AN ANIMAL LAW CASE?)

Hurricane Katrina compelled America to accept one fundamental truth — people will die for their companion animals. In light of the government's insensitivity to these crises, President Bush signed the Pets Evacuation and Transportation Standards ("PETS") Act, 42 U.S.C. § 5196a-d (2006), to ensure that federal agencies consider these special family members by making accommodations during rescue efforts. Because the state and federal government showed utter disregard for the tens of thousands of dogs and cats left to die, rescuers from around the nation arrived by the vanloads, including veterinarians, animal control officers, humane society and shelter workers, and individuals of conscience. Thanks to these Good Samaritans, many animals were saved. Many were re-homed after the chain of, at times, uncertain title passed from an on-site rescuer to a local humane society to a Humane Society of the United States volunteer at Lamar-Dixon to an out-of-state adoption agency to a kind family willing to open their hearts to animals *perceived* to be abandoned. Within the year following the receding of Katrina's waters, however, Louisianans who were displaced from their homes came looking for their dogs and cats. When against unbelievable odds they managed to confirm the animal's location, they requested that the end-rescuer return the companion animal.

The fact that lawsuits proliferated as a result of rescuers refusing to honor the original guardian's requests illustrates the inherent legal difficulties in evaluating the validity and legality of the "title" asserted by the end-rescuer against the undisputed first caregiver. In this vein, the complexion of an animal law case took on new attributes not previously anticipated. A national disaster ushered in the next wave of custody-based animal law development. As developed in the pages that follow, the frequency and power of these new currents continues to increase in velocity and strength. While debate abounds, some envision conferring legal personhood on nonhumans so that they have standing to sue or, in the case of

26-year-old chimpanzee named Tommy, caged in Gloversville, New York, the right to be released from unlawful captivity.[3] Others hope to acquire damages for pain and suffering and pre-death terror, as well as protection from third parties without needing to be owned.

1.   Fugitive Slaves and Salvors

In animal law practice, one may find oneself consulting antebellum law; specifically, doctrinal direction as it pertains to fugitive slaves and jailer/catcher/kidnapper liens on the body of the slave;[4] or maritime legal works to assess the application of salvor's liens, whereby the individual who saves a ship and its cargo from sinking may retain the rescued ship's cargo. Loosely speaking, and in proper historical context, a stray companion animal is not significantly different from a runaway slave. While it is lamentable to read appellate court decisions matter-of-factly and mechanistically describing how human beings trying to escape slavery were nothing more than strays to be taken up by bounty hunters and law enforcement, our country's less shining hour may serve animals running away from abuse and neglect. In this respect, the animal rescuer resembles an Underground Railroad operator who harbors fugitive slaves at extreme personal risk.

A domesticated animal who has not successfully reverted to a feral state will face injury, starvation, fear, and possibly death when left to her own devices in the urban "wilderness." With each passing day, her fate becomes less certain and her health jeopardized by the perils of predatory wildlife, cars, other domesticated animals, and, of course, humans.

Stray dogs and cats find themselves in need of rescue from natural perils and human cruelties. While most seek to reunite the lost animal with her original caretaker, there are circumstances where returning the animal offends the consciences of good people. Ethics alone, however, does not guard against prosecution for larceny. When coupled with the legal power of the retention lien, however, one finds a valuable means of legalizing civil disobedience. Though traditionally asserted by artisans and laborers for financial compensation in the commercial context, there is no good reason to disallow application of the common law bailment lien in the animal rescuer context. Indeed, it is fortified by the nature of the bailed or salved property. After all, if courts of the 1800s acknowledged the similarity between slaves and nonhuman animals, and affirmed liens on the body of the slave, the courts of the twenty-first century can certainly extend and refine that logic to achieve humane ends for nonhuman animals. And if maritime laws predating the existence of the United States allowed for retention liens and awards beyond *quantum meruit* for ships — objects that are indisputably inanimate and nonsentient and distinguishable on many levels from both slaves and nonhuman

---

[3] Brandon Keim, *New York State Court Hears Landmark Chimp Personhood Case*, Wired.com (Oct. 9, 2014) (Attorney Steven Wise of the Nonhuman Rights Project argued before the New York Court of Appeals that "a legal person is a legal concept. It is not a biological concept."); *see also* www. nonhumanrightsproject.org.

[4] Attorney, professor, and author Steven Wise has long described himself as a "nonhuman animal slave lawyer." Mr. Wise has written *Rattling the Cage: Toward Legal Rights for Animals* and *Though the Heavens May Fall: The Landmark Trial That Led to the End of Human Slavery*, among others.

animals — it follows that salvors of animate beings should be afforded at least the same rights and rewards.

2.   Fugitive Slave Lien

No Person held to Service or Labour in one State, under the Laws thereof, escaping into another, shall, in Consequence of any Law or Regulation therein, be discharged from such Service or Labour, but shall be delivered up on Claim of the Party to whom such Service or Labour may be due.

Morgan Cloud, *Quakers, Slaves and the Founders: Profiling to Save the Union*, 73 MISS. L.J. 369, 395–396 (2003). The Thirteenth Amendment nullified this clause. It was not uncommon to find "LOST SLAVE" ads populating the newspapers and town centers, such as this one:

$300 Reward is offered for the apprehension of negro woman, RE-BECCA JONES and her three children, and man ISAIAH, belonging to W.W. Davidson, who have disappeared since the 20th inst. The above reward will be paid for the apprehension and delivery of the said Negroes to my Jail, by the attorney in fact of the owner, or the sum of $250 for the man alone, or $150 for the woman and three children alone.

Feb. 1 Wm. W. Hall, for the Attorney

Id., at 391. While the Constitution and slave state laws permitted and encouraged slave-catching activities by slaveowners, bounty hunters and private actors, anti-slavery opponents used political and legal tools, as well as civil and uncivil disobedience, to upset the recapture of fugitive slaves. Abolitionists often argued that enforcement of fugitive slave laws "frequently led to the greatest injustice; free men, women and children were captured illegally, then sold into bondage." *Id.*, at 397.

The analogy to lost and found property laws governing the return of abused companion or farm animals who have left their owners' control warrants examination. In many respects, the abolitionists of the eighteenth and nineteenth centuries objecting to human enslavement strongly resemble the abolitionists of today who challenge nonhuman enslavement. Perhaps much can be learned from the antislavery and pro-slavery activists. For instance, "[f]requently, antislavery activists in Pennsylvania and other northern states would utilize state laws and enlist the aid of politicians, law enforcers and courts in their efforts to obstruct slave catchers. Similarly, government actors in Virginia and other southern states would protect residents accused of violating the personal liberty laws of a northern state." *Id.*, at 398-399 (citing THOMAS D. MORRIS, FREE MEN ALL: THE PERSONAL LIBERTY LAWS OF THE NORTH, 1780-1861, at 8–12 (1974) (discussing both reliance on common writs and analogous legislation in efforts to free alleged slaves in northern states) and Paul Finkelman, *Sorting Out Prigg v. Pennsylvania*, 24 RUTGERS L.J. 605, 618–20 (1993)).

Following enactment of the Fugitive Slave Clause came the 1793 Fugitive Slave Law, which allowed slaveowners to seize runaway slaves in the free states and carry them back into slavery. *Id.*, at 400–401. The seized person had no entitlement to trial by jury, and no right to testify. Oral testimony was permitted to prove ownership.

Id., at 401. The case could be decided on ex parte proof by the captor. There was no statute of limitations, so capture could occur even decades after the alleged escape. *Id.*, at 402. " 'The act was in fact an invitation to kidnapping, whether as a result of honest error or easily contrived fraud.' " *Id.* (quoting DON E. FEHRENBACHER, THE DRED SCOTT CASE: ITS SIGNIFICANCE IN AMERICAN LAW AND POLITICS 41 (1978)). Fraud was furthered along by racial profiling presumptions. Blacks in the south were presumptively slaves, while whites and Native Americans were not. *Id.*, at 403. The 1793 Act included a provision prohibiting interference with slave catchers and permitted suit for damages including a statutory penalty collected from those who rescued or concealed alleged slaves. *Id.* at 404.

In 1850, Congress passed an updated Fugitive Slave Act in the face of threatened dismantling of the Union. An appalling piece of legislation that truly favored the south despite some concessions and trenchant debate, the Act created a new position of "commissioner" to be appointed in each federal circuit solely to manage fugitive slave disputes. While the commissioners could issue warrants to permit extradition of slaves, in most cases a warrant was not required. Some imagined form of due process was permitted, whether seized with or without a warrant, as explained below:

> Whether seized with or without a warrant, the captive faced a federal proceeding structured to favor the slave owner. For example, the Act not only directed the new category of federal officers — commissioners — to grant certificates "upon satisfactory proof" by the claimant, but also offered the Commissioners a material incentive to decide that adequate proof had been offered. Their fee was doubled in cases in which they ruled for the slave owner. In fugitive slave cases, the commissioners were to be paid a fee by the claimant of the alleged runaway. The fee was "ten dollars . . . in each case, upon the delivery of the said certificate to the claimant," but only "five dollars in cases where the proof shall not, in the opinion of such commissioner, warrant such certificate . . . ."

Id., at 414–415. The Act allowed the slaveowner to "prove" his claim in an ex parte and summary proceeding without a jury and with no right of appeal by the slave. The alleged fugitive was barred from testifying. *Id.* The slaveowner could prove his claim simply by submitting an affidavit, deposition or "other satisfactory testimony, duly taken and certified by some court, magistrate, justice of the peace, or other legal officer authorized to administer an oath and take depositions under the laws of the State or Territory" from which the alleged slave had escaped. Alternatively, the slaveowner could present evidence to a judge in a slave state and use that authenticated transcript of record in the federal ex parte proceeding as binding and "full and conclusive evidence of the fact of escape, and that the service or labor of the person escaping is due to the party" claiming that the seized person was a runaway. *Id.*, at 415–416.

A federal certificate would permit the slaveowner to use "reasonable force and restraint" to remove the fugitive slave to whence he escaped. A fine of up to $1,000, imprisonment of up to six months, and civil damages of $1,000 for each escaped slave applied to any person who knowingly and willingly obstructed or hindered arrest and return of the slave. *Id.*, at 416–417. Even marshals were penalized for refusing to enforce such orders and could be fined $1,000, payable to the slave owner, not the government. *Id.* Indeed, the new federal commissioners and their appointees could summon and call to aid bystanders, or *posses comitatus*, to assist in capturing and returning a runaway slave. *Id.*, at 417. It is little wonder that our country fell into Civil War a short time after passage of this Act.

Maryland passed legislation allowing sheriffs unrestrained power to imprison suspected "runaway slaves and the fees associated with their capture and disposition."

The practical implementation of this law was described in Charles Melvin Christian's book BLACK SAGA: THE AFRICAN AMERICAN EXPERIENCE: A CHRONOLOGY 30. In the jailed slave context, one finds a similar legal application to that of bailment duties of care. In *Brock v. King*, 3 Jones (N.C.) 45 (1855), a jailor received a runaway slave without a warrant of commitment and locked the slave a dungeon in the county jail from which no person had escaped, though the jail was rather insecure. The unchained slave escaped by breaking the door and making a hole in the wall of the prison. Despite liberating himself, the slave was found murdered weeks later. The slaveowner sued the jailor for lack of due care as a bailee. The court held for the jailor noting that he acted without negligence.

> A lien on the body of the prisoner guaranteed the reward to the capturer and imprisonment fees to the sheriff. A large number of sheriffs saw that it was in their best interest to apprehend and imprison many "colored persons who might be detained for a longer period than six months, whether the person [is] free or slave." If the prison term was prolonged, the fees swelled to nearly the value of the prisoner. When that occurred, the master might be unable or unwilling to redeem the slave. In this instance, the authorized sheriff's sale could easily work to the advantage of an associate working in collusion with the sheriff. Seventy-five years later, on December 22, 1792, the Maryland General Assembly passed an act "to restrain the ill-practices of sheriffs, and to direct their conduct respecting runaways."

In *Commonwealth ex rel. Johnson v. Holloway*, 1817 Pa. LEXIS 3 (Jan. 1817), a Maryland slaveowner sought a writ of habeas corpus for the return of his runaway slave, David Johnson, from Pennsylvania. Because Mr. Johnson had committed the "crimes" of fornication and bastardy (conceiving a child out of wedlock), the courts refused to return Mr. Johnson until the slaveowner paid security for the maintenance of Mr. Johnson's child. While the federal constitution expressly stated that no laws of individual states will interfere with the right of the owner to the labor and services of his slave who escapes (Art. IV, § 2), the court held that a slave may be detained and punished for committing felonies and these inferior offenses, particularly where the slave can pay nothing to support his child, leaving the state to bear the expense of caring for the offspring. In concluding that the constitution did not prohibit detaining slaves in one state for all crimes, notwithstanding demands for return by the slaveowner, the court stated:

> But it is not to be construed so as to exempt slaves from the penal laws of any state in which they may happen to be. This would be to turn them loose on society like wild beasts; and was not at all the object of the constitution.

Id., at 2. Note the animal simile.

In *Fowler v. Norman*, 1841 Tenn. LEXIS 21 (Apr. 1841), slaves committed to the custody of a jailor (Fowler) in one county broke prison less than 12 months after detention and were captured by the jailor (Norman) of another county. Fowler offered Norman $99 to return the slaves, but he refused. Fowler then sued for detinue, claiming a lien on the slaves pursuant to a Tennessee law, which provided that "in all cases where any slave shall have been committed to any of the jails in this State, as a runaway, and shall have been duly advertised by such jailer, as required by the laws of this State, and shall not be reclaimed and proven away by the owner, and shall have been imprisoned for the term of twelve months, it shall and may be lawful for the sheriff, having previously advertised the same thirty days, to expose such slave to public sale to the highest bidder, and to apply the proceeds, in the first place, to the payment of the costs and jail fees, and the surplus to pay to the county trustee." *Id.*, at 2 (Act of 1825, Ch. 77, § 1). As the statutory "contingency" of "twelve months" detention did not arrive, Fowler had no legal right to maintain detinue for the escaped slaves. This case bears remarkable similarity to laws concerning impounded animals and the right to demand impound, boarding, and redemption fees as a retention lien prior to release to the owner.

As a disturbing aside, the case of *Griffing v. Routh*, 1856 La. LEXIS 76 (Feb. 1856) provides some idea of what slaves were worth for their wrongful death. In this case, defendant's slaves attempted to capture a trespassing, runaway slave belonging to plaintiff. In the process, plaintiff's slave was killed by grossly negligent and wanton conduct of thrusting a broadsword into fodder where he was believed to be concealed. His value? $1,200.

In *State v. Williams*, 1848 N.C. LEXIS 161 (Dec. 1848), the court evaluated whether a crime of larceny may lie when a person takes and carries away a runaway slave even though the taker is ignorant of the owner's identity. The defendant argued that as the slaves had run away, the owner lost possession and lost property could not be stolen, particularly when he had no knowledge of the slave's owner. The state maintained that possessing stolen property raises a presumption of theft or felonious taking by violence or seduction. Core to the analysis was whether a slave was similar to inanimate chattel and stray beasts. It is worth duplicating the analysis in full:

> For, when it is enquired, whether a runaway slave can be stolen, if the owner be not known, it is implied that the taker knew the negro to be the slave of someone and that the taking was *causa lucri*. Admitting those points, the necessity for securing the rights of ownership in negroes imperatively requires, that such a taking of a runaway should be held to be larceny, and the *impossibility of holding that a human being has any just similitude to an inanimate chattel that is lost, or to a brute that has strayed from its pasture*, prevents an exception founded merely on the want of knowledge in the taker, who, in particular, was the owner of the slave. This subject was incidentally under consideration in *Roper's* case, 3 Dev. 473, and CHIEF JUSTICE HENDERSON expressed himself pointedly in terms, which cover the whole ground. *He said, that runaway slaves do not fall within the description of lost property; for, from their nature, being*

intelligent beings, they are incapable of becoming estrays, in the legal meaning of the word, and in their runaway state they more closely resemble that class of lost property, than any other. The same idea pervades the statutes regulating the arrest and disposition of runaway and the punishments for harboring them. For it is not only indictable to entice or persuade a slave to absent himself from the service of the owner — in which case a knowledge of the owner is implied — but also to harbor or maintain, under any pretence whatever, "*any* runaway slave," thus clearly placing the latter crime upon the state of slavery merely of the negro, without regard to the party's knowledge of the ownership. In an indictment or declaration for harboring a runaway, a *scienter* of the ownership is never laid, but only that the negro was a runaway slave, the property of some other person. For it is alike unlawful to harbor such a slave, whether the owner be known or not. Indeed, it is incorrect to say, that, for any rights or powers over the slave by one who takes him, a runaway is without a known owner. For the statutes require that the runaway shall, when taken up, be committed to jail, and if an owner do not appear in a prescribed time the slave is to be sold for public uses; so that the public, if no one else, may be regarded as the owner. At all events, the taker up can, under no possible circumstances, rightfully keep the possession of a runaway slave longer than is requisite to convey him to prison, or gain a property of the most special kind in him, but is at most entitled only to a reward for taking up. *This is a remarkable feature in the condition of a runaway slave, which distinguishes it from that of lost goods or stray beasts; for in these last the finder gets the property until the owner appears, and therefore the idea of larceny by using the property in any manner is repelled.* But that wholly fails in the case of a runaway slave, as the person, who takes him, must know that he has no interest in the slave, and that, as against him, the public at all events has the right, and that it is his duty to provide for the proper disposition of the slave, and not convert him to his own use. Therefore, in such a case, the appropriation of the slave in the manner and under the circumstances, which usually indicate a felonious intention, is as criminal as if the slave had not been runaway. Hence we believe the understanding is almost universal, in every class of the community, that slaves cannot be reckoned among lost things, and that a runaway is, therefore, as much a subject of larceny, as any other slave; and the Court so holds.

Id., at 5 (emphasis added). At that time, however, stray dogs and cats were not uniformly considered subjects of larceny. Today, in every state it is a crime to steal or feloniously take by violence or seduction a companion animal. With microchipping and other forms of identification not significantly different from tattooing or branding, the original owner may attempt to inform the public of his claim so that the finder may not plead ignorance and withhold possession interminably. This case does not address the propriety of liening the slave, but it does speak to the vigor of the analogy between runaway slaves and stray animals, notably where the court's recognition of the former as "intelligent beings" does not extend to the latter.

This proposition, of course, has not been tested in the 168 years since this decision was published. Cruelty laws recognize that nonhuman animals experience pain and suffering as do human beings. In criminalizing an owner's cruel conduct toward her animals, the legislatures have acknowledged enforceable and protectible interests inherently possessed by the victimized animal — regardless of owned status. It follows that abused animals may exercise their intentionality by escaping mistreatment, using their "intelligence" to avoid pain and seek refuge. In this regard, runaway slaves and abused stray animals have much in common.

The case of *McNeill v. Easley*, 1854 Ala. LEXIS 71 (Jan. 1854) explores the violation of a bailment for hire contract involving the services of a slave. Plaintiff's slave was loaned to defendant bailee for work, but the slave escaped and returned to plaintiff bailor. When a demand was made for the slave's return, the plaintiff refused, noting that he believed the bailee was treating the slave inhumanely. Later convinced that the slave would be treated appropriately, the bailor instructed the slave to return to the bailee. Instead, the slave ran away. Plaintiff sued defendant on the promissory note for the slave's services. The court reversed in favor of the defendant, concluding that while a bailee is in breach if he treats a slave for hire with inhumanity, a bailor is equally in breach if he keeps possession of the slave under circumstances where there has been no contractual violation and, accordingly, the bailee does not lose his right to hire. This case supports the proposition that a bailee is in breach of a bailment contract where the bailed property (or in this case, human slave) is wasted or mistreated. While saying nothing about the propriety of imposing a lien, much less a lien against a wasteful or mistreating *bailor*, it recognizes an "implied stipulation" to treat the subject of the bailment "with humanity." Might similar implied stipulations attend to animal bailments?

In *Miller v. Porter*, 1847 Ky. LEXIS 168 (Jan. 27, 1847), plaintiff slaveowner sued defendant jailor for escape of his slave from the county jail. What distinguishes this case from others is that the plaintiff hired the jailor to receive and keep plaintiff's slave safely in the public jail, delivering the slave to his custody, rather than the jailor catching a runaway slave and imprisoning him without the slaveowner's express direction. In finding the contract against public policy, on the ground that a jailor could not "appropriate the jail to the purpose of confining runaway slaves at the instance of the owner," the court explained the proper relationship between the owner of a runaway slave and public jails. The semblance to the owner of a stray dog or cat and a publicly owned or run shelter is uncanny:

> The running away of a slave is not a public but a private offence, the prevention and punishment of which the law leaves to the owner, without making any provision in aid of his rights, except that when a runaway slave is taken up by a stranger, he may be placed in a county jail where he may be reclaimed by the owner; or if not reclaimed within a certain period, may be sold for his benefit. It is undoubtedly for the public good, and therefore, a matter of public policy, that runaway slaves should be re-taken and placed in subjection to their proper owners. And the law in the provision referred to, lends its aid to the accomplishment of that object. But the law makes no provision for relieving the owner of the trouble or risk of keeping his slave actually in his possession. This is not one of the purposes for which the jail was erected or the jailer provided. The law presumes that the owner is

competent to control and manage his own slave, and leaves the trouble and expense and responsibility of so doing to be borne or provided for by him.

Id., at 1. A modern analogy to this dispute would involve the owner of a stray dog boarding the animal at the county pound through a private financial arrangement with a kennel supervisor. If "[s]laves committed to jail by the owners are not *runaways* within the contemplation of the statute on that subject," then owned animals delivered to the custody of an animal control agency are not strays. Clearly, however, where the contract is not against public policy, the resulting implication is that the private animal rescuer is filling the shoes of an unidentified member of a defined class of bailees (a Doe bailee, if you will), accepting the implied offer to enter into the open bailment contract at the behest of the owner. It may also be assumed that some reward, or at least compensation, would be afforded to the rescuer as the involuntary or gratuitous bailee. A lien for that reward or reimbursement should then apply. As the *Miller* case indicates, when the contract for bailment is against public policy, the jailor-bailee loses his right to the promised reward, but he is also immune from liability for negligent handling. Thus, the animal rescuer should be entitled to both the right of compensation and the responsibility should harm befall the rescued animal.

In *Morehead and Bryant v. State*, 1849 Tenn. LEXIS 99 (Apr. 1849), Morehead and Bryant were criminally charged for stealing the prosecutor's runaway slave named Albert. Essentially profiteers, these slave runners nonetheless argued that a runaway slave was not the subject of a larceny because at the time they found Albert, he was not in the prosecutor's actual possession (rather, he had escaped). The court evaluated whether the prosecutor was in "constructive possession in the absence of actual intervening adverse possession[.]" Prisoners' counsel argued in the negative, asserting that Alfred was, more or less, "lost property," no different from a person who takes "a lost chattel, as a jewel, watch pocketbook or the like; or a horse or cow that has strayed from the owner's premises, or accustomed range, and is lost to the owner." *Id.* at 2. Regarding this as utter nonsense, the court replied:

> This reasoning is fallacious, and proceeds upon a false analogy. Lost property is looked upon, for some purposes, as abandoned by the former proprietor, and, as such is returned into the common stock or mass of things, and therefore as belonging to the first occupant or finder. And though the former proprietor is entitled to maintain an action for the recovery, yet, as against all other persons, the title vests in the finder. Therefore, though it may have been converted *animo furandi*, by the person finding it, it is no larceny, because the first taking was lawful. But this principle properly applies, perhaps, only to inanimate things, which cannot be transferred from or cease to be in the possession of the owner without his own or another's act or default. *It cannot, certainly, to the same extent, be applied even to animals, which possess the instinct and power of motion, and can remove themselves from place to place, though these may be lost, in some instances, in the proper sense of the term.* But it would be most absurd to predicate this of a rational, intelligent being possessed of reason, of will, memory, and all the other faculties and attributes of mind, capable of forming and maturing his purposes and of electing and applying

appropriate means to the attainment of his ends. A slave may voluntarily form and carry into effect the purpose of throwing off his allegiance to his master and may transport himself beyond his reach. Still, however, he is not, and cannot be, lost in the sense in which a watch or jewel, or even a horse, may be lost. *He has always the capacity, mental and physical, to return at pleasure, dependent solely upon his own volition; such is not the case in respect either to inanimate objects or animals. And not being lost or rather being incapable of loss, in the legal sense of the term, he is to be regarded, so long as there is no actual adverse enjoyment, as in the constructive possession of his master.*

Id. (emphasis added). This passage places animals on the continuum between inanimate property and slaves, serving as a placeholder that moves the slave from the intermediate position to one beside his slaveowning counterpart. The analogy between nonhumans and slaves collapses, however, when the court concedes that the former only have the power of locomotion and instinct but not reason and sentience. In examining the doctrine of a taking by finding, the court notes, "Hence, if a horse be found straying in a common, or on a public highway and is taken *animo furandi*, it is no finding, but felony in him that so takes him." *Id.*, at 3. "With much greater reason," it adds, "does this principle apply to slave property." *Id.*

Absent from this examination is what consideration should be given to the slave's ability to "voluntarily form and carry into effect the purpose of throwing off his allegiance to his master" and "transport[ing] himself beyond his reach"? *Id.*, at 2. The slave's status as mere property resolves the moral conundrum by simply ignoring it. In the 150 years since the *Morehead* decision, however, we have learned that a stray animal is, as described of the slave, a "rational, intelligent being possessed of reason, of will, memory, and all the other faculties and attributes of mind, capable of forming and maturing his purposes and of electing and applying appropriate means to the attainment of his ends." *Id.* If the animal has escaped from an objectively abusive or neglectful situation, even if it *knows and expects no better* (as in the case of battered woman syndrome), who is to say that the taking of this straying animal "is no finding, but felony in him that so takes him"?

Alabama answered the same "runaway slave as subject of larceny" question in the affirmative. *Murray v. State*, 1851 Ala. LEXIS 227 (Jan. 1851). It explained the finder's walking the fine line of theft as follows:

The next question we propose to examine is, whether a runaway slave is the subject of larceny. Independent of any decisions upon the subject, I should not entertain a doubt but that larceny may be committed in stealing a runaway slave. If property be found in the high-way, and the finder knows the owner, but instead of restoring it to the owner, he converts it to his own use, such conversion amounts to a felony.--2 Russ. on Crimes, 102-3; Whar. Am. Crim. Law, 400. But the very point has been decided by several of our sister States. . . . In the case of *Randall v. The State*, 4 S. & M., the Court of Errors of Mississippi recognised the same principle; and, in the opinion, a runaway slave is likened to any other lost goods, the finding and conversion of which by another, if the finder know the owner, is a larceny, but no larceny, if the owner is unknown.

Id., at 2. Absent from both *Morehead* and *Murray* is the most pressing inquiry: what if the runaway slave consents to capture (in order to sever ties from his master)? Analogously, what if the rescued animal prefers rescue over return? One may refer to this as lack of *animum revertendi* (desire to return), a concept discussed in the case of *State v. Jernagan*, 1817 N.C. LEXIS 37 (Jan. 1817).

In *Tunstall v. Sutton*, 1856 Ky. LEXIS 35 (June 1856), Henry Tunstall sued Emily Sutton, who had a life estate, and other remaindermen, for $100 due to him for capturing a six-year-old boy slave named George, who was taken by his father from his owners in Kentucky to Cincinnati against their will. Tunstall sought to foreclose upon a capture lien by subjecting George to payment. Tunstall appealed dismissal. The appellate court reversed, finding that George was "of an age capable of voluntary escape, and no doubt exercised it," even though he was taken away by his father. As a "fugitive from service" owned by the defendants, they all owed Tunstall a reward for apprehension. *Id.*, at 2. The court further reasoned that even if George were a "suckling child," he, too, would be regarded as a runaway slave with his escaping slave mother:

> But suppose a mother, who is a slave, should escape from her owner, carrying with her a sucking child not capable of an agency in the escape, ought not the child, in view of the statute, to be regarded as a runaway slave as well as the mother? Both are as much beyond the power and control of the owner, as if both had exercised an equal agency in escaping; and when found in the State of Ohio, as George was, ought not, and would not, both mother and child, under the constitution and laws of the United States, be held and esteemed fugitives from service?

Id. The lien question was not addressed in this decision, but it demonstrates how offspring or adolescent strays are not materially different from their adult counterparts. Some cities do not require licensing for animals under a certain age, or permit summary euthanasia even of healthy kittens and puppies without adhering to a stray hold period. The sentiment that age and intent are immaterial was voiced by Tunstall's appellate attorneys:

> The idea of a runaway is not different from that of an "estray," which certainly includes the young as well as the old, and only requires absence without leave. Any other idea would not authorize the recapture of an infant in Ohio, taken off by its mother, while it would the mother. The mother might be reclaimed, but the child could not, because it had been passive. So it might be said of an adult slave forcibly taken off — that he had not acted with a will in absenting himself. To state the proposition is its own refutation. The idea that the slave must *choose* to go away, to constitute him a runaway within the meaning of the law, cannot be maintained.

Id., at 1.

3. Salvor's Lien

The marine salvor's lien has truly ancient origins long recognized as a part of admiralty law. The following lengthy excerpt is produced in its entirety due to its clarity and thoroughness:

The legal concept that a marine salvor is entitled to a reward for the saving of imperiled marine property has been a recognized part of the admiralty law for more than 3,000 years. The origins of the concept may be traced from antiquity, as set forth in the Edicts of Rhodes, through the laws of the Romans, as set forth in the Justinian Digest, to the Medieval Laws of Oleron, the Code of the Hanseatic League down to the founding of the Republic. *The original concept, as it has come down from the Romans, is that an individual who risks himself and his property voluntarily to successfully rescue the property of another from peril at sea and restore it to him has bestowed a benefit on the owner and should be rewarded by the owner commensurate with the magnitude of the benefit bestowed.* The concept has a sound policy basis, descending as it does from an era when the distinction between pirates and freebooters on the one hand and honest seaman and salvors on the other was often only one of motivation and expectation. While both were on the lookout for a generous reward for their efforts, at least the latter hoped to come by it honestly. The purpose was to encourage honesty by generously rewarding those who restored property safely to the owner. Of course, many modern marine insurance adjusters would argue that the distinction between freebooter and salvor continues to be a vague one. There is still, however, a sound policy basis for the concept today. The interests of maritime safety and commerce as well as the marine environment are better served by encouraging salvors to prevent losses of vessels and cargo.

From the earliest days of this country, admiralty law has followed a liberal approach to salvage. The United States rejected the English maritime salvage system based as it was on the rights of the Crown and the lord of the manor to wrecks and salvage, in favor of a system which rewarded the individual for his efforts. It has always been the well entrenched admiralty law of the United States that, as set forth by CHIEF JUSTICE MARSHALL in 1804, if property of an individual is exposed to peril or hazard at sea and is saved by the voluntary exertion of any persons whatsoever "[a] very ample reward will be bestowed in the courts of justice."

It is the fundamental public policy of the United States to encourage seamen to render prompt aid to vessels and property in peril at sea. As discussed by JUSTICE CLIFFORD in The CLARITA, "[p]ublic policy encourages the hearty and industrious mariner to engage in these laborious and sometimes dangerous enterprises, and with a view to withdraw from him every temptation to dishonesty the law allows him, in case he is successful, a liberal compensation."

It is the well-settled view of the U.S. admiralty courts that "[c]ompensation as salvage is not viewed by the admiralty courts merely as pay, on the principle of a quantum meruit, or as a remuneration pro opere et labore, but as a reward given for perilous services, voluntarily rendered."

The admiralty and maritime law of the United States has long recognized that the law of salvage rewards the voluntary salvor for his successful rescue of life or property imperiled at sea. The purpose of this policy is to promote not only humanitarian rescue of life and property, but maritime commerce as well. JUSTICE STORY summarized it well, as he so often did:

> In cases of salvage, the measure of reward has never been adjusted by a mere estimate of the labor and services performed by the salvors. These, to be sure, are very important ingredients; and are greatly enhanced in value, when they have been accompanied by personal peril and gallantry, by prompt and hardy enterprise, and by severe and long-continued exposure to the inclemencies of the winds and waves. But an enlarged policy, looking to the safety and interest of the commercial world, decrees a liberal recompense, with a view to stimulate ambition, by holding out what may be deemed an honorable reward.

Indeed, the law of salvage is so well settled that it is sometimes said to be the *jus gentium* or the international law of the sea. *Under this well settled doctrine of international law, salvage service is one which is rendered voluntarily to a vessel which needs assistance and which is designed to relieve her from some distress of danger either present or to be reasonably apprehended.* As set forth by the U.S. Supreme Court:

> Salvage is the compensation allowed to persons by whose voluntary assistance a ship at sea or her cargo or both have been saved in whole or in part from impending sea peril, or in recovering such property from actual peril or loss, as in cases of shipwreck, derelict, or recapture.

> It is necessary to draw the distinction between a salvage service and a salvage award. In order to have a valid salvage claim and be entitled to a liberal salvage award, a salvor must first establish that the services rendered were, in fact, salvage services. In order to establish a valid claim to have rendered salvage services, a salvor must establish three elements: (1) marine peril; (2) services voluntarily rendered; and (3) success, in whole or in part, with contribution to such success by the service rendered by the salvor. Of these elements, the first, that of peril, is the most misunderstood and the most frequent source of debate. Anyone who seeks to understand the American law of salvage must first comprehend the American concept of marine peril. The concept is a broad one, liberally applied.

Andrew Anderson, *Salvage and Recreational Vessels: Modern Concepts and Misconceptions*, 6 U.S.F. MAR. L.J. 203, 206–09 (1993) (footnotes omitted, emphasis added). As one can see, the language above tracks with the truest condition of a stray animal who has been recaptured, rescued from peril, and protected against the dangers of starvation, trauma, dehydration, and other harms on the "high seas" of terrestrial society. Even the doctrine of "peril" and providing a "vessel driven aground" with "safe harbor" applies to animals with little translation:

> It is well settled that the peril necessary to constitute a salvage service need not be one of "imminent and absolute danger." It is enough that the property is in danger, either presently or to be reasonably apprehended. It is important to note that it is not the degree of peril which makes for salvage service. If distress or peril is present then, accompanied by

voluntary service and success, a valid salvage service has been performed, entitling the salvor to a salvage award. The degree of peril, whether slight, moderate, or severe, affects only the amount of the award, but not the entitlement of the salvor to a salvage award.

It is also the well settled admiralty law of the United States that a vessel driven aground, on rocks, on shoals, or on reefs, must be considered to be in a state of peril. In such a situation, the vessel is exposed to the vagaries of wind, weather and waves, and it does not require extensive seagoing experience or contemplation to consider that so long as the vessel remains in that helpless situation, without further assistance, she is subject to further damage and eventual breaking up or sinking.

Id., at 209 (footnotes omitted, emphasis added).

A distinction often raised in insurance disputes is "towage" versus "salvage." Think about how this might apply to rescuing a dog or cat "adrift" in the streets of an industrial district:

The hallmark of "towage" is the absence of peril. The motivation for the towing service is convenience not safety. An example would be where a sailboat, proceeding under sail in light airs without difficulty, requests towing assistance from a power vessel to expedite the vessel's return to her mooring in order to allow the passengers to meet an appointment.

In many cases of salvage, there is no generic difference between the physical acts of towage and salvage, where towage may be a salvage service when it is rendered to property actually in danger or where danger is reasonably to be apprehended. Some courts have designated the term as either "salvage towage" or as "extraordinary towage" where salvage service has been recognized. A typical case would arise when a power vessel has run out of fuel or is disabled and adrift at sea but the only assistance required is a tow to a safe mooring. In such cases, the level of salvage services would be extremely low when the service is rendered in harbor or close to shore, in calm weather and when numerous other vessels or towboats were available to render the same service.

Id., at 212. (footnotes omitted). Presumably, collecting a stray and transporting him or her to a humane society constitutes a form of towage, but depending on the degree to which she was imperiled, it may be appropriate to contend that salvage services were also provided. The reason the distinction should be noted is that towage alone will not arguably provide for a lien, while salvage will.

Salvage services "cannot be thrust upon an unwilling vessel master or owner who refuses them," though consent will be implied if "under the circumstances, a prudent man would have accepted." *Id.*, at 217. It becomes a question of fact whether the vessel master "took affirmative steps to decline salvage services or implicitly agreed to them." *Id.* When vessels are exposed to marine peril and "no one is aboard to refuse or accept the salvage services (whether it is derelict, abandoned or has simply been temporarily left), it is not necessary for the salvor to attempt to locate the owner or to obtain permission prior undertaking salvage operations. Under such circumstances, the salvor is not a trespasser but may proceed to assist the vessel and make a claim for a salvage award." *Id.*

Assuming a right to undertake salvage operations, the salvor earns a high-priority possessory, preferred maritime lien on the vessel. *Id.*, at 217–218 (citing 46 U.S.C. § 31301(5)(F) (1993) and *The Fairfield*, 1887 U.S. Dist. LEXIS 55 (D. Ga. Feb. 22, 1887)). While improper to deny the owner or his agents access to the vessel or property to inspect or preserve it, the general rule is that the salvor may retain possession of the vessel until adequate security to cover the salvage award is posted or it is established that the owner will not. In the former case, the salvor must release the vessel. In the latter, he must surrender the vessel to the U.S. Marshal and proceed to foreclose the lien. *Id.* The salvor's lien is lost "when the vessel throws off the towline and departs." *Id.*

Salvors of abandoned vessels (known as "derelicts" or "wrecks") may claim ownership. In all other circumstances, the salvor only obtains a possessory lien. The concept of abandonment applies where the owner has left it without intention to return or hope of recovery and requires some affirmative act by the owner which clearly and convincingly establishes a positive intent to part with ownership. *Id.*, at 218–219.

As to the value of the salvor's lien, many factors inform this figure, as described below:

> In The Blackwall, JUSTICE CLIFFORD set out the six factors to be considered in determining the amount of the salvage award. The Second Circuit has arranged them in descending order of importance as follows:
>
> (a) The degree of danger from which the vessel was rescued;
>
> (b) The post-casualty value of the property saved;
>
> (c) The risk incurred in saving the property from impending peril;
>
> (d) The promptitude, skill, and energy displayed in rendering the service and salving the property;
>
> (e) The value of the property employed by the salvors and the danger to which it was exposed;
>
> (f) The costs in terms of labor and materials expended by the salvors in rendering the salvage service.
>
> In considering its award, the court must not only consider the peril immediately faced by the vessel but the dangers presented by the situation that might have forseeably developed but for the actions of the salvors.
>
> The value of a vessel to her owner is what he can obtain for her in an arm's length, negotiated sale in the open market. Thus, the value of the benefit bestowed by salvors on the vessel owner is a vessel's market value after the salvage service but before repair compared to what her market value would have been had the salvors not intervened to relieve her from her peril. However, the amount of a salvage award is not based on a precise or exact valuation of the salved property particularly when that value is high.

Id., at 225–226 (footnotes omitted, citing *The Blackwall*, 77 U.S. (10 Wall.) 1 (1869)). Public policy dictates that the salvor's award is not limited to *quantum meruit* but acknowledges an additional sum as a premium on prompt and competent assistance. *Id.*, at 227–228.

Professional salvors, rather than being short-changed in their rescuing efforts, enjoy an equitable "uplift" thanks once more to public policy:

> Public policy also provides that, in order to encourage professional salvors to relieve the taxpayers from the necessity of buying, equipping and maintaining salvage vessels as well as training and maintaining their crews, professional salvors are entitled not only to compensation for services rendered, but to a so-called equitable uplift or incentive bonus to induce both small and large salvors to remain in business, prepared to respond to the next mayday. A professional salvor is entitled to claim a special bonus award for a successful salvage. The concept that professional salvors are entitled to premium pay for successful completion of their services has been long standing and is widespread. There is strong public policy that a professional salvor is entitled to a more liberal award than an amateur in order to encourage professional salvors to maintain salvage equipment and expertise.

Id., at 228–229 (footnotes omitted). Therefore, animal rescue groups who expend tremendous capital and undergo extensive training to save stray dogs and cats may be said to enjoy, at least in principle, an enhanced lien for their "salvage" services. The precise sum of the salvage award may be expressed as a percentage or other quantum, and are always case-specific, but the following examples provide some guidance. The very quality of the animal rescued (be he a "mutt" or "purebred," "celebrity" or "street dog," service animal or police dog) may be as relevant as the distinction in maritime law between types of salved vessels (be they a yacht, a "blue water" vessel, or a $60 million tanker. *See id.*, at 231-32.[5] Indeed, determining the "vessel's value" before salvage invites a discussion into the economic value of an animal, which invites its own extensive disagreements. For instance, should the salvage award be based on the salved animal's "intrinsic" or "fair market" value? Should any emotional increment affect computation of the salvage award?

Recent cases confirming the existence of a salvor's retention lien and providing a very judicious discussion of the above topics include *R.M.S. Titanic, Inc. v. The Wrecked and Abandoned Vessel*, 286 F.3d 194, 202–05 (4th Cir. 2002), and *R.M.S. Titanic, Inc. v. Haver*, 171 F.3d 943, 963–64 (4th Cir. 1999). Be aware that with the salvor's preferred lien comes fiduciary-type duties that, if breached, negate the right to a salvage award:

> While the law of salvage provides substantial protection to salvors to encourage their saving of life and property at sea, it also imposes duties of good faith, honesty, and diligence in protecting the property in salvors' care. Thus, salvors have to exercise a trust over the property for the benefit of the owner and subject to any orders of a court. *See Cromwell v. The Bark*

---

[5] Where the animal "drifts," that is, breaks through a person's fence, and causes damage within the enclosure, a distraint lien may apply to hold the animal as collateral to pay for damages caused.

Island City, 66 U.S. (1 Black) 121, 17 L. Ed. 70 (1861). In this vein, salvors are not entitled to remove property from the wreck for their own use or to use the property for their own use. When a violation of this trust occurs, the salvage claim is forfeited. *See Danner v. United States,* 99 F. Supp. 880 (S.D.N.Y. 1951). Indeed, it has been held that even when salvors have mistakenly misunderstood their rights and have taken property for their own use, they forfeited their right to a salvage award. *See, e.g., id.; see also The Mabel,* 61 F.2d 537, 540 (9th Cir. 1932).

Haver, at 963–64. The foregoing legal history of slaves and shipwrecks teased out the common judicial threads shared with strays and may assist in understanding the curious treatment of animals as property under the law. So begins the voyage.

D. THE HERMENEUTIC OF ANIMAL LAW PRACTICE

A *hermeneutic* is an approach taken to decipher, interpret, and solve a problem. Jurists and practitioners wield various hermeneutical canons to lend meaning to statutes and produce a just outcome. Courts rely on[6] a variety of linguistic canons including *espressio unius,* meaning that the expression of one thing suggests the exclusion of others; *noscitur a sociis,* which gives meaning to words by those with which they are associated; *ejusdem generis,* holding that a specific statute will generally supersede a more general one or a general term must reflect the class of objects also reflected in more specific terms accompanying it; the ordinary usage rule, indicating that undefined terms should be given plain and ordinary meanings unless contrary to legislative intent; the dictionary definition rule, requiring a court to follow a recognized dictionary's definition unless the legislature has codified a specific one; and the "shall" rule, which instructs that the term "may" is permissive, and does not create a statutory duty, but the term "shall" establishes an obligation unless unconstitutional or counter to legislative intent. Other textual maxims instruct that each statutory provision should be analyzed by reference to the whole act; that one should construe a statute so all language used is given effect and no portion is rendered meaningless or duplicative; to narrowly construe statutory exceptions and provisos and not create exceptions not conceived of by the legislature; and to treat silence as acquiescence.

Extrinsic canons focus on the relationship of a particular enactment to the larger body of statutory law and apply a broad, harmonizing brush so that the part comports with the whole. These canons include: the borrowed statute rule (where the legislature borrows a statute, it impliedly adopts the statute's judicial interpretations); the reenactment rule (when the legislature reenacts a statute, it incorporates settled interpretations of the reenacted statute); *in pari materia* (interpret similar statutes similarly); the presumption against repeals by implica-tion; the rule requiring interpretation of provisions consistently with subsequent statutory amendments; the rule of continuity (assuming the legislature did not create discontinuities in legal rights and obligations without some clear statement); the presumption that when the legislature acts, it intends to change existing law; a

---

[6] The following is adapted from Philip A. Talmadge, *A New Approach to Statutory interpretation in Washington,* 25 SEATTLE U. L. REV. 179 (2001).

presumption in favor of following common law usage where the legislature employs words or concepts with well-settled common law traditions; a presumption that the legislature knows prior law including judicial or administrative interpretations of statutes; a presumption favoring prospective application of a statute and its corollary canon, to the end of rejecting retroactive application of statutes; and avoiding constitutional conflicts.

Such rules of interpretation impact first principles in an animal law case; for, preliminary to any inquiry on the merits, the prudent animal law practitioner must discern whether her client (or client's ward or chattel) qualifies as an "animal" or "person" under the pertinent statute. For instance, Washington State's animal trust law, Wash. Rev. Code Ch. 11.118, would not allow a testator to designate as her trust beneficiary Otto, a Blue-Ringed Octopus, although he may seasonally enjoy a few decades. Nor can Rosie, the red-kneed tarantula or the Sylvesters, a residential slug family. Why? Washington State law validates trusts to nonhuman animal *vertebrates* only.

Or consider the gourmand who eats live escargot, a common preparation of "fresh" snails. Under many state laws, this dining experience would not constitute culinary cruelty. If a brasserie in Kirkland, Washington, served snails, however, King County Code § 11.04.250 might call for misdemeanor charges of animal cruelty because an "animal" in King County is defined as any creature other than a human, insect, or worm. The issue of whether a snail or his unshelled cousin the slug may claim to hail from heartier invertebrate stock and not share the lowly status of their earthworm counterparts is a matter of first impression and may turn on the squeamishness of the particular judge. Curiously absent from the almost all state and municipal definitions of animal are fish.

If in doubt, fall back on the rule of *ejusdem generis* (a class of animals shares a common characteristic; if the animal in question does not have that characteristic, it is not in the class protected); the rule of lenity (the judicial doctrine holding that a court, in construing an ambiguous criminal statute (or statute with civil and criminal applications) that sets out multiple or inconsistent punishments, should resolve the ambiguity in favor of the more lenient one); and the doctrine of *in pari materia* (look to the neighboring provisions and general context of the statute, including legislative history and intent statements, to see what types of animals were within the ambit). How might you determine whether to prosecute a crime against a parrot sanctuary, home to more than 500 avians — many dispossessed and neglected — for emanations of thunderous screeching, barks, excited chattering, tongue and beak clicking, much to the dismay of a new neighbor, where the relevant code makes it a nuisance for:

> Any domesticated animal that howls, yelps, whines, barks or makes other oral noises, in such a manner as to disturb any person or neighborhood to an unreasonable degree.

The term *domesticated animal* is defined as:

> A domestic beast, such as any dog, cat, rabbit, horse, mule, ass, bovine animal, lamb, goat, sheep, hog or other animal made to be domestic.

And the code also defines *animal* as "any living creature except Homo sapiens, insects and worms." Note that each of the enumerated species in the nuisance law is mammalian, while the sanctuary cares for avians, belonging to an entirely different scientific class (i.e., Mammalia vs. Aves). While you might grope at the phrase "or other animal made to be domestic," one cannot divorce it from the first five words, "A domestic beast, such as . . . ." The term *beast* is not defined in the code, but the most common dictionary definition by far conjures imagery of a wild, tusked, vicious creature — not a parrot. The NEW LEXICON WEBSTER'S DICTIONARY OF THE ENGLISH LANGUAGE (1987) defines *beast* as "*n.* any four-legged animal, esp. a wild one | a farm animal | a person with savage, brutal ways." Furthermore, a vast number of the birds at the sanctuary are wild, not "domesticated." But perhaps the simplest argument to be made is that the legislature could have easily stricken the word "domesticated," leaving the broadest definition of "animal" intact.

That said, the following spoof presents a head-scratcher, forcing the use of your imagination, as the court in *Regina v. Ojibway*, 8 Crim. L. Q. 137 (Canada, S. Ct., Toronto 1965) did. The defendant rode his pony through the park using a pillow instead of a saddle. Per Native Canadian custom, he shot the pony after it broke its right foreleg. He was charged with violating section 2 of Small Birds Act, which states: "Anyone maiming, injuring or killing small birds is guilty of an offence and subject to a fine not in excess of two hundred dollars."

The lower court held the statute inapplicable, firmly committed to believing that a pony was not a bird. The Supreme Court reversed, schooling them on this unique, endangered, four-legged mutation of the flightless cormorant. Noting that section 1 of Act defined "bird" as "a two-legged animal covered with feathers," the Court showed no interest in determining "whether the animal in question is a bird or not in fact, but whether it is one in law."

> Different things may take on the same meaning for different purposes. For the purpose of the Small Birds Act, all two-legged, feather-covered animals are birds. This, of course, does not imply that only two-legged animals qualify, for the legislative intent is to make two legs merely the minimum requirement. The statute therefore contemplated multi-legged animals with feathers as well. Counsel submits that having regards to the purpose of the statute only small animals "naturally covered" with feathers could have been contemplated. However, had this been the intention of the legislature, I am certain that the phrase "naturally covered" would have been expressly inserted just as "Long" was inserted in the Longshoreman's Act.

> Therefore, a horse with feathers on its back must be deemed for the purposes of this Act to be a bird, and *a fortiori*, a pony with feathers on its back is a small bird. Counsel posed the following rhetorical question: If the pillow had been removed prior to the shooting, would the animal still be a bird? To this let me answer rhetorically: Is a bird any less of a bird without its feathers?

Id., at 139.

Humor aside, perhaps the most significant challenge to the animal law practitioner lies in deconstructing statutory and common law to its rawest elements, recognizing that legislative and judicial mandates pertaining to nonhumans are steeped in a historical, social, political, geographical, even religious context. Forty years ago, critical legal studies adherents took lessons from the civil rights, women's rights, anti-war, and environmental movements and applied them to expand dialogic engagement concerning the use of the legal system against the "oppressed" or even the "subaltern," marginalized individuals lacking a voice, standing outside the hegemonic power structure that creates, interprets, and enforces the law. Perhaps no being can better claim subalternity than the nonhuman, and no critique more pressing than the legal study of animals.

One cannot seriously deny that nonhuman animals have become "public stakeholders" given what society takes from them in its ongoing operation — their skins, organs, muscles, bones, and labor, their bodies as platforms for medical discoveries, their existence for our aesthetic enjoyment and therapy, their physical prowess for protection and entertainment, their heightened sensory abilities to deliver advanced warning, and their unconditionally loving natures for familial companionship.[7] We live and work with nonhuman animals and rely on them for managing physical and mental disabilities; work with them in war; and raise them from birth for slaughter in agribusiness. They are stars of film and sit-com.[8] But most important, like us, they are fundamentally animal. *Sentience* admits them to the community of humans and nonhumans. Together we constitute the public for whom good must be safeguarded. Regardless of intellect, capacity to communicate or use tools, business acumen or supremacy of the physical specimen, all beings share the imperatives of self-determination and self-preservation — to varying degrees and with varying

---

[7] For a captivating discussion of the evolving societal and psychological treatment of human-animal relationships in the familial context, and the therapeutic benefit of being licked by a dog and other pet-having panaceas, see James Serpell, *In the Company of Animals* (Cambridge University Press: 1996), which so happened to be one of the most influential texts in inducting the author into the field of animal law. For the next generation in academic animal studies literature on companion animals, read texts by University of Strathclyde Professor Erica Fudge, most recently *Pets (The Art of Living)* (Routledge: 2014).

[8] The federal Animal Welfare Act sets minimum care standards for animals used in television and movies, as well as advertising by regarding those who lease animals to producers as regulated "exhibitors." After producers deliberately threw a horse to his death in the 1939 movie *Jesse James*, the American Humane Association ("AHA") formed with the goal of monitoring all productions using nonhuman animals. However, the AHA has no enforcement ability as a nongovernmental organization without delegated rights to fine, arrest, or seize. It does not monitor separation of babies from mothers and gives no consideration in its six-rating scale to what happens to the animals once used by the exhibitor. To earn the "No Animals Were Harmed" end credit disclaimer requires compliance with the AHA guidelines. http://www.americanhumane.org/assets/pdfs/animals/pa-film-guidelines.pdf. Another nongovernmental organization, the Motion Picture Association of America ("MPAA"), rates movies as G, PG, PG-13, R, or NC-17. It is unclear whether the MPAA rates films more restrictively if they depict animal cruelty, for the guidelines appear to emphasize violence toward and abuse of humans. The first short segment of the three-part South Korean film *Doomsday Book* (2012) depicts what appears to be a live cow slaughter in a method that would probably not be deemed legal under the federal Humane Methods of Slaughter Act; while the gratuitous and disturbing scene might encourage viewers to stop eating meat, one does not know if the director used computer-generated imagery or obtain the relief of the AHA's end credit disclaimer or an albeit nonspecific (as it pertains to animals) MPAA rating (the film was unrated).

conflicts. Particularly relevant is the scholarly debate surrounding the expansion of the definition of "personhood" to higher primates. A *Declaration on Great Apes* has the following germane preamble:

> The community of equals is the moral community within which we accept certain basic moral principles or rights as governing our relations with each other and enforceable at law. Among these principles or rights are the following: [1. The Right to Life; 2. The Protection of Individual Liberty; and 3. The Prohibition of Torture]

SONIA S. WAISMAN & BRUCE A. WAGMAN ET AL., ANIMAL LAW, CASES AND MATERIALS, 2d Ed., Appendix A (Carolina Academic Press: 2002). *See also The Evolving Status of Chimpanzees*, Symposium at Harvard Law School on September 30, 2002, republished at 9 ANIMAL L. 1 (2003) (speakers included Alan Dershowitz, David Favre, Roger Fouts, Jane Goodall, Cass Sunstein, Steven Wise, Paul Waldau, and Richard Wrangham, who discussed the need for the law to confer some modicum of legal status on chimpanzees).

Unlike children, the elderly, immigrants, criminals, or those with severe mental disabilities, individual nonhuman animals have no representatives officially recognized at law. Systematized protocols to provide guardians *ad litem* for them do not yet exist. Those who attempt to speak on their behalf rarely, if ever, surmount the hurdle of standing. Notwithstanding statutes and regulations directed aggregately toward nonhuman animals *in toto* (i.e., as a species, subspecies, or discrete population), *individual* animals have no means of enforcing their most fundamental interests or rights, such as avoiding unnecessary pain, physical injury, dying by a means causing undue suffering, expressing their essential natures, maintaining the integrity of family and social structures (both intra- and inter-species), and evading premature and nonconsensual death.

Legislators create law. Despite their best efforts, however, laws may fail to keep pace with human-animal interactive development. Evolving social mores may render them anachronistic nullities. And acute attacks of atavism may compel modern communities to breathe new life into old laws by reverting to even older first principles. Lawyers face the task of not just accurately interpreting these laws but, most important for animal law practice, taking the added step of arguing for the excision of dying doctrines from the body of law (as recognized by *desuetude*[9]) and reconstituting others to apply to modern legal problems.

If anything stands out among the throngs of litigators, it is the entrepreneurial spirit and will of the animal lawyer to find and employ new approaches to resolving legal issues pertaining to nonhumans. In so doing, she learns to ask the right questions and wield the answers in a manner that moves the discourse into new terrain. She must master a hermeneutic model that forces decisionmakers to grapple with the cognitive dissonance arising from layer upon layer of often paradoxical, but deeply ingrained, beliefs, assumptions, and rationalizations that typify and direct society's disparate treatment of individual animals and species. Dissonance niggles for consonance to the legal problem, and the animal lawyer is

---

[9] A doctrine that renders statutes and principles obsolete due to disuse, such as early America's blue laws.

positioned to bring that case to a commensurable conclusion.

One strain of animal law contends that the best hermeneutic of the animal law practitioner is to correct unjust interpretations of the legal definition of "animal" and their interests, effectuated by avoiding the cross-species linguistic and behavioral barriers that interfere any time a human attempts to "read" the expressions, actions, and "statements" of a nonhuman, both individually and among its cohorts. Oftentimes courts will ascribe human motivations to animals by *anthropomorphosis*. With farmed animals, however, they rarely bestow human likeness but instead draw such species as pigs, cattle, and chickens into the Cartesian mire, denuding them of any quality remotely identifiable as sentient or feeling and placing them in league with the inanimate workings of a machine — known as *mechanomorphosis*.

Mary Wollstonecraft Shelley's classic *Frankenstein; or, The Modern Prometheus* (1818) chronicles the life of scientist Victor Frankenstein, whose ability to reanimate a congeries of human tissues into a humanoid form visits death upon his brother, sister-in-law, childhood friend, wife, and father, and consumes him with a drive to find and destroy his creation, who refers to himself as "the Adam of your labours" and "your fallen angel." Not merely a dumb daemon, the unnamed, eight-foot-tall being shows promising cognitive ability, able to teach himself to read and speak, and of sentience.[10] He bemoans the way others react to his perceived hideous appearance, begging Frankenstein to make him a female companion, and tormented with such guilt and grief he sets himself adrift on an ice floe and commits suicide by pyre.

In many respects, Frankenstein's "monster" and *Star Trek: The Next Generation*'s Lt. Cmdr. Data symbolize the legal condition of nonhuman animals, as described sagely by Steven Wise in *How Nonhuman Animals were Trapped in a*

---

[10] A futuristic variation of *Frankenstein* takes the form of *Star Trek: The Next Generation*'s Lt. Cmdr. Data. In the episode titled *The Measure of a Man,* android Lt. Comdr. Data faces an order from Starfleet for an "experimental refit," namely, his disassembly and the transplantation of his positronic brain into a starbase mainframe computer to assist with Federation cybernetic research and development. Data, who has striven to become human, defies the order and testifies at a hearing before the Starfleet Judge Advocate General. The Federation, represented by Data's friend and colleague Commander William Riker, characterizes Data as property of Starfleet, denied legal personhood that would afford him any of the panoply of rights accorded by the United Federation of Planets. At trial, over objection, the Judge allows Riker to remove Data's hand for inspection, while stating, "The issue before this court is whether Data is machine, and by extension property." But the most dramatic scene occurs when Riker makes his closing argument:

> The commander is a physical representation of a dream, an idea conceived of by the mind of a man. Its purpose is to serve human needs and interests. It's a collection of neural nets and heuristic algorithms. Its responses dictated by an elaborate software program written by a man. Its hardware built by a man. And now. And now a man will shut it off this man has turned him off.

At that moment, Riker is at Data's side. Without warning he leans down, presses a switch, and turns Data off. Data collapses. Riker concludes: "Pinocchio is broken, the strings are cut."

Captain Jean-Luc Picard, defending Data, asserts that he is a sentient being capable of self-determination and the right to resign from Starfleet — essentially, divesting Starfleet of its claim to ownership. Finding the analogy to slavery *apropos*, Data contends that sentience earns him freedom from what amounts to an involuntary death sentence. Deeming him intelligent and self-aware, the JAG finds Data sentient as a matter of law and bestows upon him the right to choose whether to undergo the refit.

Nonexistent Universe, 1 ANIMAL L. 15 (1995), and David Favre in *Equitable Self-Ownership for Animals*, 50 DUKE L.J. 473 (2000).[11]

But six centuries before Data's Starfleet trial, philosophers François-Marie Arouet ("Voltaire") and Rene Descartes were having a similar debate, albeit exchanged across generations. In his Nov. 23, 1646, letter to the Marquess of Newcastle, Descartes contended that birds, dogs, horses, and monkeys do not have speech for the reason that "they have no thoughts," the mimicry and mock-speech resulting not from reason, but passion. Even "madmen" can "arrang[e] various words together and form[] a discourse from them in order to make their thoughts understood; whereas there is no other animal, however perfect and well-endowed it may be, that can do the like." Descartes, *Discourse on the Method*, at 140 (1637). Voltaire responded to the "pitiful" hypothesis that "animals are machines bereft of understanding and feeling, which perform their operations always in the same way, which learn nothing, perfect nothing, etc." He continued:

> What! that bird which makes its nest in a semi-circle when it is attaching it to a wall, which builds it in a quarter circle when it is in an angle, and in a circle upon a tree; that bird acts always in the same way? That hunting-dog which you have disciplined for three months, does it not know more at the end of this time than it knew before your lessons? Does the canary to which you teach a tune repeat it at once? do you not spend a considerable time in teaching it? have you not seen that it has made a mistake and that it corrects itself?

> Is it because I speak to you, that you judge that I have feeling, memory, ideas? Well, I do not speak to you; you see me going home looking disconsolate, seeking a paper anxiously, opening the desk where I remember having shut it, finding it, reading it joyfully. You judge that I have experienced the feeling of distress and that of pleasure, that I have memory and understanding.

> Bring the same judgment to bear on this dog which has lost its master, which has sought him on every road with sorrowful cries, which enters the house agitated, uneasy, which goes down the stairs, up the stairs, from room to room, which at last finds in his study the master it loves, and which shows him its joy by its cries of delight, by its leaps, by its caresses.

> Barbarians seize this dog, which in friendship surpasses man so prodigiously; they nail it on a table, and they dissect it alive in order to show the mesenteric veins. You discover in it all the same organs of feeling that are in yourself. Answer me, machinist, has nature arranged all the means of feeling in this animal, so that it may not feel? has it nerves in order to be impassible? Do not suppose this impertinent contradiction in nature.

THE PHILOSOPHICAL DICTIONARY, *Beasts* (1764). Consider what makes an animal different from a car: volition, sentience, sensorium, or passibility (the ability to perceive the world through sensation and to feel pain or suffer), animation, and rationality. A laptop may be programmed to do many things, much like an android

---

[11] Animal law, as slave law before it, may serve as a harbinger for cyborg or android law.

or cyborg can be artificially manufactured to appear and act human. Though "fake," many develop attachments with inanimate objects or form relationships with artificially intelligent entities. If the animal is more like a laptop, then we are conceptualizing her as a machine or a car for legal valuation and custody. But if she offers a "real" as opposed to "fake" relationship with a human being, then she is more like a person.

In this respect, is it fair to saddle defendants with non-market value monetary judgments when they engage in wrongdoing with the assumption that animals would otherwise (i.e., as in the case of agricultural animals or animals bred solely for sale on a market) have a far more modest market value? On the other hand, what of the well-established "eggshell skull plaintiff" doctrine, alluding to the fictional character Humpty Dumpty, who falls off a wall and dies due to his extremely thin shell, unable to be resurrected despite all the feudal personnel then available? The doctrine allocates risk of potentially unanticipated and sizeable damage awards to the tortfeasor who takes his plaintiff as she comes. Foreseeability principles occasionally come into play, as well. For instance, where the defendant knows or should know that the plaintiff values her animal beyond market or replacement value, and would experience emotional distress should harm befall the animal, the defendant cannot justifiably shirk full responsibility for her offense. Small animal veterinary clinics informing prospective clients that "We treat your pets like family!" and employing similar advertising motifs cannot in good faith later disclaim notice that animals victimized by their clinicians' malpractice will produce more substantial damage awards than would a large animal veterinarian treating herds at a concentrated animal feedlot operation where animals are, lamentably, regarded as units of production in a commercial operation.

Courts may also judge an animal's behavior from that species' own perspective, as in the "reasonable dog" standard invoked to determine whether he righteously bit in response to provocation — a type of *automorphosis* (viewing the animal on its own terms, rather than treating it as a human or as a machine). The juxtaposition of "reasonable" with "dog," however, releases a rather astounding compliment — i.e., in the eyes of the law, a particular dog may *reason*. But not just that. For this standard assumes not that the incident dog can rationalize, but further that the species *canis lupus* is generally capable of reasoning. Furthermore, it assumes that among all canids, a consensus of appropriate perception and reaction can be found.

Applied to a specific dog bite situation, however, the standard questionably supplants human rationality for dog rationality. "The courts have consistently pointed out that it is not the view of the person provoking the dog that must be considered, but rather it is the reasonableness of the dog's response to the action in question that actually determines whether provocation exists." *Kirkham v. Will*, 724 N.E.2d 1062, 1065 (Ill. App. Ct. 2000). After citing numerous published Illinois opinions, the court adds, "These cases demonstrate that previous courts have focused on provocation from the perspective of the animal. The cases tend to focus on how an average dog, neither unusually aggressive nor unusually docile, would react to an alleged act of provocation." *Id.*, at 1066–67. The Illinois Court of Appeals affirmed the "reasonable dog" instruction given to the jury, affirming the circuit judge's instruction, "When I use the phrase [']to provoke['] or the word [']provoca-tion,['] I mean any action or activity, whether intentional or unintentional, which would be reasonably expected to cause a normal dog in similar circumstances to react in a manner similar to that shown by the evidence." *Id.*, at 1067 (court noting this definition is accurate in accounting for what a person would "reasonably expect" and "how a normal dog would react" but cautioning that the court expressed no view on the propriety of such an instruction "when the case involves an animal known to have an unusual and dangerous nature.")

But how does one determine "how a normal dog would react," or really, *should* react? Does this "reasonable dog" standard rely upon a person of average intelligence whose knowledge of dog behavior comes from watching Cesar Milan, to conclude, rightly or wrongly, whether a dog was actually provoked, instead of whether the dog was reasonably defending itself under the circumstances. Does the standard strive to unveil the *truth* of the matter or, instead, reach conclusions based on bias, ignorance, speculation, and otherwise inadmissible testimony not grounded in viable scientific methodology? Unless the "reasonable person" has insight into canine behavior, it follows that expert testimony is the best approach. Compare ER 701 (lay opinion admissible if "helpful to a clear understanding of his testimony or the determination of a fact in issue") with ER 702 (where scientific or specialized knowledge will assist trier of fact to understand evidence or decide fact in issue, qualified expert may testify). What credentials does a "reasonable person" have, without training in dog behavior, and what evidentiary foundations underlie the conclusion of that "reasonable person" that the dog was, in fact, defending himself from an actual assault? If based on observing the dog, how does one accurately interpret those observations? Through the filter of a layperson attempting to translate the actions of another species and risk anthropomorphic error? How can the court ensure that this "reasonable person" has reached a sound automorphic conclusion as to the dog's intentionality (i.e., defending or attacking)? In other words, how can a person reliably get into a dog's head and properly judge potentially exculpatory behavior (as to both the dog *and* owner)?

Such questions reveal an undeniable truth: To understand animal law, one must understand animals. That commitment may require a firm grasp of the subject animal's anatomy, physiology, and psychology, as well as how she is perceived by human society and within religious constructs.

The animal law hermeneutic pays close attention to the impact legal homocentricity has procedurally, substantively, evidentially, psycholegally, and ethically.

1. Procedural

Hypothetical: Monroe Correctional Complex inmate Shawn Greenhalgh worried about Screech, a house sparrow accidentally confined within his cell block. Screech somehow entered the Complex in November 2010. Greenhalgh claimed guards hit Screech with a toilet paper roll and struck him with an industrial rubber band, causing him to temporarily lose consciousness. Other offenders joined in the bird's abuse. No doubt due to his will to live and Greenhalgh's humanity, Screech survived the hostile prison environment for nearly half a year. Greenhalgh explained that the two became comrades, with Screech entering his cell, resting on the empty upper bunk therein, or perching on the bars in observation of his perhaps sole companion. Greenhalgh fed Screech, who acquired his name due to a persistent desire for friendly human interaction — quietly chirping in his ear to the point of screeching when tired of being ignored. Greenhalgh understood (perhaps better than most) that Screech should be set free and not sentenced to an indeterminate period of incarceration. He only desired that Screech be humanely captured and released to his natural environment. Greenhalgh feared that a band of prison employees, at the direction of MCC management, intended to kill Screech.

Screech's friend on the "inside" now had many more on the "outside." As an attorney counseling Greenhalgh, how would you take steps to remedy Screech's predicament? How do you confirm that such a "hit squad" exists, terminate any such activity, investigate the history of animal abuse by offenders and staff, take punitive action, and coordinate efforts to humanely liberate this bird from an unnatural environment? Could you ensure that Screech would not endure a fate similar to that of a female cat and her five kittens at Sing Sing Correctional Facility in Ossining, and guarantee the prosecution of those responsible, as occurred in the case of Corrections Sgt. Ronald A. Hunlock, whom the Westchester County district attorney charged with aggravated cruelty to animals? *Corrections Sergeant accused of Killing Five Kittens at Sing Sing; Faces Felony Charge under State's 1999 "Buster's Law" to Protect Animals*, Mar. 29, 2001, N.Y. Dept. Corr. Services, www.doccs.ny.gov/PressRel/2001/hunlock1.html.

Aside from reporting the matter to the Monroe Animal Control/Police Department, Snohomish County Prosecuting Attorney's Office, Seattle Post-Intelligencer, Seattle Audubon Society, and media, might you bring a temporary restraining order and "freedom writ" action styled after a writ of *habeas corpus* or writ of *de homine replegiando* on behalf of Screech? *See* Steven M. Wise, *The Entitlement of Chimpanzees to the Common Law Writs of Habeas Corpus and De Homine Replegiando*, 37 GOLDEN GATE U. L. REV. 219 (2007). What if he were a protected migratory bird species, or endangered or threatened species under the state and federal endangered species acts? Could health codes compel humane removal of Screech to protect inmates and correctional officers? But more critically, would Greenhalgh have standing to speak for Screech as his owner, caretaker, next friend, or other type of spokesperson when Screech himself may suffer from legal invisibility?

Gaining judicial audience to hear an animal's grievance requires the proverbial "foot in the door" or procedural vehicle. Various mechanisms have been utilized, such as the Administrative Procedure Act, § 702, citizen suit provisions, taxpayer standing, private prosecution, writs of habeas corpus, and writ *de homine repligiando*.

2. Substantive

Animal law encompasses every dispute or legal transaction where the nature of the animal — genetic, phenotypic/morphological, behavioral, evolutionary, social significance or totemistic/religious value, ecosystemic role, or impact — dictates or guides the outcome or handling of the matter. Admittedly, animal law touches many substantive legal disciplines, including some less anticipated, such as intellectual property (patenting life forms and chimerae), bankruptcy (nondischargeability of debts related to dogfighting and cats who allegedly vomit on carpet by command), and tax law (deductions for service animal veterinary bills and food, and for unreimbursed volunteer expenses of a cat fosterer). The more common areas include custodial interference (lost-and-found, liens, dissolution, committed intimate relationship, domestic violence), injury and death (injury to animals by animals, injury to animals by humans, constitutional injury arising from harm to animals (e.g., 42 U.S.C. § 1983), veterinary malpractice, injury to humans by animals), cruelty and neglect, rights (service animal access, landlord/tenant and condominium/homeowners association challenges with respect to number, weight, breed, and type of animals permitted on premises notwithstanding fair housing laws, dangerous dog appeals and other administrative actions changing the legal classification of an animal), estate planning (e.g., animal trusts), commercial transactions (product liability, consumer protection, and puppy lemon laws), and several others.

According to the American Veterinary Medical Association, 2012 U.S. PET OWNERSHIP & DEMOGRAPHICS SOURCEBOOK, 36.5% and 30.4% of all American households care for at least one dog or cat, respectively. The total number of dogs and cats in American households exceeds 144.1 million. The American Pet Products Association's 2011-2012 National Pet Owners Survey concluded that 62% of all American households have an animal companion. The APPA estimates that nearly $53 billion will be spent on American animal companions in 2012: $20.46 billion on food, $12.56 billion on supplies/OTC medicine, $13.59 billion in veterinary care, $2.15 billion in live animal purchases, and $4.11 billion on services like grooming and boarding. Add more than 11 million birds and seven million horses and you get a sense of the degree to which animals command our attention day-to-day, creating legal problems in virtually every nook and cranny where an animal interacts materially with another animal or human. Dwarfing this number, of course, are the billions of chickens, turkeys, bovines, pigs, and other farmed animals raised, transported, and slaughtered each year but who figure prominently in nearly every aspect of our lives, whether we are vegan, vegetarian, or omnivorous. The following chapters will explore the most common substantive aspects of animal law.

3.   Evidentiary

Evidentiary problems pertaining to animals fall into five categories: animal testimonial evidence, animal identification evidence, animal-related discovery issues, animals as evidence proper, and animal experts.

a.   Animal Testimonial Evidence

Whether the product of passion (per Descartes) or reason (per Voltaire), animals engage in inter- and intraspecies communication. When germane to a legal dispute, such articulations, gestures, and actions may come into evidence. How should courts handle their admission?

i.   Prior Animal Bad Acts

Propensity evidence, while in unspoken conflict with the character evidence rule, is routinely relied upon by courts of law when evaluating the conduct of a nonhuman animal. Although evidence rules have always held that a person's intent should be determined primarily from her present conduct, an animal's intent must often be determined from past conduct, notwithstanding the contradictory, scientific testimony of animal ethologists. Strict common law liability for dog bites requires an inquiry into the vicious predisposition of the defendant's animal. *Johnston v. Ohls*, 457 P.2d 194 (Wash. 1969); *see also Johnson v. Lindley*, 41 F. Supp. 2d 1021 (D. Neb. 1999) (dog's behavior prior to vehicular collision relevant, and evidence of dog's playfulness or maliciousness relevant to canine *mens rea*). A few renegade courts have gone so far as to assume that a dog's lineage completely dictates and predicts its behavior, declaring certain breeds "innately vicious," including the German Shepherd. *Ford v. Steindon*, 232 N.Y.S.2d 473 (1962). Of course, most courts embrace the common law rule that dogs are presumptively good, regardless of breed. *See Cook v. Whitsell-Sherman*, 796 N.E.2d 271 (Ind. 2003):

> The common law presumes that all dogs, regardless of breed or size, are harmless. *Poznanski v. Horvath*, 788 N.E.2d 1255, 1257 (Ind. 2003); *Ross v. Lowe*, 619 N.E.2d 911, 914 (Ind. 1993). This presumption can be overcome by evidence of a known vicious or dangerous propensity of the particular dog. *Ross*, 619 N.E.2d at 914.

Id., at 275. FRE 404 applies to *persons*, not nonhuman animals. Yet, in evaluating whether a dog reasonably perceived an actual assault on her, her owner, or her family members, thereby placing provocation at issue, her pre-incident behavior may have probative value. A dog's prior interactions in various contexts may also prove that the dog acted in conformity with that behavior on the occasion in question. In other words, they may provide inculpatory or exculpatory pieces of propensity evidence. They might also indicate behavioral instability or psychological soundness, cognitive defect or integrity, or shade the manner in which the dog perceives the world around her. Mining the past for evidentiary gems favoring the accused animal or disfavoring the victim animal will no doubt be met with an objection under FRE 404(a)(1) and FRE 404(a)(2), respectively, while those disfavoring the accused animal may be met with an FRE 404(b) objection, the rule prohibiting reference to prior "crimes, wrongs, or acts."

But does FRE 404 even apply to animals? In FRE 404(a) speaking of a "person's character or a trait of character" preceding the labels "accused," "victim," and "witness," evidently not. But what evidentiary rules should apply when an animal's character or trait of character, whether belonging to the accused or victim, is at issue? Prior history may prove whether the dog was "hard-wired" to react this way or, if absent, arose from an irregularity or unforeseeable idiosyncrasy — in other words, a response more probably explained as exceptional and provoked rather than par for this animal's psyche. By analogy, consider FRE 404(a)(1). Though invoked in the criminal setting, the rule allows evidence of a pertinent trait of character of the accused offered by the accused, or by the prosecution to rebut same, to prove action in conformity therewith on a particular occasion. Though not human, a dog may stand accused of inflicting severe injury through an unprovoked bite. Provocation examines the reasonableness of a particular dog's reaction to the incident stimulus, which in turn may depend on the dog's history of reaction (or nonreaction) to different stimuli. Introducing evidence of the dog's gentle and nonaggressive character may prove that the circumstances caused the dog to behave out of character in a manner that the law excuses or justifies. *See Brown v. Eberly*, 2002 U.S. Dist. LEXIS 22012 (E.D. Pa. Nov. 14, 2002) (allowing evidence of dog's friendly past behavior over objection under FRE 404, citing *Hood v. Hagler*, 606 P.2d 548, 551–52 (Okla. 1979), *Forsythe v. Kluckhohn*, 142 N.W. 225 (Iowa 1913), *Stone v. Pendleton*, 43 A. 643 (R.I. 1899); 1A Wigmore, Evidence § 68a (Tillers rev. 1983)).[12]

By further analogy, FRE 404(a)(2) allows the accused to offer evidence of a pertinent trait of character of the victim, or by the prosecution to rebut such evidence. Such efforts are often ridiculed as a tactic to "blame the victim" in rape cases — the logic being that a victim's history of promiscuity makes consent on the incident date more probable (and constitutes a defense to the crime of rape) or that her dress and sexual predisposition warranted the sexual assault (i.e., somehow the victim "asked for it"). They also no doubt attempt to prejudice the jury against the victim based on moral, not legal, judgments. Evidentiary rape shield laws, such as FRE 412, seek to restrict such character evidence. In animal cases, evidence that a human bite victim would coax dogs off their property by walking back and forth in front of their home, making strange noises and body movements calculated to agitate, might be introduced to prove a character of historical provocation and taunting or even assumption of the risk of injury.

The rule may also apply to a Chihuahua suffering from "small dog syndrome" — i.e., uncorrected dominance behaviors resulting from mistaking and encouraging aggressive and provocative traits as "cute" — to prove that she acted in conformity with the syndrome on the date in question. On the other hand, in the proper case, FRE 404(a)(2) also allows the prosecution to offer evidence of the victim's character trait of peacefulness in a homicide case to rebut evidence that the victim was the first aggressor. Thus, if a large dog kills a small dog, the absence of "small dog syndrome" may prove judicious.

The incident dog's history also provides a means to assess whether the situational reaction of "the animal" was the result of a "perfect storm" of stacked triggers. Not only will prior encounters with people and animals in different settings allow germane comparison and contrast, but they bring the details of the incident into proper focus. For instance, the fact finder will be equipped to determine whether this incident stands out as unique or innate, whether it arose from mischievousness, playfulness, or true unbridled aggression. It will allow her to construe the absence of prior aggressive behavior as evidence that this particular response was out of character and, thus, due to a stimulus exempt by code or common law.

---

[12] While the court permitted introduction of the dog Immi's prior good acts, it also refused to admit the shooting Officer Eberly's prior bad acts, specifically that he shot and killed four dogs in the past. *Id.*, citing *Brown v. Muhlenberg Tsp.*, 269 F.3d 205, 217 (3d Cir. 2001).

Remember that a dog who displayed no unprovoked aggression in prior interactions with people and animals is presumed a "good dog" until proven otherwise. *See Drake v. Dean*, 15 Cal. App. 4th 915 (1993) ("[Because] [t]he great majority of dogs are harmless . . . the possession of characteristics dangerous to mankind . . . is properly regarded as abnormal to them." (citing Rest. 2nd Torts § 509, cmt. f); "[A] dog's bad character or evil disposition is not presumed . . . . A dog is presumed to be tame, docile and harmless until the contrary appears.") Thus, it stands to reason that the dog owner should be permitted to introduce pre-incident evidence to demonstrate the accused's character of tameness, lack of vicious propensity, and absence of unprovoked aggression to prove conformity therewith. *See also* ER 404(b) (allowing prior act evidence to prove intent (or lack thereof), here meaning intent to inflict harm without provocation).

ii.   Animal Habit

Owing to the similarity between a character trait and a habit or routine practice, FRE 406 — providing that evidence of a person's habit or an organization's routine practice may be admitted to prove that on a particular occasion the person or organization acted in accordance with same — bears mention as well as FRE 404. MCCORMICK ON EVIDENCE describes the distinction as follows:

> Character and habit are close akin. Character is a generalized description of one's disposition, or of one's disposition in respect to a general trait, such as honesty, temperance, or peacefulness. 'Habit,' in modern usage, both lay and psychological, is more specific. It describes one's regular response to a repeated specific situation. If we speak of character for care, we think of the person's tendency to act prudently in all the varying situations of life, in business, family life, in handling automobiles and in walking across the street. A habit, on the other hand, is the person's regular practice of meeting a particular kind of situation with a specific type of conduct, such as the habit of going down a particular stairway two stairs at a time, or of giving the hand-signal for a left turn, or of alighting from railway cars while they are moving. The doing of the habitual acts may become semi-automatic.

§ 162, p. 340.

> Character may be thought of as the sum of one's habits though doubtless it is more than this. But unquestionably the uniformity of one's response to habit is far greater than the consistency with which one's conduct conforms to character or disposition. Even though character comes in only exceptionally as evidence of an act, surely any sensible man in investigating whether X did a particular act would be greatly helped in his inquiry by evidence as to whether he was in the habit of doing it.

§ 162, p. 341. What does MCCORMICK mean for animals?

The following example may assist the reader. In a case that factually caricatures pit bull stereotypes, *Rosenberry v. Evans*, 48 A.3d 1255 (Pa. Super. Ct. 2012), a mother sued a landlord for negligently permitting a spastic pit bull, who had just whelped a litter, to inflict a bite that removed part of her child's nose. "By all accounts, the bite herein was involuntary and nonaggressive." *Id.*, at 1259. Raven, the dog who bit 10-year-old Alexander Prince, "had a tic, or an involuntary spasm, which intermittently caused it to clench its teeth in a biting motion," a characteristic displayed from puppyhood. *Id.*, at 1260. Finding fact issues existed as to whether the tic qualified as a dangerous propensity, the Pennsylvania Superior Court nonetheless affirmed dismissal of all claims as a matter of law since Rosenberry could not prove that the landlord had actual knowledge of Raven's muscle spasm or other dangerous propensity, nor sufficient control over the leased premises to prevent injury. Specifically, "knowledge of a dog's clenching issue is not equivalent to actual knowledge of a dangerous propensity." *Id.*, at 1262. *Rosenberry* demonstrates how an involuntary, automatic act may qualify as animal habit evidence that, in this instance at least, defends against a claim of vicious propensity.

Yet, because FRE 404 does not apply to animals on its face (unless "person" means legal, not natural, person, and legislatures or courts bestow legal personhood to nonhumans), FRE 406 will not either. Remember also that the law renders moot many FRE 404- and FRE 406-type objections by making them elements of liability. Courts routinely look backward in time to test the presence or absence of vicious propensity that, in turn, creates strict or absolute civil liability.[13] Because FRE 404 is accused- or victim-specific, and FRE 406 speaks only to persons or organizations, it follows that neither common law nor FRE 404 would endorse introduction of evidence of the accused or victim's race or sex to prove action in conformity with a putative race- or sex-based trait of character. Indeed, such an argument would be met with extreme excoriation. Yet it is made frequently with respect to dogs and breed, as discussed in later sections.

iii.   Animal Experiments

Occasionally, a party will perform a test to summon and channel an animal's "testimony." Or an expert will rely upon an animal to supply data, voluntarily (vocal, as in barking; non-vocal, as in pointing or signaling) or involuntarily (as in the case of the animal sentinel, the proverbial "canary in the coal mine," frequently used to test for toxicity and pollution due to the species' greater sensitivity to the hazard) to opine on a relevant topic. Do the rules of evidence permit these animal utterances or communications if offered via an expert or lay witness?

FRE 801, the hearsay rule, prevents admission of a statement by an out-of-court declarant offered to prove the truth of the matter asserted. Will the "truth" of a matter asserted by a "nonhuman" implicate the hearsay rule, assuming that animals become legal persons? Unless formally trained in sign language or informal gestural expression, or using mimicry to duplicate the human voice, most nonhumans will speak their minds through vocalization that cannot be indexed by some scale of veracity. A grunt, bark, whine, low, mew, screech, purr, trill, or acoustically distinct call does not necessarily assert a fact. Scientific debate also

---

[13] *See* Adam P. Karp, *Causes of Action for Loss of or Injury to an Animal by an Animal* , 38 COA 2D 281 (2008) (noting the majority common law rule that strict liability extends to dog owners or keepers who know or reasonably should know that the dog has vicious propensities likely to cause injury of the type complained of, and have a duty to adequately confine or kill the dog; failure to do so will subject the owner to prima facie liability without proof of negligence).

exists on the question of whether animals make sounds to communicate or merely instinctually (reminiscent of the excited utterance exception to the hearsay rule). When a beaver slaps her tail on the water, a chickadee chirps at a homeowner who fails to refill the bird feeder, a bullfrog roars during breeding season, or coyotes howl along with a passing ambulance sounding its siren, are the animals saying, "Beware of an intruder!," "I'm hungry. Add more seed!," "I am in the mood for love," and "Join our pack. We are here!"?

If a human attempts to reference such vocalizations in order to explain his or another's behavior, such as to destroy an alibi by tying a person to a scene, or to demonstrate notice for purposes of establishing civil liability, how does the court ensure that the principles underlying the hearsay rule carry through to nonhuman declarants? Remember that the hearsay rule seeks to mitigate the unreliability of human assertions, fallibility of human memory, and risk of conjecture or outright fabrication by limiting the introduction of hearsay through recognized exceptions or requiring in-court, under-oath testimony subject to cross-examination. As discussed herein, however, animals may not understand (or need to understand) the oath, may not prove competent to testify, and cannot be meaningfully cross-examined. So how should these utterances be reconciled?

Only if the animal utterance describes an observed incident might it qualify. Animals may encode semantic (informational) or aesthetic (sensory or emotional) data that, through a biologist's expert testimony, is capable of human translation, but according to one author, the caller does not, "in the human sense," intend to provide such rich information. For instance, certain monkeys have a palette of oral warnings that vary depending on which predator lurks nearby and the degree of urgency accompanying him. *See* Seyfarth RM & Cheney DL, *Meaning and Emotion in Animal Vocalizations*, 1000 ANN. N. Y. ACAD. SCI. 32-55 (2003). And, of course, animal vocalizations may have collateral effects on the "eavesdropping" human listener depending on whether a positive or negative valence is given to it. Such "human cerebral response" may dictate or explain why a person did what he did on a particular occasion — referencing the animal's speech and potentially implicating the hearsay objection. *See* Pascal Belin et al., *Human Cerebral Response to Animal Affective Vocalizations*, 275 (1634) PROC. R. SOC. B. 473-481 (2008).

Boise lawyer Heather Cunningham experienced a once-in-a-lifetime phenomenon when she stood no more than 10 feet away from an elephant who had just given birth in the wild. The mother's trumpeting a baby announcement over several acres resulted in a ground-thundering response as dozens of the parade came to greet the calf one by one. Would such announcement, "I just had a baby. Come meet her," if offered for the truth of the matter asserted, be hearsay?

On April 24, 2006, Colleen Edwards pointed a loaded Taurus .40 cal. with rounds chambered at two construction workers preparing to excavate land she believed contained ancestral Native American remains, protected from disinterment or disturbance by state law. Accusing them of trespassing and placing them under citizen arrest, she not only had the pistol aimed and prepared to fire, but also wore a ballistics vest and across her chest an extra .40 cal. magazine with nine bullets and a disposable camera. The next day, the Kitsap County Prosecutor's Office charged her with felony assault in the second degree. On Nov. 5, 2008, on day five of a nine-day jury trial in *State v. Colleen Mulvihill Edwards*, Kitsap Cy. Sup. Ct. No. 06-1-00616-8, where Ms. Edwards represented herself pro se, an unanticipated animal law situation unfolded. Following the lunch break for that day, Ms. Edwards notified the court of her intention to call Anthony O'Grady to testify:

THE COURT: All right. Then, this afternoon we have Mr. O'Grady and Dr. Irish; is that right?

MS. EDWARDS: Yes.

THE COURT: And Mr. O'Grady is here?

MS. EDWARDS: Mr. O'Grady — and you may not like this, but Mr. O'Grady is in the courtroom. Mr. O'Grady is my service dog, and he is going to testify on the ability of a dog to do a cadaver scent by demonstration.

THE COURT: Ms. Edwards, you're right, I'm not happy with that. I think that's a bit of a deceit on the Court at this point. . . .

MR. ENRIGHT: . . . And then with — with Mr. O'Grady, I would object to having a dog testify, or any demonstrations by a dog. I don't believe that that has any relevance to this case.

THE COURT: . . . Now let's talk about the dog, Tony. The State has objected to that. What's your response, Ms. Edwards?

MS. EDWARDS: My response would be law enforcement dogs have a history of testifying and demonstrating in courts. It is more illustrative, not an evidentiary demonstration. It is usually done by video-tape, but there is a motion in limine about videotaping dog training, so my — I would like to have the jury understand that a dog can find remains, and that's really all I need to demonstrate. If you — and, um, those remains were found by dog teams. I could do that kind of testimony on my own testimony as well. So I could handle it as a handler.

THE COURT: There will be no demonstration by the listed witness, Anthony Ohrady.

MS. EDWARDS: Okay. I'll object for the record, but I understand your ruling.[14]

On Nov. 13, 2008, a 12-person jury unanimously found her guilty as charged. Was Judge Anna M. Laurie's ruling preventing O'Grady from "testifying" sound?

Questions, commands, threats, promises, words in a document carrying independent legal significance, nonassertive conduct, and even signs may not constitute hearsay unless they relate an observation by an out-of-court declarant. Thus, begging, barking aggressively as a prelude to an attack or to tell a person to back away, and emitting an alarm call would not qualify as hearsay. FRE 801 clearly applies to utterances by a "person." Thus, nothing "said" by an animal or machine

---

[14] Reported by superior court official Crystal R. McAuliffe, RPR with author's change of "Ohrady" to "O'Grady" based on clerk's minute entries. It is likely the "G" was silent.

can be regarded as hearsay. MUELLER & KIRKPATRICK, 4 FEDERAL EVIDENCE § 380 (2d ed.) (hearsay). Instead, courts purport to examine animal statements in Cartesian manner, invoking FRE 901(b)(9) to test them under the authenticity rule, rather than hearsay rule.

Machine statements, while legitimately invoking hearsay concerns, require the proponent of the statement to demonstrate a proper foundation that the machine is reliable, correctly calibrated, and that both the input and output were accurately assimilated. The concept of "garbage in, garbage out" (GIGO) applies with special force to Breathalyzers, speed radars, alarm clocks, thermometers, tape recorders, and other computer-generated documents. Although machine statements reflect human design and input, animals are not "designed" in the same way. It is for this reason that the hearsay issues involving animal statements, such as they arise, may not be analyzed in the same successful fashion as one might evaluate machine statements. Our Cartesian view of animals as machines having been discredited centuries ago, the legal procedures used to sieve this evidence require special attention.

Describing attempts to decide whether to admit animal statements under FRE 801 as "at best fatuous," Mueller and Kirkpatrick note that admissibility more frequently turns on "authenticating" the evidence under FRE 901(b)(9). FRE 901(b)(9) speaks to evidence "describing a process or system used to produce a result and showing that the process or system produces an accurate result." Though normally applied in the case of machines, the following decisions provide some guidance for applying ER 901. *U.S. v. Khorozian*, 333 F.3d 498, 506 (3d Cir. 2003) (fax machine's automatic date-stamp on each transmission was not hearsay); *U.S. v. Cowley*, 720 F.2d 1037, 1044 (9th Cir. 1983) (machine-affixed postmark not hearsay). In animal cases, dog tracking or sniffing evidence is analyzed under this authenticating rubric. *See U.S. v. Place*, 462 U.S. 696 (1983).

This approach requires additional scrutiny when animals have been *trained* to communicate assertively with humans, so that their vocal and non-vocal statements do have an intended meaning as in the case of a scent-detecting dog. One may conceptualize such revelatory animal statements like a gas detector used by a firefighter to test the ambient levels of carbon monoxide or hydrogen sulfide, a thermographic or infrared camera to report surface temperatures of an object, or even a flashlight that illuminates a scene. In so doing, the animal is no longer a "person" giving a "statement," but a tool wielded aptly by an expert witness to allow her to reliably opine. On the other hand, sometimes animals are neither trained to communicate nor are their communications logged by eavesdroppers. Instead, individuals may expose an animal to different stimuli and place them in distinct situations to observe, quantify, and interpret their reactions after an incident at bar to prove identity, ownership, or even guilt. In so doing, one seeks to verify character or habit, whether long- or short-term.

For instance, in *State v. Staveneau*, 197 N.W. 667 (Minn. 1924), the Supreme Court of Minnesota held that it was permissible to prove theft by Walter Staveneau by having Mrs. Adams, the victim, serenade her alleged pet hen by singing into the defendant's chicken house and waiting for the bird to come to her voice. However, due to an additional foundationless experiment, the Court reversed, summarizing, in relevant part to this section, its holding as follows:

> Where there is testimony that a certain animal has acquired the habit of recognizing a person and evidencing such recognition, it is proper, when the identity of the animal is in issue, to receive evidence as to the conduct of such animal toward that person.

> But it is improper to receive evidence of experiments or tests with animals to prove identity, where there is no foundation laid that those animals have acquired certain fixed traits or habits in respect to the subject of the test so that identity might be revealed with some certainty.

Id., at 667. To prove theft, over defense counsel's objection, the trial court let the prosecutor explain that one of her Rhode Island Reds "was a pet hen of Mrs. Adams," who "would come at her call and walk around her 'singing.' " *Id.*, at 668. The state then allowed Mrs. Adams to show how the hen acted and sang when she came to defendant's chicken house and called. Owing to the proper foundation, the appellate court approved this testimony because:

> The peculiar trait or habit of this particular hen had been proven. Animals do recognize their keepers. And it was shown that this hen which Mrs. Adams identified had, while under Mrs. Adams' care previous to the theft, developed a marked preference for her and a distinctive manner in which to give vent to such preference or recognition.

Id., at 668. While the court found this "singing" evidence properly founded,[15] it ordered a new trial when the state attempted to proffer evidence of an animal experiment, as described below:

> Against objection, evidence was received as to an experiment or test made with the nine chickens which Mrs. Adams identified as hers among the flock in defendant's chicken house. Mr. Adams proposed the test to defendant, but he declined to participate therein or be bound thereby. The test was this: About sunset these nine chickens were taken in crates to the Adams' farm and liberated about 55 feet south of the chicken house. They fed and scratched around for ten minutes or so working up toward the chicken house, and then, instead of seeking entrance from the front or south side, they went around to the east and entered through a small slide door at the corner where Mrs. Adam's chickens before the theft were wont to enter. A

---

[15] An in-court attempt to permit a parrot to so "give vent" while "under close scrutiny" and while "called upon . . . to indicate by name or mannerism an affinity to either of the claimed owner," bore no fruit for, "Alas, the parrot stood mute." *Conti v. ASPCA*, 77 Misc. 2d 61 (N.Y. Civ. Ct. 1974). In another custody dispute over a bird, David DeGroff wanted to "depose" an African Grey to prove identity. While FRCP 30 permits the taking of oral deposition of persons only, in essence Mr. DeGroff wished to perform a test the results of which would corroborate his extensive efforts to teach mimicry and thereby prove his ownership. *See A LouLou of a Case*, 3 No. 5 ABA Journal E-Report 6 (Feb. 2004). That University of Washington Professor Pepperberg described how Greys can whistle Brahms' Lullaby, offer a post-burp "excuse me," and have the intelligence of a four or six year old human raises such evidentiary questions as witness competency and perhaps even hearsay. For instance, if a homicide victim attempted to reveal the identity of the murderer (call him John) through her African Grey parrot, who was with her before she died, would an attempt to elicit from the parrot a statement, "John killed me!" be admissible, whether or not nobody had ever heard that phrase uttered by the bird before the date of her murder?

> half an hour after the first experiment, two of the chickens were again taken out and liberated at the same place. In four minutes they were back in the chicken house. It is sought to sustain the ruling upon the old saw that 'chickens come home to roost,' and the bloodhound cases. But all ancient sayings are not approved legal maxims, nor do they always express truths so generally accepted as to be a part of the common knowledge of which courts must take notice.

Id., at 668. The *Staveneau* court did not find sufficient foundation for this experiment and even took issue with a similar Vermont case, where the prosecution was allowed to show that a horse, driven by the accused on the date of arson, when driven along the same road, on his own accord, made a sharp turn into another road and to a place where the accused dismounted to set fire to a building. The court held that, "We cannot affirm that an animal's conduct is ruled by one or two of its prior experiences." *Id.* Stating that "all ancient sayings are not approved legal maxims," the appellate court refused to sanction the "chickens come home to roost" experiment:

> While it is true that some individual of a species often exhibits wonderful ability in finding its way home, still as to most of the domesticated animals there is no such certainty of uniform conduct that human guilt or innocence should be determined by tests with them such as here made. Every automobile driver would say that no animal displays less sense of the location of its home and place of safety in face of danger than a chicken. If the chickens experimented with were Mrs. Adams', they were accustomed to spend the night in a chicken house, and had done so with equal readiness in three different localities within the period of a few weeks; and again, if the chickens were defendant's they were equally accustomed to enter a chicken house at night. It may be readily admitted that there is probative value in tests of the sort here used. But the danger is that it may be greatly overrated by a jury, each member of which may recall some instance where some animal exhibited traits similar to that shown by the test. If experiments like the ones here may be received in evidence, the freak act of some animal, the motives of which cannot be inquired into, may often serve to convict men of heinous crimes. When animals are allowed to take the witness stand, so to speak, their testimony should be limited to those matters wherein human knowledge and experience have ascertained that they therein habitually reveal the truth; such for instance as that a colt will know and follow its dam (*Miller v. Territory,* 9 Ariz. 231, 80 Pac. 321), or that an adult dog will recognize and cling to a master who has had him under control for some considerable time, or where it is proven that a horse, or an ox has been trained to go to its stall in a barn so that a fixed habit has been acquired so to do. Of course, tests or experiments with inanimate objects stand upon a different basis. We are of opinion that no proper foundation was laid for the reception of the experiments in question, and for that error there must be a new trial.

Id., at 669; *see also Cohen v. Rodenbaugh,* 162 F. Supp. 748 (D.C. Pa. 1957) (holding that defendant's testimony that day before accident, horse threw a named woman, was not admissible to show habit of kicking, particularly since "even the most tranquil horse may on occasion give a kick"); *Broderick v. Higginson*, 48 N.E. 269 (Mass. 1897) ("It is a familiar fact that animals are more likely to act in a certain way at a particular time if the action is in accordance with their established habit or usual conduct than if it is not. There is a probability that an animal will act as he is accustomed to act under like circumstances. For this reason, when disputes have arisen in regard to the conduct of an animal, evidence of his habits in that particular has often been received.").

Elsewhere in this opinion, the court discusses bloodhound tracking cases to emphasize that the breed's character for trailing alone does not establish sufficient foundation to admit the hound's results in a criminal case. Training and demonstrated ability must complement innate talent particularly where imprisonment is at stake. Nearly a century later, the legal foundation required for scent evidence has not significantly changed by requiring proof of the dog's training and reliability in identifying contraband, qualifications of the handler, and circumstances surrounding the search. *See U.S. v. Lopez*, 380 F.3d 538 (1st Cir. 2004) (drug dog reliability based on handler's testimony of certification at time of search and no false indications ever given). Another example of animal habit evidence involves prosecution for possession of stolen property. In *State v. McAteer*, 288 N.W. 72 (Iowa 1939), evidence that a cow returned to the prosecutor's premises, entered the barn, and placed her head in a stanchion, and demonstrated familiarity with a water tank by pushing a heavy swing door, proved her identity as owned by the prosecutor.

How does one gain access to the animal to perform this test? It seems most appropriate to analyze these cases under the rubric of FRCP 34, which permits inspection, testing, and sampling of tangible things. The scope and nature of the inspection (e.g., mere observation by animal behaviorist or interaction with stimuli?), as well as degree of interference (e.g., would taking blood or some other invasive action that might cause pain and discomfort be permissible?) and impact on privacy interests (e.g., will the examination take place in the party's home, or will it require the party's presence or participation for purposes of examination?), require further examination because the FRCP 34 examination could become more analogous to a physical or mental examination of FRCP 35.

FRCP 34 requires a balancing between the benefit to the requester and burden to the resister, even in the absence of a protective order. *Gillett v. Conner*, 133 P.3d 960, 963 (Wash. Ct. App. 2006); Wash. Civ. Rule 26(b)(1). In *Gillett*, the Court of Appeals reversed and vacated the order compelling the defendants to allow the plaintiffs to photograph and test every item inside their home in pursuit of a civil nuisance claim. In fashioning such an order in an animal case, although factually novel, the balancing framework exists and should consider the privacy interests (such as they may be delineated) of the nonhuman animal, as well as the party who owns or cares for the animal.

iv.   Animal Studies

The premise that drug, toxin, and cosmetic safety or harm, proven by a wide range of involuntary and frequently cruel laboratory tests and studies on nonhuman animals, will predict the same in *humans* assuredly presents an animal law evidentiary issue, albeit once removed from its more obvious and intended application of determining how the substance affects *nonhuman* animal physiology. Irritation studies such as the Draize eye test are conducted by placing powder or liquid into a restrained rabbit's eye and observing the effects over a multi-day period. *See Hardy v. Proctor & Gamble Mfg. Co.*, 209 F.2d 124 (5th Cir. 1954) (plaintiff's experts conducted Draize tests to prove that detergent caused blindness in rabbits when left on eyes for 48 hours, avoiding directed verdict for defendant in suit over plaintiff's eye injuries). Toxicological studies range from acute exposures to determine what dose will kill half the test subjects (LD-50), while others follow the subject for life to assess teratogenicity and carcinogenicity. Indeed, animal testing figured prominently in the Bendectin birth defect litigation.

Using one species as a modeling platform for another compels adherence to sound methodological protocols in performing the test itself and calculating statistically significant outcomes for the tested species (such as testing aircraft wing damage tolerances), but more importantly, it questions the fundamental propriety of extrapolating nonhuman results to make predictive statements about human beings (such as to predict spacecraft hull damage tolerances on reentry into Earth's atmosphere). Animal studies have proven unreliable, varying by environmental and other confounding conditions. *See* Jack L. Landau & W. Hugh O'Riordan, *Of Mice and Men: The Admissibility of Animal Studies to Prove Causation in Toxic Tort Litigation,* 25 IDAHO L. REV. 521, 539 (1989); *see also* CALABRESE, PRINCIPLES OF ANIMAL EXTRAPOLATION (1983).

Cases before *Daubert v. Merrell Dow Pharm.*, 509 U.S. 579 (1993), such as *In re "Agent Orange" Product Liability Litigation,* 611 F. Supp. 1223, 1241 (E.D.N.Y. 1985) (rejecting epidemiological studies involving animals exposed to dioxin), and *Lynch v. Richardson-Merrell, Inc.*, 830 F.2d 1190, 1196–97 (1st Cir. 1987) (rejecting *in vivo* and *in vitro* animal studies attempting to link Bendectin to birth defects in absence of epidemiological data) tended to hold that animal tests lacked reliability *per se* and could not prove that the suspected toxin or product caused plaintiff's injury absent corroborative human epidemiological studies. After *Daubert*, the door opened wider to animal test evidence and the problem of extrapolation across species became less insurmountable. In *In re Paoli Railroad Yard PCB Litigation,* 35 F.3d 717, 781 (3d Cir. 1994), the Third Circuit found the trial court abused its discretion by keeping out animal test evidence. It did so by distinguishing *Agent Orange* and *Lynch* by noting that the scientific community relied on animal tests, as did the EPA, to find that PCBs are probable human carcinogens, that epidemiological data were inconclusive, and that "animals react similarly to humans with respect to the chemical in question." However, the Supreme Court found no abuse of discretion in *General Electric Co. v. Joiner*, 522 U.S. 136 (1997), focusing not on the species disparity, but deeming the test unreliable on account of age and dose where massive doses of PCBs were given to infant mice while Joiner was an adult human exposed to a much smaller concentration. *Id.*, at 144. Studies involving direct injections of silicone into rats to prove alleged dangers of intact silicone implants in women, in the context of contradictory epidemiological studies, were deemed inadmissible in *Allison v. McGhan Medical Corp.*, 184 F.3d 1300 (11th Cir. 1999).

v. Subsequent Acts

The above discussion concerning retrospective behavior excites inquiry into prospective behavior. May a jury consider evidence of an animal's post-incident aggression? In *U.S. v. Mohr*, 318 F.3d 613 (4th Cir. 2003), a law enforcement officer was convicted of intentional misuse of a police dog in 1995. The trial court allowed the jury to consider two subsequent acts of releasing or threatening to improperly release her police dog in 1997 and 1998. The Fourth Circuit found this evidence relevant to the issue of improper deployment, necessary because probative of an essential element of the crime, reliable, and admissible under ER 403. It thus follows that in a civil suit for damages inflicted by a dog to a person in May 2012, for instance, evidence that the dog again similarly attacked in August 2012 and January 2013 might prove admissible.

Animal cases that permit evidence of subsequent conduct to show identity or vicious disposition and fixed habit include *Gordon v. Mackenzie*, S.C. (Scot.) 109 (1913), holding that evidence of attacks by a dog on people after the injury at bar showed the dog's vicious disposition. On the other hand, some courts hold that because the only relevant evidence pertains to what happened during or before the incident, post-incident viciousness will not aid plaintiff, and post-incident docility will not shield defendant. *Knickerbocker Ice Co. v. De Haas*, 1890 Ill. App. LEXIS 156 (Mar. 1890); *Lachenman v. Stice*, 838 N.E.2d 451, 464–65 (Ind. Ct. App. 2005); *Crance v. Sohanic*, 496 A.2d 1230, 1233 (Pa. Super. Ct. 1985) (evidence of dog's subsequent bites admissible in dogbite case to show whether defendant knew dog was vicious and would tend to show defendants *knew* the animal was prone to bite). To learn more about the legal implications of animal actions and conduct, see *Conduct and Actions of Animals or Fowls as Evidence*, 61 A.L.R. 888 (1929).

vi. Competency

Factfinding hinges on competent testimony, from which credibility determinations can be made, exhibits authenticated and foundations laid. Historically, only nonatheistic adults of sound mind, free of conviction for perjury or any felonious activity, and without interest in the litigation, were permitted to take the stand. Indeed, in *People v. Hall*, 4 Cal. 399, 399 (1854), the court held that persons of color could not testify for or against a European American. Over time, such restrictions have fallen away provided the witness takes an oath or affirms that she will testify truthfully and can offer testimony based on personal knowledge. *See* FRE 602, 603. Generally, every person is competent except as provided by rule or statute. FRE 601. When objections to competency are made, *voir dire* aims to confirm the witness's four capacities of observation, perception, recollection, and communication with honesty while appreciating the penalty for mendacity. Using interpreters to translate for a witness does not render the witness incompetent, however the interpreter is also bound by oath to "make a true translation" and possess suitable expert qualifications. FRE 604.

Hypothetically speaking, are nonhuman animals competent to testify? Could a prosecutor call an animal liberated from a research facility to testify as to the identity of an animal rights activist charged with breaking and entering? Angela Campbell examined the four standards for competency and found them applicable to certain nonhuman primates, including the use of an American Sign Language translator, in *Comment: Could a Chimpanzee or Bonobo Take the Stand?*, 8 ANIMAL L. 243, 252 (2002). While inquiry into the cognitive and communicative ability of nonhuman species has resulted in a prodigious body of scientific research, perhaps the greatest obstacle to nonhuman animal testimony lies in proving the animal's understanding of the consequence of lying. Campbell notes that a captive chimpanzee already suffers the penalty of imprisonment occasioning a perjury conviction, rendering the threat of violating the oath illusory.

But this begs the question of whether nonhuman animals have a fifth, and related, competency — i.e., the competency to lie. Answers may be found in the work of Amotz Zahavi and his "handicap principle," *The Cost of Honesty (Further Remarks on the Handicap Principle)*, J. THEOR. BIO. 67 (3): 603–605, gazelle stotting (spirited hopping behavior displayed to a predator to dissuade pursuit by signaling the gazelle's fitness to evade capture), counterfeit alarm calls (used by swallows and thrushes to dissuade infidelity), Møller, A.P., *Deceptive Use of Alarm Calls by Male Swallows Hirundo Rustica: A New Paternity Guard*, BEHAVIORAL ECOLOGY 1: 1–6 (1990) and Wickler, W., *Mimicry in Plants and Animals* at 108 (McGraw-Hill 1968); crustacean bluffing, *Intraspecific Deception by Bluffing: A Defense Strategy of Newly Molted Stomatopods*, 221 (4610) SCIENCE 558–560 (1983), and even Koko the Gorilla, born in 1971 at the San Francisco Zoo, best known for her ability to communicate in ASL and to have her own animal companion — preferably a cat, who, according to rumor, was blamed by Koko for tearing out a steel sink from its mooring.

vii.   Nosework

Artificial selection molded the early canid into the scent dog used by law enforcement today, by harnessing the power of the dog's nose:

> The olfactory bulb in dogs is roughly forty times bigger than the olfactory bulb in humans, relative to total brain size, with 125 to 220 million smell-sensitive receptors. The bloodhound exceeds this standard with nearly 300 million receptors.

STANLEY COREN, HOW DOGS THINK (Simon & Schuster 2004). The olfactory sense bests that of humans by as many as eight orders of magnitude. Rigorous reenactment routines provide the necessary positive reinforcement and context framing to create predictable alert responses and, thus, admissibility.

In 2013, the United States Supreme Court decided *Florida v. Jardines*, 133 S. Ct. 1409 (2013), examining in a 5-4 decision, whether the use of a scent-discriminating canine as a machinelike tool for police investigation and development of probable cause required a warrant. In affirming the trial court's decision to suppress evidence of marijuana plants to which the dog alerted, thereby negating the basis for the charge of cannabis trafficking, Justice Scalia wrote, "To find a visitor knocking on the door is routine (even if sometimes unwelcome); to spot that same visitor exploring the front path with a metal detector, or marching his bloodhound into the garden before saying hello and asking permission, would inspire most of us to — well, call the police." *Id.*, at 1416. Justice Kagan added:

> For me, a simple analogy clinches this case . . . A stranger comes to the front door of your home carrying super-high-powered binoculars . . . In just a couple of minutes, his uncommon behavior allows him to learn details of your life you disclose to no one. Has your "visitor" trespassed on your property, . . . ? Yes, he has.

Id., at 1418. And another opinion:

> Therefore, if a dog's nose is just like a thermal imaging device for Fourth Amendment purposes, a search would occur if a dog alerted while on a public sidewalk or in the corridor of an apartment building. And the same would be true if the dog was trained to sniff, not for marijuana, but for more dangerous quarry, such as explosives or for a violent fugitive or kidnapped child. I see no ground for hampering legitimate law enforcement in this way.

Id., at 1426.

> The earliest known report of the canine as detective dates from 300-272 B.C. Two men had murdered a slave and fled, leaving the slave's dog, the sole eyewitness, by the body. The King, passing by on a royal progress, ordered the body buried and took the dog in as his own. After some time passed, the dog accompanied his new master on a review of his troops. As two of the soldiers marched past, the animal flew at them in a rage. "No further evidence was needed, for, in order to escape from the dog, the criminals confessed their guilt."

Andrew E. Taslitz, *Does the Cold Nose Know? The Unscientific Myth of the Dog Scent Lineup*, 42 HASTINGS L.J. 15, 24 (1990) (quoting S. CHAPMAN, POLICE DOGS IN NORTH AMERICA 9-10 (1990)).

b. Animal Identification Evidence

Renowned University of Washington Professor of Psychology Elizabeth Loftus challenged claims of repressed (and then later recovered) memory by victims of childhood sexual abuse, but she has also monitored the effect that weapon presence has on distracting a witness's focus from other things, such as a perpetrator's facial features. Elizabeth F. Loftus et al., *Some Facts About "Weapon Focus,"* 11 L. & HUM. BEHAV. 55 (1987). Of course, where the "weapon" is the face itself, such focus might enhance identification of the incident animal's head morphology and other identifying characteristics. However, focus on other features beyond the muzzle of the animal, such as tail length and curl, hair length, coloration, and other anatomical features may be lost in the traumatic experience.

Another factor also deserves mention — namely, that the witness and the suspect are not of the same species. A meta-analysis examining own-race bias ("ORB") in facial feature discrimination showed a statistically significant "cross-race impairment," although it did not detect any exaggeration by bigoted attitudes. Christian A. Meissner & John A. Brigham, *Thirty Years of Investigating the Own-Race Bias in Memory of Faces: A Meta-Analytic Review*, 7 PSYCHOL. PUB. POLICY & L. 3 (2001). What effect cross-species (or specifically human-canine) impairment may have has not been researched sufficiently, but the need for it arises in matters involving dog attacks where look-alikes may exist or where an animal control officer has given undue suggestion to the witness by presenting a single photo of the suspect animal.

No reported cases exist in which a court has applied the law of showups (i.e., law enforcement provides victim with a single photo or set of photos of the presumed offending dog only), or photo lineup in the dangerous dog context. Nor do reported cases discussing an in-court identification of a dog exist to the author's knowledge. Due process attaches to the pretrial identification procedures because the "vagaries of eyewitness identification are well-known" to the courts. *U.S. v. Wade*, 388 U.S. 218, 228 (1967), *State v. Burrell*, 625 P.2d 726, 728 (Wash. Ct. App. 1981). A pretrial identification procedure violates due process if the procedure is "so impermissibly suggestive as to give rise to a very substantial likelihood of irreparable misidentification." *Simmons v. U.S.*, 390 U.S. 377, 384 (1968). The showing of a single photograph is impermissibly suggestive, though not necessarily violative of due process in the criminal context. *State v. Maupin*, 822 P.2d 355, 356 (Wash. Ct. App. 1992). Where the line-up is formed with the defendant appearing as the only potential suspect, as the "only possible choice," the procedure is unnecessarily suggestive. *State v. Traweek*, 715 P.2d 1148, 1150 (Wash. Ct. App. 1986). Amplifying the risk of error of eyewitness identification, at a level of magnitude beyond the scientifically proved problems with cross-race identification, *see State v. Jaime*, 233 P.3d 554, 560–561 (Wash. 2010) (noting relevance of cross-racial identification on accuracy of witness identification), is the difficulty of cross-species identification.[16]

The only published case discussing the identification issue in a civil context affirmed the identification of the dogs based on a preponderance of the evidence. *In re Matter of Fugazy*, 82 Misc. 2d 135 (N.Y. Town Ct. 1974). The close proximity of the location where the two dogs disappeared and reappeared, that they were two shepherds running together without collars and with distinguishing markings, the testimony of a police officer that they looked to be the attacking dogs, that the dogs responded to the call names "Murphy" and "Kelly," the same given by the dog owner, that a humane society employee recognized them as those he frequently observed within an enclosure on the owner's property, and that the court took notice of the owner's 38 leash law convictions over the previous six years, sufficiently established their identities.

A different result of dismissal based on insufficient identification evidence obtained when the court found that neither the victim nor witness "saw where the dog came from before or went to after the attack"; that when the Defendant removed the suspected dogs from their respective crates for inspection by animal control, they found no evidence (i.e., blood on muzzles or in mouths) of the dogs'

---

[16] In the event animal control requests a photo of the client's dog from the client, an elegant solution is to provide five pictures of similar breed dogs, including the client's dog, and tell Animal Control to have the complainant identify the incident dog. This might at least require presenting a photo array to the witness. Unless the dog is impounded, or the owner is required by statute on pains of prosecution for obstructing or hindering an investigation, one might advise against allowing Animal Control to take photos of the client's dog absent a genuine issue of identification. Once a witness identifies a dog from a single photo, it may taint any subsequent, in-hearing identification requiring that both be suppressed. Unless a defendant challenges the identification procedure as impermissibly suggestive, uncertainty of the identification goes to weight rather than admissibility. If identification presents a nontrivial issue in a dangerous dog case, consider a motion to suppress.

involvement in the recent attack on the victim's dog; that identification by the victim and witness of the two dogs that attacked "were based on photos of them taken by [the animal control officer]"; that "no photos of the other mastiffs were shown . . . for purposes of the identification"; that "the dogs were crated in the house all throughout the morning except for times when they were let outside for a short period and were in sight of the Defendant at all times"; and that both dogs were shown at numerous dog shows and did not show aggressive tendencies toward other dogs at dog shows or otherwise. *City of Seattle v. Julie Lohr*, Seattle Muni. Ct. Nos. 202912969 & 202912981 (2010), available from author.

In a 2011 Delaware case, the court reversed the dangerous dog designation of a dog who allegedly bit the victim due to insubstantial evidence, given the victim's absence from the contested hearing and hearsay evidence by the victim claiming to have seen three dogs being walked earlier in the day when bitten — meaning *any* of the three (not necessarily the one declared) could have bitten. *Hobbs v. Kent Cy. SPCA, Inc.*, 2011 Del. C.P. LEXIS 1 (Feb. 4, 2011).

c. Animal-Related Discovery Issues

Statutory or common law privileges, such as the spousal, physician-patient, journalist, priest-penitent, attorney-client, and self-incrimination, may defeat admission of adverse evidence by blocking communications between the holder of the privilege and certain classes of advisors or intimates. The marital testimonial privilege bars not just the content of discussions between party and non-party spouses, but allows the party-spouse to (according to majority state rule, but not federal rule) prevent the non-party spouse from even taking the stand against him or her. Duties of confidentiality, such as privacy protections ensured by the Health Insurance Portability and Accountability Act ("HIPAA"), may arise alongside statutory communication privileges, such as psychologist-patient. However, a duty alone does not prevent compulsive disclosure under force of subpoena, court order, or questioning under oath and a motion for a protective order will have less success than were the information protected by privilege, as well. Repercussions for breach of duty may include administrative or licensing board discipline as unethical or unprofessional conduct, or whatever statutory remedies may exist, but the breach merely becomes an issue between the one holding the duty and the one to whom the duty is owed. Consider the following restrictions against divulging communication, disseminating correspondence, and testifying in animal cases.

i. Confidentiality and Privileges — Veterinary

The questions of privilege and duty in animal law cases arise with greatest frequency when prosecuting animal neglect or abuse by relying on medical records and testimony from the suspect's veterinarian. At the outset, a veterinarian may wish to notify the authorities when she suspects cruelty but fears civil or criminal liability. No state has recognized a common law veterinarian-client privilege. *See Hendershot v. Western Union Telegraph Co.*, 76 N.W. 828 (Iowa 1898), *Belichick v. Belichick*, 307 N.E.2d 270 (Ohio Ct. App. 1973). Neither do true statutory veterinarian-client privileges (i.e., impervious to subpoena or compulsion) exist. On the other hand, duties of confidentiality affect veterinary practice in Pennsylvania,

Missouri, Georgia, Kansas, Texas, and Illinois, as well as administrative regulations of several other states, all of which impose a duty not to reveal confidential information pertaining to a patient unless, in some cases, necessary to protect public health or the patient's welfare.[17]

The duty protects patient *and* client privacy, who incidentally may have divergent interests. Where a cat owner presents her feline to a veterinarian for treatment of burned paws suffered when she threw the cat on a hot range, the cat no doubt would waive any privilege to ensure safe removal from the owner's custody and the owner's incarceration. In recognition of this conflict, however, states overwhelmingly provide exceptions by mandating breach of confidentiality to prevent commission of a crime (namely, animal cruelty, animal sexual assault, animal neglect). Oregon permits reporting by veterinarians and veterinary technicians suspecting abandonment, neglect, or abuse and mandates the same when treating animals purported to have been injured by a trapping device. ORS § 686.445(1-2). Arizona mandates reporting of suspected dog fighting or animal abuse. Ariz. § 32-2239. On Jul. 28, 2013, Washington State's law immunizing veterinarians from liability for good faith reporting of suspected animal cruelty became effective. SB 5102 (2013).

Breach of confidentiality may also prove fatal. Veterinarians may take it upon themselves to chart the perceived breed composition of the patient based on nothing other than supposition. A "Pit bull mix" notation may be seized upon by animal control as a means of enforcing breed-specific legislation, using the purported expert's unsolicited opinion (who happens to also be in a veterinarian-client-patient relationship) against the client and patient. Cavalier, imprecise, or unverified charting of prior incidents or flagging the file with cautionary notes could reveal a known vicious propensity or criminally implicate the client for matters then under investigation even though the history may be vital to treatment of injury or behavioral remediation.

In veterinary medical malpractice litigation, discovery into medical records of other, former patients is often requested. Whether privilege applies to business dealings with third parties who have no involvement in the case raises difficult issues not too dissimilar from the human medical malpractice context. After all, barring a strong suspicion of transmission of a contagious disease, or charted breach of confidentiality, few situations would authorize acquiring medical records

---

[17] The following states have passed confidentiality laws with causes of action for breach: California (Cal. Bus. & Prof. Code § 4857 (1999)); Florida (F.S.A. § 474.2165 (2000)); Georgia (Ga. Code. Ann. § 24-9-29 (1986)); Illinois (225 ILCS 115/25.17 (1994)); Missouri (Mo. Rev. State. § 340.286 (1992)); Texas (V.T.C.A. Occupations Code § 801.353 (2005)). Other states, while not having a veterinarian-client privilege statute, have adopted regulations imposing a duty of confidentiality on veterinarians. *E.g.*, Alabama (Ala. Admin. Code § 930-X-1-.10(15)), Alaska (12 Alaska Admin. Code §§ 68.100, 68.910(d)), Idaho (IDAPA § 46.01.01.152); Kentucky (201 Ky. Admin. Regs. § 16:010); Massachusetts (256 Code of Mass. Regs. § 7.01(15)); Minnesota (Minn. Regs. § 9100.0800(4)); New Mexico (N.M. Admin. Code, Title 16, Ch. 25, Pt. 3, § 8.18); New York (Rules of the Board of Regents, Pt. 29: Unprofessional Conduct, § 29.6(a), Rule 29.1(b)(8)); Louisiana (Board of Veterinary Medicine Rule 1041); Oklahoma (Okla. Admin. Reg. § 10-5-15); Pennsylvania (49 Pa. Admin. Code § 31.121, Principle 7(c)). In July 2000, the American Association of Veterinary State Board's Preliminary Draft of a Model Act for Veterinary Medicine (July 2000) § 601: Privileged Communications and Exceptions, proposed to define a veterinarian-client privilege.

from a third party where the doctor has been accused of malpractice by the plaintiff only. While treatment decisions respecting third-party patients may go to the issue of notice for purposes of showing negligence or recklessness in the subsequent treatment of plaintiff, to reveal or discuss those matters requires a protective order.

Another important evidentiary issue concerns contact with treating veterinarians. In *Loudon v. Mhyre*, 110 Wn. 2d 675 (1988), the Washington Supreme Court held that although the physician-patient privilege was waived by filing a personal injury lawsuit, the defendant was not permitted to engage in ex parte communication with the plaintiff's treating physicians. Should this doctrine apply to treating veterinarians? Given that the public policy considerations underlying the *Loudon* decision likely do not apply in the animal context, and the absence of a statutory privilege, the answer would seem to be negative — unless the animal was a service animal and his treatment required the client's disclosure of sensitive medical information to the veterinarian. While the plaintiff-patient communicates with the physician about his condition, the plaintiff-dog owner communicates with the veterinarian about the animal-patient's condition, who does not traditionally enjoy a privilege.

Finally, FRE 803(4) provides a common exception to hearsay in the case of statements made for purposes of medical diagnosis or treatment. One court, however, refused to apply this exception to allow statements of a veterinarian that the dog at issue was registered to the wife. *Atkins v. Conley*, 504 S.E.2d 920 (W. Va. 1998).

ii.   Confidentiality and Privileges — Legal

While attorneys also owe duties of confidentiality, an open question remains as to whether they can or must reveal confidences that would inculpate a client who intends to commit animal cruelty. Though the ABA Model RPC 1.6(b)(1) permits disclosure to the extent the lawyer reasonably believes needed to "prevent reasonably certain death or bodily harm," Florida goes further by mandating disclosure "to the extent the lawyer reasonably believes necessary" in order "to prevent a client from committing a crime; or to prevent a death or substantial bodily harm to another." Florida RPC 4-1.6(b). Thus, under Florida's law, if serious bodily injury or death might occur to a nonhuman animal or the client will likely commit the crime of animal fighting, animal abuse, or animal sexual assault, the attorney is duty-bound to breach.

ABA Model RPC 3.3(a) requires that a lawyer not "knowingly make a false statement of fact or law to a tribunal," nor "offer evidence that the lawyer knows to be false," nor fail to disclose a material fact to a tribunal when disclosure is necessary to avoid assisting a criminal or fraudulent act. In a hypothetical child custody situation, a family law attorney who falsely states or offers evidence "in support of the abusive client's 'fitness' as a responsible, good parent" violates RPC 3.3(a). Robin A. Rosencrantz, *Rejecting "Hear No Evil Speak No Evil": Expanding the Attorney's Role in Child Abuse Reporting*, 8 Geo. J. Leg. Eth. 327, 359 (1995). In fact, the lawyer who stands silent in this situation could be deemed to have assisted a criminal act where the lawyer knows of his client's child abuse.

Should the same accusation apply in the case of animal abuse? For more on the link between animal abuse, child abuse, domestic violence, and crimes against humans generally, see Beyond Violence: The Human Animal Connection, PSYETA (Psychologists for the Ethical Treatment of Animals), Animal Legal Defense Fund (www.aldf.org), and review the decades-old findings of the FBI and law enforcement corroborating the firm existence of this animal-human violence link.

iii.   Confidentiality and Privileges — Adopters

Although no statutory privilege for this situation exists, some courts have examined ordering discovery of an adoptive family's identity in a pet adoption context. *See Johnston v. Atlanta Humane Soc'y*, 326 S.E.2d 585 (Ga. Ct. App. 1985); *Lamare v. North Country Animal League*, 743 A.2d 598 (Vt. 1999); Tiemessen & Weiner, *The Golden Retriever Rule*, 21 Alaska L. Rev. 77 (2004). *Johnston* and *Lamare* refused to compel the animal control agency to identify the new adopters on the basis that ownership had transferred to them by operation of statute (the stray hold ordinance), rendering their identities utterly irrelevant. Forced disclosure would defeat the intent of the framers in adopting the local ordinance. An Alaska Superior Court refused plaintiffs the ability to demand that Golden Retriever Rescue, a private adoption agency, disclose the names of the adoptive families. Recognizing that such disclosure "could lead to harassment and limit or curtail adoption so as to lead to the less desirable alternative of destruction," the court denied plaintiffs' motion to compel. *Wall v. Gyuricsko*, No. 4FA-01-687 CI (Sup. Ct. 4th Jud. Dist. Nov. 5, 2001).

d.   Animals as Evidence

i.   Mere Evidence Rule

Despite similarities between dogs and people, including at the neurological level, *see* Gregory Berns, *Dogs are People, Too*, N.Y. Times, Oct. 5, 2013), some law enforcement agencies so highly regard their evidentiary value as to seize, log, and store them for prosecution. Not necessarily deemed contraband (e.g., a species unlawful to possess and in whom the government has a superior property interest), fruit of crime (e.g., a stolen horse), or instrumentality of crime (e.g., a dog "guilty" of viciously maiming another), the government holds the canine pending trial as "mere evidence" of criminal activity. Does the animal's innocence or victimization prevent such forcible detention? To answer that question requires study of seminal cases concerning the right to seize houses, cars, and even animals as part of a criminal investigation.

Traditionally, the Fourth Amendment allowed search and confiscation of contraband, fruits, and instrumentalities, but not "mere evidence," the United States Supreme Court finding that a warrant seeking defendant's papers (containing self-incriminating information) violated the constitution. *Gouled v. U.S.*, 255 U.S. 298 (1921). By 1967, however, *Warden, Md. Penitentiary v. Hayden*, 387 U.S. 294 (1967) dismantled the "mere evidence" doctrine to facilitate the governmental interest in crime-solving. Provided that one articulates a "nexus — automatically provided in the case of fruits, instrumentalities or contraband —

between the item to be seized and criminal behavior," meaning that there is probable cause to believe "that the evidence sought will aid in a particular apprehension or conviction," papers concerning animals and the animals themselves may be seized without offense to the Fourth Amendment. *Id.*, at 307. However, when the criminal proceedings terminate, property not unlawful to possess should return to the rightful owner. *U.S. v. Farrell*, 606 F.2d 1341, 1343 (D.C. Cir. 1979). When held indefinitely without commencement of criminal charges or forfeiture proceedings, or before termination of criminal prosecution, the rightful owner may attempt to replevy the items through civil suit or petition the court that issued the warrant (if seized pursuant to same) to release them when their retention is no longer required. *See Serio v. Baltimore Cy.*, 115 F. Supp. 2d 509 (D. Md. 2000) for discussion of this rule in the context of retention of firearms.

Hypothetical: A macaw owner allows a humane enforcement office to enter her home based on a welfare complaint. While inside, the officer observes an emaciated Hyacinth macaw. Believing that the owner has criminally neglected the bird, the officer seizes the macaw without a warrant. At the shelter, a staff veterinarian weighs the bird, draws blood, and tests feces — again, without a warrant. Based on physical exam findings and lab results, the jury convicts. Did the state violate the owner's Fourth Amendment right against unreasonable search (of the bird's blood, feces, and weight) and seizure? See *State v. Newcomb*, 262 Or. App. 256 (2014), *rev'd*, 359 Or. 756 (2016), for an answer.

ii.   Deceased Animals as Evidence

Dead animals do tell tales, and do so with sufficient probity as to spawn an entirely new field of veterinary medicine: forensics. Melinda D. Merck, DVM, author of the seminal text VETERINARY FORENSICS: ANIMAL CRUELTY INVESTIGATIONS (2d Ed. Wiley-Blackwell, 2013), guides the veterinarian, prosecutor, and animal control or law enforcement officer through the process of preparing an airtight investigation to detect and document pathognomonic (i.e., tell-tale) features for abuse and to prove, beyond a reasonable doubt, an animal's non-accidental injury. Lawyers should develop a familiarity with the techniques utilized to process a tort or crime scene, including the crucial, potentially case-thwarting evidentiary pitfalls arising from poor evidence documentation, specimen collection, storage, presumptive and final testing, and for deceased animals — the necropsy (an autopsy performed on a nonhuman animal). Every fiber of muscle, granule of fat, inch of skin and fur, and milliliter of blood provides a wealth of forensic evidence that can significantly affect the claims brought, defenses raised, and damages recoverable.

Learn how to recognize unique nonhuman animal identifiers (such as a feline footpad print, canine nose print, dentition, tracks); to appreciate the value of insects (the field known as forensic entomology aids determination of time of death); to distinguish among various forms of blunt and sharp force trauma, poison, chemical and electrical burns, and fire-related injuries; to reenact firearm injuries by determining trajectory and distance of a bullet or projectile (and matching same to an incident weapon), among many other species-, breed-, age-, sex-, and sterilization-specific behaviors. Animal DNA evidence may come from the victim, perpetrator, and witness, through blood, cheek cells, teeth, bone, fur, organs, skin, saliva, semen, feces, and urine — each requiring distinct collection techniques.

Veterinarians can testify about cause of death as well as causation between an injury and subsequent veterinary care. Those with experience in ballistics can coordinate efforts with law enforcement to opine on trajectories, velocities, ammunition type, and weapon used to harm an animal. Imaging modalities such as single-dimension radiographs, three-dimensional computerized tomography (CT or CAT scan), and MRI may aid in positioning bullets, grading, and timing trauma (e.g., antemortem and postmortem). Where animals die by gunshot, angle and velocity can be best determined by a close examination of entry and exit wounds, rod placement, blood splatter, lividity, powder residue, and diagnostics such as radiography and testing of extracted projectiles. They may help determine whether the animal was facing or retreating from the shooter when killed, including the distance from the discharge.

When examining causes of death from suspected vehicular impact, radiographs of bone, coupled with a skin surface examination, can determine the nature of the impact in relation to the location and speed of the vehicle at the time of impact. Postmortem and *in vivo* toxicity tests may reveal toxic and controlled substances such as methamphetamine, marijuana, LSD, and antifreeze. Cruel methods of killing can be detected by a skilled forensic veterinarian with experience in examining animals slain by hunters, traps, blunt and edged weapons or tools (e.g., to rule out death by wild animal when legs are severed cleanly), or by strangulation and suffocation. Animals dying from starvation, dehydration, hypothermia, and hyperthermia may posthumously prove their case beyond a reasonable doubt through a necropsy as this is the best (and final) means available to discredit alternative theories of death.

Hypothetical: On Oct. 15, 2012, the University Apartments maintenance crew entered Ramses Jackson's unit to clear a clogged drain in his sink. Mr. Jackson and his two cats, Pinochle and Rummy, were present and healthy. At no time did Pinochle enter the bathroom while the workers were present. Minutes after they evacuated his apartment, Mr. Jackson walked into his bathroom to find Pinochle, his female Siamese, dead in the bathtub and a horrendous stench billowing into his nostrils, through his apartment and down the hallway.

Many hours after finding Pinochle deceased, Mr. Jackson called the fire department to investigate what smelled like a gas leak invading the entire floor. The local fire department sent an engine, which arrived shortly after the call. Upon entering his unit, Lt. Godfrey smelled a sulfur-like odor. Certain it was not a gas leak because the apartment was not plumbed for gas, Lt. Godfrey used an ITX portable air monitor with a display for CO, O2, H2S, and LEL. His device showed 2 or 3 ppm of H2S for several seconds when he was in Mr. Jackson's bathroom. Other tenants commented to Lt. Godfrey that they smelled the odor and had concerns on the floor. Lt. Godfrey advised Mr. Jackson to run hot water in the bathtub, and did so on scene. The tub never drained. Prior to October 15, when Mr. Jackson would drain his sink, the water would come out his tub drain.

When the crew exited, they did not tell Mr. Jackson that they had used sulfuric acid, did not instruct him or his animals to stay out of the unventilated bathroom, did not warn him of any risks associated with exposure to the chemical and the highly toxic, air-displacing gas resulting from the interaction of sulfuric acid with the clogged organic matter. Indeed, at no time prior to exiting his apartment did any official, employee, or agent of University Apartments seek consent from Mr. Jackson to use, indicate intent to use, or warn about dangers of using sulfuric acid, specifically a product called "Buster."

Mr. Jackson had Pinochle evaluated by the local veterinary college's pathology department, which concluded, "The cause of unexpected death in this cat cannot be determined following gross and histological evaluation of the tissues. Additionally the provided history suggests peracute death from potential toxin. In many cases of this nature the cause of death is unlikely to generate significant anatomcical change. There are no anatomical changes in the cat that can help explain the death."

Creating toxic fumes by failing to cap off drains that would predictably spew vapors into an enclosed, unventilated space presents a condition endangering and impairing the health of the tenant and his animals, and turns the plumbing into a delivery system for a gas chamber. How might an expert prove that the use of Buster caused Pinochle's death? How might an expert prove that the use of Buster caused Pinochle's death?

Begin by examining the product. The Materials Safety Data Sheet ("MSDS") for Theochem Laboratories's product "Buster"[18] has NFPA and HMIS ratings of 3 ("Serious") for health. An HMIS rating of "Health: 3" means "Major injury likely unless prompt action is taken and medical treatment is given." www.paint.org/programs/hmis.html. A NFPA rating of "Health: 3" means "Corrosive or toxic. Avoid skin contact or inhalation." www.ehs.neu.edu/laboratory_safety/general_information/nfpa_hazard_rating/. Section V of the MSDS states the 93% sulfuric acid-based product carries a specific contraindication: "AVOID CONTACT WITH . . . POWDERED METALS AND ALKALIES."

Unless the building used plastic piping, or installed brand-new pipes not subject to wear and flaking, then it appears that the crew used this product in direct violation of the MSDS. Furthermore, it is common plumbing knowledge not to use sulfuric acid in stainless steel, aluminum chrome, or galvanized steel pipes. Moreover, the MSDS reports that it will create "ACID VAPORS" as a hazardous decomposition or byproduct. Because the chemical is advertised and intended to be used to clear drains, it is expected to come into contact with sulfur-compound sources (e.g., perspiration, saliva, mucous, urine, fecal matter, and is also found in foods like wine, nuts, cheddar cheese, chocolate, coffee) that create hydrogen sulfide gas with the characteristic "rotten egg" odor. The Agency for Toxic Substances and Disease Registry ("ATSDR") issued a Public Health Statement on Hydrogen Sulfide (CAS No. 7783-06-4) in July 2006 indicating that "Household exposures to hydrogen sulfide can occur through misuse of drain cleaning materials."

Section VI of the MSDS specifically speaks of health hazards occasioned by "EXPOSURE TO MISTS AND VAPORS," which it characterizes as "HARMFUL

---

[18] An interesting contrast, Theochem also sells "Fumeless," a sodium and potassium hydroxide (i.e., basic, not acidic) drain cleaner that ostensibly acts without creating the toxic fumes generated by "Buster."

AND SHOULD BE AVOIDED." A competent plumber will ensure that there is sufficient ventilation in the room. Without dispute, Mr. Jackson's bathroom had no ventilation and was quite confined.

Section VIII of the MSDS outlines control measures and, aside from recommending "LOCAL VENTILATION OF WORK AREA," it calls for respirators, and NIOSH-approved, self-contained breathing apparatuses if vapors develop during use.

A board-certified veterinary toxicologist can testify to the lethal properties of hydrogen sulfide gas. Hydrogen sulfide is highly toxic. With a molar mass of 34.08 $g \, mol^{-1}$ and density of 1.363 $g \, dm^{-3}$, H2S is heavier than air (with a mass of 28.97 $g \, mol^{-1}$ and density of 1.294 $g \, dm^{-3}$) and accumulates at the bottom of poorly ventilated spaces — like bathtubs and sinks. The LC50 for humans is 800 ppm after 5 minutes of exposure. Concentrations over 100 ppm cause immediate collapse with loss of breathing, even after inhaling a single breath. And at lethal concentration, humans may not smell the odor. According to William McLeod, Howard J. Doss, et al., with the MSU Extension, in *Beware of Manure Pit Hazards* (nasdonline.org/document/1298/d001097/beware-of-manure-pit-hazards.html):

> Hydrogen sulfide is considered the most dangerous gas in manure pits because it is highly toxic and is rapidly released from decomposing manure during agitation and pumping. Concentrations of hydrogen sulfide can soar from 5 parts per million (ppm) to more than 500 ppm in seconds after agitation begins.
>
> Concentrations of hydrogen sulfide above 600 ppm can kill an individual after taking only one or two breaths. The person falls immediately, apparently unconscious and dies without moving again. A safe evacuation of the individual can be made only if the rescuer is wearing a self-contained breathing apparatus (SCBA). Generally, a rescuer has about six minutes to begin cardiopulmonary resuscitation (CPR) before brain damage/death occurs. Unless the rescuer is wearing SCBA protective equipment (see section on personal protective equipment), there is a strong likelihood that the rescuer will also succumb to the toxic gases or lack of oxygen. There have been numerous instances where several farmers have been killed while attempting to remove someone from a pit or facility.
>
> At lower concentrations, hydrogen sulfide can cause severe illness and irritate the entire respiratory track and eyes. Symptoms may include nausea, stomach distress, belching, coughing, headache, dizziness, irritation of the eyes and blistering of the lips.
>
> It is a common belief among farmers that it is safe to enter a facility or pit if they cannot smell the putrid, rotten egg odor associated with hydrogen sulfide. This is not necessarily true because high concentrations of hydrogen sulfide paralyzes the nerve cells of the nose to the point where the person can no longer smell the gas.
>
> Hydrogen sulfide, because it is heavier than air, accumulates above the liquid level of the pit. Individuals may be quickly overcome with hydrogen sulfide when working around a pit, whether it be climbing down a ladder to

make repairs or when leaning down to take a manure sample.

It is important to note that, because hydrogen sulfide will displace air, it means that the concentration in a confined space (like a bathtub) will be far more than 800 ppm and easily over 500,000 ppm. The volume of gas produced by pouring "half a bottle"[19] (per one of the crewmember's reports) down the drain (where the clog remained even two hours later) would easily exceed the 12 cubic feet that fills a standard tub to the brim. Of course, the gas would asphyxiate even if it only filled the bottom six inches of the tub, where Pinochle's nostrils were positioned upon jumping into the deadly pool of hydrogen sulfide gas.[20] With nonhumans weighing one-twentieth that of the average man, the likelihood that the acid poured down the drain literally took Pinochle's breath away, and did so almost instantaneously, is so great as to be a certainty.

iii.   Animal Abuse Evidence in Criminal Trials

The statistical link between child/spousal abuse and animal abuse has been well-documented. The APA defines "Conduct Disorder" to include "animals" as "others" in diagnostic criteria. *See* Campbell, *The Admissibility of Evidence of Animal Abuse in Criminal Trials for Child and Domestic Abuse*, 43 B.C.L. REV. 463 (2002). Cruelty laws permit and require psychiatric treatment. However, most states do not have an analog to FRE 413-415, part of the Violent Crime Control and Law Enforcement Act of 1994, which permits evidence of sexual assault and child molestations regardless of FRE 404(b). In admitting these prior bad acts, the federal rule recognizes that they furnish a "specific" propensity profile to commit certain crimes, rather than a "general" propensity to commit undefined criminal acts. A history of sexual predation provides specific propensity evidence and is rarely a one-time occurrence. Similarly, serial killers Jeffrey Dahmer, Ted Bundy, and David Berkowitz all had a history of torturing animals.

Until passage of a variant of FRE 413-415, one may still attempt to overcome ER 404(b) by noting that prior animal abuse helps to identify the victim, the perpetrator, or the "fingerprint" of injury that may serve as a "calling card" or fit the *modus operandi* of the perpetrator. Such acts also show a pattern of abuse and motive for control. Prior abuse can help document the "downward spiral" of abuse to show that chronicity negates accident. Domestic violence toward people (and animals) is often situational and shows a specific propensity for violence against identified (or identifiable) family members. In a child abuse case, one may admit violence against other children or the other parent to explain delay in reporting or

---

[19] A bottle is one quart, meaning that he dumped approximately 500 mL (or 16 oz.) down the drain.

[20] The apartment may assert that its employees never used the chemical down the bathtub, but only in the sink, so Pinochle must have died from some other contaminant. However, the physics of hydrogen sulfide gas (heavier than air), the proximity and comparative elevation of the sink and tub, and the evidence that the plumbing circuit connects the sink and tub easily overcomes such an assertion. The fact remains that strong gas odor permeated an enclosed, unventilated space (the bathroom itself is small), and in the course of its employee running water in the sink after pouring the acid, he no doubt caused the acid to migrate farther down into the piping and to a point where the sink pipe would junction with the tub pipe, allowing the hydrogen sulfide to come up through both drain openings and fill the room. As the fumes overflowed out of the sink, they would settle on the floor and in the bathtub, essentially filling the lower part of the room with toxic gas.

as a starting point for the cascade of violence. It may also demonstrate "one continuous pattern of activity" within the home.

iv.   Animal DNA Evidence

Division I of the Washington State Court of Appeals evaluated canine DNA identification head-on in its attempted use to convict an accused murderer. *State v. Leuluaialii*, 77 P.3d 1192 (Wash. Ct. App. 2003). Gang members George Leuluaialii and Kenneth Tuilefano were convicted of two counts of aggravated murder in the first degree and first degree animal cruelty based on allegations that they killed Chief, a part pit bull, Jay Johnson, and Raquel Rivera while searching their home for money and drugs. To overcome their alibi, the state introduced forensic canine hair DNA evidence tying both defendants to the scene. The strongest DNA evidence boasted a nine-marker (of 10) match, with a probability that another dog shared Chief's DNA profile of one in 18 billion. Leuluaialii and Tuilefano challenged the admissibility of the canine DNA evidence, claiming that this form of identification was unreliable and suffered from numerous procedural and statistical limitations. The trial court admitted the evidence without a *Frye* hearing (to determine its probativity or general acceptance in the scientific community). Defendants appealed, asserting that admission of forensic canine DNA evidence constituted reversible error.

Unanimously, the Washington Court of Appeals deemed dog DNA evidence unreliable and inadmissible, though, in this instance, the evidentiary gaffe was harmless, so the convictions stood. In astounding detail, the Court surveyed the science of human DNA identification along with principles of genetic diversity in canines, concluding that while they "have genetic diversity similar to that observed in humans" with highly polymorphic "loci and alleles that might be appropriate for forensic use," the court lacked faith that all loci used in the case were polymorphic. It also questioned the accuracy of the frequency estimates upon which the 1 in 18 billion probability was calculated. *Polymorphic* refers to the variability of the DNA composition at a particular location in the chain. Without polymorphisms, the DNA pattern at that position will be identical and, thus, of no value in distinguishing one from another. In human DNA fingerprinting, only about 0.1% to 0.3% are variable. These sites are polymorphic and used as "loci" or "markers" for purposes of applying the "product rule." Testing on "amorphic" or hypomorphic sites would have little evidentiary value. After all, if 99 percent of humans share the same allele structure at a particular genome site, then a match at that site would not capture a unique "fingerprint." To compute a valid probability of match requires: (1) a species with sufficient genetic diversity; (2) a species with polymorphic markers; (3) each marker chosen by the lab must be polymorphic; and (4) frequency estimates for each marker must be accurate. While canine DNA testing for paternity, breed testing, and cancer and disease research might be "sufficiently studied," canine DNA testing for forensic use was not over a decade ago. Times are changing, albeit slowly. Since *Leuluailii*, however,[21] the state of science has improved, as noted in

---

[21] Note that the DNA methodology and database used for identity-matching in *Leuluailii* is not the same as that used for modern breed-matching. *See* U.S. Patent No. 7729863 B2 (describing Mars DNA process).

Illinois v. Slover, 791 N.E.2d 568 (Ill. App. Ct. 2003) (affirming order releasing cat hair for DNA test); *Comm v. Treiber*, 874 A.2d 26, 27–33 (Pa. 2005) (allowing consideration of canine DNA to incriminate defendant for murder of daughter); *Arizona v. Bogan*, 905 P.2d 515, 520 (Ariz. Ct. App. 1995) (discussing plant DNA under *Frye*). *See also* Antoinette E. Marsh, *Paw and Order: Using Animal DNA as Forensic Evidence — Not Yet Ready for Prime Time*, 3 J. ANIMAL L. & ETHICS 53 (2009); Katie Bray Barnett, *Breed Discriminatory Legislation: How DNA Will Remedy the Unfairness*, 4 J. ANIMAL L. & ETHICS 161 (2011).

An altercation between animal and human may also leave behind evidentiary clues and present an opportunity to reenact how a victim suffered or died, as well as who bears responsibility. Trace evidence vectors run both directions: from human to animal, and animal to human. Fur and feces may attach to the suspect's shoes or person. Human DNA may be captured underneath the nails or on the teeth of a victim animal.[22]

Hypothetical: Murder cases aside, DNA evidence has other applications in the field of animal law. Consider the case of Mercury, a five-year-old, gray, intact Pomeranian. Mercury went missing July 15, 2004. For the next two weeks, his guardian, Charlotte, called the local humane society hoping he had turned up. Weeks passed until she saw dear Mercury in the arms of a passer-by. This fine gent could scarcely control the dog in his arms, who nearly injured himself trying to reach Charlotte. She exclaimed, "Mercury, I found you at least!" But Edwin Grinchly, the holder of this bundle of quicksilver, pooh-poohed the finder's claim and insisted that he had found the quite cowed furball he now called Mr. Pickleberry during an Independence Day celebration at a local park just across the street from Charlotte's house. She had made a terrible mistake, Grinchly groused. Charlotte, much chagrinned and despairing, let Grinchly go.

Something seemed off. What were the odds that a five-year-old, gray Pomeranian would be found so close to where he was lost, intact and so responsive when placed close to his former guardian? She thought back to July 4, 2004 and realized that Mercury had been with a friend across town breeding a female Pomeranian. In fact, she could prove it. She had Mercury's son, Zeus, and access to Zeus's mother, Maia.

What better way to prove identity than by performing a paternity test, much like the one employed by prosecutors against accused fathers. Typically, a court requires a probability of paternity of no less than 99.5% (or a 1 in 200 chance that another man could share the same DNA as the putative pop). Paternity tests are ones of exclusion, the null hypothesis being that the disputed sire is not the father. Most labs catering to nonhuman DNA requesters provide probabilities of paternity in excess of 99.5% based on matching over ten markers. Charlotte sampled DNA from Zeus and proved ownership by paternity.

---

[22] To learn more about DNA testing, see www.vetgen.com, www.vetdnacenter.com, www.vgl.ucdavis.edu, and www.akc.org.

e.　Breed Evidence

> *"Clothes make the man. Naked people have*
> *little or no influence on society."*
> **Mark Twain (1835-1910)**

Outward appearances often deceive, whether perception runs skin or fabric deep. Except for the overly enthusiastic guardian who has outfitted the pooch in latest canine *haute couture*, the vast majority of dogs walk, run, and play naked but for a collar. Visual first impressions synthesize numerous variables, such as head and muzzle shape, tail and ear length, coarseness and color of coat, and sex, culminating in a judgment purporting to sum up everything the dog stands for, and is predestined to be, by the label of "breed."

One might be inclined to regard such designation as merely informational, an effort to catalog the majestic diversity of the canid world. Yet the legal consequences of the breed identification are neither innocent nor trivial.

Functioning much as a scarlet letter or insignia of scorn, the label "Rottweiler" may result in immediate imposition of restraints on control, banishment from the jurisdiction, or confiscation and death due to laws declaring dogs "potentially dangerous" or "dangerous" based exclusively on breed profiling.

For instance, on Jul. 28, 1987, the City of Yakima, Washington, enacted an ordinance banning pure and mixed-breed pit bulls. David Corvo and Mark and Bonnie Johnson joined with the American Dog Owners Association to invalidate the ordinance as unconstitutionally vague in *American Dog Owners Ass'n v. City of Yakima*, 777 P.2d 1046 (Wash. 1989). In affirming summary judgment dismissal, the Washington Supreme Court found the ordinance gave the public sufficient notice as to the type of dog disallowed within city limits despite its mathematical inexactitude and although it relied on subjective assessments by officers grading suspect dogs against breed standards and illustrations. *Id.*, at 1047.

Describing a dog as "American Staffordshire Terrier" may alone put the owner, caretaker, and even landlord on notice that the law regards him as inherently vicious and, therefore, civilly liable for injuries inflicted upon people and animals.

With much fanfare, in 2012 Maryland's highest court decided *Tracey v. Solesky*, 50 A.3d 1075 (Md. 2012), which on reconsideration reined in its "gratuitous and erroneous" holding as to mixed-breed dogs in a 5-to-2 decision. In granting the motion for reconsideration in part, Judge Wilner prudently asked, "Is it intended that a dog be classified as a cross-bred pit bull if only one of its grandparents (or great-grandparents) was a pure-bred pit bull?" The "thicket" of uncertainty described in the order bears scrutiny because the decision lacks the qualitative and quantitative measures by which to classify a dog as pure. Conceding that by "imposing strict liability for cross-breds, some greater certainty is required," and excising from the original opinion any reference to hybrids, cross-breds, or mixes, the majority restricted the scope to only those dogs who undisputedly contain no trace of a non-pit bull dog.

Still, it otherwise reaffirmed its pronouncement that purebred pit bull dogs are inherently dangerous, imposing absolute (rather than strict) liability. *Tracey* dispensed with the need to prove *scienter* of vicious propensity (the traditional strict common law elements). Accordingly, bite victims need only prove the biting dog's pedigree to hold not only the dog owner, but landlord as well, liable.

The ruling will feverishly increase the use of DNA and other tests to prove, or disprove, genetic impurity in the incident dog, with results almost assuredly rendering the *Tracey* decision a practical nullity because only a tiny percentage of visually suspected dogs will be genetically confirmed as *bona fide* 100% purebred.

The designation "Pit Bull" may serve to enhance criminal penalties or furnish a necessary element to a crime that could result in imprisonment, fines, and forfeiture of the incident dog.

For instance, in *State v. Lee*, 257 P.3d 799 (Kan. Ct. App. 2011), Derrick Lee faced a charge of involuntary manslaughter in the death of 70-year-old Jimmie Mae McConnell when a family dog and stray dog cared for by Lee entered McConnell's property and attacked her without provocation, causing her to suffer a fatal heart attack. The state rested its charge on the commission of a misdemeanor enacted for the protection of human safety (i.e., misdemeanor manslaughter) — namely, a city ordinance prohibiting the keeping, harboring, or owning a "predominantly" pit bull dog. After a mistrial, but before retrial, the state had one of the dogs' DNA tested to reveal a blend of breeds, including American Staffordshire Terrier, Bull Terrier, Bulldog, Keeshond, and Collie, with the strongest breed signature matching the American Staffordshire Terrier. *Id.*, at 804. An animal control officer testified that Lee's dog had "a large, somewhat wedge-shaped head, thick neck, taller in the shoulder area, and his body tapered down shorter towards the back," and based on all characteristics was "predominantly of the breeds listed in the municipal ordinance." A veterinarian then testified that the dog found in McConnell's yard "had the head of an American Staffordshire Terrier Pit Bull or Staffordshire Bull Terrier," with a "muscular front end, a narrow waist that went into muscular rear legs, a broad head, and a wide jaw set," leading him to conclude that the dog "had at least one parent that was American Staffordshire Terrier, Staffordshire Bull Terrier, or American Pit Bull Terrier," and, thus, was "predominantly of the breeds listed in the municipal ordinance." *Id.*, at 804. The jury convicted, and the appellate court affirmed.

Resembling a "wolf hybrid" may mobilize condominium association directors to enforce CC&Rs that compel the unit owner to banish the hybrid or be fined, resulting in possible foreclosure.

Associations are quasi-governmental state actors, so when they enact bylaws and board rules restricting ownership or the keeping of certain breeds, state law may require that they bestow constitutional protections such as due process and equal protection before threatening unit owners with hefty fines and orders of removal. Cases that discuss homeowners association or condominium association governance in constitutional terms include *White Egret Condominium, Inc. v. Franklin*, 379 So. 2d 346 (Fla. 1979), *Franklin v. Spadafora*, 447 N.E.2d 1244 (Mass. 1983), and *Levandusky v. One Fifth Ave. Apartment Corp.*, 553 N.E.2d 1317 (N.Y. 1990). While a procedurally sound vote to amend the CC&Rs to impose a total ban on non-emotional support and non-service dogs will be upheld by the courts, arguments may exist to challenge the Association's decision to ban a specific breed on grounds of arbitrariness and public policy (albeit with limited success). *See San Vicente Villas Homeowners Assoc., Inc. v. Cohen*, 2003 Cal. App. Unpub. LEXIS 11780 (Dec. 17, 2003) (upholding a 15-pound weight restriction as nonarbitrary due to a building nonconducive to large dogs with narrow hallways, single elevator, narrow stairwell, generating safety concerns; nor as against public policy); *see also Ajit Bhogaita v. Altamonte Heights Condominium Assoc., Inc.*, 2012 U.S. Dist. LEXIS 178183 (M.D. Fla. Dec. 17, 2012) (finding association to have constructively denied unit owner's request for reasonable accommodation under the Fair Housing Act relative to his emotional support animal who happened to weigh more than 25 pounds, the limit set by the Association); *Scottsdale Condominium Assoc. v. Talaroc*, 2012 Ariz. App. Unpub. LEXIS 334 (Mar. 15, 2012) (ruling against Association that established board rule banning pets in contradiction to CC&R permitting them). Still, do not forget to challenge the methodology by which the Association determines that the unit owner's dog in fact is that breed.

Rumors of even looking like a pit bull could cause an insurance company to deny coverage for grievous harm inflicted from a bite by such dog. When labeling the dog a "pit bull," plaintiffs' counsel risk pleading their clients out of recovery by giving the insurer a basis to reserve rights or refuse to indemnify under a breed-specific exclusion. And defendants who boast their breed may unwittingly hoist themselves on their own petards. Carriers who seize upon the breed exclusion will invite hearty coverage and bad faith battles resulting in potential fee awards to prevailing insureds.

For instance, though it declined supplemental jurisdiction and deferred to the Maryland Insurance Commission, in *Mutual Ben. Ins. Co. v. Lorence*, 189 F. Supp. 2d 298 (D. Md. 2002), an insured sought declaratory judgment that Mutual's refusal to cover his dog's bite violated Maryland's law prohibiting insurers from canceling policies "based wholly or partly . . . for any arbitrary, capricious, or unfairly discriminatory reason." Insurers have a duty to base all underwriting decisions on actuarially sound data. LEE R. RUSS & THOMAS F. SEGALIA, COUCH ON INSURANCE, § 2:1 (3d ed. 1995); also Larry Cunningham, *The Case Against Dog Breed Discrimination by Homeowners' Insurance Companies*, 11 CONN. INS. L.J. 1 (2004).

To avoid the above results requires legal challenge at three levels:

First, the clarity and methodological soundness of the statute or rule setting the threshold to adversely label a dog by breed;

Second, the accuracy, precision, and competence of the individual making the adverse labeling decision against that threshold;

Third, the merit of the nexus between the adverse label and the public health and safety.

These challenges all turn on scientific evidence — starting with *identification* of a dog's breed and premised on some foundation *linking* that breed to some innate malevolence. Each level requires vigorous scrutiny.

Prosecutors, landlords, homeowners and condominium associations, law enforcement officers, animal control officers, and plaintiffs' lawyers will bear the evidentiary onus of sullying the incident canine with genetic and phenotypic aspersions. Unless conceded by the dog guardian, visual identification by an animal control officer or law enforcement officer remains the most widely employed method by which to do so.

i.   Meaning of Substantial or Element

A few preliminary remarks will assist the evaluation of breed specific legislation ("BSL").[23] First, many such codes embrace AKC or UKC standards as inclusionary guidelines. These kennel clubs, however, speak to *purebreds* only (i.e., without any miscegenistic deviation in pedigree). A dog bred outside its genetic pool is no longer an unadulterated member of any specific "breed." Second, there is no breed recognized by any kennel club as a "pit bull." A legal term of art, it conflates several breed standards, often the American Staffordshire Terrier, Staffordshire Bull Terrier, Bull Terrier, or American Pit Bull Terrier.[24]

In 1989, Miami-Dade County, Fla. defined a *pit bull dog* as "any dog which exhibits those distinguishing characteristics which:

> (1) Substantially conform to the standards established by the American Kennel Club for American Staffordshire Terriers or Staffordshire Bull Terriers; or (2) Substantially conform to the standards established by the United Kennel Club for American Pit Bull Terriers." Miami-Dade Cy. § 5-17.1(a) (1989).

To aid the public and law enforcement, the county incorporated the AKC and UKC standards as "Exhibit A" to the code. *Id.*, § 5-17.1(b). But they made it clear that prohibition did not require conformational perfection. "Technical deficiencies in the dogs' conformance . . . shall not be construed to indicate that the subject dog is not a 'pit bull dog' under this article." *Id.*, § 5-17.1(c). Concerningly, the code instructed that testimony by a "veterinarian, zoologist, animal behaviorist, or animal control officer that a particular dog exhibits distinguishing physical characteristics of a pit bull shall establish a rebuttable presumption that the dog is a pit bull." *Id.*, § 5-17.1(d). The code then declared that the "pit bull" dog's "inbred propensity to attack other animals" and "danger posed to humans and animals alike . . . when running loose or while running together in a pack" requires uninterrupted, secure confinement indoors or in a locked, four-sided, six-foot tall pen with conspicuous "Dangerous Dog" warning signs. *Id.*, § 5-17.2(a). Other requirements included muzzling and a 50-foot no-walk zone around public school grounds. *Id.*, § 5.17-2(b). "Pit bull" dogs were to be registered with animal control, along with proof of $50,000 liability insurance or bond. *Id.*, § 5-17.3 to .4. But the County took it one step further by commanding every veterinary office, kennel, commercial breeder, commercial animal establishment, pet shop, and dog grooming business to post signs in three languages pronouncing the danger of pure and mixed-breed pit

---

[23] Also known as breed discriminatory legislation ("BDL").

[24] BSL has been known to include the American Bulldog, Presa de Canario, and other Molossoid breeds.

bull dogs, the illegality to acquire one, and that failure to register, muzzle, confine, and insure the same subjects a person to severe penalties. It then encouraged families to inform on their neighbors by having them call animal control if "pit bull" dogs were in the vicinity. *Id.*, § 5-17.7(1).

When the dangerous dog investigator (usually, an animal control officer, not a veterinarian, zoologist, or animal behaviorist) makes rounds through a Miami-Dade neighborhood in response to individuals identifying suspected "pit bull" dog harborers, how does he determine whether the suspect dog "substantially conforms" to one of the three breed standards? And what training and experience qualifies this reviewer to make such a conformation determination, particularly where his evaluation carries presumptive force of law?

"Substantially" has no definition within the Miami-Dade Code. While one may challenge such language as void for vagueness, the likelihood of defeating the designation on that basis alone remains slim. For while the code itself may not offer the requisite clarity, courts routinely invoke the common dictionary definition and render the ordinance valid. However, even using terms like "substantially" or "predominantly" can still prove fatal if no attempt is made to specifically identify the prohibited breed, as occurred in *Amer. Dog Owners Assoc., Inc. v. City of Des Moines*, 469 N.W.2d 416 (Iowa 1991).

In 1987, the Des Moines Municipal Code, Ch. 7, subch. 2, § 7-13, (vi)-(x) defined "vicious dog" to include:

(vi)   Staffordshire terrier breed of dog; or

(vii) The American pit bull terrier breed of dog; or

(viii) The American Staffordshire terrier breed of dog; or

(ix)   Dogs of mixed breed or of other breeds than above listed which breed or mixed breed is known as pit bulls, pit bull dogs or pit bull terriers; or

(x)   Any dog which has the appearance and characteristics of being predominately of the breeds of Staffordshire terrier, American pit bull terrier, American Staffordshire terrier; any other breed commonly known as pit bulls, pit bull dogs or pit bull terriers, or combination of any of these breeds.

In severing (ix) and the second clause of (x) as unconstitutionally vague, the Iowa Supreme Court reasoned that reference to dogs "known as" or "commonly known as" pit bulls, pit bull dogs, or pit bull terriers, according to unknown persons and unknown standards, would confuse the public and grant enforcement personnel unbridled subjective discretion. *Id.*, at 418. However, the first clause of (x) passed constitutional muster, as the use of the word "predominately" came in the context of specific breeds to which one may consult published standards.

Litigation Tip: Proportion matters. Whether stated quantitatively (e.g., 25%, 50%, two-thirds) or qualitatively (e.g., substantially, predominantly), the proportional adverb tries to define which of the crossbred canine masses fall within the rule or regulation's ambit. Where no such modifying term can be found, one should restrict its scope to only purebreds. For instance, the following policy came out of a homeowners association in King County, Washington:

For purposes of this Policy, the term "pit bull dog" means any of the following: Staffordshire Bull Terrier, American Staffordshire Terrier; American Pit Bull Terrier; any dog which has been registered at any time as a Pit Bull Terrier; any dog which has the appearance of being predominantly of the breed of dogs known as Staffordshire Bull Terrier, American Staffordshire Terrier, American Pit Bull Terrier. A dog shall be deemed to have the "appearance of being predominantly of the breed of dogs" named herein if the dog exhibits the physical characteristics which substantially conform to the standards established by the American Kennel Club or the United Kennel Club for any of these breeds.

In many respects, the labeling convention seen in this Policy resembles that found in antidiscrimination law. For instance, the Americans with Disabilities Act defines a qualified disabled individual deserving of federal law protection as one who is physically or mentally impaired, has a record of being so impaired, or is regarded as having a disability (whether she has one or not). Analogizing "pit bull" status to a disability, then, the first part of this Policy speaks to those who are impaired; the second to those with a record of being impaired; and the third to those regarded as being impaired. Structural interpretation of the entire policy demonstrates that Part One addresses purebreds only (compare to Part Three and its discussion of "predominantly" and "substantially"), as does Part Two (note that it does not say registered as a Pit Bull Terrier *mix* or *part* Pit Bull Terrier). Part Three drapes the prohibition over crossbreds but without regard for actual genetic content. The phrase "appearance of being" explicitly disregards whether the dog is *actually* one of the identified breeds. Looking like a duck suffices. Thus, a dog with no genetic history as a "pit bull" dog might be banned if regarded as one according to strictly phenotypic characteristics. Accordingly, a DNA test that proves no "pit bull" dog composition might still run afoul of this rule.

In *State v. Lee*, 257 P.3d 799 (Kan. Ct. App. 2011), the defendant argued that the failure to define "predominantly" invalidated the ordinance. His attempt to distinguish the City of Kansas City's ordinance from the City of Overland Park Police Department's definition as "more than fifty percent" mattered not to the appellate court, since *predominantly* is a "common term used as an adverb and defined by the dictionary to mean 'for the most part' or 'mainly.' " *Id.*, at 1009; *see also Hearn v. City of Overland Park*, 772 P.2d 758 (Kan. 1989). Thus, where a rule or regulation fails to include such adverbial limitation or chooses ambiguous proportional language, the practitioner should break out the dictionary and examine arguments such as void for vagueness or strict construction based on the rule of lenity or forfeiture.

Where codes do not use the terms "substantially" or "predominantly," but instead speak of the word "element," as used in the phrase "an element of its breeding . . . so as to be identifiable as partially of the breed," as found in the City of Yakima, Wash. Code § 6.18.010, for instance, a vagueness challenge remains viable for a few reasons.

The term *element* means a fundamental, essential, or irreducible constituent of a composite entity — as in the 102 elements found in the Periodic Table. An element "of breeding" suggests the existence of a single genetic component as in a heritable trait, trait set, or partial DNA fingerprint, which may or may not be physically expressed. Read in isolation, this phrase could thus read so expansively as to prohibit a dog with one confirmed genetic characteristic of the prohibited breed. The words "of breeding" distinguish dogs that resemble the prohibited breed for reasons other than by consanguinity — such as surgical alteration, disease, defect, or illness.

However, the connection between the phrase "an element of breeding" and "identifiable as partially" through the bridge "so as to be" serves to restrict such an interpretation in two ways: (1) the adverb "partially" denotes a quantity more than merely a tiny fraction but less than the entirety (in other words, between 1% and 99%); and (2) the adjective "identifiable" suggests capable of being distinguished or recognized but does not specify the mode of identification — whether genetic, visual, documentary evidence, or all available. The resulting quagmire of vagary warrants close examination.

ii.   Accuracy of Examiner

As with obscenity, jurists profess to know it (here, a "pit bull" dog) when they see it. But how does one test the integrity of those epistemological moorings? Specifically, what happens when a court seeks to qualify a law enforcement officer as an expert in "pit bull" dog identification, and then allows him to state that your client's dog substantially conforms to the breed standard of an American Staffordshire Terrier? In *Cardelle v. Miami-Dade Code Enforcement*, this precise issue arose.

The Lesson of *Cardelle*

Hearing Examiner Alfredo Bared allowed Officer Fernando Casadevall to testify that Bertha Cardelle's dog, Kitty, while admittedly a mixed breed, but having never been accused of aggressively threatening any person or animal, met the definition of a "pit bull" in having physically exhibited more than 50 percent of the agglomeration of traits associated with the American Staffordshire Terrier, Staffordshire Bull Terrier, and American Pit Bull Terrier. Accordingly, Officer Casadevall subjected her to the restraints discussed above. He utilized a *"Pit Bull" Dog Breed Evaluation Form* consisting of a checklist with 47 conformation characteristics of the head, ears, eyes, muzzle, neck, shoulders, back, body, legs, tail, coat, and size. Officer Casadevall claimed to have performed the in-person, live evaluation of Kitty from a distance of two-and-one-half-feet over the course of half an hour, resulting in him scoring Kitty with 37 inculpatory characteristics and 10 exculpatory, yielding 78.7% conformation. In outlining his expertise, Officer Casadevall recited his certification with the Florida Animal Control Association, training in "pit bull" dog fighting, working with his father in treating animals (presumably his father was a veterinarian), breeding American Staffordshire Terriers, and working 15 years with the county, seven of which he investigated "pit bull" dog complaints and cruelty calls.

Litigation Tip: When faced with such a proffered "expert," charged with applying kennel club breed standards, would it not seem that the best person to make such identification is an AKC or UKC conformation judge for those breeds?[25] The AKC weeds out conformation judges through an extensive application process. Requirements include: (1) completion of six stewarding assignments at AKC member or licensed shows in three years preceding application; (2) completion of six judging assignments at AKC sanctioned matches; (3) attendance at the Basic Judging Institute at least two years before applying for judge appointment; (4) meeting AKC occupational eligibility requirements; and (5) passing the Anatomy and Procedural Exams. The application is breed-specific.

Further, the applicant must either have 12 or more years of experience in exhibiting in conformation for at least one breed applied for, have bred or raised five or more litters on the applicant's premises for each breed, and have bred four or more champions in each breed. An alternative method permits the applicant to instead prove she has 15 or more years of experience in conformation in at least one breed applied for and document four of eight components: (1) breeding and raising four litters on premises; (2) receipt of designation of AKC Breeder of Merit for the breed applied; (3) having bred at least two champion in the breed applied; (4) owning at least one dog in each breed applied who sired four champions; (5) owning or maintaining for the duration four dogs in each breed requested and who each earned championships while residing at the applicant's home; (6) personally exhibiting four dogs in each breed requested to their championships, earning all 15 points and both majors; (7) personally exhibiting two dogs in each breed requested as specials for a minimum of two years or 60 shows; or (8) documenting 25 years of experience exhibiting dogs in conformation.

Recruiting AKC judges to BSL-commissioned panels may provide a suitable expert foundation to determine whether an incident dog adheres to a visual ideal of purity, but unless those judges have a system in place to calculate degrees or percentages of nonconformity, a municipality's quest to identify, label, and restrain dogs who closely resemble, *but are not*, purebreds, will founder on the shoals of vagueness and due process. This is particularly so where the genetic fingerprint of even proven conformation champions registered as a specific breed will quite likely contain trace DNA from a non-registered breed. For this reason, many codes allow for some leeway by using such hedging terms as "substantially" or "predominantly." A quantitative or qualitative index may assist in measuring the prohibitive proportion.

A Difference in Judging

However, AKC does not use a scorecard and assign points to each entrant. Rather, judges bestow awards to the entrants who — compared *against one another* — most closely approximate the ideal. And because BSL does not judge incident dogs as a group (but instead one at a time), ring judging differs significantly from what occurs in the animal control truck or shelter run. *See* images.akc.org/pdf/rulebooks/REJ999.pdf.

In other words, animal control does not round up ten dogs in the neighborhood,

---

[25] UKC and AKC do not condone the use of their standards for enforcing breed discriminatory legislation.

trot them out one at a time with a handler, and then bestow a "Best in Breed" penalty. Rather, it views each in isolation against the breed standard. The methodological problem comes into clearer focus when one recognizes that the officer is tasked not with determining whether the dog is phenotypically *perfect* but whether it is phenotypically *passable*. Such endeavor is best described as prequalification, i.e., to see whether the dog can make the cut to even enter the show ring. Yet this furnishes yet another distinction relative to mixed breeds subject to BSL, for only avowed purebreds may compete in AKC conformation shows. Thus, all entrants may compete, barring poor training, viciousness, dyeing, or specific disqualifications found within the breed standard itself (such as height or weight).

Remember: AKC judges do not need to decide whether the entrant *is* a particular breed because mere entry into the conformation ring constitutes such an admission by the owner. Instead, the judges decide which of the entrants most conforms to the AKC ideal standard (in other words, all are presumed to substantially conform to the breed standard, but some more than others). For a description of the history, standard, and breed exam for the American Staffordshire Terrier (and other breeds), go to www.akc.org/judges/guides.

Behavioral and Kinesiological Characteristics

It should also be noted that the AKC standard depends on behavioral presentation and gait as well, not simply static physical characteristics. For instance, the American Staffordshire Terrier Breed Standard speaks of "General Impression" for the breed as follows:

General Impression

The American Staffordshire Terrier should give the impression of great strength for his size, a well put-together dog, muscular, but agile and graceful, keenly alive to his surroundings. He should be stocky, not long-legged or racy in outline. His courage is proverbial.

Accordingly, the judge must determine the dog's agility, grace, aliveness, and courage. If animal control does test for such behavioral qualities, then the breed declaration should be challenged for lack of foundation. And because the AKC does not articulate a scientifically grounded method to assess this "General Impression," to the extent the law or rule at issue incorporates the AKC breed standard by reference, the breed declaration should be challenged on that additional ground as well, mindful further that environment may contaminate behavior. After all, a dog chased down, snared by a catch pole, and stuffed in a kennel will not behave the same way a competition show dog will in the ring, accompanied by her known and steady handler. Indeed, an impounded dog will not show agility or grace.

The Bull Terrier Breed Standard bespeaks "keen determin[ation] and intelligent expression, full of fire but of sweet disposition and amenable to discipline." The Staffordshire Bull Terrier must have a "Temperament" that shows "character of indomitable courage, high intelligence, and tenacity . . . coupled with its affection for its friends, and children in particular, its off-duty quietness and trustworthy stability[.]" www.akc.org/breeds/staffordshire_bull_terrier/breed_standard.cfm. How precisely will animal control test for these behavioral traits?

Additionally, breed standards are based on kinesiology (or study of movement as it relates to physical activity, exercise, sport). Staffordshire Bull Terriers must possess a "gait" that is:

Free, powerful and agile with economy of effort. Legs moving parallel when viewed from front or rear. Discernible drive from hind legs.

Accordingly, if animal control does not evaluate the incident dog in motion, that serves as yet another basis to challenge the designation.

Disqualifications and Faults

Because every breed standard contains Disqualifications, those might be invoked as an absolute bar to an adverse declaration — for instance, if a bull terrier has "blue eyes" or "is predominantly white." www.akc.org/breeds/bull_terrier/breed_standard.cfm. Also look to Faults that, while not an absolute bar, will undermine the contention that the dog is identifiable as a member of a prohibited breed or substantially conforming to same. An American Staffordshire Terrier with "Dudley nose, light or pink eyes, tail too long or badly carried, undershot or overshot mouth" will be penalized. www.akc.org/breeds/american_staffordshire_terrier/breed_standard.cfm.

In light of the above, would Casadevall's credentials pass AKC muster? Hardly. And the Florida Circuit Court (Appellate Division) recognized as much in its decision of Mar. 30, 2010, found at 17 FLA. L. WEEKLY Supp. 923a, pet. denied, 44 So. 3d 1183 (2010), where it concluded:

The first violation of due process concerns the hearing officer's erroneous qualification of Officer Casadevall as an expert in "pit bull dog" identification. "[A]cceptance or rejection of expert testimony is a matter within the sound discretion of the lower tribunal, and such decision will not be overturned on appeal absent a showing of abuse of discretion." Gray v. Russell Corp., 681 So.2d 310, 316 (Fla. 1st DCA 1996). The U.S. Supreme Court in Daubert v. Merrell Dow Pharm., 509 U.S. 579, 594 (1993), set forth a series of criteria against which to measure scientific or technical methods and principles, which include: testing; peer review and publication; potential error rates; standards of operation; and general acceptance in the relevant community. Officer Casadevell offered nothing about the process of measuring the data for error rates, because no such statistics are kept; no objective standards for comparison exist. This Court finds that the County applies a subjective criteria and there is little or no peer review.

The hearing officer erroneously concluded, "This is a with 15 years and all of this background, so I would qualify as an expert witness."

Cardelle, at *5–*6. In dissipating the undeserved aura of veracity the Hearing Officer bestowed upon Casadevall, the court observed:

1. Casedevall freely admitted that while he performed over 1000 "pit bull" dog inspections, he did nothing to gather data, perform quality control, or validate existing data;

2. Casadevall did not have his inspections peer reviewed; and

3. Casadevall admitted that verification of his "pit bull" dog identifications falls outside his specialization as an animal control officer.

In other words, quantity does not denote quality. *Id.*, at *7–*8. This 2-1 decision remanded for a new hearing that would likely result in reversal of Kitty's designation, for without Casadevall's testimony given any weight, the examiner could only consider that of Cardelle's veterinary experts Drs. Tess Wenzl and Manuel Morales, who both did not identify Kitty as a "pit bull" dog and stated Kitty did not conform to the breed standards. *Id.*, at *3–*4, *13. As discussed below, however, it would appear that Drs. Wenzl and Morales would also suffer from the same criticisms leveled at Officer Casadevall.

The Lesson of *Michigan Wolfdog Assoc.*

In *Michigan Wolfdog Assoc. v. St. Clair Cy.*, 122 F. Supp. 2d 794 (E.D. Mich. 2000), admitted owners of wolf-dog mixes challenged Michigan's Wolf-Dog Cross Act, M.C.L. § 287.1001-.1023 as void for vagueness in lacking a qualitative or quantitative measure by which to determine the prohibited proportion of wolf or wolf-dog cross genetic material and, further, that the definitions were scientifically flawed (i.e., neither appearance nor behavior nor DNA test serves to distinguish wolf from dog). Plaintiffs' own exhibit undermined this position, however. Prepared by the U.S. American Wolfdog Association, their expert Dr. Raymond Pierotti *could* identify wolf-dog crosses within 0.25%. That Plaintiffs admitted to owning crosses additionally hampered their argument. Still, they contended that the ordinary person could not make such a studied determination and, for that reason, the Act violated the Fourteenth Amendment.

Litigation Tip: Facial challenges require proof that the ordinance in question cannot be applied constitutionally in any circumstance, a significant burden only made more onerous by holding the plaintiff to a beyond-a-reasonable-doubt standard. Most courts will only give strong consideration to the law as applied to the petitioner, which happened here.

The Act defined wolf-dog cross as "a canid resulting from the breeding of any of the following: (i) A wolf with a dog; (ii) A wolf-dog cross with a wolf; (iii) A wolf-dog cross with a dog; (iv) A wolf-dog cross with a wolf-dog cross." M.C.L. § 287.1002(p). The code further defined "dog" and "wolf." M.C.L. § 287.1002(d, o). Despite imposing criminal penalties for violation of the Act, meriting stricter scrutiny, the district court found that Plaintiffs did not have a substantial likelihood of prevailing in their argument that the Act was unconstitutional and dismissed the notion that some "mathematical certainty" was required. *Id.*, at 804 (citing to several cases that rejected similar vagueness challenges); *but see People v. Howard*, No. 93-2722, slip. Op. at 2 (Mich. Dist. Ct. Mar. 18, 1996) (Benson, J.) (acquitting man charged under at St. Joseph County animal ordinance for owning an alleged "wolf-hybrid type animal" due to a vague prohibition against possessing a "wild/exotic animal").

Though an unfavorable outcome, the decision identified features of the Act that might serve to distinguish it from other BSL. For instance, the Act states that if "the owner of the canid is unable or unwilling to verify that the canid is a wolf-dog cross, the law enforcement office, before enforcing this act, shall consult with an expert on wolf-dog cross identification," and that such expert "shall consider all relevant aspects of identification, such as behavioral characteristics, and morphological traits, including gait, and any necropsy results." M.C.L. § 287.1013(3). Said expert must have "cumulatively, at least 10 years of training and field experience in wolf and wolf-dog cross behavioral and morphological characteristics and who is recognized as an expert at the state and national levels by others in the same field." M.C.L. § 287.1002(e). The reader may wish to cite this case for the proposition that the absence of expert-based, pre-enforcement identification weighs against constitutionality.

iii   Admissibility of Scientific Evidence

Cardelle and *Michigan Wolfdog Association* illustrate the vital importance of examining the underpinnings of an adverse identification. Such an approach has fomented debate in other contexts, as in the use of visual analysis of spectrograms ("voiceprints" or "voicegrams") to convict a man of first-degree murder, kidnapping, and extortion. *See Commonwealth v. Lykus*, 2005 Mass. Super. LEXIS 686, *3 (Dec. 30, 2005). Though *Lykus* did not permit a new trial based on the trial judge's decision to permit testimony from a lieutenant who claimed that the defendant's voice exemplar matched that of the recorded ransom telephone call, it examined the shifting standard for admissibility of scientific evidence.

In 1973, Massachusetts followed *Frye v. U.S.*, 1923 U.S. App. LEXIS 1712 (D.C. Cir. 1923), a case permitting a jury or judge to consider only those opinions founded on generally accepted methodologies deemed reliable within the relevant field: those methods clamoring for, but not yet achieving, majority acceptance would fail *Frye*. In *Frye*, the federal circuit court determined whether to permit a polygraph test result as evidence by setting forth this principle:

> Just when a scientific principle or discovery crosses the line between the experimental and demonstrable stages is difficult to define. Somewhere in this twilight zone the evidential force of the principle must be recognized, and while the courts will go a long way in admitting experimental testimony deduced from a well-recognized scientific principle or discovery, the thing from which the deduction is made *must be sufficiently established to have gained general acceptance* in the particular field in which it belongs.

Id., at 47 (emphasis added). Presently, only a handful of states apply the *Frye* standard. The rest, and all federal courts, use *Daubert*.

Seven decades after *Frye*, the United States Supreme Court decided *Daubert v. Merrell Dow Pharm., Inc.*, 509 U.S. 579 (1993). It provided an alternative to the *Frye* general acceptance test where the opinion could otherwise be shown reliable or valid (i.e., even if still gaining adherents but not yet reaching the level of scientific consensus). Considerations included: (a) the ability to test the theory or technique; (b) whether the theory or technique has undergone peer review or publication; (c) the known or potential error rate; (d) presence of standards to operate the technique; and (e) degree of general acceptance in the relevant scientific community.

Lykus discussed the effect of a post-conviction, 1979 report from the National Research Council ("NRC"), titled *On the Theory and Practice of Voice Identification*, commissioned at the request of the FBI. It found that the "technical uncertainties concerning the present practice of voice identification are so great as to require that forensic applications be approached with great caution." *Id.*, at *12 (quoting *NRC Report*, at 2). The Report acknowledged that, though widely used, voiceprinting lacked a "solid theoretical basis of answers" regarding its scientific foundation and that it "probably fails the [*Frye*] test." *Id.*, at *14 (*Report*, at 42).

The reason? In 1979, voice identification science did not "stand on a thorough foundation of quantitative information describing its capabilities through forensic practice." *Id.* (Report at 69). Yet it is important not to misstate the Report's position on voiceprinting in the courtrooms: instead of calling for its prohibition, the NRC instead urged that courts instruct juries on the possibility of error inherent in deciding whether two voices match. *Lykus* provides a suitable point of comparison in answering questions of admissibility under *Frye* and *Daubert* as to the science of breed identification (visual or genetic), as well as the purported link between breed and aggression.

Cautionary observation: DNA-based breed identification products have enjoyed tremendous popularity of late, and embracing them to prove or disprove a dog's status under BSL may, in the individual animal's case, result in acquittal or release. However, to date no court has actually entertained a *Frye* or *Daubert* motion challenging its accuracy and reliability. Among professionals, however, the tests have been regarded as a gold standard and far more suitable to the task than visual identification. Yet such reliance may establish harmful precedent. If such tests garner general acceptance among scientists and judges, they will quickly become a litmus test and municipalities may go so far as compelling the dog owner to authorize blood draws or buccal swabs. Results could incriminate both canine and owner.

Whether such mandatory swabbing or blood draw violates the Fourth and Fifth Amendments to the United States Constitution remains to be seen. Where BSL does not deem certain breeds as contraband, for which possession constitutes a crime, the Fifth Amendment right against self-incrimination would not apply, but the Fourth Amendment right against unreasonable search and seizure might. Much will come down to at least seven legal questions: (1) whether to ascribe a more protective legal standard to people versus canines generally, as "effects"; (2) whether non- or minimally invasive DNA sampling meaningfully interferes with the possessory rights of the dog (i.e., is it a "seizure?"); (3) whether DNA collection through venipuncture or swabbing constitutes an unreasonable "search" (*see State v. Newcomb*, 262 Or. App. 256 (2014), *rev'd*, 359 Or. 756 (2016); *Schmerber v. California*, 384 U.S. 757, 771 (1966) (blood test intrusion insignificant as test is commonplace, quantity of blood taken is minimal, and involves virtually no risk, trauma, or pain); *Nicholas v. Goord*, 430 F.3d 652, 656 n.5 (2d Cir. 2005) (buccal swab less invasive than blood draw); (4) whether DNA processing and creation of a DNA profile constitutes an unreasonable "search"; (5) whether the DNA collection may prove overly expansive by collecting "junk DNA" that might later be used to reveal traits and other genetic details unrelated to breed profiling; (6) whether there is a right of privacy for dog owners in their dogs (it goes without saying that dogs themselves have no such right); and (7) whether to treat canines as more akin to free citizens or detainees, arrestees, and parolees (who enjoy fewer protections under the Fourth Amendment, due in part to the federal and many state DNA collection laws; note also that suspicionless or "blanket" fingerprinting of all free citizens does violate the Fourth Amendment (*Hayes v. Florida*, 470 U.S. 811, 813–18 (1985))? *Cf. Friedman v. Boucher*, 580 F.3d 847 (9th Cir. 2009) (finding that shackling detainee, chaining him to bench, forcibly opening his jaw and extracting DNA sample without warrant, court order, reasonable suspicion, or concern about facility security clearly violated Fourth Amendment rights); *U.S. v. Mitchell*, 652 F.3d 387 (3d Cir. 2011) (discussing constitutional implications of preconviction compulsory DNA extraction); Anna C. Henning, *Compulsory DNA Collection: A Fourth Amendment Analysis*, 7-5700 (R40077), Congressional Research Service (Feb. 16, 2010) www.fas.org/sgp/crs/misc/R40077pdf.

Litigation Tip: Litigators should be prepared to invoke ER 702, and the *Frye* or *Daubert* test applicable in the jurisdiction. Because turnabout is fair play, however, be prepared for the inevitable motion to disqualify a veterinarian who testifies to an exculpatory genetic identification.

An objection on grounds that the proffers of breed identification and nexus to aggression are inadmissible under ER 702, the rule limiting testimony by expert witnesses may apply. In federal court, FRE 702 states:

A witness who is qualified as an expert by knowledge, skill, experience, training, or education may testify in the form of an opinion or otherwise if:

> (a) the expert's scientific, technical, or other specialized knowledge will help the trier of fact to understand the evidence or to determine a fact in issue;

> (b) the testimony is based on sufficient facts or data;

> (c) the testimony is the product of reliable principles and methods; and

> (d) the expert has reliably applied the principles and methods to the facts of the case.

State court analogs invariably embrace prong (a) but not all adopt (b) through (d). For instance, Wash. Evid. Rule 702 says:

If scientific, technical, or other specialized knowledge will assist the trier of fact to understand the evidence or to determine a fact in issue, a witness qualified as an expert by knowledge, skill, experience, training, or education, may testify thereto in the form of an opinion or otherwise.

Oreg. Rev. Stat. § 40.410 and Idaho R. Evid. 702 duplicate the Washington rule verbatim.

A *Frye* or *Daubert* hearing to bar admission of expert testimony may follow.

The personal opinion of an expert witness, regardless of the impressiveness of credentials, is not admissible under ER 702, as "[A] trial court must 'determine whether the evidence is genuinely scientific, as distinct from being unscientific speculation offered by a genuine scientist.'" *Group Health Plan, Inc. v. Philip Morris, Inc.*, 188 F. Supp. 2d 1122, 1131 (D. Minn. 2002) (citations omitted). Focus on evidence-based conclusions rather than authority-based opinions. To learn more, read Terence M. Davidson & Christopher P. Guzelian, *Evidence-Based Medicine*

(EBM): The (Only) Means for Distinguishing Knowledge of Medical Causation from Expert Opinion in the Courtroom, 47 TORT TRIAL & INS. PRAC. L.J. 741 (Wtr. 2012); Stephen Collier, *Breed-specific Legislation and the Pit Bull Terrier: Are the Laws Justified?*, 1 J. VET. BEH: CLINICAL APPLICATIONS AND RES. 17, 17–22 (2006).

iv.   The Nexus

In 2012, the Maine Supreme Judicial Court decided *Morgan v. Marquis*, 50 A.3d 1 (Me. 2012). It refused to create a breed-specific absolute liability standard, remarking that the trial court correctly decided not to treat "pit bull" dogs as *per se* abnormally dangerous to the class of domestic dogs. Generalities as to "pit bull" dogs "are not sufficient to survive the Restatement section 509 test for common law strict liability because that test requires a showing that the Marquises knew that Beans was dangerous[.]" *Id.*, at 5. However, in deciding negligence, the jury was free to determine if breed enhanced the duty owed due to some propensity to bite and harm. *Id.*, at 4–5.

The last case to decide the question of rational basis has determined that a jury must resolve it. In *Dias v. City and County of Denver*, 567 F.3d 1169 (10th Cir. 2009), the Tenth Circuit Court of Appeals reversed a Rule 12(b)(6) dismissal of plaintiffs' substantive due process claim, concluding that the allegations construed in the light most flattering to the plaintiffs urged the conclusion that the breed ban of the City of Denver was not rationally related to a legitimate government interest:

> Specifically, the plaintiffs contend that although pit bull bans sustained twenty years ago may have been justified by the then-existing body of knowledge, the state of science in 2009 is such that the bans are no longer rational. This claim finds some support in the AKC and UKC standards themselves, to which the plaintiffs direct us. The official UKC breed standard for the American Pit Bull Terrier, for instance, states that "[American Pit Bull Terriers] make excellent family companions and have always been noted for their love of children." Official UKC Breed Standard, American Pit Bull Terrier, Appellant Br. Ex. 4. American Pit Bull Terriers are an "extremely friendly" breed "even with strangers. Aggressive behavior toward humans is uncharacteristic of the breed. . . . " *Id.* Similarly, the AKC breed standard for Staffordshire Bull Terriers states that, "with its affection for its friends, and children in particular, its off-duty quietness and trustworthy stability, [the Staffordshire Bull Terrier is] a foremost all-purpose dog." AKC Staffordshire Bull Terrier Breed Standard, Appellant Br. Ex. 2. Without drawing factual inferences against the plaintiffs, the district court could not conclude at this early stage in the case that the Ordinance was rational as a matter of law.

Id., at 1183–84. On remand, the District Court of Colorado denied the City's motion for summary judgment dismissal of the substantive due process claim, finding that on the record amassed by Plaintiffs, "a reasonable trier of fact may find that Plaintiffs' experts are correct and there exists no rational basis for a breed specific ordinance." 2010 U.S. Dist. LEXIS 103814, *20 (D. Colo. Sept. 29, 2010) (also noting that the 2000 Center for Disease Control study cannot be used to infer any breed-specific risk for dog-bite fatalities); *see also Hopkins v. McCollam*, 300 P.3d 115 (Kan. Ct. App. 2013) (quoting *Dias*).

Litigation Tip: With respect to mixed breeds, the substantive due process argument will carry even greater force.

v.   Challenging the Designation

More than two decades ago, the Massachusetts Supreme Court in *Assoc. Dog Owners Assoc. v. Lynn*, 533 N.E.2d 642 (Mass. 1989), observed that there was "no scientific means, by blood, enzyme, or otherwise, to determine if a dog is a particular breed or any mixture thereof[.]" *Id.*, at 646. Twenty-six years later, however, such means arguably do exist to challenge the uneducated and unleashed discretion of an officer eyeballing the suspected dog.

At the present time, the MARS Wisdom Professional Panel arguably yields the best results for breed identification and does not risk possible DNA contamination by the alternatively employed buccal swab test (when wielded by a person lacking adequate skill to ensure a clean specimen), since a dog who licks another dog's body, another dog's bodily secretions, or even a person's face and hands, could introduce traces of multiple DNA signatures into the mouth.

Cautionary Note: MARS explicitly disclaims the use of its Wisdom Panel by animal control officials to determine whether a particular dog should be banned due to BSL. "*Wisdom Panel®* is designed and intended to be used solely to identify the breed history of a dog and no other purpose is authorized or permitted." Furthermore, as to the bedeviled "pit-bull," MARS states:

> The term "Pit-bull" is a bit of a misnomer and does not refer to a single, recognized breed of dog, but rather to a genetically diverse group of breeds which are associated by certain physical traits. . . . Due to the genetic diversity of this group, Mars Veterinary cannot build a DNA profile to genetically identify every dog that may be visually classified as a Pit-bull. When these types of dogs are tested with the *Wisdom Panel ®*, we routinely detect various quantities of the component purebred dogs including the American Staffordshire Terrier, Boston Terrier, Bull Terrier, Staffordshire Bull Terrier, Mastiff, Bullmastiff, Boxer, Bulldog, and various other Terriers. Additionally, there are often other breeds outside of the Guard and Terrier groups identified in the mix depending on each dog's individual ancestry . . . .

www.wisdompanel.com/why_test_your_dog/faqs/#785 (Mar. 22, 2014). In 2014, MARS changed its terms of service, stating:

> Many countries and provinces have breed-specific ordinances and laws that may require special handling or prohibit the ownership of some dogs with a particular breed in their genetic background. Wisdom Panel 2.0 is not intended to be used by regulatory or animal control officials to determine whether a particular breed is legislated or banned in a particular country or province. Nor is Wisdom Panel 2.0 intended to be used in any judicial proceedings. Rather, it is intended to be used as a tool or resource in

determining a dog's genetic history. Neither Mars Veterinary nor any related company is responsible for compliance or notification regarding these matters.

That the manufacturer has refused to give a stamp of authoritativeness to its breed detection test would appear to undermine any use in court under *Frye, Daubert,* and/or ER 702. Presaging this legal evidentiary problem in *State v. Lee,* discussed above, the Kansas Court of Appeals evaluated the trial court's refusal to grant a continuance so the state or Lee could cajole a reluctant representative from MARS to testify as to the significance of the DNA results and thus lay a foundation for admissibility. Finding no abuse of discretion in denying a continuance, it added that:

> even if a witness was willing to testify, the probable testimony was not critical to establish Lee's theory of defense. As a preliminary matter, the information in the report does not support a finding that the dog falls outside the purview of the ordinance. . . . Although the report states that the dog was a mix of breeds, the analysis specifically detected the breeds of American Staffordshire Terrier, Bull Terrier, and Bulldog. To that end, the report indicates that although the dog matched strongly to American Staffordshire Terrier and Bull Terrier, the strongest breed signature match was American Staffordshire Terrier. Because the report itself did not favor Lee's theory of defense, we find it unlikely that any proposed testimony about the report would do so.

Lee. 257 P.3d., at 809. What if the DNA test made no mention of one of the prohibited breeds? Without a MARS representative willing to testify,[26] would a jury even hear the results over an objection on grounds of hearsay and foundation? On par, is it strategically preferable for the dog owner to object to the use of any form of identification (visual or DNA) as untenable under *Frye, Daubert,* and ER 702, thereby preventing the BSL enforcer from satisfying the threshold burden of production?

While anecdotal reports of inconsistently reporting the breeds of a specific dog's grandparents and great-grandparents exist, DNA has otherwise proven more reliable than visual identification. Might the dog owner find some evidentiary work-around to ensure the DNA test's admissibility? One possibility is to pass the results through an expert whose field routinely relies upon DNA-based breed evidence, using FRE 703 or FRE 807 and state analogs.

vi.　　　Shooting the Messenger

Still, such DNA-based evidence relied upon by, say, a veterinarian or an animal control officer produces an opinion that is only as reliable as its source. If the test remains impervious to critical scrutiny due to MARS's refusal to share its proprietary methodology, then one must indirectly challenge the professional qualifications of the expert who purports to testify in support of the technique

---

[26] To date, no court has compelled a MARS Representative to testify. A successful motion to quash a prosecutor's or defense attorney's subpoena may effectively negate any foundation and serve as a dispositive procedural impediment to admissibility.

under FRE 703 and FRE 807. Rule 703 permits an expert to give an opinion based on hearsay if of the type of evidence regularly relied upon by experts in that field. This technique of backdooring otherwise inadmissible evidence through an expert witness has spilled a great deal of ink. Daniel D. Blinka, *Ethical Firewalls, Limited Admissibility, and Rule 703*, 76 FORDHAM L. REV. 1229 (2007); Ian Volek, *Federal Rule of Evidence 703: The Back Door and the Confrontation Clause, Ten Years Later*, 80 FORDHAM L. REV. 959 (2011); Laura Owen Wingate, *Louisiana Code of Evidence Article 703: Is it a Hidden Exception to the Hearsay Rule?*, 53 LA. L. REV. 1605 (1993); Ronald L. Carlson, *Experts as Hearsay Conduits: Confrontation Abuses in Opinion Testimony*, 76 MINN. L. REV. 859 (1992); Laura F. Levine, *Locking the Backdoor: Revised MRE 703 and its Realized Impact on Bases of Expert Testimony*, 87 U. DET. MERCY L. REV. 505 (2010); Paul F. Rothstein, *Rule 703. Bases of an Expert's Opinion Testimony*, FED. RULES OF EVIDENCE RULE 703 (3d ed.).

Two relatively recent United States Supreme Court decisions prove instructive — *Crawford v. Washington*, 541 U.S. 36 (2004) and *Williams v. Illinois*, 132 S. Ct. 2221 (2012). In *Crawford*, a felony assault and attempted murder case, the state offered a recorded statement of Crawford's wife during a police interrogation to prove that the stabbing was not in self-defense. Due to marital privilege, his wife did not take the stand. Over his objection, the trial court allowed the recording to be heard by the jury, whereupon he was convicted. In reversing, the Supreme Court held that such ruling violated Crawford's Sixth Amendment right to confront witnesses, for the wife's statement was testimonial in nature. Typically, sworn statements in a judicial proceeding are testimonial, and include declarations, affidavits, depositions, and confessions. So do police interrogations, such as that of Crawford's wife, who was in custody, under suspicion, and answering leading questions from detectives. Business records, such as cell phone logs, are nontestimonial.

In *Williams*, a rape case, forensic specialist Sandra Lambatos, working for the Illinois State Police lab, testified that she matched the DNA profile from a sample of the petitioner's blood (run by her lab) against a DNA profile produced by an outside laboratory, Cellmark. The sum total of her knowledge about Cellmark's processes consisted of testifying that Cellmark was an accredited lab and that its business records showed that the vaginal swabs from the victim were sent to Cellmark and returned. She could not speak to the accuracy of Cellmark's profile, nor how Cellmark handled or tested the sample. Defense counsel objected on grounds that Lambatos sought to introduce hearsay evidence that Williams could not challenge, violating the Sixth Amendment's Confrontation Clause (which, incidentally, only applies to "criminal prosecutions"). The prosecutor urged that Illinois Rule of Evidence 703 permitted Lambatos to disclose facts upon which she based her opinion even if she lacked competence to testify to those underlying facts. The trial court agreed and convicted Lambatos. A 5-4 plurality affirmed his conviction on the basis that Cellmark's test results were nontestimonial (i.e., the unsworn data did not "bear testimony" against Williams in the sense of a "solemn declaration of affirmation made for the purpose of establishing or proving some fact" or made with "a primary purpose of creating an out-of-court substitute for trial testimony," and "to establish or prove past events potentially relevant to later criminal prosecution." *Michigan v. Bryant*, 131 S. Ct. 1143, 1153–55 (2011)).

However, laboratory reports and certificates presented in affidavit form will fall within the core class of testimonial statements. *See Melendez-Diaz v. Mass.*, 557 U.S. 305, 310–11 (2009) (finding analyst affidavits concerning composition, quality, and net weight of cocaine were testimonial statements and analysts were "witnesses" for purposes of Sixth Amendment; absent showing they were unavailable to testify and Melendez-Diaz had opportunity to cross-examine them before trial, his right to confront them was violated); *see also Bullcoming v. New Mexico*, 131 S. Ct. 2705 (2011) (BAC analysis report testimonial in nature). While *Melendez-Diaz* and *Bullcoming* appear to categorically exclude most lab analyses per the Sixth Amendment, remember the evidentiary bypass of Rule 703 as discussed in *Williams*.

But then one must face the inevitable challenge that the test is not recognized as probative for BSL litigation purposes by the lab itself and, furthermore, that the lab will not reveal its methodology, thereby preventing replication and objective analysis by third parties. Moreover, admission would amount to the court involuntarily and indirectly designating the lab technician or its chief scientific officer as a court-appointed expert — without the formal appointment. The court and parties, therefore, would be forced to simply take the lab's word for it. How does this compare with other attempts to introduce novel analyses and proprietary testing?

In *Cooper v. Brown*, 510 F.3d 870 (9th Cir. 2007), the Ninth Circuit refused to admit EDTA testing in a murder trial, finding that it had not gained general acceptance in the scientific community, adding that with one exception (the OJ murder trial), no court ever admitted EDTA test results, and Dr. Ballard's credibility was "soundly rejected," along with his EDTA testing as unreliable in *New Jersey v. Pompey*. The only reason EDTA made it into the Los Angeles courtroom was because, "[T]he testing protocol . . . was never called into question. It was simply a matter of interpretation." Furthermore, "[T]he results of the tests permitted both sides to claim a measure of victory." *Id.*, at 944. *Cooper* alerts the litigator to the lesson that:

> A scientific test is not automatically admissible. For example, a polygraph test can reliably measure a person's heart rate, blood pressure, and breathing. However, a polygraph test is inadmissible to show that person's veracity.

Id., at 945 (cit.om.). Similarly, assuming the Wisdom Panel can reliably measure a dog's breed composition,[27] is it admissible for legal calibration against a BSL

---

[27] Its newest test, the Wisdom Panel 3.0, does not, at this time, detect the American Pit Bull Terrier ("APBT"), placing in doubt the test's probativity where BSL excludes or includes the APBT. For instance, if excluded from the legislation, the subject dog's genetic composition might be mistakenly matched by the Wisdom Panel to other BSL-prohibited breeds for which Mars does test (e.g., Staffordshire Bull Terrier ("SBT")). The rate of a false positive for SBT might increase by the absence of APBT in the breed detection database. Accordingly, reliance on the MARS test may violate equal protection since its database excludes APBT genetic markers. Such a dog simply cannot be tested reliably, and would be erroneously reported as genetically comprised of other breeds. Further, MARS sends a form letter explaining that different specimens from the same animal may produce different

standard, merely for entertainment, or for a very limited veterinary medical purpose of identifying potential genetic predispositions?

More critically, though, can the Wisdom Panel be deemed reliable in identifying any dog breed whatsoever? *Cooper* rejected EDTA testing under *Daubert* by noting its "inherent problematic nature," described as follows:

> Like polygraph testing, the error rate of EDTA testing cannot be determined. . . . There are no industry standards that bind the testing scientist to a certain test protocol. If anything, this problem is more pronounced in the EDTA testing field, where Dr. Ballard appears to be almost the only individual who performs this type of test.

Id., at 945. The court added that EDTA testing was not scientifically accepted and not subjected to peer review or publication. Further, because there are no standard EDTA levels against which test results may be compared, results may be significantly manipulated and prevent definitive conclusions. *Id.*, at 945–47.

Other examples of scientific tests deemed inadmissible for failure to comply with *Daubert* include astronomical dating of a photograph (*U.S. v. Tranowski*, 659 F.2d 750 (7th Cir. 1981) (rejected because no evidence procedure had ever been attempted previously by anyone, no published work outlined the necessary methodology for such dating convention, no control experiments were performed to verify the technique's accuracy, and the calculations did not demonstrate indicia of reliability); topographical brain mapping (*Head v. Lithonia Corp.*, 881 F.2d 941 (10th Cir. 1989); forensic linguistic analysis, i.e., identifying authorship of a writing by comparing syntax, spelling, and paragraphing styles (*U.S. v. Clifford*, 543 F. Supp. 424 (W.D. Pa. 1983) (method not shown to be trustworthy, reliable, accurate, or conforming to a generally accepted scientific theory); silicone antibody blood test (*Cabrera v. Cordis Corp.*, 134 F.3d 1418 (9th Cir. 1998) (did not meet *Daubert* standards of reliability). By contrast, consider the admissible gold chloride microcrystalline test to determine the chemical composition of l-cocaine (*U.S. v. Luschen*, 614 F.2d 1164 (8th Cir. 1980), the oil identification technique (*U.S. v. Distler*, 671 F.2d 954 (6th Cir. 1981), and though not yet having gained general judicial recognition, the immunobead assay procedure to detect antibodies in semen samples and thus identify semen (*U.S. v. Gwaltney*, 790 F.2d 1378 (9th Cir. 1986)).

If MARS will not disclose its methodology, none other presently performs the test,[28] and the method has not been subjected to published peer-review, how can a proponent of such evidence ever hope to demonstrate general acceptance or reliability? Scrutinizing the patents and related materials may suffice if conveyed to the court by a proper expert.

On Apr. 15, 2014, the City of Yakima, Washington, amended its BSL to permit "pit bull service animals" within city limits. YMC § 6.18.030(C)(IV) seeks to provide an exclusive DNA exception to the City's labeling of a dog as a pit bull (and the sequelae of such an adverse determination, such as impoundment and criminal

---

results. The Wisdom Panel 3.0 is perhaps the only test for wolf.

[28] Biopet Vet Lab, Inc., was a competitor but since became the target of a patent infringement action by Fred Hutchinson Cancer Research Center, Argus Genetics, LLC, and Mars, Inc. *Fred Hutchinson Cancer Research Center v. BioPet Vet Lab, Inc.*, 768 F. Supp. 2d 872 (E.D. Va. 2011).

prosecution), saying that the dog will only be released "as a result of DNA testing." In so doing, however, the City narrowed the scope of admissible evidence, arguably in conflict with not only the state and federal constitutions, but the Washington Supreme Court-enacted rules for courts of limited jurisdiction and the rules of evidence. Further, where DNA evidence is almost certainly not even admissible under ER 702 and *Frye*, given that MARS Corporation recently reiterated that its tests are not to be used for enforcement or in litigation, has the City furnished an illusory exception that gives the owner just one evidentiary basis by which to challenge an also scientifically invalid and inadmissible visual identification by a Yakima animal control officer or law enforcement officer. That this DNA defense must be also borne at the expense of the dog owner only deepens the constitutional objection.[29]

Of course, turning to visual identification compounds the morass of unreliability. Dr. Victoria Voith and colleagues recently published *Comparison of Visual and DNA Breed Identification of Dogs and Inter-Observer Reliability* in 3(2) AMER. J. SOC. RES. 17 (2013). She reached these conclusions:

(a) Known crosses of purebred dogs (i.e., mixed breed dogs) may not look like either parent and may, in fact, more closely resemble other breeds.

(b) There is little correlation between DNA identification of breeds that comprise mixed breed dogs and visual identification by professionals familiar with dogs, including animal control and veterinary medical personnel. Visual identifications by people assumed to have special knowledge in breed identification of mixed breed dogs (e.g., animal control and veterinary medical personnel) are less than 50% accurate — worse than chance. Thus, visual identification of the breed composition of mixed breed dogs is frequently inaccurate.

(c) There is a low level of agreement among professionals (familiar with dogs, including personnel in animal control and veterinary medicine) as to the most predominant breed (or any breed) in a mixed breed dog. That is, they often disagree.

(d) Even if some professionals (familiar with dogs, including personnel in animal control and veterinary medicine) agree as to the breed composition of a mixed breed dog, the DNA analysis of breed composition may not verify the agreed-upon visual identification.

(e) Lists of breeds who allegedly bite, attack or injure people, as contained in some of the widely-quoted, peer-reviewed articles, are not validated and are unreliable. The majority of the lists were compiled from newspaper accounts that were not verified as to breed of dog or who identified the dogs. Indeed, most of the authors warn, in the articles themselves, that this information is derived from unverified, potentially inaccurate sources, and there was no accurate data available regarding the population of dogs, much less the representation of specific breeds. They also caution that the breeds listed in the articles cannot and should not be used to infer any

---

[29] The code may operate as an estoppel against the City where the test disproves genetic content. Thus, whether admissible or not, this provision serves as a codified stipulation.

breed-specific risk. Rather, they usually emphasize that other factors contribute to the aggressivity of dogs, such as their environment, individual histories, and circumstances in which the dogs were aggressive. Furthermore, these lists were derived before the advent of DNA breed identification and revelation of the large discrepancy between visual and DNA identification of mixed breed dogs. In summary, reports that appear to target particular breeds as being more dangerous are not based on validated breed identifications or the known proportion of those breeds in the community. Recent articles supporting the above statements include *A Community Approach to Dog Bite Prevention*, AVMA Task Force on Canine Aggression and Human-Canine Interactions, JAVMA 218(11):1732-1749 (2001) and GJ Patroniek, M Slater, A Marder, *Use of a Number-Needed-to-Ban Calculation to Illustrate Limitations of Breed-Specific Legislation in Decreasing the Risk of Dog-Bite Related Injury*, JAVMA 237:788-792 (2010).

(f) The use of the phrase "element . . . as to be identifiable" as contained in many BSL codes is ambiguous and unclear. If interpreted to mean a feature or anatomical characteristic, it cannot be concluded with any certainty that because a dog in question appears to have some or any feature that is similar to those in a purebred dog, that the dog in question is partially that breed of dog. If "element" is meant to be a portion of the dog's genetic breed make-up, this cannot be validly or reliably visually determined. Even whether or not a dog is a purebred can be difficult to determine visually. For instance, Scott & Fuller's studies and published pictures (SCOTT JP & FULLER JL, GENETICS AND THE SOCIAL BEHAVIOR OF THE DOG: THE CLASSIC STUDY. 1965 (Univ. of Chic. Press, Chicago) clearly show that mixed breed dogs of known crosses of purebred dogs (i.e., mixed breed dogs) may not look like either parent and may, in fact, more closely resemble other breeds. Further, a paper published in the *Journal of Applied Animal Welfare Science* (Voith VL et al. *Comparison of Adoption Agency Breed Identification and DNA Breed Identification of Dogs*, JAAWS 12:253-262 (2009)), a peer-reviewed scientific journal, reported that eighty-five (85%) percent, or 17 of 20, of the dogs identified by the adoption agency as having either a type or specific breed in their ancestry did not have representative breeds detected by DNA for each of these types or breeds. If "shepherd" type indicated German Shepherd Dog, then ninety (90%) percent, or 18 of 20, of the dogs identified by adoption agencies were not reported by DNA. That is, most of the time, adoption agency identifications did not match DNA identifications.

(g) The "methodology" used by many cities to declare dogs dangerous based on if a dog appears to be a specific breed or partially a specific breed is subjective, variable by different observers, is not based on solid evidence or sound scientific principles, and lacks rational basis.

vii.   Challenging the Association

Yet the use of DNA begs the question: is DNA the answer even if it exonerates in a particular dog's case? By struggling to genetically decontaminate the dog at issue through the use of DNA (i.e., "Trixie is *only* 25% American Staffordshire Terrier"), do we still end up damning the pit bull terrier-type dog with faint praise? Should not the focus be demonstrated behavior?

Many contend that BSL suffers from the fundamental, flawed presumption that breed reliably predicts vicious propensity. It draws from retrospective review of anecdotal evidence based on questionable phenotypic and genotypic identifications (not double-blind, randomized trials that follow breed-confirmed dogs till the triggering event, while controlling for confounding variables). These identifications suffer from several degrees of critique under ER 702, *Frye* and/or *Daubert*, not to mention standard objections of hearsay and authenticity. BSL proponents will point to dogbite-related fatality ("DBRF") data, but a 2013 JAVMA publication casts deep doubt on the attempt to invoke some breed association. Gary J. Patronek, Jeffrey J. Sacks et al., *Co-occurrence of Potentially Preventable Factors in 256 Dog Bite-related Fatalities in the United States (2000-2009)*, 243 J. AM. VET. MED. ASSOC. 1726 (2013) (co-occurring and owner-preventable factors forecast DBRFs; breed did not).

Be prepared to present an expert to challenge the nexus between identification and dangerousness. In 2011 litigation against the City of Moses Lake, Wash., and challenge to its BSL, plaintiff Nicholas Criscuolo retained Dr. Kristopher Irizarry as an expert. He reached these conclusions:

1. The increasing practice of defining members of some breeds of dogs (or mixes of those breeds) as dangerous or aggressive (regardless of an individual dog's temperament) is an unfortunate consequence of ignorance and misinformation regarding dog genetics that have led to scientifically invalid dog laws.

2. The biology and genetics of dogs and dog breeds have been heavily studied during the last ten to fifteen years as a direct result of genetics and genomics discoveries made possible by the genome sequencing era and, specifically, the canine genome sequence (released to the public in July 2004). Some of these discoveries include: (1) identifying the single region within the dog genome responsible for encoding small dog size, (2) the extent of genetic similarity within and between breeds, (3) the specific regions of the genome responsible for breed-associated anatomical and morphological traits, (4) methods to determine relative contributions of ancestral breed compositions in mixed breed dogs, (5) the identification of thousands of dog genes as well as the commercial development of clinical genetic diagnostics for use in canine veterinary medicine.

3. The avalanche of canine genomics research has placed the dog in the same research arena as the white laboratory mouse and, in doing so, elucidated a significant amount of knowledge regarding the evolutionary genomics of their domestication as well as the genetic basis for the production of modern dog breeds such as those represented in the American Kennel Club. These discoveries have placed age-old questions about dogs within a

21st century scientific framework backed by very large data sets (on the order of thousands to millions of data points in each genetic experiment). This means that the speculation, myths and misinformation regarding dogs and genetics can be identified and supplanted by scientifically valid findings derived from the reproducible analysis of particular dog genetics data sets subsequently published in specific high-impact, peer-reviewed journals. The authors who published these findings are some of the most well-respected and renowned today and reside at research institutions such as Harvard University, Massachusetts Institute of Technology and the NIH to name a few.

4. The biomedical literature provides a record of the discoveries and accumulated knowledge in medical and clinically related biology. One such database offered by the National Institutes of Health (http://www.ncbi.nlm.nih.gov/pubmed/) contains more than 20 million biomedical citations. These scientific publications are indexed by key words and one can search for specific combinations of keywords and retrieve the subset of citations associated with those terms. As of September 2011, there are 37,179 citations for the search of dogs and disease. There are 20,611 citations associated with dogs and a list of specific genetic terms. This is an extremely large body of scientific knowledge about dogs and genetics from which society and the law can free itself from myths about dogs and genetics.

5. The common view of dogs and dog breeds includes a number of misconceptions for which recent discoveries in the field of canine genetics provide dispositive empirical evidence demonstrating how and why these views are wrongheaded and irrational. Some of the most common and wide-held misconceptions/myths about dogs are:

Myth 1: Dog breeds were created through the selection of breed-specific behavioral traits. This is not true and not supported by the analysis of dog genomes within and across breeds. The current state of knowledge proves that dog breeds were selected for specific anatomical traits such as short hair, long legs, pointed ears, and long snout (for example), not behavior.

Myth 2: The breed composition of a mixed breed dog can be determined by visual observation. This is not true because very few genes encode breed-associated morphological traits (on the order of 50 genes), compared to all the genes in the canine genome (on the order of 19,000 genes). Consequently, the person visually observing a dog is unable to assess the contribution of the other 18,950 genes. DNA analysis provides state-of-the-art breed determination.

Myth 3: All members of a dog breed share the same traits and behaviors. This is not true as recent discoveries in the field of canine genetics have demonstrated that members of a breed have no genetic variation in breed-defining anatomical traits (i.e. German Shepherds do have the genes to make the very short snout found in French bull dogs or pugs), but do exhibit extensive genetic variation in regions of the genome associated with other traits. This "footprint" in the genome means that the only common genetics among breed members occur within anatomical (i.e., not behavioral) genes. Therefore, some members of the breed may develop a disease that other members of the breed do not. Some members of the breed may be very shy while others may be comfortable around strangers and loud noises.

Myth 4: The presence of ancestral contributions of a specific breed within a mixed breed dog "contaminate" the mixed breed dog with undesirable traits derived from that specific breed. This is scientifically unfounded and lacks validity as a breed is defined as a lack of genetic variation within specific regions of the genome (for example, in genes encoding coat texture and color or genes encoding head shape and ear morphology). The notion that "any amount of ancestral component from a specific breed" might confer stereotyped traits from that breed is illogical and not rational. The dog genome is diluted at every subsequent generation by ½. A fifth generation descendent of a specific dog would have (½ x ½ x ½ x ½ x ½) only 1/32 of its genome derived from that ancestor. In other words, 31/32 of its genome derived from dogs that are not that ancestor. Ancestral DNA is not a virus that infects all descendants and should not be used to classify dogs in terms of behavior or anticipated safety.

6. Anatomical features associated with dog breeds are found in many different breeds.

7. AKC dog breeds are defined through a closed breeding pool.

8. A mixed breed dog is not a member of a breed.

9. The defining anatomical features of dog breeds are the result of a handful of genes that have been identified and listed in peer-reviewed scientific publications.

10. The anatomical features associated with dog breeds do not encode the brain or the connections of brain cells and are not involved in encoding the behavior of a dog.

11. Unlike identical twins in humans — who have identical DNA, members of dog breeds may look the same and have very different DNA.

12. Dogs with open breeding pools, such as mixed breed dogs, cannot be considered a member of a specific breed.

13. A dog that is 25% Labrador Retriever is not eligible to compete in an AKC dog show for Labrador Retrievers.

14. Visual identification of dog breeds is inaccurate.

15. Visual identification of dog breeds differs from DNA identification of dog breeds.

16. The lack of efficacy in identifying dog breeds is the result of relatively few regions of the genome being associated with anatomical traits.

17. The anatomical similarity of dogs within a breed causes people to assume that dogs within a breed share other traits, such as behavior, health and disease susceptibility, yet this assumption is flawed.

18. Animal professionals, including veterinarians, dog breeders, dog show judges, animal control officers and others are not capable of accurately

identifying breeds in mixed breed dogs.

19. The manner in which mixed breed dogs are visually identified is so subjective as to be arbitrary and capricious.

20. An "element" is undefinable in terms of mixed dog breeds.

21. Even using DNA, an "element" is vague and unable to be intelligently applied since all dogs share 99.9975% of their DNA across breeds.

22. An element cannot be reliably visually identified in a mixed breed dog.

23. The notion that the presence of an anatomical feature, i.e., smooth coat, correlates with behavior is not rational.

24. Visual identification of mixed breed prohibited dogs does not reliably or rationally meet the purported goals of BSL (i.e., to ensure that dogs are classified accurately and banished or euthanized to protect the public safety).

25. Breed bans do not work because bite rates do not go down; thus, there is no rational basis in terms of increasing public safety.

26. There is no scientific evidence that the prohibited breeds are more aggressive or dangerous than other dogs. This is due, in part, to the problem of acquiring accurate statistics on the total number of dogs. N.B.: the CDC specifically stated that its fatal study was not to be used for breed bans.

27. Since studies regarding breeds and bites rely in the end on visual identification by lay people, they are totally inaccurate and unscientific.

28. The science of dog DNA is the most accurate method to determine mixed breed dogs and will supplant visual identifications.

29. The stratification of dogs into breeds reduces the genetic variation within a breed. Once a member of the breed is crossed with other breeds of dogs, it gains the genetic variation from these other dogs and loses the genetics associated with a single breed.

30. Regardless of whether someone inaccurately believes that a specific breed has a certain behavior or "dangerousness," a dog with moderate or minor/trace amounts of that breed has the majority of its genome derived from breeds other than the breed in question.

31. The notion that any element of some breed would make a dog dangerous is not rational and metaphorically akin to stating that "any car that has the same color as a car driven by a drunk driver is a dangerous car."

Litigation Tip: BSL assumes a connection between breed and volatility. Force proof on this point to the requisite threshold of *Frye, Daubert*, and ER 702. It might help to conceptualize viciousness or dangerousness as a disease, virus, or medical condition. Does a physiological, anatomical, genetic, or other explanation or anomaly within the prohibited breed (assuming, of course, a proper identification has and even can be made) give rise to such hazardous defect? In short, where are the peer-reviewed studies showing general acceptance in the relevant scientific community to endorse such an innate threat threshold?

Epidemiological studies provide a suitable basis for comparison, as they have attempted to establish causation or association between human health maladies and exposures to harmful chemicals. In *In re "Agent Orange" Product Liability Litigation*, 611 F. Supp. 1223 (E.D.N.Y. 1985), the court found the methodology sound but the opinion inadmissible under FRE 703 and FRE 403, because the expert did not examine any of the persons in question or their medical records but simply opined that cross-species inferences drawn from animal studies supported the conclusion that the defoliant caused human ailments. *Allen v. Pennsylvania Eng'g Corp.*, 102 F.3d 194 (5th Cir. 1996) deemed inadmissible expert testimony that ethylene oxide caused decedent's brain cancer, due to the dearth of any conclusive studies establishing a statistically significant connection or evidence of the decedent's level of exposure. *Grant v. Bristol-Myers Squibb*, 97 F. Supp. 2d 986 (D. Ariz. 2000) rejected expert testimony that silicone breast implants caused systemic disease as opinion had not gained disciplinary acceptance nor was it based on scientific methods practiced by a recognized minority in the field. Nor was it sufficient to outweigh more than 20 epidemiological studies finding no risk of autoimmune disease from implants.

Similar challenges to the breed-viciousness nexus can and should be made to any expert on grounds of ER 702, 703 and 403.

f.   Experts on Animals

Parties increasingly call upon accident reconstructionists to reenact the final moments before injury although the subject matter rarely, if ever, involves animals. Causes of action discussed herein may demand a similar level of attention to detail and expertise from nonveterinary animal behaviorists (ethologists), veterinarians (internists, surgeons, pathologists, veterinary behaviorists, and those trained in veterinary forensics), law enforcement and animal control officers, and certified dog trainers. Equipped with modern technology, these experts can utilize DNA to match hairs, blood, and saliva. Molds of paws and teeth can be obtained and measured to prove or disprove the ability of the plaintiff's animal to threaten the defendant or the defendant's animals purportedly being protected with lethal force.

Though the tide is turning, some courts may have difficulty conceiving of an animal's death, regardless how beloved, causing mental anguish so extreme as to incapacitate, create physical manifestations of anguish, and render a plaintiff unemployable. Defendants may derail discussion of the emotional impact of grief caused by the obliteration of the "human-animal bond" by denouncing it as "psychobabble." Prepare to have counselors, psychologists, and psychiatrists trained in animal loss to testify to the *bona fide* causal link between animal injury and diagnosable emotional disorders with detailed medical evidence in a nonapologetic, sincere manner.

Experts often prove pain and suffering in animal cruelty cases. Thankfully, society has come to rely on the accuracy of its lay perceptions in the case of most heinous acts, rendering expert testimony superfluous, no doubt testament to the evolving view of animal sensibility. In *Hynes v. State*, 1 So. 3d 328 (Fla. Dist. Ct. App. 2009), the appeals court reversed the trial court's determination that "there was no proof of corpus delicti because there was no veterinary testimony that the dogs suffered pain due to withholding of food." To this, the appellate court responded:

> The veterinary testimony that the dog was malnourished, dehydrated, too weak to stand and without muscle mass were [sic] sufficient. In a case such as this, the animal's pain or suffering due to starvation is a matter of common sense and ordinary experience, just as in *Bartlett v. State*, 929 So. 2d 1125 (Fla. Dist. Ct. App. 4th Dist. 2006), where it was not necessary, in order to sustain a felony conviction under this statute, for a veterinarian to testify that a possum shot multiple times with a BB gun was suffering and had to be euthanized.

Hynes, 1 So. 3d at 330; *see State v. Zawistowski*, 82 P.3d 698 (Wash. Ct. App. 2004) (accord that it is "reasonable inference" from evidence of being "pretty much a rack of bones" that horse felt extreme hunger and that this hunger was capable of at least "mild discomfort," which is "pain" under state cruelty law); *see also State v. Paulson*, 128 P.3d 133 (Wash. Ct. App. 2006) (defining "undue suffering" as "excessive or unwarranted" [undue] and "to experience or sustain physical or emotional pain, distress or injury" [suffer]; concluding that, "[i]t is difficult to imagine that any dog, especially one who had followed [the defendants] around for almost two weeks, would not suffer unduly with such a killing scheme."); and *see State v. Andree*, 954 P.2d 346 (Wash. Ct. App. 1998) (a person of ordinary intelligence would understand that killing a kitten by stabbing it nine times with a hunting knife would cause undue suffering).

4. Psycholegal

Animal lawyers will quickly discover their therapeutic role simply in the act of agreeing to represent a client seeking justice for their animal companion. Frequently, those in mourning or in a custodial tug-of-war will, upon interviewing dozens of lawyers who dismiss their concerns, internalize a perceived institutional hostility and sense of embarrassment concerning any animal dispute. They may do so by expressing chagrin for "wasting the court's time," making excuses for their own grief as "unimportant in the scheme of things," and expecting to be ridiculed for concerning themselves with such "picayune matters." Prof. David B. Wexler's "therapeutic jurisprudence," described in a paper he delivered in 1987, examines how legal actors create therapeutic and antitherapeutic mental health outcomes with those they interact in the legal process. Over time, the doctrine took root in special problem-solving courts, such as for teenagers or addicts. It also sought to instill within lawyers a care ethic that resonates with animacentric legal problem solving. *See* Wexler, *Practicing Therapeutic Jurisprudence: Psycholegal Soft Spots and Strategies*, 67 Rev. Jur. U.P.R. 317 (1998). Margit Livingston carried the notion of therapeutic jurisprudence further in *Desecrating the Ark: Animal Abuse and the Law's Role in Prevention*, 87 Iowa L. Rev. 1 (2001), contending that the law's functionaries have an opportunity to improve the emotional and mental health of society by maximizing the therapeutic value of jurisprudence, focusing reorientation on public perceptions of animal cruelty.

Animal law cases have a distinct psycholegal flavor. To diagnose and treat ailments and dispense medications to owned nonhuman animals, the veterinarian-client-patient relationship ("VCPR") frames interaction of the veterinarian with human clients and animal patients. *See* American Animal Hospital Association Position Statement, Jul. 2012; American Veterinary Medical Association VCPR FAQ. Analogously, by commencing to resolve a particular legal problem facing both owner and animal, the animal lawyer forms a lawyer-client-animal relationship ("LCAR"). As in a VCPR, the animal is not the client, and the lawyer owes no duties to the animals themselves (as if a guardian or trustee, unless appointed in such capacity). Yet the client enlists the lawyer to improve the lot of both client and animal. Occasionally, those interests may conflict, presenting ethical quandaries that may terminate the LCAR. Fundamentally, the tripartite model differs from the bipartite models of physician-patient, priest-penitent, or conventional attorney-client.

Though people vary across our diverse country, the human-animal bond remains a common denominator — rural or urban, poor or rich, Democrat or Republican, educated or not, irrespective of religion, ethnicity, gender, nationality, or sexual orientation. Relying on extrapolations from demographic data may prove dangerous and fail to predict how a jury or judge may decide an animal law issue. In the appropriate factual circumstance, *voir dire* should focus on divining the sincerely held positions and thoughts about animals, starting with the hearth and the status they keep therein — in the house or kept in a doghouse, folded in the armoire, hanging in the closet or jewelry box, tested on drugs and beauty products at cosmetics counters or in the medicine cabinet, and served on the dinner table; then venturing off-premises where animals are sources or targets of entertainment, such as those who enjoy excursions to tide flats or off-leash parks, or who flee the hunter's arrow or angler's lure; and finally, polling reactions to highly publicized topics, such as natural disasters like Hurricane Katrina, or animal-related legislation such as the Menu Foods class action that included hundreds of lawsuits and thousands of claimants and prompted reporter Emilie Lounsberry to write *Chasing Justice in Pet-food Lawsuits: Beloved Friend or Simply Property?*, PHILADELPHIA INQUIRER (Apr. 22, 2007).

Animals also serve a psycholegal role in open court, though their presence invites staunch debate between prosecutors and the criminal defense bar. For instance, in *State v. Carlson*, 2011 Wash. App. LEXIS 269 (Jan. 24, 2011), William Carlson was convicted on two counts of child molestation involving nephew C.C. (seven at time of trial). Ariah, an in-court therapy dog, accompanied C.C. during his testimony. Though counsel did not challenge the presence of Ariah in the courtroom,[30] the court took note of C.C.'s reduced attention span by the courtroom environment, including that "he left the witness chair to play with therapy dog Ariah" and at trial, "played and talked to therapy dog Ariah." The trial judge even remarked, "[Y]ou may want to take away all the distractions." Nonetheless, the court found C.C.'s answers generally responsive to both prosecutor and defense questioning.

---

[30] This became an issue of recent debate in New York. *See* www.courthousedogs.com; Dan Wiessner, *U.S. Courtroom Dogs Spark Legal Debate*, Reuters (Sept. 12, 2011), http://www.reuters.com/article/2011/09/12/us-usa-courtoom-dogs-idUSTRE78B4KN20110912.

In *State v. Dye*, 178 Wn. 2d 541 (2013), Ellie, the prosecuting attorney's office dog, aided in the conviction of a residential burglar by sitting next to the developmentally disabled "vulnerable victim." On appeal, Dye complained that Ellie lent an aura of credibility to the victim and thereby cast an unfairly prejudicial taint upon him. In affirming Dye's conviction, the Washington Supreme Court noted that the trial court may control the courtroom, including issuing a dispensation allowing particularly fearful witnesses in need of protection to hold dolls or rely on comfort canines. It rejected the assertion that Ellie impeded Dye's right to cross-examination, distinguishing it from Dye's right to face-to-face confrontation, and adding that unless Ellie sat in the witness's lap, no such right was violated. Nor did Ellie's reaction to the witness's stress constitute "testimony from an unsworn witness that the victim is upset because he or she is telling the truth," a form of oath-helping. A child or impaired witness's need for emotional support often outweighs the possibility of prejudice to the defendant occasioned by holding a comfort item or having a dog present, provided the court explicitly balances such concerns as obtrusiveness, distraction, necessity, and, yes, allergies. Concurring Justice McCloud cautioned that, like judicial robes, the flag in the courtroom, and the witness's oath, Ellie "was a powerful symbol in this case," specifically to assist Mr. Lare in testifying. but she conveyed a "silent message about Mr. Lare's status as a sympathetic and truthful victim who is worthy of support," which warranted additional measures to neutralize or level out the symbolic power of the dog, and to ensure fairness in the proceedings.

Speciesism, defined by Joan Dunayer as "A failure, in attitude or practice, to accord any nonhuman being equal consideration and respect,"[31] pervades the legal system and jury pool, creating a backlash against reasoned and humane efforts by lawyers to expose and rebuild those troubling foundations. With ample citation, Dunayer argues that favoring the interests of higher primates and some mammals to the exclusion of birds, reptiles, fish, amphibians, and the "lesser" mammals evinces speciesist bias. Her two main critiques of the early animal rights movement are that, first, it construes speciesism as a bias *in favor of humans* only (as opposed to merely showing bias in favor of *certain nonhuman species*), and, second, that it protects the interests of nonhuman animals at the *species,* but not the *individual,* level. Dunayer's book does not dwell on what necessarily appears to follow — that: (1) a person engages in speciesism by exhibiting an *anti-human bias,* and that (2) speciesism may arise where an individual *human's rights* are devalued or ignored completely when balanced against the aggregate rights of a *nonhuman species.* But Professor David Favre, former Dean of Michigan State University-Detroit College of Law and author of animal law textbook ANIMALS: WELFARE, INTERESTS, AND RIGHTS (Animal Law & History Web Center, MSU-DCL, 2003), does manage to condense Dunayer's position into a familiar and pliable legal theory — the tort of interference with nonhuman fundamental interests. *See* David Favre, *Integrating Animal Interests into Our Legal System*, 10 ANIMAL L. 87 (2004).

As becomes clear after reading *Speciesism*, the circumstances in which nonhumans enjoy an undue right or benefit at the expense of humans are virtually

---

[31] JOAN DUNAYER, SPECIESISM (Ryce Pub. 2004).

nonexistent. The degree to which humans have subjugated and terrorized nonhuman animals for every manner of "use" or "necessary purpose" can be considered without parallel even by standards of human violence against other humans. Aside from the occasional rumination that appears to assume too much, such as the assertion that a dog rescuing a child from a burning room weighs psychological pain at losing the human companion greater than the physical pain of burning flesh, Dunayer's book contains a concise and wide-ranging array of situations suitable for dissemination.

Perhaps it is the nature of the profession, but attorneys are occupationally predisposed toward using the master's tools (to appropriate the title of an essay from Audre Lorde) to dismantle the master's house. We are pragmatists bound by *stare decisis*, but who pride ourselves on winning concessions for our clients through legal argument, not political maneuvering or press releases. Steadfast efforts at achieving incremental gain are probably the best to be hoped for in a corporatized democracy saddled with the presently limited pro-animal statutes and slow-to-evolve common law. Postmodern philosopher Michel Foucault spoke of power as emanating not only from top-down movements (e.g., revolution through removal of heads of state) or bottom-up boycotts (e.g., through consumers pocketbook-voting for ethical goods), but also from unlikely pressure points in the complex matrix of social, cultural, economic, historical, and legal relationships that surround issues of animal use and welfare. Most of us, including Dunayer, are only beginning to locate these places of power and use the legal tools to reconstruct the system to fairly treat all beings. In such times and places, old, new, and/or nonspeciesist law may obtain the best result for the nonhuman animals in question. The variables noted above, however, cannot be ignored in this quest.

5.   Ethical

Animal law's prodigious impact on conventional systems of jurisprudence prompts attorneys to account for their own ethical obligations toward nonhuman animals in and out of the courtroom. Professional responsibilities begin to conform. Unique ethical pitfalls attend to nonhuman-species representation and "cause" lawyering. The aspirational implications for professional responsibility arise from the mere recognition of the field of animal law by state and county bar associations and law schools. For those drawn to animal cases by conviction to alleviate animal suffering or to improve the legal status of animals generally, encouraging conscious regard for nonhumans in day-to-day life invites no quarrel. Where the lawyer's ethical persuasion outpaces or conflicts with the client's wishes, however, certain ethical dictates must be strictly followed. More controversial, though ethically consistent, is the notion that our Rules of Professional Conduct ("RPCs") should explicitly regulate our interactions with nonhuman animals. A moral community ensures access to justice without species-based impediments.

a.   Puritanism and Best Ethical Practices

The American legal profession was sod in Puritanical thought. Perhaps the earliest hortatory treatment of the lawyer's professional responsibility came from Puritan and religious leader Cotton Mather in 1710. Aside from his infamous role in the Salem witch trials, his writing *Bonifacius* urged attorneys to practice law with an ever-active eye toward the firmament in all their dealings. In applying such ideals to attorneys, Mather stated:

> What a noble thing would it be for you to find out oppressed widows and orphans; and as such can appear only "in forma pauperis;" and are objects, in whose oppression "might overcomes right," generously plead their cause! "Deliver the poor and needy, and rid them out of the hand of the wicked" — It will be a glorious and Godlike action!

Cotton Mather, *Essays to Do Good* 152 (George Burder ed., 1815) (Bonifacius 1710). It is this sentiment of "religious jurisprudence," as observed by Susan Carle, that drove David Hoffman and Judge George Sharswood to commend their fellow colleagues "to steer the legal system toward just results." Susan Carle, *Lawyers' Duty to Do Justice: A New Look at the History of the 1908 Canons*, 24 LAW & SOC. INQUIRY 1, 10 (1999) (cited in Judith Maute, *Changing Conceptions of Lawyers' Pro Bono Responsibilities: From Chance Noblesse Oblige to Stated Expectations*, 77 TUL. L. REV. 91, 102 (2002)). While the *pro bono publico* prescriptions of today's RPC 6.1 are embryonic and nonmandatory, and far removed from the wishes of a crusading Mather, they present one of the most controversial, aspirational elements of modern professional responsibility.

The 1969 ABA Code of Professional Responsibility's Canon 2 (Ethical Consideration 25) states, "Every lawyer, regardless of professional prominence or professional workload, should find time to participate in serving the disadvantaged." The 1983 version of the ABA Model Rules Preamble identified the role of the lawyer as representative of clients, officer of the legal system, and "*public citizen* having special responsibility for the quality of justice." As ambassadors of an equitable legal system that affects all animals, human and nonhuman, one of our inherent roles should include giving a voice to its most disenfranchised and legally disabled members.

While RPC 6.1 does not compel ethical behavior by threatening to subject attorneys to discipline, RPC 8.4 does impose the genuine threat of disbarment for discriminatory professional behavior and turpitudinous, extraprofessional behavior. The lawyer *qua lawyer* faces sanctions for committing a "discriminatory act" prohibited by state law on traditional bases, including in Washington, the rare proscription of Wash. RPC 8.4(g) of not discriminating against someone due to his or her sexual orientation *even before* Washington State amended the Washington State Law Against Discrimination to prohibit sexual orientation discrimination. Wash. RPC 8.4(k) regards an Oath of Attorney violation as subject to discipline, and Wash. RPC 8.4(n) addresses "conduct demonstrating unfitness to practice law," whether the conduct is legal or illegal. Significantly, Wash. RPC 8.4(g), (k), and (n) declare "legal" behavior "unethical," thereby exposing lawyers to discipline — albeit in the attorney's *professional* capacity only.

Washington's RPC 8.4(i) takes the further step of declaring unethical and subject to discipline behavior that is "legal" in the *private* context. Acts "involving moral turpitude, or corruption . . . ," whether "committed in the course of his or her conduct as a lawyer, or otherwise, and whether the same constitutes a felony or misdemeanor or not," expose a lawyer to disciplinary review. Finding no decisions interpreting "moral turpitude" under Wash. RPC 8.4(i), one may turn to cases interpreting the phrase under the now-recodified Wash. RLD 1.1(a), which provided for sanctions where an attorney commits any act involving moral turpitude. Although not defined in the RPCs or RLDs, Washington's Supreme Court has offered some guidance:

> This definition of moral turpitude is necessarily general. In the setting of attorney discipline, its application depends upon the collective conscience and judgment of the members of this court. It is as meaningful as other phrases adopted by other courts.

In re Disciplinary Proceeding Against Heard, 963 P.2d 818, 824 (Wash. 1998). Witness tampering and assault with a deadly weapon, even without a conviction, have been deemed morally turpitudinous.

> We essentially look to the inherent nature of the act committed by the attorney to answer the following question:
>
> [D]o the acts found against the appellant, and for which he was convicted. . . , violate the commonly accepted standard of good morals, honesty, and justice? Suppose we measure his conduct in this regard, not by any puritanical standard, but by the standard of right conduct generally prevailing among our people, uninfluenced by the fact that the statute law also punishes such conduct as a crime.

Id. (citing *In re Disciplinary Proceeding Against Hopkins*, 103 P. 805, 806 (Wash. 1909)). It has also been defined as:

> [A]n act of baseness, vileness or depravity in the private and social duties which a man owes to his fellow men, or to society in general, contrary to the accepted and customary rule of right and duty between man and man.

Attorney Grievance Comm'n v. Walman, 374 A.2d 354, 358 (Md. 1977) (quoting *Braverman v. Bar Ass'n*, 121 A.2d 473, 481 (Md. 1956), *cert. denied*, 352 U.S. 830 (1956)). The guides for ferreting out moral turpitude include *collective judicial conscience* and *colloquial morality*. What acts against animals might rise to the level of morally turpitudinous? Or would rules of professional responsibility categorically exclude them from sanction?

The contemporary treatment of nonhuman animals has been regarded by some as a diurnal holocaust with profound civic complicity. While not all take this view, there can be little dispute that those wrestling with the issue of animal rights in the court of public opinion come nowhere close to honoring the tenets of fair and robust debate "in open court," as it were. When trying the matter of animal rights, deference to the principles that guide our profession appears not to exist. Ethical Consideration 7-19 to the Model Rules of Professional Conduct speaks to the benefit of "[a]n adversary presentation" to counter "the natural human tendency to judge too swiftly in terms of the familiar that which is not yet fully known." The duty of a lawyer to the client and the lawyer's duty to the legal system are the same: to represent the client zealously within the bounds of the law." EC 7-19. Much of our treatment of animals is shrouded by the near-impenetrable wall of the right to privacy, founded upon the even more stubborn belief in the inviolacy of property rights in animals and the realty on which they are used. Author Michael Pollan proposed a workaround:

> This is going to sound quixotic, but maybe all we need to do to redeem industrial animal agriculture in this country is to pass a law requiring that the steel and concrete walls of the CAFO's and slaughterhouses be replaced with . . . glass. If there's any new "right" we need to establish, maybe it's this one: the right to look.

Michael Pollan, *An Animal's Place*, N.Y. TIMES MAGAZINE (Nov. 10, 2002). Of course, no such law yet exists. In fact, recent legislative efforts only seek to obscure and punish those who take a gander. *See* Will Potter, *First "Ag-Gag" Prosecution: Utah Woman Filmed a Slaughterhouse from the Public Street*, GREEN IS THE NEW RED (Apr. 29, 2013). Harsher criminal laws governing trespass on property owned by animal production and research facilities further hamper efforts to fulfill the public's right to know.

"In order to function properly, our adjudicative process requires an informed, impartial tribunal capable of administering justice promptly and efficiently according to procedures that command public confidence and respect. Not only must there be competent, adverse presentation of evidence and issues, but a tribunal must be aided by rules appropriate to an effective and dignified process." EC 7-20. When one cannot press a colorable claim for standing, our adversarial system abandons nonhuman interests and renders efforts to comply with its ethical considerations futile. Without standing, one cannot take advantage of discovery tools that might satisfy the spirit of Pollan's "right to look." Further sabotaging the process is the partiality of the very arbiters who adjudicate the fate of nonhuman animals; the carnivorous fox, even if donned in traditional juridical garb, cannot guard the henhouse. "To safeguard the impartiality that is essential to the judicial process, members of the venire and jurors should be protected against extraneous influences. When impartiality is present, public confidence in the judicial system is enhanced." EC 7-29.

Appearances of bias damage the public's confidence in our legal system and the prescriptions emanating from the bench. The decisionmaker must not only act fairly, but *appear* fair. *Offutt v. U.S.*, 348 U.S. 11, 14 (1954). Animal rights lawyers' heightened ethical acuity helps them recognize the *actual* unfairness of common and statutory law, so cataloguing what amounts to systemic *apparent* unfairness hardly adds much to the critique. That said, lawyers who have not embraced animal rights should feel some discomfort at the procedural infirmity of a system that provides no meaningful consideration for the barest interests of the nonhuman animal. Fairness falters when the voiceless have no advocates as a matter of law, notwithstanding the cumbersome and extremely rare remedy of the private attorney general, private prosecutor, writ of mandamus/prohibition private right of action, or *ex rel.* venue. One may balk at the animal rightist's arguments on the merits, much as one might reject the points lawfully and stridently made by a Klan member at a public rally, but unlike the white supremacist, nonhuman animals do not even have access to justice by those who would take up their cause. This is organically unfair.

Our profession's august body of ethical doctrine must accommodate the interests of nonhuman animals at a comparative evolutionary pace as that seen procedurally and substantively. Our aspirational underpinnings lend themselves to "best practice." It is this inclination to err on the side of ethical purity that should govern our legal treatment of animals. At the American Bar Association's Ethics 2000 meetings in 1997 and 1998, the Committee considered drafting a "best practice" section in the Comment section of the Rules as a "helpful and good exercise," but abandoned it in part out of concerns that they would affect malpractice standards of care. Richard W. Painter, *Rules Lawyers Play By*, 76 N.Y.U. L. REV. 665, 701 n.187 (2001). The American tradition of legal ethics boasts an at times zealous but otherwise solemn and ambitious religiosity that serves to invigorate our profession. Our potential role as society's ethical leaders should not be so quickly forsaken.

b. Considering the Animal Nonclient

Client is not defined in the RPCs. Although nonhuman animals may not sue or be sued or enter into contracts, the nonhuman animal's interests will frequently be of primary importance to your client. In cases, however, where the purposes startlingly diverge, the lawyer's own ethical compass must guide where the RPCs are silent — or are they? Consider this hypothetical.

Hypothetical: Jessica Fupperwind observed Maxwell the Husky suffering from a neck injury on March 10, 1999. After picking up her children from school, she arrived home to find Maxwell lying down, convulsing and quivering. His abruptly changed condition frightened her, as he was running about and showing no signs of injury the day before. Frantic, she called her regular treating veterinarian first, but they informed her that they were too busy and could not see him. She next called Washington Veterinary Hospital and immediately brought Maxwell to their clinic for emergency treatment. The vet could not see Maxwell directly so, for half an hour, she sat on the lunchroom floor, petting and comforting him until Dr. Lorenz sedated him with Acepromazine in order to allow for easier viewing of his wound. At this time, with Maxwell virtually unconscious and weighing 70 pounds, he quoted her an estimate of $500 to complete the surgery. She explained that she was a single mother on a limited income and going to school.

Unsure what to do, she left Maxwell in Dr. Lorenz's care and called from a friend's home to discuss options to finance the surgery. For nearly half an hour, she and his receptionist strove to reach a resolution. Ms. Fupperwind offered one hundred ($100) dollars that evening, with weekly payments. Dr. Lorenz's receptionist told her that he would only accept half now ($250); alternatively, she was told that Maxwell could be euthanized. No mention was made of seeking a second opinion. Believing this to be her only option, a crying and distraught Ms. Fupperwind arrived at Dr. Lorenz's clinic around closing time and begrudgingly signed a permit to put Maxwell to sleep. After she paid the bill for the sedative and office visit, she asked to say goodbye to Maxwell one last time. Moments later, Dr. Lorenz approached her in the waiting room, put his arm around her as tears rolled down her face, and lied. Despite knowing how attached people get to their pets, he rubbed her back, apologetically saying it was "too late." Another patient gave Jessica a hug to alleviate the sorrow. Bawling, she left, buoyed only by thinking that was the end.

Around 11 a.m. on June 8, 1999, Jessica emerged from the Safeway in Port Angeles when she saw a dog strongly resembling Maxwell across the parking lot. Dumbfounded, she twice drove by the woman accompanying him. Finally, convinced of her sanity, she approached and walked up to Maxwell. She touched his head. He licked her hand and recognized her. The area of his neck where he had the gash was healed but the hair was shorter over that region compared to the rest of his coat. He looked like her dog, so she asked the woman where she found him. She said she got Maxwell from Dr. Lorenz in May 1999. The dog who Jessica had mourned daily and harbored guilt over because she could not finance his surgery was very much alive. Moreover, the woman explained that she paid nothing for the surgery for which Dr. Lorenz had demanded $500. Jessica stumbled to her truck in disbelief and drove home.

The next day, Jessica confronted Dr. Lorenz, who admitted that his veterinary intern expressed a desire to operate on Maxwell free of charge and then adopt him for a move to Texas. Lorenz said this was "not a big deal" because the intern lived out-of-state and Jessica would never learn of the subterfuge. Lorenz added that Maxwell was his to give because Jessica signed him over.

After Maxwell had been kept in small quarters for nearly six weeks, the other client of Dr. Lorenz requested Maxwell's adoption. Lorenz claims that the "most significant factor" in lying to Jessica was his perception that she was heavily inebriated, very emotional, and generally a poor caretaker.

Should you represent Ms. Fupperwind?

Although she could assert a technical breach of contract (Lorenz did not kill Maxwell), fraud, replevin, and consumer protection claim, is it ethically consonant to try to recover Maxwell from the adopter and sue this veterinarian? Some sincerely believe that ownership does not alone confer entitlement to a nonhuman animal: an owner does not always a competent guardian make. Others would never fault a veterinarian who chooses to rescue an animal or report the client to the police for animal cruelty, even if violating other obligations at professional risk. But ethics does not just protect the rich and well-adjusted. It does not play socioeconomic favorites or yield to the conspiracy of prejudice.

One cannot confirm prejudices in a half-hour meeting with a woman he had only just met, where he had not reviewed or asked for any medical records or relied even on hearsay. Decades of veterinary practice do not bestow a detective's perfect hunch or psychologist's insight into human motivation, particularly in the absence of any questioning by him or his staff into Ms. Fupperwind's history of care for Maxwell. At this time under the law, and while one might applaud efforts to let veterinarians consider the best interest of the animal patient over and against that of the human client, *this was never Lorenz's decision.*

No one suggests that Dr. Lorenz must have treated Maxwell according to the financial arrangement proposed by Ms. Fupperwind. His options were to either perform the contract for euthanasia as requested by his guardian and owner or to request a surrender of ownership for adoption to a third party. Alternatively, he could have referred her to another veterinarian who may have accepted her payment plan. Instead, he violated ethics rules and broke the law. Yet the inescapable question remains: does it matter that Lorenz had no right to do what he did when, from Maxwell's perspective, his life was spared and he was placed with a family better able to meet his needs?

For animal law attorneys seeking a fundamental shift in the status of animals, willing to engage in lengthy and costly appeals to defend this principle, one must never forget that the client's wishes reign supreme. The client, while sympathetic, may not want to litigate for years or subject himself to intrusive discovery. He may not want to risk paying the other side's attorney's fees or sacrificing even modest financial recompense on the gamble of precedent-setting a newfangled theory of liability or damages. You may have a client who wishes to redeem his companion animal from animal control despite a history of alleged neglect or abuse. Should you defend his efforts to reunite with a dog who may be better cared for by a third party? Or, for an even closer question, what should you do in the event a handler hires you to regain ownership over a service animal who you believe has suffered as an indentured slave at the aggressive and untrained hands of a disabled client? And considering the broader impact of litigation on animals not directly at issue, what of aggressively pursuing a humane society or shelter without insurance coverage, knowing that money you take for your client will likely come from the mouths of other animals in the care of the defendant?

c.   Conflicts and Withdrawal

Rule of Professional Conduct 1.7(a)(2) requires that an attorney not represent a client where a conflict with a current or former *client* exists, but also where concurrent conflicts with a *third person or the lawyer's own interests* create an irreconcilable challenge to competent representation. The lawyer's animal welfare principles or agendas must be fully disclosed to the client, and he or she should decline or withdraw representation if written consent is not obtained. Sadly, "third person" does not strictly encompass nonhuman animals, but the lawyer's interests may stand as proxy for the nonhuman animal at interest, and allow withdrawal under RPC 1.16(b), which maintains that a lawyer *may* withdraw if the client insists on pursuing an imprudent or repugnant objective or for other "good cause."

d.   Confidentiality and Candor

Many states adopt a nonmandatory confidentiality breach provision modeled after the ABA's Rule 1.6(b)(1-2), which provides that:

> A lawyer may reveal information relating to the representation of a client to the extent the lawyer reasonably believes necessary (1) to prevent reasonably certain death or substantial bodily harm; (2) to prevent the client from committing a crime or fraud that is reasonably certain to result in substantial injury to the financial interests or property of another and in furtherance of which the client has used or is using the lawyer's services.

Though animals would likely constitute "property of another," ABA Rule 1.6(b)(2)'s requirement that the client has retained the lawyer to enable criminal or fraudulent activity limits its practical application, and remains discretionary in any event.

While ABA Rule 1.6(b)(1) does not suffer the taint of the phrase "to another" as used in Florida RPC 4-1.6(b)(2), it retains the word "bodily," suggesting application to *human* corporeal bodies only. Such an interpretation would align with the holding of the Louisiana Court of Appeals in a 1988 horse hauling case.

The Bergquists hired Richard Goetz, a horse hauler, to transport three horses to a farm. Goetz's driver, Fernandez, negligently drove the van, resulting in the horse trailer overturning in a ditch. Plaintiffs sued Goetz, Fernandez, and Commercial Union (the liability insurer) for injury to the horses. Goetz's policy excluded coverage for damage to property owned or transported by the insured but did contain a bodily injury provision. While sympathetic to the assertion that no reputable transporter would secure liability insurance excluding coverage for the transported horses, the court dismissed the insurer on two grounds: the property damage exclusion applied, and by the ordinary definition of the term, the claim that the horses endured "bodily injury" was meritless given the "generally prevailing meaning" of the term indicating only "hurt or harm to the human body or some member thereof." *Bergquist v. Fernandez*, 535 So. 2d 827 (La. Ct. App. 1988).

Florida mandates breach of confidentiality if the lawyer reasonably believes necessary to "prevent a client from committing a crime" or "to prevent a death or substantial bodily harm to another." Florida RPC 4-1.6(b)(1-2). Animal and other property crimes assuredly qualify, and by calibrating the requisite degree of certainty that the client will commit a crime, or cause death or substantial bodily harm, to what amounts to probable cause, Florida exemplifies the best drafted professional responsibility rule for the benefit of nonhuman victims. However, the use of the phrase "bodily harm to another" takes a step backward by impliedly excluding nonhumans from its ambit because "another" refers to "client," who is human. Unless and until nonhumans become recognized as protected legal "others," the double standard between subsections (b)(1) and (b)(2) remains.

Hypothetical: A long-term client arrives for his appointment to examine real estate documents to close on a new residence with a browbeaten dog, tail tucked between his legs, ears mangled, several cuts on the head, and a sheepishness that leads you to suspect abuse. You know from prior discussions that the client had adopted this dog from a shelter, so you give the benefit of the doubt until you witness how the dog cowers when the client reaches over the dog's head to shake your hand. The meeting runs late, causing the client to tire and dog to fidget. In a startling explosion, your client then smacks the dog on the muzzle and stares down the dog with a wide-eyed and stern expression until he submissively rolls over, ears pinned to the side of his head, and a stream of urine expels from the dog incontinent with fear. No doubts remain. May you report your client to animal control for animal abuse?

The more pertinent question to resolve is not whether the death and bodily injury provisions of RPC 1.6 apply to nonhumans, but whether the mistreatment of the dog during a meeting to close a real estate transaction "relates to the representation" of the client. If not, then you could freely reveal these observations to law enforcement without limitation by RPC 1.6. If so, then barring a specific exception for nonhuman abuse, you might risk disciplinary action for such disclosure. After all, the duty of confidentiality casts a much wider net than the attorney-client privilege, for it encompasses all information about a client, not just communications from a client. 1 GEOFFREY HAZARD, JR. & W. WILLIAM HODES, THE LAW OF LAWYERING 168 (1990).

To date, no state mandates animal abuse reporting by lawyers, despite obvious parallels to child abuse and a readily duplicated statutory framework. For instance, except where privileged, or disclosure would detriment the client, in Oregon, generally lawyers and judges must report suspected child abuse or face civil and criminal liability. ORS § 419B.010; ORS § 419B.005(5)(m) ("public or private official" includes "attorney"); ORS § 419B.005(1)(a) ("abuse" includes psychic and physical cruelty, neglect, as well as sexual exploitation). *See also* Nev. Rev. Stat. § 432B.220(4); Ohio Rev. Code § 2151.421;

Hypothetical: Assuming the same facts as above, further consider that your client is reported to law enforcement by his neighbor, who witnesses your client strike the dog with a metal rod just as he leaves your office. He is prosecuted and you are subpoenaed by the prosecutor to testify as to your observations. Does the attorney-client privilege prevent you from disclosing what you saw?

RPC 3.3(a) requires that a lawyer not "knowingly make a false statement of fact or law to a tribunal," nor "fail to correct a false statement of material fact or law previously made to the tribunal by the lawyer," nor especially to "offer evidence that the lawyer knows to be false." Robin Rosencrantz noted that in a hypothetical child custody situation, a family law attorney who falsely states or offers evidence "in support of the abusive client's 'fitness' as a responsible, good parent" violates RPC 3.3(a).[32] In fact, the lawyer who remains silent could be deemed to have assisted a criminal act where the lawyer knows of his client's child abuse. The same RPC 3.3 obligations should apply in the context where a lawyer knows of his client's abuse of animals. For more on the link between animal abuse, child abuse, domestic violence, and crimes against humans generally, *see* BEYOND VIOLENCE: THE HUMAN ANIMAL CONNECTION, PSYETA (Psychologists for the Ethical Treatment of Animals), Animal Legal Defense Fund (www.aldf.org), and review the decades-old findings of the FBI and law enforcement corroborating the firm existence of this animal-human violence link.

e.   Prohibited Business Transaction

ABA Rule 1.8(c) prohibits a lawyer from preparing instruments that name the attorney "or a person related to the lawyer" as a beneficiary of *substantial gifts* unless the client is related to the lawyer or "other recipient" as a spouse, child, grandchild, parent, grandparent, or other relative with whom the lawyer maintains a close, familial relationship. Interestingly, RPC 1.8(c) would not appear to be violated where the beneficiary is a lawyer's 15-year-old Arabian stallion or 12-year-old cat fighting the expensive battle against cancer, because horses and cats are not "person[s]." Whether receipt of such a stallion or cat by the beneficiary lawyer from the client would constitute a "substantial gift" presents another ethical question worth examining closely.

---

[32] Robin Rosencrantz, *Rejecting "Hear No Evil Speak No Evil": Expanding the Attorney's Role in Child Abuse Reporting*, 8 GEO. J. LEGAL ETHICS 327, 359 (1995)

f. Prospective Clients·

The relatively newly minted RPC 1.18 concerns duties to a prospective client, including an obligation not to use, reveal, or share information obtained from a prospective client, and resulting in potential disqualification of counsel with conflicts between the prospective client and a former or current client. A dog bite case, for instance, is not particularly laden with ethical puzzles, except that, like all disputes, there are two sides, the biter (or party owning the biting animal) and the bitten. Frequently, plaintiff's personal injury lawyers also handle criminal defense. Analogously, animal injury lawyers often take on dangerous dog defense. The risk of a potential conflict between biter and bitten is foreseeable, and lawyers had best take inventory of the rule pertaining to precisely such inchoate conflicts. Particularly in the field of animal law, where presently so few full-time practitioners exist, the likelihood remains high that both the potential plaintiff and defendant will contact that attorney.

Example #1. Defendant's dog Sparky bites Plaintiff Marcus Powell. Powell calls you, leaving a voicemail requesting consultation and representation in a personal injury claim against Defendant Jake Doran. Moments later, Doran calls leaving a voicemail for (a) civil defense on an anticipated suit by Powell; (b) administrative defense on a Dangerous Dog Declaration involving Sparky; and (c) criminal defense on a Negligent Control of Vicious Dog charge. You take the types of cases identified by Powell and Doran. You have never represented or consulted with either gentleman. Doran's voicemail, however, leaves the following details: (1) "My dog Sparky allegedly bit Marcus without provocation." (2) "Marcus does not know this, but it was my choice not to leash Sparky the day of the attack even though I knew better, and this was not the first time Sparky acted this way." Questions: Can you represent Powell? Can you represent Doran? Can you represent anyone?

First, one must determine whether Defendant and Plaintiff are "prospective clients." Washington's RPC 1.18(a) defines a "prospective client" as one who "discusses with a lawyer the possibility of forming a client-lawyer relationship with respect to a matter[.]" If you never call back Plaintiff or Defendant, neither can claim "prospective client" status, because, "A person who communicates information unilaterally to a lawyer, without any reasonable expectation that the lawyer is willing to discuss the possibility of forming a client-lawyer relationship, is not a 'prospective client' within the meaning of paragraph (a)[.]" RPC 1.18 cmt. 2. If, however, your assistant or voicemail or webpage "invites unilateral confidential communications[,]" a reasonable expectation may arise. RPC 1.18 cmt. 10. But note that "public dissemination of general information concerning a lawyer's name or firm name, practice area and types of clients served, and contact information, is not in itself an invitation to convey unilateral confidential communications[.]" *Id.*

Second, if designated as a "prospective client," then even if no client-lawyer relationship ensues, "a lawyer who has had discussions with a prospective client shall not use or reveal information learned in the consultation, except as Rule 1.9 would permit with respect to information of a former client or except as provided in paragraph (c)." RPC 1.18(b). In addition to *informational use prohibition*, RPC 1.18 includes a *disqualification from adverse representation prohibition*. For a lawyer "shall not represent a client with interests materially adverse to those of a prospective client in the same or a substantially related matter if the lawyer received information from the prospective client that could be significantly harmful to that person in the matter, except as provided in paragraphs (d) and (e)." RPC 1.18(c). Even the swiftest intake is required to determine if a conflict exists. Be warned, however, as "[t]he duty [outlined in RPC 1.18(b)] exists regardless of how brief the initial conference may be." RPC 1.18 cmt. 3. Accordingly, "In order to avoid acquiring disqualifying information from a prospective client, a lawyer considering whether or not to undertake a new matter should limit the initial interview to only such information as reasonably appears necessary for that purpose. Where the information indicates that a conflict of interest or other reason for non-representation exists, the lawyer should so inform the prospective client or decline the representation." RPC 1.18 cmt. 4.

The simplest solution is to apply RPC 1.18(e) to the initial conference and as part of the script read by staff, on voicemail, on webpages, or on email:

A lawyer may condition conversations with a prospective client on the person's informed consent that no information disclosed during the consultation will prohibit the lawyer from representing a different client in the matter. The prospective client may also expressly consent to the lawyer's subsequent use of information received from a prospective client.

RPC 1.18(e). Even if informed consent through this *Miranda*-like instruction is not secured, informed consent after the fact may be obtained under RPC 1.18(d)(1).

But where no consent is given at any time, disqualification is only required where the lawyer received "significantly harmful" information from the prospective client. "Significantly harmful" is more than *de minimis* harm. RPC 1.18 cmt. 15. Doran's statement (1) above is *de minimis*, if harmful at all, because it merely repeats an "allegation," while statement (2) is significantly harmful, because it reveals expectation of future harm, a prior incident, and a confession as to an act of omission.

In the above example, there seems to be no obvious prohibition against representing Doran. As to Powell, one option is to ignore the voicemail or respond by stating up front the existence of a conflict and dissuading future communications.

Example #2. Defendant Jasmine Dingleberry's dog Twinkie attacks Plaintiff Mahmood Singh's bovine Bessie. Singh retains counsel and sues Dingleberry, who then calls you seeking defense in the civil suit. You speak to Dingleberry and first confirm the allegations. You learn that Singh already has retained counsel. Noting that you would not then represent Singh, you agree to speak to Dingleberry briefly and state the following: (1) Because Singh currently has counsel, you will likely not be representing Singh against Dingleberry; and (2) Dingleberry should tender the claim to insurance as, ethically, you cannot represent Dingleberry, for it could require you to take positions that would harm your other clients (e.g., arguing for market value, vet bills capped at original value, and no emotional damages). One year later, Singh calls, asking you to substitute for her original attorney and continue the case against Dingleberry. *Questions: Can you represent Singh if he fires his attorney and asks you to substitute in?*

Like Example #1, RPC 1.18 applies, except here the prohibition against adverse representation seems stronger, as an initial conference took place and you gave general legal advice. Still, merely offering such advice to a prospective client does not mean that the prospective client has imparted "significantly harmful" information to you, warranting disqualification. However, one must be careful to avoid transforming a "prospective client" into a full-fledged client. As RPC 1.18 cmt. 11 notes, "This Rule is not intended to modify existing case law defining when a client-lawyer relationship is formed. *See Bohn v. Cody*, 832 P.2d 71, 74 [ ] (Wash. 1992)[.]" Here, having declined representation due to conflict, the only difference between Example #1 and #2 is the degree of harmful information shared and the reasonableness of expectation in confidentiality.

RPC 1.7(b) requires that you not represent a client where a conflict with a current or former *client* exists, but also where conflict with a *third person or the lawyer's own interests* creates an irreconcilable challenge to competent representation. The lawyer's own animal welfare principles or agendas must be fully disclosed to the client, and he or she should decline or withdraw representation if written consent is not obtained. Sadly, "third person" does not strictly encompass nonhuman animals, but the lawyer's own interests may stand as proxy for the nonhuman animal at interest, and allow withdrawal under RPC 1.15(b), which maintains that a lawyer *may* withdraw if the client insists on pursuing an imprudent or repugnant objective or for other "good cause."

Here, you informed Dingleberry that representation would require you to take positions at odds with your own principles as well as those favorable to your other clients. RPC 1.7 cmt. 24 notes that:

> Ordinarily a lawyer may take inconsistent legal positions in different tribunals at different times on behalf of different clients. The mere fact that advocating a legal position on behalf of one client might create precedent adverse to the interests of a client represented by the lawyer in an unrelated matter does not create a conflict of interest. A conflict of interest exists, however, if there is a significant risk that a lawyer's action on behalf of one client will materially limit the lawyer's effectiveness in representing another client in a different case; for example, when a decision favoring one client will create a precedent likely to seriously weaken the position taken on behalf of the other client. . . . If there is significant risk of material limitation, then absent informed consent of the affected clients, the lawyer must refuse one of the representations or withdraw from one or both actions.

Example #3. Same as #2 except that six months after your contact with Dingleberry, her attorney calls and asks to discuss theories of liability and damages. You are not given the name of either party, but the facts are similar to those described by Dingleberry in the original phone call. You listen to Dingleberry's attorney, take no notes, and offer general advice on authority and strategy. Six months later, Singh calls as stated in #2. *Question: Can you represent Singh?*

An attorney can form an attorney-client relationship with another attorney. It stands to reason, therefore, that an attorney can be a prospective client. Thus, one must apply RPC 1.18(a) as done in Example #1. Workshopping the case with Dingleberry's attorney would give rise to a duty of implied confidentiality and classify her as a "prospective client." Whether the Defendant herself is also a prospective client may be immaterial, for her attorney is her agent and nothing within the Rule establishes a duty to a principal, disclosed or undisclosed. Here, though Dingleberry's attorney did not identify her principal, you may be held to possess knowledge of other facts that impute disclosure. On the other hand, if knowledge is not imputed, a strict reading of the Rule suggests that while you might be disqualified from using information obtained through Dingleberry's attorney against *Dingleberry's attorney*, or be disqualified from taking representation adverse to *Dingleberry's attorney*, the same may not apply as to Dingleberry herself.

The safest approach, of course, is to draw a bright dividing line at the outset of any consultation with a prospective client or an attorney asking to run facts of a case by you. Treat the attorney as you would a prospective client, clear conflicts, and then act in accordance with all other RPCs.

g. Advertising

The Florida Bar v. Pape, 918 So. 2d 240 (Fla. 2005) provides a cautionary advertising tale. John Robert Pape and Marc Andrew Chandler ran a plaintiffs'-side firm in Fort Lauderdale, Florida. To garner business, they advertised their services with a novel mnemonic and graphic device. Capitalizing on the reputation of the mighty pit bull, they used the image of this spike-collared animal in place of the ampersand for their firm name of Pape and Chandler. After working through what must have been dozens of iterations for their toll-free number, they settled upon 1-800-PIT-BULL.

Word of this cheap marketing ploy spread and the Florida Bar Association's Office of Disciplinary Counsel took action, accusing Pape and Chandler of violating RPC 4-7.2(b)(3) and (4). The referee found no violation in using the logo, noting that it described the quality of the *attorneys* but not their *services*. Perhaps the referee respected how pits were "loyal, persistent, tenacious, and aggressive," relevant factors to a consumer selecting an attorney. And the 1-800-PIT-BULL mnemonic device, while memorable, was not unprofessional. Besides, Pape and Chandler's First Amendment rights to commercial speech nullified enforcement of the RPCs, argued the referee.

The Florida Supreme Court disagreed. First, the comment to RPC 7.1 prohibited sensationalistic imagery and slogans. Second, the referee's "artificial" distinction between the quality of the attorney versus service was unconvincing. Third, the comment to RPC 7.2(b)(4) prohibited ads *appealing to emotions*. For instance, the Florida Supreme Court banned the use of a fist logo on the grounds that it conveyed an overly brutal message; remember, the law is supposed to be governed by reason, not force.

Indeed, the crux of the *Pape* dispute centered on how one regards the innate nature of this breed (or, more accurately, this catch-all term for multiple similar breeds, like the American Staffordshire Terrier). The Supreme Court rejected the referee's charitable omission of the less desirable traits rumored to be associated with pits, such as "malevolence, viciousness, and unpredictability." It went so far as to suggest that the "pit bull" embodied the FRCP 11 mongrelization of the legal profession. They supported this conclusion by invoking dog-bite related fatality reports, identifying (validly or not) pit bulls as some of the most dangerous dogs around.

On the First Amendment question, the Supreme Court noted that, historically, while commercial speech protections apply even to lawyers, legal ads were still subject to reasonable regulations. *See Bates v. State Bar of Arizona*, 433 U.S. 350 (1977). The court distinguished the Ohio case of an attorney using the Dalkon Shield image in advertisements. *Zauderer v. Office of Disciplinary Counsel of the Supreme Court of Ohio*, 471 U.S 626 (1985). In *Zauderer*, the Supreme Court held that the use of the Dalkon Shield image informed women that this attorney represented clients in cases involving this intrauterine device and, far from being misleading or appealing to emotions, was strictly factual and informative.

The Florida Supreme Court had little difficulty distinguishing a pit bull's head from a birth control device because Pape and Chandler's practice apparently had nothing to do with pit bulls or dogs in general. They cautioned that if they permitted pit bulls to dominate lawyer ads, we could all expect to see attorneys sidling up beside sharks, wolves, piranhas, and crocodiles to advertise their practices. Pape and Chandler received a public reprimand and were ordered to attend a legal advertising ethics course.

For animal law attorneys, however, the use of the pit bull would be relevant to finding counsel well-versed in litigating cases involving attacks by pit bulls or euthanasia disposition orders where pit bulls declared dangerous are fighting for their lives.

Chapter 2

END-OF-LIFE LEGAL CONSIDERATIONS FOR ANIMALS

At thousands of shelters throughout America, after public viewing hours have ended, shelter workers are responsible for making several "Sophie's Choices"[1] as to which dog or cat, old or young, ill or healthy, of good or bad temperament, will be killed the next morning for no reason other than supply exceeds demand. Each year, millions of shelter animals pass into the designated area of the facility where a technician administers a lethal injection and places their bodies in a round barrel for rendering or group cremation. Yet, dwarfing the number of animals put to sleep in shelters, slaughterhouses slay billions of birds and mammals each year. How does the law attend to the end-of-life considerations of the nonhuman?

In 2009, Washingtonians passed Initiative 1000, called the *Washington Death with Dignity Act,* codified as Wash. Rev. Code Ch. 70.245. It allows a competent adult suffering from a terminal disease, who voluntarily expresses a wish to die, to make a written request for medication that the patient may self-administer to end his or her life in a humane and dignified manner. RCW § 70.245.020. (Washington Revised Code hereinafter cited as RCW.) One should not confuse this law with the conventional physician-assisted suicides performed by Dr. Jack Kevorkian via his Thanatron (a device that delivered euthanizing drugs intravenously at the push of a button) and Mercitron (a gas mask that delivered carbon monoxide). *See* RCW § 70.245.180 (explicitly prohibiting euthanasia by lethal injection, mercy killing, or active euthanasia). Presently, only Washington, Oregon, and Montana allow some type of physician-assisted suicide.

The disparate legal treatment and societal implications between human and nonhuman euthanasia takes us through the looking-glass where the "right" to euthanasia is presumed and bestowed without the need to furnish written, verbal, or nonverbal evidence of consent. Indeed, consent is immaterial, turning "euthanasia" into a euphemism for convenience killing.

Euthanasia derives from the Greek *eu* (good) and *thanatos* (death). It describes "ending the life of an animal in a way that minimizes or eliminates pain and distress," pursuant to the animal's interest and via "rapid and painless and distress-free" technique. AVMA GUIDELINES FOR THE EUTHANASIA OF ANIMALS: 2013 EDITION, at 6. Washington defines *euthanasia* as "the humane destruction of an animal accomplished by a method that involves instantaneous unconsciousness and immediate death, or by a method that causes painless loss of consciousness, and

---

[1] William Styron's novel *Sophie's Choice,* later an award-winning film, describes the crippling tragedy of a Polish-Catholic concentration camp survivor forced by an Auschwitz doctor to pick which of her two children must die in the gas chamber.

death during the loss of consciousness." RCW § 16.52.011(1)(e).

The term *euthanasia* appears restricted to non-farmed animals given the other end-of-life term *slaughter*, as in "humane slaughter" for "livestock" such as "cattle, calves, sheep, swine, horses, mules, and goats" in Washington's Humane Methods of Slaughter Act. RCW § 16.50.110(4). Federal law mirrors this distinction in the Humane Methods of Livestock Slaughter Act, 7 U.S.C. § 1901 et seq. In substituting the word *slaughter* for *euthanasia*, the intent remains the same — to render the animal insensible to pain prior to being shackled, hoisted, thrown, cast, or cut — at least as to farmed *terrestrial mammals* (chickens, turkeys, marine mammals, and fish, for instance, earn no protection and, by all accounts, are killed inhumanely and without a swift and painless death).

The Federal Humane Slaughter Act defines *humane method* of slaughter as either a method whereby the animal is rendered insensible to pain by "(a) . . . a single blow or gunshot or an electrical, chemical, or other means that is rapid and effective, before being shackled, hoisted, thrown, cast, or cut; or (b) by slaughtering in accordance with the ritual requirements of the Jewish faith or any other religious faith that prescribes a method of slaughter whereby the animal suffers loss of consciousness by anemia of the brain caused by the simultaneous and instantaneous severance of the carotid arteries with a sharp instrument and handling in connection with such slaughtering." 7 U.S.C. § 1902(a)-(b).

Dysthanasia, *euthanasia*'s antonym, means "bad death." Examples for conscious animals include burning, decompression, drowning, exsanguination, smothering, thoracic compression, hypothermia, and use of chloral hydrate, cyanide, diethyl ether, formaldehyde (except for *Porifera* (i.e., sponges)), or strychnine. AVMA GUIDELINES FOR THE EUTHANASIA OF ANIMALS: 2013 EDITION, App. 3. Intracardiac euthanasia by barbiturate injection is also inhumane when performed on conscious animals. Euthanasia by improperly placed gunshot is, as well. *Id.*

A. CRIMINAL LIABILITY

Intentionally killing an animal by a means causing undue suffering constitutes felony animal cruelty in most states, unless resulting from accepted animal husbandry or veterinary medical practices by a licensed veterinarian or certified veterinary technician. Misdemeanor level cruelty tends to include knowingly, recklessly, or with criminal negligence killing or injuring an animal by a means inflicting unnecessary suffering or pain. Even without an explicit veterinary defense, the commonly used adjectives "unjustified" and "unnecessary" open the door to same. Many jurisdictions also excuse law enforcement officers and licensed veterinarians attempting to euthanize animals "seriously injured and would other-wise continue to suffer," by conferring immunity from civil and criminal liability "if reasonable prudence is exercised . . ." RCW § 16.52.210.

While the Federal Humane Slaughter Act has no criminal penalty provision, states like Washington do. Inhumane methods of slaughter, including use of a "manually operated hammer, sledge or poleaxe," constitute misdemeanor violations of Washington's Humane Slaughter Act, at RCW § 16.50.140,.170. Yet, a religious double-standard arises, brought to the fore in *Pasado's Safe Haven v. State of*

Washington, 259 P.3d 280 (Wash. 2011) and *Jones v. Butz*, 374 F. Supp. 1284 (S.D.N.Y. 1974), summarily affirmed, 419 U.S. 806 (1974).

Certain methods of euthanasia are also *per se* inhumane and criminalized, such as intracardiac euthanasia by injection ("EBI") on conscious animals (Cal. Penal Code § 597u(a)(2)), use of carbon monoxide gas (§ 597u(a)(1)), high-altitude decompression chambers (§ 597u(b)(1)), and nitrogen gas (§ 597u(b)(2)). *See also Tuck v. Turoci*, 656 S.E.2d 15 (N.N. Ct. App. 2008) (confirming that intracardiac EBI on conscious cats and puppies violates protocols of AHA, HSUS, and AVMA; discussing civil suit for malicious prosecution and other claims resulting from dismissed charge against humane society shelter director for unlawfully and willfully promoting animal cruelty by "instigating and promoting employees under her supervision to conduct inhumane euthanasia and thereby causing [unnecessary] pain and suffering.").

Georgia phased out CO gas chambers through the 1990 passage of OCGA § 4-11-5.1, the Humane Euthanasia Act, mandating EBI in all shelters. However, the Georgia Department of Agriculture Commissioner Tommy Irvin refused to enforce it and continued to license gas chambers. This resulted in suit by the prime sponsor of the law, State Rep. Chesley V. Morton, against Irvin in *Morton v. Irvin et al.*, Fulton Cy. Sup. Ct. No. 2007V130839. The superior court issued an injunction to prevent future licensing of such shelters, but the Department then licensed another chamber in Cobb Cy., resulting in a second court action with the court holding the Department in contempt.

Occasionally, hoarders contend they are saving animals from certain death at local shelters, reasoning that living in squalor is better than the chance of dying at a humane society. For a case involving the necessity defense to charges of animal neglect against a woman who hoarded stray cats in order to save them from euthanasia at the shelter, see *Youngblood v. Placer Cy. Prob. Dept.*, 2007 U.S. Dist. LEXIS 66418 (E.D. Cal. Aug. 29, 2007) (denying writ of habeas corpus, affirming analysis of California Court of Appeals, which stated:

> [n]ecessity is an affirmative public policy defense, in effect a plea in avoidance and justification, which comes into focus only after all elements of the offense have been established. When public policy considerations do not support a defense of necessity, the trial court need not instruct on that defense.

> Since the defense of necessity is based on public policy, we must look to public policy to determine whether the defense was available to the defendant on the facts presented here. Aside from constitutional policy, the Legislature, and not the courts, is vested with the responsibility to declare the public policy of the state.

> The duties of a facility that acts as a depositary of living animals are spelled out in the Civil Code. "A depositary of living animals shall provide the animals with necessary and prompt veterinary care, nutrition, and shelter, and treat them kindly." The Legislature has expressly stated the public policy of this state concerning euthanasia of animals. If an animal is adoptable or, with reasonable efforts, could become adoptable, it should not

be euthanized. However, if an animal is abandoned and a new owner cannot be found, the facility shall thereafter humanely destroy the animal so abandoned. Particularly relevant to this case and the defendant's assertions is a finding made by the Legislature in 1998: "The Legislature finds and declares that it is better to have public and private shelters pick up or take in animals than private citizens."

Id., at *8–*10.

Hypothetical: Euthanasia by Gunshot. What if an individual wanted to humanely kill his sickly, suffering dog by gunshot, believing himself quite the marksman and knowing how to kill his dog instantly? Unfortunately, assume he did not fire properly. That it took some time and a few more rounds to put his dog to rest. And that without doubt during this time, the dog suffered unduly.

There is clearly *intent* to kill, but not intent to kill with undue suffering. There *is knowledge* the dog would die from being shot, especially improperly, but not that the dog would suffer as a result of firing the first bullet.

In this sense, there was only a *risk* of misfiring that would not instantly kill the dog, and that the dog might needlessly suffer. But was the risk *substantial*? Based on his experience as a sharpshooter or on his reliance on perhaps incorrect instructions on bullet placement? And was it *unjustified*? This may depend on the circumstances surrounding the ebbing health of the dog and the proximity to the vet.

If substantial and unjustified, and he consciously created the risk (i.e., failing to take precautions to minimize or eliminate the risk and thereby showing indifference to the outcome), he may be found *criminally reckless*. If there were a substantial risk that he did not consciously create (i.e., inadvertently), then he may be *criminally negligent*.

For a case involving the defense of euthanasia to charges of aggravated animal cruelty by 0.45 caliber handgun, see *People v. Larson*, 885 N.E.2d 363 (Ill. App. Ct. 2008) (while euthanasia by accurately delivered gunshot is acceptable method, jury could have found Larson guilty by taking Sinai outside and away from home and shooting him three times, notwithstanding his claim that hiring a veterinarian was cost-prohibitive).

Hypothetical: Drowning Wildlife. It is hard to conceive of delivering a more abominable death than trapping raccoons and squirrels and then dunking the trap in a garbage can filled with water. The AVMA and Humane Society of the United States have both stated that drowning is not an acceptable method of euthanasia. *See* AVMA Guidelines, S3.2.2.4 (page 56); Ludders JW, Schmidt RH, Dein J, et al., *Drowning Is Not Euthanasia*. WILDLIFE SOC BULL. 1999; 27(3):1. But do animal cruelty laws override or apply alongside fish and wildlife laws that may permit the killing of "nuisance wildlife"? One should first determine whether the wildlife meets the definition of "animal" under the cruelty chapter. If so, search for noninterference language within the cruelty law, such as a legislative pronouncement that it will not impede rights to kill venomous reptiles or animals known as dangerous to life, limb, or property. Absent such exemptive language, determine if the wildlife code incorporates by reference or defers to the cruelty code by stating that killing wildlife is "subject to all other state and federal laws."

In *State v. Lipsett*, 1997 Conn. Super. LEXIS 907 (Apr. 9, 1997), Michael Lipsett, a nuisance wildlife control operator ("NWCO"), faced two misdemeanor counts for drowning two trapped raccoons. Finding that Lipsett had an obligation to destroy the raccoons trapped from a customer's property within 24 hours, and that state cruelty law did not apply to wildlife, the court concluded that "all that the State has established is that drowning is not euthanasia and that drowning nuisance wildlife is a practice many people find highly offensive." *Id.*, at *8. However, NWCOs are not "specifically required by statute or regulation to practice euthanasia or 'humane killing' of nuisance wildlife which must be destroyed." *Id.*, at *9. Thus, while euthanasia or humane killing of wildlife is "obviously preferred over drowning, that, in itself, does not make drowning nuisance wildlife a crime."

B. RELIGIOUS SLAUGHTER

Nearly four decades later, on the opposite coast, but raising a similar challenge, plaintiffs in *Pasado's Safe Haven v. State of Washington* attempted to carry the baton of *Jones v. Butz*, 374 F. Supp. 1284 (S.D.N.Y. 1974). *Butz* challenged the ritual slaughter provisions of the Humane Methods of Slaughter Act (HMSA), 7 U.S.C. § 1901 (1970), as violating the Establishment and Free Exercise clauses of the First Amendment because the pre-slaughter handling that necessarily accompanied § 1902(b), the "kosher" method of slaughter, explicitly violated § 1902(a), the provision applying to non-ritual slaughters, and that required that animals be rendered insensible to pain before being hoisted and shackled. Plaintiffs claimed standing as taxpayers and consumers in that they could not distinguish between animals slaughtered by the kosher method from other animals. This source uncertainty established standing. However, they lost on the merits. The Washington nonprofit corporation devoted to stopping animal cruelty and providing sanctuary to its victims sought to declare unconstitutional certain provisions of the Washington Humane Slaughter Act ("WHSA"), permitting packers and slaughterers (including custom slaughterers regulated by WSDA) who killed livestock in accordance with the ritual requirements of their religious faith to avoid criminal prosecution when severing the animal's carotid arteries with a sharp instrument after being shackled, after being hoisted, after being thrown, after being cast, or after being cut — and to do so without having first been rendered insensible to pain, and without guaranteeing instantaneous loss of consciousness. This identical conduct, if performed for nonreligious or nonritualistic reasons, would be a misdemeanor. RCW § 16.50.170; WAC § 16-24-012(3).

The WHSA states, "No slaughterer or packer shall bleed or slaughter any livestock except by a humane method[.]" RCW § 16.50.120. It then defines "humane method" in expressly secular and religious terms:

(a) A method whereby the animal is rendered insensible to pain by mechanical, electrical, chemical or other means that is rapid and effective, before being shackled, hoisted, thrown, cast or cut; or

(b) A method in accordance with the ritual requirements of any religious faith whereby the animal suffers loss of consciousness by anemia of the brain caused by the simultaneous and instantaneous severance of the carotid arteries with a sharp instrument.

RCW § 16.50.110(3) (emphasis added). A plain reading of RCW § 16.50.110(3)(a) bespeaks the legislative intent of prescribing insensibility as a safeguard against animal cruelty. Necessarily, insensibility renders the Secular Method "humane" as assuredly as failing to render the animal insensible makes the method "inhumane." Common sense dictates that the legislature required insensibility before shackling, hoisting, throwing, casting, or cutting, because these actions, if performed on a conscious being, cause undue pain and suffering.

Yet the Religious Method has no such protection against inhumane treatment. One might argue that the "simultaneous and instantaneous severance of the carotid arteries with a sharp instrument" creates insensibility, but this is not even acknowledged, much less mandated, by RCW § 16.50.110(3)(b), as it is in RCW § 16.50.110(3)(a). Furthermore, the "loss of consciousness by anemia of the brain" need not be itself "simultaneous" or "instantaneous" with the severing of the carotid arteries. Indeed, loss of consciousness (and, thus, insensibility) is not immediate and sometimes can take more than one minute. Finally, it defies reason and candor to assert that having one's throat slit is an experience that does not cause pain or suffering, particularly when the Religious Method does not require insensibility prior to this act, and may occur after the animal has been shackled, hoisted, thrown (in an inverted box), or cast, and may involve use of a knife that is too short, as seen in *halal* (Muslim) slaughter.

The Religious Method therefore leaves room for abuse and religiously motivated cruelty. But whether the animal can be proved to suffer is not the only question. Of additional importance is whether one person should be jailed for killing an animal by precisely the same method as another, the distinction turning solely on religious state of mind. For RCW § 16.50.110(3)(a) does not authorize nonritual packers and slaughterers to shackle, hoist, cast, cut, or throw livestock without first rendering them insensible to pain. Accordingly, when such an individual intentionally and, by definition, "inhumanely" slaughters livestock, it is both a misdemeanor under RCW § 16.50.170 and a felony under RCW § 16.52.205(1). When one knowingly, recklessly, or with criminal negligence "inhumanely" slaughters livestock, it is a misdemeanor under RCW § 16.50.170 and RCW § 16.52.207(1).

The phrase "in accordance with the ritual requirements of any religious faith" is what converts the method, otherwise defined in secular terms, from one that is humane under all circumstances to one that is humane only when religiously motivated. Those who fail to slaughter "in accordance with the ritual requirements of any religious faith" face prosecution. The various scenarios of criminal misconduct involving the "Religious Method" include:

1. Believer, Religious Slaughter, Non-Instantaneous Severing. A packer or slaughterer abides by the ritual requirements of a religious faith but uses a technique that does not involve instantaneous severing of the carotids with a sharp instrument.

2. Believer, Religious Slaughter, Non-Sharp Instrument. A packer or slaughterer abides by the ritual requirements of a religious faith but uses a technique that involves instantaneous severing of the carotids with some-

thing other than a sharp instrument.

3. Nonbeliever, Religious Slaughter, Instantaneous Severing with Sharp Instrument. A packer or slaughterer precisely goes through the motions of the ritual requirements of a religious faith and uses a technique involving the instantaneous severing of the carotids with a sharp instrument, but is not doing so "in accordance" with the common ritual requirement that the packer or slaughterer be a believer or person of the religious faith involved. For instance, in kosher slaughter, the slaughterer must be "religiously qualified."

The rub in scenarios 1 and 2 is that even a believer who engages in ritual slaughter pursuant to his own idiosyncratic interpretation of what is required by his religion may escape prosecution regardless of whether he adopts the Secular Method, for RCW § 16.50.150 states that notwithstanding any provision of Ch. 16.50 RCW, all forms of ritual slaughter are "humane." Accordingly, such actions cannot be held to violate RCW § 16.50.120 (mandating a "humane method" of slaughter) and the individual will always escape prosecution regardless of how flagrant. Thus, while Ch. 16.50 RCW purports to impose criminal penalties upon religious minorities who fail to slaughter in accordance with the tenets of their religion, the other provisions of the chapter appears to render this proscription questionable.

The same cannot be said for nonbelievers, for it takes an otherwise secular method (i.e., cause instantaneous severing of carotids with sharp instrument) and makes it a crime not to perform that method with properly pious calibration of soul. Of course, criminalization applies not just to the Religious Method, but also the Secular Method, allocating all the peril to nonbelievers and none to believers. The WHSA would not offend the constitutions if it exposed all packers and slaughterers — religious and secular — to prosecution for failing to comply with the Secular Method. Instead, the legislature has exonerated religious minorities by offering them, and only them, an exception to the Secular Method, thereby freeing them from the criminal repercussions that would otherwise apply if they shackled, hoisted, cast, threw, or cut before stunning.

If the Religious Method required that the instantaneous severing of the carotid arteries caused "immediate" or "near immediate" loss of consciousness (i.e., insensibility), or if the Religious Method proscribed shackling, hoisting, casting, or throwing before loss of consciousness, the above scenarios would no longer offend the constitutions in the respect described — except for cutting, as the act of cutting cannot render the animal insensible to the pain of being cut.

The WHSA goes much further, however, by expressly "defin[ing] as humane" both "ritual slaughter" and "the handling or other preparation of livestock for ritual slaughter[.]" RCW § 16.50.150. The term *ritual slaughter*, glaringly undefined, invites unbridled discretion to not just statutorily defined "packers" and "slaughterers" (RCW § 16.50.110(5), (7)), but to "any person" (RCW § 16.50.110(6)). The identical conduct, if part of non-ritual slaughter, or the handling or other preparation of livestock for non-ritual slaughter, would not enjoy the laissez-faire religious privilege sanctioned by the Legislature and declared holy as a matter of public policy. The far-reaching impact of RCW § 16.50.150, by its plain language, well precedes the coup de grâce to encompass every act or omission in preparation for slaughter. And because virtually all livestock are raised from birth for the express purpose of slaughter, RCW § 16.50.150 amounts to a "cradle-to-grave" religious exemption for even admittedly cruel misconduct.

This exemption invites concern over legitimately humane issues of transport, confinement, nutrition, exercise, ventilation, veterinary care, and all other aspects considered by Ch. 16.52 RCW, Washington's cruelty law. The same handling or preparation methods, performed by those not intending to slaughter by the Religious Method, would not receive the blessing of "humane" given by RCW § 16.50.150. The result? Criminal liability under RCW § 16.50.170, as it applies to "[a]ny person violating any provision of this chapter or of any rule adopted hereunder[.]" Conduct "defined as humane" irreconcilably conflicts with any prosecution as "inhumane."

Further, in declaring ritual slaughter "humane," and noting that, "Nothing in this chapter shall be construed to prohibit, abridge, or in any way hinder the religious freedom of any person or group[,]" RCW § 16.50.150 creates an express exemption to RCW § 16.50.140, which declares as "inhumane" the use of a manually operated hammer, sledge or poleaxe. Use of such implements is criminal — unless religiously motivated. RCW § 16.50.170.

"Ritual slaughter" is not defined anywhere within the WHSA, and RCW § 16.50.110(3)(b) does not use the term "ritual slaughter" or "slaughter" at all. Nor does the WHSA incorporate by reference any provision of the HMSA. Nor does it say that it shall defer to definitions found within, or the framework of, the HMSA. Rather, it states, in relevant part:

> It is therefore declared to be the policy of the state of Washington to require that the slaughter of all livestock, and the handling of livestock in connection with slaughter, shall be carried out only by humane methods and to provide that methods of slaughter shall conform generally to those authorized by the Federal Humane Slaughter Act of 1958, and regulations thereunder.

RCW § 16.50.100. Unlike the HMSA, the WHSA declares certain methods inhumane (RCW § 16.50.140) and criminalizes noncompliance (RCW § 16.50.170). Unlike the HMSA's refusal to address handling and preparation methods for ritual slaughter under 7 U.S.C. § 1902(b) by exempting them, the WHSA defines them as per se "humane."

Additionally, the WHSA allows the double standard, turning the WSDA Director into a "Grand Inquisitor," instructing his "agents" to determine whether the slaughterer was killing with impure (i.e., other than religious) thoughts, and exonerating even the most heinous acts of ritual sacrifice (e.g., Satanism) so long as done in the name of a deity or for a religious purpose.[2]

---

[2] Kosher fraud law cases like *Commack Self-Service Kosher Meats, Inc. v. Rubin*, 106 F. Supp. 2d 445 (E.D.N.Y. 2000), *Ran-Dav's County Kosher, Inc. v. State*, 608 A.2d 1353, 1360 (N.J. 1992), *cert. denied*, 507 U.S. 952 (1993), and *Barghout v. Bureau of Kosher Meat and Food Control*, 66 F.3d 1337, 1342 (4th Cir. 1995), also support the proposition that the WHSA violates the constitution. *Commack* found that the New York State laws mandating what products may be called "kosher" incorporated Hebrew religious requirements into State law, and added:

To make matters worse, "religious" is not defined, but Washington's constitution has been interpreted to confer upon even the most dubious creed a protected status, so long as "arguably religious." *See State v. Balzer*, 954 P.2d 931 (Wash. Ct. App. 1998) (high priest of the Rainbow Tribe Church of the Living Light, a religion using psychoactive drugs and plants in prayer ceremonies and utilizing marijuana as a sacrament during the ceremonies, was a "religion" protected under the Washington constitution). Even the most idiosyncratic creed (e.g., comprised of one adherent), whose self-defined orthodoxy includes torturing livestock for ritual purposes, might be "defined as humane," exempt from prosecution under the WHSA and animal cruelty laws.

In the Jewish community, much discord exists as to what satisfies the "ritual requirements of any religious faith" given rabbinical debate over whether particular practices, such as the use of the inverted box, "second cut," or Kapparos, comply with Jewish law.[3] Other examples of discord involving ritual slaughter exist with

---

> It is incontrovertible, given the context, that in order to consistently enforce the religious code adopted by the Challenged Laws, New York State is forced to rely on advisors chosen specifically because of their religious knowledge.

Id., at 458 (adding at 459, citing *Barghout*, that even if membership in the Bureau were not restricted to adherents of Orthodox Judaism or even if there were no Bureau at all, adopting Orthodox rules requires intimate involvement with members of that faith in discerning the applicable standard.) The *Ran-Dav's*, *Barghout*, and *Commack* courts all declared the kosher fraud laws unconstitutional. For although

> civil courts may resolve controversies involving religious groups if resolution can be achieved by reference to neutral principles of law, . . . they may not resolve such controversies if resolution requires interpretation of religious doctrine[.]

"[T]he State's adoption and enforcement of the substantive standards of the laws of kashrut is precisely what makes the regulations religious, and is fatal to its scheme." *Ran-Dav's*, at 155.

> Whether prosecution under the ordinance focuses on the subjective intent of the vendor, or on the vendor's compliance with the Orthodox standards of kashrut, the ordinance still fosters excess entanglement between city officials and leaders of the Orthodox faith with each and every prosecution.

Barghout, at 1344. Under the WHSA, what would prevent a person from asserting that her religion, the Church of the Holy Hamburger, which she founded and is the sole member, requires slaughter by the Religious Method. Is the government to just take her word for it and leave her be, or engage in some investigation, interpretation, and, if unsatisfied, enforcement of based on purported membership in a specific religious sect? And if the prosecution commences, will not the state enlist the help of the religious leaders of the faith in question?

While the phrase "in accordance with the ritual requirements of any religious faith" has never been interpreted under federal or state law with respect to the WHSA or the HMSA, the *Commack* court held that the phrase "in accordance with orthodox Hebrew religious requirements" and "kosher," for purposes of determining whether the kosher fraud laws violated the Establishment Clause, created an unconstitutional entanglement for the reason that, quoting *Ran-Dav's*, "The kosher regulations rely expressly on religious tenets concerning what is kosher and who should be trusted to supervise kosher food preparation." *Commack*, at 457. *Commack* further stated that the entanglements engendered by the Challenged Laws, in themselves, "violate the First Amendment, but they also, by their nature, reflect an impermissible state advancement of religion." *Id.*

[3] "The mammals and birds that may be eaten must be slaughtered in accordance with Jewish law." Deut. 12:21. The person who performs Jewish slaughter is called the *shochet*. He is not simply a butcher, but must be a devout man, well-trained in Jewish law, particularly as it relates to kashrut. www.jewfaq. org/kashrut.htm. Indeed, in the wrongful termination case of *Maruani v. AER Services, Inc.*, 2006 U.S. Dist. LEXIS 66789 (D. Minn. Sept. 18, 2006), Leo Maruani sued a kosher slaughterhouse for firing him

respect to halal, jhakta, and Santeria (described in *Church of the Lukumi Babalu Aye v. City of Hialeah*, 508 U.S. 520, 524–25 (1993)), in addition to other lesser-known practices. Washington might have evaded these ecclesiastical disputes by drafting a law that focused exclusively on the methods of slaughter, rather than the religious mental state of the slaughterer. Indeed, the Supreme Court suggested that the City of Hialeah could have effectuated its legitimate government purpose in preventing animal cruelty if it worried that the Santerians' method of ritually slaughtering chickens was inhumane, because:

> If the city has a real concern that other methods are less humane, however, the subject of the regulation should be the method of slaughter itself, not a religious classification that is said to bear some general relation to it.

City of Hialeah, 508 U.S. at 539. The state could just as easily have enacted a WHSA that established humane methods of slaughter regardless of whether the packer or slaughterer wishing to kill the animal did so with a secular or religious intention. The Washington Court of Appeals did not reach the merits of the above arguments, instead dismissing on grounds of nonjusticiability by finding that partial statutory invalidation, the result sought by Pasado's, would "bring about a result that our legislature 'never contemplated nor intended to accomplish.' "

C. CIVIL LIABILITY — EUTHANASIA AUTHORIZED/OWNER PRESENT

Where owners or authorized agents permit euthanasia and opt to be present, practitioners may be liable for injury to the observer, such as where:

1. The observer suffers emotional distress from the animal's turbulent, aesthetically disturbing death. The AVMA Report discusses two disadvantages from EBI: the terminal gasp and occasional excitatory phase. Failure to warn the observer that this may occur could lead not only to foreseeable shock, but syncopal episodes resulting in physical injury.

2. The animal becomes fractious as a result of an excitatory phase, causing direct physical injury to the observer. In the case of equines or other large animals, observers risk being pinned or crushed if not kept at a safe distance.

3. Euthanasia is performed incorrectly, such as through improper drug selection or administration. This results in distress to the observer. For instance, failure to give a high enough dose intraperitoneally may cause

---

because he "was not living a pious life in conformance with Orthodox Jewish beliefs," and, thus, could not slaughter in accordance with ritual requirements of the Jewish faith. Shlomoh Ben-David, President of the kosher slaughterhouse sued by Mr. Maruani, states: "Based on *kashruth*, the supervising rabbis require that animals be slaughtered according to strict religious rituals and that the slaughter be performed by a shochet, or specially trained ritual slaughterer and inspector. The rabbis further require, according to *kashruth*, that the shochet have a license issued by an Orthodox Jewish rabbi and be someone who lives a visibly pious life in strict conformance with Orthodox Jewish beliefs — someone who is 'God-fearing in the public's eye.' The Orthodox Jewish community's perception of the shochet as pious and God-fearing is extremely important: otherwise, the community will not be able to trust that the shochet has slaughtered the animals according to religious ritual and that the meat is fit for consumption."

undue suffering and what some describe as "popcorning," while intracardiac administration on a conscious or unanesthetized animal is per se inhumane. A technician may also fail to inject the drug intravenously, instead allowing it to go perivascular. Euthasol (sodium pentobarbital and phenytoin sodium) has a pH of 12 or 13, stronger than ammonia, the same as bleach, and approaching the causticity of lye, all of which are considered toxic. Even slight perivascular leakage of barbiturates can cause necrosis and intense pain.

4. The veterinarian leaves the euthanizing drugs with the client to administer herself, at risk of harm to her and animal, at least in the case of an equine. *See In the Matter of Tony Cortland Smith*, M2009-131 (Wash. VBOG) (issuing Statement of Allegations for violating standard of care by leaving these substances for client to give to her colicing horse in his absence; resulting in stipulation to informal disposition and lawsuit, *Baechler v. Beaunaux*, 272 P.3d 277 (Wash. Ct. App. 2012)).

D. CIVIL LIABILITY — EUTHANASIA AUTHORIZED/NOT PERFORMED AS AGREED

When clients sign consent to euthanize forms, they contract with the veterinarian to perform the procedure, paying for a "good death." If that does not occur, either because the veterinarian commits malpractice or patently disregards the agreement, breach of contract, breach of bailment, and perhaps breach of fiduciary duty principles arise. For example, a veterinarian who agrees to euthanize according to the client's wishes, but then conceals the fact that she instead treated and adopted out the patient has committed conversion. *See Fredeen v. Stride*, 525 P.2d 166 (Or. 1974). Discipline may also ensue, as discussed in *Jackson v. State Bd. of Veterinary Med.*, 2008 Pa. Commw. Unpub. LEXIS 385 (Aug. 14, 2008).

E. CIVIL LIABILITY — NO AUTHORITY TO EUTHANIZE

Finally, there are instances in which the veterinarian lacks authorization to euthanize. Consider the following:

1. A Good Samaritan brings in a dog without a microchip or collar to an emergency clinic. Believed to be severely emaciated, she seeks treatment. A veterinarian tentatively diagnoses lymphosarcoma or another life-threatening condition and opines that the dog will not live a week. He then gives the Good Samaritan the option of further testing, supportive care, or euthanization. The Samaritan authorizes euthanasia but informs the veterinarian that she is not the owner and has no authorization by the owner to elect euthanasia. The veterinarian fails to notify law enforcement, animal control, or to even hold the dog for a day to give the true owners a chance to recover him. Another veterinarian at the clinic, the office manager, and the veterinary technician who assisted the veterinarian all strongly disagree with the need to euthanize. Though put to sleep that day, the true owners spend more than a week actively searching for the deceased dog.

The Washington Court of Appeals permitted the claims of conversion and trespass to chattels to proceed to trial, emphasizing that the question of whether the veterinarian exerted authorized dominion and control over the dog remained a fact issue, and rejecting that WAC § 246-933-060 disposed of the question as a matter of law. WAC § 246-933-060 provides that the veterinarian is free to accept or reject a particular patient, but once undertaking care, the veterinarian shall not neglect the patient as long as the person presenting the patient requests and authorizes the services for the particular problem. The veterinarian argued that euthanasia was a proper "treatment" to alleviate suffering, furnishing a defense under WAC § 246-933-060. The court instead concluded that WAC § 246-933-050 and 246-933-060 raised triable issues as to whether the veterinarian endeavored to provide at least minimal treatment to alleviate suffering of an animal presented in the absence of the owner or owner's agent or was negligent in failing to search or wait for the original owners to come forward. In arbitration, Plaintiffs prevailed on a negligence theory. *Sexton v. Brown*, 2008 Wash. App. LEXIS 2530 (Oct. 20, 2008)

2. At other times, veterinarians claim the right to euthanize based on statutory abandonment. *Saffran v. Fairfield Equine Assocs., P.C.*, 2008 Conn. Super. LEXIS 1980 (Aug. 8, 2008) is instructive. Saffran placed Quincy, suffering from severe degenerative arthritis when presented and who could not move or move easily without pain, with FEA for placement in a full body sling and hospitalization. Dr. Edwards recommended euthanasia, believing the sling ineffective. After attempting to treat Quincy, FEA notified Saffran it would discharge, reiterating the need for Saffran to retrieve his horse. Saffran did not pick up Quincy but said he was waiting on locations to which he could be moved. FEA called and mailed a certified letter stating that it considered Quincy abandoned and intended to euthanize him in 15 days. Saffran strongly disputed the recommendations of FEA and persisted in believing she should be treated in the sling, with repositioning, medicating, and hoof trimming. The court urged the parties to relocate Quincy instead of litigating the abandonment claim. They could not, so the court resolved the issue by granting a TRO to Saffran and finding no abandonment.

F. CIVIL LIABILITY — VOID AUTHORIZATION

Occasionally, one procures owner authorization under duress, undue influence, or without informed consent. Consider *Greenway v. Northside Hosp., Inc.*, 730 S.E.2d 742 (Ga. Ct. App. 2012). While en route to the hospital, Michael Greenway told emergency personnel that his "dogs are in the back yard, they will be fine," and Greenway's neighbor told EMT and the police he "would look after the dogs. . . ." *Id.*, at 745. Disoriented, unable to see, and amidst chaos in the emergency room, a patient advocate, nurses, and a doctor told Greenway in the presence of deputies that a form they handed him sought to make sure his dog "would go to the Humane Society" if he died. The doctor explained that the county policy permitted him to get his animals back within seven days. Deputy Roper then told him to "[j]ust sign the damn form" and the doctor urged similarly that he should "sign the form to get these guys out of here." Greenway executed the document by inscribing an "X" without reading it entirely, but acknowledged he understood he was giving up ownership due to his medical condition. After signing and receiving his glasses, Greenway re-read the form and learned his dogs' fates included euthanasia, causing "bells, whistles and everything" to go off in his mind. Before he could rectify the matter, he became woozy and woke up in another room. On coming to, he immediately asked the charge nurse about his dogs. She tearfully returned after making inquiries, explaining they had been euthanized.

Three days after receiving his dogs, the NALAA Corporation, which operated the animal control facility by contract with the county, killed them notwithstanding the neighbor's offer to pay $100 for boarding and food and more if needed, and stating to a NALAA employee "over and over again that those dogs were not to be euthanized under any circumstances." The NALAA employee assured the neighbor "that they 'would take real good care of the dogs.'" The Georgia Court of Appeals reversed summary judgment favoring the deputy who allegedly told Greenway to "sign the damn form" by having breached his ministerial duty with respect to the decision to ask Greenway to sign, as well as manner in which he executed that decision. The court also reversed summary judgment favoring the hospital for breach of a voluntary undertaking — namely, "to help Greenway ensure the safety of his dogs during his hospitalization, to provide advice about the effect of the release he signed, and to advise him about the entity employing Deputy Roper, and to advise him about which entity would be taking custody of his dogs if he signed the release." Additionally, the court treated proximate cause as a jury issue "on whether the euthanizing of Greenway's dogs was a reasonably foreseeable consequence of Northside's conduct," incisively analogizing to *Cotton v. Smith*, 714 S.E.2d 55, 62–63(3) (Ga. Ct. App. 2011), a case holding that a jury should decide whether a school's conduct in releasing a student to an unauthorized person proximately caused her molestation by that person. Lastly, finding that Greenway's neighbor presented evidence sufficient to invoke promissory estoppel by NALAA, it reversed summary judgment in its favor and added, "While the releases provided to NALAA may have authorized it to euthanize Greenway's dogs, it was also authorized to subsequently enter into a promise *not* to do so."

G. CIVIL LIABILITY — REFUSAL TO EUTHANIZE AGAINST MEDICAL ADVICE

There may be a discord between the client's and veterinarian's desire to euthanize, leaving the voiceless patient in the middle of an ethical quandary. If the veterinarian believes that failure to euthanize constitutes animal cruelty, she may be inclined to report the client to law enforcement or animal control. In so doing, however, she risks violating ethical duties of confidentiality. And, from a moral standpoint, she may be interfering with deeply held convictions of the owner that eschew euthanasia on religious grounds. For instance, some Buddhists adhere to the view that they must abstain from destroying living beings, who are all deemed precious. Indeed, assisting the suicide of a human being can result in expulsion from a monastic community. Some Buddhist clients extend these principles to their animal companions, believing that euthanasia interferes with the karmic cycle of suffering and spiritual growth, which will release the animal from future suffering in the next life. They instead opt for hospice care. One veterinarian's struggle is discussed at www.petmd.com/blogs/fullyvetted/2010/oct/killing_and_karma-10460. *See* www.chagchen.org/2009/07/05/what-do-buddhists-with-pets-think-about-euthanasia/.

The AVMA Principles of Veterinary Medical Ethics, Section VIII(C) states, "Ethically, the information within veterinary medical records is considered privileged and confidential. It must not be released except by court order or consent of the owner of the patient." A veterinarian may terminate the VCPR if the client does not follow advice to euthanize. Choosing to terminate the VCPR may result in accusations of patient abandonment.

The AVMA Principles of Veterinary Medical Ethics, Section III(D) state:

D.   Veterinarians may terminate a VCPR under certain conditions, and they have an ethical obligation to use courtesy and tact in doing so.

1.   If there is no ongoing medical condition, veterinarians may terminate a VCPR by notifying the client that they no longer wish to serve that patient and client.

2.   If there is an ongoing medical or surgical condition, the patient should be referred to another veterinarian for diagnosis, care, and treatment. The former attending veterinarian should continue to provide care, as needed, during the transition.

In treating the client courteously, the veterinarian should consider the spectrum of ethical responses to animal suffering, short of a knee-jerk decision to euthanize. Relevant is *People v. Arroyo*, 3 Misc. 3d 668 (N.Y. Crim. Ct. 2004). Manuel Arroyo came to the ASPCA offices to meet with an animal control investigator concerning his dog with a terminal condition. After explaining that "he was familiar with cancer because a relative had had cancer and painful chemotherapy and stated that he believed that the dog should live out her life without intervention," the officer arrested Mr. Arroyo for animal cruelty for failure to provide medical treatment. The trial court dismissed the charges, finding Mr. Arroyo's decision not to provide medical care to his dog was part of a conscious decision based on his moral beliefs and limited finances. The court's comments in dismissing Mr. Arroyo's charges bear repeating:

Furthermore, the court is troubled by the imposition of a duty to provide care in light of a statute that, like § 353, is so general in its terms. Reading this duty into the statute will create a myriad of logistical problems. For instance, how is the standard of medical care that must be provided to be determined? (i.e., To what extent must treatment be provided to avoid prosecution? Is providing regular veterinary care sufficient? Or, in light of the sophisticated medical procedures that are now available for animals — chemotherapy, radiation therapy, organ transplants — will that level of treatment be required? Will mental health treatment be required?); and how would that standard be judged? (What kind of expense is it mandated to be incurred to avoid prosecution?) It will also create ethical issues that are difficult to discern in the absence of a legislative pronouncement (When is extending a pet's life permissible? When is putting an animal to death mandated? Up to what point do we respect the owners' choice to refuse invasive treatment for their pets and allow them to die at home in the company of their human and non-human companions, rather than in a strange and antiseptic environment?).

Id., at 679–80.

H.   CIVIL LIABILITY — MISCELLANY

Wrongful discharge claims due to failure to adhere to euthanasia protocol or retaliation for whistleblower complaints concerning inhumane euthanasia also emerge. Consider *Hamilton v. City of Springdale, Ark.*, 2011 U.S. Dist. LEXIS 71049 (W.D. Ark. Jun. 29, 2011), involving claims of deprivation of due process in connection with termination, age discrimination, conspiracy to violate civil rights, retaliation for whistleblowing, and violation of rights under the Family and Medical Leave Act. While the decision should be read in its entirety, highlights include a claim of age discrimination relative to a decision to cut back responsibilities and reduce pay of an older female employee for allegedly violating euthanasia protocols and showing lack of compassion in the euthanasia room, relying in part on a comment from a supervisor that "You can't teach an old dog new tricks." A claim for retaliation also arose from Hamilton's complaint that the euthanasia trainer violated state law by failing to transport a cat's head for rabies testing.

Euthanasia prior to completion of rabies hold, failing to timely secure the body for testing, or failure to perform direct fluorescent antibody testing (dFA) on the brain tissue of the euthanized animal before disposition of body may also establish liability. *See Galmiche v. The State Farm Ins. Co.*, 923 So. 2d 756 (La. Ct. App. 2006) (parish owed duty to victim of dog bite by failing to collect dog immediately on notice of death, allowing contamination of brain tissue and forcing victim to undergo rabies treatment).

Inmates facing death by lethal injection repeatedly draw parallels to animal euthanasia protocols, arguing that the method contemplated for humans violates the Eighth Amendment protection against cruel and unusual punishment. Consider *Arthur v. Thomas*, 674 F.3d 1257 (11th Cir. 2012), *Baze v. Rees*, 553 U.S. 35 (2008), and *Cooey v. Strickland*, 589 F.3d 210 (6th Cir. 2009).

Equine mortality insurance policy challenges, such as the recent case of *North Amer. Spec. Ins. Co. v. Pucek*, 709 F.3d 1179 (6th Cir. 2013) also warrant review. Affirming judgment for the insurer, the Sixth Circuit held that while the American Association of Equine Practitioners guidelines permitted euthanasia of Off Duty, a five-year-old thoroughbred suffering from a collapsed fetlock joint, because the insurer offered to pay for fetlock arthrodesis and aftercare without diminishing coverage, Pucek's decision to euthanize Off Duty failed to meet the humane destruction exception to the intentional destruction exclusion (i.e., a certified written opinion that the horse was "incurable and in constant pain").

Chapter 3

CONTRACTUAL DISPUTES INVOLVING ANIMALS AND THE UCC

Whether dropping off your Weimaraner at a daycare, consenting to anesthesia and dental extractions for your silver tabby, fostering a Pug on behalf of a nonprofit organization, selling an Arabian stallion, or entering your Jack Russell in an agility competition, you will likely sign a written contract or verbally assent to an oral contract. As with all other contracts, standard principles of offer, acceptance, consideration, and meeting of the minds apply. Attendant defenses do as well. Perhaps the largest volume of contracts involves possessory transfers involving animal shelters and rescue organizations.

A. "ADOPTATIONS"

The word *adoption* in the context of transferring property interests in nonhumans, primarily dogs and cats, denotes irrevocable placement in a lasting home. While the term *adoption* has a fairly standardized, statutorily prescribed and independent legal significance for human beings, the contours of an adoption of nonhumans admit as many permutations as there are contractual variations, or "adoptations." The following outline guides the reader in wrestling with the quirks of animal adoption.[1]

The Uniform Commercial Code ("UCC") applies to transactions in goods (Art. 2) and leases (Art. 2A). Goods include movable corporeals and expressly "unborn young of animals." It does not apply to service contracts. *Sale* is defined by the UCC as the passing of title from the seller to the buyer for a price. *Cf. Slodov v. Animal Protective League*, 628 N.E.2d 117, 118 (Ohio Ct. App. 1993) (stating SPCA's adoption of animals not "sale of goods" under UCC). That rescues take money as an "adoption fee" does not necessarily convert the transaction from sale to non-sale from which they may escape Art. 2 provisions. The real question is whether title has passed. If so, then UCC warranties and remedies apply. If not, then consult the common law.

Rescues eschew the word "sale" for many reasons, primarily philosophical, by holding that the animal is not mere chattel to be bartered as if at a livestock auction. They strive to preserve the animal's best interests within the contract, imbuing the

---

[1] I give thanks to Nadia Adawi, Esq., former ALDF-funded extern to the WSBA Animal Law Section for her excellent research on this subject in 2010, and republished in the Section newsletter (Vol. 9, No. 1: Fall 2011), portions of which inform this chapter. I also thank University of Washington Law School Prof. Kate O'Neill for her insightful handling of this topic. *See* Kate O'Neill, *It's Raining Cats & Dogs*, WSBA-CLE (Nov. 16, 2010: Seattle, WA), Contract Pitfalls, Covenants, and Remedies in Adoption, Foster, and Sale Contracts.

transaction with gravity worthy of any human adoption agency. In so doing, they hope to retain the ability to repossess the animal and remove her from harm's way. But an equally significant justification is fiscal — i.e., to avoid paying income, retail sales, and business and occupation taxes. If the rescue lets "selling" animals get out of hand, however, that practice may overshadow its mission and jeopardize its ability to enjoy the full benefit of tax-exempt, nonprofit status.

Of course, charities routinely enjoy tax exemption for "fund-raising activities." Whether called a "sale" or "adoption," they will most likely enjoy a nonprofit corporation exemption. Most 501(c)(3) rescues characterize the transfer as an "adoption" to command larger "adoption fees" with the enticement of a tax-deductible donation. However, when the adoption fee exceeds the putative market value of the animal, the organization may subject itself to state charitable solicitation laws and *per se* violations of consumer protection acts where fraud or misrepresentation attend the solicitation of the adoption fee and related donations.[2]

If a pet store constitutes a "merchant," i.e., someone holding him- or herself out as having knowledge or skill peculiar to the practices or goods involved in the transaction or to whom same may be attributed, then the buyer may invoke the implied UCC warranty of merchantability and avoid efforts to disclaim it under 2-316(4), this section renders ineffective disclaimers of the warranty of merchantability for goods purchased "primarily for personal, family or household use and not for commercial or business use," unless "set[ting] forth with particularity the qualities and characteristics which are not being warranted." Note that a similar provision does not apply to leases. *See* § 2A-214.

Where the right of possession and use, but not title, transfer for a term in return for consideration, a lease may arise under Art. 2A. Where the animal is delivered to another to hold for a particular purpose with an express or implied contract to redeliver when the purpose has been fulfilled, a bailment exists. Bailments may solely benefit the bailor, the bailee, or benefit both. In any case, a lease is a type of bailment. Adoptions will virtually never constitute bailments because one does not anticipate that the adopter will return the animal to the rescue absent breach (i.e., an adoption for a specific term with an agreed return date in ordinary course).

However, foster agreements are almost always bailments given that the rescue may seek redelivery on demand from the foster. *See Swyssgood v. Roberts*, No. 94 CV 0980 (Akron Muni. Ct. 1994) (court rejected assertion that adoption agreement involving pony was merely "a contract for bailment for hire and use," instead finding a conditional transfer where MCSPCA transferred ownership but had "reversionary interest" safeguarded by contractual right to "regain" possession through what amounts to right of first refusal, barring transfer, gift, sale, encumbrance, assignment, or disposition to any other without written permission of MCSPCA); *see also Tucker v. Mecklenburg Cy. Zoning Bd. of Adjustment*, 557 S.E.2d 631, 636 (N.C. Ct.

---

[2] In Kansas, pet adoption fees are subject to the retailer's sales tax, though a veterinarian's charge for vaccination, sterilization, health exams, and deworming are not (unless those services are included in a lump-sum charge for the animal or separately billed as line-item charges that are part of the adoption fee). Kansas Private Letter Ruling 19–2012–01 (2012 WL 2340546, Kan. Dept. Rev.). Pennsylvania takes a similar position. https://revenue-pa.custhelp.com/app/answers/detail/a_id/2949/n/are-pet-adoptions-subject-to-sales-tax%3F. Washington recently reversed its position that rescues owed sales tax.

App. 2001) (though tangential to the key issue of whether the petitioners were operating a private kennel, the court found no manifest error in determining that donation in exchange for dog subject to conditions of care is not a sale but a conditional or partial gift).

Certain transfers of goods subject to licenses are governed by Art. 2. *See M.A. Mortenson Co. v. Timberline Software Corp.*, 998 P.2d 305 (Wash. 2000). Analogizing to software licenses, University of Washington Law School Prof. Kate O'Neill surmised that the same logic (i.e., license extends from intellectual property to property in which it is embedded) might apply to "support the idea that a transferor could essentially attach a license governing treatment and transfer to a sale of an animal."

Of course, if not technically a bailment, lease, or sale, it may otherwise constitute a non-UCC contract to be evaluated according to well-settled contract formation and interpretation canons. Or it may not be a contract at all, but instead a gift — whether unconditional or conditional. Gifts lack consideration. Most adoption contracts that have repossession clauses will defeat the gift argument because the clause itself evidences that the delivery to the alleged donee does not divest the rescue of dominion and control over the property absolutely and irrevocably. Further, gifts are not presumed and the donee must prove all elements by clear, cogent, and convincing evidence. Be aware that some jurisdictions do not recognize or enforce *conditional* gifts.

Even where an adoption contract sets the price at zero, consideration may take nonpecuniary form, such as by the adopter paying for transport of a horse from the sanctuary to the adopter's pasture, promises to provide the animal with humane, safe, and loving care, and bragging rights for the rescue organization (which may obtain grant money for touting a large number of successful adoptions). One may cleverly argue that an adoption contract constitutes a sale of *services* breached when such promises of care and transfer are unmet. However, at least one court has rejected this approach. In *In re Estate of Tyler Ray Harris*, No. 4-05-0681 (Ill. App. Feb. 3, 2006), the appeals court affirmed the trial court's order commanding the Humane Society of Illinois to return a dog named Jake, formerly adopted by the Society to decedent Tyler Harris, back to the decedent's estate. When Harris died, the estate let his roommate Becky McGrew care for Jake until she moved out. Upon leaving, she took Jake with her, whereupon the estate petitioned the court to order McGrew to return Jake. Meanwhile, the Humane Society recovered Jake from McGrew.

McGrew and Harris's father then applied to adopt Jake from the Humane Society. Upon refusal, the estate petitioned the court to order the Humane Society to return Jake to it. The court found that Harris ably performed the tasks set forth in the adoption contract during his life, stating, "Tyler was not contracting with the Humane Society to perform services for the Humane Society. Tyler was contracting to adopt the dog." It refused to construe the agreement as a personal services contract or a conditional sales contract and emphasized that "the adoption contract did not include any provision stating that title of the dog returned to the Humane Society if Tyler died before the dog." While the contract did envision that Jake would return to the Humane Society if Harris could no longer provide proper care, no life estate existed, the court construed the restriction as *inter vivos* only, found no breach, and permitted the estate to lawfully take ownership of Jake.

B. PERSONAL SATISFACTION

Where the rescue retains discretion to repossess if not personally satisfied with the adopter's caretaking skills, any purported transfer of title may appear to be illusory because defeasible by subjective fiat. However, the better approach deems the transfer non-illusory yet subject to a condition subsequent. RESTATEMENT (2D) OF CONTRACTS § 228 describes when dissatisfaction with the obligee's performance or some other factor will warrant termination of the contract. Though preferring an objective test of reasonable satisfaction over the subjective one of honest satisfaction whenever practicable (meaning that the premise may be examined by independent third parties and dissatisfaction measured according to objective criteria), § 223 provides for either test depending on the language of the contract.

For instance, if a humane society adopts a cat to an individual subject to a clause that allows it to unwind the transaction and recover the feline in its "sole, exclusive and final judgment made in good faith," then it may do so without recourse by the adopter under the subjective test of honest satisfaction. *Id.*, Ill. 1 (modified). Even without the phrase "made in good faith," the implied duty of good faith and fair dealing would apply to the test of honest satisfaction. However, merely professing dissatisfaction is not always conclusive. *McCartney v. Badovinac*, 160 P. 190 (Colo. 1916).

Absent wording that places the obligee on notice that termination may occur for idiosyncratic reasons of the obligor, especially where forfeiture (e.g., repossession of animal and no refund of adoption fee) may result, courts invoke the objective test whenever possible. *Id.*, cmt. b. Consider breeders who contract to sell a puppy but reserve the right to retake the dog and keep the purchase price "on condition of satisfactory confinement on premises" by the purchaser. Finding the buyer's wood-paneled, unstained, six-foot privacy fence less attractive and at greater risk of falling into disrepair than the breeder's preferred six-foot, chain-link fence, the breeder invokes the clause and attempts to recover the dog. The buyer would have a strong argument against forfeiture under the objective satisfaction test of a reasonable person.

C. POST-ADOPTION RESTRICTIONS AND SECURED TRANSACTIONS

The adage that possession is nine-tenths of the law bears strong consideration. Relying solely on a signed or even initialed contract by the adopter should not substitute for careful adoption application screening and home-checking. If a rescue wants certain action taken by the adopter, it should ensure so before release. For instance, some rescues contractually require that the adopter spay or neuter by a date certain. One can only guarantee sterilization, however, before releasing custody and control. *See Luri v. Take Me Home Rescue*, 146 Cal. App. 4th 1342 (2012) (foster refused to spay and then withheld possession from rescue, resulting in replevin and breach of contract action).

When adopters do not comply with post-adoption restraints, courts refereeing the dispute may construe them as future rights of reversion (automatic restoration of fee simple ownership), future rights of entry (restoration subject to invocation of condition subsequent), equitable servitudes, affirmative or restrictive covenants, gift conditions, or substantively unconscionable terms. In the right circumstance, repossession may even be permitted under Art. 9 of the UCC, as discussed below.

The court will only rescind the adoption agreement and order what amounts to a forfeiture (which courts are loathe to do) if the reversionary interest or right of entry is conspicuous, unambiguous, not the result of duress, mistake, infancy, fraud, or other time-worn contractual defenses to contract formation, and prompted by a material breach. Where a contract conveys the animal for life provided ongoing compliance with specific restraints, the court may regard the restrictions as conditions subsequent, such that breach results in divestiture and restoration. Conditions may expire, so that unreasonable delay from sitting on the breach may eliminate any remedy. If construed as a reversionary interest that springs automatically by the actions of the adopter, then no invocation or other action by the rescue may be required.

If the rescue seeks to enforce restrictions, such as spaying and neutering, but does not seek return of the animal, the court will examine equitable servitudes or contractual covenants to determine whether the remedy of specific performance is appropriate, subject to procedural and substantive fairness (i.e., unconscionability). In this regard, *Houseman v. Dare*, 966 A.2d 24 (N.J. Super. Ct. 2009), finding that companion animals have a unique value warranting the equitable relief of specific performance rather than mere monetary compensation, bears mention.

If the rescue seeks liquidated damages for a contract breach (e.g., declaw results in per-paw assessment), the court may question whether those damages reasonably approximate the economic harm inflicted. Further, the sum may so exceed the adoption fee as to prove irreconcilable (for integrity of the part — i.e., the claw — cannot exceed the value of the whole cat) or even seek to exact a penalty, which courts will not enforce. On the other hand, the rescue's lifetime financial investment in and civil liability of keeping a declawed feline (e.g., litter box avoidance, biting because rendered defenseless), as well as potential future medical expenses to treat nerve damage, bone spurs, or other complications from the procedure, might justify liquidated damages.

Finally, an esoteric and judicially untested proposal structures the adoption as an Art. 9 security agreement by viewing the transaction as one secured by promises to care for the animal, allowing the rescue to invoke repossession rights under Art. 9 of the UCC. For this to occur, however, the rescue must become a creditor, the adopter a debtor, and the animal the secured collateral. A "security interest" is defined as "an interest in personal property or fixtures which secures payment for performance of an obligation" and applies to any transaction "regardless of its form." UCC § 1-201(37). Section 9-609 permits nonjudicial repossession "without breach of the peace." Where breach may occur, one should resort to judicial action in the form of replevin. To create an enforceable security interest requires attachment per § 9-203 (creditor must give value, debtor must have rights in collateral, there must be security agreement, agreement must describe collateral, and it must be in writing or otherwise authenticated) and perfection per §§ 9-308 to 9-316. A security agreement operates as both a deed (conveying property interest) and contract (giving the transferor rights in the property upon breach or default).

D. MUTUAL MISTAKE

Sherwood v. Walker, 33 N.W. 919 (Mich. 1887), dramatically affected American contract law's evaluation of the doctrine of mutual mistake. That it concerned a bovine makes it an animal law first. Theodore Sherwood sued to replevy Rose 2d of Aberlone, a female Angus, whom he believed to be infertile and for whom he offered 5.5 cents per pound live weight, or about $80. Hiram Walker also thought her barren and agreed to the price. However, when Mr. Sherwood actually made tender, Mr. Walker refused to accept or deliver Rose because he had since learned that she was with calf, and thus was worth more than 10 times the original price. As both parties may have mistakenly believed Rose to be a heifer, not a cow, and such "mistake" went to the very heart of the bargain, the Michigan Supreme Court reversed and remanded for new trial with instructions to the jury to determine whether mutual mistake indeed existed and, thus, the contract failed for lack of consideration.

E. STATUTE OF FRAUDS

The following hypothetical will illustrate the legal problems associated with the statute of frauds, illegality, and voidable title:

Hypothetical: The curator for the hypothetical wolf sanctuary Wolf Pack International ("WPI"), in Montana contacts the director of another wolf sanctuary, Grey Wolf Rehabilitation ("GWR"), in Idaho inquiring about obtaining possession of Sunga, a captive-bred, untattooed female Northern Rocky Mountain Gray Wolf (then endangered under the Endangered Species Act ("ESA")), who was then in GWR's custody. GWR rejects the curator's request.

About one week later, Cecille Jenkins, an individual residing in South Dakota who owns sufficient acreage and has skill in handling wolves, asks GWR about opening a subsidiary of GWR in South Dakota and, at the same time, to take condition subsequent possession of Sunga. GWR agrees, provided that Jenkins cares for Sunga until Jenkins dies and returns her if no longer willing or able to do so (i.e., reverter). Sunga travels from Idaho Falls, Idaho, to Sioux Falls, South Dakota, her new home. GWR obtains Jenkins' contact information and USDA number, but not her driver's license and plate number.

After Sunga settled in, WPI's curator again called GWR asking for Sunga. GWR explained that a more suitable placement had been found. One week after Sunga's arrival, without notifying GWR, Jenkins donated Sunga to WPI's agents in South Dakota. Jenkins did so despite GWR making clear that it would never want Sunga, or any of its other wolves, to go to WPI. Jenkins also repeatedly lied to GWR about Sunga's custodial location and took steps to obscure her whereabouts by coordinating her story with that of WPI. After learning of the unauthorized transfer, GWR demanded that WPI return Sunga.

WPI refused, whereupon GWR sued WPI for return of Sunga, and Jenkins for breach of contract, fraud, conversion, and, alternatively, breach of conditional gift. WPI answered with affirmative defenses that no contract between GWR and Jenkins existed, but even if there were, it was illegal as GWR was not licensed to sell wolves as required by South Dakota law, and did not comply with federal and state obligations imposed upon it. WPI also asserted the statute of frauds. Further, it claimed to be a good faith purchaser for value, taking Sunga free and clear of any claim or restriction in the transaction when GWR transferred Sunga to Jenkins.

Jenkins also raised the statute of frauds, as well as failure of consideration and failure of mutuality of obligation. Fundamentally, she and WPI contended that no contract ever existed, but rather, that GWR made an "inter vivos absolute gift" to Jenkins, who was then free to transfer Sunga to WPI or whomever she wished. As a threshold matter, the statute of frauds does not apply to gifts.

Statutes of fraud traditionally arise in the commercial code for sales of goods for more than $500, yet they also apply to agreements that cannot be performed within one year (including a lease or sale of realty), and agreements made upon consideration of marriage. Furthermore, leases terminable at will are not within the statute of frauds. *See, e.g., Aldape v. State*, 575 P.2d 891 (Idaho 1978). Further, the Statute of Frauds bars only proof of executory (i.e., unperformed) contracts, not proof of executed contracts.

Jenkins and WPI claimed the statute of frauds applied to "any alleged restriction upon Ms. Jenkins' ability to deal with the wolf as she saw fit[.]" However, because Jenkins abandoned Sunga seven days after receiving her, the one-year rule would not apply for the simple reason that Jenkins could, and, in fact, did, find herself unable or unwilling to continue caring for Sunga in less than one year's time.

Jenkins countered that either Sunga or she could have died or become unable to perform within one year, so the statute of frauds still governed. However, when an oral promise is subject to several contingencies, such as death, disability, disinterest, or financial inability, each of which can occur within one year, enforcement of the promise is not barred by the statute of frauds. *General Auto Parts Co., Inc. v. Genuine Parts Co.*, 979 P.2d 1207 (Idaho 1999). Not only was it possible that Sunga would die within one year, but Jenkins could have died or become incapacitated or insolvent within one year.

Jenkins then claimed that the agreement amounted to one for care over an indefinite period that, given the life expectancy of the average wolf, and Sunga's tender years, would well exceed one year. However, by analogy, a claim for services rendered pursuant to an oral agreement to care for a testator during his lifetime (or indefinite period) was not rendered unenforceable by the statute of frauds as an agreement for services not to be performed within a year. *Hubbard v. Ball*, 81 P.2d 73 (Idaho 1938). In essence, she had what one may argue was a free lease or care lease for Sunga until she terminated the arrangement, at will, upon her financial or physical disability or change of mind.

Undeterred, Jenkins invoked the $500 sale of good clause, which stated:

> Except as otherwise provided in this section a contract for the sale of goods
> for the price of $500 or more is not enforceable by way of action or defense

unless there is some writing sufficient to indicate that a contract for sale has been made between the parties and signed by the party against whom enforcement is sought or by his authorized agent or broker. A writing is not insufficient because it omits or incorrectly states a term agreed upon but the contract is not enforceable under this paragraph beyond the quantity of goods shown in such writing.

I.C. § 28-2-401. *Sale* is defined as "the passing of title from the seller to the buyer for a price (section 28-2-401)." I.C. § 28-2-106(1). However, I.C. § 28-2-201 does not apply because GWR did not enter into a contract for "sale" of Sunga to Jenkins for any price. In some jurisdictions, once goods are "received and accepted," the writing requirement no longer applies and the contract is enforceable in all other respects. I.C. § 28-2-201(3)(c).

Do not forget that equitable estoppel serves as a way to avoid the sting of a contract voided by falling within the statute. Part performance establishes such equitable ground. GWR fully performed by delivering possession of Sunga to Jenkins at the location and date agreed upon. Jenkins partly performed by caring for Sunga for seven days before making arrangements to transfer her to WPI. GWR thus has a right to seek specific performance of the reciprocal promise made by Jenkins.

When one party has fully performed an oral contract within the statute of frauds, he is entitled to the equitable remedy of specific performance. *See Tew v. Manwaring*, 480 P.2d 896 (Idaho 1971); *Quayle v. Mackert*, 447 P.2d 679 (Idaho 1968). In applying the equitable estoppel doctrine, the court must consider the following with respect to the party to be estopped:

> . . . (1) Conduct which amounts to a false representation or concealment of material facts, or, at least, which is calculated to convey the impression that the facts are otherwise than, and inconsistent with, those which the party subsequently attempts to assert; (2) intention, or at least expectation, that such conduct shall be acted upon by the other party; (3) knowledge, actual or constructive, of the real facts. As related to the party claiming the estoppel, they are: (1) Lack of knowledge and of the means of knowledge of the truth as to the facts in question[;] (2) reliance upon the conduct of the party estopped; and (3) action based thereon of such a character as to change his position prejudicially.

Treasure Valley Gastroenterology Specialists, P.A. v. Woods, 20 P.3d 21, 26 (Idaho Ct. App. 2001) (quoting *Tew*, at 53). When the elements are proved, estoppel bars the party making the false representation from raising the statute of frauds as a defense. *Id.* To its detriment, GWR relied upon Jenkins' representation and agreement to return Sunga if she were no longer willing or able to provide continuing care. Equitable estoppel principles assuredly apply.

F.   PAST ILLEGALITY

Having failed the statute of frauds defense, WPI turned to illegality, a contractual doctrine that leaves the parties where it finds them and is premised on the notion that both contracting parties are equally at fault, or *in pari delicto* ("in equal or mutual fault"), in which case *potior est condition defendentis* ("the position of the [defending] party . . . is the better one.") BLACK'S LAW DICTIONARY 791 (6th ed. 1990).

Note that even if technically illegal, several defenses to the doctrine exist. Courts are wary about rendering a contract unenforceable on grounds of illegality unless it is of such an immoral character as to be pernicious and injurious to the public welfare. *Meier & Frank Co. v. Bruce*, 168 P. 5 (Idaho 1917). Other exceptions include the plaintiff's innocence as to the circumstances causing the illegality, a void insurance contract where unenforceability may defeat the purpose for which a statute has been enacted, and agreements induced by fraud.

Courts will favor the party seeking relief even in the case where the parties are not *in pari delicto*, such as where the defending party commits fraud, or there is duress, oppression, or undue influence over the other — in which case the less guilty party recovers. *Trees v. Kersey*, 56 P.3d 765, 770–771 (Idaho 2002); WILLISTON ON CONTRACTS § 19:79 (Parties not *in pari delicto*) (4th Ed. 2009). Indeed, even if no exception technically applies, courts may refuse to strictly apply the doctrine where "denying a party relief would frustrate the public interest more than 'leaving the parties where they lie.' " *Id.*, at 771.

WPI claimed the court could void any contractual obligation owed by Jenkins to GWR because GWR violated federal and state wildlife recordkeeping and tattooing laws, specifically 9 C.F.R. § 2.75(b)(1) and IC § 36-712(a).

The illegality argument brings into focus the following issues: (a) standing; (b) federal preemption of state wildlife laws; (c) whether anything illegal actually occurred so as to void the contract; and (d) exceptions to illegality doctrine.

1.   Standing

WPI never entered into any contract with GWR. Jenkins did. May WPI try to void an agreement to which it was never a party? In *Long v. Noah's Lost Ark, Inc.*, 814 N.E.2d 555, 567 (Ohio Ct. App. 2004), animal shelter Noah's Lost Ark, Inc. received a lion cub from a third party in violation of a contract between Long and the third party. The court refused to consider Noah's challenge to the legality of the sale between Long and the third party, and thus, the right to demand the lion's return due to breach thereof.

Indeed, from a purely rhetorical standpoint, taking WPI's argument to its desired conclusion would exemplify the old adage of cutting off one's nose to spite one's face. For if the contract between GWR and Jenkins was "illegal," then Jenkins would have acquired no legally enforceable ownership or possessory interests in Sunga at all. Accordingly, Jenkins would be able to pass along no better title than she lawfully acquired. This means that WPI would have acquired nothing at all, and the good faith purchaser for value doctrine, which it invoked as an affirmative defense, would have no traction whatsoever, because it only applies to "voidable" title, not "void" title. Furthermore, the Animal Welfare Act's implementing regulations make it illegal to sell, transport, or offer for transportation "any stolen animal." 9 C.F.R. § 2.60. Because turnabout is fair play, it would seem that any attempt by WPI to assert its rights vis-à-vis Jenkins falters under the same doctrine raised against GWR. Of course, one must remember that illegality doctrine results in judicial inertia, a hands-off approach that lets the chips, or in this case wolves, remain where they come to rest. In this context, the illegality argument may have tactical appeal.

2. Preemption

Any illegality defense requires close examination of the purported unlawful action. WPI claimed illegality under state law. However, federal law preempts it. Sunga, at the time of transfer, was a captive-bred endangered species. The ESA broadly preempts and declares void any state law or regulation applying to the interstate commerce in endangered species. 16 U.S.C. § 1535(f) states:

> (f) Conflicts between Federal and State laws. Any State law or regulation which applies with respect to the importation or exportation of, or interstate or foreign commerce in, endangered species or threatened species is void to the extent that it may effectively (1) permit what is prohibited by this chapter or by any regulation which implements this chapter, or (2) prohibit what is authorized pursuant to an exemption or permit provided for in this chapter or in any regulation which implements this chapter. This chapter shall not otherwise be construed to void any State law or regulation which is intended to conserve migratory, resident, or introduced fish or wildlife, or to permit or prohibit sale of such fish or wildlife. Any State law or regulation respecting the taking of an endangered species or threatened species may be more restrictive than the exemptions or permits provided for in this chapter or in any regulation which implements this chapter but not less restrictive than the prohibitions so defined.

Additionally, the Animal Welfare Act ("AWA"), 7 U.S.C. § 2131 et seq., and the implementing regulations, 9 C.F.R. §§ 3.125-.142, contain specific provisions regarding the transportation of warm-blooded animals other than dogs, cats, rabbits, hamsters, guinea pigs, nonhuman primates, and marine mammals. As noted by the district court in *In Defense of Animals v. Cleveland Metroparks Zoo*, 785 F. Supp. 100, 102 (N.D. Ohio. 1991), in the context of a challenge to the transportation of a nonhuman primate:

> [T]ogether, these statutes clearly demonstrate that federal law completely occupies the field of *interstate commerce in gorillas, an endangered species*. The Court notes that the Animal Welfare Act does not, by itself, preempt state humane laws. However, as it is applied to endangered species-as it has been in this case by regulation, and specifically as it is by regulation of *this* endangered species-the AWA, in conjunction with the Endangered Species Act, clearly must be found to preempt any state laws which might be applied to attempt to regulate such commerce.

Accordingly, the court could disregard any assertion of illegality with respect to the Idaho laws claimed to have been violated by GWR.

However, a violation of state wildlife laws concerning licensing, possession, and transportation of wolves could trigger a violation of the Lacey Act, resulting in criminal and civil penalties and forfeiture. 16 U.S.C. §§ 3372(a)(2)(A) (unlawful to import, export, transport, sell, receive, acquire, or purchase in interstate or foreign commerce any fish or wildlife taken, possessed, transported, or sold in violation of any law or regulation of any state or foreign law), 3373(a) (civil penalty), 3373(d) (criminal penalty), 3374 (forfeiture). *See, e.g., U.S. v. Powers*, 923 F.2d 131 (9th Cir. 1990) (federal prosecution of hunting outfitter who illegally sold guide services and hunting permits to those who illegally killed bears and then transported bear parts in interstate commerce); *U.S. v. Romano*, 929 F. Supp. 502 (D. Mass. 1996).

3. Illegal Conduct

WPI also reasoned that GWR violated federal law, specifically 9 C.F.R. § 2.75(b)(1), by not keeping a record containing the particulars of the transaction between GWR and Jenkins. Thus, so the argument went, any promise to return Sunga was void. In actuality, GWR had Jenkins's name, address, and USDA number, but had failed to acquire Jenkins's driver's license and vehicle plate. And 2.75 did not require notifying USDA of the transfer.

WPI next argued that GWR broke Idaho's wildlife law, specifically I.C. § 36-712(a)'s tattooing requirement. However, USDA informed GWR that photographic identification of wolves suffices without the need for tattooing, and even § 36-712(b) waived the tattooing requirement if subject to permanent individual identification by another state or federal agency. Of course, the only penalty for failure to comply with § 36-712(a) related to failing to report the transfer of a captive-born wolf was a fine, not invalidation of the transfer. To be clear, no Idaho law explicitly barred suit on any contract involving transfer (much less *interstate* transfer) of wolves.

4. Exceptions

Any law violation by GWR was *de minimis* in character and no law imposed a duty to notify any state agency of the transfer. Nor was the alleged illegality so morally turpitudinous as to bar enforceability. GWR was also not *in pari delicto* given the reasonable belief and innocent state of mind concerning the legality of the transaction with Jenkins, based on GWR's interactions with the USDA inspector and various representatives of the Idaho Fish & Game Department. Such intent is determinative. *Golberg v. Sanglier*, 639 P.2d 1347, 1354 (Wash. 1982). And the fraud exception applies given the strong evidence that Jenkins induced GWR to transfer Sunga to her under false pretenses and then collaborated with WPI to perfect the ruse. Further, failure to comply with tattooing, licensing, and reporting requirements did not serve to void the initial transfer from GWR to Jenkins, but instead let the state fine or, conceivably, impound Sunga.

G. PROSPECTIVE ILLEGALITY

The court rejected WPI's position for the above reasons. WPI argued that not only was the GWR-Jenkins contract illegal, but the court should dismiss GWR's lawsuit because it would be illegal for GWR to presently possess Sunga in Idaho. WPI raised what amounted to an argument contesting justiciability, asserting:

Therefore, Plaintiff is not entitled to ask the Court to specifically enforce the agreement GWR alleges it made with Ms. Jenkins providing for the return of this wolf to its unlicensed wildlife facility. The Court should enter an order on summary judgment holding that Plaintiff is not entitled to specifically enforce the alleged contract, and is not entitled to the return of this wolf. Based on these facts, it was — and is — illegal for the Plaintiff to obtain, possess, or transfer Sunga. In seeking the Court's assistance in returning Sunga to an unlicensed wildlife farm, Plaintiff is plainly asking the Court to assist it in enforcing an illegal contract.

GWR claimed that any purported illegality would not be consummated until after the court was positioned to afford relief, relief was in fact granted, and then, upon due notice given by the Idaho Fish and Game Department ("IDFG"), GWR remained in noncompliance. Further, prospective illegality is a matter between GWR and the IDFG, not GWR and Jenkins, and collateral to the proceedings then before the court. Nonetheless, GWR demonstrated that it would not be in violation of Idaho law should it receive Sunga upon enforcement of the contractual term. The court properly exercised its powers at law and equity to deny WPI's motion.

H. VOIDABLE TITLE

Voidable Title doctrine exists at both common law and the Uniform Commercial Code. However, the UCC overrides pre-Code common law if on point. The UCC speaks to two situations — a good faith purchaser for value, and a buyer in ordinary course.

1. Good Faith Purchaser for Value

UCC § 2-403(1) states:

A purchaser of goods acquires all title which his transferor had or had power to transfer except that a purchaser of a limited interest acquires rights only to the extent of the interest purchased. A person with voidable title has power to transfer a good title to a good faith purchaser for value. When goods have been delivered under a transaction of purchase the purchaser has such power even though (a) the transferor was deceived as to the identity of the purchaser; (b) the delivery was in exchange for a check which is later dishonored; (c) it was agreed that the transaction was to be a "cash sale," or (d) the delivery was procured through fraud punishable as larcenous under the criminal law.

As a threshold matter, animals are "goods," including the "unborn young of animals." UCC § 2-105(1). Generally speaking, when a buyer who acquires colorable (but voidable) title over property delivered voluntarily to her by the original seller, the buyer may pass good (i.e., better) title to a certain type of third party — the good faith purchaser ("GFP"). "Good faith" means "honesty in fact and the observance of reasonable commercial standards of fair dealing." UCC § 1-201(20). In context, it requires that the purchaser has no awareness of the circumstances that rendered title voidable, nor a basis to inspire a reasonably prudent person to inquire further as to the ability of the buyer to transfer good title. "Purchaser" means "a person that takes by purchase." UCC § 1-201(30). "Purchase" means "taking by sale, lease, discount, negotiation, mortgage, pledge, lien, security interest, issue or reissue, gift, or any other voluntary transaction creating an interest in property." UCC § 1-201(29). A GFP is not a donee, however, due to the words "for value," defined in UCC § 1-201(44) to include "consideration sufficient to support a simple contract."

Where the third party is not a GFP, the original seller may repossess the property from any such individual. When the property is involuntarily taken by a thief, and then pawned to an innocent third party, including a GFP, voidable title doctrine does not apply because no title whatsoever transferred to the thief. Such title is void, not voidable.

The good faith purchaser doctrine applies broadly to all sales of goods, whether or not involving a merchant or dealer. Title turns "voidable" under the UCC in the case of mistaken identity (i.e., an imposter receives the property but is not the true buyer), a check returned as NSF, an unfulfilled cash sale, or larcenous fraud. Though title may have physically transferred (as in the case of a car), giving the check-bouncing transferee possession of title (and thus color of title), the bounced check permits the seller to avoid the contract and render it "voidable." However, if the transferee then sells the car to a third party innocent as to the dispute between the seller and transferee, then the third party takes the car free and clear with no obligation to return it to the seller. This doctrine often applies in the case of animal sales.

2. Buyer in Ordinary Course (Entrustment)

UCC § 2-403(2) states, "Any entrusting of possession of good to a merchant who deals in goods of that kind gives him power to transfer all rights of the entruster to a buyer in ordinary course of business." This alternative UCC theory arises in consignments and bailments of animals (think entrusting an animal to the care of another, who then breaches that trust by giving the animal to a third party). Thus, a bailee with no authority to sell the bailed property may still pass good title to a third party if the bailee regularly sells the same kind of goods (a person known as a "merchant"). Otherwise, merely entrusting an animal to a bailee for safekeeping or treatment does not confer any such authority.

It differs from the GFP doctrine in two important respects: *first*, while possession is voluntarily transferred, no purchase occurs: therefore, without a sale or contemplated transfer of title, the grounds to avoid the transfer become moot; *second*, GFP doctrine applies to all transactions between any two people, while entrustment requires that the transferee is a "merchant." Entrustment compels proof that the entrusted merchant sold or gave the property to a buyer in the ordinary course of business ("BOC").

A BOC is defined, in relevant part, under UCC § 1-201(9) as:

> A person that buys goods in good faith, without knowledge that the sale violates the rights of another person in the goods, and in the ordinary course from a person, other than a pawnbroker, in the business of selling goods of that kind. A person buys goods in the ordinary course if the sale

to the person comports with the usual or customary practices in the kind of business in which the seller is engaged or with the seller's own usual or customary practices.

Good faith means "honesty in fact and the observance of reasonable commercial standards of fair dealing." UCC § 1-201(20). This is both a subjective and objective standard. "Sale" means "passing of title from the seller to the buyer for a price." UCC § 2-106(1). And a seller who is in the business of selling goods of the kind at issue is also known as a "merchant." UCC § 2-104(1). One example includes a person who buys a horse from a stable that both breeds and boards equines and then enters into a contract with the same stable to board for three months while he is out of the country. On his return, he discovers that the stable has sold his horse to a third party. While the entruster may sue the entrustee stable for damages, he cannot recover the horse from the third party if she is a BOC. *See Prenger v. Baker*, 542 N.W.2d 805, 808–09 (Iowa 1995) (farmer raising and selling exotics for six years was regularly engaged in selling goods of the kind and deemed a merchant); *Hammer v. Thompson*, 129 P.3d 609 (Kan. Ct. App. 2006) (entrustee cattle order buyer deemed a merchant as a matter of law).

Occasionally, the series of transfers and "sales" invoke both doctrines. Thus, even where a nonmerchant bailee sells a bailor's goods to a merchant, who then sells to a fourth party, the end-purchaser is neither a BOC (as the goods were never entrusted to the merchant, but were sold) nor a GFP (as the bailor never sold the goods to the bailee or merchant). Rather, no title passed from bailee to merchant or merchant to fourth party.

But what of the more common lost dog scenario, where a Good Samaritan delivers, or animal control officer impounds, a stray, keeps the dog over the relevant stray hold period, and then adopts him out to a third-party adopter? As the Washington Court of Appeals explained in *Graham v. Notti*, 196 P.3d 1070 (Wash. Ct. App. 2008), "[I]nadvertently losing a dog does not qualify" as a "purchase transaction," for purposes of § 2-403(1), because there was no "voluntary transaction creating an interest in property." *Id.*, at 1074. Nor would the original owner have been said to "entrust" the lost dog to either such finder, thereby negating § 2-403(2) as a source of good title. *Id.*, at 1075. Finding further that the animal control agency only had jurisdiction over the city of Spokane, not unincorporated Spokane County, where a Pomeranian named Harlee had been found by a citizen, it concluded that title never transferred by operation of the city's stray hold law. For that reason, too, it had no title to pass, illustrating the maxim *nemo dare potest quod non habet* (no man can give that which he has not). Another reason exists, however, not discussed in *Graham:* the animal control authority may not be considered a "merchant" nor the adopter a BOC. But see *Slodov v. Animal Protective League*, 628 N.E.2d 117 (Ohio Ct. App. 1993) (finding that Ohio Humane Society, because organized as a nonprofit, is not "in the business of selling animals as contemplated by the [UCC]"; also league not a "merchant" because no evidence transactions are for profit); *see also* Dale Joseph Gilsinger, *Action in Replevin for Recovery of Dog or Cat*, 85 A.L.R.6 th 429 (2013).

The continuation of the foregoing hypothetical involving the wolf Sunga will guide the clarification of an animal's clouded chain of title. Remember that GWR transferred Sunga to Jenkins pursuant to a right of first refusal. Days afterward, Jenkins gave Sunga to WPI. No money exchanged hands, but WPI did travel to South Dakota to retrieve Sunga. Did WPI acquire good title as a GFP or BOC?

Did Jenkins have any title (voidable or actual) to pass to WPI? Recall that title passed to Jenkins for life (with a reversion to GWR) and also subject to a condition subsequent should Jenkins decide she no longer could care for Sunga. Accordingly, one might conclude that Jenkins only possessed the limited title to keep Sunga for herself, not full title that would encompass the right of alienability. *See* § 2-403(1) ("except that a purchaser of a limited interest acquires rights only to the extent of the interest purchased"). Thus, WPI received, at most, a life estate. However, even this was limited by the condition subsequent, which divested Jenkins of all title the moment she took preparatory steps to transfer Sunga to WPI.

However, for the sake of argument, assume that Jenkins did have title to pass. Was WPI a GFP? Jenkins acquired Sunga through a voluntary transaction with GWR. Although Jenkins did not pay GWR, a "transaction of purchase" nonetheless occurred as "purchase" includes "taking by gift." Similarly, WPI "purchased" Sunga from Jenkins, but did it do so "for value"? Though the threshold is set rather low, any consideration that would support a simple contract will qualify. However, Jenkins "donated" Sunga without any return promises or compensation given, except perhaps the value of taking Sunga off Jenkins' hands, were Sunga to have been too costly to maintain or if Jenkins were facing fines or potential criminal charges by local, state, and federal authorities if she had no legal right to keep a wolf. Finally, did WPI acquire Sunga in "good faith," i.e., without actual or constructive notice that Jenkins was transferring Sunga to it in violation of GWR's rights? Suspicions as to WPI's professed lack of notice of the GWR-Jenkins agreement evidence lack of good faith. If WPI knew of GWR's repossessory rights at the time Jenkins donated Sunga, a court could find bad faith. But what type of due diligence must WPI have performed to don the "good faith" label?

Where state or federal laws require that certain paperwork be transferred in order to ensure passing of full ownership, WPI could argue that GWR's customary failure to comply with reporting requirements would have made any search of transfers by WPI futile. Germane to this issue is *Rudiger Charolais Ranches v. Van de Graaf Ranches*, 994 F.2d 670 (9th Cir. 1993), where a buyer of branded cattle failed to confirm that title indeed passed to the seller. The original owner, Rudiger, sued the purported GFP, Van de Graaf, for return of the cattle. Van de Graaf claimed that it was customary to complete the transfer first and obtain paperwork later, even though this custom directly violated Washington state law. Accordingly, the court held that Van de Graaf was not a GFP and voided the transaction.

Hypothetical: Consider this example: Mickey and Minnie, a married couple, adopt Pluto from the Eisner Humane Society, a nonprofit corporation contracting with the City of Disney to provide core animal control services. Minnie becomes primary caregiver to Pluto. The duo fall on hard times and, in a fit of rage, Mickey separates from Minnie, stealing Chip 'n' Dale, Minnie's premarital chipmunks, in his tugboat. Mickey, through his thug-for-hire Goofy, tells Minnie that he will drown Chip 'n' Dale unless she returns Pluto immediately. Under duress, she complies. In exchange, she gets back Chip 'n' Dale.

One week after Pluto is returned to him, Mickey surrenders him back to Eisner Humane Society, claiming that Minnie, now his ex-wife (a false statement, as no decree had been entered), had an affair with Donald Duck and overworked Pluto to the point of exhaustion. Without attempting to reach Minnie to confirm or deny Mickey's statement, Eisner Humane adopts Pluto to a Mr. Jiminy Cricket.

After the divorce is finalized, Minnie learns of Pluto's whereabouts and files suit for his return. Will she be successful?

First we must assess what type of property interest Minnie had in Pluto at the time Mickey surrendered him. For purposes of this hypothetical, disregard whether a family law temporary order prohibiting transfer or sale of community property applied, and whether the Humane Society had any repossession rights by adoption contract. As community property, Pluto could not be gifted without express or implied consent per statute or common law. Conceivably, the nonconsenting spouse may attempt to avoid the transfer and regain full ownership over that property. One limiting factor may be that, after dissolution, it is arguable that Minnie can only avoid the transfer as to her half community interest in Pluto, not the entire transfer, leaving her in the position of a tenant-in-common with Mickey.

As such, Mickey had an undivided equal interest in Pluto. By delivering his co-interest in Pluto to Eisner, and Eisner to Cricket, Minnie and Cricket are now co-tenants-in-common. But even her 50% interest may be terminated under the GFP or BOC doctrines described above.

Those without notice of a competing property interest, and who give value, take the property free and clear. Eisner was likely not a GFP, because it had notice, actual and constructive, so as to excite inquiry into Minnie's property interest in Pluto. Consequently, she may have a claim against Eisner for negligent adoption on the basis that it had a quasi-fiduciary duty of care to notify Minnie before further impairment of her property interest in Pluto. Further, putting aside whether Eisner Humane gave "value" to Mickey, Minnie did not voluntarily deliver Pluto to Mickey, a requirement of GFP doctrine. Thus, Eisner passed no title to Cricket.

Turning to entrustment doctrine, it is questionable whether Eisner Humane is a "merchant." If so, and if Cricket met the other requirements of a BOC, then he may claim 100% ownership of Pluto, except that Eisner only had possession of Pluto becaise Minnie was under duress, a surrender may not be an "entrustment," and one way to defeat the GFP or BOC doctrine is to assert that the initial transfer by Mickey to Eisner was void. Historically, such statutes void transactions where the property was subject to larceny, burglary, or robbery. In this case, the law in question was enacted in 1881. Thus, was the present-day larceny, robbery, or burglary complained of by Minnie an identically chargeable offense at the time this law was enacted? There was arguably no crime of larceny for one spouse stealing *community* property. Moreover, at common law, dogs and cats were not subjects of larceny; they were deemed to have no value. It was no crime to steal what was free, as in pilfering weeds or worthless currency. Finally, Minnie might be held procedurally to have first proved that Mickey was convicted of larceny before raising this defense.

I. FRUSTRATION OF PURPOSE

Contracts may also be avoided due to impossibility and frustration of purpose. The former excuses a promisor from performing when *objectively* impossible or impracticable due to extreme and unreasonable difficulty, expense, injury, or loss from an unavoidable and fortuitous event. A common example is the great leveler — death. However, *subjective* complaints of greater difficulty or expense than originally anticipated will not justify setting aside the contract. The latter seeks to unwind a bad deal for the promisor due to changed circumstances not contemplated at the time of contracting, and that render the agreement essentially useless. Impossibility prevents the promisor from performing at all, while frustration does not impede performance, but consideration is thwarted by factors outside the control or foresight of either party. RESTATEMENT (2D) OF CONTRACTS § 265, Ill. 1 describes a contract where B agrees to pay A $1,000 to use A's window during a parade. Due to the unforeseen illness of an important official, the parade cancels and B refuses to use the window or pay the $1,000. No breach exists and B's duty to pay is discharged by frustration.

Hypothetical: A city declares a dog potentially dangerous, orders the dog muzzled at all times when outside a proper enclosure, and requires the owner to secure $250,000 in liability insurance. Due to infirmities in the declaration and factual issues abounding, the dog owner seeks a contested hearing in municipal court. Before hearing, she negotiates a settlement agreement with the city attorney. Both parties execute the contract, which amounts to a stipulated order of continuance on relaxed conditions. If no violations occur during the probationary period, the potentially dangerous dog declaration is vacated *ab initio*: an alleged violation, on the other hand, will require a review hearing in municipal court. The specific language at issue states, "Venue for adjudication of a probationary violation shall be in municipal court."

When the signed agreement goes before the judge for a consent order, she refuses to hear any future probationary violation, saying the court lacks subject matter jurisdiction. With no recourse, the city attorney contends that the judge's ruling has rendered the contract unenforceable and deems it void, indicating that the matter should be put back on for hearing. Alternatives, such as filing a separate action for breach of contract in a court of less-limited jurisdiction, are rejected. Is the city estopped by settlement? Does frustration doctrine apply to save the city from its mistake of law? Consider the RESTATEMENT:

> Where, after a contract is made, a party's principal purpose is substantially frustrated without his fault by the occurrence of an event the non-occurrence of which was a basic assumption on which the contract was made, his remaining duties to render performance are discharged, unless the language or the circumstances indicate the contrary.

RESTATEMENT (2D) OF CONTRACTS § 265 (1979).

> The rule stated in this Section sets out the requirements for the discharge of that party's duty. First, the purpose that is frustrated must have been a principal purpose of that party in making the contract. It is not enough that he had in mind some specific object without which he would not have made

the contract. The object must be so completely the basis of the contract that, as both parties understand, without it the transaction would make little sense. Second, the frustration must be substantial. It is not enough that the transaction has become less profitable for the affected party or even that he will sustain a loss. The frustration must be so severe that it is not fairly to be regarded as within the risks that he assumed under the contract. Third, the non-occurrence of the frustrating event must have been a basic assumption on which the contract was made . . . .

Id., cmt. *a.* Was not the risk that the municipal court might lack subject matter jurisdiction be *foreseeable*, and its refusal to sign the order a risk the city attorney took owing potentially to malpractice? And does lack of jurisdiction to hear a probationary violation mean that the dog owner will actually violate probation? In other words, does the dispute-resolution provision of the agreement render performance by either party *impossible* or merely *frustrated*? Is such a concern even ripe? The city's objection is perhaps more accurately stated as lack of consideration, an illusory contract that destroys the expected value of the dog owner's performance by denying it any remedy should she breach. Impossibility doctrine would not apply as the court's refusal to accept jurisdiction did not prevent either party from abiding by the probationary terms.

J. APPARENT AUTHORITY TO CONTRACT

A single mother with two dogs and two young boys is at work when her father, without her knowledge or consent, takes the dogs to the local humane society. He then surrenders both dogs, identifying himself and signing a surrender contract that indicates he is the dogs' owner and is releasing them for the reason that the owner is "too busy." When the mother returns home to find her dogs gone, she panics and goes to the shelter. Though the dogs have not yet been adopted, she is told they belong to the humane society and an adoption application is pending. She objects, shows proof the dogs are hers, but the humane society authorizes adoption to a new family. Before transfer occurs, the mother calls the adoptive family-to-be and begs them not to complete the transaction. The family refuses, stating that they believe her to be an unfit home.

Did the humane society have title to transfer? Much depends on whether it obtained void or good title from the father. In short, the animal shelter claims that the father had "apparent authority" to surrender the two dogs. However, the law is well-settled that it cannot just rely on his statements to establish apparent authority. Apparent agency is not inferred from the acts of the agent, but depends on the principal's words or conduct to believe that he authorized the agent to so act. *See Hieb v. Minnesota Farmers Union*, 672 P.2d 572 (Idaho Ct. App. 1983).

K. UNCONSCIONABILITY

Two types of unconscionability exist — procedural and substantive. As to the former, the improprieties of the circumstances surrounding the presentation and signing of the contract, the absence of any negotiations regarding these clauses (rendering it adhesive because of the "take it or leave it" presentation on a standard form printed contract), high-pressure sales tactics, misrepresentation or fraud, hidden and nonconspicuous fine print, linguistic barriers, and the lack of any course of dealing may render a contract void as unconscionable. As to the latter, some clauses are so one-sided, overly harsh, or grossly disparate as to be facially unconscionable and void. *See Adler v. Fred Lind Manor*, 103 P.3d 773 (Wash. 2004) (finding substantive unconscionability and striking clauses even without procedural unconscionability); *Woebse v. Health Care & Retirement Corp. of Am.*, 977 So. 2d 630, 632 (Fla. Dist. Ct. App. 2008) (substantive unconscionability requires assessment as to whether terms are so "outrageously unfair as to shock the judicial conscience"). The Uniform Commercial Code's bar on unconscionable terms may also apply. UCC § 2-302; *see also* RESTATEMENT (2ND) OF CONTRACTS, § 208. Historically, unconscionable bargains in actions at law were those "such as no man in his senses and not under delusion would make on the one hand, and as no honest and fair man would accept on the other." *Hume v. U.S.*, 132 U.S. 406 (1889) (quoted by RESTATEMENT (2D) CONTRACTS, § 208 cmt. *b*). In *Hollywood Leasing Corp. v. Rosenblum*, 100 Misc. 2d 120 (N.Y. Civ. Ct. 1979), the court refused to enforce a lease provision barring animals on its premises absent written consent of the landlord on grounds of unconscionability where the Rosenblums signed the lease with the dog in lap and while the landlord's agent patted the dog on the head, stating they could disregard the no-pet provision and give oral consent to the dog's presence in the unit.

Chapter 4

DANGEROUS DOG LITIGATION[1]

While presumed harmless, dogs may behave in a manner prompting enforcement action that changes the canine's legal status to *harmful*. An estimated 70 million dogs and 74 million cats cohabit with one or more of 316 million Americans. *See* U.S. Census Bureau, American Population Clock, www.census.gov/popclock/; AVMA, 2012 U.S. PET OWNERSHIP & DEMOGRAPHICS SOURCEBOOK. www.avma.org/KB/ Resources/Statistics/Pages/Market-research-statistics-US-Pet-Ownership-Demographics-Sourcebook.aspx. With such numbers, the likelihood of human-dog, human-cat, or dog-dog interaction resulting in fright, bite, trauma, or death exposes the average dog to an almost certain risk of adverse regulation. When this occurs, dogs behaving badly earn the label "dangerous" or, if not quite as offensive to public safety, "potentially dangerous."

A dog bites in four-dimensional legal space — civilly, criminally, administratively, and temporally. Consider: A client loads her dog into her car in the middle of her driveway, when a jogger passes by. The unleashed dog runs into the street barking and circling. The jogger kicks back and her calf strikes the dog's tooth in mid-bark. Immediately, the client calls the dog back, who obeys. This 30-second event results in: (a) a criminal charge for permitting a dog to run at-large; (b) a civil suit for personal injury; and (c) a declaration of the dog as "potentially dangerous" by animal control.

But there is a fourth dimension (i.e., time), which turns on the evolving events following disposition of the charge, suit, and declaration. For instance, pleading to or being found guilty of the criminal charge might permit the judge to order the dog killed, or serve as a predicate offense to declare the dog (and the client) a habitual offender. The civil suit, if triggering insurance coverage, might result in the client's carrier dropping the client or excluding future coverage for harm caused by the incident dog. And the potentially dangerous declaration, if unopposed or not successfully vacated, could impose restraints of control (e.g., muzzling, signage, fencing, five-sided enclosures, insurance/bond) that, if defied, result in mandatory impound and euthanasia of the dog, criminal charges, and fines.

When classifying canines, start with state laws and then drill down to the locality. While municipal corporations — like towns, cities, boroughs, and counties — can define dogs as good or bad within their limits, only state law crosses all boundaries. Be mindful that some states have no dangerous dog laws, leaving regulation to localities, which might impose more severe restraints of control over dangerous dogs than state law; and note that as a dog travels from one side of the state to

---

[1] This chapter is derived in part and reprinted in part from *Defending against Dangerous Dog Classifications*, 128 AM. JUR. POF 3D 291 (2012), and used with permission of Thomson Reuters.

another, he may be subject to a patchwork quilt of inconsistent laws, including criminal codes prohibiting him even setting paw into city limits if declared dangerous by any other jurisdiction. Thus, dogs (and their guardians) may be forced to travel circuitous and inconvenient routes to get from point A to B without treading upon the soil of a town with its own brand of dangerous dog justice.

Those who defend dogs on death row often consider themselves criminal defense attorneys, even if the proceeding that resolves to sentence a canine to euthanasia takes place in a civil setting. Someone has accused the dog of a capital crime — be it killing a cat off-property, biting a letter carrier in the calf, or frightening neighborhood kids by chasing them down the street on at least two occasions. If the state attempted to exact the same penalty on human beings, the constitution would demand that the prosecutor meet the highest standard of proof available and confer all due process protections at our system's disposal.

We have come a long way from medieval France where nonhuman animal defendants were garbed in men's clothes and tried for murder; yet, startlingly, they were assigned counsel. The earliest known case dates from 1266 in Fontenay, France, where a pig was burned to death for eating a child. The ecclesiastical courts also dealt with lawsuits against colonies of insects or small mammals accused of destroying crops. After summoning each class of unwanted vermin before the tribunal, due deliberation often resulted in anathema, as occurred in the Valley of Aosta in 824, when a priest excommunicated moles. Author Esther Cohen describes the piglet trial of Sauvigny:

> In December 1457 the sow of Jehan Bailly of Savigny and her six piglets were caught in the act of killing the five-year-old Jehan Martin. All seven pigs were imprisoned for murder and brought to trial a month later before the seigneurial justice of Savigny. Besides the judge, the protocol recorded the presence at the trial of one lawyer (function unspecified), two prosecutors (one of them a lawyer and a councilor of the Duke of Burgundy), eight witnesses by name, "and several other witnesses summoned and requested for this cause". Though the owner was formally the defendant, it is clear from the proceedings that he stood accused only of negligence and was in no danger of any personal punishment. Moreover he was allowed to argue in court "concerning the punishment and just execution that should be inflicted upon the said sow", if he could give any reason why the sow should be spared. The owner having waived this right, the prosecutor requested a death sentence. The judge, having heard all the relevant testimony and consulted with wise men knowledgeable in local law, ruled, according to the custom of Burgundy, that the sow should be forfeit to the justice of Savigny for the purpose of hanging by her hind legs on a suitable tree. The piglets created a more difficult problem as there was no proof that they had actually bitten the child, though they were found bloodstained. They were therefore remanded to the custody of their owner, who was required to vouch for their future behavior and produce them for trial, should new evidence come to light. When the latter refused to give such a guarantee, the piglets were declared forfeit to the local lord's justice, though they suffered no further punishment. The court brought from Chalon-sur-Saone

a professional hangman who carried out the execution according to the judge's specific instructions.

Cohen, *Law, Folklore & Animal Lore*, Past & Present 110, 10–11 (1986). Though times have changed, dogs (by and through their owner-guardians) have a right to a death sentencing (or "disposition") hearing as a matter of law. Yet what level of due process do dogs enjoy under the Fourteenth Amendment? Who has the burden of proof when the dog owner challenges animal control's declaration of dangerousness? Is the standard of proof mere evidentiary preponderance, clear and convincing, or beyond-a-reasonable-doubt? Is there a right to subpoena witnesses and records? How much time should be given to the dog owner to present her case?

A. PRELIMINARY CONSIDERATIONS

Initially, one must confirm which governmental entity has jurisdiction. Start where the offense occurred. Does the state have its own dangerous dog law, and if so, does it conflict with municipal law? Was the dangerous dog law legally enacted, self-executing, or did it require an enabling statute for enforcement?

Next, determine the nature of the proceedings: is the classification civil, criminal, judicial or quasi-judicial? What penalties or legal consequences follow an adverse determination? Will the rules of evidence apply? Who will adjudicate? These factors impact the standard of proof and the extent of process due. Animal destruction may escalate the evidentiary burden that, in a close case, could mean life or death.

Read the charge with care. Is the dog alleged to be dangerous, vicious, or potentially dangerous? Does the code define dangerous dog and words contained therein? Do the facts conceivably apply to more than one alternative definition? Also examine the statutory defenses such as provocation and trespass.

Finally, understand what court has proper jurisdiction for an appeal. Occasionally a dangerous dog statute requires the appeal to be lodged in a court without appellate jurisdiction. Some ordinances impose deferential record review while granting a *de novo* hearing.

B. COMMON ELEMENTS

The definition of "dangerous dog" usually refers to dog behavior that imperils public welfare. By increasing severity level, they tend to fit within categories that include, *inter alia*, (i) repeatedly chasing or approaching a person in either a menacing, vicious or terrorizing manner or fashion in an apparent attitude of attack; (ii) killing or severely or seriously injuring a domestic animal; (iii) killing or severely or seriously injuring a domestic animal more than once; (iv) "causing" injury to a human being; (v) injuring a human being; (vi) severely or seriously injuring a human being; (vii) killing a human being.

Some jurisdictions intermediately use the classification "potentially dangerous dog" before declaring a dog dangerous, allowing government to take a middle course by imposing restraints to protect public safety while relieving the owner of the full extent of a dangerous dog classification or euthanasia. Usually, acts classifying dogs potentially dangerous exceed the scope of those labeling dogs dangerous, such as acting in a highly aggressive manner within a fenced yard or enclosure and appearing to a reasonable person to be able to jump over or escape, or inflicting more than one non-severe bite to an animal or person.

In some statutory schemes, a vicious dog and dangerous dog are identical. *State v. Murphy*, 860 N.E.2d 1068 (Ohio Ct. App. 2006). That dangerous and vicious dog definitions overlap does not mean they present an irreconcilable conflict. *Rabon v. City of Seattle*, 957 P.2d 621 (Wash. 1998).

Certain jurisdictions also statutorily define vicious dogs by breed, most commonly American Staffordshire Terriers, Staffordshire Bull Terriers, and American Pit Bull Terriers, labeled so by birthright without any scintilla of proof of vicious animus.

C. CONSTITUTIONAL CONCERNS IN INITIAL DESIGNATION

Due process rights attach to dog ownership. *Mansour v. King Cy.*, 128 P.3d 1241, 1245–46 (Wash. 2006) Notice and meaningful opportunity to be heard (i.e., "at a meaningful time and in a meaningful manner") in a setting where the factfinder assesses the governmental determination against a defined, clearly ascertainable, and constitutionally adequate standard of proof are the backbone of procedural due process. Parties should examine whether the officer who declared the dog dangerous met the threshold requirements set by statute, including such procedures as signing a declaration or affidavit articulating the precise grounds for issuance according to a set evidentiary threshold such as probable cause, timely giving adequate notice of rights and responsibilities to the appropriate persons in the formats required by law, and specifying the correct numerical code provisions and elements of the offense upon which the designation has issued.

Ordinances must also set forth a contested hearing/appeal procedure that comports with due process. For instance, a 2006 Washington court held insufficient the first, contested factfinding hearing before the county board of appeals following issuance of a *Notice of Violation and Order to Remove* a dog from the jurisdiction. *Mansour, supra*. It held that lack of a clearly ascertainable, adequate standard and burden of proof in upholding a removal order ("an adequate standard of proof is a mandatory safeguard"), disallowance of subpoenas for documents and witnesses ("due process requires that a pet owner contesting a removal order be able to subpoena witnesses and records"), and insufficient notice as to the precise law the dog owner allegedly violated all violated procedural due process. *Id.*, at 262–64, 70, 72. The court reversed, adding that appellate review cannot cure a deficient standard and burden of proof. *Id.*, at 267–68. Five years later, following this court's lead, another Washington court deemed unconstitutional the "pay to play" requirement of paying a fee to obtain an evidentiary hearing at which the government had to demonstrate the dog's dangerousness by evidentiary preponderance. *Downey v. Pierce Cy.*, 267 P.3d 445, 451–52 (Wash. Ct. App. 2011).

D. WARRANTLESS SEIZURE AND LACK OF PROBABLE CAUSE

Many dangerous dog designations command contemporaneous seizure, triggering the Fourth Amendment's provision that "no Warrants shall issue, but upon probable cause, supported by Oath or affirmation, and particularly describing the place to be searched, and the persons or things to be seized." The Fourth Amendment guarantees that "[t]he right of the people to be secure in their persons, houses, papers, and effects, against unreasonable searches and seizures, shall not be violated . . . ." People's "effects" include their personalty. *U.S. v. Place*, 462 U.S. 696, 701 (1983). In every circuit considering the question, domestic animals are "effects" under the Fourth Amendment. *Viilo v. Eyre*, 547 F.3d 707, 711 (7th Cir. 2008), *Altman v. City of High Point, N.C.*, 330 F.3d 194, 203 (4th Cir. 2003), *Brown v. Muhlenberg Twp.*, 269 F.3d 205, 210 (3d Cir. 2001), *Lesher v. Reed*, 12 F.3d 148, 150 (8th Cir. 1994), *Fuller v. Vines*, 36 F.3d 65, 67–68 (9th Cir. 1994), *overruled on o.g.*, *Robinson v. Solano Cy.*, 278 F.3d 1007, 1013 (9th Cir. 2002). Seizures of property take place with meaningful interference in an individual's possessory interest in that property. *Soldal v. Cook Cy.*, 506 U.S. 56, 61 (1992).

Those failing to contest a dangerous dog designation may be forced to surrender the dog or satisfy onerous requirements, such as a costly annual permit, tattoo or microchip, six-figure liability insurance/bond requirement, five- or six-sided enclosure or cage, and blaze collars. Failure to comply with these registration requirements frequently results in impound and euthanasia, along with prosecution for a misdemeanor or gross misdemeanor. That the dog owner faces these sequelae even with a timely challenge to the designation raises pressing matters of constitutional import because few ordinances impose an automatic stay. Hence, the dangerous dog designation — appealed or not — constitutes a meaningful interference with a dog owner's property and liberty interest in the dog, as well as her own liberty interests arising from criminal prosecution and incarceration.

The dangerous dog designation immediately invades several sticks in the bundle of a dog owner's private property rights, including rights to exclude, use, and alienate, and being threatened with forfeiture of the entire bundle failing compliance with costly restraints or "appeal." Where the interference with possessory interests effectively limits the ability of the owner to engage in previously allowed activities for the dog's lifetime (e.g., taking dog to off-leash park, playing ball with dog without muzzle on one's own property), and not merely a brief 90-minute interval (as in *Place*), liberty interests may also be impaired.

Under the Fourth Amendment, absent specific exceptions, a seizure of personalty is "*per se* unreasonable within the meaning of the Fourth Amendment unless it is accomplished pursuant to a judicial warrant issued upon probable cause." *Place*, at 701. Warrants require a determination of probable cause by a neutral and detached magistrate. *State v. Hatchie*, 166 P.3d 698, 703–04 (Wash. 2007). Animal control officers, sheriff's deputies, and police officers virtually never have credentials as magistrates, so where they do not seek a warrant or issuance of a dangerous dog designation prior to service on the dog owner and imposition of restraints, one might successfully argue a violation of the Fourth Amendment and corollary state constitutional provisions.

E. JURISDICTION

As probable cause serves as a prerequisite to a warrant, per the Constitution, so too might it precede issuance of a dangerous dog declaration, as many ordinances require that the officer make a finding of probable cause by enumerated evidentiary predicates like a written complaint, eyewitness testimony, or other substantial evidence. This procedural first step helps to ensure due process and avoid unreasonable seizures. But it also functions as a key to the kingdom, bestowing subject matter jurisdiction on the tribunal hearing any "appeal" from the declaration. Thus, in contesting a dangerous dog designation on the merits, one must not forget to also challenge its jurisdictional precondition. For if the officer could not, at the outset, articulate objective facts and circumstances to lead a neutral and detached person to find probable cause to believe that the dog engaged in conduct satisfying the definition of "dangerous," then no jurisdiction exists.

Unless self-executing or rendered enforceable through an enabling statute, dangerous dog ordinances, even when ruggedly and persuasively applied to specific facts, may well have been spun of gossamer. In a 2006 Minnesota case, though the city had a vicious dog ordinance, it proceeded under the state's dangerous dog law. However, because state law lacked an enforcement procedure for dangerous dog declarations (i.e., statute not self-executing), and the city code never incorporated state law, the court found no jurisdiction. *In the Matter of the Disposition of Molly, A German Shorthaired Pointer Owned by William Frederick Klumpp Jr.*, 712 N.W.2d 567, 571 (Minn. App. 2006). Self-executing provisions supply "a sufficient rule by means of which the right given may be enjoyed and protected, or the duty imposed may be enforced" and provisions that "merely indicate [] principles, without laying down rules by means of which those principles may be given the force of law" are not self-executing. *Davis v. Burke*, 179 U.S. 399, 403 (1900).

Jurisdiction also turns on geography. Just being dispatched by the 911 call center does not mean the responding jurisdiction necessarily gets to apply its dangerous dog laws. For example, a county may investigate a dangerous dog incident, seize the dog, and classify it. However, where the incident itself occurred in city limits, subject to its own dangerous dog law with more favorable (to the dog) definitions, city regulations would govern. Frequently, a dog declared dangerous in one jurisdiction relocates to another, prompting animal control to notify the new jurisdiction if so informed by the dog owner.[2] Arguably, the first jurisdiction's designation only applies therein if enforcing its local (and not a state) dangerous dog law. Furthermore, the restraints imposed on the dog and owner may only apply within the first jurisdiction. In the criminal context, restraints may take the form of sentencing conditions, placing the owner and dog at jeopardy for imposition of jail time or fine, dog impoundment, or the dog's upgraded designation (e.g., potentially dangerous to dangerous) for an extrajurisdictional violation. Many localities also retain the ability to declare a dog dangerous or potentially dangerous based on a "known propensity." This permits municipalities to redeclare a dog under the second jurisdiction's dangerous dog law premised on an earlier finding of vicious-

---

[2] Some jurisdictions impose affirmative reporting obligations on the owner to disclose when the animal has died, been sold or transferred to another, or left the city or county limits, often on pains of criminal prosecution.

ness in the first jurisdiction. Questions of first impression include: (1) Whether an owner may default on the first designation but then challenge the second designation through timely appeal; this depends on whether collateral estoppel applies to an unappealed dangerous dog designation in the first jurisdiction; (2) Whether the second jurisdiction must abide by the outcome of an appeal in the first jurisdiction; (3) Whether restraints imposed by the second jurisdiction are stayed pending appeal in the first jurisdiction; (4) How to resolve the finality of dueling (i.e., simultaneous) appeals — one in each jurisdiction? What if the owner prevails in the first but loses in the second?

F.   PREEMPTION AND CONFLICT

Conflict and preemption have courted litigation in the dangerous dog law context due to different laws pertaining to dogs at each level of government. While several cases have discussed which law prevails and why, rarely finding that state statutes preempt local dangerous dog regulations, only one case found preemption by state law. *State v. Smith*, 685 A.2d 73 (N.J. Super. Ct. Law Div. 1996), held that the legislature intended the state dangerous dog law to exclusively occupy the field of dangerous dog regulation. Conflict challenges center around whether a county or municipality may expand the dangerous dog definition contained in state law. *Hoesch v. Broward Cy.*, 53 So. 3d 1177 (Fla. Dist. Ct. App. 2011) found that Broward County, Florida, could not reduce from more than one to one the number of domestic animal deaths that classify a dog as dangerous. *Hoesch* turned on whether county law conflicted with state statute. While a county can generally pass a more stringent ordinance than state law, supplementing it, the enabling statute giving animal control its power stated that "no county . . . ordinance relating to animal control . . . shall conflict with . . . any other state law." *Hoesch*, at 1180. Because the county and state definitions were not reconcilable, the court declared the county ordinance void. *Id.*, at 1180. *See also Lima v. Stepleton*, 5 N.E.3d 721 (Ohio Ct. App. 2013) (accord).

By contrast, *Brunotte v. City of St. Paul Office of Safety and Inspections*, 2009 Minn. App. Unpub. LEXIS 176 (Feb. 10, 2009), held that the definition of dangerous dog in a St. Paul ordinance did not conflict with state law even though more restrictive than Minnesota state law. State law required proof of *substantial* bodily injury, while the ordinance proof only of bodily injury. Because state law expressly provided for local regulation, with the exception of breed-specific legislation, the court found no conflict and upheld the local ordinance. *See also Louisville Kennel Club, Inc. v. Louisville/Jefferson Cy. Metro Gov't*, 2009 U.S. Dist. LEXIS 92328 (W.D. Ky. Oct. 1, 2009) (finding no conflict between municipal and state dangerous dog law without explicit legislative parameters of the scope and nature of municipal lawmaking). When state law remains silent on an issue, local government may enact more restrictive ordinances. Thus, *County of Summit v. Meyer*, 2004 Ohio App. LEXIS 4035 (Aug. 25, 2004), found that a statute silent as to whether a dog-on-dog attack meets the dangerous dog classification permitted the locality to so define. *See also Rabon v. City of Seattle*, 957 P.2d 621 (Wash. 1998) (state law does not speak to the classification of a vicious dog, does not preempt subject matter of regulation, and can be harmonized with city law, so municipality's ordinance regarding same does not irreconcilably conflict).

The penalty for dangerous dog classifications has also created contention. For instance, while Broward County's ordinance discussed in *Hoesch* required euthanasia if a dog killed one domestic animal, Florida state law mandated three deaths before execution. *Hoesch* found the Broward County penalties conflicted with state law for having "vitiated the framework for dealing with dog attacks on other domestic animals" set forth in state law. However, a Minneapolis ordinance that did not permit the dog owner to raise the defense of provocation when an animal bit two or more times did not conflict with state law because it merely added to and complemented state law, which permitted local action the statute did not prohibit. *Hannan v. City of Minneapolis*, 623 N.W.2d 281 (Minn. Ct. App. 2001). *Hannan* reasoned that the dispute arose not over how to define a dangerous dog, but over the penalty exacted upon a dangerous dog. Concluding that cities could enact regulations imposing harsher consequences than those provided by state law, it upheld the more severe destruction criteria and failure to exempt provoked attacks.

Whether local government can increase the severity of criminal penalties beyond those set forth by state dangerous dog laws has also been litigated. *Akron v. Ross*, 2001 Ohio App. LEXIS 3083 (Jul. 11, 2001), found that a municipal ordinance escalating the criminal penalty from a lesser misdemeanor to a first degree misdemeanor did not conflict with state law. If it had boosted the penalty to a felony, however, it would have been found unconstitutional. The court found no infirmity by the city ordinance criminalizing a dog's first bite, noting the state law's silence on the subject. It also upheld a local ordinance providing for criminal liability when the state statute only mandated civil liability.

G. PROCEDURAL DUE PROCESS AND THE DANGEROUS DOG HEARING

The constitutional propriety of a dangerous dog hearing depends on how promptly it takes place (also known as "speedy hearing"), who makes the final determination, the admissibility of evidence considered by the factfinder, who bears the burden of proof and by what standard, what confrontation and subpoena rights exist, and the clarity of the charging document.

1. Scheduling the Hearing

Many ordinances set a deadline by which the hearing must occur following a dog owner's timely challenge. Though misnamed, the first, contested, fact-finding hearing occurs after what municipalities call an "appeal," even though the term connotes that a court of appellate jurisdiction will review a record generated by a court or quasi-judicial tribunal of original jurisdiction according to the scope of appellate review. Unless the dangerous dog hearing merges with the criminal case (where a city prosecutes a person for harboring a dangerous dog but does not administratively declare the dog dangerous, in effect using the criminal matter for the dual purpose of obtaining a conviction and declaring the dog dangerous beyond a reasonable doubt), no speedy arraignment or speedy trial rights will be implicated in the ordinary dangerous dog setting. Instead, noncompliance with the deadlines set by law may prompt dismissal or issuance of a writ of mandamus to compel a prompt hearing.

The doctrine of equitable estoppel by government may also play a role. Grounded on the principle "that a party should be held to a representation made or position assumed where inequitable consequences would otherwise result to another party who has justifiably and in good faith relied thereon," *Wilson v. Westinghouse Elec. Corp.*, 530 P.2d 298, 300 (Wash. 1975), a party seeking the protection of the doctrine must establish three elements: "(1) an admission, statement, or act inconsistent with the claim afterwards asserted; (2) action by the other party on the faith of such admission, or act; (3) injury to such other party resulting from permitting the first party to contradict or repudiate such admission, statement, or act." *Id.* Application of equitable estoppel against the government is disfavored. *Dep't of Ecology v. Theodoratus*, 957 P.2d 1241, 1249 (Wash. 1998) (citing *Kramarevcky v. Dep't of Soc. & Health Servs.*, 863 P.2d 535, 538 (Wash. 1993)). A party asserting equitable estoppel against the government must establish, in addition to the three elements set forth above, that equitable estoppel (4) is "necessary to prevent a manifest injustice" and (5) would not "impair[ ]" "the exercise of governmental functions." *Id.*, at 538. All required elements must be proved by clear, cogent, and convincing evidence. *Id.*, at 538.

However, consider *Beresik v. City of New Rochelle*, 4 Misc. 3d 1017(A) (N.Y. City Ct. 2004), where a court refused to dismiss a dangerous dog declaration where the dog owner did not receive his hearing within the five-day period set by city code on grounds that it was not jurisdictional or mandatory, but merely instructional and directory, and that the dog owner contributed to the failure by not appearing. *Norton v. Howell*, 2009 Cal. App. Unpub. LEXIS 1325 (Feb. 19, 2009) similarly refused to vacate a potentially dangerous animal designation based on promptness of hearing. While the city law did not mandate a deadline for the hearing or determination following the hearing, in contrast to a 1986 California decision that invalidated a law that failed to provide notice or any hearing whatsoever (although the county did schedule an *ad hoc* "courtesy" meeting), *Phillips v. San Luis Obispo Cy.*, 183 Cal. App. 3d 372 (1986), *Norton* found that a hearing within two weeks after the second incident (though more than two years after the first incident) satisfied due process and was reasonably prompt. That said, "A hearing granted as a matter of discretion is no substitute for due process." *Phillips*, at 380 (citing *Coe v. Armour Fertilizer Works*, 237 U.S. 413, 424–25 (1915)).

Occasionally, hearings may be too speedy, such as where a dog owner receives only a few days' notice. A court found no due process violation when the owner appeared without requesting a continuance to seek counsel. *Sather v. City of Spokane*, 2010 Wash. App. LEXIS 1795 (Aug. 10, 2010). Similarly, a 2011 California court rejected the speedy hearing objection (characterized as *ultra vires* conduct) of dog owners who had a hearing 18 days after their dog's seizure even though the health code required that the hearing not occur *sooner* than 30 days following seizure; in the classic case of being careful of what you ask for, by the dog owners requesting a hearing date as soon as possible, they were said to have waived the 30-day minimum requirement set by law. *Knoller v. City and County of San Francisco*, 2011 WL 1295407 (Cal. App. 2011).

Undeniably, government must provide some hearing with adequate notice to comply with the procedural due process clause. *County of Pasco v. Riehl*, 635 So. 2d 17 (Fla. 1994), deemed a dangerous dog law unconstitutional that did not provide any hearing yet imposed consequences of physical confinement, tattooing or chipping, and muzzling. *City of Cleveland v. Johnson*, 825 N.E.2d 700, 705 (Ohio 2005) held similarly in the case of an ordinance authorizing an animal control officer to make a unilateral decision to declare a dog dangerous based on breed or behavior, without a hearing, further finding that the law imposes duties of control that, if violated, result in criminal charge. In *Johnson*, the officer made a determination of viciousness based on the dog's perceived breed. While the court severed the unconstitutional portion regarding unilateral determinations of behavior-based viciousness, it left intact the constitutionality of unilateral determinations of breed-based viciousness "given the inherently dangerous nature of pit bulls" and noting that "a pit bull dog is clearly vicious in nature. It would be unreasonable and against the public interest to first conduct individual hearings on the viciousness of pit bulls after an injury has been inflicted." And the Minnesota Court of Appeals promoted the view that even a potentially dangerous dog designation that does not impose any restraints on control mandated a hearing because it serves as a predicate classification for later deeming the dog dangerous. *Sawh v. City of Lino Lakes*, 800 N.W.2d 663 (Minn. Ct. App. 2011). A year later, however, the Minnesota Supreme Court reversed, 823 N.W.2d 627 (Minn. 2012), contending that the label "potentially dangerous" did not subject the owner to any protected property interest deprivation.

A hearing, however timely on paper, does not comport with due process absent effective and adequate service of the notice of dangerous dog. *Smith v. Caldwell*, 2000 Del. C.P. LEXIS 86 (Jul. 14, 2000) evaluated a challenge to ineffective service and denial of hearing to the true dog owner where animal control timely served the notice on the dog owner's *father*. Finding the father the statutory "owner" for purposes of service, in that he had custodial and placement rights of his son the true owner (then 17) and was the keeper, harborer, and custodian of the dog, that the seizure warrant of the dog would have been served on the father as parent, and given that by filing the appeal, the father implicitly admitted ownership, the court rejected this due process challenge.

Finally, in the cases that have examined the issue relative to dangerous dogs, a pay-to-play scheme violates procedural due process. In *Downey*, the Washington Court of Appeals declared unconstitutional Pierce County's procedural framework for dangerous animal appeals, forcing an owner to pay $250 for a first-level contested hearing before an auditor's designee, who applied an unconstitutional standard of proof, and then $500 for a *de novo* second-level contested hearing before the hearing examiner, applying an unconstitutional scope of appellate review. *Louisville Kennel Club* similarly ruled unconstitutional the prepayment of a bond for care of an impounded dog in order to get a contested hearing because it mandated forfeiture of the dog even if the indigent owner would have eventually prevailed had he the wherewithal to pay.

2. The Hearing Itself

Although administrative dangerous dog hearings do not require the same degree of due process afforded in a civil suit or criminal prosecution, bare minimums do exist. For instance, the infamous attorney couple Marjorie Knoller and Robert Noel, whose Presa Canarios Bane and Hera killed Diane Whipple, unsuccessfully challenged a dangerous dog designation as to Hera in a case that went to the California Court of Appeals. Sergeant William Herndon, who worked for the San Francisco Police Department, the entity that instituted criminal charges against Knoller and Noel, served as the hearing officer. He refused to recuse himself, found Hera dangerous, and ordered her killed. The *Knoller* case illustrates some of the perennial evidentiary and appearance of fairness issues in dangerous dog disputes. For instance, the standard of impartiality differs in administrative proceedings, often because they are typically not subject to a statutory disqualification standard, lawyer ethics code, or judicial ethical canons. *Knoller* halfheartedly applied due process by requiring the the presiding officer to be a "*reasonably* impartial, noninvolved reviewer," not a perfectly impartial one. *Knoller*, at *4. To disqualify Sgt. Herndon, Knoller needed to establish legally sufficient facts demonstrating bias that would, more probably than not, render fair trial impossible.

The *Sather* court added other elements to this list, such as that the hearing examiner must not express personal views prior to issuing a decision, must remain impartial, and not become a witness. However, it found no impropriety by the examiner's post-decision "clarification," characterizing it as a settlement of the record and partial narrative report of proceedings. *Sather v. City of Spokane*, 2010 Wash. App. LEXIS 1795 (Aug. 19, 2010). *Roberts v. Kent SPCA, Inc.*, 2010 Del. C.P. LEXIS 30 (June 4, 2010), found it "very unlikely" that remanding the dangerous dog case to the administrative panel, even with new members, would result in a fair and unbiased hearing, so the court took it upon itself to reverse, vacating the death order and releasing the dog.

Knoller rejected a *per se* prohibition on law enforcement officers serving as hearing officers in vicious/dangerous dog proceedings despite a pending criminal investigation concerning the subject dog. It also held that due process does not require a formal hearing. A "reasonable opportunity" to be heard, including notification of proposed action and reasons for it, advance notice of witnesses to be called, and right to offer response, even without the right to cross-examine, would suffice. Even so, one cannot complain afterward for being deprived of such opportunities but must actually ask for the relief during the hearing. For example, *Sather* found that because the appellant never asked to subpoena witnesses or records, nor asked the complainant questions, no due process violations occurred.

While rules of evidence rarely apply in dangerous dog hearings not pursued as a criminal action, *Stanger v. Franklin Cy. Dist. Bd. of Health*, 1991 Ohio App. LEXIS 3488 (Jul. 23, 1991) (no Sixth Amendment Confrontation Clause violation because civil in nature), "that precept is not a license to introduce irrelevant evidence." *Roberts*, at *5 (administrative panel improperly considered post-hearing letters and emails outside the record). *Brunotte*, though recognizing that failure to follow a city's own procedural requirements may render the municipality's acts void or voidable, and notwithstanding the hearing officer's refusal to consider two letters offered by the dog owner (because one bore only a typed name and neither had an address) despite the code mandating consideration of "all evidence pertaining to the temperament of the animal," the court found that the hearing officer still had good cause to reject the proffer. *Hannan* did not criticize the practice of adopting written reports over live testimony given the lack of authority prohibiting the practice. While the court ruminated that it might infringe upon the right to confront witnesses, because the dog owner never raised the issue in hearing, the court did not resolve the case on those grounds. *Williams v. Seydel*, 820 N.Y.S.2d 847 (2006) deemed harmless the reliance on an uncertified hospital report to bolster a dangerous dog conclusion in light of the overwhelming evidence that the dog bit the infant. Such *independent corroboration* justification arose in *Schwab v. Boston Municipal Court*, 2007 Mass. Super. LEXIS 270 (Apr. 26, 2007), where the court rejected a pro se petitioner's challenge to hearsay testimony of an officer on grounds of admission by a party opponent and corroboration by the dog owner and other admissions in the record.

A similar outcome obtained in *Norton v. Howell*, 2009 Cal. App. Unpub. LEXIS 1325 (Feb. 19, 2009), where the hearing officer and trial court allowed hearsay in the form of unsworn letters and notes from veterinarians rebutting the dog owner's assertion that injuries to the two dogs arose from foreign plant material and not a bite. The appellate court rejected the motion to bar those letters because the owner waived it by raising it first on appeal. It further held that agency administrative proceedings may consider hearsay, and other substantial evidence supported the findings. While acknowledging the owner's contention that no county ordinance permitted hearsay in agency proceedings (and the *ultra vires* argument that the examiner acted outside authority in doing so), the court regarded hearsay admissible when, and only when, used to supplement unobjectionable evidence. But if not so used, it still would come in unless the opposing party timely objects to the hearsay evidence "before submission of the case or on reconsideration." The California Supreme Court and sister jurisdictions afforded a common law right to introduce hearsay evidence on these conditions. Exemplifying the corroborating proof required in these cases, the court added:

> But, as also noted above, there is yet a third reason to reject appellants' hearsay argument: as respondents correctly point out, *even if* the hearsay writings of the two vets in question should have been either excluded or not relied upon by the hearing officer, the trial court was correct in implicitly ruling that there was substantial *other* evidence to support the findings of the Hearing Officer as to the injuries to the first victim-dog, Rio. This evidence included photographs of Rio's injuries, the testimony of his owner at the administrative hearing concerning the events of the October 11, 2005, incident involving Rio and Lucy, a November 1, 2005, report submitted by Animal Services Officer Bender, and handwritten notes, provided by vets and/or technicians at the vet hospital regarding the treatment of Rio. Nor do appellants assert there was *any* hearsay evidence admitted with regard to Lucy's June 2007 attack on the second dog, Buddy. This was, clearly, ample other evidence to sustain the Hearing Officer's decision and then the Department's consequent order.

Id., at *5. In a strikingly harsh result that differs from the previous decision, *Tate v. SCRAPS*, 2010 WL 4069008 (Wash. App. 2010), dismissed a dangerous dog designation upon the county's failure to comply with its own code requiring the taking of evidence by sworn testimony. The hearing examiner not having sworn in any of the witnesses mandated reversal because, excluding the unsworn testimony, virtually nothing remained in the record upon which it could conduct meaningful appellate review.

H. STANDARD OF PROOF

Most jurisdictions regard dangerous dog proceedings as civil in nature and subject to a mere preponderance standard. *People v. Kikkenborg*, 910 N.Y.S.2d 407 (2010); *Leech v. Caldwell*, 2000 Del. C.P. LEXIS 58 (Mar. 5, 2000); *Giandalone v. Zepieri*, 86 Misc. 2d 79, 381 N.Y.S.2d 621 (J. Ct. 1976); *Mansour v. King Cy.*, 128 P.3d 1241 (Wash. Ct. App. 2006). When euthanasia is the penalty, a higher standard of proof may apply, and some statutory schemes require specific findings of aggravating circumstances. *Roberts*; *Town of Hempstead v. Lindsey*, 25 Misc. 3d 1235(A) (N.Y. Dist. Ct. 2009). A minority of jurisdictions enact ordinances that provide a more stringent standard than constitutionally required by applying a clear and convincing evidence standard for a dangerous dog classification. *State v. Taffet*, 2010 N.J. Super. Unpub. LEXIS 433 (Mar. 3, 2010); *Kaiser v. Brandt*, 23 Misc. 3d 1133(A) (N.Y. Dist. Ct. 2009); *Town of Hempstead*; *State v. Smith*, 685 A.2d 73 (N.J. Super Ct. 1996).

A charge of a criminal nature requires government to prove its case beyond a reasonable doubt. *Taffet, Kaiser; Town of Hempstead; State v. Smith*, 685 A.2d 73 (N.J. Super Ct. 1996). For instance, a prosecution for owning a dog who aggressively attacks and causes severe injury or death to a human being invokes this highest standard. *State v. Bash*, 925 P.2d 978 (Wash. 1996). Where a municipality elects to criminally charge a person for noncompliance with restrictions on controlling a dangerous dog without having first given the dog owner a civil hearing to challenge the designation of dangerous dog, it must prove the dog's dangerousness beyond a reasonable doubt as well as the violation of restraints. *City of Pierre v. Blackwell*, 635 N.W.2d 581 (S.D. 2001).

I. SUBSTANTIVE DUE PROCESS

Challenges to the onerousness of restraints placed upon a dangerous dog — such as the often unattainable premium for liability insurance, adverse health impacts from penning, muzzling, and short-leashing a dog, banishment, or death — may invoke substantive due process principles. Before turning to the constitutions, however, language in the governing statute or rule may require the factfinder to exercise discretion when selecting from among numerous alternative outcomes. The Washington Supreme Court counseled as much in a 1998 decision, stating, "[Rabon] claims he is entitled to a hearing on the issue whether the dogs should be destroyed. We agree that under the local ordinances petitioner should be heard on this question," thereby dodging the issue of whether the constitution required a disposition hearing (i.e., whether the dog, found dangerous, must be euthanized). *Rabon*, 957 P.2d at 628.

The substantive component of the Due Process Clause protects fundamental rights "implicit in the concept of ordered liberty." *Palko v. Connecticut*, 302 U.S. 319, 325 (1937). They include those within the Bill of Rights and six categories that the Supreme Court has specifically identified: freedom of association; right to vote;

interstate travel; fairness in criminal process; deprivation of life, liberty, and property; and right to privacy. *See* RONALD D. ROTUNDA & JOHN E. NOWAK, TREATISE ON CONSTITUTION LAW, SUBSTANCE AND PROCEDURE §§ 15.6, 15.7 (Thomson West 4th ed. 2007). The Second Amendment also enlists substantive due process protection, as self-defense is a basic right fundamental to the Nation's scheme of ordered liberty. *McDonald v. City of Chicago, Ill.*, 561 U.S. 742, 766 (2010). As with handguns, many Americans rely on dogs to protect the family, particularly to defend and protect their homestead and those cohabiting therein. The right to liberty from incarceration is fundamental,[3] *Meyer v. Nebraska*, 262 U.S. 390, 399–401 (1923), as is the right to maintain a family (which, arguably, for millions of Americans, includes the dog). Freedom in matters of family life "is a fundamental liberty interest" protected under the substantive due process clause. *See Santosky v. Kramer*, 455 U.S. 745, 753 (1982). As the U.S. Supreme Court noted in *Troxel v. Granville*, 530 U.S. 57 (2000), "[t]he demographic changes of the past century make it difficult to speak of an average American family," and thus, "[t]he composition of families varies greatly from household to household." *Id.*, at 63. That said, courts have not yet warmed to the notion that dog-keeping is a fundamental right, even when characterized as the right to own property *sui generis*, which also protects, and cements the bonds of, family.

While *Troxel* and related cases refer to human children, we have coevolved with canines since the dawn of humanity, and did not bestow the accolade of "man's best friend" upon the dog haphazardly. Dogs have protected and served human families, whether sleeping on the owners' bed, or accompanying owners to work and on vacations — in other words, even before dogs moved from the doghouse to the fireplace, they were regarded as family. Appellate courts have recognized this shift. *Rabon v. City of Seattle*, 34 P.3d 821, 826 (Wash. Ct. App. 2001), stated:

> Rabon requests that we recognize his right in his dog as something akin to a liberty interest, like a familial relationship. He argues that an action to destroy a beloved pet calls for a more careful process than might be used to destroy an inanimate nuisance. There may be merit to the argument that a person's relationship with a dog deserves more protection than a person's relationship with, say, a car.

See also Mansour v. King Cy., 128 P.3d 1241, 1246 (Wash. Ct. App. 2006) ("We recognize that the bond between pet and owner often runs deep and that many people consider pets part of the family."); *Pickford v. Masion*, 98 P.3d 1232 (Wash. Ct. App. 2004) ("Pickford, with good reason, maintains that Buddy is much more than a piece of property; we agree."); *Rhoades v. City of Battleground*, 63 P.3d 142, 149 (Wash. Ct. App. 2003) ("Here, first, the private interest involved is the owners' interest in keeping their pets. This is greater than a mere economic interest, for pets are not fungible. So the private interest at stake is great."); *San Jose Charter of Hells Angels Motorcycle Club v. City of San Jose*, 402 F.3d 962, 975 (9th Cir. 2005) ("The emotional attachment to a family's dog is not comparable to a possessory

---

[3] While a criminal conviction extinguishes the right to freedom from incarceration, this requires first a valid conviction. The substantive component to a "valid" conviction concerns whether the criminal conduct is protected constitutionally as a fundamental right. *See Eisenstadt v. Baird*, 405 U.S. 438, 454–55 (1972).

interest in furniture."); *Womack v. von Rardon*, 135 P.3d 542 (Wash. Ct. App. 2006) (creating new cause of action to recognize that "harm may be caused to a person's emotional well-being by malicious injury to that person's pet as personal property.").

Statistics also back the common law's evolution. The American Veterinary Medical Association summarized the findings from a 2006 survey of 50,000 companion animal guardians, which revealed that "[most] people consider their pets to be family members or companions, not property. . . . The statistics reveal that almost all pet owners feel a strong human-animal bond." *Human-Animal Bond Boosts Spending on Veterinary Care*, JAVMA News, Jan. 1, 2008, http://www.avma. org/News/JAVMANews/Pages/080101a.aspx. According to the updated 2012 survey, 99 percent of pet owners regard their animals as "family members" or "companions," compared to only one percent who deem them simply "property," prompting AVMA president Douglas G. Aspros, DVM to remark, "The human-animal bond is stronger than ever. . . ." AVMA, U.S. Pet Ownership & Demographics Sourcebook (2012), www.avma.org/news/javmanews/pages/130201a.aspx. This change developed over the last 30 years, evidencing a major shift in public attitude. Recent studies show that 45 percent of dog owners take their dogs on vacation; more than half the companion animal owners would prefer a dog or a cat to a human if they were stranded on a deserted island; and 50 percent of companion animals owners would be "very likely" to risk their lives to save their companion animals, while another 33 percent would be "somewhat likely" to put their own lives in danger to save their companion animals. William C. Root, *"Man's Best Friend": Property or Family Member? An Examination of the Legal Classification of Companion Animals and its Impact on Damages recoverable for their Wrongful Death or Injury*, 47 Vill. L. Rev. 423, 423 (2002).

Though unlikely to persuade a court that keeping a dog constitutes a fundamental right, a good faith basis exists to argue that a property interest in a dog as family companion is *sui generis*. While mere economic interests do not rise to the fundamental level for purposes of substantive due process analysis, where kept for largely noneconomic, familial reasons, dogs as a special type of property may merit enhanced protection. Consider deceased children's corneas. In *Newman v. Sathyavaglswaran*, 287 F.3d 786, 789–94 (9th Cir. 2002), the Ninth Circuit agreed that next of kin had protectible property interests in those of their relatives, subject to strict scrutiny analysis, given a firmly entrenched "historical pedigree." *Id.*, at 795–96, 798. For similar good reason, the "historical pedigree" of the family dog merits at least the same protection as deceased children's corneas or other human body parts. Strict scrutiny means that legislative acts limiting a fundamental right cannot survive a substantive due process challenge "at all, no matter what process is provided, unless the infringement is narrowly tailored to serve a compelling state interest." *Witt v. Department of Air Force*, 527 F.3d 806, 817–18 (9th Cir. 2008) (quoting *Reno v. Flores*, 507 U.S. 292, 301–02 (1993)). "Few laws survive such scrutiny[.]" *Id.*

Whether or not called substantive due process, dog owners often appeal to the equitable sensibilities of the factfinder. Yet *Schwab* rejected the "general principle that an order to dispose of a dog whose vicious disposition has been established by the evidence cannot stand unless it is clearly demonstrated that no less severe alternative exists" in an effort by a dog owner attempting to save a dog from death by arguing for alternative, less severe forms of restraint. And though sympathetic to the dog owner's request for banishment as an equitable alternative remedy to death, and despite acknowledging that the vast majority of dangerous dog petitioners prefer banishment over death, *Town of Huntington v. Mazzone*, 17 Misc. 3d 546, 549–50 (N.Y. Dist. Ct. 2007) found no statutory authority or precedent to grant the request, even after consulting with New York's human-related banishment laws. It concluded, "For the same ethical reason that this Court routinely declines to accede to pro se petitioners' well-meaning requests for an intrastate banishment from one neighborhood to another, it cannot participate as a state agent in the inflicting of a dangerous instrumentality upon a sister state. Surely, such an interstate tortious act would expose the parties and possibly the State of New of New York to the violation of a myriad of Federal laws and regulations." *Id.*, at 550.

For nonfundamental rights, rational basis review applies, requiring the government to furnish any reasonable basis to tie the challenged policy to a legitimate state interest. *Witt*, at 814–15.

J. APPLICATION OF FORFEITURE LAW

Certain jurisdictions impose a higher standard of proof for "forfeitures," so construing a dangerous dog proceeding as a forfeiture may serve as a bulwark against erroneous euthanasia. Only one case directly addressed the applicability of forfeiture law to euthanasia of a dog pursuant to a dangerous dog classification. *City of Cleveland v. Lupica*, 2004 Ohio App. LEXIS 4752 (Sept. 30, 2004), found that the ordinance's use of the word "forfeit" did not demand compliance with the rules applying to forfeiture of contraband. However, a Florida case applied general forfeiture law to removal of an animal in the context of animal cruelty. *Brinkley v. County of Flagler*, 769 So. 2d 468 (Fla. Dist. Ct. App. 2000) found no significant difference between removal of a dangerous dog for euthanasia pursuant to a dangerous dog statute and removal of a dog due to alleged animal cruelty. In both instances, the dog owner suffers a final, irrevocable separation from his property. Further, *Brinkley* required the state to bear the burden to prove the allegations of neglect by clear and convincing evidence, despite the animal cruelty statute placing it on the petitioner to prove fitness by clear and convincing evidence.

Where euthanasia pursuant to a dangerous dog classification constitutes a forfeiture, one could argue entitlement to a jury trial and thus remove that decision from a police chief, hearing examiner, or judge. Florida's personal property forfeiture statute mandates a jury trial unless claimants waive it. *Department of Law Enforcement v. Real Property*, 588 So. 2d 957 (Fla. 1991). Several cases apply the clear and convincing standard of proof involving euthanasia because required by statute. *People v. Jornov*, 65 A.D.3d 363 (N.Y. Sup. Ct. App. Div. 2009); *Kaiser; Cuozzo v. Loccisano*, 832 N.Y.S.2d 744 (2007). Other courts have specifically held that the civil nature of the proceedings maintains the standard of proof in a euthanasia case to evidentiary preponderance. *City of Hornell v. Harrison*, 192 Misc. 2d 273 (N.Y. City Ct. 2002).

K. COLLATERAL ESTOPPEL

A defendant who has been convicted of a crime, or whose animal has been declared (potentially) dangerous or ordered removed from the jurisdiction may have that conviction, declaration, or order regarded as a collateral, precedent action, the outcome of which could prove germane in a subsequent civil suit arising from the same conduct by defendant's animal. For instance, *Toolan ex rel. Toolan v. Cerulli*, 2006 Pa. Dist. & Cnty. Dec. LEXIS 446 (Dec. 14, 2006), declined to apply collateral estoppel offensively against the defendants, where they were convicted of violating the summary offense of harboring a dangerous dog. Instead, *Toolan* reserved preclusive effect for more serious crimes and summary offenses that function as a necessary operative fact in a non-summary conviction. Generally speaking, for collateral estoppel (or issue preclusion) to apply:

(1) the issue decided in the prior adjudication must be identical with the one presented in the second action;

(2) the prior adjudication must have ended in a final judgment on the merits;

(3) the party against whom the plea of collateral estoppel is asserted must have been a party or in privity with the party to the prior adjudication; and

(4) application of the doctrine must not work an injustice.

Thompson v. State, Dept. of Licensing, 982 P.2d 601, 605 (Wash. 1999). A fifth requirement is sometimes imposed: "that the finding sought to be made binding involve 'ultimate facts:' those 'necessary and essential' to the judgment in the first action." *Wear v. Farmers Ins. Co. of Washington*, 745 P.2d 526 (Wash. Ct. App. 1987).

Collateral estoppel prevents relitigation of an issue where the party against whom the doctrine is applied has had a full and fair opportunity to litigate the case. It cannot preclude a party from litigating an issue in a subsequent proceeding if that party had no opportunity in the prior proceeding. *Hanson v. City of Snohomish*, 852 P.2d 295, 299–301 (Wash. 1993). Accordingly, applying collateral estoppel may be improper where the issue is determined after an informal, expedited hearing with relaxed evidentiary standards. *State v. Vasquez*, 59 P.3d 648, 650 (Wash. 2002) (administrative driver's license-suspension hearing did not collaterally preclude state from DUI prosecution).

Most dangerous dog appeals before a municipal, district, or circuit court judge, or even an administrative tribunal, may confer a full and fair opportunity to litigate the issues in question, including the right to present witnesses, cross-examine witnesses and complainants, introduce evidence, and retain a lawyer to defend their interests with the burden and standard of proof squarely placed upon the government's shoulders. An administrative decision may have preclusive effect on a later civil action where the parties had ample incentive to litigate. In most administrative appeal hearings, a nonattorney may serve as a hearing examiner or member of a board of equalization. The different procedures, policies, and practices may not be sufficiently protective of defendants' interests to permit the invocation of estoppel.

Defendants may attempt to argue that collateral estoppel can only be applied defensively (e.g., the defendant prevails in a dangerous dog appeal and seeks to raise that victory as a shield in a subsequent civil action), rather than offensively (e.g., the defendant loses in a dangerous dog appeal and the victim seeks to raise that loss as a sword in a subsequent civil action). The United States Supreme Court, however, "has given courts broad discretion to apply offensive estoppel[.]" *Parklane Hosiery Co., Inc. v. Shore*, 439 U.S. 322, 330 (1979). Thus, most states permit offensive use of collateral estoppel.

L. CANONS OF STATUTORY INTERPRETATION

Inevitably, practitioners will need to familiarize themselves with statutory interpretation canons. Courts frequently defer to administrative agency rules implementing statutory policy and opinions of the attorney general in construing statutes unless the interpretation disregards the statute's plain meaning or is patently unreasonable. So when courts appear inclined to defer to interpretations by the animal control authority or hearing examiner, especially without evidence that the entity is "charged with administering a special field of law and endowed with quasi-judicial functions because of its expertise in that field[,]", *Overton v. Wash. State Econ. Assistance Auth.*, 637 P.2d 652, 654 (Wash. 1981), objections may be appropriate.

Dangerous dog hearings may rely on ambiguous words and phrases with a dual civil-criminal application. "If a statute is ambiguous, the rule of lenity requires us to interpret the statute in favor of the defendant absent legislative intent to the contrary." *State v. Jacobs*, 115 P.3d 281, 283 (Wash. 2005). "A statute is ambiguous if it is subject to two or more reasonable interpretations." *State v. McGee*, 864 P.2d 912, 913 (Wash. 1993). Under the rule of lenity, the court must adopt the interpretation most favorable to the criminal defendant." In an effort to properly construe ambiguous, undefined terms like "provocation," "severe injury," "broken bone," "requiring," and "disfigurement/disfiguring," where they have hybrid civil-criminal applications, the court must apply the rule of lenity and interpret any ambiguity strictly in favor of the dog owner. While the lenity rule traditionally applies to criminal, not civil, proceedings, civil lenity applications have been endorsed by the United States Supreme Court. *United States v. Thompson/Center Arms Co.*, 504 U.S. 505 (1992), applied lenity to a civil statute with criminal applications, by interpreting the term "make" as used in the National Firearms Act. While it provided for a $200 tax on anyone "making" a "firearm," a "maker" of "firearms" failing to comply with any of the NFA's other requirements could be subjected to a $10,000 fine and/or 10 years imprisonment. *See also Leocal v. Ashcroft*, 543 U.S. 1 (2004) (applying lenity to resolve whether a state DWI conviction was a "crime of violence" within meaning of relevant immigration statute that had both civil and criminal applications); *Clark v. Martinez*, 543 U.S. 371 (2005) (applying lenity in civil case interpreting immigration statute and concluding that "lowest common denominator . . . must govern"); *United States v. Plaza Health Laboratories*, 3 F.3d 643 (2d Cir. 1993) (applying lenity to Clean Water Act's ambiguous statutory definition for "point source"). Strict construction and lenity canons also apply in forfeiture, quasi-criminal, and criminal settings, reaching the same result — construing ambiguities against government.

1. Severe and/or Serious Injury

Municipalities penalize for perilous canine behavior most often by focusing on the nature and degree of injury sustained by the victim human or nonhuman animal. The penalty typically is proportional to injury. "Severe injury" is traditionally defined to encompass any physical injury that results in broken bones, multiple bites, or disfiguring lacerations requiring sutures or reconstructive surgery. Fla. Stat. § 767.11(3), Rev. Code Wash. § 16.08.070(3). That said, even gruesome, albeit shocking, and commonly understood "severe" injuries will not fall within such a definition. Linguistic interpretation presents a crucial task, including the need to note the singular and plural uses of each individual word, as well as account for definitions within definitions.

For example, *In the Matter of the Appeal of Jason E. Jarrett*, Seattle Hearing Examiner No. DA-11-002 (Jul. 19, 2011), a dog who bit off a victim's lower lip could not be deemed dangerous as "severe injury" required multiple lacerations, and this bite only generated one. *People v. Jornov*, 65 A.D.3d 363 (N.Y. Sup. Ct. App. Div. 2009), found that a bite wound requiring antibiotics and a torn hamstring necessitating non-steroidal anti-inflammatories and physical therapy for six to eight weeks did not qualify as a severe injury within the meaning of the statute due to lack of evidence of "protracted impairment of health." *Leech v. Caldwell*, 2000 Del. C.P. LEXIS 58 (Mar. 5, 2000) held that a bite to a foot, a bite to a foot coupled with knocking a person down, and a bite causing a person to fall, each individually warranted a declaration of the dog as dangerous for having inflicted a "physical injury," defined as impairment of physical condition or substantial pain. Similarly, *Town of Southampton v. Ciuzio*, 866 N.Y.S.2d 96 (2008), determined that substantial swelling and scarring associated with injury to the cheek, neck, and ear, associated with long-term hearing loss, constituted protracted disfigurement, protracted loss, or impairment of a function of any bodily organ sufficient to meet the definition of severe injury. On the other hand, *Town of Hempstead v. Lindsey*, 25 Misc. 3d 1235(A) (D.N.Y. 2009), refused to find severe injury even where three Rottweilers chased a man on top of his car, leaving two large and seemingly deeply penetrating wounds to his thigh, with pieces of flesh and fatty tissue ripped from his body, blood dripping from the roof and down the windshield, with paw prints on the hood of the freshly washed car. It reasoned that the bite wounds, prescription of antibiotics, and missing several days of work do not satisfy the definition of "serious injury" because there was no protracted impairment, disfigurement, and dysfunction.

Sometimes courts evaluate "severe injury" in the context of nonhuman victims, as happened in Pennsylvania where the court vacated a conviction for harboring a dangerous dog, finding the term "requiring," as in requiring sutures, unambiguously mandated the actual use of sutures, or the need for them even if not stitched (as in such cases where the animal did not receive treatment, or, if so, suffered from malpractice). *Comm. v. Morgera*, 836 A.2d 1070 (Pa. Comm. Ct. 2003). This resulted because the veterinarian did not suture the sheep, despite his claim that suturing might increase the risk of infection and subsequent septicemia and death, but would have sutured if the sheep suffered injury by brushing up against a fence. The veterinarian also testified that flap removal from the sheep's face occurred due to "the blood supply . . . [being] damaged, destroyed, and that flap of skin ends up dying and falling off, even if you try to suture it," and not for cosmetic reasons. Thus, the court also discredited the Commonwealth's argument that the use of surgical scissors to remove a loose flap of skin constituted "cosmetic surgery," defined as surgery "in which the principal purpose is to improve the appearance, usually with the connotation that the improvement sought is beyond the normal appearance, and its acceptable variations for the age and ethnic origin of the patient." Finally, while the defendant never raised it, the court likely would have also found the government's proof of facts wanting with respect to the adjective "disfiguring" in relation to the lacerations.

2. Attack

Infrequently, jurisdictions define "attack." When they do, it usually distinguishes aggressive and non-aggressive contact, the former justifying a dangerous dog classification. An "attack" typically includes aggressive physical contact with a person or animal initiated by the dog. It may encompass, *inter alia*, the dog jumping on, leaping at, or biting a person or animal. *State of Hawaii v. MacDonald*, 200 P.3d 417 (Haw. Ct. App. 2009). Some jurisdictions define the term more broadly to mean action by a dog that might cause reasonable apprehension of harm or injury to a person, together with the apparent ability of the dog to inflict such harm: this definition renders actual biting unnecessary. *La Borie v. Habes*, 277 N.Y.S.2d 70 (J. Ct. 1967); *Brooks v. Hemingway*, 433 N.Y.S.2d 551 (N.Y. Dist. Ct. 1980).

A court may also resort to BLACK'S LAW DICTIONARY to define "attack" in the face of code silence. *Brook v. City of St. Paul*, 2010 U.S. Dist. LEXIS 115024 (D. Minn. Oct. 28, 2010) refused to equate dog bites with an "attack," in part because the code used the terms in the disjunctive (e.g., "attack or bite"); thus, it reversed the euthanasia order.

3. Propensity

Considerable litigation exists about whether a dog's single bite warrants a dangerous designation, where the statutory scheme requires proof of a dog's history or propensity to attack. *Eritano v. Comm.*, 690 A.2d 705 (Pa. 1997) affirmed the acquittal of an Akita who bit a child of tender years while lunging for chicken held by the child in one hand because the statute required evidence of a dog's history or propensity to attack. The Pennsylvania Supreme Court found a single incident insufficient as a matter of law where the code required "evidence of a dog's history or propensity to attack without provocation based upon an incident in which the dog" attacks or inflicts severe injury. It did so by parsing the phrase "an incident" to refer to the event brought to the bench for determination of dangerousness, "history" to mean "a chronological record of significant events," "propensity" to mean "an often intense natural inclination or preference," and seizing upon the word "often" to lead to the conclusion that, "[t]he incident giving rise to the filing of the complaint cannot alone establish the dog's history or propensity to attack."

In a case of first impression, *Comm. v. Hake*, 738 A.2d 46 (Pa. Commw. Ct. 1999), held that a first, unprovoked attack on a human did render the owner criminally liable for the summary offense of harboring a dangerous dog, notwithstanding *Eritano*. The court reasoned that the legislature effectively repealed *Eritano* by specifically allowing the incident at bar to permit a finding of propensity, even if only the first attack, concluding that absolute criminal liability followed, and scienter ("one free bite") was a non-essential element. With respect to propensity toward nonhumans, *Comm. v. Bender*, 1994 WL 904464 (Pa. Com. Pl. 1994), declined to deem dangerous a Rottweiler who had no history of aggression toward cats, although the dog killed a cat upon escaping from the owner's control. It found that the term "propensity" required more than a single incident (i.e., killing a cat).

Most jurisdictions, however, uphold a dangerous dog classification based on a single attack, deducing a propensity from the nature of the attack itself. *Wynn v. Rudack*, 2009 Mass. Super. LEXIS 183 (Jul. 13, 2009); *Commonwealth v. Seyler*, 929 A.2d 262 (Pa. Commw. Ct. 2007); *Commonwealth v. Austin*, 846 A.2d 798 (Pa. Commw. Ct. 2004); *Commonwealth v. Baldwin*, 767 A.2d 644 (Pa. Commw. Ct. 2001); *Commonwealth v. Hake*, 738 A.2d 46 (Pa. Commw. Ct. 1999). For instance, *Comm. v. Baldwin*, 767 A.2d 644 (Pa. Commw. Ct. 2001), found severity of injury irrelevant in deducing propensity where a dog pushed down the victim and half-heartedly bit down on a finger (i.e., dorsal, not ventral, bite marks only), thus upholding the conviction for harboring a dangerous dog.

4. Domestic Animal

Statutes routinely deem a dog dangerous who kills, maims, or bites a "domestic animal" off the owner's property or on the public right of way. "Domestic" contrasts "wild," so dogs killing wildlife are often spared the designation, unless held captive or semiwild. For instance, Pennsylvania amended its Dangerous Dog Law to define a domestic animal as "any equine animal or bovine animal, sheep, goat, pig, poultry, bird, fowl, confined hares, rabbits and mink, or any wild or semiwild animal maintained in captivity." Not all jurisdictions define the phrase, but some do plainly. A harboring dangerous dog appeal resulted in affirmance of conviction where the dog attacked another dog, the court referencing the law's definition of "domestic animal" as "[A]ny dog, cat, equine animal, bovine animal, sheep, goat or porcine animal," and rejecting as absurd that dogs would not commonly qualify as domestic given the long co-evolution of humans and canines. *Comm v. Comella*, 735 A.2d 738 (Pa. Commw. Ct. 1999); *see also State v. Leonard*, 470 A.2d 1262 (Me. 1984). On the other hand, *People v. Noga*, 645 N.Y.S.2d 268 (1996), vacated a euthanasia order and dangerous dog declaration on a dog characterized as a nonaggressive bystander to another dog's inflicting severe injury to a poodle; the court also found that a dog is not a domestic animal. *See also Vail v. Terry*, 75 N.Y.S.2d 543 (1947). It may seem curious to define a dog or cat as other than a domestic animal, but strict statutory interpretation, especially laws enacted generations ago, may prove that dog-eat-dog or dog-eat-cat encounters were not envisioned as actionable offenses. Instead, legislatures may have reserved such judgment for depredating dogs interfering with commercial livestock operations.

Hypothetical: While the victims of many dangerous dogs include "livestock" such as bovines, sheep, goats, horses, and other equines, birds (or "poultry") present a close question. For instance, the City of Lakewood, Washington, defines "animal" to *exclude* "any goat, horse, mule, cattle, swine, ass, or other livestock, and excepting any dog or cat." LMC § 6.02.010(B). It never does define "domestic animal." So when it criminally charged a dog owner for allowing her dog to kill chickens in a neighbor's outdoor coop, under a code making it unlawful for a dog to cause injury to a *domestic animal*, did its own definitions bar prosecution?

The city council expressed its intention to exclude livestock from the definition of "animal," and thus, "domestic animal." If a chicken is "livestock," then it cannot be a "domestic animal," because logic dictates that if a chicken is not a statutorily defined "animal," then it does not belong to the narrower subclass of animals known as "domestic animal" either. Chickens kept in coops (i.e., not sleeping in the bed or eating from food bowls on the kitchen floor, as in the case of household companion dogs and cats), are no less "livestock," and thus not statutorily defined "animals," than the enumerated species stated in LMC § 6.02.010(B). No good reason exists to protect birds over land mammals. Indeed, United States District Court JUDGE EDWARD J. LODGE, of the District Court of Idaho, held that dogs could be considered "livestock." *U.S. v. Park*, 658 F. Supp. 2d 1236 (D. Idaho 2009):

C. Does State Law Define Dogs as Livestock?

The Court will next determine if Idaho's statutes can shed light on the parties' intent as to whether dogs are livestock. The Court finds Idaho state law is unpersuasive in helping define the term "livestock" in this case since the easement document did not incorporate certain state definitions and the state statutes that do define "livestock" for branding purposes do not appear to be applicable to facts before the Court.

Pursuant to Idaho Code § 25-1101, "livestock" is defined as "any cattle, horses, mules or asses." This definition is limited to Title 25 which deals with the State brand board. This definition is more limited than any definition used by the experts that testified. Additionally, common sense would indicate that a branding statute would not include dogs in its definition as dogs are not animals that are branded. The Court could not locate any state statute that defined dogs as livestock, however the Court could not locate any state statute that indicated dogs were not livestock. The Forest Service argues because dogs were not included in the definition of livestock in § 25-1101, they are excluded. *The Court respectfully disagrees with this argument as it is clear from intent of the statute that the purpose of the statute was not to define an all inclusive list of livestock.* Moreover, the testimony of all the experts and Mr. Curnes (who negotiated the easement) supports a finding that "livestock" is not limited to cattle, horses, mules and asses. *Based on the expert testimony, "livestock" certainly includes goats, llamas, sheep, pigs, hogs and poultry but these animals are not normally branded so they are not included in the branding statute definition for livestock.*

. . .

D. Do Dogs Fit Under the Plain Meaning of the Term "Livestock"

Having found state statutes unhelpful, the Court will turn to the plain meaning of the word "livestock." As the Ninth Circuit noted, "[t]he term "livestock" stems from the Middle Ages, when it was used as a measure of wealth or to refer to property that could be moved, particularly to a market for trade . . . . Later, the term began to be used in a more limited sense to describe cattle . . . . *Today, dictionary definition of "livestock" is sweeping, capturing every type of domesticated animal." United States v. Park*, 536 F.3d 1058, 1062 (9th Cir. 2008) (citations omitted).

Webster's Dictionary defines *"livestock" as "animals kept or raised for use or pleasure; esp: farm animals kept for use and profit." Merriam-Webster Collegiate Dictionary* 728 (11th ed. 2003). Black's Law Dictionary defines "livestock" as "domestic animals *and fowls* that (1) are kept for profit or pleasure, (2) can normally be confined within boundaries without seriously impairing their utility, and (3) do not normally intrude on others' land in such a way as to harm the land or growing crops." *Black's Law Dictionary* 953 (8th ed. 2004).

In trying to determine the intent of the parties entering the easement in 1973, the Court also examined earlier published definitions of "livestock." In *Ballentine's Law Dictionary* 746 (3rd ed. 1969), the term "livestock" is defined as:

Domestic animals, particularly cattle, hogs, sheep and horses. Livestock includes fur bearing animals domesticated, and raised in captivity. The breeding, raising and pelting of foxes is agricultural labor as that term is used in the Social Security Act. *Fromm Bros. v. United States* (DC Wis) 35 F. Supp. 145.

Black's Law Dictionary 1083 (4th ed. 1968) defines "live stock" as: Domestic animals used or raised on a farm. *Boland v. Cecil*, 65 Cal.App.2d Supp. 832, 150 P.2d 819, 822 [(1944)]. The term in its generic sense includes *all domestic animals. Meader v. Unemployment Compensation Division of Industrial Accident Board*, 64 Idaho 716, 136 P.2d 984, 987 [1943]. It includes fur bearing animals raised in captivity. *Fromm Bros. v. United States*, D.C. Wis., 35 F. Supp. 145, 147 [(1940)]. . . .

Id., at 1243–44 (emphasis added). Even if the City were to respond that at least one dictionary defines "domestic animal" to include poultry, at most that would show the ambiguity of the partially undefined term. The rule of lenity, however, would arguably compel to court to embrace the definition that excludes poultry. And the distinction between "domestic animal" and "poultry" is hardly semantical.

Turning to Washington's State Dog Law, Ch. 16.08 RCW, provides further support. RCW § 16.08.020 justifies canicide as follows:

It shall be lawful for any person who shall see any dog or dogs chasing, biting, injuring or killing any sheep, swine or other domestic animal, including poultry, belonging to such person, on any real property owned or leased by, or under the control of, such person, or on any public highway, to kill such dog or dogs, and it shall be the duty of the owner or keeper of any dog or dogs so found chasing, biting or *injuring any domestic animal, including poultry,* upon being notified of that fact by the owner of such domestic animals *or poultry,* to thereafter keep such dog or dogs in leash or confined upon the premises of the owner or keeper thereof, and in case any such owner or keeper of a dog or dogs shall fail or neglect to comply with the provisions of this section, it shall be lawful for the owner of such domestic animals or poultry to kill such dog or dogs found running at large.

Id. (emphasis added). The 1919 version of this law did not have the words "or poultry." That came in the 1929 amendment, indicating a conscious choice by the Legislature to justify killing of dogs seen in the act of attacking chickens. *However,* in that same year, the Legislature did *not* amend RCW § 16.08.030 to make it a duty to kill a dog found killing *poultry* within 48 hours after being notified of the fact:

It shall be the duty of any person owning or keeping any dog or dogs which shall be found killing *any domestic animal* to kill such dog or dogs within forty-eight hours after being notified of that fact, and any person failing or neglecting to comply with the provisions of this section shall be deemed guilty of a misdemeanor, and it shall be the duty of the sheriff or any deputy sheriff to kill any dog found running at large (after the first day of August of any year and before the first day of March in the following year) without a metal identification tag.

Id. (emphasis added). In other words, the Legislature selectively granted rights and imposed responsibilities relative to poultry, but did not treat them uniformly throughout Ch. 16.08 RCW.

Moreover, when the Legislature enacted the Dangerous Dog Law (RCW § 16.08.070-.100) in 1987, and amended it in 2002, it did not add "or poultry" to its definition of "dangerous dog" at RCW § 16.08.070(2)(b) ("kills a domestic animal without provocation while the dog is off the owner's property"). Of note, the City of Lakewood, Washington, embraces the same definition of "dangerous dog," offering highly probative evidence of legislative intent to *exclude* chickens from the definition of "domestic animal."[4]

In a related vein, courts have spared dogs from euthanasia where the statute does not call for destruction in a dog-on-dog death context. *Motta v. Menendez,* 46 A.D.3d 685 (N.Y. Sup. Ct. App. Div. 2007). Reversal also occurred where dog-on-dog killings were not proscribed by ordinance, and the dog had not attempted to bite, attack, or endanger a person. *Ohio v. Campbell,* 2009 Ohio App. LEXIS 3071 (Jul. 23, 2009). Likewise, a court found a euthanasia order impermissible despite the dog having killed two chickens, because the statute did not prohibit such conduct. *Kaiser v. Brandt,* 23 Misc. 3d 1133(A) (N.Y. Dist. Ct. 2009).

---

[4] This example settled through compromise of misdemeanor, the defendant paying $100 to the victim, so the court did not rule on this chickens-qua-"domestic animal" argument.

5.   Chase or Approach of Person or Animal

Dogs may be held dangerous without bite or contact. Usually the statute or ordinance requires that a dog menace off the dog owner's premises. *Francis v. City of Indianapolis*, 958 N.E.2d 816 (Ind. Ct. App. 2011). A dog *fright*, as opposed to dog *bite*, whereby a dog rushes a fence and causes apprehension to a person walking on an adjacent sidewalk while the dog remains on-premises, may therefore constitute menacing. Typically, a person scared by the dog's approach suffices to change a dog's legal status if done in menacing fashion or in an apparent attitude of attack, or a vicious or terrorizing manner. Delaware's dangerous dog statute sets the bar at chasing a person in an apparent attitude of attack "on 2 separate occasions within a 12 month period." *Leech*. Courts have rejected claims of vagueness, including *Louisville Kennel Club*, at *5, with respect to defining, however circularly, "attack" as "[a]n unprovoked attack in an aggressive manner on a human that causes a scratch, abrasion, or bruising, or on a domestic pet or livestock that causes death or injury. *See also Ohio v. Cowan*, 2003 Ohio App. LEXIS 3252 (Jul. 3, 2003), affirmed on other grounds, *Ohio v. Cowan*, 814 N.E.2d 846 (Ohio 2004).

Because menacing behavior may actually cause distress to a hypersensitive, dog-phobic person but not similarly affect the general public, one must also determine whether the test is subjective or objective or otherwise vague in application. The only reported case concluded that the phrase "menacing" was not vague, because the definition in the statute required that a person "reasonably believe" that the dog would cause injury. *Cowan*, 2003 Ohio App. LEXIS at *5–8. This language would prevent an unreasonably fearful person from singlehandedly spurring an agency to issue a dangerous dog classification. In addition, a statute may require the dog to be off the owner's property and not under the control of a responsible person, thereby building in a "safe harbor" or home-guarding exception. However, once loosed into the public, even a dog approaching and attempting to bite while growling and baring teeth would suffice. A dog 12 to 15 feet away from a person, paws off the ground, barking, growling, and lunging with teeth displayed provided substantial evidence to uphold a dangerous dog classification in *Francis*. Though the minor bite does not meet the definition of "injury" in the dangerous dog statute, a dog chasing a five-year-old child in a "vicious or terrorizing manner" in an apparent attitude of attack was deemed dangerous. *Penn v. Town of Wrightsville*, 639 S.E.2d 453 (N.C. Ct. App. 2007).

Similarly, when one cannot confirm an actual bite, a dangerous dog classification may arise by pleading menacing in the alternative. *Pittman v. City of St. Paul*, 2003 Minn. App. LEXIS 1178 (Sept. 23, 2003), found a dog potentially dangerous even if it did not bite the nine-year-old boy victim, who ran down the sidewalk, tripped, and fell. It reasoned that the owner's admission of purchasing a kennel because of the dog's habitual chasing of running kids and the boy's testimony that he ran when he saw a 40-60 pound dog charging toward him, reasonably believing the dog to be chasing or attacking him, amply satisfied this alternative basis.

People ex rel. LaBorie v. Habes, 52 Misc. 2d 768 (N.Y. J. Ct. 1967), interpreted "attack" to mean "to use force against in order to harm; to start a fight or quarrel with; to take offense against; to assault" and "any hostile action." It thereafter defined "assault" as "an unlawful offer or attempt to force or violence to do corporal hurt to another." And it defined "dangerous" per BLACK'S LAW DICTIONARY as "attended with risk; perilous; hazardous; unsafe," to conclude that where a dangerous dog must "attack" a person, "Actual biting is unnecessary to an 'attack'." Rather, only reasonable apprehension of harm or injury, coupled with apparent ability to cause such harm, is required. In *Habes*, a dog approached a person growling with bared teeth, chased a solicitor, nipped at a newspaper carrier, and turned on a neighbor who tried to protect his cat — but never made contact with or bit any person. As expected, the dog was found dangerous. With similar outcome, the *Brooks* court rejected the argument "friends to most, hostile to few" as a defense to a dangerous dog designation where the dog merely chased but did not bite a 16-year-old on two occasions, focusing on apprehension of imminent contact. The court remained unwilling to endorse a "one free bite" rule, which would force the victim to await actual injury before defending against a menacing animal.

While severity of injury often serves to negate provocation where a dog's response is disproportionate to the stimulus, *Eritano* also found that the severity of a child's injuries presumed intent to harm and met the statutory definition of "attack." In *Eritano*, an Akita, who had never previously attacked or bitten a person, lunged for a piece of chicken held by Lauren, a five-year-old, causing severe injury to her face and neck. The common pleas court vacated the decision of the district justice that declared Sama dangerous, on the grounds that she merely "acted on [her] instincts when [she] bit at the meat the child was holding." The commonwealth court affirmed, adding that evidence of her "history or propensity to attack" must be determined, agreeing that Sama did not "attack" Lauren, and characterizing the injuries as accidental. The statute defined "attack" as "the deliberate action of a dog, whether or not in response to a command by its owner, to bite, to seize with its teeth or to pursue any human, animate or inanimate object, with the obvious intent to destroy, kill, wound, injure or otherwise harm the object of its action." 3 PS 459-501-A. Reversing, the Supreme Court found the legislature could not have intended the absurd result that Sama's instinctual, accidental lunge did not render her dangerous. Any other outcome would defeat public policy by allowing dogs to evade adverse designations if just "playing" or trying to recover food, stymying government efforts at proving a "history or propensity to attack." Interestingly, the court addressed intentionality, stating, "Although we cannot ascertain the intent of the animal, we presume that because the dog in fact severely injured the child, it intended to do so in order to recover the chicken she was attempting to eat." *Eritano*, at 708 (fn. om.). *Groner v. Hedrick*, 169 A.2d 302, 303 (Pa. 1961) added that dog intentionality "forms no part of an animal's assault and battery, and the mood in which it inflicts harm is immaterial, so far as the owner's duty goes."

Of notable distinction, while dangerous dog laws routinely prohibit chasing or menacingly approaching a *human* in an apparent attitude of attack, they do not proscribe such behavior with respect to an *animal*, unless the chase or approach results in harmful contact. Confusion arises where a human accompanies an animal attacked by a dog, becoming an incidental target of the dog. *State v. Campbell*, 2009 Ohio App. LEXIS 3071 (Jul. 23, 2009), reversed a dangerous dog declaration against a cocker spaniel and German shepherd who ran into the street and attacked a woman's Greyhound while she was walking the dog, causing injury to the dog but not the woman. Finding a total lack of evidence that either dog made a "qualifying approach involving a person, rather than a dog," meaning that the dogs attempted to bite, attack, or endanger the woman or any other person, rendered the dangerous dog designation improper. On the other hand, *Horvath* upheld a dangerous dog destruction order involving a Rottweiler who chased two young boys and a Pekingese, whom it killed after the children fled, the court presumably overruling the objection that the dog gave chase predominantly to the Pekingese (making the boys incidental targets).

Some statutes condition the prohibited type of chasing or approaching behavior with the words "when unprovoked." *Stanger* held that only a reasonable inference that a dog acted without provocation obviated proof by direct evidence that the dogs were not provoked to menace. Such decision implies that the burden of proof falls to the dog owner to prove provocation, not the government to disprove it. However, as described below, if lack of provocation is an essential element of the offense to be proved, then the government must prove a negative, relieving the dog owner of mustering evidence to show provocation as an affirmative defense.

6. Provocation

The provocation defense frequently applies to human victims, not animal victims. *See Wortham v. City of Chicago Dept. of Admin. Hearings*, 31 N.E.3d 915 (Ill. App. Ct. 2015) (ordinance defines provocation to apply only to human provocateurs). Traditionally, the provocation defense or exclusion excuses dogs who bite in response to taunting, teasing, tormenting — whether current or historical — by the bitee. Some define provocation to include only *intentional* acts, though one may *unintentionally* provoke a dog to bite by stepping on its tail or startling it from a deep sleep. And a few define provocation to immunize the acts of children of tender years, meaning that even if punched, mounted, or kicked, the dog must simply take it. Others provide no definition at all. Pay close attention to whether the term "provocation" or "unprovoked" is elemental, i.e., part of the definition of potentially dangerous or dangerous dog, and not an affirmative defense to the designation. The former makes it an element of the offense to be proved by the government by the proper standard, the latter a defense to be proved by the owner.

Virtually never will a dog avoid a dangerous label by claiming provocation in the case of a victim who suffers injuries or bites following third-party efforts to rescue the victim by striking or scaring the dog. *Giandalone v. Zepieri*, 86 Misc. 2d 79 (N.Y. J. Ct. 1976), found no provocation in throwing a chair to deter a 250-pound Great Dane trespassing and running toward the complainant's premises unrestrained, where many children, including a toddler, were present. Nor did it find washing a car with a pitchfork for protection provocation of the same dog who ran at the complainant and chased him inside his home. Similarly, *Town of Hempstead v. Lindsey*, 906 N.Y.S.2d 776 (Dist. Ct. 2009), found no provocation where three Rottweilers chased a man on top of his car while he washed it. It did not consider provocation from the perspective of the dog. Instead, it examined whether a rational person could assume that the man could anticipate his behavior would be regarded as violent, threatening, or tormenting to the subject dogs. *Brunotte* found no provocation where two men chased dogs from the scene of an attack with a chair and dowel because reasonable people might act similarly in responding to an unprovoked dog attack. It found meritless the dog owner's attempt to impute provocation to pre-attack conduct of the bite victim from the post-attack acts of third parties. In another roof-clambering case, the *Caldwell* court found no provocation where a woman struck the dog in defense of an apparent attack, whereupon the dog bit her foot and chased her on top of a car. Whether or not the first bite to her shoe (used to kick at the dog) caused injury, the court found that any physical injury — received after the victim takes defensive action — qualified so long as not initiated by "teasing, tormenting, abusing or assaulting."

Where victims suffer bites while trying to protect their animals, courts have found no provocation. *Koivisto v. Davis*, 745 N.W.2d 824 (Mich. 2008), reversed an order granting summary judgment to dog owners on the defense of provocation where she, in essence, suffered a bite while trying to extricate her cat from the maws of the invading dogs. Responding or reacting to a dog's vicious or aggressive behavior does not constitute provocation because the dog is already in a provoked state. In finding the defendants' logic was flawed, it hypothesized, "If plaintiff had responded aggressively to stop the dogs from attacking a sleeping baby in her care and the dogs turned their attack onto her, plaintiff would not have a claim under the dog-bite statute for her injuries. A potential claim under the statute for bite injuries to the baby would exist, but plaintiff would not have a claim because she 'provoked' the attacking dogs. This absurd result is certainly not the intent of the legislation." *Id.*, at 828–829. *State v. Taffet*, 2010 N.J. Super. Unpub. LEXIS 433 (Mar. 3, 2010) bore similar outcome in a case involving Rhodesian Ridgebacks attacking a Golden Retriever when the victim intervened and suffered bites. Trying to protect his dog to avoid serious injury was "neither unreasonable nor 'provocative' under any plausible definition of the term" and his action was "certainly not 'obvious[],' 'intentional provocation' found by the Law Division judge, who failed to buttress this conclusion with anything other than the subjective opinion, bereft of factual support in the record." Furthermore, the court refused to find the "mere act of looking at Rocky at eye level is unreasonable or sufficiently provocative, as anyone of a similar height to Rocky, with face level to the dog's would fall outside the protective shield" of state law.

Riehl affirmed a trial court's conclusion that a 12-year-old striking a dog several times with a pool stick constituted provocation. Yet *Pittman* found that a nine-year-old boy who poked sticks into the dog's kennel earlier that evening but later ran down the sidewalk, tripped, fell, and suffered a bite to his ankle, did not provoke the later chase and bite. *Downey*, in vacating a dangerous dog designation, found that the government could not possibly meet its burden of disproving provocation because "no one saw how the incident started." *McCoy v. Lucius*, 839 So. 2d 1050 (La. Ct. App. 2003), reversed a judgment awarding damages to plaintiffs whose dog suffered injury in a fight with defendants' two dogs, finding the evidence sufficient to establish that the plaintiff's dog provoked the defendants'. Though a civil damages case, *McCoy* interpreted the Louisiana code's phrase "the injured *person's* provocation of the dog" to find that provocation "may be imputed to animals as well as people[,]" and, specifically, that "A dog that aggressively charges another dog may provoke an aggressive response from the dog being charged, and that appears to be what occurred in this case." *Id.*, at 1055.

Use care in examining to which prohibited acts the provocation defense applies. In *Nelson v. City of St. Paul*, 2010 U.S. Dist. LEXIS 115024 (D. Minn. Oct. 28, 2010), the court affirmed a dangerous dog designation but reversed and remanded with respect to the destruction order where a dog twice bit an intoxicated or drugged woman who punched, slapped, beat, and mounted the dog. The court refused to read "without provocation" into an alternative "[b]itten one . . . or more persons on two . . . or more occasions" definition of dangerous animal because the legislature added "without provocation" with respect to two alternative definitions, but not the operative one.

Unintentional provocation has been argued as taking the form of reaching out one's hand intending to pet a dog. Viewing the evidence most favorably to the state following a conviction, *State v. Ruisi*, 9 Neb. App. 435, 443 (2000), found that precisely such activity did not constitute provocation. Case law in other jurisdictions embraces both intentional and unintentional acts as provocation, particularly in the context of personal injury to children of tender years. *See Toney v. Bouthillier*, 631 P.2d 557, 559–60 (Ariz. Ct. App. 1981) (three-year-old punching dog may constitute provocation, irrespective of intent to provoke); *Nelson v. Lewis*, 344 N.E.2d 268 (Ill. App. Ct. 1976) (provocation where 2.5-year-old accidentally stepped on dog's tail); *Nicholes v. Lorenz*, 237 N.W.2d 468 (Mich. 1976) (determination whether six-year-old inadvertently stepping on dog's tail constituted provocation was jury question); *Porter v. Allstate Ins. Co.*, 497 So. 2d 927 (Fla. Dist. Ct. App. 1986) (four-year-old provoked dog by pulling up on dog's ears). A party may also assume the risk of being bitten by approaching a dog without permission or introduction, and invading the dog's or dog guardian's personal space. Trespassing may also constitute provocation. In this regard, see *Stehl v. Dose*, 403 N.E.2d 1301 (Ill. App. Ct. 1980) (jury could regard crossing perimeter of dog's chain, entering protected territory and remaining while dog ate as provocation).

7. Property

Location matters, as some codes deem a dog dangerous if it "has killed a domestic animal without provocation while off the owner's property." What does "property" mean as so used, and would it extend to easements? Occasionally, the same code uses the word "premises," in the context of dangerous dog restraints like muzzling, leashing, and secure enclosure. Accordingly, "property" may encompass more physical space than "premises." "Like estates in land, [easements and profits] are property rights or interests." 17 Wash. Prac. § 2.1 (Nature of easements and profits); *Bakke v. Columbia Valley Lumber Co.*, 298 P.2d 849 (Wash. 1956). One jurisdiction defines "premises" to mean "all the real property under one ownership inside the inner line of a sidewalk or, if there is no sidewalk, inside of the curb, ditch, or shoulder marking the edge of the used public right-of-way. 'Premises' also means the inside of a closed motor vehicle." Where a dog has killed of "property," the use of the term "premises" could mean that a dog is dangerous if he kills outside the perimeter of the realty "under one ownership" up to the sidewalk or other marking of the edge of the used "public right-of-way." Property rights are not just restricted to ownership in fee simple but include licenses, permits, leases, and access agreements. In *dictum*, the *Downey* court held that an access easement holder likely would not grant the right to "reside" on that property, thereby rejecting the argument that a dog who killed another in an easement would not meet the definition of dangerous for having "inflict[ed] the injury . . . off the property where its owner resides." Where the exact location of the sidewalk vis-à-vis the parcel boundary is unknown, a survey may be warranted.

8. Kill

While the word "kill" does not need a definition, the government must prove that the dog proximately caused death. Without eyewitness evidence of a dog "killing" an animal by shaking or shredding, and a necropsy, would the mere fact that a dog held the animal in its mouth suffice? *In the Matter of the Disposition of Molly, a German Shorthaired Pointer Owned by William Frederick Klumpp, Jr.*, 712 N.W.2d 567, 572 (Minn. Ct. App. 2006), discussed the proximate cause argument with respect to the word "kill," holding that the circumstances must evidence that the attacked animal would inevitably have died despite medical intervention and that the attack was directly attributable to death. Molly, a German Shorthaired Pointer, ran to the neighbors' yard and grabbed Scooter, a six-pound dog, in her mouth, shaking back and forth to the point Scooter was taken to a veterinarian with severe head trauma, almost comatose, hemorrhaging from noise and mouth. Scooter's owners declined to stabilize and elected euthanasia. Finding the word "killed" unambiguous and having the plain meaning "to put to death" or "[t]o deprive of life," the court determined that Molly did not deprive Scooter of life. Scooter's owners did, by "preclud[ing] even basic medical treatment beginning with the attempt to stabilize Scooter's condition, as suggested by the veterinarian, and her possible recovery." To find Molly "killed" Scooter within meaning of statute, "record evidence must permit conclusions that death was the direct and inescapable consequence of the attack; that the attack rendered medical assistance futile; and that euthanasia merely hastened Scooter's inevitable, imminent death." The lack of fact or opinion evidence from a veterinarian or other witness supporting the claim of futility mandated reversal. Ruling 2-1, Judge Minge dissented, concluding that Molly killed Scooter notwithstanding the sparse record, finding adequate the testimony of Linda Mertensotto, Scooter's co-owner and a nurse, that Scooter suffered so badly that euthanasia was the most humane treatment, and that the veterinary chart notes described any non-euthanasia measures as heroic.

Practitioners should consult the veterinarian who treats an animal receiving mortal wounds and who is later euthanized. A statement, given on a more probable than not basis, that the animal would have died with or without treatment is not the same as stating that the animal had no chance of survival, or, was "all dead" as opposed to "mostly dead." Indeed, even a statement that the animal had a "very grave prognosis" is not consistent with an interpretation that the animal had no chance of survival. While an animal *might* have died even with aggressive treatment, the likelihood he would survive retains some probability. A less than 50 percent likelihood of survival, with treatment that may never have been authorized by the animal owner, is not at all the same as saying, on a more probable than not basis, that the animal was "killed."

9. Singular and Plural

During a birthday party in a public park, a Boxer runs and collides with a three-year-old, who sustains a two-centimeter laceration to his nasal bridge, which is later closed by a surgeon in two layers using 40 sutures. He also sustains a single puncture wound to his cheek. For this, the dog is declared dangerous and euthanized. The jurisdiction contends that the dog inflicted a "severe injury," defined by code as "any physical injury that results in broken bones or disfiguring lacerations requiring multiple sutures or cosmetic surgery." Is this result legally defensible? Without dispute, the child sustained one laceration "requiring multiple sutures or cosmetic surgery." But the code's plain language calls for two or more lacerations, each requiring two or more sutures or cosmetic surgery. Although other tribunals had held otherwise, per the *Jarrett* example above, the court hearing this matter concluded that the word "lacerations" was interchangeable with "laceration," affirming the designation of dangerous, citing to a rule of statutory construction contained within the first chapter of the code, and which stated:

> Words importing the singular number may also be applied to the plural of persons and things; words importing the plural may be applied to the singular; and words importing the masculine gender may be extended to females also.

It did so despite the code stating that "severe injury" is one that "results in . . . lacerations[.]" Consider the following treatises on singularization of plural terms:

> Where such a construction is needed to give effect to the legislative intent, courts construe plural words to include the singular and apply singular words to the plural of persons and things, unless it is otherwise specially provided or unless there is something in the subject or context repugnant to such construction. Such a rule is applied, however, only when it is needed in order to carry out the obvious intent of the legislature, in that the legislature's affirmative use of the singular form is not insignificant.

C.J.S. *Statutes* § 441.

> The principle does not require that singular and plural word forms have interchangeable effect, and discrete applications are favored except where the contrary intent or reasonable understanding is affirmatively indicated.

> Issues over singular or plural interpretations often arise in the form of disputes about whether the article "a" restricts the application of the term which it modifies to single objects or subjects. The usual presumption in favor of the natural application appears to be reversed in such cases. It is most often ruled that a term introduced by "a" or "an" applies to multiple subjects or objects unless there is reason to find that singular application was intended or is reasonably understood.

24 SUTHERLAND STATUTORY CONSTRUCTION 47:34 (7th ed.) Even Circuit-level cases have restricted the singularization of plural terms only where necessary to carry out the evident intent of a statute. Arguably, the Legislature's use of the adjective "severe" denotes a distinction between a lesser and worse injury. The singularization of terms undermines that intention by making a nonsevere injury into a severe one.

10. Pack Dynamics

Few jurisdictions add a guilt-by-association clause to their definition of dangerous dog, such as, "If two or more dogs jointly engage in any conduct described in this subsection, then regardless of the degree of participation by the individual dog(s), all such dogs shall be deemed dangerous dogs." Such a provision overcomes the objection that the government cannot prove *which* dog inflicted the bite, caused severe injury, or killed. It appears to codify the theory of liability known as "concerted action." *Martin v. Abbott Laboratories*, 689 P.2d 368, 377 (Wash. 1984). But it invites clearly unfair outcomes when applied to dogs.

For instance, what if three dogs running down the street unattended encounter a stray cat? One dog stands a few feet away barking aggressively. Another dog tries to bite but cannot reach him because the third dog has grabbed the cat in a death throttle. Under the above code, all three dogs would be declared dangerous. In essence, this law allows a dog to be declared dangerous for *attempted* bites and injuries, merely spectating, or, at best, serving as an accomplice. In the dog context, the analogies break down unless one resorts to anthropomorphism. Do dogs "conspire"? Do they have a "common design"? How does one assess "substantial assistance or encouragement" in accomplishing the result? Consider the case of *Foster v. Carter*, 742 P.2d 1257 (Wash. Ct. App. 1987), involving a group of boys engaging in a BB-gun battle, when one got shot in the eye. The plaintiff sued all the boys, asserting joint liability due to concerted action, yet the court found insufficient evidence that the defendants engaged in concerted action directed at the plaintiff. How, then, is a court to assess the common mind of numerous dogs? A code as described above dispenses with such questions by simply proscribing any degree of participation.

11. Cause of Injury

Where the statute or ordinance requires a dog owner "to suffer or permit" a dog to bite a domestic animal, one court held that the government must prove the owner engaged in some affirmative act or omission. *Akron v. Meissner*, 633 N.E.2d 1201 (Ohio Ct. App. 1993). Another court interpreted the word "suffer" to mean "permit" and "permit" to require consent or knowledge (actual or constructive) of the specific proscribed propensities of the dog in question. *Harris v. Turner*, 466 P.2d 202 (Wash. Ct. App. 1970). Such statutory language requires the government to show negligence on behalf of the owner in order to prevail.

City of Bexley v. Selcer, 716 N.E.2d 1220 (Ohio Ct. App. 1998) vacated the conviction of a defendant found guilty of a leash law crime when a malfunctioning Invisible Fence resulted in her dog being videotaped off-premises by an officious neighbor. At trial, the city claimed the ordinance required "no culpable mental state" and imposed strict liability. Alternatively, noting that the defendant was aware her dog left her property on a prior occasion, the city claimed she acted recklessly. The trial court found her guilty of "permit[ting her dog] to go beyond the premises" without a leash because she "knew there was a risk [the invisible fence] might fail" based on the "prior failure." Selcer argued that the court improperly applied strict liability to the ordinance, and that she was not indifferent to any alleged risk. Agreeing that the leash law crime did not impose strict liability and deeming the evidence insufficient to prove recklessness, the Court of Appeals reversed. As to whether the ordinance stated a strict liability offense, in specifically evaluating the meaning of the phrase "to permit," it stated:

> The word "permit" is defined as "[t]o suffer, allow, consent, let; to give leave or license; to acquiesce, by failure to prevent, or to expressly assent or agree to the doing of an act." Black's Law Dictionary (5 Ed. Rev. 1979) 1026. Other Ohio courts have held that this definition "connote[s] some affirmative act or omission." *Akron v. Meissner* (1993), 92 Ohio App. 3d 1, 4, 633 N.E.2d 1201, 1203.

Id., at 1223. Reading the term "permit" in conjunction with "at large" conduct, the court ruled that the city must prove the owner "'permitted' the dog to go beyond the premises of the owner, i.e., by an intentional or negligent act." As Selcer had not "acquiesced in the dog's leaving the premises[,]" she had no guilt in the matter.

Alvarez v. Ketchikan Gateway Borough, 91 P.3d 289 (Alaska Ct. App. 2004), reached a similar result, rejecting the Borough's argument that leash law violations were strict liability offenses, agreeing with the defendant that:

> The verbs 'permit' and 'allow' are commonly understood to imply some volition on the part of the actor. And other jurisdictions having similar laws-laws providing that the owner of an animal shall not 'permit,' 'allow' or 'suffer' the animal to run at-large-require proof of at least negligence.

Id., at 291–92.

12.   Willful Trespass, Crime, or Other Tort

Certain dangerous dog statutes excuse dogs from the dangerous designation when the injured party commits willful trespass on the dog owner's premises, attempts to commit or committed a crime thereon, or is liable for some other tort. For instance, Washington's Dangerous Dog law provides:

> "Dogs shall not be declared dangerous if the threat, injury, or damage was sustained by a person who, at the time, was committing a willful trespass or other tort upon the premises occupied by the owner of the dog, or was tormenting, abusing, or assaulting the dog or has, in the past, been observed or reported to have tormented, abused, or assaulted the dog or was committing or attempting to commit a crime."

RCW § 16.08.090(3).

Though not using the word "trespass" explicitly, many dangerous dog codes distinguish between private and public property, or use the phrase "while the dog is off the owner's property" to geographically delineate the righteousness of biting, killing, or chasing. For instance, if a dog chases or approaches a person in a menacing fashion or apparent attitude of attack elsewhere than "upon the streets, sidewalks, or any public grounds," such as private property, the misconduct will not deem the dog potentially dangerous. RCW § 16.08.070(1)(b). Nor would killing a domestic animal who has strayed into territory where the owner lives. RCW § 16.08.070(2)(b). *Norton v. Howell*, 2009 Cal. App. Unpub. LEXIS 1325, at *3 fn.1 (Feb. 19, 2009), dodged the issue of trespass in a potentially dangerous animal case where the victim dog urinated on bushes planted on the property of the aggressing dog owner, stating, "We respectfully decline to address the issue of whether dogs (or cats, or any other pet) can be found legally guilty of 'trespassing'." However, *Gomez v. Broward Cy. Animal Care & Regulation Div.*, Broward Cy. Cir. Ct. Case COCE 09-15757 (51), at *7 (Aug. 31, 2010), dismissed a dangerous dog declaration and disposal order on the basis of trespass by an exterminator who entered the backyard without express or implied permission when bitten. In reversing, the court stated, "Since there is no evidence that the exterminator was given permission, either expressed (sic) or implied, to deliberately open the gate and enter the fenced yard (where Zeus was put at his request), the record reflects that the exterminator was trespassing at the time and place when the incident occurred."[5] The conflation of provocation with trespass also received treatment in *McCoy*, noting that trespass by a dog, Jody, "tends to corroborate Mrs. Lucius' testimony that Jody provoked the incident by charging her two dogs on their territory," even while "the fact that Jody was on the Luciuses' property is irrelevant to this portion of the inquiry." *McCoy*, at 1055 fn.2.

The phrase "other tort" at first blush appears to include all shades of culpability from simple or comparative negligence to malicious injury, though the word "other" relates back to articulated defenses such as provocation, criminal activity, and willful trespass. *McCarthy v. Daunis*, 167 A. 918 (Conn. 1933), affirmed judgment for the plaintiff, who suffered injury by defendant's dog when freeing his small dog from a fence between both parties' premises. It interpreted "committing a trespass or other tort," as used in the statute, to excuse the owner from liability for a dog bite, by construing it as "confined to trespasses or torts committed upon the person or property of the owner or keeper or his family, which the dog would instinctively defend and protect, other torts of like nature, and torts against the dog itself of a nature calculated to incite it to defensive action by use of its natural weapons of defense." It then expressly rejected that contributory negligence would trigger an exception to fault.

M. DECLARATORY AND INJUNCTIVE RELIEF

Litigants seek injunctions with varying effect in dangerous dog classification cases, most commonly to stave off euthanasia or compel release of the dog pending resolution. *Folkers v. City of Waterloo*, 2007 U.S. Dist. LEXIS 84214 (N.D. Iowa

---

[5] While the court believed that the "exterminator's sudden entry into the family's private backyard wearing a mask and gloves, carrying a large hose, metal wand, and deadly chemicals, provoked Zeus," having applied the "ordinary usage and meaning of the word 'provoked'," the court felt constrained by the ordinance's more restrictive definition of provocation, which did not permit consideration of provocation from the point of view of the reasonable dog. *Id.*, at *4.

Nov. 14, 2007); *Rabon v. City of Seattle*, 957 P.2d 621 (Wash. 1998); *County of Pasco v. Riehl*, 635 So. 2d 17 (Fla. 1994). They often couple the action with a demand for declaratory relief by challenging some aspect of a dangerous dog statute or ordinance. When doing so, consult the state's declaratory judgment act, which may require notification to the attorney general whenever a municipal or state law faces constitutional attack.

Hypothetical: The City of Francophilly, in the County of Xenophobia, State of Nebraska, a town of 1,500 citizens, 95% of whom are French émigrés with dual citizenship (France, America), has passed a new dog law, Ch. 17.89 FMC, as follows:

§ 17.89.010:

WEIGHT RESTRICTION: No dogs over 22 pounds are permitted in city limits, PROVIDED THAT French Bulldogs and dogs commonly known as French Poodles over 22 pounds are exempt from this provision.

§ 17.89.020:

NUMERIC RESTRICTION: Each household may only keep 1 dog, regardless of lot area or zoning; EXCEPT THAT one may keep as many as 10 French Bulldogs.

§ 17.89.030:

POTENTIALLY DANGEROUS DOGS — DEFINED:

    (A) Dogs may be declared potentially dangerous if they, without provocation:

        (1) urinate or defecate on the private property of a person of French descent without permission by that person;

        (2) bite a domestic animal or human being causing injury, regardless of whether sutures are required or indicated;

        (3) approach a person in a menacing fashion or apparent attitude of attack; or

        (4) fail to respond with reasonable promptness to the following doggie commands (e.g., "Reposez-vous" (sit), "Sejour" (stay), "Venez" (come), "Roulement plus de" (roll over), and "Jeu mort" (play dead)) given in French by the Francophilly Mayor.

    (B) There is no requirement for keeping a potentially dangerous dog in the city.

§ 17.89.040:

DANGEROUS DOGS — DEFINED:

Dogs may be declared dangerous if they, with or without provocation:

(1) take, bury, or consume a single French fry, Croissant, or piece of French Toast without permission of the person preparing, serving, selling, or eating such an item PROVIDED THAT French Bull-dogs are exempt from this provision AND any person who refuses such breed its take of these items shall be guilty of a misdemeanor;

(2) kill a domestic animal or human, PROVIDED THAT dogs killing German Shepherds or Rottweilers or Doberman Pinschers shall not be declared dangerous in any circumstance;

(3) have been previously declared potentially dangerous, who then:

   (a) approach a person in a menacing fashion or apparent attitude of attack;

   (b) are unleashed on public property and not under the owner's control; or

   (c) shed more than one clump of hair on a person who is neither the owner, keeper, nor caretaker of the dog; OR

(4) weigh over 22 pounds in violation of FMC 17.89.010.

§ 17.89.050:

DANGEROUS DOGS — REQUIREMENTS:

(A) Dangerous dogs may only be kept in the city if:

   (1) they are neutered or spayed within 48 hours of being so declared;

   (2) the owner maintains a surety bond or insurance no less than one million dollars to cover injuries sustained by the danger-ous dog;

   (3) the dog is renamed with a "prenoms Francais" (i.e., French first name, e.g., "Antoine" instead of Anthony or "Victoire" instead of Victoria); AND

   (4) the dog owner bequeaths his dog to former French President Nicolas Sarkozy or Sarkozy's agent.

(B) If the dog owner does not comply with the conditions listed in FMC 17.89.050(A) within 48 hours of being declared dangerous, the dog shall be seized and immediately euthanized in a humane fashion PROVIDED THAT English Bulldogs and Cocker Spaniels shall be killed by guillotine in the public square. If an owner appeals as provided by FMC 17.89.060(A) below, the requirements for keeping a dangerous dog, and the penalty of death for not complying, will be stayed pending the appeal outcome.

§ 17.89.060:

DANGEROUS DOGS — APPEAL:

(A) The owner of a dangerous dog shall receive a notice providing rights of appeal at the time the dog is declared dangerous. The owner shall waive all right to appeal if she does not do the following within 24 hours of notice, regardless of whether the next day is a holiday or weekend:

(1) In writing, deliver to the Mayor a Notice of Appeal explaining the substance of the challenge to the designation and the relief requested;

(2) Pre-pay 180 days of boarding the dangerous dog at an expense of $15 a day (or $2,700); AND

(3) Provide proof of dual American-French citizenship.

(B) A hearing to contest the dangerous dog designation shall be scheduled within 90 days of the notice of appeal being filed. Presiding shall be local resident Captain Jean-Luc Picard. Picard will:

(1) apply court rules of evidence strictly;

(2) permit cross-examination of all witnesses; AND

(3) allow the dog owner to subpoena witnesses and documents only after a showing has been made to Picard that the witness and document is material and the examination is not over-broad in scope.

(C) At the hearing, the burden of proof will be on Francophilly Animal Control to prove that the dog in question is dangerous as defined, under the following standards of proof:

(1) For French Bulldogs, beyond a reasonable doubt.

(2) For French Poodles, as commonly known, by clear and convincing evidence.

(3) For German Shepherds, Rottweilers, English Bulldogs, and Cocker Spaniels, by a scintilla.

(4) For all other breeds, by a preponderance of the evidence.

You represent Mr. Colm Meaney, a 28-year-old, Irish-American soybean farmer living in unincorporated Xenophobia County. Meaney owns a hybrid or "designer" dog named "Sweet William La Paz" (a.k.a. Bill) a 10-year-old, intact male "Franglais Bulldog" — part French Bulldog and part English Bulldog. Bill also suffers from a herniated disc causing him to lose control of his bladder. Meaney intends to breed Bill before he dies.

Meaney lives on the city-county line and enters Francophilly City Limits each day when he walks Bill. On April 1, 2006, Meaney was walking Bill in Francophilly City Limits when, due to his incontinence, Bill relieved himself on the edge of Marie Antoinette's lawn. Ms. Antoinette is of French descent and dislikes Meaney for the reason that he has allowed dog breed miscegenation and tainted the noble French Bulldog lineage. Antoinette reports Meaney to animal control, who declares Bill a potentially dangerous dog. At that time, Bill weighed 21 pounds.

On July 25, 2008, Meaney drove Bill into Francophilly to sell soybeans at the Saturday Farmer's market. Twenty yards away was "Claire's Cruisin' Croissants," an immensely popular vendor selling all varieties of French fare, including, predictably, croissants. While distracted by customers, Meaney did not notice that Bill had trotted over to Claire's and proceeded to eat an entire bag of day-old croissants. The bag was leaning against the Claire's trailer about 10 feet from the cash register. Claire caught Bill in the act and notified animal control.

Bill Declared Dangerous: Animal control weighed Bill on their portable scale at 23 pounds. They declared him dangerous under FMC § 17.89.040(1), (3)(b), (4) and impounded Bill at the scene. After he relieved himself at Francophilly Animal Control, Bill weighed exactly 22 pounds.

Meaney received the notice of dangerous dog on Saturday, July 26, 2008. He tried to file his notice of appeal on Sunday, July 27, 2008, but the Mayor's Office was closed, so he delivered it on Monday, July 28, 2008. With the notice of appeal, he tendered a check for $450, all he could afford for pre-paid impound fees.

Because he filed the appeal after 24 hours, however, Francophilly Animal Control refused to process Meaney's appeal. They also noted that he was not of dual citizenship, as required by FMC § 17.89.060(A)(3).

Meaney wants you to save Bill's life by obtaining an order to halt the execution and permission to wage the appeal. The Francophilly City Attorney blithely remarks that even if you get the execution stayed pending an appeal and Meaney is entitled to a hearing, all animal control has to do under FMC § 17.89.060(C)(3) is to prove their case by a scintilla of the evidence.

Bill will be guillotined at noon tomorrow, Friday, August 1, 2008 — unless you can convince the Xenophobia County Superior Court judge that serious errors of law exist.

(1) TRUE OR FALSE: The lack of an appeal procedure (*see* FMC §§ 17.89.030(B), 17.89.060) for a dog declared potentially dangerous is unconstitutional.

Answer: Arguably true, because a potentially dangerous dog is one step closer to being deemed dangerous. Failure to provide an opportunity to be heard to challenge the predicate designation will prejudice the dog and owner by depriving them of the chance to contest the underlying event that gave rise to the potentially dangerous dog declaration. *But see Sawh v. City of Lino Lakes*, 823 N.W.2d 627 (Minn. 2012) (designation of dog as potentially dangerous did not subject owner to deprivation of constitutionally protected property interest, obviating the need for appeal hearing).

(2) Assume you succeed in convincing the court to grant Meaney's motion to process his appeal, and a hearing is scheduled. Identify each fact you would use at the hearing to defeat the assertion that Bill is dangerous, and then briefly explain how you would apply the law to that fact. [You are not being asked to invoke constitutional challenges in this question, but to assume that Ch. 17.89 FMC is otherwise legal and enforceable as written. You are only asked to examine the legal issue of dangerousness, not conditions for keeping a dangerous dog, or penalties for failing to comply with those requirements. Do your best to argue your case within the framework of the municipal code. Relying on an appellate court to help you win on a procedural technicality is dicey, as you cannot always guarantee the safety of

the animal or the infiniteness of client's funds while the appeal is pending.]

Answer: Various arguments may include that Bill is part "French Bulldog" and thereby excused from the Croissant transgression based on implied permission; that he did not menacingly approach, go unleashed, or shed hair in violation of FMC § 17.89.040; that the croissant he consumed was not being prepared, served, eaten, or sold; that he rarely enters city limits; that he urinated accidentally (not intentionally) due to a herniated disc or other neurological disorder, or was engaging in an natural act not abnormal to his species; that he urinated at the edge of the yard, which may have been on public property; that Mr. Meaney may not have known that Antoinette was of French descent; that Bill's weight oscillated with each bowel movement, and that the scale may not have been properly calibrated, rendering the results inadmissible.

(3) Assume that Picard upholds Francophilly Animal Control's order declaring Bill dangerous. Meaney chooses to try to comply with the restrictions but wants you to eliminate or mitigate as many of them as possible. What arguments (both factual and legal) might you make to challenge the restrictions imposed by FMC § 17.89.050(A)?

Answer: The city has no extraterritorial jurisdiction; insufficient time has been given to perform the neuter, which may jeopardize his life due to medical conditions, and the neuter lacks a rational relationship to dangerousness; the bond is excessive and violates substantive due process; the renaming requirement interferes with the autonomous decisionmaking and perhaps the privacy rights of the owner, may implicate the First Amendment, may cause injury to an animal whose prior name has become ingrained and he will not respond to the new name in moments where immediate recall is required; the bequeathing requirement may violate public policy, substantive due process, and constitute an unlawful taking.

(4) Assume that Bill is declared dangerous and Meaney cannot comply with the restrictions for keeping a dangerous dog. Explain how the facts at bar affect Meaney's ability and chances to plead for an alternative disposition to death by guillotine.

Answer: Bill is part Frenchie so the euthanasia provision does not apply; breed-discriminatory legislation of this irreversible nature may violate substantive due process and equal protection; banishment may prove to be the more suitable alternative given that Bill does not reside in city limits.

(5) Assume Bill is "acquitted" and a declaratory judgment is entered that Bill is a full-blooded (or honorary) French Bulldog. He is renamed Guillaume and outfitted with a suitable French uniform that proudly displays the name "Gendarme." Commissioned as an honorary member of the Francophilly K-9 police dog force, one day he encounters an aged German Shepherd named Zeus. Due to unexpected circumstances, he manages to inflict a lethal bite on this dog. The Shepherd's owner-guardian, Friedrich von Leitz, wants to sue for Zeus's death. May Leitz sue the City of Francophilly based on FMC § 17.89.040(2)? How?

Answer: FMC 17.89.040 does not address civil liability. If anything, it demonstrates a strong municipal policy in favor of German Shepherd slayings by French

Bulldogs and may serve as an affirmative, albeit unsuccessful, defense to any such litigation.

(6) You represent Wilton Chamberlin, a citizen and property owner of Francophilly who has kept his Cocker Spaniels in hiding for fear of impound and guillotine per FMC § 17.89.050(B). Would he have standing to challenge this provision? Explain.

Answer: Mr. Chamberlin would likely have standing as a taxpayer and owner of canines subject to the Francophilly dog code, even though his Cocker Spaniels are not at risk of guillotining if they are not deemed dangerous, which is negligible given that they will likely not exceed 22 pounds, and will not have the opportunity to run at large or shed on objecting strangers if holed up in his residence.

Chapter 5

SECTION 1983[1]

Animal-related litigation against government officials and private parties acting under color of state law owes a debt to the Civil Rights Act of 1871, 42 U.S.C. § 1983. After the American Civil War, Congress enacted 42 U.S.C. § 1983 to furnish a civil remedy for emancipated African-Americans suffering at the hands of publicly installed officials who still served as rank-and-file Ku Klux Klan members. In the last 140 years, litigants have applied § 1983 to those inflicting harm of constitutional magnitude on animals and their owners. Section 1983 provides:

> Every person who under color of any statute, ordinance, regulation, custom, or usage, of any State or Territory or the District of Columbia, subjects, or causes to be subjected, any citizen of the United States or other person within the jurisdiction thereof to the deprivation of any rights, privileges, or immunities secured by the Constitution and laws, shall be liable to the party injured in an action at law, Suit in equity, or other proper proceeding for redress, except that in any action brought against a judicial officer for an act or omission taken in such officer's judicial capacity, injunctive relief shall not be granted unless a declaratory decree was violated or declaratory relief was unavailable. For the purposes of this section, any Act of Congress applicable exclusively to the District of Columbia shall be considered to be a statute of the District of Columbia.

Not until 90 years after passage did § 1983 arise from dormancy to enjoy revitalization and serious jurisprudential treatment, commencing with the disturbing treatment of the Monroe family. Police officers conducted a warrantless raid of the Monroe household, forcing the parents to stand naked in the living room while officers ransacked the house searching for evidence related to a two-day-old murder case, and then detained and held them at the police station for interrogation without the right to counsel. They were eventually released and never charged. *Monroe v. Pape*, 365 U.S. 167 (1961) (overruled by *Monell v. Department of Social Services of City of New York*, 436 U.S. 658 (1978)), held that actions of any state actor at any level of state or local government fulfill the "state action" language of § 1983, the court reversing dismissal of the complaint against the officers for violating their civil rights. However, the Supreme Court affirmed dismissal of the city, finding that Congress did not intend the word "person" to apply to municipalities. In 1978, the Supreme Court retreated from this holding of *Monroe* in *Monell*, holding the municipality liable if the official committed the violation pursuant to a policy or

---

[1] Portions of this chapter were taken from, and with permission of, the Thomson Reuters publication, Adam P. Karp, *Cause of Action Under 42 U.S.C.A. § 1983 for Death of or Injury to Animal*, 48 Causes of Action 2d 527 (2011).

custom of local government. In so holding, it did not establish *respondeat superior* liability.

Virtually all animal-related § 1983 suits piggyback the federal Constitution, though § 1983 creates a federal cause of action arising from violation of federally protected statutory, as well as constitutional, rights. Significantly for the animal law practitioner, a liberal construction applies to § 1983. *Dennis v. Higgins*, 498 U.S. 439, 443 (1991).

A. FOURTH AMENDMENT CLAIMS

As corporeal, animate property who can be detained, withheld, moved, transferred, sold, given, injured, or killed, most animal-based § 1983 cases assert a Fourth Amendment violation of *unreasonable seizure*. A concomitant Fourth Amendment *unreasonable search* claim tends to join it because mishandled animals often live, are kept, or are harbored, in areas protected by expectations of privacy. Thus, state actors may conduct a Fourth Amendment search prior to entering the curtilage or residence from which they then perform a Fourth Amendment seizure of the animal. The three essential elements of a § 1983 Fourth Amendment cause of action are (1) an act under color of law, (2) that constitutes a "search" or "seizure," and (3) is objectively unreasonable. *Brower v. County of Inyo*, 489 U.S. 593, 599 (1989). The Fourth Amendment ensures security in one's person, home, papers, and effects:

> The right of the people to be secure in their persons, houses, papers, and effects, against unreasonable searches and seizures, shall not be violated, and no Warrants shall issue, but upon probable cause, supported by Oath or affirmation, and particularly describing the place to be searched, and the persons or things to be seized.

U.S. Const. Amend. IV.

A Fourth Amendment "search" occurs whenever local or state officials intrude upon a person's reasonable expectation of privacy. Courts treat *de minimis* intrusions, even if technically violative, as "reasonable," negating § 1983 liability. *Katz v. U.S.*, 389 U.S. 347 (1967). As noted above, a "search" frequently presages the "seizure." The two most reported instances of Fourth Amendment animal-based seizures concern law enforcement officers' use of lethal force against dogs, so prevalent and geographically uniform as to produce its own body of § 1983 case law, and cruelty raids. In every circuit faced with the legal question, killing a dog is clearly established to be a Fourth Amendment seizure of property:

> "The destruction of property is 'meaningful interference' constituting a seizure under the Fourth Amendment . . . ." *Fuller I*, 36 F.3d at 68 (*citing U.S. v. Jacobsen*, 466 U.S. 109, 124–125, 104 S. Ct. 1652, 80 L. Ed. 2d 85 (1984)). Shooting and killing a dog clearly constitutes "destruction" of that dog. In 1991 it was apparent in light of preexisting law that shooting and killing a dog constituted a seizure within the meaning of the Fourth Amendment.

Fuller v. Vines, 117 F.3d 1425 (9th Cir. 1997); *see also Maldonado v. Fontanes*, 568 F.3d 263 (1st Cir. 2009) (government raid of public housing to seize dogs and cats and kill them without the person's consent is a "seizure" within the meaning of the Fourth Amendment); *Brown v. Muhlenberg Tp.*, 269 F.3d 205 (3d Cir. 2001) (shooting of Immi, a Rottweiler, was a seizure); *Altman v. City of High Point, N.C.*, 330 F.3d 194, 206 (4th Cir. 2003) (dogs are effects and their destruction triggers a seizure); *Viilo v. Eyre*, 547 F.3d 707 (7th Cir. 2008); *Lesher v. Reed*, 12 F.3d 148 (8th Cir. 1994).

To prove an actionable claim under § 1983, however, requires proof that the seizure was unreasonable, as discussed in the slaying of Bubba in Wisconsin. Virginia Viilo sued the City of Milwaukee and two police officers for the shooting death of her dog, a seven-year-old Labrador Retriever/Springer Spaniel mix. The evidence painted an unsympathetic picture of the defendants, strongly depicting them as executioners of a dog who presented no credible threat while responding to an anonymous tip that a wanted felon had entered Viilo's home with a pit bull. As officers surrounded the house, Bubba ran from the backyard — where he was relaxing with Viilo and her family — toward the front yard when Officer Carter shot him twice with a shotgun. Bubba hid under the bushes for nearly 10 minutes, bleeding, while officers prevented Viilo and others from rendering aid or rushing him to a veterinarian. Sergeant Eyre then approached the bushes, causing Bubba to exit toward the backyard. Ignoring the pleas of the crowd, Eyre ordered Carter to shoot twice more, killing Bubba. *Viilo v. Eyre*, 547 F.3d 707 (7th Cir. 2008). The defendants appealed the district court's denial of qualified immunity for the Fourth Amendment seizure (i.e., killing Bubba). Though the Circuit Court concluded it lacked jurisdiction, it nonetheless found the use of deadly force against Bubba avoidable, as he posed no immediate danger. In *dictum*, the appellate panel held that had it reached the merits of the appeal, "there would be a strong case for affirm[ance]."

The Fourth Amendment does not necessarily require that "seizures" be fatal. Instead, it examines the degree of "meaningful interference" with a person's "effects" (or animal companions). *See McCarthy v. Kootenai County*, 2009 U.S. Dist. LEXIS 105439 (D. Idaho Nov. 12, 2009) (rejecting defendants' argument that merely injuring or maiming a dog does not constitute a seizure, noting the reduction in value and significant alteration of plaintiff's possessory interest). Thus, withholding possession, euthanizing, throwing from a bridge, hanging, or permanently dispossessing (e.g., by adopting or selling to a third party) likely qualify as Fourth Amendment seizures. Further, acts of omission as well as commission raise Fourth Amendment concerns, such as where death results from deprivation of sufficient food, water, ventilation, temperature control, and medical attention. *Beckerman v. Susquehanna Tp. Police and Admin.*, 2007 U.S. App. LEXIS 26746 (3d Cir. Nov. 19, 2007), presents an example of insufficient, or meaningless, interference, where a police officer told Beckerman that he might walk his dog on back trails around his home instead of within town limits to avoid future conflict. This statement alone did not constitute a Fourth Amendment seizure as a restriction on movement.

Only those with ownership or possessory rights in the animal may assert a Fourth Amendment seizure claim. For instance, after a police dog bit a small child, officers went to the K-9 officer's home to remove and kill his canine partner. James

Lesher expressed his desire to reclaim the dog he donated to the department pursuant to an agreement to reclaim if the dog became unsuitable for police work. Threatened with termination, he relinquished custody of the dog, but sued for a Fourth Amendment violation. The Eighth Circuit found a violation, but appeared to base this on the deprivation of Lesher's livelihood by terminating his employment if he refused to surrender his canine partner. Public employees cannot be forced to relinquish constitutional rights under such threat, the court noting that who owned the dog then in Lesher's possession mattered not. However, "If James [Lesher] were not an LRPD employee, the dog would obviously have been 'seized' within the meaning of the Fourth Amendment," a course of events it found to be presumptively unreasonable. *Lesher v. Reed*, 12 F.3d 148, 151 (8th Cir. 1994). Of further interest is the related First Amendment § 1983 claim alleged after the department transferred Lesher from the canine squad after protesting the decision to kill the dog.

A colorable property interest in the animal "seized" remains a *sine qua non*. In *Wagner v. Waitlevertch*, 774 A.2d 1247 (Pa. Super. Ct. 2001), the government charged a rancher with theft and trespass after cattle rustling. Police then seized ten bovines by warrant. Though charges for theft were later dropped, Wagner claimed violations of his Fourth and Fourteenth Amendment rights, including malicious prosecution. However, because Wagner did not unambiguously state the cattle he took were, in fact, his, the court found no Fourth Amendment liability. Property interests include non-ownership possessory rights, as determined in *Agazio v. Commercity City, Colo.*, No. 10-cv-01895-RPM (D. Colo., 2012) (Judge Richard P. Matsch holding that minor child can sue for violation of her constitutional rights based on possessory interest in family dog, even though not owner).

Even class action-type § 1983 cases require a verifiable property interest by at least one of the plaintiffs. Though acknowledging that cats, like dogs, are "effects" under the Fourth Amendment, the seizure claim failed in *Akron ex rel. Christman-Resch v. Akron*, 825 N.E.2d 189 (Ohio Ct. App. 2005). In the summer of 2002, the City of Akron criminalized the act of permitting a cat to run at large. It also allowed the animal warden to seize and impound such cats. In practice, however, animal control officers issued humane traps to civilians who lodged complaints about cats roaming at large. Only cats trapped by these civilians were impounded; officers did not routinely sweep the neighborhoods for roaming felines. In August 2004, several residents filed suit, seeking a judgment declaring the law unconstitutional and seeking money related to seizures of cats since 2002. With support from Alley Cat Allies, the appellants challenged the ordinance as violating several constitutional protections, including substantive and procedural due process, equal protection, Fourth Amendment searches and seizures, as well as on the basis that the law improperly delegated police authority to private citizens as cat trappers. The old "trap and kill" versus "spay/neuter-return (SNR)" debate on how best to handle feral cat colonies thus became a subject of litigation before the Summit County Court of Common Pleas, which dismissed the complaint. The cat owners appealed. Without evidence that officers were trespassing on cat owners' properties to seize free-roaming cats, the court affirmed dismissal, finding appellants' arguments meritless.

A person possessing stolen animals may, surprisingly, assert a Fourth Amendment claim, according to *Stanko v. Mahar*, 419 F.3d 1107 (10th Cir. 2005). After refusing to produce proof of ownership of five cattle, a state brand inspector conducted a warrantless search of Stanko's property, seizing two cow/calf pairs and one yearling, then transporting them to the livestock exchange for sale. The court applied Wyoming law to justify treating the cattle as estrays because Stanko failed to provide sufficient evidence of ownership on inspection and because he expressed an intention to move them across county lines. The court also recognized the "urgent state interest of preventing trafficking in lost or stolen cattle." *See U.S. v. Biswell*, 406 U.S. 311, 317 (1972) (authorizing warrantless regulatory searches). Though unable to substantiate ownership, Stanko had just enough of a possessory claim to enjoy due process protections prior to seizure and sale. *See Wolfenbarger v. Williams*, 774 F.2d 358, 362 (10th Cir. 1985) (pawnbroker had interest in stolen property adequate to warrant due process protection). Those predeprivation and postdeprivation processes, however, were deemed appropriate to protect Stanko from erroneous deprivation after properly balancing the private and government interests. *Cf., Bowden v. Davis*, 289 P.2d 1100 (Or. 1955) (*en banc*) (declaring unconstitutional statute giving owner of horse found on public lands two days to pay roundup charge or see animal abandoned and forfeited to state).

B.   ACT UNDER COLOR OF LAW

Generally speaking, private individuals do not act under color of state law. *Gomez v. Toledo*, 446 U.S. 635, 640 (1980). Purely private conduct, no matter how egregious, does not fall within § 1983. *Ouzts v. Maryland Nat. Ins. Co.*, 505 F.2d 547, 559 (9th Cir. 1974). While the vast majority of § 1983 defendants work for state or local government, willful participants joining in action with the state or its agents, including private persons, act "under color of" state law. *Dennis v. Sparks*, 449 U.S. 24, 27–28 (1980). Four different tests determine whether private individuals are, in essence, deputized as state actors: (1) public function, (2) joint action, (3) governmental compulsion or coercion, and (4) governmental nexus. *Sutton v. Providence St. Joseph Medical Center*, 192 F.3d 826, 835–36 (9th Cir. 1999). Private conduct carries a presumption against government action. "Something more" must be present. *Id.*, at 838. Satisfying any one test meets the "state action" element, provided no countervailing factor exists. *Kirtley v. Rainey*, 326 F.3d 1088, 1092 (9th Cir. 2003). Should the plaintiff nonetheless prove application of any of these four tests, the "finding of state action 'may be outweighed in the name of some value at odds with finding public accountability in the circumstances.' " *Id.*, at 1095 (*quoting Brentwood Academy v. Tennessee Secondary School Athletic Ass'n*, 531 U.S. 288, 303 (2001)).

"Under the public function test, when private individuals or groups are endowed by the State with powers or functions governmental in nature, they become agencies or instrumentalities of the State and subject to its constitutional limitations." *Id.*, at 1092. The function at issue must be "both traditionally and exclusively governmental." *Lee v. Katz*, 276 F.3d 550, 555 (9th Cir. 2002). Joint action exists if "the state has so far insinuated itself into a position of interdependence with the private entity that it must be recognized as a joint participant in the challenged activity. This occurs when the state knowingly accepts the benefits derived from unconstitutional behavior." *Id.* at 1093 (*quoting Parks School of Business, Inc. v. Symington*, 51 F.3d 1480, 1486 (9th Cir. 1995)). The court may consider the degree to which the state controls the private individual's independent judgment. *Id.*, at 1093–94. In *Brunette v. Humane Society of Ventura County*, 294 F.3d 1205 (9th Cir. 2002), as amended on denial of reh'g and reh'g en banc, (Aug. 23, 2002), the court rejected the argument that media defendants were state actors absent substantial cooperation or intertwined activity between them and the Humane Society. as the media never participated in preraid briefings, media came in their own vehicles, and they acted independently. "The compulsion test considers whether the coercive influence or 'significant encouragement' of the state effectively converts a private action into a government action." *Kirtley*, 326 F.3d at 1094. And the nexus test requires "such a close nexus between the State and the challenged action that the seemingly private behavior may be fairly treated as that of the State itself." *Id.*, at 1094–95.

Where private persons use state enforcement schemes to take possession of animals, such as attachment, they may subject themselves to § 1983 liability. *Lugar v. Edmondson Oil Co., Inc.*, 457 U.S. 922 (1982); *cf.*, *Kuleana, LLC v. Diversified Wood Recycling, Inc.*, 383 Fed. Appx. 601 (9th Cir. 2010) (misuse of state lien foreclosure procedures not sufficient to establish state action by private party). Calling police might also implicate state action in the proper case. *See Ginsberg v. Healey Car & Truck Leasing, Inc.*, 189 F.3d 268, 272 (2d Cir. 1999) (calling police not to report offense but to resolve private dispute might trigger § 1983 liability); discussed in *Bloom v. Town of New Windsor Police Dept.*, 234 F.3d 1261 (2d Cir. 2000).

Animal-based examples examining the question of private § 1983 liability include *Daskalea v. Washington Humane Society*, 480 F. Supp. 2d 16, 27–28 (D.D.C. 2007) (humane society performed distinctive, traditional governmental functions and acted under color of state law); *Brown v. Wilson County*, 1999 U.S. Dist. LEXIS 23806 (W.D. Tex. Mar. 31, 1999) (veterinarians who participated in seizure acted under color of state law); *Boutte v. San Francisco SPCA Animal Hosp.*, 2008 U.S. Dist. LEXIS 8903 (N.D. Cal. Jan. 23, 2008) (no nexus between state and actor and SPCA); *Suss v. American Soc. for Prevention of Cruelty to Animals*, 823 F. Supp. 181 (S.D. N.Y. 1993) (SPCA was state actor during attempted rescue of trapped cat); *Schindler v. French*, 2007 U.S. App. LEXIS 941 (2d Cir. Jan. 12, 2007) (nonprofit animal protection organization not a state actor but individual defendants working for the organization were, when seizing animals and arresting owner on cruelty charges, with respect to nonconspiracy claims); *Brunette v. Humane Society of Ventura County*, 294 F.3d 1205 (9th Cir. 2002) (humane society was "state actor" given quasi-public function and ability of officers to investigate cruelty, impound, lien property, and bring criminal charges), as amended on denial of reh'g and reh'g en banc; *Chambers v. Doe*, 453 F. Supp. 2d 858 (D. Del. 2006) (humane society not state actor in context of disposal of body of dog shot by police); *Fabrikant v. French*, 691 F.3d 193 (2d Cir. 2012) (private animal rescue and its employees and agents were state actors when sterilizing dogs seized by warrant in animal neglect raid); *Crawford v. Van Buren Cy.*, 678 F.3d 666 (8th Cir. 2012) ("mere presence during the search was not sufficient to prove a conspiracy existed" between the private humane society defendants and government).

A feline § 1983 case with private actor considerations, *Giaconia v. Delaware County Soc. for the Prevention of Cruelty to Animals*, 2008 U.S. Dist. LEXIS 76765

(E.D. Pa. Sept. 29, 2008) deserves discussion. Kathryn Giaconia's cat Whiskers ran away from home, was impounded by animal control officers the same day, and delivered to the Delaware SPCA. Two days later, Giaconia found Whiskers there. Animal control officer Morgan told Giaconia she could return after 12:30 p.m. the next morning to redeem Whiskers. Morgan explained that cats were held a minimum of four days. Despite these reassurances, Giaconia called 911 twice that day, posted a message on the DCSPCA's front door, and left a message on DCSPCA's answering machine requesting assistance in retrieving Whiskers. The next morning at about 12:40 p.m., Giaconia arrived to find that Whiskers had been killed earlier that morning after being held only 60 hours. The two DCSPCA workers responsible for killing Whiskers, Soxman and Marchetti, completed a state form indicating that Soxman had been bitten by Whiskers, thereby requiring euthanasia for rabies testing of the brain. Two weeks later, DCSPCA managing director Vernon told Giaconia this was a lie. Giaconia sued the DCSPCA, Morgan, Soxman, Marchetti, Vernon, and Patricia Cotter on claims of fraud, conversion, negligence, emotional distress, and § 1983. The court found that killing a cat amounts to a Fourth Amendment seizure although § 1983 case law had customarily examined the proposition in the *canine* context. Nonetheless, it held that DCSPCA and its employees were not state actors at the time they euthanized Whiskers while ostensibly complying with state law mandating quarantine, euthanasia, and testing of any domestic animal suspected of having rabies who later bites a human being.

Veterinarians frequently face § 1983 claims arising from their assistance with law enforcement in warrant execution and triaging animals for removal from the scene. The Fifth Circuit exonerated one such veterinarian in *Brown v. Tull*, 218 F.3d 743 (5th Cir. 2000). An animal activist and animal control officer allegedly planned a covert search of the property of the Browns, who raised dogs and cats for sale. After preparing affidavits based on their observations, activists, deputies, and media executed a seizure warrant at the Browns' farm. Of the many defendants, veterinarian Catherine Tull sought dismissal. Focusing on causation, Tull's lack of participation in the specific actions depriving Brown of her constitutional rights, and Tull's lack of supervisory authority over those who so participated, the court found Tull not liable. However, it might have if:

> (1) it was Tull's idea to secure a warrant and seize of [sic] the animals, (2) Tull was physically present at the raid or personally participated in it, (3) Tull participated in drafting the seizure warrants or the affidavits supporting the warrants, or supplied any information to the court that issued the warrants, (4) Tull had any legal authority to request or order a seizure of the animals, or ever purported to have such authority over law enforcement officials, (5) Tull, a veterinarian with no legal training, had any duty under state law to ensure that law enforcement seizures are conducted legally, or (6) Tull had any control over who would participate in the raid or the manner in which the seizure of the animals was conducted[.] . . . [T]angential involvement in the raid . . . was too remote to impose § 1983 liability.

Id., at *4. Citizens calling 911 may face a § 1983 claim for triggering dispatch of law enforcement, who then inflict constitutional harm to an animal. The Tenth Circuit released the caller from liability in *Bewley v. City of Duncan*, 149 F.3d 1190 (10th

Cir. 1998). Animal control inadvertently killed a Doberman by tranquilizer dart, retrieving his body for veterinary attention from inside Bewley's home (to which the dog retreated after allegedly being darted) upon responding to a call that the dog roamed at large and menaced people at an auction nearby. Bewley brought a § 1983 action against the city, officers, and even the 911 caller on several constitutional grounds. No state action arose where the private defendant's sole involvement was to call the authorities to report Bewley's dog loose.

C. REASONABLENESS OF SEARCH OR SEIZURE

The Supreme Court established "a 'basic principle of Fourth Amendment law' that searches and seizures inside a home without a warrant are presumptively unreasonable." *Welsh v. Wisconsin*, 466 U.S. 740, 749 (1984) (*citing Payton v. New York*, 445 U.S. 573, 586 (1980)). Overcoming the presumption requires an exception to the warrant requirement. For instance, "[I]t is well settled constitutional law that, absent exigent circumstances, probable cause alone cannot justify an officer's warrantless entry into a person's home." *LaLonde v. County of Riverside*, 204 F.3d 947, 954 (9th Cir. 2000). Exigency without probable cause renders entry unreasonable as a matter of law. *U.S. v. Johnson*, 256 F.3d 895, 905 (9th Cir. 2001).

Neutral magistrate review of a search warrant permits independent assessment of the existence of probable cause. Depriving the magistrate of contradictory evidence or full facts impairs this sober and critical function. "The point of the Fourth Amendment, which often is not grasped by zealous officers, is not that it denies law enforcement the support of the usual inferences which reasonable men draw from evidence. Its protection consists in requiring that those inferences be drawn by a neutral and detached magistrate instead of being judged by the officer engaged in the often competitive enterprise of ferreting out crime." *Johnson v. U.S.*, 333 U.S. 10, 13–14 (1948). "Good-faith" does not excuse warrantless entries. *U.S. v. Warner*, 843 F.2d 401, 404 (9th Cir. 1988). Most significantly, the home possesses the greatest expectation of privacy and the highest degree of insulation from government intrusion. *Kyllo v. U.S.*, 533 U.S. 27 (2001). "With few exceptions, the question whether a warrantless search of a home is reasonable and hence constitutional must be answered no." *Illinois v. Rodriguez*, 497 U.S. 177, 181 (1990).

Traditional exceptions to the warrant requirement include:

- Entry to fight a fire and investigate cause. *Michigan v. Tyler*, 436 U.S. 499, 509 (1978).

- Entry to prevent imminent destruction of evidence. *Ker v. State of Cal.*, 374 U.S. 23, 40 (1963) (plurality opinion).

- Entry to engage in "hot pursuit" of fleeing suspect. *U.S. v. Santana*, 427 U.S. 38, 42, 43 (1976).

- Entry due to "exigencies of the situation." *Mincey v. Arizona*, 437 U.S. 385, 393–94 (1978) (also discussing exigency of rendering emergency assistance to injured occupant or to protect occupant from imminent injury); *see also People v. Chung*, 185 Cal. App. 4th 247 (2010) (extending exigent circumstances exception to permit warrantless entry of condominium to protect dog).

- Open fields. *Oliver v. U.S.*, 466 U.S. 170 (1984).

- Search of person and surrounding area incident to arrest. *New York v. Belton*, 453 U.S. 454 (1981).

- Plain view where officer is legitimately in position to observe object, incriminatory evidentiary value of object is immediately apparent to police, and officer has lawful right of access to object itself. *Texas v. Brown*, 460 U.S. 730 (1983).

- Entry as part of fulfilling the "community caretaking exception" traditionally applied to vehicle searches, not dwellings. *Cady v. Dombrowski*, 413 U.S. 433 (1973); *Colorado v. Bertine*, 479 U.S. 367 (1987).

Most animal-related warrantless entry cases invoke the warrant exceptions of plain view, consent, open fields, and exigent circumstances. Even if state actors search and seize pursuant to warrant or to a warrant exception, a § 1983 violation may arise if conducted unreasonably.

1. Hot Pursuit

Sometimes animal control officers chase down a loose or vicious dog and follow him back to the owner's premises. Does such hot pursuit violate the Fourth Amendment? The California Court of Appeals answered the question partly in the negative through a fascinating discussion in *Conway v. Pasadena Humane Society*, 45 Cal. App. 4th 163 (1996). In *Conway*, a humane society officer apprehended a dog running at large by following him into the homeowners' backyard and through the rear door of the house (open about two feet) without consent or warrant. Though first seeking police assistance for a possible burglary, officers found no criminal invasion and only Toby, the dog, lying on a bed in one of the bedrooms. The windows were closed with no means of escape. After pleading no contest to misdemeanor leash law violations, four months later, the city returned Toby to the Conways.

In reversing dismissal of Conway's later § 1983 lawsuit, the court of appeals found a Fourth Amendment violation through physical entry without a warrant. Probable cause to believe articles subject to seizure exist in a dwelling would not, in and of itself, justify a warrantless search. *Payton v. New York*, 445 U.S. 573, 588 (1980). Absent consent, the court reasoned, exigent circumstances must exist to believe that a crime was committed or incriminating evidence may be found inside. Exigent circumstances mean an "emergency situation requiring swift action to prevent imminent danger to life or serious damage to property, or to forestall the imminent escape of a suspect or destruction of evidence." *See People v. Ramey*, 545 P.2d 1333, 1340 (1976). Two primary considerations for determining exigency include (a) the gravity of the underlying offense and (b) the threat to police or public safety by delay in seeking the warrant. Exigency does not confer *carte blanche* access but still requires a strictly circumscribed search. *Id.*, at 173. Conceding for the sake of argument that initial exigency may have existed to permit the warrantless entry to search for the burglar, once the officers confirmed no burglary had taken place, and that Toby posed no danger to anyone or anything at the time, that the underlying offense was minor, and that there was adequate time to get a warrant — the justification to remain disappeared, resulting in an illegal seizure. In other words, an initial emergency ceasing to exist before warrantless reentry does not justify that second warrantless entry. *Id.*, at 175.

Observation: The government in *Conway* argued that state and local law permitted entry onto premises to impound without a warrant (namely, Cal. Gov't Code § 53074 and Pasadena Municipal Code 6.08.110). Though finding the codes suggested as much, the court held that even state and local ordinances cannot override the constitution. *Id.*, at 176. Nonconsensual entry into a home "is simply too substantial an invasion to allow without a warrant, at least in the absence of exigent circumstances, even when it is accomplished under statutory authority and when probable cause is clearly present." *Payton v. New York*, 445 U.S. 573, 589 (1980). Qualified immunity did not save the officers, either, as they are presumed to know clearly established law. That the humane society officers did not understand "basic Fourth Amendment principles" mattered not. While municipal codes are relevant in determining qualified immunity, no reasonable officer would interpret the state and local law to dispense with the Fourth Amendment's warrant requirement. That said, evidence from animal control officers in other state jurisdictions interpreting Cal. Gov't Code § 53074 (including animal control associations on state and national levels) "may also be of assistance." Reserved for a later day was whether an officer needed a warrant to take up a stray seeking refuge in someone's home. *Id.*, at 179.

2. Exigent circumstances

Some jurisdictions apply the *Dorman* test to determine exigent circumstances. *Dorman v. U.S.*, 435 F.2d 385, 393 (D.C. Cir. 1970) (noting in footnote 20 that for night search warrants, Fed. R. Civ. P. 41(c) requires that affiant be "positive" on whereabouts of property or person). The *Dorman* factors that guide a determination of exigent circumstance in the case of arrest include "the gravity of the crime which the suspect is believed to have committed, the reasonable belief that the suspect is armed, the degree of probable cause for the arrest, the likelihood that the suspect is in the premises, the risk of escape, the manner of entrance by the police." *U.S. v. Blake*, 632 F.2d 731, 733 (9th Cir. 1980). There must be a "strong reason" to believe that the suspect is on the premises. The Ninth Circuit defined exigent circumstances as "those in which a substantial risk of harm to the persons involved or to the law enforcement process would arise if the police were to delay a search [or arrest] until a warrant could be obtained." *U.S. v. Salvador*, 740 F.2d 752, 758 (9th Cir. 1984) (*quoting U.S. v. Robertson*, 606 F.2d 853, 859 (9th Cir. 1979)). Defendants bear the heavy burden of showing the existence of exigent circumstances making warrantless entry or arrest imperative. Despite a showing of immediacy, less restrictive alternatives may also exist to justify a warrantless arrest or search, such as by procuring a telephonic warrant. "Additionally, as a finding of exigent circumstances necessarily presupposes inadequate time to acquire a warrant, the government's burden is not satisfied unless it can demonstrate that a warrant could not have been obtained in time even by telephone under the procedure authorized by Federal Rule of Criminal Procedure 41(c)(2)." *U.S. v. Manfredi*, 722 F.2d 519, 522 (9th Cir. 1983).

The Seventh Circuit found volunteer department of agriculture investigator David Severino's barn search illegal in *Siebert v. Severino*, 256 F.3d 648 (7th Cir. 2001). Severino seized three of Pamela Siebert's horses 72 hours after searching a barn owned by her and her husband. While returned to the Sieberts, the court found that the horses' removal constituted a seizure under the Fourth Amendment and that the lack of warrant required Severino to prove an exception justifying removal. Severino invoked the Illinois Humane Care for Animals Act. But the court found that either Severino failed to trigger the statute's authorization to impound by not calling the department until after he took custody of the horses, or he misrepresented the horses' condition to the department to achieve sham authorization. A "government officials' procurement through distortion, misrepresentation and omission of a court order to seize a child is a violation of the Fourth Amendment." *Siebert*, 256 F.3d at 659 (quoting for comparison *Brokaw v. Mercer County*, 235 F.3d 1000, 1022 (7th Cir. 2000)). Alternatively, it held that the weight of the evidence did not support Severino's claim of exigent circumstances. Nor did the court grant Severino qualified immunity because no reasonably informed government worker authorized to ensure humane care would believe that temperatures between four and 42 degrees would justify exigent removal without a warrant.

Observation: Exigency doctrine allows law enforcement to bypass strict compliance with standard search warrant execution protocols. But not all claimed exigencies pass muster, as found in the case of *People v. Riddle*, 630 N.E.2d 141, 146 (Ill. App. Ct. 1994), where the court held that the mere presence of "pit bulls" at a residence did not create exigent circumstances dispensing with a "knock and announce" rule before conducting a search pursuant to a warrant.

3. Emergency doctrine

The relevant two-part test for the emergency doctrine asks whether (1) considering the totality of the circumstances, law enforcement had an objectively reasonable basis to conclude that there was an immediate need to protect others or themselves from serious harm; and (2) the scope and manner of the search reasonably met the need. *U.S. v. Snipe*, 515 F.3d 947 (9th Cir. 2008). Other circuits have similarly prescribed. *See U.S. v. Huffman*, 461 F.3d 777, 783 (6th Cir. 2006); *U.S. v. Najar*, 451 F.3d 710, 715, 718 (10th Cir. 2006). Traditionally, this medical emergency, or community caretaking, exception to warrantless searches requires the presence of persons faced with imminent death or harm; objects likely to burn, explode, or otherwise cause harm; or information that will disclose the location of a threatened victim or the existence of such a threat. Consequently, the officer must be able to articulate specific facts and reasonable inferences drawn therefrom that justify the warrantless entry. A key distinction between emergency aid doctrine and exigent circumstances doctrine is that they latter requires probable cause to believe a crime has been committed, while the former does not. Animal cruelty laws tend to supply the basis for probable cause, which so happen to codify most community-caretaking concerns that would justify the emergency exception (i.e., warrentless entry to prevent imminent animal cruelty). *See State v. Fessenden*, 258 Or. App. 639 (2013), *aff'd*, 355 Or. 759 (2014) (leaving question of emergency aid exception for "another day," though prelude to comment suggests answer would be yes).

U.S. v. Mickle, 886 F.2d 1320 (9th Cir. 1989), illustrates how a higher court assessed animal-based exigency. An officer responded to a call "that a gunshot had been fired in the apartment and that a dog had possibly been injured" and "that the occupants of the apartment had been arguing and sounded intoxicated." Additionally, the neighbor who made the report and spoke to the officers repeated "his claim that he had heard a gunshot and a woman exclaim that her dog had been shot." One of the officers testified to having "passed an open window through which he heard a stereo playing" but that "the second time he passed the window, the stereo was no longer playing." The officers also knocked and announced but heard no response prior to entry. Finding that a gunshot was fired in an apartment during a hostile argument between intoxicated residents and that the officers immediately dispatched could not evoke any response despite some indications that a person or persons remained in the unit, the court found a "sufficient degree of probability that a crime had taken place in the apartment and that evidence of such a crime, including seriously injured persons, would be found therein."

The Ninth Circuit affirmed not out of concern that a nonhuman animal was likely injured or killed but that "they reasonably could have remained uncertain whether a dog had been the *only victim* of the violent altercation and shooting reported by Mickle's neighbors." The court uses its own italics, no doubt to relate back to its earlier definition of exigent circumstances to include "those circumstances that would cause a reasonable person to believe that entry (or other relevant prompt action) was necessary to prevent physical harm to the officers *or other persons*, the destruction of relevant evidence, the escape of the suspect, or some other consequence improperly frustrating legitimate law enforcement efforts." Note the emphasis on "persons," not "animals."

Decided more than a decade later by the California Court of Appeals, consider the other exigency case of *People v. Chung*, 195 Cal. App. 4th 721 (2010), as modified on denial of reh'g, (July 1, 2010) and review granted and opinion superseded, 238 P.3d 1252 (Cal. 2010) (deferring action until disposition of related issue in *People v. Troyer*, 246 P.3d 901 (Cal. 2011)). *Chung* involved involving law enforcement hearing incessant, "high pitched" whining of an animal as if in pain or "being tortured"; entering Chung's home without a warrant; and asserting justified entry through the exigent circumstances exception to the warrant requirement. Preceding entry, officers knocked and announced themselves as law enforcement, causing Chung to open the door slightly and poke his head out. Though Chung denied owning any dogs, officers asked him to step outside. He complied, leaving the door open about an inch. While speaking, they heard the "faint sound of a dog whimpering inside." When the officers asked permission to enter, Chung refused, so they detained and handcuffed him outside and placed a call to the watch commander to ascertain probable cause. Without obtaining a telephonic warrant, the officers entered to find a glass pipe on the kitchen counter with residue of what appeared to be an illegal substance. Searching for the dog, an officer found canine hair and blood on the floor and walls of a bathroom, as well as knives. A small dog lay on a towel on the patio in a plastic toolbox, "injured and weak," "not responsive but . . . still breathing." *Id.* at 725. Citing *Brigham City, Utah v. Stuart*, 547 U.S.

398 (2006), the court deemed the officers' subjective motivation to enter irrelevant and affirmed the trial court's denial of the suppression motion.

Whether emergency entry to rescue animals has achieved "clearly established" status for purposes of bestowing qualified immunity upon law enforcement officers remains in flux. In 2007, the Second Circuit recognized this evolving question of law in *Shapiro v. City of Glen Cove*, 2007 U.S. App. LEXIS 12138 (2d Cir. May 22, 2007). Without a warrant, Glen Cove officers entered Shapiro's uninhabited, dirty, partially renovated home lacking heat and electricity on a cold day with many dogs seen and heard within. In affirming the grant of qualified immunity, the Second Circuit held that at the time of entry (and the opinion), it was not clearly established whether law enforcement may enter a dwelling to render emergency assistance to nonhuman animals. *See also Siebert v. Severino*, 256 F.3d 648, 657 (7th Cir. 2001) (suggesting, but not holding, that "[e]xigent circumstances may justify warrantless seizure of animals"); *DiCesare v. Stuart*, 12 F.3d 973, 977–78 (10th Cir. 1993) (same); *People v. Rogers*, 708 N.Y.S.2d 795 (2000) (warrantless search of closed pet store justified to rescue animals needing medical attention); *People v. Burns*, 593 P.2d 351 (Colo. 1979) (exigency justified search to find missing calf at risk of malnutrition and death due to maternal separation); *Tuck v. U.S.*, 477 A.2d 1115 (D.C. 1984) (warrantless removal of rabbit from closed display window in pet store to provide emergency care for heat prostration held lawful); *Brinkley v. County of Flagler*, 769 So. 2d 468 (Fla. Dist. Ct. App. 2000) (emergency exception warranted entry onto property and farmhouse resulting in seizure of hundreds of dogs and a bird); *Morgan v. State*, 656 S.E.2d 857 (Ga. Ct. App. 2008) (exigency justified warrantless entry into backyard to seize dogs). Shapiro also sued private individual Weiss-Horvath for entering her property, but the district court dismissed that claim, finding the entry privileged under common law principles. The appeals court affirmed dismissal of Weiss-Horvath including the award of attorney's fees for frivolous suit under 42 U.S.C.A. § 1988.

Scott v. Jackson County, 403 F. Supp. 2d 999 (D. Or. 2005), *judgment aff'd in part, rev'd in part on other grounds*, 2008 U.S. App. LEXIS 22685 (9th Cir. Oct. 24, 2008) bears mention because animal control actually observed dead rabbits, filthy cages sitting in direct sunlight, inoperable water dispensers, and piles of feces that prevented the rabbits from accessing their food. The extremely dire, and plainly visible, conditions supplied more than reasonable grounds to search using the emergency doctrine. *See Yates v. City of New York*, 2006 U.S. Dist. LEXIS 54199 (S.D.N.Y. Aug. 4, 2006) (emergency-doctrine warrantless entry necessary to remove a Siberian tiger and an alligator from a fifth-floor apartment.)

State v. Christenson, 45 P.3d 511 (Or. Ct. App. 2002), serves as a counterpoint. Holding a warrantless entry into a residence unauthorized under the community caretaking statute (Or. Rev. Stat. § 133.033) or the constitutional emergency aid exception, *Christensen* assumed the following as true: (1) a neighbor called to report the front door open under "suspicious" circumstances, and the resident's two pit bulls at large; (2) officers found the front door open; and (3) when the officers called out, none responded. The court concluded that it was "simply too common an event to create concern of harm in the absence of other signs of trouble, such as evidence of a forced entry or a medical emergency[.]" It then cited to two other cases that did not satisfy under the community caretaking exception under "more suspicious circumstances than those that existed here." (*citing State v. Bramson*, 765 P.2d 824 (Or. Ct. App. 1988) (open front door, 30-degree temperature, vehicle in driveway, and report of residents being out of town did not give police officers probable cause to believe that burglary had been or was being committed); *State v. Apodaca*, 735 P.2d 1264 (Or. Ct. App. 1987) (open front door and broken screen do not constitute "strong showing" that a seriously injured person might be inside the house or that a burglary was in progress or had been committed)). The court also noted that silence, following announcements by police at the threshold to the residence, does not evoke a reason for concern or lack thereof. Rather, the completely neutral scenario did not generate any reasonable belief to necessitate entry so as to prevent harm to persons or property.

Similarly, *State v. Swenson*, 799 P.2d 1188 (Wash. Ct. App. 1990), found the emergency doctrine inapplicable where a neighbor called to report her neighbor's front door open, a dog barking in the front yard, and no one home. Police searched and found drugs. Applying a reasonableness standard, the court held that the police could not invoke the emergency doctrine to justify entry for:

> [t]he barking dog was ambiguous, and by itself could not suggest an individual in medical distress. In short, the only evidence of an emergency was a door left open late on a summer night. In these circumstances, regardless of what the officers may subjectively have thought, a reasonable person would not believe an emergency existed.

In *Suss v. American Soc. for Prevention of Cruelty to Animals*, 823 F. Supp. 181 (S.D.N.Y. 1993), the court found that breaking through walls of a business without a warrant to rescue a cat trapped between the walls of that business and another building was not justified under the emergency exception to protect and preserve life where the ability to seek a warrant, at least by telephone, existed, yet police made no such attempt.

Warrantless entry to investigate rotting animal corpses did not violate the constitution in *Broden v. Marin Humane Society*, 70 Cal. App. 4th 1212 (1999) (entry into place of business due to stench of decomposing remains); nor to rescue alive animals in imminent danger in *Jackson v. Silicon Valley Animal Control Authority*, 2008 U.S. Dist. LEXIS 98521 (N.D. Cal. Dec. 5, 2008) (entry into mobile home under exigent circumstances exception), which extended exigent circumstances doctrine to nonhumans. Plaintiff's attempt to distinguish *Broden* and *Jackson* in the context of residential entry and removal of animals suspected of suffering from life-threatening conditions failed in *Anderson v. Smith*, 2009 U.S. Dist. LEXIS 58804 (E.D. Cal. Jul. 10, 2009).

Observation: Itinerant (i.e., mobile) animal abusers enjoy fewer constitutional protections. When performed curbside, such as in a van where a plaintiff resides with his animals, the subjective expectation of privacy does not match that of a residence. *Adams v. Connors*, 2002 U.S. Dist. LEXIS 14664 (N.D. Ill. Aug. 8, 2002), agreed that probable cause existed to believe that Adams committed animal cruelty. It justified the warrantless search of his van and subsequent impound of the abused dog found therein.

4. Plain View, Open Fields, and Curtilage

"Open fields" and "plain view" exceptions to warrantless search and seizure are commonly litigated in large animal (e.g., horses, bovines) cases because these species are kept outdoors, turned out to pasture for all passersby to see.

To satisfy the plain view doctrine, and authorize warrantless seizure, officers must prove that (1) the item is in plain view; (2) the officer is lawfully located in a place from which the item can plainly be seen; (3) the officer has a lawful right of access to the item itself; and (4) it is immediately apparent that the seized item is incriminating on its face (i.e., probable cause to believe it is criminal evidence or contraband). *Winters v. Board of County Comm'rs*, 4 F.3d 848, 854 (10th Cir. 1993); *see also Horton v. California*, 496 U.S. 128, 136–37 (1990). Some circuits collapse the first three prongs into one, by stating the rule that "the officers must be lawfully searching the area where the evidence is found." *U.S. v. Stafford*, 416 F.3d 1068, 1076 (9th Cir. 2005). It is an "essential predicate to any valid warrantless seizure of incriminating evidence that the officer did not violate the Fourth Amendment in arriving at the place from which the evidence could be plainly viewed." *Horton*, at 136. Thus, plain view doctrine serves to expand the seizure powers of an officer once she has justifiably intruded into the area where the item comes into plain view, whether by "a warrant for another object, hot pursuit, search incident to lawful arrest, or some other legitimate reason for being present unconnected with a search directed against the accused." *Id.*, at 135–36 (*quoting Coolidge v. New Hampshire*, 403 U.S. 443, 465–66 (1971)). "[N]o amount of probable cause can justify a warrantless search or seizure absent 'exigent circumstances.' " *Id.*, at 137 n. 7. And while exigency may exist while the item is in plain view, it may also dissipate after passage of time, rendering later entry, or reentry, unconstitutional. *Michigan v. Tyler*, 436 U.S. 499, 511 (1978) (when reentry detached from initial exigency, warrant required). However, the doctrine has not been extended to require law enforcement officers to shield their eyes when passing by a home on public thoroughfares. *California v. Ciraolo*, 476 U.S. 207, 213 (1986).

While the plain view doctrine permits *seizure*, the open fields doctrine permits *search*. One has no legitimate expectation of privacy for effects kept outside the curtilage of dwellings and outbuildings (i.e., no Fourth Amendment protection). *Oliver v. U.S.*, 466 U.S. 170, 177–79 (1984) (even fence or no-trespassing sign does not create legitimate expectation of privacy in open fields). A four-part test aids in distinguishing curtilage from noncurtilage. *U.S. v. Dunn*, 480 U.S. 294 (1987) (proximity of area claimed to be curtilage to the home whether area fits within enclosure surrounding home, nature of uses to which area put, and steps taken by resident to protect area from observation of people passing by). The two doctrines work hand in hand, by relying on open fields to obtain a lawful vantage point from which the officer may later make a plain view seizure.

For example, the Seventh Circuit found David Severino's barn search (and thus seizure) illegal in *Siebert v. Severino*, 256 F.3d 648 (7th Cir. 2001). Severino seized three horses three days after searching a barn owned by Siebert and her husband. In reversing summary judgment for Severino, the Seventh Circuit found his warrantless search of the barn illegal, though outside the curtilage and not within the actual residence, for the Sieberts nonetheless had some legitimate expectation of privacy therein. *Id.*, at 654 (*citing U.S. v. Wright*, 991 F.2d 1182, 1186 (4th Cir. 1993) (legitimate expectation of privacy in barn) and distinguishing *U.S. v. Dunn*, 480 U.S. 294, 300 (1987) as Severino entered the barn instead of just peering inside an open door. Classifying this scenario as one falling into the "obvious" category, it also denied qualified immunity to Severino, adding, "Even if Severino nosed around in the Sieberts' barn, there appears to be little or no damage, so what's the harm? The harm is that Severino violated the Sieberts' constitutional rights. Had the Sieberts been doing something illegal in the barn and Severino's search uncovered evidence, the Supreme Court mandates that such evidence be excluded (unless, of course, there is some exception to the exclusionary rule)." *Id.*, at 655.

Joining *Siebert* is *DiCesare v. Stuart*, 12 F.3d 973 (10th Cir. 1993). Responding to a stray horse call, and a last-identified location at the DiCesare property, the county sheriff and undersheriff climbed over DiCesare's gate and walked down the driveway where they came upon three horses in pens and eight dogs running loose. They left a note. While exigency may have justified that initial entry, the next day's reentry generated a constitutional problem. When the sheriff returned, he climbed the gate and found dogs eating a dead horse. Disturbed by what was seen, the sheriff came back with the undersheriff and observed several more dead horses, a dead dog, emaciated animals and one who could barely walk. The next morning, law enforcement and a veterinarian entered the property and seized several horses. They then obtained an order directing care and treatment of the horses and sale to satisfy the lien. DiCesare, incarcerated, received notice of the sale but did not redeem the horses before the actual sale, which netted a loss to the sheriff's office. The Tenth Circuit reversed and remanded to the district court following DiCesare's appeal from summary judgment dismissal on the Fourth Amendment seizure claim, rejecting the argument that the "plain view" doctrine justified the immediate warrantless seizure of the horses. It held that "the officers were neither in a place lawfully from where they could see the horses nor did they have a lawful right of access to them." It also reversed as to the due process claim since the statutory scheme did not allow DiCesare a hearing at any time before disposition of the horses. Nor did the notice of impending sale inform him of a chance to object. On remand, the district court dismissed all claims once more, this time on the basis of standing (the land on which the horses were kept, and the horses themselves, belonged to a corporation, not DiCesare). The Tenth Circuit affirmed dismissal. 82 F.3d 425 (10th Cir. 1996). *But see DiCesare v. Stout*, 992 F.2d 1222 (10th Cir. 1993), a related case (affirming dismissal of complaint alleging Fourth Amendment violation in seizure of horses, resting its decision on open fields doctrine and exigent circumstances in situations involving mistreatment of animals, rather than plain view discussed in 12 F.3d 973).

Dunham v. Kootenai County, 690 F. Supp. 2d 1162 (D. Idaho 2010), played one doctrine off the other, holding the warrantless search of horses from a pen lawful per the "open fields" doctrine, and subsequent seizure of same lawful per the "plain view" doctrine. Having found the *search* lawful under "open fields" doctrine, the court recycled that ruling to satisfy the first part of the "plain view" test — e.g., the officers lawfully searched the area where they found the inculpatory evidence. *Id.*, at 1173–1174. As to the second part of the test, thereby justifying the warrantless *seizure*, the court concluded that "visible signs of malnutrition, neglect and/or cruelty" made the association between the horses and criminal activity immediately apparent. *Id.*, at 1174.

Daugherty v. Costello, 2001 U.S. App. LEXIS 25335 (9th Cir. Nov. 5, 2001), involved animal control officers seizing 110 poodles from Daugherty's mobile home and barn. State regulation authorized the search of a probationer's home without a warrant where one parole condition was not to possess animals (the mobile home, licensed to Daugherty's mother, on parole for felony cruelty to animals). Citing *Griffin v. Wisconsin*, 483 U.S. 868 (1987), the court found no Fourth Amendment violations resulting from the merger of state law, open fields, and plain view doctrines. Further, having given Daugherty notice and a chance to be heard on return of the poodles following the seizure, the court concluded that she obtained all the due process deserved.

Observation: Pay close attention to whether the officer positioned herself from a lawful vantage point to initially view the animal, and then whether she had a legal route to access the animal at its location. *See, e.g., Gall v. City of Vidor, Tex.*, 903 F. Supp. 1062, 1066 (E.D. Tex. 1995) (an animal control officer may enter private property without a warrant to seize abused dogs where he first views their abuse from outside the premises).

5. Consent

Consent obviates the need for a magistrate-issued warrant. *Oase v. City of Tucson, Ariz.*, 103 F.3d 140 (9th Cir. 1996), examines what happens when law enforcement fails to obtain consent to search. Oase challenged warrantless inspections of his home to evaluate his cats' health. While affirming summary judgment to the county for failure to identify a policy or practice authorizing officials to perform unconstitutional searches, the court reversed summary judgment for the inspectors on the disputed question of whether Oase voluntarily consented to the warrantless search of his premises. Oase explained that he begrudgingly authorized inspection based on the threat that law enforcement would "go over [to Oase's home] and break down the door and [Oase's] cats would be taken to the county pound and destroyed," concluding that "[he] could not allow [him]self to sacrifice [his cats] just to stand on the principal (sic) of the Fourth Amendment." *See also Engsberg v. Town of Milford*, 601 F. Supp. 1438, 1442–43 (W.D. Wis. 1985), *aff'd*, 785 F.2d 312 (7th Cir. 1986) (upheld warrantless entry onto private property to investigate complaint about dogs running at large where the lessee of the property consented to the search).

Discussed throughout this section is the stolen horse case *Reid v. Hamby*, 124 F.3d 217 (10th Cir. 1997). The sheriff, without a warrant, searched Reid's pasture, visually confirming the identity of the stolen horse, and then threatening to arrest him if he did not immediately surrender it. Reid consented to entry and removal, though with obvious dismay as he innocently purchased the horse two years earlier. While warrantless searches of residences raise presumptive unreasonableness, where evidence of consent exists, the burden shifts to the property owner to prove that either consent was not given or that it was given involuntarily. *Valance v. Wisel*, 110 F.3d 1269, 1278 (7th Cir. 1997).

6. Scope of Warrant Exceeded or Unreasonably Executed

A warrant does not always confer absolute immunity if executed unreasonably or exceeded without justification. In *Stack v. Killian*, 96 F.3d 159 (6th Cir. 1996), Stack operated Aid to Animals, a nonprofit, "no-kill" shelter housing about 300 dogs and cats. Due to alleged neglect, deputies executed a search warrant. With media present, they seized 77 animals and euthanized them. Stack subsequently pleaded no contest to one count of animal cruelty and was found guilty on counts of improper burial of animals. She then sued the deputies, humane society, and veterinarians participating in the removal and euthanasia under § 1983. In 1994, the Sixth Circuit affirmed dismissal of the veterinarians under qualified immunity. *Stack v. Killian*, 30 F.3d 134 (6th Cir. 1994). Thereafter, other defendants moved for summary judgment and achieved dismissal. Stack appealed a second time, emphasizing the defective nature of the warrant and inability to contest euthanasia of the animals after removal. Because the court had already determined that execution of the warrant did not violate clearly established rights (granting immunity to the veterinarians), consistency required the same result as to the other defendants. As to the television crew, the court held that officers may be found to have exceeded the scope of their authority (and, thus, acted illegally) when in "unquestioned command" of a dwelling by permitting unauthorized invasions of privacy by third parties having no connection to the search warrant or officers' purposes for being on the premises. *Bills v. Aseltine*, 958 F.2d 697, 704 (6th Cir. 1992). On the other hand, officers may also call upon private citizens to render aid of a warrant without overstepping constitutional bounds. *Id.*, at 706. Here, the police properly solicited help from the media as the warrant authorized "videotaping and photographing" during the execution.

Observation: *Stack* teaches counsel to closely parse the language of the warrant to ascertain the legitimate scope of soliciting third party, non-law enforcement involvement in its execution. One should also undertake a detailed examination of the pre-warrant execution communications, correspondence, and contractual arrangements between governmental and nongovernmental persons and entities to assess what degree of "unquestioned command" the police had over physical entry, search, assessment, photographing, videotaping, and removal of animals.

Though conceded as valid, the Eighth Circuit nonetheless examined the manner of execution of a search warrant to seize 23 horses not ill with strangles, not weak, and not malnourished in *McClendon v. Story County Sheriff's Office*, 403 F.3d 510 (8th Cir. 2005). Except as to two animal control officers, the district court granted summary judgment. It denied qualified immunity, observing that a jury could conclude the officers seized *all* the horses (including healthy ones) to punish McClendon for removing some horses prior to seizure. In so doing, the officers might be found to have intentionally disregarded the search warrant's limitation to seize only those horses "sick and in immediate need of critical care," to include those "exhibiting signs of a disease known as strangles . . . or are weak and malnourished." The district court rejected qualified immunity, focusing on what arguably proved their subjective, malicious intent to seize the entire herd as payback for McClendon's attempt to thwart the seizure. But in so holding, the district court erred, for the relevant inquiry is whether the officers' actions were *objectively* reasonable. "An officer's evil intentions will not make a Fourth Amendment violation out of an objectively reasonable use of force." *Graham v. Connor*, 490 U.S. 386, 397 (1989). Indeed, two professionals recommended removal of all the horses, warranting reversal on that basis alone. *See Id.*, at 516.

Additionally, the seized horses fit the description in the warrant, as an independent professional determined that all either had strangles or were weak and malnourished. Further, because the warrant did not specify the number to seize but instead used qualitative criteria like disease, wellness, and body condition scoring, the officers reasonably relied upon expert opinions of those present during seizure. The statements "inadequate feed" and "deprived of necessary sustenance" meant "malnourished" for purposes of authorizing seizure. Besides, officers executing search warrants are "not obliged to interpret it narrowly." *Id.*, at 517. A dissenting judge disputed that the veterinarian used terminology that satisfied the warrant restriction only to seize horses "(1) sick and in *immediate need of critical care* and (2) either (a) showing signs of the strangles or (b) weak *and* malnourished." *McClendon*, at 521 (emphasis in original).

As in *McClendon*, the Ninth Circuit found that the officers properly interpreted the scope of a warrant in *Scott v. Jackson County*, 2008 U.S. App. LEXIS 22685 (9th Cir. Oct. 24, 2008), dismissing § 1983 claims related to the seizure of rabbits.

Observation: Officers must mind warrant boundaries. But the warrant itself must meet particularity and staleness requirements. *Massachusetts v. Sheppard*, 468 U.S. 981 (1984) (search conducted pursuant to warrant failing to conform with particularity requirement of Fourth Amendment unconstitutional). This manifestly prevents general searches. *Maryland*, 480 U.S. at 84 (1987). *Armon v. McHenry County*, 2008 U.S. Dist. LEXIS 104553 (N.D. Ill. Dec. 29, 2008), examined a particularity challenge to a warrant in a mass animal cruelty raid. It declined to declare it unconstitutional even though it did not specify every animal to be seized, due to the huge number of animals involved and inability to readily distinguish one from another. The *Armon* court also rejected the claim of staleness of probable cause, another argument raised to undermine the lawfulness of the warrant, noting that a delay of approximately one month between the last inspection of the plaintiff's premises and the issuance of the warrant did not render it stale as "it was highly likely that animal control officers still would discover evidence of multiple violations of the animal control ordinances and statutes identified in the warrant." *Maryland*, 480 U.S. at 84 (1987).

Lastly, particularized and ripe warrants still compel reasonable methods of execution. The shooting-during-execution case of *Coffelt v. City of Glendale*, 2007 U.S. Dist. LEXIS 87009 (D. Ariz. Nov. 26, 2007) found that "the officers executing the warrant had no plan for dealing with the Rottweiler save the one which was employed — shooting it," establishing a colorable violation of the Fourth Amendment not amenable to qualified immunity in light of *San Jose Charter of Hells Angels Motorcycle Club v. City of San Jose*, 402 F.3d 962 (9th Cir. 2005).

7. Seizure by Excessive Force; Shooting Dogs

Police-shooting-dog case outcomes turn on the quantum and nature of force used to stave off an alleged threat of imminent physical harm to the officer, her canine, or a bystander. The hallmark cases describing when force crosses the constitutional line are *Graham v. Connor*, 490 U.S. 386, 395 (1989), which examined nondeadly force, and *Tennessee v. Garner*, 471 U.S. 1, 11 (1985), examining deadly force. "[A]ll claims that law enforcement officers have used excessive force — deadly or not — in the course of an arrest, investigatory stop, or other 'seizure' of a free citizen should be analyzed under the Fourth Amendment and its reasonableness standard." *Graham*, at 395. "A police officer may not seize an unarmed, non-dangerous suspect by shooting him dead." *Garner*, at 11. Though the Fourth Amendment facially applies with equal vigor to both "effects" and "persons," as discussed below, courts tend to regard nonhumans as second-class citizens (or, rather, second-class "effects" in whom only a qualified or imperfect property interest exists). The doctrine nonetheless translates, albeit with some cross-species error, to nonhumans.

Nondeadly excessive force depends on the balancing factors stated in *Graham*, at 396, by:

(1) Assessing the gravity of the particular intrusion on Fourth Amendment interests by evaluating the type and amount of force inflicted;

(2) Assessing the importance of the government interest at stake by evaluating the (a) severity of the crime at issue, (b) whether the suspect posed an immediate threat to the safety of the officer or others, and (c) whether the suspect was actively resisting arrest or attempting to evade arrest by flight; and

(3) Balancing the gravity of the intrusion on the individual against the government's need for that intrusion to determine constitutionality.

Additional considerations when assessing "reasonableness" under the *Graham-Garner* rubric include:

• Was the owner-guardian present to control her (i.e., looking on eager to reassert control)?

• Was the officer called to the scene in response to a dog bite, chase, approach, or attack or just passing through the area?

• Did this dog have a reported history of aggression, and did the officer have independent, personal knowledge of same? In other words, was there probable cause to believe that the dog presented an imminent threat of serious bodily injury or death based on current as well as historical facts?

• Did the officer follow procedure by waiting a reasonable time for animal control to arrive?

• Did the officer's own actions provoke the necessity of using lethal force?

• Were less-lethal force modalities available (e.g., OC spray, Taser, baton)?

Observation: Regardless of the answers given, a law enforcement officer should possess rudimentary knowledge of dog behavior. For instance, some officers shoot dogs running at large after allegedly having threatened the public or officer with death or serious injury. Under *Garner*, deadly force may only be used against fleeing felons to prevent escape of a dangerous suspect. Whether a dog may be likened to a "fleeing felon" raises interesting philosophical issues germane to our treatment of nonhuman animals, especially canines, and presents a curious paradox — we unleash upon them a level of force typically only reserved for human criminals of sane mind brandishing weapons to kill the arresting officer, yet dogs are not "criminal-minded" and cannot be prosecuted. And while their nakedness prevents them from hiding weapons within garments and surprising officers by discharging them through a jacket pocket or pulling them from the waistband, they are possessed with sharp rows of teeth with bite forces that may exceed 300 pounds per square inch. By comparison, humans average 150 psi, hippopotamuses more than 1,800 psi, and saltwater crocodiles 3,700 psi. *See* Brian Handwerk, *"Extraordinary" Study Hints Crocs Are "Force-generating Machines" Rivaling T. rex.*, NATIONAL GEOGRAPHIC NEWS, news.nationalgeographic.com/news/2012/03/120315-crocodiles-bite-force-erickson-science-plos-one-strongest/. Of course, the comparison of a dog's maw to a thief's shiv requires further modification because the force generated by the mouth might be greater than that by the arm swinging or jabbing a blade. And, further, a single blade does not grip and hold, which bears study in light of the long-standing rule that "where a suspect threatens an officer with a weapon such as a gun or a knife, the officer is justified in using deadly force." *Smith v. City of Hemet*, 394 F.3d 689 (9th Cir. 2005).

a.   Pit Bull Rule

Though not appearing to create a "pit bull" rule, which would tilt the Fourth Amendment reasonableness calculus in favor of the shooting officer, several district courts have tenaciously focused on breed to deem slayings reasonable. For instance, canine officer William Proulx shot and killed Stacy Warboys' "pitbull dog" Blitz when he approached Proulx and his police dog Dakota as they were tracking a fleeing car theft suspect. As Proulx described it, an unrestrained, 90-100 pound pit bull, whose propensities — gentle or vicious — were unknown, closed a short distance in a matter of seconds while Dakota was identifying a pool of scent. Warboys, on the other hand, claimed Blitz had no history of aggression, approached "in a friendly mood" "with his tail wagging" when killed, which occurred after she yelled to the officer that he would not attack. In finding no Fourth Amendment violation, federal district court Judge Janet C. Hall focused not on the lack of evidence that Blitz harmed an animal or person before, but instead on his presumed breed. *Warboys v. Proulx*, 303 F. Supp. 2d 111, 118 & n.13 (D. Conn. 2004); *see also Vanater v. South Point*, 717 F. Supp. 1236, 1240–41 (S.D. Ohio 1989) (upholding anti-pit bull municipal ordinance).

Other courts go so far as to deem it reasonable to kill an unknown dog due to the "latent threat" they pose. *Powell v. Johnson*, 855 F. Supp. 2d 871, 875–76 (D. Minn. 2012) (*quoting P.M. ex rel. Whitworth v. Bolinger*, 2011 U.S. Dist. LEXIS 134130, *20 (W.D. Mo. Nov. 21, 2011)). *Whitworth* plucked the "latent threat" notion out of thin air, defying common law and Restatement comment. *See Drake v. Dean*, 15 Cal. App. 4th 915, 921 (1993) (*quoting* RESTATEMENT (2D) OF TORTS, § 509, cmt. f ("[Because] [t]he great majority of dogs are harmless . . . the possession of characteristics dangerous to mankind . . . is properly regarded as abnormal to them." and "[F]rom time immemorial [dogs] have been regarded as the friends and companions of man."); *Olson v. Pederson*, 288 N.W. 856 (Minn. 1939) ("[A] dog's bad character or evil disposition is not presumed. . . . A dog is presumed to be tame, docile and harmless until the contrary appears."); *Morgan v. Marquis*, 50 A.3d 1, 4 (Me. 2012) (affirming summary judgment on strict liability claim as "the law does not recognize that pit bulls are *per se* abnormally dangerous to the class of domestic dogs").

b. Split-second Decision

Split-second determinations made under rapidly evolving conditions render such seizures reasonable. *Altman v. City of High Point, N.C.*, 330 F.3d 194 (4th Cir. 2003), exemplifies this doctrine. Four fatal shootings of at-large dogs resulted in § 1983 claims against the animal control officers for violating the plaintiffs' Fourth Amendment right against unreasonable, warrantless seizures of their dogs with known propensities for aggression. On the date of the shooting, the dogs displayed varying degrees of hostility toward the officers and the public. Each was killed by gunshot:

(1) "Heidi," a purebred Rottweiler, allegedly beaten off by a citizen with a stick when the animal control officer shot her, but not in self-defense;

(2) "Bandit" and "Tut-Tut," seven-month-old puppies, shot as they ran with a pack of strays after attacking an animal control officer;

(3) "Sundance," a golden retriever/Labrador mix, shot after charging an officer responding to a call about biting a citizen;

(4) "Hot Rod," a part pit bull, killed after allegedly charging the officer twice but then running away without attacking.

One issue concerned whether dogs were "effects" who may be "seized" under the Fourth Amendment, such that failure to use available, nonlethal means of force when trying to impound dogs violates the owners' constitutional property right in them. The court also considered whether governmental immunity protected the officers' seizures in these circumstances. Though three justices found no Fourth Amendment violation, the court unanimously held that dogs were "effects" "seized" without a warrant under the Fourth Amendment (thereby aligning with the Third, Eighth, and Ninth Circuits). The dissenting justice held that the officers violated a clearly established Fourth Amendment right in each instance and were not entitled to qualified immunity.

Attention was given to the City of High Point's ordinance instructing animal control officers to kill at-large dogs who could not be safely "taken up and impounded," a factor that influenced the court's reasonableness assessment of the shooting of Hot Rod. It undertook to "balance the nature and quality of the intrusion on the individual's Fourth Amendment interest against the importance of the governmental interests alleged to justify the intrusion," *U.S. v. Place*, 462 U.S. 696, 703 (1983), mindful that it must allow officers to make split-second judgments. *Graham*, 490 U.S. at 396–97. Further, reasonableness focuses on actual harm to the dogs, not potential peril to third parties (undercutting "The officer could have hit a bystander"-type arguments). *Howerton v. Fletcher*, 213 F.3d 171, 175 (4th Cir. 2000) (risk to third parties not considered). Characterizing the case as presenting "both interests at their zenith," the majority had no reservation deeming the shootings reasonable even as to the closer question of Hot Rod, who was shot while fleeing, and who had not attacked or threatened anyone, perhaps because he was allegedly part pit bull and showed sufficient aggression to cause a meter reader to call the police.

Altman recognized that certain factors modify the standard reasonableness analysis, such as whether the dogs were running at large, uncontrolled, and with no owner looking on, as discussed in *Brown v. Muhlenberg Tp.*, 269 F.3d 205 (3d Cir. 2001) (State may not, "consistent with the Fourth Amendment, destroy a pet when it poses no immediate danger and the owner is looking on, obviously desirous of retaining custody"); *Fuller v. Vines*, 36 F.3d 65 (9th Cir. 1994), *as amended on denial of reh'g and reh'g en banc*, (Nov. 23, 1994) and *overruled by, Robinson v. Solano County*, 278 F.3d 1007 (9th Cir. 2002) (owners standing in front yard when Great Dane shot).

Dissenting Judge Gregory argued that the officer's "[f]lagrant disregard" of several local ordinances and police department regulations was "relevant from an evidentiary perspective to show that a reasonable officer confronting the same situations as the defendants would have acted differently" and rendered the seizures unreasonable. *Id.*, at 208–09. Finding Judge Gregory's dissent suffered from a "logical flaw . . . l[ying] in its unspoken premise, namely that the standards set by local law in fact coincide with the reasonableness standards set by the Fourth Amendment," the majority added that "[t]he Constitution is not a 'font of tort law' to be 'superimposed upon whatever systems may already be administered by the States.' *The officers' conduct violated police regulations as well as state law and was dealt with under those provisions.* But not every instance of inappropriate behavior on the part of police rises to the level of a federal constitutional violation." *Id.*, at 208 (*quoting Robles v. Prince George's County, Maryland*, 302 F.3d 262, 271 (4th Cir. 2002) (internal citation omitted, former emphasis added)).

At the time of the shootings, only two circuits found that dogs were "effects" under the Fourth Amendment: *Lesher v. Reed*, 12 F.3d 148 (8th Cir. 1994) and *Fuller v. Vines*, 36 F.3d 65 (9th Cir. 1994). As this hardly represented a consensus, the majority deemed the law not then clearly established so as to admonish an officer not to shoot and kill a family pet presenting no danger when nonlethal methods of capture would succeed. This nascent state of the law served as a basis to grant qualified immunity to the shooting officer.

The law nonetheless holds that an officer's personal views regarding the most effective methods of neutralizing canine threats or a demonstrated history of cavalier shootings "are irrelevant as a matter of law" to the question of qualified immunity, which instead depends on whether the officer acted in an objectively reasonable manner in this particular case, evil intentions aside.

Other courts have excused split-second dog slayings. *Ivey v. Hamlin*, 2002 Tenn. App. LEXIS 404 (June 7, 2002) dismissed a case against an officer who executed a bulldog. Though at large and purportedly vicious, the dog did not present an imminent danger to any person or property. The officer then dragged his body to the nearby woods. While state law mandated that the officer seize the collarless dog and confine him, Hamlin failed to take such a step as the county had no impound facility. The Court of Appeals affirmed dismissal on grounds of qualified immunity as the law was not clearly established that shooting a pet animal gives rise to a *due process* violation. Had a Fourth Amendment *seizure* claim been pleaded, the outcome probably would not have differed. *Id.* at *5–*6. *U.S. v. Gregory*, 933 F.2d 1016 (9th Cir. 1991), generated a similar outcome, finding the shooting of a dog during execution of a search warrant for marijuana at a private residence constitutional given the split-second reaction by an officer reasonably believing it to be an attack dog. *See also Brandon v. Village of Maywood*, 157 F. Supp. 2d 917 (N.D. Ill. 2001), where officers fired 19 rounds at plaintiff's dog, injuring him, after arresting a drug dealer in the plaintiff's yard. The court granted qualified immunity based on the rapidly evolving scenario.

To justify split-second decisions, courts resort to simple math to compute average speed. For instance, calculating a rate of three feet per second (fps), the district court in *Dziekan v. Gaynor*, 376 F. Supp. 2d 267, 271–72 (D. Conn. 2005), found reasonable the shooting of a 55- to 60-pound Catahoula leopard dog positioned 15 feet from the officer when it had closed from 30 feet, although this was half the speed of the dog slain in *Warboys v. Proulx*, 303 F. Supp. 2d 111, 118 (D. Conn. 2004) (holding that "[a]n officer who encounters a 90- to 100-pound pit bull dog — a dog which is demonstrably not able to be restrained by its owner or guardian and which is approaching the officer at a rate of six feet per second and is at a distance of no more than 10 feet — does not act unreasonably in shooting the dog to protect himself and his canine companion"). Consider, however, that most humans walk at a speed of four feet per second. *See* LaPlante and Kaeser, *A History of Pedestrian Signal Walking Speed Assumptions*, 3RD URBAN STREET SYMPOSIUM (Jun. 24-27, 2007), Seattle, Wash. (citing Manual of Uniform Traffic Control Devices (MUTCD) (using four as recommended walking speed to set time for pedestrian clearance phase for pedestrian signal installations) and National Committee on Uniform Traffic Control Devices (voting to reduce to 3.5 fps for pedestrian clearance phase and three fps for entire walk/flashing don't walk interval)). Would the Fourth Amendment warrant shooting a person merely walking toward an officer?

Andrews v. City of West Branch, Iowa, 454 F.3d 914 (8th Cir. 2006) sits in contrast to *Altman*. The Eighth Circuit upheld a jury verdict of an unreasonable Fourth Amendment seizure based on an officer's disregard of an ordinance counseling passivity in taking up dogs. Police chief Dan Knight responded to a call of a large black dog running loose and molesting the complainant's dog. Failing to apprehend the canine after driving through the neighborhood and losing sight of him, Knight ended up at the Andrewses' residence. Observing a large black dog in the fenced, enclosed backyard, he approached with a leash, then shot the dog twice, immediately thereafter realizing that he had injured the wrong animal. Jana Andrews had just let her dog Riker outside to relieve itself. Traumatized by the gunshots, Knight shot Riker a third time to end his suffering. When killed, Riker was not wearing a collar with tags, though his vaccinations were up-to-date. Knight shot without warning, without inquiring as to whether Riker had run loose prior to the shooting, or asking whether the backyard was completely enclosed by a fence.

Unless the jurisdiction provided for seizure and impoundment, Iowa Code Ann. § 351.26 stated that any person could (and every peace officer should) kill any dog failing to wear a collar with a rabies vaccination tag attached, adding that dogs not provided with a rabies vaccination tag "shall not be deemed property." The municipal West Branch Code defined an animal as not at large if "on the enclosed premises of the owner." The Animal Control Section of the West Branch Police Policy Manual advised that officers "should utilize all available methods to obtain capture of animals running at large," that "discharging of a firearm at an animal should be considered as a last resort," and that "animals taken into custody should be taken to the animal shelter." Finding the seizure and impoundment policy logically extended to fenced-in, passive dogs not wearing vaccination tags, the court held that a reasonable jury could deem Knight's shooting of an apparently at-large dog premature and a Fourth Amendment violation. To be clear: a violation of state or local law does not, in and of itself, establish a § 1983 claim; the Fourth Amendment seizure cause of action must stand on its own merits based on federal common law. Citing *Brown v. Muhlenberg Tp.*, 269 F.3d 205, 211–12 (3d Cir. 2001), the court declined to extend qualified immunity to Knight as no objective officer could have possibly concluded "that he could lawfully destroy a pet who posed no imminent danger and whose owners were known, available, and desirous of assuming custody."

c. Owner Present to Control

Officers deploying lethal force in the presence of an owner attempting to reassert control over an animal court failure under the Fourth Amendment. *Brown v. Muhlenberg Tp.*, 269 F.3d 205 (3d Cir. 2001) is the watershed decision stating this rule. Immi, a Rottweiler, escaped while the Browns were in the process of moving. She wandered to a nearby parking lot. As she reached the curb, an officer parked his patrol car and approached, clapping his hands and calling to her. Immi barked several times, then withdrew, circling around a vehicle in the parking lot approximately 20 feet from the curb. The officer crossed the street and walked to a position 10 to 12 feet away. Immi was stationary, and neither growling nor barking. Kim Brown looked out an open, screened window of her house seeing the officer reach for his gun. Screaming as loudly as she could, "That's my dog, don't shoot!" the officer hesitated a few seconds before pointing his gun at Immi. Desperate to protect Immi, she tried to break through the window's screen. The officer then fired five shots at Immi, four of them entering her hind end. Finding a genuine issue of material fact sufficient to overcome the motion for summary judgment, the court held that a jury could determine that the officer violated the Browns' Fourth Amendment rights when killing Immi, stating, "the state may [not], consistent with the Fourth Amendment, destroy a pet when it poses no immediate danger and the owner is looking on, obviously desirous of retaining custody." In rejecting qualified immunity, the court added that it would have "been apparent to a reasonable officer that shooting Immi would be unlawful" where her owners were known, available, and eager to assume custody. The dissent, on the other hand, asserted that the decisional law in the Eighth and Ninth Circuits pertained to dogs seized within the property of their respective owners, not those unleashed, at large, and beyond the owner's voice or signal control, leading to the conclusion that the law of this case was not clearly established, for purposes of qualified immunity, in the Third, Eighth, or Ninth Circuits.

Newsome v. Erwin, 137 F. Supp. 2d 934 (S.D. Ohio 2000) reached a similar result as the majority in *Brown*, finding that despite having tranquilized a pet lioness and informing the officer she was declawed and safe, he nonetheless shot her in the head. The court found that no reasonable officer could claim that he did not know that shooting a tranquilized pet lioness point-blank several feet away from her barn in front of the owner would violate the owner's rights.

d. Contrived Necessity

Police officers may meet the threat of deadly force with like force, subject to necessity. "Necessity" is the second prerequisite for the use of deadly force under *Garner*. "The necessity inquiry is a factual one: Did a reasonable non-deadly alternative exist for apprehending the suspect?" *Brower v. County of Inyo*, 884 F.2d 1316 (9th Cir. 1989), *on remand from Brower v. County of Inyo*, 489 U.S. 593 (1989). However, police officers cannot justify a contrived use of deadly force. *See Billington v. Smith*, 292 F.3d 1177, 1189 (9th Cir. 2002) (creating the "police liability based on provocation" doctrine).

Virtually all state and local dangerous dog codes provide a provocation defense where the animal fears an actual assault to itself, its offspring, or its owner. So, if a police officer entered a home by surprise, without introduction, brandishing a weapon and an aura of fearsomeness, would not a dog living on the premises be within its "rights" or "sensibilities as a dog" to defend its territory and guardians? In other words, should law enforcement give strong consideration to the fact that a dog will "act like a dog," and wield that knowledge to erect safeguards to accommodate its predictable behavior? Precisely such thought process underlay the Ninth Circuit's decision in *San Jose Charter of Hells Angels Motorcycle Club v. City of San Jose*, 402 F.3d 962 (9th Cir. 2005).

In rejecting qualified immunity, the Ninth Circuit found the shooting of dogs belonging to Hells Angels members an unreasonable seizure, resulting from the unreasonable execution of search warrant. No exigent circumstances existed, and the purported necessity of discharging firearms was due to law enforcement's failure to use the week before to prepare nonlethal means of neutralizing dogs rather than to kill them if they got in the way. The unlawfulness of such conduct would have been glaringly apparent to any reasonable officer. Citing *Fuller* for the proposition that killing dogs constitutes the clearly established law of a Fourth Amendment seizure, the court proceeded to examine the reasonableness of the killings, remarking that a seizure becomes unlawful when it is "more intrusive than necessary." *Florida v. Royer*, 460 U.S. 491, 504 (1983). Calling them "more than just a personal effect," the court classified the intrusion of killing three dogs "severe." It added, "[t]he emotional attachment to a family's dog is not comparable to a possessory interest in furniture." *Id.*, at 975.

Responding to the excuse that the officers' plan to engage the known guard dogs was required to preserve stealth, the court held that the officers themselves "compromised their ability to effectuate a quiet entry" as the shotgun blasts woke the residents, not the barking of dogs. Citing *Fuller*, *Brown*, *Lesher*, as well as

Chew v. Gates, 27 F.3d 1432, 1440 n.5 (9th Cir. 1994), and *Gutierrez v. City of San Antonio,* 139 F.3d 441, 450 (5th Cir. 1998), cases holding that reasonableness under the Fourth Amendment depends on whether officials contemplated alternatives before undertaking intrusive activity implicating constitutional rights, the court found that:

> These cases should have alerted any reasonable officer that the Fourth Amendment forbids the killing of a person's dog, or the destruction of a person's property, when that destruction is unnecessary — i.e., when less intrusive, or less destructive, alternatives exist. A reasonable officer should have known that to create a plan to enter the perimeter of a person's property, knowing all the while about the presence of dogs on the property, without considering a method for subduing the dogs besides killing them, would violate the Fourth Amendment.

San Jose Charter of Hells Angels Motorcycle Club v. City of San Jose, 402 F.3d 962, 977–78 (9th Cir. 2005). This was not a case requiring split-second judgments made under tense, uncertain, and rapidly evolving circumstances typically seen in matters granted qualified immunity. Practitioners may learn a great deal from *Hells Angels*'s distinction of split-second deployment of lethal force from premeditated force, as well as the inverse relationship between time to plan and reasonableness of deploying deadly force.

A California federal district court examined *Hells Angels* in the context of a warrantless entry where officers responded to an emergency 911 call and, upon entry, shot and killed the plaintiffs' dog in *Silva v. City of San Leandro,* 744 F. Supp. 2d 1036 (N.D. Cal. 2010). On account of differing renditions of whether Boo Boo threatened the shooting officer and whether the plaintiff signaled to the officers to wait so he could restrain the dog, the court cited to *Hells Angels* to deny summary judgment and qualified immunity. However, in another dog-shooting case, the California federal district court in *Perez v. City of Placerville,* 2008 U.S. Dist. LEXIS 83172 (E.D. Cal. Sept. 9, 2008), distinguished *Hells Angels* on the following grounds:

> To the contrary [refusing to extend Hells Angels], in this case, exigent circumstances were present. The officers did not have weeks to plan this search; they acted on the arrest warrant the same day they received it. At best, the facts suggest here that the officers suspected a dog might be present at the scene but they had no confirmation of that fact. Officer Algers acted reasonably in attempting to confirm the presence of a dog by making sounds to elicit a response from a dog and looking over the back fence. When there was no response and he did not see a dog, he opened the gate slightly. He was immediately attacked by Harley. Beyer responded first with pepper spray. Only once that did not work did he use his weapon to shoot Harley. After two shots the dog was still not subdued so Beyer shot the dog a third time. Within twenty minutes of the shooting, the officers transported Harley to the nearest veterinarian's office. San Jose Charter of Hells Angels Motorcycle Club v. City of San Jose, 402 F.3d 962, 977–978 (9th Cir. 2005) (recognizing that the governmental interest in safety of law

enforcement officers may well provide a "sound justification" for the killing of a dog, particularly where officers are surprised by the presence of a dog).

e. Secondary Seizure

Owners present during the seizure of an animal will often react to the horror of witnessing a beloved animal companion executed in front of them. The heightened tensions place not only the owner on edge, but law enforcement as well, leading to predictable secondary uses of force against the distraught owner. Such Fourth Amendment sequelae emerged in the Sixth Circuit case *Smoak v. Hall*, 2009 U.S. App. LEXIS 19978 (6th Cir. Sept. 2, 2009).

On January 1, 2003, the Smoak family was returning home to the Carolinas after a New Year's Eve celebration in Nashville, Tennessee. Accompanying the family in their green station wagon were their two dogs, General Patton, an adolescent bulldog/pit bull mix, and Cassie. Minutes after James Smoak accidentally left his wallet atop the car and drove away from the gas station, a woman notified the police that she witnessed the Smoak vehicle traveling at a high rate of speed down the interstate with "money flying all over[.]" The dispatcher sent state patrol to the scene and notified local law enforcement of a "recent robbery." Shortly thereafter, the dispatcher learned of the small amount of money at issue and the find of Mr. Smoak's wallet.

Based on this new information, the dispatcher concluded that no crime had occurred, yet he failed to rescind his "be on the lookout" notification. Meanwhile, state patrol executed a felony stop of the Smoak vehicle on the interstate. The Smoaks exited the car, hands behind their heads, and were handcuffed. The officers pointed assault rifles and shotguns at the family, an admittedly significant departure from accepted professional protocols. Mr. Smoak repeatedly asked that the car doors be shut because General Patton and Cassie might jump out, reiterating they presented no danger. The officers refused to shut the car door. Patton bounded out, tail wagging, and approached Officer Hall, who then killed Patton in front of the Smoak family. Mr. Smoak jumped up in shock. Officers then forced him down to the ground, causing a knee injury that required surgical repair. *Smoak v. Hall*, 460 F.3d 768 (6th Cir. 2006). The Smoaks were then put in separate patrol cars when the officers learned from dispatch that no robbery had occurred. They released the Smoaks after being cuffed for nine minutes. As the Smoaks drove away, the patrol car camera captured Officer Bush lamenting, "I wish I had never stopped that f__king car."

While the Smoaks settled with the defendants concerning the shooting of Patton, at issue in the 2009 appeal remained the $210,351.52 jury award ($9,102.80 compensatory, $192,248.72 attorney's fees) related to Officer Bush's excessive force when driving Mr. Smoak to the ground with the weight of three men landing on his left knee and one officer kneeling on his head, pinning him. In affirming, the Sixth Circuit found the use of force unreasonable under the circumstances including the "visceral reaction to Officer Hall's horrifying shotgun blast to the dog's head — Smoak stood up when he was ordered to kneel. But, in the totality of the encounter, Smoak had been fully compliant." That Mr. Smoak was sobbing and grief-stricken at just having seen Patton's head explode "in a mist of blood, bone, and brain" without any justification did not warrant the conclusion that Bush was "reasonably mistaken" and entitled to immunity for the misuse of arrest force.

The Seventh Circuit examined similar owner-reactivity issues in *Bailey v. Andrews*, 811 F.2d 366 (7th Cir. 1987), where an arrestee, who believed the officer shot his dog Lucy, asking "Did you shoot my dog?" and stating that he wanted his "damn dog," received an $80,000 jury award ($25,000 punitive) against the arresting officer under § 1983. On appeal, the Seventh Circuit affirmed on liability but remanded for a new trial on damages as excessive given the limited actual harm to Bailey.

Observation: A jury and court concluded that no reasonable officer would have found Bailey's plaintive (though perhaps overly assertive and annoying) pleas for information about his dog to constitute fighting words prohibited by the disorderly conduct statute, to be legally obscene, or to be inherently inflammatory; accordingly, the officer had no immunity for arresting Bailey on grounds of disorderly conduct. Though unspecified, the jury award of punitive damages signaled a belief that he acted with deliberate indifference to Bailey's constitutional rights under the First Amendment (arresting in response to speech or petitioning an agent of government for redress of grievances), the Fourth Amendment (conducting a warrantless search of Bailey's vehicle without consent, exigent circumstances, or other exception to the warrant requirement; and unreasonable seizure through arrest made in bad faith and without probable cause), and the Fourteenth Amendment substantive due process doctrine (kicking Bailey, inspired by malice, and representing a completely unjustified use of force), but not the Eighth Amendment (applying only to cruel and unusual punishment of sentenced criminals).

Finally, the Ninth Circuit addressed both the seizure of a dog by shooting and threatening the dog's owner at gunpoint after a potential postshooting altercation with the shooting officer in *Fuller v. Vines*, 36 F.3d 65 (9th Cir. 1994), *as amended on denial of reh'g and reh'g en banc*, (1994) and *overruled o.g. by Robinson v. Solano County*, 278 F.3d 1007 (9th Cir. 2002). Officers investigating another matter passed by the Fullers' yard. Champ, a Great Dane, merely stood up from where he was lying, near father and son. The officers contended that Champ growled and barked. The father pleaded not to shoot and said he could control Champ, yet they killed him, shooting him once in the shoulder and the other in the head to "finish him off." Officers then wrestled the son to the ground after an officer allegedly cocked the gun to his head and threatened to send him to the morgue. On appeal, the Ninth Circuit reversed, allowing the Fullers to amend the complaint to allege Fourth Amendment seizure relative to slaying Champ, but not as to the son. Three years later, in *Fuller v. Vines*, 117 F.3d 1425 (9th Cir. 1997) (Fuller II), the court rejected qualified immunity for the shooting officer. A jury awarded $143,000 compensatory and $10,000 punitive damages in relation to Champ and $77,000 compensatory and $25,000 punitive damages in relation to the assault tort claim for the son. In *Fuller I and II*, the U.S. Supreme Court refused certiorari both times (first, when the Ninth Circuit held that the shooting of a dog was an unreasonable seizure and, second, when the appellate court held that officers were not entitled to qualified immunity because the law was clearly established).

8.   Seizure from Failure to Surrender Dog

Transfer of an animal to government custody commonly precedes a claim of that animal's wrongful death by the government. Frequently, transfer occurs after warrant execution or warrantless entry and seizure, but sometimes officers demand that the owner surrender the animal. When they refuse (fearing, no doubt, that the state will kill their animal), they sometimes face arrest, as happened in *Quackenbush v. County of Santa Barbara*, 182 F.3d 927 (9th Cir. 1999). Animal control ordered Quackenbush to surrender his dog, who allegedly recently bit a young child, potentially exposing her to rabies. He refused, and the officers cited him for misdemeanor failure to produce an animal on demand of the local health officer. Qualified immunity may apply as the existence of a statute "authorizing particular conduct is a factor which militates in favor of the conclusion that a reasonable official would find that conduct constitutional." *Grossman v. City of Portland*, 33 F.3d 1200, 1209 (9th Cir. 1994). At the time of citing him, no cases interpreted the statute. However, *Camara v. Municipal Court of City and County of San Francisco*, 387 U.S. 523 (1967), overturned Camara's conviction for refusing to allow inspectors to enter his home without a warrant. But unlike the ordinance in *Camara*, which permitted inspectors to search any building, the California law did not suffer from such fatal broadness, and the officers could have reasonably questioned whether it was appropriate for Quackenbush to refuse to turn over a dog previously placed in residential quarantine and under the supervision of animal control. Thus, though his constitutional rights were violated, the arresting officer enjoyed qualified immunity. While holding Quackenbush for 49 hours before his first criminal court appearance, the officers meanwhile procured a warrant and seized the dog following his arrest, evidencing the feasibility of acting within the confines of a reasonable search requirement, a point raised by the dissenting judge.

Even if not arrested, the mere threat of arrest or criminal prosecution to achieve compliance may create a Fourth Amendment malicious prosecution claim as discussed by the Sixth Circuit in *Jones v. Gilmore*, 884 F.2d 579 (6th Cir. 1989). The poundmaster mistakenly sold a husky dog, impounded for running at large, to Scott Jones before the husky's owners arrived to redeem. The police chief tried to encourage Jones to surrender the dog after indicating his attempt to secure a reward from the owners. Jones acquiesced. He then changed his mind when the owners refused to pay. The sheriff then arrived at Jones's home to retrieve the Husky, only to be greeted by an ultimatum "no money-no dog." This prompted the sheriff to threaten Jones with criminal charges if he did not return the dog. Thereafter, law enforcement arrested Jones on a warrant, charged him with fourth-degree felony theft, and took the dog. A jury acquitted. Jones then sued under § 1983, claiming a procedural due process violation. On appeal, the Sixth Circuit affirmed dismissal on grounds of qualified immunity, but commented on the propriety of even criminally charging Jones, stating:

> There is little doubt that if Jones had not been so totally uncooperative, a criminal charge of this nature would probably not have been filed. We agree with Jones also that disputes of this nature are better left to civil resolution. We see a certain element of personal vindictiveness, albeit born of

frustration, involved in the decision to press criminal charges. Difficult though it may be at times, public officials, particularly police officials, must develop a thick hide or else find themselves constantly answering to charges of this nature.

Had the property at issue been inanimate, one doubts whether any criminal, or the subsequent civil, suits would have ensued.

Martin v. Columbia Greene Humane Soc., Inc., 17 A.D.3d 839 (N.Y. Sup. Ct. App. Div. 2005), had a different outcome. Dog breeders sued the humane society and Matthew Tully, a peace officer (also an attorney) who volunteered as a cruelty investigator with the society, when he threatened to arrest them on misdemeanor charges unless they surrendered all 15 puppies for willfully selling dogs with contagious diseases. After the Martins surrendered the puppies (worth an estimated $9,000), Tully filed criminal charges, later dismissed without prejudice by the prosecutor. Shortly thereafter, Tully notified the Martins' defense attorney that he intended to reinstate the criminal charges unless they agreed not to sell dogs for three years. The Martins responded by suing for malicious prosecution, abuse of process, tortious interference with business relations, and § 1983 violations. The appellate court affirmed denial of the motion to dismiss.

Where the plaintiff claimed a violation of her right to due process in the form of extortion when officers allegedly threatened to charge her with felony animal cruelty if she did not immediately sign a document surrendering her animals to law enforcement, the court dismissed the Fourteenth Amendment claim. It found that she did not deserve any predeprivation process because the officers removed the animals from emergent conditions and afforded her a postdeprivation hearing. *Engel v. Barry*, 2006 U.S. Dist. LEXIS 41912 (E.D. Cal. June 22, 2006), *dismissed*, 2010 U.S. App. LEXIS 2820 (9th Cir. 2010).

9. Wild versus Domestic Distinction

Courts and regulators distinguish domesticated and wild animals, rarely construing the latter as lawful to keep. Accordingly, those caring for an orphaned possum or injured flying squirrel, or assimilating captured wildlife into a domestic herd, may find themselves asserting a right of possession and, possibly, "ownership" in defiance of prohibitive wildlife laws. Are such claims sufficient to prevail in a § 1983 Fourth Amendment seizure action when agents take back animals purportedly owned by the state?

Fourth Amendment seizures arise in the context of governmental restraints on commercial breeding and sale operations, such as game farms. Take *Wright v. Department of Natural Resources*, 562 S.E.2d 515 (Ga. Ct. App. 2002). In 1963, Wright fenced a pond on his property, capturing alligators in the hope he could breed and sell their offspring. DNR denied his application, claiming they belonged to the state as wildlife. Later, he acquired Florida brood stock, keeping them separate from the Georgia alligators. Years passed and the two populations blended, causing DNR to halt Wright's further egg collection. When Wright hired a trapping service in 1996 to sell all 650 alligators on his property, DNR intervened. Wright claimed a taking under § 1983 based on his asserted property interest in the original Georgia alligators he fenced and fed in 1963. The Georgia Court of Appeals affirmed summary judgment to DNR on several grounds, including fundamentally that Wright did not own the Georgia alligators.

A contrary result came in *Blue Ridge Mountain Fisheries, Inc. v. Department of Natural Resources*, 456 S.E.2d 651 (Ga. Ct. App. 1995). In 1990, pursuant to a search warrant, DNR officials seized as contraband 1,223 white sturgeon held for breeding and caviar production. They also arrested Cochran, president of BRMF, by asserting that the sturgeon were "exotic fish" illegally possessed. BRMF sued to recover the sturgeon under state law, contending they were not wildlife owned by the state. The superior court declared the seizure illegal and sturgeon not "exotic fish." Following this ruling, the prosecutor dismissed the criminal charges. Thereafter, Cochran and BRMF sued DNR and officials for having conspired to create the crime of unlawful possession of white sturgeon by private agreement, raising state and § 1983 claims (retaliation, procedural due process, and Fourth Amendment seizure). The appellate court rejected that government defendants enjoyed qualified immunity when they prosecuted Cochran for a criminal violation based on a definition of "exotic fish" different from generally accepted definitions or codified in any promulgated regulation. *Id.* at 655. It also reinstated the Fourth Amendment unlawful seizure and Fourteenth Amendment due process claims, notwithstanding the existence of a meaningful postdeprivation remedy, for DNR seized the sturgeon pursuant to an established state procedure and not a random, unauthorized act, as discussed further in *Zinermon v. Burch*, 494 U.S. 113 (1990). *Id.* at 656. The First Amendment retaliation claim was also resurrected.

In the noncommercial context, no case better illustrates the importance of confirming lawful possession and ownership prior to bringing a § 1983 claim for wrongful animal injury or death than *Bilida v. McCleod*, 211 F.3d 166 (1st Cir. 2000). Claire Bilida rescued an orphaned raccoon whom she named Mia, raising her at her Rhode Island home for seven years before the Department of Environmental Management (DEM) seized and killed her, ostensibly for rabies testing though Mia had not bitten or scratched a human. They did so without a warrant after confirming that Bilida had no permit. The state then prosecuted Bilida for misdemeanor illegal, permitless possession of a raccoon. Bilida defeated the charge upon a successful motion to suppress evidence of a law enforcement officer seeing Mia in the cage in Bilida's backyard while responding to a false security alarm signal at her residence. The criminal court found that the officers violated her Fourth Amendment right against warrantless entry and seizure of an already caged animal absent exigent circumstances. *Id.* at 169–70. Thereafter, Bilida sued the seizing officers, the DEM director and deputy chief, and state of Rhode Island under § 1983, asserting violations of her rights to "privacy," due process, and protection from unreasonable search and seizure, as well as parallel common-law claims. The federal district court dismissed her lawsuit in *Bilida v. McCleod*, 41 F. Supp. 2d 142 (D.R.I. 1999). She then appealed to the First Circuit Court of Appeals.

In finding a Fourth Amendment violation, the court reiterated that warrantless searches are presumptively unconstitutional and extend to the curtilage (areas adjacent to the home). The court then rejected the exceptions to the warrant — exigent circumstances, plain view, and extension of earlier entry and sighting of

Mia. While justifying the *initial* entry based on exigent circumstances (e.g., responding to security alarm), the First Circuit did not find grounds to justify the *new entry* for a different purpose. *Id.* at 172 (*citing Mincey v. Arizona*, 437 U.S. 385, 393 (1978)) (exigent circumstances must be strictly circumscribed); *but see Michigan v. Tyler*, 436 U.S. 499, 510–11 (1978) (second entry by fire investigators hours after firefighters extinguished fire and seized evidence in plain view upheld). Two other warrantless entry justifications were acknowledged but not evaluated because the officers did not seriously urge them at the trial level — public health emergency from a caged raccoon and imminent credible threat that "evidence" would disappear. *Id.* at 173.

"[W]ith little enthusiasm," the appellate court found that Bilida had no property interest in Mia, for she did not possess a permit for a wild animal, rendering Mia *per se* contraband. *Id.* at 173. Despite recognizing a Fourth Amendment violation, qualified immunity excused the final reentry and seizure of Mia as a reasonably anticipated (and thus protected) extension of the original lawful entry. Reaching a contrary result on the lawfulness of the reentry "only by a very close margin" compelled the court to grant qualified immunity, which leaves "ample room for mistaken judgments" and protects "all but the plainly incompetent or those who knowingly violate the law." *Malley v. Briggs*, 475 U.S. 335 (1986). Immunity came with one "unusual caveat" — if the seizing officers knew nothing about the prior lawful entry and plain view observation of Mia in the cage, "it might seem odd to grant them immunity based solely on the opacity of the law governing warrantless reentry."

Because qualified immunity only shields officers from damage suits, not those seeking declaratory relief, the appeals court expressed its view of the constitutionality of events. It also concluded that Bilida could still pursue her state law claims, adding that "it need hardly be said that this outcome is not an endorsement of the state's procedures for treatment of pet raccoons."

10. Wrongful Detention of Dog at Undisclosed Location

Wrongful detention of animals might present a constitutional claim of deprivation of property without due process or meaningful interference with possessory rights (i.e., seizure). However, a suit against a municipality for refusing to identify an animal's location or to allow inspection by the dog owner may not meet the threshold, and could backfire on the plaintiff, as seen in *Halfond v. County of Bergen*, 652 A.2d 250 (N.J. Super. Ct. App. Div. 1995). Under state law, animal control declared the Halfonds' dog Taro vicious. Following impoundment, under mysterious circumstances Taro escaped (or was stolen) from the shelter and found at the Halfonds' home, whereupon Taro returned to municipal custody. Pending the outcome of the vicious dog proceeding, the County of Bergen refused to disclose where it held Taro. Meanwhile, the Halfonds sued the county for failure to identify Taro's location as they wanted to have their animal behaviorist evaluate him prior to giving expert testimony at the vicious dog hearing. Three days before they filed the complaint, the county made him available for examination and confirmed his health. Still, the *Halfond* suit proceeded till dismissed on summary judgment, followed by an award of fees for frivolous action.

The government may lawfully detain an animal with statutory authority subject to constitutional protections, as may arise in the case of impound, rabies quarantine, stray hold, preconviction cruelty hold/protective custody, evidentiary hold, and predetermination dangerous dog hold. However, where the animal languishes in the pound for weeks, if not months, before any decision is made to file criminal charges or administratively declare the dog vicious, pinpoint authority should be sought that gives the city or county the right to so detain. Though the traditional rule stated in *Warden, Md. Penitentiary v. Hayden*, 387 U.S. 294 (1967), may superficially favor the government's position that it can hold the animal as "mere evidence" of the crime, even where photographs or live testimony will suffice, and especially where the code does not expressly warrant euthanasia or forfeiture of the animal upon conviction, plaintiffs may test this principle by emphasizing the distinction between inanimate and animate evidence, the latter deteriorating and changing in psychological (and sometimes physical) character during the period of separation from the owner. Many states provide for a preconviction (even precharge) forfeiture hearing for animals seized for suspected animal abuse or neglect. Nonetheless, the Fourth Amendment continues to treat "mere evidence" like instrumentalities, fruits of crime, and contraband. *Id.* That said, the government must still prove that the animal will actually be used in trial *as* evidence.

11. Administrative Entry and Seizure

Many jurisdictions require that citizens permit inspections on demand whenever the government allows them to keep animals in excess of a specific number, as in the case of a kennel license. Others allow animal control officers to enter residences and commercial buildings for purely administrative, noncriminal purposes with or without a warrant. One should carefully evaluate the constitutionality of these administrative searches and seizures in the shadow of *Camara v. Municipal Court of City and County of San Francisco*, 387 U.S. 523 (1967) (overturned conviction for refusing to allow inspectors to enter his home without a warrant) and *See v. City of Seattle*, 387 U.S. 541 (1967) (reversing conviction for refusal to permit fire department representative to enter and inspect locked commercial warehouse without a warrant). In *Harkey v. de Wetter*, 443 F.2d 828 (5th Cir. 1971), residents sued when the City of El Paso attempted to pass a law allowing animal control officers to conduct warrantless searches as a condition of keeping certain animals within city limits. In affirming dismissal, the Fifth Circuit distinguished *Camara* and *See* after a case-specific analysis under general Fourth Amendment principles as required to pass on this particular ordinance where no plaintiff applied for a permit, no inspection had yet been conducted, and no animals had yet been impounded.

Where officers take the time to procure a warrant, administrative searches and seizures are rarely found unconstitutional. In *Bielenberg v. Griffiths*, 2003 U.S. App. LEXIS 5354 (7th Cir. Mar. 11, 2003), the Seventh Circuit assessed the constitutionality of building inspectors and police entering the Bielenberg residence with an administrative warrant to find a clowder (211 to be exact) of cats with the volume of urine and feces one would expect from such number, along with decaying bodies. Though psychiatrically committed and later released, but ordered to temporarily vacate while sanitizing the house, the Bielenbergs sued under § 1983 (unreasonable search and seizure of persons and cats, due process (related to civil commitment and order to vacate pending cleanup)). Meanwhile, the city lodged an animal control complaint against them, resulting in a stipulated resolution whereby the city waived fines but obtained reimbursement for the expense of removing and euthanizing the cats, and whereby the Bielenbergs were prevented from keeping cats or dogs in the house. Passing on the merits, the court held that the defendants bore no liability for entry into the Bielenberg home based on a facially valid warrant. In 2005, the Seventh Circuit again heard appeal from the Bielenbergs and, again, affirmed dismissal — conferring qualified immunity for the warrant execution and housing code inspection. *Bielenberg v. Griffiths*, 2005 U.S. App. LEXIS 7787 (7th Cir. May 4, 2005).

Contrasting *Bielenberg*, consider the warrantless raids described in the ghastly opinion of *Maldonado v. Fontanes*, 568 F.3d 263 (1st Cir. 2009). Twenty-seven named plaintiff families, all residents of three public housing complexes, sued under 42 U.S.C. §§ 1983, 1985, and 1986 for the summary seizure and cruel killings of their pet cats and dogs, asserting violations of Fourth, Fourteenth, and Fifth Amendment rights. In 1999, Congress passed 42 U.S.C. § 1437z-3, allowing public housing residents the right to have in their dwelling one or more household pets. In 2000, the Municipality of Barceloneta passed Ord. 33, disallowing residents to have pets in the town center, housing developments, or urbanizations. In 2007, the Puerto Rico Public Housing Authority approved a pet policy consistent with federal regulations. Yet shortly after the municipality began managing the three public housing complexes where plaintiffs resided, they received a letter instructing them to remove all pets or be in breach of their lease contracts. Five days later, the mayor visited each complex and executed an operation to seize the pets. On Oct. 8, 2007, the Mayor and municipal staff knocked on residents' doors, and 50 to 80 animals were seized and injected with yellowish-green colored liquid, causing some to be sedated or paralyzed. All the animals were put in one van containing six to eight plastic crates. Some were beaten against the van. Others were thrown from a bridge known as the Paseo del Indio with several dead dogs spotted at the bottom amidst scattered tree limbs. One dog was found hanging from a tree. On Oct. 10, 2007, a nearly identical incident occurred. The trial court found that some of the plaintiffs were entitled to a predeprivation hearing under the Fourteenth Amendment; that the animal companions were "effects" protected against unreasonable seizure under the Fourth Amendment; and that the Mayor's door-to-door conversations preceding "consensual" relinquishment of the pets, was a "trial-worthy issue" to determine whether the mayoral acts were limited to "knock and talks," as well as the method of killing the seized animals.

After the district court denied the Mayor's motion to dismiss for qualified immunity, he appealed. The First Circuit Court of Appeals affirmed as to the seizure and procedural due process claims but reversed as to substantive due process. As a matter of first impression, the court rejected the Mayor's assertion that the Fourth Amendment does not protect an individual's interest in his companion animal, joining all other circuits in finding that both the seizure and killing infringed upon the Fourth Amendment. *Id.*, at 270–71. Though not established in the First Circuit prior to the raids, a "consensus of persuasive authority" from other circuits amply satisfied the "clearly established" standard and, thus, barred a finding of qualified immunity. *Id.*, at 271.

With respect to substantive due process, the court reversed based on lack of a nexus between the Mayor's conduct and the conscience-shocking seizing and killing of the animals, criticizing the district court for incorrectly focusing on the grouped acts of "government officials" and not the Mayor personally. *Id.*, at 273. While the complaint alleged the Mayor's joint participation in and executing of the raid with others, the court found "bare assertions" amounted to nothing more than a "formulaic recitation of the elements" of a constitutional tort insufficient to prevent dismissal. *Id.*, at 274. Nor did a claim of supervisory liability succeed given the absence of an "affirmative link" between the subordinate's behavior and action or inaction by the mayor so as to say that the supervisor's conduct inexorably led to the constitutional violation. *Id.*, at 275. Promulgating a no-pets policy without specifying the manner of collection and disposal, and merely attending the raid, failed to establish a strong enough "link."

Remember that administrative search warrants, like criminal warrants, require probable cause. "[A]dministrative searches generally require warrants." *Michigan v. Clifford*, 464 U.S. 287, 291 (1984). "[P]rivacy interests are especially strong in a private residence." *Id.*, at 296–97. Though not requiring the same showing of probable cause in the administrative context as in the criminal context, "[f]or purposes of an administrative search such as this, probable cause justifying the issuance of a warrant may be based not only on specific evidence of an existing violation but also on a showing that 'reasonable legislative' or 'administrative standards' for conducting an inspection are satisfied with respect to a particular [establishment]." *Marshall v. Barlow's, Inc.*, 436 U.S. 307, 320 (1978) (*quoting Camara v. Municipal Court of City and County of San Francisco*, 387 U.S. 523, 538 (1967)).

Yet in finding no probable cause, a court nonetheless granted qualified immunity in *Cahill v. Montgomery County*, 528 A.2d 527 (Md. Ct. Spec. App. 1987). Thanks to a tip from a confidential informant, animal control procured an administrative search warrant and searched the plaintiff's home for unvaccinated dogs. Judith Cahill, executive director of Rescue, Inc., a nonprofit dog rescue organization, claimed lack of probable cause, rendering the search unconstitutional, and sued under § 1983 for violation of her Fourth Amendment rights. Because animal control had not been conducting an area-wide inspection based on established standards, it needed to provide specific data proving that violations existed on Cahill's property. At most, the informant offered that approximately 40 dogs were kept on the premises, although county records only showed three dogs licensed to Cahill. And while the officer procuring the warrant drove by the Cahill home to see many dogs on the premises not matching those described in the licenses, the court found no probable cause existed that Cahill had unlicensed or unvaccinated dogs illegally kept on her property for, as a nonprofit, benevolent society, Rescue, Inc. need not license strays. Further, the affidavit also did not contain one allegation that any of the dogs was unvaccinated. Thus, the improper attempt to establish probable cause from inferences arising from nonviolations of the law rendered the warrant invalid. Despite agreeing that no probable cause existed, the appeals court granted qualified immunity to the officers, for it believed the county had "the better of this argument" and realized that the officers did not have the benefit of 20/20 hindsight. In other words, it did not find the information "so lacking in indicia of probable cause as to render official belief in its existence unreasonable." *Michigan v. Clifford*, 464 U.S. 287, 289 (1984) (*quoting U.S. v. Leon*, 468 U.S. 897, 923 (1984)).

As to the *Monell* claim against the municipality for violating her constitutional rights, that this was the first time the county procured an administrative search warrant to enforce an animal control ordinance did not dispose of the matter, for "municipal liability may be imposed for a single decision by a municipal policymakers (sic) under appropriate circumstances[.]" *Id.*, at 291 (*quoting Pembaur v. City of Cincinnati*, 475 U.S. 469 (1986)). Conceding that the evidence could go either way as to whether the county had a policy to initiate petitions for administrative searches of homes based solely on complaints of a large number of animals on private premises, the court reversed summary judgment and remanded for a preliminary determination of whether "the decision maker possesses final authority to establish municipal policy with respect to the action" in question. If not, then no municipal liability would exist.

12. Fourteenth Amendment Claims — Procedural Due Process

The Fourteenth Amendment's Due Process Clause states:

> [N]or shall any State deprive any person of life, liberty, or property, without due process of law; nor deny to any person within its jurisdiction the equal protection of the laws.

U.S. Const. Amend. XIV, § 1. For animals' interests to come within the protections afforded by this amendment requires a qualifying relationship to a "person," whether as the individual's "liberty" or "property." Without exception, humans may hold *property* interests in animals. "Due process rights attach to dog ownership." *Mansour v. King Cy.*, 128 P.3d 1241 (Wash. Ct. App. 2006) (*citing Rabon v. City of Seattle (Rabon II)*, 34 P.3d 821, 825–26 (Wash. Ct. App. 2001) (applying *Mathews v. Eldrige* due process factors); *Phillips v. San Luis Obispo County Dep't of Animal Regulations*, 183 Cal. App. 3d 372, 376 (1986) (accord)). Animal companionship has also been described as a *liberty* interest. *Rabon v. City of Seattle*, 34 P.3d 821 (Wash. Ct. App. 2001), intimated that due process protection against deprivations of liberty may more appropriately speak to the nature of the right infringed when a companion animal has been killed or withheld by government after being declared dangerous. "There may be merit to the argument that a person's relationship with a dog deserves more protection than a person's relationship with, say, a car."

Procedural due process minimally requires an opportunity to be heard when the government seeks to restrict a protected liberty or property right. *Boddie v. Connecticut*, 401 U.S. 371, 377 (1971). To this end, the Supreme Court applies the balancing test of *Mathews v. Eldridge* whenever the government constrains a liberty or property interest protected by due process. *Mathews v. Eldridge*, 424 U.S. 319 (1976). The three factors weighed include:

- The private interest affected by the official action;

- The risk of an erroneous deprivation of such interest through procedures used and the probable value, if any, of additional or substitute procedural safeguards; and

- The government's interest, including the function involved, and the fiscal and administrative burdens that the additional or substitute procedural requirement would entail.

In *Siebert v. Severino*, 256 F.3d 648 (7th Cir. 2001), the Seventh Circuit found a department of agriculture investigator's barn search and horse seizure illegal. After accepting that she had a protected property interest in the three horses, and that the seizure was neither random nor unforeseen, the court found sufficient facts to support a claim for a due process deprivation even though their removal was temporary. To avoid the risk of erroneous deprivation, the court found that Siebert deserved a predeprivation hearing, which was entirely feasible given the 72-hour delay, lack of exigency, and thwarted attempts by Siebert to discuss the matter with Severino prior to seizure. Qualified immunity again did not excuse Severino for his behavior even though he might have mistakenly interpreted the Illinois Humane Care for Animals Act as providing only for a postdeprivation hearing.

By contrast, consider *Reams v. Irvin*, 561 F.3d 1258 (11th Cir. 2009). With a warrant, defendants inspected Reams family farm to ascertain whether the plaintiff had provided inadequate food and water in violation of state equine neglect law. A veterinarian present during execution of the warrant determined that 49 equines required removal to protective custody. Reams, then out of state, never learned of her right to challenge the impoundment, though weeks later she did request a hearing. Nevertheless, the defendants did not advise her then of her right to petition for return under state law. Instead, they insisted she agree to a consent order, limiting the number of equines she could keep and ordering her to pay fines. Later, defendant Irvin issued an administrative order fining her in the sum of $74,000 and ordering her to reduce her herd to 30. Only after receiving the order did Reams learn of the right to petition for agency review, which she promptly sought, albeit beyond the 30-day window set forth by statute. Upon securing an emergency order staying the threatened sale of her horses from the impound facility, Reams brought a § 1983 suit claiming deprivation of due process before and after seizure.

Though acknowledging that Reams's interest in the impounded equines was "not insubstantial," the inspection and impoundment procedures rendered the risk of erroneous deprivation rather low, and did not necessitate a predeprivation hearing. In reaching this conclusion, the court took note that added procedural safeguards before the seizure would further jeopardize the health and safety of the animals, an "undeniably substantial" state interest "significantly compromised" if predeprivation hearings became mandatory. Reams's claim that the defendants denied her adequate notice of her right to petition for return of the equines also failed given precedent. "For 100 years, the Supreme Court has declared that a publicly available statute may be sufficient to provide [constitutionally adequate] notice because individuals are presumptively charged with knowledge of such a statute." *Grayden v. Rhodes*, 345 F.3d 1225 (11th Cir. 2003). Finally, though delayed for several months and arguably not "meaningful," the postdeprivation process provided Reams with "means to present her allegations, demonstrate that the impoundment was wrongful, and receive redress from that deprivation." Furthermore, if dissatisfied with administrative agency review, the "judicial safety valve provided by the Georgia [APA] foreclose[d] any constitutional challenge to the procedural adequacy of the hearing-and-appeal procedure set forth in the Humane Care for Equines Act." *Id.*, at 1267. Only where "the state refuses to provide a process sufficient to remedy the procedural deprivation" can a plaintiff act on a § 1983 due process claim, which evidently did not apply under these facts. *McKinney v. Pate*, 20 F.3d 1550, 1557 (11th Cir. 1994).

13. Fourteenth Amendment Claims — Substantive Due Process

In addition to procedural constitutionality, government regulation must also pass substantive muster. This component of the Due Process Clause protects fundamental rights "implicit in the concept of ordered liberty." *Palko v. State of Connecticut*, 302 U.S. 319, 325 (1937) (*overruled by Benton v. Maryland*, 395 U.S. 784 (1969)). Most, but not all, rights enumerated in the Bill of Rights are fundamental, as well as certain unenumerated rights such as the right to privacy. Such rights include "the rights to marry, to have children, to direct the education and upbringing of one's children, to marital privacy, to use contraception, to bodily integrity, and to abortion." *Washington v. Glucksberg*, 521 U.S. 702 (1997). However, the doctrine "does not purport to supplant traditional tort law in laying down rules of conduct to regulate liability for injuries that attend living together in society." *Daniels v. Williams*, 474 U.S. 327, 332 (1986). An absolute prerequisite to bringing a substantive due process claim requires proof that the plaintiff suffered a deprivation of an established life, liberty, or property interest. *See Clark v. Boscher*, 514 F.3d 107, 112 (1st Cir. 2008). "[I]dentifying a new fundamental right subject to the protections of substantive due process is often an uphill battle, as the list of fundamental rights is short." *Does v. Munoz*, 507 F.3d 961, 964 (6th Cir. 2007).

While analogizing the right to have children to the right to adopt or purchase animal companions as immediate family members, in order to prove the existence of a *liberty* interest, may not be well-received (*see Ramm v. City of Seattle*, 830 P.2d 395 (Wash. Ct. App. 1992) (rejecting argument that constitutional right of privacy protects cohabitation choices with nonhuman family members)), plaintiffs may find better success arguing for the existence of fundamental *property* rights. While the Third Circuit found a fundamental interest in realty, interests like "a low bidder's entitlement to state contract" or entitlement to public tenured employment are not fundamental interests. *Nicholas v. Pennsylvania State University*, 227 F.3d 133 (3d Cir. 2000); *Leib v. Hillsborough County Public Transp. Com'n*, 558 F.3d 1301, 1306 n.4 (11th Cir. 2009) (right to earn a living not a fundamental property interest). And though the Third Circuit found that "ownership is a property interest worthy of substantive due process protection," *DeBlasio v. Zoning Bd. of Adjustment for Tp. of West Amwell*, 53 F.3d 592, 600 (3d Cir. 1995) (abrogated on other grounds by, *United Artists Theatre Circuit, Inc. v. Township of Warrington, PA*, 316 F.3d 392 (3d Cir. 2003)), the *Nicholas* court held that "we have so far limited non-legislative substantive due process review to cases involving real property ownership." *Nicholas* at 141 (emphasis added). For further discussion, see Krotoszynski, Jr., *Fundamental Property Rights*, 85 GEO. L.J. 555 (1997); Wells & Snedeker, *State-created Property and Due Process of Law: Filling the Void left by* Enquist v. Oregon Department of Agriculture, 44 GA. L. REV. 161 (2009).

Substantive due process challenges depend on which court-woven "thread" the parties follow. Legislative acts (i.e., enacting laws and broad executive regulations applying to large segments of society), as opposed to nonlegislative or executive acts (i.e., typically applying to one person or a limited number), follow different analytic avenues. *Nicholas*, at 139 (*citing Planned Parenthood of Southeastern Pennsylvania v. Casey*, 505 U.S. 833, 846–847 (1992)). Legislative acts limiting a fundamental right survive a substantive due process challenge only if narrowly tailored to promote a compelling governmental interest; if not a fundamental right, then rational basis review applies. Executive acts cannot arbitrarily infringe on a fundamental right, but when this occurs, only the "most egregious official conduct can be said to be 'arbitrary in the constitutional sense.'" *Boyanowski v. Capital Area Intermediate Unit*, 215 F.3d 396, 400 (3d Cir. 2000). The abuse of power must "shock[ ] the conscience." *Id.*, at 401.

Property interests arise from independent sources, such as state law rules and administrative codes, not by the Constitution. When legislatures expand property rights, they may also widen Fourteenth Amendment due process protections. *See Board of Regents of State Colleges v. Roth*, 408 U.S. 564, 577 (1972). For example, the Ninth Circuit expanded the scope of ownership rights in *Newman* when finding that a coroner violated parents' due process rights by removing their childrens' corneas without notice or consent. *Newman v. Sathyavaglswaran*, 287 F.3d 786, 789–794 (9th Cir. 2002). Not till then did the court have occasion to determine whether the right to possess and control one's own body is a property interest protected by the Due Process Clause. Here, one finds a disconnect between the procedural and substantive components of the Due Process Clause, for while "the property interests protected by procedural due process extend well beyond actual ownership of real estate, chattels, or money," *Board of Regents of State Colleges v. Roth*, 408 U.S. 564, 571–72 (1972), the same cannot be unequivocally said with respect to substantive protections. Siding with the Sixth Circuit, but rejecting the supreme court holdings in Florida and Georgia, *Newman* agreed that next of kin had protectable property interests in the corneas of deceased relatives given a firmly entrenched "historical pedigree." *Id.*, at 789–94. That the California law labeled the interests of the plaintiffs "quasi-property" had "little meaningful legal significance," for the Supreme Court only used the term "quasi-property" once in *International News Service v. Associated Press*, 248 U.S. 215, 236–42 (1918) (holding that news "must be regarded as quasi property"). Further, even without positive economic or market value, *Newman* held that the parents maintained a property interest in the corneas. *See also Phillips v. Washington Legal Foundation*, 524 U.S. 156, 169 (1998) (physical item still deemed "property" even absent value). Currently, the fundamental property interests protected under the substantive Due Process Clause likely extend only to realty, human body parts, and corpses. Animal law development may depend on building a conceptual bridge between deceased humans to nonhumans.

The Fourth Amendment may be the better one to apply rather than the "open-ended" substantive Due Process Clause, so the Connecticut District Court noted in *Dziekan v. Gaynor*, 376 F. Supp. 2d 267 (D. Conn. 2005), in dismissing the plaintiff's substantive due process claim arising from the shooting of his dog. Although it is tempting to invoke the Fourteenth Amendment's "shocks the conscience" standard for executive acts, where the Fourth Amendment provides explicit protection against unreasonable dog shootings, "that amendment is the guide for analysis of the claim rather than the generalized notion of substantive due process." *Id.*, at 270 (D. Conn. 2005) (*citing Albright v. Oliver*, 510 U.S. 266, 273 (1994)).

a.   Procedural Due Process — State Law-created Interests

State statutes may create parent substantive rights giving birth to constitutionally protected liberty or property interests. *Vitek v. Jones*, 445 U.S. 480, 487 (1980). Even administrative regulations can spawn a due process liberty interest. *Meachum v. Fano*, 427 U.S. 215, 229 (1976). Nonstatutory sources create them, as well. *Shango v. Jurich*, 681 F.2d 1091 (7th Cir. 1982). Further, the existence of state procedural protections may aid in deciding the existence of a substantive interest because "A state often provides for specific procedures to ensure the realization of a parent substantive right[,]" and it is "not inconceivable that substantive protections could be inferred from the existence of procedural safeguards . . . ." *Shango*, at 1100 (*citing Hughes v. Rowe*, 449 U.S. 5, 15 (1980), *quoting Lombardo v. Meachum*, 548 F.2d 13, 16 (1st Cir. 1977)).

In *Shango*, prison regulations set forth the procedure to transfer a prisoner "for whatever reason or for no reason at all." These protocols, however, did not allow the Due Process Clause to attach, "quite simply, because there is no substantive liberty interest at stake." *Id.*, at 1100. A liberty interest "cannot be the right to demand needless formality. In order to establish such an interest, a 'plaintiff must show a substantive restriction on the (official's) discretion . . . .' " *Id.* (*quoting Suckle v. Madison General Hospital*, 499 F.2d 1364, 1366 (7th Cir. 1974)).

For a counterexample, see *Oviatt By and Through Waugh v. Pearce*, 954 F.2d 1470 (9th Cir. 1992), specifically evaluating *Monell* liability with respect to deficient policies. Arrestee Kim Oviatt languished 114 days in a county detention center before being arraigned when a court clerk inadvertently omitted his name from the docket sheet, in violation of speedy arraignment and speedy trial statutes ORS 136.290 and ORS 135.010. A jury found for Oviatt, awarding $65,000, and the court granting $45,385.65 in fees upon finding a violation of his due process rights. In affirming, the Ninth Circuit examined whether the state statutes created parent rights that spawned an enforceable liberty interest under § 1983 and, further, whether the county acted with deliberate indifference in failing to implement a policy to ensure that arrestees were promptly processed.

"State laws 'create[ ] a protected liberty interest by placing substantive limitations on official discretion.' " *Id.*, at 1474 (*quoting Olim v. Wakinekona*, 461 U.S. 238, 249 (1983)) (plaintiff must show that state law contains particularized and objective standards or criteria). "In other words, 'the . . . law must direct that a given action will be taken or avoided only on the existence or nonexistence of specified substantive predicates.'" *Id.* (*quoting Toussaint v. McCarthy*, 801 F.2d 1080, 1094 (9th Cir. 1986)). "[T]he word 'shall' alone is not sufficient. Rather, the liberty interest is created when the word 'shall' is used to mandate certain procedures . . . ." *Id.*, at 1474–75 (*quoting Toussaint* at 1098). Based on this analysis, the *Oviatt* court found that state statutes created constitutionally protected liberty interests to rapidly commence trial of a defendant in custody and arraign within the first 36 hours. *Id.*, at 1475. Having determined that the plaintiff possessed a liberty interest, *Oviatt* evaluated what process was due under the Fourteenth Amendment. "When a state . . . creates a liberty interest [it] must follow minimum due process appropriate to the circumstances to ensure that liberty is not arbitrarily abrogated." *Id.*, 1475 (*quoting Haygood v. Younger*, 769 F.2d 1350, 1355 (9th Cir. 1985)). Applying the *Mathews v. Eldridge*, 424 U.S. 319, 335 (1976), factors, it found the private liberty interest great, the risk of erroneous deprivation of that interest similarly significant, and reasonable procedures for decreasing it readily available. "Under *Mathews*, [the] County's minimalist approach to jail procedure failed to provide inmates with the protection that they were due, and therefore contravened the 14th Amendment." *Id.*, at 1477.

The court next determined whether *Monell* liability attached based on the county's custom or policy. The "decision not to take any action to alleviate the problem of detecting missed arraignments constitutes a policy for purposes of § 1983 municipal liability." *Id.*, at 1477 (9th Cir. 1992). Accordingly, "[t]he fact that Sheriff Pearce did not believe a strong enough pattern existed to warrant an 'affirmative policy' does not weaken our conclusion that he had established a *policy* with regard to handling missed arraignments." *Id.* (emphasis in original). The official policy (of having no policy) evinced "deliberate indifference" to the plaintiff's constitutional rights. The jury reasonably found that the need for more or different action was "so obvious, and the inadequacy [of the current procedure] so likely to result in the violation of constitutional rights, that the policymakers . . . can reasonably be said to have been deliberately indifferent to the need." *Id.* at 1477–78 (quoting *City of Canton, Ohio v. Harris*, 489 U.S. 378, 389–90 (1989)). "Whether a local government entity has displayed a policy of deliberate indifference is generally a question for the jury." *Davis v. Mason Cy.*, 927 F.2d 1473, 1482 (9th Cir. 1991).

As to the nexus between this "policy" and the ultimate injury to Oviatt, the court determined that the defendants "misunder[stood] the law" in believing that the "true 'cause' of plaintiff's missed arraignment and prolonged incarceration was the court's clerical error." Rather, the plaintiff needed only to prove that "'the identified deficiency . . . [is] closely related to the ultimate injury.'" *Id.*, at 1478 (*quoting Harris*, at 391). "Specifically, plaintiff must prove that the injury would have been avoided had Multnomah County instituted some affirmative procedure designed to discover inmates who had missed arraignments." *Id.*

Consider these other "idle hands" nonextant policies that nonetheless amount to policies for purposes of § 1983. In *Burton v. Spokane P.D.*, 2007 U.S. Dist. LEXIS 42101 (E.D. Wash. June 11, 2007), *rev. o.g.*, 2010 U.S. App. LEXIS 12117 (9th Cir. June 14, 2010), JUDGE WHALEY found that the City's claim that it had no policy regarding strip searches, leaving it to officer discretion, was itself a policy sufficient for *Monell* liability:

At oral argument, the City argued that there is no City policy regarding strip searches; rather, whether to conduct a strip search is left up to the officer's discretion. The Court does not accept the argument that the City does not have a policy. It clearly has a policy. The policy is to leave to the officers in the field the discretion to conduct a strip search in the field without a warrant. The Court finds that the City of Spokane has a policy that allows police officers to perform strip searches in the field without a warrant, and to only seek a warrant if a body cavity is to be opened. The Court finds that Defendant Bowman was acting pursuant to the City of Spokane Police Department policy or custom of conducting strip searches in the field without a warrant.

Id., at *5 (emphasized). And also consider *Richards v. Janis*, 2007 U.S. Dist. LEXIS 77929 (E.D. Wash. Oct. 17, 2007). JUDGE SHEA denied summary judgment to the City of Yakima based on the excessively broad nature of the City's Taser policy, along with ratification and acquiescence to the Tasering officer's behavior by the City:

Plaintiffs presented sufficient evidence to establish a genuine issue of material fact as to whether the City of Yakima had a policy or custom serving as the moving force behind Officer Cavin's taser usage. As stated earlier, the Yakima Police Department's taser policy provides in pertinent part: "Extra caution shall be given when considering use of a Taser on the following individuals: juveniles under 16 years of age, pregnant females, elderly subjects, handcuffed persons, and persons in elevated positions." (Ct.Rec.3, Ex. 1.) Chief Granato interpreted the Department's taser policy as allowing tasering suspects who are handcuffed as long as they are not standing. (Ct.Rec.20, Ex. A.) Officer Cavin cannot recall any YPD restrictions on tasering handcuffed individuals and, in fact, used his taser on two prior occasions (1) firing a probe into a dog on July 12, 2005, and (2) stunning a handcuffed individual on July 21, 2005. (Ct. Rec. 37 ¶ 16.) By contrast, the National Law Enforcement Policy Center's model policy prohibits tasering a handcuffed prisoner "absent overtly assaultive behavior." (Ct.Rec.37, Ex. D.) . . . Based on Officer Cavin's taser usage history, the Department's apparent acquiescence to Officer Cavin's taser usage, and the Department's broad taser policy, the Court concludes a genuine issue of material fact exists regarding whether the Department had a well-settled policy serving as the moving force behind Officer Cavin's taser use.

Id., at *7. Finally, consider *Garner v. Memphis Police Dept.*, 8 F.3d 358 (6th Cir. 1993), finding a *Monell* violation where the city's "decision to authorize use of deadly force to apprehend nondangerous fleeing burglary suspects was, therefore, a deliberate choice from among various alternatives" and that adopting "a more permissive deadly force policy by, for example, eliminating the requirement that an officer give notice of an intention to arrest before employing deadly force" was unconstitutional. *Id.*, at 364. "The Police Department taught Officer Hymon that it was proper to shoot a fleeing burglary suspect in order to prevent escape. That was their policy." *Id.*, at 364–65.

Animal law practitioners should evaluate the existence of mandatory statutory duties pertaining to procedures involving detention, seizure, and disposition of animals. Consider, for example, Or. Rev. Stat. §§ 167.325–.350, an Oregon state law mandating when and how animals should be impounded for suspected animal cruelty and subsequently euthanized. Oregon's use of "shall" language compels certain procedures, arguably creating a constitutionally protected property interest in having such animal spared from death or adoption pending a forfeiture hearing. Assume that an Oregon county fails to adopt policies and procedures distinctly addressing the need to take affirmative steps to comply with this forfeiture procedure (i.e., permitting the killing of any cruelty-confiscated dog after the shelter's hold period expires only with an order from the court), but instead abides by an unwritten policy inviting the opposite result (i.e., without an order from police or the court, any dog may be killed when the shelter's hold period has expired). As a result, a cruelty-seized dog dies without a forfeiture hearing. In such case, a due process violation may spring from municipal disregard of state-mandated process.

Inadequate and nonexistent policies create a substantial risk of erroneous deprivation to a companion animal that could be cured easily by clear guidelines. Per the logic of *Oviatt*, a jury could determine that the need to establish a policy and custom protecting owners of cruelty-confiscated animals from premature forfeiture was of such obvious importance and so readily remedied, that its absence would quite foreseeably result in violation of plaintiffs' constitutional rights under the Fourteenth Amendment. A jury may also reason that the county's policy amounted to having none at all, leaving to its employees the overbroad discretion to disregard or follow state law. In so finding, deliberate indifference would be established. Undoubtedly, the inadequate county policy would be the driving force behind the animal's demise. Approached differently, a jury might also reasonably find that the killing of the dog without the statutory hearing afforded by state law would amount to an "unreasonable" Fourth Amendment seizure. Accordingly, a *Monell* violation would lie with respect to either or both a Fourth Amendment seizure and Fourteenth Amendment due process deprivation.

b. Shooting Animals as Due Process Violation

Though most instances involving use of lethal force against animals invoke Fourth Amendment principles, the Fourteenth Amendment Due Process Clause may also apply. This situation typically arises where law enforcement encourages, expressly or tacitly, private citizens to take up firearms against trespassing animals. In *Cathey v. Guenther*, 47 F.3d 162 (5th Cir. 1995), bird lover Dennis Guenther shot and killed neighbor Dottie Cathey's stray cat at the direction of the Town of Granite Shoals's police chief Lance Van Horn, contrary to local ordinances. After the trial court denied Van Horn qualified immunity, he appealed. The Fifth Circuit reversed and dismissed the procedural due process claim under the *Parratt/Hudson* doctrine, concluding that Van Horn's giving private citizens legal advice contradicting laws he enforced was a random and unauthorized act, for which postdeprivation remedies were available under Texas common law. *See Hudson v. Palmer*, 468 U.S. 517, 531–32 ("[W]e hold that an unauthorized intentional deprivation of property by a state employee does not constitute a [constitutional] violation . . . if a meaningful post-deprivation remedy for the loss is available.") Cathey's clever argument that Van Horn's advice placed her in indirect peril did not create § 1983 liability under the danger-creation doctrine of *DeShaney v. Winnebago County Dept. of Social*

Services, 489 U.S. 189, 199–200 (1989) because she failed to allege that the town restrained her personal liberty in a manner that distinguished her from other members of the general public. *Id.*, at 164.

With similar effect, in *Bombliss v. County of Lee*, 23 F.3d 410 (7th Cir. 1994), the Seventh Circuit dismissed a myriad of claims arising from the shooting of Bombliss's dog by a neighbor given a deputy's prior authorization. For instance, it rejected that the defendants discriminated against a class of "dog owners" (finding they were not protected as a suspect class); that the deputy's authorization created an affirmative link to the later unconstitutional deprivation by the neighbor (rejected as, at best, a single "random and unauthorized act" for which meaningful postdeprivation state remedies existed, given that the county law did not permit shooting dogs when not in defense of the shooter's domestic animals or did when dogs were unsupervised by the owner — as occurred here, citing *Parratt/Hudson*); and that in allowing "summary execution" of trespassing dogs, the county violated *state* anticruelty laws and discriminated against the class of dog owners (rejected because § 1983 only provides relief for deprivation of *federal* constitutional rights).

The random and abrupt nature of the injury primarily explains why most shooting claims fail under the Fourteenth Amendment, as exemplified by the Third Circuit case of *Brown v. Muhlenberg Tp.*, 269 F.3d 205 (3d Cir. 2001). The *Brown* court found a viable Fourth Amendment seizure claim when Officer Eberly shot Immi, a Rottweiler, several times. But it rejected the procedural due process claim per the *Parratt/Hudson* doctrine, described below. Though Immi was property, Eberly deprived the Browns of her, and the Browns were entitled to due process prior thereto, in describing his behavior as "random and unauthorized" (i.e., preventing the state from predicting the timing of the unauthorized deprivation), postdeprivation state remedies sufficed. And, thus, while Eberly acted willfully and intentionally, the court found no material distinction from *Hudson*.

Property and liberty interests protected by the Due Process Clause may spring from municipal or state statutes as in *Ammon v. Welty*, 64 F.3d 662 (6th Cir. 1995). The county dog warden shot the family dog Hair Bear in the head before expiration of the statutorily mandated hold period. Accepting the Ammons' allegations as true, the court assumed that he violated Ky. Rev. Stat. Ann. § 258.215 (requiring a seven-day hold period prior to euthanasia) after having been knowingly delivered to him by a third party who acquired Hair Bear through deceit. Despite agreeing that the Ammons established a constitutionally protected property interest born from Ky. Rev. Stat. Ann. § 258.215 (creating a substantive limitation on state action), it nonetheless affirmed dismissal of the procedural due process claim under the *Parratt/Hudson* doctrine. While describing Hair Bear's death as unauthorized and predeprivation process unavailable, because state law furnished an adequate postdeprivation remedy, no § 1983 claim would lie.

The Indiana Court of Appeals examined nonlegislative, executive action (police killing a dog), among other claims, in *Zane v. City of Portage*, 886 N.E.2d 116 (Ind. Ct. App. 2008). John Zane sued the City of Portage, its chief of police, and several officers for killing his dog upon warrantless, armed entry into his home. It began when police responded to a 911 call that W.G., an armed and drunk friend of Zane, had threatened to kill himself while holed up in Zane's weapon-filled bunker (situated in his residence). Zane, who was also inside, informed law enforcement that his beloved dog was with him. For hours, negotiations ensued. Tear gas was deployed, but Zane and W.G. did not exit. Finally, police entered with a battering ram. Before crossing the threshold into the home, the American Staffordshire terrier emerged. Feeling threatened, one officer shot and killed the dog. Another accidentally shot a round into the ceiling. On entry, they found several firearms and W.G. unconscious, whereupon they took him to the hospital. The trial court dismissed the § 1983 claims under the Fourth, Fifth, and Fourteenth Amendments. As to the Fourth Amendment, though warrantless entries are *per se* unreasonable, exigent circumstances permitted exception where the lives and safety of officers and others were in jeopardy. Here, though not a danger to anyone else, police had probable cause to believe that W.G. "himself was in imminent danger" because he threatened suicide, was intoxicated, and had many weapons at his disposal. The court also found that the amount of force to gain entry and access to W.G., including that employed in killing the dog, was not excessive or unreasonable. *Id.*, at *5.

As the court had rejected the Fourth Amendment claim, it also dismissed the substantive due process claim because Zane could not then show that the "level of executive abuse of power is that which 'shocks the conscience' or which exhibits a deliberate indifference to a person's life, liberty, or property." *Id.*, at *9. "All evidence points to an officer shooting the dog in response to a perceived threat to the officers' safety. This was not deliberate indifference to Zane's property." *Id.*, at *9. The procedural due process claim, predicated on the risk of erroneous deprivation of his private interest to be free from unreasonable searches and seizures under the Fourth Amendment, failed due to exigent circumstances, which justified the lack of a predeprivation hearing, as well as the presence of suitable postdeprivation state court remedies — even though negated by state immunity doctrines. *Id.*, at *10 (*quoting Logan v. Zimmerman Brush Co.*, 455 U.S. 422, 432 (1982)). The § 1983 claim against the city for inadequate training and policy also failed, because as Zane could not prove a single constitutional violation, he could not demonstrate that the city's purported deficiencies were the moving force behind his constitutional injuries.

c. Animal Cruelty Raids and Due Process

Numerous § 1983 cases concern the removal of animals from suspected abusers. While a Fourth Amendment claim commonly comes to mind, do not disregard the Fourteenth. For instance, in *Snead v. Society for Prevention of Cruelty to Animals of Pennsylvania*, 929 A.2d 1169 (Pa. Super. Ct. 2007), *appeal granted in part*, 966 A.2d 548 (Pa. 2009) and *order aff'd*, 985 A.2d 909 (Pa. 2009) and *appeal denied*, 992 A.2d 890 (Pa. 2010), the court found a colorable due process violation arising from the seizure of several dogs allegedly used for dog fighting, who were subsequently euthanized without giving her adequate notice of the right to redeem them. The Society claimed it had "no hard-clad policy" to return animals to a known owner after the grounds for holding them evaporated, and, further, no safeguards existed to notify the owner that her animals were ready for redemption except for a door-knock when she was not home (i.e., no doorhanger notification given, no voicemail left, no certified mail sent, and no other means of assuring notification). Thus, the court held that a jury could find the SPCA:

had inadequate procedures/policies in place to safeguard Snead's property interest in the dogs. Although unlicensed dogs are only held for 48 hours after they are no longer needed as evidence in a criminal investigation, there is no standard procedure by which to notify an owner that charges have been dismissed or withdrawn and his or her dogs are available to be reclaimed. Although Snead was known to SPCA and her phone number was in its computer, she was never contacted by telephone, nor was notice sent by mail.

929 A.2d at 1182–83. Specific "additional safeguards such as notice by mail or telephoning the owner, where her identity and address/phone number are known or ascertainable, would not be overly burdensome or costly." *Id.*, at 1183.

Porter v. DiBlasio, 93 F.3d 301 (7th Cir. 1996) yielded a similar outcome. After nine thoroughbred horses seized by county officials found their way into the custody of the humane society, without a hearing for Porter, it took ownership of the equines and adopted them out to new owners for nominal sums. Porter filed procedural due process, takings, and substantive due process § 1983 claims, resulting in reversal of dismissal on appeal. On the procedural due process claim, the court agreed that Porter had a protected property interest in the horses and that the dispute centered on what process was due. In that Wis. Stat. § 951.15(3) already provided for a five-day redemption period for stray animals, the court concluded, "Wisconsin must provide an owner notice and an opportunity for a hearing prior to permanently terminating an individual's interest in seized animals." *Id.*, at 307 (citing other jurisdictions reaching the same conclusion). Further, the absence of a formal requirement that the county provide an opportunity to be heard evidenced the county's custom of not doing so. This translated into an informal but otherwise established state procedure for purposes of *Monell* liability. Because terminating Porter's property interest after five days was eminently foreseeable, and as providing an opportunity to be heard within that five-day period was neither impossible nor excessive, the county's custom of depriving individuals of such recourse stated a viable procedural due process claim against the municipality.

Some jurisdictions fail to offer any right to a hearing prior to forfeiture of seized animals, but those who do may still face liability when those procedures fail to pass constitutional muster. *Latiker v. City of Council Bluffs*, 720 N.W.2d 191 (Iowa Ct. App. 2006), examined the actions of an animal control officer seizing Latiker's puppy after he admitted to beating the dog. Subsequently convicted of simple misdemeanor animal neglect, the city deemed the dog forfeited. Latiker appealed, but lost. He then posted a bond to stay the forfeiture to seek appellate review. On procedural due process grounds, Latiker asserted that the ordinances did not provide for forfeiture, written notice to the owner, or a procedure to demand an explanation or receive a hearing. However, as he received oral notice of impoundment of his dog at the time of removal, additional written notice of the city's intent to forfeit through adoption, and the opportunity to appeal to the board of health (in which he and his attorney participated), the court found that the city gave Latiker due process. The substantive due process challenge met a similar fate, for the city ordinance allowed the director to "take such actions as he may deem appropriate," including to impound and forfeit abused animals. This did not render the ordinance unconstitutional as applied and certainly did not "shock the conscience" as an unduly oppressive exercise of government discretion. The court also rejected Latiker's assertion that state law, which did not permit forfeiture in a simple misdemeanor case, preempted city ordinance, which did, finding that the city may establish more stringent rules (i.e., forfeiture on simple misdemeanor conviction).

Where a plaintiff repeatedly disregards an opportunity to be heard concerning the forfeiture of an animal, she cannot later complain about lack of due process. *Root v. County of Fairfax*, 2010 U.S. App. LEXIS 6381 (4th Cir. Mar. 26, 2010), *cert. denied*, 131 S. Ct. 655 (2010), held that the plaintiff could not complain after abandoning several chances to exercise her due process rights afforded by state law. Animal control officers seized nine dogs and one horse from Louise Root's residence due to suspected animal neglect. After eight individuals adopted the seized dogs, Root sued the county under § 1983, claiming due process violations. The Fourth Circuit affirmed dismissal, holding that Root received adequate notice under Va. Code Ann. § 3.1-796.115(A). Further, despite several opportunities, she failed to stay their adoption. Accordingly, she could not later complain that the county deprived her of due process.

d. Euthanasia and Due Process

When cities fail to afford due process protection, the irreversible sanction of euthanasia does not suffer deficiencies gladly. *Van Patten v. City of Binghamton*, 137 F. Supp. 2d 98 (N.D. N.Y. 2001), determined that the city denied a dog owner due process in deciding to euthanize before the owner received notice. As the owner had a significant property interest in his dog, providing love, friendship, and companionship, the potential for erroneous deprivation of property was equally significant. The hearing was not held before a municipal judge or justice, and the officer's decision did not include a written statement with supportive evidentiary summary. Moreover, Van Patten was not allowed to appeal the decision, even though judicial review might conceivably have resulted in a reversal. In balancing the burdens between the city and owner, the court found that the dog's confinement eliminated the threat to the public, and the cost to hold the dog pending appeal would have been modest.

e. Killing Animals for Rabies Testing and Due Process

Decapitation and focal brain pathology presents the only way to confirm rabies. Necessarily, such post-mortem testing produces death. Opting for a less morbid diagnostic method, jurisdictions frequently permit 10- or 15-day quarantines during which the owner or government observes the isolated animal for clinical symptoms of rabies with or without proof of rabies vaccination in accordance with accepted veterinary protocols. Familiarity with the latest science on rabies control is a must, including purported vaccine efficacy and breakthrough rates notwithstanding high rabies antibody titers in canines, felines, hybrids, and other species. A veterinary vaccinologist, for instance, may assess the scientific foundation of claims by local government that wolf-dog hybrids receive no protection from rabies vaccinations. Because local health officials tend to make decisions to perform a terminal brain study with rapidity, potential constitutional violations abound.

Such concerns arose in *Clark v. City of Draper*, 168 F.3d 1185 (10th Cir. 1999). When a four-year-old suffered a skin abrasion while viewing two miniature blue foxes at Clark's petting zoo on a school field trip, animal control impounded and euthanized them to test for rabies. The results were negative. Under the 14th Amendment, Clark claimed a violation of procedural and substantive due process. Whether her property right in the foxes was perfect or imperfect mattered not. Nor that she domesticated them as the Compendium of Animal Rabies Control explicitly stated that rabies vaccines had not been tested on foxes, thereby subordinating her property right to death-mandating state rabies laws and regulations. That city law required quarantine instead of euthanasia did not render their deaths illegal in this case as municipal ordinances could not permit what state law prohibited, or vice versa. Utah regulations required that the wild animal who bites or scratches a person "shall be killed at once . . . and the brain submitted . . . for examination for evidence of rabies." Utah Admin. Code § 386-702-6(2.4). Clark received an adequate postdeprivation (but predestruction) hearing in front of a local magistrate the morning after the late-night impoundment. Applying the *Mathews* balancing test, the court found that the government's strong interest in public health and rapid rabies testing trumped the private interest of Clark and the risk of erroneous deprivation (i.e., foxes testing negative).

While virtually nonexistent in the United States, except for bats, skunks, and raccoons, and the occasional equine bitten by the same, rabies primarily presents a problem in Asia and Africa, where dogs remain one of the most significant reservoirs of the disease. Other infectious diseases sweeping through densely populated areas, such as endemic Newcastle disease or avian influenza, may require mass quarantines and euthanasias under color of state law. For instance, the Connecticut District Court dismissed a poultry farmer's § 1983 action in *Webster v. Moquin*, 175 F. Supp. 2d 315 (D. Conn. 2001), under procedural due process, substantive due process, and Fifth Amendment takings when State Department of Agriculture officials ordered all birds at his property killed to prevent the spread of avian influenza.

f.   Trapping Cats and Due Process

Akron ex rel. Christman-Resch v. Akron, 825 N.E.2d 189 (Ohio Ct. App. 2005), discussed above, also implicates the Fourteenth Amendment. On the substantive due process claim, the city furnished a reasonable basis for its trapping ordinance based on evidence that free-roaming cats spoiled flower beds, marked windows, scratched cars, and carried disease. Even if the city did "not adopt the perfect solution," it was rational to trap and euthanize free-roaming cats after the hold period expired. On the procedural due process claim, absent evidence that healthy cats were euthanized within 24 hours of impound, the court instead accepted that the 72-hour redemption period did not violate due process. It gave adequate time for the owner to reunite with a lost cat. As to equal protection, appellants claimed that the ordinances, as applied, treated dog owners more favorably than cat owners by (1) euthanizing cats (but not dogs) for treatable, minor conditions; and (2) euthanizing feral cats (but not feral dogs) within 24 hours. Unable to prove that, in fact, dogs and cats received disparate treatment, either in policy or in practice, and where redemption periods were identical, the court found for the city.

14. Municipal Liability

Municipalities face § 1983 liability only if "there is a direct causal link between a municipal policy or custom and the alleged constitutional deprivation." *City of Canton, Ohio v. Harris,* 489 U.S. 378, 385 (1989). Direct, causal links include "a policy statement, ordinance, regulation, or decision officially adopted and promulgated by that body's officers," or a custom, "even though such a custom has not received formal approval through the body's official decisionmaking channels." A "custom, or usage, of [a] State" for § 1983 purposes requires "the force of law by virtue of the persistent practices of state officials." *Adickes v. S. H. Kress & Co.,* 398 U.S. 144, 167 (1970). Municipal liability for informal customs or practices under § 1983 received detailed treatment in the "throw down" case of *Webster v. City of Houston,* 689 F.2d 1220 (5th Cir. 1982), *on reh'g,* 735 F.2d 838 (5th Cir. 1984), *on reh'g,* 739 F.2d 993 (5th Cir. 1984). Evidence in *Webster* sufficiently established the informal policy of officers placing a weapon at the unarmed suspect's side after having killed or wounded him, in order to justify the shooting.

However, § 1983 municipal liability is not vicarious liability as typically understood by the doctrine of *respondeat superior.* Rather, it is predicated only on "acts for which the municipality itself is actually responsible . . . " *City of St. Louis v. Praprotnik,* 485 U.S. 112, 123 (1988). Further, "only those municipal officials who have 'final policymaking authority' may by their actions subject the government to § 1983 liability." *Michigan v. Clifford,* 464 U.S. 287, 291 (1984) (*quoting Pembaur v. City of Cincinnati,* 475 U.S. 469, 483 (1986)). Occasionally, a single decision by the sheriff or a police chief may expose the municipality to § 1983 liability. *See Larez v. City of Los Angeles,* 946 F.2d 630 (9th Cir. 1991); *Fuller v. City of Oakland,* 47 F.3d 1522, 1534–1535 (9th Cir. 1995), *as amended,* (Apr. 24, 1995) (municipal liability established for chief's failure to implement adequate procedures to investigate misconduct allegations). Municipal liability may also arise where the city ratifies employee action, thus creating a *de facto* governmental policy or custom. *See Praprotnik* and *Larez.*

An example of a plaintiff failing to specify a municipal policy or custom, and thus facing dismissal of his § 1983 action, arose in *Ghaderi v. City of San Jose,* 2006 U.S. App. LEXIS 15485 (9th Cir. June 12, 2006). Ghaderi claimed that the city illegally towed an unregistered motor home and caused harm to cats therein, but he failed to demonstrate that this resulted from an unconstitutional municipal policy or custom.

Occasionally, municipalities face § 1983 liability for so inadequately training their officers as to foreseeably endanger the public's constitutional rights when they come into police contact. These failure-to-train cases, however, must reflect a "deliberate" or "conscious" choice (namely, a policy) of institutionalizing incompetency. *See Harris,* at 388, 390. As the Ninth Circuit explained:

> The issue is not whether the officers had received any training — most of the deputies involved had some training, even if it was minimal at best — rather the issue is the adequacy of that training. . . . More importantly, while they may have had some training in the use of force, they received no training in the constitutional limits of the use of force.

Davis v. Mason County, 927 F.2d 1473, 1483 (9th Cir. 1991) (citations omitted). Where policymakers know to a moral certainty that the need to train officers on constitutional limitations of the use of deadly force is "so obvious" that failure to do so is properly characterized as "deliberate indifference" to individuals' civil liberties, failure-to-train liability will also arise. *See Harris*, at 390 n.10, 392 (1989).

In 2013, the Colorado Legislature passed SB 226, the Dog Protection Act, requiring law enforcement officers to undergo training in canine threat neutralization. Prior to its enactment, what if the City of Denver offered no education in canine behavior or the use of non- or less-lethal means of force despite dozens of questionable slayings of dogs over the past five years? Aside from a possible failure-to-train claim under § 1983, having a policy that explicitly permits officers to shoot stray pit bulls, regardless of threat, would establish custom-or-policy municipal liability under § 1983. But what if the city produced a manual that carefully prescribed when, and what degree of, force could be used against *humans* but otherwise left it to the unbridled discretion of the officer to decide when and how much to use against *nonhumans*? Or, what if it authorized deadly force as a "first resort" unfettered by constitutional restraints, tacitly teaching that deputies may shoot retreating, nondangerous dogs if merely at-large? In *Kaiser v. U.S.*, 761 F. Supp. 150 (D.D.C. 1991), the trial court found a Capitol Police officer acted unreasonably when shooting a Great Dane/Lab whom he believed presented an imminent danger to his own safety as it went for his police dog. *See* 152–53. "The Court finds that Miller was negligent in shooting Kal as quickly as he did. It is apparent that the policy of the Capitol Police is to use a weapon only as a last resort. Although the use of the weapon may have become necessary as the confrontation escalated, there were alternative measures that a reasonable officer concerned about his own safety and the safety of his K-9 would have taken to avoid being attacked by Kal." *Id.*, at 156.

Municipalities may also face § 1983 liability where a supervisor fails to implement existing policies or customs to ensure that a subordinate does not violate constitutional rights. A failure-to-supervise claim requires proof as follows:

> (1) identify the specific supervisory practice or procedure that the supervisor failed to employ, and show that (2) the existing custom and practice without the identified, absent custom or procedure created an unreasonable risk of the ultimate injury, (3) the supervisor was aware that this unreasonable risk existed, (4) the supervisor was indifferent to the risk, and (5) the underling's violation resulted from the supervisor's failure to employ that supervisory practice or procedure. We emphasized that "it is not enough for a plaintiff to argue that the constitutionally cognizable injury would not have occurred if the superior had done more than he or she did." . . . Rather, the plaintiff must identify specific acts or omissions of the supervisor that evidence deliberate indifference and persuade the court that there is a "relationship between the 'identified deficiency' and the 'ultimate injury.'"

Brown v. Muhlenberg Tp., 269 F.3d 205, 216 (3d Cir. 2001) (cit.om.) (*quoting Sample v. Diecks*, 885 F.2d 1099, 1118 (3d Cir. 1989)). *See also Larez v. City of Los Angeles*, 946 F.2d 630 (supervisory liability imposed against supervisory official in individual capacity for his own culpable action or inaction in training, supervising or controlling his subordinates).

Brown, discussed above, rejected the policy-or-custom liability claim under § 1983 by finding that no official policy endorsed Ofc. Eberly's conduct (in fact, the policy manual prescribed a progressive use of force against animals inconsistent with shooting Immi), nor a custom of looking the other way when subordinates employed excessive force against dogs at-large. It found no failure-to-train liability either, in that the need for more or different training was neither so obvious nor so likely as to lead to a violation of constitutional rights as to charge indifference by the policymaker. Indeed, the presence of policy manual guidance overcame the lack of formal training in canine neutralization. As of 2015, however, failure-to-train claims of this nature may enjoy greater rates of success in light of the developing consensus among police departments and sheriff's offices to implement dog-specific field protocols, particularly where more than half of the officer-involved shootings involve discharges at canines. *See* Bathurst & Cleary et al., *The Problem of Dog-Related Incidents and Encounters*, U.S.D.O.J., C.O.P.S. Dept., Aug. 2011, www.nationalcanineresearchcouncil.com/police-resources/#problem; Police & Dog Encounters video series, www.cops.igpa.uillinois.edu/resources/police-dog-encounters; Colo. Rev. Stat. § 29–5–112 ("Colorado Dog Protection Act"). Finally, absent proof that the police chiefs knew of Eberly's alleged practice of excessive force against animals and failed to take appropriate disciplinary action, and that they allegedly failed to train on proper use of force against animals, no supervisory § 1983 liability attached. *Brown v. Muhlenberg Tp.*, 269 F.3d 205, 216–217 (3d Cir. 2001).

A municipal § 1983 violation frequently requires considerable proof given the culpable mental state standard of deliberateness. A breeder claiming that a policy or custom to decimate her stock and financially oppress her violated her constitutional rights lost in *Stanley v. Kirkpatrick*, 592 S.E.2d 296 (S.C. 2004). Animal control seized and impounded Stanley's Shar Peis. Despite explaining that the unidentifiable dogs (who had no tag or license) would be held only five days before euthanasia or adoption, Stanley never came to the shelter to redeem them by paying $129 per dog as the fee for impound, spay/neuter, rabies vaccination, and at-large fine. Accordingly, the shelter euthanized the dogs due to aggression and skin problems. Surprisingly, the appellate court reversed the trial court's decision to grant the city's motion for summary judgment on the § 1983 claim that the city's policy or custom was to "oppress and financially hobble her by charging fines without lawful citation, by destroying her animals without time restrictions, and by entering her enclosed backyard without a warrant[.]" In reversing the South Carolina Court of Appeals, thereby reinstating dismissal, the South Carolina Supreme Court found that Stanley failed to show "a deliberate choice to harm her or that the City was deliberately indifferent to the alleged constitutional violations by Kirkpatrick and the shelter." *Id.*, at 177 (*citing Pembaur v. City of Cincinnati*, 475 U.S. 469, 483 (1986)). While § 1983 liability may exist whether motivated by *de facto* or *de jure* policies, the *Stanley* court found neither. The former is established by omissions where unreasonable failure to make rules causes employees to engage in unconstitutional conduct through "tacit authorization" or "deliberate indifference" to constitutional violations. *Id.* (*citing Moore v. City of Columbia*, 326 S.E.2d

157 (S.C. Ct. App. 1985)). Unable to show such a widespread custom of condonation as to have force of law, the court found that Stanley's § 1983 claim was insufficient to withstand summary judgment. Additionally, she failed to show that the city deliberately became the "moving force" behind the officer's alleged seizure of the dogs and the shelter's euthanizing them.

Stanley thoroughly examined precisely who had authority to set municipal policy. Finding that the city adopted a council/manager form of government and that all legislative powers vested in the council, with each member, including the mayor, having one vote, the court held that the shelter and its employees could not set city policy. Thus, their acts could not represent official policy as a matter of law. *Id.*, at 176. In all § 1983 policy-or-custom cases, litigants must make a similar assessment of who actually has final policymaking authority. Even the most damning written policy or unwritten custom from the director of the city animal control division may not bind the municipality where either the director acted *ultra vires* (the city not delegating to her that power) or the city implemented a superseding policy or custom.

Where the sheriff dictates policy for the county, he may qualify as the "final policymaker" for purposes of *Monell/Pembaur* liability, as found in the Tenth Circuit horse rustling case, *Reid v. Hamby*, 124 F.3d 217 (10th Cir. 1997). Sheriff Dale Wren allegedly threatened to arrest Charles Reid if he did not release a stolen horse he innocently purchased two years earlier. The Reids' *Monell* claim failed due to lack of evidence that the sheriff and undersheriff acted pursuant to an unconstitutional, established policy, or that the county lacked adequate training programs regarding seizures. Finding the sheriff qualified as a "final policymaker" for purposes of *Monell* liability concerning law enforcement activities within his county, and that a single act of a policymaking officer acting within his authority may expose the municipality to liability if the act "constitutes an act of official government policy," the court found error in the trial court's dismissal of the county commissioners. For purposes of summary judgment, a material issue of fact existed as to whether he personally authorized and participated in the events in question.

15. State of Mind

Though § 1983 has no explicit "state of mind" or culpable mental state requirement, federal common law draws form a palette of several judicial glosses depending on the federal violation at issue. For instance, proof of negligence does not suffice for Fourteenth Amendment procedural due process challenges. "We conclude that the Due Process Clause is simply not implicated by a negligent act of an official causing unintended loss of or injury to life, liberty, or property." *Daniels v. Williams*, 474 U.S. 327, 328 (1986). Instead, the plaintiff must show deliberate indifference to, or actual knowledge of, a substantial risk of serious harm, along with a failure to take reasonable measures to abate it. *Farmer v. Brennan*, 511 U.S. 825, 835–36 (1994) (in Eighth Amendment context; *deliberate indifference* lies somewhere between the "poles of negligence at one end and purpose or knowledge at the other," with "Courts of Appeals routinely equat[ing] deliberate indifference with recklessness"). Gross negligence may not qualify, either. *Clifton v. Schafer*, 969 F.2d 278, 281 (7th Cir. 1992) (equating recklessness with criminal law definition). In an open range cattle seizure case, the court found that alleged lack of due care alone did not state a claim against a sheriff due to the "mere negligence" bar of *Daniels*. *Copelan v. Ferry County*, 2009 U.S. App. LEXIS 12260 (9th Cir. June 2, 2009). While *Daniels* bars federal due process claims for "mere negligence," it remains an open question whether negligent conduct will fail to establish a Fourth Amendment seizure claim. The Ninth Circuit has clearly distinguished the holding of *Daniels* and its progeny from Fourth Amendment cases. *See Borunda v. Richmond*, 885 F.2d 1384, 1391–92 (9th Cir. 1988); *Davidson v. Cannon*, 474 U.S. 344, 356 (1986).

In the context of failure to train or supervise, juries may infer deliberate indifference where, "in light of the duties assigned to specific officers or employees the need for more or different training is so obvious, and the inadequacy so likely to result in violation of constitutional rights, that the policymakers of the city can reasonably be said to have been deliberately indifferent to the need." *City of Canton v. Harris*, 489 U.S. 378, 390 (1989); *Board of County Com'rs of Bryan County, Okl. v. Brown*, 520 U.S. 397, 409 (1997). Substantive due process challenges to nonlegislative, executive acts must satisfy the "shocks the conscience" test. *County of Sacramento v. Lewis*, 523 U.S. 833 (1998).

Campbell v. Chappelow, 95 F.3d 576 (7th Cir. 1996), demonstrates how a nonculpable state of mind can exonerate a defendant. Execution of a search and seizure warrant, procured due to suspicions of animal cruelty, resulted in removal of 12 cattle to the custody of the humane society. Though the neglect charges were later dismissed, the caretakers of the cattle filed liens on the animals and sold them to obtain reimbursement. Apparently, Campbell never received notice of the auction. The Seventh Circuit affirmed dismissal of the state troopers involved in the warrant execution, finding they had nothing to do with the actual mechanics of seizure and turnover to the humane society, followed all policies to the letter, and , in the case of one officer, did not realize she was even executing a warrant.

16. Qualified and Absolute Immunity

Section 1983 "creates a species of tort liability that, on its face, admits of no immunities." *Imbler v. Pachtman*, 424 U.S. 409, 417 (1976). Nonetheless, the Supreme Court imparts qualified immunity to government officials whose conduct did not violate constitutional rights of which a reasonable person would have known. *Harlow v. Fitzgerald*, 457 U.S. 800, 818 (1982). Thus, it shields an individual from civil liability and creates immunity from suit. *Mitchell v. Forsyth*, 472 U.S. 511, 526 (1985). A court hearing a motion for dismissal based on qualified immunity may choose the order in which it answers two questions: (1) Do the facts establish a *prima facie* claim of a constitutional violation? and (2) Was the constitutional or statutory right at issue clearly established on the date of the alleged violation? *Pearson v. Callahan*, 555 U.S. 223 (2009). The "clearly established" test applies an objective reasonableness standard. Subjective belief is irrelevant, even if malicious. *Anderson v. Creighton*, 483 U.S. 635, 641 (1987). If the court cannot answer yes to both questions, then it should grant qualified immunity and dismiss.

An appeals court reviews a district court's decision to grant summary judgment on grounds of qualified immunity *de novo*. *Sorrels v. McKee*, 290 F.3d 965, 969 (9th

Cir. 2002). A jury, not judge, decides disputed "foundational" or "historical" facts underlying a determination of qualified immunity. *Acosta v. City and County of San Francisco*, 83 F.3d 1143 (9th Cir. 1996). The court decides whether the law was clearly established. *Elder v. Holloway*, 510 U.S. 510 (1994). The more abstractly stated the violation, the less likely it will have been "clearly established" for, "[t]he right allegedly violated must be defined at the appropriate level of specificity before a court can determine if it was clearly established." *Wilson v. Layne*, 526 U.S. 603, 615 (1999). Cases need not be directly on point or "materially similar" to defeat qualified immunity. *Flores v. Morgan Hill Unified School Dist.*, 324 F.3d 1130, 1136–1137 (9th Cir. 2003) ("In order to find that the law was clearly established, however, we need not find a prior case with identical, or even 'materially similar,' facts."). Rather, the plaintiff must establish "sufficiently clear" contours of the right violated. *Anderson*, at 640.

Fish v. Lyons, 1998 Mass. Super. LEXIS 544 (Sept. 3, 1998), presents an example of the law not being sufficiently established to impose § 1983 liability. Jack, an allegedly vicious dog, bit an officer who tried to subdue him. Jack was killed in the attempt, and the officer sent Jack's remains to the state lab for rabies testing. Later that day, Fish asked for the dog's remains and the name and address of the lab. The officer refused and ordered Fish to leave the station. The mayor also failed to take action to ensure the return of Jack's body. Days later, Jack was cremated. Stating that it "can find no authority on the issue of what notice and other procedural safeguards in order to satisfy due process must be given to the owners of an unlicensed dog who bites a person, dies in the process of being captured by the animal control department, and is sent to the state lab for rabies testing," the court found the area of law not "clearly established" and, therefore, granted qualified immunity. A similar result obtained in *Bloom v. Miami-Dade County*, 816 F. Supp. 2d 1265 (S.D. Fla. 2011), where the plaintiff could not identify any caselaw or other source of authority establishing that confiscating animals to protect them from suspected animal cruelty was prohibited by the constitution. *Id.*, at 1278.

Municipalities do not enjoy qualified immunity from § 1983 suits. Only individual state actors may invoke the defense. *Owen v. City of Independence, Mo.*, 445 U.S. 622 (1980). Thus, even if a court dismisses an individual defendant on grounds of qualified immunity, the suit can continue against the municipality so long as the plaintiff maintains the other elements of proof. *See Gibson v. County of Washoe, Nev.*, 290 F.3d 1175, 1186 (9th Cir. 2002).

Some defendants have greater protection against § 1983 suits than others. For instance, judges and prosecutors may enjoy absolute immunity, in contrast to qualified immunity. Judicial immunity sweeps widely and excuses even actions driven by malicious or corrupt motives or "flawed by the commission of grave procedural errors." *Stump v. Sparkman*, 435 U.S. 349, 359 (1978). Prosecutorial immunity flows from performing activities intimately associated with judicial process. *Imbler v. Pachtman*, 424 U.S. 409 (1976). However, the prosecutor achieves only qualified immunity when acting as an investigator or administrator (essentially functioning as a police officer or detective). *Buckley v. Fitzsimmons*, 509 U.S. 259, 273 (1993). For instance, the Fifth Circuit reversed the grant of prosecutorial immunity to the county attorney who participated in an animal seizure, by allegedly entering and inspecting the property, joining in the decision to execute the seizure by rendering legal advice, planning the seizure, and physically removing the animals. Such conduct, if believed true, did not fall within the ambit of prosecutorial immunity. *Hoog-Watson v. Guadalupe Cy.*, 591 F.3d 431, 438 (5th Cir. 2009); *see also Kalina v. Fletcher,* 522 U.S. 118, 123 (1997) (prosecutor swearing out affidavit of probable cause may cause her to lose immunity).

17. *Rooker-Feldman*, Res Judicata, and Collateral Estoppel

Occasionally, a prevailing defendant prosecuted by the government plaintiff in a criminal or adjudicative proceeding will return the favor as a plaintiff in a later federal civil rights action against the former nonprevailing plaintiffs. They may file actions first in state court and try again in federal court, or vice versa (such as where the federal court declines to exercise supplemental jurisdiction over state claims). When dancing this litigation two-step, practitioners must be mindful of *Rooker-Feldman*, res judicata, and collateral estoppel.

Consider *Roch v. Humane Society of Bedford County, Tenn., Inc.*, 2005 U.S. App. LEXIS 10774 (6th Cir. June 8, 2005). In 2001, the state filed more than 250 counts of animal cruelty and other crimes against the Rochs and seized hundreds of animals from neglectful conditions. Each of the Rochs entered into a Memorandum of Understanding agreeing to pay fines and costs and promising to "forfeit any interest they may have in all animals previously seized by the Bedford County Humane Society." While the criminal cases proceeded, the humane association and the state filed a joint civil petition for relief against the Rochs, seeking a hearing to plan for care of the seized animals. Specifically, they requested euthanasia of those beyond rehabilitation and removal of the rest. The court acquiesced. Never appealing this state court order, the Rochs nonetheless sued under § 1983 (seizure, taking) and other state claims.

The Sixth Circuit affirmed dismissal of the Rochs' federal case under *Rooker-Feldman*, a Supreme Court doctrine drawing from *Rooker v. Fidelity Trust Co.*, 263 U.S. 413 (1923) and *District of Columbia Court of Appeals v. Feldman*, 460 U.S. 462 (1983) and "bar[ring] attempts by a federal plaintiff to receive appellate review of a state-court decision in federal district court." "[A] federal district court may not hear an appeal of a case already litigated in state court. A party raising a federal question must appeal a state court decision through the state system and then directly to the Supreme Court of the United States." *U.S. v. Owens*, 54 F.3d 271 (6th Cir. 1995). The Sixth Circuit utilizes a "rough guide" to distinguish between *Rooker-Feldman* and res judicata:

> [I]f the federal plaintiff was the plaintiff in state court, apply res judicata; if the federal plaintiff was the defendant in state court, apply Rooker-Feldman . . . A defendant who has lost in state court and sues in federal court does not assert injury at the hands of his adversary; he asserts injury at the hands of the court, and the second suit therefore is an effort to obtain collateral review. It must be dismissed not on the basis of preclusion but for lack of jurisdiction [under Rooker-Feldman].

Garry v. Geils, 82 F.3d 1362, 1367 (7th Cir. 1996).

For a collateral estoppel illustration, consider *Hoog-Watson v. Guadalupe County*, Tex., 591 F.3d 431 (5th Cir. 2009), discussed above. The county attorney and other county officials entered Hoog-Watson's home without a warrant and seized 47 dogs and cats inside. Thereafter, the county prosecuted Hoog-Watson but dropped charges when she entered into a plea agreement, including payment of some of the county's costs and allowing periodic inspections. Following dismissal of her federal suit due to collateral estoppel and prosecutorial immunity, the Fifth Circuit later reversed. The county argued that *Heck v. Humphrey*, 512 U.S. 477 (1994) disposed of her § 1983 claims against all defendants. *Heck* held:

> [W]hen a state prisoner seeks damages in a § 1983 suit, the district court must consider whether a judgment in favor of the plaintiff would necessarily imply the invalidity of his conviction or sentence; if it would, the complaint must be dismissed unless the plaintiff can demonstrate that the conviction or sentence has already been invalidated. But if the district court determines that the plaintiff's action, even if successful, will not demonstrate the invalidity of any outstanding criminal judgment against the plaintiff, the action should be allowed to proceed, in the absence of some other bar to the suit.

Heck, 512 U.S. at 487. *Heck* applies only to prior *criminal* proceedings. *See Ballard v. Burton*, 444 F.3d 391, 397 (5th Cir. 2006) ("The policy undergirding the favorable termination rule is based on 'the hoary principle that civil tort actions are not appropriate vehicles for challenging the validity of outstanding criminal judgments.' "). *Hoog-Watson* stated:

> When this question-the existence of a prior criminal proceeding-is viewed as a question of fact to be proven by a plaintiff, the Circuit's Heck decisions fit comfortably within typical summary judgment practice. Jackson represents the easiest case: the plaintiff pleads herself out of court by alleging facts that fall directly within Heck's bar. *See* Hernandez-Ramos v. U.S. Parole Com'n, 49 F.3d 177 (5th Cir. 1995). Brandley represents a more developed case: the plaintiff's pleadings do not include a Heck trigger but a defendant's motion for summary judgment does, and the plaintiff is forced to muster proof of Heck's favorable termination requirement to avoid dismissal. *See* Brandley v. Keeshan, 64 F.3d 196 (5th Cir. 1995). Hoog-Watson's case is between the two: The plaintiff pleads an otherwise valid § 1983 claim that may or may not implicate Heck's factual triggers; the defendant moves for summary judgment and points to evidence of the Heck trigger. If the plaintiff does nothing, the defendant may be entitled to summary judgment. But if the plaintiff introduces evidence sufficient to convince a reasonable jury that the prior proceeding was civil, the plaintiff survives summary judgment. Thus, we evaluate the defendants' motion for summary judgment by determining whether Hoog-Watson's evidence created a genuine question of fact with respect to the animal cruelty proceeding's criminal or civil nature.

Hoog-Watson, 591 F.3d at 436. Concluding that Hoog-Watson presented evidence sufficient to create a genuine issue of material fact as to whether the prior animal cruelty proceeding was criminal (*Heck* bar applies) or civil (*Heck* bar does not apply) in nature, the Fifth Circuit reversed and remanded. *Id.* It did not, however, reach the next question of whether she benefited from a favorable termination of the prior criminal case.

A case involving the offensive use of collateral estoppel, *Bilida v. McCleod*, 211 F.3d 166 (1st Cir. 2000), evaluated the effect of a prior criminal suppression order, which decisively resolved the constitutionality of the search and seizure in Bilida's favor, in her subsequent federal suit. Applying Rhode Island collateral estoppel law to find that the adverse criminal case ruling would bind *the state* in the federal case, it refused to bind the *individual officers* due to lack of privity. Disparate incentives and lack of control by the officers over the course of the criminal proceeding justified this outcome. *Allen v. McCurry*, 449 U.S. 90, 170–71 (1980). Indeed, most precedent states that determinations adverse to the state do not bind individual state officials. *See Kraushaar v. Flanigan*, 45 F.3d 1040, 1050 (7th Cir. 1995); *see generally Wright and Miller's Federal Practice and Procedure, Jurisdiction and Related Matters* §§ 4458 *et seq.*

In the administrative warrant context, failure to move to quash or appeal issuance of the warrant itself did not have preclusive effect on a subsequent § 1983 claim in *Cahill v. Montgomery County*, 528 A.2d 527 (Md. Ct. Spec. App. 1987). The county invoked collateral estoppel against Cahill when she did not appeal the circuit court's issuance of the order authorizing the search. In rejecting this argument, the appeals court emphasized that the factual issues involved in the § 1983 case pertain to the warrant *application*, not the circuit court judge's *issuance* of the warrant; that seeking to quash a warrant the applicant already executed would render her appeal moot; and that to estop Cahill would undermine the holding of *Malley v. Briggs*, 475 U.S. 335 (1986), which held that a judicial finding of probable cause to issue an arrest warrant does not allow the procuring officer to avoid the consequences of illegal behavior.

18.   *Parratt/Hudson* Defense

In *Parratt v. Taylor*, 451 U.S. 527 (1981) (overruled on other grounds by *Daniels v. Williams*, 474 U.S. 327 (1986)), an inmate ordered $23.50 worth of hobby materials by mail, which prison officials *negligently* lost. Resulting from a "random and unauthorized act by a state employee," the court dismissed any procedural due process claim. Three years later, *Hudson v. Palmer*, 468 U.S. 517 (1984), extended the *Parratt* doctrine to *intentional* deprivations of property (a correctional officer deliberately destroyed the prisoner's contraband during a cell search). Consequently, the *Parratt/Hudson* doctrine established that where a predeprivation hearing is rendered impracticable by a random and unauthorized act by a state employee, and an adequate postdeprivation remedy exists, no Fourteenth Amendment claim may lie.

Attempting to bring clarity to and rein in the doctrine, in 1990, the United States Supreme Court decided *Zinermon v. Burch*, 494 U.S. 113 (1990). State hospital staff abused the statutory scheme for admitting mental patients by depriving Zinermon his liberty through involuntary admission procedures. In allowing him to bring a due process claim, the court focused on three key distinctions: (1) his deprivation was not "unforeseeable"; (2) the predeprivation process was not "impossible" to furnish; and (3) the hospital personnel could not characterize their conduct as "unauthorized" within that term's meaning in *Parratt* and *Hudson*. *Id.*, at 136–38. The *Zinermon* exception to the *Parratt/Hudson* doctrine applies where the plaintiff seeks to hold "state officials accountable for their abuse of their broadly delegated, uncircumscribed power to effect the deprivation at issue." *Id.*, at 136. Thus, where employees have sweeping authority to effect deprivations and a duty to provide predeprivation procedural safeguards, *Parratt/Hudson* does not apply.

Bogart v. Chapell, 396 F.3d 548 (4th Cir. 2005) is instructive in the animal context. Law enforcement seized and euthanized more than 200 dogs and cats from Bogart's property, resulting in a § 1983 predeprivation procedural due process claim. In dismissing it, the trial court relied in part on a finding that the officers failed to abide by mandatory procedures set forth in the South Carolina Code, specifically, they denied Ms. Bogart a hearing at which she could seek the return of the seized animals before their humane disposition. S.C. Code Ann. §§ 47-1-120, 47-1-140, 47-1-150, 47-1-170. Yet the trial court distinguished *Zinermon* by observing that the defendants had no authority to destroy Bogart's animals immediately after seizure. Bogart then tried to offer new evidence that a York County policy allowed officers to immediately euthanize sick or injured animals prior to such hearing. Though rejected as untimely, the appeals court affirmed summary judgment dismissal notwithstanding the county policy, because it did not sanction the officers' conduct (no exigent circumstances [sickness or injury] existed to warrant summary euthanasia). Because Ms. Bogart had a sufficient postdepreviation remedy at law, she could not maintain her § 1983 claim.

The majority resolved the *Zinermon* questions of foreseeability, impossibility, and authorization against Bogart. The deprivation of her animals was "unforeseeable" as the state code prescribed precisely the manner in which the defendants would act once they seized. They could not euthanize until after the state court adjudicated possessory rights; thus, the actions of the officers were *not predictable*. Further, predeprivation process was *impossible*, as the South Carolina statute eliminated completely the officers' discretion to do otherwise until a preliminary hearing was afforded. It would be absurd to assert that the state should prevent a deprivation by enacting a rule imposing, for instance, a "preliminary" hearing — "prior to the court proceedings already provided for by statute — to determine whether the Defendants should destroy Bogart's animals in violation of their mandate to care for them." Finally, the acts of the officers were *unauthorized* within the meaning of *Parratt/Hudson* as the defendants lacked discretionary powers to affect the deprivation; rather, state law bound them to nondiscretionary duties, which they breached unlawfully.

Dissenting Judge Williams remarked that if the state procedural scheme provided for the summary killing of all seized animals, it would be patently unconstitutional; while the scheme did not compel this result, this outcome followed necessarily when the officials responsible for initiating the statutory hearing failed to do so. Thus, as she received no predeprivation process at all, Williams contended that Bogart had a viable § 1983 claim.

19. Prerequisites to Filing a Claim

A plaintiff need not exhaust state remedies before filing a § 1983 suit. *Heck v. Humphrey*, 512 U.S. 477 (1994). Nor can the state require that a litigant follow a notice of claim procedure as a prerequisite to suit. *Felder v. Casey*, 487 U.S. 131 (1988). The Maryland Court of Appeals acknowledged as much in *Ransom v. Leopold*, 962 A.2d 1025 (Md. Ct. Spec. App. 2008). The Ransoms sued the county executive, chief of police, and an "unnamed police officer" for the shooting death of their pit bull dog. Due to mismailing of the notice of claim and failure to timely and substantially comply with the *ante litem* notice provisions of state law, the court dismissed all state tort claims. Noncompliance did not derail the federal § 1983 claim, however.

While *ante litem* notice provisions imposed by the state cannot prevent prosecution of § 1983 claims, those imposed by federal government can. For instance, in *Cave v. East Meadow Union Free School Dist.*, 514 F.3d 240 (2d Cir. 2008), the East Meadow Union Free School District denied John Cave, Jr., a disabled high schooler, access to school facilities with his service dog, resulting in a myriad of federal and state claims, including those under § 1983. Finding no subject-matter jurisdiction, the appeals court held that Cave failed to exhaust administrative remedies. Normally, § 1983 does not impose any such requirement. However, the Individuals with Disabilities Education Act (IDEA)'s exhaustion requirement does extend to § 1983 pursuant to broad language of 20 U.S.C. § 1415(l) (". . . before the filing of a civil action under such laws seeking relief that is also available under this subchapter, the procedures under subsections (f) and (g) of this section shall be exhausted . . .").

Practitioners should try to select clients whose cases do not "bid[ ] fair to bring constitutional litigation into disrepute." That is how the Seventh Circuit described *Wall v. City of Brookfield*, 406 F.3d 458 (7th Cir. 2005). Wall's notorious Doberman had several run-ins with animal control, resulting in numerous fines. Undeterred, the dog escaped again. When the humane society impounded the dog, though it knew the owner's identity, it characterized the dog as a stray and withheld the canine from Wall for 60 days, prompting Wall to bring a § 1983 procedural due process claim for two months' loss of animal companionship. In affirming judgment dismissing the case, the court described the suit as "nuisance litigation that the federal judiciary does not need," citing *Parratt/Hudson* as grounds to reject the procedural due process claim and ordering her to show cause why she should not face sanctions for "making a frivolous argument in a meritless case."

20. Statute of Limitations and Venue

The statute of limitations applicable to a § 1983 claim turns on state statutes of limitations governing personal injury actions. Where multiple statutes of limitation apply, the court should borrow the state's general or residual personal injury statute of limitations rather than the statute of limitations for enumerated intentional torts. *Owens v. Okure*, 488 U.S. 235 (1989); *see also What Statute of Limitations Is Applicable to Civil Rights Action Brought under 42 U.S.C.A. sec. 1983?*, 45 A.L.R. FED. 548.

Plaintiffs may commence suit in either state or federal court, subject to the strictly controlled right of the defendant to remove the case to federal court under 18 U.S.C. § 1343(3). A 30-day time limit runs from the defendant's first notice of suit. *See* 28 U.S.C. §§ 1331, 1441, 1446. While state courts often allow for nonunanimous verdicts, federal courts mandate unanimity, which can present a proof problem depending on who carries the burden on the particular question of fact. Further, state court tends to lack the formalism of federal court. On the other hand, federal judges have far greater familiarity with § 1983.

There is no right of immediate interlocutory review for denial of qualified immunity in state court, though such remedy exists in federal court. *Johnson v. Fankell*, 520 U.S. 911 (1997). Further, state and federal courts can hear state and § 1983 claims, though the latter may do so only by exercising supplemental jurisdiction; dismissal of the federal claims, however, almost assuredly results in dismissal of the pendent state claims, creating a potential statute of limitations trap. 28 U.S.C. § 1367. Upon dismissal, Section 1367(d) allows plaintiffs a tolling period of 30 days to refile state claims in state court. A word of caution about federal court, however: parties dismissing claims without prejudice under Fed. R. Civ. P. 41(a) may lose any right to appeal at the litigation's end. *See* Schackmann and Pickens, *The Finality Trap: Accidentally Losing Your Right to Appeal (Part I)*, 58 J. Mo. B. 78 (2002) and Schackmann and Pickens, *The Finality Trap: Accidentally Losing Your Right to Appeal (Part II)*, 58 J. Mo. B. 138 (2002).

Observation: Avoid flagrant forum-shopping as admitted by the plaintiff in *Doukas v. County of San Mateo*, 2008 U.S. Dist. LEXIS 93473 (N.D. Cal. Nov. 10, 2008), who filed a state action in superior court one year before the federal action. Although the federal court retained jurisdiction over the Fourth Amendment claim involving the alleged wrongful euthanasia of plaintiff's dog at the direction of an animal control officer, it stayed the federal case to let the state matter proceed to trial. It then chastised Doukas for seeking to justify "the considerable waste of judicial resources in allowing two parallel matters involving the same parties and arising from the same facts." Though federal courts have an "unflagging obligation" to assert jurisdiction when parties seek relief under § 1983, it must discourage forum-shopping and avoid piecemeal litigation. Practitioners may avoid such an outcome by either filing federal and state claims in federal court at the outset or, if filing federal and state claims in state court without removal by the defendants, to dismiss the state suit without prejudice and refile in federal court. The latter approach, however, risks an order to pay costs under Fed. R. Civ. P. 41(d) before the refiled action may proceed.

21. Damages

Damages are not presumed under § 1983. *Memphis Community School Dist. v. Stachura*, 477 U.S. 299 (1986). As with the statute of limitations, cognizability of certain classes of damage derives from the common law of torts in the state where the incident occurred. *Id.*, at 305–06. A liberal rule of compensation applies to § 1983 claims, as noted in *Carey v. Piphus*, 435 U.S. 247, 254–55 (1978).

Where no actual injury can be proved, nominal damages not to exceed one dollar may be awarded. Prevailing plaintiffs will typically not recover reasonable attorney's fees under 42 U.S.C. § 1988 where the court awards nominal damages for a constitutional deprivation. *Farrar v. Hobby*, 506 U.S. 103 (1992). As with other claims, the plaintiffs have a duty to mitigate damages, but the duty arises only after injury. *Hill v. City of Pontotoc, Miss.*, 993 F.2d 422, 426 (5th Cir. 1993). Plaintiffs may recover emotional distress, embarrassment, anxiety, and loss of reputation damages through their testimony alone. *Chalmers v. City of Los Angeles*, 762 F.2d 753, 761 (9th Cir. 1985). However, supporting testimony from family, and medical evidence, helps. The collateral source rule also applies to § 1983 cases. *Perry v. Larson*, 794 F.2d 279, 285–286 (7th Cir. 1986). Other damages available include wage loss, past medical care, future medical care, and other predictable future expenses (lost earning capacity, out-of-pocket expenses, property damage, funeral expenses, pain, and suffering).

Punitive damages may be recovered against individuals only, not municipalities. *City of Newport v. Fact Concerts, Inc.*, 453 U.S. 247 (1981). In assessing punitive damages, the plaintiff should give an instruction to the jury about the defendant's wealth. The threshold for awarding punitive damages is reckless or callous disregard of, or indifference to, the rights or safety of others. *Smith v. Wade*, 461 U.S. 30, 46–47 (1983). To obtain a punitive damage award, the plaintiff must show not only that the defendant acted intentionally but also with intent to violate the plaintiff's federally protected right or in reckless disregard for whether it would violate such rights. *Iacobucci v. Boulter*, 193 F.3d 14, 26 (1st Cir. 1999). Actual malice need not be found. *Davis v. Rennie*, 264 F.3d 86, 115 (1st Cir. 2001). Punitive damages may be fixed even absent compensatory damages, provided that the plaintiff proved violation of a federally protected right. *Passantino v. Johnson & Johnson Consumer Products, Inc.*, 212 F.3d 493, 514 (9th Cir. 2000).

Punitive damage awards are not without limitation, as seen in *Snead v. Society for Prevention of Cruelty to Animals of Pennsylvania*, 992 A.2d 890 (Pa. 2010), where the appellate court granted *remittitur* to eliminate the punitive damage award of $100,000 on the basis that the evidence did not support the conclusion that the defendants intended to kill or maliciously killed Snead's dogs. Despite vacating the punitive damage award, Snead was entitled to recover her attorney's fees under § 1983 on top of the approximate $54,000 compensatory damages award. The court of appeals found that the trial judge abused his discretion, in denying Snead fees on the basis that Snead allegedly abused the dogs and received "a fair result" of $54,000. *Snead v. Society for Prevention of Cruelty to Animals of Pennsylvania*, 929 A.2d 1169 (Pa. Super. Ct. 2007), *appeal granted in part*, 600 Pa. 372 (Pa. 2009) and *order aff'd*, 985 A.2d 909 (Pa. 2009) and *appeal denied*, 992 A.2d 890 (Pa. 2010).

22. Costs and Attorney's Fees

Upon winning a § 1983 case, the court may also award reasonable attorney's fees to the prevailing plaintiff. *Kirchoff v. Flynn*, 786 F.2d 320 (7th Cir. 1986). Anita Kirchoff sued police officers for assault, battery, false arrest, and malicious prosecution after they caught her feeding pigeons with seed and walking her dogs off-leash in a Chicago area park. When she refused to identify herself to police (who knew her already), they arrested her and returned to her home to confine the dogs and a parakeet who accompanied her that day. Anita locked herself in the house and refused to let the officers in. Eventually, they kicked down the door and took her into custody. She spent nine hours in jail before release. Though prosecuted for littering, feeding a bird, allowing her dogs to run unleashed, and resisting arrest (locking herself in the house), the judge convicted her only of a leash law violation. The § 1983 suit resulted in a jury award of $25,000 to Anita, $17,000 less than the defendants' offer to settle a month prior. *See also $25,000 for the Birds*, 71 A.B.A.J. 31 (1985). Describing the matter as an "easy case to try," no need for two lawyers to prosecute it, that the contingency arrangement between the attorneys and the Kirchoffs provided for a 40/60 split, and the requested judgment of $50,000 unsupportable, the trial court ordered the defendants to pay 40 percent of the $25,000 jury award, or $10,000 in fees. In reversing and remanding, the Seventh Circuit instructed the trial judge to compute fees based on the "market rate" reasonably required to produce victory and not to arbitrarily apply a percentage based on a contingent fee contract.

Santhuff v. Seitz, 2010 U.S. App. LEXIS 13783 (11th Cir. Jul. 5, 2010), *cert. denied*, 131 S. Ct. 1021 (2011), provides an example where a prevailing defendant recovered fees. A turtle dealer brought a § 1983 action against a Department of Natural Resources officer, claiming that an allegedly unconstitutional, warrantless search preceded procurement of a warrant, resulting in seizure of turtles and later criminal charges for possessing protected species. Acquitted on all counts, Santhuff aggressively pursued the civil suit, claiming Fourth and Fourteenth Amendment violations. Trouble arose when Santhuff testified in deposition that he did not "have any evidence . . . that Steve Seitz walked on [my] property and took turtles from me before the search warrant." After Seitz moved for summary judgment, Santhuff then offered the "unexpected recollection" of a friend who submitted an affidavit claiming to have recognized Seitz as having entered the property and illegally searched, a recollection refreshed after seeing a photograph taken the day of the seizure. Yet the photo did not show Seitz. In later deposition, the friend contradicted his earlier declarations concerning an out-of-court identification of Seitz. Predictably, the court rejected the friend's testimony as a sham and granted summary judgment. It also awarded fees under § 1988 for a frivolous lawsuit in the sum of $38,235 in fees and $6,135.62 in costs. A district court may award reasonable attorney's fees to a prevailing defendant under Section 1988 if it finds the claims frivolous, unreasonable, and without foundation, regardless of bad faith. *Christiansburg Garment Co. v. Equal Employment Opportunity Commission*, 434 U.S. 412, 421 (1978). Counsel cannot be held responsible for fees under Section 1988. *Roadway Exp., Inc. v. Piper*, 447 U.S. 752, 761 n.9 (1980) (authorizing fees against a party).

Chapter 6

CUSTODIAL DISPUTES[1]

Looking first to background principles, then, the Fourth Circuit has endorsed the truism "[t]hat possession is nine-tenths of the law." *Willcox v. Stroup*, 467 F.3d 409, 412 (4th Cir. 2006) (determining the ownership of Civil War-era documents). As such, the common law in Virginia recognizes "a rebuttable presumption . . . that those in possession of property are rightly in possession" — that is, "actual possession is, prima facie, evidence of a legal title in the possessor." . . . That presumption undoubtedly favors Fuqua on the facts presented here. She claims to have purchased the Painting in good faith at a flea market in West Virginia, and she possessed the painting until the FBI seized it. . . . The burden thus lies with BMA, as the claimant out of possession, to rebut Fuqua's presumptive proof of ownership by "produc[ing] evidence of superior title." . . . BMA does so by way of a detinue action, alleging that the Painting was stolen from its collection in November 1951.

U.S. v. Baltimore Museum of Art (In re "Paysage Bords De Seine," 1879 Unsigned Oil Painting on Linen by Pierre-Auguste Renoir), 991 F. Supp. 2d 740, 742 (E.D. Va. 2014) (favoring BMA in concluding that Fuqua did not acquire title as a good faith or bona fide purchaser on account of Painting having been stolen).

Ms. Boyles claims nothing in the record establishes that taking the dog constituted theft. She argues the mere act of rescuing the dog off a slick road established she did not intend to deprive the owner of the dog. She points out she contacted a radio station, had contact with the dog's alleged owner, and tried to return the dog, until it ran away from her. At trial, however, the evidence established Ms. Boyles told Ms. Johnson she would return the dog to Colville the 'next day.' RP at 155. She did not return the dog. When Deputy Wanzenried contacted her about returning the dog, Ms. Boyles told him she did not think she had to return it. She told the deputy the dog was in bad shape, 'possession is 9/10ths of the law,' 'finders/keepers, losers/weepers,' and he could not prove she had the dog. RP at 59–60. Ms. Boyles also asked him what would happen if she did not return the dog. One hour before she was to return it to Ms. Johnson, Ms. Boyles told the deputy she had lost the dog in a park. But she could not provide him with any details about the park. Based on this evidence, the jury could reasonably infer that Ms. Boyles intended to deprive Ms. Johnson of her dog. The evidence was sufficient to support the second degree theft conviction.

---

[1] This chapter is derived in part and reprinted in part from Adam P. Karp, *Proof in Animal Custody Disputes*, 141 AM. JUR. *Proof of Facts* 3d 349 (2014), and used with permission of Thomson Reuters.

State v. Boyles, 2006 Wash. App. LEXIS 2541, *1 (Sept. 7, 2006, unpub.).

The nine-tenths precept, and related possessory maxims — e.g., "finders keepers, losers weepers," the capture rule of *ferae naturae* debated over the broken body of a fox in *Pierson v. Post*, 3 Cai. 175 (N.Y. Sup. Ct. 1805) — apply to realty and corporeal objects. Possessory attachments to *objets d'art* or necessities, to subjects-of-a-life such as animal companions, and even to biological or adopted human children, fuel extensive litigation. When attachments concern minors, family courts apply detailed custodial statutes that express concern about their best interests. But with respect to everything else, the laws of claim and delivery, abandonment, gifting, equitable distribution, liens and mortgages, distraint and impoundment govern. As many disputes claim breach of oral, written, and implied contracts, litigants must also focus on defects in execution and performance, and the appropriate remedies that follow. And in reconciling competing claims, one must remember that ownership does not exclude another from having a right to possession in the same property, a distinction worthy of attention in the case of a lease, bailment, or lien.

A. REPLEVIN

Derived from Middle English and Late Latin, the term *replevin* means recovery of personalty wrongfully held by another. Also referred to as "claim and delivery" or detinue, the gist of this cause of action turns on the plaintiff's superior right of possession (not ownership). Instead of seeking monetary damages for the property's value, as one might in a trover claim (modernly known as conversion and trespass to chattels), the plaintiff in a replevin action instead seeks the property *in specie*.

Replevin actions almost exclusively arise in state court. But Fed. Rule Civ. Proc. 64 explicitly provides that federal district courts may confer such relief in the manner of law of the state in which the district court sits. *See Granny Goose Foods, Inc. v. Brotherhood of Teamsters and Auto Truck Drivers Local No. 70*, 415 U.S. 423 (1974). With state court trials often scheduled more than a year after commencing suit, possessory disputes typically resolve at the show cause hearing for an order of prejudgment replevin. Even if the plaintiff loses at the show cause hearing, he still may prevail after a full trial. In *Long v. Noah's Lost Ark, Inc.*, 814 N.E.2d 555 (Ohio Ct. App. 2004), the appellate court rejected the contention that Long was statutorily barred from replevying Boomerang because he never obtained a prejudgment order of replevin, possession remained with Noah's until final judgment, and Boomerang was capable of passing by delivery. Such a result would prove unfair and inequitable, "especially in cases involving one-of-a-kind property or property with sentimental value," for to side with Noah's would mean that "a person could take someone else's property, post a bond, and keep the property."

Where adverse parties have equal rights of possession, replevin cannot lie. This principle arose in *Prim v. Fisher*, 2009 Vt. Super. Lexis 19 (Dec. 22, 2009). Patricia Prim sued Peter Fisher for equitable access to a golden retriever named Kaos, whom they jointly bought while cohabiting. Specifically, she sought an order establishing shared custody and expense. In denying her request for a preliminary injunction, the court stated, "The question becomes: what relief is available to one co-owner of personal property — not capable of division — where the other co-owner claims exclusive use and possession for himself?" In a footnote emphasizing this legal problem, the court cited to *Tubbs v. Richardson*, 6 Vt. 442, 447 (1834), where the Vermont Supreme Court warned, "It is a very inconvenient mode of owning personal property, to be tenants in common . . . ." It found that Kaos could not be physically divided, so he would need to be assigned or sold. Nor did the court want the task of "overseeing joint custody of a pet." *See also Sullivan v. Ringland*, 376 A.2d 130 (N.H. 1977) (ex-husband gifted dog to friend without ex-wife's permission, prompting court to find, "The gift was effective to transfer the husband's interest," and the law clearly states that "replevin against the donee of a cotenant will not lie."); *Barham v. Perry*, 171 S.E. 614 (N.C 1933) (appellate court rejected contention that conversion will not lie between cotenants, noting exception of imminent destruction or loss of property). Replevin, the injunctive counterpart to conversion, requires proof of an unconditional right to possession. This explains why actions between co-tenants, who each have an undivided right to possession, must fail. *Aronson v. Aronson*, 2013 WL 1859288 (Ill. App.), drew from this principle to rule for the defendant, finding that the ex-husband's daughter was deemed "at least a co-owner of the dog."

B. EQUITY VERSUS LAW

Courts tend to reject the equitable best interests doctrine in replevin actions due to its incompatibility with remedies at law. The maxim that equity does not intervene in the presence of a complete and adequate remedy at law is long-established. Replevin is a remedy at law. *See* C.J.S. *Replevin* § 3 ("Replevin is generally considered a remedy at law, and in tort. . . . If replevin is a complete and adequate remedy at law in a particular case, a court may not exercise its equitable powers."). Thus, while replevins almost universally present as matters at law, *Arguello v. Behmke*, 2006 N.J. Super. Unpub. LEXIS 2977 (Jan. 6, 2006), arose in the chancery division of the court given its jurisdiction over property of "peculiar artificial value" for which "adequate compensation cannot be obtained at law." With genuine compassion and appropriate seriousness, it ordered Chopper returned to Arguello even though Behmke did no wrong. Boldly, the court stated that "even it were to find all of the contracts valid insofar as they allowed for the dog's transport and adoption, they would be invalidated by this court of equity. Even a contract fairly procured must not advance injustice or hardship."

C. SUBJECT MATTER JURISDICTION

By and large, small claims courts only vest in the judge the authority to enter a money judgment, not to grant injunctive or declaratory relief. In *Mongelli v. Cabral*, 166 Misc. 2d 240 (N.Y. City Ct. 1995), the Mongellis bought Peaches, a baby Molluccan Cockatoo, from a pet store and raised her for five years, when medical difficulties prompted them to board her with the Cabrals. Mr. Cabral, an exotic bird breeder, took Peaches with the understanding the Mongellis were giving her away due to intolerable screeching. Finding for the Mongellis, the court held that the Cabrals failed to meet their burden of proving a gift due to lack of any written evidence that "even remotely suggested that Peaches was given or sold to the

Cabrals," that the Mongellis and the witness all testified that Peaches was placed for temporary boarding only, and that the "Cabrals' position defies the logic of self-interest" (i.e., why give away an exotic bird worth $2,700 when she could be sold?). Lacking equitable subject matter jurisdiction to order return of Peaches, the small claims court awarded damages of $3,000 (the statutory limit) and noted that the judgment would be set aside if Peaches and her cage, bowls, and toys were returned to the Mongellis within 10 days of entry.

D. MISJOINDER

Indispensable parties to any civil action must be joined. For replevins, this means the parties in actual, unlawful possession. While misjoinder may unnecessarily increase litigative burdens, it presented an argument for reversal in *Coomes v. Drinkwalter*, 149 N.W.2d 60 (Neb. 1967) and 162 N.W.2d 533 (Neb. 1968). In this cattle replevin action, Coomes prevailed and obtained a judgment of replevin and damages of one penny. Defendant Drinkwalter's son and sister were also joined, as the son asserted ownership of some cattle, the father others, and the sister the rest. While acknowledging that a misjoinder exists where a single replevin action is brought against two or more defendants each having exclusive possession of a portion of the chattels to be replevied, the Nebraska Supreme Court held that a defendant claiming title or right to possession is not a necessary party. As Roland Drinkwalter acquired the cattle and placed them on his own, his sister's, and his son's lands, exercising supervision over them so as to make him the party in actual possession (even if son and sister had constructive possession), he remained the only necessary party; they could have intervened if desired. Absent substantial prejudice, the misjoinder did not result in reversal.

E. STATUTE OF LIMITATIONS

Dismissal may occur if the statute of limitations for replevin has run. For instance, assume that a foster contract between an animal rescue and a foster states that the foster has no obligation or right to keep the animal beyond one year from execution of the contract. More than four years after execution, the rescue demands the animal's return and sues for replevin. The foster argues that a three-year statute of limitations for replevin applies, which ran on the rescue's claim, having accrued and commenced the day after the first anniversary of execution of the contract. *See Krussow v. Stixrud*, 205 P.2d 637 (Wash. 1949), and *Edison Oyster Co. v. Pioneer Oyster Co.*, 157 P.2d 302 (Wash. 1945), for this view that a plaintiff cannot just extend out the statute of limitations by sitting on the claim until she demands return (and defendant refuses to comply). In this foster contract, for example, the trial court nonetheless ruled for plaintiff, finding that the clause in question did not prejudice the rescue in any way, but merely provided that the foster had a right to foster for one year or could return the animal at any time. Whether the six-year statute of limitations for breach of written contract took precedence over the three-year replevin statute of limitations was not reached by the court, but the careful practitioner should research the disparate periods potentially applicable. As with other claims, the discovery rule may toll the statute of limitations. *See Free v. Jordan*, 10 S.W.2d 19 (Ark. 1928) (applying a three-year statute of limitations, the trial court dismissed the dog replevin case; reversing, the Arkansas Supreme Court held that the period tolls pending fraudulent concealment of the cause and does not run until discovered).

F. PROVING OWNERSHIP

Licensing records, kennel club registrations, microchip registries, and veterinary records may provide presumptive evidence of ownership, but are rarely dispositive. Contrasted with other highly regulated forms of property, such as realty, motor vehicles, or branded livestock, the law generally does not require formal recording, microchipping, certification, or other formality to pass "title" to a companion animal.

While litigants have asserted that noncompliance with dog licensing laws negates ownership, these meritless arguments serve only to distract, as no known licensing ordinance explicitly divests the transferee of ownership simply because the animal has no current license. Rather, they present a regulatory condition that permits fines — e.g., if ownership is transferred, the animal must be licensed. For instance, though answering the question of whether the owner of a deceased Pomeranian could sue the owner of the responsible Airedale where the Pomeranian was not licensed as required by law, the California Court of Appeals ruled for the plaintiff in *Roos v. Loeser*, 41 Cal. App. 782 (1919). At page 786, it refused to find Roos comparatively at fault by her failing to license her dog, discerning no causal connection between that failure and the injury. In 1942, the Court of Appeals for the District of Columbia decided *Scharfeld v. Richardson*, 133 F.2d 340 (D.C. 1942). JUSTICE VINSON and Rutledge, relying on *Roos*, rejected defendant's contention that he was not liable in damages for the death of a Pomeranian named Little Bits under a code that held the defendant civilly liable for injury or death to a dog wearing a tax tag (which, the Court noted, identifies the dog as "personal property"). Even though Little Bits did not wear such a tag, he was still determined to be personalty. A similar restraint on statutory literalism was imposed by the Iowa Supreme Court in the horrific case of *Mendenhall v. Struck*, 224 N.W. 95 (Iowa 1929).

In *Mendenhall*, the defendant came onto plaintiff's property. Without consent, he maliciously killed a female dog named Bird when she was then mother to five unweaned pups. Returning six weeks later, he forced himself into the plaintiff's house, drove out the five pups and killed them all (including tossing up one of the pups in the air and shooting him as he came down). *Id.*, at 96. His only defense was that the dogs did not carry a license tag, in violation of the statute that provided, "It shall be lawful for any person, . . . to kill any dog for which a license is required, when such dog is not wearing a collar with license tag attached as herein provided." *Id.*, at 97. In reversing the jury verdict for the defendant, the court concluded that "the Legislature never intended by this statute to permit an illegal or wrongful act in order to exercise the privilege granted."

Those endeavoring to persuade a court of their superior right of possession or ownership should also consult cases involving parties doing their utmost to avoid the title of "owner" and thereby sever any possible connection with the animal at issue and thereby avoid civil or criminal liability. Assume a dog subject to a custody dispute between two individuals bites a third party, who sues the two as parties-defendant on the theory they co-own the biting dog. Would the court grant or deny one defendant's motion to dismiss on grounds that she is not an "owner"? Consider *Beeler v. Hickman*, 50. 746, 752–53 (III, 1988), which declined to grant summary judgment dismissal to parties asserting they did not purchase the dog; the dog's alleged true "owner" never relinquished ownership; and they expressly disclaimed ownership. However, because they "resided with, cared for, and had exclusive possession of the dog for 3 years," the appellate court held that the jury needed to decide the material fact of ownership under Washington's strict liability dog bite statute.

A bill of sale or proof of purchase serves as strong evidence of ownership in the absence of post-purchase acts, omissions, or representations to dilute it. In *Decorso v. Saksa*, 2011 Conn. Super LEXIS 1461 (June 1, 2011), Gail Decorso tried to recover Anna, a pit bull terrier, from Kathleen Saksa. Decorso and Saksa cohabited when Decorso offered to buy Anna from a third party who had allegedly neglected the dog. That party reneged when learning Decorso had filed a report against her with animal control. In an effort to safeguard Anna, Saksa met with the party, expressed her concern for Anna's welfare, and convinced her to sell Anna to Saksa. Saksa paid $250, obtained a receipt, and provided food, shelter, medical treatment, leashes, muzzle, crate, and all necessities. She hired a trainer, paid to have Anna bathed, walked and fed her. Decorso cared for Anna when Saksa was at work. However, Saksa grew concerned with the imprudence of some of Decorso's caretaking decisions. A few months later, Decorso and Saksa's relationship began to falter and Decorso expressed a desire to remove Anna from the home. Saksa beat her to it, placing Anna in a kennel. Decorso then obtained Anna's veterinary records under false pretenses, and licensed her in Decorso's name only. Thereafter, Saksa followed suit and licensed Anna in her name. Decorso then sued Saksa for replevin and conversion. In refusing to enter an order of replevin, the court found she failed to establish probable cause of any general or special property interest in Anna as Saksa "bought the dog, paid for its care, food, medical treatment and incidental expenses." Though "sympathetic to the fact that Decorso discovered Anna, assisted in bettering Anna's circumstances and clearly loves this Anna," that Saksa also had a license, also resided with Anna, and that Decorso obtained a license by acquiring medical records under false pretenses, compelled the court to conclude that "Saksa has far greater rights of possession of Anna."

AKC registration, while probative, does not dispose of the question of ownership. In *Buczkowicz v. Lubin*, 399 N.E.2d 680 (Ill. App. Ct. 1980), Diane Buczkowicz sued Albert and Ruth Lubin for return of Tuf, a Shetland sheepdog. The Lubins raised, bred, showed, studded, and judged dogs as a hobby. Tuf was born at their kennel and sold to Buczkowicz, who raised him to maturity. Four years later, Buczkowicz boarded Tuf with the Lubins when she took a vacation. Finding vast show potential in Tuf, the Lubins asked if Buczkowicz would agree to letting the Lubins "own the animal." Lubin explained that AKC rules would not permit a judge to show any animal unless owned. The parties orally agreed that the Lubins could show and stud Tuf. Though Buczkowicz signed over the AKC registration naming Mrs. Lubin as a co-owner, Buczkowicz testified she only signed to facilitate his being shown. In affirming judgment for Buczkowicz on her replevin claim, and against the Lubins on their claim for injunctive relief (to hold Buczkowicz to her alleged verbal contract concerning studding for an indeterminate period of time), the appellate court rejected the argument that the AKC registration "showed a bona fide transfer of co-ownership," as, "Mere documentary title is not conclusive of ownership." *Id.*, at 202–03. Instead, the certificate created "only a prima facie presumption of title[.]"

In *Dubin v. Pelletier*, 2012 R.I. Super. LEXIS 175 (Nov. 21, 2012), the court set forth several rules of animal custody: certification of registration is *prima facie* evidence of ownership, and registration in one person's name supports the conclusion she is the exclusive owner, creating a presumption overcome only by clear and convincing evidence; ownership of mother (*partus sequitur ventrem*) supports the view that the "brood of all tame and domestic animals belongs to the owner of the dam or mother"; exclusive possession (even for one year), payment of stud fees, and exercise of control also favor ownership; no single indicia of ownership is dispositive, however, and parties' intent also governs. As Dubin was listed as the sole owner on the dog's AKC registration, chipped him in her name, and was listed at AKC shows as his owner, supervised his breedings and collected his stud fees, she established *prima facie* ownership. Pelletier failed to rebut the presumption, for she could not prove that Dubin exhibited donative intent at the time of delivering the dog, a point bolstered by Pelletier's confession that Dubin could have taken Mr. Big back at any time.

Pelletier also argued that she was the dog's "guardian" and "owner keeper," as defined by state law, claiming she satisfied the guiding indicia of the statutory definition, namely, exclusive possession, length of possession, care, and feeding, including daily responsibility for his love, affection, veterinary care, food, shelter, training, and handling. In rejecting this argument, the court concluded that Pelletier served much like a "licensed boarding kennel," statutorily exempt from the "owner keeper" definition. But even if Pelletier satisfied either definition, the court continued, it would prove immaterial to the question of ownership as the statute pertained to licensing, regulation, and liability for dog bites.

Jockey Club papers (registration documentation for thoroughbreds through The Jockey Club) and racing entries do not create ownership either, according to *Swann v. Alleva*, 45 Pa. D & C. 3d 630 (1987), and *Simpkins v. Ritter*, 204 N.W.2d 383 (Neb. 1973). Finding that it "tests credulity to believe that under the circumstances she would give the horse to Kate for its entire racing life," a five-justice majority of the Nebraska Supreme Court found a bailment only and criticized the trial court for "ignoring the bailment characteristics of the transaction," erring by "[r]elying on the foal certificate and the racing entry," as they were in the appellate court's estimation "entirely consistent with the delivery of possession for bailment purposes." *Id.*, at 384.

A recent trend of forming an animal trust as a type of ownership proxy to gain possession over the nonhuman beneficiary failed in *Mittasch v. Reviczky*, 2013 U.S. Dist. LEXIS 83677 (D. Conn. June 14, 2013). Robin Mittasch, trustee of a New York animal trust for the benefit of two Rottweilers owned by Michelle Chapman-Avery, claimed the illegal seizure and detention of the dogs by municipal and state authorities. The trust consisted of $100 for the dogs' care, was established eight months after the dogs Stella Blue and Tazzy were seized and 10 days before suit was filed. Mittasch never possessed, cared for, or even laid eyes on the dogs, yet the dogs were named "Beneficiaries," Mittasch "trustee" by "grantor" Chapman-Avery, with Richard Rosenthal as the "trust protector." Mittasch is President of The Lexus Project, Inc. and Rosenthal its General Counsel. In dismissing the case for lack of standing, the court found that Mittasch had no property interest in Stella or Tazzy, for the trustee does not "own" the beneficiaries of the trust. Instead, she had title to the Trust property — i.e., the $100 principal and interest. And Stella and Tazzy had equitable ownership of the Trust property. Even trust language ostensibly providing the right to sue on behalf of the dogs did not manufacture standing, for it is "not a matter of the parties' intent, and it does not arise by *ipse dixit*."

Signing an adoption contract as adopter might appear to convey ownership, but *Placey v. Placey*, 51 So. 3d 374 (Ala. Civ. App. 2010), did not make such an assumption in this mother-daughter custody dispute over a dog named Preston. Though Jill solely signed an adoption contract with the humane society at the time of adopting Preston, the court remained unpersuaded that the contract of adoption necessarily decided the question of ownership because the mother took primary care of Preston, who always lived with the parties "as a *family* pet." The trial court found Preston would receive better care where he spent the last six years of his life rather than in a hotel with Jill. The appellate court did not disturb the trial court's consideration of Preston's best interests.

G. PROVING IDENTITY

A court will only order replevin of property identified with specificity, a principle explored in *Prenger v. Baker*, 542 N.W.2d 805 (Iowa 1995). As to the female and juvenile ostriches, while there was "no question the plaintiffs are entitled to possession of the birds as purchasers in the ordinary course of business; the question is one of identification." Because "the record [was] replete with contradictory testimony involving the identity of the juveniles and the two female ostriches," even as to alleged microchipping, the failure of MRC and the Prengers to reliably describe with particularity *which* birds allegedly in the Bakers' possession were theirs caused the appellate court to also affirm the trial court's refusal to replevy the female or juveniles. Citing *Lyons v. Shearman*, 62 N.W.2d 196, 197–98 (Iowa 1954), involving a farmer trying to replevy his own cattle from an adjacent farmer to whose property the cattle wandered, it reasoned that a right to present possession is not enough, for that right "means nothing" unless "[h]e can show *what* he is entitled to possess."

Animals may be replevied, dead or alive. But they must exist in either form. In *Vantreese v. McGee*, 60 N.E. 318 (Ind. Ct. App. 1901), Plaintiff sued for return of a beloved dog's remains for proper burial, valuing the body at $2-$1 for the skin, and $1 for the remainder of the dog's body for fertilizing purposes. Finding that replevin lies "for every species of personal property, animate or inanimate," the appellate court reversed judgment for the defendant, rejecting the contention that where the defendant "admits the property in appellant, its value, and wrongful taking," the owner "by the mere facts of [the dog's] death, loses title to whatever of value remains in the body." The change from ante-mortem to post-mortem form "does not deprive the owner of title to, or right of possession of, property." As the property sought in this action existed in tangible form at the commencement of the action, it was error to dismiss the case.

In resolving that question of mistaken animal identity, courts look to such factors as unique identification, chain of custody, physical marks, behavior, and DNA. In *Arguello v. Behmke*, 2006 N.J. Super. Unpub. LEXIS 2977 (Ch. Div. Jan. 6, 2006), Behmke argued that "Pluto," the Great Dane she adopted, was not Arguello's "Chopper." But the court rejected this contention for a few reasons: HSUS tracked dogs by unique animal identification tags, and chain of custody proved Chopper was delivered to People for Animals (despite a data-entry error on petfinder.com); that the Dane did not respond to the name "Chopper" when called by Behmke did not prove he was a different dog as she may not have spoken loudly enough, or he could have simply been "tired, untrained, or just unfamiliar with [her]"; and that the adoption agreement lists him as a three-year-old male named Pluto while Chopper was half that age was explained by the fact that water damaged his paperwork and the satellite rescue may have just manufactured a name and age. Arguello also proved the existence of identifying features on Chopper's legs.

In *Augillard v. Madura*, 257 S.W.3d 494 (Tex. App. 2008), New Orleans resident Shalanda Augillard claimed that Tiffany Madura and Richard Toro converted her black cocker spaniel Jazz and sued for Jazz's return. Madura countered that her dog, Hope Floats, was not the same. At trial, Augillard testified to Jazz's medical conditions (she had raised Jazz for eight years) and offered two DNA test results to prove identity. According to Dr. Halverson, Augillard's expert:

> [T]he [first] test showed a complete match at all seventeen DNA markers with a likelihood ratio exceeding one trillion, meaning that "it is a trillion times more likely that the samples match because they came from the same dog" than because the samples "came from different dogs and match by chance."

Id., at 499. The second mitochondrial DNA test showed that Hope Floats and Madison, a cocker spaniel born to Jazz's mother, were maternal relatives. The trial court found Augillard's witnesses noncredible, the DNA evidence had too high a potential for tampering, and that she failed to prove her case by evidentiary preponderance. In reversing, the Court of Appeals agreed that Augillard's evidence legally sufficed, especially with respect to uncontroverted DNA evidence, and rendered judgment in her favor.

In *Barham v. Perry*, 171 S.E. 614 (N.C. 1933), Annie Barham sought to replevy "two mouse-colored mules" and other personalty from H.G. Perry. A jury found that Barham was entitled to "one of the mules described in the complaint and one-half of the other personal property." Perry appealed, claiming that the jury failed to specify which mule Barham could repossess, rendering the judgment "indefinite, uncertain, and incapable of execution." In reversing, the North Carolina Supreme Court agreed that the judgment failed to sufficiently specify which mule and what property would go to Barham, notwithstanding Barham's assurance that the parties could "readily agree on a division of the property" when the time came.

H. LOST AND FOUND

The maxim "Finders keepers, losers weepers," is not law. Instead, finders are involuntary bailees who must exercise care to locate the true owner before staking their claim of ownership by find. Unless stolen, those losing their nonhuman companions share some degree of responsibility for their predicament for, unlike inanimate objects such as a cell phone that cannot just get up and move on its own, animals enjoy the gifts of perambulation and volition, meaning they can lose or mislay themselves. Thus, lost *animate* property introduces three new concepts to the traditional manner of framing lost *inanimate* property disputes: i.e., *containment* (as a means of safeguarding from escape), *identification* (as a way to notify finders of the true owner), and *perishability* (without necessities of survival, the animal will die). Add further that those who assume the role of Good Samaritan expect to be thanked, not sued, and deserve compensation for rescue and care. Critical litigation issues include: (1) the duration of loss, (2) the original owner's efforts to find the animal, (3) the finder's efforts to locate the original owner, (4) the involvement of humane society/animal control or another third party, and (5) evidence of abuse/neglect.

Many states have lost property statutes outlining the procedure by which a finder may claim ownership of, for instance, a bejeweled necklace plucked from high grass abutting a heavily-trafficked sidewalk. Proving they belong to a different order, however, courts have refused to apply these statutes to companion animals, instead resorting to the common law, and considering whether the finder and true owner took steps to create a substantial probability of reunion. The Vermont Supreme Court, in *Morgan v. Kroupa*, 702 A.2d 630, 634 (Vt. 1997), affirmed the trial court's decision that the finder "substantially [complied] with the [Vermont lost property statute] and was therefore entitled to possession." Notably, *Morgan* held that the state lost property statute does not apply to lost companion animals.

Mary Morgan sued Zane Kroupa for return of Max, a dog she found at-large and kept for more than a year before Kroupa located him in her care. He then tried to negotiate the dog's return without success. As Kroupa drove off, Max jumped in his truck. He then left with the dog. In affirming judgment for Morgan, the Vermont Supreme Court rejected that the lost property statute applied to dogs, holding that, "No decision has ever applied the lost-property or other impounding statutes to any kind of 'beast' other than a farm animal of considerable value." Yet it recognized that it applied to agricultural animals, such as a those put into "labor" and sold at "auction" (language contained in the lost-property statute), and that it might include a "working sheep dog." Instead of engaging in statutory analysis, it drew from finder's common law, applying a balancing test that stated, "Where, as here, the finder of a lost domestic animal diligently attempts to locate its owner and provides care, shelter and companionship to the animal for over a year, a trial court does not abuse its discretion in awarding possession to the finder." Posting notices, placing newspaper advertisements, contacting the humane society, and arranging for radio announcements sufficed to "preclude[] the unscrupulous from asserting rights in a stolen pet." A single dissenting justice worried that the majority would give an advantage to scoundrels who would develop a black market in stolen pets.

Morgan concisely states the common law for lost animals:

The value of a pet to its human companions has already been noted. Accordingly, apart from providing care and shelter, finders of stray pets should also be encouraged to make every reasonable effort to find the animal's owner. Although circumstances will vary, this might include contacting the local humane society, veterinarians, or the police department, posting notices near where the animal was found, and placing newspaper or radio advertisements. Additionally, owners of lost pets should be enjoined to undertake reasonable efforts to locate their animals by contacting local humane societies and other appropriate agencies, printing and placing notices, or taking out appropriate advertisements. Together these requirements provide an incentive to finders to care for stray pets and attempt to locate their owners, and place the onus on owners to conscientiously search for their pet.

When confronted with a case of this nature, therefore, courts should factor these practical and policy considerations into any decision.

Indeed, this was essentially the approach taken by the trial court here. Although couched in terms of "substantial compliance" with the lost-property statute, the court basically held that *where the finder of a lost pet makes a reasonable effort to locate its owner, and responsibly cares for the animal over a reasonably extensive period of time, the finder may acquire possession of the animal.* As the court explained, "The court's going to decide this case on the basis that [plaintiff] found a stray dog, cared for it for a year, [and] did put up notice when she found it . . . . If you pick up a stray which does not have a market value to speak of, if you have put up notices . . . . I think that's what the law requires and after a passage of time you're entitled to keep the dog."

Having found that plaintiff diligently attempted to locate the dog's owner and responsibly sheltered and cared for the animal for over a year, the trial court was clearly within its discretion in awarding possession to plaintiff. We will not set aside findings made by a trial court unless clearly erroneous, nor disturb its conclusions if they are supported by its findings. *Cameron v. Double A. Services, Inc.*, 156 Vt. 577, 581–82, 595 A.2d 259, 261–62 (1991).

Id., at 633–34 (emphasis added). *See also* Eric W. Neilsen, *Comment: Is the Law of Acquisition of Property by Find Going to the Dogs?* 15 T.M. Cooley L. Rev. 479, 505 (1998) (*citing Morgan*, 702 A.2d at 634). *Graham v. Notti*, 147 Wn. App. 629, 638–39 (Ill. 2008), also endorses this view.

Morgan and *Graham* buttress public policy because: (1) legislatures have impliedly rejected a continuing ownership interest in lost dogs, (2) encouraging finders to take in strays adjuncts the state's police power, and (3) a plaintiff does not deserve a heightened protection of the ownership interest if she failed to meet historical threshold requirements of registration and identification. Moreover, allowing finders to take in stray dogs "may reduce hazards to traffic, prevent the spread of contagious or infectious disease, prevent damage to property and persons from dangerous canines, and reduce the overpopulation problem among the stray-dog population." Neilsen, at 504.

In *Thomas v. City of Minneapolis*, 2014 U.S. Dist. LEXIS 140844 (Minn. App. Sept. 30, 2014), Pauline Thomas left her granddaughter's dog with a friend, who then lost the dog. Two days later, the dog was impounded, kept at the Animal Control Shelter for the City of Minneapolis ("ACS"), and adopted out to Shannon McKenzie with Underdog Rescue eight days later. One day after receipt, Underdog Rescue adopted the dog to Carolyn Keller. Thomas sued ACS, McKenzie, Underdog, and Keller to recover the dog and for damages. Finding that ACS never acquired good title to pass to McKenzie/Underdog, because it failed to comply with the public posting requirement of state law, it further held that McKenzie/Underdog could pass no good title to Keller, and ordered the dog returned to Thomas.

In *Conti v. ASPCA*, 77 Misc. 2d 61 (N.Y. Civ. Ct. 1974), the ASPCA's educational parrot Chester flew away during an exhibition in a park, settling in a tall tree. The ASPCA spent hours trying to coax him down, without success. A week later, Edward Conti lured him into his residence by offering food. He then called the ASPCA for advice on raising the bird. ASPCA representatives came to his home and took him. Conti then sued in replevin. Ruling for the ASPCA, the trial court found that the law of capture might apply were Chester truly wild, extinguishing the ASPCA's property rights in him. But tamed animals enjoy greater protection for they cannot "regain their natural liberty," a distinction made in the case of *Manning v. Mitcherson*, 69 Ga. 447, 450–51 (1883), where plaintiff successfully recovered his pet canary, prompting the court to hold:

> To say that if one has a canary bird, mocking bird, parrot, or other bird so kept, and it should accidentally escape from its cage to the street, or to a neighboring house, that the first person who caught it would be its owner, is wholly at variance with our views of right and justice.

Though the ASPCA claimed Chester was the lost bird, emphasizing his ability to say "hello" and dangle by the legs, under judicial scrutiny the bird "did not exhibit any of these characteristics." While the court asked the bird to indicate "by name or mannerism an affinity" to either party, "Alas, the bird stood mute." Yet it found credible evidence that the bird was the same given size, coloration, and chronology.

In *Feger v. Warwick Animal Shelter*, 59 A.D.3d 68 (N.Y. Sup. Ct. App. Div. 2008), an unidentified person stole Kisses, Darlene Feger's cat. Ten days later, the Warwick Animal Shelter posted her picture and named her Lucy. Feger learned that Lucy had been offered for adoption. The shelter refused to divulge the identities of the donor and adoptive owner. And though it disputed that Lucy was Kisses, Feger sued for over $86,000 (related to value of Kisses and future progeny) and for the return of Kisses. Following dismissal of suit against the shelter, Feger appealed. Affirming in part, the appellate court agreed that public policy warranted not disclosing the adopter's identity for fear it "could lead to the collapse of what the Supreme Court called the 'animal adoption infrastructure.' " Reaching this conclusion, it favorably cited to similar cases from other jurisdictions. It also chronicled the change in law pertaining to animals, from enhanced anticruelty protections, animal trusts, inclusion in protective orders, to their recognized "cherished status" justifying consideration of the "best interest of the animal." As to the donor's identity, the court modified the lower ruling to require disclosure only if the donor were an employee of the shelter, employee of a service provider of the shelter, or person employed by the law firm that Feger believed may have had a role in taking Kisses. A single judge dissented from that part of the ruling, reasoning that the circumstances by which the cat came to the shelter were "highly relevant to resolution of the dispute," and clearly discoverable absent privilege (which did not exist).

I. MUNICIPAL STRAY HOLDS

Once a finder delivers the lost animal to a government shelter, or an animal control officer impounds a stray, the custody dispute enters the realm of constitutional law. When a municipality asserts ownership of another's property, it must do so in accord with procedural and substantive due process, and not engage in an illegal taking. By operation of law, many jurisdictions involuntarily forfeit ownership rights in known or assumed (but unknown) owners of cats and dogs, licensed and unlicensed, after a number of days. *Lamare v. North Country Animal League*, 743 A.2d 598, 603 (Vt. 1999), evaluated the constitutionality of a seven-day hold on lost dogs, finding the ordinance gave adequate procedural due process to the original owner. Holds shorter than two days may raise legitimate due process challenges, especially if the municipality fails to strictly comply with mandated protocols to locate and notify the owner.

Chasidy Lamare and Charles Arnold sued North Country Animal League ("NCAL"), among others, for adopting out Billy, their five and one-half year old female German Shepherd to Jane and John Doe, who were also named in the suit. While licensed, Billy was not wearing her Town of Wolcott license tags when she broke free from her tether at the plaintiffs' residence. For a month, the plaintiffs searched intermittently for Billy until Arnold's mother spoke with Gilbert Goff of Wolcott Animal Control. Goff received Billy hours after her escape from an employee at Lamoille Kennel, who, in turn, received her from a couple of Good Samaritans. Goff abided by the township's ordinance in placing notices at the village store, post office, and town clerk's office. He held Billy for nine days from impoundment before transferring her to NCAL, where she stayed for three weeks.

The plaintiffs called NCAL to demand Billy's return and offered AKC papers as proof of ownership. They also offered to pay all boarding costs. NCAL told them they needed to fill out an adoption application, as legal ownership had transferred from Wolcott Animal Control to NCAL. They complied, but NCAL denied their application, citing Billy's "best interests." In fact, NCAL had approved Jane and John Doe's adoption application two days before plaintiffs submitted theirs. *Lamare* held that, between private parties:

> When the finder of a lost dog makes a reasonable effort to locate the owner and responsibly cares for the animal over a reasonably extensive period of time, the finder may be awarded possession of the dog.

Id., at 600. Plaintiffs argued that the notice requirements under the local ordinance were insufficient and failed to guarantee due process in the taking of Billy. Thanks to an amicus curiae brief filed by the Humane Society of the United States, the Supreme Court of Vermont concluded that seven-day holds prior to transfer or sale were constitutional, even though lost and found property laws, which most commonly apply to inanimate property like rings and watches, may give the original owner 30 or as many as 60 days to come forward with satisfactory evidence of ownership before losing the right to demand its return:

> . . . [A] dog is an inherently social creature whose 'value derives from the animal's *relationship* with its human companions.' *Id.* Thus, while municipal shelters or pounds may provide temporary safety for the public and security for the animal, long-term residence in such facilities is decidedly not in the public's or the animal's interest. . . . long-term confinement is severely detrimental to the health of dogs and a considerable expense to the impounding agency.

Id., at 602–03 (*citing Morgan v. Kroupa*, 702 A.2d 630, 633 (Vt. 1997)). Colorado and Georgia have deemed three-day holds constitutional, Missouri five days, and Texas a mere 48 hours. *Thiele v. City & County of Denver*, 312 P.2d 786 (Colo. 1957); *Johnston v. Atlanta Humane Soc.*, 326 S.E.2d 585 (Ga. Ct. App. 1985); *Professional Houndsmen of Miss., Inc. v. County of Boone*, 836 S.W.2d 17 (Mo. Ct. App. 1992); *Jenkins v. City of Waxahachie*, 392 S.W.2d 482 (Tex. Civ. App. 1965).

Graham v. Notti, cited above, involved a custody dispute over Harlee, a Pomeranian, pitting his original guardian against an adopter who acquired Harlee from the municipal humane society SpokAnimal upon expiration of the City of Spokane's stray hold period. Though the suit involved a private plaintiff and private defendant, Graham argued that Notti acquired no ownership through SpokAnimal since Harlee was lost and found in the *county*, and SpokAnimal only had jurisdiction within the *city*. Although Notti was an innocent adopter, the court found that SpokAnimal lacked jurisdiction over county strays, and held that Spokane's stray hold ordinance did not effectively transfer ownership of Harlee to SpokAnimal, and from it to Mr. Notti. *Graham*, 147 Wn. App. at 636–37.

Private nonprofit rescue organizations that do not serve as the contracted animal control authorities for municipalities with such stray hold laws may not claim ownership of animals held by them over that minimum period. Like private finders, they must still strive to find the original owner. Regarded as individual Good Samaritans, the court will ultimately compare the rescue's against the original owner's search efforts, including notification to police or animal control, licensing, tagging, and microchipping. Finders should adhere to the following best practices, which may prove germane to whether the finder may claim ownership of rights extinguished in the loser:

- Scan for microchips, check for current or past licenses, and scrutinize all tags on the collar for leads (including rabies vaccination tags, which may reveal a veterinary record with owner contacts).

- Conduct a thorough intake of the person who found the stray, getting name, address, phone, email, and copy of driver's license.

- Put the animal on view for a significant period of time.

- Create both lost and found dog/cat logs.

- If there is a hotline, identify the animal on the hotline, including date of receipt, breed, relative age, color, sex, sterilization status (if known), location where found.

- If there is a website, log the animals there, too.

- Cross-report to other rescues contracting with government in the jurisdiction where the animal was found, including animal control, so they can have the information available. *If they do nothing with the information, that is not the fault of the finder.*

- Post a flyer indicating the animal was found and include a photo — ideally at no fewer than two public locations, such as the post office, library, sheriff/police, and shelter.

- Hold for more than five days (the period set by 7 U.S.C. § 2158, discussed below) and fewer than 60 (the period set by most lost property statutes), leaning toward more.

A narrowly drafted *federal* stray hold law exists, 7 U.S.C. § 2158, entitled the Federal Pet Theft Act, part of the Animal Welfare Act. *See* 4 Am. Jur. 2d *Animals* § 38. It states in relevant part:

> In the case of each dog or cat acquired by an entity described in paragraph (2), such entity shall hold and care for such dog or cat for a period of not less than five days to enable such dog or cat to be recovered by its original owner or adopted by other individuals before such entity sells such dog or cat to a dealer.

7 U.S.C. § 2158(a)(1). This pet protection component of federal law requires that shelters (governmental and private contractors) hold all cats and dogs a minimum of five days before selling them to a USDA-licensed dealer. In actuality, this becomes a six-day hold. *See* 9 C.F.R. § 2.133(a). The law also applies to purchasers of dogs or cats "alive or dead (including unborn animals, organs, limbs, blood, serum, or other parts)[.]" 9 C.F.R. § 1.1. Implementing regulations define the word "sell" to also mean to provide, so adoptions qualify.

Unless adopting to out-of-state individuals or transferring to out-of-state rescues, the Act likely will not apply in the ordinary case due to the "in commerce" element. But where a shelter gives dogs or cats to a veterinary school, which uses them in live animal laboratories (e.g., spay/neuter) or continuing education seminars soliciting attendance by out-of-state veterinarians, whereupon the animals are "resold" to individuals across state lines "for use as a pet," it is arguable that the school becomes a "dealer," rendering § 2158 applicable to the shelter.

Exemplary stray hold cases follow.

In *Stoddard v. VanZandt*, 975 N.Y.S.2d 712 (Sup. Ct. 2013), Debbie Stoddard and Zachary Murray sued to replevy Freedom, an 11-year-old cat adopted to Brian VanZandt and Stephane Fay by the Mohawk Hudson Humane Society following expiration of the five-day stray hold period. Ruling for the defendants, the trial court held that in New York, animals are not personalty, but "companion animals," entitled to special protection, including the right to be estate and protection order beneficiaries. Because the plaintiffs did not check the Society's webpage (which displayed Freedom's image), chip or collar him, and allowed him to roam the neighborhood freely, the "indeed heartbreaking event" did nothing to persuade the court to order Freedom's return.

In *O'Keefe v. Gist*, 908 F. Supp. 2d 946 (C.D. Ill. 2012), police officer Harold Gist gave Patrick O'Keefe's dog Boomer to David Hagan without a hearing or his consent. In so doing, he violated the local ordinance, which required impoundment of strays and delivery to the pound. O'Keefe sued Hagan in replevin and prevailed. Thereafter he sued the officer and city for violating his procedural due process rights. Though unauthorized, Gist's actions did not state a claim under 42 U.S.C. § 1983 because O'Keefe had been afforded an adequate post-deprivation remedy (i.e., replevin). Alternatively, even if his actions were authorized by city ordinance, because O'Keefe did not outfit Boomer with an identification tag observable upon visual inspection, Gist was prevented from providing O'Keefe pre-deprivation notice (e.g., a phone call, personal contact, or letter informing him that Boomer was found). While Boomer was microchipped, the court concluded that, "Requiring all municipalities to scan every stray dog for a microchip would create fiscal and administrative burdens that would outweigh the burden on pet owners to place identification tags on their pets or else rely on post-deprivation remedies to recover their lost pets." *Id.*, at 953. Such a holding may seem out of touch with modern shelter management practices. Perhaps it reached this conclusion because the city did not have a scanner, requiring Gist to travel to a different city to arrange a scan or to hire a private veterinarian to do so.

In *Webb v. Amtower*, 178 P.3d 80 (Kan. Ct. App. 2008), Chantelle Heath Webb sued Kansas residents Susan and Doug Amtower for replevin and conversion of her dog Buddy after the destruction of her hometown, Gulfport, Mississippi. Webb's right to recover Buddy turned on the strength of her title, not the weakness of the Amtowers'. The Court of Appeals reversed summary judgment to the Amtowers and remanded, acknowledging that factual issues existed as to whether at-large and lost property laws in Mississippi and Alabama applied and, if so, what legal effect they might have (it was unknown where Buddy was picked up). Furthermore, the Amtowers could not necessarily rely on passing of title by operation of stray hold laws when agents of a private humane society held Buddy for more than seven days, as it was unclear whether he was taken into custody by an "impounding officer" of a "county pound."

Factual issues also existed as to whether the Amtowers actually obtained ownership of Buddy through a purported adoption contract executed by the Amtowers and the Humane Society of Escambia County, Alabama, from where Buddy was transferred to the Amtowers. The "adoption certificate" prevented Amtower from selling Buddy or giving him to another for medical experimentation by stating, in bold type, **"If circumstances become such that I cannot keep this animal, I agree to return it to HSEC."** Failing to abide by its restrictions would result in forfeiture of the dog and the adoption fee. By denying the Amtowers the right of alienation and by imposing other continuing controls, the court questioned whether a sale even occurred under Kansas or Alabama law so as to vest in the Amtowers "ownership rights." Accordingly, the certificate did not represent a "complete and unambiguous contract" and the trial court erred granting them summary judgment.

In *Young v. Gostomsky*, 1978 Ohio App. LEXIS 10874 (Oct. 20, 1978), Donald Gostomsky bought a Walker Coon dog. While running the dogs to hunt raccoons, the unlicensed dog disappeared, only to be found in a truck and impounded. Four days later, animal control sold the dog to Willie Jones for $5, who then sold him to Bill Young for $20 and a shotgun. A month or so later, Gostomsky found the dog in Young's kennel and took the dog with aid of the sheriff. Young sued to replevy the dog from Gostomsky. In affirming judgment for Gostomsky, the appellate court explained that animal control denied Gostomsky due process when it sold the dog to Jones with knowledge that he was in "good physical condition, was gentle and well trained, and . . . well-bred and valuable," all without posting any notice that the dog was so found. Thus, no title passed by operation of the stray hold to Jones, or to Young.

J. LIENS

Liens permit creditors to attach and sell specific property as collateral to satisfy a debt. Some liens are consensual, as in a person obtaining a loan by voluntarily giving the bank a security interest in a dwelling, car, or other item. Others are nonconsensual and arise unilaterally from a lienor's demand for compensation. Nonconsensual liens are either possessory or nonpossessory. Possessory liens exist only as long as the lienholder maintains possession of the liened property. Lien creditors lose the lien when voluntarily and unconditionally released to the lien debtor. Nonpossessory liens, as the name suggests, survive despite such dispossession. A lien, however, merely entitles a lienor to force sale of the liened property in an effort to retire the debt on which the lien is predicated. Because personalty may be encumbered by multiple lienors or mortgagees, disputes as to which claimant has priority often arise. Generally, whoever impounds a breachy animal takes position ahead of even previous lienholders. Finally, one must appreciate the difference between the right to a lien and the right to retain the liened property (known as a "retention lien"). Having one does not necessarily imply the other.

Liens originally existed at common law. Statutory liens later expressly pre-empted or limited common law liens. Many were codified in derogation of the common law, requiring strict construction in order to perfect and enforce the lien against the lien debtor. So long as the law continues to regard nonhuman animals as mere personalty and does not invoke guardianship law principles, animal law practitioners have resorted to statutory liens such as the generic chattel lien, veterinary lien, and, in the right circumstance, agister lien. Others rely on consensual liens at time of service per written contract.

More than half of the states have codified veterinary liens. Some limit their scope to livestock or large animals. Others expire once the veterinarian loses possession. Examples of states with veterinary liens for companion animals include Tennessee, Florida, Alabama, Kansas, North Carolina, and Georgia. Tenn. § 63-12-134; Fla. Liens F.S. § 713,655; Ala. § 35-11-390; Kansas § 47-836; N.C. Gen. Stat. § 44A-2(c); Ga. § 44-14-490. Massachusetts expressly prohibits veterinarians from refusing to return an animal on grounds of nonpayment for veterinary services. 256 CMR § 7.01(4)(1).

Chattel liens grant the artisan or mechanic a retention lien over any personal property "repaired" through "labor" performed or "material" furnished at the request of its owner. Arguably, these liens apply just to inanimate property "constructed" or "repaired," not animals, though some have attempted to expand their coverage, which necessitates close examination of the operative statute and legislative history. Some assert that an animal owner constructively requests that a rescuer use labor and material (as in food, water, shelter, supervision) to repair and protect against ongoing disrepair to the stray animal, so that the rescuer obtains a chattel lien over the animal. However, at least in Delaware, the common law mechanic's lien depends on consent, express or implied, of the owner, and no lien is created for repairs made at the instance of the wrongdoer. *Universal Credit Co. v. Spinazzolo*, 197 A. 68 (Del. 1938).

Most agister liens apply only to farmers, ranchers, herders of cattle, livery and boarding stable keepers, veterinarians, and other persons to whom horses, mules, cattle, or sheep are entrusted for feeding, herding, pasturing, training, caring for, or ranching. They provide a possessory lien that attaches at the time amounts are due until paid, but expires a period (sometimes 180 days) after attachment. Read the statute closely as it may just apply to traditional livestock species and not every class of animal. For instance, see RCW § 60.56.035 (expires after 180 days); Tenn. Code § 66–20–10 (pasturage lien for six months); N.H. Stat. § 448:2 (lien on horses, cattle, sheep, other domestic animals).

Some states permit owners of damaged or destroyed fencing to impose a statutory retention lien on stray farmed animals. For instance, see RCW § 16.04.010 (trespassing animals); RCW § 16.60.015 (animals breaching fencing). In the absence of "breaking into an enclosure" or trespassing in a way that causes damage, however, it is highly unlikely these statutes would provide for a lien on a stray dog or cat found at-large on public property.

In the case of cruelty or neglect, some statutes bestow upon animal control officers and third-party caretakers a retention lien to cover the cost of care, boarding, and veterinary rehabilitation for cruelty-seized dogs and cats. *See, e.g.,* RCW § 60.56.025; Okla. Stat. § 21-1685. They are typically foreclosed upon as with other personalty liens.

At common law, subclasses of bailees enjoyed a retention lien on bailed property:

> To entitle a bailee to a lien on the thing bailed, it is clear that more is necessary than the mere existence of the bailment relationship. . . . Moreover, while it seems evident that some right on the part of the bailee to compensation or reimbursement, either expressed in, or implied from, the contract of bailment is essential in order to entitled him to a lien, nevertheless, at common law it is not every bailee for hire who has a lien on the article bailed. In general, except for bailees in such special classes as pledgees, factors, and brokers in certain instances, a lien exists in favor only on such a bailee as (1) has by labor or skill contributed to the improvement of the thing bailed, by which its value is increased, or (2) is engaged in some trade or occupation regarded as a public employment, in which the law leaves him no choice but to accept the bailment when offered. Therefore, except where a bailee falls within the latter class, as, for

example, in the case of common carriers, innkeepers, and possibly farriers, warehousemen, and wharfingers, no lien for simply keeping and taking care of property exists, unless one is created by contract of the parties or by statute; . . .

Nielsen v. Drager, 208 P.2d 639, 639–40 (Wash. 1949) (*citing* 6 Am. Jur., *Bailments*, § 274, p. 362 and 39 L.R.A., N.S., 1164 and Ann. Cas. 1913D, 1300). At common law, such liens were lost upon surrender. *See Sensenbrenner v. Mathews*, 3 N.W. 599 (Wis. 1879).

A lien is predicated on the value of reasonable expenses incurred by the bailee. In many cases, the bailee will be entitled to restitution but not necessarily a lien (retention or otherwise) for that sum. The following cases virtually all take place in the 1800s and do not involve companion animals: *Tome v. Four Cribs of Lumber*, Taney 583 (U.S. 4th Cir. 1853) (restitution allowed, no lien); *Amory v. Flynn*, 10 Johns. 102 (N.Y. 1813) (restitution allowed, no lien); *Baker v. Hoag*, 7 N.Y. 555 (1853) (restitution allowed, no lien); *Meekins v. Simpson*, 96 S.E. 894 (N.C. 1918) (restitution allowed, no lien); *Etter v. Edwards*, 4 Watts 63 (Pa.1835) (restitution allowed, no lien); *Nicholson v. Chapman*, 2 H. Bl. 254 (1793) (restitution allowed, no lien); *Bryan v. Akers*, 7 S.W.2d 325 (Ark. 1928) (no restitution); *Burns Motor Co. v. Briggs*, 160 N.E. 728 (Ohio Ct. App. 1928) (no restitution); *Holmes v. Hard*, Harper's Rep. 133 (S.C. 1824) (no restitution, no lien); *Wood v. Pierson*, 7 N.W. 888 (Mich. 1881) (no lien unless reward offered); *De La O. v. Acoma*, 1 N. M. 226 (1857) (no lien). A finder was held entitled to a lien if a reward was offered. *Wentworth v. Day*, 44 Mass. 352 (1841), *Wood v. Pierson*, 7 N.W. 888 (Mich. 1881), *Grady v. Crook*, 2 Abb. (N.C.) 53 (N.Y. 1876). Where claimed expenses are excessive, illegal, or unauthorized, or where the services were rendered gratuitously, the lien will vanish. Wrongfully liening property can invite a frivolous lien challenge and replevin action, potentially exposing the defendant to attorney's fees and damages.

In reading the following inanimate examples, consider whether a person who saves a lost cat, and then feeds, shelters, waters, grooms, and provides basic first aid, is entitled to a lien, restitution, or both. In *Fields v. Steyaert*, 515 P.2d 57 (Ariz. Ct. App. 1973), petition denied, 111 Ariz. 1 (1974), a plaintiff automobile owner sued a defendant garageman for replevin to recover his car. Defendant countered for towing and storage charges, asserting a lien. The appellate court held that the defendant who removed plaintiff's damaged car from the street after an accident and on sheriff's order was entitled to restitution prior to the date of plaintiff's demand for return but no valid lien existed. In *American Consumer, Inc. v. Anchor Computers, Inc.*, 402 N.Y.S.2d 734 (1978), a computer service company that enhanced the value of computer tapes by data manipulation, modification and assembly was entitled to an artisan's lien on those tapes. Similarly, one who dismantled, crated, and removed an elaborate shrine, to be reconstructed in a public place for inspection and study by the public, could claim an artisan's lien because this work was a step in the process of altering and enhancing the shrine's value. *In re Harriss' Estate*, 18 N.Y.S.2d 842 (1940). However, placing additional floor joists, timbers for shaft hangers and reeves, and cutting an opening in the building, in connection with machinery installation, were held nonlienable tasks because no additional value was imparted to the machinery. *Johnson v. Brizendine*, 18 P.2d 247 (Or. 1933). Also, wrapping and mailing newspapers for the publishers does not create an artisan's lien. *New York Democrat Pub. Corporation v. Laing*, 229 N.Y.S. 45 (1928).

A person who provides services *gratis* has no lien, at least according to the following non-companion animal cases. *In re Herman Hassinger, Inc.*, 41 B.R. 787 (Bankr. E.D. Pa. 1984); *Postell v. Val-Lite Corp.*, 51 S.E.2d 63 (Ga. Ct. App. 1948); and *G. A. Crancer Co. v. Combs*, 145 N.W. 863 (Neb. 1914).

Exemplary animal lien cases follow.

In *Carney v. Wallen*, 665 N.W.2d 439 (Iowa Ct. App. 2003), Joan Carney signed a "board and training" agreement with Dick Wallen Training Stables for Rodney, a horse owned by Joan's daughter. Months later, Carney purchased Lovely Looken from Dick Wallen, who offered to board that horse as well. Thereafter, Joan orally agreed that Dick's son James Wallen would train Lovely Looken. For about a year, Dick billed for boarding and training of Lovely Looken in one invoice. Thereafter, James would bill separately for training. He stopped for about three years, telling Joan to continue making payments for training directly to his father. She did not. When Joan received a bill for nearly $20,000 from James, she refused to pay and demanded the return of Lovely Looken. The Wallens refused, asserting a lien. Joan and her daughter sought a writ of replevin. James counterclaimed to foreclose the lien on the horse, but the trial court dismissed it as precluded by an Iowa state law that expressly precludes counterclaims in replevin proceedings. The court also ordered him to return Lovely Looken. In affirming, the appellate court concluded that the written agreement concerning *Rodney* did not apply to *Lovely Looken*. The "unilateral addition of Lovely Looken's name to the contract by the Wallens was insufficient to modify the contract formed to control the boarding of Rodney," if only because at the time of signing, the Carneys did not own Lovely Looken. Further, as James did not keep, herd, or feed Lovely Looken, but only trained her, the agister lien statute did not apply. Nor did the common law bailment lien apply in favor of James as "possession is a necessary element in the establishment and preservation of the common law lien." When training and transporting her to shows, he had a bailment lien, but once he relinquished custody of Lovely Looken to his father's stables, he lost it. Although Dick might have had a common law bailment lien had money been due and owing, the Carneys ensured that all boarding fees were paid in full.

In *Dairy Herd Management Corp. v. Goodwin*, 144 A.D.2d 870 (N.Y. Sup. Ct. App. Div. 1988), plaintiffs sought to recover a herd of bovines placed on defendant's farm. Though early in the proceedings the plaintiffs posted a $15,000 replevin bond, the court later granted their motion to cancel the undertaking as the defendant had no conceivable basis in law or fact to have retained possession. Specifically, he did not have a statutory bailment lien for two reasons: he was employed by the plaintiffs, and he did not furnish animal-related services as an independent contractor. In reaching this conclusion, the court focused on defendant's own allegations that plaintiffs hired him to operate the farm pursuant to a lease agreement where they would pay all operating expenses of the farm and furnish all feed for the herd.

In *Reeder v. Warner*, 112 A.D.2d 677 (N.Y. Sup. Ct. App. Div. 1985), Wendell Reeder boarded 34 thoroughbreds with Robert Warner, intending them to be sold.

Warner, however, claimed he was only promising to board, not sell. A year later, Warner served Reeder with a notice of sale per the state lien law, asserting owed boarding fees of more than $110,000. Reeder obtained a $125,000 bond and then sued to replevy the horses, but Warner refused to release any of the horses till the entire bill was paid. The appellate court considered two issues: *first*, what amount of security was appropriate to compel release of all horses and, *second*, whether the lien was *per quod* or *en masse* (i.e., whether the defendant must release individual horses upon payment of the respective board bill). On the first issue, the court found that posting an adequate bond (set by the court at $150,000) would entitle Reeder to repossession. On the second issue, it held that while the stableman's lien has been interpreted as specific to each animal, in the instant case it declined to find it "anything other than general as to the entire group of horses involved," for to rule otherwise would allow Reeder to cherry-pick five of the 34 horses with significantly higher values, thereby permitting him to undermine Warner's lien and create inequity.

In *Vaughn v. Nelson*, 62 S.E.2d 708 (Ga. App. 1908), Nelson sued Vaughn for reimbursement of the purchase price of "a white and liver and ticked pointer bitch named Maud," whom Nelson attached and bought at a court-ordered sale. Vaughn responded that he owned Maud and because "dogs are not property under the laws of Georgia," they are "not liable to attachment, levy, and sale." In affirming, the appellate court held that dogs "are as much the subject of property right as are other domestic animals, and therefore, as property, may be levied on and sold." "[W]hether he be a remote descendant of the small spaniel who changed the current of modern history by saving the life of William of Orange, or carries in his veins the blood of the faithful St. Bernard who rescues the lost traveler from the storm-swept crest of the beetling Alps," the court was compelled to hold that the dog may be sold "to satisfy even the humblest debt of his owner."

In *Tillotson v. Delfelder*, 276 P. 935 (Wyo. 1929), Louise Tillotson sued Evelyn Delfelder for delivery of horses by replevin pursuant to a chattel mortgage, creating a lien upon them. At the time the mortgagor John Peterson promised her these horses to secure a loan she gave him, they were on her pasture being fed and cared for by her. Thereafter, they were turned out. Unable to round them up due to illness, Peterson sought aid by Delfelder, who gathered 130 horses. The fraction of these 130 horses actually owned by Peterson remained disputed. Delfelder claimed an agister lien for her expenses incurred to pasture and care for the rounded-up equines. Feed became scarce, nobody came for the horses, and Peterson died, so Delfelder turned loose all but 11 — the same 11 that Tillotson sought to replevy to satisfy the debt owed by Peterson. The mortgage only spoke to horses aged three to eight, weighing 900 to 1,100 pounds, yet Tillotson demanded that Delfelder deliver to her, for instance, a 9-year-old mare weighing 1,150 pounds, a nine-year-old buckskin horse, and a 10-year-old black horse weighing 1,150 pounds. Delfelder refused, asserting that the mortgage did not identify the remaining 11 horses. Further, she claimed that, by statute, the agister lien takes priority over chattel mortgages. In reversing for new trial, the Wyoming Supreme Court held that Tillotson had no right to replevy horses not included in the mortgage; nor that Delfelder's failure to give a redelivery bond prior to a sheriff's seizure resulted in waiver of her lien, because they were taken from her involuntarily (only voluntary relinquishment extinguishes the agister lien).

In 2006, the Oregon Court of Appeals permitted a rescue organization to practically transform its status as lienor into a fiduciary utilizing a conservatorship statute in an unconventional manner. In *Cat Champion Corp. v. Primrose*, 149 P.3d 1276 (Or. Ct. App. 2006), a veterinarian reported that Jean Primrose neglected her cats. The sheriff acted on the report and seized 11 due to suspected neglect, transferring them to rescue organization Cat Champion. Several months later, the trial court dismissed the second-degree animal neglect charges against Primose after a psychological evaluation concluded she could not aid and assist in her own defense due to cognitive impairment. This left Cat Champion with incurred expenses of $32,510 for food, veterinary care, and boarding. Though it had a lien per state law, the cats were not forfeited, and Primrose remained the cats' owner. While unclear why Cat Champion did not foreclose on the lien when Primrose was deemed psychologically incapable of caring for the cats, Cat Champion instead applied for a limited protective order to obtain dispositive control over them under ORS § 125.650. It did not seek to become guardian over Primrose herself, but as a conservator needed to safeguard personalty, namely the cats, by implementing a protective order "determining the best legal, permanent placement for the cats." While acknowledging the trial court's reluctance to permanently divest Primrose of her cats, the appellate court reversed, stated that, "in some situations, such as here, protecting property means more than just holding the property for safekeeping. Each day that the cats remain in Cat Champion's care the expenses incurred in caring for them increase, and thus the debt owed by Primrose also increases. The end result is that Cat Champion seeks to protect Primrose's interests as well as its own." *Id.*, at 214.

K. BAILMENTS AND FREE LEASES

The law recognizes that animals may be subjects of bailments. *Hatley v. West*, 445 P.2d 208 (Wash. 1968) (agistment of horse is kind of bailment); *Anzalone v. Kragness*, 826 N.E.2d 472 (Ill. 2005) (recognizing claim of professional negligence and breach of bailment in veterinary medical malpractice action concerning dog). A bailment "arises generally when personalty is delivered to another for some particular purpose with an express or implied contract to redeliver when the purpose has been fulfilled." *Gingrich v. Unigard Sec. Ins. Co.*, 788 P.2d 1096, 1100–01 (Wash. Ct. App. 1990). A bailment for mutual benefit arises when both parties to the contract receive a benefit flowing from the bailment. 8 C.J.S. *Bailments* § 16 (1988). "To constitute a bailment for mutual benefit, therefore, it is not necessary that the bailee receive compensation in cash. If he derives a benefit to himself by taking possession of the bailor's property, that in itself constitutes sufficient consideration." *White v. Burke*, 197 P.2d 1008, 1013 (Wash. 1948).

One type of bailment for mutual benefit is known as a free lease or care lease. In exchange for love, affection, and enjoyment of the animal, the bailee agrees to provide supervision, shelter, food, water, and medical attention at no charge to the bailor. Owing to the lack of compensation, however, such gratuitous lease agreements, particularly those not in writing, may be misconstrued as gifts. This occurred in *Adams v. Wallace*, 2011 WL 1886580 (Conn. Super.2 011). In 2007, Kylie

Wallace explained that she would give up her horses to a good home as she could no longer afford to keep them. She conditioned transfer to Lisa Adams on her keeping the horses together, not selling them, not showing them, and granting Kylie access to the horses whenever desired. Adams agreed. Lisa Wallace, Kylie's mother, then spoke to Adams and stated she would keep the registration papers to prevent the horses from being shown or bred. Adams recalled no discussion of free leases, and was familiar with the concept, having entered into one when younger. When Adams came to pick up Sassy and Romeo, Kylie broke down. Adams assured her that if she had cold feet, she could change her mind, but intended to extend a right of rescission for hours or days, not years. No writing memorialized the transfer. For the next three years, Kylie intermittently visited and rode the horses at Adams's pasture. Meanwhile, Adams paid for all feed, veterinary care, and grooming expenses. After three years elapsed, Lisa Wallace left a message with Adams saying she planned to move Sassy and Romeo that weekend to another location. She prepared a note to similar effect. Without consent or knowledge by Adams, the Wallaces came to Adams's property with a trailer, trespassed, bypassed locked gates, and removed both horses. Before departing, Lisa left another note fabricating a tale that the horses would now live on two acres in a heated barn. Adams sued to replevy the horses. After a full bench trial, the court ordered their return to Adams, concluding that she acquired ownership pursuant to conditions she lived up to, thus rejecting the Wallaces' claim that they were transferred pursuant to a free lease.

In *Callaway v. Bailey*, 1996 Wash. App. LEXIS 610 (Nov. 1, 1996), Betsy Callaway sued Dr. Stanford Bailey and his wife Diane Bailey for the return of two horses Bronze and Peter. Callaway claimed a care lease existed, while the Baileys asserted a gift. When experiencing financial distress, Callaway admitted to using the verb "give" when transferring possession of the horses to the Baileys, but stated that industry custom interpreted the word to mean "free lease," not transfer of ownership. Shortly after delivery, Callaway admonished the Baileys for leaving the horses without water for a day. On threat to take back the horses, Callaway claimed Dr. Bailey agreed to "conditions." He disputed this, contending she said, "They're your horses . . . " When Callaway decided to leave the state, she tried to recover the horses from the Baileys' padlocked barn. Despite retaining an attorney to demand return of the horses, alleging that they failed to provide proper food, shelter, care and hydration. Bailey refused, suit ensued, and in ruling for the Baileys, the trial court found a gift, noting that, "Use of either a Bill of Sale or transfer of registration documents is not universally practiced in the equine community in the transfer of ownership of older horses" and that the word "give" does not have the commonly accepted meaning of "free leasing" a horse. Affirming judgment for the Baileys, the appellate court found clear and convincing evidence to sustain the finding of an unconditional gift. It rejected Callaway's attempt to void the gift by the defense of mutual mistake, remarking that the doctrine only applies to contracts and, besides, the record revealed little evidence to commend it. Also dismissed was the contention that ownership of a horse cannot transfer without a bill of sale or registration.

In *Taylor v. Welsh*, 138 Ill. App. 190 (1907), Carrie Taylor sued Julia Welsh and Mrs. L.A. Woodard to replevy Major, a highly decorated Persian male, whom she claimed to have purchased from Welsh's sister-in-law. Thereafter, Taylor left Major with her mother, Mrs. Perrigo, who, without her knowledge or permission, then sold Major to Welsh for $50. Perrigo stated that if Taylor did not want the money, she would refund the $50 and seek return of Major. Welsh then took Major to Chicago and sold a half-interest in him to Mrs. Woodard. Finding that Perrigo "was a mere naked bailee of the cat, without any authority to sell or dispose of it in any way, and appellee Welsh, at the time of her alleged purchase, knew that appellant was the owner of the cat and that Mrs. Perrigo had no authority to sell it," the appellate court reversed, concluding that no absolute or conditional sale occurred. Unauthorized sales by naked bailees are void, for they cannot convey good title against the true owner; thus, they constitute a wrongful conversion. Nor did Taylor need to make a demand for Major's return as a condition precedent to bringing a replevin action as "[b]eing wrongfully in possession, a demand was unnecessary." *Id.*, at 194. By the time the officer arrived to execute the writ of replevin, unfortunately, Major was moribund and died soon after. Accordingly, the court awarded $100 in damages as the difference in value between the date Welsh took possession and the date he was taken by writ (noting that his actual value was estimated between $100 and $150).

In *Kindig v. Wertz*, 176 A. 769 (Pa. Super. Ct. 1935), Jacob Kindig sued to replevy three mules from the estate of Jacob Warner, claiming they had been leased for 16 months, and that Warner defaulted by paying only a fraction of the amount owed for use of the mules. The agreement stated, in relevant part:

> [S]aid animals shall remain the property of the said Joe Kindig until all rental is paid; that I should not be able to make said payments I will return said animals to the said Joe Kindig and when said monthly installments are completed, then and not until then, shall said animals belong to me and become my property.

After the trial court ruled for Kindig, and the mules were returned to him, Warner's estate appealed, claiming they were conditionally sold to Warner, not bailed. The appellate court affirmed, finding this arrangement to be a bailment for use, as no conditional or qualified title passed to Warner (i.e., such as to allow him to transfer an interest in the mules to a third party), and the rental payments to Kindig were purchase money on bailed property only.

L. ABANDONMENT

Many states enacted animal abandonment statutes to provide a clear framework for disposing of deserted animals. Some explicitly identify veterinarians, boarding kennel owners, or any person who treats, boards, or cares for a nonhuman animal in a commercial capacity. Others deem an animal abandoned when not retrieved after a specified period or when the owner of the animal fails to pay reasonable or agreed-upon charges for care. Where no specified period exists by contract, an animal may be deemed abandoned if not retrieved within a certain number of days following demand for removal. *See, e.g.*, Ch. 16.54 RCW; Idaho Code § 25-3512.

Litigants in states that do not codify animal abandonment may still invoke the common law. Abandonment must be proved by clear, convincing, unequivocal, and decisive evidence. Critical to the establishment of this defense to possession is actual intent to irrevocably relinquish or part with the right or rights claimed to be abandoned. *Abandoned property* is property to which the "owner has relinquished all right, title, claim, and possession, *with intention* of not reclaiming it *or resuming* its ownership, possession or enjoyment." (Emphasis added.) BLACK'S LAW DICTIONARY 13 (rev. 4th ed. 1968). The burden will be on the claimant to prove the original owner's actual intent. In the absence of any express evidence to support this claim, and where alternative, less equivocal intentions may be reasonably inferred, abandonment cannot lie.

In *Long v. Noah's Lost Ark, Inc.*, 814 N.E2d 555 (Ohio Ct. App. 2004), William Long, an animal rights activist, sued Noah's Lost Ark, Inc. and the Whitehouses for return of a 10-month-old lion cub named Boomerang. Investigative journalist Alfred Guart accompanied Long to buy a one-week-old cub from an exotic animal breeder in Ohio for $1,000 with plans to transport him to a sanctuary in California. Before making the trip, they decided to leave the cub with Noah's Lost Ark for supervision until he was old enough to safely travel cross-country. When Guart was prepared to take Boomerang back, Noah's refused, citing concern he would die in transit because Guart and Long did not know how to board and care for a cub. Guart called the sheriff, at which point Noah's quoted a regulation prohibiting transport of dogs and cats under eight weeks of age, leading Guart to conclude that he would be arrested if he left with Boomerang and likely would miss his flight back to New York City. Thus, the cub remained with Noah's.

In affirming the trial court's judgment for Long, the appellate court found that he owned Boomerang because he signed the *USDA Record of Acquisition, Disposition or Transport of Animals* as buyer of an eight-day-old African lion and a furnished a receipt for $1,000. It rejected Noah's contention that he abandoned the cub because, other than entrusting Guart to find temporary housing and care for the cub with Noah's before the trip west, no other evidence existed to raise a question of material fact that would evidence "a virtual throwing away without regard as to who may take over or carry on." In short, Long bailed Boomerang. He did not abandon him or transfer ownership to Guart or Noah's. Even if Guart were said to have abandoned the cub, such finding would bear no relevance for the "best property right Guart could abandon was possession, not ownership of the cub." And were Guart somehow capable of transferring ownership by abandonment, Noah's could not provide any evidence of his intent to abandon. That Guart allegedly said to Mrs. Whitehouse, proprietress of Noah's, "Here, take him," when he handed her the cub, still presented no triable issue on the question of ownership as Long had not given Guart any right to transfer same.

M.   GIFTING

Occasionally, parties assert ownership via *inter vivos* or testamentary gift. The elements of the former vary slightly among jurisdictions, but they retain these common elements, as exemplified by *Brin v. Stutzman*, 89 Wn. App. 809, 825 (Ct. App. 1998) ((1) intention of donor to presently give; (2) subject matter capable of passing by delivery; (3) actual delivery; (4) acceptance by the donee). *Brin* affirmed an order replevying a computer and treadmill, rejecting Stutzman's assertion that they were intended as gifts. Gifts are not presumed, but one who asserts title by this means must prove it by clear, cogent, convincing, strong, decisive, and unequivocal evidence. *Tucker v. Brown*, 92 P.2d 221, 325 (Wash. 1939). The practitioner should pay close attention to the party alignment (i.e., plaintiff or defendant) of the one asserting ownership by gift, for some jurisdictions refuse to treat a gift as an affirmative defense. In such case, the plaintiff maintains the ultimate burden of disproving the existence of a gift by evidentiary preponderance, instead of the defendant proving the gift's existence by clear and convincing evidence.

Jane Hollander died, survived by Olive, a Bearded Collie mix whom she left with Lynne Wegman, friend and neighbor, with the understanding she would care for Olive and eventually deliver her to Jane's daughter Jill Hollander. Two months after receiving Olive, Wegman instead delivered the dog to Wegman's daughter in Iowa. *Hollander v. Wegman*, 349 Wis. 2d 789 (2013) (unpub.), in affirming judgment for Wegman, admonished Wegman for her betrayal of the decedent's wishes, but still found substantial evidence to support the claim that the decedent gave Olive to Wegman after Hollander, who was the decedent's first choice, disclaimed the ability to then care for her. Evidence favoring Wegman included corroborative testimony by Wegman's husband that Jane delivered Olive to his wife in his presence, that Jane taught Wegman how to walk Olive, and recommended specific reading materials for Wegman to review in caring for Olive.

Incapacity to gift may void a transfer as surely as it will void a contract. In *JKG v. SG*, 31 Misc. 3d 639 (N.Y. Civ. Ct. 2011), JKG sued SG for the return of a male Border Terrier/Dachshund mix named Macho. SG claimed ownership of Macho by gift, but the court found lack of donative intent. While hospitalized or otherwise incapacitated for about two weeks, JKG delivered Macho to SG for safekeeping, along with a bowl, leash, toys, and dog food. When he requested Macho's return, SG refused. SG acknowledged that at time of transfer, JKG was "stumbling; fell; appeared intoxicated; smelled of alcohol; the apartment was filled with dog excrement and smelled of it," the conditions were "sickening"; and Macho appeared not to have been walked in over a month. So when JKG said, in such delirium, "I want to give you the dog as a gift," the court found he lacked capacity, negating intent, and voiding any contended gift.

In *Leno v. James*, 2008 WL 4958360 (Ohio App. 2008), Alex Leno cohabited with Michelle James. When he vacated her apartment, he left behind a cat named Brutis, whom James refused to return. Leno and two witnesses claimed James gifted Brutis to Leno, while James and one witness refuted the contention. However, James testified:

> Neither of Plaintiff's witnesses were around when I told Alex that "If you take the cat, you are taking the dog also." Alex says, "No, I can't take the dog." And I said "then you're not getting the cat."

Leno produced no documentary evidence of ownership, though James furnished receipts for dog and cat food and a neuter appointment two days after the hearing. The appellate court nonetheless found no abuse of discretion in the order awarding Brutis to Leno, no doubt giving weight to James's own concession that she was prepared to give him Brutis and a dog. The court also remarked that James's documentary evidence was not conclusive of ownership.

In *Schneider v. Schneider*, 897 N.E.2d 706 (Ohio Ct. App. 2008), widow Lula Schneider sued her parents-in-law, Robert and Linda Schneider, for return of two dogs they claimed their late son Gary gifted to them before he died. Lula and Gary purchased a golden retriever and border collie, with whom they lived for four years until marital strife consumed the relationship, resulting in a domestic violence order of protection, a September 2004 order preventing Gary from removing or disposing of any property or animals, and a physical separation. Lula removed herself and her children from the marital home to an apartment that did not allow pets in July 2004. Three months later, in October 2004, Gary died from a drug overdose. After his funeral, Lula went to the home to recover the dogs, but found the locks changed. Her parents-in-law refused to return the dogs, whom they claim their son "begged" them to take, so she sued them for replevin. The trial court awarded permanent possession to the parents-in-law, claiming "the dogs were gifted by Gary Schneider to [his parents] in July 2004 during a time when there were no court orders in effect restricting his right to dispose of family pets."

In reversing and remanding for further proceedings, the appellate court found the decision against the manifest weight of evidence in this respect: while the in-laws testified that in July 2004, Gary allowed the dogs to remain in their custody most days and to let them take the dogs to the veterinarian as needed, in September 2004, Gary's father claimed that Gary approached them again, indicating that he wanted his parents to take the dogs so he could move to a smaller home without animals. Thus, no competent, credible evidence supported the finding that Gary relinquished permanent ownership and control by gifting the dogs to his parents in July 2004. While it may have proved a gift in late September 2004, that conversation might have taken place after entry of the Sept. 13, 2004 domestic relations court order prohibiting transfer of marital property. *Schneider* did not address what effect that order might have had on the validity of the *inter vivos* gift. Though Lula claimed that the in-laws bore the burden of proving a gift, the appellate court disagreed, rejecting that gifting was an affirmative defense for it was not of the enumerated defenses in Civil Rule 8(c), nor in the catchall provision of "any other matter constituting an avoidance or affirmative defense." Instead, it reasoned that the in-laws did not introduce a new issue into the case but "simply testified to that which disproved plaintiff's claim." That said, the in-laws still had the obligation of producing competent, credible evidence rebutting Lula's evidence. Apparently not raised was whether one spouse could gift community personalty without consent of the other.

Brown v. Rowlen, 1994 Ohio App. LEXIS 2174 (Mar. 12, 1994), took the same view of burden-shifting as stated in *Schneider*. Harry Brown sued to replevy a horse, Bay Boy Dopa, and his trailer, from Rox Rowlen. The trial court found by evidentiary preponderance that Brown gifted Bay Boy Dopa. Brown appealed, challenging the burden and standard of proof for gifting. In affirming, the appellate court distinguished the burden to prove a gift by preponderance (i.e., donee as plaintiff) from the burden to defend against an action to set aside a gift by clear and convincing evidence (i.e., donee as defendant). It also found that Rowlen's allegation of gift constituted a defense but "not an affirmative defense," so the burden of proof remained with Brown on the replevin claim.

Mongelli v. Cabral, 166 Misc. 2d 240 (N.Y. City Ct. 1995), discussed herein, took a different view as to burdens of proof in this cockatoo custody dispute, holding that the Defendants Cabral failed to meet their burden of proving a gift due to lack of any written evidence that "even remotely suggested that Peaches was given or sold to the Cabrals."

In *Casey v. Casey*, 2007 WL 1299228 (Conn. Super.), plaintiff Elaine Casey adopted Freeway, a miniature pinscher, from a rescue for $100. Freeway joined the household, consisting of Elaine, her two daughters Defendants Patricia and Kristine Casey, and Plaintiff's new husband Richard Black. Roughly two years after adopting Freeway, Patricia, then 19, left the family residence. Freeway remained with Elaine. About a year later, anticipating she would divorce Richard Black, Elaine moved into a temporary residence and gave Freeway to Patricia, who was living with her father, Defendant James Casey. Four months later, Elaine asked for Freeway's return, but Patricia refused. Elaine then sued her daughters and ex-husband in replevin. Defendants argued that Elaine adopted Freeway as a gift for Patricia, and that when Patricia moved out, Elaine punished her by refusing to let her take Freeway. Defendants further claimed that when Elaine moved out in 2005, she allegedly told Patricia "come get your dog." In finding for Elaine, the court closely assessed the weight and credibility of witness testimony, noting:

> The general principles guiding the court's consideration of these issues are well established. They include the following. No fact is determined merely by the number of witnesses who testify for or against it. In weighing the testimony of a witness, the court considers the witness' appearance and demeanor, the witness' biases or interests in the outcome of the trial, as well as the reasonableness of the witness' testimony, including the consistency or inconsistency of the testimony with other evidence. If the court finds that a witness testified falsely as to a particular matter, this finding of course should be considered in evaluating the balance of the witness' testimony, and in such a circumstance, the court may reject the testimony as a whole, but is not required to do so.

Id., at *2. One piece of evidence called Elaine's credibility into doubt — the check she used to purchase Freeway. The memo section of the actual check issued to the rescue said "Freeway," but the version offered in evidence by Elaine added the words "Elaine's Dog" and "my dog!!!" While taking note of Elaine's deceptive proffer of the check, the court found the check's probativity to be inconclusive and non-determinative of who had superior possessory rights in Freeway. Instead, it found that while Freeway was provided as an animal companion for Patricia, he was also a "family" dog and Elaine maintained ultimate control and ownership over him when Patricia left. It dismissed defendants' characterization of Elaine "simply manufactur[ing] an entire story to wrongfully regain possession" after she moved into temporary housing. Even if Patricia had a different understanding, an *inter vivos* gift depended on the *donor's* intent, not the *donee's*.

Undoubtedly a one-of-a-kind factual scenario — i.e., a gift of a dog in contemplation of marriage — *Elliott v. Hunter*, 1967 WL 90379 (Del. Super.) examined the dispute of Robert Elliott and Robert Hunter's daughter Patricia, who got engaged. A month later, a friend gifted a German Shepherd to both Robert and Patricia. The dog was kept at defendants' home until Patricia broke off the engagement three months later, where the dog remained and suit for replevin followed. Robert contends he gifted his share of the dog to Patricia on condition of marriage, which, having been thwarted, restored his ownership. Several courts have found that gifts of personalty are revocable either by express agreement that the gift is conditional or where the gift is of such symbolic significance or value that the law will imply it was given in contemplation of marriage. But as Robert could not "show an express agreement . . . to treat the dog as a conditional gift from her betrothed; nor . . . that this dog was of such nature that the law will imply that it was given in contemplation of marriage," the court denied his motion for summary judgment.

In *Saunders v. Regeer*, 50 Misc. 2d 850 (N.Y. Dist. Ct. 1966), Marvin Saunders placed an ad for sale of Misty, an Irish Setter, at $200, to which Cornelius and Leatrice Regeer responded, saying they could not afford Misty but would give her an excellent home. Saunders agreed to gift Misty conditioned on (a) being kept in a good home, (b) not being mated, (c) not being shown, and (d) being treated as a pet with adequate space to run. Allegedly, the Regeers breached or stated an intention to breach these conditions, and Saunders demanded her return. Saunders also sought an order from the court preventing Cornelius Regeer from transferring, selling, pledging, assigning, mating, or spaying Misty given her uniqueness as chattel. While generally irrevocable, the trial court held that equity may demand revocation of an *inter vivos* gift where the donee fails to comply with valid gift conditions, as here. The court also granted a temporary restraining order preventing the Regeers from removing Misty from New York, selling, or disposing of her without order of the court on the ground that Misty was unique, stating, "In this court's opinion there can be little question that a dog, particularly the Irish setter in this dispute, is a unique chattel. Without passing upon the merits of the respective claims of the parties, it would be a Pyrrhic victory if plaintiffs prevailed and 'Misty' was not available to effectuate a redelivery to the plaintiffs."

In *Gomer v. Davis*, 419 S.W.3d 470 (Tex. App. 2013), a 2-1 opinion, the Texas Court of Appeals affirmed directed verdict for the Davises, but reversed the entry of sanctions in the sum of $5,000 in a case brought by Leigh Gomer against Donald Davis, Ruby Davis, and Ann Steinlage for conversion of Gabriel, a purebred poodle. Gomer and Jane Artall, Donald Davis's mother, were long-term friends. In August 2008, Artall signed an AKC Transfer of Registration identifying Gomer as Gabriel's owner; however, Gomer did not mail the form to the AKC until after Artall's death in November 2010. In that 27-month interval, purportedly to ensure that Artall would have possession as long as possible before she died, Gomer only had possession of Gabriel about 10 percent of the time. After Artall's death, Gomer asked for Gabriel, but the Davises and Steinlage refused, whereupon Gomer sued on the basis of *inter vivos* gift and resulting conversion. In that Gomer admitted she never expected to take exclusive possession until after Donald Davis's mother died, the majority found no *inter vivos gift in praesenti* [at the present time] as there was no "immediate and unconditional divestiture" of Artall's ownership interest and, thus, no vesting of same in Gomer when she first permitted possession. Rather, "Artall intended to continue to exercise dominion and control over the dog until her death." The dissenting judge found that registration transfer contemporaneous with delivery established a gift, and Gomer was free to let Artall keep Gabriel for extended periods without losing ownership rights. Reversing the $5,000 sanction against Gomer and her attorney, the majority concluded that the "fatal flaw in her conversion claim was that she could not establish that Artall's gift of the dog was absolute and irrevocable and thus was a valid inter vivos gift[.]"

N. CONTRACTUAL DISPUTES — DEFECTS IN FORMATION

Defects in contract formation may void transfer of ownership or possessory rights in animals, such as fraud, illegality, impossibility, lack of agency, statute of frauds, failure of consideration, duress, and more.

1. Fraud

In *Arledge v. Ridge*, 12 Tenn. App. 415 (1930), widow Josie Ridge claimed fraud and deception by Tom Arledge, who traded her a purportedly sound mare for a mule. After having delivered the mule to Arledge, her young boy returned with the mare, whom she noticed "had something wrong with her hind parts, she could hardly walk, would not work and was not bridle wise and was in fact no value to [Ms. Ridge]." She tendered the mare back to Arledge, but he refused to return the mule, forcing her to feed "a practically worthless animal." Two months later, she sold the mare to make ends meet, getting $10. Thereafter, she sued to replevy the mule, valued at least six times that of the mare. Arledge asserted that her selling the mare after discovering the fraud meant she ratified the inequitable sale. In rejecting this argument as resulting in "unconscionable advantage" to Arledge, the court referenced the Uniform Sales Act, which abolished the distinction between exchange and sale, thereby allowing the price to be paid in specie or money. It also found no ratification. Although Ridge should have tendered the $10 to Arledge, explaining that a party who rescinds a contract on the ground of fraud must generally return what he received, such gesture "would have been an idle ceremony." Accordingly, the appellate court affirmed return of the mule and judgment against Ridge for $10.

In *Williams v. Logue*, 122 So. 490 (Miss. 1929), Williams's son bought a car from Moore by exchanging a truck and a check for $24. The next day, Williams convinced his son to unwind the transaction. The vehicles returned to the respective owners, but Moore did not give back the $24 check. Third party Logue then persuaded Williams that recovering the check was critically important, so Williams authorized Logue to make contact with Moore. Moore surrendered the check to Logue with the understanding that he would take half of whatever Logue could get from Williams, believing that he was "due something out of it" for having lost a trade when the boy had the truck. Logue then lied to Williams, saying he paid $12.50 for the check by taking a loan from his father-in-law and could not get the check back until the $12.50 was tendered. Williams and his wife gave Logue $4, a calf they valued at $8, and agreed to pay the other $0.50 as soon as possible. Logue agreed and delivered the $24 check. He then lied to Moore, saying he only got $9 out of the transaction, paying Moore $4.50. Three years later, Williams learned of the ruse played upon him by Logue and sued to replevy the calf, now a cow worth $75. The trial court authorized an award of $8 plus interest, the value of the calf at the time of the fraud, not the cow she became at $75. Williams argued that he acted with reasonable promptness after being cheated out of the calf and, thus, could elect to replevy her by rescinding due to fraud. In reversing, the appellate court held that rescission operates to void the transaction *ab initio*, restoring the defrauded party by returning title "as if it had never been out of him." Doing so avoids giving a windfall to the wrongdoer, and permitting a "swindler to profit by his own wrong." In so holding that Williams should recover the cow, however, the court cautioned that it only applied "with a case of active, corrupt, and conscious fraud, with a case wherein the moral attitude of the defendant is no better in substance than if he had obtained the property by larceny." The court expressly did not decide whether the rule applied to legal or constructive fraud without actual and conscious corruption deliberately intended.

2. Illegality

In *Foster v. Behre*, 146 A. 672 (N.J. 1929), Arthur Foster sued Henry Behre to replevy an Irish Setter named Red Bounce when Behre failed to pay the amount due. The sale occurred on a Sunday, a transaction forbidden by law. Leaving the parties where they were following execution of the illicit contract, the appellate court reversed judgment for Foster. Red Bounce remained with Behre.

In *Long v. Noah's Lost Ark, Inc.*, 814 N.E.2d 555 (Ohio Ct. App. 2004), discussed above, the appellate court overruled the exception that Long could not own the cub due to fraud and illegally purchasing a cub in violation of 18 U.S.C. § 1001 by lying to the seller about having property to house the cub and experience in raising exotic felids. However, Long did not provide any false information on the USDA form. And even if he did violate a law, the alleged illegality would not inure to the benefit of Noah's. In other words, Long's alleged illicit behavior would not establish ownership rights in Noah's. Besides, Noah's had no standing to challenge the sale.

3. Impossibility

In *Angrave v. Oates*, 876 A.2d 1287 (Conn. App. Ct. 2005), Shelia Oates orally agreed to place Lady Catherine, a 14-month-old Mountain Dog, with Jan Angrave in exchange for two puppies from the first litter. Thereafter, registration changed to reflect both parties as co-owners. Over the next two years, Angrave raised Lady Catherine. Radiographs revealed hip dysplasia, so Angrave returned Lady Catherine to Oates to evaluate the condition until further tests were performed. Oates then refused to return the dog; she also spayed Lady Catherine without consent or knowledge of Angrave. Oates lost at trial, and lost on appeal, the appellate court finding ample basis to enforce Angrave's possessory interest per the registration papers listing her name, the lengthy period of uninterrupted possession for most of the dog's life, and her exclusive payment for all her care, entry in shows, and medical treatment. Oates's contention that Angrave breached contract by not providing two puppies from Lady Catherine's first litter did not persuade either court for two reasons: the promise to provide future offspring still constituted valid consideration to support the oral contract, and Oates's own act of spaying Lady Catherine made it impossible for Angrave to perform the contract. *Id.*, at 1289 n.2 (citing *Bono v. McCutcheon*).

4. Agency

In *Grandi v. Thomas*, 391 P.2d 35 (Kan. 1964), Henry Grandi contacted J.E. Carlin to attend an auction and bid on a horse named Bold Charge, placed for sale by Robert Thomas. Carlin made the winning bid and paid $475, but Thomas bristled at the low amount and intended to have the clerk declare a "No Sale." To salvage the transaction, Carlin offered that Thomas could repurchase Bold Charge for $575. Thomas believed he had 90 days to repurchase, but Carlin recalled giving 30. Meanwhile, Carlin delivered Bold Charge to Grandi. The month after the auction, Thomas wrote Carlin stating he hoped to "get him back." Carlin said that about 60 days after the repurchase discussion, Thomas sought performance of the agreement, but Carlin refused. Thomas then spoke to Carlin's wife, who prepared a bill of sale conditioned on her speaking to her husband, adding that if he objected to sale, Carlin could buy the horse back from Thomas for $575 plus $1 a day for keep. Carlin's wife received $575 and a receipt for $40 cash for care of the horse over the previous months (though she claims to have never received the $40). Four days later, Carlin returned home, saw Bold Charge missing, and learned his wife sold the horse to Thomas. Carlin then tried to repurchase the horse from Thomas, explaining for the first time that his agency extended only to buying the horse for Grandi. Thomas refused to sell even when Grandi tendered $575 plus keep, prompting suit for replevin. On judgment for Thomas, Grandi appealed. In reversing, the Kansas Supreme Court found that Thomas gave up title by relying on an oral conversation sharply disputed by the parties; that Carlin's agreement to let Thomas repurchase the horse was outside the scope of his agency and did not bind Grandi; that Carlin could not have ratified the agency of his wife since neither had title to pass; but, most germanely, that Thomas was bound by the repurchase clause added in the bill of sale, making his refusal to return him on timely demand by Carlin and Grandi unlawful.

5. Statute of Frauds

In *Andersen v. Koss*, 527 N.E.2d 1098 (Ill. App. Ct. 1988), Plaintiff Anderson bred Skye Terriers. Defendant Koss, a licensed dog show judge, also bred them. Anderson sued to replevy from Koss a Skye Terrier named Sand Island Sinclair. Anderson contended that Koss was offered a co-ownership interest in Sand Island Sinclair for $500, which he verbally accepted, with an agreement to memorialize the terms in a detailed written contract months after he received the dog "on approval." Koss refused to sign, Anderson never cashed the check, and Koss kept Sand Island Sinclair, contending that Anderson offered to sell the dog for $500 per an oral contract with the terms that he would pay the purchase price in advance and absorb all shipping costs, that he could inspect the dog on delivery and, if not satisfied, would return him immediately for a refund. The only documents accompanying the dog on delivery to Koss were a waybill, health certificate, rabies vaccination certificate, and note from Anderson's agent. Koss asserted the affirmative defense of an oral contract for sale of $500. Anderson responded that any such agreement was void as falling within the statute of frauds. Though no writing existed for this sale of goods valued at $500 or more, oral contracts of sale are enforceable "with respect to goods for which payment has been made and accepted or which have been received and accepted." Anderson argued that she did not "accept" payment by retaining Koss's uncashed check, but the appellate court concluded that the goods (i.e., Sand Island Sinclair) were "received and accepted" by Koss on arrival in Chicago, which was adequate to take the contract out of the statute of frauds. Accordingly, in reversing, the appellate court found numerous fact issues warranting trial on the merits of the purported oral contract for sale.

6.   Meeting of the Minds

In *Rapuano v. Rapuano*, 2001 WL 1332431 (Conn. Super.), Rita Rapuano sued her daughter Gina-Lee Rapuano for breach of contract, *quantum meruit*, conversion, and unfair trade practices related to a horse named Cloud Pleaser. Essentially, Rita sought a prejudgment and permanent order of replevin, seeking judgment for possession of Cloud in specie instead of money. Rita claimed she arranged for temporary boarding at her daughter's farm after nursing two foals. When dissatisfied with Gina's care of Cloud, Rita demanded her return. Gina claims that Rita sold her Cloud, even though she had not actually paid the alleged sale price. She explained that Rita customarily would accept later payment on other horses. It was only when Cloud accidentally became pregnant that Rita demanded Cloud's return, so Gina claimed. Finding Rita's position more tenable, the court ruled for Rita. In reaching this conclusion, it gave strong weight to the following: Gina's nonpayment of any portion of the alleged purchase cost "seriously undermined" her case; Gina sent Rita a bill for six months of boarding and training fees; Gina demanded payment by Rita plus papers on another horse in exchange for return of Cloud; Gina profited from Cloud by using her for lessons and shows, which provided sufficient consideration for rehabilitation services.

Contracts implied-in-fact may bestow ownership or possessory rights with the same finality as express ones. In *Dubin v. Pelletier*, 2012 R.I. Super. LEXIS 175 (Nov. 21, 2012), however, the defendant failed in making this claim. Jayne Dubin sued Lori Ann Pelletier to recover Mr. Big at the conclusion of his career. A Norfolk Terrier with a reputation as a champion in the dog show circuit, Dubin also sought $16,000 in stud fees Pelletier collected. Pelletier responded that Dubin gifted Mr. Big to her. Alternatively, she claimed an implied contract to transfer ownership for Pelletier's handling services, that she was Mr. Big's guardian under R.I. Gen. Laws §§ 4-13-1.2 and -41, and that his best interests were served by remaining in her custody. She also sought nearly $75,000 in unjust enrichment. Tried to the bench, Judge Savage ordered Mr. Big returned to Dubin along with $16,000, a sum offset by $16,411.51 in dog handler fees on the theory of unjust enrichment.

The court rejected Pelletier's implied contract theory for various reasons, such as Dubin making payments to Pelletier (which she accepted) after the alleged transfer of ownership (showing an intent to maintain ownership and simply hire Pelletier to handle and show him), and that followed the prior course of dealing relative to other Norfolks handled by Pelletier. Though Pelletier had Mr. Big for several years, length of possession did not dispose of ownership, particularly when in direct conflict with other evidence. While declaring Dubin the *owner*, the court next set to the task of determining who had the right to *possess* Dubin for purposes of the replevin claim. Thus, the court examined the implied contract theory relative to both ownership *and* possession. Pelletier lost on both counts, the court finding a meeting of the minds only as to handing and showing Mr. Big through his specials campaign, not after his retirement.

7.   Duress and Undue Influence

In *Patton v. Wood Co. Humane Soc.*, 798 N.E.2d 676 (Ohio Ct. App. 2003), plaintiff Patton kept livestock outside during a bitter winter, prompting animal control to investigate animal cruelty due to lack of shelter. By warrant, an officer entered Patton's premises and found neglected and frostbitten animals, deprived of food and water, and sheep in need of shearing. Threatened with removal of all the animals, the officer provided Patton an alternative, which Patton accepted. He agreed to convey his dogs to animal control and abide by conditions of care. Thereafter, Patton's counsel revoked the agreement due to coercion. Defendants refused to return the dogs and refuted the allegations of unlawful seizure. Meanwhile, a second executed search warrant resulted in seizure of the remaining animals. In affirming summary judgment dismissal, the appellate court examined whether Patton signed under duress. Elements of such a cause of action are: (1) one party involuntarily accepted terms imposed by the other; (2) the party seeking to establish duress was operating under circumstances permitting no other alternative but to comply; and (3) the circumstances were the result of coercive acts of the other party to the agreement. *Id.*, at 680. The gist of duress involves "improper threats which deprive[] that person of any reasonable alternative but to assent to the terms of the person making the threat." *Id.* A party legally entitled to carry out the threat, however, is not held to have illegally coerced the other. Here, Patton had the ability to seek advice of counsel prior to signing and the officer could take the dogs without consent per R.C. § 1717.13, based not only on probable cause but Patton's failure to deny the dogs' poor condition or their deprivation of food and water. Accordingly, the court found Patton voluntarily signed the conveyance and had no right to replevy them.

Undue influence is unfair persuasion, where one party is under the influence or domination of another, or by virtue of their relationship, is justified in assuming the other will not take advantage. Courts look to the relationship of the parties, inequality of the resulting contract, susceptibility of the victim, and lack of independent guidance. Such relationships include minister and parishioner, and perhaps even friends. The party claiming undue influence has the burden of proving it by clear and convincing evidence. *Endicott v. Saul*, 142 Wn. App. 899 (2008). This defense might arise where a mentally infirm, homeless person signs a contract giving a shelter, run by a religious organization and countersigned by a deacon or minister, her cat.

8.   Mutual Mistake

Arguello v. Behmke, 2006 N.J. Super. Unpub. LEXIS 2977 (Ch. Div. Jan. 6, 2006), is rumored to be the first civil action for return of a Hurricane Katrina dog. Her home having been demolished, Annabelle Arguello was forced to evacuate. Unable to take her two beagles and Great Dane named Chopper, so she placed them in a temporary shelter operated by the Humane Society of the United States

("HSUS") pursuant to a bailment agreement. Arguello added a handwritten clause instructing the shelter to call her if it could no longer house Chopper; HSUS never struck this clause, and, in fact, a representative verbally assured it would notify her before transferring him. However, HSUS instead transferred Chopper to satellite shelter People for Animals per a *Memorandum of Understanding* that stated any animal not claimed by Oct. 16, 2005 would become the property of the Satellite Shelter. When Arguello returned to claim Chopper, HSUS could not locate him. After Oct. 16, 2005, HSUS found him with Pamela Behmke in New Jersey. Behmke obtained Chopper from the Satellite Shelter. Using its equitable powers to cancel the agreement and ordering Chopper's return, the court found the *Memorandum* unenforceable and void for mutual mistake, as both HSUS and People for Animals labored under the same misimpression of an essential fact, namely, that HSUS had any right to transfer Chopper before contacting Arguello per the bailment contract.

9. Lack of Consideration

In *Bono v. McCutcheon*, 824 N.E.2d 1013 (Ohio Ct. App. 2005), Gina Bono claimed to have purchased Doozie, a whippet puppy, from Matthew McCutcheon as a "show potential" dog, but when he refused to return Doozie to Bono, she sued for breach of contract, conversion, specific performance, and replevin. The McCutcheons claimed no contract existed as the "Sales Contract" she signed had no price, and money did not change hands. Granting summary judgment to the McCutcheons, the trial court deemed the omission of the price term fatal for want of consideration. Bono sought reconsideration, contending that her promises to maintain Doozie in good condition, show him at a number of contests, breed him, and permit the McCutcheons to have the second pick of Doozie's first litter constituted sufficient consideration. The trial court did not change its ruling, calling it, at best, a conditional sale contract with unfulfilled conditions. The appellate court disagreed, finding consideration in the form of "an exchange of puppies — Doozie for 'a puppy to be named later' " — a benefit to McCutcheon and "not merely a condition of McCutcheon's performance attached to a gratuitous promise that benefited only Bono." *Id.*, at 1017. The *Bono* court characterized the duty to take Doozie to a veterinarian within 48 hours at Bono's expense and sending a written statement from the veterinarian within seven days as "terms of the agreement" instead of "conditions" in a conditional sales contract." *Id.*, at 1018. While the McCutcheons asserted that Bono failed to comply with such terms, leaving the sale contract merely executory, the appellate court concluded that Bono enjoyed a right to possession upon signing the contract (even if ownership would not vest until some later time), and both parties "were immediately obligated by the terms of the contract." Thus, even if Bono had not satisfied conditions precedent for transfer of *ownership*, the right of *possession* existed from the moment of execution, and for that reason, the McCutcheons breached. *Id.*, at 1018. The court also reinstated the specific performance claim, recognizing Doozie's uniqueness and the inadequacy of monetary compensation. Finally, the court resurrected Bono's claim for tortious interference with contract against McCutcheon's mother, who induced her son to withhold possession of Doozie.

O. DETRIMENTAL RELIANCE

Occasionally, judicial inertia dictates custody. Disturbing the status quo requires a substantial showing by the plaintiff. Where vagaries attend to any purported agreement for extended care, or the defendant's family detrimentally relies on the arrangement by bonding with the animal, and serves without remuneration, a court may find for the defendant based on a hybridized rationale of laches, estoppel, gifting, and even abandonment.

For instance, Richard Brock bought a German Shepherd puppy named Kaizer as a gift for his wife Gail Brock. When he fell ill with cancer, and could no longer care for the dog, the Brocks asked their niece Pamela Gilbert to care for him temporarily until Richard recuperated. Though the parties agreed to the impermanence of the initially intended arrangement, Gilbert testified that Richard changed his mind and said she could keep Kaizer after seeing how attached her children became. Notarized letters from witnesses bolstered Gilbert's contention. Germane to the trial court's judgment for Gilbert were such variables as Kaizer residing with Gilbert for nearly a year without reimbursement or compensation, the absence of a written agreement, conflicting evidence as to the scope of the verbal agreement, and that Kaizer received more humane care with Gilbert. Affirming, *Brock v. Gilbert*, 989 N.E.2d 384 (Ind. Ct. App. 2013) (unpub.), found no procedural or substantive irregularity.

P. CONTRACTUAL DISPUTES — REPOSSESSION

The old precept that possession is nine-tenths of the law bears discussion by animal rescues and humane societies, for once possession has transferred to the adopter, repossession may prove exceedingly difficult and costly. Relying solely on a signature or even initialed contract should not substitute for prudent adoption application screening and home-checking. If a humane society or rescue wants certain action taken by the adopter, such as sterilization, it should do it before releasing to the adopter. When adopters fail to comply with post-adoption restraints, courts summoned to referee the dispute may characterize them as future rights of reversion (automatic restoration of fee simple ownership), future rights of entry (restoration subject to invocation of condition subsequent), equitable servitudes, affirmative or restrictive covenants, gift conditions, or substantively unconscionable terms. In the proper instance, repossession may even be permitted under Art. 9 of the Uniform Commercial Code.

Courts will only rescind an adoption agreement and order what amounts to a forfeiture (which courts are loathe to do) if the reversionary interest or right of entry is conspicuous, unambiguous, not the result of duress, undue influence, mistake, infancy, fraud, or other time-worn contractual defenses to contract formation, and then only arising from a material breach. Where an adoption contract states that the adopter owns the animal for his or her lifetime subject to ongoing compliance with specific restrictions, the court may regard them as conditions subsequent, in which case breach results in divestiture. Sitting on the breach may cause the condition to expire and bar the relief requested. If construed as a reversionary interest, then one need not invoke the condition, because it arises automatically by the unilateral actions of the adopter.

An esoteric approach structures the adoption as an Art. 9 security agreement. Should a rescue characterize the transaction as one secured by specific promises to care for the animal in a prescribed way, the rescue may successfully wield repossession rights under Art. 9 of the UCC. For this to occur, however, the rescue must become a creditor, the adopter a debtor, and the animal the secured collateral. *Security interest* is defined as "an interest in personal property or fixtures which secures payment for performance of an obligation" and applies to any transaction "regardless of its form." UCC § 1-201(37).

In *Cocciolone v. Nastasi*, 5 A.D.3d 529 (N.Y. Sup. Ct. App. Div. 2004), Gus Cocciolone entered into a stallion service contract with Louis Salerno to breed a thoroughbred mare for a fee payable when the foal "[s]tands and nurses," giving Salerno a security interest in the foal. Though the breeding occurred and mare foaled, Cocciolone never paid the full amount due Salerno because defendant Frank Nastasi, partner in the syndicate that owned the stallion, took the foal without permission. Without much discussion, the appellate court upheld judgment for Cocciolone in the sum of $15,000 (value of the yearling) on the basis that Nastasi had no valid security interest in the foal as he was neither a party to, nor in privity with a party to, the breeding contract between Cocciolone and Salerno. Nor did it inure to his benefit. Further, absent any valid express or implied agreement with Cocciolone, he had no valid lien on the yearling per state law.

Nonjudicial repossession is permitted under UCC § 9-609 only "without breach of the peace." Where breach may occur, the rescue that has a security interest should resort to judicial action in the form of replevin. To create an enforceable security interest requires attachment per UCC § 9-203 (creditor must give value, debtor must have rights in collateral, there must be security agreement, agreement must describe collateral, and it must be in writing or otherwise authenticated) and perfection per UCC §§ 9-308–316. A security agreement operates as both a deed (conveying property interest) and contract (giving the transferor rights in the property upon breach or default).

In *Selig v. Tribe*, 30 Mass. L. Rep. 94 (2012), Michael Selig and his wife found an abandoned dog in North Carolina and took him to Massachusetts to find a permanent home. They posted an advertisement on Petfinder and received an inquiry from Carolyn Tribe and her then-husband. Following a home visit, the Seligs found the Tribe residence satisfactory and adopted the dog to them subject to promises to provide "a stable home, be provided with adequate and nutritious food, [and] be given regular veterinary care and be properly and adequately supervised and confined." That day, Tribe named her Chloe, licensed her, and provided veterinary care with regularity. Selig's wife thereafter visited the Tribes for assurance they were complying with all adoption conditions. Five years later, Selig's wife grew suspicious of Chloe's neglect in the hands of Tribe, who had since divorced. Selig's wife was eventually arrested for assault and battery of an elderly person and agreed, as a condition of dropping charges, to stay away from Tribe and Chloe. This did not stop her husband, Michael Selig, who sued for return of Chloe (then 14 years old) by preliminary injunction. The motion failing, and facing a motion to dismiss by Tribe, he amended the complaint to assert fraud and misrepresentation by Tribe as to her intention of complying with the adoption terms set forth at time of delivery. Dismissed on statute of limitation grounds were the rescission and replevin claims, notwithstanding his effort to invoke the discovery rule. As neither of the Seligs made any effort for almost five years to determine whether Tribe still complied with the adoption terms, their own lack of reasonable diligence would not toll the statute of limitations. Furthermore, the court found no viable misrepresentation claim because based on future promises, which "are not the stuff of which a misrepresentation claim may be made."

Creating what have since been called "*Houseman* hearings," *Houseman v. Dare*, 966 A.2d 24 (N.J. Super. Ct. 2009) addressed a dispute involving Doreen Houseman suing her ex-fiance Eric Dare for breach of an oral agreement to give her possession of a jointly owned Pug named Dexter upon separation. She sought specific performance of the agreement and declaratory judgment of sole ownership. She also claimed conversion, emphasizing that money was insufficient to make her whole. Though the trial judge found Houseman to be "extremely" and "particularly credible," it nonetheless held that Dare was entitled to possession and owed Houseman Dexter's stipulated value. In reaching this conclusion, the court found that money damages were adequate and Dexter did not have a unique value requiring the exceptional equitable remedy of specific performance. The appellate court reversed, reasoning that companion animals are personalty possessing unique value essential to an award of specific performance, and remarking that there is no reason for a court of equity to be more wary resolving competing claims for possession of a pet based on one party's sincere affection for and attachment to it than resolving competing claims based on one party's sincere sentiment for an inanimate object. Refusing to characterize Houseman's "stipulation to the dog's intrinsic monetary value" as a "concession that the stipulated value was adequate to compensate her for loss of the special value," the appellate court remanded for further proceedings on the propriety of specific performance. *Id.*, at 29.

A year after *Houseman*, the New Jersey Superior Court, Appellate Division, decided *Mitchell v. Mitchell*, 2010 WL 289096 (N.J. Super. App. Div.). Ruth Ann Mitchell divorced Fred Mitchell. Among other rulings, the motion judge determined that their cat remain with Fred. In affirming, the appeals court referenced *Houseman* as warranting a hearing "to determine which party had the greater attachment" to a companion animal "when litigants each demand custody of the family pet, and one party asserts the existence of an oral agreement on that subject[.]" *Id.*, at *4. It found the allegations made by Ruth inapposite to the *Houseman* rule, for she relinquished any right to the cat when she gave him to Fred. Her claim of neglect (i.e., loss of one pound in a one or two-year period), not backed by any veterinary evidence, failed to justify disturbing the trial judge's order by a wide margin.

The Iowa Court of Appeals also cited to *Houseman* in *In re Marriage of Berger & Ognibene-Berger*, 834 N.W.2d 82 (Iowa Ct. App. 2013). After a 24-year marriage, Joe and Cira Berger divorced. Amidst several issues, one concerned the award of Max, the family's 10-year-old golden retriever, to Cira. Joe argued that Max should remain with him because Cira lived with another dog, Sophie, as well as to honor the deep attachment of Joe's oldest son to Max. The trial judge determined the "biggest issue" regarding Max involved who had more time to care for him. As Cira did not work outside the home and had primary responsibility for taking him to veterinary appointments, the district court favored her. Affirming, the appellate court concluded that equity was done absent evidence of abuse or neglect in Cira's care, with additional consideration given to the fact Max was licensed and GEO-tracked in Cira's name; she took him to training classes and to a veterinarian for treatment of a recent ear infection, even when in Joe's care at the time; and Cira cared for their youngest child, "who has known Max all of her life."

Q. BEST INTERESTS

Courts intervene to make decisions affecting minors and other legal dependents using its authority known as *parens patriae*. Even over parental objections, the court may exercise this power to compel action respecting the child. The public trust doctrine applies *parens patriae* to wildlife and shares common ground with "best interests" principles. In such instances where *parens patriae* makes a debut, the court provides injunctive and declaratory relief to fulfill its role as supreme guardian for the voiceless:

> The *parens patriae* doctrine, like the public trust doctrine, developed at English common law. The notion of *parens patriae*, or 'parent of the country,' originated as the king's ability to exercise power in certain instances. Under the king's prerogative, the king was 'the guardian of his people,' and could exercise authority to take care of people who were legally unable to take care of themselves or their property. Under this theory, people protected by the king basically fell into three classes: infants, 'idiots,' and 'lunatics.' With respect to children, the Crown's *parens patriae* role was as the 'supreme guardian and superintendent,' and derived from a 'trust' relationship.

Musiker et al., *The Public Trust and Parens Patriae Doctrines: Protecting Wildlife in Uncertain Political Times*, 16 PUB. L. & L. REV. 87, 103 (1995). Animals bear features analogous to those possessed by an infant or mentally incompetent human being. Legislatures honor the likeness by enacting animal cruelty statutes punishing an owner's failure to provide necessary veterinary care that results in unnecessary physical pain, thus acknowledging the nonhumans' right to health care and the duty of their human caretakers to so facilitate. When they falter, courts step in and ensure the fulfillment of these caretaking responsibilities, whether by issuing a warrant to seize, order of forfeiture, or sentence prohibiting future possession of that species. When so acting, the court protects the crime victim, essentially in *parens patriae*.

Immunity from criminal and civil fault for children and the mentally infirm further illustrates the strength of the analogy to nonhuman animals. Minors of tender years are fault-free from civil and criminal liability in most jurisdictions as a matter of law. *See, e.g., Graving v. Dorn*, 386 P.2d 621 (Wash. 1963) (under 6, incapable of negligence); RCW § 9A.04.050 (under 8, incapable of committing crime). The insane or those with diminished capacity may also avoid prosecution based on codifications of the old M'Naghten rules (formulated in *M'Naghten's Case*, 8 ER 718, [1843] UKHL J16), whereby a mentally disordered individual who cannot perceive the nature and quality of the act with which she is charged or tell right from wrong with regard to the particular act charged lacks the requisite *mens rea* to be convicted. "Right" and "wrong" are terms crafted by human society with cultural understandings that some species cannot likely fathom.

The unmistakable parallel of fostered animals to fostered children whose foster parents are regulated by Child Protective Services evidences the role of the state as a superintending parent. Public policy also safeguards nonhuman animal welfare in now widespread animal trust laws, making once precatory trusts enforceable, deeming the animal a trust beneficiary, and permitting a party interested in the welfare of the animal to petition the court to remove the trustee and ensure that the animal beneficiary receives her due. Such policies provide a vehicle for courts to invoke their inherent equitable powers where property law promotes an unfair outcome. Courts have also wielded public policy in the spirit of *parens patriae* by voiding testamentary destruction-on-death provisions, where the testator demands euthanasia of his surviving companion animals upon his demise. *See Estate of Howard H. Brand*, Chittenden Co. Probate Ct. No. 28473 (1999); *Capers Est.*, 34 D. & C. 2d 121 (1964).

If asked to break a custodial tie, modern jurists will exclusively award possession based on which party will best serve the animal's interests. In *Zovko v. Gregory*, No. CH 97-544 (Arlington County (Va.) Circuit Court, Oct. 17, 1997), Zovko and Gregory were roommates. Though originally belonging to Gregory, Zovko cared for the cat named Grady. Upon their separation, a custody dispute over Grady ensued. The court found "Grady's happiness took priority . . . " The reporter added, "[JUDGE] KENDRICK said he would decide 'what is in the best interest of Grady. . . . From what I have seen, Grady would be better off with Mr. Zovko'." *Id. See* Brooke A. Masters, *In Courtroom Tug of War Over Custody, Roommate Wins the Kitty*, WASHINGTON POST, Sept. 13, 1997, at B1.

There is also precedent to terminate joint custody when it becomes unworkable and inimical to the interests of the animal. In *Juelfs v. Gough*, 41 P.3d 593 (Alaska 2002), the Alaska Supreme Court found no abuse of discretion where a trial judge modified a divorce decree to award sole custody of a Chocolate Labrador Retriever, Coho, to the husband, though it originally provided for shared custody. The ex-wife, Ms. Juelfs, moved the court to review the dissolution agreement due to her ex-husband's failure to allow her allotted time with Coho. The ex-husband, Mr. Gough, opposed her motion, alleging that her residence imperiled Coho's life. He noted the injurious presence of her boyfriend, who dislocated Coho's elbow while breaking up a dogfight. Gough stated it is "in the best interests of Coho that the property settlement agreement provide that Coho be awarded to Steve Gough solely." In light of severe contention in continuing shared custody, JUDGE BEISTLINE awarded "legal and physical custody of Coho" to Gough and allowed the ex-wife "reasonable visitation rights as determined by [Gough]." The new arrangement failed, and after facing reciprocal restraining orders, JUDGE BEISTLINE later reaffirmed his grant of custody to Stephen Gough, holding, "Ms. Gough has no rights whatsoever to Coho and may not demand visitation or take the dog from Mr. Gough." *Id.*, at 595. The Supreme Court found sufficient grounds to warrant CR § 60(b) relief from the original judgment given the changed circumstances, making the original order unworkable.

In a decision that changed the discourse of animal custody, the Appellate Division of the Supreme Court of New York unanimously reversed the trial court's award of sole custody of a cat named Lovey, née Merlin. The trial court first recognized the interests of Lovey as a sentient, companion animal by ordering the parties to "work out a visitation schedule" because "it does not appear to be within the best interest of the cat to shift custody back and forth." *Raymond v. Lachmann*, 695 N.Y.S.2d 308, 309 (1999). It then changed its mind, and relied on strict property principles to award Lovey to defendant Suzanne Lachmann conditioned on her payment of all veterinary expenses incurred over the prior years. In letting him live out his years with plaintiff Susan Raymond, the appellate panel wrote:

> Cognizant of the cherished status accorded to pets in our society, the strong emotions engendered by disputes of this nature, and the limited ability of the courts to resolve them satisfactorily, on the record presented, we think it best for all concerned that, given his limited life expectancy, Lovey, who is now almost ten years old, remain where he has lived, prospered, loved and been loved for the past four years.

Id., at 308.

In 2007, court-appointed attorney Paul Royal of Memphis, Tenn. as the guardian ad litem for Alex, a 13-year-old Golden Retriever. Stephanie Francis Ward, *Canine Case is Doggone Tough: Tennessee Lawyer is Guardian to Pet Caught in a Custody Battle*, ABA eReport, 6 No. 20 ABA J. E-Report 1 (2007). see also *Young v. Rowley*, King Cy. Sup. Ct., Wash., No. 08-2-04292-8 SEA (Apr. 11, 2008), where the court asked to resolve dog custody in a dissolution stated:

> The foundation determination is that joint ownership of this dog is not acceptable. The parties cannot bond in joint ownership of this dog or some model of visitation based on the parenting plan of children. That's not going to work. It would be an aggravation to both parties and to the dog. So, I think it really comes down to the quality of life that Brie will have.

> With that, I do think that it is a fair decision on that, that Brie be in a family home where Brie is the only dog. This is superior to being in a home where there are a lot of other dogs involved. And I think that based upon that, I think that the best quality of life for Brie, not only this home with a number of other dogs that might be there, but all the ancillary aspects of that, that Brie would be a happier, more content dog in the home of Ms. Rowley. So, I will order that.

In *Arrington v. Arrington*, 613 S.W.2d 565 (Tex. Civ. App. 1981), Alfred Arrington appealed a divorce decree making his wife Ruby Arrington the managing conservator of Bonnie Lou, their dog. He did not bristle at lack of visitation. Rather, he wanted the title of "managing conservator." In overruling his exception, the appellate court noted that the office of "managing conservator" benefited "human children, not canine," and that "for all its admirable and unique qualities," a dog "is not a human being and is not treated in the law as such." Concluding that, "Love is not a commodity that can be bought and sold or decreed," and assured that "there is enough love in that little canine heart to 'go around,' " it affirmed Ruby managing Bonnie Lou for life.

Not all courts endorse the view that animal best interests have any place in the courtroom. For instance, see *Morgan v. Kroupa*, 702 A. 2d 630, 633 (Vt. 1997) ("family law provides an imperfect analogue," and regardless of strong emotional attachments, "courts simply cannot evaluate the 'best interests' of an animal"); *Angrave v. Oates*, 876 A.2d 1287, 1290 fn. 3 (Conn. App. Ct. 2005) (Oates's request that the court consider the best interests of Lady Catherine failed as well, for "replevin does not involve the best interest of the dog, which is a chattel[.]").

In *Marriage of Stewart*, 356 N.W.2d 611 (Iowa Ct. App. 1984), although gifted to Joan Wilson by Jay Stewart on Christmas, the trial court ordered as part of the dissolution decree that Georgetta, a dog, would go to Stewart, a veterinarian-in-training with whom she spent most of her time, including accompanying him to the office. It did so without considering Georgetta's best interests. He reasoned that the doctrine would not apply so long as the primary caregiver did not abuse or neglect the animal. On appeal, though sensitive to the need "not [to] put a family pet in a position of being abused or uncared for," the appellate court concluded, "[W]e do not have to determine the best interests of a pet." *Id.*, at 613.

In *Bennett v. Bennett*, 655 So. 2d 109 (Fla. Dist. App. 1995), Ronald Bennett appealed a divorce decree giving his wife Kathryn Bennett visitation with Roddy. Following hearing, the trial court awarded possession of Roddy to Ronald but let Kathryn take him every other weekend and every other Christmas. He sought rehearing, claiming Roddy was a premarital asset, and she moved for contempt when he refused to comply with the visitation order, whereupon the court denied his and granted her motion, increasing her access to every other month. Finding that the practice of according special status to family pets in dissolution proceedings charts an "unwise" course, the appellate court concluded that it "cannot undertake the same responsibility as to animals" as done in the case of "supervision of custody, visitation, and support matters related to the protection of our children." *Id.*, at 110–11. Reversing, it remanded for an equitable distribution of Roddy to either party, terminating shared custody as likely to result in "continued squabbling between the parties." Concluding that dogs are personalty and cannot be regarded as human beings for purposes of visitation, custody, and support, it completely divested the wife of any access and equitably distributed Roddy to the ex-husband's exclusive custody.

In *LeConte v. Lee*, 35 Misc. 3d 286 (N.Y. Civ. Ct. 2011), boyfriend Adam LeConte sued ex-girlfriend Kyungmi Lee for return of Bubkas, his Maltese, when she kept him after a two-week dogsitting stint. The trial court ordered shared custody till trial. In granting summary judgment to LeConte, the court took notice that LeConte's parents gifted Bubkas to him two years prior. Lee contended that she provided primary care to Bubkas and that his best interests were served remaining with her, in part because LeConte crated Bubkas. Finding no conveyance of possessory or ownership rights by contract or gift, and no assertion of abandonment, the court instead focused on the best interests theme raised in *Raymond v. Lachmann*, distinguishing it on grounds of duration (Lee had uninterrupted custody of only two one-month periods while Lovey, the cat in *Lachmann*, "lived, prospered, loved and [had] been loved" for four years in the exclusive care of Lachmann), life expectancy (Bubkas was only two while Lovey was much older), and potential harm (no evidence existed that crating endangered Bubkas or that he needed medical treatment). Though it would not entertain an application for joint custody or visitation, the court remarked, "While there is no legal obligation to do so, the court hopes the parties will find a way for Bubkas to continue to spend time with both parties."

In *Rapuano v. Rapuano*, 2001 WL 1332431 (Conn. Super.), where the mother sued the daughter for return of a horse, the daughter argued that the "best interests of the horse" criterion deserved application. To this court wittily quipped, at *3:

> Although that standard is consistent with the parties' stated views that Cloud is more valuable to them than their own relationship as mother and daughter, it is not an appropriate consideration in this case. This is not a child custody case. This is an action to recover a chattel . . . .

In *In re Marriage of Pilskalns*, 186 P.3d 877 (Mont. 2008), a rather short opinion, the Montana Supreme Court said this about the trial court's distribution of Maggie, a dog, to Kara Pilskalns's husband Andrews: "We decline to adopt the best interest of the child standard for distribution of pets, which are marital property." Furthermore, this holding reflected "settled Montana law[.]"

In *Dubin v. Pelletier*, 2012 R.I. Super. LEXIS 175 (Nov. 21, 2012), a dispute between a show dog handler and registered owner, the court rejected the "best interests" analysis as distinguishable from cases cited, ultimately holding that Rhode Island views animals as property and changes should be requested of the General Assembly, not the courts, noting that such a test "could open the floodgates to the litigation of pet custody disputes and other issues involving pets."

In *Nuzzaci v. Nuzzaci*, 1995 Del. Fam. Ct. LEXIS 30 (Apr. 19, 1995), though the parties stipulated to an order concerning visitation with Zach, a Golden Retriever, JUDGE CROMPTON refused to sign "an order which is in essence a visitation order in every respect, except as to the biological classification of the 'object d'etre.' " He then took a mocking view of applying child custody statutes to canines, bovines, ovines, and "even a guppy," concluding that the "prospect of applying the seven factors of § 722(a) to a Zach, a Tabitha or even a fish called Wanda for that matter, would be an impossible task." Regarding itself "powerless to come to their aid, except to award the entire dog to one spouse or the other," the court prevailed upon the parties' maturity.

Perhaps the most thorough, modern decision on the law of best interests, and one putting *Nuzzaci*-type sentiments in their outmoded place, comes from *Travis v. Murray*, 2013 WL 6246374 (N.Y. Sup.). New York Superior Court Judge Matthew F. Cooper authored an opinion in a dissolution case resolving competing custody claims to a two-and-a-half-year-old miniature Dachshund named Joey. The first few pages recounted a New York-based bibliography of articles pertaining to the canine-centric city: John Homans, *The Rise of Dog Identity Politics*, NEW YORK MAGAZINE, Feb. 1, 2010, at 20; Gregory Berns, *Dogs Are People, Too*, New York Times, Oct. 6, 2013, SR at 5, col. 1); and Alexandra Zissu, *After the Breakup, Here Comes the Joint-Custody Pet*, New York Times, Aug. 22, 1999, at S. It then turned to the facts.

Four months after Shannon Travis and Trisha Murray married, they bought Joey from a pet store. Two years later, Murray left the marital apartment with Joey while Travis was on a business trip, then lied, saying she lost him in Central Park. Travis filed for divorce, claiming she used her separate funds to purchase Joey, that she primarily cared for Joey parentally and financially, and that his "best interests" required he remain in her "sole care and custody."

Murray asserted that Travis intramaritally gifted Joey "as consolation" for Murray having to give away her cat at Travis's insistence. She, too, claimed involvement in Joey's "emotional, practical, and logistical needs," added that his "bed was next to [her] side of the marital bed," and that "best interests" warranted him living with her mother in Maine. Drawing from "de-chattelization" principles of *Raymond*, involving the cat named Lovey, Judge Cooper concluded that "in a case such as this, where two spouses are battling over a dog they once possessed and raised together, a strict property analysis is neither desirable nor appropriate." Decidedly "more than a piece of property, marital or otherwise," the court conducted a judicious and thorough national survey of animal custody decisions that apply a strict property analysis, take a custodial approach, or a nuanced treatment of both. It settled upon a decision hearkening from its own division, *Raymond*, noting that the term "best interests" does not appear anywhere in the decision. Instead it speaks to what is "best for all concerned."

While refusing to treat the dispute as it would a child custody proceeding, in part because, "To allow full-blown dog custody cases, complete with canine forensics and attorneys representing not only the parties but the dog itself, would further burden the courts to the detriment of children," and create an "unthinkable" drain of judicial resources, it did not mean the court would give the matter "short shrift." Rather, he stated:

> If judicial resources can be devoted to such matters as which party gets to use the Escalade as opposed to the Ferrari, or who gets to stay in the Hamptons house instead of the Aspen chalet, there is certainly room to give real consideration to a case involving a treasured pet.

Cautioning that permitting a "full hearing" meant no more than one day, the court advised the parties that he would make "unqualified" and final determination vesting sole custody and ownership in one party. JUDGE COOPER directed each to focus not on "why she will benefit from having Joey in her life," but — using the language from *Raymond*, "why Joey has a better chance of living, prospering, loving and being loved in the care of one spouse as opposed to the other." Germane questions would include, "Who bore the major responsibility for meeting Joey's needs (i.e., feeding, walking, grooming and taking him to the veterinarian) when the parties lived together? Who spent more time with Joey on a regular basis? Why did plaintiff leave Joey with defendant, as defendant alleges, at the time the couple separated? And perhaps most importantly, why has defendant chosen to have Joey live with her mother in Maine, rather than with her, or with plaintiff for that matter, in New York?"

Shifting the focus from what is ideal for the animal to the comparative suffering of the parties deprived of connection to the animal, one may attempt to invoke *in loco parentis* principles. For instance, in *In re Parentage of L.B.*, 121 Wn. App. 460

(2004), the intermediate appellate court permitted Sue Carvin, the lesbian partner of Page Britain, biological mother of L.B., to petition for co-parentage or visitation under common law and the Uniform Parentage Act (Ch. 26.26 RCW) based on her seven-year cohabitation with L.B. L.B. was conceived through artificial insemination of Britain by Britain's gay male friend, whom she later married. JUDGE KENNEDY, speaking for the court, noted that Washington courts recognize de facto parentage given the parent and child bond irrespective of "biology or statuses providing traditional parental rights." *See also In re Dependency of Ramquist*, 52 Wn. App. 854 (1988), where the court recognized the psychological bond of a foster child to a foster family, to whom custody was awarded. The Supreme Court revised the lower court's ruling by adapting the common law to "fill the interstices that our current legislative enactment fails to cover in a manner consistent with our laws and stated legislative policy" by recognizing de facto parentage and according such individuals the rights and responsibilities attached to biological parents in Washington. It agreed that individuals not biologically nor legally related to the children whom they "parent" may still be considered a child's "psychological parent." *In re Parentage of L.B.*, 122 P.3d 161, 167–68 (Wash. 2005). It allowed that the psychological parent had standing under common law, but not statute (the UPA), to petition for parental privileges. While L.B. speaks to human children, it is hard to reject the similarities to parties acting *in loco parentis* for animals where the alleged "legal parents" consent and enable the relationship between the "psychological parent" (plaintiff) and "child" (animal).

Following the logic of *L.B.*, such plaintiffs may strive to prove the viability and strength of the quasi-parent-child relationship through evidence that:

> (1) the natural and legal parent consented to and fostered the parent-like relationship, (2) the petitioner and the child lived together in the same household, (3) the petitioner assumed obligations of parenthood without expectation of financial compensation, and (4) the petitioner has been in a parental role for a length of time sufficient to have established with the child a bonded, dependent relationship parental in nature.

Id., at 285. The *in loco parentis* theory (i.e., the one who mothers, owns), will encounter further resistance given that most non-biological fathers and mothers do not even share the same constitutional rights of a biological parent absent legislative action. Such nonparents include adoptive parents, legal guardians, grandparents, and those acting *in loco parentis* capacity. *See In re Custody of S.H.B.*, 118 Wn. App. 71, 79–80 (2003).

Readers should also be prepared to compare and contrast the home environments of each party. For instance, were a court to apply the equitable doctrines above, a household where violence is committed against a spouse in the presence of minor children, where phones are ripped from the wall and doors are kicked down, would not be deemed conducive for the care of a companion animal, particularly one of advanced years, or where methamphetamine use, a highly addictive and illegal substance, controls the behavior of the inhabitants, placing the animal's welfare in heightened jeopardy. A felony record and long-term history of domestic violence would, in an equitable setting, merit serious review, particularly given the legislative recognition of the link between domestic violence and animal abuse. But for claims not sounding in equity, strict property principles govern.

R.   VOIDABLE TITLE/ENTRUSTMENT

Generally, a party may only pass as good title as previously obtained. Two rare exceptions permit the passing of even better — *voidable title* (good faith purchaser for value) and *entrustment* (buyer in ordinary course), as discussed in Section IV above.

For ease of reference, UCC § 2-403(1) states:

> A purchaser of goods acquires all title which his transferor had or had power to transfer except that a purchaser of a limited interest acquires rights only to the extent of the interest purchased. A person with voidable title has power to transfer a good title to a good faith purchaser for value. When goods have been delivered under a transaction of purchase the purchaser has such power even though (a) the transferor was deceived as to the identity of the purchaser; (b) the delivery was in exchange for a check which is later dishonored; (c) it was agreed that the transaction was to be a "cash sale"; or (d) the delivery was procured through fraud punishable as larcenous under the criminal law.

Animals are "goods," including the "unborn young of animals." UCC § 2-105(1). When a buyer acquires colorable (but voidable) title over property delivered voluntarily to her by the original seller, that buyer may pass good (i.e., better) title to a certain type of third party — the good faith purchaser for value ("GFP"). *Good faith* means "honesty in fact and the observance of reasonable commercial standards of fair dealing." UCC § 1-201(20). It requires that the purchaser have no awareness of the circumstances that rendered title voidable, nor a basis to inspire a reasonably prudent person to inquire further as to the ability of the buyer to transfer good title. *Purchaser* means "a person that takes by purchase." UCC § 1-201(30). *Purchase* means "taking by sale, lease, discount, negotiation, mortgage, pledge, lien, security interest, issue or reissue, gift, or any other voluntary transaction creating an interest in property." UCC § 1-201(29). A GFP is not a donee, however, due to the words "for value," defined in UCC § 1-201(44) to include "consideration sufficient to support a simple contract."

The original seller may repossess the property from any non-GFP. When property is *involuntarily* taken away by a thief, and then pawned to an innocent third party, including a GFP, voidable title doctrine does not apply because no title whatsoever transferred to the thief. Such title is void, not voidable. The good faith purchaser doctrine applies to all sales of goods, whether or not involving a merchant or dealer. Title becomes "voidable" in the case of mistaken identity (i.e., an imposter receives the property but is not the true buyer), a check returned as NSF, an unfulfilled cash sale, or larcenous fraud. Though title may have physically transferred (as in the case of a car), giving the check-bouncing transferee possession of title (and hence color of title), the bounced check lets the seller avoid the contract, rendering it "voidable." Yet, if the transferee then sells the car to a third party innocent as to the dispute between the seller and transferee, that third party takes the car free and clear with no obligation to return it to the seller. This doctrine often applies in the case of animal sales.

In *Frye & Co. v. Boltman*, 47 P.2d 839 (Wash. 1935), Frye & Co. sold a team of horses to Clifford Gray, who paid by forged check, and then sold them to an innocent purchaser Albert Boltman. In reversing judgment for Boltman, the Washington Supreme Court enforced Rem. Rev. Stat. § 2129, stating, "All property obtained by larceny, robbery, or burglary, shall be restored to the owner; and no sale, whether in good faith on the part of the purchaser or not, shall divest the owner of his rights to such property." Because passing a fraudulent check constituted larceny in 1935, and although the modern-day Uniform Commercial Code might have regarded Gray as having voidable (not void) title, the appellate court ordered Boltman to return the team.

In *Nelson v. Jones*, 219 P. 836 (Okla. 1923), Morrow traded a stolen horse (owned by Bud Powel) for one owned by Nelson. Morrow then sold the horse he acquired from Nelson to defendant Hall, who paid full value; Hall then sold it to defendant Jones. Nelson, Hall, and Jones all purchased in good faith. Thereafter, Powel recovered his stolen horse from Nelson, whereupon Nelson sued Hall and Jones in replevin for the horse he traded originally to Morrow. Upon judgment for the defendants, Nelson appealed. Affirming, the appellate court concluded that Hall was a bona fide purchaser who took good title from Morrow. While Nelson voluntarily parted with possession and title to his horse under fraudulent circumstances, the comparative innocence rule required that Hall prevail, for between the two, "where one of the two innocent persons must suffer by the fraud of a third he who has put it in the power of the third to commit the fraud must suffer."

UCC § 2-403(2) states:

> Any entrusting of possession of good to a merchant who deals in goods of that kind gives him power to transfer all rights of the entruster to a buyer in ordinary course of business.

This alternative UCC theory arises in consignments and bailments of animals (think entrusting an animal to the care of another, who then breaches that trust by giving the animal to a third party). Voidable title arises from voluntary transfers of *ownership* under false pretenses, while entrustment doctrine examines voluntary transfers of *possession* where no foul play is presumed or even material to the dispute. For no title is ever intended to pass between bailor and bailee. Thus, a bailee with no authority to sell the bailed property may still pass good title to a third party if the bailee regularly sells the same kind of goods (a person known as a "merchant"). On the other hand, entrusting an animal to a *non-merchant* bailee for safekeeping or treatment does not have the same legal consequence. Entrustment differs from the voidable title in two respects: *first*, while possession is voluntarily transferred, no purchase occurs; *second*, voidable title applies to all transactions between any two people, while entrustment requires that the transferee be a "merchant." Entrustment requires proof that the entrusted merchant sold or gave the property to a buyer in the ordinary course of business ("BOC"). A BOC is defined, in relevant part, under UCC § 1-201(9) as:

A person that buys goods in good faith, without knowledge that the sale violates the rights of another person in the goods, and in the ordinary course from a person, other than a pawnbroker, in the business of selling goods of that kind. A person buys goods in the ordinary course if the sale to the person comports with the usual or customary practices in the kind of business in which the seller is engaged or with the seller's own usual or customary practices.

"Good faith" has the same meaning as used with GFPs. UCC § 1-201(20). It applies both a subjective and objective standard. *Sale* means "passing of title from the seller to the buyer for a price." UCC § 2-106(1). And a seller who is in the business of selling goods of the kind at issue is also known as a *merchant*. UCC § 2-104(1). For instance, a person buys a horse from a barn that both breeds and boards equines. Thereafter, he enters into a contract to board the purchased horse for three months. The term passes when he discovers that the barn has sold his horse to a third party. While the entruster may sue the entrustee stable for damages, he cannot recover the horse from the third party if she is a BOC. *See Hammer v. Thompson*, 129 P.3d 609 (Kan. Ct. App. 2006) (entrustee cattle order buyer deemed a merchant as a matter of law).

In *Prenger v. Baker*, 542 N.W.2d 805 (Iowa 1995), Gene Baker boarded two breeding pairs of ostriches with Ron Rasmus, a farmer in the business of buying, selling, and raising exotics. Thereafter, Rasmus sold those pairs to the Missouri Ratite Center, Inc. ("MRC"), which then sold one of the two pairs to Gary Prenger. Prenger also traded two adult emus for two of Rasmus's juvenile ostrich pairs. The adult and juvenile pairs remained on Rasmus's farm during egg-laying season. Baker then removed the adult male purchased by MRC ("MRC male"), the adult pair purchased by Prenger ("Prenger female" and "Prenger male"), and several juveniles. The adult female purchased by MRC ("MRC female") could not be found.

The Prengers and MRC sued Baker for replevin. Gene Baker responded that he rightfully owned them along with Donald Baker, who intervened, claiming to have bought a pair of ostriches from Gene as a GFP. The trial court concluded that the Prengers owned the "Prenger Male" and MRC the "MRC male," to which they were entitled to immediate possession.

All parties appealed: the Bakers as to the Prenger male and MRC male, MRC as to the "MRC female," and the Prengers as to conversion of the "Prenger female." Affirming on all bases, the Iowa Supreme Court applied the UCC to hold that the birds were entrusted by Baker to Rasmus, who was a "merchant" of ratites and sold two ostrich pairs to MRC. As neither MRC nor the Prengers had knowledge of Baker's interest in the birds at time of purchase, they qualified as BOCs and took free of any claim by the Bakers. Thus, MRC owned the MRC male and the Prengers the Prenger male per entrustment doctrine.

In *Swann v. Alleva*, 45 Pa. D & C. 3d 630 (1987), Heather Swann bought a horse named Royal Whirl for $500 from Fred Alleva, who was hired by Samuel and Lois Ginsberg to turn her out in order to sell her, but not at 20 to 40 times less than her actual value. Based on her extensive experience in buying horses, including owning one worth $200,000, the court found it more plausible that Swann "executed the purported bill of sale for $500, so that she could enter the horse in a horse show in the 'amateur-owner' category, and that the transaction was not meant to transfer permanent ownership of Royal Whirl to her." Accordingly, in rejecting her claim of replevin, and confirming ownership in the Ginsbergs, the court found her not to be a BOC owing to lack of good faith. Though not clear from the opinion, the court regarded the Jockey Club papers as inconclusive.

S. EQUITABLE DISTRIBUTION IN MARITAL OR QUASI-MARITAL CONTEXT

If acquisition funds for the nonhuman animal can be traced, absent evidence of gifting, waiver, or abandonment, the initial acquirer should win sole custody. *Banner Life Ins. Co. v. Mark Wallace Dixson Irrevocable Trust*, 206 P.3d 481, 488 (Idaho 2009) states:

> In Idaho, the characterization of an asset as community or separate property depends on the date and source of the property's acquisition. . . . Property acquired during the marriage is presumptively regarded as community property. . . . The party seeking to overcome the presumption has the burden of proving "with reasonable certainty and particularity" that an asset is his or her separate property. . . . This may be accomplished "by establishing that the property was acquired by one spouse prior to the marriage, by tracing the funds used to acquire the asset to a separate property source, or by showing that the property was acquired by gift, bequest or devise during the marriage." . . . Absent such a showing, all property "acquired after marriage by either the husband or wife is community property."

Id., at 488 (citations omitted); *see also Weilmunster v. Weilmunster*, 858 P.2d 766 (Idaho Ct. App. 1993) (finding that 80 percent of cattle were husband's separate property having been owned prior to marriage).

Property acquired after marriage is presumed community-owned. Those challenging this presumption bear the burden of proof to rebut, frequently with documentary evidence tracing acquisition to expenditure of separate funds. *See Calder v. Calder*, 2010 WL 3370766 (Tex. App.—Austin) (dog acquired before marriage with respective separate income of each spouse, complicated by commingling separate funds in husband's bank account, resulted in court finding that purchase price came entirely from wife's deposit into that account); *Schneider v. Schneider*, 2004 WL 254247 (Tex. App.—Fort Worth) (neither spouse traced the source of funds used to buy dog, as they commingled assets in a joint bank account before marriage, prompting appellate court to construe them as tenants-in-common).

Intramarital gifting and inheritance serves as an exception. Premarital separate property remains so after marriage, absent a community property agreement. *See Rodriguez v. Rodriguez*, 2002 WL 1824846 (Cal. App.) (horse sold after separation for over quarter-million dollars not deemed an intramarital gift but instead community property). One spouse's contribution to insurance premiums, mortgage payments, and improvements to separate property does not transmute the property's character. *See Bliss v. Bliss*, 898 P.2d 1081 (Idaho 1995) (community funds used to enhance value of spouse's separate property allows for reimbursement of said funds unless intended as gift); *In re Estate of Borghi*, 219 P.3d 932, 938 & n.7 (Wash. 2009) (community property contributions to improvements upon property may create community right of reimbursement protected by an equitable lien, but such actions do not transmute from separate to community). If transmutation would not occur intramaritally as described in *Borghi*, it cannot conceivably do so in the nonmarital context. Rather, the expenditures of the community (or the other party) may create an equitable lien, a possible claim for unjust enrichment, or a quasi-contractual right to reimbursement, yet it does not recharacterize the essential nature of the property. *Hamlin v. Merlino*, 272 P.2d 125, 128 (Wash. 1954).

Usual homemaker chores that may increase value in the property do not necessarily establish an equitable lien. *In re Marriage of Johnson*, 28 Wn. App. 574, 579 (1981). To the extent defendant's right to reimbursement may not be satisfied, the dog's love and companionship may be said to provide a more than adequate offset. Analogizing to a car clarifies the analysis. Where plaintiff cohabits with defendant and purchases a car using his own funds, title to the car remains solely in him, although plaintiff allows defendant full use and enjoyment of the car. Defendant's payments for gasoline, oil changes, or repairs do not alter the fundamental nature of plaintiff's ownership.

An animal who comes into a marriage as a premarital asset belongs to the acquiring spouse exclusively. But if the purchase price consists of a down payment made with separate property and the balance with community funds, courts may apply the *inception of title* approach, where title is determined based on who supplied funds at the title's inception. This characterization would not necessarily change even if community funds paid the balance or were used to nurture, train, and raise (i.e., increase the value) of the animal. At best, this would confer upon the community a right of reimbursement. Though likely a matter of first impression, a court would probably imply a gift of the maintenance funds by the community. In the alternative, the court could choose to offset the community property funds by any community benefit the animal gave to the community. Occasionally, courts treat an animal as community property by finding a joint, reciprocal gift — i.e., husband gifts cat to wife and wife gifts same cat to husband. *See, infra, Whitmore v. Whitmore*. Where the purchaser refers to the animal consistently as "our dog," the court may even imply a gift of the dog to the community. Such an *appellation theory* (i.e., the one who names, owns) may evidence ownership or gifting, but alone will not be dispositive, and birthday or mother's day or father's day cards from the animal may just be a conduit to express affection between spouses, not an admission. After all, allowing someone to name a boat or child does not amount to gifting the vessel or babe to that person. During marriage, it is also customary to refer to all items (including premaritally purchased homes and vehicles) as shared commodities. It would be strange, indeed, for one spouse to remind the other to take off his shoes in "her house."

Offspring born, whelped, or foaled during marriage from parents separately owned by one spouse may, depending on the jurisdiction, bear the status of the mother (if mother is separate, offspring are separate), be deemed rents or profits of separate property, or be regarded as after-acquired marital property. In *Williams v. Williams*, 2008 WL 5194227 (Tex. App.—Fort Worth), a dissolution case, the trial court awarded Pflamenco, a horse, to Danielle Williams. Jerry Williams appealed, asserting that he was community property because foaled during the marriage. Finding that animal offspring born postmaritally are community property — even if the parents are separate property — the appellate court agreed with Jerry on that legal point, but did not reverse the award since the mischaracterization had only *de minimis* effect on the division of the community estate, in part because neither Danielle nor Jerry estimated Pflamenco's value. In *Corley v. Corley*, 594 P.2d 1172 (N.M. 1979), Gene Corley and Carol Jo Corley divorced. One issue pertained to horses foaled at the family farm after the date of marriage yet coming out of parents Gene purchased before marriage. Deeming the offspring "rents, issues and profits" of the parents, the New Mexico Supreme Court deemed "[a]ll the horses are patently the separate property of Corley." *Id.*, at 1175.

Occasionally, the divorce decree inadvertently omits animals. When this oversight occurs, the animals (along with other unidentified property) will pass through the dissolution as jointly owned, the now ex-spouses becoming tenants-in-common. *See, e.g., Haas v. Otto*, 392 S.W.3d 290 (Tex. App. 2012); *Ambrose v. Moore*, 90 P. 588, 589 (Wash. 1907). In *Akers v. Sellers*, 54 N.E2d 779 (Ind. Ct. App. 1944) (en banc), a married couple adopted a Boston Terrier. The dissolution decree did not speak to the dog, though the wife received the house in which the dog resided. The ex-husband sued for replevin under strict property principles and the dog's interests and desires. Deeming the dog intramaritally gifted to the wife by the husband, making the dog her separate property and divesting him of any residual property interest, the court rejected his assertions of best interests and tenancy-in-common.

The issue also arose in *Isbell v. Willoughby*, 2005 Cal. App. Unpub. LEXIS 6500 (July 26, 2005). Before marriage, Daniel Willoughby bought a beagle named Emmit for himself using his own money. Eight months later, Alice Isbell moved in, and about six months after that, they wed. One year after judgment of dissolution was entered, Daniel filed an order to show cause why Emmit, a postjudgment unadjudicated asset, should not be deemed his separate property. Alice responded that the court should deem Emmit hers based on his best interests. Upon the trial court finding Emmit belonged to Daniel, who let Alice only temporarily care for the dog, and ordering her to release Emmit, she appealed. The marital settlement agreement ("MSA") did not mention Emmit specifically, so the court turned to the catch-all provision of personalty "now in the possession of" Daniel or Alice. The trial court concluded that Alice was not in her possession (meaning "[t]o have as property; own"), but rather was possessed by Daniel at the time he signed the MSA. Although Emmit was with Alice when she signed the MSA one month later, as well as four months later when judgment was entered, the appellate court affirmed, regarding her a mere dogsitter until Daniel returned from flight school in Florida.

In *Ballas v. Ballas*, 178 Cal. App. 2d 570 (1960), Shirley Ballas filed for divorce from Maurice Ballas, who was awarded the family Pekingese. Shirley claimed she bought the dog six months after they married using her own funds, registering the dog in her name, and having possession of the dog more than a year after the parties separated. Nonetheless, the trial court gave Maurice the dog because he furnished an exhibit under the heading "Community property," listing the dog as the fourteenth of 14 items. However, his answer did not mention the dog, nor his cross-complaint. Nor did he discuss the dog at the pretrial hearing. Reversing, the appellate court found that whether the dog was community or separate property mattered not, and Shirley was entitled to keep the canine.

In *Walash v. Kilgour*, 938 N.Y.S.2d 230 (Sup. Ct. 2011), Neil Walash sued Nikki Kilgour in replevin to recover an English bulldog named Mo after Walash's ex-wife Samantha Walash surrendered him to Pet Spa and Resort, Inc. in New Jersey. Kilgour adopted Mo from the Resort, signing an adoption contract where the Spa claimed it had full ownership rights (not mentioning that Mo came to it in the midst of a divorce). Despite promises to return Mo to Neil, Samantha in fact knowingly gave him away without his consent, causing the family court judge to order her to notify the Spa and Kilgour that she had none. Kilgour was prepared to return Mo until she viewed text messages between Neil and Samantha convincing her that he delayed taking any steps to retrieve Mo from the spa by several months. The court made a number of significant rulings. First, it found that Mo, as "unique chattel," was properly subject to a replevin action under state law. Next, it found that the UCC would not apply to Kilgour as a BOC given lack of consideration, and no value paid. Third, Neil's timely demand for Mo's return did not violate the statute of limitations or laches doctrine (i.e., though he learned of Mo's whereabouts in a text message on Sept. 5, 2010, he undertook considerable efforts to recover Mo from Samantha over the following months; Samantha's deception caused excusable delay of six months before he made demand on Kilgour). Fourth, though Samantha committed no larceny in giving away Mo, who constituted marital property, she did violate the family court's automatic orders, resulting in a finding that she unlawfully disposed of marital property. It mattered not that Mo was licensed solely in Samantha's name, calling it axiomatic that property acquired after marriage is presumptively marital property. Identifying several factual issues warranting further proceedings, the court ordered counsel to address steps taken to give Neil access to Mo pending final adjudication, including determining how to weigh the equities relative to a claimed "blameless adoptive pet owner."

Though uncommon, courts may award temporary possession of an animal pending final distribution, as occurred in *CRS v. TKS*, 746 N.Y.S.2d 568 (Sup. Ct. 2002). The husband purchased a Chocolate Labrador Retriever as a 35th birthday gift for his wife, who remained home while caring for the dog. Barred entry to her New York residence, she relocated to her Florida residence without the dog, whose whereabouts were not disclosed at the time and who was kept by the husband as a form of punishment. He contended that to order temporary transfer of the dog to the wife would amount to an impermissible prejudgment distribution of marital property as the dog is "no different than [sic] a sofa, home or bank account." Because the husband could assign no monetary value to the dog, nor assert that it produced income or was a durable asset that would increase in value, nor even that a credit value of the dog could be established as an offset, the trial court exercised its discretion to award temporary possession to the wife pending judgment and to credit any proven value of the dog at that juncture, adding, "The court notes that the time and money expended litigating this issue could have been used to negotiate and fund a settlement."

In *Oldenburg v. Oldenburg*, 2012 WL 858645 (Tex.App.—Fort Worth), the court distributed the dog to Lisa Oldenburg even though Peter Oldenburg testified he provided primary care, took the dog to work with him daily, and that Lisa testified she did not know who cared for the dog while she served 40 days in jail for assault. Still, Peter admitted he wrote letters saying he would never take the dog away from her. Accordingly, the appellate court found no abuse of discretion in the trial court awarding the dog to Lisa, for she "selected the dog, adopted it, brought it home, and had at least a part in its care."

In *Whitmore v. Whitmore*, 2011 WL 588497 (Va. App.), Scott Whitmore appealed the award of a Welsh Corgi to his wife Barbara Whitmore, a dog purchased during marriage and registered with AKC in both their names. Three years later, Scott moved out and left the dog with Barbara in the marital residence (owned by Barbara) except for short periods of possession during their first year of separation. Barbara claimed Scott gifted the dog to her, though he characterized the purchase as joint. Both worked during the marriage and cared for the dog, yet Barbara spent more time taking her to the veterinarian and visiting her several times a day while hospitalized for nearly a week (while Scott "chose not to do so because he did not want to excite the dog while she was ill.") Barbara paid the $4,000 hospital bill and most subsequent veterinary bills, while Scott incurred the rest. Barbara hired a dog walking service when gone from the home and when not traveling, and worked in her home office to be with the dog. Acknowledging that both parties presented evidence of a strong bond and love for the dog, and referring to the issue of valuation as "problematic" given her "intrinsic value," the trial court deemed the canine a gift "between the parties" and, thus, a marital asset to be equitably distributed to Barbara with offset of $750, the purchase price, to Scott to acquire another dog "of like kind." Finding no abuse of discretion, the appellate court affirmed.

In *Bush v. Bush*, 336 S.W.3d 722 (Tex. App. 2010), Tracy Bush divorced Michael Bush. In appealing the trial court's finding that Pepper, Lady, and two unnamed bay mares were Michael's separate property, the appellate court evaluated whether they were gifts to Michael or to the entire family, placing additional emphasis on the fact that Lady was bought with funds from settlement or insurance proceeds arising from harm to Pepper. Tracy argued that to overcome the community property presumption, Michael needed to offer supportive documentary evidence. However, this rule would not apply to gifted horses. Though Tracy testified that Gail Ray gifted Pepper to the family, Ms. Ray stated she gave Pepper to Michael specifically, thus establishing donative intent to Michael as his separate property. As to the two bay mares, Michael testified that his uncle gifted them to him alone, while Tracy stated they were familial gifts. Though no other evidence was presented, the appellate court refused to disturb the weight given to the testimony by the trial court. Finding Lady was purchased with either insurance or settlement proceeds from injury to Pepper, and that insurance and settlement proceeds retain the character of the casualty loss or property to which the claim is attributed, the court confirmed Michael's ownership of Lady as his separate property.

In *Calder v. Calder*, 2010 WL 3370766 (Tex. App.—Austin), Daniel Calder filed for divorce from Brooke Calder with the only contested issue concerning ownership of Clementine, acquired before marriage. Each claimed to have purchased Clementine with his or her respective separate income, an assertion complicated by Daniel and Brooke commingling separate funds in Daniel's bank account before marriage. While normally the party claiming separate property in the disputed item bears the burden to rebut the community presumption, in Clementine's case, the rule did not apply as neither was married at time of purchase. Affirming, the appellate court deferred to the trial court's assessment of credibility and resolution of evidentiary conflict, finding substantial evidence to support the conclusion that Brooke used her own money to buy Clementine for $500, namely, that Daniel deposited Brooke's paychecks into his account and either immediately withdrew the money for her or held it until requested; and that Brooke deposited at least $948 into his account several days before Daniel withdrew $600 in cash, $400 going to the breeder to purchase Clementine. Further, Brooke testified that Daniel said she could have a dog only if she paid for her, with money coming from her paycheck. Finally, the court rejected Daniel's citation to a repealed statute providing that the holder of an account owns the funds therein as his separate property.

In *Schneider v. Schneider*, 2004 WL 254247 (Tex.App.—Fort Worth), Susan Schneider divorced Scott Schneider two years after he was sentenced to 30 years for felony assault. Appealing from an award of the couple's three dogs — Lucky, Dusty, and Trixie — to Susan, Scott contended that Lucky was his separate property. Susan, however, claimed she bought Lucky before marriage using cashed bonds she received as gifts from her grandmother. Scott argued that Susan gifted Lucky to him. Rebutting the community property presumption requires the party claiming the item as separate property to trace ownership by clear and convincing evidence. Because neither could do so as to Lucky — because they commingled assets in a joint bank account before marriage — the appellate court refused to characterize him as the separate property of Scott or Susan, instead construing them as tenants-in-common as Lucky was clearly obtained prior to marriage. Though erring in finding Lucky to be Susan's separate property, such was harmless as the trial court had authority to equitably distribute community property to either party and, in addition, Scott could not possess Lucky in prison.

Bruce Rodriguez and Dana Rodriguez married in 1983, separated 11 years later, and filed for divorce a year after that. In 1992, Dana claimed that Bruce bought her a horse named Sublime as a Christmas gift. In fact, he also bought her Egoiste, since she was indecisive. Bruce later intended one horse to be an investment, decided by which horse she rode. Though both Sublime and Egoiste were registered in her name, Dana primarily rode and showed Egoiste. After separating, she sold Sublime for $267,500 and earned show winnings of $15,000. Finding substantial evidence that Sublime was community property, the appellate court also remarked that Bruce did not prepare any writing (as required by statute) that would transmute Sublime into Dana's separate property. Dana claimed that the statute did not impose a writing requirement in the case of intramarital gifts of articles of *insubstantial* value; evidently, Sublime's value was quite high. Yet were the court to find he lacked substantial value, that would only waive the writing requirement, not compel a conclusion that he gifted Sublime to her. *Rodriguez v. Rodriguez*, 2002 Cal. App. Unpub. LEXIS 7511 (Aug. 8, 2002).

In *Desanctis v. Pritchard*, 803 A.2d 230 (Pa. Super. Cit. 2002), Anthony Desanctis sued his former wife Lynda Pritchard for return of Barney, a dog adopted from the SPCA by Pritchard during marriage. A few months before they divorced, they signed an Agreement stating, "Barney is [Pritchard's] property and she will have full custody," but allowing Desanctis visitation. However, the Decree never incorporated or merged this Agreement. When Pritchard moved and discontinued visitation, Desanctis sued for court-mandated "shared custody." Losing at the trial level, he appealed. Affirming, the appellate court found the Agreement, relative to visitation with Barney, was "void to the extent . . . [it attempted] to award custodial visitation with or shared custody of personal property." Desanctis was, improperly, "seeking an arrangement analogous, in law, to a visitation schedule for a table or a lamp," a result "clearly not contemplated by the statute." Furthermore, the Agreement set forth that "Barney and his social schedule belong exclusively to Appellee."

In *Van Arsdale v. Van Arsdale*, 2013 WL 1365358 (Conn. Super.), pro se litigants filed for divorce. After a short trial, but without reasoning, the court awarded "joint legal custody of the Labrador retrievers but the Labrador retrievers' principal place of residence shall be with the plaintiff," each sharing reasonable costs of feeding, grooming, and veterinary care." In contrast, *Clark v. McGinnis*, 298 P.3d 1137 (Kan. Ct. App. 2013) refused to permit such an arrangement. Dixie McGinnis appealed judgment awarding her ex-husband Douglas Clark one of the three dogs acquired during marriage, named Dinky, claiming error in the trial court not applying child custody principles, or addressing her interest in not separating the dogs for their own health. She urged that "[a]s in child custody, divided custody rarely works and is often detrimental to each dog's health." Affirming, the appellate court found no abuse of discretion and dispensed with the analogy to child custody by stating, "One relevant difference between children and dogs is that children are human beings and dogs are domestic animals. Does not the great difference between children and dogs bar all comparison or inference?" By contrast, in *Aho v. Aho*, 2012 WL 5235982 (Mich. App. 2012), the appellate court found no abuse of discretion in the trial court awarding custody of Finn, one of the family dogs, to Tina Aho "in order to keep all of the animals together." Nor did it credit David's assertion that the trial court improperly applied the best-interest standard for David was the party invoking "custody-like terms" relative to Finn, and the trial court nonetheless acknowledged the dogs were chattel.

In *Wolf v. Taylor*, 224 Or. App. 245 (2008), Toni Wolf and Sharon Taylor reached a settlement agreement concerning the dissolution of their domestic partnership. A month later, however, Wolf rescinded and moved to reinstate the matter, claiming it was impossible to perform the agreement relative to visitation with the dog named Mike. First, Wolf argued that the visitation provision was unlawful for there is no "authority in this state or the entire country . . . for a trial court to grant 'custody' or 'visitation' to personal property." Second, Wolf claimed the agreement was "incompatible with principles of ownership" and "there is no reasonable or legal way for them to succeed in accomplishing" such private arrangement for visitation. The trial court denied the motion to reinstate, and the appellate court affirmed. While finding the illegality of a dog visitation agreement "an interesting question," the appellate court did not answer it except to say that illegality would not warrant rescission of the entire separation agreement (whether based on common law or the savings clause contained within the agreement). And because Wolf only sought rescission in its entirety, and not just that part of the agreement related to Mike, the trial court properly denied her motion.

In *Tevis-Bleich v. Bleich*, 939 P.2d 966 (Kan Ct. App. 1997), Roxane Tevis-Bleich and Michael Bleich reached an agreement to grant Michael visitation with the dog named Cartie. Later incorporated into the divorce decree, it explicitly precluded modification. Thereafter, Roxane moved post-trial to modify the decree and terminate his access due to her claim of

> serious dissension [sic], misunderstandings and arguments as a result of the continued and ongoing contact by the parties with each other in regard to visitation with the dog and by the continued insistence of the Respondent in his 'rights' to the dog.

Finding the motion insufficient to justify modification, the trial court dismissed the motion and awarded fees to Michael. In affirming, the appellate court found that Roxane failed to present adequate grounds to reopen the decree and that the trial court lacked jurisdiction due her specific agreement not to modify.

In *Kennedy v. Kennedy*, 256 A.D.2d 1048 (N.Y. Sup. Ct. App. Div. 1998), divorcing after 18 years of marriage, Kevin Kennedy contended that Ima Flashy Zipper, a horse, was a marital asset, while Barbara Kennedy claimed he was a gift to their daughter. Kevin's expert valued the horse at $12,500 and Barbara's at $5,500. As title to Ima Flashy Zipper remained in Barbara's name, and she acknowledged her continued use of the horse, the appellate court upheld the trial court's conclusion that he was equally owned marital property, entitling Kevin to half his value, found to be $5,500. A different result came in *Stufft v. Stufft*, 950 P.2d 1373 (Mont. 1997), also a dissolution action, where the trial court awarded the horse to David Stufft and vehicle to Mayla Stufft. Reversing, the Montana Supreme Court held that the distribution of the equine to David lacked substantial evidence, for none knew who actually owned the animal. If by their daughter, the horse could not be distributed as a marital asset. The court reversed and remanded for determination of value and redistribution.

T. BREACHY ANIMALS AND IMPOUNDMENT LAWS

Historically referred to as laws for distraint of livestock, modern-day private impoundment statutes apply when animals breach fences or rowdily trespass, causing damage to the landowner's structures, crops, or even other animals. To enjoy the privilege of retention and sale of the encroaching creatures requires strict compliance with statutory procedure.

For instance, in *Hadden v. Fisher*, 7 P.2d 488 (Okla. 1932), E.A. Hadden bred Aberdeen-Angus cattle. A Jersey bull belonging to his neighbor, K.E. Fisher, passed through a fence separating the parcels and entered Hadden's pasture with cows present. Hadden then distrained the bull and enclosed him in another county. Fisher sued to replevy the bull, and Hadden posted redelivery bond. In affirming judgment for Fisher, the Oklahoma Supreme Court found that the trial court lacked jurisdiction as Hadden failed to strictly comply with the conditions of the distraining statute, which required that he notify Fisher of the trespass, try to settle for damages claimed, and if no settlement were reached, to notify a disinterested justice of the peace, in writing, within 24 hours of the need to come to the premises and view the damages. Therefore, Hadden lost any right to hold the bull. The court quashed the redelivery bond and remarked that mere proof of damage by the wrongful trespass (without strict compliance with statute) "does not entitle the defendant to hold possession of the property of the plaintiff[.]"

In *Sheeder v. Moseby*, 74 Pa. Super. 161 (1919), Jesse Sheeder sued for return of his cow from Robert Moseby after she broke into his enclosed lands and gave birth after impoundment. Moseby asserted a lien for shelter, care, and feeding of mother and calf and distrained both until compensated for same and damage to his herbage. But having failed to strictly comply with the statutory obligation to give notice to Sheeder or file a description of the stray cow with the town clerk were Sheeder not readily located, the trial court entered judgment for Sheeder in the sum of $320. Affirming, the appellate court added that Sheeder's election to proceed via writ of replevin instead of under the Stray Act (upon which Moseby claimed a lien, but which stated that failure to give notice would result in forfeiture of all right and title to or recovery of any sum for the trespass and compelling the delivery of the stray to the true owner without any compensation) made no conceptual difference. As wisely stated, Sheeder could have recovered the cow and calf via replevin without depriving Moseby of his lien, if lawfully acquired and kept by giving proper notice, for Moseby could have simply "transferred [the lien] from the chattel to the bond which stood in lieu of it."

In *Nielsen v. Hyland*, 170 P. 778 (Utah 1918), despite knowing his bay horse had been deceased for more than a year, A. J. Nielsen sued F. Hyland and his son in claim and delivery for the no longer extant equine that not even legal fiction could resurrect. Defendants contended they had legal right to keep the trespassing horses pursuant to state stray law. However, failing to strictly comply with the 24-hour notice provision, they lost any right to distrain and were properly treated from the beginning as wrongdoers. At no time did Nielsen formally demand return of the individual horses prior to filing suit, but instead sought the "team." Treating this as a "technicality without merit," and recognizing that more specific demand would have been met with the same resistance, the court deemed the demand futile. While true that where the defendant does not have possession of the chattel at issue, replevin cannot lie, for a court cannot order defendant to return what he does not have, the Utah Supreme Court affirmed judgment for plaintiff for return of the one living horse and $1 for the deceased.

In *Howard v. Burke*, 157 N.W. 744 (Iowa 1916), Howard's pigs entered Burke's land and began damaging his crops. Burke distrained two of the trespassers. However, Howard procured an assignment of a chattel mortgage on the animals from his lessor and asserted that the chattel mortgage took priority over the trespassing lien. Losing at trial, Howard appealed. Affirming, the Iowa Supreme Court parsed the statute and found it gave the owner of the land "the right to distrain any such animal found doing damage, regardless of prior liens of record." Otherwise, no matter how much the crop damage dwarfed the chattel mortgage sum, the landowner and crop owner would have no recourse against livestock running at large. Such reading would improvidently permit animals to maraud through pastures with their owners' impunity. The court also rejected the constitutional argument that the statute impaired contractual obligations by finding that it did not disrupt any duties between mortgagor and mortgagee. "It simply provides that trespassing animals may be distrained, and the method for collecting damages. . . . If plaintiff was the owner of the animals, instead of simply a mortgagee, and they were trespassing upon defendant's premises and destroying the crops, the defendant would have a right under this statute to take the property itself."

U. DOMESTIC VIOLENCE PROTECTION ORDERS

According to Rebecca F. Wisch, as of 2013, 25 states (inclusive of District of Columbia and Puerto Rico) enacted legislation providing for companion animals in domestic violence protection orders. www.animallaw.info/articles/ ovusdomesticviolencelaws.htm. Upon a finding of domestic violence, courts in those jurisdictions purportedly have the authority to award exclusive custody of an animal to the petitioner irrespective of the traditional in-depth analysis afforded in a replevin action. In one recent case, the appellate court in one state collaterally attacked the effect of such a trial court order entered in another state.

In *Placey v. Placey*, 51 So. 3d 374 (Ala. Civ. App. 2010), Laurie Placey sought a protection-from-abuse ("PFA") order against her daughter Jill Placey, alleging that she threatened to kill her and her husband and engaged in acts of violence against her. Upon entry of a PFA order barring Jill from Laurie's home, where a dog named Preston also resided, Jill asked the court to order return of a snake, Preston, and quarter horse, among other items. In the interim, Jill's fiancé took Preston from Laurie by force and delivered him to Jill, causing the court to enter a formal order stating, "that [the mother and the father] have OWNERSHIP of Preston." On appeal, Jill contended that the trial court lacked authority to determine permanent disposition of personalty (i.e., Preston) or to declare Laurie as Preston's owner. The appellate court found that the trial court "acted within its discretion in entering an order definitively determining the ownership of Preston so as to protect the mother from the daughter's continued, yet prohibited, contact with the mother." While the PFA Act did not expressly contemplate determining possessory rights in property like dogs, because mother and daughter brought the issue of ownership of Preston and other personalty before it, the issue was "tried by the implied consent of the parties."

In *Herren v. Dishman*, 1 N.E.3d 697 (Ind. Ct. App. 2013), Defendant Dishman acquired Sofie, a dog, from his former girlfriend. He and Plaintiff Herren dated thereafter and cohabited intermittently. Their relationship lasted 20 months. He moved out and allegedly forcibly removed Sofie. A North Carolina court granted Herren a DV protection order when Dishman threatened to "slit [Sofie's] throat" and to "gut [Herren] and throw her in a canal," giving immediate custody and possession of Sofie to Herren. Though he had since moved to Indiana, police retrieved Sofie from his apartment and returned her to North Carolina. Dishman filed for return of Sofie and $1,000 in Indiana small claims court. The court rejected as irrelevant Herren's proffer of the "whole case file" from the North Carolina DV proceeding as evidence she had "legal custody of the dog." Herren argued that before their first break-up, occurring five months after they began dating, Dishman agreed she could keep Sofie, a claim he denied. The Indiana trial court issued an order of replevin favoring Dishman, and Herren appealed. The appellate court affirmed though finding (1) that the small claims court erred in excluding the DV file, regarding it relevant to the assessment of whether the protective order conferred possessory rights entitled to full faith and credit; (2) that it misinterpreted the order as only applying to animals residing in Herren's household at the time the DV petition was filed ("This court established long ago that a person may have the right to possess a chattel 'without having the ultimate legal title to the property.' "); and (3) concluding that even if Dishman were the legal owner, Herren might have a right to *possession* per the protective order. Though giving full faith and credit to the DV order, the appellate court upheld the finding of fact that Dishman never gave Sofie away to Herren, so she never became the owner. The "pivotal issue" was whether "because the Protective Order went into effect more than one month after Dishman and Sofie returned to Indiana, Sofie could *still* have been considered 'owned, possessed, kept or held as a pet by' Herren at that time." Answering in the negative — as Herren furnished no evidence that she had a right to custody of a dog no longer in her possession for over a month before entry of the Protective Order — the court upheld the replevin order.

Raynes v. Rogers, 955 A.2d 1135 (Vt. 2008), examines a dog custody dispute within the legal crucible of an emergency abuse-protection order proceeding. Mary Raynes sought and obtained an emergency abuse-prevention order, which she later successfully converted into a permanent order, against Earl Rogers. After being romantically involved for six years, the parties separated and Rogers left Raynes's home. Four months after separation, Rogers invited Raynes to his home for dinner and to visit the horse when they got into an argument. As Raynes was leaving, she picked up Rogers's dog and took the dog to her car. In order to retrieve his dog, Rogers kicked in the door to Raynes's car and used force against Raynes personally by allegedly chasing and grabbing her, and hitting her in the face with a closed fist. Rogers admitted to placing his elbow on her neck and prying her hands apart to release his dog. Following return of the dog, Rogers drove by Raynes's home for a number of days to ostensibly prove she was "fraudulently obtaining disability benefits." On appeal, Rogers argued that he justifiably abused the plaintiff by using only the amount of force necessary to prevent her from stealing his dog. Referring to defendant's argument as attempting to equate apples and oranges, the Supreme Court rejected Rogers's novel assertion that the common law defense of property doctrine be imputed to the abuse-prevention statute, thereby operating as a complete bar to injunctive relief where reasonable force is employed. Finding no abuse of discretion by the family court, particularly because the focus was not only on the force used to free his dog, but also the reasonable fear of future harm, the court affirmed entry of the permanent order. JUSTICE BURGESS filed an impassioned dissent, condemning Raynes for essentially admitting to converting Rogers's dog, and the majority for punishing Rogers for exercising reasonable force to obtain release of his dog. The dissent's opening paragraph follows:

> Just to be clear: the majority holds that when an ill-meaning relative, or past or present disgruntled lover, dating partner, roommate or housemate enters your home and, in front of you, grabs your property and runs off with it, or even destroys it, you may not lawfully resist. If you do, says the majority, you are liable to be branded an abuser by the court and subjected to a relief-from-abuse order. This flies in the face of common sense and the centuries old recognition of our right to defend property at common law.

This author encountered a similar issue involving the conflict between a domestic violence protection order and replevin in a matter in Washington following the 2009 amendment to RCW § 26.50.060. His client, petitioner-daughter, sought a DV protection order against respondent-mother, arising from the mother's attempt to take a dog back from her daughter. Representing herself, the daughter lost at the hearing. The commissioner, *sua sponte*, ordered her to deliver the dog back to her mother within 90 minutes or face contempt. The daughter complied, and then retained counsel, who sought revision of that ruling and obtained reversal on the basis that the commissioner had no authority to order the petitioner to deliver the dog to the respondent unless the respondent asserted domestic violence by the petitioner (she did not) and, further, unless the court found the daughter engaged in domestic violence (she did not). The judge did not address the other questions concerning the prudence and authority of the commissioner, in essence issuing a writ of replevin in a summary proceeding without due process.

Chapter 7

VETERINARY MALPRACTICE[1]

On every level, the way in which people relate to animal companions on a day-to-day basis — from spending billions per year on veterinary care, specialty products, animal-care services like doggie daycare, herding retreats, agility competitions, and postmortem animal-care services such as private cremation and pet cemeteries, to lobbying legislatively and commercially for increased animal-friendly access to off-leash parks, hotels, apartments, and places of public accommodation — similarly motivates demands for accountability from veterinarians. Board grievances and civil litigation are the primary tools of deterrence to achieve a modicum of justice through a finding of fault, compensation for as near the actual loss suffered, and license sanction.

A. VETERINARY MEDICAL ERRORS AND OMISSIONS; HISTORICAL OVERVIEW

Chris Green's article, *The Future of Veterinary Malpractice Liability in the Care of Companion Animals*, 10 ANIMAL L. 163, 172–74 (2004), charted the history of malpractice claims from the times of Hammurabi, with relevant excerpt below:

> Notwithstanding this economic impact of companion animals in American society, some critics still attempt to characterize veterinary malpractice litigation as simply the latest perversion of a modern tort system run amok. Quite to the contrary, however, codified statutes specifying both compensatory and punitive damages for veterinary negligence were included in some of humanity's earliest recorded laws and have existed on the books for over 3,800 years! As the Mesopotamian Code of Hammurabi from 1800 B.C. prescribed, "The animal surgeon who has performed a successful operation on a beast or an ass should be given six shekels as a fee. If, however, due to the operation, the animal dies, the surgeon must pay compensation for 1/4 of the animal's price to the owner."
>
> In ancient India, around 2,250 years ago, the edicts of King Asoka also addressed veterinary malpractice and compensation for negligence, mandating, "If a veterinarian was careless in providing treatment to a horse, or found to have used improper medicines, and the condition of the horse worsened, he could be fined double the cost of treatment."

---

[1] This chapter is derived in part and reprinted in part from Adam P. Karp, *Litigation Concerning Veterinary Medical Malpractice*, 123 AM.JUR. *Trials* 305 (2012), and used with permission of Thomson Reuters.

Along with such early statutory provisions, common law courts in England awarded damages in suits for negligent veterinary care as early as 1370, with two such actions predating that country's first documented *human* medical malpractice case. In parallel, American courts formally recognized the concept of veterinary negligence liability as far back as 1625, yet did not record their first human medical malpractice case until another 170 years later. Beyond merely compensating these animals' obvious economic utility value, U.S. state courts have been awarding punitive or emotional damages for animal harm since 1817, and American pet owners have been suing for emotional distress from the killing of family dogs since the mid-1800s.

Given that the legal theory of civil compensation for veterinary malpractice is as old as written law itself, and that courts have considered the emotional impact of pet loss for nearly 200 years, the first relevant issue to address is the state of such litigation today.

B. DISPARATE TREATMENT OF VETERINARIANS AND PHYSICIANS AND THEIR PATIENTS

While one presumes that veterinary board oversight and discipline alone will improve the quality of veterinary care and minimize adverse health events, or that civil litigation and the threat of a monetary judgment will operate as a "failsafe" when boards fail to meet their statutory mandates, certain legislative and judicial distinctions between veterinary and human care providers bear reflection. For instance, a state's adverse health event and incident reporting system (e.g., for Washington, RCW § 70.56.010 *et seq.*) may not apply to veterinarians or veterinary hospitals; a state's closed malpractice claim reporting system (e.g., RCW § 48.140.010) may not apply to veterinarians or will only apply to claims over $10,000, as in California; a state's health-care claims act (e.g., Wash. Rev. Code Ann. § 7.70 *et seq.*) may not apply to veterinarians.

A good example of drawing the line between humans and nonhumans is *Goodby v. Vetpharm, Inc.*, 186 Vt. 63 (2009). The Goodbys sued Vetpharm, Inc., manufacturer of the antibiotic amlodipine, and several veterinarians, for the death of their cats, raising claims of negligent infliction of emotional distress (NIED), loss of companionship and society, breach of implied warranty of merchantability, breach of express warranty of merchantability, breach of implied warranty of merchantability for a particular purpose, negligence and wantonness, breach of the Vermont Consumer Fraud Act, and breach of contract. Noting the inconsistency in allowing emotional distress damages for animal companions but not for nonrelatives like stepchildren, fiancés, or other close companions under the Wrongful Death Act, the court told the plaintiffs to present their "dramatic alteration to the law" to the general assembly. On the question of NIED, because the Goodbys were not targets of the allegedly negligent acts and not in physical danger themselves, the court held that no liability attached. Even assuming that the cats "qualified as 'someone' close to plaintiffs who faced physical peril by virtue of defendants' negligence" and that the Goodbys suffered emotional injury with physical manifestations, NIED did not lie because they were not within the "zone of danger" of acts imperiling their cats and they were not subject to "a reasonable fear of immediate personal injury." The court rejected the Goodbys' contention that they were within the "zone of danger" when they administered the fatal antibiotic to their cats because NIED case law focused on the plaintiff being within the zone "of an act negligently directed at him by defendant." Nor were the Goodbys able to allege reasonable fear for their own safety, another critical element of an NIED claim.

In *Phillips v. Baus*, 2007 Conn. Super. LEXIS 1555 (May 24, 2007), the plaintiff contended that the defendants, equine veterinarians, negligently administered a betamethasone compound into the coffin joint of a bay gelding show horse named Walter, in violation of the Federal Animal Medicinal Drug Use Clarification Act of 1994, causing him to lose all value as a show horse. The defendants moved for summary judgment on the plaintiff's fourth claim involving violation of the Connecticut Unfair Trade Practice Act (CUTPA). At issue was whether veterinary medical malpractice can constitute a statutory consumer-protection claim. Finding that the defendants' actions did not deal with the "entrepreneurial aspects" of practice, the court granted the defendants' motion. Of curiosity was the plaintiff's oral argument that the CUTPA claim should survive because the treatment was provided to a nonhuman, not a human being, arguing that a malpractice claim could not apply to chattel or personalty. As a matter of first impression, the court extended the CUTPA bar on legal and medical malpractice claims to veterinary claims based on the "sufficiently analogous" treatment of humans and nonhuman animals. Had the defendants produced or distributed betamethasone, a CUTPA claim might lie, but not under these facts, according to the court. An identical decision granting the defendants' motion for summary judgment dismissal of a CUTPA claim under similar facts involving a horse named Aspen was made in *Salko Farm & Stable, LLC v. Baus*, 2007 Conn. Super. LEXIS 1580 (May 24, 2007).

In *McMahon v. Craig*, 176 Cal. App. 4th 1502 (2009), as modified on denial of reh'g, (Aug. 31, 2009), Gail McMahon sued veterinarian Diane Craig; Veterinary Surgical Specialists, Inc.; and Advanced Veterinary Specialty Group, LLC for malpractice, negligent failure to inform, intentional misrepresentation, constructive fraud, conversion, NIED, and intentional infliction of emotional distress (IIED). After performing a surgery to correct laryngeal paralysis in a Maltese named Tootsie, the veterinarian instructed a technician to give her a mixture of water and baby food to test her ability to swallow. Tootsie developed aspiration pneumonia and, despite the veterinarian's promises to provide her the best care and close monitoring, died after being left without supportive care. Of first impression was whether to apply NIED to a dog. While California imposes a duty to avoid causing emotional distress in "bystander" and "direct victim" contexts, it does not extend to the veterinarian-client relationship. Because McMahon was absent from the scene of the injury-producing event, no "bystander" NIED liability existed. Nor did "direct victim" NIED exist because the malpractice directly harmed the nonhuman animal patient, not the human client. Distinguishing the plaintiff's analogy to obstetrics malpractice NIED cases (with negligent harm to the child during birth), the court concluded that "care of Tootsie would not directly impact McMahon's health," and "unlike a mother and child, a pet owners' emotional well-being is not traditionally 'inextricably intertwined' with the pet's physical well-being."

The "direct victim" NIED theory indicates a shift in tactics by the plaintiffs seeking general damages from negligent injury or death to an animal. Most jurisdictions considering the question of NIED in a case of animal injury or death adjudicate only the "bystander" variant. Though unspoken, and untested in *McMahon v. Craig*, one predicts that the court of appeals would have found that the nonhuman animal patient herself would have been capable of bringing a "direct victim" NIED claim — if she possessed standing, a topic separately covered in this book.

C. IMPLICATIONS OF PATIENTS AS PROPERTY

Unlike human medical malpractice claims, where doctors treat human patients possessing legal personhood, veterinarians treat nonhuman patients regarded by law as personalty. As property, tort and contract claims specific to loss, damage, and destruction of objects apply: those pertaining to humans do not. Except for parasitic claims raised by the property's owner, every action involving injury or death to an animal companion starts as a property-based action that may, if the facts and law align, extend to personal injury. Patients characterized as property owned by a client establish the tripartite veterinarian-client-patient relationship unseen in the human health care context, except where the patient requires the aid of a legal guardian to make informed health-care decisions due to incompetence or incapacity.

D. OVERVIEW OF VETERINARY CLAIMS

Claims against veterinarians for harm to animals fall into six general categories, with analogs to human medical malpractice cases — (1) conversion or lack of consent (analogize to medical battery), (2) negligent misrepresentation by omission (analogize to lack of informed consent), (3) professional negligence or lack of skill (analogize to standard malpractice), (4) breach of warranty/contract/bailment, (5) fraud (altering records with intent to defraud or deprive client of animal), and (6) unfair business practices. Where veterinarians harm animals intending to cause, or recklessly causing, severe emotional distress to the owner-guardian, the tort of outrage (also known as intentional infliction of emotional distress) may arise. Malicious harm may trigger a stand-alone claim. Statutory causes of action may also exist depending on the animal's species (e.g., livestock) and use (e.g., service animal).

Veterinarians may owe fiduciary duties to clients (such as fair dealing, honesty, loyalty, trust, confidentiality). Claims for breach of fiduciary duty may arise if harm or dispossession results from unauthorized disclosure to a third party, who injures or seizes the animal, as in the case of animal cruelty, violation of numeric limitations in zoning codes, breed bans, or custody disputes. For example, a veterinarian who haphazardly and wrongfully identifies a dog as American Pit Bull Terrier, then shares that information with animal control, in a jurisdiction making it illegal to possess such a breed, may cause the client's dog to be seized and euthanized. Alternatively, a false report of suspected animal cruelty by the veterinarian, based on imperfect information, may result in seizure and mishandling of the animal by law enforcement, and malicious prosecution. Such claims fall into the realm of dignitary torts such as defamation, tortious interference with business expectancy, and invasion of privacy (species of false light and intrusion upon seclusion). If the veterinarian is a state actor, then a civil rights claim under the Fourth and Fourteenth Amendments may lie.

Finally, veterinarians who withhold possession of the patient until the client pays the bill in full may face a lawsuit for a frivolous lien, conversion, or even a consumer protection act violation. The practitioner must consult with statutes, common law, and veterinary administrative codes to determine the viability of abandonment laws, as well as veterinary and chattel liens.

E.   TESTIMONIAL PRIVILEGES AND DUTIES OF CONFIDENTIALITY

Where veterinarians serve as parties or witnesses, the practitioner should determine whether affirmative duties of confidentiality or reporting,[2] testimonial privileges, and immunities exist. The duty of confidentiality is found in the veterinary practice acts of Pennsylvania, Nebraska, Kentucky, Missouri, Georgia, Kansas,[3] Texas, and Illinois, as well as administrative regulations of several other states, all of which impose a duty not to reveal confidential information pertaining to a patient unless, in some cases, necessary to protect public health or the patient's welfare. Such a duty protects patient and client privacy, much like the HIPAA rules applicable to human patients. Despite imposing this duty, however, some jurisdictions carve out an exception that mandates breach of confidentiality to prevent commission of a crime.[4] In July 2000, the American Association of Veterinary State Board's Preliminary Draft of a Model Act for Veterinary Medicine, in section 601 regarding Privileged Communications and Exceptions, proposed to define a veterinarian-client privilege.[5]

---

[2] The following states have passed confidentiality laws with causes of action for breach: California (Cal. Bus. & Prof. Code § 4857); Florida (Fla. Stat. Ann. § 474.2165); Georgia (Ga. Code. Ann. § 24-9-29); Illinois (225 Ill. Comp. Stat. Ann. § 115/25.17); Missouri (Mo. Ann. Stat. § 340.286); Texas (Tex. Occ. Code Ann. § 801.353). Other states while not having a veterinarian-client privilege statute have adopted regulations imposing a duty of confidentiality on veterinarians. E.g., Alabama (Ala. Admin. Code Rule 930-X-1-.10(15)); Alaska (Alaska Admin. Code tit. 12, §§ 68.100, 68.910(d)); Idaho (Idaho Admin. Code § 46.01.01.152); Kentucky (201 Ky. Admin. Regs. 16:010); Massachusetts (Mass. Regs. Code tit. 256, § 7.01); Minnesota (Minn. R. 9100.0800); New Mexico (N.M. Admin. Code tit. 16, § 16.25.3); New York (N.Y. Comp. Codes R. & Regs. tit. 8, § 29.1(b)(8)); Louisiana (La. Admin. Code Title 46, §§ 1041(A), 712(C)).

[3] The Kansas Client Privilege statute keeps all records confidential unless the disclosure fits within five limited exceptions: (1) reporting cruel/inhuman treatment; (2) information needed for emergency care; (3) disclosing vaccination status for public health; (4) the client places the veterinarian's treatment or nature and extent of animal's injuries at issue; and (5) related to any board investigation or discipline. Kan. Stat. Ann. § 47-839.

[4] See , e.g., Or. Rev. Stat. §§ 686.445 to 686.455. While not mandatory, permissive reporting statutes that confer immunity from suit do exist. In 2013, Washington passed RCW § 16.52.330, providing that a veterinarian who reports suspected animal cruelty in good faith and the normal course of business faces no civil or criminal liability provided she receives no financial benefit from the incident beyond charging for services rendered prior to making the initial report.

[5] Special thanks to Greg M. Dennis, J.D., for his extensive research into the subject matter of this section. Mr. Dennis is working with the Kansas Veterinary Medical Association to iron out details in

F. CONVERSION, LACK OF CONSENT, AND MEDICAL BATTERY

When a veterinarian performs a procedure, operation, or manipulation, uses an apparatus, administers a drug, medicine, or treatment, collects a specimen, or euthanizes an animal without lawful authorization or consent of the owner or owner's agent — and such performance, use, administration, treatment, or collection causes harm — a veterinary medical battery occurs. If styled as a battery, however, such cause of action against a veterinarian will fail for failure to state a claim unless, perhaps, the patient is a *service animal* tantamount to a physical extension of the disabled handler. In the absence of consent, a physician commits battery. *See, e.g., Physicians' and Dentists' Business Bureau v. Dray*, 8 Wn. 2d 38 (1941). At this time, the common law legally classifies nonhuman patients as property. Thus, it follows that when a veterinarian operates without consent, she has committed conversion or trespass to chattels. If the conversion is willful (as opposed to innocent), emotional damages may follow.

The Illinois courts examined the tort of conversion in *Loman v. Freeman*, 890 N.E.2d 446 (Ill. 2008). The defendant veterinarian performed an allegedly unauthorized right stifle surgery on the plaintiffs' racehorse, causing permanent incapacitation. The Illinois Court of Appeals reversed dismissal of the conversion claim, noting that materially altering the physical condition of chattel so as to change its identity or character states a claim and that "permanent deprivation" of possession is not a necessary condition to sustain conversion. The Illinois Supreme Court affirmed.

Also consider *Fredeen v. Stride*, 525 P.2d 166 (Or. 1974), a case of conversion by a veterinarian of a German Shepherd dog the client authorized euthanasia rather than pay for treatment, and the veterinarian assured client this would occur when, in fact, the dog had been given away to another person. The plaintiff claimed mental anguish because her children might see the dog with the other person and because she feared the dog would be injured by any attempt to return to her home, as she lived in the same neighborhood as the new owners. The court held mental distress was an element of damages the direct and natural result of the conversion. The court further commented that the act need not be "inspired by fraud or malice" for mental suffering to be recoverable "where evidence of genuine emotional damage is supplied by aggravated conduct on the part of the defendant." In addition to awarding general damages for mental anguish, the court awarded punitive damages for the veterinarian's course of conduct in giving the dog to another person without the plaintiff's consent, calling the veterinarian's conduct a "sufficiently aggravated violation of societal interests to justify the sanction of punitive damages as a preventative measure."

Though not a veterinary malpractice case, *LaPlace v. Briere*, 962 A.2d 1139 ((N.J. Super. Ct. 2009), evaluated a conversion claim involving a quarter horse boarded at

---

Kansas's SB 148, attempting to refine the Kansas Client Privilege statute. *See* Skernvitz, *Kan. veterinarian-client confidentiality bill stalls* (May 1, 2011), http://veterinarynews.dvm360.com/dvm/Veterinary+news/Kan-veterinarian-client-confidentiality-bill-stall/ArticleStandard/Article/detail/717872?contextCategoryId=45468.

the defendant's stable. While at an out-of-state horse show, a fellow boarding stable customer took the plaintiff's horse out for exercising, allegedly without authorization, and the horse suddenly reared, collapsed, and died. Without timely authorization of a necropsy, no cause of death could be determined. The plaintiff sued the stable and the horse handler under theories of breach of the bailment agreement, breach of contract, conversion, and negligence. As to conversion, the court held that exercising a boarded horse did not meet the essential element of the claim because the handler, who was not an employee of defendant, failed to exert sufficient control and dominion over the horse so as to interfere with the plaintiff's ownership rights. Further, the court found no evidence linking the horse's death to her alleged mishandling.

Hypothetical: Conversion may also arise where consent, previously given, is withdrawn. Hypothetically, consider an adult female who signs a euthanasia consent form for her cat at a veterinary clinic that she and the cat had seen for years. Due to scheduling, euthanasia could not be performed that day. Instead, they calendared a home euthanasia for the next evening. A veterinarian and technician arrive at plaintiff's residence the next night at about 5:30 p.m. At about 5:35 p.m., in her presence, the veterinarian administers a sedative to the cat. The plaintiff inquires if it (the drug) were harmful and whether she could still change her mind about euthanasia. The veterinarian responds that the sedative was neither lethal nor harmful and that the cat would merely "go to sleep." As he administered the injection, however, the cat leapt into the air and off the bed to the ground, exiting the bedroom. He appeared to be in pain. The veterinarian tells the plaintiff that the technician will follow the cat around and make sure he does not injure himself, and return him to bedroom.

At this point, the vet tells the plaintiff to leave the bedroom (to get "fresh air and breathe"), noting it would be easier on the cat if she were absent. He surmised that the cat was too familiar with her and her presence would upset him. Plaintiff honored his request and left the room for about five minutes. When she re-entered the bedroom (shortly after 5:40 p.m.), she turned off the overhead light and turned on a small dim light on the dresser. The veterinarian then "directed" the plaintiff with his hands on her arms to kneel and assume the technician's "former" position. He placed her arms on either side of the cat — her left bicep passively cradling the cat's head while her right bicep passively cradled the cat's rear. The catheter was in the cat's left forearm. Plaintiff was crying. The veterinarian then asked if she were "ready." Plaintiff responded, "Have you given the lethal injection yet?" He replied, "No." Without hesitation, and plenty of time before he administered the euthasol, she yelled, "Don't! I have changed my mind!" The vet nonetheless persisted, "I want to take your cat and finish the procedure elsewhere." Plaintiff retorted, "No, you can't!"

The plaintiff stood and said, "I don't know what's wrong with me. I don't know why I am having such a hard time." She then explained that she had a late-term abortion and was reliving the trauma. Emotions welled, causing her to double over in grief. She felt her uterus move. But the vet did not relent. Instead of honoring her unambiguous command to stop the procedure, he urged her to let him euthanize. As a persuasive measure, he hinted that the cat was terminal (although no diagnostic test definitively stated this) and asked her to think about whether she wanted to put him through the stress of repeat sedation and fear. In her highly compromised state, she crumpled. Then, as if it were his decision to make, the vet addressed the cat directly, saying, "I have decided that it is time for you to go." Plaintiff admonished him, "Please do not say such things." The vet clammed up at that point and said nothing further until he left.

Did the veterinarian have lawful consent, revived upon withdrawal by the client? Did the vet and technician commit medical battery, of the most irreversible and injurious kind? The veterinarian may claim that the plaintiff had given written consent for euthanasia, but this does not permit him to disregard her revocation of that consent, as clearly communicated before the injection of euthasol. *See Pugsley v. Privette*, 263 S.E.2d 69 (Va. 1980) (consent for Dr. Pugsley to perform laparotomy deemed withdrawn though patient signed written consent, when, the next morning, while on the operating table, Mrs. Privette said, "I do not want to be put to sleep until [Dr. Hall] gets here," only to at that moment "fe[el] the sodium pentothal hit my vein, and I remember nothing else.") The veterinarian may also persuasively argue that the plaintiff relented upon further discussion and assented to the euthanasia after all. But was there undue influence?

Undue influence is treated in law as a species of fraud. *McCutcheon v. Brownfield*, 467 P.2d 868, 874 (Wash. Ct. App. 1970). "Undue influence involves unfair persuasion that seriously impairs the free and competent exercise of judgment." *Kitsap Bank v. Denley*, 312 P.3d 711, 717 (Wash. Ct. App. 2013) (cit.om.). Not only did the veterinarian arguably have a fiduciary relationship with the plaintiff (a significant factor giving rise to a rebuttable presumption of undue influence), but he tried to overcome her unambiguous order to halt euthanasia without regard for her then highly agitated mental state, the special nature of the relationship between her and her cat, and the extremely emotionally valenced nature of the event itself, not to mention the location where the event took place (i.e., her home, not in a sterile clinic with strange animals and people). *Id.*, at 717.

Should it have been fairly evident to the veterinarian that the plaintiff was temporarily incapacitated from then reviving lawful consent? Consider the legal impact had the veterinarian in this hypothetical charted that she "screamed and requested we stop." Would a reasonably prudent veterinarian have concluded that "consent" to euthanize was at best indeterminate, contradictory, nonfinal, and thus *not authorized*? Though no case law is on point in the veterinary context, revocation of consent to relinquish a child for adoption may provide a suitable analogy. *See* RCW § 26.33.190.160 (permitting revocation within 48 hours after birth of child or consent signed); RCW § 26.33.160(3) (permitted within one year after consent to adopt has been court-approved except for fraud, duress by person, department, or agency requesting consent, or lack of mental competency on part of person giving consent at time consent given).

Furthermore, the procedure had not yet commenced (as in the middle of inflating a blood pressure cuff or pulling blood). Even had that been the case, courts have generally accepted the view that a patient can bring an action for medical battery if the patient revokes consent during a procedure when directing the physician to stop in language that is unambiguous, so long as medically feasible to desist without any harm to the patient. *See Pallacovitch v. Waterbury Hosp.*, 2012 Conn. Super.

LEXIS 1962 (Aug. 13, 2012) (citing several authorities); *see also Coulter v. Thomas*, 33 S.W.3d 522, 524 (Ky. 2000).

G.   NEGLIGENT MISREPRESENTATION BY OMISSION, LACK OF INFORMED CONSENT

At common law, the doctrine of informed consent developed as part of the intentional tort of battery. If the patient consented to bodily touching, no action for battery could lie. To prevent doctors from bypassing tort responsibility by strong-arming unknowledgeable patients into assenting to treatment, the courts required consent to be "informed." *See Keogan v. Holy Family Hosp.*, 622 P.2d 1246 (Wash. 1980). Much like the driver leaving his car at the mechanic for an expensive and experimental repair of the transmission, the dog's owner-guardian, before spending many times over the purchase price of the animal for a procedure that could conceivably kill the dog, has a right to know all material facts pertaining to his treatment options. "Meaningful choice is at the heart of the informed consent doctrine." *Schiff v. Prados*, 92 Cal. App. 4th 692, 706 (2001).

The burden of proving lack of informed consent rests with the plaintiff — at least initially. While it is the patient's province to evaluate all treatment risks, the function of the health care provider is to furnish the patient only with risks of a serious nature, high risks, grave risks, medically significant risks, or reasonably foreseeable risks. A material risk is sometimes bounded at the lower end as seen in *Mason v. Ellsworth*, 474 P.2d 909 (Wash. Ct. App. 1970) (finding 0.75% risk of perforation of esophagus not "material"); *Ruffer v. St. Frances Cabrini Hosp. of Seattle*, 784 P.2d 1288 (Wash. Ct. App. 1990) (0.002-0.005% risk not material); *Luke v. Family Care & Urgent Medical Clinics*, 2007 U.S. App. LEXIS 20410, at *3 (9th Cir. Aug. 7, 2007) (1 in 25,000 "idiosyncratic" reaction to drug immaterial).

As explained in *Ruffer*, at 230, materiality involves a two-step test. The plaintiff must first determine the "scientific nature of the risk and the likelihood of its occurrence." In ascertaining the quality and probability of the risk, expert testimony is required. Such include "[t]he recognized serious possible risks, complications, and anticipated benefits involved in the treatment administered and in the recognized possible alternative forms of treatment, including nontreatment." Next, the plaintiff must demonstrate that such a risk is one that a reasonable patient would consider in deciding on treatment. This second step does *not* require expert testimony, which is of "secondary importance" in considerations of patient sovereignty.

A lack of informed consent claim in the veterinary context presents a matter of first impression in many jurisdictions. Some courts have recognized this claim. *See Lawrence v. Big Creek Vet Hosp., LLC*, 2007 Ohio App. LEXIS 4169, P10 (Sept. 7, 2007) (citable per Ohio Supreme Court Rules for Reporting of Opinions, Rule 3.4) ("The informed consent doctrine is not codified in Ohio. However, such practice is clearly indicative of the veterinarian's duty of care. This is an evidentiary issue that goes directly to the standard of care in a malpractice case. . . . Informed consent is part of and necessary to a veterinarian's duty of care."). Though *Lawrence* held that the cognizability of such a claim was not presently before the court, it nevertheless found that the trial court improperly granted a motion in limine to bar plaintiff's expert from testifying about lack of informed consent. *See Henry v. Zurich Amer. Ins. Co.*, 107 So. 3d 874, 882 (La. Ct. App. 2013) (applying lack of informed consent doctrine to veterinary malpractice case); *Loman v. Freeman*, 874 N.E.2d 542, 547–548 (Ill. App. Ct. 2006) (discussing veterinary duties of care, including obtaining consent, and citing law review article stating that "Effective client communication includes securing informed consent from the client before performing a procedure"); *Ullmann v. Duffus*, 2005 Ohio App. LEXIS 5463 (Nov. 15, 2005) (insinuating that material risks must be conveyed by veterinarian herself); *Ladnier v. Norwood*, 781 F.2d 490 (5th Cir. 1986) (no lack of informed consent by failure to warn racehorse's trainer of possible fatal reaction to administering vitamin E to treat anhydrosis where equine specialists unequivocally do not consider the risk (1:25,000) substantial enough to disclose); *Emes Stable v. University of Pennsylvania*, 1988 U.S. Dist. LEXIS 2972 (E.D. Pa. Apr. 4, 1988) (finding that veterinarian properly advised owners, in advance of operation, of procedure, risks, and alternatives); *Gonzalez v. S. Tex. Veterinary Assoc., Inc.*, 2013 Tex. App. LEXIS 15215 (Tex. App.—Corpus Christi-Edinburg Dec. 19, 2013) (citable under TRAP 47.7(b)) (memorandum opinion recognizing that informed consent as it relates to vaccination of small animals, due to risk of vaccine-associated sarcoma, was a type of malpractice).

H. VETERINARY LACK OF SKILL

Veterinarians must employ reasonable skill, diligence, and attention as ordinarily expected of careful, skillful, and reputable persons engaged in veterinary medicine. *Price v. Brown*, 680 A.2d 1149 (Pa. 1996). Accordingly, they owe a heightened standard of care to the patient and client. *Carter v. Louisiana State Univ.*, 520 So. 2d 383, 388 (La. 1988). Courts tend to treat veterinary negligence actions like any other professional negligence action. *See Fackler v. Genetzky*, 595 N.W.2d 884 (Neb. 1999) (malpractice standards apply to veterinarians); *Staples v. Steed*, 52 So. 646 (Ala. 1910); *Levine v. Knowles*, 197 So. 2d 329 (Fla. Dist. Ct. App. 1967); *McNew v. Decatur Veterinary Hosp.*, 68 S.E.2d 221 (Ga. Ct. App. 1951); *Folsom v. Barnett*, 306 S.W.2d 832 (Ky. Ct. App. 1957); *Dyess v. Caraway*, 190 So. 2d 666 (La. Ct. App. 1966); *Boom v. Reed*, 23 N.Y.S. 421 (1893); *Turner v. Sinha*, 582 N.E.2d 1018 (Ohio Ct. App. 1989); *Kerbow v. Bell*, 259 P.2d 317 (Okla. 1953); *Bartlett v. MacRae*, 635 P.2d 666 (Or. Ct. App. 1981); *Erickson v. Webber*, 237 N.W. 558 (S.D. 1931); *Baechler v. Beaunaux*, 272 P.3d 277 (Wash. Ct. App. 2012). For all intents and purposes, the law of the 21st century places veterinarians in the same company as their human health-care counterparts. *Mazon v. Krafchick*, 144 P.3d 1168 (Wash. 2006) (noting "familiar standard of care for professionals," quoting RESTATEMENT (2D) OF TORTS § 299A).

In *Price v. Brown*, 545 Pa. 216 (1996), the plaintiff claimed breach of bailment following a prolapsed urethra surgery on her English Bulldog occasioned by failure to monitor the dog's condition and failure to return the dog in good health, but Price did not allege professional negligence. The trial court dismissed the case without prejudice for failing to state a claim. The superior court reversed, finding that the existence of breach of bailment agreement was an issue of fact. The Pennsylvania Supreme Court reversed, swapping the breach of bailment cause of action for professional negligence as to the veterinary procedures performed on the dog. In doing so, it held that professional negligence concepts extend to veterinary medicine. The court articulated the elements of such a cause of action as:

1. The plaintiff employed veterinarian or created another basis for duty of care;

2. Veterinarian failed to exercise appropriate standard of care;

3. Veterinarian's departure from standard was proximate cause of animal's injury or death;

4. The plaintiff must specifically allege that the veterinarian was negligent in performing professional services.

Similar to legal or medical practice, the court in *Price* stated that the profession of veterinary medicine "involves specialized education, knowledge, and skills." The court also recognized substantial regulation by the Department of Health as a reason to so analogize. The court added that the plaintiff may claim breach of bailment agreement where the animal is delivered for a "particular purpose of surgical procedure" if negligence is also pled and proved. Because the plaintiff did not plead negligence, however, the court held that the trial court properly dismissed that claim. The rationale for this holding follows, at page 224:

> We agree with the trial court that the purpose for which an animal is entrusted to the care of a veterinarian is a material fact that must be considered in determining whether a plaintiff's complaint states a cause of action as a matter of law, and that Price's complaint failed to state a cause of action for professional negligence. The allegations relating to the professional services rendered by Dr. Brown cannot be deliberately excised from the complaint as if the veterinarian's services were no different than those offered by a kennel operator or dog groomer. There are significant differences between surgical services provided by a veterinarian and grooming or caretaking services.

In *Hoffa v. Bimes*, 954 A.2d 1241 (Pa. Super. Ct. 2008), *appeal denied*, 967 A.2d 960 (Pa. 2009), the court held similarly, dismissing all claims against equine veterinarians per the Good Samaritan provisions of Pennsylvania's Veterinary Immunity Act. It dismissed the bailment and trespass claims as a matter of law, invoking *Price*, and describing them as nonviable absent a claim of negligence. In *Hoffa*, employees of a training facility caring for the plaintiff's horse presented the horse in emergent condition to the defendant veterinarians. Attempts to reach the plaintiff were unsuccessful. The plaintiff sued the veterinarians for death of the horse, allegedly resulting from a negligently performed abdominal tap, bringing claims of lack of informed consent, bailment, and trespass to chattel. The trial court granted the defendants' motion for compulsory nonsuit on all claims per the Veterinary Immunity Act, which immunized from civil damages all veterinarians who, in good faith, rendered "emergency care" to an animal discovered "at the scene of an accident or emergency situation" or whose condition had "immediately prior to the rendering of such care been brought to such individual's attention at or from the scene of any accident or emergency situation." Finding that the circumstances surrounding care of this horse triggered the Act, the appellate concluded that consent was not required before the veterinarians treated the horse.

In *Mazella v. Fairfield Equine Assoc., P.C.*, 2005 WL 2452908 (S.D.N.Y. 2005), the plaintiff alleged veterinary malpractice by misdiagnosis of equine protozoal myeloencephalitis (EPM) and failure to warn of the dangers of riding a horse suffering from that condition. The plaintiff cared for an Oldenburg gelding, intended for use in hunter-jumper training and later for sale at a profit. When the owner noticed the horse's lack of coordination and lethargy, he brought the horse to the veterinarian for examination and treatment. No diagnosis was given at that time. The veterinarian, however, recommended use of a magnetic blanket and informed the owner that the horse could still be ridden, but could not compete. The day after the third visit to the veterinarian, who still had not offered a diagnosis, the plaintiff suffered severe, permanent brain injury when the horse collapsed beneath him. Supported by expert testimony, the plaintiff sued the veterinarian for misdiagnosis of EPM. The defendants moved for summary judgment. The federal district court denied the motion due to a factual question as to whether the horse had EPM. Notably, the court stated that veterinary and human medical malpractice standards of care are largely indistinguishable. Animal health-care providers owe owner-guardians that degree of skill and learning commonly associated with the prudent member of the veterinary profession, the court explained.

The next relevant question pertains to geographical variations in the standard of care. Historically, medical professionals enjoyed the protection of the locality rule, holding them to the standard of similarly situated professionals in the same city or town. However, some states have abolished this hometown preference. For instance, *Pederson v. Dumouchel*, 431 P.2d 973 (Wash. 1967), held that physicians were subject to the standard of care in an "area co-extensive" with, or in the "community" of, the physician. *See also* James Duff, Jr., *Malpractice Testimony: Competency of Physician or Surgeon from One Locality to Testify, in Malpractice Case, as to Standard of Care Required of Defendant Practicing in Another Locality*, 37 A.L.R.3D 420. In refusing to impose a statewide geographic restriction, the court explained, at 978:

> The "locality rule" has no present-day vitality except that it may be considered as one of the elements to determine the degree of care and skill which is to be expected of the average practitioner of the class to which he belongs. The degree of care which must be observed is, of course, that of an average, competent practitioner acting in the same or similar circumstances. In other words, local practice within geographic proximity is one, but not the only factor to be considered. No longer is it proper to limit the definition of the standard of care which a medical doctor or dentist must meet solely to the practice or custom of a particular locality, a similar locality, or a geographic area.

See also Stone v. Sisters of Charity of House of Providence, 469 P.2d 229, 232 (Wash. Ct. App. 1970) ("The national minimum standard is one established 'in an area coextensive with the medical and professional means available in those centers that are readily accessible for appropriate treatment of the patient.'") Examples of standard of care violations include:

- Misdiagnosis

- Lack of informed consent
- Failure of skill in surgical procedure
- Incorrect kind or amount of medication
- Violation of commonly accepted protocols
- Inadequate supervision ("captain of ship")
- Dereliction of duty (patient abandonment)
- Failure to provide preventative care
- Inadequate record-keeping propagating error
- Leaving foreign object in body

I. CONSUMER PROTECTION VIOLATIONS AND FRAUD

While a client may sue a veterinarian for malpractice related to lack of professional skill, grounds may also state a claim for shady entrepreneurial practices (i.e., unfair or deceptive advertising, marketing, prescribing, treating) like charging for unauthorized surgeries, obtaining sham (because uninformed) consent for a costly procedure, or advertising 24-hour care by an "on-site" veterinarian when the veterinarian is, in fact, only "on-call." *See Wright v. Jeckle*, 16 P.3d 1268 (Wash. Ct. App. 2001) (permitting consumer protection claim against medical doctor for lack of informed consent where health-care activities motivated solely by financial gain).

In *Prince v. Veterinary Specialty Emergency Center of Kansas City, Inc.*, 195 P.3d 291 (Kan. Ct. App. 2008, unpub.), the plaintiff asserted a violation of the Kansas Consumer Protection Act (KCPA), as well as professional negligence and breach of fiduciary duty, when the defendant veterinarian allegedly failed to timely and competently diagnose and treat gastric dilatation and volvulus (GDV), resulting in the death of Bear, a 10-year-old Rottweiler. The KCPA claim was dismissed before trial. The jury returned a no-fault verdict on the remaining claims. On appeal, Prince was held not to be an "aggrieved consumer" for purposes of the KCPA in part because she could not prove a causal link between the alleged misrepresentations (i.e., having an affiliation with the Missouri College of Veterinary Medicine; having affiliations with other veterinarians; exaggerating the size of its facility; and falsely claiming that it had access to a 24-hour pathology lab) and Bear's death.

J. BREACH OF BAILMENT; *RES IPSA LOQUITUR*

When a bailed item (i.e., an animal) is lost, destroyed, or compromised while in the bailee's possession (e.g., veterinarian, boarding facility, groomer, walker, sitter), the bailor (i.e., animal owner) makes a *prima facie* case and enjoys a presumption of negligence. *See, e.g., Chaloupka v. Cyr*, 387 P.2d 740 (Wash. 1963). Where the bailee "can show that he has exercised due care or can show the loss was caused by burglary, larceny, fire, or other causes which of themselves do not point to negligence on the part of the bailee, he can rebut the presumption." *Id.*, at 742.

Contrast this to human medical malpractice litigation, where the patient[6] modernly[7] holds the status of a legal person and not property, and no bailment exists. For this reason, plaintiffs often plead both professional negligence (sounding in tort) and breach of bailment (sounding in contract) in a veterinary malpractice action.

Res ipsa loquitur is akin to the presumption of negligence offered in a bailment action. This rule of evidence permits an inference of negligence, shifting to the defendant the duty to come forward with an exculpatory explanation by which to rebut or overcome the inference. "The inference which the doctrine permits is grounded upon the fact that the chief evidence of the true cause, whether culpable or innocent, is practically accessible to the defendant but inaccessible to the injured person." *Covey v. Western Tank Lines*, 218 P.2d 322, 327 (Wash. 1950). The doctrine is inapplicable where "there is direct evidence as to the precise cause of the injury and all the attending facts and circumstances appear." *Id.*

The test for *res ipsa loquitur* traditionally turns on the following factors:

1. The accident or occurrence producing the injury is of a kind that ordinarily does not happen in the absence of someone's negligence;

2. The injuries are caused by an agency or instrumentality within the exclusive control of the defendant; and

3. The injury-causing accident or occurrence is not due to any voluntary action or contribution on the part of the plaintiff.

Zukowsky v. Brown, 79 Wn.2d 586, 593 (1971).

As noted in the following cases, however, *res ipsa loquitur* has frequently been rejected where the negligence claim turns on the application of esoteric knowledge or specialized training. In *Pette v. Burton*, 2005 Cal. App. Unpub. LEXIS 10980 (Nov. 29, 2005) (unpub.), a 10-year-old Yorkie named Monte was brought in for exam and vaccinations. Dr. Burton recommended tooth cleaning, to which the plaintiff consented. Bailey, an unlicensed veterinary assistant, anesthetized Monte. Another unlicensed assistant, Durham, cleaned. Monte survived, but collapsed hours later and died *en route* to the emergency room. Necropsy suggested collapsed trachea or alveolitis. The plaintiff's expert, Dr. Emswiller, stated that aspiration was the probable cause of death with aspiration pneumonia and anaphylaxis as alternative explanations, adding it was unusual for this to occur. The trial court rejected a *res ipsa loquitur* instruction and directed a defense verdict. On appeal, the court held that *res ipsa loquirtur* applies only if the rarity of occurrence can be linked to evidence that the outcome occurs more likely than not due to negligence. Paucity alone will not suffice without corroborating evidence indicating negligence. Inadequate record-keeping and monitoring and use of unlicensed veterinary technicians in and of itself did not illuminate cause of death. The court noted that Dr. Emswiller also failed to causally link the lack of licensing to Monte's death. *See also Downing v. Gully*, 915 S.W.2d 181 (Tex. App. 1996) (*res ipsa loquitur* does not apply in

---

[6] A bailment would arise, however, where a patient's durable medical equipment needs adjustment and is delivered to the custody of fabricator or repairer of such items. A denturist is also a bailee.

[7] Legal research might disturbingly unveil bailment disputes between slaveowners and physicians who maim or kill slaves during surgery or treatment.

negligence action against veterinarians for neuter operation resulting in death of dog since administration of anesthetic and surgical technique are no in common knowledge of laypeople); *Hight v. Dublin Veterinary Clinic*, 22 S.W.3d 614 (Tex. App. 2000) (accord); *Losier v. Ravi*, 362 S.W.3d 639 (Tex. App. 2009) (accord, in medical malpractice context); *Milke v. Ratcliff Animal Hosp., Inc. ex rel. Ratcliff*, 120 So. 3d 343 (La. Ct. App. 2013) (*res ipsa loquitur* does not apply as neuter death not type of injury that ordinarily occurs in absence of negligence; and that 99.95% of healthy dogs recover from surgery does not alone imply 0.05% mortality by negligence)

K.   STATUTORY ABROGATION OF COMMON LAW

Any practitioner handling a veterinary malpractice case should first determine whether the state's medical claims statute applies. For instance, in 1976, Washington drastically altered the common law for actions against health-care providers by changing the statute of limitations and providing an exclusive statutory mechanism for actions involving lack of informed consent, breach of promise, and standard of care violations, including other procedural impediments such as a letter of intent to sue and mandatory mediation. Ch. 7.70 RCW Whether this chapter applies to veterinarians was resolved in the negative in the landmark case of *Sherman v. Kissinger*, 195 P.3d 539 (Wash. App. 2008).

In *de Mercado v. Superior Court*, 148 Cal. App. 4th 711 (2007), plaintiffs sued a veterinarian for fraud, negligent misrepresentation, and suppression of fact with respect to a horse he passed off as suitable for jumping. The defendant asserted that the statute of limitations had run prior to their filing suit, citing the Medical Injury Compensation Reform Act's (MICRA) one-year statute of limitations. He also challenged the plaintiffs' inclusion of a request for punitive damages in the complaint without having first obtained a court order, pursuant to the MICRA. On appeal, the court found that MICRA applied to acts involving nonhuman health-care providers because the statutory definition broadly encompassed those licensed under a specific chapter of the business and professions code, in which veterinarians were listed. However, the court did not go further to hold that the MICRA punitive damage provisions applied in this case of "professional negligence" as plaintiffs made no claim for personal injury or wrongful death: instead, they prayed for the purchase price of the horse and related costs. As to the statute of limitations, the court held that MICRA did not apply in this instance as plaintiffs did not claim personal injury resulting from professional negligence. *See also Scharer v. San Luis Rey Equine Hosp., Inc.*, 204 Cal. App. 4th 421 (2012) (plaintiffs could not rely on MICRA's letter of intent to sue provisions to toll the statute of limitations in a veterinary medical malpractice case involving only property damage).

L.   SUBSTANTIAL FACTOR TEST

Occasionally, either one of two or more causes may produce the identical harm, imposing an impossible burden on the plaintiff to prove "but for" causation. For instance, a series of errors and omissions by more than one veterinarian (or more than one clinic) may cumulatively result in animal injury or death. At other times, similar but not quite identical results will follow with one, but without the other, defendant's act. In such case where one defendant makes an undeniably insignificant contribution to an outcome, like tossing a lighted match into a conflagration that consumes a building, courts apply the alternative definition of proximate cause, also known as the substantial factor test. *See Daugert v. Pappas*, 704 P.2d 600, 605 (Wash. 1985).

In *Mavroudis v. Pittsburgh-Corning Corp.*, 935 P.2d 684, 689 (Wash. Ct. App. 1997), the Washington Court of Appeals applied the substantial factor test where the plaintiff suffered asbestosis but could not pinpoint which asbestos fibers produced from any number of asbestos suppliers caused his condition. The court found: "This is exactly the kind of situation that calls for application of the substantial factor test, in order that no supplier enjoy a causation defense solely on the ground that the plaintiff probably would have suffered the same disease from inhaling fibers originating from the products of other suppliers." Thus, the act need not, in itself, produce the injury; it is enough that it is a substantial factor in bringing it about. *Scott v. Salem County Memorial Hosp.*, 280 A.2d 843, 845 (N.J. Super. Ct. 1971).

While no known appellate decision discusses the substantial factor test in the veterinary medical malpractice context, sound analogies can be made, warranting the reader's familiarity. In *Reynolds v. Gonzalez*, 798 A.2d 67 (N.J. 2002), the New Jersey Supreme Court refused to eliminate the substantial factor test in increased-risk medical malpractice cases, where a plaintiff contends that medical negligence exacerbated preexisting conditions. In *Reynolds*, tried twice to a jury, the defendant was found to have violated the standards of medical care by failing to test for a particular syndrome, thereby increasing the risk of ultimate harm to the patient; however, the juries determined that the increased risk was not a substantial factor in plaintiff's later paralysis and other complications. Instead, they concluded that a preexisting dirt bike accident caused his foot problems. Following two defense judgments, the plaintiff sought appellate review. The Supreme Court first inquired whether evidence exists "demonstrating within a reasonable degree of medical probability that negligent treatment increased the risk of harm posed by a preexistent condition." *Id.*, at 76 (*quoting Scafidi v. Seiler, M.D.*, 574 A.2d 398, 405 (N.J. 1990)). The second inquiry required the jury to determine whether the increased risk substantially caused the ultimate harm. In reversing and remanding for a *third* trial, the court clarified the jury charge to state that "a defendant's deviation need not be the only cause, nor a primary cause, for the deviation to be a substantial factor in producing the ultimate result. However,

> defendant's negligent conduct cannot be a remote or an inconsequential contributing factor. It must play a role that is both relevant and significant in bringing about the ultimate injury. The relative weight of an increased risk that is found to constitute a substantial factor can be reflected by the jury in the apportionment of damages between the increased risk and the pre-existing condition. The trial court should also explain to the jury that:
>
>> [s]ome other event [that] is a contributing factor in producing the harm may have such a predominant effect in bringing it about as to

> make the effect of the actor's negligence insignificant and, therefore,
> to prevent it from being a substantial factor.

Id., at 80 (quoting *Restatement* s 433 cmt. d.). This test may arise in cases where a veterinarian's delay in diagnosing malignant cancer decreased the likelihood of survival by depriving the animal the benefit of anticancer treatment.

M.   LOST CHANCE OF SURVIVAL

Hastening death or reducing an animal's chance of survival may establish veterinary liability. Thus, instead of alleging that but for malpractice the animal's *death* would not have occurred, the plaintiff pleads that the animal's *chance of survival* would not have plummeted. In assessing "loss of chance," the plaintiff must prove by evidentiary preponderance that the acts or omissions of the veterinarian reduced the likelihood of survival by a sufficient degree to warrant a jury to find that the veterinarian's error or omission was a substantial factor in the animal's demise.

In *Herkovits v. Group Health Co-op. of Puget Sound*, 664 P.2d 474, 476–479 (Wash. 1983), the Washington Supreme Court found a misdiagnosis reducing the decedent's survival chance from 39% to 25% sufficient to meet the substantial factor test and allow a jury to decide whether the physician's failure proximately caused death. *But see Brome v. Pavitt*, 5 Cal. App. 4th 1487 (1992) (holding that unless decedent had greater than 50% chance of survival before the alleged malpractice, no cause of action for wrongful death arising from medical malpractice due to "loss of chance" exists). This California position has been criticized as denying justice to survivors of potentially terminally ill patients regardless how blatant the negligence.

N.   COLLATERAL ESTOPPEL IMPACT ON AND BY DISCIPLINARY PROCEEDINGS

When a veterinarian injures or kills an animal without just excuse, she may face not only a civil suit but an administrative disciplinary action or criminal charge, as well. Practitioners must account for the preclusive effect among the proceedings. As the client may not serve as a party in the administrative or criminal proceedings, may the client use a finding of fact or conclusion of law in the administrative or criminal action against the veterinarian in the subsequent civil suit? This attempt to pay forward an adverse ruling is known as nonmutual, offensive collateral estoppel: *nonmutual* because the parties are not identical (i.e., *State v. Veterinarian, Client v. Veterinarian*); *offensive* because the prior determination becomes a sword in the latter proceeding.

While a veterinarian may try to invoke collateral estoppel defensively (as a shield) where the prosecuting authority in the administrative action is the same as, or in privity with, the one in the criminal action, she may not apply it against her client — meaning that exoneration by the disciplinary board or a jury in a criminal action cannot insulate the veterinarian from a contrary finding of fault in a later civil action. *See Bassett v. State Bd. of Dental Examiners*, 727 P.2d 864 (Colo. Ct. App. 1986) (approving offensive nonmutual collateral estoppel where prior dental malpractice action by patient resulting in finding of liability was used against dentist in subsequent disciplinary proceeding); *Jeffreys v. Griffin*, 801 N.E.2d 404 (N.Y. 2003) (refused to apply collateral estoppel despite adverse disciplinary finding to a physician prior to civil suit for assault and battery).

The lesson for practitioners: Give serious consideration to the timing or propriety of a board complaint. While acts and omissions occasioning civil liability often overlap with unprofessional and unethical grounds, subjecting a licensed veterinarian to discipline, the civil action will typically result in a money judgment only (and possible loss of business and goodwill should word of judgment spread). The disciplinary action, however, could (though normally does not) result in license revocation or impairment of the privilege to practice veterinary medicine. If the plaintiff believes strongly enough to pursue discipline and the statute of limitations does not threaten to run, then file the board complaint first. Whether or not the board takes disciplinary action, the veterinarian and staff will normally respond to compulsory questioning by an investigator, turn over documents, and cooperate fully (failure to do so may provide grounds for further discipline). Public disclosure may reveal these admissions and evidentiary leads for further evaluation prior to initiating civil action.

O. EXCULPATORY CLAUSES

Virtually all veterinary hospitals in the United States require clients to sign a consent, release, or financial authorization form. These documents seek to protect the hospital (a) from a claim of conversion or lack of consent, by identifying the procedures to be performed and giving authorization to the hospital staff to use its discretion to make medical decisions without notifying the owner prior to each test or treatment; (b) from a claim of lack of informed consent, by having the client assume the risk of any disclosed complications arising from the authorized procedure; (c) by having the client release it of all liability, including negligence; (d) by guaranteeing payment prior to release of the animal; and (e) by providing for attorney's fees and costs in any action to collect on the bill.

May a veterinarian disclaim liability for her own negligence? The answer depends on whether such a contract would violate public policy on one hand, and whether the veterinarian constitutes a "professional bailee" on the other. Human health-care providers may not typically enforce a hold harmless clause against their patients because it would violate public policy. *Vodopest v. MacGregor*, 913 P.2d 779, 789 (Wash. 1996); *Eelbode v. Chec Medical Centers, Inc.*, 984 P.2d 436 (Wash. Ct. App. 1999); Managed Care Reform and Patient Rights Act, 215 ILCS 134/95 (2000) (no person or health care provider may be indemnified for its own negligence in the performance of his, her, or its duties); *Olson v. Molzen*, 558 S.W.2d 429 (Tenn. 1977) (exculpatory clause signed by patient as condition of receiving medical treatment invalid as against public policy). "Professional bailees," such as garage persons, may similarly not exempt themselves from liability for their own negligence. *American Nursery Products, Inc. v. Indian Wells Orchards*, 797 P.2d 477 (Wash. 1990); *Liability of Garageman for Theft or Unauthorized Use of Motor Vehicle*, 43 A.L.R. 2d 403 at § 8(a). The resulting conundrum faced by those litigating the enforceability of veterinary exculpatory clauses requires determining whether veterinarians more closely resemble medical doctors or parking lot attendants, or if they belong to some other category entirely.

The legal maxim that voids a contract made in violation of a statute, as in the case of state regulation delegating to supervisory boards or commissions right to suspend or revoke a veterinarian's license for "unprofessional conduct," which may include failure to exercise reasonable skill and safety, would prevent such a professional from exempting himself from that duty imposed by law. *See* AM. JUR. 2D, *Negligence* § 57; RCW § 18.130.180(4) (incompetence, negligence, or malpractice resulting in injury to a patient or creating an unreasonable risk that patient may be harmed). Accordingly, when a veterinarian endangers the nonhuman animal through lack of reasonable skill or safety, she violates a duty imposed by statute. Any effort to disclaim liability for such conduct should be void as against public policy as in the case of human health-care professionals.

While not all states recognize a statutory or common-law claim for veterinary malpractice, breach of bailment remains cognizable. A bailment is: "A delivery of personal property by one person (the *bailor*) to another (the *bailee*) who holds the property for a certain purpose under an express or implied-in-fact contract. Unlike a sale or gift of personal property, a bailment involves a change in possession but not in title." BLACK'S LAW DICTIONARY (9th Ed.). As discussed above, bailment claims carry a presumption of negligence whenever the bailee fails to redeliver the bailed property as contracted. For this reason, many bailees attempt to limit their liability through exculpatory clauses.

Courts across the country have adopted the general rule stated in 43 A.L.R.2D 403, that *professional* bailees cannot disclaim liability for their own negligence. Professional bailees include "persons who make it their principal business to act as bailees and who deal with the public on a uniform rather than on an individual basis, including primarily owners of parcel checkrooms, owners of parking places, garagemen, and warehousemen." Whether a veterinarian is a professional bailee is a matter of first impression. At least one court has agreed that in "tak[ing] his clients' animals, pets often as deeply revered as members of the family," the veterinarian puts himself "in a position of a bailee for hire and a fiduciary as far as the care and protection of the personalty is concerned." *Thorpe v. Board of Examiners*, 104 Cal. App. 3d 111, 117 (1980) (affirming revocation of veterinarian's license following conviction for smuggling 12,000 pounds of marijuana and defrauding insurance company).

To determine whether a bailee for mutual benefit (the relationship that characterizes most business transactions) becomes a *professional* bailee turns on whether the exclusionary clause violates public policy. Aside from the historically settled exceptions identified above, courts often look to whether:

1. The transaction concerns a business of a type generally thought suitable for public regulation.

2. The party seeking exculpation is engaged in performing a service of great importance to the public, which is often a matter of practical necessity for some members of the public.

3. The party holds himself out as willing to perform this service for any member of the public who seeks it or at least for any member coming within certain established standards.

4. As a result of the essential nature of the service, in the economic setting of the transaction, the party invoking exculpation possesses a decisive advantage of bargaining strength against any member of the public who seeks his services.

5. In exercising a superior bargaining power, the party confronts the public with a standardized adhesion contract of exculpation and makes no provision whereby a purchaser may pay additional reasonable fees and obtain protection against negligence.

6. Finally, as a result of the transaction, the person or property of the purchaser is placed under the control of the seller, subject to the risk of carelessness by the seller or his agents.

Wagenblast v. Odessa Sch. Dist. No. 105, 758 P.2d 968, 971 (Wash. 1988).

Given the developing judicial recognition of the companion animal as a member of the family, heavy regulation of veterinarians, and anticruelty laws criminalizing failure to provide medical attention to a nonhuman animal, most courts will likely agree that veterinarians are professional bailees. The Rockingham County Circuit Court in Virginia decided this matter of first impression in the consolidated cases, *Washington v. Equine Reproductive Concepts, LLC*, 2002 Va. Cir. LEXIS 431 (Va. Cir. Ct. Dec. 18, 2002). Based on the above logic, the court rejected as invalid an exculpatory clause that stated: "The owner of the horse understands there is risk involved with handling and managing horses and agrees to release Equine Reproductive Concepts, its employees and representatives from any liabilities associated with the horse while at Equine Reproductive Concepts." The case acknowledged the possibility that Equine Reproductive Concepts could be a professional bailee. On the other hand, in *Dow-Westbrook, Inc. v. Candlewood Equine Practice, LC*, 989 A.2d 1075 (Conn. App. Ct. 2010), the court held that a boarder agreement, releasing and holding harmless the veterinary clinic for injuries except those resulting from gross negligence or willful misconduct of clinic, did not violate public policy and could be enforced. Despite the general view in Connecticut disfavoring such provisions, this result likely obtained because both parties were commercial entities with equal bargaining power and contract savvy. Further, one may argue that the decision is limited to the facts of horse breeding and semen collection.

If your state authorizes exculpatory clauses in veterinary contracts, read with a fine-toothed comb, for they construed strictly against the party seeking relief from liability. For instance, Florida disfavors the use of exculpatory clauses "because they relieve one party of the obligation to use due care, and shift the risk of injury to the party who is probably least equipped to take the necessary precautions to avoid injury and bear the risk of loss." *Tatman v. Space Coast Kennel Club, Inc.*, 27 So. 3d 108 (Fla. Dist. Ct. App. 2009). Accordingly, "exculpatory clauses are strictly construed against the party seeking to be relieved of liability." *Murphy v. Young Men's Christian Association of Lake Wales, Inc.*, 974 So. 2d 565, 568 (Fla. Dist. Ct. App. 2008). Exculpatory clauses must unambiguously state that a customer releases the party from liability for its own negligence. *Kitchens of the Oceans, Inc. v. McGladrey & Pullen, LLP*, 832 So. 2d 270, 273 (Fla. Dist. Ct. App. 2002) (finding hold-harmless provision must "specifically and clearly" provide that a customer agrees to release a business "from their own negligence"). A general release from all liability will be construed to exclude harm caused by negligence. *Goyings v. Jack and Ruth Eckerd Foundation*, 403 So. 2d 1144, 1146 (Fla. Dist. Ct. App. 1981) (finding exculpatory clause "ineffective because it did not explicitly state that the [defendant] would be absolved from liability for injuries resulting from its negligence.") Further, if the release protects the veterinarian from injuries resulting from unspecified "complications," questions still arise as to whether they were foreseeable and disclosed as a material risk prior to treatment, or, rather, unforeseen until the midst of surgery. It goes without saying that a negligent veterinarian is not a complication, and certainly not a risk assumed by the client.

Be mindful of the distinction between presuit and postsuit releases as discussed in *Abis v. Tudin, D.V.M., P.A.*, 18 So. 3d 666 (Fla. Dist. Ct. App. 2009). Plaintiff Abis took her two dogs to Dr. Tudin, who recommended ProHeart 6, a heartworm medication. After administration, Sophie was diagnosed with thyroid failure, and Yogi exhibited physical ailments progressing to the point that Abis sought euthanasia. Abis then contacted Fort Dodge Animal Health, the maker of ProHeart 6, to pay the diagnostic expense to identify the cause of the deterioration. Though tests were inconclusive, Dr. Tudin allegedly told Abis that the results did not show that ProHeart 6 caused the ailments. Abis asked that Fort Dodge make new labels for the drug, buy a replacement dog, pay all veterinary bills, and pay to train a new dog. Though denying fault, Dr. Swan, Abis's contact at Fort Dodge, offered a "customer relation gesture" of $7,000 and the balance of veterinary expenses, along with a release. The release stated:

> For the sole consideration of $8,363.20, ILA ABIS . . . hereby releases and forever discharges WYETH, and their respective division, FORT DODGE ANIMAL HEALTH divisions and their employees, directors, officers, subsidiaries, affiliates, insurers, agents, successors and assigns, and all other persons, firms, corporations and entities . . . from all claims, demands, expenses, attorneys' fees, causes of action or suits of any kind or nature, resulting from or claimed to have resulted from the sale, use or administration of PROHEART 6 INJ at any time prior to the date hereof, including any injuries resulting therefrom or claimed to have resulted therefrom.

> It is expressly understood that this Release is a full, final and binding settlement and final discharge of all claims arising out of or relating to the allegations made in the claim . . . . This Release is intended to cover all claims, demands, expenses, attorneys' fees, causes of action or suits of any kind or nature, civil or otherwise, past, present or future, which may have been, or may ever be asserted by [Abis] as a result of the claimed injuries and/or other damages or effects or consequences to [Abis] of the use or administration of the subject product at any time prior to the date hereof. This Release is intended to cover any and all future injuries, damages or losses not currently known to [Abis], but which may later develop, or be

discovered in connection with the use or administration of the subject product.

Abis signed the release and negotiated the check. She then sued Dr. Tudin for malpractice, breach of contract, and negligent infliction of emotional distress. Dr. Tudin prevailed on summary judgment by asserting that the release barred her action. On appeal, the court rejected Abis's contention that because the release did not expressly reference acts of negligence, she was free to proceed against Dr. Tudin for malpractice. It reached this conclusion by distinguishing a postclaim release from a preclaim exculpatory clause. As to the argument that the release was unenforceable because it did not specifically cover Dr. Tudin, the court held that the completely typewritten document clearly applied to "all other persons, firms, corporations and entities" in relation to "the sale, use or administration of ProHeart 6." Despite affirming dismissal of all claims pertaining to ProHeart 6, the appeals court reversed the blanket summary judgment of claims not necessarily within the scope of the release — misdiagnosis and mistreatment of conditions.

P. EXPERT TESTIMONY

Proving a standard of care breach utilizes similar legal techniques as in a human medical malpractice case. Expert testimony, presented with reasonable medical certainty, must (a) define the standard of care, (b) examine how the defendant breached this standard, and (c) explain how this breach proximately caused the patient's injury. In the absence of this showing, the plaintiff will fail. *Baechler v. Beaunaux*, 272 P.3d 277, 280 (Wash. Ct. App. 2012). It is imperative to have an expert witness who can testify to the standard in the locality or region of the defendant and in the field of expertise relevant to the dispute. *McKee v. American Home Products Corp.*, 782 P.2d 1045 (Wash. 1989) (expert must practice in same profession); *Walker v. Bangs*, 601 P.2d 1279 (Wash. 1979) (expert need not be licensed in Washington to testify); *Sanderson v. Moline*, 499 P.2d 1281 (Wash. Ct. App. 1972) (locality rule rejected in favor of those "similarly situated" within state). However, if your expert can testify to the existence of a national standard of care that mirrors that of the state where the tortious conduct occurred, then her extraterritorial domicile, place of business, or license will prove unobjectionable., then out-of-state experts may be sufficient. For instance, in *Hill v. Sacred Heart Medical Center*, 177 P.3d 1152 (Wash. Ct. App. 2008), the appellate court reversed an order dismissing a medical malpractice case on summary judgment, based, in part, on declarations from physicians offered by the plaintiff claiming that the Washington doctors violated the standard of care in their treatment of heparin-induced thrombocytopenia. While Plaintiff's experts were from Wisconsin and Massachusetts, they noted that a national standard of care applied. The *Hill* court held:

> Dr. Willard's and Dr. Bauer's affidavits show that the applicable standard of care is the national standard. The standard of care in Washington is, then, the same standard as in their states. The same standard that applies to Dr. Willard in Wisconsin and to Dr. Bauer in Massachusetts applies to physicians here in Washington.

Id. It was also noted that the defendants did not challenge the procedures required by the applicable standards of care. *Id.*, at 454. Finding that plaintiff's affidavits raised genuine issues of material fact, summary judgment was reversed and the matter remanded in a unanimous decision. *Id.*, at 455. *See also Avivi v. Centro Medico Urgente Medical Center*, 159 Cal. App. 4th 463 (2008) (Israeli orthopedist could testify to standard of care for treating fractures in Los Angeles).

In *Lauderbaugh v. Gellasch*, 2006 Ohio App. LEXIS 2792 (June 8, 2008), plaintiff Lauderbaugh brought her dog to Drs. Gellasch and Heldmann to treat a disc problem. After Dr. Gellasch performed a laminectomy and inserted a urine catheter, the dog ran a fever and had malodorous urine. Dr. Heldman administered the antibiotic Clavamox, which had no effect. She then gave another antibiotic, without benefit, and the dog had a seizure and heart problems leading to death. Despite lack of a necropsy, Lauderbaugh's expert opined that the dog died from a massive infection. Lauderbaugh sued Drs. Gellasch and Heldman for malpractice arising from misdiagnosis and mistreatment (namely, performing a urinalysis and immediately administering antibiotics rather than waiting 48-72 hours for a urine culture). The trial court granted the veterinarians' summary judgment motion on the grounds that Lauderbaugh's expert failed to create an issue of material fact on proximate causation. In affirming, the court of appeals noted that failure to conduct a urinalysis did not contribute to the dog's death since it would not allow identification of the type of bacteria present in the urine sample, which were antibiotic-resistant. Because Lauderbaugh's expert conceded that the antibiotics used were appropriate under the circumstances, her assigned errors were overruled.

In *Ullmann v. Duffus*, 2005 Ohio App. LEXIS 5463 (Nov. 15, 2005), the plaintiff sued her veterinarian for professional negligence, breach of warranty, lack of informed consent, and infliction of emotional distress relating to the death of five cockatiels and parakeets. She alleged that the veterinarian poisoned her birds with Panacur. The case ultimately resolved against the plaintiff based on the insufficiency of her expert's affidavit. The Ohio Court of Appeals also addressed two points of general interest. First, the court acknowledged that the informed consent claim against the veterinarian was a question of first impression, but it did not reject the theory as a potential basis for recovery. Second, the court relied on earlier precedent with respect to animal loss or destruction to deny the plaintiff's attempt to recover damages under a negligent infliction of emotional distress theory. The court observed that the plaintiff's recovery was limited to the fair market value of the animal.

The plaintiff in *Diakakis v. W. Res. Veterinary Hosp.*, 2006 Ohio App. LEXIS 164 (Jan. 20, 2006), took her dog to a veterinary hospital for surgery, whereupon the dog died. To support her claim of negligence and breach of contract, the plaintiff submitted a personal affidavit stating that another veterinarian told her the defendant was "completely negligent." She also submitted an unsworn letter from this veterinarian stating "[the] most likely reason left [for the dog's death] is the aspiration of gastro-intestinal contents into the lungs while the animal was under anesthesia, especially in the post-operative recovery time." The defendant produced an affidavit from the veterinarian who performed the surgery, stating that the veterinarian's conduct did not fall below the standard of care. The court granted defendant's motion for summary judgment, and the appellate court affirmed, holding that the defendant's affidavit was admissible because it was from a licensed veterinarian who could testify to the standard of care. While the plaintiff submitted her affidavit in an effort to create a genuine issue of material fact, because she lacked personal knowledge of certain critical facts and was not a veterinarian, the court held that she failed to meet her burden in responding to the motion for summary judgment. The unsworn letter of the veterinarian, submitted with the plaintiff's affidavit, was deemed inadmissible hearsay.

In *Ruden v. Hansen*, 206 N.W.2d 713 (Iowa 1973), Dr. Hansen was sued by Ruden for lost piglets following administration of modified live vaccine to pregnant sows ("gilts"). Dr. Conley (from same county) testified that this did not meet the standard of care and did cause the deaths and deformations. Dr. Conley relied upon lab results from the Diagnostic Laboratory at ISU-Ames and the deposition of Dr. Hansen, as well as other facts concerning dates of being bred, born, and farrowing. In ordering a new trial, the appeals court rejected the locality rule in favor of the similarly-situated rule. The court also rejected the testimony of William Mills, a hog farmer who lost piglets after Dr. Hansen gave the vaccine (because he lacked expert credentials to speak authoritatively as to causation), declared Dr. Conley's reliance on the diagnostic laboratory results hearsay, and found he could not opine on causation due to lack of factual foundation. Yet he could testify to standard of care.

Q. STATUTES OF LIMITATION AND VENUE

While courts tend to treat veterinary and medical malpractice actions alike, the period of time within which to file suit, and where to file it, varies significantly, owing largely to the fact that animal cases frequently pair elements of property damage to parasitic noneconomic emotional damage (i.e., personal injury). The dilemma created by the disparate run periods illustrates the legal problem.

The statute of limitations may vary between personal injury and property damage. In New Mexico, standard personal-injury cases must be filed within three years, but only one year is permitted to commence such actions against any municipality or municipal officer (which may prove relevant if the veterinarian works at a municipal shelter). N.M. Stat. Ann. §§ 37-1-8, 37-1-24. In Georgia, such cases must be filed within two years. Ga. Code Ann. § 9-3-33. In New Mexico, actions for fraud, mistake, property damage, or conversion accrue at the time the aggrieved party has discovered the fraud, mistake, injury, or conversion, and must be filed within four years. N.M. Stat. Ann. §§ 37-1-4, 37-1-7. Property damage cases against New Mexico municipalities must be commenced within three years. N.M. Stat. Ann. § 37-1-24. Property damage cases sounding in conversion or replevin and injuries to personalty must be filed in four years in Georgia. Ga. Code Ann. §§ 9-3-31, 9-3-32.

Accordingly, plaintiffs seeking damages for the animal's "value" (property damage) and emotional distress or pain and suffering (e.g., as a claim of "bodily injury" where the disabled plaintiff loses the assistance of a service animal must recall that some jurisdictions have a shorter statute of limitations for personal-injury claims than for property damage. Thus, a suit against a veterinarian who euthanizes a cat without consent, causing mental anguish to the owner, would need to commence within three years (personal injury) in New Mexico; and within two years (personal injury) and in Georgia.

Additionally, as discussed earlier, many jurisdictions enacted statutes specific to malpractice actions, granting the health-care provider the benefit of even shorter than typical limitation periods. The practitioner must prepare to equate or distinguish mice from men to determine whether to apply such a medical malpractice time-limiting statute where it does not expressly exclude veterinarians.

Generally, venue remains in the county of the defendant's residence or where the defendant transacts business. This is true unless an express statutory provision provides otherwise. C.J.S. *Venue* §§ 5, 81. When the statute gives the plaintiff the option of multiple venues, he has complete discretion in choosing. *Id.*, § 62. For instance, in *Baker v. Hilton*, 395 P.2d 486, 487 (Wash. 1964), the Washington Supreme Court denied defendant's motion for change of venue, stating that "[w]here the relevant statute provides several places where venue may be proper, the choice lies with the plaintiff in the first instance." The court's statement accords with case law from other states. *See Soloman v. Excel Marketing, Inc.*, 682 N.E.2d 724, 726 (Ohio Ct. App. 1996); *Mills v. Dickson*, 129 Cal. App. 728, 733 (1933); *Washington v. Illinois Power Co.*, 581 N.E.2d 644 (Ill. 1991); *Bradley v. Valmont Indus., Inc.*, 701 P.2d 997, 998 (Mont. 1985); *Vallone v. Power*, 35 A.D.2d 655 (N.Y. App. Div. 1970). When an action raises alternative property- and personal injury-based causes of action that invite multiple venues, the plaintiff, not the defendant, elects. An animal law practitioner may encounter this issue where, for instance, a client on vacation in County X, leaves her dog with a pet sitter in County Y, who takes the dog to a veterinarian transacting business in County Z. The veterinarian commits malpractice in County Z, the dog succumbs thereafter to the negligence in County Y, and the plaintiff suffers emotional distress in County X upon hearing the bad news.

Hypothetical: Margareth Mendoza's cat Feliz, a 17-year-old neutered male Siamese, began developing gastrointestinal symptoms of concern when he turned 13, such as frequent vomiting, diarrhea, and voracious appetite. Between the ages of 13 and 16, Mendoza took him to The Polydactyl Clinic, where Jake Fender, DVM, attended to his general veterinary needs. Instead of recommending endoscopy or referring her to a specialist, Fender told her Feliz had "no issue of any real concern," that his "mild" issues were idiopathic (i.e., unknown origin) and could be addressed by diet (for which prescription foods were sold), and that he was just "aging" and "doing quite well for his age." Fender rebuffed and naysaid her concerns, instead assuring her that Feliz was simply growing old. He even charted, "doesn't want cat to age!" Last seen by Fender on his sixteenth birthday, April 1, 2012, it was not until April 15, 2012 that Feliz was seen again by any veterinarian — this time, by Awesome Veterinary Specialists ("AVS"), to investigate a ligament injury in his back left leg.

The AVS internist, Pinky Randall, DVM, DACVIM, recommended a complete workup for Feliz's vomiting, which occurred on April 23, 2012. Thereafter, Randall performed an endoscopy on May 6, 2012. Even then, Randall only expressed to Mendoza a "concern" that he had underlying infiltrative bowel disease such as IBD or GI lymphoma. Five days later, on May 11, 2012, two pathologists at DDx

Laboratories confirmed a diagnosis of small cell lymphoma. Mendoza had difficulty accepting this diagnosis, for no critical or acute event occurred that would have led her to believe that Feliz's health profile had dramatically changed. Further, she had assumed that Fender would not mislead her. Additionally, terrified at the meaning of, and treatment for, a cancer diagnosis, she urged Randall to run immunohisto-chemistry to confirm the diagnosis further. Those results were communicated to Mendoza on May 26, 2012. Before April 1, 2012, Mendoza abided Fender's advice and did not have contrary evidence to even suspect that he had made ongoing and serious errors in Feliz's care until after the definitive diagnosis of small cell lymphoma on May 26, 2012.

Mendoza had no real idea or understanding of the damage the Fender caused Feliz even after receiving the results of Feliz's abdominal ultrasound, for at that time there was no diagnosis, nor even a tentative one, but just an unconfirmed suspicion of IBD or GI lymphoma. The only way to know, she learned, was to conduct a biopsy study. Though she discovered Feliz's cancer in May 2012, the complete nature and degree of damage done to Feliz was not defined until late December 2012.

Marcus Inouye, DVM, DACVIM, expressed the expert opinion that Fender violated the standards of due care of a small animal veterinarian practicing in the state of California. He explains:

1. Despite the fact that Ms. Mendoza frequently sought veterinary medical assistance for Feliz's gastrointestinal symptoms that she documented, she was repeatedly rebuffed for her concern. It is well-known that chronic inflammatory conditions in certain felines can transition to malignancy (particularly IBD). An ordinary, prudent veterinarian in California should have known that hepatopathy, vomiting, diarrhea, abdominal pain, and appetite changes in a feline patient warrant a complete investigation.

2. Endoscopy is a highly effective, noninvasive procedure that should have been recommended to Ms. Mendoza as soon as the gastrointestinal symptoms were consistent. The failure of Dr. Jack Fender of The Polydactyl Clinic to adequately investigate (or refer) in a timely manner is inexcusable. The transition to malignant lymphoma could, with reasonable medical certainty and on a more probable than not basis, have been avoided if accurate diagnostics and treatment were effected.

3. Though Ms. Mendoza remained concerned about Feliz's gastrointestinal health, it was not until May 26, 2012 when her worst fears were confirmed. This is the first documentation of the disease that would eventually cause Feliz's demise.

4. Thus, it was on May 26, 2012 that Ms. Mendoza could have first been aware of sufficient facts (not just suppositions, concerns, or suspicions, but confirmed diagnoses) to put her on actual or inquiry notice that the veterinarians at The Polydactyl Clinic committed malpractice as alleged.

Ms. Mendoza filed her lawsuit against Fender and The Polydactyl Clinic on April 23, 2013, one year to the date of the ultrasound, but one year and 22 days after the last contact with the defendants. Citing Cal. Code of Civ. Proc. § 340(c) ("CCP 340"), the Defendants move for summary judgment dismissal, claiming that the statute of limitations has run on Ms. Mendoza's claim. The code states:

> Within one year: (c) An action for libel, slander, false imprisonment, seduction of a person below the age of legal consent, or by a depositor against a bank for the payment of a forged or raised check, or a check that bears a forged or unauthorized endorsement, or against any person who boards or feeds an animal or fowl or who engages in the practice of veterinary medicine as defined in Section 4826 of the Business and Professions Code, for that person's neglect resulting in injury or death to an animal or fowl in the course of boarding or feeding the animal or fowl or in the course of the practice of veterinary medicine on that animal or fowl.

Cal. Code of Civ. Proc. § 340.5 ("CCP 340.5"), which does not apply per *de Mercado* and *Scharer*, discussed *supra*, states:

> In an action for injury or death against a health care provider based upon such person's alleged professional negligence, the time for the commencement of action shall be three years after the date or injury or one year after the plaintiff discovers, or through the use of reasonable diligence should have discovered, the injury, whichever occurs first.

Defendants contend that the last possible date that they could have caused harm to Feliz was the last day that they rendered any professional service to Ms. Mendoza concerning Feliz. They identify April 1, 2012 as the operative date.

Is Ms. Mendoza's lawsuit time-barred under CCP 340(c)?

As noted in Weil & Brown, concerning the human medical malpractice statute, CCP 340.5:

> [T]he three-year period runs from the date of injury, not from the time of defendant's wrongful act. And, for this purpose, 'injury' means both the negligent cause and the damaging effect of the alleged wrongful act . . . not the act itself. The date of 'injury' could be much later than the date of the wrongful act, where plaintiff suffers no physical harm until sometime after the wrongful act — in some cases, years!

Weil & Brown, Personal Injury, ch. 5-B, § 5:161 *Three-year Statute Commences upon Discovery of Injury*; *McNall v. Summers*, 25 Cal. App. 4th 1300 (1994) (no cause of action until damages are manifest; damages are manifest when they become evidenced in some specific fashion).

CCP 340 was first enacted in 1872. Before the legislature enacted CCP 340.5 in 1970, CCP 340 applied to human medical malpractice disputes. Interestingly, cases involving veterinary malpractice did not fall within the ambit of CCP 340 until 1953. Compare Cal. Stats. 1953, Ch. 1382, § 1, subsection (3) with Cal. Stats. 1949, ch. 863, § 1. In *Huysman v. Kirsch*, 6 Cal. 2d 302 (1936), the California Supreme Court examined an earlier version of the statute at issue here. CCP 340(3) (1929) stated, "Within one year: (3) An action for . . . injury to or for the death of one caused by the wrongful act or neglect of another[.]" Cal. Stats.1929, ch. 518, § 1. The court held:

(1) It is the settled law in this state that an action by a patient against a physician and surgeon for injuries sustained by the former, by reason of the negligent or unskilled treatment of the latter, is an action sounding in tort and not upon a contract. Such an action is therefore barred by the provisions of subdivision 3 of section 340 of the Code of Civil Procedure one year after the date of the injury. (*Harding v. Liberty Hospital Corp.*,177 Cal. 520 [171 Pac. 98]; *Kershaw v. Tilbury*, 214 Cal. 679 [8 Pac. (2d) 109].)

Huysman, at 306. Over appellee's objection, the court reversed and revived the patient's claim by invoking the equitable delayed discovery rule as a gloss upon CCP 340(c) (1929). In reaching this conclusion, the *Huysman* court favorably cited to *Gillette v. Tucker*, 67 Ohio St. 106 (1902), to hold that failure to remove a surgical sponge from within a patient, which was used as part of the operation, presented a continuous obligation upon the physician, and "each day's failure to remove the sponge was a fresh breach of the contract implied by the law." *Id.*, at 309.

This holding is clearly akin to the argument made in the instant matter, where a malignant condition grows within the patient as it remains untreated. Cases since *Huysman*, but before enactment of CCP 340.5, are in accord. No doubt recognizing the logic of *Huysman*, the California legislature codified the delayed discovery rule when it enacted CCP 340.5 in 1970. Awareness of the factual cause, without actual or constructive knowledge of the tortious cause, does not commence the one-year statutory period under CCP 340.5. *Hills v. Aronsohn*, 152 Cal.App.3d 753, 759-60 (1984).

As urged by Ms. Mendoza, the earliest that she had reason to discover her claims against the Defendants was when she received the definitive diagnosis that Feliz in fact had lymphoma, a condition missed and not treated by the Defendants despite numerous opportunities. Judicious is *Steingart v. White*, 243 Cal.Rptr. 678, 683 (1988), involving a patient suffering from some physical symptoms, but who was never really aware of either the injury or the cause until properly diagnosed. The California Supreme Court found that the statute of limitations tolled until the second physician diagnosed breast cancer, not when the first physician discovered the lump in plaintiff's breast.

While CCP 340 admittedly does not explicitly include a delayed discovery clause as found in CCP 340.5, common law has fashioned such an equitable tolling rule in the case of medical malpractice (*Huysman v. Kirsch*, 6 Cal.2d 302, 306-313 (1936)), progressive occupational illness (*Marsh v. Industrial Acc. Com.*, 217 Cal. 338, 351 (1933)), legal malpractice (*Neel v. Magana, Olney, Levy, Cathcart & Gelfand*, 6 Cal. 3d 176, 190 (1971)), liability for defective drugs (*Jolly v. Eli Lilly & Co.*, 44 Cal.3d 1103, 1109 (1988)), invasion of privacy (*Cain v. State Farm Mut. Auto Ins. Co.*, 62 Cal. App. 3d 310, 315 (1976)), libel (*Manguso v. Oceanside Unified Sch. Dist.*, 88 Cal. App. 3d 725, 731 (1979), underground trespass (*Oakes v. McCarthy Co.*, 267 Cal. App. 2d 231, 255 (1968), breach of contract committed in secret and without immediately discoverable harm (April Enterprises, Inc. v. KTTV, 147 Cal. App. 3d 805, 832 (1983)), negligent breach of contract to ship personal goods, *Allred v. Bekins Wide World Van Services*, 45 Cal. App. 3d 984, 991 (1975)), and negligent breach of contract to conduct termite inspection (*Seelenfreund v. Terminix of Northern Cal., Inc.*, 84 Cal. App. 3d 133, 136-139 (1978)). See Curtis T. v. County of

Los Angeles, 123 Cal. App. 4th 1405, 1416-17 (2004)(quoting the foregoing authorities). Though no case can be cited that has specifically extended the equitable accrual rule to veterinary malpractice cases, there is no good reason not to think that the mostly analogous case, i.e., human medical malpractice, brought under virtually the same statutory section, resulted in the California Supreme Court tolling the statute of limitations. Indeed, later decisions have embraced the association between veterinarians and human health care providers, for *Williamson v. Prida*, 75 Cal. App. 4th 1417, 1425 (1999)("veterinary malpractice cases are treated like medical malpractice cases for purposes of statute of limitations"); *Clark v. United Emergency Animal Clinic, Inc.*, 390 F.3d 1124 (9th Cir. 2004) (likening veterinarians to physicians for purposes of the Fair Labor Standards Act).

R. ECONOMIC LOSS RULE

"The economic loss rule marks the fundamental boundary between the law of contracts, which is designed to enforce expectations created by agreement, and the law of torts, which is designed to protect citizens and their property by imposing a reasonable duty of care on others." *Berschauer/Phillips Const. Co. v. Seattle Sch. Dist. No. 1*, 881 P.2d 986, 989 (Wash. 1994). Courts have applied the economic loss rule to negligent misrepresentation claims against home sellers and builder-vendors, defective product claims, and negligent construction/design claims against architects, structural engineers, project inspectors, and others in the building industry.

At the outset, litigators must decide whether to construe a veterinarian's services as the type of contractual relationship subject to this rule or, instead, akin to other professional services governed by independent legal and fiduciary duties and a special relationship not subject to it. The economic loss rule only applies to damages that are purely economic in character. *Alejandre v. Bull*, 153 P.3d 864 (Wash. 2007). Any losses suffered as a result of veterinary malpractice rarely are considered purely "economic" in character, meaning "commercial loss," and reserved for "resolving purely commercial disputes" as distinguished "from an injury to the plaintiff's person or property (property other than the product itself), the type of injury on which a products liability suit usually is founded." *Miller v. U.S. Steel Corp.*, 902 F.2d 573, 574 (7th Cir. 1990).

Negligent performance of an elective neuter, implantation of a microchip, and postoperative monitoring of a beloved companion animal are decidedly not a type of "purely commercial dispute." Indeed, most veterinarian-client-patient relationships are fundamentally noneconomic in that such patients are not kept as a commercially gainful tool or profit-bearing item, damaged inventory, or equipment belonging to a retailer or wholesaler. As with most transactions involving veterinarians, companion animals receive treatment because guardians regard them as family members, not as sources of income. However, with respect to those owned by a commercial operation such as a laboratory, commercial breeding kennel, or agricultural operation, the damages may truly fit the definition of "economic loss."

> The key inquiry is the nature of the loss and the manner in which it occurs, i.e., are the losses economic losses, with economic losses distinguished from personal injury or injury to other property. If the claimed loss is an

economic loss, and no exception applies to the economic loss rule, then the parties will be limited to contractual remedies.

Alejandre, at 869. Such "exceptions" include (1) independent legal duty and (2) special relationship. However, the exceptions are arguably unnecessary because the rule does not apply where (3) the animal is "property" not constituting an "economic loss." Consider *A.J. Decoster Co. v. Westinghouse Elec. Corp.*, 634 A.2d 1330 (Md. 1994), an animal-related case excluding application of the economic loss rule. A farmer lost more than 140,000 chickens when a defective transfer switch failed to activate a backup ventilation system in his chicken house. The farmer sued in tort to recover his losses. Maryland's highest court held that deaths of the chickens constituted loss of physical property, but not economic loss, and refused to bar the farmer's tort claim under the economic loss rule doctrine.

1.   Independent Legal Duty

In *National Union Ins. Co. of Pittsburgh, Pa. v. Puget Sound Power & Light*, 972 P.2d 481, 487 (Wash. Ct. App. 1999), the court refused to apply the economic loss rule where the duties arose by statute or regulation and not by contract, stating:

> Moreover, National Union's claims against Puget Power are for breaches of statutory and regulatory duties independent of Boeing and Puget Power's contract. Therefore, National Union's claims are better described as sounding in tort.

> In contrast, tort law is designed to secure the protection of all citizens from the danger of physical harm to their persons or to their property. Tort standards are imposed by law without reference to any private agreement. They obligate each citizen to exercise reasonable care to avoid foreseeable physical harm to others. As such, tort law primarily is concerned with enforcing standards of conduct.

The Washington Court of Appeals analogized to legal and medical malpractice claims. Its elucidation proves instructive:

> Analogies to legal malpractice or medical malpractice claims are also apt. If an attorney agrees to draft a will for a client and fails to do so, the client would be able to claim breach of contract and recover under an applicable contractual fee provision. "However, if the attorney drafts the will and negligently omits having its execution properly witnessed, the attorney would be liable in tort for professional malpractice." (citation omitted) The same would be true for a doctor who performs a medical procedure pursuant to a contract but is negligent in doing so.

Boguch v. Landover Corp., 224 P.3d 795 (Wash. Ct. App. 2009). Most veterinary malpractice claims account for losses resulting from breaches of duties that veterinarians assume by common law, statute, and regulations, not those explicitly set forth by contract, and rest on the assumption that practitioners will comply with the obligations imposed by extracontractual laws.

2. Special Relationship

Several jurisdictions have enacted the "special relationship" exception to the economic loss rule and extended it to professionals like veterinarians. *See Simpkins v. Connor*, 150 P.3d 417 (Or. Ct. App. 2006) (plaintiff could bring negligence claim against hospital for failing to produce medical records, despite economic loss doctrine, where hospital owed plaintiff duty to produce records under former statute); *Congregation of the Passion, Holy Cross Province v. Touche Ross & Co.*, 636 N.E.2d 503, 514 (Ill. 1994) ("Where a duty arises outside of the contract, the economic loss doctrine does not prohibit recovery in tort for the negligent breach of that duty."). In *Passion*, the court found that the economic loss rule did not apply to a case of professional malpractice by an accounting firm, characterizing the duty as extracontractual. In Goble, *All Along the Watchtower: Economic Loss in Tort (The Idaho Case Law)*, 34 IDAHO L. REV. 225 (1998), Goble focuses on the historical exception to the economic loss rule for the category of "special relationships involv[ing] professionals and others with special knowledge, judgment, or skill." Goble adds that the difference between a contract for sale and contract for service "appears to lie at the core" of the "conclusion that service contracts can form the basis for a relationship between the parties that is sufficiently 'special' to give rise to a tort duty to act with care in providing the service." *Id.*, at 1331.

The most recent appellate word on the economic loss rule (modernly known in some jurisdiction as the independent duty doctrine) in the veterinary context refused to apply it against a plaintiff. In *Hendrickson v. Tender Care Animal Hosp. Corp.*, 312 P.3d 52 (Wash. Ct. App. 2013), the Washington Court of Appeals evaluated Julie Hendrickson's claims against Tender Care Animal Hospital and Dr. Kristen Cage for reckless breach of bailment, professional negligence, and negligent misrepresentation/lack of informed consent relating to the death of her four-year-old Golden Retriever mix named Bear. Diagnosed with gastric dilatation, but discharged without discussion of the need to decompress his stomach, Bear collapsed and died in Ms. Hendrickson's driveway a few hours after returning home. Invoking the economic loss rule, the trial court dismissed all of her tort claims and her claim for emotional distress damages under RESTATEMENT (2D) CONTRACTS § 353. Mindful of the Washington Supreme Court's prohibition against lower courts applying the economic loss doctrine to a particular tort unless the Supreme Court previously endorsed the practice, the appellate court reinstated Ms. Hendrickson's tort claims by finding that the economic loss rule, since renamed the "independent duty doctrine," had not previously been applied in the veterinary tort context. However, it rejected her attempt to extend RESTATEMENT (2D) CONTRACTS § 353 to veterinary service contracts generally, and specifically such contracts recklessly breached, noting that no Washington court had previously permitted the theory. Though acknowledging Washington and Ninth Circuit case law corroborating the cherished place companion animals keep within human families, the panel did not address the central question of foreseeability of serious emotional disturbance arising from a veterinarian's breach (reckless or otherwise) of a contract causing harm to an entrusted animal, particularly by those clinics using emotive marketing techniques to solicit clients and profit from the human-animal bond. Instead, it adopted a sky-is-falling premise that to permit such an extension would throw open the floodgates of general damage claims in animal-related contract cases.

Another appellate decision concerning the economic loss rule, *Loman v. Freeman* 874 N.E.2d 542 (Ill. App. Ct. 2006), *judgment aff'd*, 890 N.E.2d 446 (Ill. 2008), held that Illinois's "economic loss doctrine" did not apply in the veterinary context. The trial court in *Loman* invoked the doctrine to dismiss the negligence claim, but the court of appeals reversed, holding as follows:

> Although the parties in this case explicitly agreed that defendant would refrain from operating on the right stifle, defendant's duty to refrain from doing so did not arise exclusively from the service contract. The parties' agreement in this respect was nothing more than an acknowledgment of defendant's preexisting common-law duty to refrain from altering the horse in any manner except as authorized by plaintiffs . . . . Contract or no contract, if one cuts, carves, lacerates, incises, or otherwise alters someone else's property except as authorized by that person, one commits a classic tort: either trespass to chattels or conversion, depending on the extent of the alteration.

Id., at 551–552.

3. Patient Not an Economic Loss

It should be noted that with rare exceptions, veterinary malpractice suits are not product-liability cases, and the patient animal is not a defective product or defective property. The veterinarian does not construct or sell the animal to the client. Rather, the client hires the veterinarian to provide *services* to care for "property" she already owns. Accordingly, one may argue that harm to the companion animal constitutes "damage to property *other than the defective product or property.*" This interpretation is supported by *King v. Rice*, 191 P.3d 946 (Wash. Ct. App. 2008), which involved suit by a vendor against purchasers of realty for the purchasers' destruction of a modular living unit situated on the property, asserting that the structure was personal property. The court of appeals concluded that the economic loss rule did not apply, stating: "But the rule does not bar recovery for personal injury or damage to property other than a defect in the property." *Id.*, at 951. If a court construes "product" as a "service," then the "product purchased" would be professional veterinary services. Alleged to be "defective," the service "product" would have caused damage to "other property" — namely, the patient.

S. DAMAGES

Compensatory damages fit within two general categories — personal injury and property damage. Personal injury presents most commonly in the form of emotional distress to the grieving guardian, but practitioners may find secondary physical injuries at play where the injured animal bites while in painful delirium or psychosis from an overdose or incorrect prescription. Emotional distress response, even if not independently recoverable, may reflect a high property value and lost use. A counterfactual example illuminates.

If a person witnessed her "beloved" cat being ripped to pieces by a neighbor's dog in her front yard, but continued reading her Sunday paper, sipping her coffee, going inside to freshen up before running errands while her cat's agonal breaths fade into the background, then left home an hour later without taking even a momentary glance at her cat's macerated body, then allowed it to decompose on her lawn, picked at by crows for the following week, one would be quite justified arguing that her *lack of emotional reaction* would undermine any claim that the cat possessed an immense intrinsic value. The same can be said for a father who learns that his three-year-old has escaped from day care in a dangerous and congested part of town, but instead of initiating a search, continues watching the football game, playing pool with his buddies, and sleeping off a rousing evening of beer-drinking before turning attention to his son the next day. If the *absence* of emotion is probative of value, then the *presence* thereof is permissible.

Should the defendants assert that the existence of numerous animal shelters, breeders, and pet stores for consumers to purchase pets demonstrates that a fair market or replacement value exists for the animal, such a contention would buckle under sustained analysis. Time of death or injury is the relevant temporal milepost for assessing value. Most plaintiffs seek recourse for the injury or death to an adult animal, not viable (though unborn) offspring or recently birthed animals. Breeders and pet stores sell kittens, not full-grown cats. More important, these entities pride themselves on selling animals who have not yet imprinted on a select individual and are *tabulae rasa*, unbesmirched by bad habits, inculcated traits, or special training particular to one caretaker over a lengthy period.

Even if a court permits intrinsic value, the defendant may still attempt to completely sanitize the relationship between the plaintiff and her animal, restricting her from describing the actual value and the loss of use in terms other than the stale, emotionless recitation of a technical repair manual describing the specifications of a toaster oven. Distinguishing them from appliances, the plaintiff's attorney might emphasize how the animal was sentient, could give and receive affection, and possessed the faculties of reason, autonomy, affection, loyalty, and bonding. While the plaintiff may give testimony indubitably emotive, speak to distress in losing the animal, and offer features of sentimentality, such remarks completely describe the animal's characteristics and uses.

People who share their lives with companion animals expect such a sentimental characterization as within the normal limits of human-animal experience, not unusual or excessive sentimentality that most jurisdictions prohibit. Furthermore, not all animals become instant companions. Nor is their potential fully harnessed or expressed. Some revert to a wild or dysfunctional state while others never receive training or love, resulting in value stagnation or depreciation. Abandoned, neglected, and abused animals, in being regarded by their owners no differently than trash, have a negligible or nonexistent intrinsic value. Evidence may show maximization of value through labor and attention or, rather, reveal the disingenuousness of a greedy plaintiff. Recovery should not be restricted to the value ascertained by some unknown individual as if he were combing a flea market for bargains. A jury can decide what is appropriate for this type of personalty. To espouse these views with respect to a file cabinet, for instance, might strike most as excessive, but not for a companion animal.

While most jurisdictions have eliminated recovery of emotional damages for negligent harm to an animal, the majority permit them for malicious or intentional injury. In the right circumstance, mental anguish might be recoverable for breach of certain types of veterinary contracts, and certain types of breaches of contract, per RESTATEMENT (1ST) CONTRACTS § 341 and § 351, in those jurisdictions that follow the Restatement. The only courts to date to directly address the application of this doctrine to veterinarians are *Smith v. University Animal Clinic, Inc.*, 30 So. 3d 1154, 1157–58 (La. Ct. App. 2010), *writ den'd*, 36 So. 3d 247 (La. 2010) and *Hendrickson v. Tender Care Animal Hospital*, *supra* (rejecting the doctrine). *Smith* found that the contract between the plaintiffs and the animal clinic for boarding their cat was made for the gratification of a nonpecuniary interest and that the clinic knew or should have known that its failure to perform would cause a nonpecuniary loss. Advertising by the clinic, describing pets as "like our children" and stating the importance of keeping boarded pets "happy and active," furthered the holding. The clinic's Web site even included a section dealing with the loss of a pet, noting how devastating it can be to lose a companion animal. The court concluded:

> Because of the nature of the business the Clinic was in, and more clearly, the manner in which it held itself out to the public, the Clinic certainly knew that the boarding services it provided were rooted in reasons of a sentimental nature and that a failure to render services properly would result in a non-pecuniary loss. As such, the Smiths are entitled to recover non-pecuniary damages from the Clinic under La. Civ. Code art. 1998 for the Clinics breach of the boarding contract.

Finally, veterinarians risk paying punitive damages when maliciously failing to meet the standard of care or patently ignoring client instructions. *See Silverman v. Animal Medical Clinic*, 41 CONN. L. RPTR. 226 (2006), involving death to a one-year-old English bulldog. The court denied defendant's motion to strike punitive damages. *See also Fredeen v. Stride*, 525 P.2d 166 (Or. 1974) (allowing punitives where veterinarian gave plaintiff's dog to another without consent); *Carroll v. Rock*, 469 S.E.2d 391 (Ga. Ct. App. 1996) (reversed punitives in case where veterinarian lost cat); *Levine v. Knowles*, 197 So. 2d 329 (Fla. Dist. Ct. App. 1967) (punitives available where veterinarian allegedly willfully cremated body to avoid consequences of autopsy and probable malpractice claims overriding client's contrary instructions to hold body).

T. EXTRA-LABEL DRUG USE

When a veterinarian uses a drug other than permitted by Food and Drug Administration ("FDA") regulations, such as for an unapproved species or disease indication or at an unapproved dose, frequency, or route of administration, but still pursuant to the Animal Medicinal Drug Use Clarification Act of 1994 ("AMDUCA"), amending the Federal Food, Drug, and Cosmetic Act, 21 USC § 301 *et seq.*, and 21 CFR Pt. 530, she engages in off-label or extra-label drug use ("ELDU").[8]

---

[8] The AVMA has prepared an online ELDU algorithm. www.avma.org/KB/Resources/Reference/Pages/AMDUCA2.aspx.

AMDUCA made ELDU legal for non-"food producing" animals and for certain drugs in "food producing" animals, giving veterinarians discretion occasionally needed to treat nonhuman animals when the few per-label medications on hand would not aid the patient.

Topical ectoparasiticides, like imidacloprid (found in Advantage® and K9 Advantix®) and permethrin, are not regulated by the FDA.[9] Rather, the Environmental Protection Agency ("EPA") controls them as pesticides under the Federal Insecticide, Fungicide, and Rodenticide Act ("FIFRA"),[10] 7 USC § 136 et seq.[11] The Department of Agriculture's Center for Veterinary Biologics regulates vaccines and autogenous biologics. Veterinarians may produce autogenous biologics when non-autogenous products are unavailable or ineffective, and then only under sterile and safe conditions in compliance with USDA regulation 9 CFR §§ 101.2 and 113.113, as well as VS Memos 800.69 and 800.103. http://www.aphis.usda.gov/animal_health/vet_biologics/vb_cfr.shtml   and   http://www.aphis.usda.gov/animal_health/vet_biologics/vb_vs_memos.shtml.

Whether "prescription" or therapeutic diets are regulated by the FDA as food, drugs, or nutraceuticals remains unclear, though the intended marketing message that they cure, treat, or prevent animal disease certainly gives the FDA considerable regulatory leeway. On Sept. 10, 2012, the FDA-CVM published a draft compliance policy guide titled Labeling and Marketing of Nutritional Products Intended for Use to Diagnose, Cure, Mitigate, Treat, or Prevent Disease in Dogs and Cats, § 690.150 (77 FR 55480), recommending a soft regulatory touch against therapeutic food producers provided they comply with nine enumerated factors (including, most notably, limiting distribution to veterinarians where disease indications are labeled, and stripping the label of disease indications if sole outside veterinary clinics) and clarifying its position that such diets constitute "drugs" as defined by 21 U.S.C. § 321(g)(1)(B) and "food" under 21 U.S.C. § 321(f) which may further be deemed "adulterated" under 21 U.S.C. § 351(a)(5) and 21 U.S.C. § 351(a)(2)(B).

ELDU depends on a valid veterinarian-client-patient relationship. It cannot be delegated to a veterinary technician or assistant, and is authorized only after examining, diagnosing, and evaluating the patient to confirm that his or her health is threatened, or that suffering or death will occur without treatment. Furthermore, the veterinarian engaging in ELDU must be prepared to demonstrate that (1) no approved drug for such species-condition exists; (2) no on-label drug with the same active ingredient in the required dosage and concentration exists; or (3) an on-label drug exists for the species, condition, and in the required dose and concentration

---

[9] However, other parasiticides like selamectin (key ingredient in Revolution ®) are regulated by the FDA and require a prescription.

[10] Unlike AMDUCA, FIFRA does not permit ELDU and all uses contrary to label are illegal.

[11] Prescribing ectoparasiticides for an unapproved species, dose, frequency, or route of administration is not ELDU because off-label use of pesticides is per se illegal. Of course, many parasiticides need not be "prescribed" by a veterinarian at all, as they find their way onto pet supply retail shelves for over-the-counter sale. That said, the EPA gives some latitude to veterinarians repackaging and prescribing topical parasiticides, as discussed in 44 FR 62940 (Nov. 1, 1979) *Pesticide Use and Production by Veterinarians; Statement of Policy on the Applicability of the Federal Insecticide, Fungicide, and Rodenticide Act to Veterinarians.*

but will not prove clinically effective for the intended use. The veterinarian must also carefully maintain knowledge of the identity of the treated animal, and strictly comply with record and label requirements. State regulations may compel veterinarians to obtain informed consent prior to resorting to ELDU, prompting discussions with the client about the reasons for deviating from on-label use and potential risks involved. Because the duty of care applies to every stage of the VCPR, including in diagnosing a patient, prescribing and dispensing a medication, and compounding mediations in-house, the veterinarian must remain attentive. Writing or filling a prescription without a VCPR may be unlawful, as in Alabama and California: Arizona requires a preliminary physical examination.

Many veterinarians run in-house pharmacies to maintain quality control and avert the risk that an independent, human patient pharmacy may err in filling the prescription. Provided the veterinarian has accurately and precisely prescribed a medication for the particular patient or herd, complied with AMDUCA for ELDU, and discussed administration instructions with the client, veterinarians probably have little to fear from downstream pharmacist malpractice. However, since pharmacists do not typically receive training in veterinary pharmacotherapy, veterinarians should ensure that the pharmacy possesses satisfactory credentials and accreditation through the Pharmacy Compounding Accreditation Board (www.pcab.org) before having compounded prescriptions filled by human-grade pharmacies. Compounding[12] of finished form animal drugs is ELDU, so the veterinarian should follow AMDUCA and implementing regulations, as well as state pharmacy and veterinary practice acts. See also FDA Compliance Policy Guide § 608.400 Compounding of Drugs for Use in Animals (http://www.fda.gov/ICECI/ComplianceManuals/CompliancePolicyGuidanceManual/ucm074656.htm). Financial savings to the client does not justify ELDU.

---

[12] Compounding includes flavoring, mixing injectables, and converting a drug to a form administered by a different route (e.g., pill to injectable, oral suspension, or transdermal gel).

Chapter 8

NONNEGLIGENT AND STATUTORY TORTS AGAINST ANIMALS[1]

Accidents happen. But grossly negligent, reckless, intentional, and malicious acts are of a different conceptual order. The spectrum of a defendant's culpability expands the remedies afforded to the injured plaintiff. Legislated tort claims, premised on a violation of an ordinance or statute instead of common law principles, may also furnish special rights of recovery.

A. STATUTORY TORT CLAIMS

Legislatures provide recourse to plaintiffs whose animals suffer injury or death on account of animal abuse[2]; in the operation of railroads[3]; operating motor vehicles[4]; failure to report death or injury and to render aid to negligently injured or killed animal[5]; willful and malicious use of aircraft in stunting or diving over livestock in manner calculated to frighten or stampede[6]; and negligent boarding of horses.[7] In addition to creating statutory torts based on *conduct*, enhanced protections specific to the *type of animal harmed* also exist, as in the case of service animals[8] and enumerated livestock[9] While many ordinances and statutes establish rights and remedies in derogation (or even abrogation) of common law — in which

---

[1] Portions of this chapter are taken with permission of, and from the Thomson Reuters publication Adam P. Karp, *Cause of Action in Intentional Tort for Loss of or Injury to Animal by Human*, 44 COA2d 211 (2010).

[2] *See* Ala. Code §§ 3-1-11.1(b), 9-11-264; Ariz. Rev. Stat. § 3-1307(C); Conn. Gen. Stat. § 22-351; 510 Ill. Comp. Stat. Ann. § 70/16.3; Kan. Stat. Ann. § 29-409; Me. Rev. Stat. Tit. 7, § 3953; Mo. Ann. Stat. § 537.330; Mont. Code Ann. § 27-1-222; N.C. Gen. Stat. § 14-165; Ohio Rev. Code § 1717.11; Okla. Stat. Ann. Tit. 23, § 68; R.I. Gen. Laws § 4-1-5; Tenn. Code Ann. § 44-17-403; Wash. Rev. Code § 4.24.320; Wyo. Stat. Ann. § 11-30-112.

[3] *See* Ala. Code § 37-2-83; Ariz. Rev. Stat. §§ 3-1703, 3-1704; Ark. Const. Art. 17, § 12; Ark. Code §§ 23-12-902, 23-12-904, 23-12-907, 23-12-909; Colo. Rev. Stat. § 40-27-103; Conn. Gen. Stat. § 53-252 (regarding transporting animals); Ind. Code Ann. § 8-6-14-3; Kan. Stat. Ann. § 66-295; Mont. Code § 69-14-707; Nev. Rev. Stat. § 705.150; N.D. Cent. Code § 49-11-30; Or. Rev. Stat. § 608.360; Vt. Stat. Ann. Tit. 5, § 3645.

[4] *See* Ark. Code § 27-51-1406; Me. Rev. State. Tit. 7, §§ 1313, 1420-B; Mont. Code § 49-4-216; N.M. Stat. § 28-7-4; S.C. Code § 43-33-30; Tex. Agric. Code § 143.103; Va. Code § 46.2-932.1.

[5] N.H. Rev. Stat. § 207.39-c.

[6] Mont. Code § 67-1-204(5).

[7] Ky. Rev. Stat. § 422.280.

[8] *See* La. Rev. Stat. § 46:1956; N.Y. Gen. Oblig. Law § 11-107; Tenn. Code §§ 44-17-403(2), 44-17-404; RCW § 49.60.370.

[9] RCW § 4.24.320.

instance they must be construed strictly — others merely codify the common law. As a result, be mindful of arguments that the code may prompt the common law or force an election of remedies.

B. GROSS NEGLIGENCE

Where the tortfeasor fails to exercise even slight care, a claim for gross negligence arises:

> Gross negligence may be more readily understood if anchored to or guided by other more understandable concepts and ought to be directly related to the hazards of the occasion in which it is invoked. *Palsgraf v. Long Island R. Co.*, 248 N.Y. 339, 162 N.E. 99, 59 A.L.R. 1253 (1928). A gentle push of one window washer by another may be merely a playful gesture and of only the slightest negligence when both are standing in a basement window well but put the same two men on the window ledge of a skyscraper 30 stories above the ground and the same playful gesture becomes an act of the grossest negligence, if not one of wanton depravity.

Nist v. Tudor 407 P.2d 798, 803–804 (Wash. 1965). As further guidance, consider *Knowles* and *Johnson*, two Florida appellate cases permitting emotional distress damages related to gross veterinary malpractice. *Knowles Animal Hospital, Inc. v. Wills*, 360 So.2d 37 (Fla.App.1978); *Johnson v. Wander*, 592 So. 2d 1225 (Fla. Dist. Ct. App. 1992). *See Petco Animal Supplies, Inc. v. Schuster*, 144 S.W.3d 554 (Tex. App. 2004) (plaintiff's dog escaped from groomer, entered traffic, and died; court denied mental anguish damages for negligence but noted that higher degrees of culpability with evidence of ill will, animus, or desire to harm plaintiff personally might support general damage recovery). However, some jurisdictions have abolished the distinction between ordinary and gross negligence liability. See *Scott v. Rizzo*, 634 P.2d 1234 (N.M. 1981). In others, the distinction remains one without a difference given no clear right to recover enhanced or different damages (e.g., emotional distress). Yet, gross negligence remains a basis for punitive damages in certain jurisdictions. *Ruiz v. Southern Pac. Transp. Co.*, 638 P.2d 406 (N.M. Ct. App. 1981). Gross negligence also serves as the disciplinary standard for veterinarians in some states. *N.M. Bd. of Veterinary Medicine v. Riegger*, 137 P.3d 619, 623–624 (N.M. Ct. App. 2006), *aff'd in part, rev'd in part o.g.*, 164 P.3d 947 (N.M. 2007).

C. INTENTIONAL INFLICTION OF EMOTIONAL DISTRESS

Intentional infliction of emotional distress (IIED), conversion, trespass to chattels, and malicious injury share a common thread of intentionality resulting in harm to a nonhuman animal. Such torts open up categories of damage not typically available for mere negligence. In the case of nonhuman victims, the bar for general damages is raised several levels higher. Thus, to obtain compensation for mental anxiety associated with grief over an animal's untimely injury or death, certain aggravating factors must exist. In the last few decades, appellate opinions have accelerated the transition that approves recovery of emotional damages in the instances of outrageous conduct evincing evil motives, as well as "good faith" yet intentional interference with possession and control of an animal. Except for the rare jurisdiction, simple negligence has never allowed recovery of emotional harm to the animal's guardian.

In contrast to the high degree of failure that negligent infliction of emotional distress (NIED) claims face throughout the nation,[10] animal-victim intentional infliction of emotional distress (IIED) claims, also known as outrage, enjoy much greater success. Judiciaries suffer less discomfort stretching common-law doctrines to encompass outrageous mistreatment of animals. Perhaps this represents the earliest cross-pollination from the criminal to the civil justice system, where animal cruelty law development seeds a tandem civil theory in tort. This signals a change from a property-based to a morality-based view of animals consistent with the reaction the average civilized person has when presented with heinous details of animal victimization intending to cause or recklessly causing another *human* severe emotional distress. This is the most crucial distinction between the tort of outrage

---

[10] A few jurisdictions still allow a bystander NIED claim in the case of harm to a nonhuman animal. *See, e.g., Barrios v. Safeway Ins. Co.*, 97 So.3d 1019 (La.App.2012)(upholding award of $10,000 for emotional distress arising from witnessing motorist strike and kill dog based on common law permitting mental anguish damages to be recovered in the loss of corporeal movable property "when the owner is present or nearby and suffers psychic trauma as a result"); *Gill v. Brown*, 107 Idaho 1137 (Id. App. 1985) (acknowledging claim cognizability in animal death case but only where evidence of physical injury accompanying distress can be proved, which Idaho courts thereafter clarified to include sleep disorders, headaches, stomach pain, fatigue, loss of appetite, irritability, anxiety). In appropriate instances, mental anguish damages may be recovered under an NIED theory when plaintiff's life and limb is endangered by an imminent and direct threatened invasion of her personal security (as in the case of nearly being bitten by one's own panicking dog enduring excruciating pain from a recent trauma; or when nearly being run over by a passing vehicle that kills the dog attached to the short leash held by the plaintiff).

The majority position denies recovery of NIED arising from injury or death to a nonhuman. For an excellent summary of the rationale against, *see Rabideau v. City of Racine*, 627 N.W.2d 795 (Wis. 2001); also see *Pickford v. Masion*, 124 Wash. App. 257 (2004). In *Medura v. Town & Country Veterinary Assoc., P.C.*, 2012 Conn. Super. LEXIS 2078 (Aug. 10, 2012), a malpractice suit alleging acute renal failure of a nine-year-old cat secondary to Metacam toxicity, the court conducted a searching analysis of noneconomic damage law in human and nonhuman applications to resolve the open question left unanswered by the seminal case *Myers v. Hartford*, 84 Conn. App. 395 (2004), of whether a plaintiff who witnesses the fatal injury to an animal companion can sustain a claim for bystander NIED. In answering the question negatively, the court opted not to follow the logic of Judge Rubinow in *Vaneck v. Cosenza-Drew*, 2009 Conn. Super. LEXIS 1056 (Apr. 20, 2009), where a plaintiff witnessed the fatal impact of defendant's motor vehicle striking her dog. The *Medura* court held that Connecticut law would not warrant recovery by Medura for the mental anguish experienced over the course of her cat's decompensation. The court wrote: "A rule that would allow for a plaintiff to recover damages for emotional distress due to the alleged malpractice of a veterinarian that resulted in the loss of a pet, but not allow recovery for a person due to the alleged malpractice of the injured party's treating physician would defy common sense." *Medura*, at *5.

The New Jersey Supreme Court followed this trend of categorically excepting nonhumans from NIED claims, reaffirming embrace of only those who "share a close familial relationship or intimate, marital-like bond with the victim," in *McDougall v. Lamm*, 211 N.J. 203, 207 (2012). The implication: nonhumans can never fit this mold unless the legislature says so. When McDougall watched Angel, her Maltipoo for whom she paid $200 as a puppy and had for nine years, get mauled to death in front of her by Lamm's large, unrestrained dog, the court nonetheless felt compelled to deny general damages from Lamm's negligent control, yet it upheld the award of $5000 intrinsic value for Angel, based on "the loss and [plaintiff's] expectation of having the benefit of these . . . tricks and desirable behaviors in a companion over the course of many years," and that replacement cost would "not compensate plaintiff for the loss of a well-trained pet." *Id.*, at 210.

and the other intentional causes of action (e.g., conversion and malicious injury), for IIED will not lie absent a desire or deliberate indifference to *indirectly* inflict emotional harm on another through cruelty *directly* visited upon the animal.

Virtually all jurisdictions adopt several of the following elements of IIED:

1. "Extreme and outrageous" conduct going beyond all possible bounds of decency and considered utterly intolerable in a civilized community, causing shock of conscience;

2. Defendant intended to cause severe emotional distress in the plaintiff;

3. Defendant knew or should have known that actions taken would result in serious emotional distress to the plaintiff;

4. Defendant was reckless in causing severe emotional distress in the plaintiff;

5. Defendant's actions proximately caused the plaintiff's psychic injury;

6. Severe emotional distress or distress of such nature that no reasonable person could be expected to endure it; and

7. Plaintiff was the "object" of defendant's actions (i.e., direct IIED); present at time outrageous conduct was directed at a close family member (i.e., familial bystander IIED); or present at time outrageous conduct was directed at any other person if distress results in bodily harm (i.e., perfect stranger bystander IIED).

If there ever were an instance where this cause of action would apply, the facts of *Womack v. Von Rardon*, 135 P.3d 542 (Wash. Ct. App. 2006) seem exemplary. Defendants took Max, a feline cared for by plaintiff, to a middle school, doused him in gasoline, and then set him on fire. Good Samaritans rescued Max, but not before he suffered extensive burns. His dire injuries resulted in euthanasia. Both minor defendants were found guilty of first-degree animal cruelty. One set of defendants (i.e., parents and minor child) settled out of court, and plaintiff obtained a default judgment against the remaining duo of parent-child defendants. The trial court awarded $5,000 for the value of Max and plaintiff's emotional distress but dismissed various claims, including one for outrage. Plaintiff appealed. The court affirmed dismissal of the IIED claim.

This outcome may strike the reader as incredible. One can hardly fathom the level of brutishness to which one would have to descend to methodically torture a family's companion with gasoline and a match without transgressing social tolerances. Defendants' deeds unquestionably subjected the plaintiff to abuse, fright, and shock. Their violent, antisocial conduct easily appeared to meet the standard for the tort of outrage — *except* for the specific intent requirement. The plaintiff unsuccessfully argued that had the defendants encountered Max as a feral cat on public rangelands, they might not have intended to cause severe emotional distress to a human being; however, they happened upon Max resting on the plaintiff's porch, protected from the elements and set back far from the street to avoid cars and intruders. Defendants knew or should have known that Max was the ward and domesticated property of the plaintiff who would and did foreseeably suffer dramatic mental anxiety following their actions. Any reasonable person may assume that, on the night in question, Max had an owner who would serve as the potential plaintiff in any action concerning his demise. Max was neither stray nor feral. Rather, he was healthy, obviously well cared-for, and sitting on private residential property. The focus, plaintiff argued, was not whether the defendants *desired* that Max's owners and guardians suffer emotional distress but either (1) that they knew or should have known with substantial certainty that severe emotional distress would result from their action (intent as "substantial certainty") or (2) that they behaved in reckless disregard of probable, severely emotionally unsettling consequences.

To deny the plaintiff recovery under these circumstances would sanction the type of argument a defendant might make that robbing a house or breaking into a business does not give rise to IIED damages if he did not know the identities of the residents and proprietors. IIED, plaintiff reasoned, should not be precluded because the subject of the conduct had the legal status of property; rather, the conduct itself determines whether the act was heartless, flagrant, and outrageous so as to establish fault. The appellate court agreed with this contention, but not the result urged by counsel:

> The summary judgment required Ms. Womack to establish she suffered severe emotional distress and the defendants intended, rather than negligently brought about that distress. The required emotional distress "must be more than 'transient and trivial emotional distress' which is 'a part of the price of living among people.' "

> What happened to Max was deplorable, but the record does not sufficiently establish the required intent or the necessary severity.

> Moreover, the trial court, after an evidentiary hearing not before us, did find liability among the remaining liability theories. We are not persuaded the damages awarded would differ under a different liability theory except for treble damages in the case of statutory waste. While distressing, the trial court could have decided the harm was not intended or was not sufficiently severe. Thus, the court did not err in dismissing the outrage claim.

Id., at 545 (citations omitted). Though rejecting the outrage claim, the court did something innovative and breathed life into the doctrine of evolving common law: it created a new cause of action (malicious injury to a pet) described in a later section.

The tort of IIED typically requires proof of three elements: (1) extreme and outrageous conduct, (2) intentional or reckless infliction of emotional distress, and (3) actual result to plaintiff of severe emotional distress. *Reid v. Pierce Cy.*, 961 P.2d 333 (Wash. 1998). The elements were adopted from the RESTATEMENT (2D) TORTS, § 46. IIED damages have been recognized in the killing of nonhuman animals. *See Richardson v. Fairbanks North Star Borough*, 705 P.2d 454, 456 (Alaska 1985) (intentional or reckless killing of pet animal); *Gill v. Brown*, 695 P.2d 1276 (Idaho Ct. App. 1985) (reckless or negligent killing of donkey, causing extreme mental anguish and trauma). Some jurisdictions add refinements to the standard three-pronged test. Section 46 of the *Restatement*, for instance, follows:

(1) One who by extreme and outrageous conduct intentionally or recklessly causes severe emotional distress to another is subject to liability for such emotional distress, and if bodily harm to the other results from it, for such bodily harm.

(2) Where such conduct is directed at a third person, the actor is subject to liability if he intentionally or recklessly causes severe emotional distress

    (a) to a member of such person's immediate family who is present at the time, whether or not such distress results in bodily harm, or

    (b) to any other person who is present at the time, if such distress results in bodily harm.

The court in *Reid* embraced the "immediate family member — present during conduct" limitation in comment l of the RESTATEMENT as a basis to exclude plaintiffs who experience severe emotional distress but do not share this consanguineous or marital connection. *Reid*, at 337. Comment l, however, states:

> Furthermore, the decided cases in which recovery has been allowed have been those in which the plaintiffs have been near relatives or at least close associates of the person attacked. The language of the cases is not, however, limited to such plaintiffs, and there appears to be no essential reason why a stranger who is asked for a match on the street should not recover when the man who asks for it is shot down before his eyes at least where his emotional distress results in bodily harm.

RESTATEMENT (2D) TORTS, § 46, cmt. l. Id., cmt. f, ill. 11. Plaintiffs often founder on this requirement by not conceptually distinguishing defendant's *harmful act* (inflicted upon the nonhuman victim) from the defendant's *specific intent* to cause severe emotional distress in the human caretaker. Typically, act and intent unite behind a singular purpose — namely, to torture an animal, with unintended, purely incidental, or merely passing concern for the animal's guardian. Such a scenario, however, does not establish IIED. Rather, the intent must at least be dual in nature — i.e., while the act targets the animal herself, the intent contemplates harm to the animal's guardian. While no doctrine expressly prevents a plaintiff from recovering in the case of mixed motives (i.e., the tortfeasor harbors enmity toward the animal *and* the guardian and seeks to hurt the guardian through the animal's death or suffering), the plaintiff must prove that the defendant injured or killed the animal to, at least in substantial part, turn the guardian into a quivering mass of fear, angst, or extreme mental trauma. Absent that specific intent, IIED fails.

Some defendants protest the application of IIED to nonhuman animal death cases, citing to comment l. This reference, however, does not invalidate a plaintiff's claim since the same section includes Illustration 11, which clearly sets forth an example where outrage applies to the intentional killing of a pet dog:

> A, who knows that B is pregnant, intentionally shoots before the eyes of B a pet dog, to which A knows that B is greatly attached. B suffers severe emotional distress, which results in a miscarriage. A is subject to liability to B for the distress and for the miscarriage.

The precise basis of liability presented in the Restatement illustration remains unclear, though the emphasis on distress causing bodily injury (i.e., miscarriage) appears to construe the "pet dog" as either an "immediate family" member to B (in which case bodily harm resulting from anguish is immaterial under RESTATEMENT (2D) TORTS, § 46(2)(a)), or the "third person" (invoking § 46(2)(b)). Either way, the RESTATEMENT commentators had to construe the nonhuman canine as a legal person. Alternatively, it might bypass § 46(2) entirely and just conclude that intentional harm to one's property is a very foreseeable way to cause another severe emotional distress (applying § 46(1)). For a more detailed discussion of the nuances of the tort, see *Modern Status of Intentional Infliction of Mental Distress as Independent Tort; "Outrage,"* 38 A.L.R.4TH 998.

Brown v. Muhlenberg Tp., 269 F.3d 205 (3d Cir. 2001), presents a real-life example that resembles Illustrion 11, finding that a short hesitation prior to discharging a firearm can create a triable inference of intent to cause distress and support IIED. A Rottweiler named Immi, owned by the plaintiff, escaped during a residential move and wandered to a parking lot adjoining the plaintiff's property. A police officer parked and approached, clapped his hands and called. Immi barked several times and withdrew, circling around a vehicle in the parking lot about 20 feet from the curb. The officer crossed the street to a position between 10 to 12 feet away, where Immi was stationary and not growling or barking. The plaintiff screamed out an open, screened window, "That's my dog, don't shoot!" The officer hesitated a few seconds before pointing his gun. He then killed Immi with five shots (four in her rear). The district court granted summary judgment dismissal to the defendants, but the court of appeals reversed and remanded, concluding that IIED was cognizable, in part because the plaintiff was present, looking on, and desiring to reassert control over her dog at the time she was executed. It also remarked that Immi presented no imminent threat. Further, the court held that the record "clearly support[ed] a finding that Officer Eberly intended to inflict or knew he would inflict severe emotional distress on Kim Brown." *Id.*, at 218.

Where the defendant knows the plaintiff, proving IIED is easier than in the "perfect stranger" scenario. A prehistory between the parties may reveal the defendant's nefarious motivation to harm plaintiff's animal companion. However, even perfect strangers may leave hints putting the defendant on notice that harming the animal victim will generate severe emotional distress in the guardian. A service animal assisting a disabled handler presents a straightforward example. Shooting a dog in front of apparent family members is another. In *City of Garland v. White*, 368 S.W.2d 12 (Tex. App. 1963), the plaintiff's three-year-old Boxer was killed after being chased by law enforcement into the plaintiff's garage and fired upon at the step leading into the house. The premeditated intentional shotgun blast also made several small holes in the door opening from the house into the garage and nearly hit the plaintiff and his mother, who were eating lunch at the time in the dining room. With respect to the award of $200 for Mr. White's mental suffering, the court affirmed, but did not clarify the doctrinal basis for recovery (e.g., IIED, NIED, conversion).

Contractual privity between the parties makes proving causation less difficult. Where free-lease boarders of horses lied to the owners about selling them to slaughter, the IIED claim survived, the court focusing on the defendant's conduct, not the subject of the conduct (i.e., animal vs. human as primary victim). *Burgess v. Taylor*, 44 S.W.3d 806 (Ky. Ct. App. 2001). That said, formal (but impersonal) privity with a large corporation or common carrier having no or minimal prior involvement with a patron or passenger may not result in a finding of liability under IIED principles, as seen in *Gluckman v. American Airlines, Inc.*, 844 F. Supp. 151 (S.D.N.Y. 1994). In *Gluckman*, the plaintiff's dog died from heat stroke in the cargo hold of an airplane; the IIED claim failed because there was no evidence that the airline's conduct was directed intentionally at the plaintiff.

1. Outrageous Conduct

Mere annoyance, inconvenience, and temporary irritation do not rise to the level of outrageous conduct. *Miller v. Peraino*, 626 A.2d 637 (Pa. Super. Ct. 1993) ("[It] has not been enough that the defendant has acted with an intent which is tortious or even criminal, or that he has intended to inflict emotional distress, or even that his conduct has been characterized by malice, or a degree of aggravation which would entitle the plaintiff to punitive damages for another tort."). According to the RESTATEMENT (2D) TORTS, § 46, comment j, the distress must be so extreme that "no reasonable person could be expected to endure it." "Transient or trivial" or "exaggerated and unreasonable" emotional discomfort does not suffice.

Many IIED cases concern defendants directly targeting the plaintiff as the primary and sole victim. Animal-based IIED suits, however, involve at least two victims — the nonhuman animal (who often suffers extreme physical injury or death) and an eyewitness or bystander to the outrageous conduct, frequently the owner/guardian of that animal. Such instances may require the plaintiff to overcome an unspoken evidentiary hurdle — that conduct otherwise outrageous if directed at a human is equally condemnable if directed at a nonhuman. Thanks to a relatively recent national push to enact stronger animal cruelty laws, convincing a court to traverse this parallel should not present too much difficulty. The more germane challenge, rather, relates to proving that a normally constituted individual may suffer severe emotional distress from observing shocking mistreatment of an animal as arising from a legitimate and foreseeable, profoundly impactful emotional connection. Few would question whether a mother watching her human child intentionally run down by a car would justifiably experience severe emotional distress, but in some benighted jurisdictions, swapping a cat or a hamster for the human being in this example might not be conceded as juridically equivalent.

Plaintiffs have the best chance of surviving the assertion that conduct was not sufficiently outrageous at the motion to dismiss stage. *Matvejs v. Martin Cy. Sheriff's Off.*, 2006 U.S. Dist. LEXIS 91715 (S.D. Fla. Dec. 19, 2006) (because outrageousness could not be decided at the motion to dismiss stage, IIED claim remained). *DeVita v. Sirico*, 2001 Conn. Super. LEXIS 360 (Conn. Super. Ct. 2001), also provides an example of an IIED claim adequately pleaded to overcome a motion to strike. In *DeVita*, the defendant served as an imposter, claiming to the humane society to be the plaintiff's conservator, then attempting to have the family dog killed, and later forcing the dog to be removed from the house.

One would think that deliberately shooting someone's animal companion without the need for self-defense would satisfy the outrage prong of IIED. However, in

Ivey v. Hamlin, 2002 Tenn. App. LEXIS 404 (Tenn. Ct. App. June 7, 2002), the court found the facts not sufficiently atrocious to warrant liability under IIED where a deputy killed plaintiff's English bulldog. A similar outcome obtained in *Kaiser v. U.S.*, 761 F. Supp. 150 (D.D.C. 1991), a Federal Tort Claims Act case involving a U.S. Capitol police officer shooting and injuring the plaintiff's dog. Despite acknowledging the senselessness of the slaying, the court dismissed the IIED claim because it did not rise to the level of an atrocity and the plaintiff did not fear for his own safety. In *Ammon v. Welty*, 113 S.W.3d 185 (Ky. Ct. App.2002), the county dog warden shot the family dog in the head before expiration of the statutorily mandated hold period. In dismissing the IIED claim, the court focused on the facts that the dog was not shot in the plaintiffs' presence, and that no positive identification of the dog's owner existed (thus negating intent to inflict severe emotional distress on identifiable plaintiffs). In *Kautzman v. McDonald*, 621 N.W.2d 871 (N.D. 2001), dog owners sued the county, deputies, state, and highway patrol for shooting their dogs, raising claims of IIED and seeking more than $50,000 for intentional, wrongful, negligent, grossly negligent, and willful acts. In dismissing the IIED claim, the court held the allegations were not sufficiently outrageous, emphasizing how the distance between the officers and the dogs necessitated the shooting. Further, the officers were undisputedly unaware that the dogs belonged to the plaintiffs, negating intent. As an aside for those desirous of exploring cutting-edge causes of action, consider that the plaintiffs undertook a failed effort to litigate an implied private right of action for willful cruelty to animals.

In *Clark v. Brien*, 59 F.3d 1082 (10th Cir. 1995), an insured sued the insurer of plaintiffs' homestead for IIED, alleging personnel hired by insurer to conduct surveillance shot plaintiff's dog. Defendant appealed the jury award for plaintiffs. The Tenth Circuit Court of Appeals reversed, noting that surveillance alone would not constitute IIED, and to prevail, the jury would need to reasonably believe that the insurer was vicariously liable for both surveillance and shooting through an agency relationship or ratification; further, the jury would have to find that the guards intentionally or recklessly caused the plaintiffs' severe emotional distress so outrageous in character as to go beyond all possible bounds of decency.

IIED claims against humane societies often arise from decisions to impound, seize, and euthanize allegedly neglected or abused animals. Routinely faltering on the outrageousness prong, dismissal hinges on the inverse relationship between atrocity and legal justification (i.e., the more evidence that the act was justified by law, the less likely the act will be deemed atrocious). *See Daskalea v. Washington Humane Society*, 480 F. Supp. 2d 16 (D. 2007) (failure to allege facts demonstrating that the Humane Society's conduct was "outrageous" or "beyond all possible bounds of decency"). In *Hegarty v. Addison Cy. Hum. Soc.*, 848 A.2d 1139 (Vt. 2004), a warrantless seizure of a horse by the humane society led to claims of conversion and IIED. The plaintiff appealed summary judgment dismissal, but the Vermont Supreme Court found the warrantless seizure of a geriatric horse for 12 days did not deny due process, was statutorily authorized, and, thus, not outrageous. In *Ghaderi v. Hum. Soc. of Santa Clara Valley*, 2005 Cal. App. Unpub. LEXIS 4910 (June 3, 2005), a pro se complainant sued the humane society for "[a]buse, injury, death, and cruelty to animals," specifically his 35 to 40 cats, when they were towed away in the complainant's impounded motor home. His claims for negligence, IIED, and conversion were dismissed in pretrial dispositive motions. Finding the seizure lawful by statute and that the complainant statutorily abandoned the cats by failing to pay boarding charges to the humane society, the court affirmed dismissal of the negligence and conversion claims. The IIED claim was dismissed on the pleadings, having run aground on the outrageousness element, for if they were not negligent, they certainly were not acting outrageously.

In *Thompson v. Lied Animal Shelter*, 2009 U.S. Dist. LEXIS 96383 (D. Nev. Oct. 14, 2009), the plaintiff's 13-month-old dog, who refused to eat, was left with the plaintiff's contact information at an animal hospital by an unidentified dog sitter while the plaintiff was in California. After the dog became uncooperative, the animal hospital called Animal Control to ask that the dog be taken to the shelter. Plaintiff was not contacted. Three days later, the animal hospital called the plaintiff, who then called the animal shelter. The shelter's employee told the plaintiff that the dog would be held for 10 more days and then adopted if not claimed. The plaintiff explained that the dog was "all he had, and the only thing close to a child he'd ever had," and would arrange to get the dog as soon as possible if any emergency arose. The animal shelter employee assured him the dog would be safe 10 more days. Upon plaintiff's return from California, he went to the shelter on the eighth day after impound. He was told the dog was euthanized four days earlier, explaining that the dog had "a 72-hour outdate" because of his demeanor. The plaintiff, proceeding pro se, sued the shelter for negligence, NIED, IIED, and wrongful death in the amount of $15 million. Despite no case on point, the federal district court dismissed Thompson's NIED and IIED claims. As to IIED, the court stated that "euthanization of an animal outside the presence of the owner cannot be found to be 'unquestionably violent and shocking,' such as to support an IIED claim[.]" Further, the dog was not a "close relative" by blood or marriage, thereby negating recovery under both theories. *See also Jackson v. Silicon Valley Animal Control Auth.*, 2008 U.S. Dist. LEXIS 98521 (N.D. Cal. Dec. 5, 2008) (several animals seized due to suspected neglect and cruelty, but plaintiff failed to pay board and care charges required by law (rendering them abandoned); IIED, conversion, and NIED claims dismissed because animal control officers' actions were lawful and proper and hardly outrageous).

IIED has also been claimed where neighbors find straying dogs or cats and take them to animal control under false pretenses. In *Alvarez v. Clasen*, 946 So.2d 181 (La. Ct. App. 2006), the plaintiff adopted a cat who later went missing from her residence. During her search, the plaintiff asked the defendants if they had found the cat. The defendants denied knowledge of her whereabouts. Actually, the defendants had trapped the cat and taken her to the animal control shelter where she was later euthanized. The trial court dismissed plaintiff's suit for conversion and IIED, and plaintiff appealed. The appellate court affirmed, noting that no conversion occurred in the absence of a wrongful act of dominion or control. Defendants' trapping of the cat at their residence was not unlawful in light of local impoundment ordinances for stray animals. As to the claim that defendants allegedly lied to plaintiff about the cat's whereabouts, such alleged conduct failed to meet the prerequisites for an outrage claim. *See also Damiano v. Lind*, 2011 Wash.

App. LEXIS 2049 (Aug. 25, 2011) (no IIED under similar circumstances, except here defendant trapped neighbor's cat and allegedly killed or abandoned same far from home).

2. Defendant's Conduct as Proximate Cause of Plaintiff's Emotional Distress

As noted above, some jurisdictions require that the plaintiff witness the tortious event and that defendant's primary victim be a "family member," two refinements on the IIED doctrine that serve to rein in recoverable emotional harms by applying spatial, consanguineous, and temporal limitations that deem certain injuries unforeseeable as a matter of law. For instance, in *Vaneck v. Drew*, 2009 Conn. Super. LEXIS 1056 (Apr. 16, 2009), the IIED claim survived because the plaintiff witnessed the injury. Yet contrast *Vaneck* with other Connecticut cases that dismissed on this ground. *See Silverman v. Animal Medical Clinic*, 2006 Conn. Super. LEXIS 1135 (Apr. 11, 2006) (IIED dismissed); *Baton v. Sousa*, 2005 Conn. Super. LEXIS 2642 (Oct. 6, 2005) (IIED dismissed despite allegation that cat died after eating antifreeze-laced cat food fed by the defendant); *Pantelopoulos v. Pantelopoulos*, 49 Conn. Supp. 209 (Super. Ct. 2005) (former wife moved out of family home leaving dog to die from starvation in garage; ex-husband's IIED claim barred); *Myers v. City of Hartford*, 853 A.2d 621 (Conn. App. Ct. 2004) (dismissing IIED based on failure to witness tort); *Coston v. Reardon*, 2001 Conn. Super. LEXIS 3188 (Oct. 18, 2001) (dismissing IIED as unrecognized claim in case of animal victim, instead focusing on direct IIED elements (for example, whether plaintiff feared for her own safety).).

Practitioners should be mindful of IIED's spatial-temporal limitation, as that factor alone has often mandated dismissal. For instance, in *Bakay v. Yarnes*, 2005 U.S. Dist. LEXIS 39473 (W.D. Wash. Dec. 30, 2005), animal control and the sheriff seized 68 cats from plaintiffs' cattery pursuant to a warrant, but then euthanized 40 of them that evening, many through intracardiac injection on conscious cats and kittens. Plaintiffs raised numerous tort claims, including outrage. Finding that the actions taken by the county's law enforcement were not outrageous in any way, that there was no credible evidence the plaintiffs suffered severe emotional distress, and that neither plaintiff was present when the cats in question were euthanized, the IIED claim failed as a matter of law.

Similarly, in *Daughen v. Fox*, 539 A.2d 858 (Pa. Super. Ct. 1988), the appellate court dismissed IIED claims against veterinarians and an animal hospital as insufficiently outrageous (i.e., performing an operation to remove a needle from a dog's intestine when the basis for the diagnosis was the radiograph of a different dog, the radiograph was cropped to remove the names of the owners of the dog, and the veterinarians said that the dog would die without surgery). One year prior to this decision, the court of common pleas dismissed the IIED claim on another basis, namely that a dog was not an immediate member of the family. *Daughen v. Fox*, 1 Pa. D. & C.4th 422 (C.P. 1987).

In *Krasnecky v. Meffen*, 56 Mass. App. Ct. 418 (2002), sheep owners sought emotional distress damages under NIED and IIED when dogs slaughtered their sheep on their property. While limiting the class of persons allowed such recovery to a parent or person closely related to the primary victim, the court of appeals nonetheless did not reach the "novel question" of whether the class may include those suffering the loss of a companion animal. Instead, it highlighted plaintiffs' failure to satisfy the spatial and temporal proximity restrictions of common-law NIED:

> Putting aside the broader issue of noneconomic damage for injuries to companion animals, under the pragmatic position taken by our case law, the plaintiffs' absence at the time of the killing of their sheep and the fact that they did not learn of the slaughter until the following day alone preclude any recovery for the emotional distress suffered by them.

Id., at 422. The IIED claim failed on similar grounds.

In *Jackson v. Placer Cy.*, 2007 U.S. Dist. LEXIS 70426 (E.D. Cal. Sept. 24, 2007), animal control issued the plaintiff a preseizure notice informing her of intent to take her underweight horses. The parties reached an accord that allowed her to retain custody provided she adhered to a tentative feed plan, only to result in Jackson violating it. Thereafter, police procured a search warrant and took the horses. She was then convicted of three felony cruelty charges. Meanwhile, some horses were euthanized and others transferred to third parties. Jackson brought a variety of claims, including IIED, NIED, and conversion. The IIED claim was dismissed as to the euthanasia based on lack of evidence, and as to the transfers based on an unproved causal nexus to severe emotional distress.

3.   Severe Emotional Distress Suffered by Plaintiff

Typically, an IIED plaintiff need not prove physical injury manifested by emotional distress nor produce medical evidence of a diagnosable emotional disorder. However, when the plaintiff is not the "object" of the outrageous conduct, courts must perform an analysis similar, in part, to that of a bystander NIED claim by invoking such restrictions as consanguinity or affinity, spatial proximity, and temporal immediacy. Even assuming that a plaintiff may overcome these limitations, the plaintiff must still prove severe emotional distress. Thankfully, some jurisdictions presume severity based on outrageousness of misconduct. *Browning v. Slenderella Systems of Seattle*, 341 P.2d 859 (Wash. 1959) (outrageousness "self-proves" distress, obviating need for independent evidentiary showing of severity). On the other hand, consider *Dittrich v. Seeds*, 2005 U.S. Dist. LEXIS 22078 (E.D. Pa. Sept. 28, 2005), involving the shooting death of plaintiffs' dogs by a law enforcement officer. Though the officer "exacerbated [the male plaintiff's] psychiatric symptoms" to include suicidal/homicidal ideation, major depression, tearfulness, and hopelessness, because he provided no medical evidence of physical manifestations, the court dismissed his IIED claim. However, the female plaintiff, who was diagnosed with PTSD, major depressive disorder, and panic attacks, submitted enough medical evidence to substantiate the claim.

In other circumstances, causation exists, but not severity. In *Richardson v. Fairbanks North Star Borough*, 705 P.2d 454 (Alaska 1985), the borough's animal shelter mistakenly killed the plaintiffs' dog by violating a municipal ordinance requiring a 72-hour hold before euthanasia. The borough offered judgment for

$2,000, which the plaintiffs rejected, obtaining a jury verdict of $300 (as limited by the court's order limiting damages to fair market value or replacement cost). Resultantly, the court awarded $3,763 to the borough in costs and fees under the state's offer of judgment rules. On appeal, the court determined that the plaintiffs could not recover for their own pain and suffering, punitive damages, or actual value of the dog, but recognized a cause of action for IIED or reckless killing of a pet animal in appropriate circumstances. Still, the court left undisturbed the trial court's assessment that plaintiffs' emotional distress lacked the severity to warrant an IIED claim.

Schmidt v. Stearman, 253 S.W.3d 35 (Ark. 2007), provides another example of nonseverity. Plaintiff sued the defendant for conversion, trespass, and outrage resulting from the ransacking of his home and shooting deaths of his five dogs, whom he considered "children," while he was on vacation. The defendant admitted to the forced entry and shooting, claiming it was part of the process to evict the plaintiff. The defendant believed the property had been abandoned but admitted that he

> shot [the plaintiff's] dogs and "slung them over the brush," even though he acknowledged that he was acquainted with the dogs, knew they were pets, and had never had any trouble with them.

Id., at 39. The defendant claimed he killed the dogs because they could turn "wild." The trial court directed verdict for the defendant on the trespass and outrage claims. The jury issued a defense verdict on the conversion claim. Plaintiff's motion for new trial was denied, and appeal followed. On the outrage claim, although the court agreed that a jury might consider the defendant's actions "heartless and gratuitous, exceeding all bounds of decency," the directed verdict was proper because the plaintiff failed to prove he sustained emotional distress so severe that no reasonable person could be expected to endure it. Recurring depression and fear of staying on the farm did not suffice.

Few jurisdictions require the proffer of objective medical evidence to corroborate claims of severe emotional distress. For instance, in *Van Eaton v. Thon*, 764 S.W.2d 674 (Mo. Ct. App. 1988), plaintiff sued for assault and battery, IIED, and damage to property arising from riding her horse along a disputed public right-of-way, prompting the landowner defendant to punch the horse in the jaw with a closed fist. In addition to the horse becoming "head-shy," defendant threatened to shoot plaintiff and her horse and gave her the finger. The jury award of $1,000 actual damages and $7,500 punitive for the plaintiff was reversed with respect to the part of the award pertaining to the IIED claim, which failed due to lack of expert medical testimony that the mental injury was diagnosed and sufficiently severe to be medically significant — introducing a unique twist on the traditional IIED elements found in other states. *See also State ex rel. Benz v. Blackwell*, 716 S.W.2d 270, 273 (Mo. Ct. App. 1986).

Consider also *Miller v. Peraino*, 626 A.2d 637 (Pa. Super. Ct. 1993), where a veterinarian sued dog owners for, *inter alia*, defamation, IIED, and intentional interference with contractual relations. The dog owners counterclaimed, alleging IIED as well, which was dismissed due to failure to support the alleged distress by competent medical evidence. Of note was the court's application of RESTATEMENT (2D)

TORTS, § 46 to bystander IIED claims, where the primary victim is a nonhuman.

4. Conduct Not Intentional or Reckless

Specific intent matters. Failing to prove the motivation behind the defendant's action will nullify an IIED claim. In *Whalen v. Isaacs*, 233 Ga. App. 367 (1998), a neighbor left a message on the plaintiff's answering machine saying the dog would die in 24 hours if not treated immediately for consumption of a poisonous chemical. Upon rushing the dog to the veterinarian, the plaintiff learned that the dog was likely not harmed. The court dismissed the IIED claim due to lack of evidence proving the call was a hoax instead of the act of a Good Samaritan.

D. CONVERSION AND TRESPASS TO CHATTELS

Conversion typically involves the wrongful possession of, or dominion over, personal property in defiance to the owner's right thereto, unauthorized and injurious use of another's property, or wrongful detention after demand has been made. *Nosker v. Trinity Land Co.*, 757 P.2d 803 (N.M. Ct. App. 1988). In Illinois, the elements include: (1) defendant's unauthorized or wrongful assumption of control, dominion, or ownership over a plaintiff's personal property; (2) plaintiff's right in the property; (3) plaintiff's right to immediate possession of the property, absolutely and unconditionally; and (4) plaintiff's demand for possession of the property. *Cirrincione v. Johnson*, 703 N.E.2d 67 (Ill. 1998). Narrow interpretations of the doctrine (e.g., limited to refusal to deliver on demand) have been criticized. *See Case Credit Corp. v. Portales Nat. Bank*, 966 P.2d 1172, 1174–1176 (N.M. 1998) (Minzer, J., dissenting). JUDGE MINZER noted that the RESTATEMENT (2D) TORTS, § 223 lists *seven* types of conversion, including abrogation of a security interest. Section 223 provides:

A conversion may be committed by intentionally:

(a) dispossessing another of a chattel as stated in §§ 221 and 222;

(b) destroying or altering a chattel as stated in § 226;

(c) using a chattel as stated in §§ 227 and 228;

(d) receiving a chattel as stated in §§ 229 and 231;

(e) disposing of a chattel as stated in § 233;

(f) misdelivering a chattel as stated in §§ 234 and 235;

(g) refusing to surrender a chattel as stated in §§ 237 to 241.

In contrast, a trespass to a chattel may be committed by intentionally:

(a) dispossessing another of the chattel, or

(b) using or intermeddling with a chattel in the possession of another.

RESTATEMENT (2D) TORTS, § 217. Both are intentional torts. Comment c of § 217 explicates the type of intent required:

The intention required to make an actor liable for trespass to a chattel is similar to that necessary to make one liable for an invasion of another's interest in bodily security, in freedom from an offensive contact, or confinement . . . Such an intention is present when an act is done for the purpose of using or otherwise intermeddling with a chattel or with knowledge that such an intermeddling will, to a substantial certainty, result from the act. It is not necessary that the actor should know or have reason to know that such intermeddling is a violation of the possessory rights of another. Thus, it is immaterial that the actor intermeddles with the chattel under a mistake of law or fact which has led him to believe that he is the possessor of it or that the possessor has consented to his dealing with it . . . So too, a mistake of law or fact which leads him to believe even upon reasonable grounds that he is privilege to meddle with the chattel without the consent of the possessor does not prevent his act from being a trespass if the privilege is one which does not depend upon his reasonable believe, as where he acts to abate a private nuisance.

Comment b to § 223 further provides:

Conversion is always an intentional exercise of dominion or control over the chattel. Mere non-feasance or negligence, without such an intent, is not sufficient for conversion . . . If the actor has the intent to do the act exercising dominion or control, however, he is not relieved from liability by his mistaken belief that he has possession of the chattel or the right to possession, or that he is privileged to act.

Conversion may lie even if the defendant never takes custody of the property. On the issue of deprivation, the Washington Supreme Court held:

It is not necessary to a conversion that there should be a manual taking of the thing in action by the defendant; it is not necessary that it should be shown that he has applied it to his own use. . . . Does he exercise a dominion over it in exclusion or defiance of the plaintiff's right? If he does, that in law is a conversion, be it for his own or another person's use. . . .

Martin v. Sikes, 229 P.2d 546, 550 (Wash. 1951).

1. Acting without Lawful Justification

A defendant acts with "lawful authority" or "legal justification" when he has not exceeded the limits of permitted use of the property, express or reasonably implied from the terms of a contract or other agreement between the parties. Statutes also protect defendants from conversion or trespass to chattels liability by expressly permitting the type of property interference complained of. "Good faith," however, does not excuse or justify the intentional interference. Indeed, it is immaterial to whether the defendant had "lawful justification." The case of *In re Marriage of Langham and Kolde*, 153 Wn.2d 553 (2005), undercuts any assertion to the contrary:

Despite his aversion to the term "conversion," Velle describes his actions using almost the precise definition of conversion: "[The question is what is the appropriate measure of damages] when one former spouse, believing in good faith that property belongs to him, exercises dominion and control over that property, but a court later rules that the property belonged to the other spouse." Answer and Cross-Petition of Velle Kolde at 15. Velle recognizes that options are property, and that he exercised control over them wrongfully, albeit in good faith. Since good faith is irrelevant in a conversion action, we find no difference between Velle's statement and the tort of conversion.

Id., at 566, n.8. In *In re Litzinger*, 340 B.R. 897 (B.A.P. 8th Cir. 2006) (applying Missouri law), defendant's good-faith belief that she had a right to funds in a bankruptcy estate held jointly with her estranged husband was irrelevant to a conversion claim. Plaintiff needed only to prove that the defendant intended to do the act that deprived the other person of his property. *Id.*, at 904; *see also Federal Inv. Co. v. Fries*, 78 Misc. 2d 805 (N.Y. Civ. Ct. 1974) (citing RESTATEMENT (2D) TORTS, § 229); *Wiseman v. Schaffer*, 768 P.2d 800 (Idaho Ct. App. 1989) (citing RESTATEMENT (2D) TORTS §§ 222-224); *Luciani v. Stop & Shop Companies, Inc.*, 15 Conn. App.407 (1988).

Where law enforcement exceeds statutory authorization, conversion occurs, as seen in *Kay v. County of Cook*, 2006 U.S. Dist. LEXIS 61394 (N.D. Ill. Aug. 29, 2006). Ian Kay sued Deputy Raymond Greve for attempting to serve a summons on a person listed at Kay's address. After finding the doors to the apartment unlocked, Greve made a warrantless entry into his home, ostensibly on community caretaking grounds, whereupon Kay's dog grabbed Greve by the sleeve. Greve responded by kicking and then shooting the dog once in the face, killing him. Animal control arrived, and then sedated and impounded Kay's other dog. The trial court refused to grant summary judgment on Kay's Fourth Amendment § 1983, conversion, and trespass claims to maintain logical consistency, for one cannot simultaneously violate the Fourth Amendment and yet be said to seize property rightfully and with legal authorization.

Consider also the success of the plaintiff overcoming a citizen's attempt to commit lawful conversion with statutory justification in the quest to halt animal cruelty. In *Elliott v. Hurst*, 817 S.W.2d 877 (Ark. 1991), the plaintiff sued the defendant for the conversion of his wolf-hybrid dog. Responding to the plaintiff's ad to sell purebred Arctic tundra wolves, the defendant observed plaintiff's dog with a seriously infected leg. She notified a humane organization and a veterinarian, who previously treated the dog. Later, the defendant, the organization, and a deputy prosecutor threatened to prosecute the plaintiff and take the dog from him. The plaintiff acquiesced to transport the dog to the veterinarian. Meanwhile, cruelty charges were filed and a seizure warrant obtained. The vet released the dog to the defendant. Thereafter, the plaintiff sued the defendant for conversion. Finding her liable, the trial court awarded $1,400 compensatory, and $25,000 punitive damages, as well as fees of $2,500. Defendant appealed, but the appellate court rejected her first defense to conversion in the form of statutory immunity under Ark. Code Ann. § 5-62-111, providing agents or members of a humane society the right to lawfully interfere to prevent the perpetration of animal cruelty. Her second argument, that the plaintiff abandoned the dog, similarly failed.

Finders of lost animals may also face conversion claims. While Good Samaritanism frequently serves as legal justification for taking up a stray, it has limits. In

Lincecum v. Smith, 287 So.2d 625 (La. Ct. App. 1973), a man who found an ill puppy in his father's front yard took the dog to another city for medical treatment. When informed of the puppy's blindness and great expense for treatment, the man authorized euthanasia. The court found the finder liable for conversion, adding that it was not necessary for defendant's motive or intent to be wrongful, willful, or corrupt. It was enough that the owner was deprived of his property "by the act of another who had assumed an unauthorized dominion and control over it." Further, the defendant did not do "what the law expected of him under the circumstances." Specifically, he should have realized the puppy was a stray and taken action to determine whether someone had reported the dog missing, a course of action consistent with the statutory duty imposed upon finders of lost things. *Id.*, at 628 (quoting La. Civ. Code Ann. Art. 3422, and requiring that the finder do "all that was possible to find out the true owner"). Even though the result of a "humanitarian act," "when he authorized the veterinarian to 'put this dog to sleep,' he asserted both dominion and a right of ownership which he did not legally possess." *Id.* For a discussion of a conversion claim against *the veterinarian* who euthanizes a stray at the direction of the Good Samaritan, see *Sexton v. Brown, infra.*

Another common example includes the defendant's assertion of a statutory retention lien. While strict compliance may serve as legal justification to withhold the animal, noncompliance has an equally determinate impact. In *Lewis v. Ehrlich*, 20 Ariz. App. 363 (Ct. App. 1973), the plaintiff sued for conversion of his horse, an Arabian stud, following sale of the horse to satisfy an accrued, but unpaid and past due, board and feed bill. Finding the defendants did not follow the statutory sale procedure of giving due notice to the plaintiff, the court reversed and remanded for a new trial and held that the sale constituted a conversion. In *Tarantino v. Martin*, 602 P.2d 906 (Colo. Ct. App. 1979), the plaintiffs sued a ranch operator for selling their horse without adequate notice. The trial court dismissed the case, finding abandonment. Assuming without deciding the correctness of this ruling, the appeals court still reversed, holding that the defendant failed to send notice by registered or certified mail as required by statute, making him liable for the sale of the horse and tack as a conversion. In *Walters v. Weaver*, 226 P.2d 931 (Okla. 1950), a suit for conversion of a horse, the supreme court directed verdict for plaintiff because the publication notice to enforce the agister's lien failed to comply with statutory requirements.

A common example of statutory justification, providing a complete defense in a conversion or trespass to chattels action, is shooting a marauding dog. By illustration, Jennifer Mitchell sued Susan Heinrichs for shooting her Husky when he was trespassing on her land and allegedly running near her livestock pen containing chickens and a goat who had recently given birth and was still bloody. Heinrichs retrieved a shotgun from her home and approached the dog, who allegedly turned his attention to her. Fearing for her safety, she shot and killed the Husky and returned inside. Minutes later, Mitchell found her dog deceased. *Mitchell v. Heinrichs*, 27 P.3d 309, 310 (Alaska 2001). Mitchell sued for compensatory damages representing the value of her dog, emotional distress damages on claims of conversion and IIED, and for conduct giving rise to punitive damages. A first summary judgment dismissal of the IIED and punitive damage claims and order capping damages at market value preceded by a second summary judgment dismissal of the conversion claim on the grounds that the plaintiff conceded her dog had "zero" value "because other people are not interested in buying someone else's dog." On appeal, the court affirmed dismissal of the IIED and punitive damage claims on the basis that Mitchell presented no material facts challenging the contention that Heinrichs acted justifiably according to community standards while defending her livestock and herself from increasingly bold incursions by Mitchell's dog.

Legal justification frequently favors animal control officers, law enforcement officers, and government agents (e.g., veterinarians) who impound and euthanize strays. In *Ratliff v. City of Bessemer*, 88 So. 208 (Ala. Civ. App. 1920), the court found no conversion of a mule, found running at-large, and sold after impound since taken up under legal authority and disposed of in accordance with law. Further, in *Boshers v. Humane Soc. of Missouri, Inc.*, 929 S.W.2d 250 (Mo. Ct. App. 1996), the plaintiff sued the society for conversion, seeking actual and punitive damages, following the society's refusal to release 38 dogs, 23 horses, 33 chickens, three calves, three ducks, three geese, one cat, and one goat, all of whom were allegedly neglected and abused. The court found no conversion because receipt of the animals under state law through a law enforcement seizure did not bestow upon the society an independent right to determine a third party's (here, plaintiff's) entitlement to possession and, thus, its ability to release them on demand. Indeed, in a later decision within the same case, *Humane Soc. of Missouri v. Boshers*, 948 S.W.2d 715 (Mo. Ct. App. 1997), the trial court awarded the society a lien on the amount due for keeping and boarding in the sum $602,324.73, and the appeals court affirmed.

In *Studer v. Seneca Cy. Hum. Soc.*, 2000 Ohio App. LEXIS 1974 (May 4, 2000), following execution of a search warrant at the plaintiff's property, resulting in seizure of 81 cats and 78 dogs, and euthanasia of all but four, Studer was found guilty on all 14 counts charged. Studer then sued two humane societies for replevin, conversion, and due process violations, but lost all on summary judgment. On appeal, the court reversed as to the replevin and constitutional claims, noting that the record failed to demonstrate that any of the particular animals were the subject of the criminal offenses. Therefore, the court could not say as a matter of law that she lost possessory rights in same. The conversion claim, however, remained dismissed but only because of statutory immunity. Similarly, in *Boling v. Parrett*, 536 P.2d 1272 (Or. Ct. App. 1975), police seized 20 dogs pursuant to Or. Rev. Stat. Ann. § 133.377, upon good faith and with probable cause, issuing a citation to the owner for animal cruelty, taking dogs into protective custody, and transporting same to the shelter. The court held no conversion as a matter of law.

Acting with statutory authorization may negate a conversion claim against a veterinarian who euthanizes impounded strays. *Wheatley v. Towers*, 358 N.E.2d 971 (Ill. Ct. App. 1977), concerned a claim of conversion against a county veterinarian for the willful and wanton destruction of a dog impounded for running at large and not redeemed. The court of appeals affirmed dismissal, finding no intentional or reckless disregard of a known duty owed to the plaintiff given that statutes expressly allowed counties to kill impounded dogs after a reasonable time.

Though best analyzed as statutory immunity for an otherwise unjustified and illegal act, consider *San Jose Charter of The Hell's Angels Motorcyle Club v. City of San Jose*, 1999 U.S. Dist. LEXIS 21440 (N.D. Cal. Dec. 6, 1999), *aff'd o.g.*, 402 F.3d 962 (9th Cir. 2005). Law enforcement executed a warrant on the Hell's Angels' compound, shooting guard dogs dead during the process. Among other claims raised was conversion, dismissed based on state immunity found in Cal. Gov't Code § 821.6, which provided that

> a public employee is not liable for injury caused by his instituting or prosecuting any judicial or administrative proceeding within the scope of his employment, even if he acts maliciously and without probable cause.

The court reasoned that this provision applied where officers willfully destroy personal property during searches authorized by warrant. Additionally, it held that this provision protects officers from liability for injuries suffered by those who are not actual targets of the investigation but who happen to be incidental victims.

In contrast to *Lincecum*, discussed above, consider *Alvarez v. Clasen*, 946 So.2d 181 (La. Ct. App. 2006), a cat-trapping case, in which the defendant turned the plaintiff's cat over to animal control, resulting in euthanasia. The court noted that conversion involves the *wrongful* committing of an act of dominion over property of another in denial of or inconsistent with the owner's rights. Finding the act of trapping itself not "unlawful," because a statute permitted impounding of at-large cats, no conversion occurred. Another lost dog/conversion case of note is *Sexton v. Brown*, 2008 Wash. App. LEXIS 2530 (2008) (2008). Valeri Sexton and Corey Recla adopted a Yorkshire terrier, named Joe-e. During a neuter surgery, he nearly died from a congenital liver shunt condition. A month later, he underwent surgery to correct the portosystemic shunt. Though successful, he required daily medication and monitoring. Roughly one month after the shunt surgery, the plaintiffs lost Joe-e on a camping trip. Despite their vigorous search of the area, he remained missing.

That same day, a couple found Joe-e and drove him an hour away to an emergency hospital. A veterinary assistant, veterinary technician, and veterinarian testified that the dog, though very thin, had normal blood work and could be kept comfortable throughout the night. While the couple waited for test results, a new veterinarian, defendant Kenny Brown, took over Joe-e's care. Brown concluded that the dog had lymphosarcoma or another life-threatening condition and would not live a week. He then told the Samaritans that they had the choice of further testing, paying for supportive care, or euthanizing. The couple decided to euthanize, and Brown obliged. He then performed a necropsy and sent the body off to be communally cremated. At no time did he ever notify animal control or the police that Joe-e had been found, evaluated, euthanized, and then destroyed. Meanwhile, over the next ten days, the plaintiffs searched frantically for Joe-e, hiring dog rescue agencies and trackers, posting fliers and undertaking extensive efforts to find him. Upon learning that he had been killed, Sexton sought medical treatment for migraines, insomnia, hypersomulence, muscle pain, apathy, and lethargy.

The plaintiffs sued Brown and the emergency clinic for negligence, breach of bailment, negligent misrepresentation, conversion, trespass to chattels, wrongful invasion of right to custody of corpse, NIED, and violation of the Consumer Protection Act. The plaintiffs defeated Brown's motions for summary judgment dismissal of the conversion and trespass to chattels claims, and recovery of emotional distress damages as a matter of law. On appeal, the court focused on whether Brown's interference was justified under Washington's veterinary administrative code. Relying on WAC 246-933-060, Brown asserted that because his actions were legally justified, the court erred in denying summary judgment dismissal of Sexton's conversion and trespass to chattels claims. WAC 246-933-060 authorizes a veterinarian to care for a pet even if the person authorizing services is not the owner:

> The veterinarian shall always be free to accept or reject a particular patient, but once care is undertaken, the veterinarian shall not neglect the patient, as long as the person presenting the patient requests and authorizes the veterinarian's services for the particular problem. Emergency treatment not authorized by the owner shall not constitute acceptance of a patient.

Sexton argued that material issues of fact existed as to whether Brown's actions were justified under both WAC 246-933-060 and WAC 246-933-050. WAC 246-933-050 provides that: "[t]he veterinarian shall endeavor to provide at least minimal treatment to alleviate the suffering of an animal presented in the absence of the owner or the owner's agent." Viewing the evidence in the light most favorable to Sexton, the appellate court agreed with Sexton.

Legal justification may exist in the form of a personal property lien, as discussed in *Othoudt v. Addison Fur Corp.*, 262 Mich. 481 (1933). Plaintiffs ranched two foxes at defendant's farm with a contract to breed. Following a dispute, defendant refused to return the foxes, claiming a consensual contractual lien. The court found no conversion. In *Arnold v. Prange*, 541 S.W.2d 27 (Mo. Ct. App. 1976), cattle owners sued property owners for conversion. The appeals court reversed the award of actual and punitive damages, finding no tortious taking where statutes allowed landowners to keep trespassing livestock, no misappropriation contrary to plaintiffs' ownership (again, due to compliance with statutory procedures), and no improper refusal to release possession on demand (owing on statutory compliance).

2.   Nature of Deprivation or Interference

Trespass to chattels and conversion sit on the same spectrum of intermeddling. More substantial or irremediable interferences with property constitute conversion, lesser ones trespass to chattels. For example, denting a new car is to trespass to chattels what totaling a car is to conversion. As applied to animals, causing a single, nonlethal laceration on a dog's chest is a trespass, while mortally wounding a dog is a conversion. Conversion may result not only from civil theft, but also by destruction and substantial modification, including when possession remains with the plaintiff (e.g., shooting a dog being walked by the guardian). In *DeHart v. Crossen*, 2005 Conn. Super. LEXIS 1474 (June 3, 2005), plaintiff sued for dog bite injuries. Defendant counterclaimed for conversion and civil theft when plaintiff entered Defendant's property and intentionally caused physical harm to the dog, requiring euthanasia. Defendant's conversion counterclaim survived plaintiff's motion to strike; for while the dog was not taken or withheld from defendant, conversion embraced the concept of material alteration. *See also Coston v. Reardon*, 2001 Conn. Super. LEXIS 3188 (Oct. 17, 2001) (conversion claim not dismissed).

A classic example of conversion through refusal to return is *Ing v. American Airlines*, 2007 U.S. Dist. LEXIS 11716 (N.D. Cal. Feb. 5, 2007), involving a bulldog who died from heat prostration while being transported by air. After landing, the airline kept the dog from the plaintiff, preventing him from taking the dog to a veterinarian. Among other claims, conversion survived summary judgment as described below:

> Plaintiff has presented facts indicating that he was Willie's owner and that he was listed as the consignee on the waybill. Taking Ing's version of the facts as true, American refused to return Willie to allow Ing to get veterinary care, which resulted in or at least precipitated Willie's death. Furthermore, American employees have admitted that Willie was lethargic and breathing shallowly when he arrived in San Francisco. A reasonable jury could conclude that American committed conversion by not releasing the dog to Ing until after it was dead.

Similarly, *Snead v. SPCA of Penn.*, 2007 PA Super 204 (2007), *appeal granted in part*, 600 Pa. 372 (2009), and *order aff'd*, 604 Pa. 166 (2009), provides a characteristic example, where the SPCA seized several dogs from the plaintiff's residence as evidence pending resolution of dogfighting charges against her, which were later dropped. The plaintiff attempted to recover her dogs from the shelter but was told that they were all euthanized due to her failure to claim them within the 48-hour hold period. In truth, they were not euthanized until three days after she inquired. A jury found the defendant liable in the sum of $154,926.37, $100,000 of which constituted exemplary damages. The appellate court affirmed the jury's finding of conversion in depriving Snead of the use and possession of her dogs by euthanizing them, and by not giving her the chance to retrieve them after charges were dropped and they were no longer needed as evidence.

An attempt to disqualify an entire species from conversion claims failed in *Hegarty v. Addison Cy. Hum. Soc.*, 848 A.2d 1139 (Vt. 2004) (no conversion because lawful seizure). The Vermont Supreme Court rejected the trial court's reasoning that Hegarty's conversion claim failed because the horse was a pet and thus not a proper legal subject of conversion. Vermont's curious holding that pets cannot be the subject of a conversion because of the long-standing but arguably atavistic position that "the property interest in pets is of . . . a highly qualified nature" is hardly universal. This author knows of no other jurisdiction that applies this species-based distinction. The Supreme Court's discussion follows:

> On appeal, the Hegartys contest the trial court's denial of their conversion claim on two grounds. First, they assert that the trial court erred when it relied on *Morgan v. Kroupa* to characterize Paka as a pet and thus not subject to a conversion claim. 167 Vt. 99, 103–05, 702 A.2d 630, 633–34 (1997). We agree.

> The trial court correctly cited Morgan for the proposition that, in the context of a conversion claim, the property interest in pets is of such a highly qualified nature that it may be limited by overriding public interests. Morgan v. Kroupa, 167 Vt. 99, 105, 702 A.2d 630, 634 (1997). We do not quarrel with this analysis but rather with the court's suggestion that our *Morgan* ruling supports characterizing Paka as a pet. In *Morgan*, we

explicitly distinguished between pets — dogs, cats, and hamsters — and "agricultural animals with substantial economic value." Morgan v. Kroupa, 167 Vt. 99, 105, 702 A.2d 630, 634 (1997). The fact that a horse may also be considered a pet by its owner does not remove it from the category of agricultural animal with respect to the property interests at issue in a conversion claim. Morgan v. Kroupa, 167 Vt. 99, 105, 702 A.2d 630, 634 (1997). Paka is not a pet and the trial court's ruling to the contrary was in error.

Id., at 1141–1142.

Fredeen v. Stride, 269 Or. 369 (1974), presents an example of conversion by misdelivery. A veterinarian treated and then gave plaintiff's dog to another person after plaintiff authorized euthanasia rather than pay for treatment. The plaintiff claimed mental anguish because her children might be alarmed by seeing the dog with another person and because she feared the dog would be injured trying to return to her home, as she lived in the same neighborhood as the new owners. The court regarded mental distress an element of damages if it was "the direct and natural result of the conversion." Further, the act need not have been "inspired by fraud or malice" for recovery of noneconomic damages "where evidence of genuine emotional damage is supplied by aggravated conduct on the part of the defendant." In addition to general damages, the court awarded punitive damages for the veterinarian's egregious conduct in giving the dog to another person without plaintiff's consent, calling such behavior a "sufficiently aggravated violation of societal interests to justify the sanction of punitive damages as a preventative measure." The court quipped, "In other words, a veterinarian should not give a client's dog to a third person without the consent of the owner." *Id.*, at 375.

An example of conversion by incapacitation (even though the animal was not withheld from the plaintiff) is *Loman v. Freeman*, where a veterinarian performed an allegedly unauthorized right stifle surgery on the plaintiffs' racehorse, causing permanent incapacitation. The appeals court reversed dismissal of the claim of conversion, noting that materially altering the physical condition of chattel so as to change its identity or character states a claim and that "permanent deprivation" of possession is not a necessary condition for conversion. *Loman v. Freeman*, 874 N.E.2d 542 (Ill. Ct. App. 2006), *judgment aff'd on other grounds*, 890 N.E.2d 446 (Ill. 2008). In 2008, a split 4-3 panel of the Illinois Supreme Court affirmed the court of appeals with respect to the conversion, finding that permanent incapacitation of a horse through an unauthorized procedure constituted conversion even where possession of the horse was not withheld.

An example of conversion as appropriation to the defendant's own use is found in *Military Circle Pet Center No. 94, Inc. v. Cobb Cy., Ga.*, 665 F. Supp. 909 (N.D. Ga. 1987), *aff'd/rev'd o.g.*, 877 F.2d 973 (11th Cir. 1989). The Pet Center sued the director of county animal control, among others, for conversion and other claims upon execution of a search warrant premised on suspected animal cruelty. In an interesting wrinkle on conversion doctrine, the court rejected plaintiff's attempt to hold the individually named defendants liable in seizing the animals by distinguishing their official and personal capacities:

Under Georgia law "conversion is the unauthorized assumption and exercise of the right of ownership over personal property belonging to another which is contrary to the owner's rights." Plaintiff has not presented any evidence that any of the individual defendants assumed and exercised a right of ownership over plaintiff's personal property. While defendants in their official capacities may have engaged in activities which allegedly constituted conversion, no defendant *individually* converted plaintiff's property to his or her own use.

665 F. Supp. at 917 (citations omitted) (further dismissing conversion claim against the county and individual defendants in their official capacities on grounds of sovereign immunity).

Ivey v. Hamlin, 2002 Tenn. App. LEXIS 404 (Tenn. Ct. App. June 7, 2002) is in accord with *Military Circle.* Deputy Hamlin deliberately killed Ivey's English bulldog. In one short paragraph, the court found the "equitable and venerable doctrine of conversion" not implicated because Hamlin did not appropriate the dog to his own use. This holding represents a minority position that sharply deviates from the broader interpretations of conversion doctrine articulated in most other jurisdictions. However, even if killing represented an act capable of constituting conversion, the court likely would have rejected the claim on the ground of statutory legal justification.

Conversion only lies when a serious enough interference with ownership rights takes place. Trivial interferences remain noncognizable. *LaPlace v. Briere,* 962 A.2d 1139 (N.J. Super. Ct. 2009), illustrates where to draw the line of substantiality. LaPlace sued Briere, his stable, and Bridgwood, who exercised LaPlace's horse, upon learning that he died after lunging. At issue was whether one who exercises an equine without permission is liable in conversion absent evidence of cause of death or negligence. The court of appeals affirmed summary judgment dismissal, concluding that while lunging was unauthorized, it did not seriously interfere with LaPlace's ownership rights (as might in the case of removal):

> The theory behind conversion is that the actor has exerted such a major and serious interference with the plaintiff's rights to the chattel that in essence the law will force a judicial sale of the chattel upon the defendant. The Restatement (Second) of Torts describes the tort in this way: "[c]onversion is an intentional exercise of dominion or control over a chattel which so seriously interferes with the right of another to control it that the actor may justly be required to pay the other the full value of the chattel." Restatement (Second) of Torts § 222A(1) (1965). In weighing the seriousness of the interference with the owner's rights to the chattel to determine if a conversion has occurred, we should consider the following factors:
>
> (a) [T]he extent and duration of the actor's exercise of dominion or control;
>
> (b) The actor's intent to assert a right in fact inconsistent with the other's right of control;
>
> (c) The actor's good faith;

(d) The extent and duration of the resulting interference with the other's right of control;

(e) The harm done to the chattel;

(f) The inconvenience and expense caused to the other.

[RESTATEMENT (2D) OF TORTS § 222A(2) (1965).]

In light of these legal principles, Bridgwood's conduct in exercising the horse under the circumstances here, even if she was unauthorized to do so, did not constitute a conversion. While her act was intentional, in that she intended to lunge the horse, Bridgwood did not exercise such control and dominion over the horse when lunging it that she seriously interfered with plaintiff's ownership rights in the horse. She did not remove the horse from the Briere stable where plaintiff had left the horse for safekeeping. At the time, she was not interfering with plaintiff's use or possession of the horse. Lunging is part of the daily care of the horse and is not conduct that would intrinsically be viewed as cloaking the actor with the rights of an owner. Bridgwood exercised the horse in good faith, with no intent to usurp plaintiff's rights to the horse. The lunging was intended to be done for only about fifteen minutes and in fact lasted only five minutes.

Id., at 1145–1146 (citations omitted).

3. No Intent to Interfere as Negligence

In *Birmingham Hum. Soc. v. Dickson*, 661 So.2d 759 (Ala. Civ. App.1994), a jury found the local humane society negligent when it neutered a Rottweiler purportedly kept for profitable breeding after being asked by the owner not to. Although subject to a three-day statutory hold, upon expiration of which the dog became society property, the court treated the case as sounding in negligence, not as a wanton conversion. The court found no contributory negligence in Dickson's failure to control his dog, noting it had no effect on the society's negligence in neutering him. This case offers an important lesson in distinguishing ordinary from willful conversion, the former being disrobed from its conversion garb and treated as a garden-variety negligence claim. Although the society undoubtedly intentionally restrained, anesthetized, and neutered the plaintiff's dog, the intentional interference arose from inattentiveness. In this respect, one should consult RESTATEMENT (2D) TORTS, § 224, and its comment b, which states:

> For the same reason, an act which is not intended to exercise any dominion or control over a chattel but is merely negligent with respect to it is not a conversion, even though it may result in the loss or destruction of the chattel. Thus it is not a conversion negligently to drive into the plaintiff's automobile and wreck it; nor is a bailee a converter when he merely fails to use proper care in keeping the goods entrusted to him, so that they are lost or stolen.

Regardless, in this author's opinion, it appears the *Dickson* court erred, for the society did not accidentally cause the dog to be neutered (e.g., by slating the wrong dog for surgery). The intent was to neuter the dog even though it was ostensibly done in good faith and under a mistaken, even entirely reasonable belief, that the society had the legal right to do so.

4. Damages

Though black letter law in many jurisdictions is to permit emotional damages merely upon proof of an intentional tort, some contend this only applies to willful conversions. PROSSER & KEETON, TORTS sec. 13, at 67 to 68 (5th ed. 1984). "We have liberally construed damages for emotional distress as being available merely upon proof of 'an intentional tort.' " *Birchler v. Castello Land Co., Inc.*, 942 P.2d 968 (Wash. 1997); *see Comment Note — Recovery for mental shock or distress in connection with injury to or interference with tangible property*, 28 A.L.R.2d 1070; RESTATEMENT SECOND, TORTS § 929 (emotional distress damages permitted for trespass to land). An inadvertent or unintentional taking or possession of another's property is, by definition, not willful. *Fischnaller v. Sussman*, 9 P.2d 378 (Wash. 1932). To constitute wilful misconduct, there must be actual knowledge — or that which is equivalent thereto — of the peril to be apprehended, coupled with conscious failure to avoid injury. A wanton act is one performed intentionally with reckless indifference to the injurious consequences likely to result. Willful misconduct is best described as intent to injure while wantonness implies reckless indifference. *Evans v. Miller*, 507 P.2d 887 (Wash. Ct. App. 1973). The practitioner should cautiously evaluate whether the jurisdiction at bar has distinguished ordinary from willful conversions and, further, the remedies flowing from each.

Meanwhile, one starting point is the Restatement, which offers:

> Where a person is entitled to a judgment for the conversion of a chattel or the destruction of any legally protected interest in land or other thing, the damages include . . . (b) the amount of any further loss suffered as the result of the deprivation. . . .

RESTATEMENT FIRST, TORTS § 927; *see* RESTATEMENT SECOND, TORTS § 927, comment m. In interpreting clause (b), the commentators noted, "If the deprivation is the legal cause of harms to the feeling, damages may be allowable for such harms. . . ." RESTATEMENT FIRST, TORTS § 927, comment l. In *Cruthis v. Firstar Bank, N.A.*, 822 N.E.2d 454 (Ill. Ct. App. 2004), customers sued a bank for breach of contract, conversion, and consumer fraud. The trial court entered judgment on a jury verdict for plaintiffs on the conversion claim and awarded damages for emotional distress. The court affirmed, noting that with respect to a judgment for the conversion of a chattel, if the deprivation was the legal cause of harm to the feelings, damages could be allowed for the harm, citing RESTATEMENT SECOND, TORTS § 927. Responding to a similar argument made by the defendants with respect to outrage, the court held:

> In the present case, the plaintiffs did not allege that the defendant committed the independent tort of intentional infliction of emotional distress, and they need not have done so. See Sloan, 167 Ill. App. 3d at 869–70, 118 Ill. Dec. 879, 522 N.E.2d 334. Instead, the plaintiffs sought damages for emotional distress, which may be recovered from a defendant who committed the intentional tort of conversion. Accordingly, we affirm

the jury's award for the plaintiffs' emotional distress as a result of the defendant's conversion of their funds.

Id., at 467. For more information on the law concerning animal valuation and related damages, please see *Measure, Elements, and Amount of Damages for Killing or Injuring Cat*, 8 A.L.R. 4TH 1287; *Recovery of Damages for Emotional Distress Due to Treatment of Pets and Animals*, 91 A.L.R. 5TH 545; *Damages for Killing or Injuring Dog*, 61 A.L.R. 5TH 635; *Damages for Loss of Personal Property with Little or No Market Value*, 3 AM. JUR. 3D *Proof of Facts* 171.

E.   MALICIOUS INJURY

Womack v. Von Rardon, 135 P.3d 542 (Wash. App. 2006), though affirming the trial court's dismissal of the IIED claim, took the opportunity to *sua sponte* create a new civil cause of action — malicious injury to a pet. In this published opinion, the court of appeals said the following:

> For the first time in Washington, we hold malicious injury to a pet can support a claim for, and be considered a factor in measuring a person's emotional distress damages. The damages are consistent with actual and intrinsic value concepts as found in Pickford because, depending upon the particular case facts, harm may be caused to a person's emotional well-being by malicious injury to that person's pet as personal property. We do not interpret the trial court's final reference to value as limiting the measure of damages to pet fair market value.

Id., at 263–64. This decision justly evolved the common law to fill the judicial cavities that previously barred plaintiffs from recovering emotional distress damages in the case of intentional harm to animals. It did so in the following respects: (1) It confirmed societal appreciation of animals by legitimizing our emotional connection to them; (2) It created a new cause of action for a particular class of property, recognizing that pets belong to a special order not shared by washing machines and cars. There is no tort for "malicious injury to a toaster," for instance; (3) It used favorable language that conferred actual and intrinsic value to a companion animal, not fair market or replacement value; (4) It found that a person may be liable for another's emotional distress when maliciously injuring or killing a companion animal irrespective of limitations that have stymied efforts by plaintiffs to recover compensation for the emotional increment of loss, such as the many bright-line, fraud-negating limitations on bystander NIED and IIED recovery, including:

    a. Temporal proximity;

    b. Spatial proximity;

    c. Degree of relatedness (consanguinity or affinity), except being the "owner";

    d. Impact;

    e. Zone of danger;

    f. Physical manifestations of emotional injury;

    g. Medical evidence of emotional injury;

    h.   Severity of distress;

    i.   Outrageousness;

    j.   Whether the subject of the tortious behavior (i.e., the animal or property) is one for which an NIED or IIED claim can be raised as a matter of law (namely, a homocentric limitation);

    k.   Specific intent to cause severe emotional distress in a known plaintiff; or

    l.   Knowledge that the animal in question had an owner.

In sum, *Womack* provides that one who maliciously injures a pet solely to torture, and not to indirectly inflict psychic harm to the owner-guardian, will pay emotional distress damages. Readers may note, however, the doctrinal redundancy of this claim to willful conversion. Certainly, a defendant who maliciously, and therefore wrongfully and without legal excuse or justification, harms an animal will be exerting dominion and control to such a degree as to constitute a conversion — but only in jurisdictions that embrace the more expansive definition, including all seven variations contained in the RESTATEMENT. Jurisdictions requiring proof of dispossession and appropriation to the tortfeasor's own use may fail to prove conversion, such as where the animal suffers a malicious death but the defendant does not use the remains to his own ends (e.g., slaying a cow and then consuming her; shooting a bison and taking the head as a trophy). Untested is whether killing an animal for sport constitutes recreational use and cruel misappropriation of the property of another, thus satisfying the minority jurisdiction's definition of conversion even if the animal is never physically removed from the plaintiff's custody.

Finally, readers may see duplication between the tort of malicious injury to an animal and punitive damages provided in virtually all but a few jurisdictions for wanton, willful, malicious, grossly negligent, or reckless misconduct. Philosophically, the chasm separating each doctrine is wide. The former may be pleaded without leave of court, and the latter explicitly does not seek to remunerate the plaintiff for compensatory damages but instead exacts a penalty. Yet from an evidentiary standpoint, the elements to be proved vary little. In many jurisdictions, however, punitive damages hinge on proof of actual damages proved by clear, cogent, and convincing evidence. *Reed v. Central Soya Co., Inc.*, 621 N.E.2d 1069 (Ind. 1993), *modified o.g. on reh'g*, 644 N.E.2d 84 (Ind. 1994) (clear and convincing evidence required). Indeed, without compensatory damages, no punitive damages are permitted. Thus, the value of the injured or killed animal at the time of the alleged tortious activity can prove critical to assessing a defendant's exposure to punitive damages. *See, e.g., Elliott v. Hurst*, 817 S.W.2d 877 (Ark. 1991) (reversing $25,000 punitive damage award predicated on $1,400 compensatory damage award by noting that value of dog at time of conversion was likely $0; thus, no punitive damages would follow).

Only a small number of jurisdictions have fashioned a separate cause of action for malicious harm to an animal. In *LaPorte v. Associated Independents, Inc.*, 163 So. 2d 267 (Fla. 1964), a garbage collector killed Heidi, a leashed dog, by intentionally hurling a garbage can at her, then laughed and departed the scene. The court provided for recovery of sentimental value and mental suffering for the malicious destruction of a pet "irrespective of the value of the animal because of its special training such as a Seeing Eye dog or sheep dog." *Id.*, at 269. Reaching this new rule of law by way of punitive damages analysis and relying upon and extending the case of *Kirksey v. Jernigan*, 45 So. 2d 188 (Fla. 1950), the court rejected respondent's two arguments urging the contrary result — *first*, that malicious injury of a pet does not equate with the mishandling of a child's remains; and *second*, that there was contractual privity between the undertaker and the parent in the *Kirksey* case, but none between the garbage collector and the plaintiff, who did not know she was anywhere within sight nor had he ever met her or seen Heidi before. The Florida Supreme Court responded:

> As to the first of these we hasten to say that the anguish resulting from the mishandling of the body of a child cannot be equated to the grief from the loss of a dog but that does not imply that mental suffering from the loss of a pet dog, even one less an aristocrat than Heidi, is nothing at all. As for the matter of contact between the miscreant and the injured person, the attempted distinction is just too fine for us to accept.

Id., at 269. Accordingly, though not plainly stated in the opinion, *La Porte* does establish a cause of action distinct from IIED (by dispensing with such requirements as specific intent to cause harm to a known plaintiff; a severity of distress threshold; and plaintiff witnessing the injury to the animal). LaPorte's cause of action also differs from punitive damages. The jury awarded $2,000 as compensatory damages to include the dog's value and mental suffering; as well as $1,000 in punitive damages, but the respondent only complained of the element of mental suffering injected into the judge's instruction for compensatory damages. *Id.*, at 267; *see also Kennedy v. Byas*, 867 So. 2d 1195, 1197 (Fla. Dist. Ct. App.2004) (distinguishing *La Porte* by disallowing emotional damages where only negligence, not malice, was implicated); *Banaszek v. Kowalski*, 10 Pa. D. & C.3d 94 (C.P.1979) (allowing emotional damages arising from "malicious destruction of a pet" when defendant shot plaintiff's dogs in plaintiff's absence); *City of Garland v. White*, 368 S.W.2d 12, 17 (Tex. Civ. App.1963); *but see Daughen v. Fox*, 539 A.2d 858 (Pa. Super. Ct. 1988) (not expressly following or declining to follow *Banasczek*).

The case of *Zauper v. Lababit*, 2009 Bankr. LEXIS 4524 (9th Cir. Bankr., Oct. 8, 2009), *aff'd in part, rev'd in part*, 2011 U.S. App. LEXIS 3704 (9th Cir. Feb. 24, 2011) examines the question of malicious injury in the federal bankruptcy law context. The Lababits dog, Pinoy, trained for dogfighting, declared potentially dangerous, and not maintained in accordance with an animal control order and local law, killed Robert Zauper's cat Milton as he tried to intervene, in vain. Although the state court awarded more than $75,000 by default, the Cababits filed for Chapter 7 bankruptcy discharge. Mr. Zauper then launched an adversary complaint to deem the debt nondischargeable. *Zauper* provides an example of using the federal cause of action of willful and malicious injury to property (11 U.S.C. § 523(a)(6)) to obtain a nondischargeable judgment in bankruptcy. Section 523(a)(6) applied in two respects — conceptualized both as an act of commission (raising dog for fighting) and act of omission (failing to comply with affirmative duty to control dog as imposed by animal control via statute). The bankruptcy trial court deemed only $1 of the prepetition debt nondischargeable, agreeing with Mr. Zauper that the acts of commission and omission were willful and malicious, resulting in the death of his cat, but that he was only entitled to $1 for Milton's value and nothing in emotional distress. On appeal, the Bankruptcy Appellate Panel reversed and remanded for entry of Milton's intrinsic value, finding that the award of $1 clearly erroneous. The Ninth Circuit Court of Appeals then vacated the $0 emotional distress award and remanded for retrial consistent with the precepts of the claims of conversion and malicious injury to a pet, as applied per Washington law.

F.   JUSTIFIABLE CANICIDE

United States Senator George Graham Vest, also an attorney, represented a client whose hunting dog, a foxhound, was wantonly and willfully killed by a sheep farmer. Rumor has it that the jury deliberated for less than two minutes before awarding $500, although the plaintiff had asked merely for $150. Certiorari was not granted by the Supreme Court of Missouri. *Burden v. Hornsby*, 1872 Mo. LEXIS 274 (July, 1872). A classic of American courthouse oratory, this closing argument synopsizes the pathos motivating the plaintiff's case. Yet the passage proves judicious for defendants, too, since the same emotion justifies, perhaps with greater rhetorical force, the defense of animals:

> Gentlemen of the jury: the best friend a man has in the world may turn against him and become his worst enemy. His son or daughter that he has reared with loving care may prove ungrateful. Those who are nearest and dearest to us, those whom we trust with our happiness and our good name, may become traitors to their faith. The money that man has, he may lose. It flies away from him, perhaps when he needs it the most. A man's reputation may be sacrificed in a moment of ill-considered action. The people who are prone to fall on their knees to do us honor when success is with us may be the first to throw the stone of malice when failure settles its cloud upon our heads.

> The one absolutely unselfish friend that a man can have in this selfish world, the one that never deserts him and the one that never proves ungrateful or treacherous . . . is his dog.

> Gentlemen of the Jury: a man's dog stands by him in prosperity and in poverty, in health and in sickness. He will sleep on the cold ground, where the wintry winds blow and the snow drives fiercely, if only he may be near his master's side. He will kiss the hand that has no food to offer, he will lick the wounds and sores that come in encounters with the roughness of the world. He guards the sleep of his pauper master as if he were a prince. When all other friends desert he remains. When riches take wings and reputation falls to pieces, he is as constant in his love as the sun in its journey through the heavens. If fortune drives the master forth an outcast in the world, friendless and homeless, the faithful dog asks no higher privilege than that of accompanying him to guard against danger, to fight against his enemies, and when the last scene of all comes, and death takes the master in its embrace and his body is laid away in the cold ground, no matter if all other friends pursue their way, there by his graveside will the noble dog be found, his head between his paws, his eyes sad but open in alert watchfulness, faithful and true even to death.

Eulogy on the Dog, George Graham Vest. Since the founding of this country, dogs making predatory incursions into ranches either left a wake of livestock casualties behind or found themselves maimed or dead by a farmer's shotgun blast. So heavily litigated and appealed are these disputes that entire articles dedicated to the subject can be consulted. *See Civil Liability of Landowner for Killing or Injuring Trespassing Dog*, 15 A.L.R.2D 578; *Liability for Killing Dog to Protect Domestic Animal or Fowl*, 10 A.L.R. 689; *Liability for Killing or Injuring Unlicensed or Untagged Dog*, 145 A.L.R. 993.

1.   Sample Interpretation of Justifiable Canicide Statute

Though American common law provides a carefully circumscribed defense of legal justification in canicide, virtually all legislatures have also codified the privileged killing of trespassing dogs that chase, injure, harass, worry, annoy, bite, or kill certain other animals. The discussion that follows guides the reader in analytically examining the parameters in applying each statute. Consider the following illustrative deconstruction of Washington's justifiable canicide statute, as guidance to readers in any jurisdiction:

16.08.020. Dogs injuring stock may be killed.

It shall be lawful for any person who shall see any dog or dogs chasing, biting, injuring or killing any sheep, swine or other domestic animal, including poultry, belonging to such person, on any real property owned or leased by, or under the control of, such person, or on any public highway, to kill such dog or dogs, and it shall be the duty of the owner or keeper of any dog or dogs so found chasing, biting or injuring any domestic animal, including poultry, upon being notified of that fact by the owner of such domestic animals or poultry, to thereafter keep such dog or dogs in leash or confined upon the premises of the owner or keeper thereof, and in case any such owner or keeper of a dog or dogs shall fail or neglect to comply with the provisions of this section, it shall be lawful for the owner of such domestic animals or poultry to kill such dog or dogs found running at large.

RCW § 16.08.020.

First, **begin with the caption**. Arguably, RCW § 16.08.020 (formerly, 1929 c. 198 § 6) does not apply to "dog-eat-dog" scenarios, but, rather, only where a dog has chased, bitten, injured, or killed an animal kept for commercial purposes, such as livestock. While the Code Reviser's title is not law, it suggests legislative intent by stating: "Dogs injuring stock may be killed."

Second, **look to case law and Attorney General Interpretations**. The year after RCW § 16.08.020 was enacted, in 1930, Assistant Attorney General E.W. Anderson issued an opinion on whether RCW § 16.08.010 (formerly, 1929 c. 198 § 5), passed in concert with RCW § 16.08.020, applied to "dog-eat-dog" scenarios. The 1929 version of section 16.08.010 provided, in relevant part:

The owner or keeper of any dog shall be liable to the owner of any animal killed or injured by such dog for the amount of damages sustained and costs of collection, to be recovered in a civil action.

1929 c. 198 § 5. This section included a compensation schedule for animals killed or injured, including for sheep, goats, cattle, horses, mules, turkeys, other poultry, swine, and rabbits. Dogs were not mentioned. Mr. Anderson's conclusion follows:

> The classes enumerated in the schedule constitute the classes of animals usually and customarily subject to depredations by dogs. We do not believe the section was intended to apply to the situation where "dog eats dog."

30 Wash. Op. Att'y Gen. 720, 723. This law was later amended in 1985 by deleting this "schedule" but keeping the remainder of the language in its entirety. It might stand to reason that the Attorney General's interpretation of 1929 c. 198 § 5 is outdated after this amendment except that the legislature may simply have chosen to discontinue the fund that would pay farmers who lost farmed animals by dogs of unknown ownership. Moreover, 1929 c. 198 § 6 (codified as RCW § 16.08.020) was not amended; rather, it kept the same form for more than 85 years, indicative that the legislative intent to restrict "domestic animals" to commercial ones remained unchanged.

Thus, to say an animal is an animal is an animal is not necessarily so. It follows that 1929 c. 198 § 6, as originally enacted, endeavored to provide a basis for justifiable canicide only where the dog has chased, injured, bitten, or killed a commercially valuable animal, such as a sheep, goat, bovine, horse, mule, rabbit, turkey, duck, chicken, or similar class of animal — not a companion canine or feline. This interpretation is also bolstered by United States Supreme Court and Washington Supreme Court cases, which confirm that a dog is not in the same class as a "domestic animal." The language used by the United States Supreme Court in the Louisiana case of *Sentell v. New Orleans & C.R. Co.*, 166 U.S. 698 (1897), applies. The Court said:

> By the common law, as well as by the law of most, if not all, the states, dogs are so far recognized as property that an action will lie for their conversion or injury; although, in the absence of a statute, they are not regarded as the subjects of larceny.

> The very fact that they are without the protection of the criminal laws shows that property in dogs is of an imperfect or qualified nature, and that they stand, as it were, between animals ferae naturae, in which, until killed or subdued, there is no property, and domestic animals, in which the right of property is perfect and complete. They are not considered as being upon the same plane with horses, cattle, sheep, and other domesticated animals, but rather in the category of cats, monkeys, parrots, singing birds, and similar animals, kept for pleasure, curiosity, or caprice.

Id., at 701. Likewise applicable is the opinion of the Supreme Court of Washington in the case of *McQueen v. Kittitas Cy.*, 198 P. 394 (Wash. 1921):

> It is true that the legislature for the purposes of the criminal statutes, has declared dogs to be personal property (Rem.Code, § 2303, subd. 11); but, notwithstanding this, dogs do not stand on the same plane with horses, cattle, sheep, and other domesticated animals.

Id., at 396. While, admittedly, times have changed in the past 87 years such that dogs have become extensively domesticated and are subjects of larceny, the question is not whether the common law has so evolved, but whether the legislature intended to include dogs within the class of "domestic animals" when it enacted the latest version of RCW § 16.08.020, in 1929. With regard to a Missouri criminal statute prohibiting the "malicious[] expos[ure] [of] any poisonous substance, with intent that the same shall be taken or swallowed by any cattle, hog, sheep, goat, horse, mule, ass or other domestic animal or domestic fowl," the Missouri Supreme Court grappled with such a legislative intent inquiry in the case of *State v. Getty*, 273 S.W.2d 170 (Mo. 1954), noting:

> In our study of the question presented we have read a great many cases. It is true that dogs have extensively become domesticated, so that it is usual and perhaps not an improper use of language to call them "domestic animals." However, we do not think that the Legislature by the 1919 amendment intended to include them within the term "other domestic animals." The Supreme Court of Wisconsin so construed a similar statute in the case of Skog v. King, 214 Wis. 591, 254 N.W. 354. In that case the defendant shot a dog while it was fighting with his own. The trial court took the view that there was no legal justification for the killing of the plaintiff's dog because the defendant did not show that plaintiff's dog was actually "found killing, wounding or worrying any horses, cattle, sheep, lambs or other domestic animals" as provided in the statute of that state. The trial court was of the opinion that a dog is not a domestic animal within the meaning of the language "other domestic animals" found in the statute. When the case reached the upper court the latter said: "It is our opinion that the trial court was right in concluding that the Legislature did not intend to include dogs within the language 'other domestic animals.' "

> No aid can be found from the decisions of other states cited by the State in its brief. None are based upon statutes analogous to ours. For example, the Texas case cited, Manies v. State, 116 Tex. Crim. 542, 32 S.W.2d 470 (1930), is based upon a statute which specifically mentions dogs. The Georgia case, Wilcox v. State, 101 Ga. 563, 28 S.E. 981 (1897), is based upon the peculiar wording of the constitution authorizing the General Assembly to impose taxes upon "such domestic animals as, from their nature and habits, are destructive of other property." Also, the court properly held that the words "domestic animals," as there used, were intended to refer to dogs.

Id., at 173. Thus, per the logic of the Missouri Supreme Court, in that RCW § 16.08.020 does not specifically mention dogs, it cannot be used in defense of dogs. *See also McKinney v. Robbins*, 892 S.W.2d 502 (Ark. 1995) (reversing summary judgment for defendant who killed dog in defense of kitten on basis that cats were not "domesticated animals" as contemplated by legislature in passing justifiable canicide statute).

Third, **shift the burden**. Practitioners should be prepared to argue that any common law or statutory privilege or justification to kill is an affirmative defense. Defendants have the burden of proving that their actions were legally justified by evidentiary preponderance.

Fourth, **parse**. RCW § 16.08.020 should be analyzed as two alternative grounds to justifiably kill a dog — (1) while the attack is in progress, or (2) after the attack has terminated and the dog is found running at large, as follows:

"In the Act"

It shall be lawful for any person who shall see any dog or dogs chasing, biting, injuring or killing any sheep, swine or other domestic animal, including poultry, belonging to such person, on any real property owned or leased by, or under the control of, such person, or on any public highway, to kill such dog or dogs,

"After the Fact"

and it shall be the duty of the owner or keeper of any dog or dogs so found chasing, biting or injuring any domestic animal, including poultry, upon being notified of that fact by the owner of such domestic animals or poultry, to thereafter keep such dog or dogs in leash or confined upon the premises of the owner or keeper thereof, and in case any such owner or keeper of a dog or dogs shall fail or neglect to comply with the provisions of this section, it shall be lawful for the owner of such domestic animals or poultry to kill such dog or dogs found running at large.

The statute's language permits justifiable canicide only where the chase or attack is *in progress*. It does not allow for lethal force after the chase has abated, the bite or injury has been inflicted, or the domestic animal has been killed. Nor does it permit one to kill when the dog is defending its own property and inflicting injuries on a domestic animal who is trespassing and off the shooter's private property. The thrust of this statute is to permit the use of lethal force in defense of animals, not to allow cold-blooded executions after the threat ends. If this were the legislature's intention, it would not have required the person to presently "see" a dog "chasing, biting, injuring, or killing." Instead, it would have used the past tense ("saw" and "chase"/"chased," "bite"/"bitten," "injure"/"injured," "kill"/"killed").

This statutory interpretation, which draws upon themes of reasonableness and necessity, finds support in *Drolet v. Armstrong*, 252 P. 96 (Wash. 1927). The question of "reasonable necessity" is one for the jury:

Under well-considered cases and in all good reason, a person has a natural right to defend and protect his domestic fowls, and in doing so may kill dogs engaged in injuring and destroying them if there is reasonable and apparent necessity therefor, to be determined by the trier of the facts.

Id., at 97. The *Drolet* court, in evaluating the contours of this doctrine, cites approvingly to 2 Cyc. p. 415, which is cited by *State v. Burk*, 195 P. 16 (Wash. 1921), as follows:

One may kill a vicious animal in the necessary defense of himself or the members of his household, or under circumstances which indicate danger that property will be injured or destroyed unless the aggressor is killed, but it seems that such killing is justified only when the animal is actually doing injury . . . Every person has a natural right to defend and protect his animate property — as cattle, stock, and fowls — from injury or destruction by dogs, and in pursuance of that object may kill dogs engaged in doing injury to such animals owned by him; but there must exist an apparent necessity for such a course, and the destruction of the dog must be reasonably necessary under the circumstances . . . The right to kill dogs, in order to protect inanimate property, is based upon the same considerations.

Id., at 97. The *Burk* decision was reaffirmed in the context of wildlife damage, permitting lethal force when "reasonably necessary" to protect against marauding intrusions. *State v. VanderHouwen*, 177 P.3d 93 (Wash. 2008) (involving prosecution of owner of fruit orchards who shot and killed elk as they were eating his trees on his property).

Fifth, **mine the legislative history**. It is noteworthy that RCW § 16.08.020's predecessor, former Wash. Rev. Code § 3107, was extant at the time of the *Drolet* decision, and referenced by the concurring Justice Fullerton. *Drolet*, 252 P. at 97–98. The justices affirmed on the basis that the evidence supported a finding of "reasonable and apparent necessity for killing the dogs, each of which at the time it was shot being engaged in killing chickens, recently or immediately following similar trespasses at the same place." *Id.*, at 97. While the language of the predecessor statute, former Wash. Rev. Code § 3107 (1917 and 1919), is virtually identical to RCW § 16.08.020, important distinctions exist:

- Former Wash. Rev. Code § 3107 expands the class of species chased, bitten, or injured by the dog to include "any child or person." Current RCW § 16.08.020 does not speak to children or human beings and limits the class to "sheep, swine, or other domestic animal[s]" and "poultry" "belonging to such person." Thus, RCW § 16.08.020 allows canicide only where the dog is aggressing against a nonhuman. It is thus *more protective* of the dog owner.

- Former Wash. Rev. Code § 3107 applies to dogs who chase, bite, injure, or kill "any domestic animal," while current RCW § 16.08.020 restricts the class of attacked animals to those "belonging to such person." Thus, RCW § 16.08.020 allows only the owner of the domestic animal to kill the dog. It is thus *more protective* of the dog owner.

- Former Wash. Rev. Code § 3107 justifies killing a dog while the attack is in progress when the dog is "outside the enclosure of the owner or keeper of such dog," while current RCW § 16.08.020 requires that the attack occur "on any real property owned or leased by, or under the control of, such person, or on any public highway." Thus, current RCW § 16.08.020 expands the safe zone within which a dog may chase, bite, injure, or kill without giving justification to the domestic animal owner to kill the dog. It is thus *more protective* of the dog owner.

- Former Wash. Rev. Code § 3107 does not include the notification requirement found in current RCW § 16.08.020, and again provides *more protection* to the dog owner.

- Former Wash. Rev. Code § 3107 allows "any person" to kill the dog "found running at large" after that dog has previously been "found chasing, injuring or biting any domestic animal, or injuring or biting any child or person," while current RCW § 16.08.020 affords this justification only to "the owner of such domestic animals or poultry." It is thus *more protective* of the dog owner.

As explained below, litigants should be prepared to examine each component of the germane canicide statute:

1. Be prepared to prove that the dog harmed a domestic animal on real property owned or leased by the defendants. This may require a survey. RCW § 16.08.020 adds a degree of ambiguity by permitting killings on property "under [defendant's] control." This phrase is not defined, but common sense dictates that the person contemplated by the statute is one who has a controlling share in the identified parcel, some right to possession, license to use, ownership interest, or ability to remove others on demand. Adverse possession, acquiesced boundary doctrine, and implied or express easements may affect this analysis and should be given strong consideration. Another way of interpreting the phrase involves proof by contradiction — i.e., who would *not* be situated on land "under their control"? One example is a trespasser.

2. Be conscious of precisely who possesses the privilege. Under RCW § 16.08.020, only the "owner of such domestic animals" (i.e., those who have historically been chased, bitten, injured, or killed) may kill the dog "found running at-large." Thus, if plaintiff's dog chased A's livestock in March, B would not be justified in killing that dog found running at-large in May. Only A would possess the statutory privilege.

3. The present tense of the verb "to run" is critical here, as the right to kill only applies when the dog is "found running at-large." Although the phrase "running at large" is not defined in RCW § 16.08.020, it has abundant usage in nearly every jurisdiction that purports to control stray dogs. If the animal is stationary when killed (i.e., not running) and not off the owner's premises, the statutory privilege would not protect the shooter. The privilege is executory in nature, and only takes effect once the dog has left the premises without being under control.

To recap, the first ground is cast in the present, the second in the future. Any other interpretation would render the statute absurd, because it would ostensibly permit the owner of the attacked animal to kill the offending dog hours, days, and even weeks after the attack — wherever the dog may be found and regardless of whether it is running at large. This interpretation of RCW § 16.08.020 is consistent with the sound reasoning of the supreme court in *Drolet* and *Burk*, decisions that recognize the right to kill under the first prong "only when the animal is actually doing injury" and when "at the time [] shot [is] being engaged in killing[.]" *Drolet*, at 96, 97.

By way of comparison, New Mexico has codified a dog-specific defense at N.M. Stat. Ann. § 77-1-2, which provides:

> If any dog shall kill or injure any livestock, the owner or keeper of such dog shall be liable for all damages that may be sustained thereby, to be recovered by the party so injured before any court having competent jurisdiction, and it shall be unlawful to keep such dog after it is known that the dog is liable to kill livestock, and it shall be the duty of the owner to kill, or have killed, the dog upon order of the court after a finding that the dog has killed or injured livestock, and provided further, that it shall be the

right of any owner of livestock so killed or injured by the actions of any dog to kill the dog while it is upon property controlled by the owner of the livestock.

Note the statute's ambiguity: does it only permit a livestock owner to kill a dog *immediately following or in the act of* the dog injuring or killing the owner's livestock, or does it permit canicide *at any time into the future*? Must the livestock injury or death occur *on the owner's private property* to trigger the statutory justification to kill? What seems clear is that once the predicate has been fulfilled, the livestock owner may only kill the dog "while it is upon the property controlled by the owner of the livestock," and not *anywhere found running at large*, in contrast to RCW § 16.08.020 (though observe that NMS 77-1-2 does not have a notification provision).

Georgia has also codified a dog-specific defense, providing as follows:

(a) No person shall perform a cruel act on any dog; nor shall any person harm, maim, or kill any dog, or attempt to do so, except that a person may:

  (1) Defend his person or property, or the person or property of another, from injury or damage being caused by a dog; or

  (2) Kill any dog causing injury or damage to any livestock or poultry.

(b) The method used for killing the dog shall be designed to be as humane as is possible under the circumstances. A person who humanely kills a dog under the circumstances indicated in subsection (a) of this Code section shall incur no liability for such death.

(c) This Code section shall not be construed to limit in any way the authority or duty of any law enforcement officer, dog or rabies control officer, humane society, or veterinarian.

Ga. Code Ann. § 4-8-5. In interpreting this statute, note that it only permits the use of lethal, humane force to repel a canine aggressor in the act of causing injury, damage, or death. Thus, where the dog is merely trespassing and barking but not presenting a clear and imminent danger to anyone or anything, use of force would be illegal. Subsection (2)(b) likely does not create a civil cause of action for inhumane killing of dogs but instead serves as a defense to a criminal charge of cruelty to animals. Nonetheless, one should perform an implied cause of action analysis.

Below is a survey of cases invoking and adjudicating the justifiable canicide defense:

• *Mitchell v. Heinrichs*, 27 P.3d 309, 313 (Alaska 2001) (rejecting justifiable canicide defense);

• *Puckett v. Miller*, 381 N.E.2d 1087 (Ind. Ct. App.1978) (where plaintiff dog owner's two dogs, at time they were shot by defendant farmer, were "roaming unattended" in that attempts to find them had been abandoned, and were, according to defendant's uncontradicted testimony, trying to get into defendant's chicken enclosure, jumping and pouncing about and worrying defendant's chickens, defendant farmer was protected in shooting those dogs by statutes providing that any dog known to have worried any livestock or fowl or any dog found roaming over the country unattended may be lawfully killed);

- *McDonald v. Bauman*, 199 Kan. 628 (1967) (defendant's entry onto plaintiff's premises in hot pursuit, shooting and wounding dog without acquiescence by plaintiff, resulting in defense verdict, affirmed per Kan. Stat. Ann. § 47-646, which justifies landowner's killing of trespassing dog when engaged in act of depredation at time of destruction or a reasonable time thereafter);

- *Quave v. Bardwell*, 449 So. 2d 81 (La. Ct. App. 1984) (deliberate and unjustified, willful, and malicious killing of a German Shepherd resulted in affirmance of award of $2,500 compensatory damages and $120.50 medical bill);

- *Reed v. Goldneck*, 86 S.W. 1104 (Mo. Ct. App. 1905) (defendant dog killer statutorily protected when shooting plaintiff's dog who came onto property while fox hunting even though the dog was not doing anything harmful but was in front yard enclosure with 175–180 goats and 25 rabbits);

- *Frost v. Taylor*, 649 S.W.2d 264 (Mo. Ct. App. 1983) (no statutory protection for 15-year-old who shot plaintiff's dog when he heard dogs barking near sheep, due to lack of proof that dogs were in the act of harming sheep and, rather, were probably chasing coyotes);

- *Vosburgh v. Kimball*, 285 A.2d 766 (Vt. 1971) (reversing directed verdict for defense when dogs impounded by farmer were killed by constable for chasing milking cows on question of whether dogs were collared at time of impound);

- *Skog v. King*, 214 Wis. 591 (1934) (dog not a "domestic animal" in statute authorizing canicide where dog found killing, wounding, or worrying horses, cattle, sheep, or other domestic animals; thus, defendant may not kill trespassing dog simply because of fighting his dog unless reasonably necessary to do so to protect dog from death or serious harm, and here, reversal in favor of defendant appropriate given reasonable necessity under common law); Wis. Stat. Ann. § 174.01 (also provides for double damages if killing violates statutory privilege).

2. What of Defense of Wildlife?

When may one justifiably kill a dog giving chase to deer, for instance? In *State v. Long*, 991 P.2d 102 (Wash. Ct. App. 2000), Willis Long killed William Acorn's hound dogs Rowdy and Sparkle when they were out hunting bobcat near Long's property. When they chased a wild deer for a few moments across the edge of Long's property, he shot each dog three times at a distance of 90 feet with a .22 caliber revolver, then shot each in the forehead, allowing the deer to continue unharmed. Initially charged with willful/reckless killing of a pet animal (RCW § 9.08.070(1)(c)), the prosecutor amended the criminal complaint to add two counts of first degree malicious mischief, RCW § 9A.48.070, class B felonies. The first jury was hung. On retrial, the jury convicted as charged. Long claimed "wildlife protection" as a defense. While acknowledging that he had "a limited right in the wild game on his property to exclude all other persons from his . . . property for the purpose of hunting," and although his right to game is superior to that of trespassers, the state's property right to regulate wildlife trumps. "Game is not a property right appurtenant to land. Game belongs to the State." Thus, he could not claim a right to having killed Rowdy and Sparkle "in defense of wildlife or of his property." *Id.*, at 106. The court also rejected his claim to having lawfully abated a public nuisance, noting that while a dog pursuing a game animal during closed season is a public nuisance, the dogs were not specially injurious to him. Impoundment by animal control officers was the only recognized abatement measure. *Id.*, at 106–107.

G. STATUTORY IMMUNITY

Though otherwise satisfying the elements of NIED, IIED, conversion, trespass to chattels, or malicious injury, be mindful of legislative action favoring tortfeasors in admitted liability cases. State-law immunities worth considering[11] include:

- emergent care immunity.[12]
- emergency shelter immunity.[13]
- state of emergency immunity.[14]
- SPCA immunity from misdeeds of municipal actors, and vice versa.[15]
- disposition of abandoned animal immunity.[16]
- shelter immunity for disposition based on false representations of third party.[17]

---

[11] Do not forget federal qualified immunity doctrine. *See also San Jose Charter of The Hell's Angels Motorcycle Club v. City of San Jose*, 1999 U.S. Dist. LEXIS 21440 (N.D. Cal. Dec. 6, 1999), *aff'd o.g.*, 402 F.3d 962 (9th Cir. 2005) (dismissal of conversion claim against law enforcement based on state immunity in Cal. Gov't Code § 821.6).

[12] *See* Cal. Bus. & Prof. Code § 4840.6; R.I. Gen. Laws § 5-25-17; Vt. Stat. Ann. Tit. 26 § 2405; Ga. Code Ann. § 43-50-80; 42 Pa. Cons. Stat. Ann. § 8331.1; Tenn. Code Ann. § 63-12-142; N.Y. Educ. Law § 6705-a; Va. Code Ann. § 54.1-3811; 510 Ill. Comp. Stat. Ann. 70/16.5; Md. Code Ann., Cts. & Jud. Proc. § 5-614; Me. Rev. Stat. Ann. tit. 32, § 4874; Mo. Ann. Stat. §§ 340.287, 340.328; Tex. Occ. Code Ann. § 801.358; Tex. Health & Safety Code Ann. § 826.047; Ind. Code Ann. § 25-38.1-4-7; S.C. Code Ann. § 47-1-75.

[13] *See* Vt. Stat. Ann. tit. 20, § 29; La. Rev. Stat. Ann. § 29:773.1.

[14] *See* Ky. Rev. Stat. Ann. § 67.082(2) (no liability for good-faith execution of animal population reduction program in response to epidemic).

[15] *See* N.J. Stat. Ann. § 4:22-56.

[16] *See* 225 Ill. Comp. Stat. Ann. 115/18.

[17] *See* Va. Code Ann. § 18.2-144.2.

Chapter 9

THOSE HARMED BY ANIMALS

The science of human ecology examines the way humans interact with their natural world. This includes fellow humans and nonhumans and, to some extent, seeks to develop and remedy Samuel von Pufendorf's insight in *The Whole Duty of Man According to the Law of Nature* (1673), where he wrote, "More inhumanity has been done by man himself than any other of nature's causes." Excluding pathogens, nonhuman-mediated causes of injury, death, and disturbance are probably second in prevalence to human-mediated traumas contemplated by von Pufendorf. The class of nonhuman agents divides into wild and domesticated species. Some, like rhinoceroses and American Staffordshire Terriers, are deemed inherently dangerous. RCW § 16.30.010(2)(a)(ii) (rhinoceros); Sumas Muni. Code § 6.02.020 ("pit bull" irrefutably presumed to be dangerous dog). Individual animals may also exhibit behavior metamorphosing their legal status from benign to malevolent. Finally, one must draw a distinction between animals acting on their own volition and animals acting at the direction of a human caretaker.

A. ANIMAL AS DEADLY WEAPON

Likening a pit bull to a bar glass or pencil, the Washington Court of Appeals held that a "large, powerful dog that, by training or temperament, attacks a person [by charging, lunging at throat and chest, barking and growling] when intentionally released or directed to do so by its handler, meets the instrumentality 'as used' definition of deadly weapon." *State v. Hoeldt*, 160 P.3d 55, 57 (Wash. Ct. App. 2007). An entire annotation devotes itself to the subject. *See* Fern L. Kletter, *Dog as Deadly or Dangerous Weapon for Purposes of Statutes Aggravating Offenses such as Assault and Robbery*, 124 A.L.R. 5TH 657 (2004).

In the civil context, consider *Brewer v. Furtwangler*, 18 P.2d 837 (Wash. 1933). When Florence Brewer ended up disoriented at the end of a private driveway leading to a clearing where the Furtwanglers' admittedly vicious watchdog laid in wait on a 24-foot chain, she became the victim of a significant mauling. The Furtwanglers denied liability, pointing out conspicuous "Beware of the dog" and "Keep out" signs and that Brewer trespassed when bitten. The jury thought otherwise, finding them strictly liable in keeping a known, dangerous dog, excusing Brewer's wholly innocent and temporary meandering, and awarding $2,600 (in 1931 dollars) — a sum reduced to $1,800 by the court in a motion for judgment notwithstanding the verdict. Affirming, the court authored a lengthy opinion, copied in substantial part below as it handily explains when bark may not legally come to bite:

If it is established that a dog is of a vicious nature and that the owner of such dog has knowledge, actual or constructive, of that fact, the owner keeps that dog at his peril, and is chargeable for any failure to so keep it that it cannot do any damage to any person who, without essential fault, is injured by it. The owner must restrain such vicious animal even as against a trespasser on the owner's premises.

"The authorities almost unanimously hold that the owner of a domestic animal, known by him to be vicious and disposed to attack mankind, is bound to restrain it even as against a trespasser on his own premises, and that he will not be permitted to set up the commission of the trespass as a defense. The trespasser here referred to, however, is not one who enters another's premises with the intention of committing a crime thereon, but is one who is a mere technical or unintentional trespasser, although even as against criminal trespassers one is not permitted to employ any greater force than is reasonably necessary to repel invasion. This rule is upheld upon the well-established principle that the safety of human life may not be unnecessarily endangered in the protection of property, and is analogous to the rule denying to landowners the right to set spring guns as a protection against intruders, or to make other traps endangering the lives of any persons who may come in contact with them. The principle finds its most frequent application in the case of vicious dogs kept on one's premises for purposes of protection." 1 R. C. L. 1097, § 40.

The mere fact of trespassing upon the grounds of another is not, in and of itself, contributory negligence which will defeat an action to recover damages for injuries inflicted by a vicious animal belonging to the defendant and allowed to be at large upon the premises. *Eberling v. Mutillod*, 90 N. J. Law, 478, 101 A. 519.

"The principle seems well established that a man may keep on his grounds any defensive animal as a necessary protection, but the fact that a person is a trespasser does not constitute him an out-law and warrant another in negligently or wantonly injuring him. Therefore, to relieve himself from liability to a trespasser for injuries inflicted by a ferocious dog, the owner must prove that in the manner of keeping such an animal, and in its employment as a protective measure, he confined himself to strict necessity. As to just what comes within the pale of necessity the authorities are not altogether clear, but there seems to be little doubt that one is not justified in keeping, untied, on his premises in the daytime a vicious dog, and that for any injuries thereby occasioned to a voluntary or an involuntary trespasser who chances to be exposed to its ferocity, he is responsible. Where, however, one is bitten while trespassing or even negligently or incautiously coming on another's premises at night, the view has been entertained that the owner is not liable, as loosing dogs at night is deemed necessary and proper for protective purposes. Other courts, out of regard for the sanctity of human life, take the view that, as a savage dog is a dangerous instrument of protection, the owner's keeping it on the premises to protect them against trespassers is unlawful and that the owner has no right to keep such a dog for any purpose, unless it is kept in an inclosure or building, in the night-time, with caution, and as a protection against criminal wrongdoers, and if its size and ferocity are such as to endanger life, then only as a protection against a felony by 'accident or surprise." 1 R. C. L. 1123, § 66.

The respondent was a mere technical or unintentional trespasser upon the land of the appellants. While there, she was injured by appellants' dog, which appellants knew was vicious. The land was not inclosed, and the dog allowed to roam at large thereon, it is true. The land was unfenced or unenclosed as described above, but the dog was chained; his radius of travel being limited to twenty-four feet, the length of his chain. A dog chained on the unfenced property of his owner is as much at large on the premises of his owner *within the arc of his chain* as an unchained dog permitted to run at large on fenced property of his owner. The one is confined to all of the premises inclosed by the fence. The chained dog is confined to the area within the radius of his chain. *One is no more justified in keeping a vicious dog chained on uninclosed land in the daytime, as in the case at bar, than he is in keeping a vicious dog untied on fenced land in the daytime.* In either case, for any injury thereby occasioned to a voluntary or involuntary trespasser who chances to be exposed to its ferocity, he is responsible.

Id., 838–839 (emphasis added). One may conclude from reading *Brewer* that the days of guard dogs were numbered in light of the economic liability they posed even when doing their jobs of protecting family and property. Concurring Justice Holcomb anticipated such a consequence and, though *dictum*, since Brewer never entered with criminal design, wrote:

I concur in the result, but in so doing do not wish to be considered as subscribing to the doctrine that an owner cannot maintain a dangerous dog upon his own premises for the protection of himself and his property, under proper restraint and warning. Had respondent in this case been an intentional invader and wrongdoer, instead of an unintentional trespasser, no liability should be allowed, under the state of things shown.

Id., at 839. *Brewer* addresses use of force from the perspective of a landowner using dogs to repel human invaders, the inverse to the discussion of the allowable use of force to repel vicious canine invaders. The court's reference to spring guns bears further discussion, because it shows an unwillingness to allow landowners to kill to protect realty.

Brewer found liability because two variables favored the plaintiff: (1) innocent trespass and (2) known viciousness. Without both, the Furtwanglers would likely have prevailed. Knowledge of vicious propensity presumes a prior, unprovoked incident, placing the owner on notice that the dog possesses characteristics requiring utmost control. The prior incident did not historically impose liability, allowing the dog owner to escape unscathed by judgment in what many jurisdictions describe as the "one free bite" doctrine. Louisiana law, like Washington, endorsed this rule by only imposing strict liability in the case of the second bite. But efforts to legislatively and judicially repeal the rule gained traction in the late twentieth century. *See* RCW §§ 16.08.040-.060 (expressly abrogating common law by eliminating scienter requirement and holding owners strictly liable for the first bite, provided there was not implied or express consent to enter, or provocation); *Beeler v. Hickman*, 750 P.2d 1282 (Wash. Ct. App. 1988); *see also Holland v. Buckley*, 305 So. 2d 113 (La.1974) (completely reinterpreting Civ. Code art. 2321 to abandon "one free bite" rule); *Allen v. State Farm Fire & Cas. Co.*, 828 So. 2d 190 (La. Ct. App. 2002) (accord, even after legislative revision to art. 2321).

In the guard dog scenario, because the dog has been trained to act on its aggressive impulses (or represented to the public as having been so trained, even if not), scienter is almost always admitted, rendering the "one free bite" rule dialogue moot. *See, e.g., Frederickson v. Kepner*, 82 Cal. App. 2d 905 (1947) (reversing dismissal where dog threw customer over bank of a terrace, drawing inferences of scienter from fact dog was tied, a watchdog, and of large size and notorious breed); *Gerulis v. Lunecki*, 1 N.E.2d 440 (Ill. App. Ct. 1936) (affirming judgment for customer bitten by police dog kept by butcher to protect chickens from thieves and intruders, and who was allowed to roam the rear of the meat market (instead of being chained to a post in the garage and inside a 5-foot wire enclosure)); *Goode v. Martin*, 57 Md. 606 (1882) (reversing judgment for defendant, court held black-smith who overslept and failed to tie up his Newfoundland and terrier (whom he would set loose at night) liable for attack on boy waiting on smithy's porch Sunday morning as expected).

But even with scienter, guard dog owners may avoid liability by posting proper warnings. In *Frostin v. Radick*, 397 N.E.2d 208 (Ill. App. Ct. 1979), the Illinois Court of Appeals recognized that a customer bitten by a guard dog at a used car lot was not liable because she entered an area closed to the public, outfitted with warnings of the dog's presence, and she admitted she saw the dog inside the area before the attack. With similar outcome, *Belcher Yacht, Inc. v. Stickney*, 450 So. 2d 1111 (Fla. 1984) excused owners of a marina guard dog who inflicted severe bites to a customer given their placement of "Bad Dog" warning signage. When warned, a patron who intentionally disregards the obvious danger of a guard dog assumes the risk of injury (described as "invitation to injury"), as discussed in *Brown v. Barber*, 174 S.W.2d 298 (Tenn. Ct. App. 1943) (customer proceeded past posted warning sign, employee verbal warnings, and barks into service station area and bitten). Inadequate warnings, however, may expose guard dog owners to premises liability, as explored by *Villarreal v. Elizondo*, 831 S.W.2d 474 (Tex. App. 1992). To learn more about this subject, see Cheryl M. Bailey, *Liability for Owner or Operator of Business Premises for Injury to Patron by Dog or Cat*, 67 A.L.R. 4TH 976.

B.   VETERINARIAN'S AND KENNEL WORKER'S RULE

Traditionally, the firefighter's rule exempted private landowners from premises liability. As professionals trained to manage dangerous emergencies, firefighters are held to assume the risks associated with the normal, foreseeable hazards of their work. The rule is generally regarded as an application of primary assumption of risk and operates as a complete bar to liability. Over time, the rule has been examined with respect to pleas for extension to veterinarians, kennel workers, and animal control officers. In *Priebe v. Nelson*, 39 Cal. 4th 1112 (2006), the California Supreme Court invoked assumption of risk to bar a kennel worker's strict statutory liability claim for a job-related dog bite. Interestingly, the *Priebe* court was careful to stress that the assumption of risk rationale would not apply to common law strict liability claims where the risks associated with an abnormally dangerous dog were not disclosed to the kennel worker. If the owner of an animal is aware of its unusually vicious tendencies and does not disclose them, the owner is subject to potential liability. A recent decision distinguishing *Priebe* is *Harris v. Anderson Cty. Sheriff's Office*, 381 S.C. 357 (2009) (declining to follow *Priebe* in creating "kennel worker exception" to statutory strict liability).

The veterinarian's rule is a variant of the firefighter's rule and subject to the same analysis. The first court to announce it was *Nelson v. Hall*, 165 Cal. App. 3d 709 (1985), stating that vets and their assistants assume the inherent risk that any dog, even if apparently docile, might bite in course of treatment. *Id.*, at 715. "[T]he veterinarian determines the method of treatment and handling of the dog. He or she is the person in possession and control of the dog and is in the best position to take necessary precautions and protective measures." *Id.* Thus, "the risk of being attacked or bitten in the course of veterinary treatment is an occupational hazard which veterinarians accept by undertaking their employment. . . ." *Cohen v. McIntyre*, 16 Cal. App. 4th 650, 655 (1993). Importantly, Nelson noted that the rule "does not mean dog owners could never be held liable for injuries to veterinarians or their assistants . . . emphasiz[ing] that the defense of assumption of the risk extends only to the danger which the injured person has knowingly assumed; i.e., the danger the dog will bite while being treated." *Nelson*, 165 Cal. App. 3d at 715 n.4.

Since 1992, California cases applying the veterinarian's rule have focused on the relationship with the vet, and "defendant's conduct in entrusting the animal to the professional care and control of the veterinarian," not whether the vet subjectively agreed that dog bites were foreseeable hazards of the job. *Adams v. Lewis*, 2004 Cal. App. Unpub. LEXIS 8986 (Sept. 30, 2004) (quoting *Neighbarger v. Irwin Indus., Inc.*, 8 Cal. 4th 532, 541 (1994)). The *Adams* case extended the veterinarian's rule to an animal behaviorist. "[T]he veterinarian, like the firefighter, cannot recover for injuries arising out of the very conditions he or she was hired to confront." *Rosenbloom v. Hanour Corp.*, 66 Cal. App. 4th 1477 (1998) (summary judgment affirmed for plaintiff sued for injuries sustained in moving shark into larger aquarium). Exceptions have been said to exist where the dog owner conceals knowledge of vicious propensity or where the "conduct was so reckless as to fall totally outside the range of behavior ordinarily expected of those who avail themselves of veterinary services." *Cohen*, 16 Cal. App. 4th at 655; *Lipson v. Superior Court*, 31 Cal. 3d 362, 366, 371 (1982) (firefighter's rule does not apply where defendant misled plaintiff as to nature of risk presented by chemicals). *Davis v. Gaschler*, 11 Cal. App. 4th 1392 (1992), refused to extend the fireman's rule to a dog handler not specially retained by the defendants to manage their dog but who, rather, rendered aid to their dog who had been hit by a car and was bitten in the process. *Prays v. Perryman*, 213 Cal. App. 3d 1133 (1989), refused to extend the rule to a dog groomer who had not yet assumed control over a skittish dog when bitten.

In *Cole v. Hubanks*, 272 Wis. 2d 539 (2004), law enforcement officer ("LEO") Julia Cole was on duty when she came upon the Hubankses' dog wandering in the street, dragging a snapped chain. The Akita approached her. Without warning, the dog lunged, knocked her down, and bit her face and neck. She required 30 stitches to close her wounds. On summary judgment, the trial court dismissed her claim, invoking the firefighter's rule (which the state adopted in 1970). On appeal, the Wisconsin Supreme Court reversed by refusing to extend the rule from firefighters to police officers. It reasoned:

> There are many differences between firefighters and police officers. For example, firefighters know they are exposed to danger when they are called to fight a fire. As we noted in Hass, "[t]he call to duty is the warning of the hazard." . . . By contrast, police officers usually are out on patrol from the start of their shift until its end. Their efforts are not directed to one hazard, but rather they are often required to address varied circumstances, the responses to which may not always be apparent simply from the fact that they are police officers. Furthermore, firefighters and EMTs receive specialized training in fighting fires and in moving injured people at the scene of an accident, on a regular basis. While capturing stray dogs can fall within police officers' duties on occasion, they receive no specialized training to do so and it appears not to be a central focus of their day's activities. And finally, focusing too heavily on the plaintiff's occupation has the danger of permitting assumption of risk to be an absolute defense to a negligence claim, without expressly saying so. Therefore, any limit on the right to sue may also evaluate relevant public policy concerns in light of the particular claims made. As we have explained above, the public policy factors are the basis of the firefighters rule; therefore, they form the basis for our analysis here. We now turn to Cole's claims.

Id., at 553. One justice dissented from the holding of the high court. For a national treatment of the veterinarian's rule, see John C. Williams, *Liability of Owner of Dog for Dog's Biting Veterinarian or Veterinarian's Employee*, 4 A.L.R.4TH 349 (1981).

In *Delaire v. Kaskel*, 842 A.2d 1052 (R.I.2004), the Rhode Island Supreme Court was apparently the first in the nation to address whether the firefighter's rule should be extended to animal control officers ("ACO"); it held that the rule should not be applied. Id., at 1056. DeLaire slipped and fell on the Kaskels' property in response to a stray cat call. Kaskel argued that DeLaire's injury resulted from a risk of his employment and invoked the Public Safety Officer Rule. Kaskel urged the court to treat ACOs as the equivalent of LEOs given that: (a) DeLaire drove a vehicle with police license plates, (b) he carried a police-issued firearm, (c) he was a police constable, (d) he reported to a police sergeant, and (e) he used an office in the East Greenwich Police Department. DeLaire rebutted by noting that: (1) ACOs do not enjoy state law benefits given to LEOs and firefighters injured in the line of duty (such as full salary with medical and related expenses), (2) LEOs get police academy training, but DeLaire did not, (3) while the local chapter of the police union represented both ACOs and LEOs in East Greenwich, ACOs were non-police members of the union and had separate contracts, (4) LEOs had a significantly larger salary, pension, and benefit program, (5) LEOs were a statutorily protected class of employees in Rhode Island enjoying the Law Enforcement Officer's Bill of Rights. Siding with DeLaire, the court found that ACOs were not bound by the constraints of the Public Safety Officer Rule.

In February 2006, the Tennessee Court of Appeals in *Jamison v. Ulrich*, 206 S.W.3d 419 (Tenn. Ct. App. 2006), decided otherwise, holding that the firefighter's rule should apply to ACOs. The animal control officer alleged that the dog owner failed to warn about the dog's dangerous nature. He was bitten as a result. Id., at 420. Dismissing the lawsuit, the trial court reasoned that the rule barring police officers and firefighters from recovering for injury suffered in the line of duty should apply to animal control officers. Id., at 421. On appeal, the *Jamison* court stressed that animal control officers should expect to encounter aggressive dogs given the nature of their work. *Id.*, at 424-25. The *Jamison* decision is in line with several others in which animal care personnel, such as commercial kennel workers, have tried unsuccessfully to overcome the assumption of risk rationale underlying the firefighter's rule.

In *Fetchko v. Morgan*, 2008 Ky. App. LEXIS 195 (June 27, 2008), Ronald Fetchko, a Louisville metro animal control officer, suffered extensive head wounds from Bandit, a pit bull terrier-type dog cared for by Ashley Edmunds and Jonathan Morgan. Fetchko responded to a call that Bandit had attacked Edmunds and Morgan's infant child the night before, but he did not know any details beyond the fact that there was a dog bite and that he was to pick up the owner-released dog. When he arrived two blocks from the home, he was informed by dispatch that the dog owner's mother (K. Morgan) would arrive to meet him shortly. He was then approached by Morgan's mother, who was walking one dog on a leash and had another (Bandit) walking at her feet unrestrained. Not knowing that this was his contact, he engaged in a discussion with the mother, noting that both dogs "'appeared to be calm and docile,'" but he intended to tell the mother it was unlawful to walk dogs unleashed. *Id.*, at *1. As he climbed out of the truck, the mother told him "'that the unleashed dog was the [one] [who] had bitten her grandchild the previous evening.'" At this moment, Bandit began circling and then took him to the ground, attempting to get at his neck. Bandit bit him on the face many times and grabbed his left arm before he could climb back into his truck.

Fetchko sued for negligence, negligence per se, and strict liability against Edmunds, Morgan, and K. Morgan. The trial court dismissed the case on summary judgment; although Morgan's mother was an "owner" of the dog pursuant to statute, the court noted, Fetchko had assumed the risk of being injured by one of the animals he transports, so the court declined to extend the Firefighter's Rule to animal control officers. *Id.*, at *2. Fetchko appealed. In a 3-0 decision, the appellate court affirmed on the question of ownership, reversed on the question of assumption of risk, and concluded that the Firefighter's Rule would not apply under these facts. *Id.*, at *4. The case was accordingly remanded for trial. Although Edmunds and Morgan had traditionally understood "ownership" rights in Bandit, Kentucky's strict liability statute states that an "owner" includes keepers and harborers, which she certainly became. Distinguishing the matter from a case involving a groomer bitten in the face while carrying a dog, the court held that Fetchko never accepted custody of Bandit before being bitten and thus did not assume any risk of that injury. *Id.*, at *3. After all, he was merely exiting his truck and had not attempted to assert any custody or control over Bandit before being attacked.

The Firefighter's Rule bars public employees like police officers and firefighters from suing individuals when they call a public protection agency and the employee is harmed after arriving at a given location to engage a specific risk (e.g., a resident calls 911 asking for assistance with a house fire, and the firefighter comes to the residence and engages the fire, suffering injury). The court did not address the merits of whether the doctrine should extend to animal control officers but, for the sake of argument, reasoned that because Fetchko had not yet arrived at a "given location" to engage a known risk (he did not know at the time of exiting his vehicle that Bandit was the dog he was there to capture), it did not apply. *Id.*, at *4.

Even where the Rule applies, exceptions do exist. In *Gonzales v. Kissner*, 24 So. 3d 214 (La. App. 2009), ACO Toni Gonzales was repeatedly attacked by a 100-pound GSD owned by the Kissners. She had visited their residence to investigate a bite complaint from the day prior. While talking to Mrs. Kissner by her truck, the dog escaped the house by forcing open the back door and mauled the officer on her head, face, and neck. The appellate court discussed the professional rescuer doctrine, which states that firefighters, police officers, and those whose professions protect life and property necessarily endanger their safety. However, they do not assume the risk of all injuries without recourse. The Gonzales court did not decide whether the duties of an ACO fall within the Rule, but noted that they are hired to protect the public from harmful animals and can reasonably expect to encounter such beasts, who may respond aggressively during apprehension, and inflict bites in the course of employment. Indeed, the risk of being bitten arises from a specific problem the ACO is hired to remedy. Assuming arguendo that the Rule applied to ACOs, the court found application of an exemption. Under Louisiana's Rescuer Doctrine, the Rule does not apply if: (1) the dependent risks encountered by the rescuer are so extraordinary that it cannot be said the parties intended the rescuer to assume them; or (2) the defendant's conduct was so blameworthy that tort recovery should be imposed for punishment or deterrence. Despite known prior escapes and vicious propensities, the Kissners failed to secure their vicious dog. Gonzales had every reason to believe the dog would be restrained. Accordingly, the second exception would have saved Gonzales from the immunizing effect of the Rule.

C. LIABILITY FOR ANIMALS BITING OR INJURING OTHERS[1]

Nonhuman animals who sink their teeth into, or rake their claws over, another may expose their owner, keeper, or harborer to liability. In addition to statutory strict or absolute liability, three common law theories frequently take hold — negligent control, strict common law liability, and nuisance. Depending on the jurisdiction, the claims may be pleaded in the alternative, or cumulatively. In most states, a plaintiff need not elect between a statutory and common law claim, or common law negligence and common law strict liability claim, but can raise both (or all) simultaneously. *Murdock v. Balle*, 696 P.2d 230 (Ariz. Ct. App. 1985) (permitting simultaneous suit by statute and common law); *Swerdfeger v. Krueger*, 358 P.2d 479 (Colo. 1960) (accord); *Trager v. Thor*, 516 N.W.2d 69, 72 (Mich. 1994) (accord); *De*

---

[1] Copious portions of this section were taken from, and with permission of, the Thomson Reuters publication Adam P. Karp, *Causes of Action for Loss of or Injury to an Animal by an Animal*, 38 COA.2d 281 (2008).

Robertis by DeRobertis v. Randazzo, 462 A.2d 1260 (N.J. 1983) (negligence and strict liability pleadable regardless of statutory liability); *Owens v. Coury*, 614 S.W.2d 926 (Tex. App. 1981) (strict liability and negligence); *Arnold v. Laird*, 621 P.2d 138 (Wash. 1980) (strict liability and negligence); *Borns ex rel. Gannon v. Voss*, 70 P.3d 262 (Wyo. 2003) (strict liability, negligence, and negligence per se). In jurisdictions that do not permit this practice, defendants should raise appropriate objections where a plaintiff improperly proceeds under dual, alternative theories (e.g., strict common law liability and strict statutory liability) and move to strike the one most likely to succeed.

1. Strict Common Law Liability

Strict common law liability exists where the owner or keeper of an animal knows or should know of the animal's dangerous propensities. Regardless of the level of care exercised (i.e., even if nonnegligent), if the plaintiff can establish knowledge (called *scienter*), the owner or keeper will be held strictly liable.

The elements of a strict liability claim for injury caused by a dangerous domesticated animal are:

(1)   the defendant owned or possessed the animal;

(2)   the animal had dangerous propensities abnormal to its class;

(3)   the defendant knew or had reason to know the animal had dangerous propensities; and

(4)   those propensities were the cause of plaintiff's injury.

In other words, the plaintiff's injury must have resulted from a particular dangerous propensity known to the defendant.

a. Animal's Dangerous Propensities

Generally, any particular domestic animal's characteristic, habit, tendency, or proclivity to cause injury of the type complained of will be considered a "dangerous propensity." *See* RESTATEMENT THIRD, TORTS: *Liability for Physical Harm* § 23; *Collier v. Zambito*, 807 N.E.2d 254 (N.Y. 2004). The plaintiff must demonstrate rough factual equivalency between the historical *victim(s)* of the vicious propensity and the *victim* identified in the civil action. Thus, a propensity to attack large men wearing hats or to chase motorcycles may not prove a dangerous propensity to bite kittens. That said, in the hierarchy of propensities, an antihuman propensity might subsume an antianimal propensity, though not vice versa. The tendency of a domestic animal to menace or fight with other animals generally has not been deemed a dangerous propensity to harm a human being. The animal's subjective "intent" to engage in deleterious behavior, if determinable, is legally immaterial. Indeed, overly affectionate behavior may be a "dangerous propensity" if it results in injury to a person. *Pollard v. UPS*, 302 A.D.2d 884 (N.Y. App. Div. 2003).

Parity between the historical *injuries* inflicted by the vicious animal and *injuries* identified in the subsequent civil action are germane, but need not be identical. Indeed, the "one bite rule" has given way to the modern notion that an animal need not have actually caused physical harm to a person in order to show dangerous propensity. *Custer v. Coward*, 667 S.E.2d 135 (Ga. Ct. App. 2008). Past behavior evidencing an impulse to engage in the conduct at bar often suffices, such as a dog's tendency to bark, growl, and snap menacingly at a fence whenever people passed, although the dog had not actually bitten anyone before biting the plaintiff. *See Petrone v. Fernandez*, 53 A.D.3d 221 (N.Y. App. Div. 2008). *But see Carter v. Ide*, 188 S.E.2d 275 (Ga. Ct. App. 1972) (owner's knowledge of dog's propensity to attack other animals did not establish owner's knowledge that dog might attack people); *Lee v. Weaver*, 237 N.W.2d 149 (Neb. 1976) (mere fact of prior bite insufficient to establish danger to people).

A person injured when knocked down by a frolicking dog will recover only upon proof that the animal had a habit of running into or jumping on people, illustrating that the term "dangerous" embraces more than just those canines seething with animus. It includes even their hyperstimulated, highly uncoordinated, and lovingly rude, mouthy, and jumpy counterparts. A well-intended Boxer utterly lacking in training may habitually and spiritedly run up to children and the elderly only to inadvertently knock them down or cut them with her toenails as she seeks attention. She is no less a danger (or hazard) than were she seeking blood.

Courts have awarded damages for injuries resulting from friendly or playful behavior. *See Farrior v. Payton*, 562 P.2d 779 (Haw. 1977); *Owen v. Hampson*, 62 So. 2d 245 (Ala. 1952). The circumstances of the injury will convey the operative behavior of the animal, such as unprovoked injury to humans and small animals; menacing and aggressive actions like barking, snarling, growling, lunging; chasing vehicles; jumping on people or animals; the purpose for which the animal was kept or used; physical ailments causing irritability; proof of abuse or neglect; size — but what about breed?

The predominant view regards a dog's pedigree alone as insufficient to establish dangerous propensity. *See Montiero v. Silver Lake I, L.P.*, 813 A.2d 978 (R.I. 2003) (plaintiff argued that defendants should have known of a dog's viciousness because it was a pit bull — a dog "with a well-deserved reputation for viciousness," but the court disagreed, finding that "the creation of a species-specific standard of care is a policy matter that is better left to the legislature"). Yet a few renegade courts have assumed that a dog's lineage completely dictates and predicts her behavior, declaring certain breeds "innately vicious," including the German Shepherd. *Ford v. Steindon*, 35 Misc. 2d 339 (N.Y. App. Term 1962). Of course, most judiciaries adhere to the common law presuming dogs are good, regardless of breed. *See Cook v. Whitsell-Sherman*, 796 N.E.2d 271 (Ind. 2003):

> The common law presumes that all dogs, regardless of breed or size, are harmless. *Poznanski ex rel. Poznanski v. Horvath*, 788 N.E.2d 1255, 1257 (Ind. 2003); *Ross v. Lowe*, 619 N.E.2d 911, 914 (Ind. 1993). This presumption can be overcome by evidence of a known vicious or dangerous propensity of the particular dog. *Ross*, 619 N.E.2d at 914.

Id., at 275.

In the last five decades since *Ford*, the breed-specific poster dogs are the pit bull terrier-types (often identified as the genuine article or amalgamation of an American Staffordshire Terrier, Staffordshire Bull Terrier, American Staffordshire

Bull Terrier, or American Pit Bull Terrier), Rottweilers, Cane Corsos, and Presa de Canarios. *But see Knapton v. Monk*, 379 Mont. 1 (2015) (refusing to deem purebred pit bulls inherently vicious). In ascertaining propensity, courts have also looked to the animal's custodial care conditions, possible exposure to canine disease in the community, recent whelpings, and the presence of warning signs on the owner's premises as indicators of increased likelihood of attack — even where the animal in question had no prior episodes of unbridled aggression or hazardous potentiality.

Accordingly, evidence of an animal's predisposition for kindness, eagerness to please, nonthreatening and quite submissive demeanor, docile nature, custom of running away from conflict, and tendency not to redirect aggression from an animal to an intervening human (e.g., a person attempts to break up a dog fight and suffers no injury), is pertinent to a jury's determination of what occurred where the only "witnesses" to the incident were the dog and the alleged bite victim or defendant who has killed the dog in anticipation of harm. Evidence that the dog never growled or acted aggressively and would urinate while on her back in a submissive pose would be relevant to show a "hard-wired" and predictable reaction to a specific fear stimulus.

For an excellent discussion of habit, trait, and demeanor evidence, see Geordie Duckler, *On Redefining the Boundaries of Animal Ownership*, 10 Animal L. 63 (2004). The author begins by distinguishing animate tangible personalty from other forms of property, examining how an animal is animated by "intentionality" rather than "automation," as in the case of a machine. Animals have the ability to replicate, relocate on their own volition, and may "abandon" their owner. Duckler asserts that one may divine an animal's intent through propensity. While FRE 404 *excludes* most propensity evidence informed by a person's prior bad acts, strict liability doctrine *requires* its inclusion. In so doing, it endorses a double standard besaddling the poor dog with an unshakable label for life: once a bad dog, always a bad dog (and, thus, possessed of a "vicious propensity").

But is the seeming incongruity truly irreconcilable? Consider that the dog herself is not actually a party to the lawsuit and will never become a judgment debtor. Instead, much like a parent whose minor child goes on a rampage of malicious mischief whacking down mailboxes with a baseball bat and breaking windows with a well-aimed slingshot, a dog owner bears responsibility for the destructive escapades of his nonhuman ward. To hold the parent (of the human or nonhuman) liable, in what amounts to a negligent supervision claim,[2] the plaintiff must prove that the parent knew or should have known of the abnormally dangerous propensity of each. Accordingly, otherwise inadmissible propensity evidence *pertaining to the parent* never comes in evidence; but that *pertaining to the child/dog* does.

---

[2] Interestingly, some jurisdictions abrogate the common law scienter requirement in negligent parental supervision cases. RCW § 4.24.190, for instance, provides, "The parent or parents of any minor child under the age of eighteen years who is living with the parent or parents and who shall willfully or maliciously destroy or deface property, real or personal or mixed, or who shall willfully and maliciously inflict personal injury on another person, shall be liable to the owner of such property or to the person injured in a civil action at law for damages[.]" In eliminating the need to prove prior dangerous proclivity known to the parent, the legislature capped damages at five thousand dollars, but still explicitly allowed the plaintiff to pursue in excess of that figure for the parents' own "common law negligence."

Liability, therefore, comes down to how well the parent/guardian knows (or should know) his child/companion animal and what supervisory precautions he takes to avoid foreseeable tragedies. On this point, Duckler notes, "The principal danger of [an animal's] escape comes from human error," which itself comes from "an ignorance of an animal's personality." *Id.*, at 76. To the "animals-in-the-yard" scenario, he likens examples involving inanimate, yet quite potentially dangerous instrumentalities such as the "gun-in-the-drawer" or "keys-in-the-ignition" scenarios. The responsibility for the human child/animal bad actor almost always returns to the parent/owner who has failed to be aware of the propensity and intentionality of the child/nonhuman animal.

Of course, one must not oversimplify animal behavior. Are animal personalities not "variable"? Do only human beings suffer from dissociative/multiple personality disorder? Is "breed personality," therefore, like racial profiling in that it overemphasizes genetics to the point of completely dismissing learned behaviors? Does a single vicious "act" make for an immutable vicious "demeanor"? If a dog bites a nighttime jogger, can this be attributed to instinct or intent, genetically programmed "propensity" or learned "character?" Do these distinctions matter?

Perhaps in the area of provocation, these nuances are critical. When a court evaluates provocation to establish liability or deem a dog dangerous, the mindset of the allegedly provoked animal matters. Accordingly, even if the bite victim did not *intend* to provoke, a "reasonable dog" might be expected to interpret the victim's conduct as provocative, rendering the biting response to the provocative stimulus completely normal. More important, a person who understands (or should understand) animal propensity would anticipate and avoid such a foreseeable reaction. Provocation doctrine thus excludes a subset of righteous reactions from the universe of aggressive and harmful behaviors, which would otherwise serve as predicates for a finding of vicious habit or propensity.

b. Knowledge of Animal's Dangerous Propensities

The plaintiff must prove that the defendant knew or should have known of the animal's dangerous propensities prior to the time of injury to the plaintiff, a standard determined from the perspective of a reasonable person in the defendant's position. Specific knowledge of the particular behavioral trait resulting in the plaintiff's injury must be demonstrated, whether by inferred knowledge, actual awareness, or as imputed by virtue of a relationship with a person having actual knowledge. That said, some states hold that landlords of owners, keepers, or harborers who have even actual knowledge of vicious propensity are generally never liable. *See Frobig v. Gordon*, 881 P.2d 226 (Wash. 1994) (inherently vicious mammal, here a tiger, known to reside on commercial premises, did not expose landlord to liability when child injured).

Traditionally, no liability attached unless the owner of a dog knew or should have known of its vicious propensities of the type to cause plaintiff's injuries. *Wells v. Wynn*, 311 A.2d 829 (D.C. 1973). The doctrine extended to other species as well. *Durden v. Barnett*, 7 Ala. 169 (1844) (hog known to eat chickens); *Van Houten v. Pritchard*, 870 S.W.2d 377 (Ark. 1994) (cat's propensity toward violence); *Dubois v. Myers*, 684 P.2d 940 (Colo. Ct. App. 1984) (horses); *Allen v. Cox*, 942 A.2d 296 (Conn.

2008) (negligent control of cat causing injury); *Singleton v. Sherer*, 659 S.E.2d 196 (S.C. 2008) (domesticated raccoon); *Jividen v. Law*, 461 S.E.2d 451 (W. Va. 1995) (rambunctious horse). Infrequently, certain canine breeds are presumed inherently dangerous, providing constructive knowledge of propensity. *Edgar v. Riley ex rel. Riley*, 725 So. 2d 982 (Ala. Civ. App. 1998) (owner-guardians of pit bull who never attacked may, based solely on the dog's breed, be held to have knowledge of vicious propensity); *but see Morgan v. Marquis*, 50 A.3d 1 (Me. 2012) (no presumption). The foreseeable tendency of otherwise normally gentle dogs and cats to attack human beings when caring for their young may establish knowledge of vicious propensity during the nursing process. *Whitmer v. Schneble*, 331 N.E.2d 115 (Ill. App. Ct. 1975).

Dogs wont to kill or injure sheep are nuisances and may furnish scienter. *Miller v. State*, 63 S.E. 571 (Ga. Ct. App. 1909). Common canine behavior, on the other hand, often does not. *Mech v. Hearst Corp.*, 496 A.2d 1099 (Md. Ct. Spec. App. 1985) (guard dog injures trespasser); *Hiner v. Mojica*, 722 N.W.2d 914 (Mich. Ct. App. 2006) (barking, growling, jumping, or approaching strangers in a somewhat threatening way ordinarily insufficient to show abnormally dangerous or unusually vicious). Without further examination into the circumstances, a single prior bite does not confirm vicious propensities. *Frazier v. Stone*, 515 S.W.2d 766 (Mo. Ct. App. 1974); *Lee v. Weaver*, 237 N.W.2d 149 (Neb. 1976). Though not essential, prior complaints from victims aid in proof of liability. *Davis v. Bedell*, 123 Vt. 441, 442–43, 194 A.2d 651 (1963).

2. Negligence and Negligence Per Se

A dog slips its leash, a fence board breaks, an invisible fence fails, a child leaves the front door ajar, a teenager takes on more dogs than he can physically handle — all serve as examples of negligent control where the dog leaves the custody of the owner or keeper and causes injury. A *prima facie* case of negligence requires proof of the standard elements of duty, breach, causation, and damages. Defendants may overcome allegations of negligence by demonstrating they owed no duty of care to the plaintiff (e.g., where the defendant was not the owner, keeper, or harborer of the animal); or where they exercised reasonable care to prevent injury (e.g., through confinement, muzzling, leashing, supervision, or other restraint, warning signs, fencing); or, where appropriate, defendant's alleged misconduct did not cause the injury suffered (e.g., noting intervening, superseding causes by the plaintiff herself, the plaintiff's parents, due to negligent supervision (if a minor), and other sequelae not directly the result of negligent control, such as an injury not caused by physical contact between the plaintiff and the animal but instead the evasive overreaction of a plaintiff to a dogfight). The defenses of contributory and/or comparative negligence, assumption of risk, and provocation may also apply (e.g., defendant's *leashed* dog reacts to unsolicited lunge by plaintiff's *unleashed* dog while passing on a narrow sidewalk). Additionally, the animal's propensities and defendants' knowledge thereof are material to determining the level of reasonable care defendant should have exercised.

An argument that animal neglect alone states a claim for negligent control failed in *King v. Breen*, 560 So.2d 186 (Ala. 1990), the court rejecting that injuries resulting from negligent care or mistreatment of animals (leading the animal to bite) were actionable, for the reason that the theory omitted the long-standing scienter requirement of vicious propensity. In this respect, some courts treat strict liability actions as though they were negligence claims. *See Gretkowski v. Coppola*, 26 Conn. Supp. 294 (1996) (referring to claim as one of common law "negligence").

Strategically, plaintiffs may lead with common law strict liability and follow with negligence as a fallback position should they fail to prove scienter. Some jurisdictions only ever impose liability for harm inflicted by domesticated animals where scienter of dangerous propensity can be demonstrated, resulting in a curious hybrid of common law strict liability with negligence principles. *See Carr v. Case*, 380 A.2d 91, 92 (Vt. 1977) (*citing Godeau v. Blood*, 52 Vt. 251, 254 (1880)). In proving liability for negligent control, keeping, or maintenance, a plaintiff should survey all related animal control statutes and ordinances, from federal to local levels. Statutory duties, if breached, may either proffer evidence of negligence, or state a claim for negligence per se, which in essence transforms an ordinance (otherwise lacking an express private right of action) into an implied cause of action.

For instance, in *Jaffray v. Stamas*, 2005 Del. C.P. LEXIS 58 (Del. C.P. 2005), the defendant violated Decl. Code Ann. Tit. 7, § 1705(a) when he permitted his dog to run at large, constituting negligence per se, and deeming him liable to the plaintiff for the veterinarian's bill that resulted. *See also Sinclair v. Okata*, 874 F. Supp. 1051 (D. Alaska 1994) (violation of city ordinance "unequivocally aimed at preventing attacks and bites by dogs" supported negligence per se when dog caused harm while not under voice control); *Novak v. Craven*, 195 P.3d 1115 (Colo. Ct. App. 2008); *Boitz v. Preblich*, 405 N.W.2d 907, 912–913 (Minn. Ct. App. 1987); *Villaume v. Kaufman*, 550 A.2d 793 (Pa. Super. Ct. 1988); *Gough v. Shaner*, 90 S.E.2d 171, 174 (Va. 1955); *Endresen v. Allen*, 574 P.2d 1219 (Wyo. 1978). However, the statute must correspond nearly precisely to the incident at bar. *Lachenman v. Stice*, 838 N.E.2d 451 (Ind. Ct. App. 2005) examined a statute making it a misdemeanor for an owner to recklessly, knowingly, or intentionally fail to take reasonable steps to restrain her dog, from which results unprovoked bites or attacks upon another person, causing bodily injury. As the statute did not apply to harm to other animals (just people), the fatal attack on a neighbor's dog did not constitute negligence per se.

Instead of finding a per se violation, some courts ascribe an inference of negligence, applying the four-part RESTATEMENT test to determine whether to adopt a legislative enactment as the standard of care. In *Schneider v. Strifert*, 888 P.2d 1244 (Wash. Ct. App. 1995), the Washington Court of Appeals found that Franklin County's "at-large" dog ordinance established a duty to confine a Doberman Pinscher who tunneled out of a chicken pen, entered the interstate, and then collided with a motorcyclist, causing serious injuries. *Id.*, at 61–62 (applying *Restatement (2nd) Torts*, § 286 (1965)). In Arkansas, a leash law violation may supply evidence of negligence, but does not constitute negligence per se. *Bolstad v. Pergeson*, 806 S.W.2d 377 (Ark. 1991); *Slack v. Villari*, 476 A.2d 227, 231 (Md. Ct. Spec. App. 1984); *Chadbourne v. Kappaz*, 779 A.2d 293 (D.C. 2001) (rejecting argument that violating D.C. Code § 6-1008(a), the "leash law," mandated a negligence per se instruction for a man injured while trying to break up two dogs).

Where strict liability elements do not supplant those for negligent control, the defendant is bound only to the standard of care for keeping such an animal under the incident circumstances (and based on known or readily knowable historical facts) to which he was given constructive or actual notice. The defendant's compliance with relevant animal control regulations (e.g., leash law, voice control, muzzling) may defuse a negligence per se claim. A defendant may succeed in dismissing a negligent control claim on summary judgment by persuading the court that compliance with *statutory* duties cannot be reconciled with a finding that she also breached the *common law* duty of care.

Taking a thorough factual accounting may identify every failsafe employed by the defendant, every third party who may share in creating the foreseeable opportunity for an animal-on-animal injury to arise, and any details of the interaction that can be recharacterized to show due care. For instance, defendant's dog breaks free for the first time from a chain firmly staked in the ground on defendant's property or from a collar rated to restrain a dog of such weight and strength. A third party then captures the dog and keeps him in a backyard, at which time the dog attacks and kills a cat who entered that kenneled area. The defendant may consider a third-party complaint against the chain or collar manufacturer and the "dogknapper," emphasizing the lack of foreseeability of escape and viciousness (if applicable), and bring attention to the intervening, superseding causal influences that allowed this tragedy to unfold.

In Maryland, statutory violations do not constitute negligence per se but do provide evidence of the same under certain circumstances. Two Maryland cases invoke leash law ordinances with different outcomes, both turning on a close factual examination. Consider *Slack v. Villari*, 476 A.2d 227 (Md. Ct. Spec. App. 1984). The Slacks opened a fence gate to their property, allowing their unleashed Doberman named Gideon to enter their residence through a kitchen door. When Gideon walked past the door and raced toward the sidewalk, snarling and growling within inches of Dorothy and Carl Villari, who were taking their evening stroll, Mrs. Villari injured her back in an attempt to avoid a confrontation. Gideon did not leave the Slacks' property or touch either of the Villaris. The jury found the Slacks liable, but the appellate court reversed in a 2-1 decision, adding, "Mere accidental escape of an animal, without proof of the owner's knowledge or negligence, is insufficient evidence to constitute a violation of similar statutes couched in identical terms." *Id.*, at 232. The statute at issue was the Prince George's County leash law, which said, "No owner of any dog shall allow such animal to be at large in the County. . . . " *At large* meant "not under restraint and off the premises of his owner." *Under restraint* meant secured by leash or lead and under control of a responsible person, confined in a vehicle, or within the real property limits of the owner. As the dog did not venture off the Slacks' property, it was "under restraint," not "at large," and they could not be found negligent.

By contrast, consider *Moura v. Randall*, 705 A.2d 334 (Md. Ct. Spec. App. 1998). After bolting after a cat, Diesel, Randall's Rottweiler, attacked four-year-old Alex Moura three blocks away from where he walked Diesel, off-leash, in the common area of his townhouse development. The trial court dismissed the lawsuit, finding no violation of the Montgomery County animal control ordinance and no issue of material fact for negligence or strict liability. The appellate court reversed, distinguishing *Slack* in several respects: (1) Randall walked his dog on the common grounds of a multi-family development in which he lived where others had right of access, while the Slacks' Doberman was on the exclusive grounds of a single-family residence; (2) Diesel left the premises, while Gideon did not; (3) Randall conceded that Diesel had chased a cat before, showing foreknowledge of Diesel's propensity to escape his control at a moment's notice yet Randall failed to take prudent countermeasures, particularly where Diesel did not respond to commands and was too far away from Randall to be quickly restrained.

Common law defenses apply to a negligence claim. *Ross v. Golden State Rodeo Co.*, 530 P.2d 1166 (Mont. 1974) (contributory negligence and assumption of risk); *Marshall v. Ranne*, 511 S.W.2d 255 (Tex. 1974) (contributory negligence no defense in strict liability action but may apply to negligent control); *Mitchell v. Cunningham*, 2006 Mich. App. LEXIS 714 (Mar. 16, 2006) (comparative negligence applies to reduce liability). Permitting dead animals to remain unburied on the plaintiff's premises may not constitute contributory negligence because the average person does not reasonably infer that dogs coming to devour the carcasses would also kill sheep. *Peeler v. McMillan*, 1902 Mo. App. LEXIS 272 (Jan. 6, 1902).

Typically, negligence principles fault defendants for their inattentiveness *before* injury occurs; occasionally, their failure to intervene *after* an attack commences also establishes liability. In *Bushnell v. Mott*, 254 S.W.3d 451 (Tex. 2008), Genevia Bushnell, a seller of health and wellness products, was attacked by Janet Mott's three dogs when she knocked on the door to Mott's mobile home to deliver products that Mott had ordered. As Mott opened the door, her three dogs pushed through and mauled Bushnell, and Mott failed to make any attempt to stop the attack. Bushnell sued, alleging negligence, premises liability, and strict liability. The court granted Mott's motion for summary judgment, and Bushnell appealed. Affirming, the appellate court held that Bushnell could not state a claim against Mott without proving her knowledge of her dogs' vicious propensities. Bushnell sought review by the Texas Supreme Court, which reversed as to the claim for negligent handling of dogs (even those not known to be vicious) in doing nothing to halt the attack once it began. Bushnell swore that she "never once heard [Mott] scold the dogs." *Id.*, at 453 (also quoting RESTATEMENT (2ND) TORTS, § 518 cmt. j (1977), stating that while privileged to allow a dog to run at large and not exercise care to keep the animal under constant control, "he is liable if he sees his dog or cat about to attack a human being . . . and does nothing to exercise reasonable care to prevent it from doing so.") This sufficiently raised an issue of material fact on whether the post-attack handling of the dogs exposed Mott to liability.

What of wild animals, insects in particular? In *Belhumeur v. Zilm*, 949 A.2d 162 (N.H. 2008), Dennis Belhumeur sued his neighbors, the Zilms, for negligence and nuisance in allowing wild bees to nest in their tree and subsequently attack him on his own property. The trial court granted the Zilms' motion for summary judgment, and Belhumeur appealed. The New Hampshire Supreme Court affirmed dismissal, noting that the Zilms were not liable for nuisance "for wild animals that exist on their land as a natural occurrence[,]" as the "established common law rule [is] that a land owner is under no affirmative duty to remedy conditions of purely natural origin upon his land even though they are dangerous or inconvenient to his neighbors." As the wild bees were *ferae naturae* and, thus, owned by no one, the

Zilms could only be responsible for Belhumeur's injuries if they "actually reduced the wild animals to possession or control, or introduced a non-indigenous animal into the area." The court refused to "impose an enormous and unwarranted burden" of requiring landowners to abate all harms potentially caused by noxious and harmful indigenous plants, insects, and animals naturally located on their property.

3. Statutory Liability

Virtually all states set forth the circumstances by which owners or keepers of domestic animals face liability for injuries caused by animals. Frequently in derogation of common law, courts strictly construe the statutory elements. *See, e.g.,* *Pippin v. Fink*, 794 A.2d 893 (N.J. Super. Ct. App. Div. 2002). Most commonly, they abrogate the common law requirement of proving scienter of dangerous propensity. Cal. Civ. Code § 3341; Ga. Civ. Code § 51-2-6; Haw. Rev. Stat. § 663-9(a); Utah Code Ann. § 18-1-1; *but see* Ala. Code § 3-1-1 (requiring scienter). Such strict liability approach shifts the risk of loss onto the shoulders of the animal owner or guardian. While some enactments focus only on injuries inflicted by *dogs*, others expand the class of animal predators to *all animals*, either explicitly or by judicial interpretation. They also occasionally enumerate the class of victims, most typically farmed animals. *See, e.g.,* Ariz. Rev. State. Ann. § 3-1311(B-C); Ga. Code Ann. § 51-2-6; Idaho Code § 25-2806; Ind. Code § 15-5-7-1.

a. Human Victims

Due to the inconsistent and potentially misleading usage of the term "strict liability," the practitioner should familiarize herself with the precise elements of the applicable statutory and common law variants. Simply using the term "strict" does not mean that the plaintiff need not also prove negligent conduct. Specifically, confirm the following:

1. Scienter as a necessary condition;

2. Contemporaneous negligent acts or omissions as a necessary condition;

3. Availability of any defenses (if none, then "absolute liability," not "strict liability" may apply);

4. Availability of common law defenses in statutory claims.

For instance, Haw. Rev. Stat. § 663-9(a) states:

§ 663-9 Liability of animal owners.

(a) The owner or harborer of an animal, if the animal proximately causes either personal or property damage to any person, shall be liable in damages to the person injured regardless of the animal owner's or harborer's lack of scienter of the vicious or dangerous propensities of the animal.

(b) The owner or harborer of an animal which is known by its species or nature to be dangerous, wild, or vicious, if the animal proximately causes either personal or property damage to any person, shall be absolutely liable for such damage. [L 1980, c 218, § 2.]

First note the distinction between the language "shall be liable" and "shall be *absolutely* liable." Why the adverb? Does § 663-9 abrogate the common law by the phrase "regardless of . . . lack of scienter"? In 1986, the Hawaii Court of Appeals provided some answers, holding that subsection (a) "merely eliminates the necessity to prove 'scienter' as an element of an animal owner's negligence." *Hubbell v. Iseke*, 6 Haw. App. 485, 489 (1986). Subsection (b) established per se liability by dispensing with both proof of scienter and negligent conduct only in the case of inherently dangerous, wild, or vicious animals — a class not typically shared with dogs as *a species*; however, a particular dog who *by nature* comes to be known as dangerous, wild, or vicious, will create such irrefutable liability. *Id.*, at 489–90 (citing from Conf. Comm. Rep. No. 36-80). Thus, if the defendant dog owner exercises reasonable care, there will be no negligence or liability under § 663-9(a), but if the dog by nature is known to be vicious, "absolute liability" under § 663-9(b) may lie. Contrast Idaho, which establishes common law strict liability without proof that the defendant failed to exercise reasonable care: the plaintiff need only demonstrate scienter. *McClain v. Lewiston Interstate Fair & Racing Ass'n*, 104 P. 1015 (Idaho 1909).

Although satisfying the common law or statutory strict liability elements will certainly establish a *prima facie* case, exonerating or blame-allocating doctrines such as comparative fault, contributory negligence, provocation, trespass, and assumption of risk may prevail. Yet questions remain, such as whether the defensive doctrine is an element of the claim negated by the plaintiff, or an affirmative defense sustained by the defendant; and whether the legislature expressly or impliedly repealed any such common law defense.

A recent example hails from the New Castle County Superior Court of Delaware in the case *Russo v. Zeigler*, 67 A.3d 536 (Del. Super. Ct. 2013), asked to decide whether a guest had the burden of disproving all exceptions to strict liability under the state dog-bite statute. Very early one morning, the Zeiglers' Akita named Drift bit Anthony Russo in the face while he entered Ellen and Michael Zeigler's home with their daughter Stephanie. In response to allegations of strict liability and negligent control, the Zeiglers' argued that Russo assumed the risk of harm by placing his face near Drift's muzzle without having been introduced to the dog; alternatively, they contended he provoked Drift. The Delaware legislature enacted 7 Del. C. § 1711 in 1998, imposing "strict liability" on dog owners unless the person bitten trespassed, committed a crime on the owner's property or against any person, or provoked the dog. In 2010, the General Assembly redesignated 7 Decl. C. § 1711 as 9 Del. C. § 913, legislatively repealing the scienter element of vicious propensity. The legislation stated:

> The owner of a dog is liable in damages for any injury, death or loss to person or property that is caused by such dog, unless the injury, death or loss was caused to the body or property of a person who, at the time, was committing or attempting to commit a trespass or other criminal offense on the property of the owner, or was committing or attempting to commit a

criminal offense against any person, or was teasing, tormenting or abusing the dog.

Whether the victim or dog owner bore the burden to prove (or disprove) the aforementioned exceptions presented a matter of first impression. Embracing holdings by appellate courts in Massachusetts and Connecticut, which interpreted similar dog-bite statutes, *Russo* held:

> Given the consequence for a dog owner to whom the statute applies, placing the burden of proving this element on the one who seeks such application is appropriate. This Court simply can find neither statutory support nor any justification for placing that burden on defendant dog owners.

Id., at 540. In characterizing these exceptions as elements of the cause of action to be disproved by the plaintiff, rather than an affirmative defense borne by the defendant, the court nonetheless leveled the playing field by limiting the defendant to only those exceptions stated in 9 Decl. C. § 913. "Allocation-of-fault statutes are not applicable in dog-bite actions under liability statutes like 9 Del. C. § 913 unless expressly stated." *Id.*, at 541. Moreover, "When Delaware's dog-bite statute is read together with the Delaware's comparative negligence statute, it is clear the latter cannot be used in defense of an action under the former," for the phrase "liable in damages for *any* injury" does not permit any "diminution by finding of comparative fault." *Id.* at 542. That said, it held that two defenses, "external to § 913," might apply — primary (or express) assumption of risk, and possibly a public policy exception, neither of which the Defendants pleaded. Further, secondary assumption of risk (or comparative negligence) might have served as defense to claims other than strict statutory liability under 9 Del. C. § 913 — if Defendants had pleaded it.

Other cases addressing the right to invoke affirmative defenses in strict liability actions include *Hale v. O'Neill*, 492 P.2d 101 (Alaska 1971) (no liability if plaintiff unreasonably and voluntarily confronted risk of harm posed by animal); *Franken v. City of Sioux Center*, 272 N.W.2d 422, 424–25 (Iowa 1978) (assumption of risk available based on strict liability); *Mech v. Hearst Corp.*, 64 Md. App. 422, 496 A.2d 1099 (1985) (trespasser injured by guard dog trained to protect property does not raise issue of strict liability, but premises liability standards apply); *Hood v. Waldrum*, 434 S.W.2d 94 (Tenn. Ct. App. 1968) (assumption of risk applies to strict liability and gross negligence); *Tidal Oil Co. v. Forcum*, 116 P.2d 572 (Okla. 1941) (assumption of risk).

Tort reformation may allow for these defenses, and others, to be raised under the banner of "contributory fault," regardless of whether the action sounds in negligence or strict liability. It is worth scrutinizing the comparative fault statute's definition of "fault," as it may expressly include actions sounding in strict liability, statutory or otherwise. *See, e.g.,* RCW § 4.22.015 ("fault" includes negligent or reckless acts or omissions (though not intentional) or those subjecting a person to strict tort liability or liability on a product liability claim, and includes breach of warranty, unreasonable assumption of risk, unreasonable failure to avoid injury or to mitigate damages, and misuse of a product) and RCW § 4.22.005 (noting that effect of contributory fault proportionally diminishes the award by claimant's fault, but does not bar recovery).

The defense of provocation, in traditionally focusing on the interaction between the injured person and the injuring animal, turns on the intentionality of the provoking person. *Paulsen v. Courtney*, 277 N.W.2d 233 (Neb. 1979) (intentional provocation is bar); *Leiner v. First Wythe Ave. Service Station, Inc.*, 121 Misc. 2d 559 (N.Y. Civ. Ct. 1983) *summarily aff'd*, 127 Misc. 2d 794 (N.Y. App. Term 1985); *Panzer v. Harding*, 500 N.Y.S.2d 328 (1986) (assumption of risk and provocation doctrines apply to strict liability, although contributory negligence does not); *Smith v. Sapienza*, 496 N.Y.S.2d 538 (1985) (unintentional provocation a defense); *Mitchell v. Cunningham*, 2006 Mich. App. LEXIS 714 (Mar. 16, 2006) (willful provocation or gross negligence excuses owner or keeper of common law strict liability). Such a defense, however, may not readily correspond to provoking animals, given the difficulty in accurately perceiving a nonhuman animal's subjective intentions. Furthermore, the doctrine of human provocation may not mesh with the cognitive and psychological world of nonhumans, who quite likely lack the desire or capacity to purposively engage in torturous, abusive, taunting, or tormenting conduct.

b. Nonhuman Victims

A minority of states have passed strict liability laws as part of their dangerous dog codes. Dogs adjudicated as dangerous or vicious who later cause injury to animals expose their owners to stiffer civil penalties or punitive damages, in addition to the actual loss value. *See, e.g.,* R.I. Gen. Laws § 4-13-16(double damages in second action involving same predatory dog); Wis. Stat. Ann. § 174.02(1)(b) (double damages upon notification or knowledge that dog had injured or killed before); N.Y. Agric. & Mkts. Law § 121(10) (dogs deemed dangerous subject owners and lawful custodians to strict liability for injury or death to companion, farm, and service animals).

With the greater social awareness and respect for the utilization of service animals, a minority of states have passed laws permitting a statutory tort arising from merely negligent injury to a service animal — whether inflicted by a human or through a human's dog or other animal. *See, e.g.,* RCW § 49.60.370 (allowing reasonable attorney's fees and civil penalty of $1,000 for even negligent injury); Nev. Rev. Stat. § 426.810 (criminalizing the use of a dog to cause injury or death to a service animal or service animal in training and imposing penalties in addition to civil suit remedies of Nev. Rev. Stat. § 426.820; restitution includes veterinary bills, replacement cost of the animal, and all costs for aides, assistance, transportation, and other hardships incurred during the absence, and until the replacement, of the animal).

Many of the strict statutory liability regimes involving injuries to animals were enacted quite early in a state's history, when the most common animal-on-animal interaction involved dogs running at-large and killing livestock. When the farmer or rancher could not identify the culprit (or, more importantly, the party responsible for the depredating dog), government stepped in to indemnify the loss. While some states have repealed this avenue for indemnification, others have outlined a detailed, claim-noticing procedure for recovery from a county or city's dog license fund. Such government claims often demand strict or substantial compliance with statutory requirements, provide the government a right to seek contribution from the dog owner or guardian, and offer a series of appeals (resulting in trial) to the owner of the animal victim. N.J. Stat. § 4:19-5; Ohio Rev. Code § 955.29; N.H. Rev. Stat. § 466.21; Ark. Code § 20-19-102; Conn. Gen. Stat. § 22-355; 510 Ill. Comp. Stat. 5/19; Mass. Gen. Laws Ch. 140, § 157 *et seq.*; Va. Code § 3.1-796.116; Vt. Stat. tit. 20, § 3742; R.I. Gen. Laws § 4-13-19; 3 Pa. Stat. § 459-701; Or. Rev. Stat. Ann. § 609.170 (sheep only). A few states require that the claimant, at the time of the date of loss, have all dogs licensed in order to obtain reimbursement from the dog license fund. Mass. Gen. Laws Ch. 140, § 151A.

Permitted statutory damages typically include the fair market value of the injured or deceased animal. Some states, however, allow more significant remedies as part of the strict liability regime. *See, e.g.*, Miss. Code Ann. § 273.020 (daily penalty until payment made by dog owner to owner of victimized animal); Or. Rev. Stat. Ann. § 609.140(1) (double damages); S.C. Code § 47-3-230 (double damages involving sheep only); Vt. Stat. tit. 20 § 3748 (double damages and double costs involving sheep only); Ala. Code §§ 3-1-1, 3-1-2 (double damages); Ariz. Rev. Stat. Ann. § 3-1311b (treble damages); Cal. Food & Agric. Code § 31501 (double damages); Ga. Code § 4-8-4 (including consequential damages); N.J. Stat. § 4:19-8 (treble damages after failure to kill dog within 24 hours of notice being given to owner that dog had killed, worried, or wounded sheep, lamb, domestic animal, or poultry). The most liberal states award mandatory reasonable attorney's fees to the prevailing plaintiff. *See, e.g.*, Miss. Code § 95-5-21; Ind. Code § 15-5-7-1.

Because *animal* injury or death cases have historically spurred litigation over smaller damage ranges than those involving *human* injury or death, the paucity of judicial interpretation of strict liability statutes involving animal-on-animal injuries is unsurprising. Accordingly, the practitioner must anticipate the following:

1. The class of animal victims may not extend to unenumerated animals, or service or companion animals at all. *See, e.g.*, Ark. Code § 20-19-102 (domesticated animals are defined to include, but are not limited to, sheep, goats, cattle, swine, and poultry) and *McKinney v. Robbins*, 892 S.W.2d 502 (Ark. 1995) (kittens not "domesticated animals"); Idaho Code § 25-2806 (livestock or poultry, kept for domestic or commercial purposes); 510 Ill. Comp. Stat. 5/19 (livestock, poultry, and equidae); Cal. Civ. Code § 3341 (restrictive enumeration); 510 Ill. Comp. Stat. 5/18.1 (sheep, goats, cattle, horses, mules, poultry, ratites, and swine only); Me. Rev. Stat. Ann. tit.7, § 3962-A(1) (includes "pets").

2. The courts may not have determined if the "shall be liable" or "is liable" language abrogates or codifies the elements of common law strict liability, without additional language expressly dispensing with certain elements. *See, e.g.*, Cal. Civ. Code § 3341; Haw. Rev. Stat. § 663-9(a-b); Ward Miller, *Modern Status of Rule of Absolute or Strict Liability for Dogbite*, 51 A.L.R.4TH 446.

3. The class of animal predators may only extend to enumerated animals. *See, e.g.*, Ark. Code § 20-19-102(a)(2) (dogs only); Fla. Stat. § 767.01 (dogs only); Haw. Rev. Stat. §§ 663 to 9 (animals); La. Civ. Code Ann. art. 2321 (strict liability as to dogs only; negligence standard as to all other animals).

4. The class of potential defendants may also vary widely. *See, e.g.*, Ala. Code § 3-1-2 (owner or person in charge); Cal. Civ. Code § 3341 (owner, pos-

sessor, or harborer); Idaho Code § 25-2806 (owner, possessor, or harborer); 510 Ill. Comp. Stat. Ann. 5/18.1 (owner or keeper). Law enforcement may also enjoy statutory exemption from strict liability for acts by canine units. *See, e.g.,* Wis. Stat. § 174.02(4) (no liability if damage to crime suspect while on-duty); Wash. Rev. Stat. § 4.24.410 (dog handler immune for all damages if acting in good faith in line of duty).

5. The conduct of the predatory animal also determines liability under the statutory language. *See, e.g.,* Ind. Code § 15-5-7-1 (liability only while livestock is in care of owner and, presumably, not at-large or trespassing); Ala. Code § 3-1-2 (scienter of owner or person in charge of dog exposed to rabid dog, who then becomes rabid and bites); Ariz. Rev. Stat. § 3-1311 (chasing); Cal. Civ. Code § 3341(2) (immune to suit for accidental or unavoidable death or injury to any bovine, swine, horse, mule, burro, sheep, angora goat, cashmere goat, or poultry while driving or herding same from the property of the dog owner, even if injury or death occurs on or off dog owner's premises); Idaho Code § 25-2806 (kill, worry, or wound); 510 Ill. Comp. Stat. 5/18.1 (pursue, chase, worry, wound, injure, or kill); W. Va. Code § 19-20-13 (merely being "at-large"); N.H. Rev. Stat. Ann. § 466.19 (no liability if plaintiff is trespassing or committing other tort); Mich. Comp. Laws § 287.279 (mere entry by dog into field or enclosure owned by another, outside of a city, without supervision, constitutes a trespass and imposes strict liability); Iowa Code § 351.28 (exempts those whose dogs are "affected with hydrophobia" (i.e., rabies) at the time of the incident unless the owner had cause to know the dog was afflicted and could have reasonably prevented injury); Ala. Code § 3-1-1 (no liability if dog known to kill or worry sheep or other stock does so after "being set upon" by same).

6. Exceptions to statutory liability for harm to human victims may not meaningfully translate to nonhuman animal victims. For instance, "trespassers" are presumptively human. Further, how may one distinguish innocent from willful trespassing by a nonhuman? Does the court impute the animal owner's mental state to the animal? Is the animal an agent of the owner or guardian? The same interpretive difficulties arise with respect to provocation and engaging in tortious conduct. After all, can an animal (like an infant or insane person) be deemed legally competent to commit a tort or to intentionally provoke? Practically speaking, do the statutory exceptions of trespassing, provoking, and tortfeasing apply to nonhuman animal victims at all?

7. Explore applicable municipal ordinances, which may impose statutory liabilities more favorable to plaintiffs than state statutes. For instance, Clallam County, Washington's CCC 17.01.020 holds the owner of any animal liable to the owner of any animal killed or injured for the amount of damages sustained and costs of collection.

Remember that statutes are not presumed to abrogate common law unless expressly stated or by unmistakable implication, so one should review all relevant statutory provisions before drafting the complaint to ensure strict compliance. Implied abrogation of common law exists where the enacted statute undertakes to cover the entire subject and was clearly designed as a substitute for common law.

It also abrogates in the case of irreconcilable conflict. An action for damages caused by a dog may be instituted under both statutory authority and the common law. A close inspection of statutory language and applicable legislative history is warranted when drafting.

Common law defenses may apply unless the statute or case law specifically provides otherwise. *Kilpatrick v. Sklar*, 548 So. 2d 215 (Fla. 1989), held that traditional common law affirmative defenses applicable to negligence actions were unavailable against a claim under Fla. Stat. Ann. § 767.04 (strict liability statute for bites to humans); whether such is the case for Fla. Stat. Ann. § 767.05 (strict liability statute for bites to animals) remains unclear. *But see Hall v. Ricardo*, 297So. 2d 849 (Fla. App. 1974). Typically, most defenses at common law apply to statutory actions, except for contributory negligence. *See Brady v. White*, 2006 Del. Super. LEXIS 390 (Del. Super. Sept. 27, 2006) (but no elimination of common law defenses); *cf. Borton v. Lavenduskey*, 486 N.E.2d 639, 642 (Ind. Ct. App. 1985) (contributory negligence and assumption of risk apply).

Some statutes enumerate specific defenses. For example, Ariz. Rev. Stat. § 11-1027 identifies reasonable provocation as a defense, though it appears to only apply to animals injuring people. *Mulcahy v. Damron*, 816 P.2d 270 (Ariz. Ct. App. 1991); *see also* Del. Code Ann. Tit. 7, § 1711 (trespass, criminal offense on owner's property, provocation as statutory defenses). Iowa Code § 351.28 provides a single defense of "doing of an unlawful act." *See Collins v. Kenealy*, 492 N.W.2d 679 (Iowa 1992) (assumption of risk inapplicable; common law defenses appear not to apply in such statutory action). La. Civ. Code art. 2321 excuses provoked attacks, and expressly does not preclude application of *res ipsa loquitur*. Minn. Stat. § 347.22 states that provocation defeats strict liability, but does the defense extend to inadvertent, involuntary conduct? Not necessarily when a person engages in a scuffle, steps back, and inadvertently crushes a dog's tail, causing him to be bitten. However, courts have interpreted § 347.22 to permit unintentional, though voluntary, provocation. *Bailey by Bailey v. Morris*, 323 N.W.2d 785 (Minn. 1982) (jury verdict for defendants upheld in split decision of Minnesota Supreme Court, finding provocation where minor child voluntarily reached out to pet dog and suffered a bite to forehead while disregarding defendant's and defendant's child's warning to the minor plaintiff about the dog being nervous, growling, and with the dog's puppies nearby).

4. Nuisance

It is first imperative to distinguish common law from statutory nuisance causes of action, as the former tends to be unduly restrictive in two regards — (1) it is limited to interference with interests in realty; (2) it requires that the plaintiff be an owner or possessor of the land on which the interference is said to have occurred. *See, e.g.*, C.J.S., *Nuisances* § 10. For obvious reasons, these requirements negate most plaintiffs' bases to state a claim. Increasingly, however, statutory nuisance actions permit recovery of damages for interference with personalty on the land, including animals. *See, e.g.*, C.J.S, *Nuisances* § 9. At common law, plaintiffs who could prove "special injury" from a public nuisance enjoyed a private right of action without needing to prove ownership of any interests in land. *See, e.g., Institoris v. City of Los Angeles,* 210 Cal. App. 3d 10 (1989). Some statutes, like Washington's, define nuisance to include interference with use and comfortable enjoyment of "property" or "the life," clearly going beyond the common law realty-based focus. Wash. Rev. Code Ann. § 7.48.010. Indeed, the use of the word "property," without the qualifier "personal" or "real," conveys a broader meaning. Property is defined as: "1. The right to possess, use, and enjoy a determinate thing (either a tract of land or a chattel); . . . " BLACK'S LAW DICTIONARY 1232 (7th ed. 1999). Thus, property may be either realty or personalty. Statutory private nuisance claims may unambiguously provide for a cause of action by any owner where the defendant has so interfered.

At common law, an action for a private nuisance could be maintained by an individual for interference with the use and enjoyment of land. *See Northern Pac. R. Co. v. Whalen,* 149 U.S. 157, 162 (1893). A public nuisance is generally a criminal offense, but it also may be actionable in tort if the plaintiff can show that he suffered harm that was particular to him, i.e., harm distinguishable from that suffered by other members of the general public. *See* generally C.J.S., *Nuisances* §§ 133, 149. A private nuisance statute may not be merely declaratory or remedial in restating the common law (making it derogatory, rather than deferential to, the common law). This may be the case where the statute goes beyond traditional common law provisions by adding enumerated nuisances or expanding the definition beyond strict interferences with land. Dog-eat-dog cases involve the rendering insecure and essential interference with the comfortable enjoyment of both plaintiff's life and her property, the companion animal. Private nuisance contemplates substantial and unreasonable interference resulting in termination of the plaintiff's use and enjoyment of personalty or realty. Other states have construed private nuisance as extending to personalty, independent of and apart from any injury to real estate or the use and enjoyment thereof. Thus, if a plaintiff owns or possesses the realty on which her companion animal convalesces after injury or is slain, a nuisance claim may still lie even without harm to the land. In *City of Uvalde v. Crow,* 713 S.W.2d 154 (Tex. App. 1986), the Texas Court of Appeals found a private nuisance where the plaintiff suffered veterinary bills and loss of animals at his greyhound breeding facility when the animals drank and played in slough water contaminated by the city's sewage plant. The court held that "recovery for damages to property is not limited to realty but applies to personal property and special damages as well. AM. JUR. 2D, *Nuisances* § 120 (1971)." *Id.,* at 159. A Massachusetts appeals court, in the same spirit, held:

> It is not a defense to a private nuisance action that the property damaged was personal property and not real property. . . . Thus, a private person could bring an action against another even if he was a tenant and the claimed damage was to his personal property.

H. Sacks & Sons, Inc. v. Metropolitan Dist. Com'n, 493 N.E.2d 878 (Mass. 1986); *see also* AM. JUR. 2D, *Nuisances* § 457; C.J.S., *Nuisances* § 27 (fact that personal property damaged and not real property no defense to private nuisance action); *but see Womack v. Von Rardon,* 135 P.3d 542 (Wash. Ct. App. 2006) (rejecting nuisance claim involving teenagers abducting cat from private property and setting him on fire on public property).

Irrespective of any claims involving interference with realty, a plaintiff might assert a public nuisance especially injurious to the plaintiff but not others. A party may bring a private action for public nuisance even where he has no property right or privilege in land:

> In cases where special damage has resulted from a public nuisance, invasions of interests of private persons other than interests in the use and enjoyment of land are actionable. Thus, a person who suffers bodily harm from an obstruction of a highway may maintain an action therefor, although no property rights or privileges of his have been invaded. So, also, one who suffers bodily harm as the result of the keeping of explosives in a locality where their presence is declared by statute, or found in a judicial proceeding, to be a public nuisance, may recover therefor, although he has no property rights or privileges.

RESTATEMENT FIRST, TORTS § 10, 40 SC NT (1939). In many dog-eat-dog cases, the municipal or county law will declare such behavior a public nuisance. Common law supports many counties and cities' positions that harboring dangerous dogs that inflict bites constitutes a nuisance. *Patterson v. Rosenwald*, 6 S.W.2d 664 (Mo. Ct. App. 1928); *Woodbridge v. Marks*, 5 A.D. 604, 605 (N.Y. App. Div. 1896) ("vicious dog running at-large is a nuisance, because dangerous to mankind"). In *State v. Long*, 991 P.2d 102, 106 (Wash. Ct. App. 2000), a man was prosecuted for the unlawful killing of a dog who was chasing a deer out of season so that the deer could be captured and killed by his owner-guardian. Unlawful use of dogs to capture endangered species or game animals during closed season was regarded by state law as a public nuisance, so Long raised the nuisance abatement defense. The difficulty for Mr. Long was that while the code explicitly described the dog's behavior as a public nuisance, he could not prove special injury to himself as a result of the chase. True, the deer faced imminent harm, but defenses on their behalves had to be raised by the state.

Where a litigant must show equal impact to the rights of an entire community or neighborhood to sustain a public nuisance claim, proof that the animal constituted an ongoing nuisance to bicyclists, solicitors, letter carriers, and other residents may assist. One may also argue that the violation of any ordinance declaring such behavior as a public nuisance amounts to a per se finding without further proof of impact on the neighborhood. In other words, its community-wide undesirability is presumed by codification. Special injury to the plaintiff himself obviously occurs when defendant's dog seizes upon an opportunity to capture his defenseless quarry. Codified, prohibited behaviors may also state a nuisance per se, i.e., strictly without regard to any carelessness or intention of the defendant. Consider this discussion of a Utah Supreme Court case by the Washington Court of Appeals:

> The treatise cites *Branch v. Western Petroleum, Inc.*, 657 P.2d 267 (Utah 1982). There, a landowner sued a neighboring landowner whose oil wells, in violation of statute, polluted groundwater that supplied plaintiff's well. The appellate court sustained the judgment in favor of the plaintiff, holding the facts established a nuisance per se. It reasoned:
>
>> When the conditions giving rise to a nuisance are also a violation of statutory prohibition, those conditions constitute a nuisance per se,

and *the issue of the reasonableness of the defendant's conduct* and the weighing of the relative interests of the plaintiff and defendant *is precluded because the Legislature has, in effect, already struck the balance in favor of the innocent party. Defendant's violation of § 73-14-5 . . . and § 76-10-801 removed the issue of the reasonableness of its conduct compared with the nature of the injury inflicted from consideration in this case.* The declaration of the Legislature is conclusive, and its determination will not be second guessed. The result for practical purposes is the same as strict liability.

Branch, 657 P.2d at 276 (citations omitted, emphasis added).

Tiegs v. Boise Cascade Corp., 922 P.2d 115, 119 (Wash. Ct. App. 1996) (italicized emphasis in original).

Theoretically, animals may also be deemed attractive nuisances, creating premises liability for those whose nonhuman inhabitants or guests lure trespassing children to their peril. Also known as the "turntable doctrine," the "infant trespasser," "dangerous instrumentality," the "playground" rule, the "trap" or "implied invitation" theory, an attractive nuisance traditionally has four elements: (1) a structure or condition on the defendant's premises which the defendant knew or should have known in the exercise of due care involved a reasonable risk of attraction and harm to children, (2) the structure or condition maintained or permitted on the property was peculiarly or unusually attractive to children, (3) the structure or condition was such that the danger was not apparent to immature minds, and (4) the plaintiff was attracted onto the premises by such structure or condition. Catherine Palo, *Attractive Nuisance Cases*, 80 Am. Jur. *Trials* 535.

Yet not everything attractive to a child is an attractive nuisance, a point made in *Dykes v. Alexander*, 411 S.W.2d 47, 49 (Ky. Ct. App. 1967), which refused to hold the owner of a history-free dog liable after a five-year-old boy entered through a closed gate and suffered a bite. The court added that while ordinarily trespassing children occupy the same position as trespassing adults, except in the case of attractive nuisance, it as "unable to find where it has ever been held that a dog is an attractive nuisance and is per se of a dangerous character[.]" *Id.* Typically, attractive nuisance doctrine concerns artificial structures that a landowner knows or should know pose an unreasonable risk of death or serious bodily injury to trespassing children. In *Gowen v. Willenborg*, 366 S.W.2d 695 (Tex. App. 1963), an 11-year-old boy who fell from a billboard after being attacked by wasps that emerged from a concealed nest could not recover against the owner as the insects did not transform the sign into a hazardous artificial structure. In addition to finding that generally owners and possessors of land have no duty to anticipate the presence of, or guard against harm from, wild animals unless reduced to possession, harbored by, or introduced as nonindigenous species onto his premises, the court stated:

> The nest built by wasps is a natural condition and is not in itself dangerous. Knowledge of the location of a wasp nest at most would be knowledge that wasps are likely to be found at that location. Destruction of the nest would not necessarily remove the danger of an attack of the stinging insect at that location. It would remove the warning sign and might or might not cause the wasps to remove themselves to another scene of activity.

Id., at 697. As noted, the vast majority of courts decline to find that nonhuman animals constitute attractive nuisances. Also consider *Baugh v. Beatty*, 91 Cal. App. 2d 786 (1949), which held *in dictum* that a caged chimpanzee who bit a four-year-old boy while on display in a circus tent was not an "artificial and dangerous contrivance" and the trial court did not err in refusing to give an attractive nuisance jury instruction:

> An animal in a cage is not artificial and it does not fall within the definition of the word 'contrivance' which is defined in Webster's New International Dictionary, 2d Ed. (1947) page 580 as 'a mechanical device; an appliance.' Whether the attractive nuisance doctrine could be extended so far as to include a caged animal is not necessary for us to determine, since the doctrine is not applicable to the facts in the present case. It is conceded that plaintiff was a business invitee and not being a trespasser there is no need to invoke the doctrine, which is but an exception to the rule that the owner of premises is under no obligation to keep it in a safe condition for trespassers.

Id., at 791; *see also Clea v. Odom*, 714 S.E.2d 542 (S.C. 2011) (refusing to find that dog is "artificial condition" for purposes of holding landlord liable under theory of attractive nuisance).

5. Provocation

In most civil applications, Defendants bear the burden of proving the affirmative defense of provocation; in administrative settings, such as where a dog is declared dangerous, however, the prosecuting authority typically must disprove provocation as an element of the offense. Courts have examined provocation either from the perspective of the provoking injured victim as well as that of the provoked animal, each approach varying by such factors as intent, degree of disturbance or pain inflicted, recency to biting event. Provocation may even be found by completely unintentional conduct. The construct of provocation as applied to human victims may not sensibly apply to animal victims, except where the victim animal's owner or a third party instigates the melée.

Consider the following scenario: a heeled, seated, and leashed dog is declared potentially dangerous (PDD) for biting off a stranger's lip after she leans into the dog's face on a public sidewalk without permission or introduction by the dog's guardian. The stranger's husband then leans down and moves the guardian's foot to retrieve his wife's lip, an action that does not incite the dog to bite the husband. Although the injury is assuredly regrettable and quite significant, did the wife provoke the bite by the otherwise well-behaved dog who was not running at large, lunging on the leash, or doing anything other than sitting quietly before an unknown adult came into his space from above? Does your assessment change if considered from the reasonable dog's perspective? Placing undue emphasis on the outcome, while ignoring the bitee's causal role in choreographing her own injury, might result in an injustice.

Assume that for the entire life of this old, spayed female German shepherd mix with cataracts, she had never been declared potentially dangerous or dangerous.

Prior to this occurrence, assume she was never cited for any animal control violation, that there was no evidence she had been neglected or abused or that she had a propensity to escape, chase, attack, or kill any being. In essence, the potentially dangerous dog designation designates her as a "first-time offender." If she were your dog, would you challenge the PDD designation? What if you were forced to acquire liability insurance in the amount of at least $250,000, to build a secure, locked, six-sided enclosure in which to keep her, to muzzle her at all times when outside the enclosure, were forced to register her as a potentially dangerous dog for the rest of her life, and ran the risk of her being declared dangerous if she so much as chased a person on public property without making contact? Should the law not recognize extenuating circumstances that predictably trigger instinctual, self-preservational reactions from our canine companions?

While most animal control agencies regard "provocation" as involving taunting, teasing, beating, or other harmful behavior, many ordinances do not define the term. Because it admits more than one reasonable interpretation, the rule of lenity may require that ambiguous drafting be construed in the light most favorable to the defendant.

To interpret the acts of a person quickly approaching and staring into a strange dog's face at her level, her visage made blurry and image multiplied by the cataracts, while restrained by a leash and unable to flee, as provocation is a defensible position. Though not harboring any animus toward the dog, the stranger in the above example should still have been aware of the unreason in approaching an unknown dog in this fashion, without introduction by the dog's handler standing nearby. From the dog's perspective, the stranger created an apprehension of unprivileged, harmful or offensive contact — e.g., a perceived (though not actual) assault. Regardless, it shows poor canine etiquette. Animal ethologists and veterinary behaviorists can serve as potent experts in this regard.

Case law arising in the context of personal injury litigation may prove judicious. *See Toney v. Bouthillier*, 631 P.2d 557, 559–560 (Ariz. Ct. App. 1981) (finding that act of three-year-old punching dog may constitute provocation, irrespective of whether the child intended to provoke the dog and noting that "[p]rovocation is a matter of whether particular actions are likely to cause a dog to react by biting and to disregard whether the actor intended to perform the act."); *Nelson v. Lewis*, 344 N.E.2d 268 (Ill. App. Ct. 1976) (finding provocation where 2.5-year-old accidentally stepped on dog's tail and noting that unintentional acts may constitute provocation, as in "an act or process of provoking, stimulation or incitement."); *Nicholes v. Lorenz*, 237 N.W.2d 468 (Mich. 1976) (recognizing that determination of whether six-year-old inadvertently stepping on dog's tail constituted provocation was jury question); *Bradacs v. Jiacobone*, 625 N.W.2d 108 (2001) (12-year-old dropping football near dog while eating not provocation). Proportionality also affects the analysis of provocation. *Smith v. Pitchford*, 579 N.E.2d 24 (Ill. App. Ct. 1991); *Kirkham v. Will*, 724 N.E.2d 1062 (Ill. App. Ct. 2000) ("it is the reasonableness of the dog's response to the action in question that actually determines whether provocation exists," and "not the view of the person provoking the dog.").

From an equitable standpoint and practically speaking, the stranger in the above hypothetical may have assumed the risk of being bitten by approaching the dog without permission or introduction by the dog's handler, invading her personal space, and from the dog's standpoint, threatening her and her guardian. But what to make of the fact that the dog did not redirect her aggression toward the husband who made contact with the guardian's leg? A plaintiff may argue that such post-bite behavior proves that the dog did not bite to defend her guardian. A defendant may argue that the dog's failure to attack the husband proves her docile nature and that provocation incited her to bite the wife. Though not on point, consider *Stehl v. Dose*, 403 N.E.2d 1301 (Ill. App. Ct. 1980). The court found that the evidence supported a jury verdict that the dog was provoked into attacking where a prospective new owner of a German shepherd came near the dog to feed the dog scraps and pet it, but when he turned his back the dog bit him; in reaching this conclusion, the court noted that the jury could regard crossing the perimeter of a dog's chain, entering protected territory, and remaining while the dog ate as provocation. *See generally* Jay M. Zitter, *Intentional Provocation, Contributory or Comparative Negligence, or Assumption of Risk as Defense to Action for Injury by Dog*, 11 A.L.R. 5TH 127.

Certain salient factors to evaluate in any dog bite scenario such as the above one include:

1. Did the dog bark, growl, or show physical manifestations of aggressive posture at the time the stranger was bitten?

2. Was the dog restrained by a leash and unable to retreat from the stranger's rapid, warning-free advance?

3. Was the dog in a heeled position and seated at the time the stranger approached her face without warning or permission by the handler?

4. Did the dog lunge or attempt to follow the stranger after the bite, showing evidence of this being a "kindling" event for an instant conflagration of vicious behavior? Or did she keep heel position, without tugging on the leash or vocalizing?

5. Did the dog bite the handler or any third-party eyewitnesses who may have approached the dog's personal space (e.g., the stranger's husband)?

6. Did the stranger admit to habitually getting down on all fours with unknown dogs in an understandable but misguided effort to be loving (as was the case in the above example)?

7. Was the attacking dog suffering from a physical (e.g., cataracts, deafness, tenderness, or sensitivity in certain areas from disease, trauma, or prior abuse, hot spots) or mental (e.g., "insanity," prior abuse or neglect) ailment or disability?

Based on the rule of lenity, expert testimony, and certain undisputed facts, your dangerous dog defense case, or civil dog bite defense case, could turn on the successful transformation of the bitee into an agent provocateur.

Now, consider that the provocateur in the above example was another dog. Immediately, the question becomes far more difficult. To evaluate animal provocation, look to statutes and ordinances without expectations, as most apply only to human provocateurs explicitly, or by necessary implication. Occasionally, jurisdictions will define provocation to insinuate the inclusion of animal provocateurs. *See* Ala. Code § 3-1-1 (noting that person may not keep dog known to kill or worry sheep or other stock without being set upon by same, such that phrase "set upon" suggests provocation). Other codes do not identify the species of provocateur, leading to awkward attempts at anthropomorphization that may require expert testimony to avoid errors in "translation." *See, e.g.,* Kitsap Cy., Wash., Code § 7.04.020(27) (defining *provoke* as "to intentionally agitate, harass, or excite an animal," without specifying who may be said to provoke). Some codes do not define the term at all. In the absence of a definition section, the parties will have to turn to common law or the dictionary.

Clearly, not every occurrence that stimulates a dog to bite an individual exonerates. On the other hand, provocation should not be required to rise to the level of intentional torture. *Stroop v. Day*, 896 P.2d 439 (Mont. 1995), overruled o.g., *Giambra v. Kelsey*, 162 P.3d 134 (Mont. 2007); BLACK'S LAW DICTIONARY, 5th Edition, defines "provocation" as "inciting," and "that which arouses, moves, calls forth . . ." It defines *provoke* as "to excite, to stimulate, to arouse, to irritate or enrage."

How may one nonhuman animal be said to "intentionally agitate, harass, or excite an animal"? Can the court divine intentionality in a canine or equine or other species? That dogs share the faculty of sentience with us does not alone render the average layperson competent to offer an opinion on the canine psyche. Thus, without testimony from an animal behaviorist, such lay opinion that attempts to interpret the acts of the victim dog as intentionally or unintentionally provocative will likely fail to possess the requisite and sound foundation to meet ER 702. Consider: can a horse desire to agitate, harass, or excite a dog? How do we know this without interrogating the horse? An instinctual or trained response to a particular stimulus is not necessarily "intentional." Consider the case of *Montgomery v. United Services Auto. Ass'n*, 886 P.2d 981 (N.M. Ct. App. 1994) (finding that wild bobcat who tore apart tenant's belongings did not commit "malicious mischief" or "vandalism" for purposes of renter's insurance coverage).[3]

Vagueness confuses the inquiry at several levels: *first*, does provocation only refer to "intentional" conduct?; *second*, does provocation apply to nonhuman

---

[3] When a wild bobcat tore apart Sharon Montgomery's belongings, she made a claim under her renter's insurance for malicious mischief and vandalism. The trial court lyricized from the bench:

> The scarecrow wanted a heart. He wanted it from the start.

> The tin man wanted a brain. So he could be the same.

> And it was courage asked for by the lion, even though he was always crying.

> In this case the bobcat needs "intent." Or did he just rely on his scent?

> Alas, it is written in the law that the animal with the paw does not have the mind to do the damage of this kind.

> And so, I'm sorry, the plaintiff won't get paid. That's how the contract was made.

> This policy does not apply when the bobcat runs awry.

The appeals court agreed, noting that the wild animal could not form the requisite intent or malice to commit "vandalism" or "malicious mischief," covered perils under the policy. This was even the case where the plaintiff cited to dictionary definitions defining "vandalism" to include "ignorant" destruction of personalty. Other courts having considered ignorance in relation to nonhuman animals concluded that only human actors can perpetrate such acts. The foundation of this court's opinion was that, "An animal, nonhuman, acts or reacts instinctively without knowledge of right or wrong as defined by man."

provocateurs?; *third*, if so, may an animal's natural, habitual, species-appropriate, expected, or instinctual reaction suffice to prove provocation?; and *fourth*, does one focus on the conduct of the injured person or animal only, or the presence or interference of third parties?[4] Such vagaries lead to inconsistent outcomes and fail to apprise citizens of reasonable intelligence precisely what constitutes provocation. After all, experts are frequently offered to explain animal behavior to aid the jury in understanding provocation. *See Rodgers v. Dittman*, 2002 Iowa App. LEXIS 285 (Iowa App. Mar. 12, 2002). Giving a lay human interpretation of a dog's reaction may prove at odds with animal science and what ethologists would conclude is reasonable dog behavior. Holding a canine response to the legal expectations and standards for a human response may reveal a deep misunderstanding as to what provokes a dog, the type of anthropomorphic fuzziness that exposes constitutional vagueness and overbreadth.[5]

But see *McCoy v. Lucius*, 839 So. 2d 1050 (La. Ct. App. 2003) *writ den'd*, 871 So. 2d 344 (La. 2004), a case finding that the defendants' dogs were provoked when the plaintiff's Maltese, named Jody, approached defendants' two larger dogs barking and running onto their property (which the court refers to as "their territory"). While La. Civ. Code art. 2321 spoke of "the injured person's provocation of the dog," the court imputed this element to animals, stating, "A dog that aggressively charges another dog may provoke an aggressive response from the dog being charged, and that appears to be what occurred in this case." *Id.*, at 1055.

6. Owners, Keepers, and Harborers

Keepers and harborers remain accountable for the actions of animals in their care, custody, control, even if they hold no ownership interest. Owners, on the other hand, bear responsibility even if they lack immediate care, custody, or control. But incidental feeding of a stray or granting temporary permission for a dog to remain on one's premises does not an owner, keeper, or harborer make. The definition of *owner* has received elaborate discussion elsewhere in this text. A *harborer* is typically one who gives "something more than a meal of mercy to a stray dog or [suffered] the causal presence of a dog on someone's premises." *Verrett v. Silver*, 244 N.W.2d 147, 148 (Minn. 1976). It envisions affording lodging, shelter, or refuge

---

[4] For instance, at least one litigant argued (albeit unsuccessfully) that otherwise innocent, nonprovocative human conduct became provocative by the scent of a cat impregnated in the woman's hair, which passed before the dog's face. *Hunt v. Scheer*, 576 P.2d 1190 (Ok. Civ. App. 1976).

[5] Dogs are provoked to bite in seven distinct situations. While not all will satisfy the standard for legal excuse or justification, they provide insight into the canine mind:
  (1)   dominance aggression — directed to those who take something away from a dog;
  (2)   defensive aggression — directed to those who approach a dog too quickly or too closely;
  (3)   protective/territorial aggression — directed to small, quickly moving animals and children;
  (4)   predatory aggression — directed to small, moving animals or children, especially with more than one dog involved;
  (5)   pain-elicited aggression—directed to those who approach a dog when a dog is in pain;
  (6)   punishment-elicited aggression — directed to those who kick, hit, or assault a dog; and
  (7)   redirected aggression — directed to those who approach a dog when it is already in an aggressive state.

Epstein, *There are No Bad Dogs, Only Bad Owners: Replacing Strict Liability with a Negligence Standard in Dog Bite Cases*, 13 Animal L. 129, 137 (2006).

for a limited purpose or time. Where the animal owner resides on real property owned by a blood relative, who lives in a separate dwelling on that same parcel of land, does the label "keeper" or "harborer" properly befit the blood relative? *Carr v. Vannoster*, 281 P.3d 1136 (Kan. Ct. App. 2012) found the property owner, father to the dog owner, not to be a "harborer" in what it called a "strikingly apropos scenario" nestled within REST. (2ND) OF TORTS § 514, cmt. a. The comment stated: "Thus a father, on whose land his son lives in a separate residence, does not harbor a dog kept by his son, although he has the power to prohibit the dog from being kept and fails to exercise the power or even if he presents the dog to his son to be so kept." *Id.*, at 1143–44.

Some states have defined "keeper," as discussed in Connecticut's *Auster v. Norwalk United Methodist Church*, 943 A.2d 391 (Conn. 2008) (negating liability of church for dogbite sustained by guest from dog owned by church employee, who resided on premises in the rear of the parish house):

> We turn first to the plaintiff's contention that, contrary to the conclusion of the Appellate Court, the evidence was sufficient to support the jury's finding that the defendant was a keeper of Salinas' dog within the meaning of § 22–357. Under General Statutes § 22–327(6), a keeper is defined as "any person, other than the owner, harboring or having in his possession any dog. . . . " "To harbor a dog is to afford lodging, shelter or refuge to it." *Falby v. Zarembski*, 221 Conn. 14, 19, 602 A.2d 1 (1992). "[P]ossession [of a dog] cannot be fairly construed as anything short of the exercise of dominion and control similar to and in substitution for that which ordinarily would be exerted by the owner in possession." *Hancock v. Finch*, 126 Conn. 121, 123, 9 A.2d 811 (1939). "One who treats a dog as living at his house and undertakes to control his actions is [a] . . . keeper. . . . " *McCarthy v. Daunis*, 117 Conn. 307, 309, 167 A. 918 (1933); *see also Buturla v. St. Onge*, 9 Conn.App. 495, 497–98, 519 A.2d 1235, cert. denied, 203 Conn. 803, 522 A.2d 293 (1987).

Id., at 396. Courts split on whether a landlord not residing on premises with the aggressing animal remains liable. *Frobig v. Gordon*, 881 P.2d 226 (Wash. 1994) (where tiger mauled child on commercial premises, nonresident landlord not liable); *Stokes v. Lyddy*, 815 A.2d 263 (Conn. App. Ct. 2003) (not liable); *Tran v. Bancroft*, 648 So. 2d 314 (Fla. Dist. Ct. App.1995) (not liable); *Colombel v. Milan*, 952 P.2d 941 (Kan. Ct. App. 1998) (not liable); *Boots ex rel. Boots v. Winters*, 179 P.3d 352 (Idaho Ct. App. 2008) (not liable); *Strunk v. Zoltanski*, 468 N.E.2d 13 (N.Y. 1984) (landlord liable); *Uccello v. Laudenslayer*, 44 Cal. App. 3d 504 (1975) (landlord liable). On-site landlords may be deemed keepers or harborers of their tenants' dogs. *Bailey v. DeSanti*, 414 A.2d 1187 (Conn. Supp. Ct. 1980); *Edelstein v. Costelli*, 1967 Ill. App. LEXIS 1500 (June 27, 1967). *See also Landlord's Liability to Third Person for Injury Resulting from Attack on Leased Premises by Dangerous or Vicious Animal Kept by Tenant*, 87 A.L.R.4TH 1004 (1991).

In *Hill v. Hughes*, 2007 Ohio App. LEXIS 3520 (June 28, 2007), minor Cyrus Hill was airlifted to a children's hospital after being mauled by a Lab and Rottweiler mix named Pete, owned by the defendant Jerry Hughes Jr. The evening of Apr. 14, 2005, Cyrus's father visited his cousin Jerry Jr.'s home to play with model airplanes. After their wives purchased hamburgers, Pete jumped up and took a hamburger from Cyrus. Jerry Jr. then put Pete in his house. Thereafter, Cyrus opened the front door and Pete attacked. The plaintiffs sued Jerry Jr. and his father, Jerry Hughes Sr., from whom Jerry Jr. rented a home on a month-to-month tenancy. The trial court dismissed Jerry Sr., noting that he was not an owner, harborer, or keeper of the dog. The appeals court also concluded that he was not a "keeper" because he did not have "physical control" over Pete at the time of Cyrus's injury. The closer question concerned whether he was a "harborer" in having possession and control of the premises where Pete lived and silently acquiesced to his presence. While traditionally a landlord will not have sufficient possession over leased premises to be deemed a harborer, the plaintiffs argued a unique relationship between Jerry Jr. and Jerry Sr. For instance, they were father and son living on contiguous properties both owned by the father. Furthermore, no written lease existed, and the son worked for the father on the premises where he lived. In deposition, the father acknowledged that he had authority to make his son "get rid of" the dog. This exchange merited reversal. *See also George v. Paffen*, 957 So. 2d 861 (La. Ct. App. 2007), *writ granted*, 966 So. 2d 562 (La. 2007) (plaintiff father sued defendant dog owners and landlord for injuries inflicted to his son by tenant's dogs; held: 2-1 decision affirming dismissal of landlord).

In the context of animal product superstores, consider *D.C. ex rel. Christian v. Petco Animal Supplies Stores, Inc.*, 847 N.Y.S.2d 895 (N.Y. 2007). A five-year-old sustained injuries when bitten by a dog recently adopted by another patron, while shopping at Petco with her mother. The trial court dismissed all claims against the adopter of the dog and the store, and the plaintiff appealed. Although the store had an implied duty of care to its customers to prevent harm from third parties, and while its animal-friendly policy permitted this third-party customer encounter, the incident was not foreseeable as a matter of law. Statistics of 80 million customer transactions in 2005 and only five dog bite incidents reported to the store's management overcame statistics from the Centers for Disease Control and American Veterinary Medical Association of 4.6 to 4.7 million dog bites in that same year, convincing the appellate court that the store's animal-friendly policy "was not inherently dangerous by its undisputed statistical analysis and the fact that it is an industry-wide practice." The court also rejected the arguments by plaintiff that the store was negligent for failing to warn customers at its entrances or failing to check each customer and the companion animal for in-store etiquette and nonvicious demeanor.

7. Other Factors Affecting Liability

The classification of the attacking animal, the injured victim, and the situs of the attack all affect liability:

Where the attacking animal was previously declared, cited, or found vicious or dangerous, or the owner or keeper of the biter was charged or convicted of harboring or improperly controlling a, potentially dangerous, dangerous, vicious, or hazardous animal, that condition will assuredly enhance plaintiff's attempt to establish strict common law liability (scienter of propensity) and negligent control.

Where the attacking animal is an alleged pit bull-type dog, or breed allegedly genetically predisposed toward viciousness, plaintiffs will try to prove constructive scienter. With much notoriety, *Tracey v. Solesky*, 50 A.3d 1075 (Md. 2012) in a 5-to-2 reconsideration ruling, reaffirmed its declaration that purebred pit bull dogs are inherently dangerous, creating an absolute (rather than strict) liability regime. Thus, plaintiffs need not prove scienter of vicious propensity (the traditional strict common law elements), but merely the dog's pedigree. The ruling generates more problems than solutions, primarily due to the intractability of proving breed purity, because only purebred pit-bull type breeds will carry the judicial presumption of dangerousness. In granting the motion for reconsideration in part, Judge Wilner prudently asked, "Is it intended that a dog be classified as a cross-bred pit bull if only one of its grandparents (or great-grandparents) was a pure-bred pit bull?" The "thicket" of uncertainty described in the order bears scrutiny because the decision lacks the qualitative and quantitative measures by which to classify a dog as pure. Conceding that, "In imposing strict liability for cross-breds, some greater certainty is required," and excising from the original opinion any reference to hybrids, cross-breds, or mixes, the majority reined in the scope of its earlier opinion.

Decided a few weeks before, and contrary to, the amended *Tracey* decision is *Morgan v. Marquis*, 50 A.3d 1 (Me. 2012), where the Maine Supreme Court refused to create a breed-specific absolute liability standard, remarking that the trial court correctly decided not to treat pit bulls as per se abnormally dangerous to the class of domestic dogs. Generalities as to pit bulls "are not sufficient to survive the Restatement section 509 test for common law strict liability because that test requires a showing that the Marquises knew that Beans was dangerous[.]" *Id.*, at 5. However, in deciding negligence, the jury was free to determine if breed enhanced the duty owed due to some propensity to bite and harm. *Id.*, at 4–5.

Where the injured animal is a service or police animal, be mindful of special statutory remedies and criminal penalties that single out those victimized classes for unique treatment.

Where the injured person is an innocent or technical trespasser, mind *Brewer v. Furtwangler*, 18 P.2d 837, 839 (Wash. 1933), as discussed herein.

Where the bite occurs on the dog owner's property and the injured person is neither a licensee nor invitee, trespass defenses may apply even if the trespasser is a bounty hunter, as discussed in *Mota v. Gruszczynski*, 968 N.E.2d 631 (Ohio Ct. App. 2012). Thomas Mota, a licensed bounty hunter, was trying to apprehend Jerome Gruszczynski inside the residence of his parents. Affirming dismissal, the court found Mota criminally trespassed into the Gruszczynskis' back yard and on the porch where Buckshot bit him repeatedly, meeting the basis for immunity from strict liability under R.C. 955.28(B). At most, the privilege operated as a shield to criminal or civil trespass liability, not a sword to negate Mota's status as a trespasser or licensee. The court also rejected the common law negligence claim that Mota held the status of an invitee, rather than a licensee, for two reasons — *first*, the Gruszczynskis did not invite him onto their property, and *second*, even law enforcement and firefighters entering private property to perform their duties without invitation are licensees. *Id.*, at 636. The court found nothing reckless about permitting Buckshot to remain in an enclosed, screened-in porch to care for her puppies.

Where the bite occurs near (but not on) the dog owner's property, according to at least one court, premises liability exists. In *Benningfield v. Zinsmeister*, 367 S.W.3d 561 (Ky. 2012), the Kentucky Supreme Court evaluated landlord liability facing the Zinsmeisters, who lived next door to, and owned, the Harrison property, from which a Rottweiler escaped and mauled eight-year-old boy Brandon Benningfield across the street on the sidewalk. The trial court granted summary judgment to the Zinsmeisters on the premise that the attack occurred off the leased premises, and the Court of Appeals affirmed, as did the Kentucky Supreme Court. Holding that while landlords can be statutory owners under KRS 258.235(4) in "permit[ting] [the dog] to remain on or about premises owned . . . by him," to avoid "absurd consequences" rendered by overbreadth (such as holding the landlord liable where the tenant "takes the dog along on vacation and an attack occurs 500 miles away") and underbreadth (such as restricting liability to the four corners of the leased property so that a dog who "steps a few inches away from an invisible property line, which has the appearance of being a continuation of the yard, and attacks a young child" would not expose the landlord to liability), it articulated a spatial limitation of "on or about" the premises at issue. *Id.*, at 567–68. Specifically, "on or about" meant "on the property or so close to it as to be within immediate physical reach."

Where the injured party is an invitee and seeks to hold the possessor of land liable based on failure to discover and defuse or warn of a dangerous condition, even if the danger is patent (such as where the possessor should not expect the invitee to be able to protect against the hazard, even if known), be prepared to litigate whether a dog can be a "condition" on the land. This attempt to create premises liability appears as an alternative way to prove strict common law liability since the plaintiff must still show that the defendant knew or should have known that the dog's "dangerousness" posed an unreasonable risk of harm. The only benefit to a plaintiff pleading premises liability appears to be that it relieves her of the burden of proving the defendant is the owner, keeper, or harborer of the dog; instead, she need only prove that the defendant possessed the land upon which the dog was found, as defined in REST. (2ND) TORTS § 328E (though in most cases, a "possessor" will constitute a "keeper" or "harborer"). In *Giacalone v. Housing Authority of the Town of Wallingford*, 51 A.3d 352 (Conn. 2012), the Connecticut Supreme Court surmised that known vicious dogs may constitute dangerous conditions on the land for purposes of premises liability analysis. As such, landlords must address these known canine hazards by maintaining the premises in a reasonably safe condition, remarking:

> Whether a dangerous condition is created by rats, snow, rotting wood or vicious dogs, these differing facts present no fundamental ground of distinction. What defines the landlord's duty is the obligation to take reasonable measures to ensure that the *space* over which it exercises dominion is safe from dangers, and a landlord may incur liability by failing to do so.

Id., at 357–358.

Chapter 10

LANDLORD-TENANT DISPUTES

America's pre-Civil Rights era witnessed the ghettoization of people of color through a system of *de facto* and *de jure* exclusionary practices, such as overtly biased racial residency statutes prohibiting African Americans from living in European American neighborhoods,[1] content-neutral (but still disparately impacting) municipal zoning laws (minimal building lots, minimum floor space, maximum density limitations, and smaller apartments allowing only for one or two bedrooms, thereby excluding families with minor children), red-lining by the Federal Housing Administration, steering by the Department of Housing and Urban Development in implementation of the Section Eight Housing Assistance Program, and, of course, intentional acts of prejudicial mistreatment by landlords, realtors, and management companies, whether by simply refusing to rent or sell to minorities, lying about vacancies, quoting less favorable conditions of tenancy (higher rent, excluding from rent the cost of utilities, parking, and access to other facilities; higher deposits; fewer incentives to sign; imposing an application fee not required of others), or conspiring with other homeowners to pass restrictive covenants discriminating on the basis of race,[2] all in an effort to maintain what New Jersey Supreme Court Judge Pashman described in *NAACP v. Township of Mount Laurel*, 336 A.2d 713, 736 (N.J. 1975) as "enclaves of affluence or of social homogeneity." *See* Marc Settles, *The Perpetuation of Residential Racial Segregation in America: Historical Discrimination, Modern Forms of Exclusion, and Inclusionary Remedies*, 141 J. LAND USE & ENV. L. 89 (1996).

Though the twenty-first century has seen great strides in dismantling residential segregation based on race and religion, except for those lucky few dogs, cats, birds, and smaller nonhuman animals who happen to serve or ameliorate the medical conditions of their disabled owners, animal apartheid in residential settings persists in the United States, with irreversible consequences.[3] Blanket "no pet" clauses, and less categorical prohibitions restricting occupation by certain species or breeds, stature or heft, significantly contribute to the problem of animal homelessness[4] and

---

[1] A practice ended by *Buchanan v. Warley*, 245 U.S. 60 (1917) (striking Louisville, Ky. ordinance forbidding sale of realty to blacks as violating freedom of contract provision of Fourteenth Amendment).

[2] This practice, too, ended by *Shelley v. Kraemer*, 334 U.S. 1 (1948) (preventing enforcement of restrictive covenant barring "people of the Negro or Asian race" from occupying property in a St. Louis, Mo. neighborhood as violating the Equal Protection Clause of the Fourteenth Amendment).

[3] According to the ASPCA, about five out of ten dogs in shelters and seven out of ten cats are destroyed because none can adopt them. An estimated 2.7 million dogs and cats lose their lives annually in America's shelters. www.aspca.org/about-us/faq/pet-statistics.

[4] The most common reason people surrender their animals at shelters is because their place of residence forbids them. *Keeping Pets (Dogs and Cats) in Homes: A Three-Phase Retention Study, Phase*

the abandonment of animal companions on moving day. Does it help to conceptualize the seemingly irreconcilable problem of unyielding demand (of homeless pets in need of shelter and guardianship) with private and public prohibitions on supply (of dwellings that permit animal and human cohabitation), the way courts and government institutions have grappled with religious[5] and racial segregation?

Despite the recent attempt to persuade a California district court to extend constitutional protections to cetaceans, few dispute that the Bill of Rights and its protections against unequal treatment, privilege, and immunity do not apply directly to nonhuman animals. Any remedy bestowed upon a nonhuman by the federal constitution is, therefore, derivative from ownership or lawful possession by a human being in whom an enforceable right vests. She may then cast her shadow of benevolent stewardship over the rightless animal, enjoying the safeguards against eviction, impoundment, and involuntary execution by proxy. The potentiality of ownership and lawful possession has consequences, as in the case where a shelter declines to adopt to an individual applicant for discriminatory reasons. *See Sims v. Humane Society of St. Joseph Cy., Indiana Inc.*, 758 F. Supp. 2d 737 (N.D. Ind. 2010).[6]

Some have argued that the constitution disallows intermeddling with the composition of one's family. But the constitutional right of privacy protects cohabitation choices "only insofar as family members are involved," and will not afford "general protection to an individual's choice of unrelated household companions." Because the federal right will not protect the right of "two unrelated persons living together, it is certainly not violated by restrictions against a person living with small animals." *Ramm v. City of Seattle*, 830 P.2d 395, 399–400 (1992) (citing *Bedford v. Sugarman*, 772 P.2d 486, *Belle Terre v. Boraas*, 416 U.S. 1 (1974) and *Moore v. East Cleveland*, 431 U.S. 494 (1977)). In the two decades since *Ramm*,

---

I: Reasons for Not Owning a Dog or Cat www.americanhumane.org/aha-petsmart-retention-study-phase-1.pdf

[5] *See Bd. of Educ. of Kiryas Joel Village Sch. Dist. v. Grumet*, 512 U.S. 687 (1994) (finding First Amendment violation by government's excessive entanglement in fashioning school district coinciding with neighborhood boundaries of Satmar community, a Hasidic Jewish minority).

[6] Racial, religious, and sexual orientation intolerance in *human* child adoption discrimination claims are not particularly novel, but when bigotry operates to deny equal treatment to those applying for *nonhuman* adoptions, they become noteworthy. *Sims* exemplifies such trend. Alleging racial discrimination, an African-American couple sued the humane society and their veterinary hospital for violating their civil rights in denying their application to adopt Gabby, a purebred English Mastiff puppy in excellent health. When not approved the next day, the Simses were told Gabby might develop costly hip dysplasia and it could cost $6000. When the Simses responded that they earned over $100,000 a year and owned two acres and asked how the humane society concluded that the Simses could not afford Gabby's treatment, the employee remained silent. Thereafter, the humane society contended the reason for declining to adopt Gabby related to the statement made by the Simses' veterinary hospital that they provided only "minimal care" to their animal companions. The Simses filed their nine-count complaint pro se, and defendants moved to dismiss for failure to state a claim. The court found plausible the 42 U.S.C. §§ 1981–1982 claims of racial discrimination against all defendants except the president, secretary, and director of the humane society in the making or enforcing of a contract and interfering with property rights even though "[i]t seems more likely that plaintiffs' application for animal adoption from the Humane Society was rejected because the Humane Society questioned plaintiffs' ability to adequately care for an animal based on information it received from plaintiffs' veterinarian, rather than because plaintiffs were African-Americans."

appellate decisions have reaffirmed the familial status of certain animal companions; how those rulings may affect residential segregation by species who associate with (i.e., are owned or possessed by) nondisabled handlers remains to be seen. While in principle the prospect of the equal protection, privileges and immunities, and freedom of religion clauses passing indirectly to nonhumans may seem promising, as the reader will swiftly appreciate, only a minority subclass of individuals suffering from qualifying physical or mental disabilities may effectively invoke meaningful protections *under federal statutory law*, such as the Americans with Disabilities Act and Federal Fair Housing Act.

For the rest of Americans who cannot assert the right to a reasonable accommodation in the form of a service or emotional support animal, what legal defenses to unlawful detainer arise for nondisabled owner and non-service/emotional support animal alike?

Hypothetical: Drawing from the Francophilly hypothetical from Chapter 4, Dangerous Dog Litigation, *supra*, assume that Bill is nevertheless killed. Devastated by his loss, Meaney becomes a Franciscan priest, taking in all stray dogs. His church is situated in Francophilly city limits and sits on five acres. Meaney is harboring a total of 11 strays in the church basement at the time he is investigated by Francophilly Animal Control, based on a noise complaint from a Jesuit seminary across the street. Ten are French bulldogs. Has Meaney violated FMC § 17.89.020?[7]

A.   NO-PET CLAUSES

Though landlords have increasingly catered to those with animal companions in order to expand the pool of potential applicants, settled common law permits them to categorically prohibit the presence of any nonhuman, regardless of how decorous in comportment or attractive in appearance — except emotional support or service animals. While virtually all American jurisdictions permit landlords to ban animal companions across the board, there are a few dissenting judicial voices. Consider *Nahrstedt v. Lakeside Village Condo. Ass'n, Inc.*, 878 P.2d 1275 (Cal. 1994). This oft-cited decision confirms the right of condominium and homeowners association to banish even inconspicuous and harmless cats, such as Natore Nahrstedt's three "noiseless" indoor felines who "created no nuisance." In reversing the Court of Appeals, the California Supreme Court held that the restriction could be enforced regardless of proof that the cats would interfere with the right of other homeowners "to the peaceful and quiet enjoyment of their property." Dissenting Justice Arabian begins, "There are two means of refuge from the misery of life: music and cats." *Id.*,

---

[7] First, a church arguably does not qualify as a "household," so the section may not apply. Second, the ordinance is vague with respect to whether the term "keep" includes temporary possession. The Free Exercise claim under the First Amendment will likely fail, for while FMC 17.89.020 materially interferes with the Franciscan monk's spiritual quest endeavoring to save homeless strays, several United States Supreme Court decisions do not allow an individual's religious beliefs to excuse him from complying with an otherwise valid general law prohibiting conduct the state may freely regulate. *See Employment Div., Dept. of Human Resources of Oregon v. Smith*, 494 U.S. 872, 878–79 (1990). Whether the Religious Land Use and Institutionalized Persons Act of 2000, 42 U.S.C. § 2000cc (2000) would compel a different result were Meaney able to challenge the land use regulation as failing to provide the least restrictive means of furthering a compelling government interest (again, assuming that restricting numbers of animals per household is such an interest) warrants deeper analysis.

at 1292. His impassioned rejection of the majority's "chary" view of the law that "eschews the human spirit in favor of arbitrary efficiency" is worth reading. A highlight:

> Our true task in this turmoil is to strike a balance between the governing rights accorded a condominium association and the individual freedom of its members. To fulfill that function, a reviewing court must view with a skeptic's eye restrictions driven by fear, anxiety, or intolerance. In any community, we do not exist in vacuo. There are many annoyances which we tolerate because not to do so would be repressive and place the freedom of others at risk.
>
> In contravention, the majority's failure to consider the real burden imposed by the pet restriction unfortunately belittles and trivializes the interest at stake here. Pet ownership substantially enhances the quality of life for those who desire it. When others are not only undisturbed by, but completely unaware of, the presence of pets being enjoyed by their neighbors, the balance of benefit and burden is rendered disproportionate and unreasonable, rebutting any presumption of validity. Their view, shorn of grace and guiding philosophy, is devoid of the humanity that must temper the interpretation and application of all laws, for in a civilized society that is the source *397 of their authority. As judicial architects of the rules of life, we better serve when we construct halls of harmony rather than walls of wrath.
>
> I would affirm the judgment of the Court of Appeal.

Id., at 396–97; *see also* Armand Arabian, *Condos, Cats, and CC&Rs: Invasion of the Castle Common*, 23 PEPP. L. REV. 1 (1995). In 2001, no doubt infected by Arabian indignation, the California legislature reined in *Nahrstedt* by enacting section 1360.5 of the Davis-Stirling Common Interest Development Act, (now Cal. Civ. Code § 4715), which prevents condominium and homeowners associations from enacting covenants or rules prohibiting the keeping of at least one well-behaved pet, defined as a bird, cat, dog, or aquatic animal kept in an aquarium, or species as otherwise agreed by the association and unit owner. The City of West Hollywood's Rent Stabilization Ordinance restricts limitations landlords may impose on seniors, disabled persons, or those living with HIV/AIDS who wish to reside with an animal companion, and permits tenants to replace permitted pets after their loss. WHMC 17.52.010(2)(f-g). France and Belgium ban no-pet clauses. And in 1997, the Canadian province of Ontario passed the Tenant Protection Act of 1997. Section 15 states, "A provision in a tenancy agreement prohibiting the presence of animals in or about the residential complex is void." 1997, c. 24, s. 15.

In very few American jurisdictions, however, the political will has yielded statutory bars to, or waivers of, no-pet clauses. For instance, New York City enacted what amounts to a 90-day prescriptive pet easement. New York City Administrative Code § 27-2009.1 provides that once a companion animal resides in a multiple dwelling for at least three consecutive months, openly and notoriously, the no-pet clause of a lease may no longer be enforced. In a challenge arising under the open and notorious elements, *Matter of Robinson v. City of New York*, 579 N.Y.S.2d 817 (1991) found that while Cindy Robinson did not take Miss Muffy, her small dog, on regular walks, 27-2009.1 applied, for any other interpretation

> would lead to a conclusion that all small dogs or other animals whose masters elected to treat only as house pets could not have the benefit of the [Pet L]aw's waiver even though they had been seen and noted by management personnel . . . Such a reading is arbitrary and capricious also because it would seem to work most harshly against tenants who are house bound for one reason or another, such as age or disability, and who choose to have small dogs (or cats) as a companion without the need to walk them.

Id., at 819. Disputes have arisen as to whether 27-2009.1 applies to condominiums. *See Board of Managers v. Lamontanero*, 206 A.D.2d 340 (N.Y. App. Div. 1991) (applies); *Board of Managers of the Parkchester North Condominium v. Quiles*, 234 A.D.2d 130 (N.Y. App. Div. 1996) (does not apply).

In jurisdictions that do not have superseding legislation, how does a court analyze the threshold question of whether residential segregation by species is reasonable? Generally, clauses prohibiting animal companions in leased premises are valid on the basis that they seek to confer an overall benefit of comfort and maintenance of quality in housing, though they may be expressly or impliedly waived. *East River Housing Corp. v. Matonis*, 312 N.Y.S.2d 461 (1970); *Capital View Realty Co. v. Meigs*, 92 A.2d 765 (D.C. 1952). Efforts to characterize such clauses as unconscionable or unreasonable have failed. *Blakely v. Housing Auth. of County of King*, 505 P.2d 151, 156–157 (Wash. Ct. App. 1973) (not an adhesion contract); *Housing Auth., Atlantic City v. Coppock*, 346 A.2d 609, 611 (N.J. Super. Ct. 1975) (suggesting outright ban of pets reasonable regulation, yet later decision regarded it as *dictum*, see *Royal Associates v. Concannon*, 490 A.2d 357, 360–361 (N.J. Super. Ct. 1985)).

In *Young v. Savinon*, 492 A.2d 385 (N.J. Super. Ct. 1985), the court examined the conduct of a new landlord, Young, who bought an apartment complex in December 1981 with the intention of forcing tenants to move or relinquish their pet animals (including a fish) despite having knowledge that the previous landlord explicitly allowed defendants Possumato, Savinon, and Brosonski to keep their dogs, a German Shepherd, Scottish Terrier, and Chihuahua, for a period of four, one, and eight years before trial. Expert testimony suggested that such a compelled surrender or move would inflict severe psychological and physical harm. Young claimed an absolute right to change the lease provisions to ban pets regardless of any prior deal with his predecessor. The first trial court dismissed the unlawful detainer action on procedural grounds; a retrial resulted in judgment for Young. A stay of execution of writ entered pending appeal, resulted in reversal and dismissal, and overruling of a prior case. The appellate court reasoned that the New Jersey Anti-Eviction Act provided additional protections for tenants than existed prior to its enactment, when they could be evicted or denied lease renewal for basically any nondiscriminatory reason. The new act provided something of a "just cause" procedure requiring "reasonable" restrictions in rules and regulations, lease covenants, and changes in terms and conditions in a renewal lease, as here. *Terhune Courts v. Sgambati*, 1978 N.J. Super. LEXIS 1357 (D. N.J. Oct. 13, 1978), *aff'd o.b.*, 406 A.2d 1330 (N.J. Super. Ct. 1979) assumed outright bans to be reasonable, looking at the issue from the landlord's perspective only. The *Young* court reversed

Terhune and this one-sided understanding, stating that trial courts may now consider reasonableness from both landlord and tenant standpoints. Given that the implied-in-fact contract between the prior landlord, who knew the defendants had dogs and would grow attached to them over time, transferred to Young, and no greater rights could be transferred to him than the transferor possessed at time of transfer; granting deference to expert testimony; and noting that compliance through attrition was imminent, the appeals court held that the no-pet ban, under these facts, was unreasonable.

In *Downey v. Tolmie*, 1982 Conn. Super. LEXIS 498 (June 3, 1982), lessee-defendant George Tolmie was bound by a clause stating, "You will not keep any dogs, cats or other animals on the premises," although keeping a cat strictly indoors and cleaning up after him with no neighbor complaints. Nonetheless, the landlords told Tolmie to remove the cat or vacate the premises. He refused, arguing that cat-keeping did not constitute a material breach. The court rejected this materiality defense, in part because of the "reasonable and substantial basis for the prohibition" (e.g., preventing roaming about common areas, tenant allergies, tenant choice to live in environment without animals). The court also rejected the equitable argument seeking to guard against forfeiture of tenancy and infliction of disproportionate harm since Tolmie had sufficient time to relocate the feline. Further, the lease's non-waiver clause (i.e., failure to enforce does not waive right to enforce future violations) was held to override the assertion of waiver by the landlord's employees who knew of his cat but took no action for an extended period. Finally, though the lease gave landlords the "option" of termination upon the occurrence of certain events — of which animal prohibition was not listed — the court still found the violation to be material, and termination permissible, under state statutory law.

In *Guilford Housing Auth. v. Gilbert*, 2011 Conn. Super. LEXIS 85 (Jan 10, 2011) the Housing Authority tried to evict 62-year-old Catherine Gilbert for failing to pay a $500 pet deposit and to obtain general liability insurance of $300,000 for her declawed, indoor house cat. The court ruled for Ms. Gilbert, finding no material noncompliance with any valid rule, and holding that the $500 pet deposit, in exceeding her monthly rent of $475, violated state law. It also rejected the Authority's contention that Ms. Gilbert needed to acquire a $300,000 liability *insurance* policy, observing the omission of the word "insurance," and stating that she was only required to have "general liability coverage" or "a $300,000 general liability policy."

Clauses that permit certain animals with prior consent of the landlord have also been upheld. In *Mill Pond Village v. Villamarin*, 1999 Conn. Super. LEXIS 2732 (Sept. 21, 1999), Manuel Villamarin faced eviction for bringing two Rottweilers into his unit after establishing tenancy in violation of a pet clause contained in the lease (i.e., only prior written consent by lessor); that he paid $300 as a pet deposit for, and disclosed possession of, a diminutive Chihuahua (permitted by the size clause) did not permit him to bring in two other dogs without landlord permission.

B.   SPECIES-, SIZE-, AND WEIGHT-LIMITING CLAUSES

Clauses favoring one species over another have been upheld. In *Bogan v. New London Housing Authority*, 366 F. Supp. 861 (D. Conn. 1973), the federal district court upheld a housing authority's no-dog (but not no-cat) policy as neither arbitrary nor capricious, nor in violation of equal protection, as it reasonably related to a legitimate government interest in preserving the peace and well-being of its tenants. It added that "even well-attended dogs create a health and safety threat by barking, biting, fouling public areas, and attracting other, ownerless dogs," rendering the species discrimination legitimate because cats "serve a 'mousing' function, and . . . do not create health and safety problems of the same magnitude as do dogs." Further, that "plaintiffs deem their arguments as to the merits of dog ownership to be more reasonable than defendant's arguments to the contrary [] does not render defendant's action arbitrary." But see *Prisco v. Forest Villas Condominium Apartments, Inc.*, 847 So. 2d 1012 (Fla. Dist. Ct. App. 2003) (reversing and remanding due to selective enforcement of no-pet condominium association covenant that says "no pets whatsoever" except fish or birds yet, in practice, the board would enforce only against dogs, not cats); *City of Philadelphia v. Tirrill*, 906 A.2d 663 (Pa. Comm. 2006) (though not addressing merits, discusses injunction issued in favor of city to enjoin residents from keeping a Vietnamese potbellied pig at their home in violation of the City's health code barring possession of "farm animals"); Jay Zitter, *Effect, as Between Landlord and Tenant, of Lease Clause Restricting Keeping of Pets*, 114 A.L.R.5TH 443 (2003).

Size and weight restrictions also have resulted in litigation. In *City of Marion v. Schoenwald*, 631 N.W.2d 213 (S.D. 2001), the Supreme Court of South Dakota upheld the Marion ordinance limiting households to four dogs, only two of which could weigh more than 25 pounds. Finding a rational basis to support the claim that "large dogs" possess "a greater potential to kill, injure, and intimidate," and that when housed together may develop a "pack mentality" that "increas[es] their lethality," and, further, that big dogs produce excessive dog feces and foul odors, the ordinance did not violate the Schoenwalds' substantive due process rights under the South Dakota Constitution, Art. VI, § 2. Diane Schoenwald and her husband owned three dogs — a shepherd-collie mix weighing 75 pounds, a male golden retriever weighing 30 pounds, and a female golden retriever weighing 20 pounds. Presumably, the city contended that the female in fact weighed more than 25 pounds, otherwise it would not have had any colorable argument for violation. Though conceding that no other similar weight restriction for dogs had been upheld by any court in the country, that no empirical evidence proved or disproved the assertion of disparate impact based on weight, and that the restriction "carries certain troublesome exactions" due to its mutability, the court held, "If the city can lawfully restrict the number of pets per home, then it seems hardly a stretch to say that it can also limit the size of those pets — at least some of them." *Id.*, at 218. Had it used the terminology "large" and "small," instead of definite poundage, the court likely would have stricken that part of the code for indefiniteness. Because a scale could determine compliance without resorting to speculation, and since the ordinance did not ban over-25-pound dogs altogether but permitted considerable freedom in keeping two dogs of any size, the court held for the municipality. *See also State v. Maynard*, 673 S.E.2d 877 (N.C. Ct. App. 2009) (ordinance limiting dogs over five months of age to three constitutional; rejecting argument that law "should have considered and regulated pets 'by weight or other characteristics" rather than just by the number of pets, citing *Schoenwald*); *Majestic View Condominium Association, Inc. v. Bolotin*, 429 So. 2d 438 (Fla. Dist. Ct. App. 1983) (implicitly accepting reasonableness of one-pet-under-25-pounds restriction).

C. HOMEOWNERS AND CONDOMINIUM OWNERS ASSOCIATION COVENANTS

An invigorating debate among a split California Supreme Court, *Nahrstedt v. Lakeside Village Condo. Ass'n*, 878 P.2d 1275 (Cal. 1994), provides a judicious overview of the law concerning the keeping of animals and enforceability of restrictions imposed by landlords and associations, ending with Justice Arabian's oft-quoted dissent. *Id.*, at 390; *see also Construction of Contractual or State Regulatory Provisions Respecting Formation, Composition, and Powers of Governing Body of Condominium Association*, 13 A.L.R.4TH 598; *Cause of Action to Enforce, or Declare Invalid, Restriction on Use of Condominium Property*, 14 COA.2D 315; 1 LAW OF CONDOMINIUM OPERATIONS § 4:67.

Natore Nahrstedt bought a condo at Lakeside Village, moving in with three cats who allegedly caused no disruption or interference to neighboring condo owners. Upon learning of her feline companions, the Association assessed numerous fines and demanded immediate removal pursuant to the declaration of CC&Rs containing a pet restriction (banning all except domestic fish and birds). Nahrstedt sued the Association, asking for injunctive and declaratory relief (i.e., the pet restriction was "unreasonable" as applied to indoor cats, who would not be permitted to run free in common areas), termination of assessments, invasion of privacy, and negligent infliction of emotional distress. The Association defended the restriction as reasonable as a matter of law given its furtherance of the collective interest of all unit owners in health, happiness, and peace of mind.

The trial court dismissed the case for failure to state a claim, only to be reversed by the Court of Appeals on the basis that Nahrstedt stated a claim for declaratory relief because the reasonableness inquiry was "as applied," not "as to whole." It also revived her claims for invasion of privacy, to invalidate the assessments, afford injunctive relief, and seek NIED damages. The Supreme Court, however, reversed the demand for declaratory relief and remanded the remaining state claims. It reasoned that recorded condominium use restrictions contained in the declaration of a common interest development are presumed reasonable as determined by reference to the development "as whole" ("common interest"), not "as applied to complaining homeowner." Invoking "deferential standards of equitable servitude law," a reasonableness presumption may be rebutted by proving (1) arbitrariness, (2) that the burdens imposed on use substantially outweigh the restriction's benefits to the development, or (3) violation of public policy. The majority found the pet restriction "rationally relate[d]" to health, sanitation and noise concerns in the high-density condo project. Because Nahrstedt failed to address how the policy, applied uniformly to all residents, substantially burdened the development *as a whole*, her complaint was facially deficient.

Dissenting Justice Arabian writes an eloquent and impassioned plea to affirm the Court of Appeals on the basis that the majority overemphasized the semantic change in former Section 1355 of the California Davis-Stirling Act ("where reasonable") to latter Section 1354 ("unless unreasonable") to apply an overly deferential equitable servitude framework. In short, he believed that Nahrstedt stated a claim to defeat the demurrer, for use restrictions that invade and burden the privilege of cohabitation with companion animals maintained without any detriment to the neighbors' quiet enjoyment of their private property and common areas substantially outweighs any benefit to the community, and are unreasonable. Arabian also argued that such restrictions could violate antidiscrimination law, and thereby serve to rebut presumptive reasonableness on grounds of public policy. Benefits of the Association's policy, he added, were nonuniform, particularly given the greater likelihood of noise and nuisance from domestic birds and fish (aquarium leakage), species who were explicitly permitted by the policy, and where additional rules and regulations set forth a procedure to deal with bird and fish incompatibility problems, thereby rebutting reasonableness on the ground of arbitrariness. As noted above, in 2001, the California legislature amended the Davis-Stirling Act to protect condominium unit owners by restraining the reach of blanket no-pet provisions.

The next significant post-*Nahrstedt* decision was *Villa de Las Palmas Home-owners Association v. Terifaj*, 90 P.3d 1223 (Cal. 2004). A 24-unit HOA known as Villa De Las Palmas adopted an unrecorded rule stating, "Pets of any kind are forbidden to be kept in the apartment building or on the grounds at any time." Paula Terifaj, DVM, bought her unit after the enactment of this rule and visited the property with her dog Lucy, who died three years after date of purchase. She then acquired another dog, while trying unsuccessfully to persuade the Association to amend the rule. Her willful refusal to obey the rule prompted litigation and an amendment to amend the Declaration to state, "No pets or animals of any kind, including without limitations, dogs, cats, birds, livestock, reptiles or poultry, may be kept or permitted in any Apartment or anywhere on the Property." Deeming the amendment an enforceable equitable servitude, the court entered a permanent injunction against Terifaj and $15,000 in attorney's fees. The Court of Appeals affirmed, as the no-pet rule made its way from an unrecorded rule into the recorded Amended Declaration passed by a majority of the unit membership; as such, it enjoyed presumptive reasonableness per the Davis-Stirling Act and *Nahrstedt* — even though amended and recorded subsequent to Terifaj's purchase. The California Supreme Court unanimously affirmed, noting that the 2001 amendment to the Davis-Stirling Act, Cal.Civ. § 1360.5 (now Cal.Civ. § 4715), did not aid her, because it only applied to governing documents entered into, amended, or modified on or after Jan. 1, 2001. Here, Villa de las Palmas amended its Declaration a year earlier.

Occasionally, state law mandates that all use restrictions be reasonable. For instance, Idaho's Condominium Property Act, Ch. 55-15 IC, provides that only those "agreements, decisions, and determinations lawfully made by the management body shall be deemed to be binding on all condominium owners[.]" IC § 55-1516. Use restrictions not set forth in the declaration must be contained in the bylaws, and those restrictions cannot be "unreasonable." IC § 55-1507(j); see also 55-1505(2)(q). Washington's Condominium Act, Ch. 64.34 RCW, requires that the board of directors shall, in performing their duties (which includes adopting rules and regulations, and imposing and collecting charges for late payment of assessments and levying fines), exercise "ordinary and reasonable care." RCW § 64.34.308(1)(b). Further, certain restrictive covenants adopted by an HOA or COA impose obligations on the board to pass "reasonable" rules or not to "unreasonably withhold" approval of a unit owner to keep an animal. Such language may disfavor the Association, as seen in *Scottsdale Condominium v. Talaroc*, 2009 Ariz. App. Unpub. LEXIS 71 (Mar 26, 2009). The COA's CC&R Section 7.5 refused to permit animals or birds of any kind "except that usual and ordinary small household pets such as dogs, cats, or birds, may, upon approval of the Association, be kept," with the proviso that, "Approval for such pets will not be unreasonably withheld, nor will the removal of such pets be unreasonably applied." Despite this clear covenant, the Board enacted rules that initially prohibited only members in certain buildings from keeping any animals, and those in other buildings to two small animals not to exceed 20 pounds. After years of complaints, the board then enacted a blanket no-pet rule throughout the entire development. Joy Talaroc signed a contract to buy her condo after implementation of the no-pet rule. Due to the inconsistency between Section 7.5 and the Board rule, she confirmed with the management company that she could have dogs weighing less than 20 pounds. Assured of the right to cohabit with her dogs, she closed the sale, only to be cited by the HOA for violating its no-pets rule.

Following a board hearing, which unanimously refused to honor her request for an exception to the no-pet rule, it sued her for breach of the restriction and sought an injunction. Talaroc cross-moved for partial summary judgment, arguing that a supermajority of the members never amended CC&R Section 7.5 to incorporate the inconsistent board rule change, rendering it invalid. She also urged the court to find equitable estoppel. In reversing the trial court's issuance of a permanent injunction and award of fees and costs, the appellate court found the rule unenforceable as conflicting with Section 7.5. It added that the board's reliance on the no-pet rule to deny her request to keep her dogs was unreasonable as a matter of law, for the Board failed to exercise its discretion in making decisions possessed of reason, and that failed to reflect that the overwhelming majority of current membership did not want to live in a pet-free community. Further, the court alternatively found that the oral representations of what the HOA referred to as an accounting vendor (but whom Talaroc argued was the speaking agent and property manager to the HOA) nonetheless bound the Association as an apparent agent and created an actionable equitable estoppel defense.

Hypothetical: Condo Association (with 40 units) orders Unit Owner to remove her over-25 pound dog, whom she adopted after the Board enacted Rule 6.2 (below), passed ostensibly in accordance with covenant 11.10 (below). Unit Owner bought her unit in 2000. The new rule went into effect in 2009. She acquired the well-behaved 50-pound dog two months after the rule went into effect. There was no public hearing on the proposed rule, and it passed by three board members (less than 10 percent of the units).

> **Covenant 11.10** Pets. Domestic household pets, such as dogs and cats, may be kept by Unit Owners; provided, that the keeping of pets shall be subject to such reasonable rules and regulations as the Board may from time to time adopt. The Board may require the removal of any animal which the

Board in the exercise of reasonable discretion finds disturbing other Unit Owners unreasonably, and may exercise this authority for specific animals even though other animals are permitted to remain.

Pets will not be allowed on any Common Elements (or Limited Common Elements allocated for the use of more than one Unit) unless they are on a leash or being carried and are being walked to or from the Unit to a public walk or street. At all times the Common Elements shall be free of any pet debris, including food and feces matter. At no time is pet feces to be deposited in garbage. No livestock, poultry, rabbits or other animals whatsoever shall be allowed or kept in any part of the Condominium, nor may any animal be bred or used therein for any commercial purpose. Any outside facility for pets must be kept clean on a daily basis and no waste products or food be left in either the facility or on the Property.

Rule 6.2: No more than two dogs or two cats or one of each shall be permitted in any one unit (City Code). Weight of each pet not to exceed 25 pounds. (This rule applies to animals acquired after the date of adoption of Rules and Regulations.)

May the Condo Association enforce Rule 6.2 against the Unit Owner?

Use restraints imposed by a board but not amended to the Declaration may be unenforceable. For instance, were this hypothetical to occur in the state of Washington, RCW § 64.34.216(1)(n), in requiring that the Declaration list "Any restrictions *in the declaration* on use, occupancy, or alienation of units," would trump the Board's attempt to change pet rules by three-person vote instead of supermajority amendment. Amendments to the Declaration require a unit owner vote of at least 67 percent. RCW § 64.34.264(1); see also *Shorewood West Condo Ass'n v. Sadri*, 992 P.2d 1008 (Wash. 2000) ("use" restrictions must be contained in declaration, under 1963 Horizontal Regime Act [the old Condo Act]). Para. 11.10 of the *Declaration* was never amended by an Association vote to reflect the 2-dog/cat and 25-pound limitations, rendering Regulation 6.2 invalid. Other courts have held similarly. *See Granby Heights Assoc., Inc. v. Dean*, 647 N.E.2d 75 (Mass. Ct. App. 1995) (condo rule enjoining owners from using common areas to exercise dog and from allowing dog access to common areas was invalid as it effectively prohibited owners from keeping large dog in unit though restriction was not contained in bylaws or master deed); *Johnson v. Keith*, 331 N.E.2d 879 (Mass. 1975) (rule prohibiting keeping of animals in units invalid and not enforceable against owner with respect to her dog as rule was not bylaw and two-thirds vote of unit owners was not obtained); *Parkway Gardens Condominium Ass'n, Inc. v. Kinser*, 536 So. 2d 1076 (Fla. Dist. Ct. App. 1988) (board rule conflicting with declaration specifically allowing pets is unenforceable).

The Board might argue that the Rule is permitted because § 11.10 expressly delegates the task of rule-making to the Board. However, this attempt to bypass the statutory protection of Ch. 64.34 RCW lacks justification. Further, the plain language of § 11.10 conflicts with Rule 6.2, for the former says that dogs (i.e., of all breeds, weights, colors) "may be kept by Unit Owners[.]" While § 11.10 provides that the "keeping of pets shall be subject to such reasonable rules and regulations as the Board may from time to time adopt," it adds that, "No livestock, poultry, rabbits or other animals whatsoever shall be allowed or kept in any part of the Condominium. . . . " In this context, "reasonable rules" pertain not to whether a specific breed or weight of dog may be kept, but, rather, what limitations on use may be reasonably applied to dogs of any breed or weight (e.g., not allowing dog to act viciously, to bark annoyingly, to defecate in the common areas without removal, to run at-large). The second paragraph bolsters this interpretation, which defines which species are categorically banned (livestock, poultry). The Board's attempt to create a rule banning a *type* of dog (i.e., more than 25 pounds) conflicts with § 11.10, which expressly says "domestic household pets, such as dogs and cats, may be kept."

In the final assessment, "dogs" are allowed, and the Board may establish reasonable rules pertaining to *how* (not *which* of) those dogs must be kept and controlled. Considered another way, the rule must apply to a type of animal. If that animal is not allowed to exist, then there is no animal upon which the rule can operate. Para. 11.10 specifically excludes from allowable species livestock, poultry, rabbits, or other nondomestic household pets, but permits canines without limitation.

Additionally repugnant is the lack of notice and an opportunity to be heard. Due process principles frequently have been found to apply to condominium associations. At no point did the Board notify the Association of its intent to modify the pet rules, much less submit proposed modifications for public input. Instead, a decision by three individuals (out of 40 unit owners and scarcely a quorum of the Board of six) carried the day, resulting in notification to the Association in an Apr. 1, 2009 letter telling the members that the rules had changed and they had better come into compliance or face penalties for substantial violations. While Washington has not yet adopted a standard to review condominium rules, other jurisdictions have invoked constitutional principles like due process (*Majestic View Condominium Ass'n v. Bolotin*, 429 So. 2d 438 (Fla. Dist. Ct. App. 1983)), equal protection (*White Egret Condominium, Inc. v. Franklin*, 379 So. 2d 346 (Fla. 1979)), and have regarded condo association governance as "quasi-governmental" state action (*Franklin v. Spadafora*, 447 N.E.2d 1244 (Mass. 1983); *Levandusky v. One Fifth Ave. Apartment Corp.*, 75 N.Y.2d 530 (N.Y. 1990)). In failing to give the owners a chance to be heard on these changes, to vote on same, or even to lobby their board representatives, due process protections were willfully discarded, rendering Rule 6.2 invalid.

Para. 11.10 says that keeping of pets "shall be subject to such *reasonable* rules and regulations as the Board may from time to time adopt." Further, the Board "may require the removal of any animal which the Board in the exercise of *reasonable* discretion finds disturbing other Unit Owners *unreasonably*. . . . " Aside from the above dispositive arguments, one wonders whether Regulation 6.2 is *reasonable* as it bears no rational basis to nuisance, disturbance, or dangerousness. Most dogs are more than 25 pounds, yet several breeds of that weight are well-behaved. The obverse also obtains. *But see* Section B of this Chapter.

Unless the property manager is physically incapable of lifting heavy loads and in the habit of raising unit owners' dogs over her head as part of her job, or a structural engineer has documented that the foundations and ceilings would crack and buckle handle the added weight of a heavier canine, or that an animal science authority or veterinarian has justified a weight threshold for household animals, or any other empirical data to prove a distinction between large and small dogs, particularly given that weight is mutable depending on health, diet, and age, it should be evident that Regulation 6.2 is irrational. Notably, the city code to which the rule refers has not banned any specific breeds or dogs over a particular weight.

The Court of Appeals in *Shorewood* discussed the standard of judicial review to test rules adopted by a governing body — e.g., reasonableness, as opposed to presumptive validity of restrictions in recorded documents, like § 11.10 of the *Declaration. Shorewood West Condo Ass'n v. Sadri*, 966 P.2d 372, 374 (Wash. Ct. App. 1998). Specifically, where a governing body promulgates a rule restricting use, as here, the body must show the use is "antagonistic to . . . the health, happiness and peace of mind of the individual unit owners." *Id.* (quoting *Hidden Harbour Estates, Inc. v. Basso*, 393 So. 2d 637, 640 (Fla. Dist. Ct. App. 1981)). More to the point, however, when such a rule is adopted by a tiny elected board instead of a supermajority of owners, a court engages in less deferential review (i.e., stricter scrutiny), which was the position taken in *Sadri* respecting review of bylaws. *Id.*, at 375 (citing *Ridgely Condo Ass'n v. Smyrnioudis*, 660 A.2d 942 (Md. Ct. Spec. App. 1995), *aff'd*, 343 Md. 357 (1996)). That § 11.10 demands a reasonableness standard furnishes added support for this test.

Finally, there may be evidence that Rule 6.2 has been wielded to target the Unit Owner. In addition to violating equal protection principles, the rule lends itself to the position, stated above, of being unreasonable in application. *See White Egret Condominium, Inc. v. Franklin*, 379 So. 2d 346 (Fla. 1979) (restriction on occupancy of children unreasonable as applied due to nonuniform enforcement); *Prisco v. Forest Villas Condominium Apts., Inc.*, 847 So. 2d 1012 (Fla. Dist. Ct. App. 2003) (where association, which allowed cats but not dogs, despite prohibition in declarations against pets other than fish or birds, selectively enforced declarations, resident who was prohibited from keeping her dog was entitled to raise affirmative defense of selective enforcement). However, the Association's insertion of a clause that tries to defeat this argument by expressly stating that inconsistent enforcement of the pet rule cannot be used as a defense to enforcement against the aggrieved homeowner, might override a selective enforcement claim. *But see Chateau Village North Condominium Ass'n v. Jordan*, 643 P.2d 791 (Colo. Ct. App. 1982) (otherwise facially valid pet restriction that gave board discretion to permit pets on *ad hoc* basis deemed unenforceable when board refused to exercise its discretion by instead imposing blanket prohibition).

D.   EMOTIONAL SUPPORT ANIMALS AND SERVICE ANIMALS

Not all animals receive the same homecoming. Those whose owners suffer from qualifying disabling mental or physical conditions enjoy tenancy by proxy. Federal and many state laws confer upon such nonhuman animal servants rights of cohabitation as if they were live-in nursing assistants. Aware of these laws, management companies and landlords use selective language to differentiate mere "pets" from "service animals" or "emotional support animals." For while all labels may describe the same individual animal, the last two possess independent legal significance that grant access to the domicile that the first one does not (except in Section 8 housing), at least as a matter of law. The broadest and most permissive access comes to those taking corporeal form as an "emotional support animal," for the disabled handler need only prove a diagnosable emotional affliction mitigated by the animal's innate quality: no training is necessary. By definition, all mental health service animals are emotional support animals. The inverse is not always true. Individualized training sets apart the service animal from all peers, performing inculcated tasks or functions that ameliorate the disabling condition beyond just being present and through training that sets apart the animal from an ordinary animal companion. Such drills may prove taxing and costly to handler and animal alike, but they open doors to locations other than the owner's abode.

In 1973, Congress enacted the Rehabilitation Act of 1973, 29 U.S.C. § 701 et seq. to "empower individuals with disabilities to maximize employment, economic self sufficiency, independence, and inclusion and integration into society . . . [and] to ensure that the Federal Government plays a leadership role in promoting the employment of individuals with disabilities, especially individuals with significant disabilities, and in assisting States and providers of services in fulfilling the aspirations of such individuals with disabilities for meaningful and gainful employment and independent living." 29 U.S.C. § 701(b) (1–2).

In *Crossroads Apartments Assoc. v. LeBoo*, 152 Misc. 2d 830 (N.Y. City Ct. 1991), a matter of first impression, the court concluded that Kenneth LeBoo could invoke § 504 of the Rehabilitation Act of 1973, 29 U.S.C. § 794, because the landlord accepted federal funds under Section 8 of the Housing Act of 1937, 42 U.S.C. § 1437f, notwithstanding New York's position that a "no-pet clause" was enforceable, even selectively. Finding him to be a "handicapped person" due to mental illness, and that he was an "otherwise qualified person for tenancy except for the pet," the court nonetheless refused to grant either of the cross-motions for summary judgment as to liability under the Rehabilitation Act, given the factual question of whether Mr. LeBoo's disability made the cat necessary to his use and enjoyment of the apartment. The tenant introduced affidavits from his treating psychiatrist, his clinical social worker, and a certified pet-assisted therapist, confirming the benefits received from the cat in helping him cope with day-to-day mental illness. Crossroads countered with a psychiatrist claiming "no significant clinical evidence that the cat is necessary or required for LeBoo to be able to fully use and enjoy his apartment," adding that he filled a prescription for Prozac at about the time he acquired the cat, so the drug, not the cat, should be credited with mitigation of disability. For another reason, the court refused summary judgment: letting LeBoo keep the cat might place "undue financial and administrative burdens" on Crossroads, including health problems for other tenants.

Until 1988, the protections of the Rehabilitation Act only applied to federally funded or operated housing projects; with passage of the 1988 amendments to the Civil Rights Act of 1968 (also known as the Fair Housing Act), which sought to "[p]rovide, within constitutional limitations, for fair housing throughout the United States," 42 U.S.C. § 3601, antidiscrimination provisions based on disability and use of a service animal or guide applied to almost[8] every other landlord. Two years later, the Americans with Disabilities Act of 1990, 42 U.S.C. § 12101 et seq. nationally mandated the comprehensive elimination of discrimination against individuals with disabilities complete with enforceable standards, including in housing.

1. Fair Housing Act

The Civil Rights Act of 1968, P.L. 90-284, 82 Stat. 73, 42 U.S.C. § 3601-3619, is also known as the Fair Housing Act, and served to extend the protections of the Civil Rights Act of 1964, P.L. 88-352, 78 Stat. 241. The Fair Housing Act makes it unlawful to discriminate against any person in the terms, conditions, or privileges of rental of a dwelling, or in the provision of services or facilities in connection with such dwelling, due to a person's handicap. 42 U.S.C. § 34604(f)(2)(A). Failing to reasonably accommodate an emotional support animal as an exception to rules, policies, practices, or services, when such accommodation is necessary to afford the handicapped person equal opportunity to use and enjoyment of a dwelling violates 42 U.S.C. § 3604(f)(2)(A). The FHA defines "handicap," or disability, as "a physical or mental impairment which substantially limits one or more of such person's major life activities." 42 U.S.C. § 3602(h)(1). "Major life activities" mean functions such as caring for oneself, performing manual tasks, walking, seeing, hearing, speaking, breathing, learning and working. 24 CFR 100.201(b). This list is illustrative, not exhaustive. Indeed, at least one circuit has also found that sleeping and thinking are major life activities. *Head v. Glacier Northwest, Inc.*, 413 F. 3d 1053, 1060 (9th Cir. 2005).

To prevail on a reasonable accommodation claim under the FHA, the plaintiff "must prove the following: (1) that she is handicapped under 42 U.S.C. § 3602(h); (2) that the Defendants knew or should reasonably be expected to know of the handicap; (3) that accommodation of the handicap may be necessary to afford her an equal opportunity to use and enjoy the dwelling; (4) that the accommodation is reasonable; and (5) that Defendants refused to make the requested accommodation." *Dubois v. Ass'n of Apt. Owners*, 453 F. 3d 1175, 1179 (9th Cir. 2006). Notably, unlike disparate treatment claims, "Denial of reasonable accommodation claims do not require that the Plaintiff show intent." *Howard v. Gutierrez*, 405 F. Supp. 2d 13, 15 (D.D.C. 2005). "[T]he plaintiff need only show that an accommodation 'seems reasonable on its face, i.e., ordinarily or in the run of cases.' Once the plaintiff has made this showing, the burden shifts to the defendant to demonstrate that the accommodation would cause undue hardship in the particular circumstances." *Giebeler v. M&B Assocs.*, 343 F. 3d 1143, 1156 (9th Cir. 2003) (citation omitted).

The burdens on defendants are balanced against the benefits to plaintiffs by any accommodation. *See Groner v. Golden Gate Gardens Apartments*, 250 F. 3d 1039, 1041 (6th Cir. 2001). In the Ninth Circuit, the interactive process is mandatory. *Zivkovic v. S. Cal. Edison Co.*, 302 F. 3d 1080, 1089 (9th Cir. 2002). Indeed, it is

---

[8] For instance, the FHA does not apply to "Mrs. Murphy" or the granny flat, i.e., a landlord who owns a building with four or fewer units, provided she resides in one of them, does not own more than three single-family homes, does not use a real estate agent or employ any discriminatory advertising or notices, and is not in the business of selling or renting dwellings. 42 U.S.C. § 3604(b) (1–2).

essential to achieving the goals of anti-discrimination laws protecting persons with disabilities. Where a landlord or homeowners association takes a zero-tolerance policy toward certain breeds, for example, an accommodation short of outright removal may be appropriately demanded if the subject animal presents no risk of harm.

In 2008, the United States Department of Housing and Urban Development ("HUD")[9] enacted a clarifying Final Rule titled, "Pet Ownership for the Elderly and Persons with Disabilities." 73 FR 63834 (Oct. 27, 2008). It provided that untrained animal companions who by mere presence ameliorate disabling conditions must be accommodated under the FHA. This publication does an excellent job setting the parameters of access and protection furnished by the FHA and ADA. For instance, it responds to the comment, "Proposed elimination of training component is inconsistent with the regulations implementing the Americans with Disabilities Act" as follows:

> *HUD Response:* . . . There is a valid distinction between the functions animals provide to persons with disabilities in the public arena, i.e., performing tasks enabling individuals to use public services and public accommodations, as compared to how an assistance animal might be used in the home. For example, emotional support animals provide very private functions for persons with mental and emotional disabilities. Specifically, emotional support animals by their very nature, and without training, may relieve depression and anxiety, and help reduce stress-induced pain in persons with certain medical conditions affected by stress. Conversely, persons with disabilities who use emotional support animals may not need to take them into public spaces covered by the ADA.

This Rule has been recently relied upon by federal courts, who grant considerable deference to HUD interpretations of the FHA. HUD's guidance contained in the commentary to the 2008 final rule reflects HUD's fair housing enforcement stance on emotional support and service animals, and at least one federal court has found HUD's guidance persuasive, holding that animals for disabilities in housing need not be trained. Moreover, HUD and DOH are actively pursuing enforcement actions based on this position. *See Overlook Mutual Homes, Inc. v. Spencer*, 666 F. Supp. 2d 850, 859–60 (S.D. Ohio, 2009); *U.S. v. Kenna Homes Cooperative Corp.*, 557 S.E.2d 787 (W. Va. 2001) (consent decree agreeing to permit disabled residents to have service or emotional support animals); *Sak v. City of Aurelia*, 832 F. Supp. 2d 1026 (N.D. Iowa 2011) (preliminary injunction granted against city attempting to enforce a breed ban against a service pit bull, invoking ADA principles).

In 2010, the federal government amended the regulatory preamble to Title II of the ADA, explaining that law's relationship to other laws, such as the FHA and the Air Carrier Access Act, stating, "emotional support animals that do not qualify as service animals under the Department's title II regulation may nonetheless qualify

---

[9] Federally funded rental housing for the elderly and disabled must permit "common household pets" subject to reasonable rules, and without impairing the right of landlords to remove those who constitute a nuisance or threat to health and safety of other occupants or persons in the housing community. 12 U.S.C. § 1701(r)(1). See also 24 CFR 5.350–.380 for regulations concerning pet rule violation procedures, rulemaking, pet protection, and lease provisions.

as permitted reasonable accommodations for persons with disabilities under the FH Act and the ACAA." Preamble to Title II of the ADA, Amended Regulations, *Relationship to Other Laws* (Sept. 15, 2010).

Landlords may test bald assertions of disability but in most cases cannot demand actual medical records or engage in overly invasive inquiry. Further, the investigative quest must keep sensitive medical information confidential. See the USDOJ-HUD Joint Statement on Reasonable Accommodation (May 17, 2004) (http://www.hud.gov/offices/fheo/library/huddojstatement.pdf), which restricts the landlord to asking for information necessary to verify that the plaintiff satisfies the definition of disability, that articulates the needed accommodation, and shows the relationship between both.

Hypothetical: A 73-year-old widow named Tabatha Imwinkelreid resides with her two neutered and declawed male service felines named Smokey (age 7) and Sammy (age 11). Tabatha was diagnosed with Type II diabetes in 1993, hypertension in or about 1999, and hypercholesterolemia several years ago. As further evidence of her compromised physical condition, in 1999, she had a cardiac stent placed. Today she takes the following medications: Lisinopril 20 mg and Hydrocholorthiazide 25mg for hypertension; Glyburide 10 mg BID, Metformin 1000 units BID, and insulin for her diabetes; and Simvastatin 40 mg for hypercholesterolemia. Her diabetic condition frequently causes her, sometimes up to three times a night, to check her blood sugar levels and avoid falling into a diabetic coma. As a result of these long-term physical disabilities, she also suffers secondary mental disabilities in the form of situational stress reaction and anxiety, including panic attacks, as noted by her physician, Dr. Jacobs. These anxiety-producing situations recur with some frequency.

For example, Tabatha's blood sugar plummets while sleeping. She is awakened by her cats, Sammy and Smokey, who jump on her bed and rouse her in response to her jeopardized health status. Entering a dissociative fog, hardly able to see and shaking appreciably, her condition progresses to panic until she is able to hold her cats close, stroking them, using them as a focal point to reduce or stall the anxiety and normalize her sensorium. This allows her to recognize and take immediate steps to rectify the hypoglycemia. As a result, her cats assist her both physically and mentally.

Panic reactions are also neutralized by Sammy and Smokey when she is seized with fear that her stent may close or that her high blood pressure will cause a cardiac event. Her cats sense her anxiety and respond, permitting her to hold them tight, maintain tactile contact, thereby relieving her distress. Finally, due to her bona fide cardiovascular disability, Tabatha relies upon her cats to reduce heart rate and blood pressure by stroking, holding, massaging, preening, grooming, and communicating with one another. The physiological benefits of pet-assisted therapy on hypertension and other disabilities have been well-documented. *See, e.g.*, Cole et al., *Animal-Assisted Therapy in Patients Hospitalized with Heart Failure*, 16 AM. J. CRITICAL CARE 575–85 (2007) and 54 scientific journal references; M. L. Morrison, *Health Benefits of Animal-Assisted Interventions*, 12(1) COMP. HEALTH PRACTICE REV. 51–62 (2007); K. Allen, *Are Pets a Healthy Pleasure? The Influence of Pets on Blood Pressure*, 12(6) CURRENT DIRECTIONS IN PSYCHOLOGICAL SCIENCE 236–39 (2003);

Allen, Shykoff et al., *Pet Ownership, but Not ACE Inhibitor Therapy, Blunts Home Blood Pressure Responses to Mental Stress*, 38 HYPERTENSION 815 (2001). Stress is a risk indicator for diabetic shock. So, in addition to managing her hypertension, Sammy and Smokey provide a prophylactic benefit to forestall hypoglycemic unawareness and help stabilize her blood sugar level.

Tabatha purchased a unit (and share) within Arbor Park Estates, a rare community development corporate form known as a cooperative. Para. 5.14 of the Stock Subscription Agreement provides that the Shareholder agrees to abide by the house rule "to only keep such animals as are approved by the Corporation." Further, on Feb. 13, 1989, long before she bought the unit, the Board adopted a phase-out of "pets." Other long-term shareholders replaced their companion animals in clear violation of the 1989 phase-out, yet the Board took no action. Before moving in, Tabatha knew of Para. 5.14, but did not seek approval to reside with Smokey and Sammy. About four weeks after commencing residency, nosy neighbors saw her quiet cats peering out her kitchen window. They had not disturbed any other shareholder, as might be the case with a barking or vicious dog, or one whose feces are not collected on common grounds.

In response to the Board telling Tabatha to remove Smokey and Sammy, she submitted a letter from her physician, Dr. Jacobs, who noted that Tabatha "needs her cats for her health" and they "provide important therapy for her" in addressing her "situational stress reaction" and "anxiety." Further, Tabatha noted having these cats for years preceding her purchase of a share, and that they were "fixed and declawed," "never go outside," and they "are important to my health." In response to this letter, the Board President wrote Tabatha, noting a split among the Board and an intention to raise the question of amending the by-laws at the next Annual Shareholders meeting. Tabatha attended, but at no point was the question of amending the animal policy put to a vote, much less discussed, as promised.

Perhaps this is because the Board changed its mind, without explanation, refusing to "deviate from the bi-laws or amended bi-laws," and giving Tabatha two months to relocate her cats or move. Within her rights, she refused to vacate or rehome Sammy and Smokey. Then came a *Notice to Comply or Vacate* from the cooperative's law firm.

While the FHA would undoubtedly deem Smokey and Sammy emotional support animals in the residential context, if they ventured outside her unit and accompanied her to a local hotel, would they also qualify as service animals, garnering protection under the ADA?

Arguably, by providing individualized training to each cat through positive reinforcement of desired behaviors — specifically, rewarding her cats with attention and stroking when they sense her imminent and endangering condition, alert her by awakening, and respond to the disabling condition by allowing her to reassociate to reality and take necessary steps to avert a potentially fatal adverse health event — Tabatha converted Smokey and Sammy into service felines. They also assisted her in managing the secondary emotionally disabling sequelae. Note that the cats do not routinely sleep with Tabatha. Rather, they awaken her only when she is suffering from hypoglycemia. They come to her when they observe her dissociating and panicking — whether during waking hours (when consciously fearing a cardiac event) or when sleeping (as her blood sugar reaches critically low levels and she is struggling to bring those subconscious alerts to present consciousness).

Instead of hiding, scratching, or biting Tabatha, Sammy and Smokey allow her to rely upon them when she seeks their contact, no differently than a medical appliance or prescription medication taken as needed to manage a disabling health condition. Far from regarding their conduct as misbehavior, for which the cats would be disciplined (e.g., kicked off the bed, shooed away, sprayed with a water bottle, scared), she encourages the conduct. Over time, Sammy and Smokey learned to pay attention and respond to her anticipatory cues that precede critical and disabling physical and mental events. This is also known in animal behavioral learning theory (also known as the field of ethology) as "backchaining," a training process facilitated by Tabatha. A certified applied animal behaviorist was consulted to interview Tabatha and review the medical history. In her opinion, Sammy and Smokey were *bona fide* service and emotional support cats for they were trained in a way that set them apart from ordinary felines.

Some contend that species other than dogs, particularly cats, cannot be trained; alternatively, they state that teaching a cat to be loving does not qualify as the type of training contemplated by federal law, for it does not set the subject animal apart from an "ordinary pet." But here the practitioner should examine with greater scrutiny the distinction between ordinary dogs and ordinary cats. Certain expectations attend the notion of "training" a dog. Organizations such as the Association of Professional Dog Trainers (APDT) and thousands of certified and noncertified "dog trainers" bear witness to the prevalence of such endeavor, providing a benchmark by which to legally compare non-service dog training against service dog training. But except for a few persistent individuals who showcase their cat's clicker-trained marvels of agility on YouTube, no comparable institution of cat training exists. Petsmart and Petco advertise dog obedience training and seek to fill enrollment in their puppy classes, but they do not similarly offer training for cats. And aside from Jackson Galaxy, of Animal Planet's *My Cat From Hell*, who focuses on environmental variables and training distraught owners, hiring cat behaviorists is the exception, not the rule, for millions of cat lovers. This does not mean cats are not trained, for federal law does not require proof of formalized or professional training, nor certification by any governmental or nongovernmental entity.

It does mean, however, that cats are not ordinarily trained in the typical sense of the term (i.e., canine-centric). Indeed, *any* training of cats would set them apart from the ordinary cat. Training has not been defined in any great detail, but there are several recognized approaches that seek to maximize operant conditioning, whether through positive reinforcement or deterrent punishment. Of course, the 2011 amendment to the ADA moots this inquiry for no cat (at least under federal law) may boast "service animal" credentials.

2.   State Antidiscrimination Laws

Various tiers of antidiscrimination regulation apply to rental housing disputes. Consider, for example, the Iowa Civil Rights Act of 1965 ("ICRA"), Ch. 216 Iowa Code, and IC § 216.8A(3)(c)(2) (2005), which provide that landlords must make reasonable accommodations to "afford the person equal opportunity to use and enjoy a dwelling." A woman previously victimized by domestic violence, who obtained a Doberman for protection, invoked the ICRA in *State ex rel. Henderson v. Des Moines Municipal Housing Agency*, 791 N.W.2d 710 (Iowa Ct. App. 2010). Carol Henderson leased a duplex unit with her daughter. The pet policy permitted one, under-20 pound animal subject to a permit granted by the Agency. Months after commencing tenancy, her duplex faced two attempted break-ins. Ms. Henderson hid until the police arrived. The incident dredged up memories of abuse by her ex-husband and prompted her to obtain a Doberman Pinscher named Sam. Her daughter acquired a dog named Otis. Both dogs weighed more than 90 pounds. Three years later, the Agency gave Henderson a 14-day notice to comply or vacate for violating the pet policy. She identified Sam and Otis as her service animals, for they tempered her traumatic distress and allowed her to leave the unit to work or simply be outside. She also obtained a letter from her physician stating that she needed the dogs "for safety reasons and protections secondary to PTSD." The matter escalated with the Agency rejecting her contention that the dogs met the definition of service animal and threatening her with eviction. Another physician and the Iowa Division of Persons with Disabilities came to her aid. Dr. Lundberg stated that her patient had "self trained a service dog to assist her with tasks around the home such as turning on the lights when she enters a room and retrieving her light instrument as well as acknowledging suspicious persons on the property. She has had one circumstance already in which her service dog has chased away a potential offender." The Agency nonetheless rejected the request for a reasonable accommodation, and then filed a forcible entry and detainer action.

Settling with the agency, Henderson agreed to remove Otis and the City worked to expedite her Section 8 housing application so she could avoid an eviction on her record, which would render her homeless and prevent her from obtaining future public housing. The state then sued the Agency for violation of Henderson's civil rights under Ch. 216 IC. The district court granted summary judgment to the Agency, though the Court of Appeals reversed, stating that the trial court "improperly considered whether Henderson met the requirements of the pet policy given that she was requesting a waiver of that pet policy as a reasonable accommodation for her disability," and that "reasonable minds could differ as to whether Henderson's requested accommodation of a service animal was reasonable in light of her claimed mental illness." On remand, the matter was tried to a jury. However, the trial court directed verdict for the defendants. The second appeal again favored Henderson. Though brought under the Iowa Code, the court recognized the parallels to the FHA and ADA and relied upon federal law interpretations. Its recitation of legal standards and persuasive precedents from other jurisdictions offer the reader a helpful overview of the body of emotional support and service animal antidiscrimination law in America. After detailed analysis, the appellate court remanded for a new trial to allow the jury to resolve the genuine issues of material fact as to whether the requested accommodation was reasonable and necessary; Henderson's psychiatric impairment entitled her to protection; and whether she waived her claim by settling the unlawful detainer matter and removing Sam from the premises.

E.   EVICTION BASED ON NUISANCE ANIMAL

A landlord who does not implement or enforce a "no pets" clause nonetheless reserves the right to address socially inappropriate behavior by curtailing tenancy. When nonhuman tenants unreasonably disturb neighboring residents — such as overly exuberant early morning and late night vocalizations, odoriferous emissions that foul common areas, and vicious interludes — landlords may feel compelled to evict them (and their human guardians) to quell discord and avoid liability. *See Starrett City Inc. v. Cabrera*, 18 Misc.3d 1115(A), 856 N.Y.S.2d 503 (Civ. Ct. New York County 2008) (summary holdover proceeding authorizing eviction of tenant for harboring dog in violation of lease and for creating nuisance from constant barking); *Brodcom West Development Co. v. Best*, 23 Misc.3d 1140(A), 889 N.Y.S.2d 881 (Civ. Ct. New York County 2009) (dog who constantly barks, roams public areas unleashed and urinates and defecates in public areas in building constitutes nuisance, warranting eviction if dog not permanently removed in ten days); *Brolin v. Bauers*, 712 N.W.2d 87 (Wis. Ct. App. 2006) (failure to remove feces from front yard and quieting dog to avoid disturbing other tenants, among other non-animal related nuisance conduct, furnished good cause for eviction).

While ordinarily canines receive the largest share of notices to leave or timely comply with lease terms seeking to stem nuisances, cats also have provoked judicial inquiry. In *Lemle v. Adjamine*, 2003 N.Y. Misc. LEXIS 228 (Mar. 21, 2003), odors wafting through the common area caused by the Lemles' numerous cats did not rise to the level of objectionable nuisance, based on a fair interpretation of record evidence. On the other hand, *Morningside Housing Assoc. v. Barinas*, 819 N.Y.S.2d 849 (2006), upheld the landlord giving the tenant 20 days to permanently remove cats from the apartment premises, refusing to disturb the trial court's on-site determination that the tenant committed nuisance by harboring a "cadre of cats" who caused "nauseating" and "offensive" odors in the premises. A parasitic landlord-tenant action, to be sure, consider the case of nuisance fleas, discussed by *Boice v. Emshoff*, 1998 Ohio App. LEXIS 6015 (Dec. 3, 1998). Though after the physical departure of the tenant and her cat, Emshoff left behind fleas that had taken up residence on Emshoff's cat. Accordingly, the court found that Emshoff constructively occupied the house for at least another month until they were exterminated. As a result, Emshoff had to pay Boice additional rent.

A must-read case, one of the few landlord-tenant disputes concerning avians, is the New Jersey case of *K.G.O. Construction Co. v. King*, 1934 N.J. Misc. LEXIS 6 (Feb. 23, 1934). King refused to pay the landlord for rent due on an unexpired lease when vacating the premises "on account of the screechiness and annoying loquacity of a parrot owned and kept by another tenant adjoining his apartment which disturbed the peace and quiet of his home life," even though the lease contained a clause forbidding domesticated animals. King argued that KGO had a duty to evict the neighbor or neighbor's parrot to suppress the annoyance and its failure to do so constituted a constructive eviction. The landlord contended that a bird is not a "domesticated animal" subject to the operative clause and that the clause did not inure to the benefit of all other tenants. Having found that the parrot "was very screechy, querulous, and extremely loquacious, though not given to indulging in profane or indecent language," the court found him "ill-mannered, in disrupting the train of thought of the card players, and that when the parrot attempted continuously to speak above the voices of the players themselves, he brought himself within the realm of judicial censure." Humor aside, the court found for the plaintiff, holding that it was not responsible for the acts of a third-party tenant, and that the defendant was not a third-party beneficiary of the lease provision concerning domesticated animals.

Nuisance behavior of sufficient quality may even warrant such extreme remedy as removal of emotional support and service animals. The "direct threat" exception to the general prohibition against discrimination in the sale or rental of housing, 42 U.S.C. § 3604(f)(9), states "Nothing in this subsection requires that a dwelling be made available to an individual whose tenancy would constitute a direct threat to the safety of other individuals or whose tenancy would result in substantial physical damage to the property of others." The "direct threat" assessment, however, must be based on an individualized assessment that relies on objective evidence about the specific animal's conduct — *not* mere speculation about the harm or damage the animal might cause and *not* based on evidence of harm or damage other animals have caused. John Trasvina, *Service Animals and Assistance Animals for People with Disabilities in Housing and HUD-Funded Programs*, FHEO-2013-01 (Apr. 25, 2013), at 3. Accordingly, a service or emotional support animal found potentially dangerous, dangerous, or vicious under local or state law might lose its federal antidiscrimination protection and permit the landlord to withdraw an earlier reasonable accommodation.

F. HOTELS AND MOTELS

The FHA does not apply to hotels and motels lodging transient guests. *But see Red Bull Assoc. v. Best Western Intern, Inc.*, 686 F. Supp. 447 (S.D.N.Y. 1988), *aff'd*, 862 F.2d 963 (2d Cir. 1988) (FHA assumed to apply to motel providing long-term lodging to homeless persons). However, the ADA does cover "places of lodging," and thus a "place of public accommodation." ADA TAM § III-1.2000. Apartments and condominium units are not "public accommodations" under the ADA. *Indep. Housing Services of San Francisco v. Fillmore Center Assoc.*, 840 F. Supp. 1328 (N.D. Cal.1993). Accordingly, hotels and motels typically must permit guests to bring their service animals at no additional charge. Emotional support animals do not enjoy the same pass. Nor do companion animals. Yet many chains promote the amenity of pet-friendly accommodations. Nightly turndown and daily housekeeping service requires access to the room sometimes more than once a day, a distinct feature of transient lodging not offered in rented dwellings; indeed, most landlord-tenant laws prohibit entry without 48 hours' notice. While guests may consent to more or less frequent access by the innkeeper or staff, a question emerges as to what liability the hotel faces should the guest's companion animal escape or suffer grievous harm while on premises.

Hypothetical: The Cricket Inn advertises a welcoming atmosphere to all patrons, including the four-legged variety. This prompted the Jenkins family to book a room for an extended stay of one week while their house was undergoing renovation. They brought Tiny, their eight-year-old spayed female Yorkshire Terrier with them. As they checked in, a customer service representative discussed the pet policy. Mrs. Jenkins explained that they would leave Tiny in the room during the day and to suspend maid service until explicitly requested. During this discussion, she held Tiny, who weighed all of two pounds. When set down, her back rose no more than six inches off the floor. She was just too small to even put down outside.

Before checking her in, the representative handed a *Dog Waiver* to Mrs. Jenkins, stating that she agreed to "release and discharge The Cricket Inn," together with all past and present officers, directors, employees, agents, attorneys, insurers, affiliated companies, successors and assigns, "from all actions, suits, debts, bills, contracts, controversies, agreements, promises, trespasses, damages, judgments, claims and demands whatsoever," but not limited to, any claims relating in any way to her "stay at the Inn relating to the presence of [her] dog on or about the Inn premises or relating to the Inn." Mrs. Jenkins signed, paid the extra pet deposit, and retired to her room.

Monday morning, the Jenkinses briefly left Tiny in the room as they visited with the contractor to observe what progress had been made at their residence. When they returned about an hour later, Tiny, who had a happy (but not overly excited) affect, was overwrought to the point she seemed abnormally stimulated. She would not calm down despite the Jenkinses' best efforts. Thinking she had fleas, they rushed her to a groomer for a bath. Her hyper state prevented the staff from being able to work on her, so the Jenkinses next took her to the veterinarian. Benadryl, antianxiety medication, and flea treatment did not quiet her. The next stop took Tiny to the emergency hospital, where they tested her blood and urine and found her positive for methamphetamine. After two days on IV fluids and in an oxygen chamber, Tiny died.

As the Jenkinses were responsible adults and not drug users (whether illegal or prescribed, as in the case of Ritalin or Adderall, which contain amphetamine), they quickly identified the Inn as the only plausible point source — more particularly, the filthy floor of their room. They found plenty of debris, including white dust, littered beneath the bed and couch and it appeared as though it had not been vacuumed in over a year. They also found a single Advil tablet. When confronted with Tiny's death, the Inn denied fault and, adding to the burden, charged the Jenkinses despite their protest.

Is the Inn Liable for Tiny's Death?

Certainly, the Jenkinses had a contractual right to a safe, private room. Unrestricted access to controlled substances that could kill toddlers and nonhuman animals, like methamphetamine, do not constitute safe accommodations. Innkeepers owe guests the duty to exercise reasonable care to protect them from injury at the hands of the innkeeper (and innkeeper's agents) and fellow guests, limited to the dangers foreseeable to the innkeeper. An oft-reported example involves one guest using a firearm to kill or maim another. *See Miller v. Staton*, 365 P.2d 333 (Wash. 1961); *Bernethy v. Walt Failor's, Inc.*, 653 P.2d 280 (Wash. 1982). In Tiny's case, one guest's *drugs* killed another.

Whether in crystalline or tablet form, manufactured illegally or prescribed as Desoxyn, the Inn arguably had a duty to ensure that no such hazard remained after the last patron in that room checked out. Indeed, the same obligation would exist in the case of over-the-counter drugs that carry significant risk to animals, such as in the instance of acetaminophen toxicosis. Any competent and thoughtful hotelier advertising for guests to stay with their companion dogs and cats, whose mouths will be no more than inches or a few feet off the floor at any time and whose propensity to sniff, root, and ingest most anything at ground level is common knowledge, will foresee the substantial peril to which they place their patrons by failure to remove all latent hazards from under beds, under the skirt or apron of a chair, and in areas obscured from view by those who do not see the world from boxspring-height.

On the other hand, much may depend on whether it was forseeable that meth addicts were commonly staying and using at the Inn. Admittedly, the advent of pet-friendly hotels is new, so case law involving the standard of care to pets is likely nonexistent. What steps might you take to explore foreseeability? A public records request to local law enforcement could reveal multiple 911 calls and police contacts involving tenants possessing and trafficking methamphetamine, and other drug-related crimes.

At common law, innkeeper are *insurers* (i.e., strictly liable) for property kept in the rooms of their patrons. They may avoid liability by strictly complying with the statute that pertains to theft or loss of items from the room. *See Featherstone v. Dessert*, 22 P.2d 1050, 1052–1053 (Wash. 1933); *Goodwin v. Georgian Hotel Co.*, 84 P.2d 681 (Wash. 1938). Note that this premises liability theory is even more demanding than the duties owed by possessors of land to business invitees (i.e., discover, defuse, and warn of, latent dangerous conditions). Indubitably, metham-phetamines hidden from the view of the average patron (i.e., one who does not first determine whether the bed sits on a pedestal and, second, if not, looks underneath to determine what nefarious objects may thereunder lie) are "latent" and "danger-ous." Accordingly, the Inn might have been liable for Tiny's death.

What statutes, if any, apply to the death of Tiny?

In Washington, look at RCW § 19.48.030 and RCW § 19.48.070. They state:

§ 19.48.030. Liability for loss of valuables when safe or vault furnished — Limitation.

Whenever the proprietor, keeper, owner, operator, lessee, or manager of any hotel, lodging house or inn shall provide a safe or vault for the safekeeping of any money, bank notes, jewelry, precious stones, ornaments, railroad mileage books or tickets, negotiable securities or other valuable papers, bullion, or other valuable property of small compass belonging to the guests, boarders or lodgers of such hotel, lodging house or inn, and shall notify the guests, boarders or lodgers thereof by posting a notice in three or more public and conspicuous places in the office, elevators, public rooms, elevator lobbies, public corridors, halls or entrances, or in the public parlors of such hotel, lodging house or inn, stating the fact that such safe or vault is provided in which such property may be deposited; and if such guests, boarders or lodgers shall neglect to deliver such property to the person in charge of such office, for deposit in the safe or vault, the proprietor, keeper, owner, operator, lessee or manager, whether individual, partnership or corporation, of such hotel, lodging house or inn shall not be liable for any loss or destruction of any such property, or any damage thereto, sustained by such guests, boarders or lodgers, by negligence of such proprietor, keeper, owner, operator, lessee or manager, or his, her, their or its employees, or by fire, theft, burglary, or any other cause whatsoever; but no proprietor, keeper, owner, operator, lessee or manager of any hotel, lodging house or inn, shall be obliged to receive property on deposit for safekeeping exceeding one thousand dollars in value; and if such guests, boarders or lodgers shall deliver such property to the person in charge of said office for deposit in such safe or vault, said proprietor, keeper, owner, operator, lessee, or manager, shall not be liable for the loss or destruction thereof, or damage thereto, sustained by such guests, boarders or lodgers in any such hotel, lodging house, or inn, exceeding the sum of one thousand dollars, notwithstanding said property may be of greater value, unless by special arrangement in writing with such proprietor, keeper, owner, operator, lessee or manager: PROVIDED, HOWEVER, That in case of such deposit of such property, the proprietor, keeper, owner, operator, lessee or manager of such hotel, lodging house, or inn, shall in no event be liable for loss or destruction thereof, or damage thereto, unless caused by the theft or gross negligence of such proprietor, keeper, owner, operator, lessee, or manager, of his, her, their, or its agents, servants or employees.

§ 19.48.070. Liability for loss of baggage and other property — Limitation — Storage — Disposal.

Except as provided for in RCW § 19.48.030, the proprietor, keeper, owner, operator, lessee, or manager, whether individual, partnership, or corporation, of a hotel, lodging house, or inn, shall not be liable for the loss or destruction of, or damage to any personal property brought or sent into such hotel, lodging house, or inn, by or for any of the guests, boarders, or lodgers thereof, unless such loss, destruction, or damage is occasioned by the gross negligence of such proprietor, keeper, owner, operator, lessee, or manager, or his, her, their, or its agents, servants, or employees; but in no event shall such liability exceed the sum of two hundred dollars, unless such proprietor, keeper, owner, operator, lessee, or manager, shall have contracted in writing with such guest, boarder, or lodger to assume a greater liability: PROVIDED, HOWEVER, That in no event shall liability of the proprietor, keeper, owner, operator, lessee, or manager, or his, her, their, or its agents, servants or employees, of a hotel, lodging house, or inn exceed the following: For a guest, boarder, or lodger, paying twenty-five cents per day, for lodging, or for any person who is not a guest, boarder, or lodger, the liability for loss, destruction, or damage, shall not exceed the sum of fifty dollars for a trunk and contents, ten dollars for a suitcase or valise and contents, five dollars for a box, bundle, or package, and ten dollars for wearing apparel or miscellaneous effects. For a guest, boarder, or lodger, paying fifty cents a day for lodging, the liability for loss, destruction, or damage shall not exceed seventy-five dollars for a trunk and contents, twenty dollars for a suitcase or valise and contents, ten dollars for a box, bundle, or package and contents, and twenty dollars for wearing apparel and miscellaneous effects. For a guest, boarder, or lodger paying more than fifty cents per day for lodging, the liability for loss, destruction, or damage shall not exceed one hundred fifty dollars for a trunk and contents, fifty dollars for a suitcase or valise and contents, ten dollars for a box, bundle, or package and contents, and fifty dollars for wearing apparel and miscellaneous effects, unless in such case such proprietor, keeper, owner, operator, lessee, or manager of such hotel, lodging house, or inn, shall have consented in writing to assume a greater liability: AND PROVIDED FURTHER, Whenever any person shall suffer his or her baggage or property to remain in any hotel, lodging house, or inn, after leaving the same as a guest, boarder, or lodger, and after the relation of guest, boarder, or lodger between such person and the proprietor, keeper, owner, operator, lessee, or manager of such hotel, lodging house, or inn, has ceased, or shall forward or deliver the same to such hotel, lodging house, or inn, before, or without, becoming a guest, boarder, or lodger thereof, and the same shall be received into such hotel, lodging house, or inn, the liability of such proprietor, keeper, owner, operator, lessee, or manager thereof shall in no event exceed the sum of one hundred dollars, and such proprietor, keeper, owner, operator, lessee, or manager, may at his, her, their or its option, hold such baggage or property at the risk of such owner thereof; and when any baggage or property has been kept or stored by such hotel, lodging house, or inn, for six months after such relation of guest, boarder, or lodger has ceased, or when such relation does not exist, after six months from the receipt of such baggage or property in such hotel, lodging house, or inn, such proprietor, keeper, owner, operator, lessee, or manager, may, if he, she, they or it so desires, sell the same at public auction in the manner now or hereinafter provided by law for the sale of property to satisfy a hotel keeper's lien, and from the proceeds of such sale pay or reimburse himself or herself the expenses incurred for advertisement and sale, as well as any storage that may have accrued, and any other amounts owing by such person to said hotel, lodging house, or inn: PROVIDED, That when any such baggage or property is received, kept, or stored therein after such relation does not exist, such proprietor, keeper, owner, operator, lessee, or manager, may, if he, she, or it, so desires, deliver the same at any time to a storage or warehouse company for storage, and in such event all responsibility or liability of such hotel, lodging house, or inn, for such baggage or property, or for storage charges thereon, shall thereupon cease and terminate.

RCW § 19.48.030 likely does not apply because the Jenkinses would not be stuffing Tiny in a safe or vault and she was not "money, bank notes, jewelry, precious stones, ornaments, railroad mileage books or tickets, negotiable securities or other valuable papers, bullion, or *other valuable property of small compass*."

However, RCW § 19.48.070 might apply because Tiny was "personal property brought . . . into such . . . inn . . . by . . . guests . . . thereof." Statutory interpretation may be required to divine whether R.C.W. 19.48.070, when first enacted in 1915 and amended through the 1920s, ever intended to include living animals within its ambit. For instance, note that the inn is only statutorily liable for gross negligence up to $150 for "trunk and contents," $50 for "suitcase or valise and contents," $10 for "a box, bundle, or package and contents," and "$50 for "wearing apparel and miscellaneous effects," barring some other contractual agreement to pay more. Tiny was not a trunk, suitcase, valise, box, bundle, package, wearing apparel, or even a miscellaneous effect — though federal law does regard dogs as "effects" for purposes of the Fourth Amendment. The only upshot of RCW § 19.48.070 is that it seems to implicitly prevent innkeepers from disclaiming gross negligence. No statute probably applies to this situation, meaning we return to the contract and standard duties of care.

What about the *dog waiver*? Does it change this analysis?

The release's all-encompassing reach extends to "any claims relating in any way to my stay at the Inn relating to the presence of my dog on or about the Inn premises[.]" Clearly, Tiny ingested toxic substances while present on Inn premises. However, innkeepers, like professional bailees, generally cannot disclaim negligence. In *Wagenblast v. Odessa Sch. Dist. No. 105–157-166J*, 758 P.2d 968, 970 (Wash. 1988), the Supreme Court of Washington held that "an agreement discharging the defendant's performance will not ordinarily be given effect" where the defendant is a "professional bailee" or "innkeeper." *Id.*, citing REST. (2D) TORTS § 496B, cmt. g (1965) and KEETON & DOBBS, PROSSER & KEETON ON TORTS § 68, at 482–83 (5th ed. 1984). Undoubtedly, the Inn is an "innkeeper." Cases cited in *Wagenblast* are instructive, such as *Thomas v. Housing Auth.*, 426 P.2d 836 (Wash. 1967), rendering invalid a lease provision that exculpated the housing authority from injuries caused by the authority's negligence, and *McCutcheon v. United Homes Corp.*, 486 P.2d 1093 (Wash. 1971), invalidating a landlord's exculpatory clause relating to common areas in the multi-family dwelling complex. Aiding the Jenkinses in invalidating the *Dog Waiver* is that the Inn confronted them with a standard adhesion contract of exculpation, making no provision by which they could pay more to obtain protection against negligence; indeed, they paid more yet acquired less protection than common law requires.

The advent of pet-friendly hotels is relatively recent, but chains like Cricket Inn profit by the expanded scope of accommodation. With income, however, comes added responsibility. In failing to warn the Jenkinses of the risk that toxic (and perhaps illicit) items may not have been retrieved by housekeeping from underneath their bed, or to detect and remove those latent items, Inn arguably acted with gross irresponsibility.

Mental anguish is further recoverable for reckless breach of contract based on RESTATEMENT OF CONTRACTS § 341, and RESTATEMENT (2D) OF CONTRACTS § 351, allowing for general damages arising from reckless breach of a contract where it was foreseeable, at the time of executing the contract, that emotional distress would ensue for nonpecuniary reasons. Indeed, contracts of innkeepers with passengers and guests are one of the enumerated examples of the types of contracts that give rise to this element of damage:

> While at first glance section 353 might appear to support the creation of a new theory of recovery, the comments, illustrations and cases cited belie this reading. Comment *a* demonstrates a strong intent to maintain the

traditional focus on types of contracts, not types of breaches. Comment *a* provides:

> In the second exceptional situation, the contract or the breach is of such a kind that serious emotional disturbance was a particularly likely result. Common examples are contracts of carriers and innkeepers with passengers and guests, contracts for the carriage or proper disposition of dead bodies, and contracts for the delivery of messages concerning death. *Breach of such a contract is particularly likely to cause serious emotional disturbance. Breach of other types of contracts, resulting for example in sudden impoverishment or bankruptcy, may by chance cause even more severe emotional disturbance, but, if the contract is not one where this was a particularly likely risk, there is no recovery for such disturbance*

(Emphasis added.) Restatement (Second) of Contracts § 353, at comment *a* (1981).

Gaglidari v. Denny's Restaurants, 815 P.2d 1362, 1371–72 (Wash. 1991).

In the final analysis, assuming the release is rendered unenforceable, the Jenkinses would still have to prove that failing to detect and remove the medication/illicit drug from under the bed was the cause of Tiny's death and further, that such failures showed lack of reasonable care. Not an easy task, for how does one define the standard of hotelier care? Perhaps by scrutinizing trade journals or innkeeper organization customs, particularly those that market to guests with pets. It is unlikely that the Inn's actions rose to the level of gross negligence, willful and wanton misconduct, or recklessness unless the Inn was a known refuge for meth addicts.

G. DISTRESS FOR RENT

At common law, landlords had the right to distrain a tenant's personal belongings for unpaid rent, meaning they could withhold a tenant's personalty to satisfy debts owed. The terms "distrain for rent" and "distress for rent" are used interchangeably. Distrainment also arises in the context of fence damage caused by unruly animals, allowing the injured party to hold the animal as collateral for repair costs. Blackstone commented on this ancient doctrine:

> 'A fifth case in which the law allows a man to be his own avenger, or to minister redress to himself, is that of *distraining* cattle or goods for the nonpayment of rent * * * or distraining another's cattle *damage-feasant*, that is, doing damage or trespassing upon his land. The former intended for the benefit of landlords, to prevent tenants from secreting or withdrawing their effects to his prejudice; the latter arising from the necessity of the thing itself, as it might otherwise be impossible at a future time to ascertain whose cattle they were that committed the trespass or damage.

> 'And first it is necessary to premise that a distress, *districtio*, is the taking a personal chattel out of the possession of the wrong-doer into the custody of the party injured, to procure a satisfaction for the wrong

committed. 1. The most usual injury for which a distress may be taken is that of non-payment of rent. It was observed in the former book that distresses were incident by the common law to every *rent-service*, and by particular reservation to *rent-charges* also * * *. So that now we may lay it down as a universal principle, that a distress may be taken for any kind of rent in arrear; the detaining whereof beyond the day of payment is an injury to him that is entitled to receive it. * * * 4. Another injury for which distresses may be taken is where a man finds beasts of a stranger wandering in his grounds *damage-feasant*; that is, doing him hurt or damage by treading down his grass or the like; in which case the owner of the soil may distrain them till satisfaction be made him for the injury he has thereby sustained. * * *

'Secondly, as to the things which may be distrained, or taken in distress, we may lay it down as a general rule, that all chattels personal are liable to be distrained, unless particularly protected or exempted. Instead therefore of mentioning what things are distrainable, it will be easier to recount those which are not so, with the reason of their particular exemptions. * * * But, generally speaking, whatever goods and chattels the landlord finds upon the premises, whether they in fact belong to the tenant or a stranger, are distrainable by him for rent * * *. There are also other things privileged by the ancient common law; as a man's tools and utensils of his trade, the axe of a carpenter, the books of a scholar, and the like: which are said to be privileged for the sake of the public, because the taking them away would disable the owner from serving the commonwealth in his station. * * *

'In the first place then, all distresses must be made *by day*, unless in the case of *damage feasant*; an exception being there allowed, lest the beasts should escape before they are taken. * * *

'When the distress is thus taken, the next consideration is the disposal of it. For which purpose the things distrained must in the first place be carried to some pound, and there impounded by the taker. * * *'

BLACKSTONE COMMENTARIES, LEWIS ED., Vols. 3–4, p. 1024 (quoted in *Smith v. Chipman*, 348 P.2d 441, 442–43 (Or. 1960)). For an interesting twist on distraint between a landlord and tenant, where the *tenant* distrained the *landlord's* trespassing animals, see *Kelly v. Easton*, 35 Idaho 340 (1922). Statutory distraint for rent laws still exist, though many jurisdictions have curtailed the common law practice. Thus, in most jurisdictions, landlords may not seize a tenant's companion animals as a means of coercing payment.

But consider Pennsylvania's Landlord and Tenant Act of 1951, 68 P.S. Pa. St. Ch. 8. Art. III of the Act expressly permits recovering rent by assumpsit and distress. "Personal property located upon premises occupied by a tenant shall, unless exempted by article four of this act, be subject to distress for any rent reserved and due." 68 P.S. § 250.302. No exemption specifically identifies animals except § 250.404(8), which excludes "cattle or stock taken by the tenant to be fed or cared for on the leased premises for a consideration to be paid by the owner." However, the tenant may claim an exemption for personalty valued up to three hundred dollars (68 P.S. § 250.401) and other express exemptions set forth in § 250.402

(wearing apparel, Bibles, school books, sewing machines and tools of trade, uniforms, arms, ammunition), § 250.403 (property on premises under lease or conditional sale contract subject to a security interest), and § 250.404 (personalty placed in tenant's possession in course of business, held for another in course of trade, as agent or consignee, sold before distress to a bona fide purchaser, and others listed). But what of a highly valuable domesticated animal such as a macaw, French Bulldog, or savannah cat worth more than three hundred dollars?

In *McLain v. Willey*, 1910 Del. LEXIS 93 (Dec. 13, 1910), tenant John E. McLain sued his former landlord Jennie E. Cornelius to recover muskrat pelts caught on the marsh lands leased to Mr. McLain. Cornelius contended that she rented farm land to McLain for two years as part of a tenancy on shares, meaning that he would pay her one-half of all grain and fruit crops raised on the farm, one-half of all pelts of muskrats taken from that land, and one-half of all muskrat flesh if she furnished him the traps. When McLain fell into arrears, she had Willey, as bailiff, seize the pelts. McLain denied such agreement, insisting that he was permitted to save all muskrats for himself and that they could not seize them in satisfaction of any debt owed. In charging the jury, the court sided with McLain, holding that "we do not think that muskrats are property, within the meaning of the law, out of which rent can be recovered, or for which a distress will lie." Because the muskrats were free to roam throughout Cornelius's riparian lands as *ferae naturae*, and did not come out of her land (similar to crops seeded and grown exclusively on her property), and because her rights were "incorporeal and merely appurtenant to the land," any rights in hunting them were "a mere license, for which a distress does not lie." The jury held for plaintiff, awarding him six cents. While *McLain* refused to regard deceased *wild* animals as proper subjects for distraint, it did not address *domesticated* animals.

In *Weber v. Vernon*, 1899 Del. LEXIS 47 (Dec. 11, 1899), landlord Edgar Vernon distrained his tenant Frederick Weber's dairy cows for unpaid rent. Weber claimed that Vernon did so unreasonably and maliciously, causing injury to the bovines. The jury found for Weber in the sum of $66.77, following the court's charge that distraint for rent cannot occur until it is due, and that attachment of personalty for rent not yet due turns on the statutory remedy requiring the landlord to swear out an affidavit believing that he has good grounds to believe the tenant intends to remove his effects from the county or dispose of same to defeat distress for rent. The court added that if no such good grounds truly existed, the jury could infer malice. Further, even if distraint were permitted, the law requires a landlord to use reasonable care in safekeeping the animals, as described at 538:

> A person taking and holding the goods as a distress is bound to use such reasonable care as a prudent and reasonable man would use in regard to his own property of like character. If the property be cattle and horses, they should be fed and watered, and be given such attention as may be required to keep them in as good condition as when distrained; but the person taking and holding goods distrained is not bound to exercise extraordinary care of them. If milch cows be distrained, they should be milked, as without this they would suffer, and be injured. If the person holding cows so distrained uses or sells the milk, he is liable for its value, less the cost and value of the milking, keeping, feeding, and care of the animals. As a general rule, a

person taking or holding goods distrained has no right to use them for his own benefit, but, in case a horse and wagon are lawfully distrained, he may harness the horse to the wagon for the purpose of their removal to the place where they are to be impounded; and if, during such removal, the wagon is broken or damaged without negligence on the part of the landlord or his bailiff or agent, and while in the exercise of due and reasonable care, he is not liable for such damage; but, if such damage be occasioned by the negligent conduct of the landlord or his bailiff or agent, he is liable for such damage. Where the property distrained is injured or damaged while in the custody of the landlord or his bailiff or agent, the burden is on him to rebut the presumption of negligence; but the jury are to judge and determine from the evidence whether such injury or damage was occasioned by the negligence of the landlord, his bailiff or agent.

In *Smith v. Chipman*, 348 P.2d 441 (Or. 1960), the Oregon Supreme Court held that the self-help common law remedy of distress coexists with, and is not rendered null or displaced by, legislative remedies given to landlords, and even innkeepers, whose tenants and guests remain in arrears (e.g., former ORS § 87.5250.530 (hotel keeper lien on baggage, clothing, jewelry, and other property brought into inn by guest or boarder), former ORS §§ 87.535–.551 (apartment house landlords have similar lien without need to record, file, or write anything)), nor by attachment statutes that exempt from levy of writ of execution certain species of personalty. "The fact that a landlord upon instituting an action against a tenant for overdue rent, may attach the tenant's property possibly causes landlords to prefer that remedy to distress when the sums are large; but the creation of the remedy left unimpaired distress, as we shall presently see." *Id.*, at 444. Title 87 ORS has since been repealed. The new landlord-tenant act abolished distress for rent. ORS § 90.420(2).

Yet what rights does a landlord have to distrain property for reasons *other than nonpayment of rent*? According to *Sollenberger v. Cranwell*, 614 P.2d 234 (Wash. Ct. App. 1980), none. Apartment building owner Betti Cranwell appealed from judgment for $1400 for violating RCW § 59.18.230(4) of Washington's Residential Landlord-Tenant Act, which abolishes the landlord's right of distress for rent. Cranwell bought the building and immediately sought to evict the resident managers, the Sollenbergers. On May 31, 1977, she served a three-day notice to vacate. The Sollenbergers complied but were unable to gain access to their storage unit containing their furniture. Despite proof from the previous building owner that the Sollenbergers were owners of the property in the storage unit, Cranwell denied access. She claimed that the bar on distress for rent only applies where the landlord withholds property for nonpayment of rent. In affirming, the appellate court held that while RCW § 59.18.230(4) abolished the remedy of distress for rent, it also uses "clear language" to create a "cause of action for the taking or detention of a tenant's personal property. It does not limit the availability of the remedy to those circumstances in which the landlord exercises the abolished right of distress for rent." *Id.*, at 236.

H. ABANDONED OR DYING ANIMALS ON PREMISES

Occasionally, the tenant vacates the premises voluntarily or by force after issuance of a writ of restitution, leaving the nonhuman cohabitants behind. In other instances, though the tenant still has possession, she departs the premises for so extended a period as to generate concern that companion animals secured therein may die from starvation or dehydration. What becomes of them?

Statutes outline circumscribed rights for landlords to access the dwelling unit. For instance, RCW § 59.18.150(2), the subsection of the Residential Landlord-Tenant Act ("RLTA") dealing with a landlord's right of entry, allows the landlord to enter a tenant's dwelling unit in the event of emergency, abandonment, or, as subsection 59.18.150(3) obscurely sets out, "if it is impracticable to give the tenant at least two days' notice of intent to enter." At all other times, without a court order, arbitrator ruling, consent of the tenant, or notice as described in 59.18.150(3), the landlord who enters does so on pain of fines up to $100 per violation. Thus, the tenant has a qualified expectation of privacy, and may plausibly have no expectation of privacy (and, thus, no constitutional protection from warrantless searches) in the event of emergency or abandonment or proper notice. *See Kalmas v. Wagner*, 943 P.2d 1369 (Wash. 1997) (dismissing civil rights suit against police officers who accompanied property manager into residence at request of one of the tenants and following compliance with 24-hour notice requirement of RLTA informing tenants of intent to exhibit the dwelling). Emergency typically means a fire or broken water pipe. It may be "impracticable" to give even one day's notice in situations that fall short of an emergency, but in such instances, the landlord should give some warning. Abandonment of the premises is typically evidenced by a clear intent of the once-present tenant to relinquish all interest in the unit. Aside from the access rights provided by the landlord-tenant law, a landlord may have an independent ground to enter per the animal cruelty laws. For instance, RCW § 16.52.100 provides:

> If any domestic animal is impounded or confined without necessary food and water for more than thirty-six consecutive hours, any person may, from time to time, as is necessary, enter into and open any pound or place of confinement in which any domestic animal is confined, and supply it with necessary food and water so long as it is confined. The person shall not be liable to action for the entry, and may collect from the animal's owner the reasonable cost of the food and water. The animal shall be subject to attachment for the costs and shall not be exempt from levy and sale upon execution issued upon a judgment. If an investigating officer finds it extremely difficult to supply confined animals with food and water, the officer may remove the animals to protective custody for that purpose.

Some landlord-tenant acts articulate what steps must be taken. For instance, Oregon's ORS § 90.425(7)(b)(B) provides that after giving written notice to the tenant as required by subsection (3), the landlord may allow animal control to remove the abandoned pets or livestock. If such agency refuses to cooperate, then the landlord "shall exercise reasonable care for the animals given all the circumstances, including the type and condition of the animals, and may give the animals to an agency that is willing and able to care for the animals, such as a humane society or similar organization."

I. ZONING ISSUES

Residential apartheid takes form by code as well as lease. Most jurisdictions impose limitations on the number and species of animal permitted in a particular zone. The astute practitioner will evaluate the following five sources of restriction: licensing and kennel/cattery laws, zoning laws, exotics laws, covenants running with the land, and HOA/COA restrictions (for renters, lease restrictions). Because the department of planning and development frequently operates separately from animal control and licensing, that the former department might grant a permit does not mean the latter will issue the requisite license. Answers to the following screening questions will help to assess whether it is premature to roll out the red carpet for the client and her animal companions at the situs property:

(1) **Species Screen:** Is the species permitted at the situs, under local, state, and federal law? Under deed, CC&R, contract or lease?

(2) **Licensing (*per quod*) Screen:** Is each individual animal required to be licensed — by the local, state, federal authorities — at the situs?

(3) **Zoning Screen:** Is each individual animal permitted to be kept in the zone — whether characterized as hobby kennel/cattery, private (breeding kennel/cattery, commercial kennel/cattery, shelter, agricultural use? *In this respect, see U.S. v. Park,* 658 F. Supp. 2d 1236, 1245 (D.Idaho 2009) (dogs are "livestock"). Note that permitted uses may vary by lot size as well as zone. Where the code does not expressly permit the use of such organized or collective nonhuman residency, procuring a variance or obtaining a permit for a conditional use may remain viable.

(4) **Licensing as a Group (*in toto*) Screen:** Does the total number of animals exceed a threshold requiring a separate permit to operate a kennel, cattery, foster care, shelter, rescue *in addition to* individual licenses? Note that many jurisdictions count each cat and dog toward a "kennel/cattery" total, so that a law requiring a kennel permit with "four or more cats or dogs" would include the permutation of two cats and two dogs.

(5) **Spay/Neuter Screen:** State cruelty laws may include a numeric limitation having nothing to do with zoning or licensing, but instead, welfare. For instance, see RCW § 16.52.310(1) (prohibiting owning, possessing, controlling, or having charge or custody over 50 intact dogs over six months of age).

Hypothetical: Carmen, a single woman, has lived at a two-bedroom, one-bathroom home situated on a 6,300-square-foot lot in West Seattle for the last 11 years. Except for one year in 2002, she lived and lives alone. Her front yard has a white picket fence about four feet high. Her backyard is fully enclosed by a fence made of wood, chain link, or wire at least six feet high and flanked by very tall hedges. It is three times as large as the front. Her doggie daycare business, Wigglebutt, provides free pick-up and free drop-off, meaning she collects and returns her clients' dogs. This eliminates foot traffic by patrons into her home and vehicular traffic on her street. On an average week, she provides doggie daycare to no more than three clients for four to five hours a day, four to five days a week. Also on average, she provides overnight boarding to no more than two clients for one to five days a week. In any given week, however, she may have no daycare clients or overnight boarders. These clients remain in her residence at all times except for, at most, 30 minutes, and at least, 10 minutes, per day. The 10 to 30 minutes that they are outside, Carmen provides constant supervision of them in her fenced yard so they can relieve themselves. Over that time, she monitors them to ensure they do not disturb the neighbors by barking or escape. At all other times, they play, sleep, eat, drink, are groomed and medicated, as needed, inside her home.

Carmen presently owns seven dogs and two cats and regards them as her family — a 20-year-old male feline named Marcus, 15-year-old feline named Dinah, 16-year-old Dalmatian/Pointer named Barkley, 12-year-old Beagle named Samantha, 11-year-old Flat-coat Retriever named Rufus, 11-year-old Border Collie named Claude, 10-year-old Beagle named Pickles, five-year-old Black Lab/Border Collie named Tango, and a nine-month-old Papillon named Molly, all of whom, except two, are geriatric and likely unadoptable. Carmen has owned each animal virtually his or her entire life, except Barkley and Tango, whom she acquired 13 and two years ago, respectively. Some animals have special medical needs. Others sleep on her bed. Carmen spends about half her income on the animals. When deceased, she pays for private cremation. One of the reasons she opened her business about seven years ago was to be close to her family instead of traveling one to two weeks a month away on business.

The City of Seattle has allowed Carmen to license all nine animals in her name at her present address. It is believed, based on records provided by Seattle Animal Shelter ("SAS"), that the City has allowed Carmen to repeatedly relicense these animals from as far back as a decade ago. Indeed, the City let Carmen license five more animals just four months ago, including Victrola, a 20-year-old dog. The City repeatedly cited Carmen for failing to license 16 animals, accruing penalties of $2,000, yet at no time until late February 2011 did any employee of the City tell Carmen that she could have no more than three dogs, three cats, or a combination thereof. Instead, the City continued fining her for failing to license, knowing full well she had more than three. Not until late February 2011 did any representative of the Department of Construction and Land Use ("DCLU") ever tell Carmen that she had too many animals at her residence. All her dealings concerning those animals were with SAS.

About two years ago, animal control officer Dirk Petersen contacted Carmen at her commercial space in downtown West Sandlewood, in-person, while he was on the job, in his capacity as a representative of the City, repeatedly asking her to foster SAS dogs who were likely unadoptable and would face euthanasia. He knew where she lived and that she already owned dogs and cats. He licensed them for her in her business name initially and then changed them to her residential address. At no time did he say she could not legally possess more than three dogs, three cats, or a combination thereof. He urged Carmen to take five dogs, all aged canines to whom Carmen opened her heart and home.

As with the boarding dogs, Carmen's owned dogs play, exercise, sleep, eat, drink, are groomed, teeth brushed, and medicated inside her residence. She lets them outside in her fenced yard at most three times a day for five to ten minutes, along with the daycare and boarder dogs, under direct supervision. Thus, all dogs — owned and boarded — are outside at most 30 minutes a day and as few as 10. Only one of her dogs, Jasper, is a barker, so she monitors him and takes steps to ensure he does not disturb neighbors.

Carmen's two cats live strictly indoors and are not let outside at any time except to sit on cat posts in a tiny, five-sided, wire enclosure (cat yard) attached off her kitchen, only 3' x 7' in dimension.

DCLU cited Carmen for having too many animals and ordered her to reduce her numbers to four immediately or face fines, a potential criminal charge, and forcible removal of animals in excess of the permitted number allowed by SMC 23.42.052, which states:

23.42.052 Keeping of animals

The keeping of small animals, farm animals, domestic fowl and bees is permitted outright in all zones as an accessory use to any principal use permitted outright or to a permitted conditional use, in each case subject to the standards of this Section 23.42.052.

A.   Small Animals. Up to three small animals may be kept accessory to each business establishment, other than an urban farm, or dwelling unit on a lot, except as follows:

1.   In no case is more than one miniature potbelly pig allowed per business establishment or dwelling unit (see subsection 23.42.052.B).

2.   In single-family zones,

a.   accessory dwelling units shall not be considered separate dwelling units for the purpose of this Section 23.42.052

b.   up to four small animals are permitted on lots of at least 20,000 square feet; and

c.   one additional small animal is permitted for each 5,000 square feet of lot area in excess of 20,000 square feet. Accessory structures, including kennels, for four or more animals must be at least 10 feet from any other lot in a residential zone.

B.   Miniature Potbelly Pigs. That type of swine commonly known as the Vietnamese, Chinese, or Asian Potbelly Pig (Sus scrofa bittatus) may be kept as a small animal, provided that no swine that is greater than 22 inches in height at the shoulder or more than 150 pounds in weight may be kept in the city.

C.   Domestic Fowl. Up to eight domestic fowl may be kept on any lot in addition to the small animals permitted in subsection 23.42.052.A.

1. On lots greater than 10,000 square feet that include either a community garden or an urban farm, one additional fowl is permitted for every 1,000 square feet of lot area over 10,000 square feet in community garden or urban farm use.

2. Roosters are not permitted.

3. Structures housing domestic fowl must be located at least 10 feet away from any structure that includes a dwelling unit on an adjacent lot.

D. Farm Animals. Cows, horses, sheep and other similar farm animals are permitted only on lots of at least 20,000 square feet. The keeping of swine is prohibited, except for miniature potbelly pigs allowed under subsection 23.42.052.B.

1. One farm animal for every 10,000 square feet of lot area is permitted.

2. Farm animals and structures housing them must be kept at least 50 feet from any other lot in a residential zone.

E. Beekeeping. Beekeeping is permitted outright as an accessory use, when registered with the State Department of Agriculture, provided that:

1. No more than four hives, each with only one swarm, are allowed on lots of less than 10,000 square feet.

2. Hives shall not be located within 25 feet of any lot line except when situated 8 feet or more above the grade immediately adjacent to the grade of the lot on which the hives are located or when situated less than 8 feet above the adjacent existing lot grade and behind a solid fence or hedge six (6) feet high parallel to any lot line within 25 feet of a hive and extending at least 20 feet beyond the hive in both directions.

F. Miniature Goats. The types of goats commonly known as Pygmy, Dwarf and Miniature Goats may be kept as small animals, provided that male miniature goats are neutered and all miniature goats are dehorned. Nursing offspring of miniature goats licensed according to the provisions of this Code may be kept until weaned, no longer than 12 weeks from birth, without violating the limitations of subsection 23.42.052.A.

You have been hired to defend Carmen and her animals. What arguments would you raise?

The City contends that boarded animals, unowned by Carmen, apply toward the numeric limitation of SMC 23.42.052 since the undefined term "keep" means "to take care of or tend." Carmen does not dispute that keeping means caring for, tending, retaining in one's possession, or holding as one's own, but notes that the word lacks the necessary level of temporal and geographic specificity to meaningfully inform the person of average intelligence as to where compliance ends and noncompliance begins. For instance, the *Random House Dictionary* recognizes that keeping may depend on duration (KEEP (v.) (2) to hold or have the use of *for a period of time*) and location (KEEP (v.) (3) to hold *in a given place;* store; and (35) to remain or stay *in a particular place: to keep indoors*). Dictionary.com Unabridged, based on Random House Dictionary, 2011 (emphasis added). So, even accepting the definition used by the City, it leaves unanswered the qualifiers of "how long?" and "where?" rendering it vague on its face and as applied to Carmen. Recognizing its ambiguity, in 1982 the Director of DCLU enacted a rule to interpret SMC 23.44.14(e) and SMC 23.45.148,[10] stating:

> Effective immediately, the following animals will be subject to regulation by the standards for small animals:
>
> 1. Dogs;
>
> 2. Cats;
>
> 3. Rabbits;
>
> 4. Other similar animals which are customarily kept outdoors all or part of the time.
>
> . . .
>
> Effective immediately, the following animals will not be subject to regulation by the standards for small animals:
>
> 1. Hamsters, gerbils, mice and other similar animals which are customarily kept within a dwelling unit, *unless* such animals are kept outdoors;
>
> 2. Reptiles, including snakes, lizards, and turtles, which are customarily kept within a dwelling unit, *unless* such reptiles are kept outdoors;
>
> 3. Birds, such as parakeets and pigeons, which are not considered "domestic fowl;"
>
> 4. Fish.

DCLU Director's Rule 32–82 (emphasis in original). It is unclear whether DCLU properly put this out for public comment before finalizing, but the nearly 30-year-old rule does not account for the evolving relationship of Seattleites with nonhuman family members, nor the proliferation of dog culture periodicals and dog-related businesses such as Carmen's. *See, e.g., The Bark: Dog is my Co-Pilot* (1997-), *Modern Dog: The Lifestyle Magazine for Modern Dogs and their Companions* (2002-), *City Dog Magazine.* Importantly, neither SMC 23.44.14(e) nor SMC 23.42.052 speaks of dogs, cats, rabbits, hamsters, gerbils, mice, reptiles, snakes, lizards, turtles, fish, or birds like parakeets and pigeons. Rather, the code identifies the miniature potbelly pig, domestic fowl, cows, horses, sheep and other similar farm animals, swine, bees, and miniature goats. That the Director thought the code required more specificity proves its ambiguity and need for interpretation.

---

[10] There is no evidence the rule was updated to apply to SMC 23.42.052 and SMC 23.44.048 (referencing SMC 23.42.052, Keeping of Animals, for single-family zoned residential areas).

Keeping *indoors* vs. *outdoors*

The first ambiguity concerns *where* one keeps small animals. DR 32-82 distinguishes indoor from outdoor locations, exempting the former from the reach of SMC 23.44.14(e). Of note, the rule applies only to animals "customarily kept outdoors all or part of the time." The phrase "other similar animals" evidences the intent to apply the rule only to dogs, cats, and rabbits kept outdoors all or part of the time, per the interpretive canons *ejusdem generis* and *noscitur a sociis. Silverstreak, Inc. v. Wash. State Dept. of L & I*, 154 P.3d 891, 899 (Wash. 2007) ("The rule of ejusdem generis requires that general terms appearing in a statute in connection with specific terms are to be given meaning and effect only to the extent that the general terms suggest similar items to those designated by the specific terms. . . .'[S]pecific terms modify or restrict the application of general terms, where both are used in sequence.' "); *Port of Seattle v. State Dep't. of Revenue*, 1 P.3d 607, 611 (Wash. Ct. App. 2000) ("Under the doctrine of noscitur a sociis, 'the meaning of words may be indicated or controlled by those with which they are associated.' ")

Bolstering this interpretation is the second part of the rule, which categorically excludes species like hamsters, gerbils, mice, "and other similar animals which are customarily kept within a dwelling unit" save individual members of those species "kept outdoors." Thus, it matters whether the individual animal is customarily kept within the single-family residence or outside in either a separate structure, or in no structure at all (e.g., on a chain or run). Most Seattle residents live with dogs and cats as part of the family. While many have indoor-outdoor cats who roam freely during part of each day, few have indoor-outdoor dogs, especially those who live in high-rises or apartment complexes.

The most reasonable and fairest interpretation of SMC 23.42.052, therefore, applies the numerical limit only to those cats, dogs, and other small mammals who spend most to all their time outside the dwelling unit, not those animals kept strictly indoors or indoors the majority of the time. Arguably, the rule would apply to those who let their cats outside at night to return later the following day and dogs who sleep in an outside doghouse, live on a chain or tether, are left loose in a fenced yard, and who eat, drink, urinate, and defecate outdoors most or all the time. It would not apply to apartment dwellers and homeowners whose cats and dogs do most of their living inside the dwelling unit, who sleep with their owners, eat in the kitchen or dining room, and lounge on the couch in the privacy of one's home.

Accordingly, questions of fact arise as to where Carmen keeps her animals, whether owned or boarded. As noted above, her cats are *always* kept indoors, her owned dogs and overnight boarders are kept indoors 98 to 99 percent of the time (23.5 to 23.75 hours per day), and her daycare dogs are kept indoors 88 to 97 percent of the time (3.5 to 4.83, of 4 to 5, hours per day). When outdoors, the dogs are supervised by Carmen at all times in a fully-enclosed backyard with obstructing hedges and tall fencing so they can relieve themselves and return inside. Aside from urination and defecation, every other aspect of tending and caring for the dogs takes place indoors.

In construing SMC 23.42.052, one may wish to consider the ordinance's purpose. The Director rationalized DR 32-82 as follows:

Reason

The land use code regulates the keeping of animals accessory to residences in order to limit the impact that domestic animals will have on neighboring property. This intent is demonstrated by the types of restrictions placed on the various categories of animals. For example, beehives are permitted only if there is sufficient separation or screening between the hives and adjacent lots, additional small animals are permitted on single family lots which have significantly more square footage than the minimum required in the zone, and farm animals are allowed only on very large lots.

Distinguishing between animals which are commonly kept outside and those commonly kept indoors is consistent with the intent to limit the impact of pets in residential neighborhoods. Since animals, including reptiles, which are kept exclusively within a residence should have no effect on neighboring property, they should not be regulated by the land use code.

. . . Fish, whether kept in an aquarium or in an outdoor pool, do not impact neighboring properties and therefore are also not restricted.

This logic appropriately contrasts "animals which are commonly kept outside and those commonly kept indoors," noting that those "kept exclusively within a residence should have no effect on neighboring property" and "should not be regulated by the land use code." *Id.* The same applies to fish kept exclusively outdoors "in an outdoor pool," because they do not impact neighboring properties. Thus, where Carmen's cats are kept exclusively within her residence, SMC 23.42.052 does not apply to them. Nor does it apply to dogs "commonly kept indoors" except for fewer than 30 minutes a day to relieve themselves, as one group, over three 5-to-10 minute periods per day, while steps are taken by Carmen to limit any impact to neighboring properties.

Keeping limits tied to lot, not dwelling, size.

The code increases the limit of animals based on lot size, not dwelling size. This is consistent with a law that restricts the number of animals who may be kept outside. Lumberjack Paul Bunyan may live in a 400 square foot log cabin with five cats and dogs left outside and allowed to roam freely on five acres. A college student may keep the same animals inside a 1,000-square-foot stick-built home on 0.15 acres, yet Bunyan could cause more of a neighborhood impact. No law requires dogs and cats to be kept inside on one's own property, which explains why larger lots (not larger dwelling units) serve as a mitigating buffer to accommodate more outdoor animals.

DR 32-82 agrees with this concept. The purpose of limiting "the impact that domestic animals will have on neighboring property" only makes rational and nonarbitrary sense if applied to lots where the animals' noises, odors, aggressive tendencies, hazardous presence, and other nuisance-type behaviors actually waft, or trespass onto, contaminate, disturb, or endanger neighboring properties. Where contained inside a dwelling virtually all the time, enforcement against Carmen defies the purpose of DR 32-82 and SMC 23.42.052. For instance, cats kept outside without restraint may fight and disturb the peace, litter property with feces, tear into garbage bags, knock over garbage cans, scratch fences or other personalty, walk on cars, spread disease, or cause roadway hazards. Dogs kept outside without restraint for extended periods present similar hazards except they may also bark, bite, or attack. A person who keeps just one vicious, unrestrained, and unruly large dog outside the family residence at all times will likely cause more impact to neighboring properties than a dozen well-behaved dogs kept inside except for brief forays into a fenced yard to urinate and defecate.

The Kansas Supreme Court recognized the importance of distinguishing character of animals and purpose, as well as the manner and consequences of keeping same, in finding void a city ordinance limiting the number of cats to be kept inside a man's residence. *Smith v. Steinrauf*, 36 P.2d 995 (Kan. 1934). In *Smith*, the City of Topeka attempted to force Mr. Smith to reduce his cat numbers from eight to five or face arrest and fine. "The cats were reared as pets, were well trained, and neither interfere with nor annoy any person living within 250 feet of plaintiff's residence." *Id.*, at 996. They were all "born in the residence described, were never permitted to run at large, and had not been at any time outside the residence." *Id.* In finding the ordinance void, the court resorted to math:

> In framing the ordinance, the city applied the principle of classification by number; five cats, no nuisance; six cats, nuisance. Surely none but the most sensitive ear and nose could tell the difference, and the difference may not be determined on the basis of what may offend the fastidious. So the problem of nuisance or no nuisance was solved as if according to the following mathematical formula: X=maximum amount of nuisance ordinary folks must endure. To find the value of X, multiply the quantity of discomfort one cat produces by five. This computation gives the cat the benefit of the doubt, because the increment produced by associate relation is disregarded.

> Number is often a proper basis of classification. Cities are classified in that way, not because a city having a population of 19,990 should be governed differently from a city having a population of 20,010, but because a large city should have powers not possessed by a small city, and a line must be drawn. We have no such case here. There is no sound basis, independently of actual conditions and consequences of keeping, for making a discrimination between keepers, and the ordinance is void.

Id., at 998; see also Camille Nohe, *My Cat, Sam, and the Pursuit of Happiness*, 74 Aug. J. KAN. B.A. 8 (2005). Pennsylvania courts have similarly found:

> Ordinances regulating or forbidding the keeping of more than a certain number of animals have, however, usually been held invalid . . . The more possession or keeping of dogs, or the maintenance of a dog kennel, does not constitute a nuisance, or a nuisance per se, since it is a lawful business. The question whether the keeping of dogs, or maintenance of a dog kennel, constitutes a nuisance depends on the circumstances, extent of annoyance and discomfort caused, and whether there is a continuous or recurring injury. . . .

From the foregoing we conclude that it is a question of fact to be judicially determined after hearing held, whether or not the keeping of animals within a certain location is a nuisance or not a nuisance, and that it cannot be arbitrarily stated by the borough council or the court that the keeping of five dogs is not a nuisance, while the keeping of six dogs is a nuisance.

Comm. v. Gardner, 1950 Pa. Dist. & Cnty. Dec. LEXIS 58, 10–13 (Dec. 7, 1950) (citations omitted); *see also Comm. v. Creighton*, 1994 Pa. Commw. LEXIS 139 (Nov. 18, 1994) (ordinance arbitrarily limiting number of cats or dogs which person could keep within borough to five was beyond delegated power to prohibit and remove any nuisance). Such logic applies to Seattle's ordinance.

A fair interpretation, one molded by the rule of lenity, would only apply the numeric limitation to those individual animals kept outdoors more than 50 percent of the time, meaning that none of Carmen's owned animals, nor her daycare or overnight boarders, are "kept" by her.

Keeping for More than 30 Days

The second ambiguity concerns *how long* one keeps small animals. If a homeowner invites over several friends and their dogs for a "puppy party," a technique encouraged by trainers to introduce a very young dog to as many different types of people and animals as possible, thereby minimizing fear and future aggression, and encouraging bite inhibition, the number would quickly exceed three. If her guests were present for one full day, would she violate SMC 23.42.052? Or consider those who temporarily foster dogs and cats on behalf of a rescue organization, humane society, or animal control. Should those animals count toward the numeric limitation?

A person of normal intelligence reading the zoning code would find no guidance to interpret the phrase "keep small animals" in the context of duration, so she might turn to the animal code for guidance, which only requires a license when the animal is at one location for more than 30 consecutive days. "Any owner of a cat or dog over the age of eight (8) weeks must obtain a valid license for each such animal . . . [w]ithin thirty (30) days of entry . . . into The City of Seattle[.]" SMC 9.25.051. "Keeping" lacks a definition in the animal code, but it defines "harboring" as "allowing any animal to remain, be lodged, fed, or sheltered on the property one owns, occupies or controls, for more than twenty-four (24) hours." SMC 9.25.021(C). Accordingly, one may interpret "keep" in the context of SMC 23.42.052, bespeaking an intent to limit neighborhood impacts that would be more than transitory or trifling, of a duration no shorter than 24 hours and no longer than 30 days.

Carmen's doggie daycare clients remain on her premises far fewer than 24 hours a day (i.e., four to five), so she cannot be deemed a "harborer." Hence, she cannot be regarded as their "keeper." The overnight boarders, if they stay for more than one consecutive night, would render Carmen a "harborer" but not necessarily a keeper, since the duration would fall far short of mandating licensure (i.e., 30 days), and Carmen's overnight boarders do not stay more than five consecutive days at a time.

A fair interpretation, again molded by the rule of lenity, would set a 30-day floor on SMC 23.42.052, meaning that none of Carmen's daycare or overnight boarders are "kept" by her.

Estoppel through Licensing and Entrapment

Also consider the defense of estoppel, grounded in the principle:

> that a party should be held to a representation made or position assumed where inequitable consequences would otherwise result to another party who has justifiably and in good faith relied thereon.

Wilson v. Westinghouse Elec. Corp., 530 P.2d 298, 300 (Wash. 1975). As noted above, Carmen reasonably relied upon the representations, acts, and omissions of numerous animal control officers. Further, contacts between Carmen and the City were not merely commercial in nature. They were far more precious — e.g., liberty and property interests sanctified by the state and federal constitutions, resulting in severe limitations on her ability to share her life with her aged, bonded, unadoptable animal companions whom she quite understandably regards as her "family," or forcing her to make "Sophie's choices,"[11] and exposing her to criminal prosecution. Her dealings with the City have involved numerous costly citations related to her failure to license her many animals, yet not once (until late February 2011, after she had been fined) did the citing officer or any other officer with Seattle Animal Shelter inform her that instead of licensing her dogs and cats, she needed to get rid of them. To the contrary, Officer Petersen urged her to take *more* animals from the shelter and licensed them in her name at her residence, again without invoking SMC 23.42.052.

The City cites to *City of Mercer Is. v. Steinmann*, 513 P.2d 80 (Wash. Ct. App. 1973) in an attempt to negate the estoppel argument by analogizing to the holding that the City of Mercer Island's issuance of a building permit did not estop it from later claiming a violation of the zoning code. Key distinctions can be made here.

1. First, the City, through Officer Petersen, actively solicited Carmen's assistance in taking several animals that the City now claims put her in violation of SMC 23.42.052. She did not go to SAS and ask to acquire more animals. Rather, the City approached her, allowed her to develop attachments to them, and now seeks to take them away. Such conduct rises to the level of entrapment not contemplated by *Steinmann*.

2. Second, the City found Carmen in violation of licensing laws and cited her, repeatedly, despite knowing full well she had more than the purported limit of SMC 23.42.052. Indeed, the number of counts per citation alone would have put the City on notice that she was approaching or exceeding that limit. In other words, instead of using a permit as a basis to estop the City, Carmen is relying on a penalty.

---

[11] A 1982 American romantic drama cataloguing the story of a Polish immigrant, Sophie, who, after arrest by the Nazis and arrival to Auschwitz with her two children, was forced to choose which of the two would be gassed and which would go to the concentration camp.

The implication is that if she keeps them, she must license them; and by citing her for failing to license (instead of for having too many), the City made an election to pursue compliance in one vein but excuse the other. It cannot fairly have it both ways and must be bound by that election, *Steinmann* states, at 482, "Estoppel will not be applied against a municipal corporation acting in a governmental capacity *unless it is clearly necessary to prevent obvious injustice.*" *Id.*, 83 (*citing Bennett v. Grays Harbor Cy.*, 130 P.2d 1041, 1045 (Wash. 1942) (emphasized)):

> In the *Bennett* case, the court noted that those who deal with public officers must ascertain the extent of their authority, and public officers cannot permit citizens to act contrary to law. The evidence must present unmistakable justification for imposition of the doctrine when a municipality has acted in its governmental capacity.

Id. (cit.om.) This assumes the mandate is clear (which it is not, for the reasons stated above). The evidence presented by Carmen exemplifies the extent and nature of this *Bennett* justification. The only just outcome under these circumstances is that Carmen should be permitted to keep those animals presently licensed until the animals die. Otherwise, the Examiner will permit the City to expose Carmen to a manifest injustice, which relates to the special nature of the property at issue.

SMC 23.42.052 is ambiguous and requires strict statutory construction in favor of Carmen, with respect to her own dogs and cats, as well as boarders. SMC 23.42.050 on its face has not been violated in light of the plain language of subsection (E). Furthermore, the City's campaign of repeatedly citing Carmen for failing to license animals while at the same time urging her to take on more presents the classic case of estoppel by government.

J. PRISONS

Incarcerated individuals can spend their entire lives behind bars. Having been stripped of many of their rights as free persons, do they also lose the liberty to cohabit with nonhumans of their choosing? Putting aside the obvious security concerns, such as the potential use of animals as weapons or the fundamental alteration of the prison environment arising from management of, and interference from, animals, and also for the moment suspending concerns about the morality of forcing imprisonment on a guiltless animal merely by association with a convict, could a disabled inmate who relies upon a service animal demand access under the ADA or FHA? At least one court has held that prison cells are dwellings for purposes of the FHA. *Garcia v. Condarco*, 114 F. Supp. 2d 1158 (D.N.M. 2000). The ADA antidiscrimination provisions, as modified, apply to jails and detention and correctional facilities. 29 C.F.R. 35.152(b); *Pennsylvania Dept. of Corrections v. Yeskey*, 524 U.S. 206 (1998) (ADA Title II applies to inmates in state prisons). But no known case to date has addressed whether an inmate with a qualifying disability may obtain a service animal as a reasonable accommodation while jailed.

If the Gig Harbor, Washington-based Prison Pet Partnership Program ("PPPP") at Purdy, an all-female prison, is any indication, a test case may favor the inmate. For decades, the PPPP has supervised inmates raising service dogs for mobility assistance. They matriculate through a 12-to-18-month class, training the dogs at least five hours a week, including out of class time where they live with the dogs as part of the training regime. The minimum class time training is 264 hours, exclusive of the round-the-clock period with the inmate in "lockup." Cats also have found their way into maximum-security prisons, as observed with the Indiana State Prison cat program called FORWARD (Felines and Offenders Rehabilitation with Affection, Reformation, and Dedication), http://wishtv.com/2015/04/10/shelter-cats-find-freedom-at-pendleton-prison/. *See also* www.seattletimes.com/seattle-news/cats-bringining-out-the-soft-side-of-inmates/.

Chapter 11

CRIMINAL LAW

Modern-day, substantive criminal animal law derives from statute or ordinance, less frequently through administrative regulation, rarely in constitutions. Historically, common law set the boundaries of criminal animal law.[1] In 2002, the state of Florida passed Art. X, § 19, the "Animal Cruelty Amendment: Limiting Cruel and Inhumane Confinement of Pigs During Pregnancy," making it a misdemeanor of the first degree to "confine a pig during pregnancy in an enclosure, or to tether a pig during pregnancy, on a farm in such a way that she is prevented from turning around freely." It took until 2014 for South Dakota to enact a felony animal cruelty law, joining the other 49 states. In 2011, Guam became the latest United States territory, district, or possession to do so, leaving only the American Samoas and the Northern Marianas islands without felony provisions.

The then-comparatively progressive states of Massachusetts, Oklahoma, and Rhode Island enacted their felony animal cruelty laws in the nineteenth century (1804, 1887, and 1896, respectively), but it took about another century for a legislative resurgence through the rest of the country. The drive to geographically broaden the felonization of animal cruelty was embryonic just 30 years ago, with Wisconsin becoming the fourth state to enact such legislation in 1986, California the fifth in 1988, and Florida the sixth in 1989. Twenty states followed suit in the 1990s; 19 more, and three districts and territories in the 2000s; and this decade the final holdouts joined the ranks — with Guam (2011), Mississippi (2011), Idaho (2012), North Dakota (2013), and South Dakota (2014).

Felonization of crimes against animals signals more than just moral rigidification. The expansion of crimes *mala in se* (i.e., evil in itself as determined by a civilized society)[2] reflects the increasingly conservative and punitive criminal justice system as it pertains to animals. It elevates the legal status of nonhumans as *victims*, recognizing their many forms of suffering as legitimate subjects of prosecution, and warranting punishment on the same or similar order to that

---

[1] Common law created the felonies of murder, suicide, manslaughter, burglary, arson, robbery, larceny, rape, sodomy and mayhem, as well as misdemeanors of assault, battery, false imprisonment, libel, perjury, and intimidation of jurors. Jackson, *Common Law Misdemeanors*, 6 CAMB. L.J. 193 (1937).

[2] Early animal cruelty laws sought to protect the property rights of the animal's owner, not the sensibilities of the victimized animal. For instance, in *U.S. v. Gideon*, 1856 Minn. LEXIS 9 (1856), the Minnesota Territory Supreme Court vacated a conviction of a man who shot another's dog, finding not only that the dog was not a "beast" for purposes of 101 Rev. Stats. § 39, but that the dog possessed only nominal value with a property interest wholly insufficient to maintain a civil action for loss, criminal action for theft, or prosecution for willful and malicious killing, maiming, or disfiguring horses, cattle, or "other beasts of another person," as charged here. Further, whether Gideon harbored malice against the dog was legally immaterial and no substitute for the element of the crime charged, which required proof of malice toward the animal's owner as the impetus for killing, maiming, or disfiguring his beast.

involving human victims, carrying penalties that may land the convict in state prison for a year or longer, fines in the five-figure range, and extensive, life-changing, disenfranchising consequences. For instance, felons convicted of animal cruelty will lose right the to vote (except in Maine and Vermont); to hold public office; to serve as a juror; to possess firearms, to maintain a professional license or permit (including, for instance, architects, attorneys, health care providers, accountants, insurance agents); to care for a foster child; to find gainful employment; to avoid eviction based solely on conviction; to be eligible for federal assistance for higher education expenses; to receive public benefits such as food stamps or welfare; to freely travel across United States borders; and, for non-citizens committing aggravated felonies or crimes, to avoid deportation by obtaining a waiver under the Immigration and Nationality Act, § 212(h).[3]

A tiny subset of felonies levy the most extreme and irreversible penalty — capital punishment. Was a crime against an animal ever punishable by death? As discussed below, aside from bestiality, no. In 1688, England prosecuted 50 capital crimes, a number higher than during enforcement of the "Bloody Code" through 1818. Harry Potter, *Hanging in Judgment: Religion and the Death Penalty in England from the Bloody Code to Abolition* (1993); Brian P. Block & John Hostettler, *Hanging in the Balance: A History of the Abolition of Capital Punishment in Britain* (1997). "Even stealing fruit from trees and damaging ponds to allow fish to escape became capital crimes" during that period. Block, at 21. However, execution was typically reserved for crimes against persons, with the "only property offence for which the capital sentence was regularly executed and rarely commuted [being] forgery." Potter, at 9. Come passage of the Reform Act of 1832, the list of capital crimes dwindled to "rape, buggery, murder, robbery, some types of forgery, attempted murder resulting in injury and housebreaking with larceny to any value." Block, at 49.[4] By 1837, 15 offenses remained. "By 1841, seven. By 1861, four — murder, treason, piracy with violence, and arson in Her Majesty's dockyards." Block, at 43, 49, 57; Potter, at 42–43. In 1965, Britain passed the Murder Act, abolishing the death penalty.

The Capitall Lawes of New-England, codified in 1636 as part of the Massachusetts Bay Colony, cited to the Jewish scriptures to identify capital offences, including idolatry, witchcraft, blasphemy, murder, assault in sudden anger, sodomy, buggery, adultery, statutory rape, rape, man-stealing, perjury in a capital trial, and rebellion. Hugo Adam Bedau, General Introduction to THE DEATH PENALTY IN AMERICA 5 (1967). By the time of the Revolutionary War, however, the colonies

---

[3] In *Madrid v. Holder*, 2013 U.S. App. LEXIS 20487 (9th Cir. Oct. 8, 2013), a Mexican national Carlos Madrid pled guilty to the felony of maliciously and intentionally harming a poodle under Cal. Penal Code § 597(a). In refusing to waive deportation, the Ninth Circuit held that though crimes against persons are "more likely" to be deemed "potentially serious crimes" for purposes of deportation, sometimes crimes against property count. It was fair to conclude that harm to a living animal made him "a danger to the community."

[4] Section 61 of Britain's Offences against the Person Act of 1861, titled "Sodomy and Bestiality," abolished the death penalty for the crime of buggery, whether committed with human or nonhuman, and imposed a sentence of ten years to life. Common law defined it as either anal intercourse by a man with a man or woman or animal, or vaginal intercourse by a man or woman with an animal. *See* Larry Cata Backer, *Raping Sodomy and Sodomizing Rape: A Morality Tale about the Transformation of Modern Sodomy Jurisprudence*, 21 AM. J. CRIM. L. 37, 50 fn. 36 (1993).

limited capital offenses to murder, treason, piracy, arson, rape, robbery, burglary, sodomy, counterfeiting, horse-theft, and slave rebellion. Bedau at 6. By the twentieth century, the Supreme Court wielded the Eighth Amendment to decapitalize certain crimes, such as rape, that do not result in death (*Coker v. Georgia*, 433 U.S. 584 (1977)), and aiding or abetting a felony in the course of which a murder is committed by others but the defendant does not intend himself to kill, attempt to kill, or intend that a killing take place or lethal force employed (*Enmund v. Florida*, 458 U.S. 782 (1982)). It also restricted the use of the penalty against the insane (*Ford v. Wainwright*, 477 U.S. 399 (1986)) and juveniles (*Roper v. Simmons*, 543 U.S. 551 (2005)). Debate aside as to whether the death penalty should be abolished, what more defining way exists to value life than to exact such an ultimate penalty when it has been taken? And what clearer example of the double standard between humans and nonhumans exists? Aside from buggery and certain forms of theft, abuse or neglect of animals has never to this author's knowledge been a crime punishable by death.[5]

Of ardent animal welfare proponent Mark Twain's many pithy sayings, one captures the defect that drives many intentional animal cruelty crimes: "Man is the only creature that inflicts pain for sport, knowing it to be pain." Most felonies speak to such a circumstance where one specifically intends to cause undue suffering in a nonhuman, whether or not for sadistic gratification. Twain grew up in Missouri and lived through the American Civil War. The last shot was fired roughly five months before his thirtieth birthday. He lived through the calamitous and cathartic transformation of his country's moral and geopolitical landscape that ended with reunification and the abolition of slavery, rendering moot such laws as the Black Code of Louisiana. As Judith K. Schafer notes in *"Details are of a Most Revolting Character" Cruelty to Slaves as Seen in Appeals to the Supreme Court of Louisiana*, 68 CHI.-KENT L. REV. 1283 (1993), that lawmakers passed an act in 1821 mandating "a fine of $200 or imprisonment for six months for a person convicted of 'wantonly or maliciously kill[ing] any horse, mare, gelding, mule, or jack-ass,'" but merely "a fine of between $200 and $500" for maiming or killing slaves by their owners or others, was "indicative of legislative sentiment concerning cruelty to slaves." *Id.*, at 1285.

At the conclusion of the Civil War, Henry Bergh founded the American Society for the Prevention of Cruelty to Animals. Early child protection laws owe their thanks to animal protection legislation and the efforts of ASPCA founder Henry Bergh in the well-publicized case of Mary Ellen Wilson, an abused nine-year-old girl

---

[5] At least in the United States. Tokugawa Tsunayoshi, the fifth shogun of the Tokugawa dynasty of Japan, also known as *Inu-Kubō* ("the dog shogun"), enacted animal protection laws with emphasis on canines, including a number of *Edicts on Compassion for Living Things*, which imposed the death penalty for killing a dog. Louis-Frederic Nussbaum, *"Tokugawa, Tsunayoshi"* in *Japan Encyclopedia* (Cambridge: Harvard Univ. Press (2005)); Bodart-Bailey, Beatrice, *The Dog Shogun: The Personality and Policies of Tokugawa Tsunayoshi* (Honolulu: Univ. of Hawaii Press (2006)). A 21st century example of harm to animals qualifying as a death-eligible offense came in the form of an order from Tanzania's Minister for Natural Resources and Tourism Khamis Kagasheki, who said, "There will be no forgiveness when it comes to cases of poachers terrorizing innocent wildlife like elephants, rhinos and other species in this country," giving the order to all wildlife rangers to arrest poachers within its national parks and game reserves and shoot them "on the spot." David Smith, *Execute elephant poachers on the spot, Tanzanian minister urges*, The Guardian (Oct. 8, 2013).

victimized by whippings and shear-slashings, removed from her foster home thanks to a petition by an ASPCA attorney Elbridge Gerry who argued that she was a member of the animal kingdom and deserved protection akin to her fellow nonhumans. Bergh later co-founded the Society for Prevention of Cruelty to Children. *See* Robert M. Murphy, "Random Overview of Issues in the World of Child Protection," *ABA Children's Rights Litigation Newsletter*, http://www.abanet.org/litigation/committees/childrights/content/newsletters/childrens_summer2006.pdf (accessed March 30, 2007). Twain admired Bergh, writing of his efforts to save a pig from being punched with sticks, chased and harassed in an effort to "contrive all manner of means to make him unhappy" much to the entertainment of theatregoers watching *Griffith Gaunt* at Wallack's Theatre. After commenting on Mr. Bergh's ability to persuade the manager to release the pig, he comments on a particular species of animal cruelty, religiously motivated slaughter:

> Mr. Bergh does everything in the behest of the Society with the very best of intentions and the most honest motives. He makes mistakes, sometimes, like all other men. He complained against a Jewish butcher, and required his arrest, for cutting the throat of an ox instead of knocking it on the head; said he was cruelly slow about terminating the animal's life. Of course, people smiled, because the religious law which compels Jewish butchers to slaughter with a consecrated knife is as old as the Pyramids of Egypt, and Mr. Bergh would have to overthrow the Pentateuch itself to accomplish his point.

"Letter from 'Mark Twain'," San Francisco *Alta California*, Apr. 30, 1867 (quoted in SHELLEY FISHER FISHKIN, MARK TWAIN'S BOOK OF ANIMALS (Univ. of Cal. Press 2009). Twain, who befriended antivivisectionists, also observed with dismay the problem of overdriven animals:

> Probably there is no law against it. A large truck wagon, with a load on it nearly as heavy as an ordinary church, came to a stand-still on the slippery cobble stones in front of the Russ House, yesterday, simply because the solitary horse attached to it found himself unable to keep up his regular gait with it. A street car and other vehicles were delayed some time by the blockade. It was natural to expect that a 'streak' of lightning would come after the driver out of the cloudless sky, but it did not. It is like Providence wasn't noticing.

San Francisco *Daily Morning Call* (Sept. 18, 1864, p.1) (from *Clemens of the "Call,"* ed. Edgar M. Branch, p. 520) (quoted in Shelley Fisher Fishkin, *Mark Twain's Book of Animals* (Univ. of Cal. Press 2009). Lacking from this scenario is the driver's taking delight in overburdening the equine "for sport, knowing it to be pain." Presumably, the rebuked owner sought only to move a heavy load through town. If the horse collapsed in the throes of agony despite the urging of the lash, a crime might lie. *See* N.J. Stat. Ann. § 4:22-17(a)(1),(2) (crime to overdrive, overload, abuse or needlessly kill living animal); N.Y. Agric. & Mkts. Law § 353.

Criminal animal laws typically reach the following misconduct: (1) abuse, torture, or neglect (animal cruelty); (2) sexual animal assault or bestiality; (3) animal fighting; (4) animal slaughter; (5) wildlife protection including prohibitions on forms of poaching and baiting; (6) trapping; (7) theft, concealment, tampering with identification;[6] (8) poisoning; (9) improper confinement and transport in vehicles and agricultural operations; (10) abandonment; (11) hoarding and breeding restrictions;[7] (12) artificial coloring and sale of animals;[8] (13) injury inflicted by dangerous dog;[9] (14) depictions of animal cruelty, (15) forms of mutilation, such as docking and cropping and devocalization;[10] and (16) interference, harassment, and antiterrorism laws that seek to protect research facilities, agricultural operations, breeders, and hunters.

A. ANIMAL CRUELTY PROSECUTION

James F. Tweedie challenged his conviction for animal cruelty on grounds of vagueness after he admittedly placed a cat in a microwave oven, turned it on, and left the cafeteria. The feline survived shortly after removal but with agonizing and extensive burns. His only concern was "he might have jeopardized his job." The Rhode Island Supreme Court affirmed his conviction under R.I. Gen. Laws 4-1-2 (1976). *State v. Tweedie*, 444 A.2d 855 (R.I. 1982). About 20 years later, without substantively criminalizing prohibited conduct,[11] Rhode Island amended its animal cruelty law to interchangeably define owners as "guardians," becoming the first state in the country to make the semantic shift, following Boulder, Colo., the first city to swap "pet owner" with "guardian." Boulder, Colo. Code 6-1-2; *see also* West Hollywood Code tit. 9, art. 4; R.I. Gen. Law 4-1-1(a)(4); see also Susan J. Hankin, *Making Decisions about Our Animals' Health Care: Does it Matter Whether We Are Owners or Guardians?*, 2 STANFORD J. ANIMAL L. & POL'Y 1 (2009). Replacing the technological anachronism of the microwave with a century-appropriate device, would Mr. Tweedie have committed animal cruelty had he similarly tortured a stray feline in Providence in 1792, two years after statehood was granted to Rhode Island? Would it matter if the victim were an office cat owned by Mr. Tweedie's employer?

At the time of the founding of the United States, as well as two centuries later, nonhuman animals were legally deemed personalty regardless of whether "owned," or "controlled," "in custody," or "possessed" by a person "responsible" for the "animal's safety and well-being." However, early America's criminal justice system strictly characterized offenses against animals from a chattelizing perspective, indicting those who engaged in unlawful interference with the owner or guardian's property rights in the animal. In other words, those who took the lives of animals belonging to another would face punishment as thieves and malicious mischievers — without even a legal afterthought given to the animal's suffering. Occasionally,

---

[6] *See* Ohio Rev. Code Ann. § 935.18 (A)-(C), (E)-(G); W. Va. Code § 19-20-12(b) (intentional theft of companion animal).

[7] 5 L.P.R.A. 1680 (felony to breed animals without a license); RCW § 16.52.310 (limiting breeding operation sizes).

[8] See Fla. Stat. Ann. § 828.1615; 18 Pa. Cons. Stat. Ann. § 5511(g) (cruelty to cow to enhance appearance of udder); 5 L.P.R.A. 1680 (felony to sell animals on streets, roads or public places).

[9] Va. Code Ann. § 3.2-6540(J)(3).

[10] 18 Pa. Cons. Stat. Ann. § 5511(h)(1) (limitations on cropping ears of dog); (h)(2)(limitations on debarking); (h)(3)(limitations on tail docking); (h)(5) (limitations on dewclaw removal).

[11] P.L. 2001, ch. 72.

courts looked to the public disturbance caused by visually noxious behaviors in order to prosecute abusers on grounds of criminal nuisance or breach of the peace. As insightfully surveyed in David S. Favre & Vivien Tsang, *The Development of Anti-Cruelty Laws During the 1800s*, 1993 DET. C.L. REV. 1 (1993), " 'while the brutes had no legal rights, to inflict cruelty on animals in the public 'injur[es] the moral character of those who witness it — and may therefore be treated as a crime.' " *Id.*, at 6 (quoting Elbrige T. Gerry, *"The Law of Cruelty to Animals,"* Address Before the Bar of Delaware County (Aug. 16, 1875) (quoting Lord Campbell, 9 Lives Lord Chancellors 22–23)); *see also* Thomas G. Kelch, A *Short History of (Mostly) Western Animal Law: Part II*, 19 ANIMAL L. 347 (2013) (quoting Puritan Body of Liberties from Massachusetts Bay Colony in 1641). Except for a narrowly drafted Maine statute, legislation of the nineteenth century abided this narrow property-based model by only prosecuting those who willfully and maliciously killed, maimed, injured, or disfigured certain species "of another," without any regard for the animal's anguish. Favre, at 7–8 (citing 1846 Vt. Laws 34 (restricted to equines, cattle, sheep, swine); Mich. Comp. Laws 181.45 (1857) (limited to horses, cattle, or other beasts); Me. Laws ch. IV, § 7 (1821) (crime to "cruelly beat any horse or cattle")). Thus, to revisit the ailurosadistic Mr. Tweedie of 1792: had the feline instead been his boss's *bovine* set aflame with oil and torch, he likely would have served penance in the gaol. However, he would face no penalty for burning a cat to death, whether stray, kept by his neighbor, or even his own, unless made into the nuisance of a public spectacle.

Not until what Professor Favre describes as the "Bergh Era" did a conceptual transformation occur, breathing Benthamite[12] principles into stale legislation, and extending the mantle of police power to protect not only the unowned animals living according to their own instinct and intellect, nor only beasts of burden or animals in whom a purest property interest might be asserted, but also those harmed by the hands of their putative caretakers. One such manifestation is found in N.Y. Rev. Stat. tit. 6, § 26 (1829), expanding the crime to punish those who maliciously harm a "horse, ox or other cattle, or any sheep, belonging to another" to those who "maliciously and cruelly beat or torture any such animals, *whether belonging to himself or another* [.]") (discussed in Favre, at 9). Were the ignominious Mr. Tweedie to have plied his malevolence in the state of New York in 1829, with passage of the first, true anti-cruelty law, again, only farmed animals would find vindication.

Early anticruelty laws would occasionally enumerate the protected class of animals to include the term "beast," but because dogs, cats, songbirds, and other traditional animal companions were not even subjects of larceny, courts refused to bring such species within the ambit of the law's protection. For instance, *U.S. v. Gideon*, 1856 Minn. LEXIS 9 (1856) refused to characterize a dog shot by Mr. Gideon as a "beast" for purposes of a Minnesota law making it a crime to "willfully and maliciously kill, maim or disfigure any horses, cattle or other beasts of another person." It found that canines "have, in law, no value, were not intended to be included in that general term." Rather, "beasts may well be intended to include

---

[12] An English barrister, utilitarian Jeremy Bentham is best known for *Introduction to the Principles of Morals and Legislation* (Oxford: Clarendon Press 1781), where he eloquently observed at 310-11 n1, "The question is not, Can they *reason*? Nor, Can they *talk*? But *Can they suffer*."

asses, mules, sheep and swine, and perhaps, some other domesticated animals, but it would be going quite too far to hold that dogs were intended." *Id.*, at 296.

In the century and a half since Twain, Bergh, and *Gideon*, the moral and scientific[13] mandate to stem animal cruelty has rapidly evolved to encompass human behaviors under heinous circumstances that failed to garner political traction due to the philosophical impediments of an earlier time. Despite the surge in regulation, not all crimes against animals are created equal. For instance, some jurisdictions felonize only acts of commission (such as setting a cat on fire), while others include acts of omission (such as depriving a dog of food and water).[14] Some require heightened *mens rea* like malice or wantonness, while others see fit to punish criminal negligence. In an effort to take the monetary gain and bragging rights out of cruelty, at least one state has criminalized derivative acts by those not directly involved in the abuse or neglect. Illinois recently enacted an antidepiction law, punishing those who purvey, promote, advert, and thereby promote animal cruelty even where they had no hand in the torture. Merely creating, selling, marketing, offering to market or sell, or possessing images of animal cruelty constitutes a crime, even if the conduct took place outside of Illinois. 510 Ill. Comp. Stat. 70/3.03-1.

Other variations in animal cruelty laws turn on such factors as:

Inducing Children: Inducing children to engage in animal cruelty, or what Kansas calls criminal sodomy, carries a greater penalty than were the adult perpetrator alone to have raped the animal. Cf. Kan. Stat. Ann. § 21-5504(a)(2) (Class B nonperson misdemeanor) and Kan. Stat. Ann. § 21-5504(b)(2) (level 1 person felony). *See also* Minn. Stat. § 343.31 (gross misdemeanor for sexual assault committed in presence of another person); and RCW § 16.52.205(1) (felony to force a minor to inflict unnecessary pain, injury, or death on an animal).

Aiding and Abetting Abusers: Occasionally, victimized animals are seized by animal care and control. A person who obtains that "previously abused, neglected or abandoned animal" and "knowingly allows the person from whom the animal was forfeited to possess the animal" is guilty of a Class C misdemeanor for encouragement of animal abuse. Or. Rev. Stat. § 167.349.

Repeat Offenders: Though most jurisdictions treat first-time offenders as felons, others like Idaho use a three-strikes model. Idaho Code § 25-3520A(3)(b) (felony only if found guilty or pled guilty to two prior violations for intentional and malicious infliction of pain, physical suffering, injury or death upon an animal, within 15 years of the first conviction).

---

[13] While religious and secular humane considerations no doubt motivated the development of animal welfare crimes, the role of science in dismantling the Cartesian model of animals as machines and diagnosing causes of human pathology (e.g., hoarding, the link to serial killing) and the psychological afflictions of animals (e.g., stereotypy) cannot be discounted.

[14] On July 24, 2005, Washington's felony animal cruelty law was amended to include criminally negligent acts related to starving, dehydrating, or suffocating an animal. The misdemeanor law was also amended. The practical effect was to felonize animal neglect related to lack of food, water, and ventilation, but regard as misdemeanors animal neglect related to lack of shelter, rest, sanitation, space, and medical attention. RCW § 16.52.205(2).

Species: Certain species curry greater favor. In Alabama, dogs and cats have their own anticruelty law, conferring protection against first or second degree cruelty or torture. Ala. Code § 13A-11-241. In Pennsylvania, one who shoots, maims or kills any Antwerp or homing pigeon, while on flight or at rest, or detains or entraps any such pigeon which carries the name of its owner is guilty of a crime. 18 Pa. Cons. Stat. Ann. § 5511(l). Most states exclude fish and invertebrates entirely. See Ariz. Rev. Stat. § 132910(H)(1) ("[M]ammal, bird, reptile or amphibian"); Del. Code Ann. Tit. 11, § 1325(a)(11) ("Animal" excludes fish, crustacean, molluska); N.M. Stat. Ann. § 30-18-1 ("'Animal' does not include insects or reptiles"). In South Carolina, "fowl" are not covered. S.C. Code Ann. § 470-1-40(C). Other statutory definitions are quite broad. Md. Code Ann., Crim. Law § 10-601(b) ("[A] living creature except a human being"). Pay close attention to those that vary by section within the same chapter. For instance, Washington's general definition of "animal" encompasses "any nonhuman mammal, bird, reptile, or amphibian," yet the definition used for felony animal cruelty includes "every creature, either alive or dead, other than a human being." RCW §§ 16.52.011(2)(b), 16.52.205(8)(a).

Mandatory Reporting: Unless eyewitnessed by a law enforcement officer, most cruelty cases are complaint-driven. Because veterinarians, like pediatricians, will tend to see signs of animal cruelty more frequently than other practitioners, some states confer immunity for permissive or mandatory reporting of suspected illicit fighting or abuse. Ariz. Rev. Stat. § 32-2239 (mandatory); Cal. Bus. & Prof. Code §§ 4830.5, 4830.7 (mandatory); Colo. Rev. Stat. § 12-64-121 (mandatory); 225 Ill. Comp. Stat. 115/25.19, 510 Ill. Comp. Stat. 70/3.07, 510 Ill. Comp. Stat. 70/4.01, 70/4.02, 5/26-5; Utah Code Ann. §§ 58-28-602, 76-9-301(13) (permissive); 9 Guam Code Ann. § 70.11(f) (physicians, health care professionals, and veterinarians must report dogfighting or risk loss of license). Kentucky, on the other hand, actually bars veterinarians from voluntarily reporting suspected animal cruelty or fighting without a court order, subpoena, or client waiver. Ky. Rev. Stat. Ann. § 321.185. In Maine, reporting obligations vary by severity. Me. Rev. Stat. Ann. Tit. 7, § 4018 (permissive for cruelty or neglect; mandatory for aggravated cruelty).

Euthanasia: While nontherapeutic euthanasia remains a deeply unfortunate though necessary practice, some laws have something to say about the *manner* of killing. In Alaska, Arkansas, California, Delaware, Idaho, Indiana, Maryland, Minnesota, New Jersey, New York, and Wyoming, euthanasia by high-altitude decompression chamber is a crime. Alaska Stat. § 11.61.140(a)(3); Ark. Code § 5-62-117; Del. Code § 8005; Idaho Code § 25-3516; Ind. Code § 15-5-17; Ann. Code of Maryland § 10-611; Minn. Stat. § 343.37; N.J. Stat. § 4:22-19; N.Y. Agr. & Mkts. § 26-374; Wyo. Stat. § 6-3-203. In California and New Mexico, it is a crime to kill an animal by intracardiac injection on a conscious animal unless heavily sedated or circumstances justify it, as well as by decompression and nitrogen gas. Cal. Pen. Code § 597u; N.M. Stat. § 30-18-15; *see also* Cal. AG Op. 01-103 (2002). Maine permits euthanasia by gunshot only where the shooter is 18 or older, using a weapon requiring only a single shot, causing instant death, and the animal is not restrained in a way to cause undue suffering. Maine Rev. Stat. § 4011.

Banning Animal Products: Though not a crime, in 2004, the California State Legislature codified Cal. Health & Safety Code 25980-25984, making it unlawful and imposing a fine of $1000 a day to produce and sell foie gras in California. However, one could lawfully consume, gift, or import the enlarged goose or duck liver, artificially increased in size by inhumanely jamming a pipe down the bird's throat and filling it with food for nonnutritive purposes. The day after it went into effect, Jul. 2, 2012, two foie gras producers and a California restaurant group sought to overturn the law in federal district court. They failed in their challenge. *Association des Eleveurs de Canards et D'Oies du Quebec v. Harris*, 729 F.3d 937 (9th Cir. 2013) (affirming trial court's refusal to issue temporary restraining order and preliminary injunction, finding statute neither vague nor in violation of dormant commerce clause), *cert. denied*, 2014 LEXIS 5114098 (2014). For further commentary, see *Kristin Cook, The Inhumanity of Foie Gras Production — Perhaps California and Chicago Have the Right Idea*, 2 J. Animal L. & Ethics 263 (2007). False advertising lawsuits have also arisen. *ALDF v. HVFG, LLC*, 939 F. Supp. 2d 992 (N.D. Cal. 2013) (foie gras producer slogan "the humane choice" could be subject to claim under the Lanham Act, and Regal Vegan, Inc., a vegan food producer had standing).

Animal "Purpose": Though not enrolled in vocational training by choice, animals raised and/or trained to take on a human-desired *raison d'etre* may find special criminal protections not afforded their other-focused counterparts.

Law Enforcement Animals: Estimates ranging from 9,000 to 15,000 identify the number of patrol and detection dogs working for law enforcement. Dignitary rites, such as full police burial for those killed in the line of duty, designations as officers who have "sworn" an oath, and outfitting chosen canines with body armor may reflect respectful institutional attitudes and an investment-protecting sentiment, but such canines remain property in the eyes of the law. The vast majority of states make it a felony to harm a law enforcement dog or horse. Conn. Gen. Stat. § 53-247(d) (intentionally kill a law enforcement animal); 510 Ill. Comp. Stat. 70/4.04 (felony to injure or kill police animals, service animals, or search and rescue dogs); N.H. Rev. Stat. Ann. § 644:8-d (killing law enforcement dog or horse is Class B felony); RCW § 9A.76.200 (class C felony for harming police dog, accelerant detection dog, or police horse by maliciously injuring, disabling, shooting, or killing); W.Va. Code §§ 19-20-24, 61-3E-6 (intentional harm to law enforcement animal or injury to explosives-detection animal a felony). Those who willfully and maliciously harm federally commissioned law enforcement animals face up to a year in prison; if permanently disabled, disfigured, seriously injured or killed, the defendant may be imprisoned for up to a decade. 18 U.S.C. § 1368.

Service, therapy, and assistance animals: Hy Cohen, a 24-year-old blind man, could hardly make it down the street before a neighbor's aggressive dog running at large would accost him and his guide dog Layla. Vicious altercations made Layla reticent and substantially impaired her ability to work safely with Hy. At the time, the most the city could do was cite the dog owner with a civil infraction for dog off-leash. Frustrated by the weakness of the then-existing suite of animal-related crimes, Mr. Cohen lobbied strenuously for passage of what later became codified in Washington State as Layla's Law, making it a crime (varying from gross misde-meanor to Class C felony) for a person (or person's dog) to interfere, obstruct, intimidate, or jeopardize the safety of a dog guide or service animal. RCW § 9.91.170 (2001). Other states have also enacted such laws. Or. Rev. Stat. § 167.352 (Class A misdemeanor to interfere with assistance, search and rescue, or therapy animal); 18 Pa. Cons. Stat. Ann. § 5511(a)(1) (owning a dog who kills, maims, or disfigures a guide dog is a third degree misdemeanor); Tenn. Code. Ann. § 39-14-216 (maiming service animal is Class A misdemeanor; interfering with service animal is Class C misdemeanor); Tex. Penal Code § 42.091 (felony for injuring or killing assistance animal); Haw. Rev. Stat. § 711-1109.4 (injury or death to service dog or law enforcement animal is Class C felony).

Farmed animals: The most numerous and, sadly, the least protected, animals languishing in agricultural operations have seen increased criminal regulation in the form of restrictions on confinement of calves raised for veal and pregnant pigs (Ariz. Rev. Stat. § 13-2910.07; Me. Rev. Stat. Ann. Tit. 17, § 1039; Colorado 2008; Oregon 2007) and mishandling or trading of nonambulatory livestock (RCW § 16.52.225, ORS § 167.351, Cal. Penal Code § 599f).[15] Likely motivated by a spate of satanic ritual sacrifices and cattle mutilations,[16] cruelty to livestock and theft of livestock laws have taken root in some jurisdictions, even though seemingly duplicative of crimes involving non-farmed animals. For instance, in 2011, Washington enacted RCW 16.52.320, making it a Class C felony to with malice, kill or cause substantial bodily harm to livestock belonging to another person.

Zoo animals: Animals removed from their families and ecosystems, forced to spend their lives in captivity, cannot be said to lead an existence at all on par with their uncaught wild relatives. While accreditation standards and industry-accepted husbandry practices purport to enhance the well-being of those kept in zoos and marine parks, those protocols also serve to exonerate would-be abusers. An apparent rarity, Pennsylvania made it a third-degree felony to "willfully and maliciously kill[], maim[] or disfigure[]" or "administer[] poison to or expose[] any poisonous substance with the intent to administer such poison to" any "zoo animal in captivity." 18 Pa. Cons. Stat. Ann. § 5511(a)(2). This nod to the caged tiger appears progressive were it not for further examination of the definitions found in subsection (q). For while Pennsylvania does not categorically exempt customary zoological husbandry practices, it does so *impliedly* by criminalizing only that behavior which no reputable zoological association would endorse (i.e., willful and malicious harm). Furthermore, "zoo animals" only include members of the classes of mammalia, aves, amphibia, or reptilia kept in a confined area by a public body or private individual for purposes of observation by the general public, meaning that the arachnid, invertebrate, and aquarium exhibits (except for dolphins, whales, and other cetaceans — who belong to the class of mammals) lack protection.

Wildlife: If the criminal statute itself does not exclude wildlife,[17] then take care to examine whether fish and wildlife laws preempt anticruelty legislation, whether expressly or as a practical allocation of enforcement jurisdiction between game officers and animal control officers. This traditional hierarchy is slowly upending. In 2013, California enacted AB 789, prohibiting cruel wildlife killing methods. Codified as an amendment to Cal. Fish & Game Code § 4004, the law proscribes the use of

---

[15] See Animal Welfare Institute, *Legal Protections for Nonambulatory (or "Downed") Animals*, https://awionline.org/sites/default/files/uploads/documents/fa-legalprotectionsfordownedanimals-12262013.pdf

[16] To learn more about cult-inspired animal crimes, see www.vactf.org/manul/chap5/section4.php.

[17] In *State v. Cleve*, 127 N.M. 240 (1999), the Supreme Court of New Mexico held that the animal cruelty statute did not apply to wild animals, namely, two deer ensnared by Charles Cleve.

body-gripping traps for recreation or commerce in fur, certain conibear traps, and killing trapped mammals "by intentional drowning, injection with any chemical not sold for the purpose of euthanizing animals, or thoracic compression, commonly known as chest crushing." In 2001, Washington voters passed Initiative 713, codified as RCW § 77.15.194, making it illegal to buy, sell, barter, exchange or offer to buy, sell, barter, or exchange any raw fur of mammal trapped with a steel-jawed leghold trap or other body-gripping trap, whether or not pursuant to permit. Violation of the law constitutes a gross misdemeanor. Crimes also define certain forms of illicit hunting, such as unlawful bear exploitation (Ark. Code Ann. § 5-62-124), using dogs or bait to hunt black bears or cougars (ORS § 498.164), unlawfully using dogs to pursue black bears, cougar, bobcat, or lynx (RCW § 77.15.245), or hounding deer or elk (RCW § 77.15.240). In 2013, Vermont enacted HB 101, taking steps to rein in captive hunts of feral pigs. 10 VSA 4709. In 2014, a coalition of state and national groups launched a ballot initiative to stop bear hounding, baiting, and trapping. Titled the Maine Fair Bear Hunting Act, the proposal sought to preserve "fair-chase bear hunting" and eliminate the last bastion in America that permits these practices. www.fairbearhunt.com.

Exemptions abound: Along the perimeter of every anticruelty law one cannot help but observe find gaping exclusions, permitting abominable abuses premised on industrial standards, not necessarily social consensus. Most commonly, the following cruel practices find refuge from punishment: agricultural farmed animal husbandry, slaughter, rodeos and fairs, zoos and circuses, research, fishing, hunting, and trapping; pest control, training and discipline, and veterinary practice. Georgia, for instance, excludes "any pest that might be exterminated or removed from a business, residence, or other structure" from its definition of "animal" as used in its animal cruelty chapter. Ga. Code Ann. § 16-12-4(a)(1)). Arkansas explicitly exempts training devices, anti-bark collars, and invisible fences, and, despite its lethal capacity, even goes so far as to justify a person shooting a dog or cat with a BB gun "not capable of inflicting serious injury" when the animal "is defecating or urinating on the person's property." Ala. Code § 13A-11-246(4-5). Alaska permits otherwise cruel acts "necessarily incidental to lawful fishing, hunting or trapping activities." Ak. Stat. § 11.61.140(c)(4). Arizona excludes the standard activities but curiously adds "security services." Ariz. Rev. Stat. § 13-2910.05. Arkansas furnishes an Acts of God defense to deflect allegations of aggravated cruelty to a dog, cat or horse. Ark. Code § 5-62-126. Some states, like Washington, employ language that delegates to a vague group of individuals the task of determining what constitutes cruel treatment, without parameters or guidelines. In the end, this ill-defined band of private citizens and corporations decides who is exempt from prosecution for nonspecific "practices," "uses," and "rights." No bounds are placed on such exemption terminology as the following:

- "accepted husbandry practices used in the commercial raising or slaughtering of livestock or poultry, or products thereof" (RCW § 16.52.185);

- "the use of animals in the normal and usual course of rodeo events" (RCW § 16.52.185);

- "the customary use or exhibiting of animals in normal and usual events at fairs as defined in RCW § 15.76.120" (RCW § 16.52.185);

- "accepted animal husbandry practices" (RCW § 16.52.205(6)); and

- "accepted veterinary medical practices by a licensed veterinarian or certified veterinary technician" (RCW § 16.52.205(6)).

These exclusions and limitations beg the following questions:

1. What is an "accepted animal husbandry practice," "normal and usual" rodeo event, "customary use or exhibit[ion] of animals in normal and usual" fairs, and "accepted veterinary medical practice"?

2. Who decides what is "accepted"?

3. What geographical, philosophical, scientific, medical, or moral standard, if any, applies in making such a decision?

The Supreme Court of New Jersey examined such concerns in *New Jersey SPCA v. N.J. Dep't of Agriculture*, 955 A.2d 886 (N.J. 2008). In 1996, the New Jersey Legislature amended its 1898 animal cruelty law to vest in the New Jersey Department of Agriculture ("NJDA") the authority to establish "humane" standards for the treatment of domestic livestock. The NJDA was given six months to act, but it took seven years for the agency to publish proposed regulations for public comment. Ultimately enacted were regulations that, among other concerns, created an exemption for "routine husbandry practices." The New Jersey Society for the Prevention of Cruelty to Animals ("NJSPCA"), the organization historically charged with enforcing the animal cruelty law, challenged the NJDA regulations as deficient in several respects, primarily that they sanctioned cruelty to farmed animals. The appellate court approved all NJDA regulations, and the NJSPCA appealed.

In a 7-0 decision, the New Jersey Supreme Court reversed in part. The court expressly refused to evaluate whether specific practices were objectively inhumane but, instead, considered whether the NJDA's actions, to which the high court gave due deference for agency expertise, complied with the legislative mandate. In this respect, the court invalidated certain NJDA regulations that used "unworkable standards and an unacceptable delegation of authority to an ill-defined category of presumed experts." NJSPCA prevailed in its argument that the agency's definition of "routine husbandry practices" and the phrase "performed in a sanitary manner by a knowledgeable individual and in such a way as to minimize pain" did not pass muster. NJSPCA also prevailed in asserting that tail docking was inhumane. Unlike New Jersey, Washington did not even attempt to delegate to anyone (much less an administrative body) the task of implementing regulations that defined acceptable and unacceptable practices.

The Seattle, Washington-based Northwest Animal Rights Network took the position that such regulation removes any objectivity from the governing process, incentivizing a self-serving approach for industry to institutionalize any cost-saving practice, regardless of how cruel, and to increase the number of exempt methods available by formulating new ones until a critical mass embraces (i.e., "accepts") it. By defining acceptable animal husbandry practices according to what the majority, or possibly the substantial minority of a group or industry, does, might such statutory exemptions court abuse by the very individuals they mean to regulate? Or is self-regulation the least offensive and most practical means of allowing those who work directly with animals to decide what practices best fit the prevailing bounds of decency and humane treatment? The Washington Court of Appeals did not reach the merits of NARN's nondelegation violation contentions, instead affirming dismissal on grounds of nonjusticiability, failure to join indispensable parties, and raising a political question. *Northwest Animal Rights Network v. State of Washington*, 242 P.3d 891 (Wash. Ct. App. 2010). A similar challenge to religious exemptions under Washington's Humane Slaughter Act failed due to nonjusticiability and the court's discomfit with seeking partial statutory invalidation; it did not address the merits. *Pasado's Safe Haven v. State of Washington*, 259 P.3d 280 (Wash. Ct. App. 2011). To read more about broad anticruelty exemptions, see William A. Reppy, Jr., *Broad Exemptions in Animal-Cruelty Statutes Unconstitutionally Deny Equal Protection of the Law*, 70 LAW & CONTEMP. PROBS. 255 (2007).

Rarely do scientists face prosecution under a state's animal cruelty law. Vivisector Dr. Edward Taub, chief scientific investigator for primate research, performed somatosensory deafferentation on 17 macaque monkeys at the NIH-funded Institute for Behavioral Research. PETA co-founder Alan Pacheco was apparently a plant working with Taub when he took photos and notes to the Silver Springs prosecutor to arrest Taub on 119 counts of animal cruelty and neglect. Taub raised various defenses, including a challenge to the constitutionality of Maryland's anticruelty law, preemption by the federal Animal Welfare Act, and disputed evidentiary rulings. His conviction on six counts of failure to provide veterinary care and, on appeal to circuit court, failure to provide necessary veterinary care to Nero, were vacated by the Maryland Court of Appeals in *Taub v. State*, 463 A.2d 819 (Md., 1983). The appellate court held that the legislative intent of Maryland's law did not contemplate vivisection for medical research, reasoning that failing to provide necessary veterinary care was neither "unnecessary" nor "unjustifiable" and was "purely incidental and unavoidable" as part of "normal human activities." The court bolstered its conclusion by observing that the AWA governed research facilities and provided a "comprehensive plan for the protection of [those animals] . . . while at the same time recognizing and preserving the validity of use of animals in research." It also alluded to various CFRs regulating the AWA and NIH Grants. *See also Applicability of State Animal Cruelty to Medical or Scientific Experimentation Employing Animals*, 42 A.L.R. 4TH 860.

Sentencing: Penalties upon conviction vary, as some felonies are ranked offenses with mandatory sentencing ranges for incarceration; unranked felonies, on the other hand, leave open the potential for no jail time regardless of the number of priors. For instance, not until 2006 did Washington rank its first felony animal cruelty offense, and then only for felony animal sexual assault under RCW § 16.52.205(3), not any other form of felony animal cruelty (which remain classified as an unranked Class C felony). RCW § 9.94A.515, Table 2 (Rank III).

Ranking also matters to juvenile offenders. Consider the case of Max. As midnight approached on July 20, 2003, three teenagers abducted Max Womack, a two-year-old tabby in good health, from the front porch of Bernadette Womack, a Spokane Valley resident. After driving him to Centennial Middle School, the teenagers took Max to the ball field, doused him in gasoline, and set him on fire. Max suffered severe and extensive burns, causing excruciating pain and terror. At her veterinarian's behest, Max was euthanized a few days later due to the extent of his injuries. Two of the three culprits, teenagers Rusty von Rardon and Jason Brumback, were arrested and charged with first-degree animal cruelty (RCW § 16.52.205). The juveniles pled guilty to the felony charge in September. The former's deferred disposition was revoked based on too numerous modifications. The latter completed his deferral. Sentenced to no detention, Spokane County Superior Court Judge Schroeder ordered the young men to pay restitution, submit to community supervision, and to complete community service with animal control agencies (which promptly refused to allow them to serve time in their facilities). Public outrage at the light penalty spread across the nation.

Aside from media pressure, one legislative response swiftly emanated from Senator Bob McCaslin's office. In December 2003, he introduced SB 6105. This juvenile sentencing bill proposed significant changes whenever minors faced charges of felony animal cruelty. Within three months, after a House amendment and substitution in the Senate, the final bill changed the rules for minors: (1) the juvenile court may require the offender to submit to a mental health evaluation; (2) the court may order mental health treatment as a condition of community supervision; (3) upon conclusion of the period for the order of deferral, the conviction is nonexpungeable; (4) the seriousness ranking for first-degree animal cruelty increases from C to B, changing the standard range disposition from local sanctions for the first, second, and third offense (15–36 weeks confinement only for fourth offense of animal cruelty) to local sanctions only for the first and second offense (with 15–36 weeks for the third offense; and 52–65 weeks for the fourth offense). RCW § 13.40.127(9) and RCW § 13.40.0357 (2004).

To learn more about legal challenges to animal cruelty laws, *see* Sonja A. Soehnel, *What Constitutes Offense of Cruelty to Animals — Modern Cases*, 6 A.L.R. 5TH 733; and M.L.C., *Indefiniteness of Penal Statute or Ordinance Relating to Cruelty, or Similar Offenses, against Animals*, 144 A.L.R. 1041.

B. EVOLVING LAWS CHANGING WITH HUMAN MISBEHAVIOR

Animal-based crimes enacted in the last few years would have been inconceivable a mere decade or two ago.

1. Hoarding

One example involves animal hoarding. In 2008, Hawaii became the first state to tackle the problem, outlawing animal hoarding. It defined the offense as intentionally, knowingly, or recklessly possessing more than 15 dogs and/or cats, failing to provide necessary sustenance to each, and failing to correct conditions under which they are living, where the conditions harm the animals' or owner's health. Haw. Rev. Stat. § 711-1109.6. Public health literature only began documenting the pathological accumulation of animals in 1981, with a formal profile in 1999. Vibrant debate recently erupted among psychologists and psychiatrists on the question of whether hoarding disorder is distinct from obsessive-compulsive disorder. The fifth edition of the Diagnostic and Statistical Manual of Mental Disorders (DSM-V), published in 2013, has a new chapter on Obsessive-Compulsive and Related Disorders, with a specific section devoted to hoarding disorder, which it characterizes as "persistent difficulty discarding or parting with possessions, regardless of the value others may attribute to these possessions."

Warehousing of inanimate objects alone, even to the extent of causing them to fall into disrepair or waste, does not necessarily endanger other beings, except when the accumulation solicits disease-carrying colonies of rodents, invites insect infestation, or presents a fire hazard, one of many concerns raised in 2012 by the city of Orange Village, Ohio, when it made maintaining uninhabitable dwellings a misdemeanor offense. The first big-city to pass a hoarding law was Houston, Tex. in July 2014, prohibiting the unlawful accumulation of "objects or substances of a nature or in a quantity reasonably likely to create a hazard to the safety of the health of an occupant or another dwelling unit on the same or a contiguous property[.]". Hous. Code Ch. 10, Art. XX, § 10-753 (2014). Nonhumans do not qualify as "occupants." Nor do minor children. Hous. Code Ch. 10, Art. XX, § 10-751 ("occupant"). Based on its drafting, animal hoarding would not violate the ordinance unless overwhelming odor, noise, or concentration of disease vectors spilled over to neighboring units or jeopardized the very health of the animals' owner. Because objects do not feel or suffer, and as nonvulnerable adult humans of sound mind can simply walk out the front door, hoarding is rarely criminalized. Those who cannot just leave, and are forced to live in squalor, such as the elderly and children, find refuge in child and elder abuse criminal laws, as do nonhumans under animal cruelty laws. Of those jurisdictions starting to enact antihoarding laws, the few that focus on animals take note of the distinction between nonhumans and inanimate objects, and the kinship they share with children and vulnerable adults.

While Illinois's Humane Care for Animals Act defines "companion animal hoarder" and mandates psychological counseling, it does not prohibit animal hoarding itself. Instead, it requires proof that the hoarder acknowledges deteriorating conditions of the animals and household environment, as well as failure to recognize the harmful effect hoarding has on the person's own health and well-being. 510 Ill. Comp. Stat. Ann. 70/2.10. *See* Victoria Hayes, *Detailed Discussion of Animal Hoarding*, Animal Legal & Historical Center (2010). While not an antihoarding law *per se*, North Carolina's progressive Civil Remedy for Protection of Animals law, N.C. Gen. Stat. § 19A-1 et seq. (2005), confers standing to private parties and organizations, even those who have suffered no injury, allowing them to obtain injunctive relief to protect animals in neglectful circumstances, as occurred in a case of more than 300 dogs in defendants' home. *See ALDF v. Woodley*, 640 S.E.2d 777 (N.C. Ct. App. 2007) (affirming injunction prohibiting defendants from violating anticruelty law, requiring them to properly maintain property where animals kept, and giving plaintiff access to property to care for animals; ultimately entering temporary custody order); David S. Favre, *Living Property: A New Status for Animals Within the Legal System*, 93 Marq. L. Rev. 1021 (2009–10) (describing the North Carolina law and resulting litigation as examples of "strong legal rights" for animals).

With DSM-V recognition of hoarding as a disorder, legal issues on the horizon include (1) whether such a disabled individual could demand the right to keep emotional support animals under the FHA, or bypass municipal ordinances limiting the number of animals one might keep due to OCD;[18] and (2) the extent to which a landlord's hands may be tied to evict the tenant for animal hoarding, if the animals do not behave in a way causing risk or constitute a nuisance to neighboring tenants.

2. Bear Wrestling, Kangaroo Boxing

Retired at the age of 25, and in his prime weighing nearly 700 pounds and towering seven feet tall, the Canadian wrestler "Terrible Ted" was an American black bear abducted from the Gaspé peninsula in Quebec. Despite being declawed, detoothed, and forced to travel with a bankrupted carnival, Dave McKigney "adopted" Ted and began advertising him in the wrestling circuit, where his mat card reveals he competed against (and defeated) several hundred human adversaries, including future World Wrestling Federation (WWF) champions. Litigation followed McKigney, who was sued for failing to pay a successful challenger John Szigeti, who pinned Ted "for maybe 15 seconds," and later by Ed Williams, who did not get his match as promised, resulting in Ted being held on a writ of attachment at the Lowndes County jail. *Bear Wrestler Sues Promoter*, THE PHOENIX (May 7, 1968); *Fighting Bear Chickens Out?*, BEAVER COUNTY TIMES (Oct. 16, 1970). In 1978, McKigney left the door to another bear's cage open, allowing Smokey to enter his home and kill his girlfriend Lynn Orser. The Ontario Humane Society seized Ted and Smokey. Bear wrestling is a Class A misdemeanor in Mo. Ann. Stat. § 578.176. Since 1992, it has been a crime to promote, engage in, sell, buy, possess, or train bears for bear wrestling matches in Louisiana. La. R.S. § 14:102:10. Other states have similar proscriptions. 21 Okl. St. Ann. § 1700 (extends to claw and teeth removal, tendon severing, doping; as well as horse tripping); Ala. Code 1975 § 13A-12-5 (class B felony); Ark. Code § 5-62-124 (class D felony); Tenn. Code § 70-4-402 (3) (defining "circus" to exclude wrestling bears).

Though popularized in Australia, kangaroo boxing fortunately remains an infrequently billed act within the United States. In 2011, however, former circus acrobat Javier Martinez advertised three-round matches with a kangaroo named Rocky in a traveling series of Florida exhibitions. PETA filed a complaint with the Florida Fish and Wildlife Conservation Commission and the Florida State Boxing Commission, but the latter claimed no jurisdiction over nonhuman pugilists, and the former took no action to discontinue the event. North Dakota has explicitly banned kangaroo boxing and other jurisdictions' animal fighting laws might be broadly construed to eliminate such events. See N.D. St. 36-21.1-07 (rendering illegal cockfighting, dogfighting, bearbaiting, kangaroo boxing and bear fighting). In an uncomfortable melee between women's and animal rights, read Hilary Golder and Diane Kirkby, *Mrs. Mayne and Her Boxing Kangaroo: A Married Woman Tests Her Property Rights in Colonial South Wales*, 21 LAW & HIST. REV. 585 (2003). To learn more about the many unsavory permutations of nonhuman animal competition, such as orangutan kickboxing, camel wrestling, and other exploitative practices throughout the world, *see* MARK HAWTHORNE, BLEATING HEARTS: THE HIDDEN WORLD OF ANIMAL SUFFERING (Changemakers Books: 2013).

---

[18] See http://www.parjustlisted.com/evicting-compulsive-hoarders-may-violate-fair-housing-laws/.

3.   Devocalization, Declawing, Cropping, Docking, Cosmetic Mutilation

Whether for conformational, aesthetic, or nuisance mitigation, animals endure various types of involuntary physical alteration. Most states criminalize, by measure and method, ear cropping and tail docking.[19] Anticropping laws seek to ensure surgeries only on unconscious animals and operated upon by a licensed veterinarian. *Elisea v. State of Indiana*, 777 N.E.2d 46 (Ind. Ct. App. 2002) (cropping puppies' ears with office scissors, without anesthetic, or sutures amounts to animal cruelty); N.J.S.A. § 4:22-26(s) [no more than one inch from tip of sheep or bovine ear]; Conn. G.S.A. 22-366 [must have veterinarian perform dog ear cropping under anesthesia]; 10 Guam C.S.A. 34205(d) [veterinarian must certify canine ear cropping's necessity for health and comfort]; RCW § 16.52.095 [crime to cut more than one-half of ear of any domestic animal, unless a customary husbandry practice]; RCW § 16.52.090 [crime to cut solid part of tail of any horse]. Such forms of mutilation have existed for hundreds of years. But what of those procedures showcased in a Mar. 9, 2012 episode of *20/20* titled "Pet Crazy: Pet Plastic Surgery," reporting on such procedures as ear piercing, creative styling, dyeing, tattooing, braces, face lifts, liposuction, nose jobs, Botox injections, and neuticles (artificial dog testicular implants). *See* http://abcnews.go.com/2020/video/pets-pampered-dogs-cats-dancing-crazy-wild-animals-15891140.

Holly Crawford decided to make her three kittens "goth," by, without anesthesia, piercing their ears with 14–gauge barbell earrings, a small submission ring on the back of their necks, and a barbell earring on the end of a docked tail (resulting from nonsurgical banding). The appellate court affirmed her conviction of cruelty to animals, finding nothing vague about the statute and noting that even "declawing a cat with a pair of pliers without anesthesia would be an inappropriate action and would constitute torture and the infliction of intense pain" under 18 Pa. C. S. A. § 5511. *Comm. v. Crawford*, 24 A.3d 396 (Pa. Super. Ct. 2011).

On Mar. 12, 2014, New York State Senator Martin J. Golden introduced SB 6798, seeking to prohibit the subjection of any dog, cat, or companion animal to a surgical procedure with no medical benefit to the animal, for cosmetic or aesthetic purposes. As of Jun. 20, 2014, it passed out of the Agriculture Committee and moved to Rules. Sponsors justified the new law as follows:

> Cosmetic procedures on companion animals have become increasingly common as people seek to alter the physical appearance of their household pets. Pet owners are resorting to unnecessary cosmetic procedures such as tattoos, piercings, rhytidectomy, abdominoplasty, and the removal of incisor teeth to achieve the desired result.

> This legislation would protect companion animals from being subjected to such treatment. While the psychological effect on these animals is an area of debate, the fact remains that each of these procedures requires an application of general anesthesia which poses a health risk in itself. The

---

[19] While dogs undergo cosmetic alteration, equines do as well. See Sandra Tozzini, *Hair Today, Gone Tomorrow: Equine Cosmetic Crimes and Other Tails of Woe*, 9 ANIMAL L. 159 (2003).

animal must then go through the pain of recovery and possible infection or post-surgery complications. These non-medical cosmetic procedures are not just odd and unnecessary, they amount to animal cruelty.

This legislation would also cover the sale of companion animals who have been subjected to certain cosmetic procedures. This would remove the impetus for retailers to physically modify an animal in the hopes of increasing its value to prospective buyers.

Conviction would result in a misdemeanor, punishable by no more than one year imprisonment, a fine of no more than $1,000.00, or both. This penalty would be not unlike similar animal rights violations.

Not to be confused with machines that strip bark off logs, a ventriculocordectomy (or "debarking" procedure) involves the excision of tissue from the vocal cords of an animal. *See* www.hsvma.org/assets/pdfs/devocalization-facts.pdf. In 2010, nontherapeutic devocalization of dogs and cats became punishable by no more than five years' incarceration in state prison or two and a half years in a correctional facility, and/or fine of not more than $2,500. Mass. Gen. Laws ch. 272, § 80½. Ohio only prohibits debarking of dangerous dogs. Ohio Rev. Code § 955.22(F)(1). New Jersey makes it a disorderly persons offense to knowingly fail to provide true information as to whether a dog has been surgically debarked or silenced. N.J.S. § 4:19-42. It also makes it a crime of the third degree to surgically debark or silence a dog for reasons "other than to protect the life or health of the dog as deemed necessary by a duly licensed veterinarian." N.J.S. § 4:19-38. Pennsylvania criminalizes debarking unless performed under general anesthesia by a licensed veterinarian. 18 Pa. C.S.A. § 5511(h)(2).

Though Minnesota has no anti-debarking law, a controversy over the procedure arose when a county board of commissioners issued a conditional use permit to a commercial Cocker Spaniel breeder who proposed to mitigate noise by devocalizing all dogs kept outdoors. After issuing the permit, the county learned that "surgical debarking is overwhelmingly disfavored within the veterinary community and that many allege it is inhumane," and thus the county attorney and administrator encouraged (but did not mandate) the use of shock collars instead of debarking. The Minnesota Federated Humane Society sought appellate review of the permit, which required, "All dogs which have access to the outside be debarked." The Minnesota Court of Appeals remanded for further assessment of whether the debarking condition should be stricken as arbitrary and capricious or, more plainly, cruel. *In re Block*, 727 N.W.2d 166, 180 (Minn. Ct. App. 2007).

At the behest and intense criticism of Jennifer Conrad, DVM, founder of The Paw Project (www.pawproject.org), on Apr. 21, 2003, the City of West Hollywood became the first American municipality to ban nontherapeutic declawing, much to the consternation of the California Veterinary Medical Association ("CVMA"), which failed in its suit seeking to neutralize the law on the theory of preemption. *CVMA v. City of West Hollywood*, 152 Cal. App. 4th 536 (2007). In 2009, other California cities followed — Los Angeles, San Francisco, Burbank, Santa Monica, Berkeley, Beverly Hills, and Culver City. To stem the tide, the CVMA lobbied for passage of SB 762, which prevented municipalities from regulating any procedure out of existence that fell within the professionally recognized scope of practice for that licensee. Cal. Bus. & Prof. Code § 460 (2010). In 2012, seeking to discourage the practice of nontherapeutic devocalization and declawing, California forbade landlords from discriminating against or discouraging applicants who refuse to declaw or devocalize their animals, where the property owner permits animal companions generally. Cal. Civ. Code § 1942.7. Rhode Island followed suit in 2014. R.I. Gen. Laws § 4-1-41. Cal. Penal Code § 597.6 makes it a crime to perform onychectomy or tendonectomy (also known as "declawing") on a member of an exotic or native wild cat species. On the other hand, 510 ILCS 70/3.03(b)(3) expressly exempts from the animal torture statute the alteration of an animal "for any legitimate purpose, including, but not limited to: . . . declawing, defanging, ear cropping, . . . tail docking."

4.   Renting and Time-Sharing Animals

In 2007, New York City-based FlexPetz, marketed as the ZipCar for animal lovers, offered a canine rental service in the United States and Britain. www. nytimes.com/2008/03/30/nyregion/30dogs.html?_r=0. This modern business model faced strident criticism, prompting legislation declaring it illegal to cause psychological damage to animals, promoting the concept of "disposable pets," and crossing "an ethical line," said Republican Massachusetts Representative Paul Frost, sponsor of the bill. Caitlin McDevitt, *Pet Rentals: Activists and Lawmakers Take Action*; see also animallawcoalition.com/boston-bans-pet-rentals for discussion on history of bills and talking points. Renting or leasing dogs is prohibited by Mass. Gen. Laws ch. 272, § 80I(b).

What about controlled interaction with dogs and cats for a fee, where possession and ownership remains with the proprietor but the patron has access to them for comfort and entertainment? Due to strict no-pet clauses for apartment dwellers, for at least a decade, cat cafés have become popular in Japan, with nearly 150 as of 2012. Amy Chavez, *Some Breaking mews on cat cafes*, JAPAN TIMES (Mar. 24, 2012); en.wikipedia.org/wiki/Cat_café. The phenomenon has attracted the attention of enterprising Brits as well, such as the owner of Lady Dinah's Cat Emporium. www.ladydinahs.com; Bethan McKernan, *Have a Cat with Your Coffee at London Café*, SEATTLE TIMES (Apr. 4, 2014). And in 2014, North America will see the opening of two cafes in San Francisco, one in Vancouver, B.C., two in Southern California, and Purrington's Cat Lounge in Portland, Ore. Provided they address any health and safety concerns, such as by ensuring that all cats are disease-free and kept away from food production locations, posting hand washing stations and sanitizer dispensers extensively throughout the cafe with instructions to wash and sanitize before and after handling the cats, and loaning slippers for wearing inside the café to avoid tracking in and exposing the animals to toxins from the outside, animal welfare concerns may still arise. For instance, rough handling or boisterous noises could create undue stress and trauma.

While patrons may complain about coffee quality, some cafés use automatic, commercial-grade coffee dispensers instead of traditional barista equipment to avoid loud noises. They also implement house rules to maintain low indoor volume levels, disallow minors, and immediately intervene to protect a cat who wishes to be undisturbed. Although mishaps can occur in the evenings, cafés solicit volunteers or hire overnight monitors to ensure their well-being. And to avoid the quite common practice of sacrificing animal welfare for profit, the felines are not acquired from breeders, declawed, or disciplined; in many settings, they are up for adoption, giving the patron-applicant the opportunity to interact before signing a contract. A new business phenomenon, cat café regulation essentially consists of enforcing existing anticruelty legislation and ensuring acquisition of appropriate permits and licenses. Japanese regulators have had the greatest opportunity for oversight, including "cracking down on 24-hour cat cafés" to avoid cat service-worker exploitation. And in Ottawa, certain animal rights activists questioned whether the cafés were actually fronts for pet stores and sought to ban animals from public display after 8:00 p.m.

Hannah the Pet Society represents a modern example of companion animal leasing, using a business model that maintains ownership in the Society but grants to the Pet Parent lifetime veterinary and emergency care, boarding, expert behavioral guidance, and customized pet food (Total Lifetime Care®) for a single monthly fee. www.hannahsociety.com. Criticism includes that the "Parent" cannot dictate what treatments the animal will receive, or make end-of-life decisions, which are vested in Hannah's Medical Standards Board after consultation with the Pet Parent. www.wweek.com/portland/article-19896-rent_a_pup.html.

5. Canine and Equine Racing Events

The plight of greyhounds has received much deserved scrutiny. Erin N. Jackson, *Dead Dog Running: The Cruelty of Greyhound Racing and the Bases for its Abolition in Massachusetts*, 7 ANIMAL L. 175 (2001). Thirty-nine states have banned commercial dog racing outright. In the four states that have not enacted legislation to stop the practice, the tracks remain closed. But seven states still permit pari-mutuel racing — Arizona, Texas, Iowa, Arkansas, Alabama, West Virginia, and Florida. Colorado made in-state dog racing illegal (but permitted simulcasting received by an in-state facility authorized and operated pursuant to law) in 2013. C.R.S. 12-60-602 (2013). Though conventionally prosecuted under gambling codes, the cruelty infesting various stages of the dog racing enterprise also warrants invocation of the animal abuse laws, *provided* exemptions do not apply, as in Kentucky. KRC 525.130(2)(e) (exempting sporting activities, not limited to horse racing). Criticism has also hounded the treatment of thoroughbreds, again for good reason. William C. Rhoden, *Race's Aftermath Shows Sport's Brutal Side*, 157 N.Y. TIMES (May 4, 2008); *Filly's Death Brings Issues to Fore, but Where Is the Accountability?*, http://www.nytimes.com/2008/05/07/sports/othersports/07rhoden. html?_r=0 (accessed Aug. 21, 2014); Edward McClelland, *Is Horse Racing Immoral? How We Should Think about Deaths on the Racetrack*, http://www.slate. com/articles/sports/sports_nut/2012/05/kentucky_derby_2012_is_it_time_to_ban_ horse_racing_.html (May 4, 2012); Walt Bogdanich, Joe Drape et al., *Mangled Horses, Maimed Jockeys*, N.Y. TIMES, Mar. 24, 2012. For a historical overview of this event, see Joan S. Howland, *Let's Not "Spit the Bit" in Defense of "The Law of the Horse": The Historical and Legal Development of American Thoroughbred Racing*, 14 MARQ. SPORTS L. REV. 473 (2004); HOWLAND AND HANNON, A LEGAL RESEARCH GUIDE TO AMERICAN THOROUGHBRED RACING LAW FOR SCHOLARS, PRACTITIONERS AND PARTICI-

PANTS (Hein 1998). Injury of a race horse is a felony in Maryland. Md. Code Ann., Crim. Law. § 10-620.

While virtually every jurisdiction categorically excludes customary and usual fair and rodeo events, certain pastimes will no longer be countenanced. For instance, equine tripping has been banned in Arizona, Florida, Nevada, Oklahoma, and Oregon. Ariz. Rev. Stat. § 13-2910.09 (horse tripping is misdemeanor); Fla. Stat. Ann. § 828.12(4) (horse tripping third degree felony); Nev. Rev. Stat. § 574.100(5) (no intentional horse tripping allowed); ORS § 167.383; 21 Ok. St. Ann. § 1700.

6.   Crush Videos

In 1999, Congress passed 18 U.S.C. § 48, making it a felony to "knowingly create[], sell[], or possess[] a depiction of animal cruelty with the intention of placing that depiction in interstate or foreign commerce for commercial gain[.]" Impermissible depictions included "conduct in which a living animal is intentionally maimed, mutilated, tortured, wounded, or killed, if such conduct is illegal under Federal law or the law of the State in which the creation, sale, or possession takes place, regardless of whether the maiming, mutilation, torture, wounding, or killing took place in the State[.]" Legislative history reveals the Act primarily targeted "the interstate market for 'crush videos,'" which "often depict women slowly crushing animals to death 'with their bare feet or while wearing high heeled shoes,' sometimes while 'talking to the animals in a kind of dominatrix patter' over '[t]he cries and squeals of the animals, obviously in great pain,' to 'appeal to persons with a very specific sexual fetish[.]'" *U.S. v. Stevens*, 559 U.S. 460, 465–467 (2010) (quoting H.R.Rep. no. 106-397, pp. 2–3 (1999)). The common practice of masking the identities of the perpetrators depicted in the videos rendered prosecution extremely difficult, allowing the anonymous criminal acts to be enjoyed by purveyors and disseminators with impunity.

The law only survived 11 years before the United States Supreme Court dismantled it at the urging of Robert J. Stevens, proprietor of "Dogs of Velvet and Steel," who profited from selling videos of dogs fighting one another and gruesomely attacking a domestic pig, and who was indicted and convicted of three counts of violating § 48. The Third Circuit Court of Appeals vacated his conviction, finding the Act unconstitutional in violation of the First Amendment on grounds of vagueness and overbreadth, and refusing to apply the analogy between animal cruelty and child pornography or to treat animal cruelty depictions as belonging to their own category of unprotected speech such as obscenity. *U.S. v. Stevens*, 533 F.3d 218 (3d Cir. 2008). In affirming the Third Circuit, the United States Supreme Court deemed the Act overbroad, as it would force "[t]hose seeking to comply with the law" to face "a bewildering maze of regulations from at least 56 separate jurisdictions," given that § 48(a) in essence allows the one state or territory, for instance, to export its animal cruelty laws to the rest of the country. Using the no-hunting jurisdiction of District of Columbia as an example, the majority noted that a magazine depicting images of elk slain by bowhunters might showcase conduct legal in every jurisdiction *except* the Nation's Capital and, thus, expose the hunter, photographer, and entire magazine staff to criminal prosecution if the periodical made its way onto the shelves of a D.C. drug store. *U.S. v. Stevens*, 559 U.S. 460,

476 (2010). It developed the objection further by contrasting variations among jurisdictions that do not outlaw hunting altogether, but do impose restrictions as to the time, place, manner, and species, such as Missouri's permitting canned hunting of ungulates held in captivity, or Idaho's allowing the pursuit of sharp-tailed grouse, but not in Washington. *Id.* Having nullified the 1999 law, Congress expeditiously passed the Animal Crush Video Prohibition Act of 2010, amending 18 U.S.C. § 48 to cure the infirmities of the earlier version by narrowing the scope of the proscribed depiction from "animal cruelty" to "animal crush video" and increasing the penalty to a maximum of seven years imprisonment, rather than five. It is unlawful to knowingly create or distribute an animal crush video, defined as

> any photograph, motion-picture film, video or digital recording, or electronic image that (1) depicts actual conduct in which 1 or more living non-human mammals, birds, reptiles, or amphibians is intentionally crushed, burned, drowned, suffocated, impaled, or otherwise subjected to serious bodily injury (as defined in section 1365 and including conduct that, if committed against a person and in the special maritime and territorial jurisdiction of the United States, would violate section 2241 or 2242); and (2) is obscene.

18 U.S.C. § 48(a)(1)-(2) (2010). Note that unlike most traditional anticruelty laws, this federal statute does not require proof of pain or suffering; as much is implied by the focus on the malevolent acts themselves. Observe also the limitation to vertebrates and exclusion of fish and insects. Subsection (e) excepts the standard spate of "customary," "accepted," and "normal" uses and abuses of animals, such as in the veterinary, agricultural husbandry, slaughter, hunting, trapping, and fishing contexts. More information is available at: www.pet-abuse.com/pages/animal_cruelty/crush_videos.php.

Hypothetical: Michael Garcia awakened Emelie Martinez at 3:00 a.m., while holding the family's fishtank over his head. He then threw it into the television set, causing both to shatter and the goldfish to fall to the floor, gasping for air. "That could have been you," he warned. The commotion awakened Emelie's three children, ages nine, eight, and five, after whom the three goldfish were named. After Garcia ripped a VCR out of the wall, the children filed into the living room, where he then asked Juan, "You want to see something awesome?" and stomped on Juan's fish, killing him. In appealing his conviction for, inter alia, felony animal cruelty, Garcia argued that the goldfish was not a "companion animal" or "pet" for purposes of N.Y.Agr. & Mkts. § 353, nor that his stomping rose to the level of "aggravated cruelty." Inferring "that the Legislature's concern was with the state of mind of the perpetrator rather than that of the victim [goldfish]," and noting the link between violence against animals and violence against humans, the appellate division did not lend much credence to Garcia's contention that the fish died instantaneously without experiencing extreme pain. It affirmed his conviction, further finding that while goldfish differ in certain respects from the traditional mammalian animal companion, goldfish remain "one of the most common household pets." *People v. Garcia*, 29 A.D.3d 255 (N.Y. App. Div. 2006). If Garcia had mounted a tripod in the hallway to document his stomping on Juan the goldfish, with the intent of earning bragging rights (but not money) by uploading it to a website hosting company in the

Honduras, from which it would promote and broadcast such offensive content throughout the United States, would he have violated 18 U.S.C. § 48? That Garcia would not turn a profit does not matter under the 2010 Act, which removed the commercial element found in the 1999 predecessor. And subsection (c) addresses extraterritorial attempts to sell, market, advertise, exchange, distribute, or create animal crush videos outside the United States if there is an intent that it will find its way back to America. Yet the answer is decidedly no, for goldfish are not within the protected class of nonhuman animals. However heinous his behavior, its nonprurient nature would not render it "obscene."

Hypothetical:[20] Omak, Washington, is a small town of a few thousand people, in many ways typical of rural communities in Eastern Washington. But Omak is atypical of other rural towns in Washington, where residents revere the majestic animals that top the farm-animal pyramid. Omak's main attraction regularly, routinely, and blatantly kills horses. Every year the local rodeo, called the Omak Stampede, boasts of its main attraction "The World-Famous Omak Suicide Race." Over a span of four days and nights, riders repeatedly send horses off "Suicide Hill" with a 120-foot full-galloping start, plunging blindly 210 feet downhill, at a slope organizers have bragged is an "almost vertical . . . 62 degree angle." At breakneck speed, horses then meet (with concrete force) the rocky Okanogan River. After a panicked swim more than a football field in length, the horses face a final, grueling uphill sprint to the finish line.

In the decades that the Lynnwood, Washington-based Progressive Animal Welfare Society has been monitoring the race, at least 22 equine deaths have been documented; in 2004, three horses were killed in the first heat alone. Because practice runs were not official parts of the race, additional deaths went unreported. The total number in the last 30 years could be well over 35.

These horses, many "on-loan" for the event, have suffered heart attacks from overexertion, broken bones from collisions and shocking tumbles, and even horrifying death by drowning in the Okanogan River.

The Suicide Race was founded in 1935 by the Stampede's non-native, European American publicity chairperson. While its idea is loosely based on traditional mountain races, the Suicide race itself bears little resemblance to these traditional undertakings. In a culture where animals, especially the horse, are revered and respected, this event is a clear abuse of this heritage of trust between native peoples and their environment. The race has been denounced by former County officials, Native rights advocates, veterinarians and *Indian Country Today*, the leading American Indian news source. Commerce, not culture, is the real bottom line.

Is this event exempt under RCW § 16.52.185's clause "normal and usual course of rodeo events," even though there is no rodeo or stand-alone event in the United States similar to the Omak Suicide Race?

In 1993, the year before the Washington Legislature enacted the felony anticruelty *Pasado's Law*, in honor of Pasado, a donkey hanged and beaten to death

---

[20] This example quotes heavily from the summary provided by PAWS (www.paws.org/omak-suicide-race.html).

at Kelsey Creek Petting Zoo in Bellevue, Washington, PAWS attempted to privately prosecute Omak Stampede Director Cactus Jack Miller. In 1994, the Okanogan Superior Court dismissed motions by PAWS and Okanogan County Prosecutor Barnett Kalikow. Kalikow's attempt to revoke PAWS's charter through a writ of quo warranto failed while PAWS was barred from prosecuting Miller for allegedly violating state law in "causing injury to animals for gain and amusement." Dr. Michael Fox of the Humane Society of the United States called the Suicide Race "the most barbaric, inhumane spectacle of the twentieth century . . . an affront to all cowboys, equestrians and humanitarians."

What legal avenues might you take to address the abuses endured by the equine participants? And which prosecuting authority would have jurisdiction? The race takes the horses over tribal, nontribal municipal, and federal lands at various stretches. Might the Clean Water Act apply to halt the event due to activities involved in preparing the course for the race, given that it runs through the Okanogan River?

Hypothetical: It is July 3, 2011. Several junior high school-aged boys light sparklers and throw bang snaps at the asphalt. With them is Duncan, a three-year-old Golden Retriever, owned by a married couple who live down the street. Though initially scared, he is drawn to the colorful display. Another neighbor kid then arrives, having covertly smuggled in his older brother's M-80 firecracker, also known as a cherry bomb. Categorized as a Class C firework, it is presently legal to possess one that contains less than 50mg of flash powder, but it is unclear if this one did. With great anticipation, the boys encourage the kid to light the M-80. He sets it in a manhole cover, lights it, and he and the crowd back away to a safe distance. However, Duncan is drawn to the sizzle of the fuse and mouths it like a chew toy. Before the children can get Duncan to drop it, the M-80 goes off, causing Duncan's head to explode. He dies instantly without evidence of suffering or pain. Have any animal cruelty laws been violated?

Most animal cruelty laws require proof of a death causing undue suffering or physical pain. However, the killing of a dog owned by another in a criminally negligent fashion might violate other laws, such as malicious mischief or destruction of pet animal. Depending on whether this M-80 exceeded the limits set forth by the Child Protection Act of 1966, 15 U.S.C. 1261, and other ATF regulations, federal law may have been violated. *See U.S. v. Chalaire*, 316 F. Supp. 543 (E.D. La. 1970) (prosecution under CPA for sale of cherry bombs to teenagers, causing 13-year-old to nearly die and lose almost all his fingers on his left hand, most of the vision in his right eye, and a hole in his leg "big enough to put a baseball through").

Hypothetical: Tacoma, Washington's Point Defiance Zoo & Aquarium advertises Stingray Cove, where patrons may touch live stingrays without being stung by their barbs. How is this possible? Aquarists clip the barbs every few weeks with clippers like those used on dogs' toenails. www.pdza.org/stingraycove. Putting aside whether stingrays are considered "animals" under the applicable animal cruelty statutes,[21] do stingrays experience pain from the procedure? Do the American Zoo Association

---

[21] Many animal cruelty laws exclude fish. Stingrays (*D. pastinaca*), while vertebrates, are related to sharks and other cartilaginous fish.

and American Veterinary Medical Association regard debarbing as a generally accepted animal husbandry or veterinary practice exempt from such law?

C.   ABANDONMENT, HIT-AND-RUN, EXPOSURE AND OTHER VEHICULAR CRIMES

1.   Abandonment and Hit and Run

New York State may have enacted the first animal abandonment law. In discussing N.Y. Rev. Stat. § 682.2 (1866), Professor Favre recollects that "in the City of New York it was often the case that, when a work animal reached a point of age, disease, or exhaustion, so as to no longer have economic value, it was simply abandoned in the streets[.]" Favre, 1993 Det. C.L. Rev. at 15. Since 1866, abandonment of a disabled animal in such fashion has been deemed a crime in other jurisdictions. Nev. Rev. Stat. § 574.110 (maimed, diseased, disabled or infirm left to die in public street, road or public place, or to lie in public street, road or public place more than three hours after receiving notice left disabled). In Rhode Island, the penalty depends on whether the animal survives. R.I. Gen. Laws § 4-1-26 (felony for death, misdemeanor otherwise).

The traffic-related crime colloquially known as "hit-and-run" evokes images of mangled cars or unconscious pedestrians. But recently, the concept has extended to nonhuman animals struck by motor vehicles. Though not quite the type of Bad Samaritan law enacted after the murder of Kitty Genovese,[22] Puerto Rico enacted an animal hit-and-run law making it a misdemeanor to fail to call the animal round-up center or police upon running car over dog, cat, horse or head of cattle and failing to take necessary measures to tend to the injured animal. 5 L.P.R.A. 1666(d). See also Federal Way, Washington's FMC 9.18.020(2) (making it a crime to willfully run down an animal with a vehicle, and requiring the person to stop at the scene and render assistance, make an effort to locate and identify herself to the owner or keeper of animal, and report accident immediately to the police).

2.   Extreme Temperature Exposure

Though Henry Ford's Model T hit the showrooms in 1908, nonhuman animals did not become routine automobile passengers until long thereafter. Instead of leaving them at home, numerous people run errands with their animal companions.

---

[22] In 1964, this 29-year old woman was beaten to death outside her home while thirty-eight Queens residents failed to call the police or otherwise respond to her cries for help. In 1983, 21-year-old Cheryl Araujo was gang-raped on a pool table in a New Bedford, Mass. tavern as patrons stood by indifferently. For further analysis, see Anthony D'Amato, *The "Bad Samaritan" Paradigm*, 70 N.W. Univ. L. Rev. 798 (1976); Ken Levy, *Killing, Letting Die, and the Case for Mildly Punishing Bad Samaritanism*, 44 Ga. L. Rev. 607 (2010). Four states presently have Bad Samaritan Laws – Minnesota (Minn. Stat. Ann. § 604A.01), Rhode Island (R.I. Gen. Laws 11-1-5.1), Vermont (Vt. Stat. Ann. Tit. 12, § 519), and Wisconsin (Wis. Stat. Ann. § 940.34) – which variably impose a duty on a person at the scene of an emergency or crime to assist "another person" or "exposed person" suffering grave physical harm, or victimization of sexual assault, manslaughter, or armed robbery to the extent the person can do so without endangering oneself or others, including a duty to call the police. Wisconsin's law speaks nonspecifically to aiding the "victim," leaving open to judicial interpretation whether it applies to nonhuman animals.

Because nonservice animals cannot join them at the supermarket or other places of public accommodation, they remain inside an enclosed and locked vehicle. Under temperate conditions, and provided adequate airflow, such short-term confinement does not raise animal welfare concerns. But where the thermometer reaches either polar extreme, an animal may die or suffer irreversible brain damage from hypothermia or hyperthermia in a matter of minutes.

Leonard Lopez and his wife decided to take in a movie at a theater in San Antonio on Jul. 21, 1985. They left their dog in the automobile parked in direct sun, with the windows down about 1.5" on each side. The vehicle had a tinted glass "T-Top" permitting the sun to shine through the roof into the car's interior. While Mr. Lopez checked on his dog once during the show, an officer testified that "it was hot, very hot inside the car," far greater in temperature than outside the vehicle, and it was a quite warm, sunny, and dry day to begin with. Convicted of animal cruelty under Tex. Penal Code § 42.11(a)(4) (1986), for having "intentionally or knowingly transport[ed] or confine[d] an animal in a cruel manner," Mr. Lopez asserted lack of sufficient evidence and vagueness, grounds both rejected by the appellate court. *Lopez v. State*, 720 S.W.2d 201 (Tex. App. 1986)

To prevent what have been referred to as "hot dog" crimes, leaving animals unattended in a vehicle during extreme heat or cold, a number of states have imposed criminal penalties. Nev. Rev. Stat. § 574.195; N.H. Rev. Stat. Ann. § 644:8-aa; N.Y. Agric. & Mkts. Law § 353-d. W. Va. Code § 61-8-19(a) not only prohibits the dangerous confinement of an animal in a vehicle, but also forbids riding an animal when she is physically unfit, cruelly chaining or tethering an animal. Federal Way, Washington's Muni. Code § 9.18.020(4) makes it unlawful to "leave or confine an animal in any unattended motor vehicle under conditions that endanger the health or well-being of an animal due to heat, cold, lack of adequate ventilation, or lack of food or water, or other circumstances that could reasonably be expected to cause suffering, disability, or death to the animal." It adds that a "law enforcement officer or animal services officer is authorized to take all steps that are reasonably necessary for the removal of an animal from a motor vehicle, including, but not limited to, breaking into the motor vehicle, after a reasonable effort to locate the owner or other person responsible." Reflecting a new trend, Washington State enacted § 16.52.340 conferring full immunity on law enforcement and animal control officers who break and enter to save an animal from imminent harm due to extreme temperatures. An excellent survey of such laws may be found at the Animal Legal & Historical Center in Rebecca F. Wisch, *Table of State Laws that Protect Animals Left in Parked Vehicles* (2014) (www.animallaw.info/topic/table-state-laws-protect-animals-left-parked-vehicles).

Hypothetical: Jason Mulroy takes a road trip with his 10-year-old Jack Russell Terrier named Lucas. The hot weather prompts him to run the air conditioner as he travels 100 miles. The cabin temperature, though not measured, is approximately 75. Wanting to get a quick bite en route to the coast at Lincoln City, Mulroy parks his 2005 Mitsubishi Eclipse at the Whole Foods Market in Salem, Ore. in direct sunlight. The ambient outdoor temperature is 90, the time 1:15 p.m. on a quite warm summer day. He cracks all windows by 2", fully opens the sunroof, and runs inside. Though he was drinking from a water bottle, he forgets to pour it into Lucas's collapsible water bowl. After making his purchase, he returns to his vehicle at 1:30

p.m. to see it surrounded by two law enforcement officers and bystanders. Lucas barks loudly. One of the officers tells Mulroy to enter his vehicle and turn on the air. He obeys. For the next 30 minutes, they detain him. Probing an infrared thermometer through his passenger side tinted window just as Mulroy exits the store, one officer records a temperature of 98 degrees F. The same officer probes a nearby vehicle and records 113 degrees F. Lucas, meanwhile, has calmed down and sits alertly on Mulroy's lap. Officers note that Lucas was not panting furiously or barking in a fashion unusual to his breed. No rectal temperature is taken. Instead, he is released at the scene and cited with animal cruelty in the second degree for having willfully tormented, tortured, or injured a dog.

Should the charges against Mulroy be dismissed?

According to the Tufts Animal Care and Condition Scale (Patronek, GJ, *Recognizing and Reporting Animal Abuse — A Veterinarian's Guide*, American Humane Association (1997)), Mulroy would arguably have exposed Lucas to a "potentially life-threatening risk" for which "immediate intervention" was required. Predisposing factors that affect scaling include endogenous factors such as dog size, age, obesity, cardiovascular disease/abnormality, neurologic or neuromuscular disease, thick haircoat, upper airway abnormalities (brachycephalic) and exogenous factors like lack of acclimatization, confinement with limited ventilation or shade to avoid direct and full sunlight, water deprivation, medications such as diuretics, beta blockers, and phenothiazines. *Id.*; Carey Hemmelgarn & Kristi Gannon, *Heatstroke: Thermoregulation, Pathophysiology, and Predisposing Factors*, 35(7) VETSTREET, INC. COMPENDIUM (July 2013). The degree of window opening and vehicle color may also impact cabin temperature. I.R. Dadour & I. Almanjahie et al., *Temperature Variations in a Parked Vehicle*, 207 FORENSIC SCI. INT'L 205 (2011). For purposes of proving pain or suffering or significant risk of heatstroke, Lucas's core body temperature would need to rise above 105.8 degrees F., and he would have to show symptoms of excessive panting, elevated heart rate, hypersalivation and weakness, dry gums, nausea, and vomiting. Mariarita Romanucci & Leonardo Della Salda, *Pathophysiology and Pathological Findings of Heatstroke in Dogs*, VET. MED: RES. & REPORTS 2013:4 1-9.

Because no rectal temperature was taken, Lucas did not show symptoms of heat prostration or any diagnosable injury or suffering, and the evidence hardly supports a willfulness to harm Lucas, charges should be dismissed.

3. Unsafe Transport/Seatbelt Law for Animals

Vehicular cruelty crimes also include the prevalent problem of traveling with animals unrestrained in an open, uncanopied flatbed. Readers may be familiar with "Cover Your Load" traffic laws that require drivers to ensure debris does not dribble out from their vehicle or fly onto the roadway. What about *canine* loads?

Case Study: In summer, the sight is common. Dogs roving unrestrained in open pickup truck beds at freeway speeds, and people nearly striking such a dog when the owner hits his brakes. Though thrown clear from the vehicle and not hanged by a chain, the dog may suffer tremendously for several agonizing moments after hitting the asphalt. It may not die immediately from the wounds, but it defecates and urinates all over the road while trying in vain to crawl across the highway to its owner amidst the speeding cars. It may have been an incident of this type that prompted the Spokane Humane Society to prepare this flyer:

LAST EXIT

It's always been dangerous to carry a dog in the back of an open pickup truck. Traffic is unpredictable. Sudden stops and swerves can send dogs flying out to death and injury.

It's always been dangerous. And now, in the state of Washington, it's against the law. (RCW § 16.52.080)

It's easy to obey this law. Keep your dog in the cab with you, or use a crate or cross-tie. Call the Spokane Humane Society for more information.

Don't make the next stop your dog's last.

The law referred to by the Spokane Humane Society was first enacted in 1881 and amended four times, last in 1982. The law states:

RCW § 16.52.080. Transporting or confining in unsafe manner — Penalty.

Any person who wilfully transports or confines or causes to be transported or confined any domestic animal or animals in a manner, posture or confinement that will jeopardize the safety of the animal or the public shall be guilty of a misdemeanor. And whenever any such person shall be taken into custody or be subject to arrest pursuant to a valid warrant therefor by any officer or authorized person, such officer or person may take charge of the animal or animals; and any necessary expense thereof shall be a lien thereon to be paid before the animal or animals may be recovered; and if the expense is not paid, it may be recovered from the owner of the animal or the person guilty.

The 1982 amendment, however, aimed at prohibiting a person from transporting animals in the open bed of a truck. Changes made to the language of the statute demonstrate this, as well as two other documents found in the bill files in the Archives office. First, the wording of the statute was changed from prohibiting the transport or confinement of an animal "in a cruel and unnecessarily painful manner" (the thrust of the 1974 amendment) to prohibiting transport or confinement of a domestic animal in a "manner, posture, or confinement that will jeopardize the safety of the animal or the public" (the 1982 amendment). This change altered the focus of the statute from concern for the animals' comfort to one of animal and public safety.

A letter from the Washington State Federation of Humane Societies, dated March 9, 1981, stated that the amendment to RCW § 16.52.080 was necessary because "an increasing number of animals are injured/killed by being transported in the back of pickup trucks. In most cases, these animals are not securely caged, tied, etc. Amending this section should be helpful to humane officers, animal control personnel by permitting them to require the person who is transporting the animal to take appropriate safety precautions."

State Representative Shirley Winsley, one of the sponsors of the 1982 amendment, in response to a letter written by a citizen who opposed the amendment, stated initially that "there is no provision in the bill that states specifically that transporting of an animal in the back of a pickup is illegal." But she went on to explain that "'Section 5 does make it illegal to transport an animal in a manner'. . . that will jeopardize the safety of the animal or the public. . . . " She further explained that the provision making it illegal to transport an animal unsafely was unopposed. Then, after professing ignorance as to whether the manner in which the writer transported his animals was unsafe, she described a situation she personally observed in which a pickup stopped in front of her and a black Labrador dog jumped out of the open truck bed and ran into traffic, endangering both the dog and other drivers. Thus, despite her initial statement that there was no specific prohibition against transporting a dog in an open truck bed, the remainder of the letter, coupled with the statements in the Washington State Federation of Humane Societies' letter, made it clear that prohibiting dog owners from traveling with dogs in the open bed of a truck was the primary impetus behind the amendment.

Many years ago, NPR radio station KUOW interviewed Captain Tim Braniff with the Washington State Patrol, who said that transporting dogs in pickup truck beds is not illegal, although if the animal was on the running board, hood, roof, or bumper, then a citation under RCW § 46.61.600 may issue. Essentially, the animal was treated as a load that has been dropped or poorly covered, but aside from the fine, Braniff was apparently resolute in stating that it was not a criminal act.[23]

A potential unintended consequence of aggressively enforcing RCW § 16.52.080 is that, like the "mud flap" law police often use as a pretext to stop a truck to search for more serious crimes, law enforcement could use RCW § 16.52.080 for pretextual stops and selective enforcement. If the driver is then arrested far from home and unable to post bail, what would become of his dog while he or she was imprisoned?[24]

D. HORSE SLAUGHTER

Horsemeat consumption by the French, Belgians, and Japanese prompted the creation of three equine slaughterhouses in the United States — Dallas Crown, Inc. in Kaufman, Tex.; Beltex Corp. in Fort Worth, Tex., and Cavel International in DeKalb, Ill. — all owned by Belgians. In 1998, California voters passed Proposition 6, later enacted as Cal. Pen. Code § 598c, making it a felony to possess, import or export, sell, buy, give away, hold, or accept any horse with the intent of killing, or having another kill, that horse, if the person knows or should know that the horse will be slain for human consumption. Those who sell horsemeat are guilty of a

---

[23] Ross Reynolds, 94.9FM KUOW, The Conversation, "Drive You Crazy" (10/21/2003). http://www2. kuow.org/program.php?id=4647.

[24] To that end, the author initiated a "Letter from Your Dog" campaign. Upon seeing a person violating RCW § 16.52.080, he takes down the license plate, uses public disclosure to identify the driver, and sends a letter to the registered and legal owner from "their dog." Written from the canine perspective, it kindly reminds its owner-guardian of the law and asks that she "buckle [the dog] up" as she would a small child or human friends and family who might be inclined to hitch a ride in the back. The letter is nonthreatening and intended to educate. The lives of innocent dogs and passengers could depend on it.

misdemeanor. Cal. Pen. Code § 598d. See http://vote98.sos.ca.gov/VoterGuide/
Propositions/6.htm for arguments favoring and opposing the law. Other jurisdictions have joined in the ban. Miss. Code § 75-33-3; 63 Okla. Stat. § 1-1136. On Jan.
17, 2007, with the telling introduction, "The lone cowboy riding his horse on a Texas
trail is a cinematic icon. Not once in memory did the cowboy eat his horse[,]" the
Fifth Circuit Court of Appeals vacated the district court's permanent injunction
prohibiting the prosecution of slaughterhouses for processing, selling, and transporting horsemeat for human consumption, thus permitting Texas to enforce Tex.
Agric. Code § 149.002-.003. *Empacadora de Carnes de Fresnillo, S.A. de C.V. v.
Curry*, 476 F.3d 326, 336–37 (5th Cir. 2007). In so ruling, the Fifth Circuit
terminated horse slaughter operations at two slaughterhouses in Texas.

Months later, on May 24, 2007, Illinois amended its Horse Meat Act, 225 ILCS
635, making it illegal to slaughter horses, or import and export horse flesh, for
human consumption. Cavel International, a foreign corporation operating one of
three American horse slaughterhouses, sought a preliminary injunction to halt
enforcement of the amended act on the ground that it was preempted by the federal
Meat Inspection Act and was unconstitutional under Article I, section 8, of the
federal Constitution (commerce clause). The trial court denied Cavel the injunction.
In a 3-0 decision, a three-judge panel on the Seventh Circuit Court of Appeals,
Judge Richard Posner authoring, affirmed denial of the preliminary injunction
sought by Cavel and dismissed the suit with prejudice. *Cavel International v.
Madigan*, 500 F.3d 551 (7th Cir. 2007). The Federal Meat Inspection Act includes a
preemption clause, barring states from enacting additional or different laws than
those established in the federal statute and regulations addressing the production
of horse flesh. However, the Act does not require states to permit horse slaughter.
Rather, if the state allows horse slaughter, it must defer to federal regulations of the
practice.

Accordingly, Cavel "confuse[d] a premise with a conclusion," and their preemption argument was rejected. As to the commerce clause challenge — namely, that
banning Illinois horse slaughter impacts interstate and foreign commerce (the
primary purveyors of horse flesh reside outside of the United States) — the court
held that the Illinois law arose from a sufficiently rational state interest to justify
the ban, and that the minimal interference with foreign commerce did not justify
invalidating an otherwise nondiscriminatory (i.e., local businesses get no privilege
over foreign operations like Cavel) law. Responding to Cavel's claim that "the horses
will be killed anyway when they are too old to be useful and what difference does
it make whether they are eaten by people or by cats and dogs?", the court
responded, "The option of selling the animal for slaughter is thus financially more
advantageous to the owner, and this makes it likely that many horses (remember
that Cavel slaughters between 40,000 and 60,000 a year) die sooner than they
otherwise would because they can be killed for their meat." Accordingly, the specific,
legitimate interest recognized by the court was "in prolonging the lives of animals
that the population happens to like," remarking that the public "can ban bullfights
and cockfights and the abuse and neglect of animals."

It is worth noting that Cavel was the last horse slaughterhouse for human
consumption in business in the United States. As a result of the Seventh Circuit's
decision, Cavel closed its operations and ended horse slaughter for human

consumption in America. While horses in Illinois may no longer be killed for *pot au feu de cheval* (horse stew), slaughterhouses are free to kill horses for zoos, from which the court noted a pronounced demand. The result may be that Cavel and former human-consumption horse slaughterhouses will supply zoos only or relocate to states other than Texas or Illinois without similar prohibitions.

On Jan. 18, 2014, President Obama signed an appropriations bill that explicitly prohibited using federal funds to pay for USDA inspections of horses under the Federal Meat Inspection Act and the Federal Agriculture Improvement and Reform Act. Because uninspected meat may not be sold, unless privately butchered for personal consumption, it effectively crippled the domestic horse slaughterhouse model.

E. DOWNED ANIMALS

On January 1, 2009, California criminalized the sale of meat or meat products from "nonambulatory" (or downed) animals for human consumption, and mandated immediate euthanization of same. Two voluntary membership-based trade associations, the National Meat Association and the American Meat Institute, sued the state of California, Governor Schwarzenegger, and Attorney General Brown to prevent enforcement of Calif. Penal Code § 599f against swine slaughterhouses. By amending the law in 2009 to apply to federally inspected slaughterhouses, Plaintiffs argued, California imposed more expansive restrictions and penalties than otherwise permitted by federal law. The Federal Meat Inspection Act, 21 U.S.C. § 601 et seq. ("FMIA"), so they argued, preempted and rendered illegal Calif. Penal Code § 599f. California federal district court judge Lawrence J. O'Neill granted the Association's motion for a preliminary injunction and halted enforcement of § 599f against federally inspected swine slaughterhouses. *National Meat Ass'n v. Brown*, 2009 U.S. Dist. LEXIS 12523 (E.D. Cal. Feb. 19, 2009).

The FMIA was enacted by Congress in 1907 to address worries over meat safety by creating a system of pre- and post-slaughter inspection, marking, labeling, and packaging. As does Section 599f, the FMIA regulates "non-ambulatory disabled livestock." Unlike California law, however, the FMIA does not require immediate euthanasia (i.e., death by mechanical, chemical, or electrical method rapidly and effectively rendering the animal insensitive to pain) but permits, in certain circumstances, the animal to be held pending evaluation by an inspector or veterinarian, who may decide to condemn the animal or permit slaughter. Also unlike California law, the FMIA allows nonambulatory animals to be delivered to the slaughterhouse, rather than be refused and returned to the shipper.

While the FMIA expressly permits states to pass laws with respect to any other matters regulated under 21 U.S.C. § 601 et seq., it equally precludes states from interfering in areas explicitly covered by the Act. The question for the court was whether Section 599f improperly encroached upon areas regulated by the FMIA. Judge O'Neill held, at page 9:

> Thus, a state rightly could preclude different types of meat for human consumption, such as horse meat or dog meat or rat meat, for that matter. A nonambulatory pig is not a "type of meat." A pig is a pig. A pig that is

laying down is a pig. A pig with three legs is a pig. A fatigued or diseased pig is a pig. Calling it something else does not change the type of meat produced. Thus, the exception discussed in *Empacadora* does not apply.

Pursuant to *Empacadora* and *Cavel*, California could prohibit all pigs from being processed for human consumption and not be preempted by FMIA. However, California permits pigs to be produced for human consumption. Therefore, California is barred from imposing additional or different inspection requirements on animals to be produced for human consumption. Having allowed pigs and swine to enter the food supply, California cannot alter the federally mandated requirements of inspection.

The Ninth Circuit reversed, finding that the FMIA did not preempt or conflict with California law banning downer slaughter. Following *Cavel* and *Empacadora*, it held that FMIA preemption applies to meat inspection and labeling requirements, not the *type of meat* that may be sold in the first place. Here, California law states that nonambulatory cattle may not be slaughtered. Thus, the FMIA has nothing to act upon. While the Ninth Circuit Court of Appeals reversed Judge O'Neill in *National Meat Ass'n v. Brown*, 599 F.3d 1093 (9th Cir. 2010), the United States Supreme Court reversed, thus reinstating the holding of the trial court. *National Meat Ass'n v. Harris*, 132 S.Ct. 965 (2012); *National Meat Ass'n v. Harris*, 680 F.3d 1193 (9th Cir. 2012) (vacating 2010 ruling and affirming trial court).

Section 599f, while leaving much to be desired as far as humane pre-slaughter handling of livestock is concerned, took important steps to criminalize the transport and presentation of downed animals to slaughter. By requiring immediate "euthanasia" (a term that would appear to permit electrocution and death by gunshot, in addition to sodium pentobarbital or other euthanizing solution), Section 599f protected suffering animals from the added indignity of being dragged, forklifted, or prodded as they make their way to the killing floor.

Other states enforce nonambulatory cattle laws. Whether they suffer from the preemption argument embraced by in *Brown* remains to be seen. For instance, RCW § 16.5a.225 makes it a crime to knowingly transport or accept delivery of live nonambulatory livestock to, from, or between any livestock market, feedlot, slaughtering facility, or similar facility that trades in livestock. It also requires euthanasia of these animals before transportation. *See also* Ore. Rev. Stat. § 167.351 and Animal Welfare Institute's *Legal Protections for Nonambulatory Animals* report at https://awionline.org/sites/default/files/uploads/documents/fa-legalprotectionsfordownedanimals-12262013.pdf.

F. SEXUAL ASSAULT OF ANIMALS

Many do not realize that manual ejaculation (digital stimulation), electroejaculation, artificial vaginas, and other semen collection techniques are routinely employed by dog and horse breeders, and in the farm setting for boars, rams, stallions, cows, chickens, and turkeys. Wild captive animals such as lions are often anesthetized before electroejaculation. In the film *Blackfish*, viewers observe an orca named Tillikum, held captive by SeaWorld and trained to present his penis to be manually ejaculated for purposes of artificial insemination.[25] Aside from the distasteful purpose of performing captive orca breedings for evidently commercial purposes (i.e., as future performers), do such acts violate bestiality laws?

In 1533, bestiality, the "detestable and abominable vice," became a felony without benefit of clergy and was punishable by death. The next century brought the coevolution of Christian and European legal condemnation of bestiality as a crime against God's law and the "natural order." Erica Fudge, *Monstrous Acts: Bestiality in Early Modern England*, 50(8) History Today (Aug. 2000). Christians reacted harshly to bestiality for multiple reasons, including: its supposed connection to witchcraft; its reversal of God's natural hierarchical order (with humans, and males more specifically, at the top); its undermining the reproductive intent of sex (along with sodomy and masturbation); and the belief that cross-species procreation would produce centaurs and mermaids and other human-nonhuman chimerae. *Id.*, and Piers Beirne, *Rethinking Bestiality: Towards a Concept of Interspecies Sexual Assault*, 1(3) Theoretical Criminology 317 (1997). Immanuel Kant described bestiality, homosexual sex, and masturbation as "the most disgraceful and the most degrading [conduct] of which the human being is capable," putting one's self "below the level of animals." Kant, *Lectures on Ethics*, at 170. He reflected the sentiment of his time that all non-procreative sex was "unnatural," i.e., against God's will.

In the last several centuries, moderate views have prevailed. No state regards bestiality as a capital offense. Beirne writes, "Recently, the social control of bestiality has formally passed from religion and criminal law to psychiatric discourse. . . . However, at once subverting this psychiatrization and also echoing certain aspects of the spirit of decriminalization, there has gradually emerged a pseudo-liberal tolerance of bestiality." Beirne, at 319. This tolerance took root in the pro-sex feminist movement of the late 1970s and early 1980s, in which such (still) controversial writers as Gayle Rubin and Pat Califia called for feminists to embrace, or at least tolerate, sexual diversity "on the fringe of society,"[26] such as pedophilia, sado-masochism, and public sex acts. Similarly, Dutch biologist Midas Dekkers's 1994 book *Dearest Pet: On Bestiality*, possibly the only sustained, book-length academic exploration of the subject, equivocally posits that bestiality should in certain circumstances be celebrated, not discouraged, as one of many types of sexual expression on the human sexual continuum, adding that "as long as none of those involved suffers pain, no form of sex should be seen as pathological, bad or mad." *Id.*, at 148. Throughout, Dekkers repeatedly supports this project of pseudo-liberalism with an array of paintings, photographs, and writings from popular folklore, literature, cinematography, religion, biology, sexology, penology, and law. Both pro-sex feminists and Dekkers make the same mistake as the religious, philosophical, and legal discourses they critique by ignoring or eliding the subjectivity of those animals who find themselves subjected to human sexual coercion.

---

[25] For more info, go to http://arbl.cvmbs.colostate.edu/hbooks/pathphys/reprod/semeneval/collection.html; for a clinician's assessment, read Hani Miletski, MSW, Ph.D., *Understanding Bestiality and Zoophilia* (2002)(www.drmiletski.com/information.html).

[26] Gayle Rubin, *Sexual Politics, the New Right, and the Sexual Fringe*, in The Age Taboo (Alyson, 1981), 108, at 115.

In 2005, Douglas Spink was arrested en route to British Columbia off the I-5 interstate with 328 pounds of cocaine in his trunk. After his release from federal prison in 2010, federal agents raided his Sumas, Wash. residence, finding bestiality paraphernalia, and described by some[27] as an animal brothel where nonhuman animals were abused by at least one individual, a Welsh tourist named Stephen Clarke (later prosecuted and deported). The animals were seized and Spink was imprisoned on federal drug charges, then released in 2012, only to be arrested again on several state felony animal sexual assault charges in 2014. Reporter Carreen Maloney, formerly a writer for the *Winnipeg Free Press* and *Ottawa Citizen*, turned her attention to what Spink calls "heterospeciesism" in her upcoming book, *Uniquely Dangerous*. Ms. Maloney explains:

> My investigation began after the home of a man I had never heard of was raided by the federal government in northern Washington State. Douglas Spink was accused of running a bestiality brothel. His animals were seized and landed at my local shelter, an organization I had been writing for—and about—for more than 10 years. When I heard about it from shelter workers, what concerned me most was whether the animals had been harmed.

> At first I wasn't sure if I was going to write anything. The subject seemed shadowy and complex. But when the facts I uncovered didn't match the official storyline being presented by authorities and the media, I felt a responsibility to find the truth.

> What started out as an investigation into the life of one man uncovered a worldwide community of people called zoos who knew they were different in a way that caused them to be reviled by society. They communicated mostly by the internet, often encrypted, with their identities usually hidden behind online nicknames.

> Yet here was one man who wanted to speak out publicly about zoophilia.

> Despite the fact that Doug Spink wanted to talk, none of the other journalists who covered the raid story would speak with him. From prison, he phoned, emailed and wrote letters to journalists asking to tell his side of the story. For years his appeals went unanswered. To me, it was unsettling how the media handled the story, but even more troubling was how people felt about the animals. Many expressed to me that they thought the animals of zoos had to be killed. In their minds, the only way to erase the offense to human dignity was to snuff out the animals, which would thereby redraw the line that divides man from beast.

> The lives of Doug Spink's four horses were spared, but the fates of his seven dogs are still not known by this investigator.

> It is interesting to note that many of the activities that cross the species line, such as manual stimulation of an animal's penis, are perfectly legal and considered standard practice when collecting semen for commercial breed-

---

[27] Formal evidence that money changed hands does not appear to exist, according to reporter Carreen Maloney, discussed below.

ing purposes by veterinarians and others. The thoughts behind the act are what define the crime. Officially, sex with animals is not illegal in every state, unless the animals are physically injured, although the legal system often finds other ways to punish zoos.[28]

Spink has described himself as an ardent species-equality activist, moved by images from PETA depicting factory farm horrors, and convinced that spaying and neutering has surgically mutilated nonhumans in a way that creates "socially crippled versions of themselves." Mark Hay of Vice.com asked Spink, "Historical precedent or not, critics of heterospecies relationships say it's impossible for animals to give consent for a sexual relationship, so human-animal intimacy is at least coercive, but more often abusive. What do you say to that?" Spink's response excites further inquiry in *Animals Can Consent to Sex with Humans, Claims Humans Accused of Running Animal Brothel* (Jul. 14, 2014), http://www.vice.com/read/apparently-animals-consent-to-sex-in-the-beastiality-brothel. Spink argues that heterospeciality is a legitimate sexual orientation, which should receive no less protection than that enjoyed by homosexual or transgendered individuals. He revived the controversy over zoophilia a mere five years after 45-year-old Boeing engineer Kenneth Pinyan died after being anally penetrated by an Arabian stallion at a farm in Enumclaw, Washington. The documentary *Zoo*, which debuted at the Sundance Film Festival in 2007, described his life and death. http://www.imdb.com/title/tt0874423/. James Michael Tait, who collaborated with Pinyan and a third man to visit a farm to have sexual intercourse with equines none owned, was charged and convicted of criminal trespass only, resulting in a one-year suspended sentence, a fine of $300, one day of community service, and a strict prohibition never to return to the Arabian stallion breeding compound. http://www.thestranger.com/seattle/Content?oid=30811.

Why not a stronger penalty? King County prosecutors could not charge Tait with promoting, videotaping, or otherwise facilitating sexual animal assault due to the absence of any physical evidence of harm to any horse. And because the sex acts did not occur in public view, nor could indecent exposure apply. Passed on Feb. 11, 2006, Washington became the 37th state to criminalize bestiality (for the second time, as discussed below). A class C felony, RCW § 16.52.205(3) made it illegal to knowingly engage in sexual conduct or contact with an animal; knowingly cause, aid, or abet another person to do so; knowingly permit same on premises under one's control; knowingly organize, promote, conduct, advertise, aid, abet, participate as an observer, or perform any service in furtherance of such act for a commercial or recreational purpose; or knowingly photograph or film, for purposes of sexual gratification, same. Note the similar reach of animal fighting laws, which contemplate prosecution of the constellation of many other individuals and entities in such animal abuse enterprise. The state need not prove physical injury. Further, penetration is but one of many acts giving rise to felony conviction, for merely "touching or fondling" the sex organs or anus of an animal (defined to include "every creature, either alive or dead, other than a human being"), whether "directly or through clothing," suffices. The Washington law also addresses Mr. Pinyan's fatal

---

[28] Email communication with Carreen Maloney (July 3, 2016).

experience, whereby the animal's sex organ makes contact with the anus of the person.

Washington enacted its first bestiality law in 1909.[29] It read:

§ 9.79.100. Crimes against nature.

Every person who shall carnally know in any manner any animal or bird; or who shall carnally know any male or female person by the anus, or with the mouth or tongue; or who shall voluntarily submit to such carnal knowledge; or who shall attempt sexual intercourse with a dead body, shall be guilty of sodomy and shall be punished by imprisonment in the state penitentiary for not more than ten years. (L. '09 p. 950, § 204.)

RRS § 2456 (1932). In 1937, the statute was amended to impose a maximum penalty of 20 years for an offense committed against a child, while in all other cases incarceration was limited to a decade. Session Laws of the State of Washington 25th Session, Laws of Washington pp. 321-2, 1937. In 1975, the legislature enacted a Revised Criminal Code. In the process, it decriminalized previously proscribed sexual acts. By revamping former RCW § 9.79.100, it repealed the "sodomy" statute without replacing it. Unfortunately, it struck the language prohibiting bestiality and necrophilia. However, the drafters acknowledged this point directly as follows:

. . . Finally, the extremely rare cases of bestiality and necrophilia currently prohibited by the sodomy statute, RCW § 9.79.100, are not covered in this chapter. If such conduct does occur, and no question of mental defect or disorder is raised, prosecutions may still be brought under the section in the other titles of RCW concerning cruelty to animals or abuse of corpses.

Revised Washington Criminal Code, Published by the Legislative Council's Judiciary Committee, Without Prior Approval of the Contents, and Submitted to the People of the State of Washington for the Purpose of Obtaining Their Comments, p. 181, Dec. 3, 1970. Many did not share the optimism regarding animal cruelty laws' ability to punish nonconsensual contact that did not result in physical injury. It took another three decades for the legislature to amend the felony cruelty law to address

---

[29] Forty-four years earlier, the Iowa Supreme Court decided whether words imputing bestiality to a female constituted actionable slander *per se*. *Cleveland v. Detweiler*, 1865 Iowa Sup. LEXIS 20 (June, 1865). While at common law, implying unchastity to a female gives rise to civil liability without proof of special damage, and though the term "implies actual, unlawful commerce with *the other sex*," not another *species*, the court refused to reverse, holding:

We would not like to decide that a female, guilty of the charge imputed in the case at bar, was chaste. The charge involves unchastity of the highest, grossest and most flagrant character. An *ordinary* accusation of unchastity is mild and gentle, as compared with the one for which the action is brought. We must abandon the rule, or else hold that it extends to such a case as the one before us.

Id., at 302–03 (affirming $700 judgment against Detweilers when Cynthia Detweiler said, among other statements, "Mary Cleveland killed the dog, and that she (meaning Mary) had been caught in the act with the dog, and the dog had died from the effect of it.") See also *Ausman v. Veal*, 1858 Ind. LEXIS 865 (1858) (reversing judgment for defendant and remanding for further proceedings in suit accusing Veal of slander in stating, as to Mary Ausman, "Thank God if my daughters did have bastards they never had pups. She did have pups in Ohio, and It can be proved. She had two pups by a haystack.")

bestiality, thanks in large part to the publicity surrounding the Enumclaw equine sexual assault case in 2005.

The Substitute Senate Bill Report noted the following testimony:

> Testimony For: A broad array of interest groups have helped with this legislation, to make sure a fair bill was developed. The Grange was involved, as well as agricultural interests, veterinarians, other legislators, animal welfare groups, and prosecutors. This bill protects creatures that cannot give consent. The case in south King County that occurred last July brought to light the abuse that some animal protection groups knew was occurring, but zoophilia, or sex with animals, is not currently illegal in Washington. The Legislature has attempted to take a comprehensive approach to sexual offenses. This bill falls in line with that approach. The conduct focused on in this bill is the kind of conduct that often escalates, after victimization of animals, children, or others become victims. This is really a public safety issue. Another concern is the transfer of animal to human disease.

> Testimony Against: None.

The Substitute House Bill Report took a similar position:

> Testimony For: This bill is a result of a heinous case that happened in the 31st district. Zoophilia (or bestiality) is considered a paraphilia just like pedophilia, sexual masochism, and sadism. Earl Shriner was a pedofile who admitted to practicing bestiality. They view animals and others as lesser than themselves. Currently, it is illegal to make an electronic production or reproduction of bestiality, but it is still legal to practice the act of bestiality. This bill would close that loophole. There was a case in New York where mentally ill homeless women were taken off the street and held hostage. In exchange for food they would have to perform sexual acts with the animals. Since it was illegal in that state those men were prosecuted. Another negative outcome as a result of having sexual contact with an animal is zoonotic diseases. These are diseases that are transmitted between animals and humans. The most prevalent disease today is bird flu which is a disease that will pass to the general population if this type of behavior continues. This type of behavior is not only animal cruelty, but also an animal welfare issue. It is an issue of conduct that can escalate and become harmful and dangerous to humans. This is also a common behavior among sex offenders especially among juvenile offenders who are known to start their deviancy with family pets. This bill should be considered part of the Legislature's comprehensive approach to dealing with sex offenders.

> Testimony Against: None.

The Bill Reports demonstrate concern that the animal herself have the freedom to permit or reject interspecies sexual contact. Legislators have also examined the degree to which bestiality is a gateway sexual assault crime to child molestation and adult rape. Why do we pass laws criminalizing child rape if not to value the right of the child to consent to such contact, whether or not there is physical injury? Why do we pass laws criminalizing adult rape if not to value the autonomy of the victim to reject the sexual (and/or aggressive) advances of the rapist? The same can be said for the mentally ill. There is no good reason not to extend the continuum of consent to all sentient beings, regardless of (or, better yet, because of) their incapacity to accept or reject the sexual assault. In many respects, nonhuman animals are analogously legally classified as "incapable" of giving consent due to minority or mental defect. The disturbing and conclusory argument raised by some, that consent is a non-issue because nonhuman animals do not consent to the myriad other ways in which we use and abuse them against their will, disrespects the subjectivity of the those animals who are subjected (often forcibly) to human sexual coercion. Aside from the general interests of the state to curb what it regards as "self-destructive" activities (e.g., drug abuse, self-mutilation, suicide), or to halt the escalation of sexual aggression from nonhumans to humans, bestiality harms a third party — the sentient being who has been violated sexually, whether or not she sustains physical or psychological injury (a point not distinctly regulated by existing cruelty laws).

While the law does not prohibit all human contact with animals, it can restrict its manner, time, and place. In some cases, bestiality causes incidental physical injury and pain to the animal. But where death is immediate and painless, and there is no fulminating disease process or delayed onset of injuries from the sex act itself, how does one overcome the anticipated retort that this sexual use (much like a use for entertainment, food, labor, industry, or science) is "necessary" given a supposed hierarchy of humans over nonhumans? Peter Singer, author of *Animal Liberation*, notes:

> Some men use hens as a sexual object, inserting their penis into the cloaca, an all-purpose channel for wastes and for the passage of the egg. This is usually fatal to the hen, and in some cases she will be deliberately decapitated just before ejaculation in order to intensify the convulsions of its sphincter. This is cruelty, clear and simple. (But is it worse for the hen than living for a year or more crowded with four or five other hens in barren wire cage so small that they can never stretch their wings, and then being stuffed into crates to be taken to the slaughterhouse, strung upside down on a conveyor belt and killed? If not, then it is no worse than what egg producers do to their hens all the time.)

Peter Singer, *Heavy Petting*, http://www.utilitarian.net/singer/by/2001----.htm,

Peter Singer took tremendous criticism for writing what some animal rights activists and religious conservatives regarded as an apologia for zoophiles. Although disturbing in detail, Singer did recognize that while animals may be subjects-of-a-life, they are also be subjects-of-a-*sexual*-life, who might solicit sexual contact from humans. Take, for instance, the story of Birute Galdikas, "the Jane Goodall of orangutans," who was the object of sexual interest to a large male orangutan, or the dog who makes an appearance at a dinner party by gripping the leg of household guests and "vigorously rubbing [his] penis against them." Some might argue that such overtures suggest that nonhuman animals, if they have the capacity to withhold consent, also have the capacity to give consent. And this distinction could be material in the Enumclaw case were it not for the fact that instances of seeming consent may, in fact, result from manipulation and coercive power.

Does Singer anthropomorphize to the extreme in regarding a sexually frustrated animal's action as consent? In response to the argument that a dog humps a human leg because it enjoys this act, Karen Davis, Ph.D., asks: "What . . . is a sexually mature male dog deprived of a normal sex life with a member of his own species supposed to do with his sex drive?" *UPC Letter to The New Republic re: Bestiality/Peter Singer* (Mar. 25, 2001). Might it also signify sexual maladjustment, a symptom of domestication and comprehensive control over the animal's environment, and the animal's coping mechanism? For at the heart of bestiality (as in rape) lies power: in virtually all cases of human-nonhuman sexual interaction, a power differential exists. Nonhuman animals are "owned" property. They could not consent to sex any more than a human slave could completely consent to sex with his or her owner: their interests are usurped by their property status.

We control exactly what happens to animals, whether they are companion, farm, or feral beings. We must interpret their "affection" or "solicitous behavior" through the lens of their environment and its influences, which we largely, if not solely, prepare. Even if the sex act appears solicited by the nonhuman animal, the solicitation cannot be read clearly as sexual desire for *that* partner, but more a solicitation for *a* partner. Parallels may be drawn to the pubescent teenager yearning for his or her adult teacher, or a sexually abused (and confused) adolescent who acts out sexually with her guidance counselor or psychologist. Humans attempt to discern sexual motivations and consensual contact as juries must frequently decide in rape trials, such as whether the racily clad sorority sophomore was "asking for it" during a drunken evening at the frat house. But our ability to do the same with nonhumans is, at best, limited by a language barrier, not to mention cross-species dissimilarities. Perhaps only where the human enters the nonhuman animal's own natural realm (i.e., wild, undomesticated, feral, e.g., the Galdikas example), could meaningful consent be determined. So long as animals are domesticated for introduction into the human environment, their actions remain conditioned by our influences.

Notably, bestiality is a non-wild animal phenomenon, occurring among animals who have been domesticated for submissiveness. Whether as companions or as agricultural commodities, animals are thoroughly dependent upon humans for food, shelter, and exercise. An animal's sexuality is often manipulated, as is his or her physical space. We castrate males and perform hysterectomies on females, inoculate and inseminate cows, breeders and veterinarians manually ejaculate animals as a common breeding practice, electrically induced ejaculation is conducted on primates for tests and we decide if, when, and with whom an owned animal mates. Thus, humans always maintain coercive control over animals, from the moment of conception to nonconsensual termination of life. Only the willfully naïve would examine the question of sexual animal assault and consent divorced from this cultural anthropological context.

G. CRIME OF CARING — MAINTAINING A NUISANCE BY SUPPORTING FERAL COLONIES[30]

State statutes define felines as domestic animals, not wildlife.[31] Thus, most free-roaming cats are not covered by state wildlife agency jurisdiction and, in many cases, cannot legally be hunted. On the other hand, cats classified as feral, nuisance, predatory animal, pest, and wildlife may be hunted or killed by methods customarily prohibited for use on domestic animals. Wyoming, Minnesota,[32] and South Dakota allow cats to be hunted as non-protected animals.[33]

In 2005, under the guise of bird protection, the Wisconsin Conservation Congress (WCC), a public advisory group, proposed defining "free-roaming domestic feral cats" as an "unprotected species."[34] If adopted, this reclassification would have allowed hunters to shoot collar-less cats who roamed outdoors.[35] Public outrage criticized the proposal as crossing "the line from wildlife management to people's pets."[36] Although the WCC voted for reclassification, the executive committee overrode the vote.[37]

Other legislative attempts to categorize cats as an invasive species or overpopulated would also expose cats to traditional hunting and trapping. For example, in 2012, constitutional amendments proposed in New Jersey[38] and Mississippi[39]

---

[30] Credit for several segments in this subsection is given to Laura M. Nirenberg, Legislative Attorney, Cat Initiative, Best Friends Animal Society.

[31] Most wildlife laws do not address ferals. E.g., Colo. Rev. Stat. Ann. § 33-1-102(51) (2003) (excluding domestic animals from wildlife); Fla. Stat. Ann. § 585.01(10) (2001) (defining domestic cat as a "domestic animal" and excluding it from wild animals); Md. Code Ann., Crim. Law § 10-621 (2002) (prohibiting cats, other than domestic cats, from importation); Vt. Stat. Ann. tit. 20 § 3541 (2002) (having a separate code section for domestic pets).

[32] Telephone Interview by Heather Mackinnon, Valparaiso University Law School student, with Jason Abraham, Furbearer Season Specialist, Wildlife Management at Minnesota DNR, St. Paul, MN (Mar. 3, 2012). Minnesota DNR takes the position that roaming feral cats can be taken, and thus freely hunted and killed, by anyone. It is the responsibility of the person doing the taking to correctly establish whether the cat is wild or owned.

[33] Wyo. Stat. Ann. § 23-1-101(a)(viii) (2010) (Wyoming's statute defines "[c]oyote, jackrabbit, porcupine, raccoon, red fox, wolf, skunk, or *stray cat*" as "predatory animals") (emphasis added). The statute states that "[p]redatory animals and predacious birds may be taken without a license in any manner and at any time." *Id.* § 23-3-103(a). *See also* Mitsuhiko A. Takahashi, *Cats v. Birds in Japan: How to Reconcile Wildlife Conservation and Animal Protection*, 17 Geo. Int'l Envtl. L. Rev. 135, 149 (2004); Associated Press, *Wisconsin Residents Back Hunting Feral Cats*, Apr. 14, 2005, http://www.msnbc.msn.com/id/7475469 (last visited Mar. 1, 2012).

[34] Madison Audubon Society, Inc., *Accomplishment Report July 2004-June 2005*, http://madisonaudubon.org/audubon/docs/AnnualRpt04_05.pdf (last visited June 12, 2012).

[35] Dean Schabner, *Wisconsin Voters Back Plan to Hunt Cats*, ABC News, Apr. 12, 2005, http://abcnews.go.com/US/LegalCenter/story?id=662272&page=1#.T5aVdqtDuHc (last visited Apr. 24, 2012).

[36] Taimie L. Bryant, et al., *False Conflicts Between Animal Species*, Animal Law and the Courts: A Reader, 253–297 (Thomson-West, 2008). *See* Dean Schabner, *Wisconsin Voters Back Plan to Hunt Cats*, ABC News, Apr. 12, 2005, http://abcnews.go.com/US/LegalCenter/story?id=662272&page=1#.T5aVdqtDuHc (last visited Apr. 24, 2012).

[37] Madison Audubon Society, Inc., at 14.

[38] NJ ACR 40; NJ SCR 16 (2012) ("The taking of fish and wildlife by fishermen, hunters and trappers,

stipulated that hunting and trapping were the preferred methods of "controlling all invasive or overpopulated species."[40]

Regulatory efforts to reclassify sub-populations of the cat species have also taken effect. In 2011, the term "feral cats" was included as an example in the Occupational Safety and Health Standards (OSHA) for Shipyard Employment regulation definition of "vermin."[41] Agency personnel repeatedly asserted that feral cats did not create a hazard and could not explain how or why this language was included.[42] In fact, in 2011, the state of Washington moved to adopt this same language,[43] but after confirming with OSHA that removal of this term would not present a problem, decided against doing so due to the subjectivity of the term "feral cats" and the legal ramifications that could arise by ignoring statutory protections for cats.

Feral cat colonies have become a source of tension in urban areas, pitting not only bird conservancies and Audubon societies against no-kill advocates and feral cat trap-neuter-release volunteers,[44] but also property owners who resent the noise, property damage, and disease vectors that may follow such populations. In response, municipalities began to enact criminal nuisance laws seeking to prohibit individuals from in any way supporting feral colonies. For instance, Donald Zimmerman was charged with one misdemeanor count of maintaining a public nuisance arising from his feeding a clowder of feral cats, who, in turn, "befoul[ed] the air with their urine, littering the ground with their excrement, caterwauling, and damaging flowerbeds and shrubbery." Zimmerman was convicted first in a bench trial, from which he appealed, and was again convicted by a six-person jury. Testimony included two neighbors who trapped 30 to 40 cats and "disposing of

---

by traditional means and methods, shall always be a preferred and available way of controlling all invasive or overpopulated species.").

[39] MS HCR 29 (2012) ("Hunting, fishing or trapping by sportsmen shall always be a preferred and available means of controlling all invasive or overpopulated species.").

[40] NJ ACR 40; NJ SCR 16 (2012); MS HCR 29 (2012).

[41] 29 C.F.R. § 1915.80(b)(33) (2012).

[42] Personal communication between Laura Nirenberg, Esq., Legislative Attorney, Cat Initiative, Best Friends Animal Society, and Dale Cavanaugh, Deputy Regional Administrator, OSHA Region 10 Headquarters (Mar. 1, 2012) (confirming that it is unknown why "feral cats" was listed as an example in the "vermin" definition, removing this term would not raise an "effectiveness issue," and given the elusive nature of feral cats, their mere presence is not a hazard); Personal communication between Laura Nirenberg and Amy Wangdahl, Director, Office of Maritime and Agriculture, OSHA, (Mar. 25, 2012) (stressing that in five years of site visits, Ms. Wangdahl had never seen one feral cat and does not deem them to be a workplace hazard).

[43] WAC 296-304-01001; see Letter from Michael Silverstein, MD., Assistant Director, Occupational Safety and Health to Laura Nirenberg, Esq., Legislative Attorney, Cat Initiative, Best Friends Animal Society (Feb. 15, 2012) ("The Department of Labor and Industries is withdrawing WSR 11-24-062, filed on December 6, 2011. The Department of Labor and Industries will be filing a separate, expedited rulemaking which removes the example of 'feral cats' from the definition of 'vermin' in the proposed amendments to Chapter 296-304 WAC, Safety Standards for Shipbuilding, Ship Repair and Shipbreaking.").

[44] See Urban Wildlands Gp. v. City of Los Angeles, 2010 Cal. App. LEXIS 2226 (Feb. 23, 2011) (denying motion to intervene by two animal protection groups seeking to reopen lawsuit to dispute that the California Environmental Quality Act applied to the City's TNR program); County of Cook v. Village of Bridgeview, 8 N.E.3d 1275 (Ill. App. Ct. 2014) (village anti-TNR ordinance conflicted with county ordinance regulating feral colonies).

them" at farms outside town, and another neighbor who altered nine and placed them in homes. Despite these efforts, the cat population rebounded. Zimmerman testified in his own defense, admitting he left food outside for ferals to eat so they would not starve and because he loved animals, who are "God's creation." At sentencing, the district court ordered him to remove his house pets — three kittens, two cats, and a 15-year-old poodle, even though he was charged for feeding outdoor ferals. Zimmerman appealed, claiming no nexus between his conviction and the removal order. The Supreme Court found no abuse of discretion by the district court sentencing judge, focusing, in part, on the distinction between a forfeiture and a removal order. *State v. Zimmerman*, 228 P.3d 1109 (Mont. 2010); see also *Cottongame v. State*, 2014 Tex. App. LEXIS 7813 (Jul. 17, 2014) (affirming conviction of woman who fed more than two dozen feral cats on her property for violating ordinance limiting to three the number of cats a person may keep).

H. AG-GAG

Dairy farmers Douglas and Mary Jane Burdick had recently joined the federal government's Dairy Termination Program ("DTP"), a congressional effort to increase dairy prices by restoring market equilibrium through what amounted to a generous severance package. DTP participants agreed to discontinue milk production and stop acquiring dairy cattle for a period of five years (a prelude to exiting the dairy business). As a condition of acceptance into the DTP, however, the USDA issued Notice LD-249, imposing a 15-day deadline to ensure that "All female dairy cattle [will] be branded with a hot branding iron. Freeze, chemical, or other branding methods are not acceptable."

Finding hot-iron facial branding to violate New York's animal cruelty law and the prohibition against alternative, more humane methods like cold branding arbitrary, the Burdicks and the Humane Society of Rochester and Monroe County for the Prevention of Cruelty to Animals, Inc., sought an injunction against enforcement of LD-249. On Apr. 16, 1986, federal district court Judge Michael Telesca of the Western District of New York granted the relief requested. *Humane Soc. et al. v. Lyng*, 633 F. Supp. 480 (W.D.N.Y. 1986), did not resolve the conflict between LD-249 and New York cruelty law by trampling states' rights under the heel of the federal government, nor by ignoring the scientific question of whether LD-249 endorsed a cruel method of branding. Instead, Judge Telesca found:

> On the testimony before me, the hot-iron face branding of cows appears to constitute a violation of the state anti-cruelty laws which the Humane Society is sworn to prevent. In addition, by branding their cows, the Burdicks would expose themselves to prosecution for violation of New York Agriculture and Markets Law § 353. Even more important is the prospect of not qualifying for the program if they fail to brand their cows within 15 days of acceptance. Membership in the program is limited to those applicants accepted as of April 1, 1986.

Decided nearly 30 years ago, at a time when the legislative attitude toward animal cruelty would be best described as anemic, Telesca accusatorily wrote, "Most importantly, if cruelty to animals were indeed a consideration, LD-249 would not be drafted the way it is." Since *Lyng*, some businesses continue to see animal cruelty as economically advantageous, thanks in large part to recent legislative efforts to close the curtains to eyes of not only consumers, but also competitors pushed out of the market because they refuse to let profit interfere with compassion and do not view animals as purely units of production.

Many contend that a business model striving for economies of scale by embracing a mechanistic view of animals is incompatible with, and inimical to, animal welfare. Indeed, the approach inevitably becomes diseconomic. Neglectful, restrictive, and anxiety-producing conditions reduce productivity, often in the form of herd disease and increased mortality. At this point, industry resorts to subclinical antibiotics as a prophylactic measure to counter the abusive conditions in which they force the animals to wallow. And in so doing, a vigorous debate has picked up steam not only on the role of such countermeasures in the creation of antibiotic-resistant super-bugs and their harm to human health, but also the widespread environmental impacts of concentrated animal feedlot operations. As the public learns more about the origins of the meals on their plates, a care ethic has taken its rightful place among the other traditional consumer considerations like price, taste, quality, and variety. One would think the government would listen to its citizens.

Yet instead of arresting animal abuses at farmed animal operations or phasing out practices that European farmers abandoned years ago — and what the Pew Commission on Industrial Farm Animal Production[45] said in its 2008 examination of American farmed animal practices "prevent the animal from a normal range of movement and constitute inhumane treatment" (speaking of veal crates, hog gestation pens, restrictive farrowing crates, and battery cages for all poultry) — states are attempting to enact laws that not only obscure what happens to farmed animals, but criminally target those who seek to bring cruel practices to light.

One such law punishes those who record animal abuse at an agricultural operation without consent of the farmer and do not turn over those recordings to law enforcement within 24 hours of recording. This serves the industry's agenda to out undercover investigators, hamper newsgathering efforts, and prevent the public and government agencies from knowing risks to consumer, occupational, environmental, and animal health and safety. Without such recordings, prosecutors would rarely be able to make animal cruelty charges stick. It should strike the reader as oddly coincidental that the day the fifth Butterball employee pled guilty to animal cruelty — charges brought because of an undercover video showing workers stomping and kicking birds, throwing them by the necks into metal cages, and beating them with metal bars — that North Carolina Senate introduced the Commerce Protection Act, a law that, in part, created the crime of "employment fraud," which would have the practical effect of ensuring that such videos would never again see the light of day. N.C. S.B. 648 (filed Apr. 2, 2013).

Such a law also would have prevented the 2012 animal cruelty charges brought by Twin Falls County Prosecutor Grant Loebs against three workers at Betten-court Dairies' Hansen facility. This is precisely what proponents of Idaho Senate Bill 1337 appeared to want. This new bill criminalized merely entering an agricultural production facility and making audio or video recordings of the most

---

[45] www.ncifap.org

heinous acts of animal cruelty if done "without the facility owner's express consent or pursuant to judicial process or statutory authorization." Idaho Code § 18-7042 (enacted Feb. 28, 2014).

Given what society takes from them from the cradle-to-slaughter process — their skins, organs, muscles, bones, and labor — one must question why industry needs any law to deter, much less punish, those who record undisputed, heinous, and universally objectionable acts involving the brutalization of animals? If everyone agrees on what the video depicts, then why not focus on the perpetrator rather than the whistleblower? Why only permit amnesty to the videographer if he delivers a copy to law enforcement within one day, but offer no refuge in *two* — where prosecutors could charge animal cruelty *one or two years* after the act? Why make it a crime to capture images of criminal activity at the workplace, when that activity creates a hostile and illicit work environment for an employee who is striving to make a living (while at the same time showing compassion to the animals with whom he works), but not to make it a crime for that same person to share, verbally or in writing, what he observed? And why create a mandatory reporting law for the *employee* but not the *employer*? No trade secrets or proprietary information risk being exposed, unless industry implements abusive protocols as a cost-saving measure to outperform more conscientious competitors.

Instead of getting ahead of the issue by promoting transparent operations and honoring what the public considers important — namely, treating animals humanely — industries fuel the fox-guarding-the-henhouse image, spawning deep suspicion and rising consumer diffidence. They do so despite several economic indicators warning that animal cruelty is bad business. Mega-corporations like McDonald's realized this, dropping Sparboe Farms after Mercy for Animals showed horrific acts of cruelty — more commonplace than anyone in industry cares to admit — at five facilities in Iowa, Minnesota, and Colorado. Target Corp. followed suit, pulling their eggs off its shelves.[46] On April 25, 2012, Burger King Corp. pledged 100% cage free eggs by 2017 and elimination of gestation crates for breeding pigs.[47] Dozens of other restaurants have made similar game-changing moves.

Misleading advertising used to make consumers believe they are buying products not sullied by mistreatment invites fraud and securities litigation. In the race to court the more conscientious consumer, akin to efforts of contractors to boast "LEED-certified" and orchardists "100% organic," most American egg producers labeled their cartons "Animal Care Certified." This empty (and misleading) slogan resulted in a Sept. 30, 2005 announcement by the Federal Trade Commission ("FTC") that the United Egg Producers' logo would, by consent, be removed nationwide in 2006 and replaced with a revised "United Egg Producers Certified" seal.[48] That same year, UEP paid a $100,000 fine to settle false advertising claims

---

[46] Cynthia Galli et al., *McDonald's, Target Dump Egg Supplier After Investigation*, ABC via 20/20 (Nov. 18, 2011).

[47] Chris Isidore, *Burger King to use eggs from cage-free hens*, CNN Money (Apr. 25, 2012).

[48] See Letter from FTC to Meier and Dillard re *Complaint Seeking Action Against the United Egg Producers for Deceptive Advertising in Connection with the "Animal Care Certified" Program* (Sep. 30, 2005). http://www.ftc.gov/sites/default/files/documents/closing_letters/united-egg-producers-uep/uepstaffopinionlettercok.pdf

by 16 state attorney general offices and the District of Columbia attorney general.[49]

In addition to pressure from consumers, industry has seen recent challenges from within (its own shareholders). In 2009, HSUS filed Securities and Exchange Commission ("SEC") and FTC complaints against IHOP and DineEquity, Inc. for making misleading claims that they served "cruelty-free" food per "dignified, humane" animal care standards.[50] And in 2011, the SEC overruled Columbus, Ohio-based restaurant chain Bob Evans's petition to block HSUS's proposal encouraging a phase-in of cage-free eggs in the company's 2011 proxy materials.[51]

As an additional example, the 2009 Westland/Hallmark False Claims Act lawsuit brought by HSUS resulted in the largest beef recall in history.[52] Undercover video showing the abuse and slaughter of downed cows prompted a half-billion dollar settlement and bankruptcy following accusations that the California slaughterhouse defrauded the federal government's school lunch program by signing contracts promising humane treatment of animals.

The message is clear: business must embrace, not oppose, animal welfare. Idaho's (and similar) legislation, coupled with arrests of those like Utahan Amy Meyer, have fueled societal distrust of the agricultural industry. On March 17, 2014, 16 organizational and individual plaintiffs sued Idaho Governor "Butch" Otter and Attorney General Lawrence Wasden in an effort to overturn IC § 18-7042. *ALDF v. Otter*, 2014 U.S. Dist. LEXIS 147539 (D. Idaho Oct. 14,2014). The litigation raised several constitutional claims under the First and Fourteenth Amendments, the Supremacy Clause (preempted by the False Claims Act, 31 U.S.C. §§ 3729, 3730, the Food Safety Modernization Act, 21 U.S.C. § 399d, and the Clean Water Act, 33 U.S.C. § 1367(a)). *ALDF v. Otter* followed the first agricultural gag lawsuit, *ALDF v. Herbert*, U.S.D.C. C.D. Utah No. 2:13-cv-00679-RJS, challenging Utah's Code 7§ 6-6-112 on similar grounds on July 22, 2013.

I. TERRORISM

In 1992, Congress passed into law the Animal Enterprise Protection Act, 18 U.S.C. § 43, creating the crime of "animal enterprise terrorism" to be enforced against those traveling in interstate or foreign commerce, "or us[ing] or caus[ing] to be used the mail or any facility in interstate or foreign commerce" with the goal of "causing physical disruption to the functioning of an animal enterprise" and "intentionally damag[ing] or caus[ing] physical disruption to the functioning of an animal enterprise by intentionally stealing, damaging, or causing the loss of, any property (including animals or records) used by the animal enterprise, and thereby causes economic damage exceeding $10,000 to that enterprise, or conspires to do

---

[49] http://cok.net/camp/victories/animal-care-certified-eggs-exposed/

[50] *IHOP and DineEquity Face SEC, FTC Complaints Over False Animal Welfare Claims*, http://www.humanesociety.org/news/press_releases/2009/10/ihop_trade_complaints_101409.html   (Oct. 14, 2009).

[51] Kristie Middleton, *SEC Rules Bob Evans' Proxy Must Include Animal Cruelty Resolution*, http://www.triplepundit.com/2011/06/sec-bob-evans-animal-cruelty/ (Jun. 14, 2011).

[52] Tracie Cone, *Westland/Hallmark Meat Settlement Reached After Major Meat Recall*, Huffington Post (Nov. 16, 2012).

so." An "animal enterprise" included commercial or academic enterprises using animals for food, fiber, agriculture, research, or testing; zoos, aquariums, circuses, rodeos, lawful competitive animal events; and fairs or similar events seeking to advance agricultural arts and sciences. 18 U.S.C. § 43(d)(1)(A)-(C) (1992). Few prosecutions followed passage of the AEPA. With considerable publicity and anticipation, the federal government prosecuted Stop Huntingdon Animal Cruelty USA, Inc. and six associated individuals related to operation of a website disclosing names and addresses of individuals associated with a laboratory, while calling for "direct action" and lauding illegal activity as "accomplishments." The website also promoted electronic civil disobedience through transmission of "black faxes." *U.S. v. Fullmer et al*, 2009 U.S. App. LEXIS 25747 (3d Cir. N.J. Oct. 14, 2009); convictions for conspiracy to commit interstate stalking and to use a telecommunications device to abuse, threaten, and harass, affirmed in a 2-1 decision, 584 F.3d 132 (3d Cir. 2009);[53] see also *U.S. v. Young; U.S. v. Samuel*, 467 F. Supp. 990 (W.D. Wis Mar. 26, 1979) (two individuals sentenced to 2.5 years for liberating thousands of mink from fur farms).

Save sole opposition by U.S. Representative Dennis Kucinich (D-OH), 14 years later, a 2006 amendment and change in the title from "Protection" to "Terrorism" conferred upon the Department of Justice what the sponsors contended was "necessary authority to apprehend, prosecute, and convict individuals committing animal enterprise terror." The Animal Enterprise Terrorism Act of 2006 encompassed a broader range of targets, i.e., affiliates and associates of animal enterprises, including their immediate family members, spouses, or intimate partners. 18 U.S.C. § 43(a)(2)(A)-(B) (2006). The AETA also imposed criminal penalties absent proof of any "economic damage"; intimidation, criminal trespass, and harassment would suffice. "Economic damage" is defined as the cost to replace lost or damaged property or records, repeating interrupted or invalidated experiments, profit loss, and other increased costs and losses with the exception of "any lawful economic disruption (including a lawful boycott) that results from lawful public, governmental, or business reaction to the disclosure of information about an animal enterprise." 18 U.S.C. § 43(d)(3)(A)-(B). Where "economic damage" accompanies conduct that violates the AETA, the court may exact more severe penalties in proportion to the harm. For instance, the maximum period of incarceration rises from one year (in the case of $0–$10,000 "economic damage") to five years (for the range of $10,000–$100,000) to 10 years (in excess of $100,000) to 20 years (in excess of $1,000,000). 18 U.S.C. § 43(b)(1)(A)-(B), (b)(2)(A), (b)(3)(A), (b)(4)(B) (2006).

One of the earliest prosecutions under the AETA failed in *U.S. v. Buddenberg*, 2010 U.S. Dist. LEXIS 78201 (N.D. Cal. 2010) (indictment against four protestors targeting University of California researchers dismissed without prejudice due to defective indictment); see also *U.S. v. Bond*, 2011 U.S. Dist. LEXIS 23702 (D. Colo. Feb. 22, 2011) and *U.S. v. Bond*, 10-cr-00844 (D.Utah) (defendant charged with arson and an AETA violation for burning down a leather store and a restaurant that served foie gras); *U.S. v. Viehl, U.S. v. Hall*, 2:09-cr-00119, 2010 WL 148398 (D.Utah)

---

[53] Huntingdon Life Sciences, Inc. also sued SHAC and individual members civilly. *Huntingdon Life Sciences, Inc. v. SHAC*, 129 Cal. App. 4th 1228 (2005); see also 2006 WL 4055411 (Cal.Sup.2006) (fees awarded to SHAC attorneys on successful anti-SLAPP motion).

(defendants charged with AETA violations for releasing animals from fur farms); *U.S. v. DeMuth*, 3:09-cr-117, 2010 WL 3712966 (S.D.Iowa) (defendant charged with violating the AETA for liberating ferrets from a breeding facility).

Activists and civil libertarians took an offensive posture by filing a facial challenge to the AETA in *Blum v. Holder*, 930 F. Supp. 2d 326 (D.Mass.2013). Dismissed due to lack of Article III standing, the court found that all individual plaintiffs, including SHAC defendant Lauren Gazzola, did not face a reasonable risk of prosecution under the statute, concluding that "[w]here Plaintiffs seek to engage in lawful and peaceful investigation, protest, public-speaking, and letter-writing, the court cannot reasonably conclude that these actions fall within the purview of a statute requiring intentional damage or loss to property or creation in an individual of a reasonable fear of death." *Id.*, at 337.

Minnesota enacted the first animal terrorism law in 1988. Minn. Stat. Ann. § 346.56. Various state animal enterprise terrorism legislation followed. For instance, RCW § 9.08.090 makes it a felony to, without authorization, knowingly take, release, destroy, contaminate, or damage any animal kept in a research or educational facility where the animal is to be used or is used for medical, research, or educational purposes; as well as to destroy or damage records, equipment, research product, or other things pertaining to such animal. A civil counterpart exists, RCW § 4.24.570–.590, providing for civil liability (i.e., reasonable attorney's fees, civil fine, and costs). In Oregon, interference with animal research facilities is a crime whether or not the facility suffers damage. ORS § 167.312(3)(b). The code does not define "damage." *But see State v. Borowski*, 220 P.3d 100 (Or. Ct. App. 2009) (deeming Oregon's animal agricultural operation interference law, ORS § 164.887, unconstitutional on equal protection grounds). For further state-by-state assessment, see Cynthia F. Hodges, *Detailed Discussion of State Animal "Terrorism"/ Animal Enterprise Interference Laws* (Animal Legal & Historical Center, 2011).

Hypothetical: Spay and Neuter Alliance, a nonprofit rescue organization, learned that Corky's, a pet store in the same city in which SNA is headquartered, decided to sell puppies purchased from local breeders, contradicting earlier promises made to work with area rescue groups instead. Corky's sells mixed-breed puppies for $495 to $695, which it calls an adoption fee. SNA calls for a boycott, and prints a 6" x 9" educational postcard about puppy mills. The front of the card states in large print, "PUPPIES AREN'T PRODUCTS! BOYCOTT CORKY'S PETS!" and cites shelter euthanasia statistics. The back encourages readers, "Don't Shop . . . Adopt" and adds, "Never Buy a Puppy Online or in a Pet Store!" Smaller print describes how "[m]ost pet store puppies and online puppies come from puppy mills," followed by a description of the neglectful conditions, health and behavioral issues that flow from procuring such puppies. In June, 10 SNA volunteers line the sidewalk in front of Corky's — without blocking the entrance, or pushing or shoving patrons — and hand out these cards while chanting, "Puppies Aren't Products! Boycott Corky's Pets!" Corky's loses at least $1,000 in profits that day alone. The protests continue weekly to the point that Corky's must lay off employees due to reduced business. Police are called.

What criminal and civil liability do the activists potentially face?

Lawful picketing in front of a pet store, even causing a loss in sales or business goodwill, does not implicate the AETA. See 18 U.S.C. 43(d)(3)(B) and (e)(1), stating that the law shall not be construed "to prohibit any expressive conduct (including peaceful picketing or other peaceful demonstration) protected from legal prohibition by the First Amendment to the Constitution." Furthermore, none of the protestors traveled in interstate or foreign commerce for the purpose of interfering with Corky's, so the very first element of § 43(a) cannot be proved.

The back of the postcard strongly implies that Corky's is selling from "puppy mills," and all the horror and risk that phrase connotes (not to mention the assertions made in the postcard as to cramped housing, neglect, bad genetics, lack of socialization, several congenital/hereditary disorders, parasites, and communicable diseases like parvovirus and other maladies). One concern is that SNA has insinuated that puppies sold by Corky's will be ill, deaf, blind, and infected. Such statements could expose SNA to civil liability unless they have firm evidence. For future reference, SNA might add a statement that clearly indicates it is not accusing Corky's of actually selling such animals but requests that readers ask Corky's where the puppies come from, if they come from puppy mills, and if Corky's takes steps to personally inspect where the breeding dogs are maintained and where the puppies are whelped (to ensure a hygienic, humane, non-cramped, behaviorally enriched, disease-and-parasite-free environment).

Corky's might threaten litigation based on tortious interference with business expectancy, but this requires proof that the store had a valid contractual relationship or business expectancy; that SNA knew it; that SNA intentionally interfered to induce or cause breach of the contract or to terminate the relationship or expectancy; that SNA did so for an improper purpose or using improper means; and that there was damage. *See, e.g., Leingang v. Pierce Cy. Med. Bureau, Inc.*, 930 P.2d 288, 300 (Wash. 1997); but also see *Caruso v. Local Union No. 690 of Teamsters*, 107 Wn. 2d 524 (1987). *Caruso* involved suit against a union alleging interference and defamation arising from articles encouraging union members not to patronize Caruso's business. The Washington Supreme Court held that publishing "do not patronize" articles calling for a boycott was constitutionally protected and could not support a tortious interference claim, citing *NAACP v. Claiborne Hardware Co.*, 458 U.S. 886 (1982). However, if the information upon which the "do not patronize" request was based was false, it would subject the publisher to a defamation claim.

In any high-visibility and close-contact venue where demonstrators may assemble, the following guidelines may enhance communication and avoid arrest:

(A) Notify law enforcement in advance of any intention to picket and leaflet and address any concerns they might have. One should present oneself as reasonable, willing to make minor concessions that will not impact effectiveness, and prepared to educate so that police understand the issue and that the thrust of the protest is completely nonviolent. This draws law enforcement to the side of the peaceful protestor, teaches that what is being done is legal and why, and minimizes unpleasant surprises the day of the event.

(B) Have an observer at such events who remains on the sidelines to provide an independent assessment, using video (but be mindful of state laws that prevent interception and recording of private conversations).

(C)   Prepare a Code of Conduct that counsels participants to stay on public property, not block store entrances, not to disrupt business, not to vandalize or engage in illegal conduct, and not to use profanity or threats or harassing language.

J.   ANIMAL FIGHTING

Nobel Prize winner Gabriel Garcia Marquez's novella *El Coronel No Tiene Wuien Le Escribe* centers around a gamecock, described as the protagonist's deceased son Agustin's "legacy," who represents economic salvation if he wins upcoming fights. Literary critic George R. McMurray writes, "The cock, then, not only symbolizes hope, but ultimately emerges as a symbol of the absurd hero's (the colonel's) fight against fate." Marquez also created the character Jose Arcadio IV, who ironically enjoys cockfighting while railing against other injustices in *One Hundred Years of Solitude*. Latin American culture embraces a "sport" rendered illegal in every state in the United States. Journalist Marvin West writes in *Leo Loves a Good Cockfight*, WESTWORDS IN MEXCONNECT (Oct. 1, 2003):[54]

. . . Cockfighting may be the world's oldest spectator sport. It almost certainly predates another blood game, human gladiators in the Roman Coliseum, fighting to the death for the entertainment of the rich and drunk.

Cockfighting was once the national sport in England. America's founding fathers raised and fought roosters. Legend has it that President Lincoln earned the nickname "Honest Abe" as a fair and honorable judge of cockfights.

Massachusetts banned the sport in 1836. Delaware put it away in 1852, long before PETA. Vermont outlawed cockfighting in 1854, Connecticut in 1862, Iowa in 1868, Pennsylvania a year later, District of Columbia and Minnesota in 1871, Nebraska in 1873, Arkansas in 1879, Mississippi and New Jersey in 1880, New York, Tennessee and North Carolina in '81. Animal rights rolled on and on. State after state outlawed cockfighting. Only Louisiana is holding out.

Cockfighting is not only legal in Mexico, but widely accepted, relished, even honored. Fathers bring young sons to introduce them to tradition. Leo has heard that when an earthquake shakes a Mexican home, the man of the house first rescues his gamecocks, then his wife, then his children. If he has time, he moves his pickup truck.

Critics lash out at cockfighting, calling it cruel and brutal. Defenders say chickens dying is part of the game, just as chickens dying is part of Kentucky Fried Chicken. One features plump breasts, meaty thighs, white gravy and biscuits, the other gorgeous plumage, arrogant posture, a perfect fighting machine with a surly disposition, eyes burning, feet clawing at the ground.

---

[54]   http://www.mexconnect.com/articles/1378-leo-loves-a-good-cockfight.

Broilers live 42 days, until beheaded. Gamecocks live until they die in the arena. Think about it.

Dogfighting has a similar pedigree, having originated in England, gaining popularity among the working class, and then falling out of legal favor in the nineteenth century. Sociologists Rhonda Evans, DeAnn Gauthier, and Craig Forsyth studied "dogmen" in the South, the name self-bestowed by fighting dog breeders and competitors, opining that dogfighting provided an outlet for "expression of masculinity," particularly among those of the lower class who lacked sufficient esteem-building occupational successes. Francesca Ortiz, *Making the Dogman Heel: Recommendations for Improving the Effectiveness of Dogfighting Laws*, 3 Stan. J. Animal L. & Pol'y 1, at 11–12 (2010) (quoting *Dogfighting: Symbolic Expression and Validation of Masculinity*, 39 Sex Roles: J. Res. 825, 829 (1998)). Of course, celebrity sports figure Michael Vick dashed the common perception that only the economically disadvantaged participate in dogfights. Kevin Van Valkenburg, *Dogfight Fans Aren't So Easy to Categorize, Experts Say Interest Tends to Cross Lines of Race, Geography*, Balt. Sun at 1D (Jul. 29, 2007).

Federal criminalization of dogfighting commenced with 1976 amendments to the Animal Welfare Act, 7 U.S.C. § 2156 (prohibiting ventures that involve interstate or foreign commerce). Thanks to Michael Vick, P.L. 110-22, the Animal Fighting Prohibition Enforcement Act of 2007 amended it by prohibiting interstate or foreign commerce in knives and gaffs and raised penalties for animal fighting ventures. It was again subject to a recent amendment in 2014 by P.L. 113-079, Sec. 12308(b), which further implicated spectators and adults who cause a minor under the age of 16 to attend a fight between any live bird or live mammal. To learn more about enforceability of animal fighting laws, see Tracy Bateman Farrell, *Validity, Construction, and Application of Criminal Statutes and Ordinances to Prosecution for Cockfighting*, 69 A.L.R. 6th 207; Fern L. Kletter, *Validity, Construction, and Application of Criminal Statutes and Ordinances to Prosecution for Dogfighting*, 68 A.L.R. 6th 115; and, for a novel civil approach, Rachel Blumenfeld, *Dog Baiting Abatement: Using Nuisance Abatement to Regulate Dogfighting*, 17 Sports L. J. 1 (2010).

K.   DEFENSE TO CRUELTY CHARGE — MISTAKE OF FACT

Ervin Tilbury, his wife, and four children lived in a mobile home surrounded by countryside. Frequently wild dogs would enter his property, occasionally in large packs, relieving themselves, ripping out insulation from under his home, and digging up the vegetable garden. At times they would threaten him, prompting a call to the sheriff's office, which regarded loose dogs as a low priority. According to Tilbury, the evening of June 10, 1991, his four-year-old son Michael went outside to play as he worked at his desk. Five minutes later, his child came in with tears streaming, talking about "mean" dogs. Mr. Tilbury emerged to see a Labrador and Malamute urinating and defecating in his yard. He yelled and threw gravel to get them to leave. Instead, they stood their ground and snarled with tail lowered. Normally he would reach for his BB gun and fire into the air or ground to scare the dogs. This time, the BB gun was misplaced, so he loaded a. 22 cal. rifle and came back outside to hear the dogs making a commotion near his shed. They were breaking and knocking over items. When they saw him, they bared their fangs and growled, coming after him. He fired twice, hitting both. He then executed the Labrador "to put him out of his misery." After the humane society refused to retrieve the body, Tilbury then placed it in a dumpster and reported the shooting to law enforcement. That night, the Malamute died.

Sheriff's Deputy Morgan recalled a different explanation — that Tilbury killed both dogs at a distance of 25 feet while they were sniffing around a metal building and did not threaten him at any time. The Labrador had seven entry wounds and wore a collar. The jury convicted Tilbury of cruelty to animals, for which he was sentenced to six months in jail and 12 months' probation. Tilbury appealed, raising two defenses — mistake of fact and necessity. He claimed the evidence did not suffice to show he knew the dogs were "domesticated living creatures," the type of animal protected by Tex. Pen. Code 4§ 2.09, as opposed to ferals. *Tilbury v. State*, 890 S.W.2d 219 (Tex.App.—Fort Worth 1994). This mistake of fact defense may also arise in prosecutions of cats mistakenly believed to belong to feral colonies. *See* Jeremy Masten, *Don't Feed the Animals: Queso's Law and How the Texas Legislature Abandoned Stray Animals, a Comment on HB 2328 and the New Tex. Penal Code § 42.092*, 60 Baylor L. Rev. 964 (2008) (two Baylor University students acquitted after shooting, decapitating, and skinning a feral cat named Queso on basis that the cat was not an "animal" under the earlier version of the law; the 2007 amendment now includes "any stray or feral cat or dog"). It may also apply in wildlife enforcement actions, such as where a hunter kills a domesticated dog by mistake, believing her to be a wolf, at a time when it was illegal to hunt wolves.

L. UNITS OF PROSECUTION AND VALUATION OF ANIMALS

If a perpetrator tortures multiple animals, should he or she face one combined count of animal cruelty or one count for each animal? Courts have closely examined whether to treat individual animals as units of prosecution for purposes of counting charges. *State v. Nix*, 334 P.3d 437 (Or. 2014), vacated, 356 Or. 768 (2015), applied ORS § 161.067, the "anti-merger" statute, to ORS 167.325, the second-degree animal neglect statute, when Arnold Nix faced 20 counts arising from his mistreatment of farmed animals. Nix contended that each animal was not a discrete "victim" for purposes of the statute, so he should only face one merged count. In affirming the Court of Appeals, *Nix* acknowledged the historical recognition of nonhumans as "victims":

> In that light, it can be seen that defendant's contention that the "plain meaning" of the word "victim" refers only to persons, and not to animals, is predicated on a selective reading of the dictionary definitions. The first sense listed in the definition, for example, refers broadly to "a living being," not solely to human beings. And the synonymy gives as an example of the word "victim" the sacrifice of animals. The ordinary meaning of the word "victim," then, is capable of referring either to human beings, animals, or both.

Illustrative examples of the plain meaning of "victim" to refer to animals are not difficult to locate. Especially in the context of animal cruelty, it is common to refer to animals as "victims." As far back as the mid-nineteenth century, John Stuart Mill referred to the "unfortunate slaves and victims of the most brutal part of mankind; the lower animals." John Stuart Mill, 2 *Principles of Political Economy: With Some of Their Applications to Social Philosophy* 579 (1864). Rachel Carson complained of cruelty to all, "whether its victim is human or animal." Letter from Rachel Carson to Oxford University Press, (undated) (on file with Yale University Library). A headline from an early New York Times article referred to "Animal Victims of Railroad Trains." NY Times, Oct 11, 1914, at 77. A more recent article from 1982 on a series of hunting photographs from India mentioned pictures of "animal victims *Images of India,* N Y Times, April 25, 1982. A 1992 article from the Chicago Tribune similarly is headlined, "Pair Heading to Bosnia to Aid Animal Victims of War." Chi Trib, Oct 6, 1992. Closer to home, an article in the Oregon State Bar Bulletin reported that, "[t]he Oregon Legislature has repeatedly and consistently articulated a strong public policy favoring the aggressive prosecution of animal cruelty cases by enacting statutes requiring police officers to make arrests in cases of animal abuse and to pay for and provide care to victim animals." *Full–Time Prosecutor to Litigate Animal Cruelty Cases Statewide,* Or State Bar Bulletin, May 2013.

Having concluded that animals could generally hold the status of "victim" under ORS § 161.067, the court then queried whether the legislature intended to treat each animal as a victim for the substantive offense of second-degree animal neglect. Again, it held that the "phrasing of the offense reveals that the legislature's focus was the treatment of individual animals, not harm to the public generally or harm to the owners of the animals." *Id.,* at *8.

Jason Yon had a taste for black bear gallbladders, buying four of them for a total price of $800 in 2008. For this, the state charged him with two counts of unlawful trafficking of wildlife in the first degree, a class C felony (RCW § 77.15.260(2)). After resting its case, Yon moved for dismissal on the basis that the state could not aggregate the value of the bear gallbladders to exceed the $250 threshold set by statute, instead requiring him to be charged separately for "each individual animal unlawfully taken or possessed," as provided by RCW § 77.15.030. This maneuver would help Yon avoid felony charges. The trial court denied his motion and found him guilty as charged. In reversing and remanding, the appellate court determined that RCW § 77.15.030 mandates a *per animalis* (*per quod, per partem*), not *in toto,* assessment. Finding that the contraband consists of parts of big game animals instead of the whole mattered not and would lead to "absurd results" inconsistent with the statutory scheme. For instance, RCW § 77.08.010(55) defined wildlife to include bodily parts. Unlike the Lacey Act's unit of prosecution measure discussed in *U.S. v. Senchenko,* 133 F.3d 1153 (9th Cir. 1998), the unit of prosecution under Ch. 77.15 RCW is the animal, not the conduct. "Accordingly, a trafficking transaction involving the purchase of two black bear gallbladders, which necessarily came from two different bears, amounts to two distinct crimes under the legislature's chosen unit of prosecution." *State v. Yon,* 246 P.3d 818, 821–22 (Wash. Ct. App. 2011); *see also State v. Norman*, 358 Mont. 252 (2010) (grouping animals to obtain felony conviction proper in unlawful possession of game animals prosecution); *State v. Siliski*, 238 S.W.3d 338 (Tenn. Crim. App. 2007) (each individual animal mistreated formed basis for separate conviction of animal cruelty).

Pamela Deskins confined 39 dogs for 147 days, resulting in various casualties, such as dogs killing one another and victimizing animals off her property. The state charged her with one count each of second-degree animal cruelty, harassment, evidence tampering, and confining domestic animals in an unsafe manner, in violation of RCW § 16.52.080, which states:

> Any person who wilfully transports or confines or causes to be transported or confined any domestic animal or animals in a manner, posture or confinement that will jeopardize the safety of the animal or the public shall be guilty of a misdemeanor. And whenever any such person shall be taken into custody or be subject to arrest pursuant to a valid warrant therefor by any officer or authorized person, such officer or person may take charge of the animal or animals; and any necessary expense thereof shall be a lien thereon to be paid before the animal or animals may be recovered; and if the expense is not paid, it may be recovered from the owner of the animal or the person guilty.

The state claimed Deskins violated RCW § 16.52.080 for a period of 147 days, bookended by an attack on a neighbor's dog on May 6 and the killing of the her own dog on September 30. While Deskins challenged the conviction based on lack of a unanimity instruction (i.e., the jury could have found her guilty only if all agreed on which specific act (of potentially dozens or hundreds) furnished the basis for the conviction), which the Court of Appeals rejected, it did ruminate on the proper "unit of prosecution." *State v. Deskins*, 2012 Wash. App. LEXIS 2100 (2012) Remaining unresolved was how to characterize the RCW § 16.52.080 charge — was it one "best viewed as a single ongoing offense," 39 offenses (one for each dog), 147 offenses (one for each day), or 5,733 offenses (one for each dog for each day)?

Prosecutors learned to closely read the definitional instruction and elements instruction to ensure they matched the charging document. The amended complaint alleged Deskins's failure to "confine or separate" dogs in her care, implicating the "shelter" and "space" alternative elements of RCW § 16.52.207, the second-degree animal cruelty law, not the other alternatives of "rest, sanitation, [and . . .] medical attention." Yet the jury instruction permitted a finding of guilty for failure to provide "necessary shelter, rest, sanitation, space or medical attention." Only two of the five methods were charged, a "mistake . . . unfortunately common in these days of word processing and standardized instruction forms, but has long been recognized as prejudicial error." *Id.*, at *5.

Aside from aggregation concerns discussed above, individualized valuation of subject animals may impact the severity of crime charged. For instance, defendants convicted of felony theft of chickens earned a reversal and remand as the court failed to instruct the jury that if it found the chickens were worth less than two dollars apiece, then they might find the defendants guilty of petit larceny; if worth more than two dollars, then they could convict on a felony. *Saylor v. Comm.*, 214 S.W. 826 (Ky. Ct. App. 1919) (conflicting evidence supported a finding of value between 75 cents and one dollar and over two dollars); *see also State v. Duncan*, 268 P. 139 (Wash. 1928) (affirming conviction of man charged with grand larceny for stealing eleven chickens valued over $25; though market value of chickens sold for food consumption would be valued less than $25, but much more for breeding purposes, "[t]here was no evidence controverting the testimony of the state as to the value of the chickens for breeding purposes, and we think it clearly sufficient to base a verdict thereon").

How valuation of animal companions currently affects prosecution of theft or death crimes presents a developing legal problem where the civil justice system frequently finds that dogs and cats have no market value but an exceptional "intrinsic" or "special" value.[55] Contrast this with the criminal law of the nineteenth century, which refused to even treat a canine as the subject of larceny, thus rendering the indictment charging Robert Lymus with breaking and entering a stable with intent to steal a dog not valid for burglary. *State v. Lymus*, 1875 Ohio LEXIS 425(1875). Nor can taking honey of wild bees constitute larceny, at least when the hive is located on another's land but the pollen from which it was fashioned may have been made from flowers, fruits, and vegetables situated elsewhere. *People v. Hutchinson*, 169 Misc. 724 (1983).

M. CHARGING ISSUES — WEAPON ENHANCEMENTS

Mike Meiser let Chief, his two-year-old Labrador retriever, out of his home around noon on Mar. 23, 2000. Unfortunately, he did not supervise Chief closely enough, because he wandered off. Five gunshots rang out, and Chief yelped, flinched, and dragged himself up the driveway of a home along the road, where he collapsed and died. Bradley Hackenberger admitted to shooting Chief, asserting that he appeared rabid and had attacked him and his cocker spaniel Lucky. The jury disbelieved Hackenberger and convicted him of second-degree misdemeanor cruelty to animals. The trial court applied a sentencing enhancement for the use of a deadly weapon and ordered Hackenberger imprisoned for six months to two years, less one day. Even though the unenhanced cruelty conviction alone carried no provision (in ordinary circumstances, and in this case) for jail time, the Pennsylvania Supreme Court affirmed the deadly weapon sentencing enhancement. *Comm v. Hackenberger*, 836 A.2d 2 (Pa. 2003). Mr. Hackenberger argued that the enhancement provision did not apply to animal cruelty "because the purpose behind the provision is to punish only those offenses in which the defendant has used a deadly weapon against *persons*."

In a 7-2 decision, the majority agreed with the Commonwealth that the "plain language permits its application to any offense in which the defendant has used a deadly weapon to commit a crime, as long as possession of a deadly weapon is not an element of the offense itself." Two dissenting justices held, "No matter how much empathy one may have for an animal killed for no justifiable reason, . . . this

---

[55] Some courts use the replacement value less depreciation test if no market value exists. *State v. Jacquith*, 272 N.W.2d 90 (S.D. 1978) (valuing prescription sunglasses stolen from inside vehicle). Typically, the peculiar value set upon the item by the owner is not considered. 3 Wharton's Criminal Law § 345 (Grades of larceny-Determination of value).

provision was enacted to penalize someone for possessing or utilizing a deadly weapon intended to do harm to a person." *Id.*, at 202–03 (quoting *Comm v. Hackenberger*, 795 A.2d 1040, 1048 (Pa. Super. Ct. 2002) (Del Sole, P.J., concurring and dissenting)). See also *Comm v. Kneller*, 999 A.2d 608 (Pa. Super. Ct. 2010) (affirming application of weapon sentencing enhancement to defendant's conviction for conspiracy to commit cruelty to animals and rejecting as meritless Kneller's assertion that her case is distinguishable from *Hackenberger* since she owned one of the victims) and Erika Farkas, *Animal Owners in Pennsylvania Are Not Afforded an Absolute Right to Kill Their Healthy Animal: Commonwealth v. Kneller*, 2 Duq. Crim. L.J. 63 (2011). Note also that some sentencing enhancement laws only apply to ranked offenses. *See State v. Soto*, 309 P.3d 596 (Wash. Ct. App. 2013) (statutory firearm enhancement does not apply to conviction of felony animal cruelty that does not involve animal sexual assault, an unranked Class C felony; Washington's bestiality law is a ranked felony).

N.   CHARGING ISSUES: *BLAKELY* AND AGGRAVATORS

The Sixth Amendment guarantees a criminal defendant the right to a trial by jury and, as explained by the United States Supreme Court in *Apprendi v. New Jersey*, 530 U.S. 466 (2000), also implicates sentencing where aggravating factors warrant deviation from the statutory maximum range. "[A]ny fact that increases the penalty for a crime beyond the prescribed statutory maximum must be submitted to a jury, and proved beyond a reasonable doubt." *Id.*, at 490. In 2004, the Court decided *Blakely v. Washington*, 542 U.S. 296 (2004), refining *Apprendi* to define "statutory maximum" as the maximum sentence a judge "may impose solely on the basis of the facts reflected in the jury verdict or admitted by the defendant [in a guilty plea]." *Id.*, at 303. Thus, if a judge relies upon post-verdict facts to find aggravating, sentence-enhancing factors, they must have been sieved first through jury deliberation. However, "the fact of a prior conviction" is an exception to this rule.

On Mar. 27, 2003, Donald Hedger stabbed and slit the throat of his son's dog. He pleaded guilty, and the prosecution recommended 18 months incarceration in county jail with work release privileges. At sentencing, the trial court found several aggravating factors — prior criminal history, two outstanding arrest warrants, great risk of recidivism, mutilation and killing of his three-year-old son's animal companion in front of his son, and fleeing the jurisdiction. It then sentenced Hedger to twice the recommended time to state prison — the maximum for a Class D felony. The Indiana Court of Appeals upheld the sentence, observing that a single aggravating circumstance supports imposition of an enhanced sentence and adding that, while neither party addressed the impact of *Blakely*, at least two aggravators did not implicate its holding (criminal history and pattern of criminal activity making the likelihood "great" that he would commit additional crimes). *Hedger v. State*, 824 N.E.2d 417, 418 and n.2 (Ind. Ct. App. 2005); see also *U.S. v. Romero*, 432 Fed.Appx. 790 (10th Cir. 2011) (no error in using prior convictions to increase presumptive maximum sentence for aggravated animal cruelty from 18 to 36 months).

O. SELF-DEFENSE IN ANIMAL CRUELTY CASES

Customarily, criminal defendants facing murder or assault charges may raise self-defense and demand an appropriate jury instruction, thereby increasing the likelihood of acquittal. But does it apply where a nonhuman has been killed or maimed? Kevin Pegues was convicted by jury of two counts of assault in the second degree and one count of harming a police dog when he stabbed at the canine.

> Either just before or just after Pegues was tased, a K-9 handler, Officer James Sturgill, released a police dog. The dog ran toward Pegues, who was temporarily immobilized by the taser, and bit him around the head and neck. Pegues brought his hands to his head in an effort to protect himself and then wrestled with the dog for several seconds. While still on his knees, Pegues stabbed the dog with the knife, severing a muscle in its neck. Pegues then began to get up, lunging toward the officers as he did so. An officer yelled "knife'" and a different officer fired two rounds into Pegues' torso. RP (April 15, 2010) at 64. Pegues is permanently paralyzed as a result.

State v. Pegues, 2011 Wash. App. LEXIS 2902 1 (Wash. Ct. App. 2011). The four-inch deep wound missed vital organs and major blood vessels, permitting the dog to survive after emergency surgery. The trial judge denied his request for a self-defense instruction, reasoning that it applied to use of force against persons, not dogs. Finding that a large, powerful dog, who happens to work for the police department, may constitute a "use of force" by law enforcement and be wielded as a weapon for purposes of the criminal code; and that no meaningful difference exists between deploying a police dog or any other force modality for purposes of ascertaining a defendant's right to a self-defense instruction, the appellate court vacated his conviction for harming a police dog. It set parameters, however, stating, "Any person upon whom a police officer trains a firearm is in actual danger of serious injury or death, and pursuant to Pegues' proposed standard, such a person would be justified in slaying the officer in order to protect himself. This, of course, is not the law. Instead, where an officer's use of force is not excessive, a person has no right to resist an arrest by any means." *Id. at* 8. See also *People v. Lee*, 131 Cal. App. 4th 1413 (2005) (self-defense can apply to attack by animal, and failure to give instruction warranted reversal of conviction of retired deputy sheriff who fired handgun to scare two unleashed dogs while walking her dog); *U.S. v. Clavette*, 135 F.3d 1308, 1311 (9th Cir. 1998) (conviction of man who killed grizzly bear in violation of Endangered Species Act affirmed since jury could reasonably have found that he did not kill in self-defense); *Devincenzi v. Faulkner*, 174 Cal. App. 2d 250 (1959) (self-defense and defense of third person instruction warranted where defendant drove car into Great Dane who was about to attack teenager and had just harmed defendant's cocker spaniel); *Grizzle v. State*, 707 P.2d 1210 (Okla. Crim. App. 1985) (reversal of conviction of animal cruelty where defendant shot and killed dog who was biting his son); *What Constitutes Offense of Cruelty to Animals— Modern Cases*, 6 A.L.R. 5TH 733, §§ 12(b), 28 (1992).

P. PRE-AND POSTCONVICTION FORFEITURES AND POSTCONVICTION RESTITUTION[56]

Animal cruelty forfeitures do not differ significantly from drug forfeitures, as law enforcement can seek forfeiture in a civil action as well as a criminal action. One primary distinction, however, pertains to the nature of the property seized. Forfeited property in the drug context typically lacks volition, sentience, and the ability to suffer, but in the animal cruelty context, the confiscated animate "property" embodies those qualities to the fullest extent. As a practical matter, and unlike their inanimate counterparts, this means that seized animals require ongoing supervision, board, veterinary attention, and protection from the owner, all at a cost that more often than not exceeds the value of the seized animal herself. Perhaps unexpectedly, the current of jurisprudence that recognizes the familial-type bond between a person and animal companion, and, thus, the status of the animal as more than mere property, creates a doctrinal riptide in the forfeiture situation. It serves to protect the animal from the owner, while at the same time guarding the owner against summary termination of a quasi-parental relationship.

As a threshold matter, due process requires notice and an opportunity to be heard prior to forfeiture. In *Com. v. Gonzalez*, 403 Pa. Super. 157, 588 A.2d 528 (1991), before being convicted of 23 counts of cruelty to animals related to cockfighting, the SPCA euthanized the seized roosters after allowing them to fall ill allegedly stemming from the SPCA's neglect, all without notice or a hearing. Agreeing with his contention that the cruelty statute violated due process, the Superior Court of Pennsylvania held that the provisions of 18 Pa. Cons. Stat. Ann. § 5511 permitting destruction of seized animals without an opportunity to be heard beforehand or afterward violate both state and federal constitutions. Despite so holding, the court refused to reverse his convictions, finding that the violation in no way affected the adjudication of guilt.

This means that impediments to the right to a contested hearing, such as prepaying boarding or coercing surrender, may fail to pass constitutional muster. In *Louisville Kennel Club, Inc. v. Louisville/Jefferson County Metro Government*, 2009 U.S. Dist. LEXIS 92328(W.D. Ky. Oct. 2, 2009), the court struck down part of an ordinance mandating permanent forfeiture of the seized animal upon a judicial finding of probable cause that the owner violated one of the humane treatment requirements, where the owner failed to post bond for care of the animal in 30-day increments. In that the ordinance divested a person of his dog *even if* he was ultimately found innocent of the underlying charge, the kennel club presented a legitimate due-process claim. The court explained that due to the likelihood that a judge might find probable cause, the defendant might then not be able to afford to post the $450 upon the probable cause finding, and a jury might later acquit him of charges, the risk of erroneous deprivation of the property interest in the animal remained significant. As the city has "little interest in keeping ownership of pets belonging to innocent citizens," absent an additional hearing, appeal, or late-payment process, the court found that the ordinance suffered irredeemably.

---

[56] Copious sections of the following were taken from Adam P. Karp, *Challenges to Pre- and Post-Conviction Forfeitures and to Postconviction Restitution Under Animal Cruelty Statutes*, 70 A.L.R.6th 329 (2011), with permission from Thomson Reuters.

The actual hearing itself cannot adjudicate vague terminology, nor can it rely on insufficient evidence to satisfy the preponderance standard. In *State ex rel. Connors v. Nineteen Horses*, 2010 Conn. Super. LEXIS 149 (Jan. 15, 2010), following *State ex rel. Gregan v. Koczur*, 287 Conn. 145 (2008), the court found that Conn. Gen. Stat. Ann. § 22-329(a) did not utilize unconstitutionally vague language with respect to the meaning of "neglect," resulting in a finding of neglect of two horses, forfeiture of same, and an award of restitution for all veterinary costs and care from date of seizure through date of forfeiture.

In *In re 8 Horses, 22 Dogs*, 297 S.W.3d 125 (Mo. Ct. App. S.D. 2009), after describing Mo. Ann. Stat. § 578.018 (2000) as "a well-intentioned law so poorly drawn that it raises more questions than it answers and gives inadequate guidance to nearly everyone affected thereby," and inviting the general assembly to "perform a valuable service by redrafting this law," the Missouri Court of Appeals reversed the judgment awarding custody of the animal owners' horses and dogs to the humane society "for disposition as necessary" due to insufficiency of the evidence and other statutory infirmities. Twelve business hours after learning that authorities executed two search warrants and seized 23 dogs and eight horses from the owners' farm based on suspected abuse and neglect, the court heard a motion to "determine the immediate disposition" of their animals. The prosecutor called a deputy who executed the warrant and the humane society president, but no veterinarian, to provide expert testimony to establish alleged cruelty. Setting bond at $20,000 to care for the animals for at least 30 days, the court failed to make a necessary finding of abuse or neglect. Accordingly, the appeals court reversed, highlighting the insufficient evidence to link the animals' conditions to any acts of abuse or neglect.

The equitable "innocent owner" defense, commonly raised in drug forfeiture proceedings, merits passing consideration. In *People v. Henderson*, 282 Mich. App. 307 (2009), *appeal denied*, 485 Mich. 871 (2009) *appeal denied*, 771 N.W.2d 793 (Mich. 2009), two defendants — one who was the owner, and the other who was the primary caretaker of, horses — faced felony animal torture and misdemeanor failure to provide adequate care charges. The owner contemporaneously defended a civil forfeiture action pertaining to the horses. In reinstating the order of forfeiture of 69 horses, quashed by the circuit court on innocent-owner grounds, the court of appeals held that whether the caretaker was supposed to take care of the horses is of no consequence, because he did not.

In *Russu v. State*, 2005 Tex. App. LEXIS 3862 (May 19, 2005), upon seizure of 43 cats and one dog from the plaintiffs' residential homes, the trial court found cruel treatment and ordered the animals forfeited to the humane society. When the plaintiffs appealed that order to the county court, the state moved to dismiss on grounds of no appellate jurisdiction, citing Tex. Health & Safety Code Ann. § 821.025. As the legislature only permitted appeal of orders involving sale of animals at public auction, and not an order to forfeit and convey animals to the custody of the humane society, the county court lacked jurisdiction to hear their appeal, and the court of appeals accordingly dismissed for want of jurisdiction.

Initiating a criminal prosecution does not serve as a precondition to preconviction forfeiture, though in one case, the court held that the forfeiture action must be initiated at least two weeks prior to final disposition of the related criminal charge. In *People v. Kasben*, 2006 Mich. App. LEXIS 3251 (Oct 31, 2006), prior to conviction on 13 (and acquittal on five) counts of misdemeanor animal neglect, the owner's 53 horses were seized and a civil forfeiture proceeding filed. That he only faced charges with respect to 18 of the 53 horses did not nullify the seizure of the other 35 as state law mandated seizure of "all animals" then being used or held for use in violation of the applicable statutes. That the owner failed to pay the cost of care pending criminal trial to avoid sale of the horses, even though he offered to post realty as a bond, did not negate the basis for forfeiture as his property was encumbered. Further, that the civil forfeiture action was not brought to hearing before disposition of the criminal charges did not eliminate the statutory basis to forfeit because the statute permitted the prosecutor to file a civil forfeiture action at least 14 days before the final disposition of the criminal action. While a prompt disposition hearing guards against runaway costs and an increasing bond, that it did not occur in this case was excusable because the prosecutor satisfied the statutory requirement that the hearing take place within 14 days thereafter or "as soon as practicable." For a variety of unique reasons, it could not occur until after the criminal case's disposition (because the defendant delayed proceedings by firing his attorney and claiming ownership of the horses by third parties).

Thus, even if acquitted of charges, the civil forfeiture remedy may still exist. In *State v. Sheets*, 112 Ohio App. 3d 1 (4th Dist. Highland County 1996), the court of appeals found no abuse of discretion in the trial court's probationary condition that Sheets surrender 121 horses even though he was convicted of cruelty with respect to only 10, and notwithstanding the defendant's argument that Ohio Rev. Code Ann. § 959.99(D) allowed only for forfeiture of "the animal or livestock" cruelly treated rather than all the horses kept by the defendant. In *State v. Burrell*, 71 Ohio App. 3d 507 (6th Dist. Wood County 1991), having been acquitted on two charges of animal cruelty, Burrell sought return of the horse and cow seized prior to being charged. The trial court refused, claiming them forfeit, but on reconsideration agreed that he could repossess the horse and cow upon payment of $750 in boarding charges. In reversing, the court of appeals found, first, that the trial judge had no statutory authority to order payment of boarding as a precondition to release, and second, the court had no right to keep the horse and cow from the owner upon dismissal of charges against him.

Still, where the government does not commence a preconviction forfeiture process, either by choice or because no statute permits it, forfeiture can only occur as a condition of criminal sentencing or probation. In such context, disputes emerge over the lawful scope of forfeiture — i.e., encompassing all animals seized prior to filing criminal charges, all animals then in possession of the defendant at time of sentencing, or only those animals subjected to criminal activity upon which the defendant was convicted. *State v. Martin*, 378 S.C. 113 (2008) examined this question. Upon execution of a search warrant, a magistrate ordered sixty horses placed in on-site, protective custody with an equine rescue organization, allowing access to the horses at the owner's property with the option of removal in the organization's sole discretion. S.C. Code Ann. § 47-1-150(C)(2) required a postseizure hearing within three days to assess if the owners were "fit to have custody of the animal." Instead, the hearing took place over two weeks following removal of the horses, the day after the owners were arrested on ill treatment of animals charges. While acknowledging that the rescue organization failed to timely schedule the postseizure hearing, the magistrate refused to order the immediate return of the horses "to an environment that could potentially be harmful to them."

Instead, the court commanded the rescue organization to arrange for the § 47-1-150 hearing within 24 hours. Prior to that hearing, the owners appealed the magistrate's ruling declining to direct the horses' return, indicating that they had no intention of attending any such hearing. While the appeal was pending, the owners were indicted on 60 counts each of ill treatment of animals. Months later, they were each convicted on four of 60 counts. While the court ordered forfeiture of the four horses to which the convictions pertained, no decision had been then made on the other 56. The circuit court subsequently found that the horses were properly removed, that the owners did not deserve a postseizure hearing, and besides, the owners had "declined" the hearing that the magistrate ordered (choosing instead to appeal). The Supreme Court of South Carolina ruled *in favor* of the owners with respect to their right to a postseizure hearing within three days of seizure, pursuant to § 47-1-150(C)(2) (in essence affirming the magistrate's order), but *against* the owners with respect to automatic return of the 56 horses that were the subjects of the acquittal counts. While reading S.C. Code Ann. § 47-1-170 as not allowing forfeiture of all animals seized as a penalty upon conviction, it instead remanded for a fitness hearing under S.C. Code Ann. § 47-1-150(F)(1). If deemed capable of adequately providing for the horses, then they would return to the owners upon payment for their care.

Similar questions permeate the proper scope of restitution, including whether a rescue organization or humane society constitutes a proper "victim" entitled to restitution at all. In *State v. Ham*, 2009-Ohio-3822 (Ohio Ct. App. 3d Dist. Wyandot County 2009), the defendant was convicted on one charge of animal cruelty, whereupon the court ordered the defendant to pay restitution to the humane society in the sum of $3,126.72 for the care of a Great Dane, whom the court also ordered forfeit. In vacating restitution, the court of appeals interpreted Ohio Rev. Code Ann. § 2929.28(A)(1) to only require the offender to pay restitution to "the victim of the offender's crime or any survivor of the victim." Finding neither the humane society nor the dog a proper "victim" or "survivor of the victim," and citing the plain language of the statute, the court refused to require the defendant to pay for food, board, transportation, veterinary evaluations, vaccinations, and other administered medications. In reaching this conclusion, the court relied upon *State v. Angus*, 2006-Ohio-4455 (Ohio Ct. App. 10th Dist. Franklin County 2006).

In *People v. Henry*, 2009 WL 1314823 (Mich. Ct. App. 2009), the defendant appealed that part of the judgment and sentence on his conviction for one count of animal abandonment or cruelty and four counts of owning an unlicensed dog that pertained to $9,642.10 in restitution arising from the cost of housing and veterinary care for all dogs seized from his home. The appellate court agreed that he only should pay the costs associated with the seized dog forming the basis for his conviction of animal cruelty, reversing the restitution order and remanding with respect only to the dog(s) the defendant was convicted of mistreating or abandoning, not all dogs seized. In so ruling, the court embraced the reasoning of *People v. Nichiow-Brubaker*, 2007 WL 2713417 (Mich. Ct. App. 2007), which focused on the phrase "the animal" and its use of the definite article to limit restitution.

Another wrinkle in cruelty seizures concerns the potential conflict between demanding restitution for the cost to care for victimized animals pending final disposition of the criminal case when they have been forfeited prior to conviction. Some jurisdictions refuse to award restitution past the date of surrender or forfeiture. In *People v. Speegle*, 53 Cal. App. 4th 1405 (3d Dist. 1997), the California Court of Appeals determined that the defendant's conviction on eight counts of felony animal cruelty authorized an award of restitution in the sum of $265,000 (rounded) for the care of 200 poodles, one cat, and three horses seized from her property in 1993. Animal control officers delivered the animals to the Northwest Society for the Prevention of Cruelty to Animals (NWSPCA) whose care burden nearly bankrupted the nonprofit and left it virtually unable to take in other animals. The NWSPCA also faced seven lawsuits by the defendant, and her relatives threatened NWSPCA employees. Finding unpersuasive her claim that she only owed restitution relative to the eight animals to whom each conviction pertained, not the other 196, the court rejected and concluded that the phrase "costs of impoundment" refers to "all animals lawfully seized and impounded with respect to the violation," the words "with respect to" focusing temporally on the moment of seizure and having general import, not contingent on those animals identified in the criminal charge or even those charges resulting in conviction. It reached this conclusion by distinguishing the general phrase "with respect to" from the more limited phrases "for," "from," or "as a result of," which the court held "would require a direct connection." *Id.*, at 1417. The court gave further attention to the defendant's position that upon the court's order of abandonment of the impounded animals, she no longer owned them and, therefore, had no duty to reimburse the NWSPCA. Noting that the duty to pay costs of care extends through "the time of proper disposition," and that a subsequent forfeiture does not operate *nunc pro tunc* by rendering the animals abandoned at the moment of impound, the court ordered the defendant to pay restitution from date of impound through date of forfeiture. Lastly, the court rejected the defendant's contention that the NWSPCA had a duty to mitigate her cruel behavior by euthanizing the animals instead of accruing $8,000 to $20,000 per month in costs of care.

Because cruelty seizures typically result in parallel civil and criminal actions, clever defendants will attempt to invoke estoppel and constitutional principles to bar subsequent action after the former action (most commonly the civil forfeiture case) concludes. *Scott v. Jackson County*, 244 Or. App. 484 (2011) took up such argument made by animal control. The state court held that the federal court's grant of summary judgment dismissal of Scott's § 1983 claim against county officers who seized her rabbits was not automatically preclusive of Scott's state conversion or trespass to chattels claims in the state court filing. In *Bradley v. State*, 2009 WL 1688200 (Tex. App. Houston 1st Dist. 2009), petition for discretionary review refused, (Oct. 21, 2009), the court ordered the forfeiture of the owner's 45 dogs and that he pay $9,020 for boarding and care of same. Thereafter, the state charged him with animal cruelty. In rejecting the owner's double jeopardy argument — that the forfeiture and order to pay constituted a fine and "punishment" placing him in jeopardy and barring reprosecution on "identical facts" — the appellate court refused to find the forfeiture-payment disposition "so punitive either in purpose or effect as to transform the civil action and remedies imposed into a criminal punishment."

Others invoke the Fourth Amendment exclusionary rule to suppress evidence introduced in the civil forfeiture hearing as might occur in a criminal case. In *Pine v. State*, 921 S.W.2d 866 (Tex. App. Houston 14th Dist. 1996), writ dismissed w.o.j., (Sept. 26, 1996), the plaintiff was convicted by a jury of cruelty to animals under the penal code (Tex. Penal Code Ann. § 42.11(a)(2)) and found to have cruelly treated his livestock under the health and safety code (Tex. Health & Safety Code Ann. § 821.023. The county court ordered the plaintiff's animals forfeited to the county. Pine asserted that the state's failure to procure a valid warrant at the outset required suppression of all evidence of mistreatment and dismissal of the forfeiture action (no differently than it might require acquittal of criminal charges). While agreeing that forfeiture proceedings have a "quasi-criminal" character in which the exclusionary rule invoked under the Fourth Amendment may apply, the appeals court stated that "unlawful seizure of the res will not defeat its forfeiture where the state submits lawfully acquired evidence of its forfeitable character." Specifically, a procedural error committed by the state while initially securing temporary possession of animals whose cruel treatment and forfeitable status is proven by competent evidence should not override the statute's primary goal of protecting the welfare of the animals. Again, so long as legitimately obtained evidence independently furnishes the basis for forfeiture, an admittedly unlawful seizure will not terminate forfeiture proceedings.

Routinely rejected are claims that animal forfeitures constitute an excessive fine in violation of the Eighth Amendment to the U.S. Constitution and state constitution counterparts. In *State v. Tarnavsky*, 84 Wash. App. 1056 (Div. 3 1996), upon seizure of more than 100 equines, the state charged the owner with two counts of animal cruelty. Found guilty on one count, the court ordered forfeiture of the seized animals, and the owner appealed, claiming postconviction forfeiture violates due process, constitutes double jeopardy, and an excessive fine. In rejecting all three contentions, the court found that Wash. Rev. Code Ann. § 16.52.085, and Wash. Rev. Code Ann. § 16.52.200 provide adequate notice and opportunity to be heard; that imposing criminal penalties (here, suspended jail time) *along with* forfeiture did not constitute a multiple punishment as the latter merely imposed a remedial sanction and could not be deemed punishment for purposes of double jeopardy; and that while forfeiture can serve remedial and punitive purposes and receive scrutiny as a fine, here, the forfeiture's overriding goal sought to protect abused animals from further abuse by the person convicted of having abused them — rendering it nonexcessive in any event.

Subject-matter jurisdiction necessitates consideration, but particularly where the fates of animals taken into protective custody depend on not losing control (actual or constructive) over the *res* (i.e., the animals), a contention raised against a justice of the peace who ordered forfeiture of animals valued far beyond the amount-in-controversy limits of the court. In *Chambers v. Perry*, 2010 WL 1052909 (Tex. App. Dallas 2010), reh'g overruled, (Apr. 22, 2010) and review dismissed w.o.j., (Aug. 27, 2010), after seizing 121 dogs and one cat from the pet owner's residence, followed by her conviction for animal cruelty, and order of forfeiture of all animals, the pet owner appealed, claiming that the animals' value (alleged to range between

$60,000 and $350,000) exceeded the amount-in-controversy cap of the justice of the peace court (then $5,000) and that the court lacked jurisdiction over "a suit in behalf of the state to recover a penalty, forfeiture, or escheat." The appellate court rejected these two arguments, noting that the legislature expressly vested justice courts with "special and limited jurisdiction over actions alleging cruel treatment of animals" as well as "over forfeiture of animals found in situations constituting cruelty to animals." Additionally, the court found that the forfeiture arose not under the code of criminal procedure, but the health and safety code, which did not require allegations of criminal activity.

Animals, as property, may have more than one owner. Co-owners not criminally charged or given notice of the right to challenge forfeiture, such as spouses, breeders, secured parties, and promoters, may attempt to collaterally attack any forfeiture order. In *State v. Siliski*, 2006 WL 1931814 (Tenn. Crim. App. 2006), convictions on nine misdemeanor counts of animal cruelty resulted in forfeiture of more than 200 animals to animal control. Thereafter, third parties claimed ownership of some of the forfeited animals and sought their return. Informally adjudicating their claims with unsworn testimony, the trial court denied the third-party applications. The Tennessee Criminal Court of Appeals reversed, concluding that the criminal court lacked jurisdiction to resolve third-party claims of this nature. Rather, it only possessed authority to order transfer of custody of the animals to the humane society. Looking to those parts of the code addressing judicial forfeiture procedures, the court reasoned that only a separate civil action could resolve the dispute of ownership in animals seized and placed with animal control as part of a criminal case.

In *State v. Zimmer*, 166 Wis. 2d 3 (Ct. App. 1991), the defendant having been convicted on two counts of negligently failing to provide shelter to dogs and rabbits, two counts of negligently failing to supply food and water to them, and obstruction of an officer, the trial court ordered forfeiture of the animals. The owner argued that the court could not forfeit his wife's ownership interest in same, particularly where she was acquitted of similar offenses. Not having herself appealed, however, the court affirmed the trial court's order, noting that her husband lacked standing to assert her putative interest but did acknowledge that she might seek a declaratory judgment under the statute and invoke due process principles.

For further analysis, see Fern L. Kletter, *Propriety, Measure, and Elements of Restitution to Which Victim is Entitled Under State Criminal Statute — Cruelty to, Killing, or Abandonment of, Animals*, 45 A.L.R.6TH 435.

Q. MANSLAUGHTER AND MURDER THROUGH ANIMAL

As discussed earlier, dogs may constitute deadly weapons. When they maim or kill, criminal repercussions follow. Most readers may recall Diane Whipple.[57] Attorneys and Aryan Brotherhood associates Marjorie Knoller and Robert Noel's

---

[57] *See* Richard H. Polsky, Ph.D., CAAB, *The Case of Diane Whipple* [www.sfdogmauling.com/CaseofWhipple.html]; The Death of Diane Whipple, SFGate.com [www.sfgate.com/news/article/The-Death-of-Diane-Whipple-3311937.php] (Mar. 22, 2002); Bill Hewitt, *Unleashed Fury: A Dog Attack in*

two Presa Canarios mauled Whipple to death in a San Francisco apartment building. In 2002, Knoller and Noel were found guilty by a Los Angeles jury of involuntary manslaughter, owning a mischievous animal causing death of a human being, and, for Knoller, second-degree murder. The trial court granted Knoller a new trial on the second-degree murder conviction. The People, Knoller, and Noel appealed. Holding that the trial court applied an incorrect standard for subjective awareness when considering implied malice, the California Court of Appeals remanded. *People v. Noel*, 128 Cal. App. 4th 1391 (2005). In reversing the Court of Appeals, the California Supreme Court reasoned that "the trial court set the bar too high, ruling that implied malice requires a defendant's awareness that his or her conduct had a *high probability* of resulting in death," and that the Court of Appeals set it "too low, permitting a conviction of second degree murder, based on a theory of implied malice." *People v. Knoller*, 158 P.3d 731, 732–33 (Cal. 2007) (remanding to Court of Appeals to return case to trial court with proper instructions). The trial court, before a reassigned judge, denied Knoller's motion for a new trial and sentenced her to 15 years to life in prison, from which she unsuccessfully appealed a second time. *People v. Knoller*, 2010 Cal. App. Unpub. LEXIS 6668 (Aug. 20, 2010). On Jul. 3, 2014, federal judge Jon S. Tigar denied Knoller's petition for a writ of habeas corpus. *Knoller v. Miller*, 2014 U.S. Dist. LEXIS 91146 (N.D. Cal., Jul. 3, 2014). Murder prosecutions for death by dog continue to draw media scrutiny. Corina Knoll and Debbie Truong, *A Savage Death, an Unusual Trial*, L.A. TIMES A1 (Aug. 29, 2014) (discussing death of 63-year-old Antelope Valley woman killed by four dogs with sidebar describing seven other murder charges involving dog-related fatalities from 1987 to date).

R.   PRIVATE PROSECUTION

Citizens may also seek resolution through the rare but still surviving avenue of private prosecution. Private parties, in fact, prosecuted all state and territorial criminal cases in English and American common law, before the divergence of tort and criminal law and the creation of the public prosecutor's office. Wainstein, *Judicially Initiated Prosecution: A Means of Preventing Continuing Victimization in the Event of Prosecutorial Inaction*, 76 CAL. L. REV. 727 (1988); *see also Steel Co. v. Citizens for a Better Environment*, 523 U.S. 83 (1998) (Stevens, J., concurring) ("private persons regularly prosecuted criminal cases" at time of nation's founding). Only the Attorney General or a U.S. attorney may initiate a criminal prosecution in federal district court. *See Mikhail v. Kahn*, 991 F. Supp. 2d 596 (E.D. Pa. 2014), *aff'd*, 2014 U.S. App. LEXIS 12927 (3d Cir. July 9, 2014); *Inmates of Attica Correctional Facility v. Rockefeller*, 477 F.2d 375 (2d Cir. 1973); *U.S. v. Banuelos-Rodriguez*, 215 F.3d 969 (9th Cir. 2000); *Temple v. Geroulo*, 2011 U.S. Dist. LEXIS 4344 (M.D. Pa. Jan. 18, 2011); *U.S. v. Panza*, 381 F. Supp. 1133 (W.D. Pa. 1974); *Connecticut Action Now, Inc. v. Roberts Plating Co.*, 457 F.2d 81 (2d Cir. 1972); *N.Y. v. Muka*, 440 F. Supp. 33 (N.D.N.Y. 1977) (private citizen has no right to prosecute federal crime); *U.S. v. Bryson*, 434 F. Supp. 986 (W.D. Okla. 1977) (only Attorney General and duly authorized U.S. Attorneys may prosecute criminal

---

San Francisco Kills a Beloved Lacrosse Coach and Stirs Outrage Coast to Coast, 55(7) People (Feb. 19, 2001).

actions in federal courts); *U.S. v. Panza*, 381 F. Supp. 1133 (W.D. Pa. 1974).

Pennsylvania ranks first in the prodigious development of private criminal complaint case law, thanks to fastidious interpretation of a rule of criminal procedure staging both the manner by which individuals may seek to persuade a district attorney to file charges and, if such endeavor fails, the appropriate appellate scope of review. *See Commw. v. Brown*, 550 Pa. 580 (1998); *Commw. v. Benz*, 523 Pa. 203 (1989); *Commw. v. Metzker*, 442 Pa. Super. 94 (1995); *Commw. v. Pritchard*, 408 Pa. Super. 221 (1991). Other states permitting variations of private initiation of prosecution (whereby the baton passes from the complainant to the public prosecutor to continue within her discretion) or private prosecution from charge to verdict include, but are not limited to, New Hampshire (*State v. Martineau*, 148 N.H. 259 (2002)); New Jersey (*State v. Avena*, 281 N.J. Super. 327 (1995); Ohio (*State ex rel. Rodriguez v. Hofner*, 2011-Ohio-4142 (2011); Rhode Island (*Cronan ex rel. State v. Cronan*, 774 A.2d 866 (R.I. 2001); Washington (CrRLJ 2.1(c)); West Virginia (*Harman v. Frye*, 188 W. Va. 611 (1992)); Wisconsin (*State v. Unnamed Defendant*, 150 Wis. 2d 352 (1989)).

The court in *Seeton v. Adams*, 50 A.3d 268 (Pa. Commw. Ct. 2012), *affirming Seeton v. Adams*, 17 Pa. D. & C. 5th 341 (Pa. C.P. 2010), held that a writ of mandamus could not be issued to "correct" the district attorney's allegedly "mistaken view" of the Animal Cruelty Law when withdrawing the citations that the county's humane society police officer issued to a sporting association arising from its live pigeon shoot. The district attorney had the final word on a decision to prosecute or not to prosecute, and exercised his authority as chief law enforcement officer for the Commonwealth in Berks County, whether he was correct in his interpretation of the Animal Cruelty Law or not.

In *In re Private Criminal Complaint of Clein Against Graf*, 862 A.2d 596 (Pa. Super. 2004), the complainant and his dog suffered a mauling by the defendants' unrestrained Rottweiler. His attempt to file a private criminal complaint under the Pennsylvania Dangerous Dog Law resulted in the district justice referring him to the district attorney, who refused to permit the complaint and sent him to the dog warden — who took no action. The complainant appealed to the court of common pleas, naming the district attorney as respondent and urging the court to compel him to permit prosecution. It refused, and the complainant appealed yet again. First, the superior court held that the district justice "erroneously refused to accept appellant's private criminal complaint," since 3 Pa. Cons. Stat. § 459-502-A expressly permitted the person attacked by a dog or a person whose animal suffered injury by a dog to bring a complaint before the district justice without needing to ask for permission from the district attorney. Similarly, the court of common pleas erred in barring the complaint when asserting that the matter remained under investigation by the dog warden, pointing to the plain language of 3 Pa. Cons. Stat. § 459-502-A, which did not require vetting by either district attorney or dog warden. The appeals court affirmed the court of common pleas because the complainant named the wrong respondent — the district attorney, not the district justice who erred in refusing to accept the complaint.

Most prosecuting attorney associations oppose statutes or rules allowing private prosecution (or initiation thereof), raising primarily a separation of powers objection. By way of example, the author has brought several private citizen criminal complaint petitions under Washington's CrRLJ 2.1(c), which provides an avenue for private initiation of misdemeanor or gross misdemeanor charges by any person filing an "Affidavit of Complaining Witness" found within the rule. A judge then makes a probable cause determination, as well as considers other factors set forth by rule and may conduct a limited evidentiary hearing by examining the complainant and other witnesses under oath. CrRLJ 2.1(c). Note that, as ambiguously written, CrRLJ 2.1(c) does not delegate prosecutorial discretion to a private citizen, but uses the municipal or district court judge as the gatekeeper, who will, as an attorney, be guided by the RPCs and statutory charging guidelines, as well as consider the right for a defendant, if acquitted, to recover attorney's fees. Indeed, CrRLJ 2.1(c) expressly requires such consideration be given.

Case Study: In 2007, Spokane resident Chris Anderlik put CrRLJ 2.1(c) through its paces by filing a petition under CrRLJ 2.1(c) against Spokane County Sheriff's Deputies Ballard Bates and Duane Simmons, seeking the right to charge them with second-degree animal cruelty arising from Tasering a Black Angus male calf for cumulatively more than seven minutes, after which he died. Bill Morlin, *County Attacks Taser Ruling*, SPOKESMAN REVIEW (Jun. 30, 2007) [m.spokesman.com/stories/2007/jan/27/county-attacks-taser-ruling/. Prior to filing her petition for a citizen criminal complaint on December 4, 2006, Ms. Anderlik contacted the city and county prosecuting attorney's offices to initiate prosecution, and the Sheriff's Office to conduct an internal affairs investigation. In support of the allegations of torture, Ms. Anderlik presented several declarations, including those of world-renowned Dr. Temple Grandin, the "father of veterinary ethics" Dr. Bernard Rollin, and large animal veterinarian Dr. Holly Cheever. No action was taken, so she utilized CrRLJ 2.1(c).

At the hearing on her petition on January 22, 2007, over the prosecutor's objection, Spokane County District Court Judge Sara Derr found probable cause to charge Damon Simmons and Ballard Bates with second-degree animal cruelty and additionally found that all considerations (1) through (7) identified in CrRLJ 2.1(c) were satisfied. Specifically, the court held:

> So here's my ruling. As far as the animal cruelty, and I have fairly well-defined where I see the potential for that charge, I believe that probable cause does exist. I've satisfied the additional factors that need to be considered. I just went through one to seven. The complaining witness indicates that she is aware of the gravity of this complaint, the necessity of court appearances for herself as well as any witnesses, and several have been identified to set this up. And possible liability for any kind of false arrest.

The court instructed Ms. Anderlik to prepare a criminal complaint for review and signature by her and Deputy Prosecuting Attorney Brian O'Brien.

In the Spokesman-Review, Sheriff Ozzie Knezovich "defended his deputies" and told reporters that the officers were "completely justified." And the Prosecuting Attorney openly "refused to file charges," publicly arguing "against the filing of the citizen's petition." On January 25, 2007, the Spokane County Prosecuting Attorney's Office filed a motion for reconsideration challenging the entire citizen criminal complaint process as unconstitutional. On January 27, 2007, the Sheriff again said that "killing the animal was necessary for public safety reasons." Excerpts from the prosecuting attorney's motion were disseminated publicly in the local newspaper, voicing continued opposition to filing of charges.

On March 1, 2007, Ms. Anderlik submitted a proposed criminal complaint to the court and prosecutor Brian O'Brien, with her reply on the motion to appoint a special prosecutor and disqualify the Spokane County Prosecuting Attorney's Office. The criminal complaint was signed and appended to Ms. Anderlik's reconsideration motion.

On March 2, 2007, the court heard oral argument on the prosecutor's motion for reconsideration and Ms. Anderlik's appointment and disqualification motion. On March 12, 2007, the court issued a memorandum opinion where she concluded that the officers' actions "went well beyond reasonable prudence and crossed over to negligent cruelty," and that "[t]hese actions directly resulted in the death of the calf by the impact of the Tasers." The court upheld its findings of January 22, 2007 that Ms. Anderlik had satisfied the elements of CrRLJ 2.1(c); that probable cause existed to charge Simmons and Bates with second-degree animal cruelty; that Simmons and Bates were not immune under RCW § 16.52.210; and that the court would otherwise have permitted Ms. Anderlik to file a criminal complaint as provided by CrRLJ 2.1(c) but for the additional conclusions of law that the court had no authority to appoint a special prosecutor and that to compel the prosecutor to handle this criminal matter would violate separation of powers doctrine as applied. In the final reckoning, however, the court added:

> Under these specific circumstances, the Rule is futile for any citizen who chooses to proceed under it (should the Court reach the determination that a criminal complaint should be filed).

Further, the court remarked:

> Without the County Prosecutor's willingness to proceed with prosecution of this case, the Complainant's exercise of her claim under the Rule is meaningless.

On March 19, 2007, Ms. Anderlik filed her own motion for reconsideration and/or relief from this March 12, 2007 memorandum opinion. Argued on March 26, 2007, Ms. Anderlik's motion to finalize and certify the court's previous rulings for appeal under the RALJ and for direct review to the Supreme Court resulted in Judge Derr orally ruling that her order of March 12, 2007 was appealable as a matter of right under the RALJ. She added:

> I believe that by allowing the Petitioner to stand in the shoes of the prosecutor until such time as — as a complaint is filed, because the rule, by its — on its face, says, once the complaint's filed, in essence, it's turned over to the prosecutor to proceed. But, until that time, the Petitioner is acting in the capacity of a prosecutor.

On June 4, 2008, the Washington Supreme Court granted Ms. Anderlik's motion for discretionary review. Two weeks before oral argument, however, the court dismissed claiming it granted review improvidently. In re the Citizen Criminal

Complaint of Chris Anderlik, No. 81295-1.

Case Study: Years later, the author tried to wield CrRLJ 2.1(c) again, this time against Des Moines Police Officers Michael Graddon and Steven Wieland, who allegedly conspired to execute Deirdre and Charles Wrights' beloved female Newfoundland, Rosie, on Nov. 7, 2010, shooting her four times with an assault rifle after she was Tasered and run off her property after she escaped from the Wrights' residence. Des Moines Police officers found her in the Wrights' driveway, one officer Tasered her in a misguided attempt to put a catchpole over her head. This sent her shuttling away in fear, so the officers hunted for her, finding her in the fenced backyard of a neighbor blocks away. Rosie had hidden in blackberry bushes deep within. While sitting still, not barking, growling, or showing any aggression, Wieland gave Graddon the order to fire an M4 assault rifle at Rosie. He did, causing her to drop defenseless. He then shot her three more times before she finally died. After the first shot, an unidentified officer is heard on a dashcam exclaiming, "Nice!" and a witness claims to have seen the officers engaging in high-fiving, backpatting type of behavior. When the Wrights returned from their overnight vacation, Rosie was gone and police had not informed them that Rosie had been executed. It was only after finding a Taser dart on their property that prompted the Wrights to go to the police and inquire, at which time Rosie's death was disclosed. A vigil followed, with appearance by the Des Moines Mayor and several city councilmembers, resulting in a call for the mayor's resignation by the Des Moines Police Guild.

As neither prosecuting attorney for Des Moines or King County would prosecute the officers for misdemeanor animal cruelty and willful killing, Mr. Wright timely filed petitions under CrRLJ 2.1(c) in Des Moines Municipal Court seeking to privately prosecute them.

On Feb. 28, 2011, Des Moines Municipal Court Judge Alicea-Galvan recused herself and signed an order changing venue to King County District Court ("KCDC") Chief Judge Barbara Linde for assignment within that court. On Mar. 17, 2011, Judge Linde enter orders disqualifying the entire KCDC bench and changed venue to Pierce County District Court ("PCDC"). On Mar. 25, 2011, the court administrator for PCDC confirms that no judge will hear the case, and returns the matter to King County. On Apr. 27, 2011, Judge Linde ordered a change of venue to Snohomish County District Court ("SCDC"). On Aug. 2, 2011, the parties appeared before Judge Tam Bui, and argued the merits of the petition and the City's motion to deem CrRLJ 2.1(c) unconstitutional. who sets forth a briefing schedule to manage a supplemental motion to dismiss by the City and to otherwise consider the City's original motion to dismiss. On Sept. 19, 2011, Judge Bui rejected the City's procedural and constitutional arguments in their entirety, including that CrRLJ 2.1(c) is unconstitutional facially and as applied, but dismissed the petition, finding no probable cause. Mr. Wright then appealed her decision to the Snohomish County Superior Court, but by the time the appellate judge ruled, the statute of limitations had run on any viable criminal charge. See Mark Miller, Slain dog's owners ask judge to hold officers accountable, KVAL (Aug. 2, 2011) [www.kval.com/news/126600963.html].

Though the hot potato handling of the private criminal complaint petition would have exhausted and dismayed most victims, the Wrights then filed a federal civil rights lawsuit against the City and officers involved. *Wright v. City of Des Moines*, No. 12-CV-01962-JLR (W.D. Wash. 2012). On Apr. 24, 2013, U.S. District Court Judge James Robart awarded over $50,000 in attorney's fees on top of the $51,000 FRCP 68 Offer of Judgment made by the Defendants early in the litigation. Mike Carter, *Owners of Dog Slain by Police Are Awarded Attorney Fees*, THE SEATTLE TIMES, Apr. 24, 2013, http://www.seattletimes.com/seattle-news/owners-of-dog-slain-by-police-are-awarded-attorney-fees/.

Chapter 12

VEGETARIAN AND VEGAN LITIGATION

The 2008 *Vegetarian Times* poll, collected by the Harris Interactive Service Bureau, surveying 5,050 respondents, found that 3.2 percent of the American population is vegetarian, of which one million are vegans. In 2011, the Vegetarian Resource Group commissioned Harris to perform another survey of 1,010 adults. In three short years, the percentages jumped to approximately 5.0 percent vegetarian and 2.5 percent vegan (or nearly eight million people).[1] Dietary vegans abstain from consuming animal products. Ethical vegans extend their commitment beyond dietary choices to avoid certain cosmetics, clothing, and vaccines. Animal lawyer and named plaintiff Jerry Friedman described Ethical Veganism this way:

> Ethical Veganism extends beyond trivial dietary preferences. Diet is merely a small part of observing a non-exploitive relationship with the people and animals of this world. Ethical Veganism is a relational lens through which to view the world. Ethical Vegans are not "speciesist" and value the sanctity of all life, seeking to exclude from their life, as far as possible and practical, all forms of exploitation of, and cruelty to, animals for food, clothing or any other purpose. Consequently, Ethical Vegans do not eat meat, fish or poultry, and do not use other animal products and by-products including eggs, dairy products, honey, leather, fur, wool, soaps and toothpastes which contain lard, etc., and Ethical Vegans do not participate in the biomedical experimentation on animals and avoid activities or products which encourage it. As can be seen from this "list" of prohibited activities, being vegetarian is only one small part of being an Ethical Vegan. While being a Vegan or Ethical Vegan necessarily implies that one is a vegetarian, the opposite is not true; being a vegetarian does not imply one is an Ethical Vegan, let alone a Vegan. . . . There is a common ethical principle shared by all Vegans which is a reverence for life and desire to live with, as opposed to depending upon, the other species of the planet.

Friedman v. S. Cal. Permanente Med. Gp., 102 Cal. App. 4th 39 (2002); Pet. for Rev. at 17 (Oct. 23, 2002) (No. S110916); *see* generally Erik Marcus, *Meat Market: Animals, Ethics, & Money* (Boston: Brio Press, 2005); Sarah Soifer, *Vegan Discrimination: An Emerging and Difficult Dilemma*, 36 Loy. L.A. L. Rev. 1709 (2003); Karen Iacobbo & Michael Iacobbo, Vegetarians and Vegans in America

---

[1] In 2015, however, VRG used Harris again to poll 2017 adults 18 and over. The figure 3.4% vegetarian again arose, though the two highest subcategories of vegetarians were 18-34 year olds (6%) and households earning under $50,000 (7%). Close to 15% of the 3.4% were vegans, or about half a percent of all Americans (i.e., 1.54 million). According to the 2015 poll, 55% of vegetarians (including vegans) were female. A 2012 Gallup poll, however, surmised that 5% of Americans were vegetarian.

TODAY (Westport, CT: Praeger Publishers, 2006); Donna D. Page, *Veganism and Sincerely Held "Religious" Beliefs in the Workplace: No Protection Without Definition*, 7 U. PA. J. LAB. & EMP. L. 363 (2005).

Legal issues pertaining to vegans and vegetarians relate predominantly to accommodation — in employment, education, medical care, and institutionalized meals. Though adherents to particular faith systems may find support, and even prescription, for vegetarianism in religious canons of Buddhism, Christianity, Hinduism, Judaism, Wicca, and Spiritual Veganism, others embrace such multifaceted conscientious views from a secular, humanist, or other nonreligious perspective. Stanley M. Sapon, *Is Veganism a Religion?*, VEGNEWS (Dec. 2002); *Vegan Ethics*, at www.veganforlife.org/ethics.htmwww.veganforlife.org/ethics.htm and International Vegetarian Union, Religion and Vegetarianism, www.ivu.org/religion. www.ivu.org/religion. As discussed below, the primary vegan workplace challenges arise under Title VII, the First Amendment, and state antidiscrimination laws.

A. EMPLOYMENT

When Jerry Friedman, an ethical vegan of nearly 10 years, learned that the mumps vaccine was cultured in chicken embryo, he refused to submit to this mandatory condition of permanent employment with Kaiser Permanente Medical Group. In response, Kaiser withdrew its offer of employment. Friedman then sued, claiming religious creed discrimination under the California Fair Employment and Housing Act ("FEHA"), Govt. Code § 12940 and Regulation 7293.1, defining "religious creed" as "any traditionally recognized religion as well as beliefs, observations, or practices which an individual sincerely holds and which occupy in his or her life a place of importance parallel to that of traditionally recognized religions."

Although California decisional law had not then formally construed "religious creed" under the FEHA or administrative regulations established by the Employment and Housing Commission for purposes of implementing the FEHA, its holdings in other contexts did "point away from a strictly theistic definition of religion. A belief in a Supreme Being is not required." *Friedman*, at 49. United States Supreme Court decisions also broadened protections from those with belief in a Judaeo-Christian Creator and a system of after-death punishments and rewards to religions "which do not teach what would generally be considered a belief in the existence of God," such as "Buddhism, Taoism, Ethical Culture, Secular Humanism and others." *Torcaso v. Watkins*, 367 U.S. 488, 495 fn. 11 (1961).

After surveying California decisional authority, the hallmark United States Supreme Court cases of *U.S. v. Seeger*, 380 U.S. 163 (1965) (conscientious objection to military service); *Welsh v. U.S.*, 398 U.S. 333 (1970) (conscientious objector status applies to "all those whose consciences, spurred by deeply held moral, ethical, or religious beliefs, would give them no rest or peace if they allowed themselves to become a part of an instrument of war"); and *Wisconsin v. Yoder*, 406 U.S. 205 (1972) (Amish families convicted for refusing to allow their children to attend public high school), federal Title VII employment discrimination law,[2] and federal non-employment discrimination law, the court embraced Third Circuit Court of Appeals Judge Arlin M. Adams's objective test for determining whether a belief "plays the role of a religion and functions as such in an individual's life." Originally articulated in *Malnak v. Yogi*, 592 F.2d 197 (3d Cir. 1979), and later adopted in five other circuits, the test follows:

> First, a religion addresses fundamental and ultimate questions having to do with deep and imponderable matters. Second, a religion is comprehensive in nature; it consists of a belief-system as opposed to an isolated teaching. Third, a religion often can be recognized by the presence of certain formal and external signs.

Africa v. Com. of Pa., 662 F.2d 1025, 1032 (3d Cir. 1981). Before applying the three-pronged test, the court admitted that the EEOC definition of religion is more expansive than Regulation 7293.1 and, perhaps, than the statutory interpretation in *Seeger*, which protects strictly moral or ethical beliefs held with the "strength of traditional religious views." Reg. 7293.1 requires that said beliefs carry not only the import and weight of traditional religious views but must *occupy in his or her life a place of importance parallel to that of traditionally recognized religions.*

As applied, Friedman lost, the court determining that Friedman's veganism did not address the "meaning of human existence; purpose of life; theories of human-kind's nature or its place in the universe." Arguably, classical Darwinism would begin to address these issues. The court then found a lack of comprehensivity in that there was no "apparent spiritual or otherworldly component" and that veganism is "limited to the single subject of highly valuing animal life and ordering one's life based on that perspective." But what of parallels to the Jewish doctrine of *tikkun olam* (without the overt messianic component that is, of course, critical to this prong) or similar "reverence of life" belief systems? Because the *Malnak* test requires not just an "isolated teaching," but a full "belief system," Metaphysically tethering philosophical and ethical doctrine to a supreme being or power is critical. On the last point, Friedman's veganism did not possess sufficient indicia of religious formality and externality, having not found teachers, services, holidays, or other organizational structures. Does this suggest that no *religions of one* qualify under this statute? The court concluded that veganism inspired or required by a traditionally recognized religion or quasi-religion qualifying under *Malnak* may be protected as "religious belief" under 7293.1.

Since *Friedman*, another court examined veganism in an employment discrimination dispute. Sakile Chenzira, a hospital customer service representative working for Cincinnati Children's Hospital for more than a decade was discharged due to a refusal to receive a non-vegan flu vaccine. *Chenzira v. Cincinnati Children's Hospital Medical Ctr.*, 2012 U.S. Dist. Lexis 182139 (S.D. Ohio Dec. 27, 2012). She sued under Title VII of the Civil Rights Act of 1964, Ch. 4112 of the Ohio Revised

---

[2] Title VII renders unlawful the employment practice of discriminating against an employee or prospective employee on the basis of "such individual's race, color, religion, sex, or national origin. . . ." 42 U.S.C. § 2000e-2(a). Employers must reasonably accommodate the employee's "religious observance or practice" unless doing so would be an "undue hardship on the conduct of the employer's business." 42 U.S.C. § 2000e(j) (defining "religion").

Code, and pleaded tortious wrongful discharge in violation of public policy. At the motion to dismiss stage, the court rejected the hospital's contention that veganism was "no more than a dietary preference or social philosophy" or that Chenzira's essay response, "The Biblical Basis of Veganism," was nothing more than "strategically cherry-picked Bible verses":

> The Court finds that in the context of a motion to dismiss, it merely needs to determine whether Plaintiff has alleged a plausible claim. The Court finds it plausible that Plaintiff could subscribe to veganism with a sincerity equating that of traditional religious views. The Sixth Circuit's decision in *Spies* in no way bars such conclusion. In *Spies*, the Court found that a Buddhist inmate's dietary request was adequately met by the provision of a vegetarian diet, as the inmate himself conceded that a more restrictive vegan diet was not a religious requirement of his faith. 173 F.3d 398, 407. The Court's conclusion is further bolstered by Plaintiff's citation to essays and Biblical excerpts. Although the Code makes it clear that it is not necessary that a religious group espouse a belief before it can qualify as religious, 29 C.F.R. § 1605.1, the fact here that Plaintiff is not alone in articulating her view lends credence to her position. Accordingly, at this early stage of the litigation, the Court finds it inappropriate to dismiss Plaintiff's claims for religious discrimination based on her adherence to veganism.

Id., at 4.

On Aug. 20, 1996, the Equal Employment Opportunity Commission held that vegan beliefs rise to the level of a protected religion under Title VII. *Anderson v. Orange Cy. Transit Auth.*, EEOC Charge No. 345960598 (1996).[3] Bruce Anderson drove buses for public transit. When his strict vegan views compelled him to refuse to hand out Carl's Jr. coupons to passengers so they could claim free hamburgers, the OCTA fired Anderson for insubordination — even though he offered to place them in a basket so passengers could take them as they wished. David Haldane, *Vegetarian Bus Driver Settles Suit Against Agency for $50,000*, L.A. TIMES (Nov. 20, 1996), at A3; for further discussion, see Donna D. Page, *Veganism and Sincerely Held "Religious" Beliefs in the Workplace: No Protection Without Definition*, 7:2 U. PA. J. OF LABOR & EMP. L. 363 (2005). Title VII religious accommodation claims abide a two-part burden shifting analysis. The employee must establish a *prima facie* case by proving (1) an employment obligation interferes with her religious practice; (2) she has informed the employer of same; and (3) the employer subjected her to an adverse employment action due to her inability to perform as required. Then the burden shifts to the employer to rebut one or more elements of the *prima facie* case, show it offered a reasonable accommodation, or that accommodation would constitute an undue hardship. *See EEOC v. Union Independiente de la Autoridad de Acueductos y Alcantarillados de Puerto Rico*, 279 F.3d 49, 55 (1st Cir. 2002).

---

[3] *Friedman* acknowledged that the EEOC took a more expansive view of "religion" under Title VII than the FEHA.

State antidiscrimination laws may also protect religion-based dietary preferences in the employment context. In *Kumar v. Gate Gourmet, Inc.*, 325 P.3d 193 (Wash. 2014), the Washington Supreme Court found a prima facie case of religious accommodation claim under the Washington Law Against Discrimination where airport employees' sincerely held religious beliefs mandating a vegetarian diet conflicted with the employer's requirement that they all eat company-provided food (citing security concerns). Though informing the employer of the conflict, it responded by first deceiving the employees into eating food prohibited by their religions. It then refused to entertain any of the employees' proposed accommodations, forcing them to ingest animal products or work hungry.

Occasionally, the sexual politics of meat[4] manifest not as discrimination based on vegetarianism or veganism, but on gender. In *Catalanello v. Kramer*, 18 F. Supp. 3d 504 (S.D.N.Y. 2014), managing director of Credit Agricole CIB Robert Catalanello sued Arizona State University Associate Dean and Professor of Law Zachary Kramer for defamation and related dignitary torts for statements made in the article *Of Meat and Manhood*, 89 Wash. U. L. Rev. 298 (2011) and the lecture "Of Meat and Manhood/The New Sex Discrimination" in which Kramer examined the lawsuit by Ryan Pacifico, a former junior foreign exchange trader at Credit Agricole, who sued Catalanello, his former supervisor, for creating a hostile work environment by harassing him for not eating meat and referring to him as "gay" or "homo" in front of coworkers. When Catalanello told the traders they were dining at a Brazilian steakhouse, someone asked what Pacifico could eat there, to which Catalanello responded, "Who the fuck cares? It's his fault for being a vegetarian homo." Three years after filing suit, Pacifico nonsuited his case with prejudice. While the case pended, Kramer submitted an article on the law's refusal to treat gender stereotyping as a form of sexual orientation protection under Title VII, treating Pacifico's case as a "case study" to "highlight[] the messiness of modern sex discrimination." His concluding remarks explain how sex discrimination occasionally takes other forms, such as a "hybrid of vegetarian and sexual orientation discrimination." In 2012, Kramer presented a lecture at Western New England University School of Law, arguing that Catalanello viewed Pacifico's vegetarianism as a proxy for effeminacy and that male vegetarianism is, wrongly, an unprotected trait in federal employment discrimination law. The trial court dismissed the lawsuit, finding Kramer's statements to be nonactionable opinions and fair accounts of an official proceeding.

B. CONSUMERS

While not presenting as a free exercise or religious discrimination claim, vegans misled by health care providers and manufacturers into swallowing or implanting animal products may state a claim under unfair business practice acts. Mystie Michael, likely a vegan who also suffered from a severe Lidocaine allergy, specifically asked that no animal products or xenografting "parts" be used as part of a bone grafting procedure performed by periodontist Dr. Mosquera-Lacy of

---

[4] Carol J. Adams authored the both widely-acclaimed and reviled critical feminist/animal studies text *The Sexual Politics of Meat: A Feminist-Vegetarian Critical Theory* in 1990 (Bloomsbury Academic, Rev. Ed. 2010).

Bright Now! Dental. Months prior to the procedure, Michael specifically requested non-animal bone (allograft or synthetic graft). Moments before the procedure, Michael said, "Dr. Lacy, I said I didn't want cow bone . . . I just can't fathom the thought of animal parts being in my body. . . . Do you have human bone?" Dr. Lacy had given her seven Lidocaine capulets as an anesthetic and confirmed that she would use human bone. After the procedure, Michael vomited, lost consciousness, and was rushed to the ER for treatment of conditions arising from the Lidocaine allergy. When Dr. Lacy called to check on Michael, she admitted using cow bone because she did not have enough human bone to finish Michael's procedure.

Michael sued for negligence, medical battery, and Consumer Protection Act ("CPA") violations. *Michael v. Mosquera-Lacy*, 165 P.3d 43 (Wash. App. 2008). The trial court dismissed the CPA claim on summary judgment. Michael nonsuited her remaining claims and appealed the trial court's order. At issue was whether Michael suffered "injury to business or property," a key element of a CPA claim. She asserted that the cow bone inserted into her jaw was defective and an unlawful "substitution of products." The Washington Court of Appeals agreed that the injury was the type that, if proven, would be subject to the CPA, and added that, "If her only injury was gum swelling or complications from the bone grafting surgery, then the CPA would not apply. Here, as in *Tallmadge*, Michael thought she was purchasing one product but was given another." *Id.*, at 48. Merely proving a nonquantifiable deprivation of use and enjoyment of property (e.g., the graft and her jaw) sufficed.

The court next rejected Mosquera-Lacy's assertion that the lack of evidence of advertising or promotional activities negated Michael's claim, finding that "advertising is [not] necessary to satisfy [the unfair or deceptive act element] of a CPA claim." *Id.*, at 48. While the "learned professions" are typically not subject to the CPA except for their "entrepreneurial activities," the court found that a material issue of fact existed as to whether Dr. Lacy's representations and use of cow bone related to how Bright Now! obtained, retained, and dismissed its clients. The final element of the CPA — public interest impact — also resolved in favor of Michael, the court noting that the factors informing the traditional distinction between a "consumer transaction" or "private dispute" are not dispositive in order to demonstrate public interest, and since Bright Now! could not demonstrate that "the only reasonable conclusion from the evidence was that the transaction involved did not affect the public interest," the matter should go to the jury. *Id.* Judge Bridgewater dissented, noting that Michael's case turned on personal injury, not property damage, and did not demonstrate how cow bone was less valuable or enduring, or more prone to repair, than human bone. The Washington Supreme Court reversed, finding that the defendant's misconduct did not involve the entrepreneurial aspects of practice germane to the CPA. *Michael v. Mosquera-Lacy*, 187 P.3d 268 (Wash. 2009).

Other unfair business practice litigation revolving around nondisclosure or misrepresentation of the inclusion of animal products in items marketed to end-consumers include the use of cochineal extract (pulverized beetle carcasses) in Frappuccinos, smoothies, cakes, and doughnuts (*Anderson v. Starbucks Corp.*, Los Angeles Cy. Sup. Ct. BC485438 (filed May 25, 2012)); the sale of cosmetics as "vegetarian" (*Balser v. Hain Celestial Gp., Inc.*, 2013 U.S. Dist. LEXIS 180220

(C.D. Cal. Dec. 18, 2013)); a pharmaceutical company's failure to label its B-12 tablets, "recommended . . . for vegetarians and vegans," as coated in gelatin (*Lateef v. Pharmavite LLC*, 2013 U.S. Dist. LEXIS 51457 (N.D. Ill. Apr. 10, 2013) (dismissing claim because label did not assert a fact concerning presence or absence of gelatin in its supplements)); a tuberculosis test distributor's representation that it did not contain animal products and was "Vegan 'safe' " and "Vegan 'friendly' " (*Friedman v. Merck & Co.*, 107 Cal. App. 4th 454 (2003) (dismissed as no duty to warn existed, foreseeability of harm was too remote, and California law did not recognize negligent misrepresentation for risk of emotional harm alone)); and see *Sharma v. McDonald's Corp.*, King Cy. Sup. Ct. (Wash.) No. 01-2-12267-3SEA (historic class action lawsuit on behalf of 16 million vegetarian and Hindu consumers seeking accountability from McDonald's for false advertisement and using beef tallow in French fries).

C.   SCHOOL LUNCH

When Congress passed the National School Lunch Act of 1946, 42 U.S.C. §§ 1751–1769j, it established the National School Lunch Program, administered by the USDA. Accepting federal funding required that schools serve USDA-approved lunches, which mandated offering students dairy milk. 42 U.S.C. § 1758(a)(2). Come 2004, Congress amended the Act to require the offering of dairy substitutes to meet dietary needs of students. Child Nutrition and WIC Reauthorization Act of 2004, P.L. No. 108-265. On Jul. 19, 2012, Susan Levin, M.S., R.D., of the Physicians Committee for Responsible Medicine ("PCRM"), filed a petition with the USDA seeking to exclude dairy milk as a required component of the federal school lunch program, contending that it does not improve bone health or reduce osteoporosis risk but actually creates new ones. http://www.pcrm.org/pdfs/health/PCRM_USDA_milk_petition.7.19.12.pdf.

In 2013, Active Learning Elementary School in the Queens borough of New York City became the first public school in the country to serve only vegetarian meals for breakfast and lunch. Cheryl K. Chumley, *Where's the Beef? Bloomberg Launches Vegetarian-only School Lunch*, WASHINGTON TIMES (May 1, 2013). Compare this shift to a plant-based diet with the State of Washington's closure of a vegan-only preschool, kindergarten, and elementary school. For 20 years, Ellouise Carroll, Ph.D., directed a trilingual state-approved K-6 Early Education Center Academy in Puyallup, Wash. Dr. Carroll explained, "I couldn't, in good conscience, feed the children in my care in a way that I now knew was not healthy for them." Yet state law imposed various impediments to Carroll's vision. "We were not allowed to be vegan (in order to be licensed in the State of Washington, you *must* serve dairy products and, if you don't serve meat, you actually have to serve twice as many dairy products: one as a liquid dairy and one as a substitute for the meat)." The school closed in 2003 after she could not afford to fight the government. Karen Iacobbo and Micahel Iacobbo, *Vegetarians and Vegans in America Today* 142–43 (Praeger 2006). In the last decade, focus on the health benefits of plant-based diets and deleterious effects of animal products, coupled with recognition of lactose intolerance among non-European American students, led to codified requirements to promote dairy and meat alternatives. Monica Eng, *Lactose Intolerance: When Drinking School Milk Makes Students Feel Sick*, CHICAGO TRIBUNE (Nov. 26, 2012). For instance, the

District of Columbia Healthy Schools Act of 2010, Sec. 205(b)(2), requires that schools "inform families that vegetarian food options and milk alternatives are available upon request."

D. GRADE SCHOOL DISSECTION AND VIVISECTION

Tenth-grader Jenifer Graham, a vegetarian sophomore opposed to killing animals for scientific purposes was enrolled at Victor Valley Union High School. She objected to dissecting a frog in her biology class and received a zero for the assignment, lowering her grade from A to B. The school rejected her request to use a frog model, claiming it would give her an advantage over other students and jeopardize its academic rigor and credibility among universities and colleges. She later filed a federal lawsuit, *Graham v. Bd. of Trustees of the Victor Valley Union H.S. Dist.*, C.D. Cal. CV-87 03764 (1987), which U.S. District Court Central District of California Judge Manuel L. Real dismissed, stating, "I don't think she has any choice in this," adding, "She can't take this to absurdity. The Constitution is not meant to be absurd."[5] United Press International, *Suit on Frog Dissection Rejected*, L.A. TIMES (Aug. 1, 1988). However, he did tell the school to provide her with a frog who died from natural causes and allow her to identify internal organs from photographs. Joe Menosky, *Down in the Swamps, a "Natural" Death for a Frog Is, Well, Just Not Natural*, L.A. TIMES (Aug. 22, 1988). The school failed to provide her with such a frog, and she appealed. Subsequently, the district settled, removing all negative marks from her record, and paying her legal fees. Associated Press, *Student Who Sued School Isn't Required to Cut Frog*, N.Y. TIMES (Aug. 3, 1988).

But changes did not end with litigation. *CBS School Break* aired a special titled "Frog Girl: The Jenifer Graham Story," and the California Legislature passed a law that mandated alternatives to dissection for elementary and secondary students who object on moral grounds. Cal. Educ. Code § 32255.1. The District of Columbia and 17 other states have given students the choice — Connecticut, Florida, Illinois, Louisiana, Maine, Maryland, Massachusetts, Michigan, New Hampshire, New Jersey, New Mexico, New York, Oregon, Pennsylvania, Rhode Island, Vermont, and Virginia. http://aavs.org/animals-science/laws/student-choice-laws/. *See also* www.animalearn.org; Marcia Goodman Kramer, *Humane Education, Dissection, and the Law*, 13 ANIMAL L. 281 (2007) (discussing *Graham* and other antidissection cases). Some school districts uniformly ban vivisection in the classroom, without requiring that each individual conscientious objector opt-out. Eleven states[6] presently mandate humane education. *See* Cal. Edu. Code § 51540 and §§ 233–233.5; Fla. Educ. Code §§ 233.061(2)(j), 233.09; Fla. Stat. §§ 1003.42(2)(k), 1001.01(2); 105 Ill. Comp. Stat. 5/27-13.1, 5/27-14, 5/27-15, 5/27-18; La. Stat. Ann. § 17:266; N.Y. Educ. Law § 809; RCW § 28A.230.020; Maine Code ch. 20 § 1221; Mass. Gen. Stat. Ch. 272 § 80G; N.J. Educ. § 18A:35-4.1; N.H. Crim. Code § 644:8-c; ORS § 336.067; Pa. Public Sch. Code of 1949 § 1514.

---

[5] Judge Real was later investigated for judicial misconduct by the Ninth Circuit Court of Appeals. Terry Carter, *Real Trouble*, ABA Journal (Sept. 1, 2008).

[6] N.D. Political Code 884 (1905, ch. 108) required teaching of humane education of "not less than two lessons of ten minutes each per week." That provision appears to have been repealed.

Illustration: Humane Education Petition for Rulemaking Example

The Florida legislature charged the Department of Education and its instructional materials committee with this duty:

§ 1006.31. Duties of the Department of Education and school district instructional materials reviewer.

(2) EVALUATION OF INSTRUCTIONAL MATERIALS.—To use the selection criteria listed in s. 1006.34(2)(b) and recommend for adoption only those instructional materials aligned with the Next Generational Sunshine State Standards provided for in s. 1003.41. . . . When recommending instructional materials, each reviewer shall:

(c) Include materials that encourage thrift, fire prevention, and *humane treatment of people and animals.*

Fla. Stat. § 1006.31(2)(c) (emphasis added).

Also applicable are Fla. Stat. §§ 1003.42(2)(k), 1001.01(2), stating:

§ 1003.42. Required instruction.—

(1) Each district school board shall provide all courses required for middle grades promotion, high school graduation, and appropriate instruction designed to ensure that students meet State Board of Education adopted standards in the following subject areas: reading and other language arts, mathematics, science, social studies, foreign languages, health and physical education, and the arts.

(2) Members of the instructional staff of the public schools, subject to the rules of the State Board of Education and the district school board, shall teach efficiently and faithfully, using the books and materials required that meet the highest standards for professionalism and historic accuracy, following the prescribed courses of study, and employing approved methods of instruction, the following: . . .

(k) Kindness to animals.

§ 1000.01. The Florida K-20 education system; technical provisions.—

(1) NAME. — Chapters 1000 through 1013 shall be known and cited as the "Florida K-20 Education Code."

(2) LIBERAL CONSTRUCTION. — The provisions of the Florida K-20 Education Code shall be liberally construed to the end that its objectives may be effected. It is the legislative intent that if any section, subsection, sentence, clause, or provision of the Florida K-20 Education Code is held invalid, the remainder of the code shall not be affected.

No administrative rules were enacted to administer Fla. Stat. § 1006.31(4)(c). While the Science Specifications 2009, at 243–44, provide passing acknowledgement of humane principles, evidently amiss are rules that would otherwise have prevented the disrespectful handling of birds and animal cruelty inflicted at the hands of Florida high school students the catalyst for a rulemaking petition as more fully described below. The Specifications state:

H. HUMANITY AND COMPASSION

Portrayal of the appropriate care and treatment of people and animals must include compassion, sympathy, and consideration of their needs and values and exclude hard-core pornography and inhumane treatment.

See Florida Statutes §§ 1003.42; 1006.31(4)(c); 1006.34(2)(b).

Inclusion of compassion. When providing examples in narrative or visuals, materials sometimes depict the care and treatment of people and animals. Generally, this means showing in some way a measure of compassion, sympathy, or consideration of their needs and feelings.

Exclusion of inhumanity. In the context of personal and family values, Florida expressly prohibits material containing *hard-core pornography*. In addition, although the definition of *inhumane treatment* can sometimes appear to be controversial, as in science research, there is general agreement that instructional materials should not advocate any form of inhumane treatment.

As with the evaluation of multicultural representation, it is important to consider the context of the subject and the age and abilities of the students.

Science Specs 2009, at 243–44.

On Mar. 9, 2011, petitioners Hargreaves, UPC, and HERO filed a *Petition for Agency Action* with the Florida Department of Education, seeking the promulgation of new or clarified rules in the areas of humane treatment of animals and banning animal slaughter in K-12 classrooms, pursuant to the statutory mandates of Florida education law. Catalyzing this petition was the highly publicized criminal prosecution of Hawthorne High School students Patrick Ruebin Dougan and Robert Sylvester Gordon with the crime of cruelty to animals in relation to a chicken allegedly tortured during a classroom slaughter project in 2009. Specifically, Mr. Gordon raised a chicken over his head and then smashed her into the ground, whereupon she flapped her wings frantically and died. Mr. Dougan filmed the incident and posted it on YouTube, encouraging viewers to come to his school to see more "animal cruelty." The violent YouTube video that sparked the investigation by law enforcement can be seen at www.upc-online.org/hawthorne/.

Though dismissed by *nolle prosequi* on Dec. 7, 2009, due to ostensible lack of evidence, that Mr. Dougan and Mr. Gordon would not face criminal charges did not obviate critical consideration of the issues motivating this petition. For if the State Attorney found the misconduct sufficiently atrocious to pursue felony charges against 18-year-olds in the brutal killing of a chicken, that alone commended serious, independent examination. Hawthorne High School teacher Allen Shaw decided to offer a "Broiler Project" where he would teach children how to handle chickens from hatchlings to slaughter, raising them on campus through the moment of cervical dislocation, followed by butchering. The Activity Card completed by investigating Officer J. Ritchie[7] revealed the following important details:

> I spoke to the Principal Craig and he was unaware of the video or that there were any animals located on school grounds. . . . We spoke to Allen Shaw the teacher of the FFA program about the incident. Mr. Shaw did say that they were teaching the kids how to properly kill and prepare chicken they had raised. I explained about the video to Mr. Shaw and he was unaware that the incident had happened. . . . Mr. Shaw explained that he has 40 students in that class and that he helped each student kill their chicken and prepare it. Mr. Shaw stated that he must have been busy helping another student when the incident occurred. Mr. Shaw clearly stated that the way the chicken was killed was not an approved method taught in this class.

Though Mr. Shaw's students supposedly received written instructional materials governed by the State Instructional Materials Committee ("SIMC") and Fla. Stat. § 1006.31, state law concerning biological experiments on living subjects also applied, per Fla. Stat. § 1003.47, which states in relevant part:

Biological experiments on living subjects.

> (1) It is the intent of the Legislature with respect to biological experiments involving living subjects by students in grades K through 12 that:

>> **(a) No surgery or dissection shall be performed on any living mammalian vertebrate or bird.** Dissection may be performed on nonliving mammals or birds secured from a recognized source of such specimens and under supervision of qualified instructors. Students may be excused upon written request of a parent.

>> . . .

>> (c) Nonmammalian vertebrates, excluding birds, may be used in biological experiments, provided that physiological harm does not result from such experiments. Anatomical studies shall only be conducted on models that are anatomically correct for the animal being studied or on nonliving nonmammalian vertebrates secured and from a recognized source of such specimens and under the supervision of qualified instructors. Students may be excused from such experiments upon written request of the parent.

>> . . .

>> (g) All experiments shall be carried out under the supervision of a competent science teacher who shall be responsible for ensuring that the student has the necessary comprehension for the study to be undertaken. Whenever feasible, specifically qualified experts in the field should be consulted.

>> (h) Live animals on the premises of public and private elementary,

---

[7] This document and others referenced in this section are on file with author.

middle, and high schools shall be housed and cared for in a humane and safe manner. Animals shall not remain on the premises of any school during periods when such school is not in session, unless adequate care is provided for such animals.

(2) The provisions of this section shall not be construed to prohibit or constrain conventional instruction in the normal practices of animal husbandry or exhibition of any livestock in connection with any agricultural program or instruction of advanced students participating in advanced research, scientific studies, or projects.

Deposed as part of the criminal prosecution were two Hawthorne High School students, Samantha Faircloth and Rodney Tillman. Ms. Faircloth described Mr. Shaw's humane "method" as follows:

Q.   Okay. Did you recall your teacher, Mr. Shaw, demonstrating, before the class started, how to properly kill a chicken?

A.   Yeah.

Q.   How was that?

A.   He just like grabbed his head and his feet and just popped the head out of place and then threw it in the bucket until it died.

Faircloth Dep., at 10:9-16 (emphasis added, confirming that Mr. Shaw did not ensure prompt euthanasia). She adds, on cross-examination:

Q.   When the kids were throwing the chicken in the bucket, were the chickens alive?

A.   They were like — yeah; but they were like — I guess the nerves, like they were like —

Q.   They were flopping around; right?

A.   Yeah.

Q.   Even when Mr. Shaw popped the chicken's neck and threw him in the bucket, the chicken was flopping around?

A.   Yeah.

Id., at 12:5-14. Student Rodney Tillman comments on the class as well:

Q.   Can you please tell me what you saw?

. . .

A.   It was a project in ag class, and everybody was popping chickens' necks. It was a class grade. And it just got a little out of hand, and people started pulling heads off completely.

Tillman Dep., at 4:9-17. Noting that the decapitation by Mr. Gordon was not exclusive to him, Mr. Tillman adds:

A.   Mr. Shaw instructed us how to do it, and we just took it too far by, you know, pulling the heads off way too hard.

Q.   Okay. Where was Mr. Shaw when all these heads were popping off?
            Was he in a place where he couldn't see this?

A.   I think his back was turned.

Id., at 10:1-7. Indeed, with 40 students and more than 20 chickens to be killed in a 50-minute class, while Mr. Shaw instructed them on how to clean and dress the chickens after killing, it certainly appears that Mr. Shaw did not have sufficient time or control over the classroom, creating an environment posing a significant risk of animal cruelty.

Two world-renowned experts asked to watch the Robert Gordon and Patrick Dougan video, Dr. Nedim C. Buyukmihci, Emeritus Professor of Veterinary Medicine at University of California at Davis, and Dr. Ian J.H. Duncan, Professor Emeritus in Animal Welfare at the University of Guelph's Ontario Agriculture College Department of Animal and Poultry Science, offered comments signifying precisely why Shaw's "Broiler Project" violated Fla. Stat. § 1006.41 (SIMC humane education protocol), 1003.42 (kindness to animals component), and 1003.47 (biological experiments).

Dr. Duncan stated, in relevant part:

> I have watched the video entitled "Chicken Bashing at Hawthorne High School" several times. In my opinion, the actions shown depict gross cruelty. This opinion seems to be shared by at least one of the children observing the actions since I could hear the words " . . . terrible cruelty . . . " in the background.
>
> . . .
>
> I am shocked that school children would be given access to live animals without any apparent supervision. In my opinion the teacher "in charge" should be held at least partly responsible for this act of cruelty.
>
> . . .
>
> The usual way for farmers to kill chickens is to dislocate the neck. It is quite a skilled technique to do this properly, and I really do not think that school children should be attempting this procedure. . . . [Cervical dislocation] has always been thought [] humane i.e. that a bird so treated lost consciousness and died within a few seconds.
>
> However, recent research completed at Guelph suggests that this is not the case. . . . We are now advising all farmers (turkey and chicken) to use this non-penetrating captive bolt pistol instead of manual dislocation of the neck.
>
> . . .
>
> However, I have no idea how skilled the pupils were at dislocating necks. If necks are dislocated at a lower level than the Atlas and Axis, consciousness will last longer. . . . It is the head that is experiencing the suffering and it is the head that must be very closely observed. Our student here in Guelph relied heavily on certain reflexes including the papillary response to

light and the blinking of the nictitating membrane (the third eyelid in birds) in response to stimulation, to judge whether or not the birds were conscious and when death occurred.

Duncan Aug. 18, 2010, Correspondence to Karp. In light of Dr. Duncan's comments, there is no evidence that Mr. Shaw taught his students death verification techniques in order to assess the relative success in "humanely" killing the chickens each student learned to raise from one-day-old chicks. In this respect, Dr. Buykmihci offers highly probative observations on the effectiveness of the technique, even in skilled hands, which urbanized teenagers assuredly did not possess:

> Although cervical dislocation *may* (this is an important qualification) be an effective method of killing chickens, it has to be applied properly. *Nevertheless, there are no scientific studies to confirm that this method is truly humane.* In fact, loss of consciousness may not be instantaneous and electrical activity in the brain may persist for many seconds suggesting that the individual can continue to feel pain and suffer during this time. Even if decapitation occurs, this does not result in instantaneous death and suffering can continue for some seconds. It is reasonable to conclude, therefore, that movement on the part of the animals subjected to these procedures is not simply reflexive and indicates suffering for at least some time after the procedure.

> Because the students were being taught the technique of cervical dislocation, it should be obvious that no student likely had the skills to "properly" do this procedure. In cases such as this, professionals such as myself and my colleagues' recommend that the birds first be anesthetized. This must be done through acceptable veterinary methods. In the event of incorrect application, this would allow the instructor the opportunity to then kill the individual immediately so that suffering will not occur.

Buyukmichi Jun. 17, 2010, Letter to Davis. The last sentence is critical. Mr. Shaw was nowhere to be found when Robert Gordon slammed the chicken into the ground after allegedly dislocating the neck. How many other chickens suffered at the hands of 39 other high schoolers during Mr. Shaw's period of distraction?

UPC and HERO contended that the "Broiler Project" violated Fla. Stat. § 1003.47(1)(a) in that the forcible restraint and attempted dislocation of the neck constituted a form of vivisection. "Dissection," or anatomization, is defined as the process of disassembling and observing, cutting apart, or separating tissues. That some students ripped off the heads of chickens clearly fit within the scope of prohibited dissection. Even the act of dislocation, when "properly" performed by very skilled farmers,[8] constitutes dissection in that it, colloquially speaking, results in "breaking the neck" or "snapping the spine." By separating the spinal cord from the brain, death purportedly ensues rapidly. When performed on living animals, such dissection violates Fla. Stat. § 1003.47(1)(a).

---

[8] See, however, the Aug. 18, 2010 letter of Dr. Duncan and Jun. 17, 2010 letter of Dr. Buyukmihci, calling into doubt the humanity and effectiveness of cervical dislocation of birds.

Fla. Stat. § 1003.47(2) does not alter this analysis. First, Mr. Shaw's course was not part of an agricultural program or instruction of "advanced" students participating in "advanced" research, scientific studies, or projects. These were average high schoolers taking an entry-level course. Nor would slaughtering birds in high school constitute "conventional" instruction, given that the technique is one utilized by adult, experienced farmers, not children, and certainly not "in connection with" advanced students participating in advanced research. Finally, per Dr. Duncan, cervical dislocation has proved to be an inhumane method; instead, nonpenetrating captive bolt or controlled atmospheric euthanasia methods have become the norm.

On Apr. 14, 2011, Florida Department of Education Commissioner Eric J. Smith denied the petition, finding that UPC, Hargreaves, and HERO lacked standing and that the matter had become stale, because the incident took place in 2009. *Petition to Initiate Rulemaking, Final Order*, No. DOE-2011-2272-FOI (Apr. 14, 2011).

E. POSTSECONDARY EDUCATION

After admission to Ohio State University's College of Veterinary Medicine, student Jennifer Kissinger received an Admission Acceptance Form stating that the faculty believed "the use of live animals in the teaching program is essential" and that, "Objection to the use of live animals will not be grounds for excuse from class." In her second year, the College required that she take Operative Practice and Techniques, a surgical course involving the anesthetization, operation, and swift euthanization of healthy animals. Citing her religious beliefs, Kissinger requested an alternative curriculum to fulfill the surgical requirement. The College refused. When she enrolled in her third-year classes but did not participate in such surgeries, the College said she could withdraw from the Operative Practice class, but then no longer continue with subsequent courses, at which point she would have to petition for readmission. After filing suit on various grounds, including 42 U.S.C. § 1983 (relative to First and Fourteenth Amendment violations), state common-law and constitutional theories, the College offered an alternative curriculum. After fine-tuning, she accepted the revised offer, completed matriculation, obtained her degree, and practiced veterinary medicine.[9] Her request for prevailing party attorney's fees[10] under 42 U.S.C. § 1988, however, failed. *Kissinger v. OSU*, 5 F.3d 177 (6th Cir. 1993). Without examining whether Kissinger's veganism amounted to a religion, the Sixth Circuit appeared to assume as much, yet concluded, "Ohio State's curriculum did not violate Kissinger's right to exercise freely her religion"

---

[9] Jennifer Kissinger again became a party to litigation, resulting in an appellate decision, *Sherman v. Kissinger*, 195 P.3d 539 (Wash. Ct. App. 2008). Sued for malpractice allegedly causing the death of Arlene Sherman's toy poodle named Ruby, the appellate court reversed the trial court's dismissal of her state tort claims, which it predicated on application of Ch. 7.70 RCW, Washington's medical malpractice statute. It held that veterinarians were not covered by the Act. The appellate court also refused to limit Ms. Sherman's to Ruby's fair market value, instead outlining a three-part test to determine whether that measure, or instead replacement or intrinsic value, best applied. While an arbitrator found for Ms. Sherman and awarded $22,300 for Ruby's intrinsic value and emotional distress, Dr. Kissinger and the hospital filed a request for a trial *de novo*, nullifying that award.

[10] Rutgers University Law Professor Gary L. Francione represented Kissinger and wrote this accessible text with Anna E. Charlton, *Vivisection and Dissection in the Classroom: A Guide to Conscientious Objection* (American Anti-Vivisection Society (1992)).

and she "was not legally entitled to force Ohio State to exempt her from taking Operative Practice and Techniques." *Id.*, at 179, 181. What if OSU challenged Kissinger's views as not a bona fide religion?

Hypothetical: A second-year veterinary student, Marcus Welby was enrolled at Bovine State University's College of Veterinary Medicine. To graduate, he needed to complete Dr. Martinez's mandatory course, Small Animal Surgery, VM 553, which required his participation in one laboratory utilizing a colony dog destined for euthanasia under a terminal protocol. Future courses also would require him to dissect non-ethically sourced cadavers. Welby made a formal request to reasonably accommodate his deeply held moral convictions as a vegan, thereby affording him an equal opportunity to pursue an education in veterinary medicine. Forcing him to engage in vivisection or dissection as a prerequisite to receiving his degree or full credit for a required course jeopardized his constitutional rights to freedom of religion, so he claimed. An acceptable alternative, already kindly offered by one of his other professors in a different course, would be the use of a spay/neuter-return dog with a non-terminal protocol in lieu of the colony dog, where sterilization would coincide with anesthetization. For lessons involving deceased animals, an acceptable alternative would be an "ethically sourced" cadaver, which may be obtained through an Education Memorial Program.

The University ignored such overtures, and Welby filed a federal lawsuit against the Board of Trustees of the University, the Deans, and Dr. Martinez, associated with the Small Animal Surgery Section. In the action, he sought declaratory and injunctive relief for violations of his civil rights under the United States Constitution and Bovine State Constitution — namely, his First Amendment right to free exercise of religion; the deprivation of his property interest in his education and his liberty interests in his reputation, standing, and future educational and career opportunities, all without procedural due process under the Fourteenth Amendment; and his Fourteenth Amendment right to equal protection — as well as breach of contract. He sought compensatory damages, attorney's fees, and costs.

As the complaint explained, Welby embraced veganism, a sincerely held moral way of living seeking to exclude, as far as possible and practical, all forms of exploitation, unnecessary suffering, and cruelty to animals solely or predominantly for human purposes. He objected to the killing of healthy animals and the performance of surgical techniques on healthy animals for whom invasive surgery neither palliates, cures, nor prevents disease, when conducted solely for educational purposes, and where accepted alternatives exist. His "reverence for life" belief system related to an ultimate concern and influenced his life greatly, affecting, among other things, his diet, choice of clothing, and views about the use of animals in experimentation, entertainment, labor, and education. In short, he considered it a moral transgression to harm any animal when the primary benefit does not directly accrue to that animal. Incidental human edification was morally confluent with his belief system, but only where the animal patient derives the chief advantage. Any other scenario violated his convictions.

He was not a utilitarian, a philosophical perspective often invoked to justify repeated invasive and nonconsensual surgeries of animals for the greater good of veterinary medicine and the treatment of other animals within the species. This perspective, he argued, held no inherent claim to supremacy over deontologistic philosophies that embrace the ancient and spiritual ethics of reciprocity, as encapsulated in the "Golden Rule" and "Silver Rule." Kant's Categorical Imperative, a modern restatement of these rules, roughly stated, asks us to treat others as ends in themselves and to act so that the maxim of our action might be universal law. Welby's moral compass was set to acknowledge and honor these ethical mandates.

Welby's veganism did not engage in a utilitarian ethical calculus where one expressly or tacitly omits from the calculation the real quantities of animal patient nonconsent, discomfort, imprisonment, incapacitation, and killing. Moreover, this assessment fails to acknowledge the detriment to the veterinary student compelled to perform these superfluous surgeries. Deontologists and vegan moral actors hold fast to duty-driven obligation to avoid trespassing on the dignity and bodily integrity of all creatures except where the primary beneficiary is the animal herself. This imperative does not depart from the conventional tenets of human medicine as embraced in the Hippocratic Oath and the colloquialized directive to, "First, do no harm." Welby, rather, saw veterinary medicine as a science and art, an honorable means to heal nonhuman animals under his care and supervision. By compelling him to participate in surgeries, he argued that BSU needlessly confronted him with an unconstitutional dilemma, made additionally impermissible given the presence of numerous suitable alternatives.

The general belief system of the vegan is premised on refusing to derive any benefit from the suffering of another creature. For this reason, vegans avoid consumption of dairy, knowing that many cows suffer from repeated impregnation and nearly constant lactation and experience severe restriction of mobility and a shortened lifespan, followed by slaughter. The calves born to these cows are then sent to veal factories or killed shortly after birth.[11] Knowing the fate that may befall

---

[11] In a June 29, 2016, telephonic interview by the author with Howard Lyman, nationally known fourth-generation rancher producing dairy and meat, and victorious defendant in a lawsuit brought against him and Oprah Winfrey by the National Cattlemen's Beef Association in 1996, Mr. Lyman gave the opinion that, nationally, three to five percent of all male calves born at dairy operations are killed instead of being fed and cared for until they could be transported to auction to be sold to veal farms. Noting that "It's not all wonderful and lovely out in agriculture land. It is a dirty, tough business," Mr. Lyman described the killing process: "It is easier just to pick up a hammer, hit them in the head, and throw them in the dead pile." The killing rate significantly increases if there are no established field operations in the area and dairies must wait a week or more to auction off the newborns. "The dairy operation wants to get rid of the newborn calf as quickly as possible" because they are a burden to keep alive and transport. "By the time they take out transportation and cost of auction operation, it is much more cost-efficient just to get rid of them." Such treatment of male calves is "absolutely happening today" and is "not something they like people to know about, but it is happening."

On June 29 and July 1, 2016, the author also emailed attorney Jerold D. Friedman (who became interested in civil rights as an animal activist beginning in the 1990s). He confirmed that in 1995, several animal rights activists and he went to dairy farms in Southern California several times on Sunday nights before trucks arrived on Monday mornings to pick up dead calves placed along the side of the road. Infant mortality is high among calves so the dairy farmers pay for weekly pickups. It was believed they died from pneumonia due to weakened immunity caused by inadequate food and exposure to bad weather. They likely did not receive their mother's milk (or not enough) to build their immunity, nor their mother's warmth or protection. Such calf corpse roundups continue to this day. The activists used the dead calves at many demonstrations against McDonald's to bring awareness to the cruelty inherent in the meat and dairy industries.

the milk-producers, vegans find it ethically impermissible to seize any benefit (i.e., milk) from the suffering and future misery of that creature. Analogously, in the human context, many consumers boycotted goods produced by corporations hiring child or slave labor, in a desire not to benefit from the suffering of other moral agents. Contributing to the demand that facilitates the continued nonconsensual suffering of animals, even in the name of learning, presented Welby with an ethical quandary at severe odds with his deeply held convictions. To earn constitutional protection, Welby argued that veganism and other "reverence for life" belief systems, like that embraced and practiced by Welby, need not ground themselves in a recognized theism.*Welsh v. United States*, 398 U.S. 333, 339 (1970).

How would you rule on Welby's religious discrimination claim?[12]

Modern free exercise jurisprudence[13] requires the complaining party to demonstrate that her religious convictions are sincerely held and central to religious practice. Courts will not delve into the truth or rationality of those beliefs, so long as "arguably religious." *International Soc. for Krishna Consciousness, Inc. v. Barber*, 650 F.2d 430, 439 (2d Cir. 1981); L. TRIBE, AMERICAN CONSTITUTIONAL LAW § 14–16, at 828 (1978). To merit First Amendment protection, such beliefs need not cling to a traditional religious dogma or tenet, but "[p]urely secular views do not suffice." See *Frazee v. Illinois Department of Employment Security*, 489 U.S. 829, 833–35 (1989); *Dettmer v. Landon*, 617 F. Supp. 592 (E.D. Va.1985) (issue is not substance of belief system but function or role of it as part of a person's "ultimate concern"; ordering that prison official's refusal to give inmate access to candles, salt or sulfur, incense, kitchen timer, and white robes impermissibly infringed upon his First Amendment right).

Next, the party must demonstrate that the challenged act or legislation burdens the free exercise of religion through its coercive effect. Thus, a facially neutral, nonselectively enforced statute may still violate the constitutional right to free exercise if it indirectly constrains religious practice. The Supreme Court has rejected the indirect-direct burden dichotomy. If the government does impair religious belief, it must identify a compelling government interest that justifies such imposition and that the burden imposed represents the least restrictive means of satisfying it. See *Thomas v. Review Board*, 450 U.S. 707, 717–718 (1981).

Hypothetical: Part-time waitress and vegan Francesca Dumond learns that hunters in her neighborhood have decided to spend the weekend hunting Canada geese. Feeling obligated to protect these creatures, she approaches them in a blind and asks, "Why is it you can't admit that you get a thrill out of killing?" They pay her little attention. She continues, "You mutilate more than you kill, and leave the geese to die a terrible death." One hunter attempts to engage her in discussion but insists that she leave as her presence disrupts their efforts to concentrate and ensure that the geese do not flee the area. She refuses and is later arrested under the Hunter Harassment Act. She claims that her religious views spur her to speak

---

[12] This hypothetical involved one of the author's early clients, resolved without litigation through accommodation by the University.

[13] Note that Title VII only applies in the employment context. Hence, Kissinger could not invoke the Civil Rights Act's protection but sought a remedy under the federal constitution.

up for the animals and bear witness to their torment.

Does the First Amendment protect her right to remain near the hunters and speak her truth, even loudly?

Except for the religious gloss, the above hypothetical draws directly from the case of *Dorman v. Satti*, 678 F. Supp. 375 (D. Conn.1988) (finding the Act unconstitutional on grounds of vagueness in civil rights action filed by Dorman), *affirmed by* 862 F.2d 432 (2nd Cir. 1988); see Sharon L. Bass, *Law Shielding Hunters Put to the Test*, N.Y. TIMES 11C (Apr. 13, 1986).

An attempt to infuse hunter harassment litigation with free exercise principles arose in *Binkowski v. State*, 731 A.2d 64 (N.J. Super. Ct. 1999), where three individuals sought to declare New Jersey's Hunter Harassment Statute unconstitutional as an impermissible regulation of speech. Binkowski, Chief Veterinarian of the Associated Humane Societies' Animal Shelter in Newark, possessing a deep spiritual belief in the sanctity of life, the rejection of speciesism, and abhorrence of animal cruelty, claimed First Amendment protection, including under the Free Exercise Clause, against the restrictions imposed under N.J.S.A. § 23:7A-1 to -3. Those sections permitted civil and criminal remedies, as well as a private right of action, against those who hindered or prevented the lawful taking of wildlife through a variety of actions seeking to scare or repel wildlife and, thus, interfere with efforts of hunters to stalk their quarry. In particular, N.J.S.A. § 23:7A-2(g) prohibited persons from

> . . . mak[ing] or attempt[ing] to make loud noises or gestures, set[ting] out or attempt[ing] to set out animal baits, scents, or lures or human scent, us[ing] any other natural or artificial visual, aural, olfactory, or physical stimuli, or engag[ing] in or attempt[ing] to engage in any other similar action or activity, in order to disturb, alarm, drive, attract, or affect the behavior of wildlife or disturb, alarm, disrupt, or annoy a person lawfully taking wildlife; . . .

Though never charged with violating the statute, Binkowski feared that peaceful protest activities might result in her prosecution. She argued that the statute regulated the content of her speech by punishing only those espousing anti-hunting messages, a contention rejected by the Appellate Court by construing it narrowly as "preventing only the physical interference with hunting by those who have the purpose to interfere." *Id.*, at 75. Jacqueline Tresi, *Shoot First, Talk Later: Blowing Holes in Freedom of Speech*, 8 ANIMAL L. 177 (2002); Katherine Hessler, *Where Do We Draw the Line Between Harassment and Free Speech? An Analysis of Hunter Harassment Law*, 3 ANIMAL L. 129 (1997).

F. PRISONERS

By far, the greatest volume of vegetarian or vegan rights disputes find litigants from our nation's jails and prisons. Inmates cannot simply travel to the restaurant or supermarket of their choosing, but must rely on what the commissary and cafeteria provide. But because putatively "religious" demands might jeopardize legitimate penal objectives (e.g., a Sikh requests a ceremonial sword or dagger, named a *kirpan*), reasonable debates may arise — though it is hard to see how perishable foodstuffs could ever present a security risk.

The oft-cited *Spies v. Voinovich*, 173 F.3d 398 (6th Cir. 1999), articulates the First Amendment free exercise position typically taken as to incarcerees demanding meals without animal products. Douglas Spies, an ordained Zen Buddhist serving time at Marion, Ohio's North Central Correctional Institution, began guiding fellow Buddhists in meditation. The prison permitted him to use the chapel and religious icons, but would not honor his request for a vegan diet. A prison chaplain contacted the International Buddhist Meditation Center in Los Angeles and learned that while Buddhism counseled abstention from animal flesh, veganism was not a required tenet. Accordingly, NCCI rejected his request, and he sued. In light of Spies's admission that "a vegan diet is not a requirement for Zen Buddhist practice," and that the prison did furnish him with a vegetarian meal, the Sixth Circuit held that he had no First Amendment right to a vegan meal. *Id.*, at 406. In so ruling, however, the majority made clear that:

> [W]e are not stating that Spies's veganism is not a sincerely-held religious belief. Rather, we are stating that because the prison has already provided him with a vegetarian meal, we believe, in this instance, that the prison's decision to deny him a vegan meal is reasonably related to legitimate penological interests.

Id., at 407. Dissenting Circuit Judge Moore differed, stating that the prison's defense that veganism was not mandated by Spies's religion was "inadequate as a matter of law," for Spies was entitled to prove that accommodation of his own sincerely held beliefs would not unreasonably burden the prison resources. *Id.*, at 410.

Had Spies filed his lawsuit after Sept. 22, 2000, when the Religious Land Use and Institutionalized Persons Act ("RLUIPA"), 42 U.S.C. § 2000cc et seq., became effective, the outcome may have been more aligned with that in *Borkholder v. Lemmon*, 983 F. Supp. 2d 1013 (N.D. Ind. 2013). "It is not every day that someone makes a federal case out of ramen noodles. But unfortunately that's what Joshua Borkholder had to do" after the prison officials revoked his vegan diet upon learning that he "ordered chicken-flavored ramen noodles from the prison commissary." Borkholder became vegan while imprisoned after "continual study" of religious doctrine and concluded that it was immoral "to slaughter harmless animals for food when there [are] other natural foods being grown for human consumption." The commissary did not sell vegetarian noodles, so he resorted to buying chicken-flavored ramen noodles, discarding the flavoring packet, and adding peanut butter to the boiled noodles — or eating them plain. Judge Philip P. Simon granted Borkholder declaratory and injunctive relief to restore his vegan diet and provide him with vegetarian ramen.

Aside from the standard First Amendment analysis, the court invoked the RLUIPA. *See Koger v. Bryan*, 523 F.3d 789, 796 (7th Cir. 2008) (contrasting RLUIPA with First Amendment, which requires only that the prison provides an "adequate justification" premised on "legitimate penological interests" as opposed to the higher burden of showing that the action presents the least restrictive means to further a compelling government interest); see also *Reed v. Faulkner*, 842 F.2d 960, 963 (7th Cir. 1988) ("It would be bizarre for prisons to undertake in effect to promote strict orthodoxy, by forfeiting the religious rights of any inmate observed backsliding, thus placing guards and fellow inmates in the role of religious police.") Pursuant to the Prison Litigation Reform Act, Judge Simon narrowed the injunction to enjoin the prison from revoking Borkholder's vegan diet simply because he buys chicken-flavored ramen noodles from the commissary or a similar product with a separately packaged meat flavoring that can be readily discarded, when no vegetarian alternative exists. For an example one step beyond Borkholder — where the prison insists that the formerly vegan (then-vegetarian) inmate become carnivorous, consider *Goodman v. Carter*, 2001 U.S. Dist. LEXIS 19504 (N.D. Ill. Nov. 29, 2001). Wiccan inmate Goodman sought and initially obtained a vegan diet from prison but then tried to supplement it by purchasing items containing eggs and dairy from the commissary, at which point the defendants removed him from the vegan diet and would not offer him a vegetarian diet. Ruling for Goodman, the court explained how it "does not understand why Goodman is being denied eggs and milk products — which he is willing to pay for himself — for no articulated reason. . . . As far as appears on this record, denying Goodman the privilege of purchasing these foods from the commissary has no rational relationship to any legitimate purpose whatever."

G. CHILD ABUSE

African-American couple Jade Sanders, 27, and Lamont Thomas, 31, only gave their newborn son Crown Shakur soy milk and apple juice. He died at six weeks of age due to bronchopneumonia secondary to extreme malnourishment and starvation. At trial, Thomas volunteered that food was very expensive, to which the prosecution presented evidence of nearly empty cupboards. Sanders conceded that she did not tell her coworkers about her pregnancy. Thomas asked, "Why would I do something with his body? We are against animals being murdered, why would we be cruel to him and try to do something to his body?" Sanders attempted to justify their raising of Crown, saying "they did what they thought was right," speaking of their motivation to raise Crown as a vegan. The prosecution insinuated that Sanders and Thomas invoked veganism as an afterthought to avoid prosecution for the intentional starvation of their child. Both were convicted of malice murder and sentenced to life in prison. Associated Press, *Vegan couple will serve life sentences for starving baby to death, court rules*, N.Y. DAILY NEWS (Sept. 12, 2011); *Sanders v. State*, 715 S.E.2d 124 (Ga. 2011) (affirming convictions). After three convictions of vegan parents in four years, the *New York Times* published an op/ed by Nina Planck, entitled "Death by Veganism," claiming that vegan diets imperil infants, though not even the prosecution made such a connection in the Crown case. The American Dietetic Association and Dieticians of Canada stated in 2003 that well-planned vegan diets are "appropriate for all stages of the life cycle, including during pregnancy, lactation, infancy, childhood and adolescence." *Position of the American Dietetic Association and Dieticians of Canada: vegetarian diets*, 64(2) CAN. J. DIETETIC PRAC. & RES. 62 (2003).

H. MEDIA

In 1949, the Federal Communications Commission required broadcast license-holders to present controversial issues of public importance honestly and equitably — in short, fairly. The "Fairness Doctrine" required networks to give airtime to contrasting viewpoints on matters of public interest. *Red Lion Broadcasting Co. v. FCC*, 395 U.S. 367 (1969) (upholding doctrine's constitutionality). As of August 2011, the FCC eliminated language implementing the Doctrine. *FCC Chairman Genachowski Continues Regulatory Reform to Ease Burden on Businesses; Announces Elimination of 83 Outdated Rules*, 2011 WL 3679221 (F.C.C. Aug. 22, 2011). Before its repeal, however, complaints were lodged with the FCC concerning vegetarianism. *In re Shriver Concerning the Fairness Doctrine*, 46 F.C.C.2d 1121 (May 10, 1974) (claiming that *Merv Griffin Show* episode featuring animal protein advocates and refusing to allow her to appear because "vegetarians have been represented" did not violate the Doctrine as she failed to provide reasonable grounds proving that "the issue of an animal protein diet versus a vegetarian diet is a controversial issue of public importance"); *In re American Vegetarian Union Concerning Fairness Doctrine*, 38 F.C.C.2d 1024 (Dec. 13, 1972) (accord in context of *The Phil Donahue Show* disparaging vegetarian diet without offering vegetarian viewpoint).

Yet when criticism of meat-eating, or more accurately meat-producing, comes under scrutiny, libel litigation against television show personalities has commenced. In *Texas Beef Group v. Winfrey*, 11 F. Supp. 2d 858 (N.D. Tex. 1998), a number of cattle companies sued Oprah Winfrey, Harpo Productions, Inc., and Howard "Mad Cow" Lyman for false disparagement of perishable food products under the Texas False Disparagement of Perishable Food Products Act (T.C.P. R.C. § 96.002), common law business disparagement; common law defamation; statutory libel; negligence and negligence *per se* arising from Apr. 11, 1996 and Apr. 16, 1996 shows discussing Bovine Spongiform Encephalopathy ("BSE") and its link to a variant of Creutzfeld-Jakob Disease ("V-CJD"). Running through the program was the key assumption that the American cattlemen's feeding practices (ruminant-to-ruminant) contributed to the danger of BSE and V-CJD in the United States. Plaintiffs claimed that "malicious editing" of factual and scientific information presented through counterpoint by Drs. Hueston and Weber would have calmed the hysteria of the "mad cow" scare. Additional defamatory/disparaging comments alleged included:

(1) Winfrey's allegedly damaging "never eating a hamburger again" comment;

(2) Lyman's "Mad Cow Disease could make AIDS look like the common cold" statement;

(3) Lyman's "The United States is treating BSE as a public relations issue, as Great Britain did, and failing to take any 'substantial' measures to prevent a BSE outbreak."

On motion for summary judgment, the trial court dismissed defendants' statutory food disparagement claim, defamation, statutory libel, and negligence claims, but retained the common law business disparagement claim. As to allegedly false statements, the court held that the defendants' speech occupied the "highest rung" of First Amendment values given its coverage of "matters of public concern" and factual basis. Lyman's comments had a factual basis — ruminant-to-ruminant feeding was an existing practice in the United States. Exaggeration does not equal defamation. It deemed the Perishable Food Products Act ("PFPA") inapplicable as: (1) the statute does not apply to live "fed cattle"; (2) plaintiffs' cattle had not "perished" or "decayed beyond marketability"; and, alternatively, (3) the plaintiffs proffered insufficient proof tending to show that the defendants knowingly disseminated false information. Moreover, the statute required actual knowledge of falsity, the highest standard available under defamation law.

The submitted jury instruction for this remaining claim stated: "Did a below-named Defendant publish a false, disparaging statement that was of and concerning the cattle of a below-named Plaintiff as those terms have been defined for you?" The jury found for the defendants. The Group appealed, and lost. *Texas Beef Gp v. Winfrey*, 201 F.3d 680 (5th Cir., 2000). As to the PFPA, the Fifth Circuit examined whether the defendants knowingly disseminated false information tending to show American beef was not fit for public consumption. It concluded that while Lyman and Winfrey melodramatized the scare, it was Winfrey's nonactionable "stopped cold from eating another burger" comment that had the greatest fallout. "Lyman's opinions, though strongly stated, were based on truthful, established fact, and are not actionable under the First Amendment." As to the assertion of malicious editing:

> Stripped to its essentials, the cattlemen's complaint is that the 'Dangerous Food' show did not present the Mad Cow issue in the light most favorable to United States beef. This argument cannot prevail. . . . So long as the factual underpinnings remained accurate, as they did here, the editing did not give rise to an inference that knowingly false information was being disseminated.

Id., at 689. Concurring Judge Edith Jones nonetheless held that live, fed cattle are "perishable food products":

> While recognizing this diminution in value, the district court found that live cattle do not decay "beyond marketability" because they may still be sold for uses other than USDA prime beef — e.g., hamburger or dog food. This interpretation, however, would seem to vitiate the applicability of the statute to food products that were undoubtedly intended to fall within the protective reach of the Act. For example, bananas are undoubtedly a food product that will decay over time. Yet, bananas with brown spots have uses beyond consumption as fresh bananas — e.g., when processed in banana bread and certain non-food uses. The Act, properly construed, does reach fed cattle.

Id., at 691. She relied upon the definition of "perishable food product":

> A perishable food product is "a food product of agriculture or aquaculture that is sold or distributed in a form that will perish or decay beyond marketability within a limited period of time." Tex. Civ. Prac. & Rem. § 96.001.

Id.

> The evidence adduced at trial demonstrates that live cattle appear to decay steadily in value from their optimum date of sale (perish beyond

marketability) just as an apple hanging from a tree might rot. That the decay occurs pre-slaughter does not detract from the protections of the statute. An apple will rot on the tree as easily as it will rot in the grocer's produce section.

Id. As to the single claim going to the jury, the plaintiffs appealed the "of and concerning" language, asserting that the instruction improperly required the jurors to find (1) that defendants made false, disparaging statements regarding *specific cattle*, and (2) that defendants made false, disparaging statements "of and concerning cattle," as opposed to *beef.* The appellate court affirmed as the plaintiffs failed to object with sufficient specificity or state the grounds of their objection or offer a proposed alternate instruction.

Chapter 13

ESTATE PLANNING

Except for long-lived avians, equines, and reptiles, nonhumans ordinarily predecease their human guardians. In anticipation of life's uncertainties, individuals often take steps to ensure what they regard as humane and appropriate treatment for their beloved companions will continue after their demise — whether to provide care and necessaries or, curiously, to terminate the animal's life. When drafted ambiguously, confusion and conflict abound, compelling judicial involvement.

A. DESTRUCTION-ON-DEATH

The Tenth Codicil to Howard H. Brand's will stated, "If at the time of my death I am still the owner of any animals, including any horses and/or a mule, I direct my Executor to have such animals destroyed." Mr. Brand also directed that his Cadillac be crushed, and that the demolition take place in the Executor's presence, who was to certify to the court that the vehicle was completely obliterated. The Coalition to Save Brand's Horses — composed of a prior owner of the horses in question; the Vermont Humane Federation, Inc.; the Vermont Volunteer Services for Animals Humane Society; the Humane Organization for Retired Standardbred Equines; and the Student Animal Legal Defense Fund chapter at Vermont Law School — were granted leave to intervene in the proceeding. In Defense of Animals filed an amicus brief to protect the horses. *Estate of Howard H. Brand*, Chittenden Cy. Probate Court No. 28473 (1999).

Despite finding Mr. Brand's intent unambiguous, i.e., knowingly and voluntarily directing that his livestock be killed to avoid their victimization or suffering in his absence, the court refused to facilitate his posthumous directive as contrary to public policy, on the ground that giving literal effect to the clause would court illegality and undermine the ascendant anticruelty laws then in effect ("Consequently, public policy and Vermont law should operate to allow these animals the opportunity to continue living.") Applying the doctrine of *cy pres* in an unconventional way (i.e., it normally applies to charitable trusts), the court spared the horses' lives as it would be impossible or unlawful to give his intention literal effect. But mindful that the horses could end up in neglectful conditions that Mr. Brand sought to avoid, the court decided to "oversee the placement of Mr. Brand's horses and . . . [to] prohibit any future transfer of ownership without prior approval of the court." *Id.*, at 6–7.

Brand relied upon an earlier Pennsylvania case, *Capers Est.*, 34 D. & C. 2d 121 (1964). Ida Capers directed that Brickland and Sunny Birch, her Irish Setters, be humanely euthanized on her death. Her executors filed a declaratory judgment action to ascertain their rights and duties in relation to this put-to-sleep clause.

Even the Pennsylvania Attorney General intervened. The court found the clause to be the product of extreme risk-aversion, however well-meaning. It recognized that the dogs were not grieving but "very, very happy" and well cared for (perhaps better than by Capers), according to the testimony of a veterinarian. Similar to *Brand*, the court concluded that Ms. Capers's intentions were carried out to an equal or greater level of care to which the dogs were accustomed, rendering the destruction-on-death clause superfluous. Further, confiscating life of a healthy animal companion for no purpose was among the "clearest cases" for violation of public policy, causing the court to void the clause. Additionally, the Pennsylvania Wills Act, allowed for *disposition*, not *destruction*, of property, citing *Brown Est.*, 137 A. 132 (Pa. 1927). The Orphans' Court declared the clause void as against public policy and directed kennel keeper Thomas Miller and the Western Pennsylvania Humane Society to arrange for new guardianship of the dogs.

What of the fact that humane societies and veterinarians routinely euthanize owned or surrendered animals on demand for nontherapeutic reasons, or that animals "raised for human consumption" are put to death "personally without fear of legal reprisal"? *See Brand Order*, at 3 ("Why then, queries the Estate, should questions arise when a person directs by Will that his animals be destroyed?"). *Brand* distinguishes what one may do herself from what she may cause another to do on her behalf. It also cites to *Morgan v. Kroupa*, 702 A.2d 630 (Vt. 1997) for the proposition that property in domestic pets is highly qualified and subject to the state police power. It further finds that Brand's horses were a "unique type of 'property'" meriting special attention. *Brand Order*, at 4. Traditionally, government raises this argument to defend the right to confiscate and kill animals. Here, the court wields the doctrine to save animals from death. But is the motivation behind public policy pure altruism or materialism (i.e., conserving resources, avoiding waste)?

B. CARE-ON-DEATH

Centuries ago, probate law abided by inflexible notions that prohibited designating nonhuman animals as beneficiaries of trusts, whether because only human beings (i.e., at least those not legally classified as property) could receive a legacy of money, bequest of personalty, or devise of realty, or due to drafting insufficiencies that violated the Rule Against Perpetuities ("RAP"). Each state's RAP varied somewhat, but all sought to limit the ability of a decedent to create interminable future interests (e.g., trusts) for remote descendants. Traditionally, the RAP requires that such interests must vest, if at all, within 21 years following the death of a life in being at the creation of the interest. "In being" meant human, including those *in utero*, in relation to whom the passage of time would be measured. In the twentieth century, a small number of states partially or completely abolished the RAP by statute, including Alaska, Delaware, Idaho, Illinois, New Jersey, Pennsylvania, Kentucky, Maine, Maryland, Missouri, South Dakota, Rhode Island. Alaska Stat. §§ 34.27.051–.100; 25 Del. C. § 503, 765 Ill. Stat. 305/4; Idaho Code § 55-111; 33 Me. RSA § 101-A (does not apply if trust expressly states it does not); Md. Est. & Trust § 11-102(5) (does not apply if expressly stated); V.A.M.S. § 456.025(1); N.J.S.A. § 46:2F-9; S.D.C.L. § 43-5-8; R.I. Gen. Law § 34-11-38. Twenty-nine states and the District of Columbia have adopted the Uniform Statutory Rule Against

Perpetuities, which deems nonvested property interests invalid unless certain to vest or terminate within 21 years after the death of an individual then alive or 90 years after creation. *See, e.g.,* Va. Code § 55-12.1. Some states deviate from this 90-year rule but expanding the duration to 150 years following the effective date of the instrument. See RCW § 11.98.130. Wyoming adopts a millennium rule. Wyo. Stat. § 34-1-139(b).

Workarounds to the juridical prejudice against nonhumans and the RAP include establishing precatory or honorary (i.e., unenforceable but strongly desired by testator) trusts in the form of a legacy sufficiently large to care for the bequested animal, along with instructions for the legatee-bequestee. These so-called "Trixie Trusts" were named after the dog at issue in the *Searight* case. George Searight bequeathed his dog, Trixie, to Florence Hand, along with $1,000 in trust to compensate her $0.75 a day for Trixie's care till her death, at which time the residue would divide equally among five remainderpersons. *In re Searight's Estate*, 95 N.E.2d 779 (Ohio Ct. App. 1950). While the Probate Court found that Trixie could be taxed (at an agreed value of $5), the $1,000 legacy could not (except for the remainder). The Department of Taxation of Ohio appealed from that determination, as well as that an inheritance tax could not be levied on successions to property passing to an animal. The Court of Appeals affirmed, reasoning that while the testamentary gift for care of Trixie was not a trust "in the accepted sense in which that term is defined" (the defect being that it lacked a human beneficiary), the gift also did not violate the RAP or bar against capricious and illegal transfers (because caring for a companion animal was a worthy undertaking). As the trust could not possibly endure beyond 21 years, any RAP objection was moot, for if the money were invested, it would extinguish in 3.65 years (i.e., $0.75/day x approx. 1,332 days); if realizing 6% interest, then 4.16 years. Because only gifts to persons, institutions, and corporations were taxable, and as Trixie was neither, no tax could apply. When the money passed to the remaindermen, at that time the Department could tax the funds. This left open the question of whether one could use the care of an animal as the pretextual loophole to avoid the inheritance tax?

In the 1990s, states began enacting laws that explicitly permitted testators to create enforceable trusts for *certain* nonhumans as direct beneficiaries. *See* https://www.animallaw.info/statutes/topic/wills-and-trusts; http://www.aspca.org/pet-care/planning-for-your-pets-future/pet-trust-laws. Uniform Probate Code § 2-907 and Uniform Trust Code § 408 statutory pet trust provisions permitted pets to be direct beneficiaries. To date, 46 states and the District of Columbia have some adaptation of a pet trust law. Trusts with a pet as direct beneficiary are taxed under I.R.C. § 641(e) but as the pet does not have a Social Security number, the trust receives no income distribution deduction and must pay all taxes at the trust level. Rev. Rul. 76-486,[1] 1976-2 CB 192; Gerry W. Beyer & Jonathan P. Wilkerson, *Max's Taxes: A Tax-Based Analysis of Pet Trusts*, 43 U. Rich. L. Rev. 1219 (2009) (a comprehensive discussion of all tax issues affecting pet trusts, both statutory and common law).

---

[1] Decedent A establishes testamentary trust to care for A's animal companion. On death, trust corpus was to distribute to A's heirs, if living, or descendants. At time, trust was void in A's state due to RAP. Because trust bequest for care of A's animal was void from inception, IRS held that valid trust never came into being for purposes of imposing tax under Section 641 of Code.

Testatrix Camille F. Howells died married to an estranged husband and one next of kin (her sister), both of whom she intentionally disinherited. Her fondness for Charles Rattray led to her entrusting her two cats and three dogs to him, along with money for their care as long as they lived. *In re Howells' Estate*, 145 Misc. 557, 260 N.Y.S. 598 (Sur. Ct. Erie County 1932). Judge Wingate determined that Howells's dominant testamentary desire was to care for her animal companions as her sole immediate family, with the balance (trust income with right to invade principal upon showing of need) to Rattray — but only so long as the trustee retained a fund balance for care of her animals. Proceeding to adjudicate the "legal effect and consequences of the directions" in light of the RAP, the court deemed the trust void by statute. Because it was predicated on five *nonhuman* animal lives in being and one human life in being (i.e., Rattray), Howells was left intestate.

Novel arguments aside, the court could not construe Howells's trust as nonperpetual (and thus not voided by the RAP), as it did not absolutely terminate according to New York law, which limited the duration of a trust to two lives in being; nor did it expressly set a date for termination. The trust would not terminate upon Rattray's death because the will neither explicitly nor implicitly released the executor from his duty to care for her animals under the Eighth paragraph (it merely deducted $400 and additional reasonable sums for her headstone and grave maintenance). Nor did the fact that the trust allowed the trustee limited power of invasion of principal for Rattray's need absolutely terminate the trust within Rattray's lifetime since the condition subsequent (i.e., a demonstration of need) was uncertain on two levels — (i) as to time of invasion, and (ii) as to time of exhaustion of principal. The RAP statute required that any condition subsequent must be "so limited that in every possible contingency [the trust] will absolutely terminate within the prescribed period." Here, no guarantee existed that Rattray would exhaust the principal before his death.

Further, RAP was premised on *human* lives in being. Although identifying at least one human life (Rattray), the fact that it would continue after his death forced the executor to use *nonhuman* measuring lives, in violation of the statute. That the life expectancy of Howells's nonhuman animals was merely a decade was immaterial, for the issue was not their expected term of survival, but their species. If instead of two cats and three dogs, Howells used five sextagenarian relatives, there would be no RAP violation. To be clear, *Howells' Estate* did not forbid nonhuman animal trusts *per se*. For instance, it embraced the Irish decision *Matter of Kelley-Cleary v. Dillon* (1932 Irish Rep. 255), which allowed a 21-year nonhuman animal trust but refused to use nonhuman measuring lives:

> In the course of an elaborate opinion which upheld the validity of the trust for twenty-one years, but no longer, the [*Kelly*] court says (beginning at p. 260): 'If the lives of the dogs or other animals could be taken into account in reckoning the maximum period of 'lives in being and twenty-one years afterwards,' any contingent or executory interest might be properly limited, so as only to vest within the lives of specified carp, or tortoises, or other animals that might live for over a hundred years, and for twenty-one years afterwards, which, of course, is absurd. 'Lives' means human lives. It was suggested that the last of the dogs could in fact not outlive the testator by more than twenty-one years. I know nothing of that. The court does not

enter into the question of a dog's expectation of life. In [261] point of fact neighbor's dogs and cats are unpleasantly long-lived; but I have no knowledge of their precise expectation of life. Anyway the maximum period is exceeded by the lives even of specified butterflies and twenty-one years afterwards. And even, according to my decision — and, I confess, it displays this weakness on being pressed to a logical conclusion — the expiration of the life of a single butterfly, even without the twenty-one years, would be too remote, despite all the world of poetry that may be thereby destroyed. In *Robinson v. Hardcastle* [2 Bro. C. C. 22, at p. 30] Lord THURLOW defined a perpetuity in these words: 'What is a perpetuity, but the extending the estate beyond a life in being, and twenty-one years after?' Of course by 'a life' he means lives; and there can be no doubt that 'lives' means lives of human beings, not of animals or trees in California.'

Kelly, at 260. Had Howells's will provided for *two* lives in being plus 21 years, it would have likely survived nullification.

Some courts bypass the RAP completely by construing the instrument as creating no trust at all. John Renner died unmarried and without children. His surviving niece and nephew contested his will, which provided for maintenance and interment of his dog and parrot with the residue going to Mary Faiss Riesing, trustee and executrix. Renner also bequeathed his dog and parrot to Riesing. Specifically, he gave his residuary estate to the executrix Riesing in trust, instructing that "[u]pon the death and interment of the last of my pets to survive, I give, devise and bequeath my entire residue estate so held in trust unto the said [friend], absolutely and in fee." At audit, the residue amounted to $11,900. Renner's niece and nephew claimed the pet trust void under the RAP, which they contended would result in intestacy and their entitlement to the residuary estate. *In re Renner's Estate*, 57 A.2d 836 (Pa. 1948). The auditing judge rejected their argument, finding no RAP problem, and holding that the residuary estate vested upon Renner's death, thereby making any direction to care for his animals precatory. No trust having been created, Justice Linn affirmed the auditing judge.

In resolving Renner's ambiguous phrasing, the court employed the rule finding the estate vested rather than contingent (thereby risking intestacy). Thus, Renner's estate vested in Riesing on his death, and his dog and parrot became her property. Furthermore, the court found evidence that the cost to maintain the animals would never consume the residuary. Besides, even if the trust were voided by the RAP, Riesing would take the residue under Pennsylvania's Wills Act.

Dramatically overfunded animal trusts present another concern. Florence B. Lyon left a residuary estate of more than $1.4 million in trust to care for her four horses and five dogs until their deaths, without any provision to accelerate the gift of the residue to Princeton University. Conservative calculations placed trust income at $40,000 to $50,000 a year, yet estimated maintenance costs for the nine animals were only $5,000 a year after an initial $22,000 shelter expenditure. The executors and Princeton filed a petition for declaratory judgment to deem the noncharitable trust excessive. *In re Lyon's Estate*, 67 Pa. D. & C. 2d 474 (1974).

Although the Court found that Ms. Lyon did not name a person capable of enforcing the duties of trustee (i.e., a beneficiary), and while the equines and canines could not demand an accounting by the trustee, the court did not declare the provision invalid on that basis. "Animals being animals cannot ascertain that the provisions of the trust are being carried out." *Id.*, at 478. Nor did it void her gift as an unenforceable "honorary trust," holding that such an idea "emphasizes form over substance and neglects the responsibility of the court to ascertain the intent of the testratrix and give effect to it so far as is possible." *Id.*, at 478. Rather, though not strictly applicable, it applied the RAP rule using a measuring human life in being plus 21 years to allow for at least a 21-year trust term. To honor the public policy to "[forward] the circulation of property," and drawing from principles discussed in the above-described *Renner* case, the court found that she may not have contemplated precisely how much it would cost to maintain the animals, nor the size of her estate, and would not have directed that the fund continue to accumulate revenues far beyond the costs of care and thus have her entire estate "tied up for the lives of the animals if less than the full estate was necessary for the purpose." *Id.*, at 480–81.

Thus, based on *Renner*, the court exercised its equitable powers to reduce the trust corpus and accelerate the gift of the residue to Princeton while ensuring that the animals were looked after for 21 years following her death. Specifically, the court proposed a 21-year trust with $150,000 principal in care of animals under the supervision of the Antietam Humane Society supervision; a 21-year trust with $125,000 principal, five acres, and $25,000 for a building in care of the animals under executor supervision; or a contract with Princeton to provide life care for animals in exchange for complete, immediate transfer of the $1.4 million residue. But what if the animals lived longer than 21 years? The court assumed that the life expectancy would not exceed 20 years. But horses could easily survive into their thirties.

A modern example of the *Lyon* case involves hotelier and business magnate Leona Helmsley, who left $12 million in trust for Trouble, her Maltese. Following her death, the court reduced the bloated trust by $10 million per N.Y. Est. Powers & Trusts Law § 7-6.1(d), which permits modification of the trust fund if it "determines that amount substantially exceeds the amount required for [its] intended use." Cara Buckley, *Cosseted Life and Secret End of a Millionaire Maltese*, N.Y. Times (Jun. 9, 2011). Trouble died three years after Ms. Helmsley did. The subject of two dozen death and kidnapping threats, she spent her final days with Carl Lekic, the general manager of the Helmsley Sandcastle Hotel. Mr. Lekic estimated her annual expenses at $190,000 to compensate her security team, groomer, chefs, and veterinarians, in addition to a guardian fee of $60,000 a year.

Ms. Helmsley's Charitable Trust, executed on Apr. 23, 1999, and amended thereafter, also invited litigation in 2009, prompting the Humane Society of the United States, ASPCA, and Maddie's Fund, as well as a local rescue named D.E.L.T.A. Rescue, to challenge the trustees' decision to donate only a tiny fraction of her billions to animal welfare despite the fact that the March 1, 2004, Mission Statement identified first its intent to make grants for "(1) purposes related to the provision of care for dogs, followed by "(2) such other charitable activities as the Trustees shall determine." This Statement also revoked all prior ones. Nonetheless, the Trustees gave $136 million to help humans but only $100,000 to animal welfare. Anticipating a conflict where "dog-related charities [would] seek to challenge the Trustees' grants," the Trustees petitioned the court to determine the scope of their discretion. The Attorney General of the State of New York sided with the Trustees, arguing that the Statement had utterly no consequence as her May 11, 2004, Fourth Article, Para. B amended and restated the trust instrument to give the trustees plenary powers in no way limited by any Mission Statement. Quite simply, the Article superseded the Statement, restoring sole discretion to manage and distribute income and principal to any charitable entities as the trustees would determine. On Feb. 19, 2009, New York County Surrogate's Court Judge Troy Webber agreed and advised that the Trustees could go forth and distribute to either animal or human charity in any quantum they saw fit. *In Matter of Rosenthal*, N.Y.C. Sur. Ct. 2968/2007 (Feb. 19, 2009).[2]

Undeterred by this result, the organizations filed a motion to intervene and be heard on the merits. Surrogate's Court Judge Nora Anderson denied their motion to reopen the case and to vacate the prior order, as well as their motion to intervene. *In Matter of Rosenthal*, N.Y.C. Sur. Ct. 2007/2968/A (Apr. 15, 2011).[3] She reasoned that the organization was "no more than a class of possible beneficiaries to whom, we have assumed for argument's sake, the trustees should give 'special emphasis' in making grants." In distinguishing the facts at bar from an illustrative case that permitted intervention by a charity, the court held that Ms. Helmsley did not specifically earmark funds for their benefit nor could the organizations "expect to obtain funds simply by applying and qualifying for a distribution," nor that they were in jeopardy of categorical elimination as possible beneficiaries of the trust. More to the point, the court worried that these four organizations were likely a tiny fraction of potentially dozens of animal welfare organizations, of "unclear and problematic" proportions, who would vie for her billions, not a group "sharply defined and limited in number." The court also rejected the novel argument that the organizations themselves could serve as class representatives to determine how to divvy up the funds among appropriate dog-related charities, as well as the contention that the Attorney General suffered an irreconcilable conflict that would not permit it to properly govern the distribution among charities, dog and human-related.

The organizations appealed, and the appellate division affirmed, finding that only the Attorney General may enforce trust provisions as far as beneficiaries are concerned, and that the organizations lacked standing to intervene. *In re Rosenthal*, 99 A.D.3d 573, 952 N.Y.S.2d 194 (2012), *cert. denied*, 20 N.Y.3d 1058 (2013); *see also In re Public Benev. Trust of Crume*, 829 N.E.2d 1039 (Ind. Ct. App. 2005), *aff'd on reh'g*, 834 N.E.2d 705 (2005) (no standing for coalition of animal welfare providers to challenge Humane Society petition to pledge assets of public charitable trust).

---

[2] Decision on file with author. James Barron, *Charities Ask a Court to Direct More of Helmsley's Billions to Help Dogs*, N.Y. Times (Aug. 10, 2009). Frank James, *Dog Charities Sue for More Leona Helmsley Wealth*, N.P.R. The Two-Way (Aug. 11, 2009).

[3] Decision on file with author. This Judge was later disciplined by the Commission on Judicial Conduct for failing to uphold the integrity and independence of the judiciary, by failing to avoid impropriety, by failing to refrain from inappropriate political activity, and misusing campaign contributions for private benefit or to others. *In the Matter of the Proceeding Pursuant to Section 44, Subdivision 4, of the Judiciary Law in Relation to Nora S. Anderson, A Judge of the Surrogate's Court, New York County*, 2012 WL 5213822 (N.Y. Com. Jud. Cond.).

C. PATENT AND LATENT AMBIGUITIES

Whether pertaining to animals or not, careful drafting of wills avoids ambiguity that exposes lawyers to malpractice claims, at least according to Prof. Angela M. Vallario of the University of Baltimore School of Law, in her article *Shape Up or Ship Out: Accountability to Third Parties for Patent Ambiguities in Testamentary Documents*, 26 WHITTIER L. REV. 59 (Fall 2004). Accordingly, one must pay close attention to draft out ambiguities whenever possible. Failure to do so may invite costly will contests that disturb the testator's memory and invade the residue with avoidable litigation expenses.

Contracts are ambiguous "when there are two different reasonable interpretations or the language is nonsensical. Whether a contract is ambiguous is a question of law, but interpreting an ambiguous term is an issue of act." *Potlatch Educ. Ass'n v. Potlatch Sch. Dist. No. 285*, 226 P.3d 1277, 1280 (Idaho 2010). "A patent ambiguity is one which is evident from the face of the instrument. A latent ambiguity is not evident on the face of the instrument alone, but becomes apparent when applying the instrument to the facts as they exist." *Estate of Kirk*, 907 P.2d 794, 800–801 (Idaho 1995). Patent ambiguity leaps from the page itself through the use of insensible or contradictory language without resorting to any other source document or conversation. In some jurisdictions, a third specie of ambiguity exists, a type of latent ambiguity called equivocation, which is "an ambiguity which involves an accurate description that equally applies to two or more persons of the same name or things of the same description." *Estate of Bergau*, 693 P.2d 703, 705–06 (Wash. 1985) (en banc).

Raffles v. Wichelhaus, 1864 WL 6161 (K.B. 1864), one of the earliest cases studied by first-year law students, provides an example of latent ambiguity. Cotton was to arrive "ex Peerless" from Bombay. However, two ships sailed by the name Peerless — one leaving from Bombay in December, the other in October. When the plaintiff refused to buy the cotton from the December-departing vessel (instead wanting the earlier shipment), the defendant asserted breach. Finding latent ambiguity as to *which* Peerless the parties had in mind, the court resorted to extrinsic evidence and found no meeting of the minds, resulting in no contract.

Parol evidence that does not contradict, vary, add to, or subtract from the terms of an unambiguous written agreement may assist in clarifying a *latently* ambiguous term therein. *Knipe Land Co. v. Robertson*, 259 P.3d 595, 601–02 (Idaho 2011). Parol evidence may not come in to clarify and resolve *patent* ambiguities. *Latent* ones by their very nature require reference to evidence outside the four corners of the will. The minority position taken by Wisconsin, Arizona, New York, Maine, Minnesota, South Dakota, and Mississippi appears to permit parol evidence for patent ambiguities. *See* Vallario, fn. 212, *supra*.

Examples of patent ambiguity include: (1) "I bequeath my residual estate to the veterinarian identified in the previous paragraph." However, in that earlier provision, no such individual is identified. In such case, the ambiguous gift fails. (2) "I leave ten dollars ($10,000) to my nephew Jackson, the shelter manager at Kootenai County Humane Society."

Examples of latent ambiguity include: (1) "I give my beloved cat Orbit to Josephine," where the testatrix had both a first cousin and best friend named Josephine. (2) Equivocation: "I leave $10,000 to my favorite animal organization, PAWS." Over her lifetime, the testator volunteered for the Progressive Animal Welfare Society ("PAWS") and also donated money to the Pacific Avian & Wombat Sanctuary ("PAWS"). Extrinsic evidence will help resolve which PAWS was the intended beneficiary. (3) Misdescription: "I give my 20-acre parcel at 13501 Peekabu Ln. to the Maricopa Humane Society." While the decedent owned 15301 Peekabu Ln., she did not have title to 13501 Peekabu Ln. Such typographical error may be cured by relying on extrinsic evidence to strike "13501" from the will and revise it to state, "I give my 20-acre parcel on Peekabu Ln. to the Maricopa Humane Society." The court can then cure the ambiguity of *which* parcel through extrinsic evidence.

The addition of two small words, used to describe an individual specifically named in the bequest, can turn a patent ambiguity into a latent one. In *Sigley v. Simpson*, 131 P. 479, 480 (Idaho 1913), the Idaho Supreme Court addressed the latent ambiguity in the will of M.J. Heney, where he left "unto my friend Richard H. Simpson the sum of six thousand dollars," resulting in a will contest between Richard H. Simpson and Hamilton Ross Simpson. The trial court sided with the latter, and the former appealed, arguing that parol evidence could not be admitted to prove that Heney meant "Hamilton Ross" when he wrote "Richard H." In affirming, the Supreme Court allowed parol evidence to cure the latent ambiguity resulting from the use of the words "my friend," given that the former was his employee and not a friend, while the latter was intimate with Heney, was his personal associate, had been the subject of discussions with third parties about leaving a legacy, and that Heney did not know the latter's given name or order of his initials and always addressed him as "Mr. Simpson." *Id.*, at 73. Concurring justices found "friend" to be "a word of weight and meaning," which fit the latter contester, not the former, and permitted the use of parol evidence. Had Heney not prefaced the bequest by the word "friend," so they said, "there might be no room for construction." *Id.*, at 74.

In reaching this conclusion, *Sigley* approvingly cited to *Acton v. Lloyd*, 37 N.J. Eq. 5 (1883), which used parol evidence as to devisee identity, holding the bequest to "Dickey Lloyd" was intended for "David S. Lloyd"; to *Camoys v. Blundell*, 1 H.L.C. 77, 9 Eng. Rep. 969, in its use of extrinsic evidence to deem Thomas Weld Blundell entitled to the legacy naming Edward Weld, though Edward was his brother, by observing that the court must construe the will "with reference to the evidence of the state of the family as known to the testator," and letting the "description prevail over the name"; to *Woman's Foreign Missionary Society v. Mitchell*, 48 A. 737 (Md. 1901), quoted as saying, "It is the identity of the individual, natural or artificial, that is material, and not the name. . . . The identity being established, the name is of no importance"; and to *Reformed Presbyterian Church of N.A. v. McMillan*, 72 P. 502 (Wash. 1903), which reversed the trial court's conclusion that the legacy to a nonexistent board of disabled ministers lapsed to the heirs at law, using parol evidence.

Consider this modern example. Wendell K. Miles's passion for animals translated into generous benefaction to animal welfare organizations. Using a preprinted form, and making several specific bequests in his own handwriting, Mr. Miles included a specific, non-residuary devise of realty to the "Colville human society." Nearly one year to the day of his death on April 22, 2010, the estate filed an Amended Petition for Distribution, asking the court's permission to authorize sale of the realty and to distribute proceeds to the Red Cross, the residuary beneficiary, claiming that as no precise entity named "Colville Humane Society" existed, the gift lapsed to the Red Cross. *In re Estate of Miles*, 2013 Wash. App. LEXIS 2574 (Oct. 31, 2013).

Various organizations laid claim to the devise, including the Colville Valley Animal Sanctuary, Dog Patch Group, Inc., and Colville Pet Rescue. On Sept. 19, 2011, after finding a latent ambiguity calling for receipt of parol evidence, the trial court made findings of fact, including the following:

> On March 2, 2010, Wendell K. Miles executed his "Last Will of Wendell Kenneth Miles," making specific bequests to seven individuals and two specific charities — "SPEA" or American Society for the Prevention of Cruelty to Animals, and "PETA," or People for the Ethical Treatment of Animals. A third charity was also specified — "Colville human Society my real estate" He also designated that any "residual money to go to Red Cross" — American Red Cross. At the time Mr. Miles executed his will, Dog Patch Group, Inc. dba Dog Patch Humane dba Dog Patch, was no longer accepting animals from the general public — had not been broadly accepting animals since at least April, 2008. It had continued to accept and place dogs on a "personal level." It was located at 2307 Hickey Way, outside Colville city limits, but with a Colville mailing address. Dog Patch Humane, Inc., as of March 2010, was marketing a holistic methodology for treating humans and animals. The marketing was through a website. Local advertising using the word "humane" was mostly extant in the late 1990s's. Dog Patch Group, Inc. was listed in the yellow pages under humane societies and animal shelters in March, 2010, but the phone number was listed under Dog Patch Group, Inc.

> Colville Valley Animal Sanctuary, Inc., was located in Arden, south of Colville, with a Colville mailing address. It was formed in 2003. It used Colville Pet Refuge Humane Society, Inc., in business letters in late 2009. Since 2005, it had used the dba "The Refuge Humane Society" on business cards, thank you notes, promotional brochures, t-shirts and sweatshirts, and on parade banners. Its brochure defined "humane society" and its publication, "The Poochie Press," was put out under the dba "Colville Pet Refuge Humane Society." In 2010, it sheltered 202 cats and 103 dogs and adopted out 114 cats and 102 dogs. It also trapped and spayed/neutered 21 cats.

> The testator used smaller case letters for some proper nouns — "debbi Odion" and "Colville human Society," and "Eric olsen." All designations were as to specific individuals, no designations to a class. He had a clear intent to leave property to charitable organizations that protect and care for animals. This intention extended to all animals, not just dogs. And, the actual designation "Colville human Society" was singular.

The responding charitable organizations in the Colville vicinity that protect and care for animals were, of course, "in existence." Ambiguity arose as to which organization the testator intended to designate. He knew the names of the organizations; he knew they were not located within Colville City limits, but that they had Colville mailing addresses; and he knew of the basic services each organization was providing in March, 2010.

The trial court concluded that Mr. Miles's will gave rise to a latent ambiguity in designating the "Colville human Society," as more than one charitable organization could meet that description. *Cy pres* would not apply as he designated to a specific entity, not a class of beneficiaries. Since "The Refuge Humane Society" and "Colville Pet Refuge Humane Society" closely approximated "Colville human society," the court found that Mr. Miles intended to devise his realty to the Colville Valley Animal Sanctuary.

On Oct. 31, 2013, the Washington Court of Appeals affirmed the trial court, finding that the appellant Joyce Tasker did not have standing to contest the ruling. Thus, the trial court's reasoning stood, namely that the latent ambiguity resolved in favor of the Colville Valley Animal Sanctuary, rejecting Dog Patch Group's assertion that *cy pres* applied, and rejecting the residuary beneficiary American Red Cross's argument that the gift lapsed and the realty should go to it.

D. CY PRES

BLACK'S LAW DICTIONARY defines "cy pres" as "[t]he equitable doctrine under which a court reforms a written instrument with a gift to a charity as closely to the donor's intention as possible, so that the gift does not fail." BLACK'S LAW DICTIONARY 415 (8th ed. 2004). Like the ambiguity doctrines described above, *cy pres* achieves the goal of reforming the will to fulfill the testator's last wishes. However, ambiguity is not typically the problem that calls for *cy pres*: generality is. *Cy pres* only applies where it is evident the testator did not intend to gift to a specific person or entity, but instead to a class of beneficiaries.

Hedin v. Westdala Lutheran Church, 81 P.2d 741 (Idaho 1938), presents the doctrine of *cy pres* in the context of a will provision vesting in the executor and trustee "unlimited power of selection of the beneficiary, or beneficiaries, of [Mr. Johannesson's] bounty, so long as . . . expended for religious or charitable purposes," without designating any preference for any form of religion, specific institution or individual, or class of institutions or individuals. The sixth paragraph of Johannesson's will bequeathed the estate's residue to O. Bohman of Troy, Idaho, as trustee, to manage, sell, and distribute all realty and personalty, at such time and to such entities and individuals as he deemed fit, subjected to the eleemosynary directive stated therein.

While describing the nearly universal, general rule that private trusts must designate a beneficiary or fail, in grappling with the proper legal approach to be taken to either enforce or invalidate this sixth paragraph, the Idaho Supreme Court quoted from several sister jurisdictions, recognizing that in some states courts will uphold a trust even without a designated beneficiary. *Id.*, at 742. This exception to the rule arises from the English doctrine of *cy pres*, where the King, or his chancellor, would act ministerially to designate the beneficiary. The court then extensively quoted from Pomeroy, who describes *cy pres* as follows:

> In administering charitable gifts, the English courts have leaned so strongly in favor of sustaining the trusts, even when the donor's specified purpose becomes impracticable, that they invented at an early day, and have fully established, the so-called doctrine of *cy-pres*. The doctrine may be stated in general terms as follows: Where there is an intention exhibited to devote the gift to charity, and no object is mentioned, or the particular object fails, the court will execute the trust *cy-pres*, and will apply the fund to some charitable purposes, similar to those (if any) mentioned by the donor. 'If the donor declare his intention in favor of charity indefinitely, without any specification of objects, or in favor of defined objects which happen to fail from whatever cause,—even though in such cases the particular mode of operation contemplated by the donor is uncertain or impracticable,—yet the general purpose being charity, such purpose will, notwithstanding the indefiniteness, illegality, or failure of its immediate objects, be carried into effect.' In the first kind of cases, where the donor has specified no object, the court will determine upon some scheme which shall carry out the general intention; in the second kind, where the donor's specified object fails, the court will determine upon another object similar to that mentioned by the donor. A limitation upon the generality of the doctrine seems to be settled by the recent decisions, that where the donor has not expressed his charitable intention generally, but only by providing for one specific particular object, and this object cannot be carried out, or the charity provided for ceases to exist before the gift takes effect, then the court will not execute the trust; it wholly fails. The true doctrine of *cy-pres* should not be confounded, as is sometimes done, with the more general principle which leads courts of equity to sustain and enforce charitable gifts, where the trustee, object, and beneficiaries are simply *uncertain*. There is a radical distinction between the two, although the doctrine of *cy-pres* may be to some extent an expansion or enlargement of the other principle. In the great majority of the American states the courts have utterly rejected the peculiar doctrine of *cy-pres* as inconsistent with our institutions and modes of public administration. A few of the states have accepted it in a modified and partial form.

Finding the sixth paragraph "wanting," concerned that "such testamentary efforts have been likened unto powers of attorney to make wills, which the law does not permit," and fearful that "much mischief and evil would result in adopting in Idaho a doctrine which would uphold a will placing the disposal of a testator's property beyond the supervision of the courts," *Hedin* declared that part of the will invalid and void. *Id.*, at 745–46. Justice Budge dissented, reminding the majority that the "authorities are not in harmony" and that elementary law compels the court to indulge every intendment of the testator to prevent the will's failure:

> A careful reading and analysis of the 6th paragraph of the will carries conviction, to my mind, that it was the intention and express desire of Johannesson that the residue of his estate should be, by his trustee, paid out for charitable or religious purposes, from time to time as his trustee

should elect, negativing the payment of the residue of the estate to his heirs or for purposes other than charitable or religious.

Id., at 748.

Twenty-five years later, *In re Eggan's Estate*, 386 P.2d 563 (Idaho 1963), distinguished *Hedin* factually by upholding a will provision bequeathing Mr. Eggan's residuary estate and his home to the City of Moscow "to be used only to build and/or furnish and/or equip a Youth Center Building . . . to be used primarily for the recreation of the youth of this area." *Id.*, at 331. Finding the phrase "youth of this area" sufficiently definite to articulate Mr. Eggan's intentions, the court upheld the bequest to the City.

In *Dolan v. Johnson*, 509 P.2d 1306 (Idaho 1973), the Idaho Supreme Court again revisited the doctrine, finding that the testatrix's residuary charitable trust "for religious, charitable, literary, educational and public uses or purposes" would otherwise have failed due to lack of specificity as to the class of beneficiaries were it not for the words "as hereinafter set forth," referring to a detailed list of designations as to how the money would be used — e.g., to maintain institutions for the advancement of learning, hospitals and rehabilitation centers, churches and religious activities, and holistic development of young men and women. *Id.*, at 1310–11. Importantly, Idaho will not invoke *cy pres* to rescue a purported charitable trust from invalidation where the charitable purposes are not sufficiently definite. *Dolan*, at 389. By comparison, consider states like Washington. *Puget Sound National Bank of Tacoma v. Easterday*, 350 P.2d 444 (Wash. 1960), makes this point:

In *Horton v. Board of Education of Methodist Protestant Church*, 1948, 32 Wash.2d 99, 201 P.2d 163, 171, we quoted from Scott on Trusts as follows:

"Where it clearly appears that the testator intended that the property should be applied only to the *particular purpose which failed*, or for the benefit of a *particular association or corporation which was dissolved*, it has been held that the doctrine of *cy pres* is not applicable and that the property reverts to the heirs or next of kin of the settlor." (Italics ours.) 3 Scott on Trusts 2112.

Later, in the same opinion, we quoted from *Duncan v. Higgins*, 129 Conn. 136, 26 A.2d 849, as follows:

"The doctrine [*cy pres*] applies in situations where a testator has evidenced a dominant intent to devote his property to some charitable use but the circumstances are such that it becomes impossible to follow the *particular method* he directs, and the courts then sanction its use in some other way which will, as nearly as may be, approximate his general intent. * * *" [Italics ours.]

"Ordinarily where an organization to which a charitable gift or devise is made is incapable of taking it, the question whether its payment to another organization will be permitted is determined upon the basis of the applicability of the *cy pres* doctrine or doctrine of approximation; and that doctrine will be applied only where the court finds in the terms of the will, read in the light of surrounding circumstances, a *general intent* to devote the property to a charitable use, to which the intent that it go to the particular organization named is secondary. * * *"

Again, in *Townsend v. Charles Schalkenbach Home for Boys, Inc.*, 1949, 33 Wash.2d 255, 205 P.2d 345, 350, we said:

"* * * The doctrine does not mean that some kind of a charitable trust will be enforced every time the testator expresses a charitable intent. The settlor must have had a *broad, general* intent to aid charity as a whole, *or some particular class of charitable objects. His intent must not be narrow and particular. * * *"* (Emphasis added.)

Id., at 450.

An example of the interplay between latent ambiguity and *cy pres* emerged in *Phipps v. Barbera*, 498 N.E.2d 411 (Mass. Ct. App. 1986), which involved a testatrix who named a particular museum, rather than museums in general or the public at large, leading the court to conclude that the will lacked general charitable intent and rendered *cy pres* inapplicable. Instead, the court resolved the latent ambiguity through parol evidence:

a. *Application of cy pres doctrine.* The MFA argues that the judge committed error when he declined to apply the doctrine of cy pres to reform the bequest of the Paxton paintings. There was no error.

The cy pres doctrine has been stated as follows: "It is now a settled rule in equity that a liberal construction is to be given to charitable donations, with a view to promote and accomplish the general charitable intent of the donor, and that such intent ought to be observed, and when this cannot be strictly and literally done, [a] court will cause it to be fulfilled, as nearly in conformity with the intent of the donor as practicable." *Rogers v. Attorney Gen.*, 347 Mass. 126, 131, 196 N.E.2d 855 (1964), quoting from *American Academy of Arts & Sciences v. President & Fellows of Harvard College*, 78 Mass. (12 Gray) 582, 596 (1832). "[I]f the charitable purpose is limited to a particular object or to a particular institution, and there is no general charitable intent, then, if it becomes impossible to carry out the object . . . the doctrine of [cy pres] does not apply, and, in the absence of any limitation over or other provision, the legacy lapses." *Selectmen of Provincetown v. Attorney Gen.*, 15 Mass.App.Ct. 639, 646, 447 N.E.2d 677 (1983), quoting from *Teele v. Bishop of Derry*, 168 Mass. 341, 343, 47 N.E. 422 (1897).

We think that the cy pres doctrine does not apply here. The testatrix clearly intended to benefit a "particular," although nonexistent, institution, rather than museums in general or the public at large. *Selectmen of Provincetown v. Attorney Gen., supra*, 15 Mass.App.Ct. at 646–647, 447 N.E.2d 677. In addition, the presence in the clause that disposes of the paintings of a specific gift over to Barbera if the paintings should not be accepted points to the conclusion that there was no general charitable intent. *Rogers v. Attorney Gen.*, 347 Mass. at 134, 196 N.E.2d 855. We see nothing in this result that is contrary to G.L. c. 12, § 8K.

Id., at 414.

Mary Ericson died in 1991, creating a "death bed" will providing for Emma Brown as life income beneficiary with residue "distributed outright and free of trust to the International Wildlife Society." However, when Ms. Brown died in 2007, no IWS could be found. The testator's attorney deduced that IWS was an amalgamation of the names of two wildlife organizations — International Wildlife Conservation Society and Wildlife Society — not a specific entity or organization. Ms. Brown attested that it was Mary's intent to have the assets distributed to a local Broward County benevolent animal organization that would aid and care for animals and not consider destruction except as a last resort, adding that she "often spoke of the Humane Society [of] Broward County." *SPCA Wildlife Care Center v. Abraham*, 75 So. 3d 1271, 1274 (Fla. Dist. Ct. App. 2011). Several organizations petitioned for the residue, including the SPCA Wildlife Care Center, asking the court to invoke *cy pres*.

In reversing the trial court's order that the testamentary trust failed and would pass through intestacy, the court embraced *cy pres* by making specific Ms. Ericson's general charitable intent and remanding to the trial court to substitute another plan of administration that would approach her original scheme as closely as possible. Frequently *cy pres* cures the fatal effect of misnaming a beneficiary or the circumstance where the beneficiary ceases to exist at the time of the testator's death, as here. *Id.*, at 1276–77.

Refusing to apply *cy pres* where the trust specified an alternative disposition if the named charity no longer existed, consider *Hearing Dog Program v. San Francisco SPCA*, 2010 Cal. App. Unpub. LEXIS 6318 (Aug. 10, 2010). Specifically, the Berrys left 20 percent of the estate to the SFSPCA hearing dog training and placement program, which was discontinued after their deaths but before distribution of the bequest. Three former SPCA employees formed the nonprofit charity "The Hearing Dog Program" and claimed its entitlement to the 20 percent. The will provided that 20 percent would go to "Hearing Dogs for the Deaf," presently at the same address as the SFSPCA, which also received 20 percent. Though the SFSPCA adopted board minutes and sent out notices stating it had discontinued its program, the society still claimed entitlement to the money by providing services and having a budget, administrator, and staff. In finding the bequest unambiguous, the court held that the words "currently of 2500 16th Street" were intended to identify the program by its then-current address (i.e., SFSPCA), not to eliminate it if the SFSPCA moved its program, nor that it set conditions or minimum standards on the scope of the hearing dog program, nor that it default to a successor. As the SFSPCA continued running such a program, albeit bare-bones, it qualified for the gift. If it were not in existence and had no successor, it would, per the will, divide among the other named charities or their successors in interest.

In *In re Wolf's Estate*, 7 Misc. 2d 799, 162 N.Y.S.2d 645 (Sur. Ct. Erie County 1957), the testator left a legacy of $200 to the Animal Society of Nassau County, though no such entity existed. Using *cy pres*, and other statutory and inherent powers, the court ordered that the gift go to the North Shore Animal League & Dog Protective Association, Inc.

E. EQUITABLE DEVIATION

Unlike *cy pres*, equitable deviation reforms the administrative provisions of the trust. *Cy pres* alters the purpose to which the trust corpus may be applied. Equitable deviation gives effect to the testator's primary charitable goal and may apply even in the case of a specific charitable intent (contrary to *cy pres*, which relies on general intent).

In *Matter of Estate of Offerman*, 505 N.E.2d 413 (Ill. App. Ct. 1987), the Humane Society of Will County/Joliet (Humane) intervened as an interested party in the probate of the will of Evelyn Offerman, seeking equitable deviation related to an alleged charitable trust. The will provided a conditional gift of the estate residue to the ASPCA provided that it would, in part, build and maintain a shelter in Joliet, Ill. Finding the cost prohibitive and distance considerable (ASPCA was located in New York), the ASPCA disclaimed the gift. This triggered the gift-over part of Ms. Offerman's will, dividing the residue among seven charitable organizations where the ASPCA "fails to qualify" in meeting the stated conditions. The Humane Society was not one of the seven named but believed that it should be substituted for the ASPCA, arguing that it qualified, that "the ASPCA is only the mode, not the object of the gift," and that it could fulfill her primary purpose to benefit the stray and homeless animals in the Joliet area.

Finding that the will provided for a clear and unambiguous, conditional gift to the ASPCA which failed by disclaimer, that Ms. Offerman had no general charitable intent and did not intend a charitable trust, that Ms. Offerman could have identified an alternative organization with similar purposes (but did not), but instead inserted a gift-over provision, "indicate[d] that she had the ASPCA specifically in mind and did not have a general charitable intent to benefit the animals, irrespective of the organization involved." *Id.*, at 303. Humane introduced two letters authored by Ms. Offerman indicating a general charitable intent, but the court refused to consider them as they were executed before the will, were not part of the will, and because parol evidence would not clarify provisions of a will unless ambiguous. The court then addressed equitable deviation:

> Equitable deviation is a doctrine under the common law whereby courts have the power to order deviations from a trust instrument when compliance with them becomes impossible or illegal or, because of circumstances not known to the testator and not anticipated by him, literal compliance would defeat or impair the purpose of the trust. In order for the doctrine of equitable deviation to apply the testator must have intended to create a trust. Equitable deviation can be distinguished from the somewhat similar doctrine of *cy pres* in that equitable deviation deals only with changes in the administrative provisions of a trust, while *cy pres* involves an alteration of the purpose to which the *res* of the trust is to be applied.

> Equitable deviation is inapplicable in this case because it is clear from Mrs. Offerman's Will that she did not intend to create a charitable trust. Even if she intended to create a charitable trust the doctrine still would not be applicable because she did anticipate the possibility that the ASPCA would refuse to accept the bequest in Article Six of her will. The "fails to qualify language" and the gift-over provision in Article Seven of the will

clearly encompasses a refusal by the ASPCA to accept the gift on the terms set forth in Article Six. In addition, equitable deviation is only proper when literal compliance with the terms of the trust is impossible as a result of an unforeseen condition. Even if the ASPCA's refusal to accept is viewed as an unforeseen condition, literal compliance with the terms of the will is not impossible. ASPCA did not refuse the request because literal compliance with the conditions in Article Six was impossible, but because ASPCA decided that it was not practical or cost effective for them to accept the gift.

Id., at 305.

Chapter 14

WILDLIFE LAW

In certain ways, free-roaming wildlife are the most autonomous and liberated nonhumans on earth, coexisting with the least human involvement, which often means harassment, harm, habitat destruction, and death. This chapter surveys the most prominent statutes.[1]

A. ENDANGERED SPECIES ACT

In 1973, Congress passed the Endangered Species Act ("ESA"), 16 U.S.C. § 1531 et seq., to guard against the population decline of imperiled species to the point of extinction due to unregulated economic development and diffidence toward growth's environmental impacts. *Tennessee Valley Auth. v. Hill*, 437 U.S. 153, 184 (1978) found "the plain intent of Congress in enacting [the ESA] was to halt and reverse the trend toward species extinction, whatever the cost." The Department of the Interior's United States Fish and Wildlife Service ("FWS") and the Department of Commerce's National Oceanic and Atmospheric Administration ("NOAA") administer the ESA. *See* 50 C.F.R. §§ 23.11 et seq., 17.22. Animals and plants may be listed as "endangered" if at the brink, or "in danger of[,] extinction" or "threatened" if "likely to become an endangered species within the foreseeable future[.]" 16 U.S.C. § 1532(6), (20).

Once so listed, ESA prohibitions automatically apply under Section 9 of the Act (codified as 16 U.S.C. § 1538). The most common cause for private litigation under the ESA concerns the proscription against "taking" an endangered species, but other forbidden actions include the import, export, possession, sale, delivery, carriage, transport, shipment of unlawfully taken species and having delivered, received, carried, transported, or shipped such species in commerce in the course of commercial activity. 16 U.S.C. § 1538(a)(1)(A)-(G). "Take" means to "harass, harm, pursue, hunt, shoot, wound, kill, trap, capture, or collect, or attempt to engage in any such conduct." 16 U.S.C. § 1532(19). "Harm" includes significant habitat modification or degradation that "actually kills or injures fish or wildlife by significantly impairing essential behavioral patterns, including, breeding, spawning, rearing, migrating, feeding or sheltering." 50 C.F.R. § 222.102 (NOAA's Rule); 50 C.F.R. § 17.3 (FWS's Rule). Civil penalties up to $25,000 per violation and criminal penalties up to $50,000 and one year's imprisonment per violation follow under the ESA. 16 U.S.C. § 1540(a)-(b).

---

[1] Readers should examine environmental protection laws as well, such as the National Environment Policy Act ("NEPA"), Clean Air Act ("CAA"), and Clean Water Act ("CWA"), for they have been used to defend nonhuman animals as well as flora, streams, mountains, and other features of the landscape.

Fish and wildlife held in captivity or a controlled environment on Dec. 28, 1973 or the date the animal was listed as endangered are "captive-held" exempt from the (a)(1)(A) and (a)(1)(G) prohibitions — e.g., import or export of an endangered species, or violation of any regulation pertaining to such endangered species or any threatened species. 16 U.S.C. § 1538(b). Note that the captive-held exemption under 16 U.S.C. § 1538 does not undo the "take" prohibition of (a)(1)(B), a point of judicial scrutiny in a recent case involving Ringling Brothers, as discussed below.

If not exempted by the captive-held provision of § 1538(b), a permit must be obtained from FWS to determine whether the proposed activity bears the hallmark of "scientific" endeavor or "enhance[s] the propagation or survival of the affected species." 16 U.S.C. § 1539(a)(1)(A). Entities who fulfill the requirements of joining the captive-bred program for endangered species may obtain such permits. 50 C.F.R. § 17.21(g). Other permitted actions include those properly described as "incidental" to an otherwise lawful activity. 16 U.S.C. § 1539(a)(1)(B). The ESA also provides for United States participation in the Convention on International Trade in Endangered Species of Wild Fauna and Flora ("CITES"), T.I.A.S. No. 8249, 27 U.S.T. 1087 (1973), a 180-nation treaty to protect against extinction or endangerment due to harmful transactions in global commerce. Escalating trade restrictions vary depending on which appendix a particular species is listed. CITES, Art. III, ¶ 3 requires that Appendix I animals, who merit the greatest protection, may not be imported if "used primarily for commercial purposes." The ESA cross-references CITES in this respect at 16 U.S.C. § 1538(c)(1); 50 C.F.R. § 23.15.

1.   Standing and Private Right of Action

While the FWS and NOAA are presumptively charged with enforcing the ESA, civilians may also ensure compliance by private right of action pursuant to its citizen-suit provision, 16 U.S.C. § 1540(g). A jurisdictional prelude to litigation requires service of a written 60-day notice of intent to sue. 16 U.S.C. § 1540(g)(2)(A). To pass muster under § 1540(g), however, is far easier said than done, as illustrated by the decade-long battle between the ASPCA, the Animal Welfare Institute, the Fund for Animals, and Tom Rider, a former Ringling Brothers elephant handler, against the Ringling Brothers and Barnum & Bailey Circus and Feld Entertainment, Inc. *ASPCA v. Ringling Bros.*, D.D.C. No. 1:03CV02006 (Sept. 26, 2003). They sought declaratory and injunctive relief for alleged violations of the ESA by Defendants' harming, harassing, and wounding Asian elephants. Defined as illegal "takes," the Plaintiffs accused the Defendants of "routinely beat[ing] elephants, chain[ing] them for long periods of time, hit[ting] them with sharp bull hooks, break[ing] baby elephants with force to make them submissive, and forcibly remov[ing] baby elephants from their mothers before they are weaned," as part of their disciplinary process. *See* 16 U.S.C. §§ 1538(a)(1)(B) (prohibits the "take" of "any" endangered species), 1532(19) (defining "take" to include such conduct).

The trial court initially dismissed the case due to lack of Article III standing. Finding, for purposes of a Rule 12 motion to dismiss, that Mr. Rider's alleged strong personal and emotional attachment to the elephants would cause him psychic harm were he to attend a circus performance and witness the symptoms of their mistreatment (e.g., gashes, bruising, behavioral impact), the D.C. Circuit Court of Appeals reversed. *ASPCA v. Ringling Bros.*, 317 F.3d 334 (D.C. Cir. 2003). The court noted that other circus-goers would not share his ability to detect injuries, a point that helped establish injury-in-fact and confer standing under the ESA's citizen-suit provision.

In *HSUS v. Babbitt*, 46 F.3d 93 (D.C. Cir. 1995), the Humane Society for the United States and Milwaukee resident Kay Mannes sued Bruce Babbitt, Secretary of the Interior, for FWS's issuing a certificate exempting Lota — an Asian elephant captured in the wild in 1950 and transported to the Milwaukee Zoo in 1954 — from the CITES and ESA requirements. After 36 years in captivity, Lota left the zoo to the Hawthorn Corporation due to claimed irremediable aggression problems. The Plaintiffs strongly suspected that Hawthorn intended to use her for elephant rides and performances with the Ringling Brothers and Barnum & Bailey Circus. One year after her transfer, in 1991, FWS issued a CITES certificate deeming Lota a "pre-Convention animal" exempt from CITES's import and export restrictions; it also amended the permit to deem her a "pre-Act animal" further exempt from ESA prohibitions. Hawthorn apparently intended to show Lota within the United States and abroad[2] using the permit, even for arguably commercial purposes, which would otherwise violate 16 U.S.C. § 1538(a)(1)(A), (E).

Plaintiffs challenged FWS's interpretation of "commercial activity" to exclude transportation of endangered species between states or countries, provided ownership and control remained with the same person or entity. Such analysis worked to deny Lota any of the protections afforded her by the ESA, for while she undoubtedly met the timing criterion (she was captive for decades prior to enactment of the ESA and listing of the Asian elephant), the captive-bred ESA exemption of 16 U.S.C. § 1538(b) would only apply if "any subsequent holding or use [of Lota] was not in the course of a commercial activity." Were Hawthorn subject to the ESA restrictions, so Plaintiffs argued, it would likely fail to acquire a conservation permit, preventing her from crossing state and country lines, and saving her from an ignominious life in the circus following nearly four decades confined at a zoological park.

The appellate court never reached that question, however. Instead, it dispensed the matter on grounds of standing, holding that Mannes lacked standing as she suffered no cognizable injury. Though she may have frequented the zoo, she did not form a personalized relationship to the object of her study, i.e., Lota. Her contention that she lost the ability to study Asian elephants generally due to the diminishing supply failed to persuade, for a reduction in number from four to three could not cause Mannes to suffer any appreciable adverse impact. In addition, she had no right to view endangered species in a conservation setting as opposed to a commercially exploitative setting. That said, the "sudden departure" of an animal of individual study might constitute an injury-in-fact. As to the HSUS members, suffering distress at the prospect of Lota's absence was too generalized a harm, particularly where no member of HSUS even saw Lota before or after her removal.

---

[2] Ringling Brothers and Barnum & Bailey Circus were co-defendants, so one may reasonably conclude that HSUS believed Hawthorn intended to maintain ownership and control on paper while allowing her to spend her final years as a circus performer.

The court also found no ability to causally trace issuance of the FWS permit to Lota's removal from the zoo, as she was taken away prior. Similarly, no redress could be afforded by rescission of the permit, as it would not compel Lota's return to the zoo.

2. Covered Animals

Years into the *Ringling Bros.* litigation, the circus moved for summary judgment dismissal of the entire suit, claiming that the elephants were exempted as "pre-Act" species or, alternatively, permitted captive-bred wildlife — meaning in either case that the "take" provisions of the ESA had no bearing on what Ringling Brothers allegedly did to the elephants at issue. District Court Judge Emmet Sullivan granted the circus's motion as to the captive-bred elephants only.

Section 9 of the ESA makes it unlawful generally to "take" any endangered species by harassment or harm. Harassment means "an intentional or negligent act or omission which creates the likelihood of injury to wildlife by annoying it to such an extent as to significantly disrupt normal behavioral patterns which include, but are not limited to, breeding, feeding, or sheltering." With respect to "captive wildlife," the term "harass" is narrowed to exclude animal husbandry procedures that meet or exceed the Animal Welfare Act minimum standards, breeding procedures, and certain veterinary care protocols. Harm means an act "which actually kills or injures wildlife." This "take" prohibition is found at subsection (a)(1)(B).

Section 9(b) of the Act (the "pre-Act" exemption) holds that subsections (a)(1)(A) and (a)(1)(G) do not apply to wildlife held in captivity before December 28, 1973 or the date the animal was first added to the endangered species list. The Asian elephant was listed on June 14, 1976. Subsection 9(a)(1)(A) prohibits certain imports and exports of endangered species, and 9(a)(1)(G) makes it unlawful to violate any regulation promulgated by FWS concerning endangered and threatened species. Ringling Brothers argued that the "pre-Act" exemption applied to "takes" even though subsection (a)(1)(B) (the "take" prohibition) was not specifically listed in Section 9(b). It pointed to the implementing regulation, 50 C.F.R. § 17.4, which appears to very broadly extend the "pre-Act" exemption to "any activity involving endangered or threatened wildlife which was held in captivity or in a controlled environment on December 28, 1973." Moreover, 50 C.F.R. § 17.21(c) states that it is unlawful to "take" endangered wildlife within the United States. Accordingly, Ringling Brothers argued, even if not directly exempted from the statute's take provision found in subsection (a)(1)(B), their elephants were exempted indirectly by federal regulation. The court disagreed, holding that Congress clearly intended that the pre-Act exemption only applied to subsections (a)(1)(A) and (a)(1)(G). In not specifically referencing any other subsections, the court assumed that Congress chose to exclude subsections (a)(1)(B) through (a)(1)(F). Therefore, the pre-Act exemption did not apply.

The next issue addressed by Judge Sullivan concerned captive-bred wildlife, 21 of whom were conceived in captivity and conscripted to labor under the command of the circus. FWS issued the circus a captive-bred wildlife ("CBW") permit to allow for "takings" and other otherwise prohibited activities under Section 9 "to enhance the propagation or survival of the affected species." Ringling Brothers argued that the ASPCA did not have standing to challenge its alleged noncompliance with FWS's CBW permit. The court agreed, noting that the citizen suit provision did not reference Section 11(g) of the ESA, the provision concerning permits. *ASPCA v. Ringling Bros. & Barnum & Bailey Circus*, 502 F. Supp. 2d 103 (D.D.C. 2007).

Notably, the ESA's "pre-Act" exemption was tapered by congressional amendment in 1982, as it originally (in 1973) operated as a wholesale exemption for all violations of Section 9(a)(1). The fact that the FWS failed to update its regulations after 1982 did not create statutory ambiguity, but was the result of inattentiveness or deliberate disregard by federal regulators. Judge Sullivan applied the same doctrine in protecting the elephants forced into captivity before 1976 as he did to exempt those unfortunate enough to be conceived in captivity by them. The rule of statutory construction is called *expressio unius est exclusio alterius*, meaning, "mention of one thing implies exclusion of another thing." This is the first known decision interpreting the apparent conflict between statute and regulation concerning pre-Act exemptions. The practical longevity of this opinion for circus animals, however, is short, given that those animals excused from the exemption are already deceased or decades old.

3. Fee-Shifting

On December 30, 2009, following a six-week bench trial, Judge Sullivan dismissed the case due to lack of standing, after finding that the star witness, Tom Rider, was "pulverized" on cross-examination and "essentially a paid plaintiff and fact witness" with "a motive to falsify" the entire basis for his standing, for which his testimony was afforded "no weight." *ASPCA v. Feld Entertainment, Inc.*, 677 F. Supp. 2d 55, 67, 89 (D.D.C. 2009), *aff'd*, 659 F.3d 13 (D.C. Cir. 2011), *reh'g den'd*. Following dismissal, Feld resumed its stayed lawsuit against the plaintiffs and their attorneys, alleging violation of the Racketeer Influenced and Corrupt Organizations Act, 18 U.S.C. § 1961 et seq., among other claims. *Feld Entertainment, Inc. v. ASPCA*, 523 F. Supp. 2d 1 (D.D.C. 2007). On Jul. 9, 2012, Judge Sullivan dismissed the state law claim of champerty and the RICO action against individual attorneys Howard Crystal and Kimberly Ockene, but allowed the remaining claims for maintenance, malicious prosecution, abuse of process, the Virginia Conspiracy Act, and RICO to proceed. *Feld Entertainment, Inc. v. ASPCA*, 873 F. Supp. 2d 288 (D.D.C. 2012). The ASPCA settled with Feld for $9.3 million in 2012.

On March 29, 2013, the district court granted Feld's motion for fees against the plaintiffs under the fee-shifting provision of 16 U.S.C. § 1540(g)(4), stating:

> The Court carefully considered the testimony of approximately thirty witnesses and hundreds of exhibits in an effort to find any evidence that any of the plaintiffs had standing to pursue their claims. There was none. The voluminous decision will not be repeated here, but a summary recitation of some of the findings of fact will demonstrate the groundless nature of the claims.

AWI v. Feld Entertainment, Inc., 944 F. Supp. 2d 1, 5 (D.D.C. 2013). In 2014, the remaining twelve parties settled for $15.75 million.

4. Commercial Activity

Among the list of prohibited acts, the ESA seeks to stem the delivery, receipt, carriage, transport, or shipment of covered species in interstate or foreign commerce in the course of commercial activity, except as provided by 16 U.S.C. §§ 1535(g)(2) and 1539. 16 U.S.C. § 1538(a)(1)(E); 50 C.F.R. § 17.21(e). The term "commercial activity" means:

> [A]ll activities of industry and trade, but not limited to, the buying or selling of commodities and activities conducted for the purpose of facilitating such buying and selling: *Provided, however*, That it does not include exhibition of commodities by museums or similar cultural or historical organizations.

16 U.S.C. § 1532(2). In promulgating regulations under the ESA, the FWS defined "[i]ndustry or trade in the definition of 'commercial activity'" as "the actual or intended transfer of wildlife or plants from one person to another person in the pursuit of gain or profit." 50 C.F.R. § 17.3; see *HSUS v. Babbitt*, 46 F.3d 93, 96 (D.C. Cir. 1995). Thus, transferring a covered species to another across state lines, not receiving any money in exchange, but entering into what amounts to a free-lease, care-lease, or possessory loan for the altruistic, noncommercial motives that the animal be cared for humanely for the rest of her life may not be subject to the ESA.

Imported animals listed in CITES Appendix I may not be used for a "primarily commercial purpose." The Resolution of the Parties to CITES defines "commercial purpose" as an activity designed "to obtain economic benefit, including profit (whether in cash or kind) and is directed toward resale, exchange, provision of a service or other form of economic use or benefit." Conf. Res. 5.10. Thus, if a petting zoo were to import the Northern hairy-nosed wombat (*Lasiorhinus krefftii*), an animal listed in CITES Appendix I and 50 C.F.R. § 17.11 as endangered, promising to post educational signage around the wombat exhibit, have staff describe the animal's endangered status prior to allowing patrons to touch, and committing to contribute to the captive-breeding of wombats by loaning adults for participation in a breeding program, a court might find that the important purpose was not primarily commercial and, thus, not arbitrary or capricious or contrary to law for FWS to issue an import permit under the ESA and CITES.

5. Hybrid Species

The federal government lists protected animals by common and scientific names per binomial nomenclature — first by genus (capitalized), then species (not capitalized) and, where applicable, subsecies (not capitalized). 50 C.F.R. § 17.11. Animals may be listed as endangered or threatened at the species, subspecies, or specific population or geographic range levels. The ESA, however, does not apply to hybrids, a point examined closely in *U.S. v. Kapp*, 419 F.3d 666, 673 (7th Cir. 2005). A jury convicted William R. Kapp of multiple violations of the ESA and Lacey Act, related to killing and trafficking in endangered tigers (*Panthera tigris*) and leopards (*Panthera pardus*), both listed at the species level as endangered per

16 U.S.C. §§ 1532–33. While these listings also protected all subspecies of the tiger and leopard, Kapp argued that they would not extend to hybrids. Therefore, he reasoned, the government failed to prove beyond a reasonable doubt that the tigers and leopards at issue were not species hybrids (e.g., cross between tiger and lion) or inter-subspecies hybrids (e.g., cross between Bengal tiger (*Panthera tigris tigris*) and Siberian tiger (*Panthera tigris altaica*)).

On the first point, while the appellate court held that the ESA did not protect unlisted hybrids, the evidence at trial sufficed to demonstrate that Kapp had in fact traded in protected purebreds. *Id.*, at 673 ("But crosses between tigers or leopards (including all subspecies) and members of unlisted *species* or subspecies, such as lions, are not protected. Therefore, ligers or tigons, which are hybrids of tigers (*Panthera tigris*, listed) and lions (*Panthera leo*, not listed), are not protected."). On the second point, the court dispensed with Kapp's contention by citing 50 C.F.R. § 17.11(g) (listing of a particular taxon includes all lower taxonomic units).

Would a wolf-dog hybrid be protected under the ESA? The current list of endangered and threatened species may be found at 50 C.F.R. § 17.11(h). Presently, certain populations of grey and red wolves are endangered, who join dogs in the genus *canis*, along with coyotes, jackals, and dingos, among other canids. However, all three belong to distinct subspecies, and in the case of the red wolf, a different species entirely: common dog (*Canis lupus familiaris*), grey wolf (*Canis lupus lupus*), red wolf (*Canis rufus rufus*). The other listed wolf, the maned wolf, is the only species in its genus (*Chrysocyon brachyurus*). Per *Kapp*, a hybrid of *C. lupus lupus* and *C. lupus familiaris* would not be protected.

6. Preemption

In California, Adidas sold athletic shoes made from Australian kangaroo skin. Cal. Penal Code § 653o banned the import of products made from kangaroos. The 1970-enacted section 653o was followed in 1973 by the ESA. In 1974, the three species of kangaroo imported by Adidas were declared "threatened." In March 1995, however, these kangaroo species were "delisted" by FWS. As of 1995, federal law no longer prohibited importation of kangaroos, their body parts, or products made from their body parts. Desirous of enforcing California law, the nonprofit group Viva! International Voice for Animals sued Adidas and other retailers, alleging a violation of this penal code and commission of an unlawful business practice under Bus. & Prof. Code § 17200, entitling them to an injunction against importing kangaroo skin to California. Prior to filing suit, Viva! issued a press release from executive director Lauren Ornelas (Apr. 21, 2003), stating in part:

> Animal Cruelty: Each year, hunters are licensed to shoot millions of adult kangaroos for their meat and skins. Baby 'joeys' — worthless to the industry — are ripped from their dead mothers' pouches and bludgeoned, decapitated, or simply abandoned to die of starvation. Australia is currently in the midst of one of the worst droughts on record and bush fires are raging across the country decimating kangaroo numbers; yet the kangaroo industry continues to shoot millions more.

This law provides Californians with a way to speak out against the kangaroo massacre. Kangaroos are wildlife, not shoes, said Ornelas. Adidas needs to get in step with the times and use synthetic materials for all their shoes.

Yet superior court Judge Ronald E. Quidachay and the California Court of Appeals rejected Viva!'s argument, holding that the ESA "conflict preempted" the California penal law notwithstanding that section 653o applied to *all* kangaroos, not just those listed on the ESA lists. *Viva! International Voice for Animals v. Adidas-Salomon AG*, 2004 WL 5202033 (S.F. Cy. Sup. Ct. Apr. 28, 2004); *Viva! International Voice for Animals v. Adidas Promotional Retail Operations, Inc.*, 134 Cal. App. 4th 133, 36 Cal. Rptr. 3d 19 (2005).

Although the appeals court affirmed the interpretation of section 653o as applying even to "delisted" or "unlisted" species, it concluded that the California law conflicted with accomplishing Congress's objectives in passing the ESA, given its "strong international component" with "sovereign foreign powers," and federal agency's multi-decade efforts to work with Australian government in managing its kangaroos. This decision depicts how judges will emphasize the case law justifying what they consider a prudential outcome. Indeed, the judges acknowledged that Viva!'s position was "not unreasonable and finds support in numerous cases allowing the state regulation of species not listed under ESA." In reaching its conclusion, the appeals court did not find an "express" or "implied" preemption of state law (the two other methods of invalidating the application of a state law). Instead, it focused on the policy-driven analysis that underlies a finding of "conflict" preemption and concluded that the American policy of allowing "unrestricted importation" of Australian kangaroos was a "reward" in exchange for "effective conservation measures." How might the single "stick" wielded by one of 50 states meaningfully interfere with the much larger "carrot" of nationwide federal ESA policy? See also 16 U.S.C. § 1535(f), the ESA's specific preemption clause underscoring an intent not to interfere with state conservation laws unless in conflict with an ESA permit or exemption.

Undeterred, Viva! appealed once more. This time, the California Supreme Court reversed, finding no preemption as Section 653o did not undermine any federal policy intended to influence Australian kangaroo management practices. It specifically rejected the argument that FWS's delisting of three subspecies of kangaroo signaled a policy against state regulation. Rather, "the three species had, in Fish and Wildlife's eyes, recovered." *Viva! v. Adidas*, 41 Cal. 4th 929 (2007).

B. MARINE MAMMAL PROTECTION ACT

The Marine Mammal Protection Act ("MMPA") of 1972, 16 U.S.C. § 1361 et seq. functions similarly to the ESA, yet it focuses on aquatic mammals, whether or not threatened or endangered. Presently, the law protects approximately 125 marine mammal species, including cetaceans, sirenians, and pinnipeds. Marine turtles, marine and anadromous fish, and invertebrates are not protected under the MMPA but may find refuge under the ESA. Like the ESA, the MMPA prohibits the "taking" of marine mammals in U.S. waters and by American citizens on the high seas, as well as the importation of marine mammals or their parts into the United

States. 1994 amendments to the MMPA codified exemptions to take prohibitions such as for scientific research, Alaska Native subsistence, and small incidental takes. 50 C.F.R. §§ 216.21–.47. In addition to criminalizing harassment of marine mammals, defined to mean pursuit, torment, or annoyance with potential to injure or potential to disturb behavioral patterns, the MMPA prohibits providing sustenance to marine mammals in the wild. 50 C.F.R. §§ 216.11–.17; 50 C.F.R. § 216.3 ("Take" includes "feeding or attempting to feed").

While there is no private right of action under the MMPA, citizens may challenge actions taken under the MMPA pursuant to the APA, 5 U.S.C. § 702, such as when an MMPA permit is granted or denied by a government agency. In this vein, consider the MMPA jurisprudence in a highly-publicized context pitting children against harbor seals.

In 1930, Ellen Scripps built a 300-foot concrete breakwater in the Pacific Ocean near La Jolla to create a bathing pool for children. The state granted lands to the City in trust for this purpose, which was conditioned on being "exclusively to public park, bathing school for children, parkway, highway, playground and recreational purposes, and to such other uses as may be incident to, or convenient for the full enjoyment of, such purposes . . ." By 1997, however, harbor seal and sea lion feces had rendered the Children's Pool Beach unusable. In 2004, Valerie O'Sullivan, sued the City of San Diego, claiming it violated the statutorily created public trust by allowing higher concentrations of fecal pollution that presented a human health risk, and placing a rope barrier to further restrict public access that only exacerbated the contamination, so she claimed. O'Sullivan urged for dispersion of the marine mammals under the MMPA, specifically § 109(h). *O'Sullivan v. City of San Diego*, No. GIC 826918 (S.D. Sup. Ct. 2004). The trial judge granted her motion and ordered the city to restore the pool to its 1941 condition. Years passed in noncompliance and the uninterrupted stringing of the rope as the City appealed and lost before both the California Court of Appeals and California Supreme Court. On remand, the City moved to clarify the court's injunction and to reconsider the "rope issue." The trial judge refused to do so, saying that the rope barrier cut off public access to the Pool and breached its duties under the trust.

Three years after the injunction issued against the City, litigation commenced in federal court when the Animal Protection and Rescue League ("APRL") and Dorota Valli sued the State of California, City of San Diego Department of Parks and Recreation, and Mayor Jerry Sanders to require placement of a rope barrier during seal pupping season, in part due to the harassment (intentional or unintentional) faced by children and their parents coming close to pregnant seals, scaring them into the water, and throwing objects at them. Ms. Valli reported observing seal miscarriages. The trial judge denied the TRO and raised concerns about abstention given the-pending state action involving the Pool. *Animal Protection & Rescue League v. California*, 2008 U.S. Dist. LEXIS 8030 (S.D. Cal. Feb. 4, 2008). The Ninth Circuit dismissed the federal suit on subject matter jurisdiction grounds, concluding that appellants could not enforce the terms of the MMPA, which had no private right of action. *APRL v. California*, 282 Fed. Appx. 637 (9th Cir. 2008).

Undeterred, the animal rights groups took a new tack. In 2012, they sued the City of San Diego and its Planning Commission after it denied them a permit to maintain a year-round guideline rope at the Pool to protect the seals from humans. In its answer to the complaint, the City confessed its error and agreed to a court order vacating the denial. *See* Tony Perry, *In La Jolla People-versus-Seals Battle, Tide Has Yet to Turn*, L.A. TIMES (Jan. 8, 2012); *Judge Sides with Seals on the Beach in La Jolla*, L.A. TIMES (Apr. 12, 2013). The latest legal development involved the payment of attorney's fees in excess of $80,000. *APRL v. City of San Diego*, 237 Cal. App. 4th 99 (2015).

C. BALD AND GOLDEN EAGLE PROTECTION ACT

In 1940, Congress enacted the Bald and Golden Eagle Protection Act ("BGEPA") to protect America's winged emblem, chosen at the Continental Congress of 1782. 16 U.S.C. § 668. A 1962 amendment expanded the law to protect the Golden Eagle. It imposes a criminal penalty:

> Whoever, within the United States or any place subject to the jurisdiction thereof, without being permitted to do so as provided in this subchapter, shall knowingly, or with wanton disregard for the consequences of his act take, possess, sell, purchase, barter, offer to sell, purchase or barter, transport, export or import, at any time or in any manner any bald eagle commonly known as the American eagle or any golden eagle, alive or dead, or any part, nest, or egg thereof of the foregoing eagles, or whoever violates any permit or regulation issued pursuant to this subchapter, shall be fined not more than $5,000 or imprisoned not more than one year or both: [subsequent convictions carry enhanced penalties; providing further a pre-Act exemption]

16 U.S.C. § 668(a). It further provides a civil penalty:

> Whoever, within the United States or any place subject to the jurisdiction thereof, without being permitted to do so as provided in this subchapter, shall take, possess, sell, purchase, barter, offer to sell, purchase or barter, transport, export or import, at any time or in any manner, any bald eagle, commonly known as the American eagle, or any golden eagle, alive or dead, or any part, nest, or egg thereof of the foregoing eagles, or whoever violates any permit or regulation issued pursuant to this subchapter, may be assessed a civil penalty by the Secretary of not more than $5,000 for each such violation. Each violation shall be a separate offense. No penalty shall be assessed unless such person is given notice and opportunity for a hearing with respect to such violation. In determining the amount of the penalty, the gravity of the violation, and the demonstrated good faith of the person charged shall be considered by the Secretary. For good cause shown, the Secretary may remit or mitigate any such penalty. Upon any failure to pay the penalty assessed under this section, the Secretary may request the Attorney General to institute a civil action in a district court of the United States for any district in which such person is found or resides or transacts business to collect the penalty and such court shall have jurisdiction to hear and decide any such action. In hearing any such action, the court must sustain the Secretary's action if supported by substantial evidence.

16 U.S.C. § 668(b). Pursuant to § 668a, the Secretary of the Interior may issue permits for taking, possessing, or transporting eagle specimens for scientific or exhibition purposes of public museums, scientific societies, and zoological parks (50 C.F.R. 22.21); "the religious purposes of Indian tribes" (50 C.F.R. § 22.22), taking depredating eagles (50 C.F.R. § 22.23); falconry purposes (50 C.F.R. § 22.24: Golden eagles only); or when needed for protection of wildlife or agricultural or other interests in a particular locality. Importantly, "[B]ald eagles may not be taken for any purpose unless, prior to such taking, a permit to do so is procured[.]" *Id.* The eagle feather law, 50 C.F.R. § 22.11, allows enrolled members of federally recognized tribes to apply for an eagle permit for use in bona fide tribal religious ceremonies.

D. MIGRATORY BIRD TREATY ACT

Congress attempted to regulate the hunting of migratory waterfowl, who would travel great distances across state and international lines. States chafed against such efforts and challenged the regulations as unconstitutional. This prompted Congress to empower the State Department to negotiate a treaty with Canada (care of the United Kingdom) in 1916. Upon ratification, Congress enacted the Migratory Bird Treaty Act of 1918 ("MBTA"), 16 U.S.C. §§ 703–12, to implement the prohibitions that had previously been susceptible to successful states' rights arguments, which contended that the federal government lacked the power to regulate migratory bird hunting. When the state of Missouri took issue with the MBTA, the United States Supreme Court sided with the United States. *Missouri v. Holland*, 252 U.S. 416 (1920) declared the MBTA the constitutional product of the treaty-making power and Art. VI, cl. 2, the " supremacy clause." In 1936, the MBTA incorporated a similar convention with Mexico. Later amendments memorialized accords with Japan and Russia. This criminal law makes it

> unlawful at any time, by any means or in any manner, to pursue, hunt, take, capture, kill, attempt to take, capture, or kill, possess, offer for sale, sell, offer to barter, barter, offer to purchase, purchase, deliver for shipment, ship, export, import, cause to be shipped, exported, or imported, deliver for transportation, transport or cause to be transported, carry or cause to be carried, or receive for shipment, transportation, carriage, or export, any migratory bird, any part, nest, or eggs of any such bird, or any product, whether or not manufactured, which consists, or is composed in whole or part, of any such bird or any part, nest, or egg thereof included in the terms of the conventions between the United States and Great Britain for the protection of migratory birds concluded August 16, 1916 (39 Stat. 1702), the United States and the United Mexican States for the protection of migratory birds and game mammals concluded February 7, 1936, the United States and the Government of Japan for the protection of migratory birds and birds in danger of extinction, and their environment concluded March 4, 1972, and the convention between the United States and the Union of the Soviet Socialist Republics for the conservation of migratory birds and their environments concluded November 19, 1976.

16 U.S.C. § 703(a). Violating various parts of the Act results in criminal penalties pursuant to 16 U.S.C. § 707. The Secretary of the Interior may authorize permitted hunts, takes, captures, killings, possession, sales, purchases, shipments, transportation, carriage, or exportation of any bird, part of bird, nest or egg thereof. 16 U.S.C. § 704; *see also* 50 C.F.R. § 20.20 (hunting conducted under state hunting license); 50 C.F.R. § 21.21 (import and export); 50 C.F.R. § 21.22 (banding and marking); 50 C.F.R. § 21.24 (taxidermist permit); 50 C.F.R. § 21.25 (waterfowl sale and disposal); 50 C.F.R. § 21.26 (special Canada goose); 50 C.F.R. § 21.27 (special purpose); 50 C.F.R. § 21.28 (falconry); 50 C.F.R. § 21.30 (raptor propagation); 50 C.F.R. § 21.31 (rehabilitation); 50 C.F.R. 21.41 (depredation). Importantly, the MBTA contains a forfeiture provision. It states, "[a]ll guns, traps, nets and other equipment, vessels, vehicles, and other means of transportation used by any person when engaged in pursuing, hunting, taking, trapping, ensnaring, capturing, killing, or attempting to take, capture, or kill any migratory bird in violation of this subchapter with intent to offer for sale, or sell, or offer for barter, or barter such bird in violation of this subchapter shall be forfeited to the United States[.]" 16 U.S.C. § 707(d).

E.   COMPARING ESA TO MBTA AND BGEPA

Unlike the ESA, which protects eagles, eggs, nest, and habitat, the BGEPA and MBTA do not expressly protect habitat or indirect harm to birds. That said, a recent 2007 regulation defining the word "disturb" within the BGEPA remains as yet untested in the courts and may signal an expansion of eagle protection. Thus, a developer could remove all trees near a bald eagle nest if it did not touch the eagle, eggs, or nest. "Removal of trees is not in itself a violation of the Eagle Act." 72 FR 37363. However, cutting down a tree with an active nest would. Should the owner of the hypothetical parcel attempt to develop the land, the operative prohibition requiring analysis is "take."

The BGEPA defines "take" as "pursue, shoot, shoot at, poison, wound, kill, capture, trap, collect, or molest or disturb." 16 U.S.C. § 668c. The term "disturb," part of the definition of "take," resembles the ESA's definition of "harm." Harming and harassing may also be construed as an incidental take. FWS defined "disturb" in 2007 to mean "to agitate or bother a bald or golden eagle to a degree that causes, or is likely to cause, based on the best scientific information available, (1) injury to an eagle, (2) a decrease in its productivity, by substantially interfering with normal breeding, feeding, or sheltering behavior, or (3) nest abandonment, by substantially interfering with normal breeding, feeding, or sheltering behavior." 50 C.F.R. § 22.3, 72 FR 31139. Accordingly, activities calculated to indirectly vex, harass, or annoy the bald eagles to the point they abandon their nesting and, perhaps, roosting sites would constitute a take and summon related criminal and civil penalties. One may obtain a permit under 50 C.F.R. § 22.26 where "associated with, but not the purpose of, the activity," if it cannot practicably be avoided. One may also procure a permit to take an eagle nest. 50 C.F.R. § 22.27.

An important difference between the ESA and BGEPA used to concern the incidental take permits available under the ESA, Section 10 (16 U.S.C. § 1539), and incidental take statements under the ESA, Section 7, which allowed taking birds as an unintended consequence of other activities. The BGEPA, on the other hand, did not authorize these permits. In 2007, FWS proposed a rule authorizing it to issue incidental take permits. The current, final rule enacted in 2009, 50 C.F.R. § 22.28, 74 FR 46879, allows for incidental takes of bald eagles if the petitioner obtained a section 7 authorization or section 10 permit prior to the date of delisting in 2007.

The MBTA does not define "take." However, the Ninth Circuit interpreted the term to only apply to direct taking, such as by poisoning or hunting: it did not proscribe indirect takes by habitat modification. *See Seattle Audubon Soc. v. Evans*, 952 F.2d 297, 303 (9th Cir. 1991) (MBTA did not bar Forest Service from logging areas deemed habitat for migratory birds as "Habitat destruction causes 'harm' to the owls under the ESA but does not 'take' them within the meaning of the MBTA.") Yet at least one court found that BGEPA's definition of "take" mirrors the scope of the ESA. *Contoski v. Scarlett*, 2006 U.S. Dist. LEXIS 56345 (D. Minn. Apr. 10, 2006) (finding word *harm* under ESA tantamount to *take* under BGEPA).

F.   FERAL CATS AND THE ESA/MBTA

Eyes of environmental and animal welfare ethicists, birders and cat fanciers, and 12 jurors were all on Jim Stevenson, a 54-year-old former science teacher and founder of the Galveston Ornithological Society. Stevenson stood trial on felony animal cruelty charges for the November 8, 2006 shooting of a feline in the alleged defense of piping plovers, an endangered species[3] also protected by the MBTA. Stevenson described the cat as one of a colony of feral predators camping out under the San Luis Pass bridge and stalking the dunes to kill "tame, abiding little creatures" who "can't see or hear a cat creep up on them." Bruce Barcott, *Kill the Cat That Kills the Bird?*, New York Times Magazine (Dec. 2, 2007). At the moment he discharged the .22 rifle, the cat, who "dropped like a rock," was not in the act of attacking or killing any bird.

Above him, a tollbooth attendant John Newland heard the discharge and called the police. Newland kept photographs of Stevenson's several highly likely kills, including "a mother and a baby in their bed, splattered all over the wall." Stevenson grew quiet when confronted with the accusation, responding, "What I would say to that is that if that's so, why doesn't he have any evidence to support that accusation?" The Galveston County district attorney took the position that Stevenson killed a cat owned by Newland, *not* a feral, while Tad Nelson, Stevenson's defense attorney, argued that if that were the case, then Newland should be read his *Miranda* rights for aiding and abetting the killing of endangered or migratory birds. On Nov. 16, 2007, the court announced a mistrial. Shortly thereafter, he received death threats and was nearly killed when someone allegedly shot at his head while he stood on his porch.

The contention that those who feed feral colonies face liability under the ESA or MBTA is dubious and certainly lacks precedent, probably due to causal attenuation, lack of culpable mental state, and the fact that feeding such felines would ostensibly

---

[3] The piping plover became protected under the ESA on Jan. 10, 1986.

reduce or eliminate their need to hunt endangered species for sustenance.[4] Pamela Jo Hatley[5] promoted this hypothesis in her report to the USFWS in January 2003, titled *Feral Cat Colonies in Florida: The Fur and Feathers are Flying.* https://www.law.ufl.edu/_pdf/academics/centers-clinics/centers/feralcat.pdf. That said, knowingly managing feral feline colonies in ecologically sensitive areas designated as "critical habitat" may be grounds to exercise caution. 16 U.S.C. § 1532(5)(A) (defining "critical habitat" to include areas occupied by protected species). While letting slip the cats of TNR into endangered populations might not meet the definition of "take," they could constitute acts that "harm" or "harass" by significantly impairing essential behavioral patterns, including breeding, feeding, and shelter. Still, the federal government or private plaintiff would need to establish causation between TNR activities and the harm or harassment of protected species.

While not pertaining to TNR, the case of *Strahan v. Coxe*, 127 F.3d 155, 163–64 (1st Cir. 1997) offers an interesting parallel. It found that the Commonwealth of Massachusetts committed a take of the Northern Right whale in violation of the ESA when it licensed commercial gillnetters and lobster potters knowing that they would be deployed "in specifically the manner that is likely to result in a violation of federal law," namely, by cetaceans becoming entangled in the state-permitted gear. One evident distinction between government-sanctioned human activity that takes, harms, or harasses protected species, on the one hand, and civilian-supported nonhuman activity with the same outcome, on the other hand, is that, as pithily stated by United States District Court Judge Oliver W. Wanger of the Eastern District of California in *Coalition for a Sustainable Delta v. John McCamman*, 725 F. Supp. 2d 1162, 1168 (E.D. Cal. 2010), "A fish cannot 'take' another fish under the ESA, because only a 'person' can violate the ESA's take prohibition." Furthermore, the lethal fishing gear only jeopardized the whale's habitat thanks to state permitting, while feral cats existed within songbird habitats long before any intervention by TNR advocates. Irrespective of government endorsement or criminalization of TNR activity, because feral cats are not relocated in large numbers to critical habitats, but rather are maintained in self-established colonies, attempts to extend ESA case law will quite likely fail.

Notwithstanding the foregoing, intentionally introducing a nonindigenous predator to a critical area populated by endangered species, or intentionally failing to take steps to prevent a preexisting predator from thriving to the significant detriment of endangered prey, might constitute a taking under the ESA, a concept discussed in *Palila v. Hawaii Dep't of Land and Natural Resources*, 852 F.2d 1106 (9th Cir.1988). The Ninth Circuit Court of Appeals found Hawaii violated the ESA by allowing feral mouflon sheep to graze (and be sport hunted) throughout the critical habitat of a particular species of honeycreeper, known as the Palila bird. The Sierra Club, National Audubon Society, Hawaii Audubon Society, and Alan C. Ziegler joined the Palila species itself as named plaintiffs in this action seeking to enjoin the state to remove these habitat-destroying mammals from the Palila's

---

[4] For the following research, I give thanks to Best Friends attorneys Laura Nirenburg and Stacey McFadin.

[5] Ms. Hatley obtained her J.D. from University of Florida in 2003 and her Ph.D. from the University of South Florida in 2013.

domain. Lest government agencies overreact to the holding of *Palila* and determine that lethal solutions are preferred to ongoing and intensive management, consider *Animal Lovers Volunteer Assoc., Inc. v. Carlucci*, 849 F.2d 1475 (9th Cir. 1988), which held that permanent, large-scale reduction in population of nonindigenous species may have environmental significance for purposes of conducting a National Environmental Policy Act environmental impact statement. For instance, elimination of a population might disrupt the ecosystem balance by increasing other populations who might in turn predate on endangered species. *Id.*, and see *Coalition*, at 1193 (noting that reducing striped bass population might ultimately decrease delta smelt population by preventing the bass from preying on one of the smelt's primary predators and competitors, the Mississippi silverslide).

Hatley also contends that, like those who accidentally cause chemical leaks, apply pesticides by air, or fail to install equipment to protect birds from power lines, those who tend to feral colonies (i.e., releasing cats into the environment) may be strictly criminally liable under the MBTA:

> It is quite obvious that cats can be lethal to birds, and if the death of a migratory bird can be traced to a cat, or a cat colony, which can be further traced to an individual or organization, there may be strict liability for that person under the MBTA.

Hatley, at 20. Her premise warrants serious consideration if residing in that part of the country where the Circuit court has interpreted the MBTA broadly to prohibit acts that directly or indirectly, yet still proximately, cause migratory bird injury or death. 16 U.S.C. § 707(a) makes it a misdemeanor to violate the MBTA and does not explicitly supply any *mens rea* requirement, leading many jurisdictions to conclude it imposes strict liability. Some courts have held that direct, though unintended, poisoning of birds from toxic substances violates the MBTA. *U.S. v. FMC Corp.*, 572 F.2d 902 (2d Cir. 1978) (dumped waste water killed birds); *Corbin Farm Serv.*, 444 F. Supp. 510 (E.D. Cal. 1978) (misapplication of pesticide caused deaths).

Generally, the Eighth and Ninth Circuits have taken the narrow view that an MBTA "take" means "physical conduct of the sort engaged in by hunters and poachers[.]" *Seattle Audubon Society v. Evans*, 952 F.2d 297, 302 (9th Cir. 1991). They conclude that the MBTA does not reach those who inflict indirect and unintended avian casualties. The Second and Tenth Circuits, however, have held that liability also extends to unintended takes provided they are foreseeable: they also rely on prosecutorial discretion to select truly meritorious cases. *See U.S. v. Apollo Energies, Inc.*, 611 F.3d 679, 684–86, 689–90 (10th Cir. 2010) (discussing strict liability status of MBTA and whether failing to cap an exhaust stack or cover access holes to the heater/treater will foreseeably cause birds to become trapped). A relatively recent federal district court decision out of North Dakota discusses the circuit split and sides with the narrower interpretation:

> If the Migratory Bird Treaty Act concepts of "take" or "kill" were read to prohibit any conduct that proximately results in the death of a migratory bird, then many everyday activities become unlawful — and subject to criminal sanctions — when they cause the death of pigeons, starlings and other common birds. For example, ordinary land uses which may cause bird deaths include cutting brush and trees, and planting and harvesting crops.

In addition, many ordinary activities such as driving a vehicle, owning a building with windows, or owning a cat, inevitably cause migratory bird deaths.

. . . More important, to extend the Migratory Bird Treaty Act to reach other activities that indirectly result in the deaths of covered birds would yield absurd results.

See U.S. v. Brigham Oil & Gas, L.P., 840 F. Supp. 2d 1202, 1212 (D.N.D. 2012) (emphasis added). As with the ESA, distinctions can be drawn between releasing a harmful effluent into waters or noxious fume into the air and humanely tending to animals who happen to reside near species favored by the federal government.

G. APPLICATION TO TRIBAL LAND

While most states have their own laws regarding species of concern, whom they may classify as threatened, endangered, sensitive, or monitored, these enactments do not apply to tribes or enrolled tribal members engaging in otherwise illegal behavior on tribal lands held in trust, or even on land reconveyed back to the tribe or tribal member in fee. Because tribes are regarded much like sovereign nations, tribal land remains impervious to state or local zoning, land use, animal, or environmental regulations. As a general rule, state laws do not apply to tribal members or tribes on a reservation absent specific authorization under federal law: *federal* and *tribal* animal and environmental protection laws do. *See California v. Cabazon Band of Mission Indians*, 480 U.S. 202, 207–10 (1987) (noting that P.L. 280 does not authorize states to enforce civil/regulatory laws on tribal land). A recent case on point is *Gobin v. Snohomish Cy.*, 304 F.3d 909 (9th Cir. 2002).

In *Gobin*, a tribal member sued Snohomish County for attempting to exert land use regulatory controls over her lands. She intended to subdivide a 25-acre parcel, connect to septic, and then sell to the general public without regard to tribal affiliation. The County maintained that if the land were acquired in trust, it would approve the subdivision as proposed (leaving it to the tribe to apply its own land use/zoning/environmental assessment), but if kept in fee, it would impose its own zoning, subdivision, and development regulations, thereby limiting her to 10 homes instead of 25. In affirming summary judgment for the tribal member, the Ninth Circuit held:

1. Our Nation's deeply rooted history employs a policy to leave tribal members free of State jurisdiction on a reservation except where Congress expressly intended that State laws apply. *Id.*, at 914 (*citing McClanahan v. Ariz. State Tax Comm'n*, 411 U.S. 164, 170–71 (1973)).

2. Congress's decision to make Indian fee lands freely alienable and freely encumberable does not mean the County can enforce *in rem* land use regulations (i.e., directed at land itself, not individuals [as in *in personam*]) over those lands. *Id.*, at 916–17.

3. No "exceptional circumstances" warrant the state asserting jurisdiction over on-reservation activities of tribal members. The Court rejected the County's argument that its interest in protecting bull trout and salmon in Quilceda Creek, as required by the ESA, evidenced the "exceptional

circumstance" warranting such regulation of tribal members, since the "Tribes must also comply with the Endangered Species Act as well as its own strict laws protecting wildlife." *Id.*, at 917.

4. In acknowledging the risk that "Indians and non-Indians might conspire to transfer fee lands back and forth to avoid any County or tribal regulation," the Court characterized this enforcement problem "best handled jointly by the County and the Tribes in furtherance of their already excellent relationship." Any administrative problem did not justify undermining tribal sovereignty in favor of County regulation. *Id.*, at 918.

Five years later, the Ninth Circuit decided *In re Sonoma County Fire Chief's Application for an Inspection Warrant*, 2007 U.S. App. LEXIS 8118 (9th Cir. Apr. 5, 2007), ruling that while exceptional circumstances might justify enforcing state and county laws on-reservation against tribal members without Congress's express authorization, fire codes did not qualify. *Id.*, at 672. In *Sonoma*, the County tried to enforce the fire code on a casino on reservation land.

Hypothetical: A tribal member owned 15 acres of land in the Tulalip Nation, a federally recognized tribal reservation. Its chief inhabitants are the Great Blue Herons (*Ardea herodias*), which maintain a heronry exceeding 100 in size, and the Bald Eagles (*Haliaeetus leucocephalus*), which roost atop several snags. Development will assuredly harass and harm both species, resulting in the taking of individual birds. May the tribal member sell the land to a Canadian, non-tribal member so she can log the area and build a condominium development? What if construction commences while still owned by the tribal member?

Assuming that the federal government has classified most or all of the acreage as wetland presents three impediments to development by a tribe or enrolled tribal member: the MBTA, BGEPA, and the Clean Water Act, 33 U.S.C. § 1251 et seq. ("CWA"). A significant impact project could also trigger National Environmental Policy Act, 42 U.S.C. § 4321 et seq. ("NEPA") procedures. Though the southern populations (south of 40 degree north latitude[6]) were listed as endangered on Mar. 11, 1967 (32 FR 4001), and the Washington population deemed threatened in 1978 (43 FR 6233), the eagles were since delisted due to recovery on Jul. 9, 2007 (72 FR 37346). Thus the ESA does not afford any protection to the Bald Eagle. The Great Blue Heron is not listed as endangered or threatened under the ESA, either. Both the herons and eagles are deemed migratory birds protected by the MBTA. Only the bald eagle enjoys protection under BGEPA.

Tribal members may obtain permits to "take" bald eagles for ceremonial and religious purposes, even if it means separating eaglets from their parents, raising them to fledglings, and then killing them in a ceremony. *See U.S. v. Tawahongva*, 456 F. Supp. 2d 1120, 1125 fn.8 (D. Ariz. 2006). However, the BGEPA will not permit exceptions to the prohibitions on taking eagles for Native Americans who are not members of recognized tribes and "applying for a permit would be futile." *Id.*, at 1128. The MBTA does allow exceptions for unenrolled members. *See U.S. v. Winddancer*, 435 F. Supp. 2d 687, 693 (M.D. Tenn. 2006).

---

[6] Basically south of Denver, Colo. The Tulalip Nation is positioned generally at the 48th degree north parallel.

At least a decade or so ago, it was policy of the United States not to enforce aspects of the MBTA against members of federally recognized Indian tribes. *U.S. v. Eagleboy*, 200 F.3d 1137 (8th Cir. 1999). Eagleboy, not a member of any federal tribe, possessed hawk parts in violation of the MBTA. He claimed the government's policy not to prosecute tribal members constituted racial discrimination. In rejecting his argument, the Eighth Circuit found that policy discriminated based on tribal membership, not race. *Id.*, at 1138. Further, special treatment of tribal members has been upheld due to certain obligations toward Native Americans. *Id.* This long-standing "Morton Policy," issued in 1975 by then-Secretary of Interior Rogers C.B. Morton, commits to nonprosecution of tribal members who possess, use, carry, wear, give, loan, or exchange among other Indians, without compensation, all federally protected birds, and their parts and feathers in cultural and religious ceremonies. However, the Secretary "will continue to enforce against all persons those Federal laws prohibiting the killing, buying or selling of eagles, migratory birds, or endangered species, as well as those laws prohibiting the buying or selling of the parts or feathers of such birds and animals." *Id.*

The Secretary of the Interior created a permit system allowing limited possession of bird parts under BGEPA and MBTA. 50 C.F.R. §§ 22.11(a), 22.22. Typically, permits allow acquisition of eagle parts only from the National Eagle Repository, and only rarely from private rookeries. Further, the MBTA allows issuance of permits to possess migratory bird parts for many purposes, including for all citizens "for special purpose activities related to migratory birds, their parts, nests, or eggs," not otherwise provided for by other permit provisions. 50 C.F.R. § 21.27.

To develop wetlands would require acquisition of a Dredge and Fill Permit from the U.S. Army Corps of Engineers under 42 U.S.C. § 404. *See also* 40 C.F.R. Part 230. Section 404 regulates discharge of dredged and fill material into U.S. waters, including wetlands. With Environmental Protection Agency oversight and approval, tribes can administer 404 permitting. After applying for a permit, a public notice invites interested individuals and agencies to comment on the proposed activity. Traditionally, wetland status prohibits development unless no alternative exists to serve the project's purposes. Residential development is not a water-dependent use (such as a marina or boatyard), creating a presumption that wetland (as opposed to upland) development is not suitable. This tips against permit issuance. A myriad of factors and conditions attend CWA permit determinations and go beyond the scope of this analysis. While the CWA offers a citizen-suit provision under 33 U.S.C. § 1365(a), it only applies to violations of effluent standards or limitations (e.g., polluting waters).

This leaves a challenge to the federal government under the Administrative Procedure Act ("APA"), 5 U.S.C. § 702, granting judicial review to a person suffering a legal wrong due to agency action, or adverse effect or grievance by same, to judicial review. In an APA suit premised on a violation of the MBTA, the court determines whether the implementing agency action were "arbitrary, capricious, an abuse of discretion, or otherwise not in accordance with law." 5 U.S.C. § 706. Be mindful that the law is unsettled as to whether the federal government has waived sovereign immunity for the purpose of allowing private citizens to mount APA actions related to the MBTA and BGEPA, as neither law has an express waiver. *See Sierra Club v. Martin*, 110 F.3d 1551 (11th Cir. 1997) (no right to sue); *Newton Cy.*

Wildlife Ass'n v. USFS, 113 F.3d 110 (8th Cir. 1997) (no right to sue); *HSUS v. Glickman*, 217 F.3d 882 (D.C. Cir. 2000) (rejecting *Newton Cy.* and *Martin* to hold FWS subject to injunction under MBTA). At least in the D.C. Circuit, while "the MBTA provides no private cause of action against the United States government to enforce its provisions, . . . the law of this Circuit is clear: a plaintiff may sue a federal agency under the APA for violations of the MBTA." *Fund for Animals v. Norton*, 281 F. Supp. 2d 209, 217 (D.D.C. 2003) (quoting *Center for Biological Diversity v. Pirie*, 191 F. Supp. 2d at 175). That the BGEPA overlaps with the ESA has created a void in case law interpreting whether APA actions based on the BGEPA are viable, probably because citizens flock to the ESA. Of importance in answering such legal question may be that BGEPA carries criminal and civil penalties, while the MBTA is exclusively a criminal act. *But see Jaeger v. Cellco Partnership*, 2010 U.S. App. LEXIS 25014 (2d Cir. Dec. 10, 2010) (affirming trial court's conclusion that private plaintiffs may use APA to pursue claims against federal agencies for failing to adhere to MBTA and BGEPA, but may not sue state or municipal agencies under the APA).

One must not forget that the Tulalip Nation very likely has its own suite of environmental, animal protection, and/or land use laws. Undoubtedly, they would apply to the tribe and tribal members. This remains an avenue for further research.

While various options exist, perhaps the best involves concerned neighbors forming a nonprofit corporation under Washington law, funded by tax-deductible donations, which then purchases the parcel subject to clear restrictions and covenants never to develop the parcel and to otherwise permit uses as decided by the board of directors. Many land trusts operate this way.

H. WILD AND FREE-ROAMING HORSES AND BURROS ACT

At the turn of the twentieth century, millions of feral horses roamed the rural United States. From 1934 to 1963, however, the United States Forest Service and United States Grazing Service paid privateers to kill mustangs and sell their corpses for pet food. Ranchers could round up horses they wanted and the Forest Service would execute the remainder. See *The Fight to Save Wild Horses*, TIME (Jul. 12, 1971). Furious over the horse-culling measures, which included chasing down equines by air or motor vehicle much to their terror and injury, advocates convinced President Eisenhower to enact the Hunting Wild Horses and Burros on Public Lands Act, P.L. 86-234 (coined the "Wild Horse Annie Act" after Velma Bronn Johnston, an insurance firm secretary from Reno, Nevada). This law prohibited hunting feral horses on federal land by air or motorized vehicle.[7] Despite the Act's

---

[7] However, the Omnibus Parks and Public Lands Management Act of 1996 authorized BLM and the USFS to use helicopters and motorized vehicles for feral horse gathers on public lands. Litigation resulted in a temporary restraining order to prevent helicopters from coming too close to scared herds. On Jan. 23, 2013, the BLM issued Instruction Memorandum No. 2013-059, calling for the suspension of gather operations if the lead contracting officer representative believes the roundup is inhumane or unsafe. Further, it imposed other restrictions, such as limited use of electric prods, summoning of veterinary assistance, provision of fresh, clean water and good quality hay, and protection from inclement weather while being detained.

restriction, numbers continued to plummet, prompting passage of the Wild and Free-Roaming Horses and Burros Act of 1971 ("WFRBHA"), 16 U.S.C. §§ 1331–40. It addressed the competing interests of feral horse advocates opposed to aggressive and cruel population reduction measures, and those of ranchers and hunters who allegedly suffered from overgrazing and soil erosion by the herds, by criminalizing the harassment or killing of feral horses or feral burros on federal land. The new law compelled the Department of Interior's Bureau of Land Management ("BLM") to enforce and protect the animals, study nonlethal sterilization methods, foster adoptions,[8] and create safe harbors on public property.

The Land Policy and Management Act ("FLPMA") of 1976 and the Public Rangelands Improvement Act ("PRIA") of 1978 also amended WFRBHA,[9] resulting in the establishment of 209 herd management areas ("HMAs") dedicated to the preservation of feral horses on federal land, a number that has since declined to 179.[10] Challenges to the constitutionality of the WFRBHA have failed. *See Kleppe v. New Mexico*, 426 U.S. 529 (1976) and *U.S. v. Johnson*, 685 F.2d 337 (9th Cir.1982).

A recent clash over implementation of the WFRBHA has arisen in Wyoming. Half of Wyoming's wild equids reside in one of four HMAs — Salt Wells Creek, Great Divide Basin, White Mountain, Little Colorado — more than two million

---

[8] Several lawsuits brought by the Animal Protection Institute critiqued BLM's "adopt-a-horse" program (43 C.F.R. § 4740.2(b) (1977)) and disregard of "adopter" intent, namely, to slaughter or use as rodeo stock. The PRIA amended the Act to limit to four the number of excess animals who could be adopted unless the Secretary made a written finding that the person could humanely care for more than four. 16 U.S.C. § 333(b)(2)(B). Such an adopter needed to be "qualified" and "assure humane treatment and care." *API v. Hodel*, 671 F. Supp. 695 (1987), *aff'd*, 860 F.2d 920 (9th Cir.1988) held that BLM could no longer ignore such contradictory adopter intentions when transferring title, rejecting the federal government's assertion that it could knowingly adopt out horses to individuals who intended to put the animals to commercial use after providing humane treatment for one year:

> Viewed in light of the WHA's other statutory provisions that explicitly forbid the commercial exploitation of wild equids, see 16 U.S.C. Secs. 1333(d)(5), 1338(a)(4), and strive to insure their humane treatment, see 16 U.S.C. Secs. 1333(b)(2), 1333(c), 1338(a)(3), 1338a, it would be unreasonable to maintain that Congress intended a qualified individual to include a person who has expressed an intent to commercially exploit these "living symbols of the historic and pioneer spirit" that "enrich the lives of the American people." See 16 U.S.C. Sec. 1331.

Id., at 926. Review of legislative history supported this conclusion:

> Legislative history thus reveals that Congress intended the one-year wait for title transfer to act as a probationary period that would weed out unfit adopters. The Secretary's disregard for the announced future intentions of adopters undercuts Congress' desire to insure humane treatment for wild horses and burros. In fact, it renders the adoption process a farce, for the one-year requirement of humane treatment and care serves no purpose if on the day the one-year period expires, the adopter can proceed to the slaughterhouse with his horses or burros.

Id., at 927. However, the Burns Amendment of 2004 (2004 H.R. 4818, P.L. 108-447) largely eviscerated such considerations by changing 16 U.S.C. 1333(e) to provide that the BLM retained plenary ability to sell any "excess animal" over ten years of age or who was offered unsuccessfully for adoption at least three times, for any purpose and "without limitation" – including for sale to the highest bidder at local sale yards or livestock selling facilities. Once sold, the "excess animal" would no longer be deemed a wild free-roaming horse or burro under the Act.

[9] *See also* http://www.blm.gov/wo/st/en/prog/wild_horse_and_burro/wh_b_information_center/facts_and_stats/history_of_the_program.html.

[10] http://www.blm.gov/wo/st/en/prog/whbprogram/history_and_facts/quick_facts.html.

acres of private and public land known as the "Wyoming checkerboard." Members of the Rock Springs Grazing Association ("RGSA") control much of the rangeland in southern Wyoming, grazing about 60,000 sheep and 5,000 cattle with generous taxpayer subsidies. They have repeatedly complained that about 1,300 wild horses roaming throughout that area have interfered with their operations. On Jul. 27, 2011, the RGSA sued the federal government asking that it order the removal of all wild horses from private land and adjacent public lands in the checkerboard. Evidence strongly suggests that Deputy Assistant Secretary for Land and Minerals Management Sylvia Baca invited RGSA to sue the Department of the Interior as a means to secure funding to perform the roundups, which it did, whereupon the federal government half-heartedly resisted the suit and quickly settled in a consent decree that gave the RGSA what it demanded. Andrew Cohen, *How the Department of the Interior Sold Out America's Wild Horses*, THE ATLANTIC (Mar. 21, 2013).

The July 2011 consent decree between the BLM and RGSA authorized the zeroing-out (roundup and killing) of wild horses in the Salt Wells and Great Divide Basin HMAs, sterilization of wild horses in the White Mountain HMA, and halving of those in the Adobe Town HMA. In short, the free-roaming horses in Wyoming will be reduced from approximately 3,685 to 2,070.

I.   FOX AND COYOTE PENNING

Eighteen states permit fox and coyote penning, a barbaric practice that relies on trapping and trafficking wild foxes and coyotes to pen operators who use them to train packs of hunting dogs by setting them upon the foxes and coyotes in enclosures from which they cannot escape.[11] In May 2011, the Animal Welfare Institute, Project Coyote, and the ALDF sued the Indiana Department of Natural Resources following its decision to waive state permit requirements to allow the WCI Fohound Training Preserve to possess wildlife — for example, coyotes. Plaintiffs contended that WCI did not "possess" the animals because they could allegedly escape from the fenced enclosure. A 2012 investigation, compelled by the trial court after WCI ignored the request for inspection, confirmed the presence of no exits. Also discovered were what WCI described as safe havens for fleeing coyotes, which were in fact metal pipes large enough for hounds to enter from both ends. On Nov. 30, 2012, plaintiffs obtained a default judgment declaring WCI's possession of coyotes unlawful under Indiana law. *ALDF, Inc. v. Robert Carter*, Marion Cy. Sup. Ct. 49D04-11-05-PL-018181 (2011). Recent efforts to prohibit penning have made gains. *See* Anna Stolley Persky, *New Law in Virginia Will Ban Controversial Fox-penning Sport*, A.B.A.J. (Jul. 1, 2014).

J.   CONTEST KILLS AND ANTIGAMBLING LAWS

While some jurisdictions prohibit giving away of a live animal as a prize in a drawing, lottery, contest, sweepstakes, or other game (*see* Pa. Stat. § 5511.1(a)), what of bestowing prizes upon those who kill animals? Notwithstanding the legality

---

[11] To learn more, see http://www.projectcoyote.org/documents/IN_Penning_Report_PC_ALDF_AWI_Final_low_res.pdf.

of the type, timing, and manner of wildlife trapping and hunting, wagered hunts may violate antigambling laws. A recent example involved Duane Freilino, organizer of the JMK Coyote Hunting Contest in Crane, Or. Competitors pay an entry fee to kill as many coyotes as possible and claim cash purses for such accolades as "most kills," "largest kill" and, quite disturbingly, the greatest number of kills by a child. Freilino also promoted the event by hosting a "Calcutta" tournament, understood to mean an open auction in conjunction with a tournament where gamblers buy in, bet on outcomes, and win prize money for each place their bet advances in the tournament. The BLM had previously denied Freilino a special use permit to conduct this killing contest, so he relocated it to private land. Though no bag limits or other restrictions to the coyote hunt existed under Oregon fish and wildlife law, local resident Louann Thompson, ALDF, and Project Coyote challenged the event as a public nuisance per Oregon's Nuisance Abatement Act, ORS § 105.555, citing gambling as the nuisance as defined in ORS § 167.177. They sought declaratory and injunctive relief, as well as attorney's fees and damages.

Freilino asserted that the Eighth Annual JMK Coyote Hunting Contest was not gambling because it was not a game of chance, but instead relied on "skill and demonstration of hunting prowess." By definition, he urged, the Contest was not gambling because it was directly influenced by the participants. He counterclaimed for IIED, accusing the defendants of crank calling, threatening to harm or kill him, his wife, and four-year-old daughter, publicly berating him in the press, Internet and social media, threatening to call child protective services against him, hacking into his computer, and harming his reputation, for which he sought $100,000. *Thompson v. Freilino*, Harney Cy. Cir. Ct. No. 14-01-25CV.[12] Though the trial judge refused to issue a temporary restraining order to stop the hunt, Freilino was ordered to halt any planned betting as unlawful gambling. Meanwhile, the plaintiffs filed an anti-SLAPP motion to strike the counterclaim. Before the judge ruled on the merits, the parties entered into a Jun. 20, 2014, consent decree that enjoined Freilino from ever sponsoring, promoting, hosting, or otherwise creating any hunting contests within the state of Oregon, and for him to pay the plaintiffs $4,000 in attorney's fees and $1,252 in costs. Further, if he violated the order, he would pay stipulated damages.

---

[12] Pleadings are available on request from the author, received thanks to Jessica Blome, the lead ALDF attorney on the case.

Chapter 15

ANIMAL WELFARE ACT

Less than 50 years old, the Animal Welfare Act ("AWA"), 7 U.S.C. § 2131 et seq., has gone through several significant amendments. The AWA and the United States Department of Agriculture ("USDA") and its Animal & Plant Health Inspection Service ("APHIS")'s implementing regulations, 9 C.F.R. §§ 1.1–12.1, set the minimum standards for the treatment of certain species in research, exhibition, transport, and sale. Civil and criminal penalties apply. Businesses covered by the AWA include "dealers," typically animal breeders and brokers, auction operators, or those who sell domesticated, laboratory, exotic, or wild animals. Class A dealers deal only in animals they breed and raise; the rest are Class B. Retail pet stores selling directly to owners, hobbyists, animal shelters, and boarding kennels are not regulated. Class C licensees, known as "exhibitors," include zoological parks, marine mammal shows, circuses, carnivals, and promotional or educational exhibits. However, agricultural shows, fairs, rodeos, kennel club competitions, game preserves, and nonexhibiting private collectors are exempt.

"Animal transporters" require a registration, not a license. They include airlines, railroads, and truckers. Research facilities must register as well, and include government-run research institutions, drug firms, universities, diagnostic labs, and facilities studying marine mammals. Federal institutions, primary and secondary schools, and agricultural research institutions are exempt. If registered or licensed, the business or individual must comply with all federal regulations, including recordkeeping and standards of care. Licensing records may be accessed through the Animal Care Information System ("ACIS"). https://acissearch.aphis.usda.gov/LPASearch/faces/Warning.jspx.

A. AMENDATORY HISTORY

First enacted in 1966, the Laboratory Animal Welfare Act ("LAWA") focused on six species — cats, dogs, nonhuman primates, rabbits, hamsters, and guinea pigs used in research, with emphasis on pets stolen and sold to research facilities. LAWA was undoubtedly motivated by two articles in print media, the dog farm (modernly, "puppy mill") exposé *Concentration Camps for Dogs*, 60(5) LIFE 22–28 (Feb. 4, 1966) and Coles Phinizy's November 29, 1965 *Sports Illustrated* article on a Dalmatian named Pepper, who had been euthanized in an experimental procedure at a New York hospital after disappearing from her family's yard. LAWA required dealers of research-destined dogs and cats to obtain a license, and research facilities to register if using dogs or cats purchased in interstate commerce or receiving federal research money. President Richard Nixon signed 1970 amendments that not only renamed the LAWA as the AWA, but expanded the definition of "animal" to include all warm-blooded laboratory animals; imposed minimum care standards on in-state and interstate transported animals, not just those crossing state lines; and required anesthetics and tranquilizers during certain animal experiments.

Despite the unambiguous definition, the Secretary of Agriculture administratively exempted rats, mice, and birds from the definition of "animal," leaving completely unprotected nearly 90 percent of all creatures used and kept against their wills in laboratories. Nixon's AWA required licensing by exhibitors, defined "research facility," and exempted retail pet stores, agricultural fairs, rodeos, and dog and cat shows.

Increased public awareness of animal fighting enterprises led President Gerald Ford to sign the 1976 amendments, which added Section 26 to the AWA, thereby outlawing interstate or foreign transport of animals in fighting ventures, and revised standards imposed on "carriers" to include enterprises transporting regulated animals. They also mandated "carrier" licensure. The law passed over objection by the USDA and Attorney General, who deemed animal fighting a state and local issue. The early 1970s brought reports of animal casualties in transportation from suffocation or exposure to severe temperatures, prompting amendments to establish standards for shipping containment, food, water, rest, ventilation, temperature, and handling.

The Silver Spring Monkey Case, spurred by undercover volunteer and co-founder of People for the Ethical Treatment of Animals ("PETA") Alex Pacheco's documentation of several AWA violations by Dr. Edward Taub at the Institute for Biological Research in Silver Spring, Maryland, led to the seizure of 17 monkeys from his laboratory and his prosecution for animal cruelty, as discussed herein. Thanks to Pacheco and PETA, national concern over the mistreatment of laboratory animals reached a critical mass, prompting President Ronald Reagan to sign the 1985 Improved Standards for Laboratory Animals Act ("ISLAA"). In addition to broadly expanding the USDA's jurisdiction over animals kept in labs, used in experiments, higher education, on exhibit, or in captive marine environments, the amendments imposed exercise requirements for dogs, psychological enrichment for primates, gave rise to the Institutional Animal Care and Use Committee ("IACUC"), and established what is now known as the Animal Welfare Information Center ("AWIC"). IACUCs vet experimentation proposals at registered institutions to ensure the implementation of alternatives to experiments involving undue pain or suffering, or unnecessary duplication. The AWA was further amended in 1990, including the Pet Theft Act, which imposed a mandatory five-day hold at all shelters before permitting sale to research facilities, and prohibited dealers from selling dogs and cats they did not breed unless they could furnish certified records proving the animals' origins.

In 2000, after facing a lawsuit by the Animal Legal Defense Fund, the USDA agreed to amend the definition of animals to include rats, mice, and birds. Congress passed the Farm Security and Rural Investment Act of 2002, which President George W. Bush signed into law, thereby amending the AWA to redefine the definition of "animal" to match the regulatory definition challenged by ALDF. In so doing, the legislature arrested the regulatory transformation, reverting to a definition that excluded "birds, mice of the genus Mus, and rats of the genus Rattus, bred for use in research." On a positive note, the 2002 amendments increased the maximum animal fighting penalty from $5,000 to $15,000 and made it a misdemeanor to ship birds in interstate commerce for fighting purposes or to sponsor or exhibit a bird in a fight knowing any of the birds were so shipped (even in a state legalizing bird fighting).

In 2007, President George W. Bush signed the Animal Fighting Prohibition Act, which amended the AWA to make it a felony punishable by up to three years in prison to knowingly sell, buy, transport, or deliver, in interstate or foreign commerce, a knife, gaffe, or other sharp instrument for attaching to the leg of a bird for use in an animal fighting venture. It also made it a felony to use the mail to trade in such devices or promote animal fighting ventures. At that time, however, one could lawfully *attend* an animal fighting event. The deep criticism and spotlight on NFL quarterback Michael Vick ushered passage of the 2008 Farm Bill, which further stiffened animal fighting penalties by raising the maximum period of incarceration to five years, and adding more precise definitions to eliminate any vagueness that have stymied efforts to cripple dog-fighting enterprises. It also prohibited importation of dogs for resale unless at least six months of age, healthy, and current on vaccinations — with certain exceptions for research, veterinary treatment, and Hawaii imports from certain countries.

B.   LAX ENFORCEMENT

APHIS's Animal Care program enforces the AWA as to about 12,000 licensees and registrants. In 2012, it did so with an annual budget of only $28 million. Predictably, a USDA Office of the Inspector General May 2010 audit concluded that the Animal Care program's administration against recidivist dealers was ineffective, it misused guidelines to lower penalties for AWA violators, and some large breeders bypassed the AWA by selling animals via the Internet. APHIS AC Program Inspections of Problematic Dealers, May 2010, www.usda.gov/oig/webdocs/33002-4-SF.pdf. On Sept. 17, 2013, APHIS implemented a final rule, 78 FR 57227 (2013), which amended 9 C.F.R. Pts. 1 and 2, revised the definition of "retail pet store" to require licensing by breeders in "sight unseen" transactions that did not involve "face-to-face" delivery to customers but typically occurred over the Internet. "Brick and mortar" stores remained exempt from licensing and inspection under the AWA. Photos, Skype, webcam, and other electronic methods of communication could not evade licensing obligations by such entities. Of course, increasing the number of licensees without a concomitant boost in operational revenue was a recipe for irregular and fruitless enforcement.

The sting of the 2010 OIG report exposed the inefficacy of APHIS in the puppy mill context but was certainly not the first such rebuke of the notoriously underachieving agency. A January 1995 audit report by the OIG focused on various research facilities and licensed dealers, observing that APHIS penalties, which were often so low that violators regarded them as a cost of doing business, were not aggressively collected and were often arbitrarily reduced. Moreover, inspectors accommodated, rather than suspended, facilities repeatedly refusing access. A revisitation of deficiencies from the OIG's 1992 report proved that APHIS still did not reinspect all facilities with serious violations. USDA, OIG Audit Report No. 33600-1-CH (January 1995).

Aside from lobbying for more funds and shaming APHIS, what steps could be taken to ensure that the AWA, subject to so many significant changes that would conceivably make appreciable differences to the lives of the covered animals, would actually demand accountability among the regulated entities? Recognizing the futility of an unfunded mandate (albeit prior to the 2010 OIG report), several individuals, including Pia Salk, utilized state law as a means to enforce the AWA. By filing a taxpayer action under California's Code Civ. Proc. § 526(a), they sought a judgment against the Regents of the University of California to declare unlawful and discontinue animal research in violation of the AWA. The Regents demurred, claiming, *inter alia*, federal preemption. *Salk v. Regents of the University of California*, 2008 Cal. App. Unpub. LEXIS 10292 (Dec. 19, 2008). Finding no private right of action under the AWA, the trial court dismissed the complaint. Salk appealed. In a 3-0 decision, the California Court of Appeals affirmed. The principle of conflict preemption applied. In rejecting the presumption against preemption, the court found that Salk was trying to police and supervise compliance with federal law when Congress never intended private citizens to do so, and that to allow Salk to pursue her taxpayer action would prevent accomplishment of a federal goal — e.g., using animals in certain research to "advance knowledge of cures and treatments for diseases and injuries afflicting humans and animals." *Salk* sounded the death knell to private enforcement of the AWA, at least in California. It reasoned that a contrary ruling "would raise the specter of exposing research facilities to decisions of judges and juries that might inject inconsistency and unpredictability into laboratory research, thus increasing the costs of federally funded research[,]" as well as "might also discourage scientists from entering many lines of medical inquiry." States that incorporate federal law by reference, such that a violation of the AWA would constitute a violation of state law, might permit taxpayer plaintiffs like Salk to privatize enforcement of the AWA.

Another method to achieve meaningful public oversight of APHIS utilizes the Administrative Procedure Act ("APA"), 5 U.S.C. § 702, which confers a right of action upon a person injured by agency action. Take, for instance, the decision by the USDA and APHIS to leave rats, mice, and birds unregulated under the AWA, an official position since 1971 (36 FR 24919 (1971)), despite Congress defining "animal" as:

> [A]ny live or dead dog, cat, monkey (nonhuman primate mammal), guinea pig, hamster, rabbit, or such other warm-blooded animal, as the Secretary may determine is being used, or is intended for use, for research, testing, experimentation, or exhibition purposes, or as a pet.

7 U.S.C. § 2132(g). In 1990, USDA regulations refined the definition of animal to include the six originally identifies species but explicitly excluding "[b]irds, rats of the genus Rattus and mice of the genus Mus bred for use in research . . . " 9 C.F.R. § 1.1. That year, two animal welfare organizations and two individuals sued the Secretary under the APA, claiming that the regulatory definition disregarded the Congressional mandate to regulate other such "warm-blooded mammals." Lack of standing sidelined *ALDF v. Espy*, 23 F.3d 496 (D.C. Cir. 1994) ("ALDF I"), vacating *ALDF v. Madigan*, 781 F. Supp. 797 (D.D.C. 1992).

In 1998, ARDF and In Vitro International, Inc. filed a petition for rulemaking to amend the regulation to include the trio. Thereafter, suit commenced, seeking declaratory and injunctive relief. Beaver College psychology student Kristine Gausz claimed aesthetic injury to her interest in studying rats in a humane environment. As the USDA regulations exempted rats from the AWA, she argued having no choice but to suffer in the presence of animals receiving "inadequate housing, water, food, and veterinary care." In a departure from the *ALDF I* ruling, the district court found standing for Gausz to permit review of the USDA regulation, thereby denying the Secretary's motion to dismiss. *ARDF v. Glickman*, 101 F. Supp. 2d 7 (D.D.C. 2000). Thereafter, the parties entered into a stipulation to dismiss the action without prejudice with the full expectation that the USDA would grant the pending petition and bring much-deserved protection to those three species after 35 years of regulatory marginalization. Yet, as noted above, the legislative branch checkmated the executive branch by passing the 2002 Farm Bill, thus codifying the discriminatory agency definition that had been in place since 1971.

Animal welfare organizations again wielded the APA in *Animal Legal Defense Fund v. Veneman*, 2004 U.S. Dist. LEXIS 31333 (N.D. Cal. Mar. 2, 2004), attempting to countermand the failure of the USDA to adopt a policy guiding zoos, research facilities, and other regulated entities to ensure psychological well-being for nonhuman primates, in order to comply with ISLAA, which instructed the USDA to "promulgate standards to govern the humane handling, care, treatment, and transportation of animals by dealers, research facilities, and exhibitors." 7 U.S.C. § 2143(a) (1). Such standards were to include "minimal requirements . . . for a physical environment adequate to promote the psychological well-being of primates." 7 U.S.C. § 2143(a)(2)(B). Though the Secretary did propose a regulation in 1989 (54 FR 10897, 10917), the final version adopted in 1991 left much unsaid. ALDF challenged part of the vague rule that delegated decisionmaking authority by embracing an undefined set of "accepted professional standards, as cited in appropriate professional journals or reference guides, and as directed by the attending veterinarian," 9 C.F.R. § 3.81(a). In *ALDF v. Secretary of Agric.*, 813 F. Supp. 882 (D.D.C. 1993), the district court struck down 3.81 as arbitrary and capricious and contrary to law. The D.C. Circuit Court of Appeals reversed. *ALDF v. Glickman*, 204 F.3d 229 (D.C. Cir. 2000).

But this did not cure the interpretive difficulties of 3.81, which the USDA recognized in its proposed 1999 "Policy of Environmental Enhancement for Nonhuman Primates," which stated that "additional information on how to meet the standards in § 3.81 is necessary." 64 FR 38145, 38146. Yet in December 2002 and March 2003, APHIS employees publicly announced that the USDA would not honor the 1999 draft policy, leaving 3.81 in place. Though dismissed for lack of subject matter jurisdiction (i.e., the USDA met its statutory duty to act, leaving nothing requiring judicial review), the Ninth Circuit reversed and remanded, but not before the en banc panel vacated the three-judge ruling on ALDF's motion citing a settlement. *ALDF v. Veneman*, 490 F.3d 725 (9th Cir. 2007) (en banc), vacating 469 F.3d 826 (9th Cir. 2006).

Chapter 16

ANIMAL LAW PERTAINING TO MASS TRANSIT

A. RAILROADS

Animals who cross paths with trains rarely escape the encounter unscathed. While velocities and stopping distances vary, a locomotive's fixed route means it has nowhere to go except along the trajectory of a dedicated railroad. Even with the keenest eyesight, a train engineer who hits the air brakes at the earliest possible moment may not be able to bring a 100-car freighter to a standstill before coming upon grazing cattle. For this reason, "A railroad track is itself a warning of danger." *McBeth v. Northern Pac. R. Co.*, 204 P.2d 248, 252–53 (Wash. 1949). "Every man," and certainly nonhuman animal, "who goes upon a railroad track courts danger." *Schommers v. Gr. N. Ry. Co.*, 172 P. 848, 848–49 (Wash. 1918). But a dog, cow, or horse may not perceive the risk that a speeding train will be coming around the mountain without warning. Legal principles of train liability recognize this species distinction, with consequences for both railroad companies and animal guardians. Failure to control or confine animals who stray onto an active track may be held comparatively at fault on the assumption that, "A man who willingly abandons his property to destruction, or purposely exposes it to known danger, has no right, either in law or morals, to invoke the assistance of the courts of justice to secure pay for it." *Welty v. Indianapolis & V. R. Co.*, 4 N.E. 410 (Ind. 1886) (quoted in *Jones v. N. Pac. Ry. Co.*, 100 P.2d 20 (Wash. 1940)).

1. Collisions

A general familiarity with the relevant regulatory agencies may help the practitioner obtain historical data on railway fatalities and prior enforcement actions. In 1966, Congress passed the Department of Transportation Act, which established the Federal Railroad Administration ("FRA"). Thereafter, in 1970, Congress passed the Federal Railroad Safety Act ("FRSA"), 49 U.S.C. § 20106. FRSA preempts local regulations affecting interstate and intrastate railroad safety. The DOT's Office of Safety notes that accidents with nonhumans are not collected by the FRA (at least not as of 2011).[1] That said, data from state regulatory agencies may bear fruit. For instance, the Washington Utilities & Transportation Commission regulates railroad companies operating in Washington State investigates casualties and fatalities.

---

[1] Letter of Denise Kollehlon, FRA FOIA officer, to author on Mar. 16, 2011. See 49 C.F.R. Pt. 225 for details pertaining to railroad reportable accidents and incidents and FRA investigative protocols.

At common law in most states, tracks need not be fenced, and lack of fencing is not deemed negligent. *See, e.g., Timm v. Northern Pac. R. Co.*, 13 P. 415 (Wash. 1887). Historically, railroads had duties of care to keep adequate lookout for livestock, to slow or stop the train when not dangerous to passengers, to have working brakes and appliances, to avoid attractive nuisances, and to sound a warning of the train's approach. Further, where railroads acquire rights-of-way through enclosed lands, they cannot throw the close open without the other's consent, allowing stock to enter, trespass, and be struck. *Hubert v. Connell Northern Ry. Co.*, 129 P. 105 (Wash. 1913).

Most states have abrogated the common law by imposing statutory liability on railroads that fail to install substantial fences and sufficient cattle guards at ends of sidetracks or switches, along the right-of-way, and at each crossing. *See, e.g.*, N.M. Stat. §§ 77-16-16 (railroads, fencing of lines, damages for injury to livestock), 77-16-17 (requirements of railroad fence), 77-16-18 (report of killed or crippled livestock; inspection and removal); RCW § 81.52.050. Natural barriers along the track do not excuse liability where livestock are free to access the track by moving around the end of the barriers. *Taylor v. Spokane Falls & Northern Ry. Co.*, 73 P. 499 (Wash. 1903). Strict liability has also been imposed on railroads for failing to maintain such obstacles. *See, e.g.*, RCW § 81.52.060. Affirmative defenses to animals injured by trains include comparative fault, trespass, and contributory negligence in failure to abide by running at-large laws. Relevant New Mexico cases include *Hittson v. Chicago, R. I. & P. Ry. Co.*, 86 P.2d 1037 (N.M. 1939) and *Reagan v. El Paso & N.E. Ry. Co.*, 106 P. 376 (N.M. 1910).

Train collisions with dogs frequently yield defense verdicts. Only one such case wound its way to the United States Supreme Court. *Sentell v. New Orleans & Carrollton R. Co.*, 166 U.S. 698 (1897), examined the death of Countess Lona, a pregnant Newfoundland struck by an electric car. Decided not on the merits of whether Sentell was imprudent in allowing her to walk the streets unrestrained and cross a live track, instead it focused on the issue of damages by upholding the constitutionality of a Louisiana law that stripped Lona of any value because Sentell did not license her. Other cases, however, did look to the question of care.

Chicago, R. I. & P. R. Co. v. Reeves, 231 S.W.2d 103 (Ark. 1950) found no liability for a train striking two dogs near a bridge, where the whistle promptly sounded and the train could not stop in time. Nor was the railway company held liable where its train killed a dog crossing the tracks near the depot. Although seen, *St. Louis-San Francisco Ry. Co. v. Matlock*, 132 S.W.2d 657 (Ark. 1939) found the company bore no responsibility because the whistle was blown and bell rang as it approached the platform on which the dog was standing, and an emergency stop would have endangered passenger safety. On the other hand, the quickness of a dog relative to a slower-moving bovine may not be relied upon to absolve the railroad of its duty to exercise care to avoid running over an animal. *St. Louis, I.M. & S. Ry. Co. v. Rhoden*, 123 S.W. 798 (Ark. 1909). Where, if keeping proper lookout, the engineer and fireman could see the dog so near track as to indicate danger, failure to blow the whistle or frighten the dog was actionable negligence. *St. Louis, I.M. & S. Ry. Co. v. Fuller*, 165 S.W. 949 (Ark. 1914).

Occasionally, efforts to sonically repel animals may work too well, instilling terror and causing the animal to race away in the opposite direction toward even greater peril. *St. Louis Southwestern Ry. Co. v. Conger*, 105 S.W. 1177 (Ark. 1907) found no fault by the engineer letting off steam to frighten a straying mare from the track, when she injured herself on a winged fence extending across the track. On the other hand, needlessly blowing a whistle in the city, causing a horse to run and hurt the driver, will establish liability. *Weil v. St. Louis S.W. Ry. Co.*, 43 S.W. 967 (Ark. 1898).

Failure to remove attractants adjacent to the track may also result in blame. *St. Louis, I.M. & S.R. Co. v. Wilson*, 171 S.W. 471 (Ark. 1914) held the company liable for hurting animals drawn to the railroad by failing to empty accumulating feed stuffs on the right-of-way or maintaining fence to keep them out. And *St. Louis, I.M. & S. Ry. Co. v. Newman*, 127 S.W. 735 (Ark. 1910) deemed the railroad responsible for having left leaking raw cottonseed oil cars in an open space on the right-of-way, allowing it to fill the ditch with oil, which the cattle lapped up, causing them to die.

Train collision cases turn on the facts. In November 1938, Toppenish, Washington, herders assumed the pasture was enclosed and made camp at dusk. Their cows grazed near and on the track. Moving at 60 mph, the train first saw them 800–1,000 feet ahead. The brakes were promptly applied and all wheels locked, but no alarm sounded. The passenger train struck the cows at 40 mph and killed 13. *Jones v. Northern Pac. Ry. Co.*, 100 P.2d 20 (Wash. 1940) held the railroad not negligent for failing to keep adequate lookout, failing to stop or slow the train, failing to sound warning of the train's approach, and failing to maintain a right of way fence and private gate. Rather, the herders were deemed contributorily negligent for failure to keep cattle from trespassing on the right-of-way and failure to ascertain whether the field was securely fenced.

In May 1897, herders in Spokane camped with five horses for the night. The five-acre triangular field had fences on two sides, although a portion remained open. Before bedding down, the herders secured permission from the premises owner and turned their horses loose to graze after being told no trains come after 8:00 p.m. They were situated 375 feet from the track. No doubt mistaken as to the schedule, a train coming up the track later that evening at normal velocity and with operational air brakes caught the herders by surprise. At first sight, the horses were four to five car lengths away. Three horses died from the impact. *Dickey v. Northern Pac. Ry. Co.*, 53 P. 347 (Wash. 1898), found the railroad not negligent notwithstanding a law establishing prima facie negligence if the railroad failed to fence the track. It deemed the herders contributorily negligent for failing to ensure the track was fenced before letting them trespass on the right of way.

At 3:00 a.m. in November 1913 in Balch, Washington, the train fireman observed colts 200 feet down the track. The train was traveling 28 to 30 mph with 16 cars — a light load. The curved track prevented the engineer from seeing the horses until the engine straightened out. Though the fireman called the engineer, who immediately shut off the steam and set the air brakes, the freight train crushed three colts, who ran 400 feet before being overtaken. The trial court found the railroad negligent as a matter of law in failing to stop the train within 600 to 650 feet. The Washington Supreme Court reversed in *Benn v. Chicago, M. & St. P. Ry. Co.*, 154 P. 1082 (Wash. 1916), finding they exercised due care even though courts have held railroads negligent as a matter of law where a two-coach length train does not stop within 150–200 feet while traveling 6–8 mph or a two-coach length train traveling 35 mph does not stop within 700 to 800 feet. Benn argued that the company failed to comply with Rem. & Bal. Code 8730, 8731, which required the railroad to build cattle guards at each crossing, sidetrack, and switch, as well as fencing along the right of way. The Supreme Court found the statute incomprehensible and that the law only created a presumption of negligence, which the defendant rebutted.

In August 1902, an empty logging train was traveling 10–12 mph down a 1% grade. Rounding a curve, the engineer saw horses 250–300 feet away. The track sat on high grade. Ninety feet beyond the horses' position was a trestle 15 feet off the ground. Rafferty's horses died after being pushed 150 feet by the train onto the trestle where they fell over the side. The train never stopped, though they claimed to have done everything in their power to do so, including traveling at a customary speed, using ordinary appliances, officered by a proper crew, setting the brake as soon as possible, reversing the engine, and blowing the whistle. Rafferty argued the train could have stopped in 60 feet. A jury found for Rafferty and awarded $200. The Washington Supreme Court affirmed, adding that knowledge by the company that animals would be frequently encountered at this location and caught in such a trap favored a finding of fault. *Rafferty v. Portland, V. & Y. Ry. Co.*, 73 P. 382 (Wash. 1903).

One early morning in Lewis Cy., Washington, a four-car passenger train was traveling 25 mph to the depot. The fireman had an unobstructed view. He could have seen a horse 500 feet away coming up an embankment onto the tracks but failed to stop the train, causing it to strike the horse, carry it forward, throw it into a stationary freight car, crushing its head. The jury found for the plaintiff, and the Supreme Court affirmed. Though technically a trespasser, and while the train had no duty to fence the area so close to the depot, the evidence strongly suggested negligence, and the state law concerning stock running at large did not then apply in this county. *Willett v. Oregon-Wash. R. & Nav. Co.*, 162 P. 14 (Wash. 1916).

As can be gathered from the foregoing, particularly given technological advances in braking, alerting, and early warning systems, modern railroads have a duty to keep a lookout for animals, make sounds to scare animals off tracks, have working brakes and appliances, maintain fencing and cattle guards (if required by statute[2]), avoid attractive nuisances, anticipate problem areas and traps, and operate the train sober.[3] Animal guardians have a duty to keep animals from trespassing on the right-of-way and from running at-large.

---

[2] For instance, RCW § 81.52.050 requires every person, company, or corporation controlling or managing a railroad to build a substantial fence at every point where a roadway or other public highway cross the track, as well as a sufficient cattle guard. This law only applies outside city limits, or any sidetrack or switch. Failure to do so creates strict liability for livestock killed. RCW § 81.52.060.

[3] RCW § 9.91.020 makes it a gross misdemeanor for an engineer, motorman, gripman, conductor, switch tender, fireman, bridge tender, flagger, or signalman, to regulate or run a train on a railway while intoxicated. See also N.C. Gen. Stat. § 14-281 (class 2 misdemeanor).

2. Humane Transit

In the nineteenth century, most farmed animals moved across the United States stuffed into boxcars for several days on end, causing intolerable suffering, unsanitary conditions, and casualties. In 1873, Congress passed the Twenty-Eight-Hour Law, to require provision of food, water, and rest at various points on the line. A 1906 law replaced the 1873 version, which was later amended in 1994 to include common carrier vehicles and vessels traversing by ground. The 28-Hour Law, 49 U.S.C. § 80502 (1994) states that a rail carrier, express carrier, or common carrier (except air or water), receiver, trustee, or lessee of one of those carriers, or owner or master of vessel transporting animals from a place in one state, the District of Columbia, or a territory or possession of the United States through or to another such place, may not confine animals in that vehicle or vessel for more than 28 consecutive hours without unloading for food, water, and rest. Sheep may be confined for 36 hours when the 28-hour period ends at night. Ineluctable circumstances excuse strict compliance, or where the owner of the animals requests in writing that the period extend from 28 to 36 hours.[4]

The unloading period must last for at least five consecutive hours. 42 U.S.C. § 80502(b). The Act does not apply where the vehicle or vessel provides food, water, space, and an opportunity to rest. *Id.*, at (c); however, "opportunity for rest" means the ability to lie down. *U.S. v. Boston & M.R.R.*, 117 F.2d 424 (1st Cir. 1941) (all animals must have enough area to lie down simultaneously); *U.S. v. Powell*, 65 F.2d 793 (4th Cir. 1933) (accord). Knowing and willful failure to comply yields a civil penalty between $100 and $500 per violation. *Id.*, at (d). Most states have enacted their own transit cruelty laws, largely mirroring federal law.[5] Whether state or federal, enforcement remains lax.

By the twenty-first century, the primary mode for transporting more than 95 percent of all farmed animals was by short or long haul semi-trailer truck. U.S. Department of Transportation, Bureau of Transportation Statistics, 2002, SCTG Code: 01 — SCTG Description (2-digit): Live animals and live fish. Despite this paradigmatic shift in intermodal transport of livestock, the USDA took the alarming position that the Twenty-Eight Hour Law did not apply to trucks. 60 FR 48362, 48365 (Oct. 19, 1995). This prompted HSUS to initiate a petition for rulemaking to have the agency clarify that "common carrier" and "vehicle" include trucks based on the plain meaning of those terms. On Sept. 28, 2006, the USDA authored a letter to HSUS in response to its 2005 petition to explicitly extend the Act to truckers. The agency claimed that it had reinterpreted "vehicle" to include transportation by motor vehicle per an internal memo prepared in 2003. The public

---

[4] According to the Animal Welfare Institute, neither the USDA nor the USDOJ had investigated or prosecuted 28-Hour Law violations. www.awionline.org/sites/default/frtes/uploads/legacy-uploads/documents/FA-LegalProtections DuringTransport-081910-1282577406-document-23621.pdf.

[5] An attempt to contract around the Law was deemed void by the Washington Supreme Court in *Reynolds v. Great Northern Ry. Co.*, 82 P. 161 (Wash. 1905). A carrier received horses from a connecting carrier after being in a car for ten hours, unloaded them, reloaded them, took them to their destination while confined for over 45 hours without food, some without water, and despite requests to take them to the stockyards for care. The Washington Supreme Court found the carrier negligent independent of the Twenty-Eight Hour Law. *Pierson v. Northern Pac. Ry. Co.*, 100 P. 999 (Wash. 1909).

Statement of Policy Under the Twenty-Eight Hour Law, 9 C.F.R. Pt. 89 (2003), however, makes no such assertion.

Though the law broadly uses the term "animal," the USDA takes the untenable position that it does not apply to birds. 9 C.F.R. § 89.1 (1963) (no mention of chickens, but instead quadrupeds); Henry Cohen, *Brief Summaries of Federal Animal Protection Statutes*, 27, American Law Division (Aug. 15, 2008). Rhode Island, Wisconsin, Pennsylvania, and Connecticut, on the other hand, explicitly protect chickens and turkeys. R.I. Gen. Laws § 4-1-7; Wis. Stat. § 134.52; Pa. Stat. § 5511(e); Conn. Gen. Stat.§ 53-249.

Does each animal deprived the rest period present a separate violation, or does the law enforce violations *en masse*? Under the former version of the law, the unit of offense was not measured by number of shipments on the same train, nor was the train the unit of offense, but one penalty accrued for each period that lawful confinement expired (i.e., 28-36 hours). Subsequent penalties arose every 28–36 hour period thereafter. *Baltimore & O.S.W.R., Co. v. U.S.*, 220 U.S. 94 (1911); *U.S. v. Watson-Durand-Kasper Grocery Co.*, 251 F. 310 (D.C. Kan. 1917). No current cases interpreting the penalty provision of the law have been found.

3. Claims

When animals perish in transit, the owner may seek remuneration from the carrier. Contracts for carriage may set forth deadlines for noticing claims, filing suit, and limiting liability, so they should be reviewed with care. For purely intrastate transport, regulations impose drafting parameters. For instance, RCW § 81.29.020 prevents carriers from shortening the claim-filing deadline to less than nine months and the statute of limitation for lawsuits to less than two years. It also voids limitations of liability and damage caps, requiring payment for the full actual loss, damage, or injury, except as to baggage on commercial ferries or motor vehicles or property for which the carrier may establish rates dependent on a declared or released value. In *Wall-a-Hee v. Northern Pac. Ry. Co.*, 41 P.2d 786 (Wash. 1935), the Washington Supreme Court held that while horses were shipped in the baggage car attached to a passenger train, they were not "baggage" in the meaning of the term as articles of personal conveyance for personal use, thus entitling the tribal member to actual value without limitation. In Kansas, if a railway company or corporation fails to pay the full value of an animal killed or wounded within 30 days of demand being made, it shall also pay a reasonable attorney's fee for prosecution of the suit and litigation costs. K.S.A. § 66-296. Unlike other jurisdictions, Kansas holds such carriers strictly liable regardless of negligence for any animal death. K.S.A. § 66-295.

Hypothetical: Fernando Gomez moved to Edmonds, Washington, in late 2009 and began frequenting the off-leash dog park located at the south end of Marina Beach Park. He would visit with his four Huskies — nine-year-old female Boca, nine-year-old male Niko, three-year-old male Chalupa, and eight-year-old male Pasco. During the first visit, Gomez noticed that the southernmost portion of a fence abutted dense overgrowth collecting atop a rocky embankment proving nearly impossible for his dogs to traverse, particularly for the older Boca and Niko. Exercising due care, he examined this area. From his perspective, the tide, boulders, debris, and vegetation formed a barrier precluding any access onto the railroad tracks on the other side of the fence.

Gomez and his dogs used the park approximately two to four times a month. In the summer of 2010, he saw Burlington Northern Santa Fe adding a line and the City installing new fencing. Sometime before November 19, 2010, but after Gomez's summer visit, the barrier's characteristics (i.e., fencing and vegetation) changed. The overgrowth and rock piles were cleared, leaving an easily navigated pathway at least three feet wide immediately adjacent to the fence. In other words, the southernmost end of the fence lost any of its prior utility, permitting easy access onto the tracks. Gomez had reasonably relied upon the preexisting, unbroken natural and artificial barrier observed on dozens of previous uneventful visits to the park.

On November 19, 2010, Gomez took his dogs to the park, arriving about 12:30 p.m. On the many occasions he visited prior to Nov. 19, 2010, his dogs had not entered the tracks or even shown an interest in doing so. Content that the overgrowth of vegetation, piled boulders, and fencing were impenetrable from his dogs' standpoints, he and the dogs used the park without incident. Gomez allowed his dogs to play for about 45 minutes. During this time, he did not see any signage warning that the fence was now useless and no longer sufficiently blocked access to the tracks. He then walked to the center of the park, near a large log running east-west, where he watched the little dogs for about 10 minutes. A horn blast and sight of Chalupa running northbound toward Fernando alerted him to the fact that Boca and Niko were likely in danger. A BNSF freight train had stopped near the entrance to the park. Gomez ran to the southern end of the park, and for the very first time saw the three-foot path permitting easy access to the tracks. He traversed this path and entered the right-of-way to find his dogs trapped underneath the sixth car back from the engine. Gomez screamed, "Stop the train!" Nearly half a dozen people north of him were waving their arms and screaming to get the engineer's attention. The train came to a complete stop.

Boca was tucked down under the train, but moving. Niko appeared in shock. Gomez nearly rescued his dogs when the train began to move again. It completely cleared the scene and did not stop, forcing Gomez and his dogs to suffer an unbearable three minutes until the last car passed. During this time, Gomez watched in horror as Boca picked up her head and tried to stand to walk toward him. She failed repeatedly as the bottom of the train continued to strike her head forcefully, bloodier with each impact. Eventually, she turned, her gaze meeting with Gomez. She recognized him. Realizing she would try to come to him, Gomez screamed, "Lay down! Stay!" but the noise and fear overcame his commands. In a moment indelibly impressed in his mind, Gomez watched as she was decapitated by the wheels of the train.

Meanwhile, Niko had severely labored breathing. Gomez attempted to lift Niko into his arms to carry him to his vehicle and take him to the veterinary hospital. In his efforts to pick up the severely injured Niko, it caused such excruciating pain that Niko bit deeply into Gomez's arm and, then, into Niko's own foot to avert the agony. Police and animal control helped mount Niko on a stretcher and took him to a nearby veterinary hospital, where he was euthanized due to the severity of his injuries. Gomez never sought treatment for the wound inflicted by Niko, even though it caused temporary nerve damage. While it healed within the next few months, Gomez still has a scar, emblematic of the deep psychological harm he endured from witnessing the violent injury and death of his beloved dogs.

In April 2011, still haunted by the incident, Gomez sought counseling with a psychologist. Over the nine sessions, Gomez worked hard to manage the symptoms of depression and post-traumatic stress disorder arising from the incident, including EMDR therapy.

Other incidents having taken place at the park bear mention. On July 9, 2000, a young woman and her dog were struck by a southbound BNSF freight train near the off-leash dog park. After complaining that there was no fence or barrier between the off-leash dog park and the tracks, she told Officer Steer, "Tell your boss to put a fence up." Using rollertape, Officer Steer measured the length of cyclone fencing separating the tracks from the off-leash park as 569.4 feet. The "narrowest point" between the park and the tracks at the top of the embankment was 708.9 feet. In other words, the City permitted a 140-foot opening between the off-leash park and the tracks. Thus, nearly *10 years* before Gomez's tragic incident, the City had reason to know the importance of securing the property to the "narrowest point" to prevent dogs from entering the tracks.

On October 16, 2006, a dog was reported killed on the tracks. City Council member Buckmaster noted that pedestrians and dogs could enter the tracks where the fence ends — yet neither she nor the City did anything about it. Instead, she "still fault[ed] the owner." And the Parks Manager acknowledged that "where the fence ends and out of park boundaries, pedestrians and dogs may get onto tracks."

Also in 2006, the City became aware of a beach erosion problem, putting it on notice that any vegetation or even rocks that might temporarily block access beyond the fence could wash away, leaving a path to the tracks. No steps were taken to prevent erosion, other than to pass the buck to BNSF. The erosion concern was also noted in December 2007. Again, the City took no independent action.

On August 12, 2008, citizen Jeanne Siler emailed an animal control officer saying she saw two dogs on the tracks, describing the potential for a tragedy as "terrifying." She proposed a way to block access or use a warning sign. The officer forwarded this complaint to the director of parks and acknowledged that "dogs have been hit by trains over the years." The City still took no action on the matter.

On June 7, 2009, Jennifer Chin reported that the park was not secure and both her dogs ran onto the tracks. She complained about no secure barrier or signage. The Parks Director remarked that "with the tide out a few hundred feet, it is not and cannot be secure and dogs can wander all the way to Richmond Beach." He thus acknowledged that the off-leash park was *per se* insecure. And though he claimed he would "implement" her suggestion to "sign the park as being NOT SECURE," this in fact did not happen until more than a year later, after another off-leash dog park visitor's complaint is lodged.

In May 2010, the city installed temporary "dog proof fencing" to secure the park from BNSF work. Evidently, the City did so to keep dogs off the tracks, assuming a duty to protect them from a lethal hazard. In June 2010, the Parks Director informed the nonprofit, volunteer-run off-leash area association that it was authorized to cut grass immediately to the west of the north-south boundary fence, thereby exposing a path that would allow dogs access to the tracks.

On August 17, 2010, the Parks Director conveyed his awareness that low tide made it impossible to fence off entirely at the south end, noting in the past they extended the fence "as far as possible" to "try to discourage dogs (and people) from going up and over onto the tracks." Councilmember Buckmaster adds this happened "three or four" times in the prior five years. Indeed, her initial reaction was to do nothing other than to admonish parkgoers to "understand your pet and ensure you have control." Only after a complainant expressed disbelief at her cavalier attitude (calling the fix a no-brainer) did she agree. On this date, the Parks Department began working on a sign that alerted parkgoers the ends of the park were "not securely fenced due to high and low tides." But the signs were not placed anywhere near the south end of the park where the fence permitted dogs to access the tracks.

The City estimates that the park sees 150,000 to 200,000 users per year — or potentially hundreds of dogs and people per day. On August 9, 2007, the Parks Director confirmed there were "two to four hundred dog owners and their dogs visiting the park every day, and even more popular on weekends." Two years earlier, on January 3, 2005, a survey reported an average of "21 dogs per hour" at the beach park, even in the winter, concluding "the dog park has a steady stream of people & pets."

After the Gomez incident, the animal control officer sent an email dated November 26, 2011, stating that this was not the "first dog, or person" she was aware of being hit by a train in that part of the park. She related her conversation with Gomez, concurring with him that despite the "new black fencing," she also wondered why it was not possible "to get 5 more feet of fencing installed so another animal does not get onto the tracks." Critically, on November 26, 2011, she discouraged nearly a dozen people from going that far south.

Is the City negligent for the deaths of Boca and Niko and the bite to Mr. Gomez?

Failure to do what the officer commonsensically proposed is arguably negligent, especially when the Parks Manager acknowledged that at low tide "dogs can proceed further south and climb up rocks and enter onto tracks. . . ." This admission proves the City was aware that the risk to dogs fluctuated with the tide. What did the City do to mitigate this known risk, a latent hazard that would catch by surprise most people not carrying tide tables in their hip pocket, who would glance south and reasonably conclude that the fenceline would extend along and enclose the perimeter of the park (or at the least prevent entrance onto the tracks)? A fenceline that, from the perspective of a park user entering, reading the kiosk, or using the watering facilities, deceptively bends with the coastline and gives the illusion that it extends as far as the eye can see?

On November 29, 2010, the Parks Manager said the parks crew would add 5 to 8 feet of additional fence and new signs near the area where Boca and Niko entered the tracks. But why was this not done before November 19, 2010?[6] Even Councilmember Buckmaster admitted that "what we find is folks don't read signs sometimes." And what of people who do not read English? The City recognized the ineffectiveness of taking a minimalistic approach to guaranteeing dog and human safety, but took no additional action. Clearly, more was possible had the City exercised due care.

When balanced against the risk of harm — a risk so serious as severe injury and death from a speeding train — the cost of adding more signage, extending the fence, barricading the end of the park, or providing a more evident visual (if not sonic) warning was so modest as to compel a conclusion of negligence. The City had an obligation to undertake far more precautions than it had before November 19, 2010, commensurate with the actual peril that it knew and repeatedly acknowledged over the years, as stated above. And if the City could not or would not undertake genuine, substantial steps to ensure that even those who do not read signs will not endanger their dogs, *it should have shut down the park.*

Relevant is the unpublished case of *DeBerge v. City of Seattle*, 2000 Wash. App. LEXIS 3406 (Dec. 26, 2000). Ms. DeBerge was hit by a train when visiting Seattle's Golden Gardens Park in June 1994. The right-of-way bisected the park. She sued the City for negligently failing to discourage park patrons from using well-worn footpaths leading across the tracks from one side of the park to the other, either by erecting a fence or other barrier or warning patrons of the dangers posed by passing trains. The appeals court reversed and remanded after the trial court granted summary judgment for the City. Here, the City of Edmonds owed a unique duty to dog owners given the invitation to let their dogs run loose in a large area that deceptively appears completely segregated from the active rail line.

A landowner may be liable for harm to invitees who stray outside the area of invitation if the landowner maintains the property in way that makes the scope of invitation ambiguous. *Mesa v. Spokane World Exposition*, 570 P.2d 157, 159 (Wash. 1977). Negligent failure to prevent the invitee from straying extends the area of invitation. *Tincani v. Inland Empire Zoological Soc'y*, 875 P.2d 621, 631–32 (Wash. 1994). Thus, the City invited dogs onto the tracks, a fatal temptation.

A possessor of land is liable to the invitee by condition on the land if:

1. He knows of the condition and unreasonable risk of harm to the invitee;

2. Should expect the invitee will not discover or realize danger or will fail to protect against it; and

3. Fails to exercise reasonable care to prevent against danger.

The City may respond that it tried to avoid these outcomes, and that while a dog may not recognize the danger of a railroad, the dog's owner should. But voluntary assumption of duty through affirmative conduct can give rise to liability if not performed with reasonable care, and the failure increases the risk of harm or harm is suffered by reliance on the City's undertaking. *See Sado v. City of Spokane*, 588

---

[6] FRE 407 prevents admission of evidence of subsequent remedial measures to prove negligence, culpability, defective product or design, or need for a warning or instruction. However, it may come in to prove ownership (if disputed) control, and feasibility of precautionary measures.

P.2d 1231, 1233 (Wash Ct. App. 1979); RESTATEMENT 2D TORTS §§ 323, 135 (1965). By establishing an off-leash dog park adjacent to an active rail line and erecting incomplete fencing that gives false assurances of security, however, the City failed in its municipal undertaking. For these reasons, the City should be held negligent. However, Gomez may also bear comparative fault for failing to take reasonable steps to obey the signs that did exist, failing to confirm that the fencing in fact did protect his dogs from trains he knew would come down the tracks, and failing to remain close to his dogs before he lost sight.

Is the City strictly liable?

If the City contends that it was impossible to do more to eliminate the risk of dogs entering the tracks around the "dog-proof fence" through the "narrowest point" of the park and becoming injured or killed, then it is accepting that having an off-leash dog park sandwiched between a high-volume rail line and eroding beach with changing tides condones abnormally dangerous activity for which it might be strictly liable. The RESTATEMENT (2ND) OF TORTS § 520 sets forth six factors to consider in determining whether an activity is abnormally dangerous:

(1) Existence of a high degree of risk of some harm to the person, land, or chattels of others;

(2) Likelihood that the harm resulting from it will be great;

(3) Inability to eliminate the risk by the exercise of reasonable care;

(4) Extent to which the activity is not a matter of common usage;

(5) Inappropriateness of the activity to the place where it is carried on; and

(6) Extent to which its value to the community is outweighed by its dangerous attributes.

Washington embraces § 520. *Klein v. Pyrodyne Corp.*, 810 P.2d 917, 919–20 (Wash. 1991). "The essential question is whether the risk created is so unusual, either because of the magnitude or because of the circumstances surrounding it, as to justify the imposition of strict liability for the harm that results from it, even though it is carried on with all reasonable care." *Id.*, at 920. Though not all of the elements (1) through (6) are required to state a claim, all apply here. The active rail line mere feet away from hundreds of people and off-leash dogs passing through by the hour presents a high degree of risk of harm, as evidenced by the prior casualties and reports of dogs on the tracks. Due to the speed and frequency of train traffic, the likelihood of severe injury or death to a dog — who does not read signs — is great. The City has repeatedly asserted that it cannot eliminate the risk by reasonable care. The activity is not a matter of common usage as would be transmission of high voltage electricity through rural areas along overhead uninsulated power lines, providing power to countless numbers of citizens; instead, the park serves the needs of dog owners living or working in proximity to the City of Edmonds, a fraction of the general public. By all accounts, it is inappropriate (and the City acknowledges this through signage warning that the park is not secured) to allow off-leash dogs to roam freely just feet away from an unobstructed rail line conveying high-speed trains around a blind curve, thereby depriving the dog or person caught unawares with any reasonable opportunity to escape before impact. The value to the dog owners of Edmonds is no doubt appreciable, but the value of a *per se insecure* park that exposes their dogs to severe injury or death.

That said, no reported cases to this author's knowledge treat an off-leash park adjacent to an active rail line as an abnormally dangerous activity. Indeed, the operation of trains has been found not ultrahazardous. *Warner v. Norfolk & Western Railway Co.*, 758 F. Supp. 370 (W.D. Va. 1991); *Raymond v. S. Pac. Co.*, 488 P.2d 460 (Or. 1971).

Does the City enjoy the absolute defense of the recreational immunity statute?

RCW § 4.24.210(1) provides that public and private landowners and possessors of lands who permit the public to use them for purposes of outdoor recreation, including but not limited to:

> cutting, gathering and removing firewood . . . , hunting, fishing, camping, picnicking, swimming, hiking, bicycling, skateboarding or other nonmotorized wheel-based activities, aviation activities . . . , rock climbing, the riding of horses or other animals, clam digging, pleasure driving of off-road vehicles, snowmobiles, and other vehicles, boating, kayaking, canoeing, rafting, nature study, winter or water sports, viewing or enjoying historical, archaeological, scenic, or scientific sites, without charging a fee of any kind therefore, shall not to liable for unintentional injuries to such users.

RCW § 4.24.210(4)(a).

However, the statute does not immunize for injuries sustained to users "by reason of a known dangerous artificial latent condition for which warning signs have not been conspicuously posted."

On its face, RCW § 4.24.210 only applies to recreational users harmed on the land owned or in lawful possession of the defendant. RCW § 4.24.200, in setting forth the legislature's purpose statement, uses the word "thereon." *See also Swinehart v. City of Spokane*, 187 P.3d 345, 350 (Wash. Ct. App. 2008) ("The purpose of this statutory grant of immunity is to encourage landowners to make their lands available to the public for recreational uses by limiting their liability to those who are injured while on the property.") As described in this hypothetical, Gomez's dogs suffered grievous harm on property owned by BNSF, not the City of Edmonds. Gomez was also bitten on BNSF property, not within the park. The City did not own or have lawful possession of the BNSF right-of-way on the date of loss. Nor was the BNSF right-of-way property that members of the public were allowed to use for outdoor recreation. Indeed, the no trespass signage completely negates application of RCW § 4.24.210. The legislature also found that the purpose of RCW § 4.24.210 was to provide "property owners with immunity from legal claims for any unintentional injuries suffered by certain individuals recreating on their land[.]" Wash. Sess. Laws of 2003, ch. 16, § 1.

Further, it is questionable that the act of merely releasing dogs in an off-leash dog park constitutes "outdoor recreation." No dogs are "ridden" in the park. Indeed, while other states specifically identify "training of dogs" or "on-leash and off-leash walking of dogs" as recreational activities, Washington's statute does not. *See* N.J.S.A. § 2A:42A-2; Tex. Civ. Prac. & Rem. Code Ann. § 75.001(3). If the property is not held open for "purposes of outdoor recreation," RCW § 4.24.210 simply does not apply. Be mindful, however, of the wide arc thrown by the legislature using *inter alia* language. Also examine the common thread running through the enumerated activities. The focus of the legislature was to guard against liability "arising when individuals are permitted to engage in potentially dangerous outdoor recreational activities, such as rock climbing." Wash. Sess. Laws of 2003, ch. 16, § 1. There is no similar hazard in letting well-behaved dogs off-leash in a fenced park, except perhaps dog bites to people and other dogs, or falls from collisions with dogs running around the park. Gomez was not injured while doing anything in the park. He did not trip and fall, throw out his back while descending a child's slide, or impale himself on a piece of playground equipment.

And because the statute seeks to abrogate common law, it must be construed strictly, not liberally. *Matthews v. Elk Pioneer Days*, 824 P.2d 541, 543 (Wash. Ct. App. 1992) ("Absent a stated direction of liberal construction, RCW § 4.24.210 should be strictly construed. RCW § 4.24.210 is in derogation of the common law rules of liability of landowners and occupiers. Statutes in derogation of the common law are *strictly construed* and no intent to change that law will be found unless it appears with clarity.") The common law is altered because the statute creates a new statutory classification of "recreational user," distinct from the traditional premises liability classifications of trespasser, licensee, or invitee. *Davis v. State*, 6 P.3d 1191 (Wash. Ct. App. 2000). In *Matthews*, the Court of Appeals refused to regard festival activities (entertainment, competitions, demonstrations) as "outdoor recreation" because they did not require (a) active involvement (i.e., physical in nature) or (b) the outdoors; it thus reversed summary judgment dismissal of a spectator's suit involving injury when a canopy fell on her while she watched entertainment on an outdoor stage at a community festival.

The act of letting one's dog off-leash in a park to roam at-will may occur while the dog owner remains still, sitting on a bench, or just watching — like a spectator. While the dog's actions may be physical, the dog's owner merely needs to unhook the leash. Further, dogs permitted to be off-leash do so predominantly indoors given that the Edmonds off-leash ordinance makes it unlawful to let a dog off-leash and remain "at-large" (meaning off premises of owner and not under immediate control by leash, cord, or chain). Edmonds Mun. Code §§ 5.05.010(C), 5.05.050. By explicitly exempting Marina Beach Park South from Edmonds Mun. Code §§ 5.05.050 and 5.05.060(A) (unlawful to allow dog to stray and/or enter park or public property), the City has legislated into existence a world that permits off-leash dogs only on private property and within a secure enclosure or residence. Edmonds Mun. Code § 5.05.060(C) (the exemption), thereby proves the rule that, in Edmonds (and most of America), allowing a dog off-leash is an activity commonly conducted *indoors*.

While dog walking is an activity commonly conducted *outdoors*, dogs are not walked in an off-leash park. They are set free to run and play with other dogs or simply to explore. Dogs play within millions of Americans' apartments and dwellings. Letting a dog off-leash or allowing more than one dog to interact is an activity that may be conducted indoors or out and does not require active human involvement. Gomez was not engaged in activity (a) physical in nature at the time of the tragedy, (b) that required his participation (that is, after all, the point of an off-leash dog park; there is no need to keep the dog under control or avoid it running at large), (c) that needed to take place outdoors, and (d) that caused injury to himself. His dogs were arguably not statutory "users," "members of the public," or "persons." The only individuals subject to RCW § 4.24.200 ("the public," "toward persons") and RCW § 4.24.210(1) (applies to "members of the public" as "users"), RCW § 4.24.210(2) ("volunteer group or to any other users"); RCW § 4.24.210(4) ("sustained to users" and referencing conspicuous "warning signs" — but *dogs do not read signs*). Like *Matthews*, Gomez did not engage in outdoor recreation. He did not suffer injury while throwing a ball or Frisbee to his dogs or tripping on a log and breaking his leg. He just let his dogs do as they pleased in an area he believed, quite reasonably, was safe from trains. Assuming *arguendo* that his dogs were engaged in outdoor recreation, RCW § 4.24.210 does not apply to dog "users" as strictly construed.

Only personal injury claims are immunized, not property damage. Dogs are property. Thus, any claim involving harm to Boca and Niko falls outside RCW § 4.24.210, which plainly applies only to "injuries to such users," not damage to users' property. RCW § 4.24.210(1). The legislative finding also confirms the intent of RCW § 4.24.210 is to immunize against claims for "injuries suffered by certain individuals recreating on their land[.]" Such injuries are personal to the individual recreating, not to property owned by such an individual. RCW § 4.24.200 does not alter this analysis since in using the phrase "persons who may be injured or otherwise damaged by the acts or omissions of persons entering thereon," the word "damaged" modifies "persons," meaning harm to the person, not to property. It likely references emotional distress damages related to a physical injury.

Furthermore, strict liability claims are not immunized. RCW § 4.24.210 only immunizes defendants from liability for unintentional injuries, abrogating the law of premises liability (not strict liability). At common law, landowners or possessors of land owed a duty of reasonable care to make the premises safe for the occupant and avoid causing injury, except as to trespassers to whom no such reasonable care standard applies. Invitees merit the highest level of protection, requiring the possessor to use reasonable care and affirmatively discover dangerous conditions. A licensee/social guest may expect the landowner to use care with respect to known dangerous conditions when he can reasonably anticipate that the condition or danger is latent. In this context, RCW § 4.24.210 seeks to dispense only with the duty of care, i.e., negligence-type fault only. Strict liability, on the other hand, applies to all landowners, including trespassers. RCW 4.24.210 does not abrogate that common law duty, and no court will do so without express legislative direction. Had the legislature intended to excuse strict liability, it would have stated so. Consider *Gould v. Motel 6 Operating L.P.*, 2005 Wash. App. LEXIS 880 (Feb. 7, 2005) (noting that the law of premises liability does not impose duties beyond ordinary care, stating, "Strict liability does not apply."). *Gould* furthers the argument here that the legislature's intent in passing RCW § 4.24.210 was not to obliterate strict liability, but only to excuse ordinary duties of care. Nor does RCW § 4.24.210 guard against gross negligence, willfulness, or wantonness.

The danger presented at the park was patent, arising from a latent condition and outside the statute. Even if RCW § 4.24.210 were to apply, subsection (4) excludes known, artificial, dangerous, latent conditions for which warning signs were not conspicuously posted. First, we must identify the injury-causing condition before determining whether it was known, dangerous, artificial, and latent. *Davis v. State*, 6 P.3d 1191, 1195–96 (Wash. 2000), *aff'd*, 30 P.3d 460 (Wash. 2001). The "injury causing condition" is the "specific object or instrumentality that caused the injury, viewed in relation to other external circumstances in which the injury is situated or operates." *Ravenscroft v. Wash. Water Power Co.*, 969 P.2d 75, 80–81 (Wash. 1998). The "condition" here was the improper fencing failing to block the southernmost boundary of the park — one that was known to the City, artificial, and dangerous. The only bone of contention is whether it was *latent*.

While the danger of being struck by a train may have been patent (i.e., the specific risk posed by the injury-causing condition), the condition itself was latent, when viewed from the perspective of the plaintiff. *Van Dinter v. City of Kennewick*, 846 P.2d 522, 525 (Wash. 1993) (latency means "not readily apparent to the recreational user"). That the condition may have been patent from the dogs' perspectives does not mean it was from Gomez's, who was quite a distance from the south end of the park and did not and could not see that the City had allowed the enclosed area to be thrown open. Dogs, like children, would not understand the danger of railroad tracks, and no claim of patency can be imputed from the dogs to the dogs' owner.

This case is distinguishable from *Van Dinter* or *Swinehart*, which denied the plaintiff recovery from a patent condition that posed a latent danger. *Van Dinter*, at 526 (placement of metal caterpillar with antennae was patent condition, though the antennae may have caused a latent danger of eye-poking); *Swinehart*, at 352 (insufficiently maintained playground surface at Red Wagon slide exit was patent condition, though it may have posed latent danger to adults using slide). In both cases, the plaintiff could visually ascertain the condition, readily apparent to the average user, even if the danger thereby posed was nonobvious. Here, the fence, which runs from the entrance for nearly the length of two and a half football fields (i.e., 708'), curving eastward along the railroad right-of-way as far as the eye can see, makes it readily apparent to park users that the patent danger of trains, created by the patent condition of no barrier, was eliminated by installation of a fence, which the railroad was not required by law to erect within city limits. In other words, the City made an otherwise patent condition apparently nonexistent by erecting a fence and inviting people to let their dogs loose pursuant to an express statutory exemption to the city's dog leash law.

RCW § 4.24.210(4) does not confer immunity for the latent condition where "warning signs have . . . been conspicuously posted." The City had three signs posted that day, but none was anywhere near the latent condition. Not until after the incident did the City add two more signs close to the southernmost end of the park, on the plateau, in plain view to anyone approaching. While those post-incident signs may arguably have been conspicuous, the content of those signs remained imprecise, ambiguous, and ineffective. Saying that the "ends of dog park are not securely fenced due to high and low tides" fails to apprise the user of the danger that dogs have free access to the railroad tracks and may be struck and killed by a train. Instead, it suggests a drowning danger (due to the tides). On the date of this incident, the tide was nearly at the highest point (9'), making the condition even more nonevident (9').

Several individuals found the signage nonconspicuous, such as Karen Beauregard, who first went to the park five years ago and became a regular in 2009, going about three times a week with her dog. She never saw the signs that were allegedly posted on Nov. 9, 2010, remarking that when a user enters the park, she pays attention to the opening of the gate, to avoid letting dogs out or in, and then becomes engaged in visiting with other people and their dogs. She remarked that you would need a flashing, neon sign to get folks' attention about an insecure park. To her, the signs were clearly inadequate.

B. AIR TRAVEL

Though air carriers have transported nonhumans since the 1930s, those passengers have been restricted to traveling in the cargo hold. Noreen Lanza, *Keeping the "Live" in Live Animal Air Cargo Transport*, Live Animal Air Cargo Transport, 76 J. Air L. & Com. 229, 229 (Spr. 2011). With passage of the Air Carrier Access Act of 1986 ("ACAA"), 49 U.S.C. § 41705, flight attendants welcomed emotional support animals with in-cabin comforts as they accompanied their owners. In 2009, Pet Airways became the first pets-only airline allowing unaccompanied companion animals to travel in-cabin. Four years later, it ceased operations. Since then, major airlines have permitted dogs and cats to fly with passengers even if not ACAA-qualified. Gary Stoller, *Pet Travel Policies for Top U.S. Airlines*, USA Today (Oct. 9, 2013). They remain subject to Federal Aviation Administration ("FAA") carry-on baggage rules. FAA, Pets in the Passenger Cabin (www.faa.gov/passengers/fly_pets/cabin_pets) and 14 C.F.R. § 121.589. The AWA does not cover carry-on animals but does regulate transportation of animals in cargo, with orders and fines pertaining to extreme temperatures, escape, and inadequate ventilation. While the upgrade from cargo to cabin alone may save lives, those relegated to traveling with baggage remain at risk of depressurization and heat prostration.

1. Casualties in Domestic Air Travel

The Calk family booked a flight on American Airlines from Newark to Los Angeles in October 1997. On arrival, Mr. Calk learned that Jed, their Golden Retriever, was "not ready yet." Twenty minutes passed. He was then presented with Jed's body, covered in urine, feces, and vomit. Dying en route to the emergency hospital, an autopsy revealed death by suffocation. Erin Sheley, *Live Animals: Towards Protection for Pets and Livestock in Contracts for Carriage*, 3 Animal L. 59, 59 (2007). Two years later, TWA flight attendants rebuffed Gordon Anzalone's frantic efforts to check on Enzo, his eight-year-old Boxer, held in the cargo hold while the plane sat on the tarmac for hours in the boiling St. Louis heat. Staff wheeled Enzo out on a cart, dead. Mr. Anzalone explained to Court TV, "There was no blanket over him, and fluids were oozing out of every cavity . . . My wife just collapsed." The airline filed for bankruptcy before the case went to trial. *Id.*, at 60.

According to the database created from mandatory reports made pursuant to the Safe Air Travel for Animals Act of 2001 ("SATAA"), 49 U.S.C. § 41721, implemented by 14 C.F.R. § 234.13 (70 FR 7392) and Directive 70 FR 9217, 32 puppies and 24 dogs suffocated, respectively, on Delta Airlines and United Airlines in 1990, and there were 2,516 documented cases of dogs and cats suffering severe injury in air travel. The Act purported to require reporting, training, cargo hold redesign, and increased liability for harm. As passed, it provided only for mandatory reporting and training. The airlines thwarted efforts to increase the civil penalty from $2,500 to $5,000, and to increase civil liability to double that of the luggage. Before passage of SATAA, the Air Transport Association estimated that nearly half a million animal companions travel by air per year, but only one percent (5,000) die. Betsy Wade, *Animals by Air: It's Beastly*, N.Y. Times, Apr. 23, 2000.

A decade after passage of SATAA, the number of casualties per year remains steady. The first annual estimates provided by the USDOT's Aviation Consumer Protection and Enforcement Division, generated by compiling reports from May 2005 through December 2005, identified 25 deaths, 18 injuries, and 5 losses. The reports for 2010-2011 revealed 39 deaths, 13 injuries, and five losses. The next year tallied 35 deaths, nine injuries, and two losses. Airconsumer.ost.dot.gov/reports/index.htm. These statistics only pertain to warm- and cold-blooded animals kept as a pet in a family household, thereby excluding animals shipped as commercial cargo. *Reports by Carriers on Incidents Involving Animals During Air Transport*, 70 FR 7392-02, editing 14 C.F.R. § 234.13(c) (1). Of course, these figures only provide the numerator, not the total trip denominator, for purposes of computing the percentage of animal incidents. Aside from APHIS regulations, members of the nongovernmental organization International Air Transport Association ("ATA") have developed Live Animal Regulations ("LAR") to set a global standard for animal transport.

On July 2, 2014, the DOT cured some of the above-described limitations in Final Rule 2014-15503. The new 14 C.F.R. § 235 expanded the definition of "animal" to include not just pets but "any dog or cat which, at the time of transportation, is shipped as part of a commercial shipment on a scheduled passenger flight increased, including shipments by trainers and breeders" (14 C.F.R. § 235.1 ("animal")); SATAA's reporting requirement to every scheduled-service passenger flight on any aircraft with even fewer than 60 seats, provided that the carrier operates at least one aircraft capable of seating more than 60 passengers (14 C.F.R. § 253.2); and required carriers to produce calendar-year reports including the total number of animals transported in the calendar year (14 C.F.R. § 235.3(b)(2)).

When an airline loses, or causes injury or death to, an animal, owners should first consult with the contract of carriage. If traveling as carry-on baggage, see the passenger ticket. If as cargo, view the air waybill. Such documents will set forth the terms or carriage or refer the traveler/shipper to another form. Commonly, the liability-excluding and -limiting contract contains liability excluding and limiting conditions; temperature embargos to guard against freezing or overheating during extreme weather conditions; or brachycephalic breed advisories to reduce the risk of heat stroke or respiratory distress. Typically, they shorten the period within which, and manner by which, an owner may notify the airline of claims. *Royal Ins. Co. v. Emery Air Freight Corp.*, 834 F. Supp. 633 (S.D.N.Y. 1993) held that a faxed notice sufficed to comply with the written notice requirement set forth in the contract. Such notice typically must include the shipper's name, consignee's name, carrier's name, air waybill number, flight number, date of delivery, location where delivered, departure and destination ports, and description of goods and value. After serving the notice of claim, which airlines often limit to 14 days for damage, 21 days for delay, and 120 days for loss (though a much shorter 24-hour period for baggage), the claimant should send supporting documentation within the defined period of typically 21 to 45 days. Domestic contracts for air carriage have also reduced the statute of limitations to one or two years. They also frequently cap damages at sometimes as little as 50 cents per pound for animals shipped as cargo. When sent as baggage, federal law imposes a $3,400 minimum limit to large aircraft. 78 F.R 14913 (Mar. 8, 2013) (amending 14 C.F.R. § 254.4). Thus, in the case of a five-pound Chihuahua traveling as cargo between Miami and Los Angeles, a domestic contract for carriage that limits liability to $.50 per pound would entitle the owner to only $250.

The Civil Aeronautics Act of 1938 established the Civil Aeronautics Authority. Two years later, it split to form the Civil Aeronautics Board ("CAB"), which regulated all domestic interstate flights, set fares, rates, and schedules, and authorized tariffs (i.e., the contracts of carriage). One such CAB-era case involved Sir Michael Robert, a Golden Retriever. Elaine Klicker sued Northwest Airlines ("NWA") for the wrongful death of Sir Michael Robert when he died en route from Minneapolis to Billings as excess baggage in the cargo hold. The Klickers informed NWA of his value at $35,000 but were not permitted to declare a higher value or pay more for additional protection. NWA contended that its Tariff Rule 345(D)(3) exculpated it completely as "not . . . liable for the loss, death, or sickness" of any live animal transported. However, the rule provided that live animals could travel as baggage. Yet NWA required large dogs to fly as cargo.

NWA next challenged jurisdiction, claiming that the CAB should hear the matter, not the federal district court. The CAB deemed the rule "unlawful" and ordered its cancellation. Based on a public policy against allowing a common carrier to disclaim negligence, the court followed the CAB's lead. It then turned to the limiting Tariff Rule 370(A), which sought to cap damages at $500 for loss or damage to any "personal property, including baggage . . . unless the passenger [has declared a higher value and paid $.10 per $100]." As NWA did not let the Klickers declare a higher value, the Rule did not apply. For the same reason, the court rejected application of Tariff Rule 370(C), which held that NWA could not accept for transportation or storage any personal property, including baggage, with a declared value of more than $5,000. In reversing and remanding for a trial on damages at common law, the Ninth Circuit concluded that NWA could not say it made a mistake in accepting Sir Michael Robert for transport and then, when he died, shift the burden to an innocent shipper. *Klicker v. NWA*, 563 F.2d 1310 (9th Cir. 1977).

The federal government phased out the CAB in 1985 upon passage of the Airline Deregulation Act of 1978, ushering in an era of unregulated contracting between carriers and shippers. In such *laissez faire* context, one way to overcome such a shockingly low recovery with respect to cargo is to declare and insure for a higher value. The *released valuation doctrine* honors the right of the airline to allocate risk of loss to the shipper by releasing it from liability beyond the stated rate in consideration of the thrifty shipping cost. It binds the shipper to the per-pound recovery if given reasonable notice of the rate structure and opportunity to pay a higher rate for greater protection. Thus, if a shipper wants to insure the Chihuahua against loss at 100 times the default rate, i.e., $2,500, it must declare a value of $2,500 and pay the carrier the increased shipping cost. With respect to checked baggage, contractual limitations of value do not apply unless reasonably communicated. In applying this *reasonably communicated* test, courts look at the ticket or waybill to determine if the limitation is facially conspicuous and whether surrounding circumstances of the carrier-passenger relationship justify holding the passenger to the printed restriction.

In *Deiro v. American Airlines*, 816 F.2d 1360 (9th Cir. 1987), Thomas Deiro sued American Airlines for negligence, breach of contract, and willful and wanton behavior seeking $900,000 for the death of seven racing greyhounds and injuries to two others when they flew from Portland to Boston via Dallas/Fort Worth. During the layover, they were left in their shipping cages exposed to nearly 100 degree temperatures without ventilation or water. The airline ignored Deiro's pleas to protect them. Finding he had a full and fair opportunity to insure the dogs for a greater sum and had been informed of the rate structure, the court applied the doctrine against him. The Ninth Circuit bound Deiro to the fine print of the ticket based on both the released valuation doctrine and reasonably calculated test. Calling it a close case, the court examined the physical characteristics of the ticket and found that it fell in-between nonexistent and conspicuous, but extrinsic factors resolved the matter against Deiro given he was a sophisticated traveler and had nine days to review the ticket. Thus, Deiro's recovery was limited to $750.

When Andrew Gluckman graduated from high school in 1988, his parents bought him a round-trip ticket to the West Coast as a gift. While camping, Andrew found Floyd, a Golden Retriever. On June 22, 1988, he called American Airlines to see if he could return home with Floyd traveling with him in the cabin. Told no, he reluctantly shipped Floyd as baggage at the cost of $30. American never explained that Floyd would be forced to remain in a non-air conditioned cargo hold while the plane stayed on the ground; that the hold would not be monitored in-flight; that the crew could not control the cargo temperature; and that the outdoor temperatures could exceed the safety limits set by American. Gluckman's ticket did not reveal that Floyd was treated as baggage, that American limited its liability, or that he could insure Floyd for more. On the day of the flight, mechanical problems grounded the plane for an hour. It was 115° F outside, making Floyd's compartment 140° F.

When Andrew disembarked, he saw Floyd on his side panting, his face and paws bloodied, evidence of his panicked effort to escape. American prevented Andrew from taking Floyd to a veterinarian for 45 minutes. He was euthanized the next morning due to heat stroke and brain damage. Gluckman sued. American first claimed that the one-year statute of limitations had elapsed. Alternatively, it claimed it only owed him $1250, the contractual limit of liability per contract and 14 C.F.R. § 254.4. In *Gluckman v. American Airlines*, 844 F. Supp. 151 (S.D.N.Y. 1994), the trial court dismissed his claims for NIED, IIED, loss of companionship, and Floyd's own pain and suffering. However, it denied American's motion for summary judgment by concluding that the released valuation doctrine did not apply to Floyd, for he traveled as excess baggage, not cargo. As to the reasonably communicated test, the court observed that while the intrinsic factors favored American, extrinsic ones disfavored it.

Willie, a young English Bulldog, shipped in a kennel from New York to San Francisco on American Airlines. He arrived on August 6, 2005 in distress and breathing shallowly. Terrence Ing tried to rush him to a veterinary hospital, but the airline refused to release him, causing his death. American asserted a $50 cap per the air waybill as Mr. Ing did not declare a higher value. After suing American in state court for negligence, conversion, trespass, breach of contract, and a violation of the Animal Welfare Act through the California Business and Professions Code, American removed the case to federal court. *Ing v. American Airlines*, 2007 U.S. Dist. LEXIS 11716 (S.D.N.Y. Feb. 5, 2007) On summary judgment, the trial judge held that federal common law applied and preempted state claims related to loss of or damage to goods by interstate common carriers. It also rejected the effort to create a private right of action under the AWA through Cal. Bus. & Prof. Code § 17203. As to whether American breached its contract, the court examined the waybill for prima facie validity.

Finding that it did allow Ing to "opt out" by declaring a higher value, the court then applied the released valuation doctrine, but not the reasonable communicativeness test — for Willie shipped as "Priority Parcel," not checked baggage. Finding the limitations of liability on the reverse of the airbill satisfactory, and that the language on the front referred Ing to the back and identified a space to declare a value and pay an "excess value fee," the court concluded that American gave him reasonable notice. He also had a fair opportunity despite being purportedly rushed — i.e., having arrived one hour before his flight and asked to complete a 15-minute transaction — and not being told by American Airlines about the option to declare a higher value. However, the limitations of liability would only apply if American did not breach its contract at the outset. By not returning Willie to Ing on demand, and by transporting him in violation of American's own tariff embargo by shipping Willie above a prohibited temperature, Ing argued that the carrier could not enforce the terms of a contract it violated, citing *Coughlin v. Trans World Airlines*, 847 F.2d 1432 (9th Cir. 1988). Finding that triable issues of fact existed as to whether American breached the air waybill, the court denied summary judgment on the breach of contract claim. It further held that post-landing behavior constituted a separate actionable incident (i.e., refusing to return Willie to Mr. Ing for nearly five hours, allowing him to die).

Data worth scrutinizing in air carrier death and injury cases include pressure and temperature logs in the cargo hold; a roster of cargo loaded and unloaded with weights, size, and category; internal inspection reports; make/model of the plane; dimensions of the hold; service records for the aircraft; flight recorder and other logs; and SATAA reports.

Hypothetical: Jack Shephard's cat, Abby, a three-year-old female tabby, traveled with two littermates as cargo from New York City to Los Angeles on Oceanic Airlines flight 815 on Sept. 22, 2004. Before departure, Dr. Shephard signed the following Oceanic air waybill:

OCEANIC AIRLINES LOGISTICS

[X] Oceanic Pet First™

Shipper certifies that the particulars on the face hereof are correct and that insofar as any part of the consignment contains dangerous goods, such part is properly described by name and is in proper condition for carriage by air according to the applicable Dangerous Goods Regulations.

/s/ Jack Shephard

(Signature of Shipper or his Agent)

- -

Executed On

9/22/04 0519 JFK /s/ W. Dalton

(Date) (Time) (Place) (Signature of Issuing Carrier or Agent)

It is agreed that the goods described herein are accepted in apparent good order and condition (except as noted) for carriage SUBJECT TO THE CONDITIONS OF CONTRACT ON THE REVERSE HEREOF. ALL GOODS MAY BE CARRIED BY ANY OTHER MEANS INCLUDING ROAD OR ANY OTHER CARRIER UNLESS SPECIFIC CONTRARY INSTRUCTIONS ARE GIVEN HEREON BY THE SHIPPER, AND SHIPPER AGREES THAT THE SHIPMENT MAY BE CARRIED VIA INTERMEDIATE STOPPING PLACES WHICH THE CARRIER DEEMS APPROPRIATE. THE SHIPPER'S ATTENTION IS DRAWN TO THE NOTICE CONCERNING CARRIER'S LIMITATION OF LIABILITY. Shipper may increase such limitation of liability by declaring a higher value for carriage and paying a supplemental charge if required.

- -

Declared Value For Carriage: 0   Airport of Departure: JFK   Destination: LAX (Flight 815)

Nature and Quality of Goods: CATS   Number of Pieces and Gross Weight: 3 (89#)

Total Prepaid: $325.78

This was the first time he had ever shipped cargo, much less an animal. He had never flown with animals as checked baggage or carry-on. He had not read and was not aware of the terms contained on the back of the waybill, and had no idea that liability for the loss and death of Abby would be capped at $50. No staff member called his attention to the waybill's fine print (front or back), and there was no signage (in line at the airport, at the cargo counter, or anywhere else) that alerted him to these restrictions on carriage. He arrived at the air cargo facility at JFK International Airport around 5:00 a.m. and, within minutes, had tendered his three cats for carriage to Los Angeles. Shephard did not have to wait in line and was the only customer there at that hour. Preparing to move across the country, while delivering his cats to the agent, he carried his six-month-old child. Driven from New York City to the La Guardia airport, he left on a Continental Airlines flight to Los Angeles, where he would reunite with Abby and the other cats later that day. Unlike a seasoned traveler with days to pore over the terms of carriage and make alternative arrangements, Dr. Shephard had at most a few minutes before leaving to catch his own flight.

The reverse side of this waybill begins "CONDITIONS OF CONTRACT" and has 19 bulleted terms, including Claims Time Limits and Procedures, requiring written notification within 60 days of the date the originating carrier accepts the shipment. Damage or loss discovered after delivery must be reported to the carrier in writing within 45 days after receipt of such notice. The Liability Limits paragraph restricts damages to the lesser of actual harm sustained or the declared value. By default, this amounts to 50 cents per pound or $50.00, whichever is higher, unless a higher value is declared. Dr. Shephard did not declare or pay for a higher value for Abby.

On arrival in Los Angeles, an Oceanic handler mishandled Abby's carrier while unloading her from the airplane, causing the door to open and allowing Abby to escape. Despite significant efforts to locate her, Abby was not found. Oceanic employees notified Shephard of Abby's loss the day he arrived in Los Angeles. He was escorted onto the tarmac to try to find Abby, to no avail. Clearly, Oceanic had notice of the loss of Abby within minutes of deplaning.

He comes to your office on Dec. 30, 2004 and explains that he never submitted a notice of claim.

If you represent Dr. Shephard, how might you overcome the arguments that he has waived all claims by untimely noticing and that his damages do not exceed $50?

Anticipating the objection that the claim was not filed within 60 days of the ship date, Dr. Shephard may contend that notice was given to the delivering carrier at the destination by Oceanic's employees in Los Angeles. Accordingly, Oceanic cannot claim prejudice. The released valuation doctrine would apply only if Dr. Shephard received fair notice of the rate structure and had a fair chance to pay more for greater protection. As explained below, this doctrine overlaps with the reasonable communicativeness test. "It is quite possible, however, that the physical character-istics of the ticket might dictate that no contractual limitation exists though there might have been a full and fair opportunity to declare a higher value." *Deiro*, at fn. 4. But see *Ing*. Were the reasonable communicativeness test to apply under federal common law (it does not, because Abby flew as cargo, not checked baggage), the small, inconspicuous print containing this notice provision, as well as limitations of liability found on the reverse side of the airbill, may not "reasonably communicate" these highly restrictive terms.

Had Abby been shipped as checked baggage, what result?

Assuming that the case arises in a circuit that embraces the two-part test, and the Ninth Circuit does, consider: at no point did any Oceanic employee notify Dr. Shephard that it was limiting recovery to $50 for the loss of his cat, or that he could choose between higher and lower liability by paying a correspondingly greater or lesser charge. In other words, the "released valuation doctrine" that often operates in these contexts did not apply because these exclusionary terms were not "reasonably communicated" to Dr. Shephard. The ticket clearly does not alert the shipper to liability limitations and extremely short claim periods in any conspicuous fashion. The only mention of such terms is *below* the shipper's signature in a box executed by the carrier. It is not set apart by a different pattern, color, or demarcation, and the pitch is smaller than the corresponding font size that would be marked by checkbox (as in the Oceanic Pet First box on the right side of the waybill). The precise limitation is not even contained on the front of the airbill. Instead, it is located on the back, without further conspicuous distinction. Under the first prong of the *Deiro* test, therefore, the ticket itself may fail to reasonably communicate these restrictive terms. Under the second prong, the extrinsic factors surrounding the issuance of the waybill tip heavily in Dr. Shephard's favor. However, there is no duty for an airline employee to call attention to or explain the terms and conditions of an air waybill to a customer. *Norton v. Jim Phillips Horse Trans., Inc.*, 901 F.2d 821 (10th Cir. 1989); *Husman Constr. Co. v. Purolator Courier Corp.*, 832 F.2d 459 (8th Cir. 1987).

2. Casualties in International Air Travel

Claims involving animals leaving American airspace are subject to international treaties and conventions. The United States became a party to the Warsaw Convention in 1929, modified by the Convention for the Unification of Certain Rules for International Carriage by Air, referred to as the Montreal Protocol No. 4 to the Montreal Convention ("MP4"), in 1999. Similarly short notice periods apply to international air claims — seven days for damage to baggage, 14 days for damage to goods, 21 days for delay, and typically 120 days for loss. A two-year statute of limitations applies. Nonhumans flying as *cargo* are worth US $9.07 a pound per the Warsaw Convention, and 17 Special Drawing Rights ("SDR") per kilogram under the MP4, Art. 22(3).[7] The most that can be recovered under the MP4 for *baggage* is 1000 SDR unless the claimant can prove intentional, reckless, or knowing damage. MP4, Art. 22(2), 22(5). The Warsaw convention preempts all state law claims and all causes of action for damage to persons or cargo. *El Al Israel Airlines, Ltd. v. Tseng*, 525 U.S. 155, 174–76 (1999). Federal common law also preempts.

In the case referred to by the judges as "The Greyhounds Who Left the Driving to Delta," Patrick Dalton, an Irish citizen, sued Delta Airlines for the deaths of five racing greyhounds shipped from Shannon, Ireland, to Miami, Florida, via Boston. Despite arriving safely in Boston and boarding that evening, the dogs died from suffocation before reaching Miami. Dalton sued for $60,000 and lost profits. *Dalton v. Delta Airlines*, 570 F.2d 1244 (5th Cir. 1978). This pre-MP4 case applied the Warsaw Convention's two-year statute of limitations (Art. 29) and seven-day written notice of claim provision (Art. 26). Dalton did submit a notice, but tendered it 13 days too late. The trial court entered summary judgment for Delta, and Dalton appealed. Art. 26(2) provides that in case of "damage," complaints must be lodged within seven days of receipt of the goods. However, Art. 13(3) does not require notice at all for lost goods. Further, if the carrier admits loss, or if the goods do not arrive in seven days, the consignee may sue. Characterizing the deceased greyhounds as neither "damaged" nor "delayed," but instead destroyed, the seven-day notice provision did not apply:

---

[7] As of Oct. 5, 2014, 1 SDR equals US $1.48, or US $11.32 a pound. www.imf.org/external/np/fin/data/rms_mth.aspx?reportType=CVSDR.

A demijohn of rare brandy falling 15 feet off the conveyor belt to the airport's concrete apron is no longer that when the container is smashed and the contents run off in the view of covetous eyes. So it is with dogs, dogs bred, born and trained for kennel racing, not just for flesh, hide or hair. Recognizing, as we must, that live dogs are goods, when dead they are no longer just damaged goods. They are not at all the thing shipped.

Id., at 1247. No notice is required for destroyed goods, a fact of which the carrier is painfully aware. "Thus where destruction of goods occurs on an international flight the shipper-consignee need not give Article 26(3) notice." *Id.*, at 1248; *see also Hughes-Gibb & Co. v. Flying Tiger Line*, 504 F. Supp. 1239 (N.D. Ill. 1981) (accord relative to 130 "breeding swine" shipped from Chicago to Davao City via Manila; Art. 26(3) notice not required for deceased animals).

An MP4 era case, *Adler v. Westjet Airlines, Ltd.*, 2014 U.S. Dist. LEXIS 92332 (S.D. Fla. Jul. 8, 2014) examined whether a flight attendant's decision to unceremoniously force a disabled woman, her husband, and her service Yorkshire Terrier off a flight from Fort Lauderdale to Toronto was preempted by MP4. After acknowledging the treaty was the "supreme law of the land" and applied to this dispute, the trial judge rejected that Art. 17 required dismissal of all state law claims. They remained only subject to the treaty's limitations of liability.

Chapter 17

INSURANCE LAW

Unlike their human counterparts, nonhuman animals do not benefit from traditional insurance coverage provisions found in homeowner's, renter's, or motor vehicle policies. Despite the increasing recognition of their status as members of the family, the fairness gap generated by underwriters weighing actuarial risk against nonhuman animals and insurance law's conservative doctrinal spin has broadened. Just and otherwise viable claims are denied coverage. The gap will only be bridged through litigation, legislation, or insurance commissioner rulemaking.

Consider the case of Samantha, a border collie, who frequently accompanied the Huxleys on rides in the car. One such venture, however, resulted in an accident. Samantha was traveling unrestrained in the backseat. George's wife, Priscilla, occupied the passenger seat. This is where Samantha was sitting when George hit an invisible oil slick on the roadway. Though the car careened around a corner and nearly hit oncoming cars head-on, the guard rail absorbed the brunt of the impact and no one was killed. Priscilla suffered a punctured lung and lost several weeks from work. Samantha nearly died as she was thrown into the front windshield. Today, Samantha requires a wheelchair for mobility to protect her severed spine. A police report was filed, concluding that an unknown individual (likely a driver) illegally dumped or leaked gallons of motor oil, creating a severe road hazard.

With veterinary bills exceeding $5,000, the Huxleys turned to their automobile insurance for coverage. While Personal Injury Protection ("PIP") covered Priscilla's injuries, the same would not apply to Samantha — because she was not a "person." Uninsured/Underinsured Motorist ("UM/UIM") coverage, even if it could have applied to the phantom tortfeasor, would not pay for Samantha's "bodily injury" — again, because of her nonhuman status. The Comprehensive provision of the auto policy also did not apply to Samantha given that she was not part of the vehicle, nor did it cover on-board personal property.

The Huxleys then turned to their homeowner's insurance. The unambiguous policy exclusion of animals ended that inquiry. Not having pet insurance, a rider, or an umbrella policy, Samantha remained uninsured. Against their better judgment and wishes, they were forced to either find her a new home or put her to sleep. Despite efforts to solicit foster caregivers for a geriatric, incontinent dog with ongoing health problems and monthly physical therapy and medication bills, the Huxleys reluctantly euthanized Samantha.

Had Samantha been a service dog to Priscilla, helping her with bracing and retrieval, the result might have been different. Was injury to Samantha tantamount to bodily injury to Priscilla? If so, would PIP and UM/UIM apply? If Samantha were required for the operation of the vehicle by Priscilla, should she have been driving, might the Comprehensive provision of the auto policy govern?

Recognizing the demand for nonhuman passenger coverage, insurers have begun marketing pet injury endorsements. For instance, Nationwide provides Pet Injury Collision Coverage to reimburse reasonable expenses up to $500 for harm to a "family member's" dog or cat. Progressive includes pet injury as part of its collision coverage up to $1,000.

A. MOTORIST COVERAGE

The following cases illustrate the intersection of animal law and vehicle insurance law. Insureds injured in a motor vehicle accident with a bovine sued for UIM benefits. The Ohio Court of Appeals affirmed the trial court's dismissal based on undisputed facts that "there was a collision; the cow was not insured at the time of the collision; and that the cow caused the collision." Looking to the dictionary, the court concluded that while "designed for operation on land," a cow was not "a self-propelled, wheeled conveyance that does not run on rails" — ergo, a motor vehicle. *Mayor v. Wedding*, 2003 Ohio App. LEXIS 5947 (Dec. 5, 2003).

When a large playful dog jumped from an open window of a parked car and caused the insured plaintiff to fall off his motorbike and sustain injury, Duvigneaud sued GEICO, seeking UIM coverage. The appellate court agreed that transporting animate things, such as dogs, is an ordinary "use of a vehicle," and triggers UIM coverage for injuries "arising out of the ownership, maintenance or use of such uninsured automobile." The uninsured driver's conduct, in having negligently failed to control the dog from exiting his vehicle and causing harm, fit the policy language. Note that the analysis in *Duvigneaud v. Government Employees Insurance Co.* (GEICO), 363 So. 2d 1292 (La. Ct. App. 1979) [4-2 decision] was later disapproved.

A police officer suffered a career-ending injury from a suspected felon's dog, who leapt from the vehicle to protect the suspect, lying face down on ground per the officer's instructions. The officer sought UIM coverage, claiming that the attack arose "out of the use of a motor vehicle." Distinguishing itself from *Duvigneaud* and related cases, the appellate court concluded that because the purpose of the journey in the vehicle was unknown (was it to transport the dog?), and because the bite did not occur while the victim and/or dog were in the vehicle, the appellate court affirmed dismissal. It did so in accord with numerous other opinions that found no nexus between the animal-related injury and the vehicle use. A two-step test aided in the analysis of "use": (1) Was the conduct of which plaintiff complained a legal cause of the injury? (2) Was such conduct properly deemed use of the automobile? *Carter v. City Parish Govt.*, 423 So. 2d 1080 (La. 1982). The suspect's stop and exit from the vehicle had nothing to do with his manner of driving, but rather his status as a felon. The dog attack did not occur because he was in the vehicle, but in order to defend the suspect. One judge dissented, noting that the purpose of the uninsured driver was to use his car to transport himself and his dog, and that the attack occurred almost immediately after the driver was placed on the ground, without being called from the vehicle by the driver. *Sanchez v. State Farm Mutual Automobile Ins. Co.*, 878 P.2d 31 (Colo. Ct. App. 1994).

An automobile insurer and homeowner's insurer battled for determination of who needed to pay damages in a personal injury and wrongful death action brought against the insured when his 3½-year-old son set a visitor's car in motion. The court concluded that the little boy did not "use" the car for purposes of triggering the automobile liability policy provision for, or the homeowner's insurance policy exclusion of, injuries arising from vehicular use. Of interest is the court's reference to the scenario of a dog entering "an unoccupied automobile and, by releasing the hand brake or maneuvering the gear shift, set[ting] that vehicle in motion." *Erie Ins. Exchange v. Transamerica Ins. Co.*, 533 A.2d 1363, 1368 n.6 (Pa. 1987). To be a "user" of a vehicle requires that the individual "at least know and understand the uses to which an automobile, as an automobile, may be put." Accordingly, a dog, much like the toddler, could not be deemed a "user."

In a surprising exploration of the commonalities among perambulating drunkards, inanimate objects, and creatures great and small, a Texas federal district court found that a driver was not entitled to coverage for damage to her Chevrolet Blazer when it hit an intoxicated man with a blood-alcohol level of 0.148 on the Houston freeway late at night. *McKay v. State Farm Mut. Automobile Ins. Co.*, 933 F. Supp. 635 (S.D. Tex. 1995). It was no surprise that Gillian McKay struck this man, but was he an "object" or an "animal" for purposes of the Comprehensive part of her State Farm automobile policy? As she did not purchase collision coverage, the insurer denied her claim. The Comprehensive coverage explicitly excluded "collisions," which were defined to mean upset or contact with another "object." Exceptions to the collision exclusion were "malicious mischief and vandalism," as well as "contact with a bird or animal." McKay argued first that the drunkard was an "animal" with whom she made contact, and not an "object," both terms undefined in the policy. Alternatively, she claimed that he committed malicious mischief by recklessly darting across lanes of speeding traffic. The district court granted State Farm's motion for summary judgment by finding that a human is not an animal, but rather is an object, which raises a curious philosophical conundrum. On the one hand, the running man was more than "an inferior or irrational sentient being," what the court called an "animal," but denser than a block of wood, or an "object."

B. ANIMAL SABOTEURS AND VANDALS AS COVERED PERILS

Businesses and households victimized by burglars, robbers, prowlers, or vandals may make claims under their commercial, renters, or homeowners policies. But what if the "tortfeasor" or "criminal" is nonhuman?

A wild raccoon caused interruption in electrical service, resulting in fatal heat prostration to the insured's pigs. The insured sought a declaration that both the raccoon's sabotage and pigs' deaths were covered losses, quoting from the policy that it "shall include the peril of death to livestock caused by wild animals." Though unorthodox in presentation, the court agreed that the raccoon caused the pigs' demise when it shorted out the transformer fuse. *Lochtefeld v. Marion Mut. Ins. Ass'n*, 619 N.E.2d 1222 (Ohio Ct. C.P. 1993).

When a wild bobcat tore apart Sharon Montgomery's belongings, she made a claim under her renter's insurance for malicious mischief and vandalism. The trial court lyricized:

> The scarecrow wanted a heart. He wanted it from the start.
>
> The tin man wanted a brain. So he could be the same.
>
> And it was courage asked for by the lion, even though he was always crying.
>
> In this case the bobcat needs "intent". Or did he just rely on his scent?
>
> Alas, it is written in the law that the animal with the paw does not have the mind to do the damage of this kind.
>
> And so, I'm sorry, the Plaintiff won't get paid. That's how the contract was made. This policy does not apply when the bobcat runs awry.

The appeals court agreed, noting that the wild animal could not form the requisite intent or malice to commit "vandalism" or "malicious mischief," covered perils under the policy. This was even the case where the plaintiff cited dictionary definitions for "vandalism" that included the "ignorant" destruction of personalty. Other courts, having considered ignorance in relation to nonhuman animals, concluded that only human actors can perpetrate such acts. The foundation of this court's opinion was that, "An animal, non-human, acts or reacts instinctively without knowledge of right or wrong as defined by man." *Montgomery v. United Services Automobile Ass'n*, 886 P.2d 981 (N.M. Ct. App. 1994).

C. EQUINE LIFE INSURANCE POLICIES

Term life insurance for humans resembles mortality policies for nonhumans. Due to their potentially six- or seven-figure values, much coverage litigation has arisen in the equine context.

The valuable horse "Palatine King" was insured for $19,200 during the period of July 27, 1949 to July 27, 1950. Less than four weeks shy of the policy end date, Palatine sustained an injury requiring immediate euthanasia. Because the policy demanded veterinary consent before euthanasia as a condition precedent to extending coverage, Rosen sought the insurer's permission to put Palatine King to rest. It refused, thereby prolonging the horse's life beyond the policy end date of July 27, 1950. Rosen alleged it did so fraudulently and capriciously. The court denied the insurer's motion to dismiss, noting that Rosen's allegations, if true, stated a claim. *Rosen v. Underwriters at Lloyd's of London*, 100 F. Supp. 825 (E.D. Pa. 1951).

An anachronism, *Hinsworth & Gibbins v. The People's Mutual Live Stock Ins. Co. of Penn.*, 2 Pa. D. 541 (Pa. C.P. 1893), involved the killing of a horse by an SPCA without the insurer's written consent. The insurer denied the plaintiffs' demand for $150 for the horse's value on the basis that the policy did not apply when the horse was "destroyed" by an SPCA, even though suffering from an incurable malady. The court rejected plaintiffs' claim that the exclusion only applied when the horse could be cured, though sick, or when the horse was destroyed, or "unbuilt," by the disease, not the blow to the head care of the SPCA.

As time passed, courts embraced more humane notions. Plaintiff sought to recover from the insurer on a life insurance policy for his show mare. Though she did not sustain a complete fracture of the bone (one of the two alternative exceptions to the intentional destruction exclusion), neither did the insurer consent to her euthanasia (the second alternative). Despite frequent correspondence from the insured to the insurer, indicating, with veterinary support, that the mare was in near constant pain from having suffered a permanent injury, the insurer denied and ignored the request that it consent to her humane death. When the Plaintiff euthanized the mare and then made a claim on the policy for $3,500, it balked.

At trial, the court instructed the jury that, notwithstanding the insurer's withholding of consent, if they found "that the mare was here injured in such a manner as to cause it a high degree of pain and suffering which would to a reasonable certainty continue for such a long time as to make it inhumane to keep the mare for further treatment [and the veterinarian advised that she had an incurable injury rendering her useless for any purpose and should be euthanized], then your verdict should be for the plaintiff for $3,500[.]" *Butler v. Hartford Live Stock Ins. Co.*, 112 N.W.2d 50, 53–54 (Minn. 1961). The jury found for the plaintiff in the amount of $3500, and the insurer appealed. Citing *Rosen, supra*, the court held that the consent-to-kill exception was not absolute and must allow for destruction of the insured animal where pain is "acute," immediately follows the accident, and it would be inhumane to wait for insurer approval. Though the charge to the jury improperly focused on the utility of the horse to the insured as a basis of euthanasia, because it also instructed that the jury needed to find it inhumane to let her persist in a constant state of pain, the appellate court found at most harmless error.

D.   ANIMALS AS COVERED LOSSES AND INSTRUMENTALITIES OF LOSS

Virtually all homeowners insurance policies expressly exclude animals as covered losses for first-party claims made by the insured for reimbursement of the animal's value. On the other hand, they quite frequently will treat certain animals as covered instrumentalities for purposes of adjusting third-party claims made by the victim-claimant harmed by the insured's animal. But what of the situation where the first-party insured makes a claim for property damage caused by the insured's animal? Mr. Smith's 300-pound "gentle range cow" fell through the cover of his drained pool, causing damage to all involved. Smith sought to recover under his homeowner's policy (for the pool damage only). However, the policy excluded property damage caused by "domestic animals." Finding an ambiguity (did it apply to only household companions or all domesticated, non-wild animals?), the trial court ruled for Smith. Reversing, the appellate court delineated only two categories of animal (wild and tame), not three (wild, domestic household, domestic non-household). Given that cows are accustomed to live in or near human habitations, the hapless heifer was a "domestic animal" and Smith recovered nothing under his policy. *Smith v. State Farm Fire & Casualty Co.*, 381 So. 2d 913 (La. Ct. App. 1980).

The Gibsons owned several horses, one of whom was tied by a rope to a vertical support beam pole of the farm outbuilding. When the farrier who tied the horse began shoeing, the horse persistently pulled on the pole, causing the roof of the barn to collapse. *Gibson v. Farmers Ins. Co. of Wash.*, 2007 Wash. App. LEXIS 846 (Apr. 23, 2007). The Gibsons sued Farmers for denial of coverage for damage to their barn, claiming that loss was covered by "the weight of . . . animals" provision. They further argued that the terms "animal" and "domestic animal" were ambiguous as drafted by the insurer, and such ambiguity should be resolved in their favor. Farmers denied the claim. The Gibsons sought a declaratory judgment, which was denied, and the Court of Appeals affirmed. It reasoned that the policy treated collapsed buildings as covered losses only when there was an "accidental direct physical loss . . . caused only by . . . weight of contents, equipment, animals or people." Yet, the collapse occurred due to *force*, rather than *weight*. The Gibsons' alternative assignment of error also failed to persuade the appellate court. Whether the coverage provision applied to "animals" or "*domestic* animals" was irrelevant because only weight, not force, mattered.

What of an animal's effluvium, specifically the feces from six-year-old Cellie Dudley's dog, whom she enjoyed walking in the apartment complex common areas near insured Barbara Franz's unit? Furious with Dudley's dog's droppings, and in order to teach the young girl "a lesson," Franz smooshed Cellie's hand in her dog's poo. A lawsuit ensued and the insurer filed a declaratory judgment action claiming no liability coverage for Franz's intentional act causing bodily injury. Franz claimed she had no intent to injure, just to educate. The court rejected Franz's appeal by inferring a subjective intent to harm, thereby depriving Franz of coverage. *American Family Mut. Ins. Co. v. Franz*, 980 S.W.2d 56 (Mo. Ct. App. 1998).

E. BUSINESS PURSUITS EXCLUSION

Most homeowners policies exclude acts within the scope of the insured's business; such claims require separate commercial general liability coverage. Where the insured did not hunt and skin wild animals as a regular activity to earn a livelihood or as a profession, but rather was a person heavily invested in slaughtering and skinning defenseless animals, the court found he was not engaged in "business" and the business property exclusion did not apply. Accordingly, his claim for $3,500 under his homeowner's policy following the theft of pelts from his on-site freezer raised a question of fact for determination by a jury. *Asbury v. Indiana Union Mut. Ins. Co.*, 441 N.E.2d 232 (Ind. Ct. App. 1982). This "business pursuits" exclusion has obvious implications for those who breed animals as a side venture or even Good Samaritans who run rescues out of their homes and take donations for spay/neuter and vaccinations.

F. PET INSURANCE

Stepping back to survey the short, 30-year history of pet insurance tells us much about our relationship to animal companions. Veterinary Pet Insurance (VPI) correctly notes that it created the pet insurance market in 1982, selling its first policy for Lassie. That several other companies now compete in the U.S. market against VPI evidences the existence of sufficient demand to sustain this vital paraindustry to veterinary medicine. At a time when access to affordable health insurance for humans caused tremendous upset among the uninsured and under-insured, leading Congress and the U.S. Supreme Court to wrestle with varying plans seeking to ensure medical care to the masses, it may seem a bit profligate to perseverate over nonhuman health insurance. That said, veterinary health insurance presents an animal rights issue, because it removes the financial impediment to medical treatment, which in turn should yield a better quality of life (and prevent death by economic convenience). According to MarketResearch.com, less than one percent of American animal guardians have insurance (compared to 18% in Britain and 48% in some Scandinavian countries), but economists forecast the market expanding to $800 million by 2012 due to increased spending habits on veterinary services, strengthening of the human-animal bond, and policy awareness. Due to the numerous plan options available, a boutique insurance agent industry has grown to advise insureds on pet insurance policies. See, for instance, The GlenKirk Agency of Kirkland, Washington (www.glenkirkagency.com).

Overview. Buyers must carefully examine and understand the nomenclature of insurance coverage, specifically the terms deductible, coinsurance/copay, caps, and premiums. In a nutshell, the insured pays a premium to obtain a payout (or benefit) on claims made against the policy. Assuming the claim is not excluded by the policy, the benefit paid to the insured results from a straightforward calculation of ((Claim x Insurer's Copay) - Deductible) < Limit, where Claim = the amount of the bill to be reimbursed, Insurer's Copay = the percentage of the claim paid by the Insurer before a deductible is applied, Deductible = the fixed amount the insured must pay before pet insurance pays benefits, and Limit = the per incident/per term/per life ceiling payable under the policy. Sometimes, insurers subtract the deductible from the claim before calculating the Copay. For instance, if an insured claims $1000 for an MRI, with a deductible of $250 and copay of 20%, then the insurer will pay (($1000 x 80%) - $250) = $550.

Additional Considerations. In review of various policies, other matters worth evaluating include:

Chronic, Congenital, Developmental, Hereditary Condition, Disease, or Defect. Policies typically define each word, and each has consequences. Generally speaking, a congenital condition is one extant and discoverable at birth; a hereditary condition is one genetically transmitted but may or may not be extant and discoverable at birth (in fact, it may not ever manifest till very late in life); a developmental condition results from faulty development of the body while aging that may not be genetically triggered and could become extant and discoverable after birth during the formative stages of the animal. Unless a rider is purchased, congenital conditions are universally deemed pre-existing and not covered. Some policies refuse to cover hereditary and developmental conditions as well, absent additional coverage. And VPI is one of the few to define "chronic" condition to mean not curable; thus, even if the condition went into remission for a year, where the initial onset precedes the effective date of the policy, it will be deemed an incurable and preexisting condition and, therefore, not covered.

Limits and Nonrenewal. Astute insureds must be aware of multiple benefit caps, as an animal may reach one before another and lose out on further benefits. Generally, there are three caps in play at any one time — lifetime, period, and incident. The lifetime cap is the maximum amount the insurer will pay for the life of the insured animal. Once reached, the policy is spent. Pethealth claimed to distinguish itself by offering unlimited lifetime coverage for *accidents*, but still capped lifetime illness coverage at $72,000 for dogs and $60,000 for cats: note the distinction in covered peril, a claim may arise from an accident, illness, or injury. The period cap is the most the insurer will pay for that animal in the one-year term; and because insurers can decide not to renew the policy for any reason within typically 30 to 60 days before end of the policy term, this makes the lifetime cap largely illusory, for virtually none will exhaust the lifetime cap in one year. In addition, there is the per incident cap. And because many policies define "incident" so as to pool or stack, and therefore encompass, multiple conditions, the insurer can stop paying for those multiple conditions when the total amount claimed exceeds a single incident limit (instead of applying a per incident limit to each individual condition). Finally, be mindful of the occasional procedure, condition, and breed-specific exclusions or caps, particularly where different breeds suffer genetically predisposed afflictions. Pethealth provided an example of a condition cap, limiting reimbursement to $6,000 in certain illness categories.

Dispute Resolution. Occasionally insureds and insurers disagree about the interpretation and application of the policy, including the medical necessity of a procedure (i.e., challenging coverage) and the usual and customary expense for same (i.e., challenging the benefit amount). For this reason, one must evaluate the dispute resolution limitations and remedies set forth in the contract. Almost all policies first require submission of the complaint to an "independent" veterinary examiner (IVE) or appraiser, selected and paid for by the insurer. If the examiner/appraiser disagrees with the insured's primary veterinarian/appraiser, an umpire may be recruited to break the tie, with the cost split between the insured and the insurer. Failure to cooperate with such a review process bars suit against the insurer, since the step-by-step review process is characterized as an exhaustion-of-remedies requirement. For example, Pets Best had three levels of dispute resolution: first, sending the claim to a claim representative not involved in the initial decision; second, sending it for external review (an impartial veterinarian selected and paid for by the insurer); third, binding arbitration conducted according to the American Arbitration Association ("AAA") rules with shared costs and fees. A concern with binding arbitration under AAA is the cost. The fee for a consumer dispute under $10,000 is typically $1,000. In addition to the escalating review process, most insurers attempt to invoke a statute of limitations of one year from the date of first treatment for the condition identified in any legal action. Unless the policyholder's state's insurance laws prohibit attempts to shorten the statute of limitations, this limitation could prove fatal, particularly if the mandatory review process does not toll the period in which to file suit.

COBRA. In 1985, Congress passed the Consolidated Omnibus Budget Reconciliation Act to, among other goals, ensure that employees would not have to face new waiting periods and be denied coverage for preexisting health conditions while between jobs. Legislators reasoned that by changing insurance companies (due to changing employers), the new insurer will not want to insure for conditions that, though they developed after the date of prior employment (and thus were not barred by the prior employer's health insurer as a preexisting condition), precede the new employment commence date and, thus, are preexisting from its perspective. COBRA provided stopgap coverage for up to 1.5 years in most cases. As one might expect, there is no similar COBRA protection for employees who change jobs (and, thus, change pet insurance). Note that many policies offer employer discounts should they decide to provide pet insurance to their employees.

What is Excluded. The conditions not covered are too numerous to examine here, but insureds must pay close attention to breed-specific exclusions and almost across-the-board noncoverage for dysplasia and ligament tear repairs. Many insurers do not contribute to a risk pool that pays for cruel procedures by refusing to cover declaws, dewclaw removals, tail docking, and ear cropping. Healthy Paws will not cover dogs kept for commercial reasons, including "racing dogs." They also will not pay for injuries resulting from animal fighting. The policies also tend to bar any claims arising from intentional harm to an animal by the insured, the insured's family member, or resident of the insured's household. Keeping pace with the changing landscape of animal care and publicized by the TLC program *I Cloned My Pet*, one finds in some policies a cloning exclusion.

Hypothetical: Sol, a male Great Dane, is picked up as a stray, impounded by animal control, and adopted to the Pheasants a year later on May 1, 2009. His age unknown, the shelter nevertheless lists him as 18 months of age. On December 4, 2009, the Pheasants enroll him with Dog Gone Insurance. In early 2010, his guardians noticed how he would descend stairs on three legs, favoring his back right leg. An MRI revealed medial patellar luxation. A TPLO surgery costs $3,000. The Pheasants make a claim for reimbursement with the insurer, which rejects the claim, asserting that Sol's condition is congenital, citing Exclusion 27, which states, "Any fees associated with treatment or diagnosis of Congenital Conditions including but not limited to patellar luxation, umbilical hernia, entropion, elongated soft palate, stenotic nares, malocclusion, mitral valve defects, patent ductus arteriosis, recessed vulva, ventricular septal defect and portosystemic shunt." *Hereditary* is defined in the policy as "a condition, defect or disease, which was transmitted to the Pet(s) genetically from its parent(s). The condition, defect or disease may or may not be manifested until late in life if at all." The Pheasants obtain a letter from Sol's board-certified surgeon, who describes the condition as *developmental*, not congenital or hereditary. The insurer also invokes Exclusion 7, which excludes "Claims for Hereditary Conditions that first manifest; whether diagnosed, treated or not; in a Pet that first enrolled after its second birthday." Further consider Exclusion 5, which bars "Claims for any condition that manifested; whether diagnosed, treated or not before the policy effective date of coverage."

Must Dog Gone Insurance pay the claim?

Exclusions are interpreted narrowly as a matter of law. The policy interpretation dispute hinges on various factors: (1) despite the fact that the insurer characterizes *all* patellar luxations as "congenital," veterinary science recognizes that some luxations are *developmental* or *hereditary;* (2) the shelter's age estimate suggests that the Pheasants enrolled him after his second birthday, meaning that a *hereditary* patellar luxation will not be covered under Exclusion 7; and (3) if the *developmental* patellar luxation manifested before December 4, 2009, Sol will have no coverage due to Exclusion 5.

Most interpretation disputes first pass through several tiers of dispute resolution. Upon exhaustion of those stages, litigation seeking a declaratory judgment may ensue. Often, reasonable attorney's fees may be recovered by the prevailing party. Dog Gone Insurance, however, adds a provision to its policy that expressly prevents recovering attorney's fees. Such a provision is likely void as against public policy. The Pheasants might also consider a uniform trade practice law/consumer protection or insurance bad faith claim if the insurer persists in its denial in the face of competent veterinary evidence.

Chapter 18

BANKRUPTCY LAW

One would be remiss not to explore the intersection of animal and bankruptcy law, the fertile area of assets and liabilities, creditors and debtors. Nonhumans need not seek bankruptcy relief to discharge debts because, practically speaking, they cannot carry debts, sue or be sued, or have judgment entered against them. Indeed, legally speaking, they are deemed property under the law. While animal trust laws do recognize animals as lawful beneficiaries of trusts, who may need protection from creditors and trustees looking to satisfy debts against those assets, the field of bankruptcy-related animal law focuses primarily on animals as exempted assets and as instrumentalities of harm, creating nondischargeable debt.

Homeowner's insurance ensures payment of most dog bite claims involving negligent control or strict liability, as does automobile insurance for hapless drivers colliding with vehicles conveying animals. But insurance will not pay for some of the starkest examples of men and women's cruelty to nonhuman animals, often pled as intentional torts like fraud, outrage, and conversion. As might be expected, the likelihood of financial recovery from those who commit such acts is inversely related to the seriousness of the misdeed. The need for aggressive postjudgment collections is a foregone conclusion, and the risk of bankruptcy upending the underlying judgment an ever-present threat.

A. NONDISCHARGEABILITY

Most judgment debtors seek refuge in Chapter 7 to shake off judgment creditors whose underlying claims sound in negligence, such as a garden variety motor vehicle accident, or breach of contract. The vast majority of judgments die by operation of Chapter 7 discharge. Those that survive are then emasculated by a subsequent Chapter 13 plan, which frequently entitles the creditor to about a dime on the dollar spread out over three to five years of monthly payments. Many collection attorneys refer to this practice as filing a "Chapter 20." The three most common animal-related grounds to prevent a discharge in Chapter 7 or Chapter 13 include proving that the debtor committed larceny (11 U.S.C. § 523(a)(4)), a tort involving willful and malicious injury to persons or property (11 U.S.C. § 523(a)(6)), or by obtaining money or goods under false pretenses or fraud (11 U.S.C. § 523(a)(2)(A)). Numerous other exceptions to discharge can be found at 11 U.S.C. § 523 et seq. Practitioners must understand that, even if a plaintiff obtains a final judgment on state law claims for conversion, intentional infliction of emotional distress, fraud, or malicious injury to an animal, the elements of such claims may not fully correspond to the elements of the federal causes of action under Section 523 of the Bankruptcy Code — which must be proved to prevent discharge. In anticipation of a bankruptcy, plaintiffs may consider including in the special verdict form (if jury trial) or *Findings of Fact and Conclusions of Law* explicit reference to the elements of nondischargeability, including "actual knowledge that harm to plaintiff is substantially certain," "subjective intent to harm," and all manner of thieving or fraudulent behavior. Failure to so specify may require a new trial on the issue of nondischargeability in bankruptcy court.

1. 11 U.S.C. § 523(a)(4)

Section 523(a)(4) prevents discharge "for fraud or defalcation while acting in a fiduciary capacity, embezzlement, or larceny." 11 U.S.C. § 523(a)(4).

> For purposes of section 523(a)(4), a bankruptcy court is not bound by the state law definition of larceny but, rather, may follow federal common law, which defines larceny as a "felonious taking of another's personal property with intent to convert it or deprive the owner of the same." 4 *Collier on Bankruptcy* ¶ 523.10[2] (15th ed. rev. 2008).[1]

In re Ormsby, 591 F.3d 1199, 1205 n.4 (9th Cir. 2010); *see also In re Morris*, 229 B.R. 683 (E.D. Ky. Br. 1999) (finding that burglar's taking of property of another without his consent and with intent to permanently deprive him of possession constituted larceny for purposes of 523(a)(4) and willful and malicious injury for purposes of 523(a)(6)). In a dognapping or horsenapping case, 523(a)(4) would prove most germane.

2. 11 U.S.C. § 523(a)(6)

Section 523(a)(6) prevents discharge "for willful and malicious injury by the debtor to another entity or to the property of another entity." 11 U.S.C. § 523(a)(6). *Kawaauhau v. Geiger*, 523 U.S. 57 (1998), made clear that for this section to apply, the actor must intend the consequences of the act, not simply the act itself. *Id.*, at 60. Both willfulness and maliciousness must be proven to block discharge. However, "it is of no moment whether the [debtors'] conduct satisfied the willful and malicious standards articulated under [state] law," as federal standards apply. *In re Lababit*, 2009 Bankr. LEXIS 4524 (9th Cir. B.A.P. Oct. 8, 2009).

a. Willfulness

"Section 523(a)(6)'s willful injury requirement is met only when the debtor has a subjective motive to inflict injury or when the debtor believes that injury is substantially certain to result from his own conduct." *Carrillo v. Su (In re Su)*, 290 F.3d 1140, 1142 (9th Cir. 2002). The Debtor is charged with knowledge of the natural consequences of her actions. *Id.*, at 1146. The subjective standard is based on the debtor's "actual knowledge that harm to the creditor was substantially certain." *Id.* However, when speaking of "actual knowledge," the court is

> not suggesting that a court must simply take the debtor's word for his state of mind. In addition to what a debtor may admit to knowing, the

---

[1] [4] Felonious is defined as " 'proceeding from an evil heart or purpose; malicious; villainous . . . Wrongful; (of an act) done without excuse of color of right.' " *Elliott v. Kiesewetter (In re Kiesewetter)*, 391 B.R. 740, 748 (Bankr. W.D. Pa. 2008) (quoting BLACK'S LAW DICTIONARY (8th ed. 2004)).

bankruptcy court may consider circumstantial evidence that tends to establish what the debtor must have actually known when taking the injury-producing action.

Id., at 1146 fn. 6. Accordingly, even if "subjective intent to harm" is not demonstrated, grounds may exist to pursue a claim under the alternative "willfulness" basis of "subjective belief that harm is substantially certain."

b. Maliciousness

In addition to willfulness, the creditors must also prove maliciousness. While the "malicious" inquiry is separately analyzed from the "willful" requirement, proof of the former tends to compel proof of the latter, from which it may be inferred. *In re Thiara*, 285 B.R. 420, 434 (9th Cir. B.A.P. 2002) (noting that in case of intentional and willful conversion, malice may be inferred from the nature of the wrongful act); *In re Endicott*, 254 B.R. 471, 478 (Bankr. D. Idaho, 2000) (noting how very same evidentiary facts relate to both elements). A "malicious injury" is one involving: (1) a wrongful act, (2) done intentionally, (3) which necessarily causes injury, and (4) is done without just cause or excuse. *In re Su*, at 1146–47. The Ninth Circuit has refined the "malicious" inquiry to allow for proof that it was "reasonably foreseeable" that the debtor's actions or inactions might injure the creditor, rather than show specific intent to injure. *In re Britton*, 950 F.2d 602, 605 (9th Cir. 1991); *In re Bammer*, 131 F.3d 788, 791 (9th Cir. 1997) (does not require showing of biblical malice); *In re Trantham*, 304 B.R. 298, 308 (6th Cir. B.A.P. 2004). To infer malice, however, it must first be established that the conversion was willful. *See Thiara*, 285 B.R. at 434.

Unlawfully taking, harming, or killing an animal; or retaining possession of an animal knowing that she belongs to another who is actively searching for same constitutes both a conversion and a § 523(a)(6) violation as discussed in *In re Thiara:*

> A conversion of another's property without his knowledge or consent, done intentionally and without justification and excuse, to the other's injury, constitutes a willful and malicious injury within the meaning of § 523(a)(6).

Id., at 431 (quoting *In re Bailey*, 197 F.3d 997, 1000 (9th Cir. 1999)).

c. Encouragement of Third Parties

Section 523(a)(6) does not require that the debtor actually be the one who personally inflicts damage to the person or property. Indeed, where the debtor seeks or encourages another to commit a willful and malicious act, he may not achieve discharge. "[T]he types of encouragement which may lead to a finding of nondischargeability under § 523(a)(6) can range from overt encouragement to simply an omission, if such an omission was calculated by the debtor in a willful and malicious manner to cause injury." *In re Sintobin*, 253 B.R. 826, 830–31 (Bankr. N.D. Ohio 2000) (finding interpretive support in *Geiger* and public policy and holding that an intentional tort is "an act or omission"). In *Sintobin*, the defendants did not deter their children, who had a known propensity for vandalism, from causing serious damage to plaintiff-landlord's property. Accordingly, those who incite others to maim animals may bear accomplice bankruptcy liability.

d. Omission and Inaction

While commission of a wrongful act might satisfy both willful and malicious prongs, omission or inaction could as well. In addition to the *Sintobin* court, others acknowledge that omissions state the basis for nondischargeability under § 523(a)(6). *See In re Vestal*, 256 B.R. 326, 328–329 (Bankr. M.D. Fla. 2000). This question was analyzed in great detail by the Eighth Circuit Bankruptcy Appellate Panel in 2006, where the appellate panel expressly rejected the debtor's argument that "a passive failure to act (acts of omission), as opposed to overt conduct (acts of commission), cannot meet the standard for nondischargeability under § 523(a)(6)." *In re Patch*, 356 B.R. 450, 457 (8th Cir. B.A.P. 2006), rev. o.g., 526 F.3d 1176 (8th Cir. 2008).[2] "[T]he failure to act in the face of a duty to do so can constitute an intentional tort." *Id.*

The *Patch* court found that the debtor's knowledge that her son had been a victim of abuse for an extended period, that she continued to leave him with his abuser, that she purposefully hid that abuse from others by removing him from daycare and speech therapy, and that, on the night of his death, she prevented him from obtaining medical help when he obviously needed it, even if she did not actually intend or desire for her son to die, satisfied the alternative basis of willfulness in that she was substantially certain that her son's injury would result from her conduct. *Id.*, at 456–458. *Patch* provides a ready analogy in an animal neglect or fraud situation.

One may similarly prove malicious injury through omission or inaction where the failure to act is in disregard of knowledge that injury is substantially certain to occur. *Id.*, at 459 (citing *In re Muhammad*, 135 B.R. 294, 298 (Bankr. N.D. Ill. 1991). The *Patch* court found the debtor's inactivity both willful and malicious. A California bankruptcy court cites to the *Patch* doctrine in disagreeing with the debtor that because she "merely failed to act . . . did not commit an intentional tort." *In re Macias*, 2007 WL 2223472, at 6 (Bankr. E.D. Cal., 2007) (evaluating where allegation of *failure to render aid* set forth a basis for willful injury).

e. Illustrative Cases

In the context of animals destroying a landlord's property, consider *In re Carlyle*, 2007 Bankr. LEXIS 193 (Bankr. W.D. Mo. 2007). Debtor-renters owned a large dog and two cats. After defaulting on rent, the debtors vacated the premises and filed for Chapter 7. The landlord commenced an adversary proceeding to establish that the $7,800 in rental property damage resulting from the debtors' companion animals was nondischargeable under § 523(a)(6). Debtors denied that they intentionally allowed their animals to ruin the premises. Though convinced that the Debtors and

---

[2] On appeal to the 8th Circuit, the court reversed the B.A.P. but on grounds that "no rational trier of fact could find that Patch's action or inaction was 'willful' based on the summary judgment record and any reasonable inferences derived from that record." *Id.*, at 1182. Finding support and opposition to the B.A.P.'s interpretation of acts of omission for proving "willfulness," the 8th Circuit refused to "conclusively resolve" the issue of whether a failure to act in the face of a duty can constitute an intentional tort. *Id.*

their animals damaged the dwelling, the court was equally convinced that the landlord did not prove that the damage was done with intent to injure him, thus making the debt dischargeable. *Slip op.* at 3.

In *In re Peterson*, 332 B.R. 678 (Bankr. D. Del. 2005), judgment creditors sought to avoid discharge of Chapter 7 debts based on § 523(a)(6). They asserted that the debtor agreed orally and in writing that she would be solely responsible for damage to the premises by her dogs. They further noted strict liability under Del. Code Ann. 7:1711 (holding an owner liable for damages for any injury, death or loss to person or property caused by such dog). The court held that even a knowing breach of contract would not constitute willful and malicious injury. *Id.*, at 685. Furthermore, a finding of liability under DCA 7:1711 could not prevent discharge because it did not contemplate a particular mental state or a finding of willful and malicious injury. *Id.* (citing *In re Pourdas*, 206 B.R. 516, 520 (Bankr. S.D. Ill. 1997) (holding that failure to obtain license or insurance policy for vicious dog, violating strict liability statute, was not willful and malicious)). Wittily, the court notes that this case

> involves the keeping of dogs with a propensity towards messiness — not viciousness. Thus, plaintiffs' reliance on dog bite authorities is misplaced. It is one thing to knowingly keep a vicious dog, it is another to knowingly keep a messy dog.

Id.

In *In re Feige*, 2005 WL 3320847 (W.D. Wash. 2005), the federal court sanctioned Spoerer and his counsel $7,500 following summary judgment dismissal of an adversary proceeding to except from discharge the Feiges' debt under § 523(a)(6) and § 523(a)(2)(A). Spoerer, the landlord, rented his premises to the Feiges. Spoerer maintained that the Feiges told him that while the wife owned a pet sitting business, the debtors did not personally own pets and would not have pets in the house. The Feiges defaulted in rent, prompting an unlawful detainer action, which also sought fees for damages to the premises from the Feiges' cats and from the alleged intentional destruction of property prior to surrender of the premises. An arbitrator awarded $15,960 in back rent and late fees plus $29,224.22 in attorney fees. On a trial de novo, the state court trial judge awarded $84,911.26. Then the Feiges filed for Chapter 7.

In the adversary proceeding, the district court affirmed, stating that even if Spoerer relied upon the Feiges' misrepresentation of having no pets, he failed to establish a link between the misrepresentation and the loss suffered. "Although the Feiges' misrepresentation may have induced Spoerer to enter into the lease, there is no connection alleged between lying about cats and failure to pay the rent, nor is the withholding of rent a foreseeable result of owning pets or lying about owning pets." *Slip op.*, at 4. The district court noted that the $750 for carpet cleaning could have potentially been excepted from discharge, but Spoerer sought to attribute the entire $85,000 debt to the presence of cats. As to the § 523(a)(6) willful and malicious injury claim, the court added that the only part of the judgment arguably stemming from "willful and malicious" conduct is $1,151.76 for carpet cleaning and labor to repair the kitchen cabinets. Humorously, the court added, "Spoerer offers nothing to show that the Feiges intentionally caused their cats to stain the carpet with feces and vomit. Instead, Spoerer focuses its argument on the number of cats and that

they were not allowed, none of which are relevant to the Feiges' subjective intent."
Slip op., at 6.

3.   11 U.S.C. § 523(a)(2)(A)

Section 523(a)(2)(A) prevents discharge of debts "for money, property, sewrvices, or an extension, renewal, or refinancing of credit, to the extent obtained by — false pretenses, a false representation, or actual fraud, other than a statement respecting the debtor's or an insider's financial condition." Where the debtor falsely promises to care for a creditor's nonhuman animals, but instead slaughters them and lies about it, particularly where the debtor knows of the creditor's emotional bond to the warded animals, do not forget § 523(a)(2)(A). Defrauding creditors by misappropriating bailed animals for personal gain creates an arguably nondischargeable debt under the "false pretenses" exception, or potentially as defalcation or fraud in a fiduciary capacity (under § 523(a)(4), as in the case of free-lease arrangements with farm animals). A word of caution: if the transaction can be considered "consumer"-based, a creditor risks paying the debtor's attorney's fees if she does not prevail. 11 U.S.C. § 523(d).

B.   DOG BITES

Before *Geiger*, nondischargeable dog bites found refuge in § 523(a)(6). *See Humphreys v. Heller*, 157 Misc. 568 (N.Y. Sup. Ct. 1935) (where debtor wrongfully kept dog knowing him to be ferocious, and dog later bit creditor, willful and malicious exception satisfied); *Yackel v. Nys*, 258 App. Div. 318 (N.Y. Sup. Ct. App. Div. 1939) (though gravamen of complaint dealt with negligent control, because debtors knew dog previously bit other people, the act of harboring the dangerous dog was wrongful and malicious and done intentionally and satisfied § 523(a)(6)); *Beam v. Karaim*, 47 N.Y.S. 2d 193 (N.Y. Cty. Ct. 1944) (unlawful keeping of German police dog known to be vicious states claim for willful and malicious exception); *Jaco v. Baker*, 174 Or. 191 (1944); *Peerson v. Mitchell*, 239 P.2d 1028 (Okla. 1950). These cases, though more than 50 years old, suggest that strict statutory or strict common law dog bite liability claims are nondischargeable in bankruptcy.

After *Geiger*, however, these claims are "all bark" unless the creditor can prove the debtor intended not just the act of harboring a vicious dog, but also the desire to harm the creditor. In other words, did the debtor sic Fido on the creditor? *See Matter of Quezada*, 718 F.2d 121 (5th Cir. 1983) (finding that neither debtors' harboring pit bull within fenced premises in crowded neighborhood, nor subsequent negligence in permitting dog to escape to cause injury, sufficed to prevent discharge of the debt) (pre-*Geiger*). For more information, see 26 A.L.R.2d 1368, *Injury by Dog or Other Animal as Wilful and Malicious Injury so as to Preclude It or Judgment Procured on It from Operation of Bankruptcy Discharge.*

C.   EXCEPTIONLESS DEBTS

Debts not dischargeable even under a Chapter 13 payment plan include court-ordered restitution awards/criminal fines, certain (p)alimony/child support orders, student loans, tax liens, and death or personal injury caused by a drunk or intoxicated driver. 11 U.S.C. § 1328. It is doubtful that the "drunk driver" exception of § 523(a)(9) ("death or personal injury caused by the debtor's operation of a motor vehicle . . . ") to discharge would apply to nonhuman animals, although a service animal might be deemed an extension of the disabled handler. If maintenance decrees or agreements contemplate payments for the spouse or child's companion animals, one may argue that the incidental "puppy support" award is nondischargeable under § 523(a)(5) ("domestic support obligation"). Certainly, criminal fines related to animal cruelty would never be excused under § 1328 (a)(3).

D.   ANIMALS LOST IN CONVERSION

As property, animals may be subject to disposition by the bankruptcy trustee as part of the bankruptcy estate. The case *In re John*, 352 B.R. 895 (Bankr. N.D. Fla. 2006) instructs about the danger of converting to a Chapter 7 from a Chapter 13 after certain personal property (including a family dog) has left the possession or control of the Debtor on the date of conversion. The debtors in *John* originally filed a Chapter 13 in 2003, listing $3,660 worth of certain unencumbered, nonexempt, personal property (including clothes, jewelry, household goods, handtools, and the family dog) ("Property"). After the Plan was confirmed, the Debtors retained possession of this Property and made substantial payments toward the plan. However, they eventually defaulted and voluntarily converted to a Chapter 7 in 2006, pursuant to 11 U.S.C. § 1307(a). Upon conversion, the Chapter 13 trustee is discharged and a new Chapter 7 trustee is appointed. §§ 348(a), (e), 701(a)(1).

The Chapter 7 trustee sought turnover of the Property scheduled in the original petition. A consequence of the debtors' choice to convert to a Chapter 7, rather than pursue a hardship discharge under § 1328(b), was that § 348 controlled as to the definition of "property of the estate." It included personalty owned by the debtors at the time of the Chapter 13 petition "if, and only if, such property remained in the possession or control of the Debtors on the date of [Chapter 7] conversion." *Id.*, at 904. The Debtors asserted that the Property in their original Chapter 13 petition should "no longer" be considered property of the estate, even though it remained in the Debtors' possession on the date of conversion. They argued that the Property vested in them after they made payments under the Chapter 13 plan. The court disagreed, noting that upon conversion, it was no longer a Chapter 13 case. As property of the estate, the Chapter 7 trustee was required by law to pursue it and reduce it to money. §§ 348(f)(1)(A), 704(1). Where the dog was not listed on the Debtors' Chapter 7 schedules (but was listed on the date the original Chapter 13 petition was filed), it became the property of the estate in the converted case. Thus, the Trustee retained the power to permit or deny the Debtors the right to retain the dog by repurchasing the dog from her.

E.   FRAUD IN FAILING TO DISCLOSE "PET DOG"

In *In re Smith*, 351 B.R. 274 (Bankr. D. Conn., 2006), creditors brought an action under § 727(a)(2)(A), (2)(B), (3), (4)(A), (4)(B), and (5) and made the "patently preposterous assertion that the [Chapter 7] Debtor should be denied his discharge for failure to list as an asset on Schedule B his 'pet dog,'" prompting the remark from Debtor's counsel:

> It is a terrible thing to live for four or five years with the kind of debts that Mr. Smith had incurred, not knowing if you're ever going to get out from under. It's a particularly terrible thing if you're the kind of person as I think Mr. Smith has demonstrated he is. He isn't trying to skin anybody: he wasn't trying to gain anything: he wasn't trying to pull a fast one. He had, if anything, the misfortune of having a creditor named The Cadle Company who came after him for everything from the household account and the household and business accounts to the now infamous and, hopefully, never again to be seen in this Court of any other court around here that does bankruptcy, failure to list Buddy, the dog. . . .

Id., at 276. Given that one may assert a high intrinsic value for a companion animal, which may affect what exemptions can be taken, was it inappropriate not to list Buddy? If not, is the court saying that he is more a dependent than estate property?

F. ANIMALS AS BANKRUPTCY ASSETS

Aside from exceptions to discharge, certain classes of property are exempt from disposition as part of the bankruptcy estate. Be aware that debtors may elect either the state or federal exemption regime. The federal framework, per 11 U.S.C. § 522(d)(3), allows for a per item exemption of $525 or an aggregate exemption of $10,775 for household goods, including animals. The Washington framework permits an exemption of up to $2,700 per individual or $5,400 for the community with respect to household goods, appliances, furniture, and home and yard equipment. RCW § 6.15.010(3)(a). Other personal property, except personal earnings, not to exceed $2,000 in value (not to include more than $200 in cash, bank deposits, bonds, stocks, and securities), is also exempt. RCW § 6.15.010(3)(b). Tools of a farmer's trade (notably not identifying animals) are exempt up to $5,000. RCW § 6.15.010(4)(a), (c). Note, however, that "all professionally prescribed health aids for the debtor or a dependent of the debtor" are *per se* exempt. RCW § 6.15.010(3)(e). Whether RCW § 6.15.010(3)(e) applies to service animals as "health aids" is unknown.

Service animals present a unique exemption challenge, given that they double as trusted companions and a form of durable medical equipment or prosthetic device. *See* 11 U.S.C. § 522(d)(9) (professionally prescribed health aids are categorically exempt) and *Burnham v. State Dept. of Social and Health Services*, 115 Wash. App. 435 (2003) (service animals needed to correct physical deformity or malfunction may not be DME but are prosthetic devices, the expenses for which can be reimbursed). *See also* § 522 (d)(11)(D) (up to $17,425 exempt for payments related to personal bodily injury). It is uncertain whether the exemption would extend to service animals, but consider a New Jersey appellate division's decision stating, "[I]n view of the function of the dog as a veritable extension of the appellant's own body, an injury to the dog is tantamount to an injury to appellant's person." *In re Matter of Lillian Kline*, Superior Court of New Jersey, Appellate Division Cause No. A-1788-95TS (1996).

The federal district court of Oregon ruled that horses were domestic animals and exempt under the Oregon bankruptcy statute although kept for riding or "personal use," as opposed to agricultural or commercial gain. Rejecting the trustee's claim that the statute did not intend to define horses kept for "personal use" as "domestic animals," the court stated, "[a]ny domestic animals, including horses and dogs[,] should be included whether kept for the use of the whole family or primarily for only one member thereof." *In re Canutt*, 264 F. Supp. 919 (D.C. Or. 1967). The Oregon statute also exempted food required to maintain those animals, although the exemption limit was a mere $300. One can readily see inevitable conflict between bankruptcy exemption law and nonhuman animal valuation law (where intrinsic value far exceeds fair market value). Bankruptcy courts also draw distinctions between exemptions for commercial animals and companion animals, but how does one resolve the dual classification of, say, a debtor's beloved poodle who happens to be a Westminster icon studded out regularly at tens of thousands per breeding? See *In re Cass*, 104 B.R. 382 (Bankr. N.D. Okla. 1989) (horses used occasionally as pets or riding animals not claimable as property held primarily for personal, family, or household use, because main value was as profitable stud animal).

In *In re Glenn*, 345 B.R. 831 (Bankr. N.D. Ohio 2006), the court considered the Trustee's motion to dismiss the Chapter 7 petition on grounds of "substantial abuse" pursuant to § 707(b) with respect to the question of whether Debtor's enumerated income and expense figures, for purposes of applying the "disposable income" test, included impermissible expenditures on luxuries, for example, budgeting $350.00 a month for pet care, with Mrs. Glenn describing her pets "as her children." "Disposable income" is defined by that "which is received by the debtor and which is not reasonably necessary to be expended for the maintenance or support of the debtor of the dependent of the debtor . . . [.]" 11 U.S.C. § 1325(b)(2). *Id.*, at 836. While the court agreed with a statement made in *Matter of Wyant*, 217 B.R. 585, 588 (Bankr. D. Neb. 1998) that it was "commendable that the debtor is willing to care for these animals and to attend to their feed and medical needs[,]" it also reasoned that, "As between the debtor's elderly horses and dogs and his creditors, I think that the creditors should be paid first. The proposed expenditures on these animals are excessive, unreasonable, and not necessary for the maintenance of support of the debtor or his dependents." *Id.*, at 839. *See also In re Mooney*, 313 B.R. 709, 716 (Bankr. N.D. Ohio 2004) (noting that there is nothing wrong with "dog treats, dog dental care items and more," but there is something wrong when "these expenses continue and unpaid creditors are told by the bankruptcy court to shinny up a cactus.").

In *Matter of Wilson*, 162 F.3d 378 (5th Cir. 1998), the Fifth Circuit Court of Appeals certified to the Louisiana Supreme Court the question of whether 100 dairy cows, valued between $100,000 and $150,000, could be claimed under the Louisiana bankruptcy code as "tools" and "instruments" that are "necessary to the exercise of a trade, calling, or profession, by which [the debtor] earns his livelihood." *Id.*, at 379 (citing La. R.S. § 13:3881(A)(2)). The certified question was answered in the negative. *In re Wilson*, 734 So. 2d 1214 (La. 1999) (rejecting debtors' plea to apply the "functional test" in their favor, as used by the Tenth Circuit in *In re Heape*, 886 F.2d 280 (10th Cir. 1986) (requiring court to interpret language of exemption statute in light of function and use of property, rather than physical characteristics)). The creditors urged adoption of the Seventh Circuit logic that "to regard cows and other livestock as tools or implements" would do "particular violence to the English language." *Id.* (quoting *Matter of Patterson*, 825 F.2d 1140, 1147 (7th Cir. 1987)). The Louisiana Supreme Court concluded:

> In those instances where animals are being used to perform work on the farm, such as mules which are used to pull plows, the jurisprudence has concluded such animals are tools of the farm, even though they might not fall within a dictionary definition of tools. In this light, the function of the animal is not substantially different from a pickup truck, which is specifically listed as an exempted item in La. R.S. 13:3881(A)(2)(d). By contrast, animals being held as livestock do not perform the work of the farm. Admittedly, in the case of a dairy farm, much of the equipment of the farm is there for the purposes of milking the cows. However, the cows themselves do not perform the work of the farm; rather, they are the "raw material" of the farm, from which the finished product is made. Seen in this light, we conclude livestock on a farm are not tools and instruments as set forth in La. R.S. 13:3881(A)(2).

Id., at 1216. While it can be disputed that the cows do no "work" on the farm or that they are mere "raw material," particularly when they are being raised for subsequent slaughter, such an objection is hardly material for purposes of bankruptcy law — because whether they are "tools" or "implements" does not liberate them from their fundamental status as owned chattel.

One should also be aware that the federal lien avoidance statute of the bankruptcy code prohibits the fixing of a lien on an interest of the debtor in property to the extent that such lien impairs an exemption to which the debtor would have been entitled under 11 U.S.C. § 522(b), if the lien is a judicial lien (§ 522(f)(1)(A)) or a nonpossessory, nonpurchase-money security interest in any animals held primarily for personal, family, or household use of the debtor or a dependent of the debtor (§ 522(f)(1)(B)(i)). But see *In re Thompson*, 750 F.2d 628, 631 (8th Cir. 1984) (did not permit lien avoidance of security interest in 210 pigs worth $4,500, finding that pigs were not held primarily for person, family, or household use of the farmer).

Chapter 19

VALUATION OF ANIMALS

Hypothetical: In your mind's eye, the lynx-point Siamese sits perched atop your desk, gazing at you through half-closed eyelids, tail coiled around her front paws. Breaking from her mesmerizing stare, she launches into a tale of woe. Neighbors a few blocks over had been training their large, mixed-breed dogs in the illicit art of fighting. Small animals and unsuspecting small-breed dogs were taken and used as bait to train Bane, Tank, and Piggy. When Piggy had a litter of puppies, the neighbor drop-kicked her eight-week-old pups over the six-foot fence, forced them to drag logging chains, and run treadmills for hours until they collapsed. The poor creatures slept outside in a roofless, chicken-wire perimetered enclosure, without the benefit of shelter from the rain or cold.

One morning, Piggy and her pups were running at-large (as they are wont to do) in the small town. They scoured the neighborhood for blood. Only this time they claimed the life of the Siamese whose apparition is watching as you draft the demand package to the defendant dog owners.

Pyewacket was an older cat who had lived with a young girl and her single father for 12 years. She was lounging in the sun in the dandelions and catnip adjacent to the tulip bed of your clients' back yard when Piggy and her pups picked up her scent. The lot turned their menacing attention to Pyewacket, broke through the decorative fence, and attacked her in mid-stretch.

Within moments, the once content feline was being drawn and nearly quartered by the six dogs. The commotion attracted the teenage daughter and her father. Both ran to the sliding glass door. In horror, the daughter, who had loved the cat like a baby for 12 years, collapsed to the floor, covered her ears, and wailed for divine intervention to spare her cat's life. The father ran outside to disperse the dogs. Behind they left the Siamese, her tongue still in her mouth but with the entire lower jaw hanging by a thread of tissue. One eye was black, the other a narrow slit. Orange-colored blood poured from her nose and mouth. With nearly every bone in her body broken, the father could barely lift her into the car for the emergency trip to the vet's office. Before dying, Pyewacket heard the daughter's crying and mustered what strength she had to turn her head in the girl's direction, an effort to console her as she had done for over a decade of tears and tantrums. She died in transit after choking on her own blood.

Pyewacket licks her paw and washes her face. As you watch her, you wonder how to quantify her life. What does the law say about valuing this beloved cat who gave solace, compassion, support, and love to your minor client? An orphaned kitten, she was abandoned to a woman who gave her away for free. She sat cuddled with her littermates, mewing and scampering in a deep cardboard box until a three-year-old girl and her father approached and peered inside. She looked up at the little girl. From that moment on, for the next 12 years, she became the girl's best friend and the girl her guardian.

At 15, the three-year-old is now a depressed teenager who suffers post-traumatic stress from and recurrent, graphic nightmares of, the violent attack on Pyewacket. She still mourns daily, and occasionally breaks down completely.

(1)   Can she recover for the pain and suffering of this innocent feline?

(2)   Can she obtain emotional distress damages for her presence during the fatal attack on her beloved cat?

(3)   What is the economic value of this cat? Is she more like a pencil (i.e., fungible), a family heirloom (i.e., intrinsic value), an automobile (which depreciates over time), an antique (which appreciates over time), or a child?

(4)   What is the noneconomic value of this cat in terms of loss of utility, loss of parent-child consortium, mental anguish, deprivation of companionship, friendship, protection, and love?

By this time, Pyewacket has (in your mind) sprawled across your desk and is pawing at the mouse as you apply finishing touches to the damages section of the demand letter. You patiently explain that ailurophobic and less adventurous attorneys would shoo her out of the office, appraise her at $20, and call it a day. But you are not jaded, nor easily discouraged. You realize that the world is comprised of countless other species possessing sentience, a co-evolutionary nature, and a level of domestication deserving of judicial respect. Whether integral or incidental to your practice, you become an animal law attorney.

The disconnect between legal "objecthood" and legal personhood becomes most apparent when we consider that humans can sue for their pain and suffering, yet nonhuman animals, who unquestionably have the same capacity for pain and suffering, cannot see theirs taxed to the wrongdoer. Ethical societies wishing to rectify wrongs through civil redress may only restore equilibrium by compensating every dimension of harm unlawfully inflicted. When an evil individual intentionally pepper-sprays a dog through the mail slot of the owner's locked front door because he hates the family, he has caused a number of what should be compensable damages — emotional distress and economic loss to the family, but also retinal burn and excruciating pain and suffering to a blameless and childlike dog. By providing recourse through legal institutions, we may preserve the dignity animals deserve as sentient beings who ache, fear, and brave intolerable cruelties.

Debate exists, however, as to whether larger monetary awards will, in fact, yield this outcome. *See* Victor E. Schwartz & Emily J. Laird, *Non-Economic Damages in Pet Litigation: The Serious Need to Preserve a Rational Rule*, 33 PEPP. L. REV. 227 (2006). Commentators like Schwartz examine the similarities between animals and property that the courts have held possess no market value, such as family photographs and heirlooms. On the one hand, restricting a plaintiff to the depreciated market valuation would prove unduly harsh and not serve the paramount rule of just compensation. But Schwartz differs, contending that a higher valuation under the law would not serve animals and their owners. Ultimately, critics like Schwartz argue that the cost of veterinary services would likely increase, and owning a fully insured and fully cared-for animal companion may become cost-prohibitive. As a result, fewer animals will be adopted and more will die in shelters.

Such refrain occurs with alarming frequency despite a lack of empirical evidence. Nowhere in the article do the authors cite to one study that proves the probability (or even the very real possibility) that the sky will actually fall in the form of a mass exodus of veterinarians from the field or skyrocketing costs of care. *Burgess v. Shampooch Pet Indus., Inc.*, 131 P.3d 1248, 1253 (Kan. Ct. App. 2006) (rejected "hyperbolic[]" claims that a ruling allowing recovery of veterinary bills in excess of acquisition price would "open the proverbial 'floodgates' of high-dollar litigation on behalf of animals. . . .")

Erudite sources have acknowledged the two basic functions of the law of torts — to deter future conduct through a finding of liability and to compensate the injured person for damages sustained. RESTATEMENT (2D) OF TORTS § 901 (1979); Learned Hand, 3 A.B.C.N.Y. LECTURES ON LEGAL TOPICS 87 (1926). Yet some veterinarians disingenuously rely on the human-animal bond for their livelihoods while contending that their malpractice should be economically fixed at fair market value. To restore balance to this doctrinally unfair alignment, and to use the civil justice system to provide both compensation and deterrence, requires discipline. However, private litigation is a poor and highly costly substitute, at least until financial recoveries accurately reflect the true losses sustained by animal guardians, and the animals themselves.

The following list identifies classes of potentially recoverable damages:

1. Prudently incurred search and rescue expenses
2. Veterinary bills to effect a cure for physical injury
3. Loss of use/companionship during convalescence
4. Depreciation in (intrinsic) value
5. Reduction in enjoyment of life
6. Interference with quiet use and enjoyment of animal
7. Future veterinary bills for physical injury
8. Reduction in life expectancy of animal
9. Permanent partial disabilities/impairments of animal
10. Resocialization and retraining for psychological injury
11. Wage loss or substitute domiciliary care of convalescing animal
12. Mileage to effect cure
13. Emotional distress
14. Secondary physical injury to owner-guardian (e.g., injured animal bites rescuer or rescuer injured during rescue attempt by cause other than injured animal)
15. Punitive damages
16. Statutory civil penalties

17. Actual, incidental, and consequential damages

18. Lost progeny

For deceased animals:

1. Prudently incurred search and rescue expenses

2. Veterinary bills to effect a cure for physical injury although futile (recoverable on basis of compliance with duty to mitigate)

3. Loss of use/companionship during convalescence and between date of death and date judgment rendered

4. (Intrinsic) value

5. Loss of enjoyment of life

6. Interference with quiet use and enjoyment of animal

7. Resocialization and retraining for psychological injury, although futile

8. Wage loss or substitute domiciliary care and monitoring of animal prior to death

9. Mileage to effect cure

10. Emotional distress

11. Secondary physical injury to owner-guardian (e.g., injured animal bites rescuer or rescuer injured during rescue attempt by cause other than injured animal)

12. Punitive damages

13. Statutory civil penalties

14. Actual, incidental, and consequential damages

15. Burial, cremation, memorialization

16. Lost progeny

Hypothetical: Orbit is the author's 26-year-old, neutered male, orange tabby adopted from a shelter at the age of two for probably less than $50 in 1989. By Schwartz's calculation,[1] one would be lucky to get more than a few dollars for Orbit. But this presumes that animals can be replaced. A shelter or humane society will tell you that not only have they never had such a cat surrendered by owner or found as a stray, but if such a cat were to exist, they would likely find none to adopt him at that age — in part due to the need to treat Orbit with bidaily subcutaneous fluid therapy, oral doses of liquid and pill medication, and transdermal methimazole application to treat his hyperthyroid condition. Specifically, no replacement could ever be found who matches the phenotypic and genotypic characteristics of Orbit, not to mention his personality and the extent to which he enlivened the household, provided stability (the author's wife described him as her "rock"), and delighted with his gentle and loving manner. A true "replacement" in the genetic sense only

---

[1] In the interest of full disclosure, Professor Schwartz does appreciate felines. "Mr. Schwartz once owned two cats, Chat and Spinach. He believes that if Chat had lived the length of years of a human, Chat would have been admitted to a reasonably good law school. Spinach, on the other hand, would have been gainfully employed at a fast food chain, eating some of the profits." Schwartz, 33 Pepp. L. Rev. at fn. A1.

would require that the tortfeasor produce a clone. Such an evidentiary tack does not suffer forays into a plaintiff's emotional distress, excessive sentimentality, or human-animal bond. Therefore, if one allows replacement value to guide valuation in such animal death cases, then such proponents of replacement value may be saddled with five- or six-figure debts per nonhuman decedent, the price to clone at Sooam Biotech Research Foundation in Seoul, Korea. *See Earl v. Menu Foods Income Fund*, 169 Wash. App. 1005 (2012) (pro se plaintiff claimed $180,000 in damages to create a clone of Chuckles, his cat who allegedly died from eating food contaminated with acetaminophen and cyanuric acid).[2]

---

[2] The technology for cloning cats was developed and successfully employed in 2001 through collaboration between Savings and Clone, Inc. and Texas A&M University. Shin et al., *A Cat Cloned by Nuclear Transplantation*, 415 NATURE 859 (Feb. 21, 2002). Dog cloning feasibility followed in 2005 via the somatic cell nuclear transfer (SCNT) technique. Cells in a cat or dog can be classified as being either (a) somatic cells or (b) germ cells. Somatic cells are all cells comprising the tissues and organs of the dog (except for the germ cells). Germ cells are the specialized cells found in males (sperm precursors) and females (oocytes, commonly called "eggs") which combine together to form a fertilized embryo. The cloning technique replaces the process of sexual reproduction, in which sperm and egg combine to produce a fertilized embryo.

A study published by Yin et al., *Production of Second-Generation Cloned Cats by Somatic Cell Nuclear Transfer*, 69 THERIOGENOLOGY 1001-1006 (2008), demonstrated the feasibility of producing a cloned cat from a donor who was a cloned cat. In this particular study, the donor, a 6-month-old male cat (who was himself a clone) was successfully used to produce a "clone of the clone" cat. Oh et al., *Recloned Dogs Derived from Adipose Stem cells of a Transgenic Cloned Beagle*, THERIOGENOLOGY, Vol. 75, 1221-1231 (2011), held similarly, using a donor beagle (who was itself a clone) with a specific genetic mutation that passed to the "clone of the clone" dog. These studies provide strong evidence that a cat or dog who is cloned can serve as the donor for subsequent clones.

Gomez, et al., *Nuclear Transfer in Cats and its Applications*, 66 THERIOGENOLOGY 72 (2006), reviews cat cloning research. Yin et al., *Generation of Cloned Cats Expressing Red Fluorescent Protein*, 78 BIOLOGY OF REPRODUCTION 425 (2008), describes the successful genetic modification of a cloned cat via the introduction of a gene that encodes a red fluorescent protein into the genome of a white, male Angora cat. Two live-born, cloned cats were genetically verified to be clones of the donor cat. In addition, the cloned cats tested positive for the introduced gene. Taken together, these results demonstrate the technology feasibility of successfully cloning a genetically modified cat.

Kim et al., *Lessons Learned from Cloning Dogs*, 47(4) REPROD DOM ANIMAL (2012), reviews dog cloning research and catalogs the growth characteristics of cloned dogs. The conclusions presented in the paper state that cloned dog height, weight, embryological development, and blood properties were similar between donors and clones. Slight exceptions included some variations in body weight and dental development; however, many traits such as body weight, for example, can be influenced by factors outside of genetics, such as diet, activity level, and environment. This paper also describes studies that were done to assess if the reproductive cycle in female cloned dogs was similar to non-cloned members of the breed. The findings of the studies conclude that the reproductive traits of the cloned dogs are within the normal limits of the breed.

Choi et al., *Behavioral Analysis of Cloned Puppies Derived from an Elite Drug-Detection Dog*, 44 BEHAV GENET. 68-76 (2014), describes the behavioral analysis of scent detection working dogs and compares the behavioral properties of the cloned dogs to the behavioral properties of the donor, as well as to naturally bred dogs. The breed employed in this study was the Golden Retriever, and used the Korea Customs Detector Dog Training program to assess their capacity of scent detection. The authors report that seven out of eight cloned dogs met the selection criteria for scent detection dogs as compared to one of the naturally bred dogs, and concluded that "clones are more consistent in their behavior than naturally bred animals." Scent work is a very specific behavior set and cannot be extrapolated to imply other behavioral similarities among individuals who demonstrate this particular aptitude.

Some argue that a clone of a pet cat or dog is the closest genetic and phenotypic "replacement" for the loss of the donor. Putting aside the morality of cloning (given the overpopulation crisis that afflicts our

By way of analytical comparison, consider *Mieske v. Bartell Drug Co.*, 593 P.2d 1308 (Wash. 1979). The Mieskes brought developed movie film to Bartell Drug for splicing onto larger rolls. Dozens of canisters filled with irreplaceable memories were subsequently lost or destroyed due to the negligence of the defendant, who deemed rolls of raw negative sufficient compensation. Plaintiffs argued that the memories, while contained on the film, had no market value, and could not be replaced or restored. They added, however, that the memories were so unique that some other measure of damages must exist to ensure full compensation. The Washington Supreme Court agreed, affirming the jury's award of $7,500[3] as the actual value of the film to the plaintiffs. Wrestling with the question of establishing the "value to the owner" under the intrinsic value measure, the Court addressed the recoverability of "sentimental value." In upholding the trial court's jury instruction, it explained that:

> In essence it allowed for recovery for the actual or intrinsic value to the plaintiffs but denied recovery for any unusual sentimental value of the film to the plaintiffs or a fanciful price which plaintiffs, for their own special reasons, might place thereon.

Id., at 1311. By distinguishing "usual" sentimental value from "unusual" sentimental value, however, the Court expressly permitted some element of sentimental value. Further, the *Mieske* court was careful to narrowly interpret the phrase "sentimental value" so as not to exclude usual and customary sentiment:

> What is sentimental value? The broad dictionary definition is that sentimental refers to being "governed by feeling, sensibility, or emotional idealism . . . " Obviously that is not the exclusion contemplated by the statement that sentimental value is not to be compensated. If it were, no one would recover for the wrongful death of a spouse or a child. Rather, the type of sentiment which is not compensable is that which relates to "indulging in feeling to an unwarranted extent" or being "affectedly or mawkishly emotional . . . "

Id.

How would you compare and contrast Orbit to inanimate objects of value or apply *Mieske*?

---

country), the cloning valuation argument may gain currency. Veterinarians may also find that the standard of care will evolve to require informing owners at or near time of death of the ability to extract a DNA sample for cryogenic storage and later cloning, especially given the foreseeable and well-documented grief following loss of a companion animal. Companion animals are frequently perceived as family members, children, best friends, and confidants (Butler & DeGraff, *Helping During Pet Loss and Bereavement*, 18 VETERINARY QUARTERLY, Suppl, 1996). The impact of pet loss and intensity of grief are more profound in cases of an unexpected or sudden loss (Walsh et al., 48(4) FAMILY PROCESS (2009)). Additional feelings of blame and guilt occur when a pet death results from a potentially avoidable situation, such as being hit by a car. Id. Owners who keep their pets indoors have a stronger attachment and, subsequently, indoor pet housing correlates with anxiety and insomnia following loss of a pet (Kimura et al., *Psychiatric Investigation of 18 Bereaved Pet Owners*, 73(8) J. VET. MED. SCI, (2011)).

The foregoing material was provided courtesy of Kristopher J. Irizarry, Ph.D., a geneticist and Associate Professor of Bioinformatics, Genetics, and Genomics at Western University of Health Sciences in Pomona, Calif.

[3] In 2015 dollars, this figure approaches $30,000.

While snapshots and video clips capture and memorialize past moments, and can be spliced into a seamless track, they remain inorganic, frozen, and independent of one another. On the contrary, a cat who has lived in loving cohabitation with his owner-guardian is not the same as at the time of being adopted, but changes with age and nurturing. The prior experiences undergird the future ones. This is why the value he provides to the owner increases with each passing day. Thus, the cat who existed on the date of the tortious injury or death is actually an embodiment of that same cat the day before, and the day before that, recursively to the date he first came into the plaintiff's life. Picture the layers of an onion or the rings of a tree. Destroying historical images is tantamount to coring an onion or stumping a tree from the inside out — a form of retrograde amnesia that is occasionally so traumatic as to prove fatal. In this regard, the *Mieske* images are not laid down linearly in celluloid or some other film stock, but concentrically, within an organic, living vessel. So when one wrongfully kills an animal companion, she has not only destroyed the present manifestation, but obliterated the set of experiences that made the animal who he was that day, an animal who only existed that day because of the daily investments and value placed thereon by the owner. No other property better deserves application of, nor exemplifies, intrinsic value principles. Indeed, it would be the height of irony to permit the owner to obtain intrinsic value for destroyed photographs of the animal (per *Mieske*), but only obtain a fair market value for the genuine article (i.e., the animal himself).

An animal's value may be further enhanced by his therapeutic, hedonic, and recreational use — irrespective of the emotional fallout from his death. He may also have enhanced the value of other activities and locations, such as making "coming home" a more enriching experience, in part because it was selected with his comfort in mind and became associated with him. Excursions to locales were more valuable because they were experiences shared with the animal so that his untimely death may deprive the owner of these value-added experiences and diminish the value of place. *See* Daniel M. Warner, *No Place of Grace: Recognizing Damages for Loss of Home-Place*, 8 WIS. ENVTL. L.J. 3 (Spr. 2002) (seeking to extend loss of consortium to loss of home and to compensate for disruption of relationship to same). An animal may have enhanced the value of the owner's relationships with other people to whom he entrusted the animal's care, with whom he socialized, and in building familial bonds. In rare cases, the animal may have been closely associated with a predeceased, immediate family member, so that the death of the animal revives feelings of loss associated with the death of that human being. Indeed, the animal's death may impair the owner's very sense of identity in having become a "metaphorical extension[] of [his] owner[]." Adjunct Harvard Law Professor Steven Wise stated that "the wrongful killing of one's companion animal may threaten the way in which an owner constitutes herself: in losing her companion animal, she loses a vital part of herself." Wise, *Recovery of Common Law Damages for Emotional Distress, Loss of Society, and Loss of Companionship for the Wrongful Death of a Companion Animal*, 4 ANIMAL L. 33, 67–68 (1998).

Each act of positive and loving reinforcement, command, massage of the ear, rub on the back, activity shared with others and in new locations, what one may call "investments" over the tenure of care, may increase the animal's value the way aging wine's maturation creates a more developed and multi-layered bouquet, its flavor becomes more satisfying, and its quality increases. One New York court reasoned that a good dog's value increases rather than falls with age and training. "The dog's age is not a depreciation factor in the court's calculations, for 'manifestly, a good dog's value increases rather than falls with age and training.'" *Brousseau v. Rosenthal*, 110 Misc. 2d 1054, 443 N.Y.S.2d 285 (N.Y. Civ. Ct., N.Y. Cnty. 1980) (*quoting Stettner v. Graubard*, 82 Misc. 2d 132 (N.Y. Town Ct., Harrison 1975)). These labors of socialization, individualized training, and reciprocation make the animal more "functional" and "useful" to the owner and, thus, dramatically increase his value.

An animal may be conceptualized as a "work of art," and the owner the artist. However, this masterpiece may revert to its raw state if ignored or mistreated. That the owner does not allow this to happen bolsters value. An animal cannot be replaced as easily as one removes a SIM card from one cell phone into another. This argument simply does not mesh with human-animal experience. There is no fair market value for a pet who has been kept as a family member by a particular individual. The animal's value is optimized for personal use, like specially manufactured property or a stamp printed to advertise services of one individual with little or no use to anyone else. Many animals imprint on an owner. To create a new "stamp," as it were, would require an investment beyond just buying a generic model and would turn on the impossible task of reenacting over a decade of environmental variables and genetic characteristics. While most toaster ovens function according to rigorous specifications established both by law and manufacturer guidelines, consumers and retailers alike rely on quality controls that ensure that Toaster #1 and Toaster #1,000,001 will operate within the same tight margin of performance. However, dogs and cats are not like toasters. Though breeders may hope to create the perfect specimen, even geneticists cannot guarantee that a cloned animal will behave identically to its progenitor.

Humans are social animals. They crave companionship. While some accomplish this drive through associations with fellow humans, others develop bonds with nonhumans. Additionally, some rely on technology as a means of assuaging loneliness. However, inanimate forms of personalty cannot provide "companionship" for the reason that they do not return affection, dialogue, or sustain relationships akin to the sociologically significant dyads of husband-wife, parent-child, sibling-sibling, and friend-friend. While artificial intelligence may someday challenge this assertion, at the current state of robotics and computer science, arguably only biological, carbon-based life forms can provide companionship.[4]

---

[4] "People tend to react anthropomorphically to the unit," thanking it, praising it, and even reprimanding it if it does not behave. *See Roomba Fans Fall Hard for Robot Vacuums*, NPR The Bryant Park Project (Oct. 29, 2007), http://www.npr.org/templates/story/story.php?storyId=15721606 (discussing a boutique market to outfit Roombas in garb that make them resemble animals, as well as the field of emotional design, researched by Ja Young Sung at Georgia Tech, which coined the term "Roomba-attached individuals" for those who emotionally connect with these robots). *See* Associated Press, *Roombas fill an emotional vacuum for owners: Some have named them, dressed them — even introduced them to parents* (Oct. 2, 2007). Isaac Asimov's *I, Robot*, described artificially intelligent robots as "a cleaner, better breed than we are" governed by the three laws of Robotics: (1) the robot may not injure a human or, through inaction, allow a human to come to harm; (2) the robot must obey orders given by humans except when in conflict with the first law; and (3) a robot must preserve its existence so long as it does not conflict with the first or second law. Not all scientists, psychologists, and ethicists wish to

Recent neuroscientific research using MRI technology has confirmed that eye contact between a dog and his human guardian releases the neuropeptide oxytocin, also known as the love hormone. GREGORY BERNS, HOW DOGS LOVE US: A NEUROSCIENTIST AND HIS ADOPTED DOG DECODE THE CANINE BRAIN (New Harves: 2013).

A plaintiff's attorney will need to overcome the tendency of the jury or judge to restrain surging pathos with perceptions that pets are just property and courts should not concern themselves with such trifles. The following reflections may guide the practitioner in preparing appropriate arguments to persuade the fact finder to comfortably harmonize this inner conflict. In ascertaining value, regardless of whether market value is the court-prescribed measure, the *uses* to which the property is put bears strong relevance.

Utility of any property can be evaluated by several dynamic factors — (1) the limitations of the property itself; (2) how the owner uses the property; (3) how time affects the property; (4) how the property affects the owner; and (5) how the owner treats the property when it becomes useless. For purposes of comparison, consider (a) a car, (b) an heirloom, and (c) a human corpse. Each of the above five factors will be applied.

A. THE CAR

(1) **Product Variation**: Although subject to accepted parameters of operation, a car may be reduced to its parts. If a part falls outside specification, it may be replaced and the car reassembled for optimal operation. There is no "ghost in the machine" or free will that makes it refuse to yield to human intervention. A car and its parts are fungible. Its utility can be predicted within narrow confidence intervals according to design and that does not vary appreciably from one car to another

---

facilitate the human-robot bond, or human-robot interaction ("HRI"). See Clara Moskowitz, *Human-Robot Relations: Why We Should Worry*, livescience.com (Feb. 18, 2013). Someday service robots, such as the Toyota Human Support Robot, may replace service animals. TMC Develops Independent Home-living-assistance Robot Prototype (Sept. 21, 2012) http://www.toyota.com.hk/about/news_and_events/2012/company/0921.aspx. Perhaps courts will need to address the robot-animal bond, as showcased in the episode "Schisms" in *Star Trek: The Next Generation*, where android Data penned an "Ode to Spot," his cat, whom he also painted seated on his lap in a self-portrait. Though making the gaffe of claiming that felines lacked sentience, one can excuse Data this glitch in his ethological subroutine:

> Felis Cattus, is your taxonomic nomenclature,
> an endothermic quadruped carnivorous by nature?
> Your visual, olfactory and auditory senses
> contribute to your hunting skills, and natural defenses.
> I find myself intrigued by your subvocal oscillations,
> a singular development of cat communications
> that obviates your basic hedonistic predilection
> for a rhythmic stroking of your fur, to demonstrate affection
> A tail is quite essential for your acrobatic talents;
> you would not be so agile if you lacked its counterbalance.
> And when not being utilized to aide in locomotion,
> it often serves to illustrate the state of your emotion.
> O Spot, the complex levels of behaviour you display
> connote a fairly well-developed cognitive array.
> And though you are not sentient, Spot, and do not comprehend,
> I nonetheless consider you a true and valued friend.

(assuming the same make, model, and year).

(2) **Variation by User**: The car will not perform better for Driver A than Driver B if A and B operate the vehicle identically. It does not *prefer* one over the other.

(3) **Variation over Time**: With time, property ages. Its usable life depletes. The more the owner uses the property, aside from a "burn-in," the less useful it becomes.

(4) **Use Affects User**: A car will not fundamentally change the owner. Unless an "heirloom" (described below), its use will not cause the owner to develop an emotional attachment.

(5) **Disutility**: When obsolete or extinguished of usable life, the car will be sold for salvage value or abandoned. Most people do not bury, cremate, or give last rites to a car. When the cost to repair exceeds the cost to buy a new car, few, if any, will forego a new purchase.

B. THE HEIRLOOM

While a pocket watch, 1925 photograph, or infant's baseball outfit may be sold at a garage sale or bought at a thrift store, where these items are keepsakes or heirlooms passed down from one generation to another or imbued with personal attachments to living or deceased persons, their value to the owner is far greater than to a stranger.

(1) **Product Variation**: A pocket watch's utility will vary by the quality of its parts, design, and manufacture. However, where these factors are largely identical, utility will not vary. When the watch passes down as an heirloom from grandfather to grandson, the "utility" of that watch to the grandson does not depend on its ability to keep time. Rather, its utility lies in its ability to become an immortalizing substance, a material remembrance of a departed loved one.

(2) **Variation by User**: The utility of a 1925 photograph of a cousin's graduation from West Point may have minimal interest to historians but will be useless to the average consumer. The relative who possesses this photograph will, as in the case of the pocket watch, regard it with utmost utility.

(3) **Variation over Time**: A mother whose son is now grown and out of the house may regard his infant-sized baseball outfit with great nostalgia. "Nostalgic value" is based on a longing for the past. Items possessing this value operate as time-traveling talismans. As more time from the nostalgic event elapses, the utility increases.

(4) **Use Affects User**: By definition, an heirloom implants a nostalgic seed in the owner. Over time, this emotional attachment and special value grows and matures with life experience.

(5) **Disutility**: Far from being regarded as trash, because keepsakes appreciate in nostalgic value over time, owners undertake sometimes Herculean efforts to preserve these items in their original state.

C. THE CORPSE

Human corpses[5] *were* once human. After death, what — legally speaking — are they? If one shoots a corpse, can one be prosecuted for assault or murder? Can a corpse sue for posthumous defamation? The answer to both questions is no.

(1) **Product Variation**: Corpses, aside from their use at research institutions, have no commercial value. They vary based on an infinite number of factors as specific and rarefied as the lives the corpses led. However, there is one common denominator — they are all dead and, therefore, perishable. Biohazardous, they must be stored or destroyed. Accordingly, far from providing utility, for those not related or bonded to the corpse, the dead body imposes costs on the caretakers. The law regards corpses as unique objects, such that those who dare arrest, attach, detain, or detain any human remains for any debt or demand, or upon any pretended lien or charge, are frequently guilty of a gross misdemeanor.

(2) **Variation by User**: It is a bit incongruous to speak of "using" a corpse. However, as in the case of heirlooms, there is nostalgic value in human remains. The crematory industry is testament to this fact. While some may regard an urn containing the ashes of a deceased loved one as offering "companionship," such a reference might be best reserved for animate beings. Much of what motivates survivors to place value on a human corpse are the enhanced dignitary obligations motivated by religious or ethical mandates. Useful for comparison are nonhuman remains. A sizeable percentage of pet owners insist on private cremation or burial in a pet cemetery, often at a cost several times over its falsely termed "fair market value" at time of death.

(3) **Variation over Time**: Unless reduced to ashes or interred, the corpse will biodegrade like all other entities to the point of being unrecognizable. Once converted to a static form (whether cremated, mummified, or placed in a coffin), the corpse becomes much like an heirloom.

(4) **Use Affects User**: See the response to the heirloom hypothetical.

(5) **Disutility**: People honor their dead through ritual. These rituals create industries like funeral homes and crematories. While the value of a living person is greater than a dead person, the law and society do not regard corpses as useless trash.

D. THE COMPANION ANIMAL

(1) **Product Variation**: If the court insists on viewing animals as property, then it must acknowledge that, as classes of property go, they belong to one *sui generis* — largely because of their individual wills, intentions, and capacity to develop enmities and amities. *See* Geordie Duckler, *On Redefining the Boundaries of Animal Ownership: Burdens and Benefits of Evidencing Animals' Personalities*, 10 ANIMAL L. 63 (2004). Some animals are used for food production, others for pets.

---

[5] Some litigators insist that deceased nonhumans leave *carcasses*, not *corpses*. While the modern use of the word "corpse" tends to focus on human remains, the archaic meaning included any body, human or animal, alive or dead.

However, like people with distinct personalities and capacities, nonhuman animals possess varying degrees of *companionability*. For instance, "wallflowers" often suffer from agoraphobia and situational awkwardness, such that their ability to provide or enjoy companionship generally is more constrained than in their "social butterfly" counterparts. Wallflowers may overcome their inhibitions in the company of certain people. Individual A's ability to accompany Individual B turns on how A and B interact. To put a finer point on the analysis, the pet dog or cat's "utility" or "companionability" depends both on the identity of the human being seeking that animal's companionship and the animal's genetically and environmentally influenced demeanor. For instance, a socially appropriate, physically and psychologically sound German Shepherd (GSD #1) may provide greater companionship generally than another German Shepherd (GSD #2) raised on the streets as a feral dog and abused by vagrants. However, in the hands of a highly empathetic and calm handler who takes her everywhere with him, GSD #2 may surpass the level of companionship provided by GSD #1, who is left inside a dark apartment 10 hours a day while her 25-year-old upwardly-mobile professional bachelor sows his oats.

(2) **Variation by User**: See (1) above.

(3) **Variation over Time**: Because nonhumans belong to a different species, inherent obstacles arise in cross-species communication, as surely as they do in cross-race and cross-cultural contexts. In keeping an animal as a companion, one must always mind the cross-species barrier. In isolation or as a result of human abuse, once-tamed animals may revert to a wild state. Thus, unless the human owner continues to "use" the companion animal, it will fall into disutility. With the automobile, increased use reduces utility over time. However, with a companion animal, increased use increases utility, and lack of use may result in depreciation.

(4) **Use Affects User**: Greater use of a companion animal generates even stronger emotional attachment. Much like an heirloom or human corpse, for which the dignitary and nostalgic value distinguishes each from a car, in affiliating with a particular human owner, the companion animal's value evolves and always is owner-dependent. In this regard, the animal cannot be replaced or reproduced without turning back time. An heirloom often serves as an extant and tangible "proxy" for another person who may be deceased, disabled, or unavailable. It bridges to bring the owner to the person associated with the heirloom. The emotional attachment, though directed toward the heirloom, in fact passes through the item to the memory of a human being. However, an heirloom does not reciprocate affection or interact with the owner. It is always acted upon by the owner, not vice versa. A human corpse is the direct representation of the beloved human being, but it also serves as a proxy for the spirit that once inhabited the shell. It does not, however, reciprocate or interact with the "owner." A companion animal, on the other hand, while it may serve as a means to a nostalgic end, as in a "proxy" for another human being (e.g., the dog belonged to a widow's husband and is now cared for by the surviving widow), more commonly serves as an end in itself, a stand-alone recipient of emotional attachment. Indeed, the companion animal serves often as a proxy for the owner herself, providing a mirror for self-reflection.

Companion animals share similar qualities to certain personalty like clothing, paintings, heirlooms, and photographs sold on the open market, even at a heavily depressed rate, yet possess additional value that is strictly personal to the plaintiff, who has invested in said chattel a special significance that is not shared among other fungible, consumer goods. Humans create a bond with a companion animal based on a life imprint. They fill a void for their guardian-owners that changes their daily routine in profound ways and is of long duration. In short, pet owners imbue companion animals with an inherently personal value, much like the manner in which human parents regard their human children. Indeed, the vital connection between an animal and her guardian-owner has been classified by academician Steven Wise as vesting in the owner a type of "constitutive property." To sell the companion animal would require, at some level, a sale of the owner's identity.

(5) **Disutility**: We form relationships with companion animals, causing their value to appreciate as the bond deepens, in contrast to other market goods we purchase and use to obsolescence or destruction. Thus, even when companion animals age, their value is often many times greater than what their owners spend on veterinary care and unnecessary expenditures (e.g., toys, treats, luxuries).

E. BRIDGING THE NONHUMAN-PREHUMAN DIVIDE

The human fetus occupies a limbo status, falling outside the well-defined boundaries of existing legal definition. In wrestling with the subject, the law has attempted to draw the prehuman-human line at viability or "quickness" for purposes of treating the fetus as something other than a viable human being existing outside the mother. "Arguing that embryos and fetuses are persons in a strict sense is about as convincing as saying animals are." Parsi, *Metaphorical Imagination: The Moraland Legal Status of Fetuses and Embryos*, 4 DePaul J. Health Care L. 703, 708 (1999). Yet select members of the class of "potential humans" — preembryos/prezygotes, embryos, nonviable fetuses, and viable fetuses — have justiciable interests and, thus, standing to assert claims traditionally afforded only to sentient, autonomous human beings.

One case in point is abortion. During the preimplantation and previability stages, the mother has the right to kill the prehuman as if it were her property. She may exclude others from access to the prehuman and assert sole ownership rights. Thereafter, the prehuman's dignitary interests may be interposed, the fetus having crossed the property-person Rubicon with gestationally evolving interests that may be raised even against the mother to whom it is existentially affixed. For birthed nonhuman animals, on the other hand, though gifted with sentience and personality, conventional jurisprudence had nonreflectively relegated their status to the position of inanimate chattel dispossessed of rights or interests. In surrogate motherhood agreements, the "gestational carrier" must often act in the best interests of the intended parents *and the fetus*. Consequently, the unborn human occupies the dual status of trust property and intended beneficiary. See Yamamoto & Moore, *A Trust Analysis of a Gestational Carrier's Right to Abortion*, 70 Fordham L. Rev. 93 (2001). Legislatures discomfited by the premise that prehumans are mere property have passed "fetal protection acts" criminalizing harm to a fetus. Modern inheritance law also affords prehumans a share equal to living siblings so long as she is born alive at the time of the testator's death. Even stillborns may bring tort actions.

See Danos v. St. Pierre, 383 So. 2d 1019 (La. Ct. App. 1980), *judgment aff'd*, 402 So. 2d 633 (La. 1981).

The Tennessee Supreme Court has attributed to prehumans a status between property and full personhood. In *Davis v. Davis*, 842 S.W.2d 588 (Tenn. 1992), the court held that prefetal embryos stood on this quasi-property ground. While initially the trial court found that human life begins at conception and that the embryos are human beings deserving of the court's protection, the Tennessee Supreme Court reversed, finding instead that they deserve treatment neither as persons nor property. As such, they were entitled to "special respect because of their potential to become human life." This decision recognizes a heightened property status, imparting to such chattel consideration of its dignitary and future interests. If a prefetal product of conception from implantation with less than eight weeks of development is deemed more than property, then should courts see fit to extend additional jurisprudential courtesies to fully developed nonhumans? Or is the speciesist divide too great?

Moen v. Hanson, 537 P.2d 266 (Wash. 1975), followed the *Davis* trend in allowing a civil action for parental bereavement in the loss of a viable, unborn, human fetus. In Washington, parents may sue under Wash. Rev. Code Ann. § 4.24.010 for wrongful death of a viable fetus. The *Moen* court held that "minor child" extended to the viable unborn given the historical existence of its legal personality. Subsequent to this decision, in 1998 the Washington State Legislature amended Wash. Rev. Code Ann. § 4.24.010 (Laws of 1998, ch. 237, § 1) without disturbing *Moen's* central holding. Rather, it provided a case for a parent's loss of her child's consortium where the parent "has had significant involvement in the child's life, including but not limited to, emotional, psychological, or financial support." "By emphasizing involvement in a child's life, this language suggests that there is no cause of action for a fetus which does not yet have an independent life." *Baum v. Burrington*, 119 Wash. App. 36, 40 (2003).

Thus, while a statutory wrongful-death action may not lie for nonviable fetuses, Washington law provides fertile basis for suits by viable prehumans that have had no appreciable relationship with their human owner-guardians. In light of *Moen*, *and as an analogy only*, a viable, indeed alive, sentient cat with a present attachment to the plaintiff should confer upon the bereaving guardian a status comparable to that given a parent grieving over an unborn fetus without an extant personality. Contrast a prehuman's inherent incapacities to involve himself with a human adult on any similar cognitive or intuitive level with that of a fully conscious service animal, police dog, or mature feline. Even the brain-absent anencephalic child or adolescent in a persistent vegetative state or comatose grandparent does not have the capacity to reason or interact on any level approximating that between a companion animal and her guardian-owner. The well-documented filial and therapeutic relationship of humans to their companion animals presents an even stronger starting point to grant special consideration for this special kind of quasi-property.

F. COMPENSATORY DAMAGES[6]

The measure of damages for an injured or deceased companion animal varies by jurisdiction, as either market value, replacement value, or what has been termed actual, peculiar, intrinsic, or special value. When the market value cannot be ascertained or does not adequately compensate the owner, many courts use "a more elastic standard . . . sometimes called the standard of value to the owner." *McDonald v. Ohio State Univ. Veterinary Hosp.*, 644 N.E.2d 750, 751–752 (Ohio Ct. Cl. 1994); *see also Landers v. Municipality of Anchorage*, 915 P.2d 614, 618 (Alaska 1996) (quoting *Bond v. A. H. Belo Corp.*, 602 S.W.2d 105, 109 (Tex. Civ. App. Dallas 1980), writ refused n.r.e., (Dec. 31, 1980)) ("[T]he most fundamental rule of damages . . . requires the allowance of damages in compensation for the reasonable special value of such articles to their owner taking into consideration the feelings of the owner for such property."). Courts have awarded special value damages for companion animals for more than 100 years. *See, e.g., Hodges v. Causey*, 26 So. 945 (Miss. 1900) (allowing special value damages for owner and allowing witnesses to testify to the dog's qualities and characteristics); *Klein v. St. Louis Transit Co.*, 696, 93 S.W. 281 (Mo. Ct. App. 1906) (applying actual-value-to-the-owner standard and permitting trier of fact to award damages based on evidence that dog owner prized his dog, took pleasure in his company, and was proud of what the dog could do).

Various jurisdictions have also acknowledged a *per se* intrinsic value rule, where a plaintiff may recover the intrinsic value of certain types of property as a matter of law, without even needing to allege or prove lack of market value. *See Condie v. Swainston*, 112 P.2d 787 (Idaho 1940); *Kimball v. Betts* 169 P. 849 (Wash. 1918), *Barber v. Motor Inv. Co.*, 298 P. 216 (Or. 1931). Typically, this rule of compensation applies to household goods, kept for personal use and not sale, as well as wearing apparel. In support of a holding that reversed the lower court for limiting the claimant to the market value for pieces of galvanized syphon, *Condie* cited to *Kimball*, applying the rule to such items at a forced sale under void process, and to *Barber*, applying the rule to such converted items. Turning to New Mexico yields a nearly 80-year-old decision applying the *per se* intrinsic value rule to a dog. In *Wilcox v. Butt's Drug Stores, Inc.*, 35 P.2d 978 (N.M. 1934), the New Mexico Supreme Court upheld the trial judge's award of $150 for the value of "Big Boy," a King Charles Spaniel who died from strychnine poisoning in a pharmacist malpractice case. The defendant argued that the judgment should be limited to $10, the alleged "market" or "pecuniary" value of Big Boy. The Court disagreed with the conclusion that "damages for the wrongful destruction of a dog must be limited to market value or pecuniary value."

The RESTATEMENT OF TORTS § 911 (1939) also identifies the class of items for which there is only an intrinsic value. Comment *e* to Section 911 ties together the dog, the family portrait, and secondhand clothing and furniture (as addressed by *Kimball* and *Barber*):

---

[6] Portions of this section are derived and reprinted in part from Adam P. Karp, *Causes of Action for Loss of or Injury to an Animal by an Animal*, 38 COA 2d 281 (2008) and Adam P. Karp, *Litigation Concerning Veterinary Medical Malpractice*, 123 AM. JUR., *Trials* 305 (2012), and used with permission of Thomson Reuters.

e. Peculiar value to the owner.

The phrase "value to the owner" denotes the existence of factors apart from those entering into exchange value which cause the subject matter to be more desirable to the owner than to others.

Some things may have no exchange value but may be valuable to the owner; other things may have a comparatively small exchange value but have a special and greater value to the owner. The absence or inadequacy of the exchange value may result from the fact that others could not or would not use the things for any purpose, or would employ them only in a less useful manner. Thus a personal record or manuscript, an artificial eye or a dog trained only to obey one master, will have substantially no value to others than the owner. The same is true of articles which give enjoyment to the user but have no substantial value to others, such as family portraits. Second-hand clothing and furniture have an exchange value, but frequently the value is far less than its use value to the owner. In such cases it would be unjust to limit the damages for destroying or harming the articles to the exchange value.

With respect to animal injury, defendants have sought to cap damages at the animal's original value, by equating them to cars, using the logic that it makes no sense to spend more to repair a vehicle than to replace it. See *Wilson v. Seattle, R. & S. Ry. Co.*, 104 P. 1114 (Wash. 1909); *Keyes v. Minneapolis & St. L. Ry. Co.*, 30 N.W. 888 (Minn. 1886); *Ellis v. Hilton*, 43 N.W. 1048 (Mich. *1889)*; *Gillett v. Western R. Corp.*, 1864 Mass. LEXIS 159 (Sept. 1864). Every appellate court that has evaluated the issue as to companion animals has warranted veterinary bills in excess of a putative "market value." *See Martinez v. Robledo*, 210 Cal. App. 4th 384, 147 Cal. Rptr. 3d 921 (2012); *Burgess v. Shampooch Pet Indus., Inc.*, 131 P.3d 1248 (Kan. Ct. App. 2006), *Kaiser v. U.S.*, 761 F. Supp. 150 (D.C. 1991), *Hyland v. Borras*, 719 A.2d 662 (N.J. Super. Ct. App. Div. 1998), *Leith v. Frost*, 899 N.E.2d 635 (Ill. App. Ct. 2008), *Kimes v. Grosser*, 195 Cal. App. 4th 1556 (2011). In *Burgess v. Shampooch Pet Industries, Inc.*, 131 P.3d 1248 (Kan. Ct. App. 2006), the plaintiff took her dog to the defendant for grooming. Immediately after the grooming session, the dog limped. The defendant denied liability even though a veterinarian had given the dog a clean bill of health just two days before. After the plaintiff obtained judgment for veterinary bills related to a hip surgery, and court costs, the defendant appealed, insisting that damages should not exceed the dog's market value.

In this case of first impression, the Kansas Court of Appeals affirmed, agreeing with the trial court that "a pet is different than a motor vehicle . . . or other items of personal property in that a pet has no real market value[.]" *Id.*, at 1250. The plaintiff likened her years of companionship with her dog to "the Master Card ad—priceless." Emphasizing "long-standing, common-sense jurisprudence," the court upheld the award of damages even though the plaintiff's dog had no market value. *Id.*, at 1252 (quoting *Zager v. Dimilia*, 138 Misc. 2d 448 (J. Ct. 1988) ("it is impossible to reduce to monetary terms the bond between man and dog, a relationship which has been more eloquently memorialized in literature and depicted on the motion picture screen").) The court added that:

[T]he award of the amount Burgess spent on veterinary bills is in accord with the very purpose of the law of damages — to make Burgess whole and return her to the position she was in prior to Shampooch's tortious conduct. It can hardly be said that a lesser award — for example, Murphy's original purchase price of $175 depreciated over 13 years — would "'make good the injury done," *Kansas Power and Light Co. v. Thatcher*, 14 Kan. App. 2d 613, 797 P.2d 162 (1990), or fairly and adequately compensate Burgess or her out-of-pocket expenses.

Id., at 1253. In *Hyland v. Borras*, 719 A.2d 662 (N.J. Super. Ct. App. Div. 1998), the court permitted recovery of $2,500 in veterinary bills though five times greater than the cost of a new dog was $500, stating:

It is purely a matter of "good sense" that defendants be required to "make good the injury done" as the result of their negligence by reimbursing plaintiff for the necessary and reasonable expenses she incurred to restore the dog to its condition before the attack.

Id., at 664.

Many courts have rejected market value as the measure of damages in companion animal cases. In *Brousseau v. Rosenthal*, 110 Misc. 2d 1054 (N.Y. Civ. Ct. 1980), a plaintiff brought a negligence action against a kennel arising from the death of "her sole and constant companion." The court concluded that plaintiff was entitled to "actual value" damages because "plaintiff relied heavily on this well-trained watchdog and never went out into the street at night without the dog's protection." In an Illinois veterinary malpractice case, the court acknowledged the value of the human-animal relationship and allowed compensation for that loss. *Jankoski v. Preiser Animal Hosp., Ltd.*, 510 N.E.2d 1084, 1086 (Ill. App. Ct. 1987). In *La Porte v. Associated Independents, Inc.*, 163 So. 2d 267, 269 (Fla. 1964), the Florida Supreme Court held "that the affection of a master for his [or her] dog is a very real thing and that the malicious destruction of the pet provides an element of damage for which the owner should recover." Florida courts since *La Porte* have followed this precedent. See *Anzalone v. Kragness*, 826 N.E.2d 472, 477–478 (Ill. App. Ct. 2005) (following *Jankoski*); *Altieri v. Nanavati*, 1989 Conn. Super. LEXIS 17, 5–6 (Dec. 11, 1989) (recognizing damages beyond market value sometimes awarded); *Quave v. Bardwell*, 449 So. 2d 81, 84 (La. Ct. App. 1984) (discussing factors to calculate value of plaintiff's dog and approving discretion of trial court in determining damages); *Demeo v. Manville*, 386 N.E.2d 917, 918–919 (Ill. App. Ct. 1979) (trial court properly permitted plaintiff to testify about dog's value based on qualities and commercial value); *Wertman v. Tipping*, 166 So. 2d 666 (Fla. Dist. Ct. App. 1964) (trier of fact could consider dog's special value to owner); *Paguio v. Evening Journal Ass'n*, 21 A.2d 667 (N.J. 1941) (special damages for killing of dog); *McMahon v. Craig*, 176 Cal. App. 4th 1502, 1518–1519 (2009) (permitting peculiar economic value, exclusive of sentimental or emotional value and of loss of affection and society).

Nevertheless, other courts have held that damages are restricted to fair market value. *Richardson v. Fairbanks North Star Borough*, 705 P.2d 454 (Alaska 1985); *Mitchell v. Heinrichs*, 27 P.3d 309, 313 (Alaska 2001) (including costs of training, costs of replacement, medical care, immunizations); *Nichols v. Sukaro Kennels*, 555

N.W.2d 689 (Iowa 1996); *Soucek v. Banham*, 524 N.W.2d 478 (Minn. Ct. App. 1994); *Goodby v. Vetpharm, Inc.*, 974 A.2d 1269, 1272 (Vt. 2009) (rejecting right to recover more than market value of animal); *Lachenman v. Stice*, 838 N.E.2d 451, 467 (Ind. Ct. App. 2006) (restricting value of terrier to fair market); *Scheele v. Dustin*, 998 A.2d 697, 703 (Vt. 2010) (no recovery beyond market value). In 2013, the Texas Supreme Court resolved the circuit split of *Medlen v. Strickland*, 353 S.W.3d 576 (Tex.App. 2011), *rev'd*, 397 S.W.2d 184 (2013) and *Petco Animal Supplies, Incorporated v. Schuster*, 144 S.W.3d 554 (Tex. App. 2004). *Strickland* involved the negligent euthanasia of Avery, a mixed-breed dog, by shelter worker Carla Strickland. The court declined to depart from a "restrictive, 122-year-old precedent classifying pets as property for tort-law purposes" in order to "recognize a new common-law loss-of-companionship claim that allows non-economic damages rooted solely in emotional attachment, a remedy the common law has denied those who suffer the wrongful death of a spouse, parent, or child, and is available in Texas only by statute." *Id.*, at 185 (fn.om.). Although the court recognized the power of the human-animal bond and emotional harm sustained by survivors of beloved animal companions, it nonetheless capped damages at market value in adherence to established law. "The packaging or labeling matters not," the unanimous court concluded. "Recovery rooted in a pet owner's feelings is prohibited." *Id.*, at 198.

Courts tend to regard unborn animals as accessions, improvements upon the original property that impart extra value, and, while gestationally affixed, are alienable at birth. The court does not engage in fetal stage analysis, asking if an early stage nonhuman animal fetus (nonviable) sits in the same class of property as a late-stage nonhuman animal fetus (viable) or a newborn viable animal? Unbred (unconceived) animals, by contrast, are worthless, though the value of lost progeny can help determine the market value for the killed adult. To award lost profits or loss of future use of parent breeders has been deemed "double recovery" and not allowed as a matter of law (irrespective of speculativeness), based on the contention that the market value includes all uses to which the property may be put, including breeding. In *Covey v. Western Tank Lines*, 218 P.2d 322 (Wash. 1950), a wheel came off the defendant's trailer and struck a plaintiff's mink pen, killing two and liberating three dihybrid mink. The plaintiff sought damages for both the market value of the lost and destroyed animals as well as for their progeny. The Washington Supreme Court held that a showing of the value of lost progeny could only be used in substitution for the market value of the lost or destroyed mink and not as a second basis for recovery. Thus, in the case of killed fertile, yet barren, animals, the plaintiff's recovery is limited to the market value of the adults, whether arrived at directly by receipts or indirectly through substitute measure. See also *Bueckner v. Hamel*, 886 S.W.2d 368 (Tex. App. 1994), writ denied, Jan. 12, 1995 (distinguishing value of deceased animals from their future progeny, noting that breeding potential could be considered in value of animal).

In *Hamilton v. King County*, 79 P.2d 697 (Wash. 1938), the county's drainage ditch digging operations within five feet of mink pens disturbed the colony during whelping season, leading 67 mink to abort their offspring. The Washington Supreme Court found the county liable for trespass to chattel in the amount of $1340, or $20 for each aborted kitten, the estimated depreciation in market value for all mink due to the abortifacient disturbance. Unlike *Covey*, the plaintiff only sought damages for the difference in the value of the females before and after the abortions and not the additional value of unborn kittens. "The loss of progeny was taken into consideration only in calculating the decreased market value of the mother mink before and after the wrongful intrusion." *Covey v. Western Tank Lines*, 218 P.2d 322, 326 (Wash. 1950) (explaining *Hamilton*). *But see Cloakey v. Bouslog*, 234 P.2d 880 (Wash. 1951).

G. PUNITIVE DAMAGES

In the vast majority of American jurisdictions, plaintiffs may seek punitive damages. See *Kautzman v. McDonald*, 621 N.W.2d 871 (N.D. 2001) (punitives permitted for wrongful injury committed willfully or by gross negligence, per N.D. Cent. Code § 36-21-13); *McConnell v. Oklahoma Gas & Elec. Co.*, 530 P.2d 127 (Okla. 1974) (punitives sought where electric company workers left yard gate unlatched, resulting in dog's escape and death when hit by car). For an educational discussion on the importance of mental state in distinguishing claims of conversion and punitive damages, consider *O'Harra v. Pundt*, 310 P.2d 1110 (Or. 1957), where plaintiff sued a veterinarian for the conversion of three Malamutes picked up for being at-large. The veterinarian then euthanized them short of the five-day statutory hold. Defendant appealed the jury award of $1,000 compensatory damages and $5,000 punitive damages. The appellate court agreed with the finding of conversion, but reversed on the question of punitive damages, focusing not on the *post hoc* rationalizations and false representations made to the plaintiffs as to the reason for having killed the dogs (the veterinarian said they were ill, but the true reason was miscalculating the hold period), but instead on his state of mind at the time of euthanasia:

> In view of the instructions given to the jury on the issue of compensatory damages, it is clear that the jury by its verdict found that the defendant did not at the time of the killing have the opinion that the dogs were ill or injured to such an extent that it would be inhumane to allow them to live. But the jury may well have found that the defendant erroneously believed that the "time was up" when he killed the dogs and that thereafter when he discovered his error he sought to justify his action by falsely claiming that the dogs were ill and that he was authorized for that reason to kill them. The fact, if it be one, that defendant lied as to the condition of the dogs in an effort to escape the results of his mistake in counting time would not show that at the time of the killing he acted in wanton or wilful disregard of the rights of the plaintiff, as alleged in the complaint. We have concluded that the evidence is consistent with the theory that he killed the dogs as a result of a careless mistake in computing the time, and thereafter sought to excuse himself by claiming that the condition of the dogs was such as to authorize their destruction under the contract.

> There is no evidence whatever of any actual malice or ill will on the part of the defendant toward the plaintiff. The question of the defendant's state of mind, whether wanton and wilful or not, relates to the time when he did the act of killing. An innocent or negligent act could not be converted into a wanton and wilful one by the fact that defendant thereafter sought by improper means to justify his mistake. It follows that the state of mind of

the defendant at the time of the act became a matter of pure speculation, and the evidence was insufficient to support a verdict for punitive damages.

Id., at 1118–19.

Where government agents blatantly disregard ordinances enacted to protect property interests, punitive damages may exist as observed in *Wilson v. City of Eagan*, 297 N.W.2d 146 (Minn. 1980). The court affirmed an award of punitive damages against the warden who intentionally authorized the killing of a cat in violation of the stray hold ordinance but reversed the punitive award against the officer who actually did the killing, given he was unaware that the stray hold ordinance had not yet run. Any time a firearm is discharged at a dog, the risk of incurring punitive damages remains high. See *Webb v. Jackson*, 583 So. 2d 946 (Miss. 1991) (officer injured dog and nearly hit homeowner when shooting gun; punitive damages discussed); *Fowler v. Town of Ticonderoga*, 131 A.D.2d 919, 516 N.Y.S.2d 368 (N.Y. Sup. Ct., App. Div. 1987) (punitives discussed in case involving alleged malicious shooting and killing of dog by animal control officer).

Where animals suffer malicious harm, punitive damages have been allowed. *Parker v. Mise*, 1855 Ala. LEXIS 76 (June 1855) (allowed for malicious killing of dog); *Bradley v. Martin*, 2007 Ariz. App. Unpub. LEXIS 880 (Nov. 13, 2007) (allowed); *Jemison v. Southwestern R.R.*, 75 Ga. 444 (1885) (malicious killing of dog permits punitives); *Ten Hopen v. Walker*, 96 Mich. 236 (1893) (malicious killing of dog permits punitive damages). Even if not technically malicious, reckless disregard equates to an intentional violation providing for punitive damages. *Florida East Coast Ry. Co. v. Cain*, 210 So. 2d 481 (Fla. Dist. Ct. App. 1968) (reversed punitive damages against railroad for spraying arsenic-laden weed killer along right-of-way, causing deaths to cows due to lack of gross or flagrant character or reckless disregard that is equivalent to an intentional violation).

Those who invoke the justifiable canicide statute may avoid liability for conversion, IIED, and malicious injury, as well as punitive damages. However, the irreversible act of pulling the trigger may have lasting financial consequences, as discussed in *Propes v. Griffith*, 25 S.W.3d 544 (Mo. Ct. App. 2000), where the defendant corralled plaintiff's yellow lab and Brittany spaniel upon finding them in her sheep pen. At her request, the sheriff arrived. She said she intended to euthanize the dogs. Refusing to release the dogs to the sheriff at his suggestion, the defendant took the dogs to a local veterinarian, who would not euthanize them, knowing they belonged to the plaintiff. The defendant then drove 45 minutes out of town to a new clinic and had them euthanize the dogs. She then lied to the plaintiff about what transpired. The trial court awarded $2,000 actual and $4,000 punitive damages, which the court of appeals affirmed, finding that the punitive damages were awarded for "the precise reason" contemplated at common law. See also *Granier v. Chagnon*, 203 P.2d 982 (Mont. 1949) ($1,500 punitive award reversed based on justifiable canicide statutory defense); *Trenka v. Moos*, 168 P.2d 837 (Mont. 1946) (defense verdict reversed for new trial on actual and exemplary damages where defendant shot dog more than once, the first time to desist the attack on defendant's chickens, the second time ostensibly to put the dog out of its misery though the evidence failed to show humane motivations); *Green v. Leckington*, 236 P.2d 335 (Or. 1951) (suit involving shooting of dog while chasing chickens; reversing and revising award because jury failed to segregate actual from exemplary); *Williams v. Spinola*, 622 P.2d 322 (Or. Ct. App. 1981) (suit involving shooting of dog let out to hunt raccoons; even if not a privileged killing by statute (because dog was not actually chasing sheep when killed), no punitives permitted because not so flagrant a violation of societal interests); *Nelson v. Percy*, 540 A.2d 1035 (Vt. 1987) (discussing punitives in context of shooting of plaintiff's dogs while allegedly harassing livestock); *Mitchell v. Heinrichs*, 27 P.3d 309 (Alaska 2001) (disallowed).

Veterinarians court a judgment against them inclusive of punitive damages when they maliciously fail to follow the standard of care or patently ignore the instructions of a client. In *Silverman v. Animal Medical Clinic*, 2006 Conn. Super. LEXIS 1135 (Apr 11, 2006), the plaintiffs alleged that the defendant veterinarian's reckless and malicious behavior and negligence caused the death of their one-year-old English bulldog. Defendant's motion to strike was denied, for while Conn. Gen. Stat. Ann. § 22-351a(d) expressly barred recovery of punitive damages when the veterinarian follows accepted standards of care, the converse also applies (i.e., failure to follow the standard of care exposes the veterinarian to punitive damages). *See also Fredeen v. Stride*, 525 P.2d 166 (Or. 1974) (allowing punitive damages where veterinarian gave plaintiff's dog to another without consent); *but see Carroll v. Rock*, 469 S.E.2d 391 (Ga. Ct. App. 1996) (reversed punitive damages in case where veterinarian lost cat).

Failure to control one's dog can also result in punitive damages, as seen in *Dolan v. Pearce*, 1998 U.S. Dist. LEXIS 7182 (E.D. Pa. May 18, 1998) (applying Pennsylvania law) (finding evidence in support of punitive damages sufficient where defendant completely disregarded the dog law in permitting lethal attack on plaintiff's dog, witnessed by his two minor sons). Fraudulent concealment of wrongdoing, resulting in death or discarding of animals, has given rise to punitive damages. See *Burgess v. Taylor*, 44 S.W.3d 806 (Ky. Ct. App. 2001) (affirming $75,000 punitive award for fraudulent killing of horses under care lease); *see also Levine v. Knowles*, 197 So. 2d 329 (Fla. Dist. Ct. App. 1967) (punitive damages available where veterinarian allegedly willfully cremated body to avoid consequences of autopsy and probable malpractice claims overriding client's contrary instructions to hold body). Punitive damages have been sought against those who purport to hold a valid lien and then foreclose or sell animals rightfully owned by the plaintiff. *Molenaar v. United Cattle Co.*, 553 N.W.2d 424 (Minn. Ct. App. 1996) (punitives allowed for conversion in deliberate disregard of rights or safety of others where cattle seized and sold); *see also Mitzel v. Zachman*, 16 N.W.2d 472 (Minn. 1945) (malicious castration of two bulls who broke into pasture resulted in treble damages to plaintiff). Though recoverable, some courts have reversed excessive punitive awards. *Dreyer v. Cyriacks*, 297 P. 35 (Cal. 1931) ($25,000 punitive damage award in addition to actual damages was grossly excessive in action for killing of dog).

Hypothetical: Raymond Dokes loved his blue-lace, red Wyandottes. Occasionally, he would led the hens and chicks out of their enclosure to peck around his fenced backyard as he gardened. A Sunday afternoon, while weeding, he caught a glimpse of a cat perched atop his six-foot fence. A Norwegian forest cat peered down at the brood and their clutch. Dokes reached for his rifle, which he had sitting by the stump nearby. Slowly, he raised the weapon, looked through the scope, aimed for center mass, and pulled the trigger. The cat let out a scream and dropped, scampering off. Dokes then opened the gate to his yard, and tracked the cat about 20 yards away. He carried the body of the deceased cat back to his shed. Though knowing the cat was domesticated and likely owned by a neighbor, he proceeded to put the body in a bag of chicken feed, which he then inserted into a black garbage bag. Along with his other debris, he placed the body in his receptacle, wheeled it to the street, and waited for pick up the next morning.

The evening before collection, his neighbor Chelsea Mfume knocked on the door. She handed him a "Lost Cat" flyer for Loki (the cat that was then lying yards away in the garbage bag). She asked him about her cat. Not mentioning the feline he shot hours before, and "kind of stumbling for a second," he instead directed Mfume a few lots away to a location where he claimed he heard a "terrible cat fight." During this conversation, he became visibly angry when talking about cats that had come on his property and attacked his chickens. But, he assured her, "I don't ever shoot cats. I always throw rocks at them. That scares them away." She thanked him for this lead and spent the next three hours sitting quietly in that lot, calling to Loki, treats in hand. After talking to another neighbor, who had lost three cats in the previous two years (about the time Dokes moved in), Mfume began to listen to her intuition. At midnight, she went to Dokes's driveway and wheeled the garbage can to her driveway. She then emptied it, only to find Loki's body in the trash bag.

Mfume sues Dokes for conversion, outrage, and fraud. She also petitions the court to allow her to recover punitive damages under a statute that says, "In any action seeking recovery of punitive damages, the claimant must prove, by clear and convincing evidence, oppressive, fraudulent, malicious, or outrageous conduct by the party against whom the claim for punitive damages is asserted." Case law interprets the statute to require proof of an "intersection of bad act with bad mind."

Do the facts warrant a punitive damage instruction?

On the one hand, a court might find that while Dokes may have used excessive force (i.e., a firearm instead of a pellet rifle, slingshot, or other, nonlethal sonic or visual deterrent, such as simply yelling and running at the cat), Dokes shot Loki with intent to protect the Wyandottes. And while he discarded Loki's body without attempting to ascertain the identity of his owners, at most this may rise to the level of recklessness, creating an unreasonable risk of harm and high probability that harm would result. Remember that when he killed Loki, he did not then know that Loki was owned by Mfume, although he knew he was owned by someone. Further, he did not kill Loki or discard his body with a desire to cause distress to Mfume. The court may also interpret "outrageous" to require proof of some, if not all, of the elements found in the common law tort of outrage. Recklessness alone does not rise to the level of malice or even intentional wrongdoing. While it might meet the "reckless infliction" prong of the outrage tort, without proof that his actions were performed to cause severe emotional distress in Mfume, the court might conclude that punitive damages cannot be recovered.

Of course, the practitioner must examine whether the "outrageous" alternative really does jibe with common law doctrine. One court held:

While the conduct giving rise to a claim for emotional distress and a claim for punitive damages may be of the same quality, it does not follow that an award of damages is either duplicative or must be co-extensive. The emotional distress damages are awardable for a condition particular to the aggrieved party. Punitive damages are awardable primarily to deter future bad conduct. There need be no overlap between the two.

Walston v. Monumental Life Ins. Co., 129 Idaho 211, 220 (1996). In other words, whether Mfume experienced any harm (emotional or economic, as here, given the loss of Loki) is immaterial to whether punitive damages need be awarded. Quite simply, damage is not an element of a punitive damage claim. *Cf. Payne v. Wallace*, 136 Idaho 303, 306 (Idaho Ct. App. 2010) (four elements of outrage are: (1) intentional or reckless conduct; (2) which is extreme and outrageous; (3) causing plaintiff's emotional distress; (4) where the distress was severe). Dokes's behavior — individually and cumulatively (i.e., killing, discarding, lying) — might create a triable issue on the question of outrageousness, oppressiveness, and fraud.

Consider this further hypothetical: A man picks up a stray dog, ties her to a tree, and repeatedly shoots her with arrows until she dies. He has no knowledge that the dog is owned by the plaintiff. Such conduct is clearly outrageous, if not malicious and oppressive. At the time of torturing her, he evidently had an extremely harmful state of mind and knew with substantial certainty that his conduct would cause grievous bodily harm to the canine. While, under this court's earlier rulings, the man might not be liable for the tort of outrage as to the plaintiff (having slain the dog without intent to cause emotional harm to the owner by such acts), justice would be thwarted were the court to deny the dog's owner punitive damages. This is so because the purpose of punitive damages is to deter future misconduct to as yet unidentified or even identifiable victims, while the purpose of outrage is to compensate for emotional harms intentionally or recklessly inflicted upon a known or knowable plaintiff.

If Dokes's intent when he shot Loki was to protect chickens, then he may not have possessed the specific causal intentionality giving rise to an outrage claim. Even so, for purposes of a punitive damages motion, facts construed in the light most favorable to Mfume cast doubt on this handy pretext, where his true goal was to kill Loki and then conceal the evidence of his wrongdoing.

H.   SPECIAL CONSIDERATIONS FOR SERVICE ANIMALS

One must distinguish a companion animal's ability to provide companionship from a service animal's ability to offer, for example, seizure-alert, seizure-assistance, and mobility-assistance. While there may be moments of levity during training, the immense sacrifice of energy and time, which a disabled handler may not have in great abundance, cannot be omitted from the valuation equation. Anyone who has tried to train a dog to perform basic obedience tasks will understand the predominant periods of frustration and exhaustion punctuated by infrequent, small victories. Imagine training a dog not just to heel or sit, commands of slight consequence to the average dog guardian, but to do the following, all of which a disabled individual must spend time training, tailoring, and revising:

1. Basic Obedience Skills All Service Dogs Must Learn

Sit

Down

Stand

Stay — in all positions (sitting, lying down, standing)

Come when called

Walk at heel

Leave it

Should know voice commands and hand signals for all skills

2. Other Skills Service Dogs Learn

Reliable off-leash and distance work

Vocabulary for objects (phone, shoe, etc.)

Retrieve objects on demand and as needed (notice when things fall; without command)

Tuck (tail and feet) to stay out of the way

Tug (to help take off clothes, close doors, turn on lights, etc.)

Wait (before coming out of car, getting off bus, etc.) — basically a stay command but the dog does not have to be given the command each time

Back up (walk backwards) — useful in narrow aisles

Ignore food even if dropped/placed on face or paws

Drop (fast, instant down) — useful if someone is scared of dog, or if another dog is stalking, or if dog is upset during alert, etc.

Hup (jump up on something)

Corner (curl into corner out of the way)

Under (go under table or chair and lie down)

Drag (retrieve large objects, help bring in groceries, etc.)

Wave and bow — "ambassador" skills to show how well dog is trained; useful when store owners try to kick dog out, or when kids ask to pet the dog but are not allowed

Paws Up (put paws on counter, bed, or if little dog, up on leg to give object to owner)

"Working" and "Off Duty" commands for when people want to pet the dog, or if dog is allowed to greet a friend but must then ignore

Laundry (put clothes in or out of hamper, separate into piles)

Tidy (pick up things on floor and put them in basket)

Others specific to your client's service animal

3. Basic Socialization Skills All Service Dogs Must Learn:

Synchronicity in heeling. Dog must walk politely at "heel" at all times. If in a narrow space, the dog falls behind the owner and then catches up. The dog must modify her pace to match the owner at all times.

Reactive coping with extraordinary phenomena (multi-sensory). The dog must learn to cope with loud noises, including sudden, booming, sustained, high-pitched, and percussive (such as applause and drums, which may actually cause great discomfort). She must cope with sudden frights, like an umbrella opening in her face, or a child flapping a coat. Service dogs may need to attend fireworks displays, manage reactions to strange, threatening objects, like crutches and wheelchairs, motorcycles, kids on skateboards, children throwing items. They must properly react to strange sensations, like a bus blowing by, gum landing on her fur, or the uncomfortable flooring or table base that she must lie on in a restaurant. The service dog must handle crowds, people stepping on her paws, petting her as they pass, grabbing her (especially her tail), holding strange objects at her eye level. She must be prepared to ignore stares and be present around loud or angry conversations.

Mobility coping. Service animals must learn to traverse uneven surfaces, such as slippery tile, street grates, crackly plastic, or hot tarmac; to pass through puddles without trying to jump, over sharp gravel, as well as on stairs, ramps, and tunnels. They must negotiate moving surfaces or containments, such as elevators, escalators, airport walkways, trains, planes, and boats. Mobilizing through tight quarters is also a must, like a cramped store or on a bus, and must settle in without panicking, even if being squashed into a cab. They must enter and exit through doorways, including automatic, revolving, and those that close quickly and loudly behind them. They must not lag or forge ahead.

Ignoring stimuli. Service animals must practice ignoring other animals, such as police horses, other dogs, squirrels, or animals in captivity. Balancing being an affable dog who keeps strangers at ease while maintaining focus on the disabled handler means disregarding people who coo, offer food, whistle, and click. She must learn only to respond to the handler's voice, and to overlook balls and other moving toys, sources of fun, and playing children. She must decline food, even if offered or dropped directly on her.

Etiquette. The service dog must not scratch or lick in public, especially when they have allergies.

Advanced retrieval in social settings. Retrieving items off the kitchen counter or out of the trashcan, but only when asked, requires advanced training so as not to inhibit the retrieval drive.

Sign language. He must learn a variety of hand signals in case a command must be given in a quiet place such as at a play or in a hospital.

Potty training. Service animals learn to relieve themselves on command, and only in certain areas, such as grass or mulch so he does not get confused in an open mall, fairground, or zoo that feels like "outside" but is not a potty place.

Wear clothes such as a cape, backpack, booties for hot or icy weather, sun visor or sunglasses for bright sun, and other clothes for "ambassador" purposes, i.e., to make the dog appealing to the public and reduce access difficulties.

Ongoing stay. Service dogs must learn to stay for hours at a time without forgetting the "stay" command. Many non-service dogs doze off, awakening only to forget and rise. Service dogs remember.

On/off-duty comprehension. Like a switch, service dogs know when they are on-duty and off-duty. While they need play and rest times, service dogs are always available for work and must flip from playing to working states immediately when asked.

Seizure-assist. They learn how to behave if the handler falls unconscious, typically by lying quietly beside or on top of handler. She learns to recognize EMTs and police officers, whom she must permit to remove her from an unconscious/injured owner, and not try to protect.

Constant refining, rehabilitation, and testing. Service animals must be constantly encouraged and rewarded, even after formal training has finished. Yet, in fact, service dog never truly is "done." If the handler needs something in particular, but the dog has not yet mastered that vocabulary, the handler should be able to keep asking and the dog should keep bringing anything she can find until matching the request. She should always be willing and confident to work, which requires constant monitoring to ensure the job remains nontedious and invigorating. The handler must check constantly for developing problems (e.g., if the dog is startled by a loud noise such as a bus's airbrakes, she must return to the bus stop several times to defuse the traumatic fear response).

Creative disobedience. Many service dogs develop this skill, which should be encouraged. One watches for opportunities to train. For instance, a dog must use his own judgment in the handler's best interest, even if it countermands a direct order. The author's client's service dogs both learned to break a "stay" if they saw her sit or lie down, or if they thought she was getting sick. Both developed a behavior of not allowing her to stand up after a seizure, until they thought she was no longer seizing or she was well enough to get up. Both would lie across her and alert again if she attempted to get up before they thought she was safe.

How long would it take the average person to train a dog to perform one-tenth of the foregoing? And what if your very freedom to leave the house, drive a car, go for a stroll along the beach, buy groceries, visit a friend, go out on a date, get dressed, do your laundry, or pick up things you accidentally dropped, was completely dependent on these skills – and to a level of reliability that was virtually unquestionable?

Customization Training. Any service animal trainer will tell you that service dogs are not "ready for use out of the box" upon sale or delivery to the service animal user. The "customization," "synchronization," or "individuation" period of training personalized to the idiosyncrasies of the user is undeniable. To fully replace a service animal, one must consider all the expenditures invested in training him not just as a generic service animal, but as a unique service animal further customized to serve the handler's disabilities, preferences, and needs. Occasionally, after the death of a service animal, the disabled individual must immediately start training a new one to restore some modicum of normalcy previously enjoyed with the fully trained and "bombproofed" service animal. In so doing, she mitigates damages. Yet even after formal training and more than a year of personalization and refinement, the new dog may still not perfectly replace the old one, discrepancies for which the court will likely account.

Considerable effort and time involves establishing synchronicity. A plaintiff's schedule may include a lot of "heel-work" (the service animal matches his pace with hers while she slows to look at something, always watching to make sure he was keeping up), using escalators, crossing sidewalk grates, and ignoring public response to the "cute dog," which involves a lot of tail-grabbing. Trips out may take nearly twice as long because of devoting so much attention to assuring and educating the new dog. While learning how to cope with new situations, the new dog may interfere with your client's dates to comedy clubs or ice-skating.

The plaintiff may sacrifice meeting friends in restaurants for fear of a lack of preparedness. She may have to teach the new dog to walk through the mall without slipping on tile floors or getting distracted by shoppers. She may abstain from trips because of classes, or make an appointment at Toys 'R' Us to teach the dog to accept children groping, or to the local skate park to grow inured to whizzing objects and sudden noises. The plaintiff may end up taking many more medications due to stress and lack of rest. For those without life-altering disabilities, it may be hard to comprehend how much is expended to "connect with" a new service animal and, thereby, approximate the caliber of the old dog.[7]

Consider something as simple as going grocery shopping.

With concerted effort, Jane Doe eventually succeeded in completing a task or errand while she trained him, resulting in a doubling of time. For instance, the New Dog would stick his nose on an avocado, exploring as dogs are wont to do. This action required Jane's correction, to teach him the proper response to an avocado, her purchase of that avocado and those adjacent, and her apologizing to anyone who saw him sniff the fruits and vegetables. She might then go to the pasta aisle, where he would nose a package of spaghetti, forcing her to drop what she was holding, correct him, load the pasta into her cart, and again apologize to those staring at her from the aisle. With much more fine-tuning, she and the New Dog reached the level

---

[7] "Down Time" versus "Up Time." Plaintiffs may still train even when prostrate or not exposing the animal to outdoor stimuli. One's disability may only permit at most six to eight hours of "up time" before she has to lay down. Even so, the dog may retrieve items such as slippers, a remote control, books, socks, or get the phone. In the beginning, the service animal may only understand how to retrieve items pointed to; it may take additional training to teach him to recover items from other rooms to which the plaintiff could not point, like the telephone, a critical tool for emergencies when she cannot crawl to, or otherwise reach, the cord. While lying down, the disabled handler may also teach the service animal to jump up on the bed with retrieved items and to find items lost in couch cushions. From this position, she may train him in down-stay and vocabulary acquisition.

where her hands could be full and she could completely trust his judgment around food, including the meat section. The supermarket assistance gold standard, which he practically achieved, is walking politely next to her cart, falling behind when there is not room, and then catching back up to a heel position, standing dead-still while she takes items off the shelves, ignoring the inevitable petting from strangers, picking up items she drops while disregarding others items on the floor, and helping her walk when she gets wobbly. As you can see, a trip to the grocery store might be the single chore Jane would attempt in a day, missing out on other activities she would have been able to enjoy or complete with the Old Dog's assistance.

In addition to the arduous routine, the plaintiff may experience unnecessary emotional distress, manifested by increasing her medications and becoming ill with greater frequency while training the new and managing the stress of losing the old. The withdrawal of the old dog's support may exacerbate disabilities and cause the plaintiff to experience substantial mental anguish and bouts of extreme exhaustion for several months.

Class time alone could never be deemed sufficient to provide the training for basic obedience, behavior, and socialization techniques, much less the advanced service animal skills and commands unique to the plaintiff, who may choose to self-train or co-train (with instructor supervision while at school) where she cannot afford to be wait-listed for two to eight years for another dog with concomitant skills. The plaintiff may also not have the finances to hire a trainer at $25 to $50 an hour at a total cost of $30,000 to $50,000. Classes provide an economic and expeditious alternative to clients ideally suited to mold their new animals into a suitable replacement. Much like college, actual class time is but a small component of the overall education. In order to economize, the plaintiff may blend basic socialization, obedience, protection, support, retrieval, seizure-assistance, seizure-alert, and mobility-assistance skills with custom-tailoring to her environments and preferences.

Agencies that provide service animals invest time as follows in basic training and retrofitting to the disabled user. Guide Dogs for the Blind, Inc. ("GDB") employs ten phases of training over roughly two years at a cost of $60,000 to $65,000, and a minimum of 880 hours. Note that these dogs are only trained for helping the visually impaired or totally blind with mobility skills. For decades, the Prison Pet Partnership Program at Purdy ("PPPP") has worked with female inmates at Purdy in Gig Harbor, Washington, to train service animals for mobility, with waiting lists as long as three to five years. While free to the disabled person, these dogs have an estimated value of $15,000 to $18,000 based on Assistance Dogs International standards. The minimum class time training is 264 hours, not including round-the-clock time spent with the inmate in "lockup." Paws-with-a-cause, a national, donation-driven organization known to train seizure response dogs, has three- to four-year wait lists, and spends at least 600 hours to basic train a dog to do such tasks as stated on their website:

> PAWS Service Dogs are custom-trained to assist people with physical disabilities affecting one or more limbs. Service Dogs can enhance a person's independence by helping with tasks such as pulling a wheelchair, opening doors, turning light switches on/off or picking up objects as small

as a dime. If a client falls, the dog can even act as a brace to help them up.

PAWS has trained Service Dogs to assist people who have Multiple Sclerosis, Muscular Dystrophy, Rheumatoidal Degeneration, ALS, Cerebral Palsy, spinal cord injuries and many other conditions affecting a person's mobility or strength.

In addition to performing tasks related to a physical disability, a PAWS Dog can also be trained to assist with tasks related to a seizure disorder or hearing loss.

http://www.pawswithacause.org/i-want-a-dog/service-dogs. They claim a cost to breed/rescue, raise, train and place an Assistance Dog to ordinarily exceed $30,000. Assistance Dogs International, Inc. ("ADI"), a coalition of not-for-profit organizations, has established minimum standards of training seizure respond/alert dogs, all of which should be exceeded by any reputable training facility. For more information, go to http://www.assistancedogsinternational.org/.

Chapter 20

SERVICE ANIMALS

Considerable evidence indicates that animal companions prolong life and help reduce the frequency of serious disease. *See, e.g.,* Gregg A. Scoggins, D.V.M., Note, *Legislation without Representation: How Veterinary Medicine Has Slipped Through the Cracks of Tort Reform*, 1990 U. ILL. L. REV. 953, 973, citing several studies demonstrating the benefits of animals in the treatment of handicapped children, the mentally impaired, and the elderly, and showing that the presence of animals has the effect of lowering blood pressure and heart rates. These data further establish that companion animals provide a compensable benefit and are a unique kind of property whose loss cannot and should not be valued like inanimate items of property. The effects on people interacting with dogs has been well documented. Friedmann et al. reported that children's blood pressures decrease while resting with a dog and while reading with a dog (*Social Interaction and Blood Pressure: Influence of Animal Companions*, in J. NERVOUS AND MENTAL DISEASE, Vol 171, No. 8, 1983), and Braun et al. reported similar findings with adults (*Physiological Effects of Human/Companion Animal Bonding*, in NURSING RESEARCH, Vol. 33, No. 3, 1984). Friedmann et al. also reported a strong connection with pet ownership and survival one year after a heart attack (*Animal Companions and One-Year Survival of Patients After Discharge From a Coronary Care Unit*, in PUBLIC HEALTH REPORTS, Volume 95, No. 4, 1980).

Several U.S. colleges and universities include study of the human-animal bond in their coursework. Some offer a single course, while others offer a certificate program. All may be found in a variety of disciplines. The surprisingly large number of colleges — including highly respected institutions — reflects a growing acceptance of the key role that animals play in our lives. In 1975, the National Institutes of Health commissioned research titled "The Human Health Responsibilities of Veterinarians," which was the first official recognition of the triangular interrelationships among people, their veterinarians, and their pets. http://csu-cvmbs. colostate.edu/vth/diagnostic-and-support/argus/Pages/default.aspx. In 1999, three organizations (the American Veterinary Medical Association, the American Association of Animal Hospitals, and the Association of American Veterinary Medical Colleges) commissioned an economic study, a significant portion of which addressed the human-animal bond in depth. The study concluded that, "in veterinary practice, recognition of the human-animal bond is an important determinant of successful practice." http://csu-cvmbs.colostate.edu/vth/diagnostic-and-support/argus/Pages/default.aspx. These above examples demonstrate that the bond between a companion animal and a human animal is real and capable of empirical study and analysis. In addition, the human-animal bond has financial and business implications as well as personal emotional influence.

Research goes further in the study of this bond. We might anticipate and expect that scientists involved in laboratory animal research remain emotionally distant from their subjects, if for no other reason than self-protection. However, the INSTITUTE FOR LABORATORY ANIMAL RESEARCH JOURNAL in 2002 devoted an entire issue to the *Implications of Human-Animal Interactions and Bonds in the Laboratory*, ILAR JOURNAL Vol. 43 (1) 2002. Kathryn Bayne, D.V.M., reports in her article *Development of the Human-Research Animal Bond and Its Impact on Animal Well-being* that the bond between animal and human is based on affection and/or respect:

> In the research environment, it is not uncommon for a bond to develop between the investigator, veterinarian, and/or animal care technicians and the animals with which they work. . . . Circumstances that foster the formation of these bonds include the close and frequent contact between the researchers and their animals, . . . the dependency of the animals on the animal care staff for their daily needs. . . .

Dr. Bayne also notes that special bonds can form with certain animals. "A strong contributing factor to the development of a bond is commitment to the animal," in caring for the animal, recognizing the animal's individuality, training the animal, and talking to the animal. http://dels.nas.edu/ilar_n/ilarjournal/43_1/Development. shtml (accessed on 8/7/2007).

In fact, a 2001 American Animal Hospital Association survey reported that 44 percent of pet owners would spend $3,000 or more to save their pet's life, and 21 percent would travel 1,000 miles or more to obtain specialty care for their pet. A Pfizer Animal Health/Gallup Organization Dog Owner survey reports that more than 75 percent of pet owners say their dog's health is as important to them as their own. http://csu-cvmbs.colostate.edu/vth/diagnostic-and-support/argus/Pages/ default.aspx. These kinds of owner attitudes reflect that owners are willing to demonstrate behaviorally that they believe their relationship with their dog is one-of-a-kind. This relationship between a companion animal and a human animal is bidirectional. Tannenbaum describes this as a relationship that benefits both parties and is mutually voluntary. *The Health Benefits of Pets*, NIH Technology Assess Statement Online, Sept. 10-11, 1987 (accessed 8/7/07). From the time a person brings an animal into his/her household, the two interact with and affect each other. The training that the person provides, caring for the dog's daily needs, taking the dog with her to work and on outings, talking with the dog — all serve to strengthen the bond bidirectionally. The more attention an owner gives to a dog, the more likely that dog will behaviorally respond. This two-way interaction will mold itself into a personalized, unique relationship, and the relationship has the potential to grow with each communication.

As the bond is strengthened, so is the potential for significant grief when that bond is broken. "During a person's experience with a companion animal, the depth of attachment grows, deepening the experience of loss when the animal dies." Messam et al., *Grief Following Death of a Companion Animal, in* CURRENT ISSUES AND RESEARCH IN VETERINARY BEHAVIORAL MEDICINE 184 (2005). Grief after pet loss is not as openly acknowledged as grief after the death of a human companion. As a result, the grieving person may receive inadequate support in their grieving and may feel isolated, which can increase the recovery period. *Id.* A study performed by the University of California, Davis School of Veterinary Medicine and published in 2005, reports that in highly attached caregivers, 50 percent were still grieving after one year. *Id.* There is a wealth of popular books available on the topic of pet loss. In addition, the Association for Death Education and Counseling (ADEC), the National Hospice and Palliative Care Organization (NHPCO), and the Hospice Foundation of America (organizations designed to provide care for humans) all recognize pet loss as a valid form of grief, yet it is still considered disenfranchised grief. In fact, the entire April 2007 issue of ADEC's The Forum was dedicated to pet loss. The Association for Pet Loss and Bereavement provides not only supportive information, but also a referral list of counselors who provide pet loss counseling.

Notwithstanding the abundant foregoing evidence, the therapeutic benefits conferred upon their guardians[1] do not transform those *companion, therapy, or comfort* animals into *service* or *emotional support* animals[2] protected under such federal laws as the Americans with Disabilities Act ("ADA"), Rehabilitation Act of 1973,[3] Fair Housing Act ("FHA"),[4] Air Carrier Access Act ("ACAA"), and state antidiscrimination laws.

A. AMERICANS WITH DISABILITIES ACT

Like the FHA, the ADA prevents discrimination based on disability or use of a service animal or guide dog. While the federal statute itself does not define "service animal" or "guide dog," 28 C.F.R. § 36.104 (2008) did:

---

[1] This unidirectional focus on benefit to the disabled person, instead of burden to the service animal, begs a critical question: should the law regulate the potentially deleterious effects upon those nonhumans forced to spend their lives laboring on behalf of a highly dependent human being, especially one who may inadvertently harm, neglect, or abuse them? While some animals may thrive in such an exclusive, dyadic relationship, electing to organize and restrict their interactions according to the needs of their disabled handler, they cannot be said to have voluntarily and intelligently elected such an arrangement at the outset. Those who fail out, or create a "direct threat" to others, including the disabled handler herself (as in the case where service primates have injured or killed their users), may be engaging in uncivil self-emancipation, throwing off the mantle of involuntary servitude. That said, the overwhelming majority of service dogs, properly treated, particularly the "working" breeds, probably prefer the nearly-constant attention and closeness engendered in the life as an assistance animal, compared to the companion dog left at home most of the day, and sometimes, night while his guardian leads her life outside the home.

[2] *Grider v. City and County of Denver*, 958 F. Supp. 2d 1262 (D. Colo. 2012), remarked that "Plaintiffs appear to underestimate the degree to which non-disabled individuals might derive therapeutic value from the companionship of a pet. . . . Within these parameters, the Court can readily conceive of individuals who, while not meeting the legal definition of having a disability, nevertheless rely on the family pet in some of the same ways (if not necessarily to the same degree) as the [disabled] Plaintiffs do." *Id.*, at *4.

[3] Discussed in Chapter 10(D). Section 504 of the Act, 29 U.S.C. § 794, provides that no otherwise qualified individual with a disability in the United States, shall, solely by reason of disability, be excluded from participation in, denied benefits of, or be subjected to discrimination under any program or activity receiving Federal financial assistance or any program or activity conducted by any Executive Agency or United States postal service. Analytically, the ADA and Section 504 are identical relative to rights and obligations. *Vinson v. Thomas*, 288 F.3d 1145, 1152 n.7 (9th Cir.2002).

[4] Discussed at length in Chapter 10, Section D(1).

> Service animal means any guide dog, signal dog, or other animal individually trained to do work or perform tasks for the benefit of an individual with a disability, including, but not limited to, guiding individuals with impaired vision, alerting individuals with impaired hearing to intruders or sounds, providing minimal protection or rescue work, pulling a wheelchair, or fetching dropped items.

In 2011, however, this changed with the Sept. 15, 2010 final rule of the Civil Rights Division of the Department of Justice, titled *Nondiscrimination on the Basis of Disability by Public Accommodations and in Commercial Facilities*, 75 FR 56236-01:

> Service animal means any dog that is individually trained to do work or perform tasks for the benefit of an individual with a disability, including a physical, sensory, psychiatric, intellectual, or other mental disability. Other species of animals, whether wild or domestic, trained or untrained, are not service animals for the purposes of this definition. The work or tasks performed by a service animal must be directly related to the handler's disability. Examples of work or tasks include, but are not limited to, assisting individuals who are blind or have low vision with navigation and other tasks, alerting individuals who are deaf or hard of hearing to the presence of people or sounds, providing non-violent protection or rescue work, pulling a wheelchair, assisting an individual during a seizure, alerting individuals to the presence of allergens, retrieving items such as medicine or the telephone, providing physical support and assistance with balance and stability to individuals with mobility disabilities, and helping persons with psychiatric and neurological disabilities by preventing or interrupting impulsive or destructive behaviors. The crime deterrent effects of an animal's presence and the provision of emotional support, well-being, comfort, or companionship do not constitute work or tasks for the purposes of this definition.

75 FR 56250. Contrary to lay perception, federal law does not require training by a certified professional (self-training may suffice), nor registration of the service animal with a governmental or nongovernmental agency, nor performance of an enumerated task or function (instead, it offers illustrative examples), nor a specific degree of service — whether measured by intensity, duration, frequency, or proportion of daily activities. Rather, the question is whether the animal responds (i.e., works or performs tasks or functions) to the individual's needs in a way distinguishing it as a service animal. 75 FR 56193. And while the law never did prohibit recognition and protection of mental health service dogs, the days of proprietors, employers, and government agencies honoring only patently obvious working dogs (e.g., seeing-eye) were hopefully ended by the Final Rule's explicit embrace of psychiatric service dogs, who may perform tasks to "include reminding the handler to take medicine, providing safety checks or room searches for people with PTSD, interrupting self-mutilation, and removing disoriented individuals from dangerous situations." 75 FR 56269. To be clear, however, emotional support animals — owing either to lack of individualized training or not engaging in qualified "work" — do not qualify as service animals. "The difference between an emotional support animal and a psychiatric service animal is the work or tasks that

the animal performs," adding that "emotional support, well-being, comfort, or companionship . . . do[es] not constitute work or tasks for the purposes of this definition." *Id.*

Species discrimination pervades the 2011 amendment by limiting the label "service animal" to canines, excluding felines, reptiles, rabbits, ferrets, amphibians, rodents, and farm animals (including all horses, ponies, pigs, and goats). 75 FR 56267. However, it stopped short of breed discrimination by stating that "if an individual uses a breed of dog that is perceived to be aggressive because of breed reputation, stereotype, or the history or experience the observer may have with other dogs, but the dog is under the control of the individual with a disability and does not exhibit aggressive behavior, the public accommodation cannot exclude the individual or the animal from the place of public accommodation." *Id.*, at 56265.[5] The Department believed that a canine-centric focus would "provide greater predictability for state and local government entities as well as added assurance of access for individuals with disabilities who use dogs as service animals." *Id.* Exotic animals also were excluded. Though the Department gave serious consideration to capuchin monkeys, it rejected them due their risk of zoonotic disease transmission and unpredictable, potentially aggressive behavior. *Id.*, at 56267–68. Oddly, among the menagerie of all creation, this Final Rule allows the miniature horse to trot alongside the service dog. 75 FR 56251 (28 C.F.R. § 36.302(c)(9)); see discussion at 75 FR 56272.

The law's breadth extends to places of employment (Title I), access to public services (Title II), and places of public accommodation (Title III).[6] While the ADA protects the qualifying disabled who do not rely on service animals, this chapter emphasizes the failure to accommodate assistance species. States are not immune from the ADA under the Eleventh Amendment. 42 U.S.C. § 12202. The prevailing party bringing an action under the ADA may recover reasonable attorney's fees and litigation expenses. 42 U.S.C. § 12205.

An ADA-protected disabled person has a physical or mental impairment that substantially limits one or more major life activities; a record of such impairment; or is perceived as having such impairment (whether she does or not). 42 U.S.C. § 12012(1); 28 C.F.R. §§ 35.104, 36.104. Major life activities include such functions as caring for oneself, performing manual tasks, walking, seeing, hearing, speaking, breathing, and learning. Merely irritating, transient, or minimal impairments do not substantially limit such an activity; instead they must render the person unable to perform the major life activity that an average person could perform, or impose a significant restriction as to condition, manner, or duration under which the major life activity may be performed relative to the average person. The ADA Amend-

---

[5] Some jurisdictions have taken the position that imposing regulations on keeping certain breeds of service animal, such as leashing, sterilization, microchipping, registration, and muzzling (so as not to interfere with ability to perform), without outright banning same, does not violate the ADA. They contend that a "reasonable accommodation" does not mean the *perfect* accommodation; rather, the concept admits a level of compromise between public and private interests that such laws ostensibly embrace.

[6] Subchapter IV pertains to telecommunications. Subchapter V contains miscellaneous provisions, including coverage of Federal wilderness areas. Otherwise, the ADA does not apply to federal agencies: however, Section 504 of the Rehabilitation Act does.

ments Act of 2008 broadened the definition of "disability" to disregard the ameliorative effects of mitigating measures such as medication, medical supplies, equipment or appliances, low-vision devices (except ordinary eyeglasses or contacts), prosthetics, hearing aids or implants, mobility devices, or oxygen therapy equipment and supplies; the use of assistive technology; reasonable accommodations or auxiliary aids or services; or learned behavioral or adaptive neurological modifications. 42 U.S.C. § 12102(4)(E).

As of March 15, 2011, the federal government bestows upon only canines (and the occasional miniature horse) the label service animal provided they are individually trained to do work or perform tasks for the individual with a disability. 75 FR 56250. Be mindful that the foregoing definition of service animal applies under Titles II and III of the ADA, not Title I (pertaining to employment discrimination, and which evaluates the issue of animal access as one of "reasonable accommodation"). Arguably, a more relaxed definition of "service animal" (to encompass untrained emotional support animals) would apply in the workplace, akin to the definitions found in the Rehabilitation Act of 1973, Section 503 and the Federal Fair Housing Act. *But see Struthers v. England*, EEOC DOC 07A40043 (Jun. 29, 2006) (finding that Czar, a 33" tall Borzoi who was initially Struthers's companion animal but later certified as an assistance animal by the Tender Loving Care Service Dog organization did not meet the definition of "service animal" because she could not prove nexus between alleged disability and accommodation request to have Czar by her side); *Mennen v. Potter*, EEOC DOC 01A13112, 2002 WL 31232232 (Sept. 25, 2002) (refusing to determine if "service animal" includes emotional support animal but finding that accommodation of allowing bird to remain in facility if caged and area kept clean was reasonable).

Litigants asserting violations of their rights as disabled individuals relying upon service and emotional support animals have the initial burden of proving a prima facie case. Failure to accommodate claims predominate in the service animal access subset of federal disability discrimination cases. Reasonable accommodation claims require no showing of discriminatory intent or disability-based animus; rather, they sound in strict liability. *Higgins v. New Balance Athletic Shoe, Inc.*, 194 F.3d 252, 264 (1st Cir. 1999); Jacqueline Rau, *No Fault Discrimination?*, 27 Ohio St. J. on Disp. Resol. 241, 265-65 (2012); *Crowder v. Kitagawa*, 81 F.3d 1480, 1483-84 (9th Cir. 1996) (Title II ADA claims do not require showing of intentional discrimination); *Lentini v. California Center for the Arts, Escondido*, 370 F.3d 837, 846-47 (9th Cir. 2004) (no "intent" requirement in Title III ADA claim); *Indep. Living Resources v. Oregon Arena Corp.*, 1 F. Supp. 2d 1159, 1169 (D. Or. 1998) (Title III ADA claims encompass disparate impact as well as animus).

1.   Title I

Subchapter I, 42 U.S.C. §§ 12111–117, pertains to discrimination in the occupational setting and compels "meaningful access" and "comparable" services to nondisabled counterparts. 42 U.S.C. §§ 12132, 12143. Animal-based disputes under Title I typically involve refusal by an employer (with more than 14 employees) to accommodate the need of a disabled employee to bring an animal to work. Title I makes it unlawful for a covered entity to discriminate against a qualified individual on the basis of disability in regard to job application procedures, the hiring, advancement, or discharge of employees, employee compensation, job training, and other terms, conditions, and privileges of employment. 42 U.S.C. § 12112(a). 42 U.S.C. 12112(b)(5)(A) makes it illegal to discriminate against a qualified individual on the basis of disability, which is defined to include "not making reasonable accommodations to the known physical or mental limitations of an otherwise qualified individual with a disability who is an applicant or employee, unless such covered entity can demonstrate that the accommodation would impose an undue hardship on the operation of the business of such covered entity." Another type of failure to accommodate claim arises under 42 U.S.C. § 12112(b)(5)(B), defining discrimination as "denying employment opportunities to a job applicant or employee who is an otherwise qualified individual with a disability, if such denial is based on the need of such covered entity to make reasonable accommodation to the physical or mental impairments of the employee or applicant." Complaints under Title I should be lodged with the Equal Employment Opportunity Commission ("EEOC") within 180 days of the date of discrimination, or 300 days if filed with a designated state or local fair employment practice agency. As the ADA adopts the procedures set forth in the Civil Rights Act of 1964, 42 U.S.C. § 2000e-4 to e-9, an individual may generally only sue under Title I within 90 days after receiving a right-to-sue letter from the EEOC. 42 U.S.C. §§ 12117(a), 2000-5(f)(1); *Valenzuela v. Kraft*, 801 F.2d 1170, 1174 (9th Cir. 1986).

Title I makes it unlawful for a covered entity to discriminate against a qualified individual on the basis of disability in regard to job application procedures, the hiring, advancement, or discharge of employees, employee compensation, job training, and other terms, conditions, and privileges of employment. 42 U.S.C. § 12112(a). 42 U.S.C. § 12112(b)(5)(A) makes it illegal to discriminate against a qualified individual on the basis of disability, which is defined to include "not making reasonable accommodations to the known physical or mental limitations of an otherwise qualified individual with a disability who is an applicant or employee, unless such covered entity can demonstrate that the accommodation would impose an undue hardship on the operation of the business of such covered entity." Another type of failure to accommodate claim arises under 42 U.S.C. § 12112(b)(5)(B), defining discrimination as "denying employment opportunities to a job applicant or employee who is an otherwise qualified individual with a disability, if such denial is based on the need of such covered entity to make reasonable accommodation to the physical or mental impairments of the employee or applicant."

2. Title II

Subchapter II, Part A, 42 U.S.C. §§ 12131-132, addresses discrimination by excluding qualifying individuals with disabilities from participation in, or denial of benefits of, any public service, program, or activity of a public entity, or discrimination by that entity. Subchapter II, Part B, 42 U.S.C. §§ 12141-165, regulates discrimination in public transportation other than by aircraft or certain rail operations, as well as by intercity and commuter rail. A private right of action exists under Title II. *Barnes v. Gorman*, 536 U.S. 181, 186 (2002); 42 U.S.C.

§ 12133; *Tennessee v. Lane*, 541 U.S. 509, 517 (2004). Circuits have split as to whether the right extends to implementing regulations of Title II. Casey R. Fronk, *The Scope of Statutory Permissiveness: Private Actions to Enforce Self-Evaluation and Transition Plans under Title II of the Americans with Disabilities Act*, 74 U. CHI. L. REV. 1345 (2007).

Title II provides that "no qualified individual with a disability shall, by reason of such disability, be excluded from participation in or be denied the benefits of the services, programs, or activities of a public entity, or be subjected to discrimination by any such entity." 42 U.S.C. § 12132. A "qualified individual with a disability" is one "who, with or without reasonable modifications to rules, policies, or practices, the removal of architectural, communication, or transportation barriers, or the provision of auxiliary aids and services, meets the essential eligibility requirements for the receipt of services or the participation in programs or activities provided by a public entity." 42 U.S.C. § 12131(2). To bring a Title II accommodation claim, a plaintiff must proof (1) he has a disability, (2) he is otherwise qualified to receive the benefits of the public service, program, or activity, and (3) the defendants excluded him from participation in or denied him the benefits of such service, program, or activity or otherwise discriminated against him because of his disability. *Doe v. Bd. of Regents of University of Nebraska*, 280 Neb. 492, 525 (2010).

Kristy Pruett, a woman suffering from juvenile onset diabetes and bouts of hypoglycemic disorientation, sought the assistance of a chimpanzee[7] who sat with her when alone, helped her by retrieving candy or beverages with sugar on command, turned on lights, picked up remote controls and phones, slept with her, and provided mental stimulation. Though she previously kept a Tonkean ape for nearly a decade, the Arizona Fish and Game Department restricted private possession of chimpanzees and refused her an import permit. When she applied for, but did not receive, a USDA exhibitor permit, AFGD told her to export the chimpanzee as unlawfully possessed restricted wildlife. She refused and then filed suit under Title II of the ADA and Section 504 of the Rehabilitation Act. The court found for the State of Arizona, concluding that it did not have to reasonably accommodate her disability by waiving the possession of wildlife restriction because the chimpanzee did not *yet* meet the definition of service animal (despite being in training), nor did the training it did possess specifically ameliorate her disability. Further, she had alternatives available, such as acquiring another Tonkean ape (not banned in Arizona), implanting a continuous glucose monitor with insulin pump, or strapping a cell phone and glucose gel pack to her belt. *Pruett v Arizona*, 606 F. Supp. 2d 1065 (D. Ariz. 2009).

Autistic woman Joan Newberger faced a similar outcome to Ms. Pruett. New Orleans police officers and Louisiana Department of Wildlife and Fisheries employees stopped Ms. Newberger on Bourbon Street in the French Quarter of

---

[7] Interestingly, the court refers to Pruett's ex-husband who "deems himself Pruett's service animal such that she does not need the assistance of a primate." *Id.*, at 1068. It should also be noted that Ms. Pruett could not care for this two-year-old chimpanzee on her own, but relied on her ex–husband to change the diaper, prepare food, and feed. The chimpanzee also suffered severe allergic reactions resulting in anaphylaxis, demanding the use of an epi pen to prevent epileptic shock.

New Orleans as she and her caregiver were strolling with four small monkeys dressed in pirate attire. They seized the animals and cited her for cruelty to animals and possession of nonhuman primates in public and without a license, upon which she was convicted. The district court dismissed her ADA lawsuit in *Newberger v. Louisiana Department of Wildlife and Fisheries*, 2012 U.S. Dist. LEXIS 116356 (E.D. La. Aug. 17, 2012), premised on the notion that the monkeys did not meet the earlier (and broader) definition of service animal,[8] for she lacked "evidence to set a service animal apart from an ordinary pet," notwithstanding that the ADA does not require documentation of individualized training. Finding joy in "dressing the monkeys and that they had a calming effect on her" did not suffice. *Id.*, at *4 (citing *Baugher v. City of Ellensburg*, 2007 U.S. Dist. LEXIS 19073 at *15 (E.D. Wash. 2007)).

The ADA protects arrestees with service animals, as exemplified in the case of Richard Pena, who suffered a significant stroke in 1998, causing him to rely on Prissy, an Akita, to aid his mobility. While at the Bexar County Courthouse to research his adoption, a security officer refused him and Prissy entry, stating "dogs are not allowed in this building." After Pena explained that she was his service animal, the officer summoned a supervisor. Over the 15-minute delay, the officer forced Pena to stand for an "absolutely interminable" period due to his ataxic condition. On arrival, the supervisor demanded proof that Prissy was a service animal and interrogated Pena as to his specific disability. Though no such proof is required by federal law and questions seeking disclosure beyond mere tasks and functions that the animal performs is unlawful, Pena produced a Social Security Administration document verifying his disability and that he had a service dog. Allowed onto the third floor, he proceeded to conduct his research. *Pena v. Bexar Cy.*, 726 F. Supp. 2d 675, 679 (W.D. Tex. 2010). About half an hour later, co-defendant Brian Stanford allegedly told Pena to leave, claiming that only seeing-eye dogs were permitted in the courthouse. Pena stood his ground. Stanford threatened to arrest him and then forcibly grabbed him by the hand and cuffed him with the aid of another deputy, Humberto Hernandez. The two deputies then carried him down the hallway, causing him "excruciating pain." As Pena would not release Prissy's leash, she was choked. Charges against Pena for resisting arrest, criminal trespass, and cruelty to animals were dismissed. Pena thereafter sued under Title II of the ADA and Section 1983. The defendants did not dispute Pena had a qualifying disability.

While Title II and its regulations did not explicitly address service animals, and while Title III expressly does not apply to public entities, Title III's regulations and DOJ interpretations have been interpreted to impose upon public entities the duty to make reasonable accommodations for those with service animals. *Id.*, at 685 (citing *Rose v. Springfield-Greene County Health Department*, 668 F. Supp. 2d 1206, 1215 (W.D. Mo. 2009)). Unlike Section 1983 jurisprudence, *respondeat superior* does apply to ADA violations and does not require a policy, custom, or practice of discrimination by the public entity to establish fault. *Id.*, at 686 (quoting *Delano-Pyle v. Victoria Cy.*, 302 F.3d 567, 575 (5th Cir. 2002)). Finding that neither party adequately addressed the ADA's application to what happened on the third

---

[8] See 75 FR 56236, 56265–66 (Sept. 15, 2010), 28 C.F.R. § 36.104.

floor, the court denied summary judgment on the Title II count. Citing *Lollar v. Baker*, 196 F.3d 603 (5th Cir. 1999), the court further held that Pena could not sue the individual defendants for violations of Title II under Section 1983 because Congress had intended that ADA serve as the exclusive enforcement mechanism for deprivation of his rights as a disabled person. Following independent analysis, the court also dismissed the Fourth and Fourteenth Amendment claims against the individual officers and the County.

Reaching a similar conclusion, consider *Sears v. Bradley County Government*, 821 F. Supp. 2d 987 (E.D. Tenn. 2011), which dismissed a Title II claim against a police sergeant who temporarily prevented a woman with a seizure disorder from entering the courtroom with her service dog to testify as a witness at her son's friend's trial. Delay was occasioned by seeking permission from a judge's court officer and closure of the courthouse over the lunch hour. The court found that his refusal to allow entry was not intentionally motivated by discrimination on account of her disability but by his "genuine bewilderment at how to handle service animals." His "efforts to seek approval from Judge Randolph, including his forwarding of the papers provided by Plaintiff's husband to Judge Randolph's court officer, indicate he was not attempting to discriminate against Plaintiff."

Another notable Title II case involved Snickers, a part Pit Bull service dog certified to assist James Sak, a retired law enforcement officer who suffered from a hemorrhagic stroke, leaving him confined to a wheelchair, as the right side of his body was permanently disabled. *Sak v. City of Aurelia*, 832 F. Supp. 2d 1026 (N.D. Iowa 2011). When Sak and his wife moved from Chicago to Aurelia, Iowa, a city of 1,100 people, he was told to remove Snickers or face daily citations for violating the city code prohibiting the keeping, harboring, owning, or possessing a Pit Bull Dog. The code also threatened Sak with confiscation of Snickers. In a detailed opinion, the federal district judge issued a preliminary injunction preventing enforcement of the breed-discriminatory law against Sak upon payment of a one dollar security. 28 C.F.R. § 35.130(b)(7) requires a public entity to make reasonable modifications in policies, practices, or procedures when necessary to avoid discrimination on the basis of disability, unless the entity can show that the changes would fundamentally alter the nature of the service, program, or activity. The court rejected the City's first argument that Sak had no ADA claim because neither he nor Snickers was denied access to any public services, or even public places. It reasoned that the ADA extended to the regulation of any activity by an ordinance is, "itself, a program, service, activity or benefit of the City that Title II of the ADA will reach," further citing cases that treat municipal zoning ordinances as public "programs" or "services" the enforcement of which constitutes local government "activity." Furthermore, 42 U.S.C. § 12132 bars discrimination by the entity, independent of any services, programs, or activities — the focus being disparate administration of the pit bull ban without regard for Sak's disability. *See also Frame v. City of Arlington*, 657 F.3d 215, 225 (5th Cir. 2011) ("services, programs, or activities" have been construed to mean "all of the operations of a local government").

Aside from finding a likelihood to prevail on the merits, the court also considered the irreparable harm to Sak, to include degradation in quality of life (e.g., he had fallen from his wheelchair twice without Snickers to assist him with bracing and reseating and called 911 for assistance). Sak convincingly argued that

Snickers was tantamount to a wheelchair. Moreover, replacing Snickers with a non-pit bull service dog would still cause irreparable harm "because Snickers has been individually trained for Sak's individual needs," and would result in considerable lost time and difficulty obtaining and training a substitute animal, while Sak would suffer the loss of security and potential for injury in the interim. In balancing the private interest of Sak against the public interest in protecting health and safety, the court rejected that the former must yield where exceptions could be made to help disabled individuals, as in the case of *Crowder v. Kitagawa*, 81 F.3d 1480, 1485 (9th Cir. 1996), finding that Hawaii's rabies quarantine violated Title II as applied to the visually impaired, as Congress did not intend to separate the blind from their guide dogs. *See also Grider v. City and County of Denver* 958 F. Supp. 2d 1262 (D. Colo. Mar. 30, 2012) (finding that Title II claim against breed-discriminatory legislation barely stated an accommodation claim premised on inability to navigate public areas and use service animals in public; but dismissing disparate impact claim due to failure to allege facts that evinced a significantly adverse or disproportionate impact upon disabled owners of service pit bulls, given the absence of quantitative or qualitative evidence in the complaint).

3. Title III

Subchapter III, 42 U.S.C. §§ 12181-189, prohibits discrimination in places of public accommodation and services operated by private entities. Places of "public accommodation" are too numerous to list but include such places as inns, hotels, motels, restaurants and bars; movie theaters, concert halls, stadiums, auditoriums, convention centers, lecture halls, bakeries, grocery stores, clothing stores, supermarkets, shipping malls, amusement parks, Laundromats, barber shops, offices of an accountant, lawyer, health care provider, or hospital, museum, library, park, zoo, amusement park, schools K-12, colleges, day cares, homeless shelters, gymnasiums, spas, bowling alleys, and terminals, depots, or stations used for specified public transportation (which does not include aircraft), and cruise ships that contain public facilities. 42 U.S.C. § 12181(7)(A)-(L), (10). Certain private clubs and religious organizations are exempt. 42 U.S.C. 12187. Private businesses confused about what questions may be asked to uncover service animal fraud may benefit from consulting the United States Department of Justice guidances, such as the 1996 *Commonly Asked Questions About Service Animals in Places of Business*, www.ada.gov/qasrvc.htm; the 2002 *ADA Business Brief: Service Animals*, www.ada.gov/svcanimb.htm; and the 2015 Department of Justice FAQ about Service Animals and the ADA, http://www.ada.gov/regs2010/service_animal_qa.html.

Asserting that the guidances were contradictory and that a private membership club's creation of an animal access policy based on them violated Title III, consider *Grill v. Costco Wholesale Corp.*, 312 F. Supp. 2d 1349 (W.D. Wash. 2004), which clarified the proper scope of interrogation by a vendor of a disabled handler. Susan Grill, a member of Costco since 2000, attempted to enter a Costco warehouse with her service dog, Charlie. Its written policy admitted animals if "visually identifiable as a service animal by the presence of an apparel item, apparatus or other visual evidence that the animal is a service animal." If lacking, then "the member of guest must be prepared to reasonably establish that the animal does, in fact, perform a function or task that the member or guest cannot otherwise perform." *Id.*, at 1350. Costco personnel were then advised to "inquire of the animal's owner what tasks or functions the animal [so] perform[s]." The 1996 *Commonly Asked Questions* guidance permits asking if the animal "is a service animal required because of a disability," while the 2002 *Business Brief* contends that the business may ask "what tasks the animal has been trained to perform, but cannot require special ID cards for the animal or ask about the person's disability." *Grill* rejected the argument that the task-based inquiry indirectly compels disclosure of a person's disability, particularly invisible ones, since an individual may respond without divulging specifics, such as by stating, "the animal is trained to alert me when a medical condition is about to occur" or "the animal is trained to pick up items off the floor for me." *Id.*, at 1353. Although not codified in the C.F.R., the court gave deference to these Justice Department interpretations, as well as the DOT guidance for implementation of the Air Carrier Access Act, permitting airline personnel to obtain "credible verbal assurances" from passengers, including specifically "[w]hat tasks or functions does the animal perform for you?"

The ADA applies in settings where service dogs might conceivably endanger other ill patients. In *Pool v. Riverside Health Services, Inc.*, 1995 U.S. Dist. LEXIS 12724 (D. Kan. Aug 25, 1995), a wheelchair-bound plaintiff relied on Abraham, her 85-pound Golden Retriever who had been trained to pull her wheelchair. When attempting to visit her fiancé, who was being treated in the emergency treating area posted with a sign saying "Patients Only Beyond This Point," the hospital refused her admission with Abraham. Although she experienced pain to provide her own locomotion, as well as embarrassment, the court found no Title III violation. Sparse on analysis, the court concluded that qualifying individuals with disabilities do not enjoy unlimited access, particularly given concerns of "infection control, cross exposure, allergic reactions, patient dignity and confidentiality, [and] unpredictable behavior of the patient and the animal." Similarly, *Perino v. St. Vincent's Med. Ctr. of Staten Is.*, 502 N.Y.S.2d 921 (N.Y. Sup. Ct. 1986), found that a guide dog could not enter a hospital delivery room during childbirth, according to New York Civil Rights Law. *Albert v. Solimon*, 684 N.Y.S.2d 375 (N.Y. Sup. Ct., App. Div. 1998), determined that a physician's examination room was not a public facility under a New York Civil Rights Law barring discrimination against persons using service dogs. *But see Tamara v. El Camino Hosp.*, 964 F. Supp. 2d 1077 (N.D. Cal. 2013) (granting preliminary injunction to mobility-impaired and bipolar woman relying on service dog while staying in a locked psychiatric ward, finding that hospital did not show how presence of service dog would fundamentally alter the nature of the facility nor that dog would present a direct threat).

Rose v. Springfield-Greene County Health Department, 668 F. Supp. 2d 1206 (W.D. Mo. 2009), a Title II (against health department) and Title III (against Wal-Mart and Cox) case decided before the 2011 amendment to the definition of service animal, rejected that plaintiff Debby Rose, who claimed to suffer from agoraphobia and anxiety but made no complaints of disability, nor was diagnosed with a disability for more than 30 years over the period that she claimed impairment, was disabled. The court also denied that her Bonnet Macaque monkey named Richard, whom she allegedly self-trained in "break[ing] the spell," "break-[ing] off the focus," "crowd control," "chang[ing] the mood," "designat[ing] when

[she] ha[s] a change in [her] heart rate and blood pressure," and "keep[ing] control of what [she's] doing," but whose primary task was described by her physician as sitting with her as a comfort, was a service animal. While no codified thresholds exist as to the quantum or type of training required, nor is certification by any governmental or nongovernmental entity required, the court concluded that Richard had no such individualized training but that the "vast majority of these 'tasks' involve nothing more than the monkey providing comfort." Merely offering "reassurance is equivalent to a household pet, and does not qualify as a service animal under the ADA." *Id.*, at 1215; *see also Access Now, Inc. v. Town of Jasper*, 268 F. Supp. 2d 973, 980 (E.D. Tenn. 2003) (refusing to enjoin city from enforcing equine ban in residential neighborhood in case where Tiffany, 9, suffering from spina bifida and hydrocephalus, sought to have a miniature service horse, the court finding she did not have a qualifying disability (no substantial limitation of major life activity), nor could she claim her miniature horse, provided by the Make-a-Wish Foundation to aid bracing and retrieval, as a service animal due to lack of individualized training).

Surprisingly, more than one city council has entertained laws permitting dogs in bars. Would such law be necessary for service dogs? *Johnson v. Gambrinus Company/Spoetzl Brewery*, 116 F.3d 1052 (5th Cir. 1997) ruled in favor of a blind plaintiff denied the right to bring his guide dog on a brewery tour, which began at the wort-viewing area in the grant, then to the brewkettle where tourists could peer over the wort as it boiled. The brewery defended its position by citing 21 C.F.R. § 110.35(c) and the alleged risk of food contamination (i.e., dog hair in beer). The Fifth Circuit found the five "critical control points" on tour to have a virtually impossible likelihood of contamination by a guide dog, particularly given the filtering process and the relative risk of 5,800 tourists annually — who were not forced to wear hair nets and beard coverings. In finding for Johnson, the court held that the brewery failed to meet its burden to show that the proposed modification would fundamentally alter the nature of the accommodation or jeopardize public safety.

Quadiplegic Kathleen Lentini and her service Shih Tzu/Poodle named Jazz attended several concerts at the California Center for the Arts in Escondido, California. On two nights, Jazz yipped during intermission, yet none complained. When she returned for the performance of Tango Buenos Aires, the House Manager told Lentini she could not enter with Jazz on account of prior barking, and she refused to leave him in her car due to the cold weather and due to disruption of "the bond that was created between them as a result of Jazz's training." Law enforcement arrived, and the manager indicated his intention to sign a citizen arrest form and have her removed from the premises. At that point, Lentini left in exchange for a refund of her tickets. The federal district court found for Lentini, ordering the Center to modify its policies to confer "broadest feasible access" and not to exclude a service animal who made a noise on a previous occasion, even if disruptive, when made and intended to serve as means of communication for the benefit of the disabled owner or when it would be otherwise acceptable to the Center if engaged in by humans. *Id.*, at 842. The Center argued that the compelled modifications were neither reasonable nor necessary as Lentini had a human companion to assist her, as well as special ushers, but the Ninth Circuit overruled the objection. Nor did the appellate court find that the modification fundamentally altered the nature of the Center's services or facility, adding that it did not meet its burden to prove this affirmative defense. *Lentini v. California Center for the Arts, Escondido*, 370 F. 3d 837 (9th Cir. 2004).

B. SECTION 504 OF THE REHABILITATION ACT OF 1973

Organizations receiving federal funding violate Section 504 of the Rehabilitation Act, 29 U.S.C. § 794, if denying a qualified disabled individual a reasonable accommodation to enjoy meaningful access to the benefits of public services. *Ability Center of Greater Toledo v. City of Sandusky*, 385 F.3d 901, 909 (6th Cir. 2004). Section 503 of the Act, 29 U.S.C. § 793, requires nondiscrimination in employment by Federal government contracts and subcontractors with contracts of more than $10,000. Section 501 of the Act, 29 U.S.C. § 791, also guards against discrimination in employment by Federal agencies of the executive branch.

The 2011 definition of "service animal" applicable to Titles II and III of the ADA does not apply to Sections 501, 503, or 504. 28 C.F.R. § 35.103 (noting inapplicability to Title V of the Rehabilitation Act); Sarah K. Pratt, Deputy Assistant Secretary for Enforcement, *New ADA Regulation and Assistance Animals as Reasonable Accommodations* (Feb. 17, 2011); *Velzen v. Grand Valley State University*, 902 F. Supp. 2d 1038, 1047 (W.D. Mich. 2012) (Section 504 embraces emotional support animals). In 2013, HUD issued an FHEO Notice 2013-01 titled Service Animals and Assistance Animals for People with Disabilities in Housing and HUD-Funded Programs (confirming that the Title II and III amendments to the definition of service animal did not apply to the Rehabilitation Act). "Disability" under Section 504 has the same meaning given in the ADA. 29 U.S.C. § 705(9)(B).

Section 504 of the Rehabilitation Act of 1973, 29 U.S.C. § 794(a), states, in relevant part, "No otherwise qualified individual with a disability in the United States, as defined in section 705(20) of this title, shall, solely by reason of her or his disability, be excluded from the participation in, be denied the benefits of, or be subjected to discrimination under any program or activity receiving Federal financial assistance or under any program or activity conducted by any Executive agency or by the United States Postal Service." The Act has incorporated by reference the definition of "individual with a disability" as found in the ADA. 29 U.S.C. § 705(20)(B); *see also* 29 C.F.R. § 32.4(a). In relation to employment discrimination by federal employers or recipients of federal funding, Title I and select Title IV ADA standards apply. 29 U.S.C. § 794(d). To prevail on a Section 504 claim, a plaintiff

> must establish that (1) he is a 'qualified individual' with a disability, as that term is defined in the Rehabilitation Act, (2) he is 'otherwise qualified' to participate in the offered program or activity or to enjoy the services or benefits offered, (3) he is being denied the opportunity to participate in or benefit from the defendants' services, programs or activities, or was otherwise discriminated against by the defendants by reason of his disability and (4) the defendants, or the entity they represent, receive federal financial assistance so as to be subject to the Rehabilitation Act.

Mercer v. Champion, 139 Conn. App. 216, 230 (2012) (quoting *Mercer v. Strange*, 96 Conn. App. 123, 131 n.9 (2006)).

C.   FAMILY AND MEDICAL LEAVE ACT

The Family and Medical Leave Act of 1993, 29 U.S.C. §§ 2601–54, guarantees covered workers the right to up to two 12 weeks per year of protected, unpaid leave for qualifying medical and familial reasons. Specifically, eligible employees may take such time off for the birth of a son or daughter of the employee in order to care for such son or daughter; placement of a son or daughter with the employee for adoption or foster care; to care for the spouse, or a son, daughter, or parent, of the employee, if such spouse, son, daughter, or parent has a serious health condition; or any qualifying exigency arising out of the fact that the spouse, son, daughter, or parent of the employee is on covered active duty in the Armed Forces. 29 U.S.C. § 2612(a)(1) (A)-(C), (E).[9] As might be expected, the FMLA does not extend to nonhuman family members. *See* 29 U.S.C. § 2611(7) ("parent" means biological parent of employee or individual standing in loco parentis), (12) ("son or daughter" means biological, adopted, or foster child, a stepchild, a legal ward, or a child of a person standing in loco parentis), (13) ("spouse" means husband or wife), (17) ("next of kin" means nearest blood relative of that individual).

D.   AIR CARRIER ACCESS ACT

The Air Carrier Access Act of 1986, 49 U.S.C. § 41705, stems commercial airline discrimination against disabled passengers. Enacted after *United States Department of Transportation v. Paralyzed Veterans of America*, 477 U.S. 597 (1986), which held that the Rehabilitation Act did not apply to private air carriers because they were "indirect recipients" of federal funding, the ACAA has virtually the same mandate and definitions as the ADA. *Love v. Delta Air Lines*, 310 F. 3d 1347, 1350 n.1 (11th Cir. 2002), discusses the legislative history of the ACAA. No private right of action exists. *See Boswell v. SkyWest Airlines, Inc.*, 361 F.3d 1263 (10th Cir. 2004); *Lopez v. Jet Blue Airways*, 662 F. 3d 593 (2d Cir. 2011). As discussed in Chapter 16, *Adler v. West Jet Airlines, Ltd.*, 2014 U.S. Dist. LEXIS 92332 (S.D. Fla. Jul. 8, 2014), involved the ejection of a married couple and their service dog from a Fort Lauderdale-Toronto flight before take-off. Though they did not bring an ACAA claim, WestJet unsuccessfully argued that it preempted their negligence claim even though it might prove germane to the duty of care in a negligence action. *See also Gilstrap v. United Air Lines, Inc.*, 709 F. 3d 995, 1010–11 (9th Cir. 2013). As hinted at above, in the cabin of a plane at an altitude of 30,000 feet, Title III of the ADA does not apply. Grievances under the ACAA must be lodged with the Aviation Consumer Protection and Enforcement Division of the DOT.

A 2003 guidance expanded the definition of service animal to explicitly exclude any requirement of state or local governmental certification, and to include emotional support animals (with suitable documentation). *Guidance Concerning*

---

[9] 29 U.S.C. § 2612(a)(1)(D) was held unconstitutional by *Coleman v. Court of Appeals of Maryland*, 132 S. Ct. 1327 (2012).

Service Animals in Air Transportation, 68 FR 24874-2 (May 9, 2003), Nondiscrimination on the Basis of Disability in Air Travel, 73 FR 27614-01 (May 13, 2008), and 14 C.F.R. Part 382. The animal may sit anywhere the disabled person does so long as no aisles are obstructed and emergency evacuation remains possible; alternative seating in the same class should be provided without charge for facilities, equipment, or services required for the accommodation (if animal placed in cargo). Cleaning charges for damage, if also assessed against non-disabled passengers, are permitted. Seizure alert and emotional support animals may assist a qualifying individual with a disability without individualized training due to innate ability. Formal training ("schools") is not required so long as a reasonable explanation can be provided as to functions.

14 C.F.R. § 382.117, Must carriers permit passengers with a disability to travel with service animals?, describes when an air carrier may interrogate a passenger about the status of the animal as a service, emotional support, or psychiatric service animal. "Credible verbal assurances" alone should be accepted as evidence of service animal status, in addition to the presence of harnesses, tags, ID cards, or other documentation. 14 C.F.R. § 382.117(d). Only if uncertainty remains should staff follow with questions on what tasks the animal performs. *See* Nondiscrimination on the Basis of Disability in Air Travel, 73 FR 27614-01, 27658-27660 (also speaking to service animals in training and whether the qualified individual with a disability must accompany the service animal in the cabin). In the absence of credible verbal assurances, documentation may be required. 14 C.F.R. § 382.117(e) explains.

Service animals may be excluded from the cabin who present a "direct threat" to health or safety or cause "significant disruption," but not mere inconvenience to other passengers. "Certain unusual service animals (e.g., snakes, other reptiles, ferrets, rodents, and spiders) pose unavoidable safety and/or public health concerns and are not required to transport them." Other animals, such as "miniature horses, pigs and monkeys should be evaluated on a case-by-case basis by U.S. carriers." See Nondiscrimination on the Basis of Disability in Air Travel, 73 FR 27614-01, 27661. 14 C.F.R. § 382.21 provides that an air carrier may refuse to transport the passenger, delay the passenger's transportation, impose conditions, restrictions or requirements not imposed on other passengers, or require the passenger to provide a medical certificate if the passenger poses a direct threat. 14 C.F.R. § 382.19(c) sets forth the factors that inform the individualized assessment, one based on reasonable judgment relying on current medical knowledge or the best available objective evidence, looking at the (1) nature, duration, and severity of the risk; (2) probability that the potential harm to the health and safety of others will actually occur; and (3) whether reasonable modifications of policies, practices, or procedures will mitigate the risk. Where a direct threat is found, the carrier "must select the least restrictive response from the point of view of the passenger, consistent with protecting the health and safety of others." 14 C.F.R. § 382.19(c)(2).

E. INDIVIDUALS WITH DISABILITIES EDUCATION ACT

The United States Department of Education enforces the Individuals with Disabilities in Education Act of 1990 ("IDEA"), 20 U.S.C. § 1400 et seq., it applies to those states and local agencies accepting federal funding and requires that they offer all disabled children with a "free appropriate public education," with emphasis on special education and related services to prepare them for further education, employment, and independent living. 20 U.S.C. § 1400(c)(5)(A)(i). While IDEA itself does not have an antidiscrimination component, it creates a framework for adjudication of any disputes under the Rehabilitation Act or the ADA, both of which apply in the public school context. *Cave v. East Meadow Union Free Sch. Dist.*, 514 F. 3d 240 (2d Cir. 2008), involved a hearing-impaired student who sought to bring Simba, his service dog, to high school in order to alert him to emergency bells, people calling his name, sounds of car engines in the street, and to enhance his socialization skills. *Id.*, at 244. His parents described Simba as an "independent life tool," akin to his cochlear implants. In denying the request, the school officials determined that Simba's presence would disrupt his overall individual education program ("IEP") under which he had already functioned satisfactorily. Because the parents failed to request and attend a due process hearing to present complaints concerning the IEP, the Second Circuit held that they had failed to exhaust administrative remedies and could not file suit. The court reached this outcome despite the parents urging the court not "to treat John, Jr. . . . as a *student* who is being deprived of an appropriate public education, but as a *person* who is being denied access to a public facility by reason of his disability and his non-educational need for a service dog." It reasoned that at least in part, the parents were challenging the adequacy of John's IEP because it excluded Simba, and the IDEA encompassed "more than simply academics." *Id.*, at 248.

Sullivan v. Vallejo City Unified Sch. Dist., 731 F. Supp. 947 (E.D. Cal. 2007) granted a preliminary injunction to Christine Sullivan, a wheelchair-bound child with cerebral palsy, learning disabilities, and partial deafness to require her school district to permit her service dog to accompany her based on a clear probability of success on her Section 504 claim. It specifically rejected the contention that space and health concerns compelled exclusion of her dog or that she should ask other people to retrieve dropped objects for her. Furthermore, it concluded that the decision to create an IEP that precluded her from having a service dog likely violated Section 504 as well. *Id.*, at 960.

F. STATE ANTIDISCRIMINATION LAWS

Do not overlook antidiscrimination laws at the state level. For a list of such assistance laws, see Rebecca F. Wisch, *Table of State Assistance Animal Laws*, www.animallaw.info/topic/table-state-assistance-animal-laws. In *McDonald v. DEQ*, 214 P.3d 749 (Mont. 2009), an employee filed a disability discrimination complaint against the Montana Department of Environmental Quality for failure to provide nonskid floor coverings so her service dog, Bess, an Australian Shepherd, could maintain traction on tile floors. Bess helped with bracing and tactile stimulation during a dissociative episode — increasing mobility and alleviating barriers to personal interaction. Bess had a history of slipping, falling, and hitting her chin on the floor, causing limping and soft-tissue injuries. DEQ argued that it need not accommodate the user of a "poorly performing assistive device," analogizing Bess to a defective wheelchair. The Montana Supreme Court found that nonskid floor coverings served as an accommodation for McDonald, not Bess. Though questions of functionality were not immaterial, they were "simply misplaced here, since the functional capability of McDonald's assistive device relates to the reasonableness of the necessary accommodation, not whether DEQ had a duty to provide one in the first place." *Id.*, at 264–65. Of interest is the concurrence/dissent of Justice Patricia O. Cotter, who disputed DEQ's argument that the value of Bess (a dog who can no longer perform services as a service animal) is essentially nothing and that Bess "was nearly three-fourths finished with her service life" when she had to be retired, such that McDonald was therefore only entitled to one-fourth of the replacement fee of $500, the amount charged by CARES, the corporation that provided McDonald with Bess at the outset.

G. COMPETING DISABILITIES AND DIRECT THREAT

Fiona, a 125-pound Italian mastiff who sent a 62-year-old nurse practitioner to the hospital after Heather Morris, the disabled handler, tied her to a park bench without a muzzle in violation of animal control directives, was deemed vicious, although she also qualified as a service animal. San Francisco Police Department Sergeant Bill Herndon captured the essence of the problem of trying to classify vicious dogs as service animals:

> This is just a lack of common sense. Here we have a dog that obviously presents a danger to the public, and [Morris] wants to get service dog tags and expose more members of the public in more and more dangerous areas. I don't know about you, but I don't want to be in a restaurant next to that dog.

Joe Eskenazi, *Service with a Snarl*, SAN FRANCISCO WEEKLY, Jun. 17, 2009. The direct threat exception, however, would alleviate some of Sgt. Herndon's concerns, for it permits regulated entities to exclude even *bona fide* service animals should they nonetheless behave in a manner creating substantial risk of injury or death to others, as in the case of a service animal declared potentially dangerous, dangerous, or vicious, or where, despite not being labeled, the service animal acts in a disruptive manner that endangers staff and patrons. While some contend that the ADA overrides state and local dangerous dog ordinances, federal law does not excuse aggressive behavior or bestow upon a service dog one free mauling. But what of those who pose as disabled users of trained service dogs? Might they be increasing the risk of violent confrontations when their untrained, disobedient dogs have been permitted, under false pretenses, to enter otherwise prohibited areas? *See Service Dog Scams Putting People "At Risk,"* 5 On Your Side, WRAL.com, Nov. 18, 2013, http://www.wral.com/service-dog-scams-putting-people-at-risk-/13111411/; *see also Canine Companions for Independence petition to stop service dog fraud and online sales of service animal paraphernalia*, www.cci.org.

Public entities and accommodations need not suffer gladly animals behaving badly. Where animals present a "direct threat," or an accommodation or modification for same causes "undue hardship," or an animal is out of control, discrimination may be deemed necessary and lawful.

Where a "significant risk to the health or safety of others . . . cannot be eliminated by reasonable accommodation," the defendant agency or proprietor may raise the "direct threat" defense to a claim of failure to accommodate. 42 U.S.C. § 12111(3) defines "direct threat" for purposes of Title I, with further clarification in 29 C.F.R. § 1630.2(r), setting forth four factors by which to ascertain the existence of a "direct threat" in the employment context – viz., (1) duration of risk; (2) nature and severity of potential harm; (3) likelihood that potential harm will occur; and (4) imminence of potential harm. Of note is 29 C.F.R. § 1630.2(r)'s addition of the words "the individual or" before "others," thereby extending the "direct threat" defense to situations where the disabled individual endangers herself.

Title II's "direct threat" defense mostly mimics Title I's 29 C.F.R. § 1630.2(r) by outlining factors that govern the assessment of whether the individual (or more appropriately, the individual's service animal) presents same. Those factors are (1) nature, duration, and severity of risk; (2) probability that potential injury will actually occur; (3) whether reasonable modifications of policies, practices, or procedures or the provision of auxiliary aids or services will mitigate the risk. Unlike 29 C.F.R. § 1630.2(r), 28 C.F.R. §§ 35.104 and 35.139 offer no direct "threat to self" defense. Interestingly, the ADA itself does not codify a "direct threat" defense under Title II, yet the ADA Title II Technical Assistance Manual, II-2.8000, describes it as a basis to deem a plaintiff not a qualified individual with a disability.

Title III codifies a "direct threat" defense to a claim of failure to accommodate by describing the existence of a "significant risk" that "cannot be eliminated by a modification of policies, practices, or procedures or by the provision of auxiliary aids or services." 42 U.S.C. § 12182(b)(3). 28 C.F.R. § 36.208 is virtually identical to 28 C.F.R. § 35.139. *See also* ADA Title III Technical Assistance Manual III-3.8000.

Title II's 28 C.F.R. § 35.136(b) and Title III's § 28 C.F.R. 36.302(c)(2) provide that a public entity and place of public accommodation may ask an individual with a disability to remove a service animal from the premises if (1) the animal acts out of control and the handler does not take effective action to control him or her, or (2) the animal is not housebroken. To be "under handler's control" means to

> have a harness, leash, or other tether, unless either the handler is unable because of a disability to use a harness, leash, or other tether, or the use of a harness, leash, or other tether would interfere with the service animal's safe, effective performance of work or tasks, in which case the service animal must be otherwise under the handler's control (e.g., voice control, signals, or other effective means).

28 C.F.R. §§ 35.136(d), 35.302(c)(4).

Each Federal agency has its own Section 504 of the Rehabilitation Act of 1973 regulations. For instance, the Department of Education implemented 34 C.F.R. § 104.12(a) and (c) to discuss when an undue hardship exists relative to making a reasonable accommodation to a known physical or mental limitation of an otherwise qualified handicapped applicant or employee, in the context of a recipient of Federal financial assistance from the Department of Education and to the program or activity receiving such assistance.

In addition to Section 504 regulations that may apply to landlords receiving Federal funding through HUD, the Fair Housing Act excludes from coverage those with disabilities "whose tenancy would constitute a direct threat to the health or safety of other individuals or whose tenancy would result in substantial physical damage to the property of others." 42 U.S.C. § 3604(f)(9). The "direct threat" assessment cannot be based on fear, speculation or stereotype but requires reliable objective evidence and such considerations as (1) the nature, duration, and severity of the risk of injury; (2) the probability that injury will actually occur; and (3) whether there are any reasonable accommodations that will eliminate the direct threat. Joint Statement of the Department of HUD and DOJ, *Reasonable Accommodations Under the Fair Housing Act*, May 17, 2004, at 4, http://www.hud.gov/offices/fheo/library/huddojstatement.pdf (accessed Feb. 28, 2016). *Douglas v. Kriegsfeld Corp.*, 884 A.2d 1109, 1121 n.19 (D.C. Ct. App. 2005), held that the Joint Statement is entitled to substantial deference.

Although "undue hardship" and "fundamental alteration" defenses are not codified in the Fair Housing Act, courts have invoked them as part of the analysis of whether the accommodation request of the tenant is unreasonable. "A 'reasonable accommodation' is one which would not impose an undue hardship or burden on the entity making the accommodation." *Peabody Props., Inc. v. Sherman*, 418 Mass. 603, 608 (1994) (citing *Majors v. Housing Auth. of DeKalb*, 652 F.2d 454, 457 (5th Cir. 1981)).

> In addition, housing providers are not required to provide any reasonable accommodation that would pose a direct threat to the health or safety of others. Thus, if the particular animal requested by the individual with a disability has a history of dangerous behavior, the housing provider does not have to accept the animal into the housing. Moreover, a housing provider is not required to make a reasonable accommodation if the presence of the assistance animal would (1) result in substantial physical damage to the property of others unless the threat can be eliminated or significantly reduced by a reasonable accommodation; (2) pose an undue financial and administrative burden; or (3) fundamentally alter the nature of the provider's operations.

> For an extensive discussion of reasonable accommodation principles, see the "Joint Statement of the Department of Housing and Urban Development and the Department of Justice: Reasonable Accommodations Under the Fair Housing Act" (HUD/DOJ Joint Statement), available at: http://www.hud.gov/offices/fheo/disabilities/index.cfm.

Final Rule, *Pet Ownership for the Elderly and Persons with Disabilities*, 73 FR 63834, 63835.

How should places of public accommodation manage conflicts between a disabled individual allergic to nonhumans and another disabled individual reliant on a service animal? *Lockett v. Catalina Channel Express, Inc.*, 496 F. 3d 1061 (9th Cir. 2007), examined precisely such a legal problem. On account of a dander-free (and, thus, animal-barring) policy, Catalina Channel Express, which operated a ferry between Long Beach and Catalina Island, refused to sell a ticket to Tricia Lockett, a blind woman assisted by a guide dog, so she could access the more expensive and less crowded Commodore Lounge. Though Catalina changed its policy two weeks later, Lockett sued under Title III of the ADA for failure to modify policies to permit service animals in the lounge. The district court dismissed her lawsuit by finding that Catalina gave Lockett "different and separate accommodation" allowed by 42 U.S.C. § 12182(b)(1)(A)(iii) and, alternatively, that 28 C.F.R. §§ 36.208, 36.301(a), and 36.302(c) condoned such conduct due to health and safety concerns. While rejecting the trial court's first contention, as Catalina "did not offer Lockett a separate arrangement or facility, but relegated her to the general passenger area," the Ninth Circuit recognized the dilemma posed by Lockett and held that 28 C.F.R. § 36.208 permitted Catalina "to ask Lockett to travel in the general passenger area while it investigated the matter."

Finding that the "one-time request that Lockett accept passage in the general passenger area was a reasonable judgment under 28 C.F.R. § 36.208," the appellate court affirmed dismissal on that narrow basis. In so ruling, the court hastened to add that it did not mean to suggest that the ADA did not compel a policy change. "Indeed, CCE may well have violated the ADA had it not changed its policy." Circuit Judge Hall dissented, finding Catalina did not make the individualized threat assessment required by regulation, nor that it undertook to examine what reasonable modifications would neutralize any purported, significant health threat.

Chapter 21

CONSUMER PROTECTION LAW

Few forget Joe Camel, the cartoonized mascot for Camel cigarettes, which advertised the brand between 1987 and 1997. In 1991, the Journal of the American Medical Association published a study alleging that six-year-olds could associate him with cigarettes, thus demonstrating that R.J. Reynolds had targeted children with the "Joe Camel" campaign. Even the American Medical Association asked that Reynolds retire the caricatured dromedary. Thereafter, San Francisco attorney Janet Mangini sued the company for targeting minors. Prior to trial, the matter settled for $10 million earmarked to finance child antismoking efforts. Susceptible to such imagery, child consumers (and their parents) have been enticed by such marketing ploys.

Supported by the Center for Science in the Public Interest ("CSPI"), on December 15, 2010, Sacramento resident Monet Parham filed a class action against McDonald's on her behalf and that of Maya, her six-year-old daughter, asserting that the company's misleading marketing of "Happy Meals" to children, coaxing them with toys, contributed to the adolescent health crisis. The suit identified two classes — children under the age of eight lured by the meals, and parents who succumbed to the pestering by those children. CSPI likened McDonald's to "the stranger in the playground handing out candy to children," and added, "McDonald's use of toys undercuts parental authority and exploits young children's developmental immaturity — all this to induce children to prefer foods that may harm their health. It's a creepy and predatory practice that warrants an injunction." www.cspinet.org/litigation/closed.html. On April 4, 2012, the trial court dismissed the lawsuit, finding that parents bear exclusive responsibility for making food purchasing decisions.

While this modern approach to reining in deceptive food advertising to children does not focus on animal mistreatment, it certainly could. For instance, might a circus or zoo misleadingly market to children by encouraging them to see animals they imply have been kept humanely or, worse, enjoy the performing or exhibitionary life? Would not the adolescent audience take away all reasonable interpretations with less sophistication than an adult audience? To prevail on most false advertising claims, one must prove that the message taken away by the consumer was "reasonable" and "materially" affected their consumer decision. It has been held that where the defendant intends to convey a particular message, reasonableness and materiality are presumed (e.g., "we need to use the Happy Meal to target the adolescent market"). Does the "Animal Care Certified" logo have a tendency to mislead the consuming public? If so, would a false advertising claim lie?

March 31, 2006, was the last day United Egg Producers could use the "Animal Care Certified" logo per two agreements among UEP, the FTC, and attorneys-general in 16 states and the District of Columbia. See letter from Mary K. Engle, FTC Associate Director, Division of Advertising Practices, to UEP, Sept. 30, 2005, http://www.ftc.gov/sites/default/files/documents/closing_letters/united-egg-producers-uep/uepstaffopinionletter.pdf.

A. STATE UNFAIR PRACTICE ACTS

Every state has a consumer protection law prohibiting *deceptive* practices (also known as "little FTC" statutes, named after the Federal Trade Commission Act, 15 U.S.C. § 45 et seq.). Most also condemn *unfair* practices. According to the National Consumer Law Center's *Consumer Protection in the States* 2009 report, www.nclc. org/images/pdf/udap/report_50_states.pdf, the potency and applicability of unfair and deceptive act and practice ("UDAP") laws vary widely. It catalogs anti-consumer findings, such as judicial interpretations narrowing the scope of some UDAP laws to "almost no consumer transactions"; denying fees to a prevailing consumer; authorizing entry of fees against a defeated consumer; and exempting out lenders, creditors, and insurance companies from their ambit. Still, UDAP laws offered animal welfare litigants a tool to combat fraudulent ads duping the public into purchasing animal products represented as ethically sourced, for which they paid a premium.

One of the earliest animal-based UDAP actions arose when PETA sued a California dairy board over its "Happy Cows" campaign, alleging that the board's advertising practices contained deceptive and false representations, such as when commercials would "portray spacious, grassy pastures on beautiful, rolling hills with a few cows grazing and wandering about and 'enjoying' the ease, luxury, and contentment of life as a dairy cow in California," using the tag line "Great Cheese comes from Happy Cows. Happy Cows come from California." *PETA v. California Milk Producers Advisory Bd.*, 125 Cal. App. 4th 871, 875–76 (2005). Unfortunately, the Court of Appeals never reached the merits, having determined that the State Board was not a "person" for purposes of the UDAP. Moreover, it held deep reservations about judicial reprimands and injunctions infringing on the state's sovereign power.

In addition to animal welfare organizations challenging producers and retailers who flood the commercial discourse with statements that obscure and conceal the plight of animal suffering, what of those same organizations joining the dialogue with their own advertisements, thereby injecting a perspective that truthfully reveals what steps lead to the sale of plastic-wrapped, Styrofoam trays of flesh, cartoned eggs, or fur-lined apparel? A reverse UDAP suit against these messengers might prove colorable were the statements false, unfair, or deceptive. One such effort, brought by Huntingdon Life Sciences against PETA, failed. In *Huntingdon Life Sciences v. Rokke*, 978 F. Supp. 662 (E.D. Va. 1997), the district court dismissed a suit claiming that PETA falsely publicized lab conditions. It also rejected that the Lanham Act, 15 U.S.C. § 1125, which governs deceptive advertising in interstate commerce and concerns itself strictly with commercial or competitive injury, applied to PETA's political, noncommercial, speech. In addition, PETA did not compete with HLS. The backlash against organizations like HSUS tends to focus on misleading charitable solicitations, not the sale of goods.[1]

In fall 2001, the District of Columbia's Commission on Arts and Humanities solicited artists to participate in a public art project called "Party Animals," consisting of 200 pre-formed donkey and elephant sculptures to be installed at prominent locations. If the Commission approved the solicited design, the artist would receive an honorarium and money for supplies. The exhibit would belong to the District until sale at auction. Not allowed were "direct advertising," messages of "social disrespect," certain "slogans and inappropriate images." The Commission rejected several designs from the more than 1,000 submissions. Aside from the general artistic competition, however, prime sponsors paying more than $5,000 could design their own donkey or elephant for placement at a "prime public location." PETA did just that. Along with the check was a cartoonist's depiction of the proposed elephant design, showing an elephant with a sign tacked to its side, saying, "The CIRCUS is Coming; See: Torture Starvation Humiliation All Under the Big Top." The Commission rejected this design. PETA submitted two more designs: a happy circus elephant and a sad, shackled one poked by a trainer. It accepted the happy design. PETA submitted a third design with a shackled, crying elephant carrying a similar "CIRCUS is Coming" sign. Claiming that "PETA's proposed . . . design did not compliment these goals [of festivity, whimsy, and amusement], and indeed was contrary to the Party Animals' expressive, economic, aesthetic, and civic purpose," the Commission Director rejected the shackled elephant.

One month after the exhibit opened, PETA sued the Director and the District of Columbia for violating its First Amendment rights under Section 1983. It sought a preliminary injunction compelling the Commission to accept the rejected designs. The district court made three rulings: (1) in 2002, it issued a preliminary injunction forcing the Commission to display PETA's last elephant, where it was installed until the exhibit closed; (2) in November 2003, the court awarded PETA $4,000 in damages, essentially a "refund" for the four of five months that PETA's elephant was not displayed; there was also evidence from the district court's opinion, however, that the $4,000 was awarded for the "loss of First Amendment rights"; and (3) in December 2003, the court entered judgment for the $4,000 it awarded by memo the month before. The District appealed all three rulings.

In a 2-1 decision, the District of Columbia Court of Appeals dismissed the appeal of the court's preliminary injunction as moot and not presenting an issue "capable of repetition, but evading review." It remanded the appeal of the monetary award for the district court to clarify whether its judgment of $4,000 rested on a First Amendment violation; if not, then that issue was also moot. The majority focused on whether the Commission's refusal to allow PETA's sobbing elephant design, yet permit others, like tributes to heroes and victims of September 11, commemorations of civil rights leaders, a design chock full of political quotations and a design featuring the "butterfly ballot" used in the Palm Beach County, Florida 2000 presidential election, represented a ripe and ongoing conflict between PETA and the District when the exhibit had been closed for nearly two years by the time the

---

[1] According to humanewatch.org, "over 150 separate complaints [are] on file with the Federal Trade Commission regarding HSUS and its fundraising practices."

appeal was heard. PETA tactically argued that the District's appeals were not moot. Animal rights organizations often seek to perpetuate their gains made "on the streets," as it were, by securing a precedent-setting ruling from an appellate court. Such a decision could have wider impact than city-by-city acts of civil disobedience or, in this case, artistic stratagem. *PETA v. Gittens*, 396 F.3d 416 (D.C. Cir. 2005).

The first lawsuit in America to bring attention to the plight of veal calves, *ALDF v. Provimi Veal Corp.*, 626 F. Supp. 278 (D. Mass. 1986), asserted a violation of Massachusetts's consumer protection act (i.e., unfair and deceptive practices in nondisclosure) by Provimi Veal Corporation, a Wisconsin veal producer buying calves from Massachusetts, slaughtering them, and selling veal to meat distributors. Seeking injunctive relief to force Provimi to reveal the "cruel treatment" and "subtherapeutic antibiotic dosing" of veal calves, ALDF's state lawsuit was removed to federal court on grounds of diversity jurisdiction. Provimi defended by claiming preemption and failure to state a claim. The federal district court dismissed the lawsuit for failure to state a claim, finding that the cruelty to animals law, not the consumer protection law, was the appropriate avenue notwithstanding the absence of a private prosecutor provision and despite ALDF's assertion that it was Provimi's failure to give information, not the mistreatment itself, that was unfair and deceptive. As to subtherapeutic dosing, the court held that regardless of whether nondisclosure of antibiotic feeding was unfair and deceptive, the Federal Food, Drug, and Cosmetic Act ("FDCA"), 1 U.S.C. §§ 301–92 and the implementing regulations of the Food and Drug Administration ("FDA"), as well as the Federal Meat Inspection Act ("FMIA"), 21 U.S.C. §§ 601–95, and regulations enforced by the USDA, preempted the entire matter. Furthermore, no private right of action existed under the FDCA. In addition, ALDF never asserted that Provimi violated federal laws.

Although ALDF would never condone dining on veal parmigiana, it took the legal position that Provimi's material omissions of such practices caused harm to its Massachusetts members, who "do not want to buy veal from calves raised in this cruel and unhealthful manner." It also contended that "because this information is not available to retail consumers, ALDF members have unwittingly bought and eaten Provimi veal. Other ALDF members feel they are unable to buy or eat veal at all." While spearheading animal rights organizations toe a vegetarian or vegan line, for the sake of establishing standing to sue, they collaborate with individuals who may take a gastronomically less staunch position. Such a cross-spectrum approach allows plaintiffs to maximize the likelihood of having matters heard on the merits, as occurred in *Jones v. Butz*, 374 F. Supp. 1284 (S.D.N.Y. 1974), *summarily affirmed*, 419 U.S. 806 (1974).

In *Jones*, six individuals and three organizations sued the Secretary of Agriculture, Acting Administrator of Consumer and Market Services of the Department of Agriculture, and Rabbi Joseph Soloveitchik. Numerous Jewish organizations intervened. Plaintiffs charged that the Humane Slaughter Act ("HSA"), 7 U.S.C. § 1901 (1970) and its ritual slaughter provisions violated the Establishment and Free Exercise Clauses of the First Amendment. Section 1902, in relevant part, identifies two "humane" methods of killing: (1) rendering animals insensible to pain before being shackled, hoisted, thrown, cast, or cut; or (2) slaughtering in accordance with the ritual requirements of the Jewish faith or any other religious faith that prescribes a method whereby the animal loses consciousness by anemia of the brain caused by simultaneous and instantaneous severance of the carotid arteries with a sharp instrument. Plaintiffs argued that kosher pre-slaughter handling explicitly constitutes inhumane slaughter under § 1902(a), as the animals are hoisted and shackled before being rendered insensible to pain. Plaintiffs claimed standing as taxpayers and consumers, asserting source uncertainty (in the sense that they could not distinguish § 1902(b) and (a) meat, and were therefore forced to eat "ritually prepared" (and inhumanely slaughtered) meat.)

The district court held that the plaintiffs had standing to sue to challenge the religious exemption to the federal HSA, based, in part, on federal taxpayer status. *Id.*, at 1289 (citing criteria of *Flast v. Cohen*, 392 U.S. 83 (1968), which allows federal taxpayer standing without special injury in challenges brought under the First Amendment, and noting the expenditure of money to pay for travel and subsistence expenses of members of the advisory committee authorized under section 5 of the Act). Refusing to sit "as a super-legislature to weigh the wisdom" of humane slaughter and pre-slaughter livestock handling, and describing the alignment of § 1902(b)'s definition with ritual procedure under religious law a mere coincidence that did not "undercut its validity or propriety," the court found no First Amendment violation. That the United States Supreme Court summarily affirmed, however, has *de minimis* precedential value. A U.S. Supreme Court decision summarily affirming that federal district court decision, without signature by any of the justices, in a one sentence opinion, "Facts and opinion, D.C., 374 F. Supp. 1284. Judgment affirmed," commands little attention.[2]

---

[2] Note that no *certiorari* determination was made. This is because the Plaintiffs sought direct review by the Supreme Court. A party may appeal as of right to the Supreme Court from an order granting or denying an interlocutory or permanent injunction in any civil action, suit or proceeding required by any Act of Congress to be heard and determined by a district court of three judges. 28 U.S.C. § 1253. The reader may wonder why there are no Supreme Court briefs on the merits, argument before the court, or an opinion of any substance or signature by any justices. This is because the Supreme Court's summary affirmance fails to provide any meaningful review or explanation at all. That is, after all, what "summary" means. But what precedential value this summary affirmance carries is dubious. The Solicitor General filed a motion to affirm, noting that the matter did not raise a substantial federal question, which was joined by intervenors who framed the question as whether the kosher slaughter method was constitutional and humane (which was not the issue at all, but whether the HSA could constitutionally exempt religious groups from the "render insensible" requirement to those animals ritually slaughtered).

The Supreme Court rendered its decision, but not even *per curiam*. Perhaps the Clerk of the Supreme Court issued it at the direction of the Supreme Court, but one cannot discern from a one-line affirmance what was affirmed, and why. It is settled law that summary decisions by the Supreme Court are binding on the inferior federal courts and are decisions on the merits. *Hicks v. Miranda*, 422 U.S. 332, 344 (1975). "[L]ower court judges are left to guess as to the meaning and scope of our unexplained dispositions." *Colorado Springs Amusement Ltd. v. Rizzo*, 428 U.S. 913, 919 (Brennan, J., dissenting from denial of certiorari).

The precedential significance of the summary action in Salera [a summary disposition], however, is to be assessed in the light of all of the facts in that case; and it is immediately apparent that those facts are very different from the facts of this case.

Mandel v. Bradley, 432 U.S. 173, 176 (1977); *see also Hicks*, at 345 n.14 (applying precedent if "issues . . . [are] sufficiently the same."). Further, the Supreme Court noted "[w]hen we summarily affirm, without opinion, . . . we affirm the judgment but not necessarily the reasoning by which it was reached[,]" and "the rationale of [summary] affirmance may not be gleaned solely from the opinion below[.]" *Mandel*, at

In the 30 years since *Provimi Veal* and *Jones*, animal use industries have changed their public complexion by undergoing a paradigmatic advertising make-over. The code of silence has been broken by ethical sloganism and a race to secure brand supremacy by speaking to consumer compassion. While many vendors, manufacturers, and corporations do not exaggerate or mislead when catering to those who make spending decisions based on the moral treatment of animals, others have adverted to animal welfare concerns by tempting consumers with illusory humane certifications and other duplicitous affirmations. Responding to these tactics, animal law attorneys have resorted to the executive branch by filing complaints with federal consumer protection, animal agriculture, and securities and exchange regulators. For an excellent survey of state and federal approaches, including petitions to the FTC, FDA, and USDA, see Carter Dillard, *False Advertising, Animals, and Ethical Consumption*, 10 ANIMAL L. 25 (2004). Academics in journalism have also taken note of this recent, successful tack. PATRICIA SWANN, CASES IN PUBLIC RELATIONS MANAGEMENT: THE RISE OF SOCIAL MEDIA AND ACTIVISM (2D ED.), Ch. 3, Sec. 4 (Food for Thought) (Routledge: 2014).

B. FEDERAL REGULATORY COMPLAINTS

The Federal Trade Commission Act, 15 U.S.C. § 41 et seq., empowers the Federal Trade Commission to break up monopolies and eliminate unfair methods of competition in or affecting commerce, and unfair or deceptive acts or practices in or affecting commerce. 15 U.S.C. § 45(a)(2). No private right of action exists, but concerned parties may file complaints or petitions to initiate FTC investigations. 15 U.S.C. § 46, 16 C.F.R. §§ 2.1–2.2. On Dec. 18, 2010, following discovery that retailers sold fur-trimmed items unlabeled or mislabeled as faux fur, when in fact many contained domestic dog or wolf fur, President Obama signed into law the Truth in Fur Labeling Act, amending the Fur Products Labeling Act of 1951 ("FPLA"), 15 U.S.C. § 69 et seq. to close the $150 *de minimis* loophole, which allowed the FTC to exempt from fur-content labeling those products containing fur or fur trim with a component value of less than $150. 16 C.F.R. § 301.39(a).

False advertising claims pertain to apparel. On May 15, 2007, HSUS filed an FTC petition to enjoin false advertising and labeling of fur garments by retailers and fashion designers alleged to have violated the FPLA. Specifically, drawing from undercover investigations and mass spectrometry analysis, HSUS claimed to have scientific and testimonial evidence that entities such as Macy's were selling garments advertised as "faux fur, genuine raccoon or coyote, or rabbit fur when, in fact, the garments include fur from members of the canine family, such as domestic dog, wolf, or raccoon dog." HSUS asked the Commission to seize the deceptively advertised and labeled garments, initiate proceedings for injunctive relief, and impose penalties of up to $5,000 per violation under 15 U.S.C. §§ 69f, 69g, and 69i.

---

176 (quoting Fusari v. Steinberg, 419 U.S. 379, 391–92 (Burger, C.J., concurring) (1975)). Further, as articulated by the Supreme Court in *Illinois State Board of Elections v. Socialist Workers Party*, 440 U.S. 173 (1978), "[a] summary disposition affirms only the judgment of the court below[,]'" and the reasoning of the lower court opinion cannot be examined to determine the precedential reach of the summary affirmance. Questions that "merely lurk in the record" are unresolved and no resolution may be inferred. *Illinois*, at 182–83.

http://www.humanesociety.org/assets/pdfs/Fur-Labeling-5-15-07-Amended-FTC-Petition.pdf. HSUS supplemented the complaint on Apr. 24, 2008. On Nov. 22, 2011, HSUS lodged a petition to enjoin false advertising and labeling by 11 entities. http://www.humanesociety.org/assets/pdfs/fur/ftc_petition_fur_11-2011.pdf. In 2013, the FTC acted on HSUS's petition against Neiman Marcus, Dr. Jays, and Revolve Clothing, announcing the issuance of consent orders compelling compliance with FPLA advertising and labeling restrictions. *See* Decision & Order, *In Matter of DrJays.com, Inc.*, No. C-4408 (Jul. 18, 2013); http://www.ftc.gov/news-events/press-releases/2013/08/ftc-approves-final-orders-settling-charges-against-retailers.

False advertising pertains to meat production. HSUS, which had become a shareholder of Seaboard Corporation, one of the largest pork producers in America, filed a shareholder proposal to end the use of gestation crates, a response in part to Seaboard's 2008 "Sustainability & Stewardship Report," which courted consumers drawn to pronouncements of corporate social responsibility by asserting that its products were raised "free from cruelty" and in accordance with the "most humane practices." HSUS contended that these claims were irreconcilable with findings from a recent investigation into the use of gestation crates and surgical procedures without anesthesia, some of which resulted in piglets dying from "ruptures," where the "piglets' intestines spilled out from the opening where their testicles were removed during castration," what a farm manager described as "part of the learning process" of new employees. HSUS also argued that such remarks did not mesh with consumer opinion data. In addition to the September 2011 shareholder proposal, in January 2012, HSUS filed complaints with the FTC and SEC concerning this report. The FTC and SEC complaints mirror one another with respect to the deceptive claims contained in Seaboard's "Sustainability & Stewardship Report," demonstrating the double-barreled approach leveled against the pork producer.

The FTC complaint alleged unlawful deception relating to animal care, and unsubstantiated interpretations of express or implied claims, namely, consumers dishonestly lured by the siren song of humanely treated breeding sows. Though nonbinding, HSUS cited to reports prepared by the National Advertising Division ("NAD") of the Better Business Bureau ("BBB"), governed by the Advertising Self-Regulatory Council ("ASRC"), which invites consumers and competitors to lodge complaints with this nongovernmental body and resolve false and deceptive advertising disputes. In its petition, HSUS argued that animal welfare issues have become recognized by the NAD as important variables in purchasing choices:

> Advertising claims which tout that the advertiser is addressing particular social or ethical concerns can provide consumers with important information about their purchasing choices.

Starbucks Corp. (Free Trade Certified Coffee), NAD Case Report 4592 (Nov. 2006); *United Egg Producers, Inc. (Animal Care Certified Eggs)*, NAD Case Report 4108 (Nov. 2003); *D'Artagnan, Inc. (Foie Gras)*, NAD Case Report 4959 (Jan. 2009).

The SEC complaint emphasized the antifraud components of the Securities Exchange Act of 1934, 15 U.S.C. § 78a et seq. and Commission Rule 10b-5, 17 C.F.R. § 240.10b-5, seeking an order ceasing the dissemination of false or misleading statements in an effort to solicit stock purchases by, and thereby protect, socially responsible investors. In 2013, Seaboard Foods settled with the FTC by agreeing to alter website content to eliminate any ambiguity concerning the use of gestation crates.

In this same time frame, HSUS lodged an FTC complaint against the National Pork Producers Council for deceptive advertising through its "We Care" and "Pork Quality Assurance Plus" training and certification programs, owing to the prevalence of gestation crating. And one day after pork producer Smithfield Foods launched a corporate responsibility website claiming that pigs live in "ideal" conditions where their "every need is met," HSUS filed a similar SEC complaint. http://www.humanesociety.org/assets/pdfs/farm/smithfield_sec_complaint110211. pdf. A month after filing the complaint and issuing a demand to inspect Smithfield's records on gestation crating, Smithfield recommitted to its 2017 phase-out deadline.

C. QUI TAM

The False Claims Act ("FCA") of 1982, 31 U.S.C. §§ 3729–33, contains a *qui tam*[3] provision that effectively deputizes private sector individuals and entities, often whistleblowers, with the ability to file actions as relators on behalf of the United States in an effort to recoup federal funds from those who have defrauded government programs by making false claims. Among several prohibitions, the FCA declares it unlawful to knowingly present or cause to be presented a false claim for payment or approval; to knowingly make, use, or cause to be made or used, a false record or statement material to a false or fraudulent claim. 31 U.S.C. § 3729(a)(1)(A), (B). Successful relators may recover a reward of 15 to 30 percent of the recovered funds. A slim majority of states have "little FCA" laws to discourage certain frauds against state government, typically Medicaid only. Some cities and counties, such as New York City and Allegheny County, Pennsylvania, do as well. *See* Taxpayers Against Fraud Education Fund, www.taf.org/states-false-claims-acts.

Without question, HSUS filed the most successful and widely publicized, if not the very first, animal-based FCA action in *U.S. ex rel. HSUS v. Hallmark Meat Packing Co.*, 2013 U.S. Dist. LEXIS 126949 (C.D. Cal. Apr. 30, 2013). Filed under seal, as required by 31 U.S.C. § 3720(b)(2), HSUS tendered abundant evidence of false claims by nine defendants, including most notably Westland/Hallmark Meat Company, who allegedly made patent and material misrepresentations in their technical proposals and bids to secure approximately $150 million in National School Lunch Program contracts. Specifically, HSUS accused them of lying about compliance with humane handling protocols, a point graphically captured by undercover footage of downed cow abuses at a Chino meat processing facility in 2008. This lawsuit followed the largest meat recall in America's history, i.e., more than 50 million pounds of beef during 2006–2008. *Id.*, at *5. Though only captured on video in 2007, facility worker Ugarte Navarro deposed that during his 25 years working at the plant, he observed and personally participated in the abuses depicted therein, such as slaughtering nonambulatory cattle and using forklifts and chains to move them. He also deposed to having used electric shocks on cattle and

---

[3] From the Latin *qui tam pro domino rege quam pro se ipso in hac parte sequitur* ("[he] who sues in this matter for the king as well as for himself.")

cell phones to warn coworkers of the location of government inspectors to avoid detection of inhumane treatment and slaughter of downed cows. *Id.*, at *13. In denying Cattleman's Choice, Inc.'s motion to dismiss, the court found that Navarro's deposition presented triable issues of unlawful treatment of animals, including regulations prohibiting the use of sharp or pointed objects to drive livestock and the cavalier use of electronic prods. *Id.*, at *14 and 9 C.F.R. § 313.2. In November 2013, a final consent decree resulted in a settlement by the principal owners and investors in the sum of $3,116,802, separate from another partial settlement by the Westland owners, Donald Hallmark, Sr. and Donald Hallmark, Jr., a year earlier for $316,802. Final judgment against Westland Meat Packing Co. amounted to $155,684.827.

Chapter 22

PRODUCTS LIABILITY

Failing products may leave a stream of casualties, human and nonhuman. Did the parasiticide spray stop fleas from biting but also poison the rabbit doused in the chemical? Did a dog chew toy or plastic bone fragment into edible pieces resulting in an intestinal tear or airway obstruction? Although intended to benefit, entertain, and enrich, toys or accessories for companion animals may lead to tragic endings. Yet unlike humans, the nonhumans themselves may be the unsafe products, or render a product unpalatable.[1] Every state[2] has a body of common and/or statutory law stating the grounds to hold manufacturers, wholesalers, distributors, and retailers liable to customers, users, and even innocent bystanders[3] randomly injured due to the defective design, manufacture, distribution, and marketing (or labeling) of products.

Conceptually alluring, products liability claims offer plaintiffs a far less arduous row to hoe because they impose no-fault liability[4] for defects in the design, manufacture, or warning of the unsafe product and, in some jurisdictions, are not susceptible to the defense of comparative negligence. In addition to strict liability, products liability claims also sound in negligence, breach of express and implied warranty and, occasionally, consumer protection violations, though some jurisdictions treat products liability actions as the exclusive mode of recovery. *See Gerrity*

---

[1] The "Paisley snail" or "snail in a bottle case" ushered in the modern concept of Scottish and English tort law and imposed upon a ginger beer manufacturer the duty to exercise care to ensure the beverage's safety for those who may imbibe it. *Donoghue v. Stevenson*, United Kingdom House of Lords 100 (1932). In *Donoghue*, a woman suffered shock and gastrointestinal upset at allegedly finding a deceased gastropod in the drink.

[2] No federal products liability act ("PLA") exists, though certain federal laws preempt state PLAs, such as the Federal Biomaterials Access Assurance Act, 21 U.S.C. §§ 1601–06, the Virus-Serum-Toxin Act, 21 U.S.C. §§ 151–58, and even federal agency standards. *See Geier v. American Honda Motor, Inc.*, 529 U.S. 861 (2000).

[3] *Macpherson v. Buick Motor Co.*, 111 N.E. 1050 (N.Y. 1916), started the trend to abolish the requirement of privity between the injured party and the manufacturer (with whom no privity of contract existed) in the negligence context. Justice Benjamin Cardozo extinguished the "notion that the duty to safeguard life and limb . . . grows out of contract and nothing else." *Henningsen v. Bloomfield Motors, Inc.*, 161 A.2d 69 (N.J. 1960), abandoned privity in the implied warranty context. *Greenman v. Yuba Power Prods., Inc.*, 377 P.2d 897 (Cal. 1963), extended the *Macpherson* principle by not only allowing suit against a product manufacturer absent privity, but further by not requiring proof of negligence. It thereby made strict products liability the rule rather than the exception.

[4] While the manufacturer's conduct becomes immaterial and the burden of proving negligence lifts from the plaintiff's shoulders, she must still persuade the factfinder that the product is defective and caused her injury. Some states impose strict liability only against a manufacturer, not the product seller (except, for instance, when it provided the plans and specifications for the manufacture, marketed the product under its trade or brand name, or is a controlled subsidiary of the manufacturer).

v. R.J. Reynolds Tobacco Co., 818 A.2d 769, 773 (Conn. 2003).

Manufacturing defects focus on assembly line inconsistencies or sub-par production materials, rendering the product unsafe and nonconforming to the design specifications — which would, if followed, create a safe product. Design defects point out the flaw that renders even the perfect archetype unsafe, regardless of whether the assembly uses the finest ingredients and most meticulous labor to bring the concept into reality. In other words, no matter how well manufactured, such product's design will always render it useless and dangerous. Warn defects apply even to manufacture- and design-pure products where a proper warning would apprise the buyer of its inherent, nonobvious danger. Common defenses include statute of limitations, statute of repose, federal preemption, unavoidable danger, assumption of risk, misuse, alteration, intervening or superseding fault, and failure to mitigate. For a detailed treatment of product liability, see JOHN S. ALLEE, THEODORE V.H. MAYER, ET AL., PRODUCT LIABILITY (Law Journal Press 2014).

A. ANIMAL AS PRODUCT

Where the nonhuman causes harm to a human plaintiff, does a state's product liability act ("PLA") apply? Close examination is required, as only seven state appellate courts have directly ruled on the subject. *See Live Animal as "Product" for Purposes of Strict Products Liability*, 63 A.L.R. 4TH 127; *Animals as "Products,"* AM. L. PROD. LIAB. 3d § 111.1; Jason Parent, *Every Dog Can Have its Day: Extending Liability Beyond the Seller by Defining Pets as Products Under Products Liability Theory*, 12 ANIMAL L. 241 (2005); *Liability of Seller for Fraud or Misrepresentation as to Health or Breeding of Puppy or Adult Dog*, 74 A.L.R. 6TH 505; *Misrepresentation in Sale of Animal*, 35 AM. JUR. POF 2d 607.

While the Uniform Commercial Code regards nonhumans as "goods" under U.C.C. § 2-105(1), not all jurisdictions treat them as "products." The Model Product Liability Act invites ambiguity, defining *product* as

> any object, substance, mixture, or raw material in a gaseous, liquid, or solid state, possessing intrinsic value which is capable of delivery either as an assembled whole or as a component part and is produced for introduction to trade or commerce; but such term does not include human tissue, blood and blood products, or organs.

MPLA § 2(H). Restatement commentators suggest a more expansive definition:

(a) A product is tangible personal property distributed commercially for use or consumption. Other items, such as real property and electricity, are products when the context of their distribution and use is sufficiently analogous to the distribution and use of tangible personal property that it is appropriate to apply the rules stated in this Restatement.

(b) Services, even when provided commercially, are not products.

(c) Human blood and human tissue, even when provided commercially, are not subject to the rules of this Restatement.

REST. (3D) TORTS: *Products Liability* § 19. Though all jurisdictions recognize nonhuman animals as tangible personalty:

Courts are divided regarding whether living animals, such as pets or livestock, should be considered to be products for the purpose of determining a commercial seller's liability in tort. Frequently, as when diseased livestock are sold and subsequently must be destroyed, the claim to recover for their value involves a claim for harm to the product itself and thus represents a claim for pure economic loss not permitted by this Restatement. See § 21. But when a living animal is sold commercially in a diseased condition and causes harm to other property or to persons, the animal constitutes a product for purposes of this Restatement.

Id., cmt. b. States have denied that animals are products due to their "mutability." *Whitmer v. Schneble*, 331 N.E.2d 115, 119 (Ill. App. Ct. 1975) (Doberman not product because nature not fixed when leaving seller's control years earlier); *Anderson v. Farmers Hybrid Cos.*, 408 N.E.2d 1194, 1199 (Ill. App. Ct. 1980) (same reasoning with diseased gilts who infected other pigs); *Kaplan v. C Lazy U Ranch*, 615 F. Supp. 234, 238 (D. Colo. 1985) (accord where horse expanded chest when saddled and then relaxed, loosening saddle); *Latham v. Walmart Stores, Inc.*, 818 S.W.2d 673, 676 (Mo. Ct. App. 1991) (plaintiff contracted psittacosis from parrot); *Malicki v. Koci*, 700 N.E.2d 913, 915 (Ohio Ct. App. 1997) (parakeet infected with psittacosis not a product); *Blaha v. Stuard*, 640 N.W.2d 85, 88 (S.D. 2002); *Coogle v. Jahangard*, 609 S.E.2d 151, 153 (Ga. Ct. App. 2005) (rejecting analogy between pet dog and manufactured product due to unpredictability of performance and behavior and stating that no statutory duty applies to person transferring ownership of a dog).

Janice Sease purchased a skunk from Perfected Pets, Inc., of Portland, Ore., who bought the animal from Taylor's Pets, Inc. of Minnesota. Janice brought the skunk to the home of Nora Thayer, Paula Hill, and Bradford Hill. Though it never bit Nora,

she handled it, fed it and came into contact with its saliva. The skunk also did not bite Paula's 16-year-old brother, Brad, but he came in contact with the skunk's saliva, because he handled the skunk at a time when he had open cuts and scratches on his arms from cutting blackberry bushes. Moreover, during play, the skunk had licked Brad several times with its tongue and also had stuck its nose in Brad's mouth. The skunk bit Janice and Shirley, and Betty came in contact with its saliva.

Sease v. Taylor's Pets, 700 P.2d 1054, 1055 (Or. App. 1985). Days later, the skunk died and tested positive for rabies. Nora underwent the series of prophylactic rabies treatments and suffered a severe vaccine reaction, including welts, bruises, constant nausea and vomiting. Paula had a less marked reaction, but both she and Nora knew they might die even after taking the treatments. Brad did not take the shots on advice of his physician who said they might cause anaphylactic shock and death. The plaintiffs sued based on strict products liability under Or. Rev. Stat. § 30.920. *Id.*, at 1056. Defendants appealed judgments of $20,000 to each, arguing that a skunk is not a "product" for purposes of the PLA, and that Brad could not recover emotional distress damages as he suffered no "physical harm."

Oregon's PLA does not define "product," but it does incorporate by reference Special Liability of Seller of Product for Physical Harm to User or Consumer,

Section 202A of the RESTATEMENT (2D) TORTS, cmts. *a-m*. ORS § 30.922(3). *Sease*, at 1057–58, relied on cmt. e and its inclusion of articles that may not have undergone processing before sale, to include "poisonous mushrooms which are neither cooked, canned, packaged, nor otherwise treated," in order to find that the skunk was a "product." It rejected the mutability argument raised in other jurisdictions, like Illinois. In reaching this conclusion, it referred to the statutory defense contained in ORS §§ 30.915 and 30.920(1)(b), which protected sellers or manufacturers of products not substantially "in the condition in which it was sold or leased." It reasoned that Oregon's PLA thus anticipated that products might change somewhat naturally or by intentional alteration after the moment of sale. Here, the skunk entered commerce while incubating the fatal disease.

Sease also refused to authorize emotional distress damages under the PLA unless a plaintiff suffered physical harm. While Brad exposed himself to a rabid skunk and increased the risk of physical harm, he did not actually suffer same. *Id.* at 120. *See also Beyer v. Aquarium Supply Co.*, 404 N.Y.S.2d 778, 779 (N.Y. Sup. Ct. 1977) (breeder, distributor, or vendor who places diseased animal in stream of commerce bears same responsibility as marketer of defective manufactured product); *Worrell v. Sachs*, 1989 Conn. Super. LEXIS 2, 6–7 (Feb. 8, 1989) (puppy with parasites deemed product due to diseased condition under state PLA); *Johnson v. William Benedict, Inc.*, 1993 Conn. Super. LEXIS 2605 (Oct. 5, 1993).

Hypothetical: Ragnar, a Norwegian Buhund, was whelped in Connecticut by Brunhilda Svindal, who sold him to Floridian Aksel Blomkvist. In 2007, Blomkvist returned Ragnar to Svindal, who re-sold Ragnar to Tomas Pedersen of Seattle. Pedersen asked the rescue organization Save Every Dog ("SED") for a courtesy listing to give Ragnar away. SED also has a sheltering contract with the county in which it is headquartered and takes in all strays.

Ragnar was given to an unnamed party, who failed to control him. Upon getting loose, Ragnar was delivered to SED as a stray in 2009. The person presenting Ragnar left no contact information. Ragnar had a microchip, allowing SED to identify Svindal as the breeder. Svindal asked for Ragnar back, as had a Norwegian Buhund rescue organization in Illinois.

Five months passed. Over that time, Ragnar caused no injury to any animal or person. Nor was there any evidence that he had, in the past, bitten or otherwise injured any animal or person. He had never apparently been declared potentially dangerous, dangerous, or even cited for an animal control violation in any jurisdiction. He passed his initial temperament test in 2009. However, he received critical reports from a local animal control officer and dog trainer who both said he should be euthanized due to aggression.

SED has undergone its share of drama over Ragnar. Two board members resigned solely over the turmoil of whether to kill Ragnar, return him to Svindal, or to the Illinois rescue.

Will SED face products liability should it transfer or adopt out Ragnar only to have him bite or otherwise injure another?

Case law in Washington is well-settled that only the owner, keeper, or harborer of a dog is liable for injuries caused by the dog. The landlord of the owner, keeper, or harborer is not. *Frobig v. Gordon*, 881 P.2d 226 (Wash. 1994) (en banc); *Clemmons v. Fidler*, 791 P.2d 257, 259, *rev. den'd*, 115 Wn.2d 1019 (1990); *Markwood v. McBroom*, 188 P. 521, 522 (Wash. 1920); *Shafer v. Beyers*, 613 P.2d 554, 555–56, *rev. den'd*, 94 Wn.2d 1018 (1980). In short, liability flows from ownership or direct control. *Clemmons*, 791 P.2d at 259; *Shafer*, 613 P.2d at 555; *see also* RCW § 16.08.040 (owner of dog liable for dog's attacks). Moreover, a landlord is not liable for harm caused by his tenant's dog, even if the landlord knows of the dog's vicious tendencies. *Clemmons*.

If SED were to contend that Ragnar was a dangerous or vicious animal and, further, if a court were to conclude that as a class, Norwegian Buhunds are inherently dangerous, even then SED would have no duty to warn of vicious propensities. In *Patrick v. Sferra*, 855 P.2d 320 (Wash. Ct. App. 1993), the plaintiff was injured after falling off her horse, which she had received as a gift from the defendant. The plaintiff sought damages for negligence, breach of contract, and breach of implied warranty of fitness for a particular purpose. The court held that the racehorse's former owner and owner of stable at which he was boarded had no duty of care, such as might support a common-law negligence claim, to warn the current title holder of the fact that racehorses, as a group, may have a tendency to bolt. *Id.*, at 324.

While *Sferra*, indeed, addresses duties owed to the current owner of the animal, it also notes that where the donee/transferee is aware of the animal's dangerous propensities, the donor/transferor's failure to warn of those propensities cannot be the proximate cause for resulting injuries. *Id.*, at 326 (*citing Hosmer v. Carney*, 1920 N.Y. LEXIS 910, *75–76 (Feb 24, 1920) (stating that where the buyer or transferee "knows, or before injury ascertains, the vicious character of the animal," the seller or transferor is not liable for any injuries resulting to the transferee). The breeder (Svindal) is certainly aware of any alleged vicious characteristics of Ragnar, and the Illinois rescue is equally apprised of the propensities of this breed. Further, SED can undertake best practices by informing Svindal, or third- and fourth-parties, of any alleged "dangerous propensities" through a complete and candid disclosure. It is difficult to fathom how, under such circumstances, SED could be deemed to have breached a duty to warn.

Another theory worthy of consideration is products liability, premised on the notion that dogs are "products" for purposes of the Washington Product Liability Act (Ch. 7.22 RCW). Of course, it is doubtful that "shelter dogs" are "products" under RCW § 7.72.010(3) for the reason that Ragnar was not "produced for introduction into trade or commerce." Even assuming SED dogs are "products," SED would not be classified as either a "product seller" under RCW § 7.72.010(1) (as it is arguably not in the "business of selling dogs"), nor as a "manufacturer" under RCW § 7.72.010(2) (as it does not "design, produce, make, fabricate, construct, or remanufacture" the "dog" before "sale" to a user or consumer). Assuming that SED were a "manufacturer" or "product seller" and that dogs like Ragnar were covered "products," liability would attach only if the product was "not reasonably safe as designed or not reasonably safe because adequate warnings or instructions were not provided." RCW § 7.72.030. It cannot be said that SED "designed" their dogs, so the only plausible theory would be that the dogs were not "reasonably safe" due to failure to warn. A manufacturer's duty of ordinary care involves a duty to warn of hazards involved in the use of a product, which are or should be known to the manufacturer. *Simonetta v. Viad Corp.*, 197 P.3d 127, 131 (Wash. 2008) (en banc) (evaluating negligence under Ch. 7.22 RCW and citing to RESTATEMENT (2D) OF TORTS § 388 (1965)). "Whether a duty is owed is a question of law that generally depends on mixed considerations of logic, common sense, justice, policy, and precedent." *Id.* If a retailer knows of a product's dangerous condition, but the purchaser is aware of the condition, and furthermore the retailer warns the purchaser, the retailer cannot be held liable. With reference to the duty to disclose, the law recognized in Washington is the RESTATEMENT (2D) OF TORTS § 388 (1965), which states:

> One who supplies directly or through a third person a chattel for another to use is subject to liability to those whom the supplier should expect to use the chattel with the consent of the other or to be endangered by its probable use, for physical harm caused by the use of the chattel in the manner for which and by a person for whose use it is supplied, if the supplier
>
> (a) knows or has reason to know that the chattel is or is likely to be dangerous for the use for which it is supplied, and
>
> (b) has no reason to believe that those for whose use the chattel is supplied will realize its dangerous condition, and
>
> (c) fails to exercise reasonable care to inform them of its dangerous condition or of the facts which make it likely to be dangerous.

Id., at fn. 3 (*citing* RESTATEMENT (2ND) OF TORTS § 388 (1965)). "To have a claim under § 388, a party must satisfy all three subsections — (a), (b), and (c)." *Id.* Assuming for the sake of argument that SED is a "supplier," there is no set of facts that would impose liability upon SED upon full disclosure of any believed "dangerous conditions," as a potential transferee or third party would fail to prove (b) and (c).

B. COMMON PRODUCTS LIABILITY ACTIONS PERTAINING TO ANIMALS

Commercial products typically intended for nonhuman end-users, or those who own and care for them, fall into three broad categories: containment and restraint; food; and biologicals.

1. Defective Fences and Collars

Mary Oehler sustained personal injury when Andy Davis's German Shepherd broke free from his collar and rambunctiously, but without viciousness, jumped on her. Alleging improper casting and composition, Davis contended that the metal ring on the defective collar purchased from Puppy Palace Enterprises, Inc., allowed his dog to escape. The trial court dismissed the case, and the Pennsylvania Superior Court affirmed in a sharply divided 4-3 decision. *Oehler v. Davis*, 298 A.2d 895 (Pa. Super. Ct. 1973). Excusing Davis and Puppy Palace,[5] the majority held:

---

[5] The statute of limitations had run on suing the manufacturer of the faulty D-ring.

> In the instant case, the failure of the ring to confine the dog was in conjunction with a breach of duty by the supplier to keep the dog confined, but that breach had no legal connection with harm brought about by the playfulness of the dog. In a practical sense, it can be said that a plaintiff who has no cause of action because of the playfulness of a dog, should not acquire a cause of action because of the violation of a duty, imposed without fault, which enabled the dog to wander.

Id., at 898. While all dissenters agreed that Davis bore no liability because he lacked any knowledge of the dog's vicious propensity to harm human beings, even mischievously, the three justices refused to join in the exoneration of Puppy Palace. Citing uncontradicted testimony of the D-ring's defects, and emphasizing the distinction between common law negligence and strict products liability endorsed by RESTATEMENT (2D) OF TORTS § 402A (adopted by Pennsylvania), they criticized the majority's restrictive view of legal causation with respect to an innocent bystander. About this time, other jurisdictions were extending products liability to bystanders, albeit in the automobile (not dog containment) context. *Cf. Elmore v. American Motors Corp.*, 451 P.2d 84 (Cal. 1969) (applying strict liability on behalf of driver or passenger injured in collision with driver of defective vehicle); *Darryl v. Ford Motor Co.*, 440 S.W.2d 630 (Tex. 1969) (accord).

Peters v. Lyons, 168 N.W.2d 759 (Iowa 1969), affirmed a finding that the retail seller of a dog chain bore liability for breach of the implied warranty of fitness for a particular purpose when the dog owner told the retailer's clerk of the weight and type of dog he wished to restrain. When the product intended to restrain animals causes direct harm to the user, the foreseeability problem becomes less insurmountable. Jay Stapleton, *Conn. Firm Pays $1.3 Million After Retractable Dog Leash Malfunctions*, CONNECTICUT LAW TRIBUNE Aug. 27, 2014) (Michael Slugg lost his eye when Sally, his coonhound, "took off at a dead run," causing her short training leash to unfasten from the extended retractable Hip Hugger leash, which recoiled and struck him in the left eye).

Boomer, the Pachers' Golden Retriever, liked to walk through the neighborhood. To discourage such behavior, they purchased an invisible fence from Invisible Fence of Dayton ("IFD"). For years, the fence failed, prompting several complaints and service calls. Persistently testing and breaching containment, Boomer remained undeterred even with the change from a two-prong collar and three-volt battery to one with four prongs and a nine-volt battery. As a last resort, IFD placed both collars on Boomer. Later that day, Boomer let loose a piercing bark unlike any Mrs. Pacher heard before, came barging through the front door and collapsed, emitting a foul odor. Days later, the Pachers observed two dark black wounds, irritation, and pus from under the collar. While a PLA claim may have proved viable, the Pachers only sued for negligence and breach of contract. *Pacher v. Invisible Fence of Dayton*, 798 N.E.2d 1121 (Ohio Ct. App. 2003).

2.   Defective Foodstuffs

Animal nutrition raises products liability concerns, as in the case of defective foodstuffs. The class actions against Menu Foods, Inc., signify the most recent animal law example. In March 2007, this Canadian pet food manufacturer recalled dozens of brands of wet pet food, eventually expanding to 180 brands of pet food and treats produced by 12 different manufacturers. Adulterated pet food ingredients containing melamine and cyanuric acid led to acute renal failure and death in hundreds, if not thousands, of companion cats and dogs. On Feb. 6, 2008, following investigations by the FDA and U.S. Attorney's Office, a federal grand jury indicted two Chinese nationals, Xuzhou Anying Biologic Technology Development Co., LTD, Suzhou Textiles, Silk, Light Industrial Products, Arts and Crafts I/E Co., LTD, U.S. company ChemNutra, and its president and CEO for conspiracy to import products reputed to be wheat gluten but in fact had been contaminated by melamine. U.S. Department of Health & Human Services, U.S. Food and Drug Administration, *Charges Filed in Contaminated Pet Food Scheme*, Feb. 19, 2008, www.fda.gov/ForConsumers/ConsumerUpdates/ucm048139.htm.

Animal guardians filed more than 100 class actions against Menu Foods and other manufacturers, ingredient suppliers, distributors, repackagers, and retailers. After consolidation by the Judicial Panel on Multidistrict Litigation and transfer to the New Jersey District Court, *In re Pet Food Prods. Liab. Litig.*, 499 F. Supp. 2d 1346 (J.P.M.L. 2007), the court stayed litigation to facilitate mediation, which resulted in a $24 million settlement. Cases decided on the merits have examined such claims based on design, manufacturing, and warning defects. In *Adkins v. Nestle Purina Petcare Co.*, 973 F. Supp. 2d 905 (N.D. Ill. 2013), the district court dismissed strict products liability claims against nonmanufacturing merchant defendants who sold chicken jerky dog treats as the plaintiffs lacked any proof that they knew the treats were defective at the time of sale. *Purina Mills, Inc. v. Askins*, 875 S.W.2d 843 (Ark. 1994), applied strict liability to cattle feed allegedly in defective condition that rendered it unreasonably dangerous due to vitamin deficiencies.

Hypothetical: On April 21, 2004, Kim fed In the Raw Only Chicken to her 18-year-old, neutered male silver tabby cat named Bill. The package had no warnings concerning large pieces that might cause obstructions in cats. All it offered were the following notes:

> **SAFE HANDLING NOTE: This product contains raw meat. Please exercise precautions in handling**.

> **Ingredient List: USDA Free Range Chicken, ground including bone, gizzard, heart and liver**.

After repeated bouts of vomiting and loss of appetite, Kim took Bill to her veterinarian. Radiographs revealed an obstruction in his small intestine. Exploratory surgery located a sharp piece of chicken bone, which the surgeon removed after resecting a portion of his bowel. For the next two weeks, Kim had to push food through a feeding tube directly into his stomach.

Does In the Raw have products liability?

Generally, a product manufacturer is subject to strict liability to a claimant if the claimant's harm was proximately caused by the fact that the product was not reasonably safe in construction. A product is not "reasonably safe in construction" if the product deviates materially from the design specifications of the manufacturer or differs in some material way from identical units in the same product line. The manufacturing defect that occurred here (e.g., inadequate grinding) triggers strict liability. As an alternative grinding process was feasible and any burden of its implementation was outweighed by the seriousness and likelihood of the precise harm visited upon Bill and Kim, a design defect may also exist. Finally, because advisory instructions on the risk of obstruction for unprocessed bones was not provided or inadequately provided, a warn defect should be explored. The Safe Handling Note did not advise about choking or obstruction hazards; rather, it appeared to focus on bacterial contamination from mishandling uncooked, raw product. Precautions contemplated by the purchaser might include washing one's hands and all surfaces that the product might touch, or keeping the product frozen or refrigerated before use. "Ground" suggests that the chicken bone has been pulverized to a degree suitable for feline consumption without cooking or other intervention. This is, after all, a raw food product.

C. DEFECTIVE ANIMAL DRUGS AND VACCINES

With laws mandating rabies vaccination, and the increase in pharmaceutical research and development of drugs for nonhumans, the rise of adverse events such as injection-site sarcoma, organ failure, and occasional death introduce an area ripe for products liability litigation. The Federal Food, Drug, and Cosmetic Act ("FDCA"), 21 U.S.C. § 301 et seq. sought to regulate unsafe drugs and fraudulent marketing, including premarket approval for new drugs by the Food and Drug Administration ("FDA"). Despite such federal oversight, Congress explicitly disavowed preemption of state law in the context of prescription drugs. *Wyeth v. Levine*, 555 U.S. 555, 574 (2009) (finding that FDA approval of drug labeling did not impliedly preempt state law failure-to-warn claims asserting label inadequacy).

One of the earliest such suits pertains to Rimadyl® (carprofen), a nonsteroidal anti-inflammatory for dogs that the FDA approved on Oct. 25, 1995. On Oct. 12, 1999, Jean Townsend, individually and on behalf of all others similarly situated, sued Pfizer, Inc. for the death of George, her chocolate Labrador Retriever, on account of his taking Rimadyl for arthritis pain. *Townsend v. Pfizer, Inc.*, Hampton Cy. Ct. Comm. Pleas, No. 99-CP-25-353 (S.C.). Less than two months later, on Dec. 1, 1999, the FDA's Center for Veterinary Medicine ("CVM") issued its *Update on Rimadyl* to inform the public of reported adverse drug experiences with the drug. http:// www.fda.gov/AnimalVeterinary/NewsEvents/CVMUpdates/ucm129408.htm. Due to adverse drug experience ("ADE") reports lodged with the FDA in 1997, shortly after Rimadyl's marketing by Pfizer, the CVM asked the company to modify its adverse reaction section of the drug label. Since 1998, the FDA/CVM received 3,626 ADE reports involving the drug. Thirteen percent of the Rimadyl ADE reports were fatal. It also asked Pfizer to send a "Dear Doctor" letter to veterinarians to inform them of the adverse effects reported with its use, including death.

On Mar. 9, 2000, Pfizer began sending "Dear Doctor" letters to veterinarians prescribing to canine patients. http://www.fda.gov/downloads/AnimalVeterinary/ SafetyHealth/ProductSafetyInformation/UCM056794.pdf. It also included a Client Information Sheet ("CIS") that specifically advised that Rimadyl could cause death with   or   without   warning.   http://www.fda.gov/downloads/AnimalVeterinary/ Products/ApprovedAnimalDrugProducts/DrugLabels/UCM050404.pdf. *Townsend* settled in 2004, with Pfizer making cash offers to more than 300 plaintiffs, averaging $1000 per animal with no confidentiality provision. In 2009, however, another Rimadyl death prompted litigation. Christopher Cooper and Shelley Smith sued Pfizer, Inc. for strict products liability, negligence, breach of express and implied warranty, misrepresentation, and deceptive trade practices arising from the death of Sophie, their Golden Retriever, following suspected Rimadyl toxicity and liver failure. *See Cooper v. Pfizer, Inc.*, Boulder Cy. Dist. Ct. (Colo., filed 2011); Mitchell Byars, *Boulder Dog Owners Reach Settlement with Pfizer over Golden Retriever's Death*, Mar. 26, 2013, DailyCamera.com.

Animal immunobiologicals are licensed and monitored by USDA's APHIS and subject to the Animal Virus, Serum, Toxin, Antitoxin Act ("Virus-Serum-Toxin Act," or VSTA[6]), 21 U.S.C. §§ 151–59, and regulations, such as the *Final Rule Pertaining to Restrictions Which May Be Imposed by States on the Distribution and Use of Veterinary Biological Products*, which issued a 1992 declaration of preemption and intention to occupy the field "[w]here safety, efficacy, purity, and potency of biological products are concerned . . . [because] Congress clearly intended that there be national uniformity in the regulation of these products." APHIS took the position that "States are not free to impose requirements which are different from, or in addition to, those imposed by [the Agency] regarding the safety, efficacy, potency or purity of a product. Similarly, labeling requirements which are different from or in addition to those in the regulations under the Act may not be imposed by the States." 57 FR 38758. Thus, failure-to-warn, inadequate-disclosure, failure-to-instruct, and all labeling claims except failure to comply with labeling and packaging requirements set forth by APHIS, are preempted. *Lynnbrook Farms v. SmithKline Beecham Corp.*, 79 F.3d 620, 630 (7th Cir.), *cert. denied*, 117 S. Ct. 178 (1996).

The VSTA also bars implied-warranty claims because whether a product is fit for an intended purpose or of merchantable quality directly counters a vaccine's "safety, efficacy, potency or purity." *Id.* The same logic applies to fraudulent misrepresentation, false advertising, and consumer protection. *Id.* Because courts construe APHIS approval of vaccine content and sufficiency of design, manufacture, and testing prior to licensure as meeting the duty of care, common law negligence claims also fall away. *Murphy v. SmithKine Beecham Animal Health Gp.*, 898 F. Supp. 811, 818 (D. Kan. 1995). *But see TDM Farms, Inc. v. Wilhoite Family Farm, LLC*, 969 N.E.2d 97 (Ind. App. 2012) (VSTA does not preempt nuisance, negligence, or trespass by one hog farm against another that misused serum). Express warranties must also submit to the VSTA's preemptive reach to the extent predicated on labeling and packaging. *Behrens v. United Vaccines, Inc.*, 189 F. Supp. 2d 945, 962–63 (D. Minn. 2002) (drawing from *Cipollone v. Liggett Gp., Inc.*, 505 U.S. 504 (1992)). Further, VSTA preempts design defect strict products liability claims.[7] *Id.* Perhaps all that remains after *Lynnbrook* are those state tort claims premised on noncompliance (i.e., violation or disregard) of APHIS regulatory

---

[6] The VSTA makes it unlawful to prepare, sell, barter, exchange, ship, or deliver for shipment any worthless, contaminated, dangerous, or harmful virus, serum, toxin, or analogous product intended for use in treating domestic animals unless and until it has been prepared in compliance with USDA regulations. 21 U.S.C. § 151. Violations of the VSTA are prosecuted as misdemeanors. 21 U.S.C. § 158.

[7] One may still argue that the VSTA does not preempt *manufacturing* defect claims, given that such failure would not comply with APHIS regulations.

standards. *Id.*, at 629; *see also Brandt v. Marshall Animal Clinic, Inc.*, 540 N.W.2d 870 (Minn. Ct. App. 1995) (cattle farmers who suffered losses after administering cattle vaccine lost suit against vaccine manufacturer and veterinary clinic based on federal preemption under the VSTA); Paul LeRoy Crist, *A Legal Virus Attacks Farmers and Ranchers — And There Is No Vaccine: APHIS Has Left No Tort Remedies at Common Law*, 1 DRAKE J. AGRIC. L. 1 (1996).[8]

While the VSTA renders manufacturers virtually impervious to civil suit, veterinarians still face liability for professional negligence, lack of informed consent, and breach of warranty. Non-vaccine manufacturers do not enjoy VSTA immunity but may still invoke the learned-intermediary doctrine, which protects a manufacturer against failure-to-warn claims by the ultimate user provided it has adequately warned the "learned intermediary," i.e., the prescribing physician who is expected to "account [for] the propensities of the drug, as well as the susceptibilities of his patient." *Reyes v. Wyeth Labs.*, 498 F.2d 1264, 1276 (5th Cir. 1974). However, "[p]hysicians become learned intermediaries only when they have received adequate warnings from the drug manufacturer." *Thom v. Bristol-Myers Squibb Co.*, 353 F.3d 848, 853 (10th Cir. 2003). Courts have split on whether an animal pharmaceutical manufacturer may raise the defense in the veterinary medical context. One court concluded that a veterinarian cannot serve as a learned intermediary with respect to dangers to humans exposed to a drug in the process of administering it to nonhumans:

> Although a veterinarian receives training in pharmacology, his "patients" are animals rather than humans. A veterinarian, therefore, can be expected to have knowledge of the particular susceptibilities of the *animals* he treats, or of *animals* generally, but not of those of persons, by definition not under his care, either in general or who happen to obtain from the veterinarian a prescription drug to be used in treatment of an animal. Hence, it may have been reasonable for Rachelle to expect Dr. Swain to have particular expertise and knowledge concerning the dangers *to ani-*

---

[8] The tide may be turning, however. Consider *Franklin Livestock, Inc. v. Boehringer Ingelheim Vetmedica, Inc.*, 113 F. Supp. 3d 834 (E.D.N.C. 2015), where commercial cattle farmers Franklin Livestock, Inc. administered USDA-licensed and APHIS-tested vaccines from Boehringer Ingelheim Vetmedica Inc., causing the bovines to suffer endotoxemia, which claimed thousands of lives and diminished value of thousands more. The vaccine manufacturer moved for summary judgment dismissal of the farmers' claims for breach of warranty, negligent design and manufacture, failure to warn, failure to comply with the VSTA, as well as unfair and deceptive trade practices, premised on federal regulatory preemption. While Congress intended to establish nationally uniform standards for preparing and selling animal vaccines via the VSTA, the Act did not expressly speak to state law preemption. However, APHIS regulations did. 57 FR 38,758-38,759 (Aug. 27, 1992). In denying the motion, the trial judge held that, while cases following *Fidelity Fed. Sav. & Loan Ass'n v. de la Cuesta*, 458 U.S. 141 (1982), decided that APHIS preempted state law in this field, those opinions predated *Wyeth v. Levine*, 555 U.S. 555 (2009), an FDA case concerning pharmaceutical drug labeling. *Wyeth* held that while agency intent to preempt is partly determinative and necessary to a preemption determination, it is not dispositive and "counsels against construing APHIS's preemption proclamation so broadly as to leave plaintiff with no remedy in the instant case." *Id.*, at *3. As to whether the manufacturer failed to comply with APHIS regulations, the trial court cited well-established law that the state law claim of per se negligence, a tort paralleling federal requirements, may be brought. *Id.*, at *4. *But see Wyoming Premium Farms, LLC v. Pfizer, Inc.*, 2013 U.S. Dist. LEXIS 62476 (D. Wy. Apr. 29, 2013) (distinguishing *Wyeth*, but not ascertaining impact of preemption on state common-law remedies).

mals involved in the use of chloramphenicol and thus to communicate those dangers to persons who will directly administer the drug to an animal. But it seems unreasonable to expect a veterinarian such as Dr. Swain to have the medical expertise necessary to make him in all instances a "learned" intermediary with regard to dangers to *humans* who are exposed to a drug in the process of administering it to animals. At least this is so where, as here, the drug is properly dispensed for subsequent use by animal owners away from the direct supervision of the prescribing veterinarian. We therefore reject Rachelle's argument that the learned intermediary doctrine should apply and, consequently, its challenge to the district court's instructions regarding the scope of Rachelle's duty to warn.

Osburn v. Anchor Laboratories, Inc., 825 F. 2d 908, 913 (5th Cir. 1987). *Cf. Haste v. American Home Products Corp.*, 577 F. 2d 1122 (10th Cir. 1978) (applicable in case of bovine vaccine).

Even if a plaintiff can overcome preemption, or instead seeks recourse against the prescribing veterinarian, several material issues bear mention, such as: Did the animal need the vaccine? If so, was it prescribed in the proper form, in the proper manner and location? Was it handled properly, administered aseptically, at the proper interval, and with informed consent? Veterinarians should disclose the nature of the condition vaccinated against, and reasonable dangers within the veterinarian's knowledge that may result. Many guardians purchase vaccines from a farmers' cooperative and administer them without a veterinarian's guidance. While this approach may prove economical in the short-run, vaccine failure could result in long-term losses as the owners will almost assuredly bear the brunt of any casualty, as in the case of a puppy contracting parvovirus despite immunization against the disease.

D. ANIMAL ACCOUTREMENTS

Toys, treats, and other accessories marketed by outfitters provide yet another source for products liability. For instance, Booker, Dawn Stanley's French Bulldog, consumed a Double Action Chew Toy, marketed under the Nylabone trade name, causing intestinal injury. The chew toy packaging advised buyers to "review guidelines for more products and tips." The guidelines stated, in relevant part, that the toy was "non-edible" and, though "non-toxic," was "NOT intended for consumption." Stanley's primary objection was that they failed to adequately inform consumers of medical risks associated with the toy, e.g., "the fact that pieces of the Chew Toys often break off and are ingested by dogs, and much of the time are invisible to veterinarians." Stanley initiated a class action lawsuit against the manufacturer and its holding company, stating eight claims: strict products liability, negligence, breach of implied warranties, breach of express warranties, fraud, Maryland's consumer protection act, other States' CPAs, and unjust enrichment. Defendants filed a motion to dismiss five of the claims, including the strict liability claim premised on warn defects.

Finding that Maryland law "does not require the best of all possible warnings," but "only a reasonable warning," and that the guidelines "gave consumers a reasonable warning of medical danger if their dog ingested a large piece of the toy," the court dismissed the failure-to-warn claim in the face of the sufficient "general warning of danger." *Stanley v. Central Garden and Pet Corp. and T.F.H. Publications d/b/a Nylabone Prods.*, 891 F. Supp. 2d 757, 764 (D. Md. 2012). Defenses to such non-edible, yet ingestible item claims include that the incident product was not manufactured or retailed by the defendant; the buyer misused the product (e.g., mismatched size, lack of supervision); or that a confounding variable was to blame (e.g., a dog ingests tinsel, ribbon, or bungee cords that wad around part of the synthetic bone, causing an intestinal tear).

In 1972 Congress enacted the Consumer Product Safety Act, 15 U.S.C. § 2052, which established the Consumer Product Safety Commission ("CPSC"). Authorized to pursue recalls and ban products in rare cases, the CPSC has jurisdiction over "consumer products," defined at 15 U.S.C. § 2052(a)(5), not otherwise regulated by a myriad of federal agencies, such as the FDA or USDA. However, products that might cause incidental harm to human beings may fall within its ambit, such as aquarium heaters (CPSC Release 11-202). As the commission focuses on harm to humans, toys for nonhuman animals are not regulated by the Commission, which has not set safety standards such as appropriate phthalate or lead levels or choking hazards. Steve Dale, *First Children's Toys, Are Pet Toys Next?*, Steve Dale's Pet World Radio; Andrew Adam Newman, *For Pet Owners, Too, Toys a Reason for Concern*, N.Y. TIMES, Dec. 22, 2007.

In the early days, the CPSC believed it could regulate live animals, such as diseased pet turtles (*see* Jan. 29, 1974 advisory letter stating "non-food animals" were consumer products, http://www.cpsc.gov//PageFiles/110363/78.pdf), but on Apr. 16, 1990, it disavowed that interpretation when presented with the issue of wolf-hybrid dogs, concluding that "Congress did not intend to include live animals, as such, within the definition of a 'consumer product' subject to the CPSA." http://www.cpsc.gov//PageFiles/105750/311.pdf.

> On Nov. 29, 2012, following comment by ARDF, AAVS, HSUS, PETA, and PCRM, the CPSC codified an Animal Testing Policy to guide product manufacturers subject to the Federal Hazardous Substances Act concerning replacement, reduction, and refinement of such methods. It specifically issued this guidance "in part to encourage non-animal alternatives to testing," inviting manufacturers to "refer to *in vitro* and *in silico* methods, in general, as alternative test methods that a manufacturer may wish to consider in lieu of animal testing."

16 C.F.R. 1500.232.

Hypothetical:[9] Maggie sees a beautiful Love Story Lily at a nearby florist. A sticker attached to the plastic sheathing around the flower alerts her that the lily might stain clothing and should not be consumed by humans. She places it in a vase on her dining room table. That evening, her cat Marcus contacts and ingests parts of the flower, causing him to undergo immediate and aggressive emergency veterinary treatment for lily toxicosis. He dies. Despite industry awareness that true lilies will attract felines and prove highly toxic to them, no instructions or

---

[9] This example draws from an actual case filed by animal lawyer Dane Johnson of Karuna Law, LLC in Portland, OR.

warnings informed Maggie that the lily was unsafe for use in homes with cats present.

Do the nursery and florist bear liability for Marcus's death?

Assuming that the flower meets the definition of "product" under state law, no manufacturing or design defect would lie because nothing about the growth of the flower from seed rendered it unreasonably and intrinsically dangerous — *at least to people*. However, by placing the lily into the stream of commerce without ensuring it would not pose an unreasonable risk of harm to those using it as intended, a strict liability warn defect or negligent marketing claim may exist.

TABLE OF CASES

[References are to pages.]

[References are to pages.]

[References are to pages.]

[References are to pages.]

[References are to pages.]

TABLE OF CASES

[References are to pages.]

[References are to pages.]

I

J

[References are to pages.]

[References are to pages.]

[References are to pages.]

[References are to pages.]

[References are to pages.]

[References are to pages.]

[References are to pages.]

[References are to pages.]

[References are to pages.]

[References are to pages.]

TABLE OF STATUTES

[References are to pages.]

[References are to pages.]

[References are to pages.]

[References are to pages.]

[References are to pages.]

[References are to pages.]

[References are to pages.]

[References are to pages.]

[References are to pages.]

[References are to pages.]

[References are to pages.]

[References are to pages.]

INDEX

[References are to sections.]

[References are to sections.]

[References are to sections.]

[References are to sections.]

[References are to sections.]

[References are to sections.]

[References are to sections.]